LATIN AMERICAN HISTORICAL DICTIONARIES SERIES
Edited by A. Curtis Wilgus

1. *Guatemala*, by Richard E. Moore, rev. ed. 1973.

2. *Panama*, by Basil C. & Anne K. Hedrick. 1970.

3. *Venezuela*, by Donna Keyse & G. A. Rudolph. 1971.

4. *Bolivia*, by Dwight B. Heath. 1972.

5. *El Salvador*, by Philip F. Flemion. 1972.

6. *Nicaragua*, by Harvey K. Meyer. 1972.

7. *Chile*, by Salvatore Bizzaro. 1972.

8. *Paraguay*, by Charles J. Kolinski. 1973.

9. *Puerto Rico and the U.S. Virgin Islands*, by Kenneth R. Farr. 1973.

10. *Ecuador*, by Albert W. Bork and Georg Maier. 1973.

11. *Uruguay*, by Jean L. Willis. 1974.

12. *British Caribbean*, by William Lux. 1975.

13. *Honduras*, by Harvey K. Meyer. 1976.

14. *Colombia*, by Robert H. Davis. 1977.

15. *Haiti*, by Roland I. Perusse. 1977.

16. *Costa Rica*, by Theodore S. Creedman. 1977.

17. *Argentina*, by Ione Wright and Lisa M. Nekhom. 1978.

18. *French and Netherlands Antilles*, by Albert Gastmann. 1978.

Historical Dictionary
of
ARGENTINA

by
Ione S. Wright
and
Lisa M. Nekhom

Latin American Historical Dictionaries, No. 17

The Scarecrow Press, Inc.
Metuchen, N.J. & London
1978

R
982.003
W949
1978

Library of Congress Cataloging in Publication Data

Wright, Ione Stuessy.
    Historical dictionary of Argentina.

    (Latin American historical dictionaries ; no. 17)
    Bibliography: p.
    1.   Argentine Republic--Dictionaries and encyclopedias.
I.   Nekhom, Lisa M. , joint author.   II.   Title.
F2804. W74   982'. 003   78-7918
ISBN 0-8108-1144-8

TO

THE CHILDREN OF OUR FAMILIES

TABLE OF CONTENTS

EDITOR'S FOREWORD

Teamwork that produces anything significant is to be commended, especially if the partners are compatible and cooperative. This Historical Dictionary of Argentina is the result of a friendly and effective collaboration between a teacher and a student, continued over several years. All differences of opinion about facts to be included or excluded have been settled by amicable discussion. Their joint efforts, therefore, have resulted in a comprehensive and detailed historical dictionary that will satisfy the scholar as well as those desiring a better understanding of this great South American country. The authors, one born in the United States and the other in Argentina, have produced a guide and handbook to Argentine history since the beginning of the sixteenth century. Some items constitute brief essays concerning places and persons; biographies especially are excellent. Fortunately, Argentina has been acutely conscious of its history and the authors have been able to use many readily available sources, as is evident from the selective references and the extensive bibliography.

Dr. Ione Stuessy Wright was born in Illinois but shortly moved to Florida where she graduated from high school. Her studies were continued with a B.A. degree at the University of Richmond (1926), an M.A. degree at the University of California, Berkeley (1937), and a Ph.D. degree at the same school in 1940. Like a whole generation of graduate students at the University of California, she fell under the friendly and scholarly spell of the great historian of the Americas, Dr. Herbert Eugene Bolton. From him she received her love and enthusiasm for Latin America. Over the years, having married a Pan American Airways pilot, she has traveled widely in these countries and has written monographs and articles about many of them, winning a reputation as a competent Latin American scholar. Her teaching career has been at the University of Miami, from 1946 to her retirement in 1972 as Emeritus Professor of History. During this period Dr. Wright carried out research in several Latin American countries and attended numerous conferences at which she read papers or presided. She is a member of several professional societies and her name is listed in a number of who's who publications. From 1964 to 1972 she edited the scholarly Journal of Inter-American Studies (founded at the University of Florida, 1959) with the title later extended to include World Affairs. But Argentina has always attracted her attention and she is working on a biography of José de San Martín.

Lisa M. Nekhom, Dr. Wright's efficient associate and collaborator, was born in Buenos Aires, Argentina. She has lived for several years in Paris and has spent considerable time in the United States. Her father's family dates back to 1561 in Argentina where one of her forebears, a Spanish officer, settled and acquired property which still remains in the family. Her father was a physician. Her mother's family is descended from a Spanish noble who served as an officer in the wars for independence (1811) in La Plata. At present Mrs. Nekhom is working on an M. A. degree at the University of Tulsa, having completed her B. A. at the University of Miami where she transferred from the University of Cuyo, Mendoza, Argentina. She is a United States citizen.

The readers of this Dictionary will become aware immediately of the scholarly competence of the authors, so clearly evident in their use of sources and their treatment of facts. They have produced a work of outstanding importance and have made a real contribution to the field.

A. Curtis Wilgus
Emeritus Director
School of Inter American Studies
University of Florida

INTRODUCTION

The purpose of a dictionary is to provide useful, accurate information. An historical dictionary bears the further responsibility of placing these facts against the proper background, relating them both chronologically and geographically with the wider perspective of happenings and developments elsewhere that may have affected them. It must also, at the same time, infuse each listing, as nearly as possible, with the spirit and atmosphere of its own time and place. This we have essayed to accomplish in tribute to and in honor of a country that we both love.

Both the selections of listings and the interpretations given them have been hammered out until acceptable to both authors: one, a professional U.S. historian of Latin American history, the other a criolla descended from conquistadores in Mendoza and Corrientes, bred in the history of her country and currently a U.S. graduate student.

For the most part we have relied on the excellent historiography of Argentine scholars and writings of U.S. and British historians in that field. See Suggested Readings, Appendix III.

We count on our friends, relatives, and colleagues to inform us speedily of the mistakes of fact and interpretation that inevitably appear in a work of this kind, so that we may no longer remain in error and future editions may be corrected.

We are indebted to many who have helped us carry the burden of this project and participated in the fun of it. Our thanks go especially to Fred Greene for his computerized map work, to Marc Nekhom for his assistance on the maps and his expertise in the listings on petroleum and Y P F which he wrote, and to Margarita Pelleyá for typing the final manuscript.

Others who have helped substantially with research and clerical chores include: the students in Dr. Julian I. Weinkle's seminar on Argentine history (University of Miami), Gary Frank, Carmen Cáceres de Moyano, Molly Pando, Louise Stuessy, Rose Reque, Paleta Wright, and Deborah Lacey.

We are deeply grateful to Mildred Merrick, head of the reference department of the University of Miami Library, where most

of this work was done, for her cooperation, and to the library of
the University of Tulsa.

Here it is. Use it. We hope you like it.

Ione S. Wright
Miami, Florida
July, 1977

Lisa M. Nekhom
Tulsa, Oklahoma

- A -

ABAD, ALONSO (1526-1590). Conquistador and one of founders of San Miguel de Tucumán in 1565; contributed to the founding of Salta (1582); held public office in Santiago del Estero 1585-1590.

ABALOS. Site in province of Corrientes where General Francisco Ramírez forced a final encounter on July 24, 1820 with the fleeing Uruguayan forces under General José Gervasio de Artigas. After this defeat Artigas sought asylum in Paraguay.

ABC BLOC (or POWERS). Name applied to efforts of Argentina, Brazil, and Chile to form peacemaking agency, around 1912-14, for resolving regional disputes; acted as mediators between U.S.A. and Mexico, 1914; established permanent mediation commission in 1915 (ABC Treaty); settled dispute between Colombia and Peru, 1915; attempted, unsuccessfully, with League of Nations, to settle Chaco dispute; ended during Perón period.

ABEILLE, L'. Political, literary, commercial journal that ran for twenty-six issues and one supplement--April 25 to July 30, 1827; edited by Juan Lasserre.

ABEJA ARGENTINA, LA. Monthly publication of the Sociedad Literaria April 15, 1822 to July 15, 1823; included among its authors the most distinguished writers of that reform period; contents dealing with variety of subjects, including literature, science, agriculture, industry, the frontier, commerce, etc.

ABERASTAIN, ANTONINO (1810-1861). Public figure, liberal leader, tragic victim of political turmoil, 1861.
    Born in San Juan, educated at University of Buenos Aires, entered public life and became politically active member of the Asociación de la Joven Generación Argentina (1838); remained in Chilean exile until after Rosas' fall; returned to San Juan to become embroiled in confused, but violent political situation with national complications: President Derqui had placed an interventor, José Antonio Virasoro, in San Juan to quiet turmoil there; Virasoro was so dictatorial that Derqui, Mitre, and Urquiza asked him to resign, but citizens of San Juan had assassinated him the same day (November 16, 1860) and Aberastain, respected leader of liberal group, was made

1

governor; Derqui intervened again, sending liberal negotiators along with force under Juan Saá, governor of neighboring San Luis; Aberastain resisted but was defeated in bloody battle of Pocito (January 11, 1861) and shot the next day; his execution aroused so much controversy that it threatened the harmony that Mitre, Urquiza, and Derqui had been developing between interior provinces and Buenos Aires; in 1914 the city of San Juan erected a monument to honor its distinguished citizen.

ABERDEEN-ANGUS (or POLLED ANGUS). Breed of English cattle introduced into Argentina in 1879 by Carlos Guerrero to improve and increase beef production in Argentina.

ABIPONES. Site of Jesuit mission in province of Santiago del Estero founded in 1749, named for indigenous Indians of this area who for two centuries raided the northern provinces. Jesuit Dobrizhoffer left a complete written description of the culture of these Indians.

ABOGADO NACIONAL, EL. Newspaper in Buenos Aires giving political news, general information, and articles about literature. October 15, 1818-May 10, 1819.

ABRAMO, FERNANDO (1786-1872). Honored as national military hero of the liberation period. Italian-born, arrived in Buenos Aires as a youth, took part in all the fighting from the patricios to San Martín's expedition to Peru. Remained in the army until retirement.

ABREU, DIEGO DE (d. 1553). Conquistador and early settler of the Río de la Plata area; arrived with Pedro de Mendoza; served under Mendoza and Alvar Núñez Cabeza de Vaca but opposed government of Martínez Irala, serving briefly as governor at Asunción after overthrowing Martínez Irala's appointee during his absence on an exploratory trip.

ABREU, GONZALO DE (d. 1581). Governor of Tucumán (1574-1580); succeeded Jerónimo Luis de Cabrera; responsible for first labor regulations in that area, designed to assure the supply of Indian labor necessary for the survival of the Spanish settlements while avoiding the abuses to which the Indians had been subjected; undertook, in 1578, an unsuccessful expedition in search of the City of the Caesars (see Caesars, City of), opening up communications between Córdoba and San Juan (settled by Chileans); assassinated by his successor, Hernando de Lerma, a victim to the turbulent politics of the Tucumán frontier.

ACADEMIA NACIONAL DE LA HISTORIA, LA. Learned society formed of distinguished Argentine historians, with membership by invitation only; its purpose is to foster the writing and understanding of Argentine history; this is accomplished by a program of publication of facsimile reprints of rare historical documents, promotion of historical research and publication of its scholarly findings, the diffusion of historical and cultural information about the nation, and a sustained, cooperative effort to compile the history of the nation. It dates from 1893 when Bartolomé Mitre, Ernesto Quesada, José Toribio Medina, and others formed the Junta de Historia y Numismática Americana, with Mitre as first president; began its publications with facsimile reprints of Ulrich Schmidel's account of conquest, Pedro Lozano's early history. Its Boletín was begun in 1923 under presidency of Martiniano Leguizamón. In 1927 Ricardo Levene, then president of Junta, presented project for a complete history of Argentina, with separate volumes to be written by specialists in that field; this Historia de la nación argentina, under Levene as general editor, was first published in 10 volumes, 1936-1942; for later editions see Suggested Readings, Appendix III.

On January 21, 1938, the Junta was rechristened as La Academia Nacional de la Historia and nationalized by executive decree of President Agustín P. Justo.

ACASSUSO, DOMINGO DE (d. 1727). Spanish soldier and merchant who founded San Isidro in 1706, making good an earlier promise to bring economic aid to the wretched farm laborers in that area.

ACCION ARGENTINA see ARGENTINE ACTION

ACEVEDO Y TORINO, DR. MANUEL ANTONIO (1770-1825). Priest and missionary; public figure; signer of Declaration of Independence.
      Born in Salta; educated at Colegio de Monserrat, university, Córdoba; received his doctorate in 1793; ordained in 1795; returned to Salta 1799; cofounder and rector of School of Philosophy; then assigned to religious duties among the Calchaquí and Catamarca Indians; back in Salta, attached to the Cathedral, he enthusiastically supported the May Revolution; helped care for the wounded of Belgrano's army after the battle of Tucumán; nominated by Belgrano, was elected to membership of the Venerable Cathedral chapter of Salta (1813) but continued in his rural ministry; became member, along with his fellow priest and close friend Juan Ignacio Gorriti, of Congress of Tucumán; signed Declaration of Independence; became strong partisan of idea of restoring Inca monarchy; continued in Congress after its move to Buenos Aires; constantly worked for establishment of primary schools in rural areas; initiated the ceremony honoring San Martín after his victory at Chacabuco; took his turn as president (1817); was imprisoned briefly during the anarchy of 1820 but, after a few more years with his Indians in Catamarca, returned to Buenos Aires as a member of the Constituent Congress; died shortly afterward.

ACHA, MARIANO (1799-1841). Career military officer who participated in most of the civil and Indian wars of his period; born

in Buenos Aires, he entered the Dragones de la Patria in 1818
and remained in the military for the rest of his life; fought at
Cepeda, Cañada de la Cruz, San Nicolás, and Gamonal; later
in the Indian wars under Colonel Rauch; joining forces with
Lavalle in the civil wars, he won the victory that brought him
fame at Angaco (August 1841) but in a return engagement a
few days later with the pro-Rosas forces under Benavides, he
was defeated and later killed; romanticized by anti-Rosas
writers both because of his courage and his personality (Sarmiento: "the immortal Acha," "the chivalrous Acha," for example).

ACHAVAL, JOAQUIN DE (1792-1844).   First chief of police of Buenos Aires.
        Born in La Paz of wealthy merchant father, he moved
with his family to Buenos Aires as a child; educated in Buenos
Aires, he grew up to take a prominent place among the merchants there; became a regidor of the Cabildo in 1819, reelected in 1821 and appointed "Diputado de Policía." When the
Cabildos were abolished by law of December 24, 1821, he became the first Chief of Police, responsible for organizing the
new department so that it could function effectively. He held
this office for two years, carrying out the reforms of Rivadavia, Minister of Rodríguez' government, then retired to private life and a continued business career.

ACHEGA, DOMINGO VICTORIO (d. 1859).   Porteño Canónigo of the
Cathedral of Buenos Aires, chosen by Pueyrredón to become
the first Rector of the Colegio de la Unión del Sud, opened
July 16, 1818, in the Templo de San Ignacio.   Played active
part in the political life of the Argentine nation from the formation of the patriot government in 1810 until 1828; profoundly
interested in improving the education of the nation.

ACUERDO DE SAN NICOLAS   see   SAN NICOLAS, AGREEMENT OF

ACUERDOS DEL EXTINGUIDO CABILDO DE BUENOS AIRES.   Very
important documentary collection, forty-seven volumes, published 1907-1934 by the Archivo General de la Nación, containing the acts of the Cabildo from 1589 until its extinction in
1821.

ADELANTADOS.   Noblemen who, according to a system of government developed during the reconquest of Moslem Spain, advanced the forward line of conquest and settlement at their own
risk and expense, in return for unusual political and military
powers over the population in the land occupied, and important
economic rewards and opportunities; adelantados also had full
power over land and labor distribution; system transferred to
America in special areas; when Spain wanted to occupy the Río
de la Plata area, partly because of Portuguese pressure from
Brazil and partly in the hope of opening a shorter route to
the Andean silver mines, as well as to increase the size of

the empire, the adelantado method was used; four adelantados actually entered upon their duties: Pedro de Mendoza, 1536-37 (years in Argentina, contract signed earlier); Alvar Núñez Cabeza de Vaca, 1542-44; Juan Ortiz de Zárate, 1574-76; and Juan Torres de Vera y Aragón, 1578-87, who inherited his title by marrying Juana, the daughter of Juan Ortiz de Zárate and an Inca princess Leonor Yupanqui.

See articles on individuals mentioned for information regarding their achievements as adelantados.

ADOBE (from Arabic athob, meaning unbaked bricks). Clay mass, sometimes mixed with straw for texture and strength; basic building material used for public and private buildings in colonial Argentina until stone and other building materials began to replace it in the cities in the late eighteenth century.

ADUANA see CUSTOMHOUSE

AFRICANA ARGENTINA. A mutual aid society, or nación, of blacks established in the Barrio de Monserrat; its primary purpose was to emancipate all blacks (see Naciones).

AGENTE COMERCIAL DEL PLATA. Political news periodical published under editor Manuel Toro y Pareja, June 17, 1851 to March 31, 1852; supported Rosas; then, after battle of Caseros, Urquiza.

AGRELO, PEDRO JOSE (1776-1846). Lawyer and law professor, editor and author, public figure.

Porteño law graduate of Chuquisaca university, performed important legal and public services to patriot governments following May Revolution; edited the Gazeta of Buenos Aires (1811); served as fiscal (government attorney) for trial of leaders of Alzaga conspiracy (1812); was prominent member of Assembly of 1813 and on commission to draw up project for constitution (see Assembly of Year XIII); used pages of El Independiente and La Crónica Argentina (1816-1817) to oppose Belgrano's idea of Inca monarchy and to insist that big decisions must be made by free vote of citizens; exiled to United States, with other editors of La Crónica, by Pueyrredón in 1817 because of their journalistic attacks on his government and political activities against the directorate and favoring federal principles; after his return, devoted himself primarily to teaching and legal studies until forced by Rosas into exile where he died in poverty.

AGRICULTURE. Although agriculture rivaled stock-raising in importance in the early decades of the twentieth century and formed, with it, the core around which nearly all other economic interests developed and upon which they depended, this agricultural development, based on widespread use of fertile pampas and increased use of other areas, made possible by rail transportation to old and new ports (such as Rosario), is a modern phenomenon. On the other hand, agriculture has been a significant component of the Argentine economy, in various areas, since Indian times.

Spaniards found sedentary Indians, especially in northern areas, cultivating corn, squash, beans, cassava, and potatoes; early colonial settlements survived and continued to subsist on these, but with rapid spread of cattle on pampas, meat and the drink made from the wild mate became the staple diet of pampas dwellers, most of whom never tasted bread or cereals; in towns and on estancias during colonial period, subsistence farming areas were set aside for provisions; cabildos were always concerned with bread supply in towns; eating habits, combined with shipping restrictions and shortage of labor, contributed to lack of interest in increasing agricultural production; grapes, wine, and fruits were exported from Cuyo (then part of Chile) from the late sixteenth century, and Tucumán had sugar cane plantations and vineyards shortly thereafter.

After establishment of viceroyalty (1776) both Spanish and creole officials promoted agriculture, but to little effect; Spain offered incentives for increased cultivation of wheat (Argentina still importing it) and for planting the hemp and flax necessary for increasing naval demands for sails, cordage, etc.; Manuel Belgrano and other creoles wanted agricultural development to diversify the economy; Belgrano also hoped to use unemployed women in towns in small industries based on agricultural produce; Semanario de Agricultura and El Telégrafo pushed the project, deploring the poverty of farmers, etc., insisting that Argentina's fertile lands had more wealth to offer than gold and silver mines; British Estrella del Sur (Montevideo, 1807) offered free trade and agricultural development as enticements for Plata area to break ties with Spain.

In early national period, Rivadavia, as well as many provincial officials, attempted to encourage interest in agriculture through education and other means, but with little success; during the period 1826-1856, agriculture suffered reverses due to civil wars, drafts of laborers for military service, and increasing prosperity of pastoral industries; following Rosas' regime (1852), both Urquiza's government and that of Buenos Aires attempted to foster agriculture by attracting immigrants, establishing experimental farms, building of railroads, importation of foreign capital, etc.; government support continued during the presidencies of Mitre and Sarmiento with the establishment, 1868, of the Instituto Agrícola for agricultural education; the department of agriculture added to the cabinet, 1871 (given ministry status in 1898).

The breakthrough finally came in 1875 when the first shipload of cereal was exported; President Avellaneda publicly recognized this as the most important event of his administration; by 1880 agriculture began to overtake livestock as chief source of national income. Five main agricultural areas may be distinguished: 1) the subtropic, littoral area including Misiones, Corrientes, and Entre Ríos, where traditional pro-

ducts, such as mate, citrus and other fruits, have been supplemented by rice, tobacco, soybeans, tung, cotton, peanuts,
etc. ; 2) the Northwest around Tucumán, where sugarcane has
expanded rapidly, controlled by a few wealth planters using local and migrant workers; 3) the Andean area, centering around
Mendoza and concentrating heavily on vineyards and orchards;
4) the pampas area, including Buenos Aires, Santa Fe, Córdoba and portions of adjacent provinces--the great cereal producing area, along with such other products as hemp, flax, alfalfa; and 5) Patagonia, experimenting with cold-weather crops.
        New crops have acquired significance as technological in-
novations or social and cultural changes, both at home and
abroad, have been reflected by new or changing demands on
national and world markets, but during the half century following the 1880s agriculture had a major role in shaping the nation's society, economy, and culture into a new, more prosperous, more cultivated form that masked temporarily the
problems accompanying it.
        Since the depression of the 1930s Argentina has been at-
tempting to cope with these problems--such as need for diversification of the economy by greater industrialization, at least;
integration of immigrants (many, but not all, attracted by agriculture) into life of nation; attention to areas of neglect (pock-
ets of poverty in abandoned areas and problems of migrant
workers); freeing Argentine economy from dependence on vicis-
situdes of world markets over which it has no control; fairer
distribution of profits from agriculture--as well as to increase
production by further mechanization, better methods, opening
of new lands, etc.
        See Agropecuarian Interests; Alluvial Era; Colonization,
Cooperatives, and listings of various agricultural provinces.

AGROPECUARIAN INTERESTS. Term referring to combined ranching, agricultural, and other industries, based on land use, in
contrast to extractive, manufacturing, and heavy industry; agropecuarian interests controlled Argentine political, social, and
especially its economic life from the time of Rosas (when the
land was largely used for stockraising) to that of Perón, decades after agriculture had become a rival for primacy; other
industrial development lagged somewhat as capital sought the
higher profits to be made by selling farm products on world
market; with world-wide depression in 1930s Argentina's economy was in trouble and the traditional free trade, free capitalistic enterprise system came under attack by those who advocated government regulation, diversification and development
of industry, economic independence, wider distribution of
wealth,. etc. , and the breaking of the landed oligarchy's control; Perón succeeded in destroying much of the old system
but Argentina's economic woes continued.

AGUADO, ALEJANDRO, Marqués de las Marismas del Guadalquivir
(1784-1842). Spanish officer, banker, nobleman, friend and
financial advisor of José de San Martín in his exile.

Began his military career as cadet in infantry regiment
of Jaén in 1798; continued in military career until French
were gone from Spain (1815); moved to Paris where he rapidly
became successful banker; acted as personal banker for Ferdinand VII and performed important services for his country in
the settlement of French and British debts; for which he was
decorated and given title of Marqués de las Marismas del Guadalquivir: renewed friendship, dating from old fighting days,
with San Martín in Paris, 1830; persuaded the Liberator to
make his home in Paris; enriched the last two decades of San
Martín's life in exile.

AGUARIBAY. Name by which the indigenous Schinus molle was
known in northeastern Argentina; transplanted to the United
States, it is variously known, sometimes as the Brazilian pepper tree, or the California pepper tree; its mastic resins
were used medicinally by the Indians and introduced into Europe by Jesuit missionaries working among the Guaraní Indians.

AGÜERO, JOSE EUSEBIO (late 18th century-1864). Distinguished
Cordoban churchman, ecclesiastic public figure, and professor
of philosophy and Derecho Público Eclesiástico.
Closely associated with General Paz; exiled by Rosas
for more than fourteen years; returning to Buenos Aires after
Rosas' departure, Canon Agüero became a founder and first
rector of the Colegio Nacional by Mitre's appointment.

AGÜERO, JUAN MANUEL FERNANDEZ DE (1772?-1840). First
professor of philosophy at the University of Buenos Aires
(1821)--ecclesiastic.
Born in Spain, brought to Buenos Aires at an early age,
educated at Real Colegio de San Carlos in Buenos Aires; received degrees of bachiller, licenciado, and doctor in the
Facultad de Sagrada Teología from Universidad de San Felipe
in Santiago, Chile; ordained there; returned to Buenos Aires;
taught in San Carlos and then combined priestly and teaching
duties while quietly sympathetic to revolutionary aims; became
first professor of philosophy in the newly founded University of
Buenos Aires; served as deputy in the Junta de Representantes
1823-1824.
Author of books based on his teachings: Principios de
ideología elemental, abstractiva y oratoria.

AGÜERO, JULIAN SEGUNDO DE (1776-1851). Porteño priest and
public figure of great intellectual and forensic talent; strong
supporter of Rivadavia's ecclesiastical reforms and unitarist
ideas.
Born in Buenos Aires, educated at San Carlos, earned
doctorate in theology at University of Chuquisaca; returned to
Buenos Aires to serve as legal counsel for the royal Audiencia;
continued ecclesiastical and public responsibilities but was increasingly drawn to latter; slow to accept the May Revolution,

he walked out of the session of May 22, 1810, without voting
but five years later, May 25, 1817, he eloquently espoused
the new cause in sermon at the Cathedral, condemning Spain,
praising patriot government; became ardent supporter of Rivadavia's reform program in early 1820s as well as his centralist ideas and plan to federalize Buenos Aires; fought for these
as member of Congress 1824, continued as minister of government under Rivadavia as President; supported Lavalle against
Dorrego and Buenos Aires estanciero federalist group; forced
into exile with Rivadavia; died in Montevideo.
 As writer and intellectual, Dr. Agüero took the initiative in calling together leading Buenos Aires intellectuals January 1, 1822, to organize the Sociedad Literaria which, among
other activities, published distinguished periodicals El Argos
and La Abeja Argentina.

AGUILAR, FELIX (1884-1943). San Juan geodetic engineer, educated at the Universidad de la Plata, with postgraduate work
in France, Germany, and Italy; reorganized the Observatorio
Astronómico de Córdoba; served as director of the astronomical observatory at La Plata (1919-21; 1934 until his death) and
organized the Escuela Superior de Ciencias Astronómicas
there; initiated or participated in every scientific project related to his field in both Argentina and neighboring countries.

AGUILAR, VICTORIANO (1790-1855). Porteño military officer
whose career, largely in defense of Buenos Aires, began with
his enlistment in 1806 in the Patricios to fight against the
English Invasions and culminated after the battle of Caseros
when, as commandant of the fortaleza of Buenos Aires, he
maintained order in the city, preventing looting by the disbanded rosista troops.

AGUINALDO. Cash bonus that many commercial and banking institutions customarily gave their employees at Christmastime;
Perón's government, December 23, 1946, by law distributed
an extra month's salary to everyone on the national government's payroll as an aguinaldo; practice extended by law to all
workers throughout the nation.

AGUIRRE, CRISTOBAL DE (1736-1831). Basque merchant who
moved to Buenos Aires in 1770 and became important public
figure; elected to Cabildo in 1786; urged the establishment of
a consulado in Buenos Aires and became an official in it; attended the Cabildo Abierto of May 22, 1810, but retired without voting.

AGUIRRE, FRANCISCO DE (c. 1500-1580). Conquistador and governor of Tucumán; founder of Santiago del Estero, oldest permanent settlement in Argentina.
 Born in Talavera, Spain; became professional soldier
and received appointment as corregidor of his native city as
reward for his action in war in Italy; in 1536 Aguirre left all

that he had acquired in Spain to seek his fortune with Pizarro
in Peru; fought against Almagro forces in civil wars of Peru;
in 1540 he accompanied Pedro de Valdivia to Chile and took
part in founding of Santiago; held office of first alcalde there
1541, 1545, 1549; in 1551 he was appointed by Valdivia to
serve as lieutenant governor over the northern area, including
La Serena, Chile, and Barco (in the old Tucumán region);
Aguirre's mission was to hold the latter for Chile and to establish permanent settlements; taking Juan Núñez del Prado,
official from Peru who had founded Barco (see listing), as a
prisoner after defeating his forces, Aguirre established Santiago del Estero, moved Barco colonists there, and spent the
next few months appointing officials, building fortifications,
gathering supplies, distributing lands for cultivation, and al-
lotting 46,000 Indians in encomienda; at Valdivia's death,
Aguirre returned to Chile in unsuccessful attempt to take over
succession; in 1560s he returned to Tucumán, having been
appointed by the viceroy of Peru as governor; after having
pacified the Indians in several campaigns, he sent his nephew
Diego Villaroel to establish San Miguel del Tucumán (1565) on
the site formerly occupied briefly by the first Barco and by
Cañete; in 1566, Aguirre was succeeded by another governor;
his life for the next fourteen years was made up of incredible
adventures and misfortunes, including various political imprisonments; finally he retired to La Serena where he died in
1580.
    Outstanding among the Tucumán conquistadores,
Aguirre's impact was especially pronounced in the effectiveness with which he could deal with the Indians, commanding
both respect and fear from them to an unusual degree; and to
the fact that his settlements were made as part of a continental plan that had already included an outlet to the Atlantic
at Buenos Aires; often called one of Argentina's real founders
and builders.

AGUIRRE, JOSE MARIA (1783-1847).   Santa Fe military hero of the
    independence period; Colonel Aguirre's active fighting career
    began in the March to Paraguay under Belgrano; continued at
    siege of Montevideo; then in the Army of the North; joined San
    Martín's Army of the Andes and expeditionary army to Peru;
    remained in Peru until the fighting was over; returned to fight
    under Alvear at Ituzaingó in the war against Brazil; honors in-
    cluded silver medal, gold medal and cord of honor for Maipú,
    the Orden del Sol of Peru; honored, along with others who re-
    mained in Peru to continue the fight after San Martín's de-
    parture, for refusing to give up the wearing of the famous
    blue and white cockade identifying him as Argentine.

AGUIRRE, JUAN FRANCISCO (1758-1811).   Spanish officer in
    charge of part of the boundary commission to establish the
    line between Portuguese Brazil and Spanish La Plata area, as
    provided in the treaty of San Ildefonso (1777), Aguirre left a
    diary of his trip containing not only geographic material but

descriptions, reports of travelers, etc., very useful to anyone
studying the late colonial period of Buenos Aires and that area.

AGUIRRE, JUAN PEDRO (1781-1837).   Porteño patriot, public figure, early financier.   Son of Cristóbal Aguirre, took part in
   la reconquista, member of the patricios regiment; joined the
   patriots in the May Revolution; supported the interests of Buenos Aires in the civil wars and anarchy; served as president
   of the Banco Nacional during Rivadavia's presidency and held
   other offices and positions of responsibility and honor.

AGUIRRE, JULIAN (1868-1924).   Buenos Aires musician and composer of more than sixty works in chamber music, classical
   choral pieces, and piano; in 1916 he founded the Escuela Argentina de Música.
        As a young merchant, contributed 6500 pesos for fight
   against British; served as member of cabildo; attended cabildo
   abierto of May 1810, voting for resignation of viceroy Cisneros; sent by Supreme Director Pueyrredón to Washington to
   secure U.S. recognition of independence of United Provinces
   following the declaration of independence by the Congress of
   Tucumán (July 9, 1816) and San Martín's victory at Chacabuco
   (February 12, 1817) and to purchase naval vessels for San
   Martín's expedition to Peru, Aguirre vigorously pressed both
   missions in Washington and New York for several months
   (1817-1818); Acting Secretary of State Richard Rush expressed
   sympathy but could not act; Secretary of State John Quincy
   Adams held firm against recognition until the situation in the
   United Provinces could be clarified further with regard to the
   actual sovereignty exercised by the Pueyrredón government;
   Spanish agents secured the arrest of Aguirre in New York for
   violations of the neutrality acts by purchasing naval vessels;
   early in 1818, Aguirre, freed by the efforts of Adams (and
   President Monroe himself), and accompanied by their good
   wishes for his country, departed for Buenos Aires early in
   1818 in the Horacio, one of the frigates that he had obtained,
   to be followed by a second, the Curiacio.
        Continued to hold public offices, served as director of
   the Banco Nacional and ended his political career as minister
   of Hacienda in Balcarce's government.

AGUIRRE, RODRIGO DE.   Conquistador of Tucumán; lieutenant governor, 1557.   Nephew of Francisco de Aguirre; accompanied
   his uncle to America and throughout his campaigns and activities; became first chief justice in Santiago del Estero; when
   Spaniards revolted against Francisco de Aguirre in 1557, Rodrigo de Aguirre, by virtue of his position, took over authority
   while members of cabildo argued about which course of action
   to pursue; the arrival of Miguel de Ardiles, with credentials,
   solved the problem as his authority was accepted by all.

AGUYARI, JOSE (1840-1885).   Venetian painter, with international
   reputation in Europe, designer of court robes for Maximilian's

coronation in Mexico; accepted invitation of Spanish merchant Francisco J. Brabo to accompany him to Buenos Aires in 1871; remained there, painting the pampas, which fascinated him, and teaching. Famous paintings included El rancho en el campo, Pablo y Virginia en la selva, Bote pescador.

AIZPURUA, BENITO (1774-1833). Naval officer and cartographer. Born in San Sebastián, sailed on merchant ships plying between Spain and Río de la Plata; served as chief pilot under Admiral Brown in war against Brazil; became interested in need for accurate charts of the Río de la Plata and devoted rest of his life to this project; one of most useful of his works was the publication of his revised, annotated edition of a chart of the Río de la Plata made in 1823-25 by Andrés Oyarbide.

AL AVISADOR PATRIOTA Y MERCANTIL DE BALTIMORE. Political paper of four issues--September 2 to 29, 1817-designed to counteract the criticism of the Pueyrredón government with which the mercantile community of Baltimore was being flooded by Argentines exiled by Pueyrredón, including Pedro J. Agrelo, Manuel Moreno, and Vicente Pazos Silva.

ALACALUF. Indigenous inhabitants of the areas bordering the Straits of Magellan--probably came from Chile. Nomadic canoe men, physically and culturally similar to, but somewhat taller than, the Yámanas; never numerous, almost totally extinct now.

ALAIS, JUAN (early nineteenth century-1848). English portrait painter and engraver who moved to Buenos Aires in 1827; famous for portraits of Juan Manuel de Rosas and of General Tomás de Iriarte; engraved plates for Buenos Aires provincial paper money.

ALAMBRADO. Fenced area enclosing main buildings of an estancia to keep them safe from animals (see Richard Black Newton).

ALAMEDA. Poplar-bordered and shaded mall or public walk, often along a river; a feature of eighteenth-century European urban planning that became very popular in Argentina; sponsored by both royal and local officials; early ones in Buenos Aires and Córdoba; alameda in Mendoza planted by San Martín as governor, 1814; practice continued into nineteenth century.

ALANIS, JOSE LUIS (1798-1851). Baqueano (guide) who contributed greatly to the success of Güemes' operations and that of other gaucho armies fighting against the royalists for independence; born in San Luis, educated in Córdoba, joined the Army of the North when he was twelve years old and remained with the gauchos of Salta for the rest of his life.

ALBA, EL. Weekly literary review, Buenos Aires, 1868-1869; Mitre a contributor.

ALBARELLOS, RUPERTO (d. 1853). Spanish merchant and public
figure. Moved to Buenos Aires early in the nineteenth century; acquired wealth and position; became member of the
cabildo; married Isabel Pueyrredón y O'Doghan and founded
large and prominent family; aligned himself with patriots in
defense of Buenos Aires against the British and in the Cabildo
Abierto of May 1810; continued throughout his life to exert
leadership, particularly in projects of economic expansion and
development in the new nation.

ALBARIÑO, JOSE MARIA (1794-1867). Military hero of the Army
of the North in fight for independence under Martín Güemes
and Rondeau; returned to serve under Lavalle with rank of
colonel; remained in exile in Montevideo until fall of Rosas;
returned to serve as chief of staff in Buenos Aires in 1852
and to perform other military duties until forced by poor
health to retire.

ALBARRACIN FAMILY, San Juan. Family, dating back to early
days of colonization, whose members have contributed significantly to public life and historical development of their native
province San Juan and of the nation; best known member is
Domingo Faustino Sarmiento, whose mother, Paula Albarracín
de Sarmiento (1778-1861), came from impoverished branch of
the family; Sarmiento himself noted the Arabic origin of the
family--believed to be descended from twelfth-century Saracen
chief, Al Ben Razin, who settled down in Spain and established
a family that converted to Christianity.
     Sarmiento, visiting Arabs in Algiers (1846) and, taken
for one himself, was struck by similarities between their life
and his own in provincial San Juan, and came to feel a close
relationship between Arab and Argentine gaucho, finding this
relationship one cause for the disheartening difficulty of bringing the vaunted European "civilization" to those in Argentina
whom he called "barbarians."
     A few of the Albarracines who deserve special mention
are: José Tomás Albarracín (1779-?), who served as governor for brief intervals during the period 1829-1832, when San
Juan, like most of Argentina, suffered political unrest; Colonel
Santiago Albarracín (1800-1869) followed military career
throughout his life; joined Army of the Andes, but was assigned to garrison duty in San Juan; in 1825 joined General
Sucre's forces in Alto Perú (Bolivia) and fought in the final engagements against the royalists there; distinguished himself in
the war with Brazil, barely escaping with his life from the
battle of Ituzaingó; fought in Indian campaigns; joined General
Paz in fighting against Rosas and then spent years in exile;
returned after Caseros; when war with Paraguay broke out, he
offered his services but Mitre told him that he had served his
country long and well enough and had earned retirement; Isidoro Albarracín (1838-1889) returned to San Juan, after earning his law degree in Buenos Aires, to practice law, to devote himself to his experimental plantings of French grapes

and mulberries, and to give his services as founding member
and first president of the Franklin Library (1866); held high
judicial positions in San Juan, Mendoza, and finally in La
Plata, where he died; Juan Crisóstomo Albarracín (1841-1899)
graduated from the University of Córdoba with high honors; devoted his life to public service and education, for the most
part in San Juan, but accepting national responsibilities also;
succeeded Avellaneda (1873) in President Sarmiento's cabinet
as minister of Justice, Public Instruction, and Religion (Culto);
became president of Supreme Court of Justice, San Juan, and
presided over the provincial General Council of Education;
made important contribution through body of new laws and codification of all the laws relating to irrigation; and organized
the department of public works; Alejandro Albarracín (1849-
1899); physician and surgeon who also served as president of
provincial board of education (1877); elected governor of province 1890, by coalition of parties, becoming third governor to
complete term; rector of Colegio Nacional de San Juan; served
as national senator from San Juan, 1896-1898; Ignacio Lucas
Albarracín (1850-1926), son of Colonel Santiago Albarracín;
received his doctorate in jurisprudence from university of Buenos Aires; shunned public and political activity after return to
San Juan; became active in the Sociedad Protectora de Animales (Humane Society) when it was founded in 1879 and succeeded Sarmiento, its founder, as president in 1885, devoting
the rest of his life to furthering this cause.

ALBERDI, JUAN BAUTISTA (1810-1884).   Lawyer, writer, intellectual, father of Constitution of 1853.
    Born in Tucumán of Spanish Basque father who became
naturalized Argentine citizen, 1816, and mother of prominent
Tucumán family (Josefa Aráoz y Balderrama), orphaned at the
age of ten, made his first trip to Buenos Aires (two and one-
half months by carreta) at age of fifteen; entered Colegio de
Ciencias Morales where he met fellow students Juan María
Gutiérrez, Miguel Cané, Esteban Echeverría, Vicente Fidel
López, and others with whom he would, in another decade, become known as part of the Generation of 1837, form the Asociación de Mayo, and find exile in Montevideo (1838-43) from
Rosas, after having graduated in law from University of Córdoba; most of his adult life spent in foreign countries and
much of his writing done abroad; traveling in Europe, 1843-44,
he became attracted to the newly-published theories of Auguste
Comte, promising greater social, political, and economic progress and development through scientific aids; seeking to apply
these ideas to Argentine problems, he became one of the nation's most influential precursors of positivism.
    Alberdi shared with other members of the Generation of
1837 a determination to study the realities of the Argentine
life and scene so that effective organic institutions might be
established, and his special contribution seems to lie in his
determination to formulate juridical bases on which the entire
structure might be built; his most famous work was his Bases

y puntos de partida para la organización política de la República Argentina, the first version of which he hastily published
in time for it to serve as a guide for the Constitution of
1853; his constant preoccupation with a search for unity or
conciliation shows itself not only in this constitution which attempted to bridge the gap between centralism and federalism
but also in his earlier attempts to do the same during the
first days of Rosas' rule; in his efforts to unite the city and
rural populations into one civilization and culture; his desires
to graft the best of European and North American cultures onto Argentine society (the basis of his oft-repeated "gobernar
es poblar"--to govern is to populate); and his views regarding
the federalization of Buenos Aires in 1880; becoming increasingly pacifistic, he had opposed the Paraguayan war; took refuge from unpopularity in exile (1881) in Paris where he died
(1884) while trying to arouse interest and support for a Hispanic American league of nations which, in conjunction with
certain European countries, could peacefully arbitrate boundary
and other international disputes, making recourse to war unnecessary.
        His public career was brief: represented Argentine
Confederation to France and Italy, 1854-61, and served an un-
distinguished term as deputy from Tucumán to national congress 1878-1881; a prolific writer, his published works fill
twenty-four volumes, including poems, stories, even a manual
for piano instruction, but his fame lies in his political and
juridical essays that in many cases provided acceptable solutions to Argentina's pressing problems of that moment and
served to stimulate the thinking of intellectuals of his own and
later generations. See Jorge M. Mayer, Alberdi y su tiempo
(Buenos Aires, 1961).

ALBERTI, MANUEL (1763-1811). Porteño priest educated in theol-
    ogy in Córdoba, enthusiastically espoused the revolution from
    the beginning, adhering closely to the radical ideas of Mariano
    Moreno; voted against execution of Liniers, collaborated with
    Moreno in the Gazeta de Buenos Aires, continuing after Mor-
    eno's exile; member of Cabildo Abierto, 1810.

ALCABALA. Tax levied on every business transaction, purchase,
    or donation; from ancient Roman tax gabella in Spain; trans-
    ferred to Argentina at beginning of colonial period, varying
    from 2% in sixteenth century to 6% at time of viceroyalty;
    lowered by patriot junta of 1810 to 4% but continued to be lev-
    ied until after the reorganization of the nation in 1853; disap-
    peared in latter nineteenth century as it conflicted with popular
    ideas of free trade.

ALCAIDE. Functionary in charge of local jails and prisoners
    (from Arabic al caid--jefe or caudillo); originally--under ca-
    bildo--a regidor or appointee, after suppression of cabildos
    (1821 in Buenos Aires) the alcaide was responsible to the new-
    ly-constituted municipal authorities.

ALCALDES.   Local magistrates who were members or officials of
the cabildo (municipal council); office, dated back to Fuero de
León, 1020, transferred to Spanish America soon after discovery; first alcaldes usually appointed by founder of city; after
that elected annually by cabildo members, with interval of two
years before re-election, always subject to royal approval; in
Argentina, alcaldes of the following categories were used:
    1.   Alcaldes ordinarios (one or two, depending on im-
portance of town)--Alcalde de primer voto (highest in rank)
and Alcalde de segundo voto (second); selected preferably from
descendants of conquistadors or founding settlers (much less
important in Buenos Aires in eighteenth century); from resident citizens who were white, literate, and who owed no debt
to the royal treasury; annual elections usually held on January
1, as in Buenos Aires, but could be held at different date
(Santiago del Estero in October); alcaldes presided over cabildo meetings, unless royal administrator resided there; exercised judicial functions, both civil and criminal, and assumed
political power in absence or death of superior royal official;
had jurisdiction over both town and surrounding countryside until Alcaldes de Hermandad were added.
    2.   Alcaldes de Hermandad--because of difficulties of
administering justice and policing the rural area for which it
was responsible--extending to Córdoba on the west and Santa
Fé in the north--Cabildo de Buenos Aires in 1606 elected two
alcaldes de Hermandad, Antonio Hernández Barrios and Julián
Pavón, to perform these functions under the laws of the Spanish Hermandad; appointment thereafter usually went to wealthy
estanciero; held responsible for maintaining order and dis-
pensing justice in rural area; sometimes called alcaldes cua-
drilleros from armed forces which they maintained; number increased as settlement increased; even ten not enough to maintain order in viceregal Buenos Aires; in 1790, it was seriously proposed that a rural police force, like the Spanish Hermandad de la Mesta, be used in Argentina; instead a new position,
that of Alcalde Provincial, was created.
    3.   Alcalde Provincial--very powerful official who was
given authority over all the alcaldes de Hermandad in his
area; usually bought his position; increasingly important toward
end of colonial period in Buenos Aires.
    4.   Alcaldes de barrio--as population increased in
towns, these men were selected to oversee individual sections;
introduced around 1730, the office had varying significance during the rest of the colonial period, but assumed importance
following the 1810 May Revolution when the Junta made alcaldes
de barrio responsible for all public life and functions in their
districts.
    5.   Alcaldes Indios--Indian towns were governed by
Indian alcaldes mayores, under supervision and authority of
corregidores and other royal officials.

ALCARAZ, TRATADOS DE.   Two treaties, one secret and one open,
drawn between Urquiza and Joaquín Madariaga, governor of

Corrientes, 1846, in an attempt to establish peace between
Corrientes and the Confederación.   Rejected by Rosas, the
treaties were frustrated but the significance lies in their almost fundamental political results: Argentine historians generally point to this breakdown (and renewed interprovincial
warfare) as an important element in Urquiza's decision, May
1, 1851, to move against Rosas' Buenos Aires government.

ALCEDO, ANTONIO (1735-1812).   Author of five-volume Diccionario
geográfico histórico de las Indias occidentales o América, considered to be a major contribution to the historical data, especially geographical and political, available for Spanish America in the colonial period; born in Quito of Spanish captain-
general there, Alcedo pursued his research for twenty years
while at the same time rising to the rank of colonel in the
Spanish army; elected to the Real Academia de la Historia after the publication of the second volume; material on Argentina includes geographic, ethnographic, and scientific observations, as well as a brief historical resumé of each province,
city, bishopric, along with chronological listing of the gover-
nors and first two viceroys.   Diccionario translated into English by G. A. Thompson
(London: Printed for J. Carpenter, 1812-15); modern Spanish
edition: (Madrid: Ediciones Atlas, 1967).

ALCORTA, AMANCIO (1842-1902).   Porteño public official who
served as minister of foreign affairs and religion several
times: from April to June 1890, again during the government
of President Uriburu, and finally during the second presidency
of General Roca; honored by universities and learned academies both at home and abroad for his writings in law, including Tratado de derecho internacional (1878), Estudios sobre el
curso forzoso (1880), Las garantías constitucionales (1881).

ALCORTA, DIEGO (1801-1842).   Highly-respected porteño physician
and surgeon, teacher, and legislator of independence and courage during Rosas' period; greatly influenced the thinking of the
new generation of intellectuals, including Juan María Gutiérrez,
Félix Frías, Juan Bautista Alberdi, and Vicente Fidel López,
many of whom have paid tribute to his memory.

ALDAO BROTHERS, Mendoza.   Triumvirate of strangely passionate,
violent brothers who dominated the Cuyo area during the anarchy of the 1820s and the civil wars of the following decades
until the death of the last one, 1845; all had previously won
distinction and popular acclaim by their courageous exploits in
San Martín's liberating armies; historical role still controversial; evaluation apt to reflect emotional bias, because of their
violence, or political bias, because of their support of Rosas.
   José Félix Aldao (1785-1845), known historically as
General Aldao (from his military rank), or Father Aldao (popularly called "el fraile" by his enemies), as he had been ordained into the Dominican Order and never formally left it,

was the eldest, most prominent, the longest-lived, and the only one to die a natural death; appointed by San Martín as chaplain in the Army of the Andes, he quickly joined in the action
and never returned to his priestly duties; fought valorously--
becoming almost a legendary hero--throughout the campaigns
in Chile and in Peru, where he had been placed in charge of
recruiting and organizing guerrilla forces among the sierra Indians to fight the royalists; returning to Mendoza he became
involved in the civil wars there and quickly, with his brothers
until their early deaths, established and maintained himself in
complete control of the province and surrounding area for most
of the time until his death 1845; defended Mendoza from invading armies and encouraged settlement of southern part of province by Chilean immigrant farmers; won devotion from his
soldiers and the many poor people whom he fed and protected;
hated by others, like Sarmiento, for his use of violence and
unconventional personal life.

Francisco Aldao (1787-1829) entered San Martín's elite
mounted grenadier regiment in Mendoza, gained distinction and
promotion in the fighting in Chile (1817-19); recrossed Andes
with San Martín in 1819; became involved in military revolts,
captured and sent to Lima for court-martial; reintegrated into
the liberating army there because of his earlier achievements
and those of his brothers; fought in the battle of Ayacucho that
ended the war for independence; returned to Chile; became involved with organizing movements against Rosas but joined his
brothers on the other side after reaching Mendoza; killed in a
mix-up 1829 by shots ordered by his brother (José Félix) while
an armistice was being arranged with enemy forces.

José Aldao (1788-1830) fought under Las Heras in the
Army of the Andes; cited by San Martín for his brave action
in the Chilean campaign, including his capture of Spanish governor José Marcó del Pont there; rejoined his brothers in
Mendoza and became involved in civil wars of Cuyo; assassinated June 11, 1830 by Indians believed to be allies; sometimes called the most humane of the Aldao brothers.

ALDAO FAMILY, Santa Fe. One of oldest, wealthiest, most prominent families in Santa Fe; Casa de los Aldaos, 2865 Calle Buenos Aires, completed in 1711, now an historical monument as
authentic expression of colonial architecture; family traditionally interested in administration, providing public officials from
Spanish colonial period to modern times, and in economic development, particularly of Santa Fe area.

Dr. Pedro de Aldao (1780-1823) graduated in law from
University of Charcas (Chuquisaca); returned to practice his
profession and undertake public responsibilities in his native
town; one of the first Santa Fe leaders to acclaim the May
Revolution (1810) and to lend his active support to the first
patriot government.

His son, Tiburcio Aldao (1815-1871), spent most of his
early maturity in Montevideo, returning after Rosas' departure
in 1852 to assume his own public and personal responsibilities

in Santa Fe; presided over the supreme court; enthusiastically endorsed programs for colonies of immigrant farmers, donating land of his own for this purpose; this work carried on by his son of the same name, Tiburcio Aldao (1847-1876).

Another son, Ricardo Aldao (1860-1937), turned his attention to public administration, serving as governor of province of Santa Fe 1924-1928; the construction of public works, including highways, schools, police stations, etc.; and responsibilities in the economic life of the province, serving as president of the Bolsa de Comercio and of the Sociedad Rural, as well as bank director.

ALEM, LEANDRO NICEBRO (1842-1896). Major political leader (Radical) of the 1880s and 1890s. Born in Buenos Aires, profoundly influenced by the execution of his father as a Mazorca leader in 1853 (which he may have witnessed); dedicated himself to his law studies and the writing of poetry--one line of which might serve as motto for his life: "I do not bow my head in battle"; fought in the 1859 battle of Cepeda and at Pavón for the uniting of the nation; served throughout the war with Paraguay; returned to complete his law studies in Buenos Aires and to enter public life; elected deputy to provincial legislature of Buenos Aires in 1871; 1874 became national deputy; vigorously opposed Avellaneda's conciliation policy; eloquently argued in National Chamber of Deputies against federalization of Buenos Aires on grounds that provincial hierarchy would replace porteño one, without any gain in popular representation and that it was, in fact, a step toward stronger central government in the current European pattern; resigned his position and retired to private life when law passed (see Federalization of City of Buenos Aires); became intellectual leader and political guide to discontented groups seeking political change and greater participation in governmental processes in the 1880s; had already (1877) formed the short-lived Republican Party with his friend Aristóbulo del Valle; now in 1889, in confused events of the political and economical crises facing the nation, organized the Unión Cívica de la Juventud, out of which came the Unión Cívica Radical; Alem one of chief leaders of the July 1890 revolt which resulted in President Juárez Celman's resignation; elected national senator, prominent in every political activity during next few years--always opposing Pellegrini, the new president, fomenting revolutions in the provinces which supported him against the government; frustrated within his own party by new leaders desiring different directions, Leandro Alem committed suicide, 1 July 1896, leaving a message to his shocked followers, attributing his action to treason within the party.

Although the UCR which Alem had led was composed of diverse elements, many of them new to Argentine political life, Alem himself represented the traditional popular element in this new movement and in his person links the federalism and populism of the early and mid-nineteenth century with the reforms of Hipólito Yrigoyen (his nephew and political pupil) and Juan Domingo Perón in the twentieth.

ALEMANN, JUAN (d. 1897). Swiss journalist brought to Argentina in 1874 by President Sarmiento to help with Argentina's colonizing ventures; after brief stay in Santa Fe province where he published a German periodical--the first paper in an immigrant colony--he returned to Buenos Aires to establish a Swiss colonization office and the daily newspaper Argentinisches Tageblatt.

ALEN, LEANDRO (1792-1853). Police officer during Rosas administration; born in Buenos Aires, son of Galician shopkeeper, he entered the militia but transferred in 1830 to the police department, where he remained until his death; executed, December 29, 1853, after the fall of Rosas, for alleged crimes committed as a prominent member of the Mazorca; father of the famous political leader Dr. Leandro Alem (who changed the last letter of his surname).

ALFALFA. Leguminous green plant, Asiatic in origin, Arabic name; brought to the New World from Spain; introduced as a cultivated plant--sponsored by Sarmiento and the Sociedad Rural, among others--in 1872; quickly became most important forage crop, with significant effects on Argentine economy; responsible for opening up the interior provinces where it was widely grown.

ALFEREZ REAL. Royal herald and standard-bearer; office of greatest honor in cabildo; involved custody and public bearing of the royal banner and substituting for the alcalde when absent or dead; included double salary; in Buenos Aires this office was customarily rotated among the regidores and alcaldes by action of their colleagues.

ALGARROBO. Indigenous tree found in Argentina, given Arabic name by Mendoza's followers in 1536 because of its similarity to the Spanish locust; used by Indians and Argentines for food, drinks, wood, fences, etc.; there are many famous algarrobos under whose shade historic conferences (that of San Isidro where San Martín and Pueyrredón conferred in 1818) or other events took place.

ALGUACIL. Regidor of the cabildo who had charge of the police functions and administrative duties involving judicial decisions. This was in addition to any other functions that might be assigned to him by the cabildo.

ALIANZA DE GALARZA (1842). Alliance formed between rulers of Uruguay, Entre Ríos and Santa Fe against Rosas. Military direction entrusted to Fructuoso Rivera led to disastrous defeat of latter at Arroyo Grande.

ALIANZA DEL 29 DE MAYO DE 1851 (supplemented by that of

November 21, 1851). After Entre Ríos took over its own foreign affairs, May 1, 1851, it signed an alliance treaty with
Uruguay and Brazil to confirm Uruguay's independence in the
face of Oribe's attack and, in later treaty with Corrientes
joining to fight against the tyranny of Rosas to free Argentina.
Brazil and Uruguay, junior partners, mere allies in this venture.

ALIANZA LIBERTADORA NACIONALISTA. Perón's street fighters.
Extreme right wing group. Directed by Guillermo Patricio
Kelli. Its influence began to wane in the 1960s after episodes
in the Malvinas and La Rioja (see Tacuara).

ALIAU, ISIDRO (1829-1906). Catalonian educator who moved to Argentina in 1857 and played a leading role in the development
of the educational system and institutions of Rosario.

ALICE, ANTONIO (1886-1943). Buenos Aires artist who won national and international fame for his paintings of Argentine historical events. Outstanding are: The Death of Güemes, for
which he won the international gold medal at the centennial exposition in 1910; San Martín en Boulogne sur Mer, painted in
France and based on data furnished by San Martín's granddaughter and other family records; and Argentina, tierra de
promisión, a large scene depicting the constitutional convention of 1853 requiring twelve years of work.

ALICO, JOSE (also known as Alejandro Ferreyra). Indian baqueano
from Santiago del Estero greatly in demand in early nineteenth
century; served as guide for first liberating armies going into
Upper Peru (Bolivia); during 1830s lent his services to generals Paz and Lamadrid during civil wars; joined General Lavalle and formed part of the guard of honor accompanying the
latter's remains to Bolivia after his death in 1841; apparently
remained in Bolivia.

ALJABA, LA. Woman's magazine, November 16, 1830-January 14,
1831 (eighteen issues); edited by Petrona Rosende de Sierra.

ALJIBE (from Arabic word alchub, meaning well). Special kind of
round (in contrast to square cistern) underground container for
storing rainwater; introduced into Argentina from Spain in the
late colonial period and used extensively in the nineteenth century; some very beautiful or famous ones remaining, such as
the one built by Santiago de Liniers in the Fortaleza (1808)
following the English Invasions, and in various large private
homes, such as that of General Mitre which became the Museo
Mitre; aljibes still in use in modern times in the interior.

ALLAN, JOHN (d. 1871). British engineer who came to Argentina
in 1857 to assemble the first Argentine locomotive, La Porteña; remained to work with Ferrocarril Oeste and other railroads until his death in the yellow fever epidemic of 1871.

ALLENTIAC. Language used by Huarpe Indians living at time of
conquest in what is now southern part of San Juan province;
Spanish missionaries studied this language and used it for
their catechisms and other religious materials; milcayac,
spoken by Huarpes of Mendoza, is a related dialect.

ALLIANCE BETWEEN ARGENTINA AND COLOMBIA (1823). Alliance signed between Argentina (by Rivadavia) and Colombia
(by Joaquín Mosquera) mostly for friendship and mutual defense of independence against Spain or other threatening powers; Mosquera submitted lengthy treaty but briefer one by
Rivadavia was the one signed; later ratified by both governments.

ALLIANCE BETWEEN CORRIENTES AND PARAGUAY (1845). On
November 11, 1845, a treaty of alliance was signed between
the provincial government of Corrientes and Carlos Antonio
López' government of Paraguay, where Paraguay bound itself
to furnish a well-equipped army to support Corrientes in its
fight against Rosas and Corrientes guaranteed recognition of
Paraguay's independence and free navigation of the Paraná and
Plata rivers; Francisco Solano López (a general seventeen
years old) was sent to Corrientes with army of several thou-
sand--one of his first military ventures--but alliance soon fell
victim to civil wars of rival provincial caudillos.

ALLIANCE BETWEEN PROVINCE OF CORRIENTES AND REPUB-
LIC OF URUGUAY (1838). Signed December 31, 1838, in
Montevideo by independence hero Manuel de Olazábal for gov-
ernment of Corrientes, then under Colonel Genaro Berón
Astrada, and by Dr. Santiago Vásquez, minister in President
Rivera's Uruguayan government; treaty called for offensive
and defensive alliance against Rosas and his government; stip-
ulated that it was not against the Confederation or any of the
provinces, calling on them instead for aid in overthrowing
Rosas (see Genaro Berón de Astrada).

ALLUVIAL ERA. The name given by José Luis Romero to the
period beginning around 1880 and continuing past the mid-
twentieth century during which the flood of immigrants inundated Argentina, bringing a diversity of constantly changing
new problems throughout the society; alienation between the
masses, no longer creole but new, often non-Spanish, European, and the creole hierarchy meant for the first time that
social aims, purposes, and interests differed sharply, and traditional political institutions, rooted in a common culture, no
longer served; differences of interests brought changing political parties to confrontation and Argentina has found difficulty
in combining these into a common national objective and entity.

ALMAFUERTE (pseudonym adopted by Argentine writer Pedro Bonifacio Palacios) (1854-1917). Controversial poet, vigorous
champion of the masses; born in San Justo, Buenos Aires

province, mostly self-taught, secured a position in the provincial government and began to write poetry that captured the
imagination of the masses with its spirited defense of their
rights and belief in their potential; widely read, and, although
literary critics still debate merits of his poetry, his influence
is acknowledged on poets of the early twentieth century and
two volumes of his poems, entitled Poesías completas are included in Grandes escritores argentinos (volumes XIV and
XXI); Almafuerte voiced eloquently and effectively the aspirations of the alienated classes then demanding political and social participation in Argentina's life.

ALMAGRO, JUAN DE (1755-1843). Spanish royal official who came
to Buenos Aires in the 1780s as a judge in the royal audiencia, remained to hold other royal posts; attended the cabildo
abierto of May 1810, voting with the majority so that if a
change in government should come, it would have the support
of men of probity and of experienced officials; retired thereafter to private life, devoting himself to his properties in Buenos Aires (Barrio Almagro).

ALMEYRA, HILARIO DE (1799-1885). Buenos Aires physician and
surgeon; served in various armies against Rosas; remembered particularly for his successful, very difficult head operation on General Mitre during the siege of Buenos Aires in
1853; and for his outstanding performance during the yellow
fever epidemic in 1871 in Buenos Aires.

ALMEYRA, JUAN AGUSTIN (1748-1837). Owner of the country estate of El Talar where the battle between Lavalle and Dorrego,
followed by the latter's execution, took place (December 9,
1828); born in Buenos Aires of Portuguese father and porteño
mother; educated at university in Chuquisaca (now Sucre); held
various public positions of responsibility and contributed generously to patriotic movement in 1810, but concentrated on increasing and developing his rural holdings around Navarro,
southwest of the capital.

ALMOJARIFAZGO (from Arabic word almorif, meaning inspection
or inspector). Customs duty imposed upon the export of products and goods of Spain and upon their importation into the
colonies; usually 5% to 10%, with the latter more usual to the
end of the seventeenth century; in the regulation to free commerce (1778) the rate was set at 7% for foreign goods and 3%
for national products in the major ports, with Buenos Aires
included in this classification.

ALODIALES, BIENES. Property held free from any feudal rights
or demands; changes from European feudal system particularly
marked in Argentina, where nearly all the rural and urban
land grants to original settlers were alodial; Juan de Garay
spelled it out clearly in his grants to the new founders of Buenos Aires (1580).

ALOJA.   Strongly fermented drink made from the fruit of the alga-
     rroba blanca; popular among the Diaguitas and Indians around
     Córdoba.

ALONSO, JUAN CARLOS (1886-1945).   Spanish-born, self-taught
     artist who moved to Buenos Aires and won national and inter-
     national honors; favorite themes: Rosas period and his own
     contemporary scene.

ALONSO, MATEO (1878-1951).   Important Buenos Aires sculptor,
     best known for his Christ of the Andes (q. v.).

ALSINA, ADOLFO (1829-1877).   Political leader and public figure;
     founder of the Autonomista party; vice president under Sarmi-
     ento.
          Born in Buenos Aires, son of Valentín Alsina and grand-
     son through his mother, Antonia Maza, of Manuel Vicente
     Maza, Adolfo Alsina grew up naturally into political involve-
     ment; returning to Buenos Aires after Caseros, from exile with
     his family in Montevideo, he became active in political move-
     ments (such as pandilla group) purposing to maintain Buenos
     Aires independence from control by Urquiza's Confederation;
     belonged to national guard that fought at Cepeda and Pavón;
     after reorganization of nation, leader of the Autonomista party
     formed during Mitre's presidency to combat his plan to feder-
     alize Buenos Aires and to keep it instead as provincial capital
     (members often called Alsinistas); wielded great political power
     in both capital and nation, cultivating the support of the urban
     bourgeoisie; nominated for presidency in 1868 but, realizing
     that his support was essentially limited to Buenos Aires,
     agreed to accept the vice presidency in return for support of
     Sarmiento's nomination; appointed minister of war by President
     Avellaneda, Alsina drew up and implemented through Julio A.
     Roca a plan to push the Indian frontier back and populate the
     lands with settlements of farmers to open up the fertile farm-
     ing and grazing lands of the south that were needed for Argen-
     tina's rapidly developing economy; his death in 1877 marked
     transition to new political leadership (under Roca) and reorgani-
     zation of political parties--Autonomist party became National
     Autonomist Party.

ALSINA, JUAN DE (d. 1807).   Famous Catalonian surveyor who
     came to Buenos Aires in 1782 with the boundary commission
     to settle boundary between Portuguese and Spanish America;
     remained to establish distinguished Argentine family (including
     Valentín Alsina and Adolfo Alsina); taught in Belgrano's school
     of navigation; published the Almanaque y calendario general
     diario de cuartos de luna de acuerdo al meridiano de Buenos
     Aires, para los años 1801 y 1802, a very important and scien-
     tific publication for its time; died fighting in the streets of
     Buenos Aires against the second British invasion in 1807.

ALSINA, VALENTIN (1802-1869).   Jurist, public figure, champion

of Buenos Aires provincial autonomy in the post-Rosas period.
Born in Buenos Aires, son of Juan de Alsina, began
studies in law at the University of Córdoba under direction of
Dean Funes; married Antonia Maza, daughter of Dr. Manuel
Vicente Maza, became father of Adolfo Alsina; followed successful, distinguished law career in Buenos Aires as practicing lawyer, jurisconsult, professor, and author; taught law at
University of Buenos Aires; served on commission to draw up
code of rural law; as president of the Cámara de Justicia, approved improved prison system and was responsible for other
reforms; important legal writings include his defense of Argentina's claim to the Malvinas and a treatise on the free navigation of the Plata river system; public life began with serving
as subsecretary of minister of foreign affairs under Rivadavia
and continued until his political clash with Rosas brought him
imprisonment and exile; from Montevideo carried on active subversive campaign against Rosas in various journals, including
Comercio del Plata of which he became editor at death of
Florencio Varela.
    Returning to Buenos Aires after Caseros, he became
leader of group determined on autonomy or independence for
Buenos Aires province, refusing to join with Urquiza's Confederation; held various high positions in the provincial government, being elected as constitutional governor in 1857; confrontation between Alsina and Urquiza inevitable due to economic barriers erected by both governments in the rivalry between Buenos Aires and the rapidly developing new port at
Rosario, the charges and countercharges of interventions and
increasing political and social instability throughout the Plata
area, and primarily to the personal animosity between Urquiza
and Alsina, each refusing to talk the peace everyone wanted
until the other resigned from office; a test of arms at Cepeda
(1859) routed Mitre's troops and forced Alsina's resignation to
private life, where he remained thereafter, refusing Mitre's
invitation to become a member of the Supreme Tribunal of the
reorganized nation but emerging (1868), shortly before his
death, to swear in his son Adolfo Alsina as vice president of
the republic.

ALSOGARAY BROTHERS, ALVARO AND JULIO. Alvaro Alsogaray,
    air force engineer and successful businessman, and Julio Also-
    garay, career military officer, led groups determined to re-
    turn to a laissez-faire economy; Julio participated in unsuc-
    cessful military revolt against Perón, 1951, and played impor-
    tant role in golpe that placed Onganía in the presidency, 1966;
    Alvaro, brought into Frondizi's cabinet as minister of the econ-
    omy and acting minister of labor, attempted to carry out and
    to gain popular support for Frondizi's plan for stabilization of
    the economy and reducing inflation but met with limited suc-
    cess, 1959-61, particularly from those who suffered most un-
    der austerity program; Onganía tried different approaches to
    solving the economic problems but found it necessary, in order
    to win popular support, to sidetrack the Alsogarays by appoint-

ing Julio commander-in-chief of the army and sending Alvaro
to Washington as ambassador, 1966; by two years later, both
had been replaced; continuing in public life, Alvaro became
head of the Independent Civic party; ran unsuccessfully for
president in 1973, losing to Justicialist candidate Héctor
Cámpora.

ALTA GRACIA, ESTANCIA DE. Historic estancia in province of
Córdoba; given to Jesuits for their work by Alonso Nieto de
Herrera; stone chapel there designed by Jesuit architect
Andrés Blanqui and built around 1750; in May 1810 Santiago
de Liniers bought estancia, lived there briefly; declared a na-
tional historical monument in 1941.

ALTO PERU (Upper Peru)--modern Bolivia. Throughout first two
centuries of colonial rule, area included by present Argentine
Republic (with exception of Cuyo) had been administratively attached to the Audiencia of Charcas (Sucre); with the creation
of the viceroyalty of the Río de la Plata (1776), Alto Perú
was included and governed from Buenos Aires; attempts were
made to unite Alto Perú with the other provinces under the
patriot governments of Buenos Aires following the May Revolution of 1810, but these were dropped in 1815 after three successive revolutionary armies had been repulsed there; following the final defeat of the Spaniards at Ayacucho in Peru, Alto
Perú established itself as an independent republic taking
Bolívar's name and a constitution written by him, and selecting Antonio José de Sucre, victor at Ayacucho, as its first
president.

ALTOLAGUIRRE, JUAN DE (1770-1815). Porteño military officer
given command of southern frontier in Córdoba; in charge of
fort of Carlota while English prisoners were interned there
(1806); backed Liniers in unsuccessful counter-revolutionary
movement in Córdoba (1810); then went to Alto Perú (Bolivia)
to join royalist forces there; became governor of Santa Cruz
de la Sierra province; killed in 1815, fighting against the
patriot leader Ignacio Warnes in the war of the Republiquetas.

ALTOLAGUIRRE, MARTIN JOSE DE (1742-1813). Viceregal
treasury official interested in agricultural development; born
in Buenos Aires; held several responsible treasury appointments in the viceroyalty of La Plata; remembered, however,
primarily for his interest in agronomy and his collaboration
with Manuel Belgrano in this field; carried on extensive linseed experiments; credited with having introduced the growing
of flax and hemp to Buenos Aires. (Viceroy Pedro de Cevallos had proposed this earlier.)

ALURRALDE, MIGUEL IGNACIO DE (1782-1859). Tucumán ecclesiastic, educated at Córdoba, appointed chaplain of the patriot
armies following the 1810 May Revolution; later served in
church positions in Salta and Tucumán.

ALURRALDE, PEDRO (1816-1892). Member of Tucumán family who
moved to Buenos Aires for business reasons; then established
himself in San Nicolás de Arroyos; joined Urquiza's anti-Rosas
forces when they reached his area and his home became
Urquiza's headquarters for the negotiations and signing of the
Acuerdo reached there (see Acuerdo de San Nicolás).

ALVARADO, ROQUE (1795-1860). Principal promoter of Jujuy independence; prominent in political life of his province until his
participation in the Coalición del Norte; its defeat forced him
into exile in Bolivia; after Rosas' fall at Caseros, he returned
to become governor of Jujuy in 1853 and again in 1857-59.

ALVARADO, RUDECINDO (1792-1872). A major Argentine military
hero of the South American war of independence from Spain.
Born in Salta, Alvarado was working in Buenos Aires when the
May 1810 revolution took place; espoused the cause and returned to Salta to arouse popular support for it; joined the
Salta patricios and fought at Huaqui in Upper Peru; formed
part of the escort of Juan Manuel de Pueyrredón, retreating
from Charcas to Tucumán with the treasury of the royal mint;
joined Army of the Andes in August 1816; rose rapidly in
rank and in San Martín's favor because of his actions there:
major role in Chacabuco; cool courage at disaster of Cancha
Rayada saved large part of army; forced famous Burgos Regiment to surrender for first time at Maipú; campaigned in
southern Chile, then returned to Mendoza to refresh his troops
and get new recruits; boldly recrossed with his army into Chile
to prevent infection from the mutinies in the Cuyo area and to
save and organize an army for San Martín's forthcoming Peruvian venture; 1820, became commander of the famous
Mounted Grenadiers; in Peru joined Tomás Guido in representing San Martín at the negotiations at Punchauca (q.v.); made
San Martín's chief of staff when Lima was occupied; left as
commander of the United Army when San Martín resigned and
departed from Peru; October 1822, undertook the previously
planned expedition to the Peruvian intermediate ports with disastrous results; both the Peruvian government and Bolívar,
now in command, exonerated him, however, and Alvarado became governor of the fortifications at Callao; taken prisoner
in the mutiny of February 5, 1824, and turned over to the
royalists, he joined other patriot prisoners in escaping, after
the news of Sucre's victory at Ayacucho, to arouse the Bolivi-
ans to fight against the remaining royalists; back in Lima, with
independence won, Alvarado was given highest possible honors
by Bolívar, including rank of Grand Marshal of Peru.
        Returning to Argentina, Alvarado was given official
honors and positions but quickly ran into opposition from Rosas and local caudillos; while governor of Salta forced into exile by Quiroga (1831); returned to Salta, by special permission
of Rosas, in 1848; called back into public life after Caseros,
serving as Urquiza's minister of war and navy in 1854 under
the new constitution of 1853; resigned to take over the gover-

norship of his own province.

ALVAREZ, AGUSTIN (1857-1914). Sociologist, educator, and writer.
    One of the Argentine intellectuals to recognize (1894)
that his country had already entered a period of rapid, continuing changes bringing a sharp break with the past; accepted
the intellectual challenge involved in the creation of new institutions for the emerging new age; believed that institutions of
each society should be based on individual morality and suited
to that particular society; education, directed by a strong government of talent, would be the instrument by which a common
society, with social justice for all, would be forged from the
diverse elements--democracy would follow; to this end he devoted his life to study, teaching and writing; sharply criticizing social and political evils, he nevertheless optimistically
called for progress to higher goals for a better society.
    Born in Mendoza, he early joined in student demands
for reform, effecting changes in the educational system; after
completing his education, he held various public offices but
came to concentrate on academic duties as professor in the
University of Buenos Aires and professor, founding vice president, and lifetime chancellor of the University of La Plata;
published many articles and books, largely dealing with political and sociological themes, South America (1894); ¿Adónde
vamos? ; La transformación de las razas en América, etc.

ALVAREZ, JOSE SIXTO (1858-1903). Journalist, interpreter of social and political changes of the closing decades of the nineteenth century.
    Born and reared on estancia in Entre Ríos, education
completed at Normal school in Paraná, Alvarez moved to Buenos Aires and began his journalistic career in 1879; after several positions on major and varied publications, including
Mitre's La Nación, and an interlude (1886-1887) as head of the
detective bureau which included reorganization of police records and editing of the official journal, Alvarez became editor
of the newly founded weekly review, Caras y Caretas, and captured popular imagination with a feature in the first issue: a
column by a semicomic figure, Fray Mocho, relating, always
in colorful colloquial terms, tales of interviews with all sorts
of street characters or repeating old gaucho stories or urban
legends; through Fray Mocho (a pseudonym for Alvarez himself) and drawing on his own varied background and experiences,
Alvarez continued for five years to call Argentine attention to
the changes taking place in their country due primarily to the
enormous influx of immigrants; today honored as preeminent
literary voice and interpreter of the alluvial era, showing in his
Cuentos de Fray Mocho the processes of mixing, mingling confrontation and rejection, fusing or paralleling action between immigrants and creoles of both lower and rapidly emerging middle classes that were steadily transforming Argentine society
to a new identity.

ALVAREZ, JUAN JOSE (1820-1892).   Churchman, educator, jurisconsult, and public figure.
    Born in Paraná, ordained in 1847 after receiving law
doctorates at the University of Buenos Aires; followed active
career as ecclesiastic, jurisconsult, legislator, and educator;
served as chaplain of Urquiza's army at Caseros and honorary
chaplain of national army; member of constituent congress of
1853 and in other legislative assemblies later; cooperated in the
founding of the Colegio de la Inmaculada and became its dean;
appointed dean of the Paraná cathedral, 1865; effectively used
new legislation to establish seminaries in Salta, San Juan, and
Paraná; eulogized as valiant and indefatigable champion of his
country, the church, and the people.

ALVAREZ, JULIAN BALTAZAR (1788-1843).   Radical patriot leader
in period preceding fall of the directorate (1820).
    Born in Buenos Aires, with doctorates in theology from
University of Córdoba and law from that of Charcas, he deserted his ecclesiastical vocation for a political career; follower of Mariano Moreno and Bernardo Monteagudo; director of
the Sociedad Patriótica; his bold positions brought him both imprisonment and positions of responsibility, depending on the
party in power; in 1820 moved to Montevideo where he entered
a distinguished legal career, culminating in the presidency of
the Uruguayan supreme court.

ALVAREZ, TEODORO (1818-1889).   Beloved physician and skilled
surgeon in Buenos Aires; successfully removed aneurism from
General Bartolomé Mitre.

ALVAREZ BARAGAÑA, DIEGO (c. 1750s-1807).   Born in Gijón,
Asturias; came to Buenos Aires with establishment of the viceroyalty; amassed a fortune; contributed generously to public
projects; gave both his life and much of his fortune to the fight
against the British invasions, 1806-1807.

ALVAREZ CONDARCO, PEDRO NOLASCO (1800-1835).   Career military officer; fought in war for independence.   Born in Tucumán,
younger brother of José Antonio Alvarez de Condarco; joined
Army of the Andes in Mendoza; fought at Chacabuco; accompanied his brother to London but returned to Chile to join San
Martín's liberating expedition to Peru; fought in many battles
including the final one at Ayacucho; returned to Buenos Aires,
remaining in army until his early death.

ALVAREZ DE CONDARCO, JOSE ANTONIO (1780-1855).   Manufac-
turer of gunpowder and explosives, cartographer, important
collaborator in success of San Martín's army's crossing of the
Andes (1817).
    Born in Tucumán, son of alcalde, Alvarez Condarco be-
came deeply interested in the making of gunpowder and other
explosives; supported the Buenos Aires Revolution of May 1810;
by 1812 was director of gunpowder and explosives factory in

Córdoba; joined San Martín in Mendoza, in charge of manufacturing munitions for the training of the Army of the Andes as well as for the proposed liberating expedition into Chile; served also as cartographer in amazing exploit: unwilling to send his army into the difficult Andean passes without the best, latest information possible, San Martín sent Álvarez Condarco on a special mission to the Spanish governor of reconquered Chile to inform him officially that the United Provinces had formally declared their independence from Spain; counting on the fact that the governor would correctly send the emissary safely home, despite his feelings, San Martín directed Alvarez to take the longer Paso de los Patos over to Chile, believing that Marcó del Pont would send him back by the most direct route, Uspallata Pass: the scheme worked and a few weeks later (February 1817) the army crossed safely over into Chile to defeat the royalist forces at Chacabuco, using the maps that Alvarez Condarco had compiled from his memory of the two passes traversed; served as San Martín's aide-de-camp; fought heroically at Chacabuco; then was sent to London to buy ships for the first Chilean naval squadron; persuaded Lord Cochrane to accept command of it; returned to spend the rest of his life, independence won, in Chile, teaching mathematics.

His son, José Antonio Alvarez de Condarco, Jr., returned to Argentina to serve in several ministerial capacities in governments of the 1850s and 1860s.

ALVAREZ JONTE, ANTONIO (1784-1820). Patriot official, diplomat, close personal friend of San Martín and collaborator in his fight for independence.

Born in Madrid, moved as young boy to Buenos Aires; educated at the Colegio Monserrat de Córdoba, then graduated in law at the Universidad de San Felipe in Santiago, Chile, 1809; returned to Buenos Aires and supported the May Revolution; sent back to Chile by the junta to report on the revolution in Buenos Aires and to secure cooperation of the Chileans in their mutual efforts toward autonomy; returned to Buenos Aires because of illness; chosen, as eloquent orator, to make official address at anniversary of May Revolution, 1812; elected, October 1812, along with Juan José Paso and Nicolás Rodríguez Peña to form the Second Triumvirate; member of commission sent to establish order in Upper Peru (Bolivia) and served on board that reviewed disasters at Vilcapugio and Ayohuma and exonerated General Belgrano; exiled because of his activities in April 1815 uprising in Buenos Aires, Alvarez Jonte went to London where he quickly involved himself with those British statesmen and others interested in the independence of Argentina; supported financially by San Martín, he aided in creating the Chilean fleet that Lord Cochrane had agreed to command, and returned to Chile with Cochrane, 1818; gravely ill, he continued to discharge duties assigned him by San Martín, arousing the enmity of Lord Cochrane who resented his loyalty to San Martín and felt, also, that Alvarez Jonte's illness prevented his carrying out his responsibilities effectively;

embarked for Peru with San Martín liberating army, as auditor of the Army of the Andes, but died in Pisco; buried later in the Pantheon in Lima with honors by San Martín, who also placed his children under the guardianship of the government, with lifetime pensions.

ALVAREZ THOMAS, IGNACIO (1787-1857).   General, interim director of La Plata, diplomat.
       Born in Arequipa, Peru, son of the Spanish governor of that province, began military career in Buenos Aires in 1799; seriously wounded and captured in the fight against the British in Montevideo (1807) but freed and sent to London for medical care; back in Buenos Aires he offered his support to the May Revolution; April 3, 1815, on his way to confront the forces of Artigas, led revolt of officers against Director Alvear, forcing latter out of office; appointed interim director of the United Provinces (until Rondeau could assume post); convoked the congress of Tucumán to meet in 1816; forced to resign April 1816; considered to have been one of early representatives of national, rather than porteño, spirit; sent as minister plenipotentiary to Peru and Chile in mid-1820s, returning to Buenos Aires in 1827; spent most of Rosas period in residence and travel outside Argentina; left unpublished book of memoirs.

ALVEAR, CARLOS MARIA DE (1789-1852).   Public, military, diplomatic figure.
       Socially prominent and wealthy; passionate, eloquent, and personally talented and charming; courageous, with distinguished military record; Alvear's inordinate ambition to play effective role, both politically and militarily, in directing the nation's course and deciding its destinies constituted a force that had to be reckoned with, and could be counted on, from his return to Argentina in 1812 until his death.
       Born in Santo Angel, in eastern Misiones, October 25, 1789, son of Diego de Alvear, Spaniard, and María Josefa Balbastro, porteña; began military career as cadet in Buenos Aires, then in 1804 accompanied his family on tragic voyage to Spain (see Diego de Alvear); after fighting with distinction against Napoleonic forces in Spain, returned to Buenos Aires by way of England, sailing on the George Canning with San Martín, Zapiola, Chilavert, Baron de Holmberg and others; with San Martín offered his services to Triumvirate March 9, 1812; accepted, Alvear plunged into political and military activity; helped organize the powerful Logia Lautaro and eventually gained full control of it; promoted resolution of October 1812; became president of the Assembly of Year XIII, influential in the direction and actions taken (see Assembly of Year XIII); as commander of patriot forces received surrender of Montevideo from royalists (1814); balked by military uprisings in his attempt to replace Rondeau as commander of the Army of the North, he became Director of the government of Buenos Aires, instead; disillusioned by events from some of his earlier ideals, Alvear resorted to military

force to carry on his program and approached the British
seeking a protectorate; these and other unpopular acts
brought his overthrow and exile after less than four months
in office (April 1815); later returned, joining forces with
Chilean José Miguel Carrera and littoral caudillos Ramírez
and López in attempt to overthrow Buenos Aires government and establish federalism, with Alvear as governor of
Buenos Aires province; even after success at Cepeda (1820),
Alvear prevented from governorship by defeat by Dorrego,
backed by Rosas; after exile in Uruguay, served briefly as
minister to the United States during President Monroe's administration, then as minister to Bolivia; called back to be Rivadavia's minister of war and then placed in command of the
forces fighting against the Brazilian empire; won several victories, ending the war successfully with that of Ituzaingó
(1827); retired to private life for nearly nine years, then became minister plenipotentiary to the United States (1838) where
he represented the interests of Rosas' government, fighting
particularly hard, but unsuccessfully, to get support from President Polk for Argentina against the Anglo-French intervention;
died in New York in 1852; his remains transported with honors
to Buenos Aires in 1854 in ship commanded by Admiral Guillermo Brown.

See Thomas B. Davis in Suggested Readings, Appendix
III.

ALVEAR, DIEGO DE (1749-1830).   Career naval officer, royal official, author.

Born in Mantilla, Spain; educated to become royal officer and official; sailed with scientific expedition to India,
China, the Philippines, in 1771; accompanied Pedro de Cevallos' expedition to Río de la Plata, 1776; remained on duty
there for several years, marrying prominent porteña, Josefa
Balbastro, in 1782; appointed director of one division of the
boundary commission provided for by the Treaty of San Ildefonso, he left Buenos Aires late in 1783 to begin the difficult work
of establishing the boundary between Portuguese and Spanish
territory; assigned the eastern portion from the Atlantic to the
Uruguay River, he devoted several years made difficult by terrain and Indian hostility, to this task; reestablished his home
in Buenos Aires, then decided in 1804 to return to Spain;
armed squadron, in which he was sailing, was surprised off
Cádiz coast by British attack and forced to surrender; Alvear's
wife and seven children lost in the Mercedes, which burned and
sank; he and son Carlos, in another vessel, captured and taken
to London, where George III freed them and restored their
property; Diego de Alvear (with English wife by whom he later
had several children) returned to Spain where he was received
with high honors and resumed his career, culminating in his
appointment as brigadier; died in retirement in Madrid; author
of numerous works on Argentina largely based on his diary and
records as boundary commissioner, including his description
of the natural history of Misiones, Relación geográfica e his-

tórica de la provincia de Misiones, published by Pedro de
Ángelis in 1836.

ALVEAR, MARCELO TORCUATO DE (1868-1942).   President, 1922-
28, and Radical political leader.
     Born in Buenos Aires of aristocratic family (grandson
of Carlos María de Alvear); graduated in law, 1889, and took
part in Radical activities of that year and the next; spent several years traveling in Europe, returning to serve as Buenos
Aires deputy in congress, 1912-17; went back to France as
Yrigoyen's ambassador for five years, also representing Argentina in Geneva at the organization meetings of the League of
Nations; returned to Buenos Aires in 1922, having been elected
president as Yrigoyen's hand-picked choice as his successor;
his administration (1922-28) was marked by continued prosperity; a stronger orientation toward constitutional, rather than
personal government--resulting in a schism in the Radical
party (UCR), with Alvear leading the Anti-Personalists; Buenos
Aires beautified; strong cabinet gave able support; relatively
peaceful administration in spite of strikes, etc.; no great
changes made; in troubles that erupted during Yrigoyen's second term Alvear was exiled briefly, but after Yrigoyen's
death, became leader of the Radical party, twice again being
presented, unsuccessfully, as its candidate for the presidency;
strong supporter of Allies in World War II until his death in
1942.

ALZAGA, MARTIN DE (d. 1812).   Wealthy Basque merchant and
founder of prestigious landed family, leading cabildo member,
powerful public figure in events of 1807 to 1812 in Buenos
Aires; eventually tragic victim of them.   Within ten years after arriving in Buenos Aires as a twelve-year-old Basque boy,
Alzaga had learned Spanish and accumulated enough capital,
credit, and commercial success to move toward public life;
became member of cabildo in 1785, head alcalde ten years
later; first in consulado (1799) to voice the protests of peninsu-
lár merchants against the liberalized trading regulations demanded by creole hacendados, with viceregal support; 1806-
1807, joined with Liniers and Pueyrredón in defeating the British invasions, becoming the hero of Buenos Aires' successful
defense against General Whitelocke's forces (July 5, 1807);
as head of Buenos Aires cabildo, controlled events with little
opposition until Liniers received appointment as viceroy in
1808; Alzaga and cabildo resented Liniers' demand that viceregal powers be returned to him, with cabildo fulfilling its own
more limited functions; estrangement between Alzaga's group
and Liniers increased as Spaniards became suspicious of the
French Liniers' actions toward events in Spain; showdown in
power struggle came January 1809 when cabildo (probably at
Alzaga's suggestion) called for a cabildo abierto to force the
viceroy to resign and to form a junta government; Liniers
lacked force to resist but, in a dramatic last minute move,
Cornelio Saavedra, commander of the Patricios regiment, and

other creole officers placed their military forces and creole
public opinion behind Liniers; revolution disintegrated and
Alzaga and other leaders were deported to Patagonia for a
time; revolution had clearly drawn lines of power struggle between peninsulares and creoles and had produced a model with
which the successful Revolution of May 25, 1810 could be undertaken; Alzaga, emerging from private life in 1812, and his
Republic Party (for independence under peninsular control) determined to wrest control of the patriot government away from
the creole second Triumvirate; counting on the fact that Buenos Aires was practically without a garrison (troops having
been sent to the Army of the North) and that Princess Carlota
had promised to send men, arms, and supplies from Brazil,
in her hope of being crowned in the Plata area, and that other
forces were promised from Montevideo, the "Conspiracy of
Alzaga" (as it came to be known) was ready for action by July
1, 1812, with success apparently assured; by combination of
circumstances--Alzaga's sentimental desire to strike on July 5
(the anniversary of his glorious actions against the British),
the fact that the Portuguese forces had been persuaded by the
British to return to Brazil, and above all, the viceroy's discovery of the conspiracy--the revolution was aborted; the
leaders, including Alzaga, were captured, tried, executed, and
their bodies exhibited in the Plaza de la Victoria for three
days; among spectators was a fifteen-year-old boy who was
later to be accused of ruthless methods during his own rule--
Juan Manuel de Rosas.

ALZOGARAY, ALVARO JOSE DE (1811-1879). Naval and military
officer who began his career as a secretary under Admiral
Guillermo Brown in the war with Brazil (1826); continued to
hold positions of responsibility including the command of the
first steamship in the Argentine navy, La Merced, 1849.

AMADEO, MARIO (1911-   ). Leader of right-wing Catholic nationalist group in civil conspiracy against Perón; joined forces
with Lonardi and military to overthrow Perón, 1955; held
strong position in Lonardi's short-lived government; continued
as leader of rightist political Catholic group.

AMALIA. Romantic novel written by José Mármol while in exile;
an emotional novel of real historical value because it depicts
the passions and emotions as well as the customs of the Rosas
period; first part published in Montevideo 1851, completed
work published in 1855 when the author had returned to Buenos
Aires; translated into English by Mary Jane Serrano, N.Y.,
1919.

AMBAS AMERICAS. Illustrated journal published in New York,
1867-68, by Domingo Facundo Sarmiento, then Minister to the
United States; articles dealt with education, agriculture and
other practical and cultural matters that he thought would be
of interest to Spanish-speaking people; interested also in

counteracting U.S. sympathy for Paraguay in the Triple Alliance war.

AMBROSETTI, JUAN BAUTISTA (1865-1917). Archaeologist, ethnologist, folklorist, natural scientist.

Born in Gualeguay, Entre Ríos, educated in Buenos Aires; at age of twenty joined group of naturalists making field studies in the Chaco; published his observations under pseudonym Tomás Bathata; named director of the zoological section of provincial museum of Paraná; from then until his death, his professional career included writing, studying, directing research and teaching, representing Argentina in scientific congresses throughout the world (first to represent Argentina at Scientific Congress in New York, 1902); considered to be the founder of Argentine archaeological studies, as well as the first to study Argentine folklore on a scientific basis; among his important scholarly publications are Arqueología argentina (Buenos Aires, 1920) and Supersticiones y leyendas, in many editions.

AMEGHINO, CARLOS (1865-1936). Younger brother (and collaborator) of better-known Florentino Ameghino, and scientist in his own right; conducted extensive searches for fossils in the Chaco and northern area, then concentrated on Patagonia; left large collections of fossils and scholarly studies regarding them.

AMEGHINO, FLORENTINO (1854-1911). Born in Luján, largely self-educated; became one of Argentina's most creative and most widely known scientists, with the degree of Doctor honoris causa conferred by University of Córdoba; geologist and paleontologist, he was especially interested in probing the background of man in the pampas; best-known work, La antigüedad de hombre en el Plata.

ANADON, LORENZO (1855-1927). Public figure who performed variety of services. Born in Rosario Talla, Entre Ríos, educated in the river provinces, and with a doctorate in laws from the University of Córdoba; after career combining teaching and journalism, elected to legislative positions in both Córdoba and Santa Fe provinces, and as national senator from Santa Fe; became professor and dean of the new Faculty of Philosophy and Letters at the University of Buenos Aires; distinguished himself as member of the Argentine delegation to the Pan American Conference in Mexico, 1901; held directorships and other positions in various national banks and private corporations; served as minister to Chile 1905-13 and minister of finance under President Roque Saenz Peña; 1917, elected president of Central Junta of the Workers of the Republic; and in 1919 became president of Unión Popular Católica Argentina.

ANARCHY. Term sometimes used generally for periods of disorder and civil war during early decades of Argentine national life

but applied specifically and accurately to the "terrible year
1820" in which all semblance of government broke down, symbolized in the "day of three governors" (June 20, 1820) on
which three different governmental entities in Buenos Aires
were each appointed as governor, no one of which had legal
status or power enough to hold the position; civil war, begun
by provincial caudillos desiring a federal republic based on
democratic principles and opposing Buenos Aires elitism, sec-
recy and centralism in government (and apparent willingness
to establish monarchy under foreign prince), aided by ambitious political leaders opposing the directorate government for
their own purposes, succeeded in overthrowing the government
(see Cepeda), only to reveal the fact that there was no underlying political institutional framework left to take over; ten
years of Buenos Aires leadership had succeeded in destroying
much of the hated colonial political framework, but, accepting
the essential priority of winning independence, had not yet been
able to construct new structures; provinces, especially Buenos
Aires province, now turned attention to task of creating new
organic and viable institutions for every aspect of life within
each province; postponed until later was the difficult problem
of integrating these autonomous regional patterns into the national system of which they all inherently felt a part.

    Argentine intellectual José Manuel Estrada has charac-
terized the 1820 victory for democracy as "barbarous but fecund.   Fecund, I say, because it was an assertion of democracy as the immutable formula of our political being; barbarous because the social nucleus which produced it was barbarous, because its methods were barbarous, and the roads into
which it drove the people were bloody" (quoted in Ricardo Le-
vine, A History of Argentina, page 353).

ANCHORENA FAMILY.   Dating from late eighteenth century in Buenos Aires, name still stands for landed wealth and power;
founded by Spanish father Juan Esteban de Anchorena and criollo
mother Ramona Josefa de Anayo in the early days of the viceroyalty of La Plata; active in the consulado, the family quickly
began to amass a fortune based on commerce and cattle; members of family continued to be more interested in their own
participation in the economic development of Argentina than in
politics, but were ready to accept public responsibility when
needed: fiercely independent and attached to their own original
landbase, the province of Buenos Aires.

    Among prominent members are three brothers of the
first generation: 1.   Juan José Cristóbal Anchorena (1780-
1831), born in Buenos Aires but educated in Spain; returned to
devote himself primarily to commerce, but imprisoned briefly
by Lavalle as a follower of Dorrego; 2.   Tomás Manuel de
Anchorena (1783-1847), porteño, received doctorate from the
University of Charcas (Sucre), returned to play prominent role
in Cabildo of Buenos Aires until exiled for refusal to recognize
Regency government; accompanied Belgrano's army to Bolivia
as secretary; elected to Congress of Tucumán (1816) in which

he was noted as one of the most active members; signed the
Declaration of Independence; strongly supported federal system
of government as the one best suited to the Argentine political
realities; supported Rodríguez' government at first, but broke
with Rivadavia over latter's centralism; as follower of Dorrego, imprisoned by Lavalle; became strong adherent of political group supporting his relative Juan Manuel de Rosas; retired from public life, refusing to accept the provincial governorship offered him (1834), to devote himself to his financial interests: one of Argentine directors of bank founded with
British funds. 3. Nicolás de Anchorena (1785-1856), educated
at San Carlos in Buenos Aires, devoted himself to commerce
and cattle-raising but entered public life whenever his very
strong federalist convictions dictated such action; partisan of
Dorrego, he fled into exile when his two older brothers were
imprisoned by Lavalle; refused governorship of Buenos Aires
province twice (1834, after Tomás had refused it, and 1853);
supported Rosas with his money and his counsel; after Caseros
and the setting up of the Confederation, he urged the independence of Buenos Aires province, against Mitre's desire for an
eventually reunited Argentina; later served at the constitutional
convention of 1860 at which the 1853 constitution was modified
to suit the newly united nation.
    Later generations included such figures as the sons of
Tomás Manuel: 1. Tomás Severino de Anchorena (1827-1899)
selected by President Luis Sáenz Peña to act as Foreign Minister during the difficult time of tension with the British because of the Baring Crisis; and his son Tomás E. de Anchorena (1853-1916), medal graduate of the University of Buenos
Aires who devoted himself to improving the quality of his
herds, establishing at Lobos one of the most famous cattlebreeding ranches (cabañas) in Argentina; director of Sociedad
Rural Argentina and the Cooperativa de Hacendados. 2. Juan
de Anchorena (1829-1895) successfully increased his enormous
inherited fortune, importing better breeding cattle and sheep;
known as largest wool producer of the nation; greatly increased his landholdings.
    In the twentieth century Aaron Anchorena made his
mark as an early aeronaut; brought back from France a balloon (1200 cu. meters) which made a two-hour flight from Palermo (in Buenos Aires) to Colonia, Uruguay; a founder of
Aeroclub Argentino (1908).

ANDEAN AREA. May be considered Argentina's far west; includes
    Mendoza, San Juan, Catamarca, La Rioja, Salta, and Jujuy;
    petroleum, orchards and vineyards are main products; dry
    climate, semidesert soil, needs artificial irrigation; mild win-
    ters, hot summers, little rainfall. Mendoza is one of the
    most advanced provinces of the country.

ANDEAN RAILROAD. Railroad extending west from Buenos Aires;
    started in 1870s, and finally reached its goal, Santiago, in
    1910; service suspended for several years when section

washed away in 1934. Tunnel section used for motor vehicles
for period after 1940; returned to normal service in 1948.

ANDES, CROSSING OF THE. San Martín's successful crossing of
the Andes from his encampment in Mendoza to San Felipe in
Chile, to begin his continental plan of liberation with the winning of Chilean independence, was a dramatic military achievement in which Argentines still take legitimate pride (Juan D.
Perón, for example, deeply interested in military history submitted a paper on this subject to the Second International Congress of History of America in Buenos Aires, 1937); involved
in this feat were about 4000 soldiers, another 1400 militia
auxiliaries to aid in transport and supplies, 9000 mules and
1500 horses, 18 cannon, other artillery and munition supplies;
with planned precision the Army of the Andes moved into the
cordillera in mid-January 1817; small, diversionary units having already been dispatched by northern and southern passes,
on January 18, General Juan Gregorio de las Heras led his division of 800 men into the direct but difficult Uspallata pass
(more than 10,000 feet high); the following day the rest of the
main army, with San Martín in command of two divisions
headed by Miguel Estanislao Soler and Bernardo O'Higgins,
started through the somewhat longer but easier northern Paso
de los Patos; after eighteen days of braving and surviving the
difficulties and dangers of the terrain, the wild winds and
freezing nights, the soroche or puna (mountain sickness)
that attacked both men and beasts, the unexpected clashes with
royalist patrol forces, the two major sections of the army
came down the western slopes to their Chilean rendezvous exactly on schedule and with minimal losses, and on February
12, 1817, crushed the royalist forces at Chacabuco; as planned,
on that same day, Ramón Freire's small force, having successfully come through the Paso de Planchón, took possession
of Talca in the south; and in the north, Nicolás Dávila took
Copiapó, and Juan Manuel Cabot occupied Coquimbo. (See
Bartolomé Mitre and Leopoldo R. Ornstein in Suggested Readings, Appendix III, for further reading.)

ANDONAEGUI, JOSE DE (1685-1761). Colonial governor and military commander of Buenos Aires; during the thirteen years of
his administration, following appointment in 1745, Adonaegui
provided for the survey of the Patagonian coast by fathers Catriel and Quiroga; established stable government in Montevideo
and brought Indians of that area, as well as southern Argentine frontier, under control; faced with responsibility for carrying out the provisions of the treaty of 1750 between Spain and
Portugal, he was forced to subdue the Guaraní Indians who refused to accept cession to hated Brazilian slave-traders; Andonaegui fostered the development of the settlement at Luján,
raising its legal status to that of villa and building a bridge
across the Luján river to provide easier access between the
rural areas and the town; turned over his responsibilities to
Pedro de Ceballos and returned to Spain, died in Madrid, hav-

ing reached rank of lieutenant general; left numerous descendants in Buenos Aires.

ANDONAEGUI DE VALDEPARES, MARIA DE LA ENCARNACION (1769--after independence was won). Woman patriot of independence period who defied her royalist father and husband (executed for conspiracy in 1812) to use her home in Buenos Aires as a base from which to aid the cause of independence.

ANDREU, PEDRO JUAN (1697-?). Jesuit missionary; educator and administrator.
        Born in Palma, Majorca; received his doctorate in theology and canon law; determined to become a missionary to the uncivilized Indians, he arrived in Buenos Aires in 1734, completed his novitiate in Córdoba, and was ordained in Buenos Aires; by 1737 he was working with the Lules of Tucumán and among the hostile Indians of the Chaco; his work met with some success but he was often harassed by the hostile Indians of the area; in 1761 he became the Jesuit Provincial of Paraguay and continued to send missionaries into the Chaco area; when the Jesuit expulsion order came in 1767, it found him serving as rector of the Colegio Máximo de Córdoba de Tucumán; Father Andreu reached Italy where he died.

ANDREWS, JOSEPH. British merchant who visited South America in 1818, sold the Windham, of which he was owner and captain, to become the Lautaro of the Chilean navy; returned to Buenos Aires (from London) in 1825 on business trip for Chilean and Peruvian Mining Association, in which he was a stockholder; spent months traveling through interior into the mining areas and published a full account of his observations, notable for keen observation of detail and for understanding of social customs and life styles on every level: Journey from Buenos Ayres Through the Provinces of Cordova, Tucumán, and Salta to Potosí (2 vols., London, 1827); Spanish translation by Carlos A. Aldao, Viaje de Buenos Aires a Potosí y Arica (Buenos Aires, 1920).

ANGACO. Victory won by Mariano Acha over José Félix Aldao in the civil wars of Cuyo, mid-August 1841; Acha, on his way from San Juan to unite his force with that of Gregorio A. de La Madrid, was confronted by a much larger force under Governor Aldao; bloody fighting lasting one whole day resulted in defeat of Aldao; battle remembered historically as heroic feat, but results were nullified by Acha's defeat and death at the hands of Aldao's allies a few days later.

ANGELIS, PEDRO DE (1784-1859). Italian intellectual who met Bernardino Rivadavia in Paris and was persuaded to return with him to Buenos Aires to aid in developing its cultural life; became co-editor with J. J. Mora of La crónica política y literaria de Buenos Aires; a man of great prestige in the literary and intellectual world, he served Rivadavia's government

well, continuing to do the same for his successors, being remembered as almost the only intellectual to support Rosas;
wrote many historical essays and his Colección de obras y
documentos relativos a la historia antigua y moderna de las
provincias del Río de La Plata (5 vols., Buenos Aires, 1910)
is a valuable contribution to the study of Argentine history.
A new, more complete edition, with prologue and notes by
Andrés de Carretero, appeared several decades later, with the
final volume 8 (in two parts) being published by Editorial Plus
Ultra, in Buenos Aires in 1972.

ANGOLA. Black nación or mutual aid society formed in Buenos
Aires and named for country of origin of most of its members (see Naciones).

ANTARCTIC ARGENTINA (Antártida Argentina). Argentina claims
an Antarctic wedge of territory extending from the 60° S.
parallel to the South Pole between meridians 25° and 74°
west; incorporated this into the newly created territory of Tierra del Fuego (q.v.); Argentina's claims, based primarily on
its proximity and prior exercise of sovereignty de derecho y
hecho (in law and in fact) over this area, as well as inherited
Spanish claims, are disputed by Chile (with similar basis for
its overlapping claims) and by Great Britain, which claims the
entire area on grounds of discovery, formal filing of claims,
and the establishment of local administration, much of it governed as Falkland Islands Dependencies; all three nations have
established bases and meteorological stations in the area; Argentine claims are legally tied in with its claim to the Falkland Islands but legally separate from it; Antarctica offers
limited possibilities for settlement but is important strategically (especially for air travel) and for scientific observations;
holds promise of exploitable mineral wealth; Argentina's interest, strongly reinforced by considerations of national pride
and security, has persistently pressed its claims, with increasing vigor since the late 1940s, Perón's government demanding U.S. and OAS hemispheric backing of its position;
when Great Britain presented the case to the International
Court at The Hague, 1955, Argentina refused to recognize the
court's jurisdiction; finally, December 1, 1959, in Washington,
D.C., Argentina joined with eleven other interested nations
(including Great Britain, Chile, and the United States) in signing a thirty-year Antarctic Treaty (including the Falkland Dependencies, but not the Falkland Islands) that agreed to: 1)
suspend all territorial claims and disputes; 2) guarantee free
use of whole continent for scientific research; and 3) set up
an inspection system to prevent military activities in violation
of treaty.

ANTIPERSONALISTA. Name commonly used for schismatic group
of Radical party; formed in 1918 and generally acknowledged
Marcelo T. Alvear (q.v.) as its leader; Antipersonalistas
were determined to avoid political conflicts based primarily

on personal differences of leaders; they emphasized party programs of action rather than personalities of leaders; in contrast to Irigoyenist left-wing radicals, Antipersonalistas were
tied in with the international economy and shared many of the
social and economic ideas of the oligarchy, although somewhat
more given to reform than most of the latter; they were especially active and influential during the 1920s and 1930s (see
Political Parties).

ANTI-SEMITISM   see   JEWS

ANTULA, SOR   see   PAZ Y FIGUEROA, MARIA ANTONIA DE LA

ANUARIO DE HISTORIA ARGENTINA. Begun in 1939 as official organ of the Sociedad de Historia Argentina; contains interesting
original historical studies, including those on La diplomacia de
Belgrano en Paraguay; Orígenes del correo; Temas de historia
jurídica; Brown-Cochrane; La conferencia de Guayaquil; El
nacionalismo de Rosas; El cabildo.

ANZOATEGUI, CIRO (1845-1915). Called by Carlos S. Cornejo "the
popular gaucho of the North"; a salteño who made a career of
typifying the gaucho, his life, and culture; collected anecdotes
and information about them; rode on horseback, with a company of horsemen, from Tucumán, Salta, Jujuy, Catamarca,
and La Rioja to Buenos Aires to represent officially the gaucho
spirit of Argentina at the Centennial of the May Revolution.

ARAMBURU, PEDRO EUGENIO (1903-1970). Army general; provisional president, 1955-58.
        Loyal military supporter of Perón's government until he
joined conspiracy led by General Eduardo Lonardi and Mario
Amadeo to overthrow Perón in October, 1955; then, in November, led move to replace Lonardi, who was considered too len-
ient with Peronistas, with junta government; Aramburu, as
provisional president, determined to de-Peronize government,
economy, and society; restored constitution without Perón
amendments; maintained order, brought businessmen into government instead of labor; returned La Prensa to owners; improved economy but large balance of trade deficit created;
Aramburu belonged to increasingly large number of military
officers who wanted more civil, less military, government;
turned government over to elected president Arturo Frondizi in
1958; kidnapped and murdered by Peronist guerrillas, 1970, in
what latter called an act of justice for the summary trial and
execution of military leaders of revolt of 1956.

ARANA, FELIPE (1786-1865). Foreign minister in Rosas' government 1835-52.
        Born in Buenos Aires of prominent merchant-landholding
family; received law degree in Chile; returned to Buenos Aires
in time to join the patriotic group in Cabildo Abierto of May
1810; continued in public service while practicing his profession

until his retirement following the fall of Rosas, 1852.

As minister of foreign affairs following Rosas' return to office in 1835, Arana served his country well by his stubborn insistence on Argentine sovereignty combined with skill in negotiating agreements; the Arana-Mackau treaty, 1840, ended the first French intervention on terms considered favorable to Argentina, and the Arana-Le Predeur agreement brought the second French blockade to an end along with the question of Rosas' intervention in Uruguay; unsuccessful in his earlier demands for reparations regarding U.S. actions and incidents in the Falkland Islands, Arana finally succeeded in establishing friendly working relations with the United States, including agreement about the opening of the Plata river system after Paraguay came under the freer control of Carlos Antonio López.

Due to the fact that internal preoccupations had resulted in foreign relations being somewhat neglected during the two decades preceding Arana's accession, his work is regarded as very important and his collected papers serve as a valuable source for the study of this period.

ARANA-MACKAU, TREATY OF.   Treaty ending the first French intervention, signed October 29, 1840, by Felipe Arana, for Rosas' government, and Baron Mackau (Vice Admiral Angel Armando de Mackau) for France; ratified shortly afterward by both nations; provisions: Argentina to pay indemnities (to be decided by joint commission) to French subjects for losses or injuries due to actions of Rosas' government; France to lift blockade and to return Martín García Island and captured Argentine naval vessels; exiles to be permitted to return to Argentina, with amnesty, if they agreed not to oppose Rosas-- generals not included in amnesty, except for General Juan Lavalle who had been supported and supplied by the French and was now protected by them; neutrality with regard to Uruguayan internal affairs agreed.

Although both Rosas and France claimed treaty to be a victory, it failed somewhat in its purpose; Lavalle refused to accept it; unitarists denounced it; and Argentine involvement with Uruguay continued for another decade.

ARAOZ FAMILY of Tucumán (and Salta).   Prominent Tucumán family dating back to colonial period; has contributed independence heroes, public officials, ecclesiastics, educators, and men of medicine and science to Argentine public life; among them: Bernabé Aráoz (1782-1824) supported the May Revolution and organized the Tucumán militia to accompany Belgrano's army to the North; fought in battles of Tucumán (1812) and Salta; became governor of Salta, then (1814) appointed governor of the newly created province of Tucumán; ousted temporarily by political rivals, he seized possession of the government, November 1819; proclaimed himself supreme president of the autonomous republic of Tucumán (1820); called congress to meet; but in civil wars that followed, he was overthrown and

executed, 1824; his brother, J. Miguel Francisco de Aráoz
(1785-?) had also fought with Belgrano, held various public
offices in Tucumán and Salta, and served as official in Bernabé's government. Pedro Miguel Aráoz (1759-1832), ecclesiastic with theology doctorate from Córdoba, was delegate to
the Congress of Tucumán and signer of the Declaration of Independence (July 9, 1816); member of Congress called by his
cousin Bernabé and supporter of the latter; founder of El
Telégrafo Imparcial, first newspaper in Tucumán (1820), in
which he campaigned vigorously for free public education.
Lucía Aráoz (d. 1862) affectionately remembered in provincial
legend as the belle ("La Rubia de la Patria") of the ball held
in Tucumán to celebrate the signing of the national Declaration
of Independence and honored for her life of dedication to public service and charities; married Francisco Javier López
Molina, enemy of Aráoz government in early 1820s. Diego
Aráoz (b. 1785) supported the May Revolution and fought with
Belgrano's army, being promoted to lieutenant colonel; opposed vigorously the seizure of Tucumán government by his
cousin Bernabé. Miguel Moisés Aráoz (1823-1883) ecclesiastic;
consecrated as bishop of Berissa (1872); became auxiliary bishop in Salta. Benjamin Aráoz (1856-1895) journalist who used
pen name of Argos; physician who became surgeon, first of
navy, then of army, also in the expeditions of 1878-80 into
the Río Negro and southern Patagonian areas; died while serving as governor of Tucumán. Guillermo Aráoz (1843-1914)
organized Tucumán's public archives; made topographical field
studies of the Salado and Bermejo rivers, reporting especially
on their more effective use for river transportation in national
development. José S. Aráoz (1829-1886) was born in Tucumán
but moved to Salta where his uncle, Bishop of Berissa, Miguel Moisés Aráoz, was living; divided his attentions as provincial administrative official between the organization of Salta
provincial archives and public health duties; published several
reports on public sanitation, including a full description of the
dreaded cholera, and ways and means of avoiding or treating
it (1867); commissioned in 1880 to compile a financial history
of the province from the documents in the archives, Aráoz was
still working on this project in 1886 when a cholera epidemic
attacked Salta; fleeing from it to Tucumán, taking with him the
major portion of the public archives, to save them from the
fires in cholera areas, he himself died of cholera and most of
the documents were lost or destroyed. Ricardo Aráoz (1865-
1950) fought this same 1886-87 cholera epidemic in Salta as a
young medical student and returned to the university in Buenos
Aires to write his doctoral thesis on it; spent most of his life
practicing medical profession and directing public health projects in Salta. José Luis Aráoz (1874-1945), after gaining
medical degree, thesis on mental health problems, 1899, returned to Tucumán to devote himself to teaching, public service, and medical research; co-discoverer of intestinal para-
site "la filaria tucumana." Miguel Aráoz Sola (1858-1896),
older brother of Ricardo Aráoz, engineer, active in railroad

construction; organized company to promote gold mining operations in Jujuy; father of Dr. Ernesto M. Aráoz, governor of
Salta (1942-43).

ARAUCANIANS. Originally Chilean Indians, farmers and herders of
llamas (replaced after the conquest by Spanish animals), living
between Bío Bío River and Valdivia area; called themselves
Mapuche ("people of the land"); shared much of the Central
Andean culture but fiercely prevented conquest by Incas or integration into their empire; offered same intransigent opposition to Spanish conquistadors in Chile; gradually, however,
Spanish pressures and changes in settlement and labor patterns
combined with economic opportunities offered by wild cattle and
horses on the Argentine pampas to bring thousands of Araucanians through the Andean passes to occupy the grasslands and
then spread southward; by eighteenth century, southern Mendoza, Neuquén, and Buenos Aires provinces largely filled with
Araucanians or with pampas Indians who had accepted Araucanian culture and way of life; no longer farmers but cattlemen
and horse traders, they posed a continuing threat, from viceregal times on, to estancias and frontier settlements by their
sudden, successful, violent raids, driving off herds of cattle
or horses, often to Chilean markets; securing the frontier
against them became essential; finally accomplished by the military campaign of 1879-80 (the "Conquest of the Desert") in
which Julio A. Roca, minister of war, destroyed the Araucanian settlements on the Río Negro and dispersed the inhabitants.

ARAUJO, JOSE JOAQUIN (1762-1835). Treasury official of the
viceroyalty in Buenos Aires. Deeply interested in Argentine
history; 1803, edited a Guía de forasteros del virreinato de
Buenos Aires, showing a vast knowledge of the political, military, and ecclesiastical history of the country, based on thorough research in public and private archives. Possessed a
magnificent library. Died just as he was preparing the second
edition of his Guía for publication.

ARBITRIOS. The two resources that the cabildos had for appropri-
ating funds for their expenses were propios (q. v.) and arbitrios. Latter were special purpose taxes, imposed at will or
necessity of the cabildo for such emergencies as equipping an
expedition against the Indians or financing the construction of
a public building. Eventually, however, they took on an almost permanent character and the administrative reforms of
Charles III attempted to suppress them. Innumerable examples
exist of their continued imposition by Argentine cabildos until
they themselves were suppressed.

ARCHEOLOGY. In contrast to the full development of archeology in
Europe, the study of archeology in Argentina has confined itself primarily to a study of indigenous peoples. Its beginnings
in the 19th century were in the hands of foreign and Argentine
scientists--naturalists, at first, among the most important be-

ing Florentino Ameghino and Francisco P. Moreno. Juan B. Ambrosetti, Entre Ríos, is considered to be the father of Argentine archeology, properly speaking.

ARCHIVO AMERICANO, EL. Periodical subsidized by Rosas, designed to give information about the political, moral, and economic situation of the Argentine Confederation; published in Spanish, English, and French; published in two series, of thirty-two and twenty-nine issues; second series, begun in March 1847, ended December 24, 1851.

ARCHIVO GENERAL DE LA NACION. Created by Rivadavia in 1821, while minister in Rodríguez' government of province of Buenos Aires, to bring together all the various archives of the capital, including those of the cabildo; first director, Francisco de Paul Saubidet; after federalization of Buenos Aires in 1880, joint commission of the nation and Buenos Aires province placed archives under national control, with its present name (1884); important function of the Archivo has been extensive scholarly publication program based on its materials.

ARCHIVO HISTORICO DE LA PROVINCIA DE BUENOS AIRES. Created during the governorship of José Luis Cantilo, 1925, under the directorship of Ricardo Levene, this archivo has become one of the most important historical centers in the country, not only because of its important collection of material but also because of the fine editorial policy of publication of collections, monographs and special studies.

ARDILES, MIGUEL DE (1515-1586). Early conquistador of Tucumán; lieutenant governor, 1556-1557. Ardiles accompanied Diego de Rojas in expedition that discovered Tucumán and, with Francisco de Mendoza, reached the Paraná in 1545; returned to Peru, fighting against Gonzalo Pizarro in the civil wars; coming back to Tucumán with the expedition of Juan Núñez de Prado, Ardiles was present at the founding of Barco II in the valley of the Calchaquí and at that of Barco III among the Juríes; he left descriptions of the sufferings endured by the settlers from hunger, cold, and other deprivations, as well as from the Indian attacks on both towns; he also aided in the establishment of Santiago del Estero (1553) and served as member of its cabildo for several years; later he assisted in the founding of San Miguel de Tucumán, 1565, and in that of Salta, 1582; Ardiles seems to have died around 1586; his son, also Miguel de Ardiles (1547-1603), inherited his father's ability as well as his estate and became equally important as conquistador, government official, and encomendero; in the seventeenth century the grandson and son, Miguel de Ardiles, continued the family tradition of public service and leadership in Córdoba, his native city.

ARENALES, JOSE ILDEFONSO ALVAREZ DE (1798-1862). Military engineer; author of historical and topographical studies.

Born in province of Cochabama (Bolivia), son of General Arenales; brought up in Salta where his mother's family lived; completed military education as engineer and artilleryman in Buenos Aires and became San Martín's ayudante major in Army of the Andes; in Peru, served as artillery commander under his father; returned to Salta with him from Peru; continued his own military career, leading Salta forces to Buenos Aires for Brazilian war, fighting against Santa Cruz in Bolivia; more and more hampered by deafness, which became complete, he refused to accept the generalship offered him after Caseros; devoted himself to topographical studies, president of the Topographical Department, 1834-1852; and historical works, such as his Segunda campaña a las Sierras del Perú en 1821, published in 1832, in which he meticulously detailed the operations (in which he had participated) and refuted other writings about the campaign--notably, those of General Miller; as his political life was nonpartisan, he managed to live peacefully during the Rosas period, commanding respect, and honored by scientific organizations.

ARENALES, JUAN ANTONIO ALVAREZ DE (1770-1831). Military hero of war of independence; governor of Salta.

Born in Spain, educated by relatives to become a priest, chose military career instead; came to Buenos Aires as member of the garrison, 1784; after completing his military studies, transferred as lieutenant colonel to Bolivian area; became champion of Indians against government oppression and mistreatment; joined patriots in Chuquisaca revolutionary rebellion, May 25, 1809, becoming commander of patriot forces; movement put down by royalist forces under Goyeneche, Arenales saved from execution by previous distinguished record, sent as prisoner to Callao dungeons; escaped and returned to his home in Salta, espoused the Buenos Aires Revolution, assisted Belgrano brilliantly in defeat of royalists at Salta (February 20, 1813), and requested that the Assembly (Year XIII) issue him a letter making him a citizen of the United Provinces of the Río de la Plata; appointed governor of Chuquisaca, found himself isolated by patriot defeats of Vilcapugio and Ayohuma; organized guerrilla warfare, so successfully that Pezuela was forced to abandon northern provinces of Argentina to protect royalist rearguard; Arenales reoccupied Chuquisaca, then joined Rondeau's forces in third attempt to take over Alto Perú (Bolivia) for revolution; after defeat at Sipe Sipe, Arenales led retreat to Tucumán, where he remained until civil war broke out; then crossed Andes into Chile where San Martín was preparing Liberating Expedition into Peru; Arenales welcomed by San Martín and made division commander; after arrival in Peru was placed in command of two important campaigns into the sierra to gain control of that area before royalists could use it as a base of operations; won several victories but unable to complete missions with full success; in April, 1821, after Peruvian independence had been declared, Arenales became governor of northern

province of Peru with responsibility for training forces and
preparing for the Ecuadorian campaign; following San Martín's
departure from Peru in 1822, Arenales requested retirement;
granted by Peruvian government, with rank of Grand Marshal;
became governor of Salta, 1823, where he attempted to establish liberal government like that of Rivadavia in Buenos Aires;
sent troops to aid in war against Brazil; 1827, revolt led by
José Gorriti deposed Arenales who moved to Bolivia, where
he died December 4, 1831.

AREQUITO, REVOLT OF. Revolt, January 8, 1820, of major portion of Army of the North, that marked the beginning of the
end of the national government; in response to Supreme Director Rondeau's command, Army of the North moved toward
Buenos Aires to strengthen Rondeau against actions of the littoral caudillos; at the post of Arequito, approaching province
of Córdoba, the widespread revulsion against the fratricidal
war in which they were involved, expressed itself in the revolt of more than half the army, led by General Juan Bautista
Bustos, seconded by Colonel Alejandro Heredia and Commandant José María Paz; to avoid bloodshed, almost certainly futile, the commanding general, Francisco Fernández Cruz, continued on to Buenos Aires with remnant of army; Bustos returned to city of Córdoba, his native town, where he soon became governor of the province; purpose of the revolt was to
make Córdoba a power base from which peace could be established throughout the provinces; Bustos believed his action
would neutralize forces of caudillos, as well as that of Rondeau; provinces of interior supported Revolt of Arequito and,
like Córdoba, declared their political relations with Buenos
Aires dissolved (see Juan Bautista Bustos and Córdoba).

ARGENTINA. The name by which La República Argentina is commonly known has had a long and varied history. Among the
various names given to the estuary discovered by Solís, that
of Río de la Plata has prevailed. The river was believed to
open the way most easily to the Sierra de la Plata, reputed
(and later found) to be in Alto Perú. The term "Argentina"
(from the Latin argentum for silver) was early used as a
synonym for the Spanish la Plata in referring to this area
(Upper Peru or one of the Silver Cities there). Apparently it
was first applied in print to its present area in a poem, written by the Arcediano Martín del Barco Centenera, with the
title Argentina y conquista del Río de la Plata, con otros
acaecimientos de los Reinos del Perú, Tucumán y Estado del
Brasil, published in Lisbon (1602). (Prior claims for Ruy
Díaz de Guzmán's use of the term in his chronicle of the Conquest seem to lack validity as its use in the title only appears
in later, not the original, period.)

        "Argentina," almost always used as an adjective substi-
tute for rioplatense, continued to grow throughout the colonial
period and became very popular in the late colonial and early
independence period coming to be applied only to what is now

Argentina and meaning "American" or "criollo." Increasing
pressure for its official use in the new nation appeared in official debates and literature, including the national hymn by
Vicente López, and it finally appeared in the Constitution of
1826 as the República Argentina (of which Rivadavia became
president). The term Nación Argentina also appeared for the
next few decades; however, various names were used as the
official name of the nation.

Finally, after Urquiza and the Constitution of 1853 had
used the title Confederación Argentina and the two Argentine
nations united, in 1860, by decree Derqui said that only República Argentina should be used to avoid confusion. Apparently, however, Nación Argentina also continued to be used
according to the Constitution for sanction of laws.

See Angel Rosenblatt, Argentina, historia de un nombre;
or Academia Nacional de la Historia, Los nombres que usó
oficialmente la República Argentina (Buenos Aires, 1951).

ARGENTINA, LA. Famous frigate, formerly La Consecuencia,
commanded by Hipólito Bouchard; with his ship armed as
privateer with 42 cannons, crew of 450, provisions for six
months, Bouchard sailed from Buenos Aires, July 9, 1817,
with letters of patent from Director Pueyrredón and instructions to sail east across the Atlantic to intercept Spanish shipping on way to Philippines; two years later, after incredible
adventures in Africa, the Philippines, Hawaii--where he recovered the Argentine corsair Santa Rosa de Chacabuco from
a crew that had mutinied, with aid from King Kamehaha I--
and an attack on the Spanish capital of Monterey, in California,
he arrived in Chile, only to become involved in trouble with
Lord Cochrane (q. v.); under its old name of La Consecuencia,
however, the frigate was taken into the fleet of the Liberating
Expedition and had the honor of transporting the Granaderos a
Caballo to Peru, 1820.

ARGENTINE ACTION. Moderate political group that attempted to
find an Argentine middle ground between radicals and militar-
ists of the right, 1940-1943; it hoped to form an inter-party
coalition for the defense of democracy in Argentina; adopted a
program combining nationalism with economic and social reform; this called for social justice, land reform, development
of mineral resources, industrialization, economic independence,
and an intermediate position between free enterprise and a
controlled economy; the movement failed to gain adequate support from either civilian or military groups and was proscribed in 1943 by the new military government as "pro-com-
munist," but many of its proposals appeared later, in slightly
different form, in Perón's program of political action and social and economic reform.

ARGENTINE CIVIC LEGION see LEGION CIVICA ARGENTINA

ARGENTINE CONFEDERATION see CONFEDERACION ARGENTINA

ARGENTINE MESOPOTAMIA see MESOPOTAMIA, ARGENTINE

ARGERICH, COSME (1756-1820). Physician and surgeon; born in
Buenos Aires, educated in Spain, returned to practice medicine
in his home country; introduced free vaccinations against
smallpox in Buenos Aires (1805); served as military surgeon
for the second squadron of Hussars against the English Invasions; participated in Cabildo Abierto that proclaimed the May
Revolution; accompanied the expeditionary army to Upper Peru
as surgeon; returned to Buenos Aires because of poor health;
spent remaining years teaching and practicing medicine, as director of the Medical Institute.

ARGERICH, FRANCISCO COSME (1784-1846). Distinguished medical
figure; born in Barcelona, son of porteño father Cosme Argerich, then studying medicine in Barcelona; reared and educated
in Buenos Aires at San Carlos and later at the University of
Buenos Aires, served in the hospitals at the time of the English Invasions; sent to aid San Martín's wounded men after the
battle of San Lorenzo (1813); at San Martín's request, served
as medical officer in the Army of Upper Peru until 1816, returned to Buenos Aires and secured his medical degree from
the newly established university. Continued active in public
and professional life until forced into exile during Rosas' period; died in Montevideo.

ARGERICH, JUAN ANTONIO (1788-1848). Porteño military hero
from British Invasions until he resigned, as colonel in 1828,
at death of his wife; entered the church; served with distinction.

ARGERICH, LUIS (1791-1839). Porteño military hero 1810-1839;
brother of Juan Antonio; author of Reglamento del Parque de
Artillería, published in La Gaceta Mercantil, October 29-No-
vember 18, 1834.

ARGIROPOLIS. Work published by D. F. Sarmiento in 1850--title
signifying "City of Silver." Anticipating Rosas' fall, Sarmiento
drew up plans for the new nation, to be called the United
States of the Río de la Plata, to include Argentina, Uruguay,
and Paraguay; with a new capital city (like Washington, D.C.)
to be built on the island of Martín García; important features
of new government: free navigation of rivers and strong encouragement of immigration. Condemned as utopian by Alberdi and others, Argirópolis nevertheless played important
role in formation of the political ideas of Urquiza and others.

ARGOS DE BUENOS AIRES, EL. Periodical designed to provide
serious information and news items; two periods of operations:
34 issues, May 12-November 24, 1821; reorganized by Sociedad Literaria de Buenos Aires, January 19-November 30,
1825, 211 issues, editors: Manuel Moreno, Ignacio Núñez,
Gregorio Funes, and Domingo Olivera; with literary counterpart

La Abeja and contemporary El Ambigú, depicts Rivadavia period clearly.

ARGÜELLO, JOSE ANTONIO (d. 1849).   Córdoban captain of the
patricios, member of Las Heras' division of the Army of the
Andes; returned to Córdoba from Chile to follow Bustos; exiled as unitarist during Rosas' period; died in Chile.

ARGUIBEL, ANDRES (1773-c. 1826).   Born in Buenos Aires, found
himself in Spain at outbreak of the fight for independence; unable to return, devoted his energies to providing Argentine
patriot leaders with information regarding government actions
in Spain; returning to Buenos Aires in 1825, he was eulogized
in La Gaceta Mercantil for his efforts, honored by his native
province, and elected to the Congreso General shortly before
his death.

ARIAS, AMARO LEONCIO, General (1849-1905).   Porteño career
military figure; served in major actions of Paraguayan war;
in national army action against General R. López Jordán;
acted as federal interventor in provinces of Catamarca and of
Entre Ríos (1891); commanded national forces in Santiago del
Estero and later in the province of Buenos Aires in the intervention overthrowing Governor Costa; held other posts of military and political responsibility.

ARIAS, FRANCISCO GABINO (1732-1808).   Salteño explorer of the
north and northwestern regions of the viceroyalty of the Río
de la Plata, sometimes accompanied by the Buenos Aires merchant Matorras.   Wrote a full account of his expeditions into
the Gran Chaco but was unable to publish it and manuscript
has not been found.

ARIAS, JOSE INOCENCIO, General (1846-1912)   Porteño career
military figure and public official: took part in more than 100
combats, including Paraguayan war, action stamping out the
rebellion of General López Jordán in Entre Ríos, forcing the
surrender of General Mitre at La Verde after his revolution in
1874.   Repeatedly called back from retirement for both military and political responsibilities, he died while serving as
governor of his native province of Buenos Aires.

ARIAS, MANUEL EDUARDO (d. 1823).   Gaucho commandant who
won distinction resisting royalist invasions on the northern
frontier.   Born in Jujuy, son of Francisco Arias and an Indian of Humahuaca, known as "la Coya," his entire life was
spent in the concerns of his provinces; one of Güemes' most
effective fighters in the war for independence; he later quarreled with him; returning to Jujuy, Arias lost his life while
supporting the governor, Colonel Agustín Dávila, against a
conspiracy that succeeded in overthrowing him.

ARIAS, MARIA BENITA (1822-1894).   Córdoba-born founder of the

new Argentine teaching and nursing order of nuns named the
Siervas de Jesús Sacramentado (1872).

ARIAS, TOMAS (1804-1863). Salteño merchant and public figure;
first constitutional governor of Salta after the fall of Rosas.

ARIAS, VICTOR J. (1888-1925). Salteño engineer and intellectual
who devoted his life to a study of the colonial art of his region and to archeological and ethnological studies of the indigenous inhabitants of that area; largely responsible for the
building ordinance that preserved colonial style in the architecture of modern Salta; enthusiastic collector of Salteño antiquities and discoverer of the culture of Candelaria, later to
be studied in detail by Alfred Metraux.

ARIAS CORNEJO, JOSE MANUEL (1817-1888). Salteño jurisconsult,
public official, teacher, and historian. After receiving his
doctorate in laws from the University of Chuquisaca, he returned to take an active part in almost every phase of life in
his native province; served as minister general (prime minister) for several of the governors; promoted the establishment
of a public library and a new building for the Colegio Nacional; served as federal judge in Salta; concerned himself in his
legal practice, and in writing, with the relationship between
public and ecclesiastical law; deeply interested in the history
of the northern region of Argentina, he dedicated himself to
the gathering of materials, research, and historical writing:
as a result of his efforts, materials relating to the founding
of Salta were sent to the historian Dr. Vicente G. Quesada,
who published them in the Revista del Paraná as well as the
Revista de Buenos Aires.

ARIAS DE SAAVEDRA, HERNANDO (1561-1634)--also known as
Hernandarias. First creole governor in the Río de la Plata
area.
          Born in Asunción of Spanish parents, he devoted al-
most his entire career to public life; served under Gonzalo
de Abreu, governor of Tucumán; then assisted Juan Torres de
Vera y Aragón in the founding of Corrientes (1588); appointed
lieutenant governor in Asunción, 1592, and then served three
times as governor of the Río de la Plata area: 1597-98,
1602-1609, 1614-1620; known as the "first patriot of La
Plata" for his achievements and statesmanship; pacified the
Indians; maintained order within the communities; established
in Buenos Aires the first public school; fostered agriculture;
explored Patagonia to the Colorado and Negro rivers, searching for the legendary City of the Caesars (1604); tried to promote the settlement of this area, to hold it from the Indians
and to prevent the Dutch--sailing in those waters--from taking it over, but found no support either in Buenos Aires or
Spain; urged that settlements also be made in Uruguay and
farther north toward Brazil but lack of interest and resources prevented this; attempted, with some success, to

break up the smuggling trade at La Plata ports; was instru-
mental in getting the Plata area divided into two jurisdictions,
with governors in both Asunción and Buenos Aires, the Jesuits established in missions among the Guaraní Indians in the
Guayrá area, and Buenos Aires established as a bishopric.

ARIAS DE VELAZQUEZ, PEDRO ANTONIO DE (1772-1834). Salteño
colonial intellectual and bibliophile, public official, precursor
and consistent supporter of independence movements. With
degrees from both the University of Córdoba and that of San
Marcos in Lima, he was named asesor (advisor, assessor) of
the Real Tribunal del Consulado of Lima, 1798; later resigned
and was called back to Salta by family affairs; from 1808 on,
active in plans and plots for independence. Totally disagreeing with Miranda's secularistic ideas, his patriotic lodges, his
reliance on England for support, Arias de Velázquez carried
on secret correspondence with the Bolivian revolutionary leaders including Dr. Mariano Michel and Lic. Pedro Domingo
Murillo. He supported the Revolution of May enthusiastically
and was influential in setting up Salta's new revolutionary government. At first a supporter of Güemes, differences between
them resulted in Arias' exile. In 1831 he joined in the fight
against Juan Facundo Quiroga. At his death left fine library.

ARIAS RENGELL HIDALGO, JOSE ANTONIO (1744-1787). Colonial
historian and public official.
        Born in Lerma, Tucumán; educated in Chuquisaca for
life of intellectual; returned to Salta de Tucumán to take up
public responsibilities and to devote himself to historical studies of his province; the first to study northern Argentine history; became involved in the expeditions into the Chaco and
wrote Información sobre el estado de las nuevas conquista del
Chaco (1780); Descripción de la Provincia del Gran Chaco
Gualamba (1781); and Crónica de la expedición al Chaco (1781);
manuscripts published nearly a century later by Pedro de
Angelis and Manuel Ricardo Trelles; moving to Córdoba as
royal treasury official, he completed his editing of the famous
Diario del Coronel José Gabino Arias sobre la expedición al
Gran Chaco, published by Pedro de Angelis in his Colección
de obras y documentos.

ARLEQUIN. Humorous, illustrated weekly periodical that appeared
in 1899, May-July, for twelve issues.

ARMAS BLANCAS, FABRICA PATRIOTA DE. Factory established
(1813) in Caroya, Córdoba, under direction of Manuel Rivera,
to manufacture sabers of excellent quality for the Mounted
Grenadiers and other weapons needed by the independence
forces.

ARMISTICE BETWEEN OLAÑETA AND SALTA. This armistice,
signed between Olañeta, commander of the vanguard of royalist troops from Upper Peru, and officials of Salta, July 14,

1821, forced the royalists to evacuate Salta and Jujuy and also served as the basis for the institutional reorganization of the province of Salta, now freed from fear of invasion.

ARMSTRONG, CLARA J. (1847-1915). U.S. educator, one of first brought to Argentina under government sponsorship; first director of the Escuela Normal de Maestra de Catamarca, 1878 (named for her in 1928); later at the schools in San Nicolás de los Arroyos and San Juan; in 1883, at request of Argentine government, brought fourteen U.S. teachers to Argentina; moved to Cuba in 1896.

ARMSTRONG de J. A. BESLER, FRANCES (1860-1928). Schoolteacher from New York, member of group brought to Argentina in 1879 by D. F. Sarmiento; 1883, founded the Normal School of Córdoba; 1888, helped establish the Normal School of San Nicolás de los Arroyos and remained its director until her retirement in 1914.

ARMSTRONG, TOMAS (d. 1875). Banker, industrialist, estanciero, philanthropist of a distinguished Irish family, arrived with his parents in Buenos Aires in 1817; for 58 years played a prominent role in the life of his adopted country; active as banker, financier in railroad building, establishment of agricultural colonies, commerce; close friend and cooperator with presidents; widely known for his generosity to both Catholic and Protestant religious institutions.

ARMY OF THE ANDES. Army formed in Mendoza by General José de San Martín, 1814-1817, with which he crossed the Andes January-February 1817 to liberate Chile as first step in continental plan of liberation; consisting of approximately 4000 men. Argentines and Chilean exiles, the army was largely a local effort of the patriotic citizens of Mendoza until late 1816, when Supreme Director Pueyrredón in Buenos Aires, convinced that San Martín's plan was the only one to promise success in winning independence, used all the power of his office to support him with men and supplies; after the Chilean independence had been won, Army of Andes returned to Cuyo area to rest and recuperate before going on to liberate Peru; ordered by Rondeau (1819) to bring his army to Buenos Aires, then threatened by anarchy and civil war, San Martín ignored the order, recrossed the Andes to Chile where the Army of the Andes became merged into the larger Liberating Expedition that sailed for Peru 1820 (see José Francisco de San Martín; Andes, Crossing of the).

ARREDONDO, JOSE MIGUEL (1832-1904). General with more than forty-eight years of active military service; born in Uruguay, took part in the battle of Caseros, defender of Buenos Aires against siege by Urquiza, served in frontier posts, fought in battles of Cepeda, Pavón, defeated the montoneras under Chacho (General Vicente Peñaloza) and captured the leader who was killed in action; fought in the major battles (1865-67) of the War with Paraguay; returned to northwest frontier service; took part in the crushing of the revolt of López Jordán; took leave in 1886 to participate in Uruguay's political conflicts but, after defeat, returned and was reinstated. Crowned his career with appointment as vocal of the Junta Superior de Guerra (1892) and commandant superior of San Luis, Mendoza and San Juan.

ARREDONDO, NICOLAS ANTONIO DE (1740-1802). Fourth Viceroy of the Río de la Plata 1789-1795: military career officer (Brigadier General in the royal army) who became royal official; after winning distinction in the wars in Italy, took part in the expedition to Florida (1780), then became military and political governor of Cuba; appointed governor-intendant of La Plata (centered in Bolivia) followed by promotion to viceroy of the United Provinces of Río de la Plata. Features of his reign: strong promotion of a diversified economy; silver mining improved by the increased importation of mercury; cattle-raising stimulated and estancieros supported in their rivalries with merchants; personal efforts given to successful establishment of the royal consulado (commercial tribunal) established by royal order in Buenos Aires, 1794; Buenos Aires improved through paving of important streets and downtown areas, authorization of the building of a permanent amphitheater for bull fights in the square of Monserrat, institution of a public health program, etc.; efforts pushed to complete the survey of the boundary between Brazil and the viceroyalty of Río de la Plata, as defined by the Treaty of San Ildefonso, 1777; strengthened northern boundary defenses against activities of cattle raiders, smugglers, and contraband traders; promoted colonization of Patagonian coast and stimulated the whale fishing industry through a large company granted royal privileges; vigorously continued new viceregal policy of co-existence, politically and economically, with the Patagonian Indians, maintaining their settlements as a matter of international policy as well as expansion of colonization.

Returned to Spain after turning over his office to his successor, Viceroy Pedro Melo de Portugal y Villena in March 1795 to fill other offices until his death in Madrid, 1802.

ARREGLO ROMERO (Romero Agreement) see JUAN JOSE ROMERO

ARRIAS DE MULAS. Term applied to mule trains used for transporting goods or supplies in the colonial period as well as (less correctly) to droves of mules being moved from breeding farms to distant markets, both especially important in the later colonial period of the Río de la Plata; arrias de mulas constituted the principal means of transport between Río de la Plata, Alto Perú (Bolivia), and Peru: especially used in transporting mercury to the mine area for silver processing--e.g., in 1780 the chief contractor (asentista general) used 1,430 mules from the Jujuy area to deliver 350 cajones (large boxes) of mercury to the mining area of Potosí. Eventually, all the mules from Salta were assigned by viceregal order to mercury transport.

According to Concolorcorvo, a mule train could make no more than one roundtrip of 200 leagues annually, allowing for rest period of at least thirty days at the final point of destination before beginning the return trip.

Coastal arrieros (mule drivers) were said to get two to four times as much use out of their mules, in contrast to the mountain mules, because of their practice of turning them out to graze every night in alfalfa fields or feeding them with ears of corn carried along for that purpose.

Mule trains provided a tax resource, each mule being taxed, usually between two and four reales; when viceroy Avilés y Fierro assigned this tax money to the Buenos Aires paving program, it amounted to 5,468 pesos in one year; practice of taxing mule trains continued into the national period, Santa Fe, for example, requiring payment of a tax for mule transports to enter the province (1858).

The increased demand for mules in Peru brought about the driving of large numbers of them hundreds of miles to market from the breeding estancias of Argentina. These droves came also (less accurately) to be referred to as arrias. According to Concolorcovo, 50,000 mules from Salta and Tucumán entered the markets of Peru in ten years.

Mule raising for Peruvian markets became a profitable enterprise along the Atlantic coastal area also; the Franciscan friar José Pedro Parras tells of encountering a drove of mules from the estancias of Buenos Aires province at the altura of the Carcarañá river (juncture with the Paraná), consisting of 3,000 two-year-old mules costing 2-1/2 pesos each, and commented on the large number of skilled mule skinners (drivers) required to maintain the drove constantly in a semi-circular formation to prevent loss.

Don Francisco Antonio Candioti made a fortune out of this traffic; beginning with a drove of 1,000 mules that left Santa Fe in May 1764 under the care of twenty highly skilled muleteers, he successfully completed his seventeenth drive in 1780, having transported up to 6,000 to 8,000 mules annually to Peru, despite the constant dangers of Indian attacks, the great skill required to handle so many animals and to keep them in good condition, not to mention the necessity of recruiting enough mule drivers with both the necessary skill and the physical stamina to withstand the rigors of the long, arduous trip. Usually these rigors were reduced by traveling during the night hours and sleeping during the heat of the day.

ARRIBEÑOS. Infantry corps of men from the northern provinces, formed under Liniers against the second English invasion; fought bravely in the defense of Buenos Aires July 5-6, 1807.
   Juan Ramón Balcarce, officer in the Blandengues (later

to become a general) was one of the first members; and the
first revolutionary expedition, under the command of Francisco
Ortiz de Ocampo, was largely formed of volunteers from this
corps.

ARRIGUNAGA Y ARCHONDO, TOMAS DE (d. 1841). Spanish royal
officer who remained in Argentina to become a prominent citizen and public figure in Salta.
      Born in Vizcaya, he came to Buenos Aires as a colonel,
attached to the corps of Cántabros. Moved to Salta where he
held various royal offices; in 1807, as head of the Government
Intendancy of Salta del Tucumán, he acted promptly and efficiently to send aid to the Buenos Aires government against the
English invasions; when the Revolution of May took place, however, he placed himself firmly on the side of the Crown and
remained, throughout the war of independence, a leader in the
royalist group of Salta opposing independence.

ARRIOLA, JOSE NICOLAS, Colonel (1793-1835). Military hero of
the War of Independence, whose career spanned the entire period from the Revolution of May to the final battle of Ayacucho.
      Born in Corrientes, he offered his services to the junta
following the Revolution of May, took part in Belgrano's expeditions, then was assigned to the Army of the Andes; fought
in Chile in battle of Chacabuco, at the siege of Talcahuano,
the surprise attack and defeat at Cancha Rayada, distinguished
himself at the victory of Maipú; accompanying San Martín's
Liberating Army to Peru, he won one of San Martín's recently
established gold medals for his action at the Battle of Cerro
de Pasco, under General Arenales; took part in the entrance
into Lima, the assault on Callao and other action there, winning a second decoration, San Martín's gold medal with dia-
monds. Remained in Peru after San Martín's departure, continuing in the fight for independence; was wounded and taken
prisoner in the final Sierra campaign; returned to Buenos
Aires, was assigned duties in his native Corrientes province
and served with General Alvear in the war with Brazil. Died
in 1835 after having been inactive for several years.

ARROBA. Spanish measure of weight and volume commonly used as
unit in colonial Argentina; name comes from either Arabic or
Hebrew word meaning quarter, as arroba equaled one-fourth of
old quintal, or twenty-five pounds (modern quintal is 100 kilo-
grams).

ARROTEA, MANUEL (c. 1793-1861). Merchant and public official in
Buenos Aires from 1818 until his retirement following the de-
feat of Rosas in 1852; born in Montevideo, moved to Buenos
Aires as a boy, became a merchant, served in Cabildo, 1818-
21; during Rosas' period served on the Publications Board
(Jurado de Imprenta), member of the Sociedad Filantrópica;
Tribunal of the Consulado (1834); and as Federalist member of
the Legislature, 1836-52.

ARROYO, PEDRO MELITON (1801-1875). Porteño who married into socially prominent Mendoza family (m. doña Trinidad Godoy) and played prominent public role in Mendoza in the 1850s and 1860s, culminating in several brief terms as governor during the 1860s.

ARROYO DE LA CHINA (today Concepción del Uruguay in Entre Ríos Province, about 150 miles north of Buenos Aires). Site of two important events in the early period of the liberation movement; Congress called by Artigas of representatives of the northern provinces as far as Córdoba to draw up counterproposals to be sent to the government of Director Alvarez Thomas; and the naval encounter between the small royalist river fleet, commanded by Captain Romarate and the patriot squadron, under Tomás Notter (i. e. the North American Thomas Nother), sent up the Uruguay River by Admiral Brown to eliminate the enemy forces, subsisting on local supplies there; the encounter, March 28, 1814, resulted in the defeat of the patriots whose action had been characterized by more boldness than caution; because of the daring conduct of the ranking officers, resulting in the death of Nother and wounding or death of several of his immediate subordinates, along with the magnificent manner in which the junior officers were able to effect a withdrawal without complete disaster, the Argentine navy views this event with great pride, especially as Hubac, who had been the second in command and forced out of action by his wounds, was the patriot naval commander to accept Romarate's surrender following the ousting of the royalists from Montevideo in July of that same year.

ARROYO GRANDE. Site, on the Entre Ríos shore of the Uruguay River, of a bloody victory by Rosas' forces, under command of the Uruguayan general Manuel Oribe, brilliantly assisted by cavalry led by the governor of Entre Ríos, General Justo José de Urquiza, over the allied Uruguayan and anti Rosas Argentine forces led by Fructuoso Rivera, December 5-6, 1842; growing out of the Uruguayan civil war and rivalry of Rivera and Oribe for the presidency, it was a vital part of the civil wars of Argentina attempting to oust Rosas and involved the largest forces of any battle yet fought in Argentine civil wars; Rivera lost more than 3,000 men (over a third of his forces) and was forced back into Uruguay for safety, while Oribe was enabled to move at once against Montevideo.

ARROYO PINEDO, MANUEL ANDRES DE (1778-1839). Public figure and banker in Buenos Aires; took part in the defense against the English Invasions, honored by the Cabildo for his efforts (supplies and recruiting, organizing; as well as active participation); member of the Cabildo Abierto of May 22, 1810, voted for the deposition of the viceroy and formation of patriotic junta; member of cabildo and elected to legislature, 1821; became director of Banco Nacional (1826) and later president.

ARSLAN, EMIN (emir) (1873-1943). Lebanese diplomat who remained in Argentina following World War I; established and edited periodical La Nota; published various historical and fic-
tional works in both Arabic and Spanish.

ARTEAGA, JOSE SERAPION DE (c. 1780-1845). Prominent and
controversial political figure in northwestern Argentina, 1810-
1844; born in Salta; educated with doctorate in law at the University of Chuquisaca; in legal or political capacity active in
public life of Salta, Tucumán, Jujuy at various times in his
career; briefly member of the Congress of Tucumán, later
played leading role in the local affairs of this area during the
period of anarchy and caudillism following the declaration of
independence.

ARTEAGA, LUISA SANCHEZ DE (1823-1883). Often called the first
porteña woman painter of Argentina; member of prominent
Buenos Aires family, she studied under the French diplomat
and artist M. Blondel; best known for her miniature of Rosas
and family portraits.

ARTICULOS DE CONFEDERACION. A constitution for a federated
type of government presented to the Assembly of the Year XIII
(1813) for consideration; authorship disputed--attributed to the
deputy from Tucumán, don Nicolás Laguna, but bears strong
resemblances both to the Articles of Confederation of the
United States (1787) and to Artigas' instructions to the Uruguayan delegates; no constitution adopted by this assembly but
way prepared for constitutional action after the declaration of
independence.

ARTIGAS, ANDRESITO (Andrés Guacurari). Mission-born Guaraní
Indian whom General José Gervasio Artigas adopted and gave
his name; fought alongside the general until 1815 when he was
made Captain of the Blandengues and placed in charge of the
government in Misiones; defended the area against Paraguayan
and Brazilian invasions; finally captured in latter (1819) and
imprisoned in Rio de Janeiro; released in 1821.

ARTIGAS, JOSE GERVASIO, General (1764-1850). Uruguayan independence hero; closely related to Argentine leaders in early
years of the struggle for independence. Born in Montevideo
of a socially prominent, wealthy family, he preferred life on
the family estancias with the gauchos; became officer in the
Blandengues; fought against the English invasions of 1806 and
1807; went to Buenos Aires to offer his aid and cooperation
after the Revolution of May: at Rondeau's invitation, he sent
representatives to the constituent Assembly of the Year XIII
(1813) with explicitly written instructions and suggestions for
a confederated constituion for which they were to work; when
the credentials of his delegates were rejected, he broke with
Rondeau and devoted himself to the formation of a federation
of the northwestern provinces of Argentina including Entre

Ríos, Corrientes, Córdoba, Santa Fe, Misiones, and the Banda
Oriental.
    In 1814 he proclaimed the Liga de los Pueblos Libres,
with himself as protector, and posted a real threat to the government of Buenos Aires through his alliance with the caudillos. A break with Ramírez, caudillo of Entre Ríos, along
with the Portuguese invasion of Uruguay from Brazil, forced
Artigas to retreat to Paraguay where he became and remained
for thirty years a prisoner of Francia.

ARZE Y ZELARRAYAN, PASCUAL (1815-1885). Ecclesiastical edu-
    cator, public figure, author, bibliophile, church administrator,
    missionary, religious historian.
    Born in Tucumán, educated in Cuyo and earning his doc-
torate at the University of Córdoba, he used his ecclesiastical
training and position to contribute to the educational and cultural life, along with the religious, of the provinces of Salta,
Tucumán, Jujuy, and Santiago del Estero. Prototype of Catholic religious, cultural, social leadership in Northwest provinces in the nineteenth century.

ASAMBLEAS CONSTITUYENTES ARGENTINAS. Extremely impor-
    tant work in 7 vols. published by the Instituto de Investiga-
    ciones Históricas de la Facultad de Filosofía y Letras de la
    Universidad de Buenos Aires, under direction of Dr. Emilio
    Ravignani. Publication completed in 1939. Definitive work,
    publishing all pertinent papers; gives a sound, detailed docu-
    mentary base (source) for study of development of Argentine
    institutional evolution from 1813 to 1898.

ASCASUBI, HILARIO (1807-1875). Early author of gaucho poems
    and active fighter against Rosas.
    Born under a cart on the road between Córdoba and
Buenos Aires, of Spanish Basque father and Córdoban mother;
ran away to sea at age of twelve, returning to Argentina after
an adventurous three years including travel in Europe and
North America (California); settled in Salta as printer and
writer; with Juan Arenales published the first periodical there,
La Revista Mensual de Salta, including his own poem celebrat-
ing the victory of Ayacucho; fought in the war against Brazil,
at Ituziangó; forced into exile (1832) because of his strong unitarist principles, he spent the next twenty years in Montevideo, engaged in various businesses while writing; established
close ties with anti-Rosas leaders; served as Urquiza's aide in
battle of Caseros defeating Rosas, then joined Mitre's government in Buenos Aires, considering Urquiza's government a
continuation of Rosas' federalism.
    A prolific writer throughout this period, his fame as
author lies in the fact that he was one of the first to express
the Argentine spirit in terms of gaucho life and language, and
his poems, especially the epic Santos Vega for which he is
best known, constitute valuable documentary descriptions of country life, customs, places, objects, people, etc., of early and

mid-nineteenth century Argentina; three volumes of these works, including Santos Vega and Paulino Lucero (story of gaucho fight against tyranny), were published in Paris, 1872.

ASCENCIO DE MALLEA, TERESA DE (born between 1525 and 1530, died 1604). Indian princess, daughter of the cacique Angaco, married Captain Juan Eugenio de Mallea, conquistador and founder of San Juan; honored by Argentines as the first Indian girl within their territory to have established a Catholic home and family following her acceptance of Christianity and marriage according to Spanish religious and civil laws.

ASIENTO DE NEGROS. Contract given by the Crown to either an individual or a company for the importation of black slaves for sale into Spanish American lands. The first asiento to affect Argentina was that given in 1595 to Pedro Gómez Reynel, including a minor provision for importation of 600 slaves to Buenos Aires annually; later asientos either omitted Buenos Aires or made slight provision for slave importation and slaves formed an important item of the contraband trade in the Río de la Plata area; the big change came in 1713 when the Treaty of Utrecht granted the asiento to England, giving it the right to import slaves into Spanish American ports, including Buenos Aires. British companies were assigned these contracts, British agents went to each port, and the importation of black slaves, selling for 80-90 pesos each at Buenos Aires, became important business, changing not only the society of Buenos Aires, but also the face of the city as accommodations for the care and sale of the influx of blacks were set up; and providing new forms of wealth and economic opportunities for porteño merchants and entrepreneurs.

ASOCIACION CATOLICA ARGENTINA (A. C. A.). Late nineteenth-century attempt by devout conservative Catholic lay leaders to strengthen the church and the religious life and education of Argentina against the increasingly powerful forces of secular liberalism; used publications, political action, organization of rural and urban laborers, evangelistic tours, etc., to accomplish purpose. Organized by Félix Frías (1876), reorganized (1883) and continued by José Manuel Estrada, it disappeared in the early twentieth century, its functions having been assumed by the various organizations that it had created; its initials A. C. A. and emblem continued to be used in Acción Católica (see Catholic Action).

ASOCIACION DE MAYO. Name by which patriotic new generation of intellectuals became known, 1837-38, because of determined efforts to implement the ideals of the May Revolution of 1810 in the Argentina of Rosas. Beginning as a literary society, meeting in the Buenos Aires hall of the well-known bookseller Marcos Sastre, Estéban Echeverría, Juan Bautista Alberdi, Juan María Gutiérrez, Vicente Fidel López, Miguel Cané and forty or fifty others met frequently to discuss the new romantic literary currents of Europe as well as its revolutionary political and philosophical ideas.   When Rosas' suspicions were aroused and the bookstore closed, Echeverría and other leaders reorganized their group, this time for political purposes, along the lines of patriotic societies of young liberals in Europe, even calling themselves "Joven [Young] Argentina"; concentrated their efforts on formulating clearly the "symbolic words" of their social creed for Argentina--Echeverría charged with the formulation, the others with listening, discussing, refining or modifying; claiming to be neither unitarists nor federalists, they called on all Argentina to join them in creating a better nation along the lines of constitutional organization, liberty, and equality; moving actively into opposition against Rosas, the group was dispersed by the government; leaders fled to Montevideo where Echeverría published the Dogma socialista, 1839.

ASPERGER, SIGISMUNDO (1687-1773).   Jesuit missionary, physician, and natural scientist.
        Born in Innsbruck, Asperger entered the Jesuit order in 1703; he had already acquired considerable repute for his success as a physician in treating illnesses before he arrived in the Río de la Plata area in 1717; his services were in immediate demand the following two years to care for victims of the virulent smallpox epidemic that swept through the eastern part of the country; was honored formally by the city of Córdoba for having saved hundreds of lives and it was said that fully half the Guaraní mission Indians would have died, had he not been there to care for them; he was also greatly interested in indigenous medicinal plants and made use of them to supplement his European medical supplies; his discovery of the use of the mastic from the aguaribay pepper tree for ointment brought a European demand for its importation in large quantities; Asperger's studies of these native medicinal plants, as shown in his Tratado de materia médica and similar writings, were later cited by another natural scientist, Amadeo Bonpland (q. v.), as a useful guide to the study of medicinal plants of the Misiones region; at the time of the Jesuit expulsion from Argentina (1767), the royal officers found Father Asperger in such a pitiful, ulcerated, paralyzed condition that they left him at Apóstoles mission (said to have been the only Jesuit not removed from Argentine territory); he died there a few years later.

ASSEMBLIES OF THE YEAR XII.   Name applied to two general assemblies that met in Buenos Aires in April and October 1812; these constituted an attempt of the 1811 Triumvirate to vest the legislative power of government in a representative assembly (its members to be elected every six months); assemblies found difficulties in working with unfamiliar political form--that of divided powers; fell victim to rivalries between provinces and Buenos Aires seeking to take over viceregal control, the varying fortunes of the military action of independence, as well as personal power conflicts and enmities; both Triumvirate and General Assembly overthrown by revolution of October 8, 1812, sponsored by the newly-formed Patriotic Society and the Lautaro Lodge.

ASSEMBLY OF THE YEAR XIII. Called by the Second Triumvirate, convoked January 31, 1813, with Carlos María de Alvear as president, this assembly has been ranked by Argentine historians as one of the four great Argentine conventions (along with the Cabildo Abierto of May 1810 that produced the revolution of that name; the Congress of Tucumán, 1816, that declared independence; and the Constituent Congress of Santa Fe that wrote the famous, enduring constitution of 1853) because, although it made no explicit declaration of independence and did not actually consider a constitution for adoption, its work assured the first and, by removing foundations of the colonial period and encouraging an awakening of national and reform consciousness in the public, paved the way for the second.

Reform leaders declared the sovereignty of the people, replaced the royal seal by a new patriot one which also appeared on the new coinage; adopted the blue and white banner first used by Belgrano (1812) as the national flag, and commissioned and then adopted the national anthem written by Dr. Vicente López y Planes; passed limited economic reforms; improved organization and discipline of the army; enacted major program of basic social institutional changes and reforms. Ecclesiastical reforms: although Roman Catholic Church was recognized as official church, religious toleration was guaranteed, and the Argentine church was declared to be independent of foreign authority; priests were forbidden to take their final vows before age of thirty; Tribunal of the Inquisition abolished; religious hospital funds secularized and ecclesiastical administration generally reformed.

New divisions were created for political administration, forming the origins of modern Argentine Provinces: slavery not abolished, but all native-born children and all slaves imported into country were declared to be free, Indians relieved from payment of tribute and forced labor, and declared to be free and equal; use of titles or heraldry of nobility forbidden, and mayorazgo abolished in favor of equal inheritance by all children; torture in criminal investigations prohibited.

One of the primary purposes of this assembly had been to draw up and adopt a formal constitution but when three constitutions were presented, one by the appointed committee, another by the Sociedad Patriótica, and a third, very similar to the United States' Articles of Confederation, drawn up by Artigas' followers and calling for provincial autonomy with minimal national power, in contrast to the other two which were strongly centralist, the Assembly decided not to consider any of them.

Increasing conflicts between Artigas' confederation groups and porteño leaders, complicated by power struggle in triumvirate, led to abolition of Second Triumvirate and vesting

of the executive power in a single director, Gervasio Antonio
de Posadas (1814).

ASUNCION.   Capital of republic of modern Paraguay (see Juan de
Garay, Domingo Martínez de Irala and other related topics for
Asunción's important role in permanent settlement of Río de
la Plata region in sixteenth century).

ASYLUM, RIGHT OF.   This ancient Spanish practice of establishing
by law certain religious places where a fugitive could find at
least temporary protection from his pursuers, especially those
bent on personal vengeance, and some assurance of legal safeguards became important only briefly in the late colonial period in Argentina when royal decrees of Charles III set up such
sanctuaries (1773) at La Piedad and San Anselmo in Buenos
Aires; quickly fell into disuse after the 1810 revolution.

ATENEO IBEROAMERICANO.   Founded in 1912 by a distinguished
group of Spanish Argentine and other Latin American intellectuals in Buenos Aires for the purpose of emphasizing the cultural ideals and achievements of the Hispanic peoples through
the sponsoring of lectures, meetings, publications and the
maintenance of a large library; originally called the Ateneo
Hispanoamericano, the name was changed to Ateneo Iberoamericano in 1927 to include Brazilian culture.

AUCAS.   Araucanian Indians who had left Chile to make their home
in the Argentine area where game was more abundant; formed
a subgroup of the Pampas Indians.

AUCHMUTY, SIR SAMUEL (1756-1822).   British general, said to be
one of the few officers who came out of the Buenos Aires expeditions of 1806-07 with distinction.   Born in New York, son
of loyalist clergyman (rector of New York's Trinity Church,
1764-77), served with the British Army against the Americans
during the Revolution; remained in British Army to see service in India and Egypt; sent in 1806 to reinforce the British
forces in Río de la Plata; took over Montevideo, 1807; published La Estrella del Sur, newspaper in English and Spanish
in which he attacked the Spanish restrictive commercial policy
in its American colonies; served as one of Whitelocke's four
division commanders in the attack on Buenos Aires, 1807,
and succeeded in capturing the Plaza de Toros, but was forced
to surrender with Whitelocke; returned to England where he
was sent on missions to Madras and Java, finally dying in Ireland where he had been sent as commandant.

AUDIENCIA.   Spanish political-judicial tribunal forming one of most
important administrative institutions in the government of Spanish America; first established in Santo Domingo, shortly after
its settlement; new ones established whenever new areas
seemed to need them; all of present Argentina was attached to
the audiencia of Charcas (in city also called Chuquisaca, La

Plata, and, today, Sucre in Bolivia) throughout most of the
colonial period; all civil, legal, criminal, political or public
security matters that could not be handled by the local authorities had to go there for settlement; briefly, 1661-71, the
first Audiencia of Buenos Aires was established under the
presidency of the military governor, Captain don José Martínez
de Salazar, with two oidores (judges); when this failed to accomplish the two purposes for which it was established: to
get rid of piracy and smuggling, and to stimulate the settlement of the Río de la Plata area, it was ended.

The second Audiencia of Buenos Aires was authorized
in 1783 and opened in 1785 under the presidency of the viceroy,
Marqués de Loreto; all of the provinces in the new Viceroyalty
of Río de la Plata were placed under its jurisdiction except
for those in the presidency of Charcas; it continued to function
until 1812 when it became transformed into the Cámara de
Apelaciones (Court of Appeals).

AUDIENCIA DE CHARCAS   see   AUDIENCIA

AUGIER, FRANCISCO RAFAEL (1762-1847). Galician who came to
Buenos Aires early in the 19th century, moved to Catamarca,
where he married and became an important citizen, acting as
one of the chief leaders in the movement to separate Catamarca from the province of Tucumán in 1821.

AUGUSTINIANS. Members of the most ancient Order of St. Augustine entered the Cuyo area from Chile in 1617; established a
convent in San Juan in 1644 and the Convent of Santa Mónica
in Mendoza in 1657; extended their activities throughout the
national area, performing educational, parochial, and diocesan
duties; greatly interested in education and the development of
craft industries (pottery); continued to work in special projects
after independence and secular reforms.

AULON. Name of an ancient Turkish Roman Catholic diocese, no
longer in existence, revived in 1829 and used by the Vatican
throughout much of the nineteenth century in Buenos Aires
(Bishop of Aulón) as part of an attempt to avoid trouble in the
controversy over the disposition of the ecclesiastical patronage
formerly held by the Crown. Used briefly again in the twentieth century (see Church-State Relations).

AUTOMOBILE CLUB, THE ARGENTINE. Begun in 1904, almost as
a sport under the leadership of Dalmiro Varela de Castrex,
the Argentine Automobile Club has played an important and
continually expanding role in twentieth century development in
transportation and industry; promoted better roads and bridges,
manufacture of parts and cars, established service stations
and resthouses, prepared maps and tourist guides, led in the
legislation necessary for importation of cars, and for licensing cars and drivers, and participated actively in international conferences.

AUTONOMIA, ACTA DE (Act of Autonomy). Document by which Catamarca seceded from the República de Tucumán and began an autonomous life as a province (August 25, 1821); act signed by fifty-two Catamarcan members of a cabildo abierto called for that purpose; elected Catamarcan General Juan Nicolás Avellaneda y Tula as first governor.

AUTONOMISTAS (also known as alsinistas from their leader, Adolfo Alsina). Member of political party formed (1860s) to keep Buenos Aires as provincial capital rather than federalize it as Mitre wished to do (see Political Parties).

AVALOS, EDUARDO. Member of G.O.U., participating in the revolution of 1943 with Perón and other colonels; during period 1943-1945, Avalos was one of important military officers who, for personal and political reasons, resisted Perón's increasing power; opposed action of 1944 placing Farrell in presidency; as commander of important Campo de Mayo garrison, invited Farrell, Perón and others to mass meeting at his headquarters, October 9, 1945; underestimating his power, Farrell, Perón and others accepted; Avalos issued ultimatum: Farrell could stay--Perón must go; Farrell agreed; Perón sent as political prisoner to Martín García; new cabinet formed October 12, with General Avalos replacing Perón as minister of war; five days later, October 17, Perón returned triumphantly to mass meeting at Plaza de Mayo; Avalos and other military commanders decided not to fire into crowd; Perón in power, Avalos arrested, released, and retired.

AVALOS, PACT OF. Pact of alliance by Corrientes, Misiones and Banda Oriental (Uruguay) to sustain the freedom and independence of the Confederated Provinces under leadership of Artigas, signed April 24, 1820, near the end of this leader's career.

AVATI (or ABATI). Guaraní word for maize, which was brought back from the Paraná by Sebastian Cabot's men.

AVELLANEDA. Industrial district settled in 19th century by Italian, Spanish, and Polish immigrants; occupies a special place in Perón's romance with descamisados' historic march of October 17, 1945, that restored Perón to power, it began in Avellaneda; ever since, the district has been a center of Peronist activity.

AVELLANEDA, MARCO M. de (1813-1841). "Martyr of Metán," leader of heroic revolt against Rosas.
          Born in Catamarca, son of Juan Nicolás de Avellaneda y Tula; brilliant and precocious, with doctorate in laws from the University of Buenos Aires; persecuted as an anti-Rosas journalist, he returned to the northwest, devoting himself to public offices in Tucumán; becoming head of the government in 1840, he formed a coalition of the northwestern provinces, including Tucumán, Salta, La Rioja, Jujuy, Catamarca; for-

mally withdrew recognition of Rosas as governor of Buenos
Aires, and the authority previously granted Rosas, of handling
the international affairs of the provinces; Oribe, sent by Rosas,
completely routed the coalition forces led by Lavalle, at
Famaillá, September 19, 1841, captured the leaders of the re-
volt--including Avellaneda who was executed in Metán, October
3, his head severed and displayed atop a lance in the main
plaza of Tucumán, ending the coalition (see Coalición del
Norte).

AVELLANEDA, NICOLAS (1836-1885).   President of the Argentine
Republic, 1874-1880; lawyer, writer, and public official.
Born in Tucumán, son of Marco M. de Avellaneda (the
"martyr of Metán"), grandson of the distinguished Catamarcan
public figure of the early independence period, Juan Nicolás
Avellaneda y Tula.   President Avellaneda completed the mold-
ing of the nation, begun by Mitre and continued by Sarmiento,
with national order consolidated; economic crisis averted and
favorable balance of trade created; Patagonian lands opened to
settlement; the traditional political rivalry between the provinces and Buenos Aires subdued, Buenos Aires federalized and
old parties gone, paving the way for new political activities.
His own personal and professional interests, largely in the
areas of education, land development, and the politics and diplomacy of conciliation, form the basis of most of his writings
as journalist (editor of El Nacional), lecturer, and essayist
(12 vols. of writings, including his book Tierras públicas) and
his activities as public official for provincial Buenos Aires government, minister of justice, religion, and public instruction
under President Sarmiento, and during his own presidency.
Important events and achievements of Avellaneda's administration include: first cargo of wheat shipped from Rosario to Great Britain, 1878 (Avellaneda considered this to be
the most important event of his term of office) and shipments
of other cereals increased greatly; immigration and agriculture
were publicly fostered and the first comprehensive public land
law drawn up in 1876 to facilitate the settlement of farmers
(both native and immigrant) on the newly-opened Patagonian
lands and elsewhere; value of wool increased to 50% of exports; remarkable continued progress in education, from elementary schools, with provisions for various minority groups,
to advanced scientific research; cultural life flourished throughout the nation; treaties to settle boundary disputes lingering
from the Paraguayan War were signed with Paraguay and Brazil in 1876, and with Chile in 1877 (involving the Straits of
Magellan and Tierra del Fuego); and the remains of San Martín
were brought back from France to Buenos Aires.

AVELLANEDA Y TULA, JUAN NICOLAS (1788-1855).   Catamarcan
who became governor-intendant (1817-19) and then, in 1821, the
first popularly elected governor of his native province.

AVENDAÑO, SANTIAGO (1820-?).   San Juan military figure who

took refuge from Rosas among the pampas Indians (1839-52);
later served as interpreter for Argentine forces engaged in
pushing the Indians farther south and west; rose to rank of
colonel; published his memoirs in various issues of the Revista
de Buenos Aires.

AVIATION. The use of aviation for transporting mail, passengers,
and cargo moved slowly until after World War II but interest
had been shown for more than a century; in 1810 a Dutch
watchmaker, who lived in Mendoza, had tried to gain Liniers'
support in Buenos Aires for constructing a dirigible that could
cruise at an airspeed of 45 miles per hour; in 1854, Guillermo Rawson seriously suggested experiment in mechanical
flight; during Paraguayan war a balloon was used for military
observation; interest in balloons and heavier than air planes
was largely stimulated by foreigners who came to Argentina for
exhibitions, etc.; Argentine interest came first from sports and
military groups; Aeroclub established in 1908; flying exhibition
and races as part of the 1910 centenary; Escuela de Aviación
Militar established shortly thereafter, developing into the Ser-
vicio Aeronáutico and school of military aviation; first military
air maneuvers in 1914; Zuloaga and Bradly crossed Andes in
1916; Italian initiative important after World War I; followed by
English, French, German, North American; French Compañía
Aero Postal opened mail and passenger flights between Buenos
Aires and Paraguay, then, in Argentine hands as Aeropostal
Argentina, opened flights from Bahía Blanca to Comodoro Rivadavia, 1929; by 1929 Pan American-Grace (PANAGRA) was flying down the West Coast and across to Buenos Aires, and in
1931, Pan American Airways opened flights to Buenos Aires on
the Atlantic side; the German Lufthansa in 1937 became closely
affiliated with the Aéropostal Argentina, German equipment and
mechanics being used but management Argentine and, after
1939, pilots also Argentine; following World War II, tremendous expansion of Argentine international and domestic airlines
under both private and government auspices; along with this
went the expansion and improvement of the infrastructure, air-
ports, mechanical services, communications, meteorological
reports, training, etc.; under Perón these various companies
were placed under government control and then nationalized;
Aerolíneas Argentinas, created, 1949; aviation industries promoted as part of Perón's first Five Year Plan--Industrias
Aeronáutica y Mecánicas del Estado (I. A. M. E.).

AVILES Y FIERRO, GABRIEL DE. Marqués de Avilés (d. 1810).
Royal official; Viceroy of Río de la Plata 1799-1801.
      Born in Spain sometime in first half of eighteenth cen-
tury; came to South America at time of rebellion of Tupac Amaru (José Gabriel Condorcanqui) in Peru; served on military
tribunal (1781) that sentenced him to death by drawing and
quartering; after serving as subinspector of army in Peru,
sent to Chile as governor and captain general; in late 1797
designated viceroy of Río de la Plata, to succeed Field Mar-

shal Antonio Olaguer y Feliú; took over duties March 14, 1799, and remained in office until May 20, 1801; particularly interested in the beautification and improvement of Buenos Aires; in stabilizing the Indian frontier; favored giving Indians individual land-ownership and more equal rights; reaffirmed Spain's claim to Malvinas Islands and to southern Patagonia; attempted to improve administration of Guaraní mission towns from which Jesuits had been expelled thirty years earlier; encouraged economic development, tax reforms and cultural progress; known as an administrator of great ability, honesty, integrity, and philanthropy, Avilés left Buenos Aires to fill the highest royal post in Spanish America as viceroy of Peru (1801-06). [Mariluz Urquijo, José María, El virreinato del Río de la Plata en la época del Marqués de Avilés (1799-1801) (Buenos Aires, 1964).]

AXIS POWERS. Term applied to alliance between Germany, Italy, and Japan opposing Allied Powers, including United States (after 1942), in World War II; Argentina accused of favoring Axis, and certainly several of its leaders did; most Argentines, however, preferred to consider their nation as neutral, unwilling to join U.S. and other American nations in declaration of war against Axis Powers until January 1944; strong German influence in military, loyalty of Italian Argentines to country of their ancestors, and traditional national desire for neutrality in international wars were among elements involved; Argentina suffered decline in inter-American relations because of its firm stand but was restored to full membership following Conference of Chapultepec and end of war (see World War II).

AYACUCHO. Sierra valley in Peru where the combined patriot forces under General Antonio José de Sucre defeated the armies of the Spanish viceroy and commanding general, José de la Serna, December 9, 1824, to win the independence of Spanish South America; approximately eighty officers and men from San Martín's Mounted Grenadiers and other parts of the Army of the Andes participated in this final victorious action and were cited by Sucre.

AYOHUMA. Site in Alto Perú (now Bolivia) of disastrous defeat, November 14, 1813, of General Manuel Belgrano's patriot army by royalist forces under General Joaquín de la Pezuela; important military and political effects: San Martín sent to replace Belgrano in command of the Army of the North; almost total destruction of army made continued fighting doubtful, if not impossible; loss of the province of Upper Peru from the United Provinces de la Plata foreshadowed; increasing pessimism among some Argentine leaders, such as Nicolás Herrera, as to nation's ability to maintain itself independently.

Mujeres de Ayohuma--honorary title conferred on Indian woman María and her two young daughters for their courage in braving the front lines of fighting to provide the wounded with fresh water and other services.

AYOLAS, JUAN DE (1510?-1538). Conquistador and explorer (1536-
37) of Paraná and Paraguay river areas; favorably impressed
by Ayolas' first report of his Paraná exploration, Pedro de
Mendoza took his expedition upriver and established a settlement named Nuestra Señora de Buena Esperanza at the port
near the mount of the Carcarañá; Mendoza returned to Spain
leaving Ayolas in charge; Ayolas set off up the Paraguay and
toward the west seeking the sierra of silver about which he had
heard; returning laden with silver and gold, before regaining
contact with Domingo Martínez de Irala whom he had left in
charge of the Spanish base at Candelaria, Ayolas and his party
were killed by Indians whom they had considered friendly.

AYUNTAMIENTO.   Another term applied to the town council (see
Cabildo).

AZARA, FELIX (1746-1821). Spanish scholar, scientific observer
and naturalist, cartographer and geographer, whose writings
based on his various official duties in La Plata area not only
provide best description of the land, flora and fauna at that
time, but provide the basis for all the land development of the
Argentine Republic during most of the nineteenth century; came
in 1778 as an officer in the commission responsible for the
boundary between Spanish and Portuguese America; after other
related commissions, returned to Spain in 1801 to continue his
writing and studies.

AZCUENAGA, DOMINGO DE (1758-1821). Author of fables, satiri-
cal, and humorous writings; collaborator, using signature
D.D.D.A., in first Argentine periodical El Telégrafo Mercantil; refrained from political involvement in critical events of
early 19th century.

AZCUENAGA, MIGUEL DE (1754-1833). Prominent, highly-respected military and public figure of the late colonial and early national period; born in Buenos Aires but educated in Spain, returned to Buenos Aires, 1773, where he saw military action
against the Indians and the Portuguese in Uruguay; became member of cabildo in Buenos Aires and held other responsible royal
appointments; fought against the British in both invasions of
Buenos Aires; became one of precursors of the May Revolution
in which he took active role; appointed to first patriot junta
but purged, as a follower of Mariano Moreno, in the revolution of April 5-6, 1811, and exiled briefly to Mendoza; returned to hold responsible political and military positions
(chief of staff, 1818, with rank of brigadier); honored for his
sincere, disinterested patriotism, his military distinction, and
his integrity and diligence in public office.

AZCUENAGA, VICENTE DE (1706-1787). Born in Vizcaya, moved
to Buenos Aires in 1748; married creole girl, amassed a for-

tune as a merchant; became member of the cabildo, 1759; generally regarded as one of Buenos Aires' most distinguished, generous citizens at the time; father of brigadier Miguel de Azcuénaga.

AZOPARDO, JUAN BAUTISTA (1774-1848). Born in Malta, worked in shipyards, came to Río de la Plata in eighteenth century; privateer against enemy and pirate ships; joined Liniers against English invaders (1806-1807); remained to support the May Revolution, 1810, and to join Cornelio Saavedra's force; given command of three ships with reinforcements for Belgrano on his campaign to Paraguay, 1811, Azopardo was surprised at San Nicolás by a Spanish squadron from Montevideo, and badly wounded, taken prisoner, leaving Belgrano isolated and forced to sign a treaty agreeing to leave Paraguay; taken back to Spain, Azopardo was imprisoned at Ceuta; freed by the Riego revolt (1820), he returned to Buenos Aires, was once more given command of a river boat, the brigantine General Belgrano, made second in command to Admiral Guillermo Brown; later became captain of the port; retired in 1827; lived quietly until his death in 1848.

AZULES Y COLORADOS. Groups within the armed forces in the 1960s that played political roles; taking their names from the Blue and Red names used in war games; both groups opposed Peronism and both gave at least lip service to constitutionalism; Azules were also known as "legalists"; favored return to constitutional government with non-political professional army men and were represented by the army elite, the cavalry; Colorados supported military supervision over political affairs, and were represented by the violently anti-Peronist officers of the army and the naval forces; feeling ran high between the two groups in confrontation for control of the government; Azules under the leadership of Onganía won, defeating the Colorados under the leadership of Admiral Isaac Rojas of the navy; the following elections (1963) brought Illia to presidency; Azules continued to be important in Onganía's administration (1966), while Colorados lost power.

AZURDUY DE PADILLA, JUANA (1781-1862). Heroine of northern border warfare in fight for independence. Born in Chuquisaca (now Sucre, Bolivia); educated in convent to become nun; left religious life and married, 1805, a soldier, Manuel Asencio Padilla; from then until his death in battle, 1816, at Viloma, they fought side-by-side; withdrew to Salta where she became valued fighter with Güemes who secured permission from Director Pueyrredón to appoint her a lieutenant colonel with uniform and all the rights and privileges of the rank, 1816; Belgrano himself bestowed the sword; after victory in 1825 she returned to Chuquisaca and a quiet life with her daughter.

- B -

BACA, JOSE TEODORO (1831-1914). Prominent medical figure;
active in fight against yellow fever and cholera; public health
officer, professor of medicine, and leader in medical research, particularly that related to childbirth.

BACACAY. February 13, 1827--site of battle during war between
Argentina and Brazil in which Juan Lavalle defeated the Brazilian forces and won his generalship.

BACHMANN, EUGENIO (1834-1896). Austrian naval officer, graduate of the Naval Academy of Fiume, moved to Argentina in
1870 where he spent the rest of his life contributing to the scientific progress of that country; served as astronomer of the
observatory at Córdoba under Gould (see Benjamin A. Gould);
member of the science faculty and received honorary doctor's
degree at the University of Córdoba; appointed director of the
national Naval Academy, and, in retirement, edited La Plata
Rundscham, to inform Germans of Argentine scientific advances. Active in Masonry, he served as Grand Master.

BACLE, CESAR HIPOLYTE (d. 1838). Pioneer printer and lithographer in Buenos Aires. French lithographer (born in Geneva
in late eighteenth century) was operating important establishment for lithography, printing, painting, and similar processes
in Buenos Aires by 1826; reproduced portraits of heroes of
War of Independence and early national period, as well as publishing books commemorating the local scenes, fashions, and
customs of Buenos Aires at that time; widely mentioned in histories of Argentine printing and art.
    Became deeply involved in politics; friendship with such
Rosas adversaries as Rivadavia and Valentín Alsina made him
suspect; found in possession of maps and charts of military interest to the enemy, Bâcle was imprisoned in Santa Fe; died
six months later; this so-called Bâcle incident was cited by
France as one cause for its intervention in Río de la Plata,
1838.

BACLER D'ALBE, ALBERTO (1789-?). Napoleonic veteran (b. in
Savoy) who played a significant role in San Martín's Army of
the Andes and expedition to liberate Peru; came to Argentina
in 1817 with rank of captain of engineers; joined San Martín's
army in Chile, participating in the assault on Talcahuano, being cited by San Martín for his role at Maipú, using his scientific training in the liberation of Peru; returned to Chile 1824;
and then to Europe.

BADLAM, ESTEBAN (1813-1834). Considered to be one of the first
victims of Rosas' dictatorship; nephew of Mariano Moreno;
Badlam shot openly in Buenos Aires, April 29, 1836, by a
group of mazorqueros bent on reducing the opposition to Rosas
before Rivadavia's return.

BAEZ, GUILLERMO FEDERICO (1810-1879). Born in Asunción,
Paraguay, he became involved for most of his life in the
troubled political and international affairs of the Plata countries and Brazil, particularly in those relating to the riverine
provinces; after the Paraguayan war, in which he had served
as chief of the Paraguayan legion formed by Mitre, returned
briefly to Paraguay to hold various offices and positions
there before returning to Buenos Aires shortly before his
death.

BAHIA BLANCA. City and port located approximately 350 miles
from Buenos Aires on a very fine harbor in southern Buenos
Aires province; today a modern city, a major military and
naval base, and one of Argentina's most important ports,
linked to rest of nation by networks of railways, highways,
and airlines, and serving the interior as outlet for its grains,
wool, cattle, etc.
        Little used during the colonial period, Bahía Blanca be-
came of interest in the late eighteenth century when military
expeditions were sent there exploring for adequate sources of
cheap, good salt to use in saladeros (beef-drying plants for
making "jerky"); as war with Brazil was threatened over Uruguay in 1820s, Rosas was sent to secure the Indian frontier
and to prepare defenses in Bahía Blanca against possible Brazilian invasion; by 1828 it was a frontier village, with fort and
trading post and, after Rosas' Indian campaign of 1833, had
improved overland communications with Buenos Aires; gradual
growth came with the settling of territories of Neuquén and La
Pampa; Indian wars of 1879-1883 permitted rush of farmers,
ranchers, and sheepmen to push southward toward Bahía
Blanca; arrival of the first railway, the Southern, in 1884
made it possible for interior produce to reach shipping point;
port construction and improvements followed; town of Bahía
Blanca became urbanized, with high percentage of European immigrant settlers; in 1905 showed political activity as Radical revolt broke out in that city simultaneously with those in Buenos
Aires, Córdoba and Rosario.

BAIGORRIA, JUAN BAUTISTA. Mounted Grenadier hero. Born in
San Luis, selected as a member of the first squadron of Granaderos a Caballo; distinguished himself in their first military
engagement--San Lorenzo, February 3, 1813--by interposing
himself between San Martín who was trying to extricate himself, with a wounded hand, from a horse that had been killed,
and the royalist soldier who was about to kill him; in saving
San Martín, Sergeant Baigorria was said to have saved "half
a continent. "

BAIGORRIA, MANUEL (late eighteenth century-1875). Cordoban who
took up arms in 1816 and continued in military career until his
death; became a kind of white cacique on the frontier, fighting
with and against Indians; served as liaison frequently between
Indians and others; also took part in formal military actions

under General Paz; later, at Pavón, under Mitre; fought at
Las Playas against El Chacho.

BAILON, AGUSTIN (1808-d. after 1854). Priest and educator. Galician Jesuit who came to Buenos Aires shortly after Rosas
had invited the Order back to the country. Sent to Salta for
relief from long-standing pulmonary ailments, he found himself to be so much healthier there that he asked for and received permission to leave the order and remain in Salta as
priest and educator; with enthusiastic backing of the lay and
clerical leaders of the community, he founded the historic
Colegio de la Independencia to educate boys in sciences, letters, and humanities; became widely known as scholar and educator; largely responsible for the intellectual distinction of the
Salteños immediately following the Rosas period.

BAIRES, CARLOS (1868-1920). Buenos Aires editor, literary figure, educator, and public official. His activities included
ministerial positions, teaching on the Faculty of Philosophy and
Letters at the university; participation in the revolution of
1893 as a member of the Radical Party, editorship of La
Prensa, authorship of several literary works, including La
propiedad literaria y artística (1905).

BALADIA, PABLO. Educator. Former Spanish official, he devoted himself after 1814 to introduction of more modern systems of pedagogy into Spain, such as the Lancastrian method
and French methods of mutual teaching; exiled in 1823, he met
Rivadavia in London and offered his services to the "Republic
of Buenos Aires"; Rivadavia brought him to Argentina where
he served as director general of all schools, laying the foundations for a modernizing educational reform in the systems
there; retired in 1828 to devote himself to his own private
Gimnasio Argentino (elementary and intermediate school).

BALBASTRO. Important family name in Buenos Aires during early
nineteenth century. María Josefa Balbastro married (1782)
naval captain Diego de Alvear y Ponce, on duty in the Río de
la Plata; returning to Spain in 1804 with their eight children,
their fleet was attacked by the British outside the port of
Cádiz; the only survivors in the family were Alvear and his
son Carlos María (later to become director of La Plata and
commander-in-chief of the army); other members of the Balbastro family played roles of varying importance in the events
of the early decades of the nineteenth century, particularly in
the defense of Buenos Aires against the British invasions and
in the war of independence.

BALBIN, RICARDO. (1904-   ). Born in province of Buenos Aires.
Leader of the UCR during the 1940s; expelled from the House
by the Peronists, jailed in 1950; presidential candidate in 1951;
formed UCRP in 1956 separating from the Frondizists; presidential candidate in 1973 election--defeated with 21.22% of

votes; candidate for president in the election of September 23,
1973.

BALCARCE FAMILY, Buenos Aires.   Family that produced several
military heroes of the independence and early national period.
       Francisco Balcarce (1745-1793), founder of family; born
in Barcelona; came to Buenos Aires as cavalry officer, 1765;
married María Victoria Martínez Fontes porteña; accompanied
Vértiz in expedition of 1773 and capture of Colonia del Sacramento, 1777; assigned to the Blandengues, made commander of
the Indian frontiers in 1784; died while fighting near Luján.
       His sons, all born in Buenos Aires and following him
in military careers included: 1. General Antonio González
Balcarce (1774-1819) the hero of Suipacha; began military career in Blandengues, under his father; defending Montevideo
against British, 1807, captured and sent to England as prisoner; released, he fought against Napoleon's forces in Spain; returned to Buenos Aires after May Revolution and was placed
in charge of revolutionary army to Córdoba and Upper Peru;
at Suipacha, November 7, 1810, won first Argentine victory
over royalist forces; defeated later; back in Buenos Aires,
held various public and military offices, becoming chief of
staff; sent to Army of the Andes where he served as second
in command to San Martín; fought in several Chilean engagements, including Cancha Rayada and Maipú, before illness sent
him back to Buenos Aires where he died, shortly after having
been reappointed chief of staff. 2. Diego González Balcarce
(1784-1816); also served in Blandengues, fought British in
Montevideo, captured, sent to England; fought in Spain against
the French; was on his way back to Buenos Aires when May
Revolution took place; accompanied Belgrano's army en route
to Paraguay, then to the North; remained with Army of the
North under command of San Martín and Rondeau, fighting in
battles of Tucumán, Salta, Vilcapugio, Ayohuma, and Sipe
Sipe; attained rank of colonel before illness and death overtook
him in Tucumán. 3. Francisco González Balcarce (1778-
1812) joined the army in 1808; accompanied first patriot army
to Upper Peru; fought at Suipacha and at defeat of Huaqui;
killed in action at Nazareno January 12, 1812. 4. José Patricio Balcarce (1779-1807), like several of his brothers,
served under his father on the frontier; fought the British in
Buenos Aires, 1806; killed in Montevideo in second British invasion during same action (1807) in which his brothers Antonio,
Diego, and Marcos were taken prisoners. 5. General Juan
Ramón González Balcarce (1773-1836) joined Blandengues under
his father on Luján frontier, 1789; transferred to command at
Tucumán; interned British prisoners, 1806; returned with
troops to assist Santiago de Liniers in defense of Buenos Aires
against second British invasion, 1807; one of military officers
opposing role of Cisneros in May Revolution; accompanied
Castelli to Córdoba to suppress counterrevolution there; had
responsibility for execution of leaders; joined Belgrano's army
in North; fought in battle of Tucumán; represented Tucumán in

Assembly of Year XIII; assigned to observation of caudillos in river provinces; second in command at defeat by López and Ramírez at Cepeda, distinguished himself by saving his force, almost intact, in retreat; in 1820, briefly replaced Sarratea as governor in Buenos Aires; served as minister of war and navy under Dorrego; sent to Brazil to work out peace; held same ministry in Rosas' first government; elected governor of Buenos Aires, 1832, but ousted by Rosas' supporters; died in Concepción del Uruguay.   6.   General Marcos González Balcarce (1777-1832) began his military career under his father; campaigned with Sobremonte against Portuguese in Misiones; fought British in first invasion, captured in Montevideo in second (1807) and sent to England; fought briefly in Spain against Napoleonic forces, returning to Buenos Aires in time to participate enthusiastically in May Revolution; sent to Chile; then to Mendoza as governor of Cuyo, being succeeded by San Martín in 1814; served briefly as Álvarez Thomas' secretary of war; later fought and was defeated by Ramírez in Entre Ríos; retired from military service for a while but returned to conduct force and supplies against riparian caudillos; captured in Santa Fe, 1819; later occupied series of official positions, usually ministerial, in governments of Las Heras, Rivadavia, Vicente López, and Rosas, until his death in 1832.

Among other members of the Balcarce family were two sons of General Antonio Balcarce: Mariano Balcarce (1807-1885), diplomat to European countries for four decades; strongly encouraged and facilitated European immigration into Argentina; married Mercedes de San Martín, only daughter of the Liberator, and they and their two daughters (who died without descendants) made their home in Paris; and Florencio María Balcarce (1818-1839), brilliant poet who spoke for the transition generation, between Rivadavia and Rosas, leaving a small but memorable collection of writings before his death at age of twenty-one.

Francisco Javier Balcarce (1807-1829), son of General Marcos Balcarce, captain of artillery, drowned when the ship on which he was being transported up the river, was wrecked in a storm; and Lucas Balcarce (1777-1812), a cousin of the generals, who fought at Suipacha and Huaqui and was killed in action, along with his cousin Francisco at Nazareno (1812).

BALDINI, LUIS (1855-1952).   Italian who moved to Mendoza in 1890; pioneered in improving and establishing prestige for local wine industry.

BALENZATEGUI, TOMAS DE (d. 1812).   Spanish merchant who established himself in Buenos Aires, 1786; held post of regidor several times; patriot; supported May Revolution.

BALLERINI, AUGUSTO (1857-1902).   Italian-trained porteño painter who specialized in historical subjects: El Paso de los Andes, etc.

BALLVE, ANTONIO (1870-1909). Director of the National Penitentiary of Buenos Aires from 1904 until his death; won international acclaim for his prison reforms and publications in that
field.

BALVIANI, CESAR. Spanish colonel who arrived in Buenos Aires
in 1806 shortly after the Reconquest; aided Liniers in defeat of
General Whitelocke, then continued on to Peru.

BAMBA. Extensive, involved legend of colonial Córdoba that Atali-
va Herrera transformed into an epic poem (Bamba, poema de
la Córdoba colonial, Buenos Aires, 1944).

BANDA ORIENTAL--"Eastern Shore" or "Bank." Colonial name for
Spanish province east of the Uruguay river; came under Buenos Aires jurisdiction and was included in the viceroyalty of
the United Provinces de la Plata when it was created (1776);
became independent (1828) as modern Uruguay (see Montevideo).

BANDOLA. Wooden box, with hinged lid, on four feet, usually two
meters long and one wide, traditionally used to store and display hardware, notions or other merchandise in the market
places by merchants licensed by the cabildo; precursors of the
modern kiosks. The merchants (popularly called bandoleros)
formed a strong security guard to protect their wares.

BANEGAS, JOSE LEON (1777-1856). Porteño priest who dedicated
his life to education; stood firm against Rosas' impositions and
later (1855) became a member of the Council of Public Instruction.

BANGUELA (sometimes Bangala). One of the most important
naciones (q.v.) formed by the numerous blacks in Buenos
Aires in the early nineteenth century; like all the others the
Nación Banguela (founded 1825) was completely organized with
its king and queen and their officials; was designed to furnish
aid to its adherents; to make it possible, above all, for the
blacks to make a good living; supervise the moral life of the
community; rescue and buy the freedom of slaves; perform religious services, particularly memorial ones, and to provide
fiestas and dances. The Banguela nation was centered around
its ranchos in Calle Méjico and the headquarters in Calle
Chile; all the nations operated under a common regulation approved by the government; during the Rosas period the nations declined into social clubs or organizations.

BANKS, BANKING. One of Rivadavia's prime concerns was to establish proper banking facilities in the new nation as a necessary component of the sound economic development of the country; the Banco de Descuentos (Discount Bank) founded in Buenos Aires, 1822, under provincial regulation, with private foreign (mostly British) and Argentine capital, was the origin of

this system; in 1826 the National Bank opened; under Rosas in
1836 this was transformed into the Casa de Moneda, with
limited banking functions; in the 1850s, following the fall of
Rosas, both the Confederation government and that of Buenos
Aires province were interested in establishing new banks;
provincial bank created from the Casa de Moneda; in the 1860s
foreign banks were established (especially British and Italian)
and the Banco Nacional was established in the early 1870s,
operating with considerable success until the crisis of 1889-
1890; in 1891, following the economic debacle that closed both
the national and provincial banks in Buenos Aires--and through
the involvement of the Baring Brothers institutions--almost
precipitated a crisis for the Bank of England, a new bank was
authorized by Pellegrini's government (December 1891), the
Banco de la Nación Argentina; inspired confidence and played
an important role in aiding Argentine commerce, industry, and
agropecuarian industries; in 1914 when the U.S. Federal Reserve Act for the first time permitted the establishment of
branch banks (under national charter) in foreign countries, the
National City Bank of New York established a branch in Buenos Aires, the first U.S. bank there, followed shortly afterwards by others as U.S. capital flowed more freely into the
country; in the mid-1930s, following the Boca-Runciman agreements, the Banco Central Argentino was created to centralize
control of currency, commercial credit, foreign exchange,
etc.; privately owned by Argentine and foreign capitalists but
supervised by the government; in 1946, following Perón's election but before his inauguration, the Banco Central was nationalized as part of the nationalist move for economic independence; during his administration the Banco de Crédito Industrial Argentino promoted industrial development and made
loans to approved businesses; following Perón's departure,
Raúl Prebisch was called in as economic consultant to the government; his recommendations that the Central Bank (of which
he had been the head) be restored to its former independence,
that Argentina join the World Bank and International Monetary
Fund were eventually accepted.

BAQUEANO (sometimes baquiano). The guides whose knowledge of
the topography, climate, water supply, and resources of the
land made possible the occupation of the trackless pampas and
desert lands, the conquest and occupation of Patagonia and
northern frontiers and successful military operations of the
late colonial period and nineteenth century; usually gauchos,
many, including at least one woman, have their names perpetuated in both literature and place-names.

BARBARIN, MANUEL MACEDONIO (1781-1836). African slave who
earned his freedom in Buenos Aires and participated actively
in the defense against the British invasions, in the Revolution
of May, and continued his military career in Buenos Aires until his death; rose to rank of lieutenant colonel.

"BARBARUCHO." Popular name given royalist Colonel José María Valdés, protagonist of the tragedy in which General Martín Miguel de Güemes fell victim.

BARCALA, LORENZO (1795-1835). Mendoza-born slave, freed by Assembly of XIII legislation; fought in independence wars; with unusual gifts of leadership and ability to organize, rose to rank of colonel, fighting in provincial wars, in Brazil, and in civil wars until his capture, courtmartial and execution by Aldao in Mendoza.

BARCO. Name given to first settlements attempted in Tucumán, or northern part of Argentina, in sixteenth century; the name Barco used in honor of birthplace of Pedro de la Gasca, governor-general and president of audiencia of Peru, who in 1549 commissioned Juan Núñez del Prado, resident of Charcas (today Sucre in Bolivia) to begin settlement of Tucumán; with about eighty soldiers, Núñez del Prado established Barco I (1550) along route previously taken by Diego Rojas; when this was threatened by Valdivia, who claimed this area as part of Chile, Núñez del Prado moved the settlement north to Barco II, within limits of modern Salta; attacks from the Diaguita Indians forced a third move, Barco III, to a location about half a league south of present Santiago del Estero; in 1553, Francisco de Aguirre was sent from Chile to establish a permanent settlement in that area; he took Núñez del Prado prisoner and moved the colonists to the new town that he was founding on the Río Dulce, Santiago del Estero, the first permanent settlement in Argentine territory.

BARCO CENTENERA, MARTIN DEL (1535-c. 1602). Priest and poet-author of La Argentina.
    Spanish priest who accompanied expedition of adelantado Juan Ortiz de Zárate, as chaplain, to Asunción (1572-1574); shared life of conquistadors in Río de la Plata, present with Garay at refounding of Buenos Aires in 1580; two years later went to Peru where he participated in various ecclesiastical activities; returned to Spain in 1592; became chaplain to Cristóbal de Mora, Marqués de Castel Rodrigo; accompanied latter to Lisbon upon his appointment as viceroy there; author of poem of 28 cantos La Argentina y conquista del Río de la Plata, con otros acaecimientos del Perú, Tucumán, y estado del Brasil, published in Lisbon, 1602, under patronage of viceroy to whom the poem was dedicated; died shortly thereafter, while hard at work on sequel.
    First writer to use "Argentina" (from Latin word for silver) to refer to both people and area; first to publish historical work on Río de la Plata; and considered to have been, with Ruy Díaz de Guzmánn (q. v.), one of first two Argentine historical writers.

BARILARI, MARIANO (1819-1867). Italian patriot, exiled after revolution of 1848, became one of founders of the fort and colony

of Nueva Roma in Bahía Blanca; took part in fighting the Indians and in other military campaigns; his son Atilio Sixto
Barilari (1857-1928) had distinguished career in navy, attaining rank of admiral; grandson Atilio Daniel Barilari (1887-
1943) held diplomatic posts in Spain and other European countries, as well as in various Latin American capitals.

BARILOCHE. Site of first Jesuit mission in Patagonia; founded
along with the one at Nahuel Huapf by Father P. Mascardi who
was killed by the Indians and the mission destroyed in mid-
eighteenth century; declared a national historical site in 1943
(see Río Negro Province).

BARING BROTHERS AND COMPANY. British banking firm that
played leading role in advancing capital to Argentina for nineteenth-century development; involvement brought Barings increased wealth and power but ended in the company's liquidation in the so-called Baring Crisis of 1890-96.
    Founded by Francis Baring (with his brother John) in
1770, it had become one of the greatest European financial
firms by 1810; first to offer capital to newly-independent Argentina, floating a loan of £1 million in 1824 for the provincial
government of Buenos Aires to finance minister Bernardino
Rivadavia's plans for modernization and development; loan in
default by midcentury as Rosas, however willing, was unable
to make payments; after fall of Rosas, Barings assisted Mitre,
in 1857, to reestablish the flow of capital for burgeoning Argentine development; Barings rode the crest of the wave and
were leading bankers concerned with marketing Argentine securities in the 1880s, becoming heavily involved with a commitment to sell £42 million of Argentine bonds for which the
company also guaranteed the interest.
    Caught by surprise by the economic collapse that ac-
companied the political revolution that replaced President Miguel Juárez Celman with his vice president Carlos Pellegrini,
1890, Barings faced disaster by the end of that year, unable to
meet its commitments or to dispose of the Argentine bonds;
emergency action by the Bank of England and the British government facilitated the orderly liquidation of the great firm,
preventing financial panic in Great Britain, while Pellegrini and
his successor, Luis Sáenz Peña, were able to reestablish Argentine credit by stringent economic measures, aided by renewed Argentine prosperity; Barings later permitted to reorganize on a limited basis. See H. S. Ferns, Britain and Argentina in the Nineteenth Century, (London, 1960).

BARRACAS. Southern port area of Buenos Aires built up by Italians.

BARRANCA YACO (in Córdoba). Site of the assassination of Facundo Quiroga (February 16, 1835).

BARRERE, AGUSTIN (1865-1952). Priest born in Buenos Aires

province of French parents; educated in Europe, returned to
Argentina in 1894 as a member of the Lourdist Congregation;
sent to Catamarca, he spent the rest of his life in ecclesiastical and educational activities, culminating in nearly 22 years
as the Bishop of Tucumán.

BARRETO, FELIX G. (1870-1948). Historian and archivist; first
director of the Archivo Histórico de Santa Fe; published the
papers of Rosas; a biographical series of Santa Fe historical
figures; played leading role in other provincial historical activities.

BARRIALES, CHACRA DE LOS. Farm outside of Mendoza given to
San Martín and his daughter Mercedes by the Cabildo of Mendoza in 1816; vineyards and olive groves; sold by Mercedes
San Martín de Balcarce in 1872 and proceeds given to various
charities in Buenos Aires.

BARROS, ALVARO (1827-1892). Colonel, governor of Buenos Aires
province, active in capital and provincial political and military
affairs throughout life; journalist, author of several books, including Fronteras y territorios federales del sud (Buenos
Aires, 1872).

BARROS PAZOS, JOSE (1808-1877). Cordoban jurist; returned from
exile after Caseros to play active judicial role in the nation;
serving as president of the nation's Supreme Court at the time
of his death.

BARRUFALDI, LUIS (1893-1921). Early pilot (won wings 1917) of
prestige and popular appeal; 1921, held record for flight with
a passenger--7,500 meters; commissioned to attempt to fly
across the Andes from Mendoza in October 1921, he was killed
in the crash of his final training flight for this venture.

BARTON, DIEGO (1781-1850). Scottish merchant who arrived in
Buenos Aires in 1809, married English Ann Mackinlay, and became an important import-export merchant; credited with having organized the first football team in the country.

BAS, ARTURO M. (1875-1935). Cordoban lawyer who fought all his
life with considerable success for his ideals of Catholicism,
provincial rights in Constitutional law, and progressive social
legislation; served as professor of law at the University of
Córdoba (retired after the Student Reforms of 1918); national
deputy to Congress; and left a large body of writings on various aspects of public law and social themes.

BASAVILBASO, DOMINGO DE (1709-1775). Spaniard from Bilbao who
moved to Buenos Aires as a youth, devoted himself to business,
which brought him both prestige and fortune; active throughout
his life in public affairs (member of Buenos Aires Cabildo);
remembered especially for his role in establishing tax support

for the newly-established (1752) frontier guard (later designated Blandengues) and other responsible positions related to colonial public finance; especially active in initiating reforms and businesslike practices; buried in the Cathedral, built during his lifetime and with whose financial operations he had been closely related.

BASAVILBASO, MANUEL (1807-1866). Born in Entre Ríos, personal friend of Urquiza, he spent his life devoted to the latter's causes; became general, held various positions of public responsibility.

BASEBALL (Béisbol). Introduced into Argentina in 1888; popular among foreigners (including Americans and Japanese) in Buenos Aires, as well as Argentines; 1950, la Asociación Deportiva Latinoamericana, first Argentine club devoted exclusively to baseball, was established.

BASES Y PUNTOS DE PARTIDA PARA LA ORGANIZACION PO-LITICA DE LA REPUBLICA ARGENTINA (Bases and points of departure for the political organization of the Argentine Republic). Important work by Juan Bautista Alberdi which served as both basis and guidelines for the preparation of the national Constitution of 1853. Similar in many aspects of its thinking to those of the United States (and especially the recently-drawn constitution of California) as well as those of other Spanish American nations, the Bases differed in its frank emphasis on government responsibility for promoting desirable immigration, thus reflecting the special immediate practical needs of Argentina. (See Enrique de Gandía, Historia de la República Argentina.)

BASILICA DEL PILAR. National monument in Buenos Aires near the Recoleta Cemetery; constructed by Jesuit architects and dedicated in 1732; contains fine sculptures, the best being that of San Pedro de Alcántara, probably done by the famous Spanish imaginero (carver or painter of sacred images) Alonso Cano.

BASKETBALL (Basquetbol). Introduced into Argentina (Buenos Aires) in 1912 by Philip P. Phillips of the Asociación Cristiana de Jóvenes [YMCA]; played by both young men and women.

BATEMAN, John G. (1810-1889). British engineer, trained in hydraulics and road construction, arrived in Buenos Aires in 1870 under contract of Buenos Aires Provincial Government to draw up plans for the construction of the port, provisions for water and drainage systems, and for the cobblestone paving of the city streets.

BATERIA, PUENTA DE LA. Site of bitterest and most decisive fighting in the city of Corrientes (May 25, 1865) during the Argentine recapture of the city from the Paraguayans who were holding it.

BATERIA "LIBERTAD." Site of the artillery battery of that name in the banks of the Paraná river in Santa Fe, near Rosario, where Belgrano flew the Argentine flag before his army for the first time, February 22, 1812.

BATTAGLIA, GUILLERMO (1872-1913). Porteño actor who gave distinction to the Argentine theater in the early 1900s.

BAUCKE, FLORIAN see PAUCKE, FLORIAN

BAZAN, JUAN GREGORIO (d. 1570). Conquistador of Tucumán; lieutenant governor 1554-1556. Early conquistador who distinguished himself in helping to establish early settlements (Barco II, 1551 and Santiago del Estero 1553); named lieutenant governor and chief justice of latter, 1554-1556; spent his time fostering the precarious growth of the new town that became the first permanent Argentine settlement; in 1560 he assisted Juan Pérez de Zorita in founding of Cañete; later he returned to Tucumán and was present at the founding of San Miguel de Tucumán (1565) and then became captain and lieutenant governor of the newly founded Talavera, 1567 (better known by its old name Esteco--q.v.); in order to fulfill its purpose as a way station on the road from Santiago del Estero to Peru, a large supply of Indian labor was essential; Bazán made this his first priority and ranged throughout the neighboring area, exploring much new country toward the Bermejo, seeking to obtain the required Indians by force, diplomacy, or incentives; he met with some success but not enough to solve this problem for Esteco permanently; leaving Esteco in 1569 to escort his family arriving from Peru, Bazán's party was ambushed by the Lules Indians of the area; most of the group escaped but Bazán, guarding the rear, was trapped; in an action that has become a proud part of Argentina's pioneer heritage, Bazán's son-in-law, Diego Gómez de Pedraza, himself already out of danger but appealed to for aid, made the historic reply: (as handed down by eyewitnesses) "Caballero soy y no voy huyendo" ("I am a caballero--gentleman of honor--and do not flee") and returned to join his father-in-law in fighting to their deaths.

BEAGLE CHANNEL (Canal de Beagle). Strait, extending east and west; separates Argentine Tierra del Fuego from part of Chilean Tierra del Fuego to south; most important Argentine town on north shore Ushuaia; name taken from British ship Beagle, captained by Robert Fitzroy, engaged in making scientific surveys and soundings, 1833-1834, as well as geologic and anthropological observations and studies by naturalist Charles Darwin, accompanying expedition; continued to be area of interest to British throughout nineteenth century.

See writings of Charles R. Darwin, especially those edited by Lady Nora Barlow; also E. Lucas Bridges, Uttermost Parts of the Earth (London, 1948; New York, 1949); Spanish translation, Buenos Aires, 1952.

BEAUCHEF, JORGE (1787-1840). French-born veteran of Napoleon's
    army from 1805 to Waterloo (including one year as prisoner of
    war in Spain); joined Army of the Andes in Chile (1817) and
    fought in most of the major engagements against the loyalists
    there and later against the Araucanians in the South. After a
    brief visit to France he returned to Chile.

BEAUMONT, J. A B. English author of biased but detailed de-
    scriptions of Buenos Aires in 1826-27; Travels in Buenos
    Aires and the Adjacent Provinces of the Rio de la Plata. With
    Observations Intended for the Use of Persons Who Contem-
    plate Emigrating to that Country or Embarking Capital in Its
    Affairs (London, 1828). When author's father, Tomás Barber
    de Beaumont, who had extended hospitality to Rivadavia in
    London, ran into difficulties with his colonization project,
    drawn up during 1825-26, to bring colonists to the province of
    Buenos Aires from Glasgow, Liverpool, and London, J. A. B.
    Beaumont came to Buenos Aires to work out the arrangements
    directly with Rivadavia. Unsuccessful in this he returned to
    write his account, colored by disillusionment and bitterness,
    but valuable in its descriptions of Buenos Aires and neighbor-
    ing provinces, recorded historical detail of political and diplo-
    matic figures and events of the mid-1820s.

BEAZLEY, FRANCISCO J. (1864-1924). Public official; educator.
    Grandson of Francisco Beazley, American friend of Guillermo
    Brown, who came to the Plata area during the war with Bra-
    zil and served as naval officer in Brown's fleet; Dr. Francis-
    co J. Beazley was born and educated in Buenos Aires, pro-
    fessor and vice rector of the Colegio Nacional; became chief
    of police in Buenos Aires 1896; modernized the service and
    introduced many innovations during his eight years in that po-
    sition.

BECA--scholarship or fellowship. Name taken from the distin-
    guished sash that students of each university were permitted to
    wear; system of fellowships tied in closely with development of
    national educational system dating from the late colonial per-
    iod.

BECK BERNARD, CARLOS (1819-1900). Dutch-born, Carlos Beck
    Bernard, with his wife Lina, came to Argentina in 1857 to
    become a founder of the first agricultural colony in Santa Fe
    province; after having lost his fortune there he returned to
    Europe but Mitre, followed by later government leaders, ap-
    pointed him as the first European to represent Argentine immi-
    gration interests in Switzerland and Germany, a charge which
    he held until 1886; author of numerous writings in French and
    German about Argentina.

BECK BERNARD, LINA (1824-1888). Alsatian-born, she accom-
    panied her husband to Argentina and wrote perceptive, memor-
    able, descriptive accounts of it. See José Luis Busaniche's

translation (with biographical introduction) of her work, entitled Cinco años en la Confederación Argentina, 1935.

BEECHE, GREGORIO (1800-1878).   Born in Salta, son of a Catalán intendancy official and the daughter of a wealthy local family, Gregorio Beeche was involved in the public life of northwestern Argentina, Bolivia, and Chile of that period; personal friend and business associate of Marshal Andrés de Santa Cruz (Bolivian); supported the Liga del Norte (League of the North) against Rosas and aided exiles fleeing from his power; an exporter of quinine, suffered serious financial losses that made him decide to move to Valparaíso, 1841, where he remained until his death serving as consul general; a dedicated bibliophile, he was constantly building his library; in close contact with such Argentine exiles as Sarmiento (who called him "the forgotten civilizer"), Alberdi, Mitre and others; his library, catalogued in 1879 by Vicuña Mackenna, became the public library of Valparaíso at his death.

BEHETY, MATIAS (1849-1885).   Uruguayan-born writer prominent in Buenos Aires' literary and journalist circles; editor of Las Novedades in 1880.

BEIRO, FRANCISCO (1876-1928).   Political figure, born in Entre Ríos, active in Unión Cívica Radical; died shortly after becoming vice president of the republic.

BELGIUM.   Established as an independent nation in 1830, sent its first diplomatic representative to Argentina in 1851.

BELGRANO, CARLOS JOSE (1761-1814).   Military officer.   Son of Domingo Belgrano y Peri; born in Buenos Aires; entered military service early and remained in it; military commander of ports of Las Conchas and San Fernando and of both when they were combined in 1810; sent, 1812, as military head and president of the ayuntamiento of Luján.

BELGRANO, CARMEN (1814-1894).   Social and cultural figure. Daughter of José Gregorio Belgrano; interested herself in intellectual and cultural pursuits from an early age; surrounded in her own family and through her engagement to Juan Thompson (broken as a result of his political involvements after 1839 and absences from Buenos Aires) with the brilliant intellectuals and cultural figures of that period; eventually her home in retirement became the center and gathering place for Buenos Aires cultural activities of the mid and later nineteenth century; without the brilliance of a great intellectual herself, she typified the porteño culture of her period, especially the feminine grace and living style most admired by the porteños and was widely known and affectionately respected; mistakenly said to have been collaborator with her uncle, General Manuel Belgrano, in translating George Washington's Farewell Address (she was highly proficient linguistically), but Belgrano had completed this in Tucumán (1813) before she was born.

BELGRANO, CONGRESS OF.   In the conflict between the national
government and that of Buenos Aires province (1880), the former took up official residence in the barrio of Belgrano (northern suburb of Buenos Aires) and, on September 20, declared
Buenos Aires to be the Federal Capital of the Argentine Republic and no longer a part of the province.

BELGRANO, DOMINGO (1731-1795).   Merchant, royal official; father
of General Manuel Belgrano.
    Born in Liguria, Italy, of ancient and honorable family,
Domingo Belgrano y Peri, moved to Buenos Aires as merchant, 1751; married porteña María González Casero, 1757,
with whom he had a very large family; performed some militia
duties but devoted himself primarily to his interests as merchant; 1778 became customs official, urged establishment of
consulado (commercial tribunal) in Buenos Aires; 1781 member
of Buenos Aires Cabildo.

BELGRANO, DOMINGO ESTANISLAO (1768-1826).   Ecclesiastic and
public figure.
    Born in Buenos Aires, son of Domingo Belgrano; edu-
cated at university in Córdoba; ordained as priest; returned to
Buenos Aires where he was named canon of the cathedral;
participated in preliminary patriotic actions and in Cabildo
Abierto that brought about May Revolution of 1810; when National Library was created, donated his library to it as part
of the original holding; gave generously of his own funds to
support patriot armies; named as executor of the will of his
brother, General Manuel Belgrano, with responsibility for care
of his schools and his daughter, Manuela Mónica, in Tucumán; died six years later.

BELGRANO, FRANCISCO (1771-c. 1824).   Merchant; public official;
military officer.
    Born in Buenos Aires, son of Domingo Belgrano; edu-
cated at Colegio de San Carlos in Buenos Aires; devoted himself primarily to his commercial interests; member of cabildo
1806, elected second alcalde in 1815; held various other public
offices; enlisted among the defenders of Buenos Aires against
the British in 1806 and took part in other engagements later,
attaining the rank of lieutenant colonel (1819).

BELGRANO, JOAQUIN CAYETANO (1773-1848).   Merchant, public
official.   Brother of General Manuel Belgrano; appointed royal
treasury official, 1804, but attended Cabildo Abierto of May
22-25, 1810 and voted to oust the viceroy; prominent in public
official life: elected First Alcalde in Buenos Aires in 1813;
Second Alcalde, 1820; held various other cabildo and consulado
offices; when office of justice was created, he was the first
appointed for the barrio of Montserrat, 1822; appointed again
in 1834; died at his home in 1848.

BELGRANO, JOSE GREGORIO (1762-1823).   Officer in militia cavalry.   Born in Buenos Aires, son of Domingo Belgrano and
brother of General Manuel Belgrano; enlisted early in the militia cavalry; fought against the British; attained rank of colonel (1816); attended the Cabildo Abierto of May 1810 and voted
with his brothers for the forced resignation of the viceroy and
resumption of rule by the Ayuntamiento.

BELGRANO, JUAN CARLOS (1848-1911).   Jurisconsult, legislator.
Born in Brazil, his parents refugees from Rosas; returned to
Buenos Aires after Rosas' fall; graduated in law; after several
judicial appointments, spent some time traveling and studying
in Europe; devoted himself to politics after returning to Buenos
Aires; served as deputy in the Buenos Aires provincial legislature, becoming its president in 1878; briefly occupied provisional governorship, 1893; elected national deputy in 1894, but
refused to serve; went back to Europe and scholarly pursuits,
dying in Paris 1911.

BELGRANO, MANUEL, General (1770-1820).   Colonial royal official; patriot leader and military hero of independence; creator
of Argentine flag.
        Born in Buenos Aires, son of Domingo Belgrano y Peri;
educated in Buenos Aires, then sent to Spain where he studied
at the universities of Salamanca and Valladolid, graduating with
law degree; deeply interested in new economic ideas then sweeping Europe, he welcomed appointment as secretary of the consulado (merchant tribunal) to be established in Buenos Aires,
1794, viewing it as opportunity to put new ideas into practice
for the development of his own country; from 1794-1810, his
annual Memorias constitute a record of the various projects
proposed for developing agriculture, improving business and
commerce, introducing new industries, building new roads and
improving old ones, bettering conditions of navigation and establishing new schools for training participants in these economic pursuits; opposition, powerful and sarcastic, blocked many
of his plans but he also received strong support from others,
especially creole merchants, intellectuals schooled in the more
liberal ideas of enlightenment, and scientists and agronomists;
convinced that his country could never progress under Spanish
rule, he became supporter of independence.
        During British invasions of 1806-1807, he fought as a
militia officer against Beresford, then fled to Montevideo to
avoid swearing allegiance to the British Crown; returned to
fight, as officer in the Patricios, under Liniers to defeat
Whitelocke in second invasion (1807); resigned from consulado
post early 1810 for rest; called back by fellow patriots to help
prepare for May Revolution in which he played a dominant role,
becoming a member of the first patriot government; when it
seemed necessary to bring all parts of viceroyalty under patriot government, Belgrano, despite his limited military experience and training was sent with army to Paraguay (September
1810); met with ferocious opposition from Paraguayans and after

defeat at battle of Tacuarí, March 9, 1811, convinced that
Paraguayans wanted independence but not Buenos Aires domination, Belgrano signed armistice with Colonel Cabañas and
withdrew; strongly criticized by Buenos Aires groups, but soon
vindicated; assigned in early 1812 to take charge of new batteries at Rosario, Belgrano made one of his greatest contributions to Argentine history by unfurling (February 27, 1812) a
blue and white banner as the official flag of the patriots; failing to receive the official rebuke sent by the government (independence had not been declared) because he was on his way
to new appointment, Belgrano called on his new army in Tucumán to swear allegiance to it after it had been formally
blessed and four years later the Congress of Tucumán made it
official (see Flag of Argentina); receiving a totally disorganized army, Belgrano pulled it together in time to win a brilliant and unexpected victory in Tucumán, September 24, 1812,
and another one at Salta February 20, 1813 (for which the government rewarded him with a gift of 40,000 pesos that he
used to establish four elementary schools); unfortunately these
victories were followed by two defeats in Upper Peru at Vilcapugio, October 1, 1813, and, retreating, at Ayohuma; replaced
by San Martín as commander of the Army of the North; sent
on diplomatic mission to Europe with Rivadavia but Ferdinand's
restoration to Spanish throne and defeat of Napoleon brought
Belgrano back to Buenos Aires, February 1816; went to Tucumán where he attempted to influence the Congress of Tucumán
to do three things: to declare independence (declaration signed
July 9, 1816); to adopt his national flag (accepted July 25);
and to establish a monarchy--form of government that Belgrano thought best suited Argentine political realities of the
time--preferably under an Inca prince; these latter ideas rejected, although many leaders of the north, like Martín Güemes, believed such a government necessary to tie northwestern
Argentina and Upper Peru to the Buenos Aires government in
a united new nation; following years--1816-1819--spent as commander again of the Army of the North but without further
campaigns into royalist areas; increasing illness had almost
incapacitated him in 1819, when he was seized by leaders of
a revolutionary movement that overthrew Mota Botello, governor of Tucumán; vigorous representations by his doctor saved
him from the pain and humiliation of having irons placed on
his swollen and painful legs, and permitted him to return to
Buenos Aires where he died on June 20, 1820.
     The best evaluation of Belgrano's place in Argentine
history is to be found in the evolution of Bartolomé Mitre's
classic biography of him; beginning in 1857 as little more than
a simple biography of a great patriot, it grew, in succeeding
editions to the final one, published in 1887, into a three-volume work entitled Historia de Belgrano y de la independencia
argentina, no longer a mere biography but a vast panorama of
events in which Belgrano appears as the prototype of his era.

BELGRANO, MANUEL (d. 1839).   Poet and writer.   Born in Buenos

Aires, son of José Gregorio Belgrano and nephew of General
Manuel Belgrano; studied law at university of Buenos Aires;
particularly interested in languages; formed part of the group
that became known as the Generation of 1837 and fled with the
first of these to Montevideo to escape Rosas; died there in
1839; widely known as poet and author among his contemporaries, controversies and lack of publication make it difficult
to evaluate his contribution.

BELGRANO, MARIO (1884-1947).   Historian.   Born in Paris, son
of Juan Carlos Belgrano; returned to Buenos Aires to study
law and social sciences at the University of Buenos Aires and
to claim Argentine citizenship; served as secretary, 1903-1910,
for the Bulletin Argentine de Droit International Privé, edited
by Estanislao S. Zeballos; concurrently, 1906-1913, edited El
Tiempo, directed by Carlos Vega Belgrano; increasingly interested in history; attended the Güemes centenary (1821) as guest
of honor because of his kinship to General Belgrano; went back
to France where he devoted himself to research in French archives on subjects related to Argentine history, publishing, in
French and Spanish, a number of scholarly historical studies,
1925-1935; returned to Buenos Aires to continue his research
as an adjunct member of the University faculty; published biography of Juan O'Brien, 1938, and rewrote and revised his
biography of Manuel Belgrano, along with a comprehensive
iconography of the general; member of the National Academy
of History; served as secretary for the II International Congress of History of America, Buenos Aires, 1937; that same
year became vice-director of National Historical Museum, post
that he held until his death.

BELGRANO, MIGUEL (1777-1825).   Soldier and poet.   Born in Buenos Aires, son of Domingo Belgrano and brother of the general;
at early age went to Spain where he studied in military academies and entered military service; produced his first poetic
work there, Rasgo histórico, a poetic chronicle of contemporary events; back in Buenos Aires in 1801 he wrote for El
Telégrafo Mercantil; later, learning of the May Revolution, he
moved permanently to Buenos Aires, supported the patriot
cause, and wrote patriotic poetry, such as Batalla de Maipú,
in which he extolled the actions of the victorious General San
Martín, whom he admired greatly; in 1823, was named rector
of the Colegio de Ciencias Morales; died two years later in
Buenos Aires.

BELGRANO RAILROAD.   Railroad extending north from Córdoba
through Tucumán to Jujuy; reached Tucumán 1876 and Jujuy
1900; built largely with European capital (see Railroads).

BELIN, JULIO.   French printer, fellow-student of Sarmiento in
France, joined him in Chile where they formed a sociedad
tipográfica [publishing company or printing press] that published most of Sarmiento's works written in Chile, as well as

several periodicals. Belín married Sarmiento's only daughter, Faustina. Six children: most famous Augusto and Eugenia, the painters.

BELIN SARMIENTO, AUGUSTO (1854-1936). Grandson of Sarmiento who throughout his life as editor and diplomat devoted himself to the collection and saving of all of Sarmiento's belongings and the editing of his writings.

BELLAS ARTES, NATIONAL ACADEMY OF. The idea of forming a national academy to foster the development of the fine arts germinated with a group of young Argentine painters who were living (1872) in the humble Buenos Aires home of Braulio Berrotarán, an authentic rural peasant and gaucho who served as their model as well as their host in the creole fashion of life in which they wanted to live while they devoted themselves to painting Argentine scenes; joined by the newly-arrived, distinguished Italian painter José Aguyary, they conceived the idea of forming a society for the fostering of pictorial representations of Argentine life; Sarmiento gave them his support, but it was not until 1876 that the Sociedad Estímulo de Bellas Artes was formally organized; during the next few decades it advanced in both scope and quality--emphasizing teaching functions and formal shows, often with government support; in 1905, at the request of the society, it was nationalized and placed under the direction of the minister of Justice and Public Instruction who was at that time Joaquín V. González; an advisory board was appointed, with Ernesto de Cárcova as president and Eduardo Sívori (a member of the original group of painters) as vice president.

BELLEMARE, GURET. French jurist who came to Buenos Aires, 1822, as part of a small French farming group but moved into Buenos Aires to become interested in law reform of the 1820s; concerned himself especially with penal reform and criminal law; proposed among other measures the adoption of the jury system used in the United States; at Dorrego's request he drew up and published in 1829 El plan general de organización judicial para Buenos Aires, in which were stated the principles that would serve as basis for a code of national laws; considered to be important contribution to Argentine legal history and republished in facsimile editions, with preliminary note by Ricardo Levene, by Instituto de Historia del Derecho en la Facultad de Derecho y Ciencias Sociales de la Universidad de Buenos Aires (Buenos Aires, 1949).

BELTRAN, FRAY LUIS (1784-1827). Mendoza-born priest who devoted his energies and skill to producing and servicing artillery; made possible many of the victories of Carrera, San Martín, and Bolívar.

BELTRES, FELIPE (?-1856). French-born engineer; fought against British in Buenos Aires in 1807; in Northern Army;

after independence settled in Tucumán where he devoted himself to scientific studies; director of first Lancastrian school
in Tucumán.

BEMBERG, OTTO. Argentine millionaire published El desquite del
oro (1934) in which he blamed the problems of the country on
mechanization. He intended to give part of Argentina to the
Germans.

BENAVENTE, MARCELINO DEL CARMELO (1845-1910). Argentine-
born priest, who became Bishop of Cuyo in 1899; credited
with having initiated the erection of the Cristo Redentor de la
Cordillera (Christ of the Andes) 1904.

BENDITO. Improved tent-like shelter on the pampas made of two
hides propped against a center pole; often used by Indians.

BENEGAS, TIBURCIO (1843-1908)   Winemaker; public figure; financier.
        Born in Rosario; studied in Santa Fe; became manager
of Banco Nacional in Rosario; moved to Mendoza in 1881; used
his banking contacts to become pioneer in development of successful wine industry of that area; acquired historic El Trapiche property in Godoy Cruz and transformed it into a vineyard and winery model for the entire area; he introduced many
modern scientific methods; important among these was the use
of the hilera planting system, in which vines are planted in
rows, trained on low wire fences, with more effective use of
irrigation ditches between the close rows; increased production
greatly; because of this and other innovations the Trapiche
Bodega was bottling fine wines by early 1900s; he continued
prominent in the banking and political careers already entered
in Rosario; founded branch of Banco Nación in Mendoza, 1884;
became National Congressman two years later and senator in
1882; resigned to become governor of Mendoza (1887-1889); during his administration he established schools, and Banco de Mendoza, ordered bridge built across the river, and contracted with
Italian engineer César Cipoletti to draw up plans for improving
irrigation and drainage systems; left office because of federal intervention due to military rebellion within province (see Mendoza);
served as senator again 1895-1899; sent to Chile as plenipotentiary minister and extraordinary ambassador, 1903-1905; resigned
because of bad health; died in Buenos Aires; left a prominent,
highly respected, and wealthy family, as well as one of the wealthiest wineries in the country, that unfortunately went into bankruptcy in 1972; among the places commemorating Tiburcio Benegas'
name in the area are a school, a street, a railroad station, the
Tunuyán river dam, and a town.

BENEGAS, TREATY OF. Treaty of "perpetual" peace to end costly
years of fighting between Santa Fe and Buenos Aires, signed
November 24, 1820, at the Cordoban estancia of Tiburcio
Benegas, with the governor of Córdoba, General Juan Bautista

Bustos, serving as mediator and guarantor; in addition to signing the pledge of peace and friendship (later made into an alliance between the two provinces), Buenos Aires agreed to
send delegates to the congress to be called in Córdoba; and
Rosas, in a correlative private agreement, pledged that
25,000 (later actually 30,000) head of cattle would be sent to
Santa Fe to replenish the herds largely destroyed by five years
of continuous fighting; treaty had important results; peace between the two provinces lasted thirty years, removed the
Entre Ríos caudillo, Francisco Ramírez, from possibility of
intervening in Santa Fe-Buenos Aires relationship, and created entirely new political alignment for the civil wars that
later broke out; Santa Fe had basis for new prosperity; and
Juan Manuel Rosas for the first time became known and made
an important political impact outside his own province of Buenos Aires.

BENGOA, JUSTO LEON.   Leader of the G.O.U. who, disenchanted
with Perón, tried to obtain his resignation in 1944; active in
the revolution of 1955.

BENOIT, PEDRO (d. 1853).   French civil engineer, veteran of Napoleon's army, moved to Buenos Aires after Waterloo; after
serving briefly in Guillermo Brown's navy (1819), and spending
some time as assistant to the French scientist Aimé J. A.
Bonpland, he was called into service of the Martín Rodríguez
government as engineer; steadily advanced in public works
projects until his appointment, shortly before his death, as
civil and naval architect and member of the Public Works
Council in Buenos Aires government of Vicente López.

BENOIT, PEDRO (son) (1836-1897).   Architect, engineer and city-
planner.   An engineer like his father, he directed the construction of large numbers of public buildings in Buenos Aires
provinces; designed the new city of La Plata, taught engineering there, and held various municipal posts.

BENTHAM, JEREMY (1748-1832).   British intellectual pensador
and philosopher, interested in all Latin America; made impact
on early years of Argentine nationality through his close
friendship and continued correspondence with Bernardino Rivadavia, minister and first president of the Argentine nation;
during the 1820s, Bentham's political theories were widely
translated, read, discussed, taught in the university and consulted in the political developments of that critical decade.

BERDUC, ENRIQUE (1855-1928).   After active role in public and
political life of his native city of Paraná, he moved to the national scene, serving as national deputy from his province, accepting the responsibility of minister of Hacienda de la Nación
(Treasury) and director of the Banco de la Nación; contributed
greatly to the development of public construction in Paraná
and public education.

BERDUGO, MARIANO (1803-1857). Spanish-born Jesuit who came
to Buenos Aires to establish Jesuit missions; eventually expelled by Rosas.

BERESFORD, WILLIAM CARR, Viscount (1768-1854). British general who captured Buenos Aires, 1806. Entered British army
in 1785; lost one eye in shooting accident in Nova Scotia; made
his military reputation under Sir David Baird in Egypt (1799-
1803) and South Africa (1805); placed in charge of armed
force of 1500-1600 men accompanying Sir Home Popham's expedition from South Africa to the Río de la Plata area; landed
his troops at Quilmes 25 June, 1806 and on June 27 at three
o'clock in the afternoon took possession of fort at Buenos
Aires; next day hoisted British flag and issued proclamation
promising administration of justice; respect for rights of private property; protection of Roman Catholic religion; and freedom of commerce equal to that enjoyed in other British colonies; he later announced that blacks and Indians would not be
aroused against residents; reduced customs charges and freed
certain trades from state monopoly to demonstrate commercial
advantages of British rule; due to fact that Popham's expedition had been undertaken without official instructions (see British Invasions) and its purpose was not clear, Beresford viewed
his operation as simple conquest and called on all citizens to
swear allegiance to the British crown; most, however, felt like
Belgrano: "El amo viejo o ninguno" ("the old master or
none") and turned to opposition.
    Santiago de Liniers, with Alzaga, Pueyrredón, and oth-
ers organized successful reconquest of Buenos Aires August 12,
1806, and Beresford was interned at Luján; there he spread
the word that the British were not interested in conquest as
much as in aiding the Spanish Americans to win their independence from Spain, to enjoy the benefits--especially economic--
of such freedom; alarmed at this propaganda, the viceroy ordered him moved to imprisonment in Catamarca but Saturnino
Rodríguez Peña and other porteños helped him to escape and
return to England, 1807.
    Assigned to the task of reorganizing the Portuguese army
during the peninsular wars, he showed such talents for organization that Wellington declared that, in event of his own death,
he would want Beresford to succeed him; in the hardfought battle of Albuera (1811) Beresford commanded the combined English, Portuguese, and Spanish forces that defeated the French;
among his Spanish officers was Lieutenant Colonel José San
Martín, Argentine future liberator of southern South America;
after the peninsular wars Beresford continued in military service until retirement in 1830, having become a viscount in 1823.

BERG, FEDERICO GUILLERMO CARLOS (1843-1902). Latvian natural scientist chosen by Carlos G. C. Burmeister to assist him
in establishing scientific activities and education in Argentina;
succeeded Burmeister as Director of the Museum of Buenos Aires;
national and international honors awarded him.

BERISSO.   A working class district and suburb of La Plata about 35
     miles from Buenos Aires; the Swift and Armour plants make
     Berisso a center of the meat-packing industry; workers in
     these plants are organized into one of the strongest unions of
     the Peronist "Bloc 62"; the streets of Berisso, low-cost hous-
     ing projects stand as tangible monuments to Peronist welfare
     policies.

BERMEJO RIVER.   River that rises in Tarija, Bolivia, at altitude
     of more than 6500 feet and flows through Argentina to empty
     into Paraguay River after meandering nearly 700 miles through
     swampy and subtropical Chaco region; Bermejo forms boundary
     between Chaco and Formosa provinces (this portion of river
     known as the Teuco); Bermejo frequently changes its channel
     and often floods large areas adjacent to it; early Spaniards at-
     tempted to use it as route from Peru and northwestern Argen-
     tina to the Chaco region and Río de la Plata area but found it
     impossible to navigate; various missions were established
     among the Toba and Mocovi Indians there and a Spanish town
     was founded in 1585 at Concepción del Bermejo (q.v.), but all
     were eventually abandoned because of Indian hostility; in late
     eighteenth century, Governor Jerónimo Matorras took expedi-
     tion into Chaco from Salta, more or less following Bermejo
     route and finally reached site of former Concepción del Ber-
     mejo; Franciscan missionaries and military commandants were
     also active in this area in closing decades of eighteenth cen-
     tury, attempting to bring Indians into reductions and to stabi-
     lize the northern border; the unnavigability of the Bermejo
     continued to tantalize and frustrate people in that area and in
     1872 Natalio Roldán took a small steamboat up the river as
     far as Tigre Colmado (see Chaco and Formosa provinces).
          Other Bermejo rivers are to be found in Catamarca,
     La Rioja, and La Pampa provinces but these eventually lose
     their identity in larger streams.

BERMUDEZ, JUSTO GERMAN (1783-1813).   Captain in San Martín's
     Mounted Grenadiers who died of wounds received in the fight
     at San Lorenzo (San Martín's first military action in Argen-
     tina).

BERON DE ASTRADA, GENARO (d. 1839).   Governor of Corrientes;
     opponent of Rosas; becoming governor of province early in
     1838 he quickly faced the armed opposition of Rosas supporter,
     General Pascual Echagüe, governor of Entre Ríos, who was
     calling on Rosas to support him; Colonel Berón de Astrada de-
     cided to challenge them both, in one of first open movements
     against Rosas' power; signed treaty with President Rivera of
     Uruguay, called on governor of other provinces to join him in
     withdrawing power to negotiate with foreign powers and other
     powers that they had delegated to Rosas; entered into collusion
     with Argentine anti-Rosas exiles in Montevideo and led his
     army against the invading Rosas-supported one of Echagüe;
     when the promised forces of Rivera never appeared, Berón

de Astrada's army was decisively defeated in the battle of Pago Largo March 31, 1839, and he himself was killed.

BERRA, FRANCISCO ANTONIO (1844-1906). Porteño writer who also lived in Uruguay; won international acclaim for his writings in pedagogy in Uruguay and Argentina; his fundamental work Apuntes para un curso de pedagogía, hailed internationally as one of the major contributions to pedagogical literature of its period.

BERRUTTI, JOSE J. (1871-1951). Porteño educator and adminstrator responsible for many innovations (including first night schools of women); author of texts and pedagogical monographs.

BERTOLE, EMILIA (1900-   ). Painter of historical subjects (including three official portraits of Hipólito Yrigoyen) which won national and international popular and critical acclaim.

BERUTI, ANTONIO LUIS (1772-1841). Patriot leader of independence period.
        Born in Buenos Aires of Spanish parents, educated in Spain, returned to Buenos Aires at time of British invasions; member of creole patriot group working for independence; collaborator of Mariano Moreno; very active in Cabildo Abierto in May 25, 1810 revolution; fought as staff officer in the Army of the Andes at battle of Chacabuco; commended by San Martín; returned shortly thereafter to Buenos Aires; became active in unitarist politics; died following the battle of Rodeo del Medio in which he had fought (1841).

BERUTTI, ARTURO. (1862-1919). Born in San Juan, grandson of independence leader Antonio Luis Beruti, became first recipient of Argentine national music fellowship; created several operas (Yapanki, Los héroes, Facundo); particularly interested in Indoamerican themes.

BERYLLIUM. Beryllium aluminum silicate, a very hard, lustrous mineral with crystals that come in many colors in precious and semiprecious gemstones (such as emeralds and aquamarines); a source of beryllium, a hard, rare metallic element, found only in combination with other elements, greatly in demand in modern metallurgy; its presence known in Argentina since the late nineteenth century; now mined intensively in Córdoba, as well as in San Luis and Catamarca.

BETBEDER, ONOFRE (1860-1915). Naval officer--vice-admiral-- from Mendoza. Devoted entire career to naval activities; often represented Argentina on naval matters abroad or in international conferences, especially those dealing with naval architecture; frequently sent as part of officer crew--or eventually as commander--to pick up ships commissioned to be built abroad; minister of Marina (Navy) 1906-1910, following death of Commodore Rivadavia; died in New York while presiding over the Naval Commission supervising the construction of the acorazados (battleships) Rivadavia and Moreno.

BETLEMITAS. Members of first American monastic religious order, founded in Guatemala in 1672; came to La Plata area in 1748 and remained there until 1850, maintaining hospitals and mental health institutions in several cities and playing an active role in medical and health services to the military; particularly active during the period of the English invasions and the wars for independence.

BEVANS, SANTIAGO (1777-1832). English engineer brought by Buenos Aires government to Argentine in 1822 to direct the newly created Department of Hydraulic Engineering; under Rivadavia's government he planned extensive projects related to modernizing the water supply of the city; constructing a port; opening new internal water routes to the capital; quarrying the riverbeds for construction rock, etc.; experimented with gas-lighting and a new prison design; retired to private life in 1828 when Dorrego took over the government and dropped the uncompleted projects.

BEVERINA, JUAN (1877-1943). Cordoban military career officer and military historian: La guerra del Paraguay (7 vols.); wrote extensively about General José María Paz; collaborator in the Historia de la nación argentina, published by the National Academy of History.

BIALET MASSE, JUAN (d. 1907). Spanish-born and trained educator; came to Argentina in 1873; taught at Mendoza, San Juan, La Rioja; professor of engineering and medicine at University of Córdoba; active both professionally and as author writing about projects and matters dealing with irrigation and agriculture.

BIANCO, GERMAN (1869-1943). Italian-born marble worker who, in 1907, imported and established the first marble-working equipment and began the exploitation of Argentine marble deposits.

BIBLIOTECA, LA. Monthly historical review published in Buenos Aires by Paul Groussac, 1886; discontinued in 1898 because of controversy its views had aroused.

BIBLIOTECA DEL COMERCIO DEL PLATA. Title given to special book section in newspaper Comercio del Plata begun by Florencio Varela, 1845; purpose was to include memoirs, historical writings, and documents of historical or cultural value, in a format that could be removed, combined with others, and bound; first issue printed Washington Irving's Vasco Núñez de Balboa; the collections of four volumes holds significant place in Argentine historiography.

BIBLIOTECA DEL CONGRESO DE LA NACION. Major national library in Buenos Aires; traditionally dated from the Constitutional Convention of 1826 but becoming important only in the modern years, after varying periods of activity and neglect; directed by a congressional administrative commission, in addition to library functions, it sponsors active research and publishing programs in fields relating to Argentine historical and social development.

BIBLIOTECA DEL MUSEO SARMIENTO. In 1938, the National Commission of Museums and Historical Monuments created an Argentine historical library in the Sarmiento museum, housed in the building in Belgrano in which the National Congress that federalized Buenos Aires had met in 1880; important collections have been added to it from the libraries of Avellaneda, Juan Bautista Alberdi, and others.

BIBLIOTECA MAYOR, Córdoba. Founded in 1818 by the governor, Manuel Antonio de Castro, in an attempt to build a public library on the basis of the few remaining volumes from what had been the very fine Jesuit library at the university before their dispersal, 1767; little progress made with it until after 1883 when it received the highly selective library of bibliographer and codifier Dalmacio Vélez Sarsfield, rich in holdings of legal, social science, historical, and political philosophy materials; other gifts followed to make it a comprehensive, well-rounded library.

BIBLIOTECA PUBLICA (National Library). Founded by the revolutionary leaders of 1810 in Buenos Aires, with Mariano Moreno its sponsor and first director (briefly); has received both popular and private support for its activities since then; important popular cultural force and center; nationalized in 1884; directors elected from group of most distinguished cultural figures; its publication: Revista de la Biblioteca Nacional.

BIBLIOTECA PUBLICA DE LA CIUDAD DE LA PLATA (La Plata Public Library). Founded in 1884, after the federalization of Buenos Aires and the nationalization of the public library there, to serve as public library for province of Buenos Aires; first director Francisco P. Moreno; with founding of the National University of La Plata, 1905, the library became nationalized as part of it; developed into major research, reference, and reading library.

BIDAU, EDUARDO L. (1862-1921). Porteño law professor and author of studies in international law; particularly interested in inter-American legal disputes; effectively upheld Argentina's rights in Patagonia, providing basis for settlement of boundary dispute with Chile; appointed rector of University of Buenos Aires in 1913.

BIECKERT, EMILIO. Born in Strassburg, trained in brewing, came

to Buenos Aires and in 1860 opened his own beer brewery
which rapidly became an important component of national industrial development.

BIEDMA, CARLOS MARIA (1878-1946). Educator, author of pedagogical works, founder and director of Escuela Argentina
Modelo, 1918; in which he put into practice many innovations,
including most modern foreign methods and theories.

BIEDMA, JOSE JUAN (1864-1933). Porteño author of historical and
biographical works, and director of National Archives. Held
various military and public assignments in the Río Negro area
as well as in Buenos Aires, 1904-1921; published (with José
Antonio Pillado) a Diccionario biográfico argentino, 1897.

BIEDMA, MARTIN (1847-1909). Won international recognition for
the quality of his printing arts; published books, periodicals,
pamphlets of every kind; credited with having given Argentine
industrial and graphic arts the direction and position of distinction that they have since enjoyed.

BIENES DE DIFUNTOS (Estates of deceased). Spanish laws regulated every phase of the handling of estates belonging to Spaniards in colonial Spanish America; high-ranking official, usually an oidor or a judge was regularly appointed to this position to ensure that the proceeds from the estates reached the
Spanish heirs properly; in Argentina, the importance of this
was shown in the immediate delegation of such responsibility
when Garay founded Santa Fe and in actas capitulares (charters) of cabildos of other towns.

BILBAO, MANUEL (c. 1828-1895). Writer and historian. Chilean-
born lawyer, brother of Francisco Bilbao, the radical Chilean writer and philosopher; after years of exile and travel in
Peru and Europe, settled in Buenos Aires where he lived for
the rest of his life; left extensive writings in law, history,
contemporary affairs, fiction, an editing of Alberdi's works,
etc.; active in attempts to settle Chilean-Argentine boundary
disputes.

BILLINGHURST, ROBERTO (1782-1841). English merchant in La
Plata area who committed himself to the fight for independence; close friend and important supporter of Admiral Guillermo Brown.

BLACKS. Role of blacks in Argentina differs from that in other
American countries; present in large numbers throughout colonial period, up until middle of nineteenth century; they have
almost completely disappeared from Argentine scene; reasons
only partially understood; role and contribution to national historical development equally hard to identify or to evaluate.
       The black population resulted from the introduction of
Negro slavery at the very beginning of colonization (see

Slavery, Slave Trade); labor was needed because of the scarcity of Indians and the impossibility of using them for Spanish labor; Negroes from Africa and Brazil seemed to be the answer; black labor, however, was not needed for field gangs as the cool climate ruled out the tropical sugar and tobacco plantation systems, while the scarcity of mines limited the demand for that kind of labor; of the thousands of blacks brought in by traders, legal or contraband, to Buenos Aires annually, many were moved up the royal highway for sale at the Peruvian or Upper Peruvian mines and plantations and others were transported across the Andes for sale in Chile, but most remained in Buenos Aires and Córdoba and scattered among the interior towns, where they formed the corps of house servants, rural workers, and municipal skilled and unskilled laborers; although usually at the bottom of the social scale, whether free or slave, blacks entered intimately into the Creole life and society, with their problems of survival, defense, and growth, with the adjacent empty plains offering blacks, as well as whites and mestizos, a gaucho's or peasant's way out; as larger number of Spaniards were attracted to the increasingly prosperous colony, lower middle class creoles were pushed even farther down the social and economic scale to the lower level where miscegenation among all groups was more common; economic changes of the eighteenth century brought concentrations of blacks to Tucumán (in the 1760s, blacks and mulattoes outnumbering others by 12,000 to 8,000), the supply base (rice, mules, wagons) for the royal highway from Lima to Buenos Aires; at Córdoba, largest city and customhouse until Buenos Aires replaced it as viceregal capital, 1776, and at Buenos Aires which became a port of entry, blacks forming from one-third to one-fourth of the population from the 1770s to 1820; blacks and mulattoes accounted for approximately 60,000 of a total population of 500,000-600,000 in 1810 in area of present Argentina.

By 1825 this number had not changed greatly although casualties had been heavy among the blacks fighting in the war for independence and in the civil wars that followed; during early national period urban and port activities drew them to Buenos Aires, especially as free or cheap meat became increasingly scarce on the pampas; blacks tended to gather into nacíones (nations), each taking the name of the African place of origin; most of these centered in Barrio Montserrat and combined the characteristics and functions of fraternities and mutual aid societies, owning property (some claims lasting into the twentieth century), working for the emancipation of those still slaves, providing benefits for the others, and holding their own special ceremonies and fiestas, the latter regularly attended by Rosas whom the blacks strongly supported.

By 1895 the number of blacks had dropped to 5,000 in a total population of four million, and since then it has dwindled to a mere trace; factors involved in this virtual disappearance of blacks seem to include: lack of new black immigration; attrition due to civil wars of Rosas' period; heavy in-

cidence of fatal pulmonary diseases among blacks; miscegenation; and migration to other areas offering greater economic
opportunities or more congenial climates.

Black contribution to Argentine historical development
seems to have been a moral one, joining with other ethnic
elements in creating Argentine identity and way of life, rather
than as a separate cultural element.

BLAMEY LAFONE, RICARDO Q. (1878-1946). Catamarcan, specialist in English language and literature, followed diplomatic
career culminating (1926) in his becoming counsellor of the
Argentine Embassy in London; turned successfully, at age of
fifty, to musical composition emphasizing themes of his homeland, among them: the rhapsody Andalgala; a suite entitled
Escenas catamarqueñas, El ombú, a symphonic poem derived
from W. A. Hudson's work; works well received in both Europe and Argentina.

BLANCO, RAMON (1855-1936). Career officer in the navy from the
age of eleven; President of Supreme Council of War and Navy
1914-1920; attained rank of admiral.

BLANCO ENCALADA, MANUEL (1790-1876). Naval hero of wars of
independence.

Born in Buenos Aires, son of oidor, educated in Spain
for the Navy, serving in Spanish Navy, decided to return to
Buenos Aires to offer his services in the independence movement; his services rejected in Buenos Aires, he went to Chile
where his naval experience was quickly recognized as needed;
served under San Martín in Chile and Peru, either in command
of the allied Chilean-Argentine naval forces, or second to Lord
Cochrane during his period of command.

BLANDENGUES   Cavalry forces that guarded the Argentine Indian
frontiers; created in 1751, they received their name from the
enthusiasm with which they brandished their arms in welcome
to the first review visit by the governor; colorful uniform and
gaucho pattern of life; popularly considered to have been the
real source of the national army, the training ground for many
of the leaders of independence (cf. Balcarces, Estanislao López, Artigas, etc.); and to have contributed greatly to the advance and civilization of the frontier, especially through the
establishment of many important towns.

BLANES, JUAN MANUEL (1830-1901). Uruguayan artist whose prolific paintings of historic events and portraits of the Plata
area received great acceptance in Buenos Aires where a large
number of his paintings may still be found in museums, etc.

BLANQUI, ANDRES. Jesuit architect who (along with Juan B. Pri-
moli) came to supervise the construction of eighteenth-century
churches and other buildings (especially estancia headquarters)
for the Society of Jesus in Argentine area.

BLASCO IBAÑEZ, VICENTE (1867-1928). Writer. Born in Spain;
important in Argentina because of his influence on Argentine
writers like Leopoldo Lugones; visited Argentina during the
centennial (1910) and wrote La Argentina y sus grandezas;
during his visit he attempted to introduce rice-growing colonies into Corrientes but his efforts failed; he also founded the
colony of Cervantes in Río Negro; Blasco Ibáñez was more admired in foreign countries than in his own; considered a re-
gionalist he started a series of novels attacking social evils set
in different Spanish areas (Fruit of the Vine, 1905); the most
popular, Blood and Sand, attacks bullfights; he wrote colorfully
and was a master in creating suspense in his works; died in
Mentone, France, where he had been exiled for attacking Primo
de Rivera.

"BLOC 62." Sixty-two Peronist-controlled labor unions in the CGT
(Confederación General del Trabajo).

BLOCKADES OF BUENOS AIRES.
        1. September 10-October 16, 1810. Spanish forces
of Montevideo imposed blockade as a result of May Revolution;
the Junta appealed to the British naval squadron in those
waters, and to Lord Strangford, minister at Rio de Janeiro in
the name of Ferdinand VII. The Spanish-English alliance, and
the fact that British commerce was suffering; blockade lifted
as a result of British pressure.
        2. 1811-March to September. Renewed blockade from
Spanish forces at Montevideo, recognized by British because
the new viceroy was sent by England's ally, the government of
Cádiz; blockade lifted due to diplomatic efforts of British and
patriot activities in Uruguay.
        3. War with Brazil, December 10, 1825-September 26,
1828. At outbreak of war, Brazil imposed complete blockade
on all ports and coast of Argentine Republic; in spite of protests of neutrals that it was illegal, and vigorous Argentine
naval action, blockade was not lifted until peace was made.
Cost: reduced shipping (from 492 ships in 1823 to 30, 41, 62
in 1826, 1827, 1828--not counting smugglers); affected credit
and financial life of both Brazil and Argentina; ruined the development and colonization plans of Rivadavia.
        4. Blockades during Rosas' period (two): First--
March 1838-October 1840--France. French blockade without
declaration of war between the two nations. Cause: Various
incidents; foreign shipping tied up; ended by Arana-Mackau
agreement. Result 1841: 662 trading vessels entered the
port, including the first Spanish ones in many years. Second--
Anglo-French--September 18, 1845-July 15, 1847. Cause:
Rosas' blockade (June 1848) of Uruguay Republic as measure
against Uruguayan leader Rivera. Events: Blockade ineffective for most part; smugglers, both Argentine and foreign, used
new ports; traffic continued; Montevideo gained by legitimate
British trade suffered; important incident: the Liberator San
Martín lashed out against this foreign attempt to conquer Argen-

tina and bequeathed his sword to Rosas in tribute of his defense of Argentine independence. Ended, first by England, then by France, because it was ineffectual against Rosas and harmful to legitimate British and French commerce.
5. Argentine Confederation against Buenos Aires, April 20-June 20, 1853. Naval action by Urquiza in his attempt to include Buenos Aires in the confederation; blockade failed when naval officials joined Buenos Aires' side.
6. Blockade of Revolution of 1880--May 8-June 22. Purely political growing out of dispute between province of Buenos Aires and nation in election of Avellaneda's successor; attempt to prevent arms from reaching Governor Carlos Tejedor of Buenos Aires; blockade broken, the revolution broke out; result: Roca, not Tejedor, elected president and Buenos Aires finally federalized that same year.

BLUE BOOK ON ARGENTINA. An 86-page book, issued by U.S. State Department, 1946, based on documentary evidence (much of it captured German material) accusing Argentina of cooperation with Nazis and subversive totalitarian, anti-democratic elements during World War II; purportedly prepared for information of American republics at forthcoming consultation; book widely circulated throughout Argentina just before February national elections; unexpected result: Argentines, as well as Perón (whose answer was the Blue and White Book), looked on it as continuation of Spruille Braden's fight against Perón and what he regarded to be anti-democratic forces in Argentina--begun in 1945 while Braden was U.S. ambassador to Argentina, now continued by him as assistant secretary of state for Latin American affairs; nationalists, resenting what they regarded as U.S. interference, swept Perón into office, with Blue Book getting some credit for his election.

BOARD OF DEMOCRATIC COORDINATION (1945). Formed by the Radical, Conservative, Socialist and Communist parties to fight the revolutionary regime. Asked the Supreme Court to take the government and call elections. It staged the September March, which was memorable in Argentine history; for first time all political parties marched together demanding immediate termination of the dictatorship.

BOCA JUNIORS. Sport club, originally devoted to football, of national and international renown.

BODEGA. In Argentina this term usually refers to a vineyard with its own wine factory.

BOEDOS OF SALTA. Family that contributed several historical figures of distinction in independence period and that of the civil wars that followed.
        Dámasa Boedo (1818-d. after 1880). Woman patriot, fighter, mystic, and educator; served in Juan Lavalle's army as soldier, fighting against Rosas, as well as nurse and

seamstress for the troops; after Lavalle's death, went as voluntary exile to Bolivia; devoted herself to religion and the education of youth in Sucre, La Paz, Coquimbo, Lima, and Guayaquil; prevented by poor health from becoming a nun; returned
to Salta in 1880; died there.

José Félix Boedo (1808-1871). Brother of Dámasa and
Mariano Fortunato; military figure who rose to rank of colonel;
took part in fighting against Olañeta on the northern frontiers,
under José María Paz, distinguished in fight against Brazil
(left for dead with seven wounds at Ituzaingó); lived in exile
in Bolivia; returned to Salta in 1843 to form militia of Orán,
became commander of the Salteño frontier forces and governor
of Orán; confirmed in his rank as colonel of Army of the Confederation, had post guarding boundaries of Córdoba and San
Luis; died in Buenos Aires in yellow fever epidemic (1871).

Juan Ramón Boedo (1783-1817). Military hero of war
of independence. Brother of Mariano Boedo and father of Dámasa, José Félix, and Mariano Fortunato; joined Belgrano's
Army of the North; fought against royalists in battles of Tucumán, Salta, Vilcapugio, and was captured at Ayohuma (1813);
imprisoned in Casemates of Callao; escaped and returned to
Argentina but left at once for Chile to join San Martín's patriot army there; killed in action in the assault on the plaza of
Talcahuano.

Mariano Boedo (1783-1819). Signer of the Declaration
of Independence. Educated in Córdoba and at Charcas where
he became a close friend of radical patriot leader Mariano
Moreno; held various public offices; elected to represent his
province (Salta) at Congress of Tucumán; was serving as vice
president of Congress when it passed the declaration of independence, July 9, 1816, which he signed; moved to Buenos
Aires where he died.

Mariano Fortunato Boedo (1803-1841). Militia officer,
fought against royalists in the north; belonged to the Cazadores
de Salta, incorporated into Manuel Rodríguez' army; disfigured
and seriously wounded by shot that destroyed his lower jaw in
battle of Ituzaingó against Brazil; hospitalized, as was his
brother José Félix, wounded in same battle; joined federalist
forces of Salta later; captured by unitarists in 1841, executed
by Lavalle's orders.

BOERR, JUAN CARLOS (1830-1908). Military officer (born in San
    Nicolás de los Arroyos) who, after long career, was sent as
    colonel to the western frontier to pacify the Indians; he divided
    the groups; found land for them to occupy; suppressed upris-
    ings; established schools; and turned the Indians to agricultural
    pursuits (1869-1872); held other military commands, retiring
    as Governor of National Penitentiary in 1895.

BOEUF, FRANCISCO (1834-1899). French scientist and writer;
    came to Buenos Aires in 1881; director of the newly-founded
    Observatorio de la Plata from 1883 until his death.

BOGADO, JOSE FELIX (1777-1829). Paraguayan (born in Villa
Rosa) who joined the Argentine cause of independence; accepted
by San Martín into the Mounted Grenadiers at San Lorenzo in
1813, he participated in all the major activities of San Martín's
army, and later that of Bolívar in Peru; returned triumphantly
to Buenos Aires 1826 as colonel in the remaining Argentine
troops of the Army of Liberation--only seven of them Mounted
Grenadiers. Participating in various military actions during
the next few years, he died of pneumonia in 1829.

BOGGIANI, GUIDO (1861-1901). Italian painter who came to Argentina in 1887 to spend six years studying and portraying the life
and customs of the fierce Guaycurüe Indians in the Chaco; returned in 1896 to gather data and make maps and sketches;
learned the language, wrote a dictionary of the languages of the
Guaycurües, collected legends; killed by Indians when he went
back (from Asunción) into the Indian territory for the last time
(1901).

BOHORQUEZ, PEDRO (c. 1602-1667). Andalusian adventurer and im-
poster whose impersonation of Inca prince led to widespread revolts of Indians that threatened survival of Tucumán settlements
in 1650s and 1660s.
        Bohórquez, whose original Spanish name was probably
Pedro Chamijo, was born in utter poverty; at early age ran
away from his rural home to Cádiz where he was befriended by
Jesuits who taught him to read and write; accompanied his
uncle Martín García to Peru in 1620; remained there for nearly
three decades, married to a mestiza, living in rural poverty;
eventually he made his home among Indians in the high Andes
where he heard tales of the fabulous hidden treasure of the
Incas; armed with purportedly ancient maps, Bohórquez engaged in numerous treasure hunts, backed by various officials,
including one viceroy; his failure to find the treasure, along
with other schemes and attempted exploits, kept him in constant trouble with royal authorities; he was finally deported to
Chile and from there (because of new difficulties) he made his
way through Cuyo to Catamarca and Salta in 1656; representing
himself to the Indians as Hualpa Inca, a royal prince who had
come to lead them to victory over the Spaniards, Bohórquez
won full allegiance from all the Calchaquí chieftains; at the
same time he persuaded Governor Alonso de Mercado y Villacorta (q. v) that, given proper authorization, he could recover
the lost treasure for the governor; in spite of warning from advisers familiar with Bohórquez' past, Mercado appointed him
captain-general, with military powers, over the northern portion of Tucumán; almost immediately, the latter led the Calchaquians in a violent revolt against Spanish settlements, missions, and garrisons; Mercado suppressed it ruthlessly and an
uneasy peace was established; Bohórquez had escaped to royal
authorities and Mercado went to Buenos Aires to assume his
duties as governor of Río de la Plata; Bohórquez, having been
freed by royal officials as gesture of goodwill to the Indians,

returned and took advantage of Mercado's absence to organize
a new and greater uprising against the Spaniards, (including
western Chaco Indians, also) but this time Mercado, who had
been reappointed as governor of Tucumán, captured and executed the false Inca in the course of stamping out the entire
revolt. Bohórquez' story was included by Father Pedro Lozano in his Historia de la conquista del Paraguay, Río de la
Plata y Tucumán written in the early eighteenth century.

BOLAÑOS, LUIS DE (c. 1550-1629). Franciscan priest, missionary,
    and linguist; known as apostle and civilizer of Paraguay and
    Río de la Plata.
        Born in Marchena, Andalucía; entered Franciscan order,
studying at Convent of Santa Eulalia; not yet ordained, joined
group of twenty-two Franciscan recruits accompanying fray
Alonso de San Buenaventura on his return to Río de la Plata
missionary work; sailed in expedition of adelantado Juan Ortiz
de Zárate (1572); after great hardships missionaries finally
reached Asunción May 30, 1575; Bolaños remained in service
in La Plata area until his death more than fifty years later; at
first accompanying San Buenaventura, Bolaños participated in
the establishment of churches, missions, towns, among the
Guaraní and in Guayrá, baptizing Indians by the thousands and
acquiring an influence and ascendancy over them that attracted
some official jealousy; ordained in 1584, he accepted presidency of Franciscan monastery in Asunción; continued missionary labors along banks of Paraná and Paraguay rivers; left his
mark on all settlements and established new ones such as
Itatí in Corrientes and Barradero in Buenos Aires; formed
close working relationships with royal officials, especially
Hernandarias, as well as with other missionaries, such as
Jesuits; not satisfied with having learned Guaraní to preach
more effectively, he compiled a book of catechism and prayers
in that language that was widely used by all missionaries until
that of Ruis Montoya was written; at first accepted by bishop
of Asunción, Martín Ignacio de Loyola, but later rejected as
heretical by Bishop Bernardino de Cárdenas because of words
used to denote deity, this little book remains an interesting
chapter in the study of indigenous languages in Argentine region; Bolaños died in Buenos Aires shortly after giving testimony regarding the martyrdom of Father Roque González de
Santa Cruz; buried there in the Convento de San Francisco.
        Legendary role of Bolaños in littoral provinces parallels
that of San Francisco Solano in the northwest. See Fray Pacífico Otero, Dos héroes de la conquista (Bolaños and Solano),
(Buenos Aires, 1905).

BOLEADORAS (often, but incorrectly called bolas). Indian weapon
    made from two or three stones (occasionally only one) at the
    end of leather thongs; thrown with deadly effectiveness in hunt-
    ing and warfare; many conquistadors, including Diego de Men-
    doza, killed by these; adopted and widely used by gauchos in
    rural pastoral life; replaced by modern weapons in warfare but,

as late as 1831, General Paz, governor of Córdoba, was captured by use of a boleadora.

BOLETIN DE LA ACADEMIA NACIONAL DE LA HISTORIA. Annual, official publication of the National Academy of History; begun in 1937-1938, it is considered to be a continuation of the bulletin of the Junta de Historia y Numismática Americana; begun in 1924.

BOLETIN OFICIAL DE LA NACION. Official publication, established by law No. 438, October 5, 1870, in which every law and decree must be published; these automatically go into effect upon the required publication.

BOLIVAR, SIMON (1783-1830). Venezuelan leader who liberated northern Spanish America; after conference in Guayaquil with José de San Martín, liberator of southern Spanish America, and San Martín's departure from Peru, Bolívar united the two armies and, with this general Sucre, defeated the Spanish forces finally at Ayacucho in 1824. Extensive bibliography exists in both English and Spanish. See especially Gerhard Masur's scholarly Simón Bolívar (2nd ed., University of New Mexico Press, Albuquerque, 1969).

BOLIVIA. Name taken after independence by new republic in area formerly known as Alto, or Upper, Peru (see Alto Perú); preoccupied with internal problems and provincial conflicts, the Buenos Aires government had sent no forces after 1822 to fight the royalists in northwestern Argentina and Upper Peru and now (1825) facing war with Brazil, offered no opposition to the separation of the new nation from the old viceroyalty; when Andrés Santa Cruz briefly (1836-1839) united Peru and Bolivia into a confederation, Rosas joined Chile in declaring war on Bolivia (1837), primarily because unitarist forces had been permitted to use that nation as base from which to attack Rosas; latter unable to send much support to Chilean forces that defeated Santa Cruz; relations between Argentina and Bolivia generally amicable; Perón strengthened ties by politico-economic agreements and close relationship between labor groups, bringing Bolivia into cooperative bloc he was attempting to create.

BOLOS. Name taken by society, or nación, of blacks in the Barrio de Monserrat (see Naciones).

BOLSA, LA. Title of a realistic novel that first appeared as a serial in La Nación, 1891; author's signature "Julian Martel" pseudonym for José Miró, young newspaperman on La Nación; novel depicts life of Buenos Aires as it centered around the wildly active, then disastrously crashing contemporary or current stock market in that period; detailed, authoritative, and well-written, the novel received immediate acclaim and continues to merit distinction as a literary document of an era.

BOLSA MERCANTIL (stock market). The institution of a stock market has its roots in early Argentine national history with Rivadavia's formal opening of a Bolsa Mercantil in Buenos Aires in 1822; short-lived, it became a casualty of the war with Brazil and the internal political struggles that followed; in 1848 an institution named Camoati took over some of the functions of a stock market, and in 1854 a group of 118 persons who made up the Tribunal de Comercio established the Bolsa de Comercio which had limited functions and was succeeded in 1883 by the modern Bolsa de Comercio.

BOMAN, ERIC (1867-1924). Swedish archeologist who devoted himself to study of ancient Indian civilizations of northern Argentina; especially interested in the Diaguitas; wrote extensively about his findings; his Antiquités de la Région Andine de la Republique Argentine et du Désert d'Atacama hailed as first important systematic archeological description of the area.

BONAPARTE, JOSEPH (1768-1844). King José I of Spain, 1808-1813.
On August 13, 1808, the Marquis de Sassenay arrived in Buenos Aires with dispatches from Napoleon; Viceroy Liniers received these in the presence of a junta; the news of the abdications of both Charles IV and Ferdinand VII in favor of the emperor and Napoleon's intention of placing his eldest brother, Joseph Bonaparte, on the Spanish throne shocked Buenos Aires; almost immediately Sassenay was asked to leave; Liniers informed the porteños of the news and announced that his government would formally recognize the sovereignty of Ferdinand VII; for some reason, however, the Spanish governor at Montevideo, Xavier de Elío became suspicious of Liniers' loyalty at this time and began intrigues against him that would later have significant political consequences. Joseph Bonaparte played no further role in Argentina, which had started on its way to independence, and very little in Spain, being overthrown in 1813 by the Anglo-Spanish forces.

BONAPARTE, NAPOLEON see NAPOLEON I

BONEO, JUAN AGUSTIN (1845-1932). Bishop monsignor Boneo of Santa Fe diocese, dean of Argentine ecclesiastical hierarchy at the time of his death.
Born in Buenos Aires; one of first Argentine students to attend the Latin American religious academy in Rome; devoted his entire life to the work of the church in his native country, held many positions of responsibility; remembered especially for his compassionate, self-sacrificing labors during the cholera epidemic in Buenos Aires in 1886.

BONEO, MARTIN L. (1829-1915). Porteño painter, Italian-trained; depicted life and land of nineteenth-century Argentina; also painted portraits; important canvases include En la enramada and El candombe (African dance) in 1848--said to be the only documentary picture of Rosas presiding over a candombe de gala in his home.

BONETTI, AMERICO JUAN BAUTISTA (1865-1931).   Porteño sculptor noted for his wood carvings and sculptured figures, especially on religious themes.

BONPLAND, AMADEO JACOBO ALEJANDRO (1773-1858)--originally named Aimé Jacques Alexandre Goujaud.   French naturalist who devoted the last four decades of his life to the study of plants, animals, and minerals of Río de la Plata area, including Buenos Aires, Paraguay, and the former Jesuit mission areas up the Paraná and Uruguay rivers.

While studying medicine in Paris he formed friendship with Alexander von Humboldt; accompanied him on scientific trip to America, 1799-1804, including northern South America, Mexico, the Caribbean, and returning by way of the United States; collaborated with von Humboldt in the organization and publication of the resulting studies; published two botanical volumes of his own; persuaded by Rivadavia, Belgrano, and Sarratea to come to Buenos Aires in 1817; warmly welcomed and appointed Naturalist of Río de la Plata to succeed Tadeo Haencke; when political anarchy (1820) frustrated his hopes of establishing a museum in Buenos Aires at that time, he decided to go to Corrientes and Misiones; deeply interested in the possibilities of cultivating mate (then harvested from wild plants); at Santa Ana, site of old Jesuit mission, surprised and captured by Francia, dictator of Paraguay, and held in Paraguay for nine years (1822-1831) despite urgent pleas for his release from rulers and scholars; permitted, while interned, to continue his scientific studies, the practice of medicine, and to engage in business ventures; after being unexpectedly released, he established himself at São Borja, another old mission (in Brazil); returned to Buenos Aires, 1832, to ship important collection of plants, animals, insects, fossils, and minerals to France, but refused to go back to his native country; also declined invitation of Governor Alejandro Heredia to make Tucumán the base for his scientific studies; after spending five more years at São Borja and shipping second collection to France from Buenos Aires (1837), he went back to Santa Ana, hoping to establish a model agropecuarian colony there; became involved in anti-Rosas activities but returned to Santa Ana and Corrientes after Caseros and accepted, in spite of his advanced age, the invitation of Governor Pujol to become director of the Corrientes provincial museum, to be established in the capital (Corrientes) 1854; died four years later, buried in the cemetery Paso de los Libres.

BOQUERON (formerly known as Potrero del Sauce).   Site of hard-fought, costly battle in Paraguayan War, July 16-18, 1866, in which the allies emerged victorious; Solano López asked for talks but negotiations broke down and war continued.

BORDABEHERE, ENZO (1895-1935).   Santa Fe political figure assassinated in national senate.
        Born in Santa Fe; educated there and in Buenos Aires as
    a lawyer; became strong supporter of Lisandro de la Torre
    (q. v.) in the League of the South and Progressive Democratic
    party; became member of national senate in 1933; when the
    heated debate between Lisandro de la Torre and minister Luis
    Duhau (q. v.) over corruption and controversial practices of the
    meat monopoly became violent (July 23, 1935), the junior sen-
    ator from Santa Fe went to his colleague's aid; several shots
    rang out and Bordabehere, attempting to shield L. de la Torre,
    was killed and Duhau received a wound in his hand; the scan-
    dal ended the debate and brought a reorganization of the cabi-
    net.

BORGES, JORGE LUIS (1899-   ). Writer.   Internationally known
    Argentine poet, essayist, prose fiction writer, considered to
    be finest stylist and one of Argentina's greatest writers; pro-
    jects whatever the theme or characters of a given literary
    work, the spirit, drama, and color characteristic of Argentine
    historical development, along with works dealing explicitly
    with historical events and traditional customs.

BORGES, JUAN FRANCISCO (1816-1897). Public official. Born in
    Santiago del Estero in same year in which his father, also
    named Juan Francisco Borges, was executed by firing squad
    following decisive action of forces of Belgrano and Bustos in
    putting down Borges' rebellion aimed at winning autonomy for
    his province; son devoted his life to public service, serving
    in appointed administrative jobs, then frequently elected to leg-
    islative posts; served as acting governor of the province sev-
    eral times; 1860 elected national senator; 1864, president of
    the provincial constitutional constitution; strongly supported
    growth of primary education in his province throughout his
    career.

BORLENGHI, ANGEL GABRIEL (1906-   ). Labor leader; govern-
    ment official.
        Early labor union leader (Commercial Employees Fed-
    eration) to join Perón's movement; became powerful official in
    his government; considered to be one of most radical of Peron-
    ists and strongly anti-church; dismissed as minister of the in-
    terior by Perón in 1955 in an unsuccessful, last minute at-
    tempt to save his government by a turn toward moderation and
    conciliation.

BOSCH, ERNESTO (1863-1951). Diplomat and public figure.
        Born in Buenos Aires, entered diplomatic service at
    early age and spent most of his life in that career; held post
    in United States, 1889-1893; various posts in Europe culminat-
    ing with appointment as Minister Plenipotentiary to France,
    1906-1910; served as minister of foreign affairs, 1910-1914;
    1930-1931; named president of the Central Bank of Argentine
    Republic in 1936.

BOSTONESES.   Term frequently applied indiscriminately to all U.S. citizens by Chileans and Argentines in the late eighteenth and early nineteenth centuries, the name deriving from the large number of Bostonian sea captains that made their way to ports of these countries seeking to engage in trade.

BOTANICAL STUDIES.   Begun in colonial period by missionaries, especially Jesuits; stimulated in late eighteenth and early nineteenth century; promoted throughout the national period by European scientists--Tadeo Haencke, Aime Bonpland, Charles Darwin, and Germán Burmeister, for example--and such presidents as Sarmiento and Avellaneda; in addition to the botanical societies and curriculums offered at the various universities, there are special centers of note, including the Miguel Lillo, in Tucumán, named for the famous botanist of that area; and the Darwinion Institute, founded by Cristóbal M. Hicken in Buenos Aires, 1924.

BOUCHARD, HIPOLITO (1783-1843).   French-born corsair who became naval hero of San Martín's liberating force to Peru; early member of the Mounted Grenadiers, resigned to join navy; disciplined by Cochrane after adventurous trip around the world (see Argentina, La), Bouchard was reinstated and promoted by San Martín; remained in Peru after war, killed on his sugar plantation there in 1843.

BOULOGNE SUR MER.   French city, in department of Calais, in which San Martín spent the last two years of his life, having sold his home in Paris in 1848 to get away from the revolutionary activities there.

BOURBON.   Dynasty that ruled Spain (and its colonies) from 1700 (Felipe V) [with minor breaks in 19th century] until 1931 when Alfonso XIII was dethroned to make way for the Spanish Republic; restored in 1975 with Juan Carlos.

BOURBON REFORMS.   Term applied to legislation by which Spanish kings in eighteenth century attempted to restructure political, economic, and social and cultural institutions of Spain and Spanish American colonies to centralize royal power, increase revenue, organize defense more effectively and to introduce and make use of new ideas of the Enlightenment; reforms called "Bourbon" because of royal family name and also because many of the reforms had previously been used by Bourbon rulers in France (see Carlos III for Bourbon reforms in Argentina).

BOVEDAS DE SAN MARTIN.   Colonial buildings near Uspallata reputed to have been used as powder factory for San Martín's Army of the Andes; now officially declared to be a national monument.

BOWLES, WILLIAM (1790-1838).   British naval officer.   Visited

Bowles 110

Buenos Aires 1813; returned as commodore of British naval
force based in Buenos Aires, 1816-1819; close personal friend,
admirer, and correspondent of San Martín; deeply sympathetic
to Argentine fight for liberation from Spain; actually collaborated as much as possible with Argentine Liberator and other
patriot leaders; correspondence with San Martín constitutes
valuable historical source material; so do his reports to British admiralty, reinforcing other British reports urging confidence in San Martín's military ability and personal integrity
as effective leader of forces for independence; contact between
Bowles and San Martín continued after Bowles returned to England, married Lord Palmerston's sister, and took his place in
Parliament, while San Martín was living in Europe.

BOY SCOUTS (Argentine Association of). After early foreign attempt (1908) to introduce Sir Robert Baden-Powell's Boy Scout
movement to Argentina showed little success, an indigenous
Argentine effort (1911-1912) led by Dr. Francisco P. Moreno,
based on nationalism, and eventually backed by national and
provincial governments, and sponsored by prominent citizens
won widespread acceptance.

BRABO, FRANCISCO JAVIER (d. 1913). Spanish-born merchant
and entrepreneur; active in Uruguayan and Argentine business
and politics; published and edited annotated work entitled
Colección de documentos relativos a la expulsión de los jesuitas
de la República Argentina y del Paraguay en el reinado de
Carlos III (Madrid, 1872); art collector and sponsor in Buenos
Aires in closing years of his life; responsible for bringing
painter José Aguyarí to Argentina.

BRACKEBUSCH, LUIS (1849-1906). German geologist, cartographer,
scientist, who centered his studies and scientific writing in
Argentina (1872-1888) and then in Germany on the geology of
central and northern Argentina; one of first to note deposits of
petroleum there (Formación petrolífera de Jujuy, 1883).

BRACKENRIDGE, HENRY M. (1786-1871). U.S. author of excellent
descriptions of Argentina in the independence period; secretary
of commission, headed by Caesar Augustus Rodney, sent to
Buenos Aires to study desirability of U.S. recognition of the
republic; Brackenridge's notes published in London (1820) under
title Voyage to South America, Performed by Order of the
American Government in the years 1817 and 1818 in the Frigate Congress.

BRADEN, SPRUILLE (1894-1978). U.S. Ambassador to Argentina,
1945-1946 (see Blue Book on Argentina).

BRADLEY, EDUARDO (1887-1951). Aviation pioneer in Argentina;
made (with Captain Angel María Zuloaga) first aerial crossing
over the Cordillera of the Andes, in a free balloon--globo
libre--June 14, 1915; stimulated Argentine interest in flight;

served with several commercial airlines, local manager of
PANAGRA; 1929 honored as comendador of the Royal Order of
Isabel la Católica.

BRAMBILLA, FERNANDO. Italian artist and architect; accompanied
Alejandro Malaspina's expedition to Río de la Plata, 1784; left
large collection of drawings of that area in that epoch.

BRAMUGLIA, JUAN ATILIO (1903-). Jurisconsult, statesman, writer.
Born in Chascomús, Buenos Aires province; legal counsel for railroad union; became early backer of Perón and
played important roles in his government; as foreign minister,
1946-1949, restored much of Argentina's prestige in international affairs; reaffirmed Argentina's adherence to the inter-
American system; won some recognition of Argentine claims in
Antarctica and to the Falkland Islands at Rio Conference of
Hemispheric Security; proved to be able exponent of Perón's
Third Position in international affairs (midway between Communist and Capitalist nations) at both Rio de Janeiro and at
Bogotá conference, 1948; as chairman of the United Nations Security Council in 1949, he acted as spokesman for the members
belonging to the six neutral nations seeking to work out a compromise solution of the Berlin blockade crisis; retired from
government service and turned to scholarly pursuits, especially
the writing of books related to legal aspects of labor and labor
movements.

BRANDZEN, FEDERICO DE (1785-1827). French nobleman, veteran
officer of Napoleonic army, came to Buenos Aires at Rivadavia's invitation, to join San Martín's army; fought in Chile,
Peru; returned to die in the battle of Ituzaingó, in Argentina's
war with Brazil.

BRAVO, MARIO (1882-1944). Tucumán member of Argentine "Literary Generation of 1880," active politically and intellectually
as Socialist, strongly sponsoring social reforms to the left.

BRAZIL. Largest nation in South America; formerly Portuguese;
Argentina's Atlantic neighbor on the northeast; for centuries
their historical developments have been related; Indians, who
later came into Jesuit Missions (q. v.), had long moved freely
about in both areas, sharing language and culture; colonial rivalry between Spain and Portugal (q. v.) for lands drained by
the Río de la Plata system and ports near its entry into the
Atlantic (see Colonia del Sacramento and Montevideo) began in
the sixteenth century and continued until mid-1800s; the con-
tested north bank of the estuary then went to new nation of
Uruguay following Argentina's War with Brazil (q. v.); the
boundary line in Paraná area was finally drawn following the
Paraguayan War (q. v.) in the 1860s and free navigation of the
rivers was assured; throughout this entire period active trade
was carried on, usually contraband during the colonial period;
both Argentina and Brazil considered it essential to satisfy

their basic needs; they continue, in 1970s, to be important trade partners; in modern times Argentina and Brazil compete for leadership of Latin America but their tradition of cooperation in mutual interests continues; in 1915 they joined Chile in ABC Bloc (q. v.) and both took part in organization of Latin American Free Trade Association (q. v.) in 1961; currently they are engaged in joint effort to use waters of Paraná River for new source of energy.

BRITISH INVASIONS.   Called las invasiones inglesas by the Argentines but British by the British themselves.

The two unsuccessful attempts of the British to take over the Río de la Plata area, in 1806 and 1807, resulted from the impulse of a British naval officer, but grew out of more than a century of increasing English interest in the area, and led directly to the May Revolution of 1810.

After the British gained the asiento for the slave trade in 1713, increasing numbers of British commercial and naval vessels in the south Atlantic caused Spanish authorities to fortify Montevideo, Buenos Aires, and other ports in the Río de la Plata area; following the establishment of the viceroyalty (1776), with capital at Buenos Aires, and the acceleration of the international wars, with Spain tied to France by the Family Compact, plans for defense of Buenos Aires called for the retirement of royal authorities to the interior to mount effective counterattack in event of enemy capture of Buenos Aires (total number of soldiers available for entire viceroyalty rarely exceeded 2,400), with final disposition of captured territory depending, in any case, on diplomacy; as nineteenth century opened, two new elements were added to situation: industrializing England needed more sources of raw materials and food, as well as new markets for its manufactures (especially since the loss of its North American colonies); and the Venezuelan revolutionary leader, Francisco de Miranda, had largely succeeded in convincing British authorities that Spanish American colonies would provide such markets in return for British aid in throwing off Spain's sovereignty.

Among those convinced was Commodore Sir Home Popham, one of the ablest, most creative officers in the British Navy who decided to take action in 1806; having secured Cape Town, South Africa, as a base of operations in the South Atlantic, and intending to cruise along the South American coast to obtain necessary food supplies for the return voyage to Europe, he determined to test Miranda's theory by seizing Buenos Aires (then a city of 40,000-50,000); with a force of 1500-1600 men under William Carr Beresford to help in the capture and to remain as an occupation force, he sailed for the Río de la Plata and, avoiding the more heavily fortified Montevideo, landed Beresford's force at Quilmes, a few miles from Buenos Aires, on June 25, 1806; the viceroy Rafael de Sobre Monte, forewarned a day or so before, fled to Córdoba, leaving Buenos Aires on its own; two days later, on a rainy afternoon at three o'clock, June 27, 1806, Beresford took over the fort,

leaving one man killed and twelve wounded; the next day the
British flag was hoisted and Beresford issued his proclamation
of regulations; within a few days both British and Argentines
had learned a great deal: Miranda's estimate of the animosity
between Spaniards and creoles as being so great as to cause
the creoles to welcome the British against the Spaniards proved
to be greatly exaggerated; the porteño leaders desiring independence (still few in number, but influential) were disappointed
to learn that the British had come to conquer (Beresford's only choice, as no official instructions had been given for this
unauthorized expedition) and not to facilitate independence; the
British promise of a freer trade under their rule antagonized
both the Spanish merchants who profited by the Spanish monopoly and the creoles who wanted completely free trade; within
a few days, Argentines and Spaniards united in the common
cause and the British found themselves facing a totally hostile
populace organizing under the leadership of Santiago de Liniers,
French-born Spanish naval officer, Martín de Alzaga, leading
Spanish merchant and cabildo member, and Juan Martín de
Pueyrredón, creole official, to recover the city; on August 3,
Liniers' troops from Montevideo started slipping through the
British fleet in the Río de la Plata, whipped by winter gales,
to join Pueyrredón's peasant troops and the hastily organized
urban militia; August 12, the Liniers forces advanced in two
columns toward the fort, where Beresford was forced after
fighting (British casualties 300, Buenos Aires 200) to surrender
all the British flags, banners, 35 cannon, 1600 muskets, and
other artillery and military equipment, along with 1200 men
as prisoners; public feeling was so high that these were interned in the interior, rather than returned to England.

Meanwhile Popham had returned to England to receive a
tumultuous welcome from the populace, especially the mercantile community, as festive wagons carried the Argentine treasure ($1,100,000 from the viceregal treasury alone) through
London streets September 20, as proof of the rich promise of
this new colony; but a very cool reception from members of
Lord Grenville's government, furious at this action so contrary
to basic British policy and facing them with deep embarrassment at having to scatter their troops to hold and increase the
Latin American conquests at a moment when Napoleon's pressure in Europe was mounting to the critical point; as a concession to public opinion, however, two forces were prepared in
the fall of 1806, one directed to the Río de la Plata under Major General John Whitelocke who was to take over as governor,
and the other to go to Chile; meanwhile British merchants and
adventurers scrambled to get their goods and themselves across
the Atlantic as quickly as possible; the arrival in November of
the news of Beresford's surrender diverted all forces to Río de
la Plata.

On August 14, 1806, two days after the Reconquest, a
formally assembled Cabildo Abierto had met in Buenos Aires;
it affirmed Liniers' victory over Beresford, censured the conduct of the viceroy, and, with Sobre Monte's reluctant acquies-

cence, placed Liniers in military command; preparations began
at once for defense against expected new British invasions; all
citizens between the ages of 16 and 50 (who had not already
volunteered) were drafted; militia companies were formed of
creoles, Spaniards (organized according to place of birth),
Indians, mestizos, blacks and mulattoes, and provincials (especially from the river provinces), and feverishly trained.
British under Gen. Sir Samuel Auchmuty (q. v.) (former
New York loyalist) took Maldonado January 5, 1807 and on February 13, after sixteen days of hard fighting, gained Montevideo
where they settled in to await the arrival of the rest of the
British troops; in Buenos Aires, Sobre Monte, who had ineffectually attempted action against the British in Uruguay, was
deposed as viceroy; Junta de Guerra (War Council) (February
10) gave Liniers full powers to cope with the emergencies and
invasion that was now only a matter of time; on June 28, 1807,
Whitelocke's forces, consisting of approximately 10,000 well-
equipped veterans of European wars, landed at Barragán cove;
Liniers, who had about 8100 hastily trained, unconventionally,
if not poorly, armed militiamen, went out to oppose him in an
ill-advised action that resulted in a rout; Martín de Alzaga immediately took control in Buenos Aires, now vulnerable, and
had order established and the defense reorganized when Liniers
returned July 3 to take over; the following day Whitelocke's demand for surrender was rejected; and on July 5, Whitelocke
began his way into Buenos Aires; having rejected a systematic
block by block razing of the city on humanitarian grounds, and
also because his orders required that he be responsible for as
little damage as possible to facilitate his government of the
city later, Whitelocke attempted to take the city by assault;
three main columns, with several smaller ones, started down
the narrow streets converging toward the plaza, holding their
fire as much as possible until they should encounter the main
forces; instead, they faced heavy fighting all the way--every
house a fort from which invisible marksmen aimed muskets,
hand grenades, brickbats, "stinkpots," and all sorts of combust-
ibles at the British soldiers trapped between their fire, trip-
ping over barriers, and falling into ditches in the street; only
the New York Auchmuty reached his assigned goal; Whitelocke
counted his losses--400 killed, 650 wounded, nearly 2000 taken
prisoners, many of these wounded--and decided to accept Liniers' offer to permit the British to leave in a total evacuation
of Buenos Aires and with the transfer of Montevideo back to
Spanish authorities; upon his return to London, Whitelocke
faced court martial and was dismissed; during the following
year, as Napoleon invaded the Iberian peninsula Spain and England became allies in the Peninsular Wars to defeat the French
forces and British interest in Latin America became almost
wholly economic, rather than imperialistic.
          The results for Argentina of the events of the British In-
vasions--in terms of pride, sense of national identity, self-
confidence in political and military matters, growing sentiment
for independence, familiarization with new ideas, and eagerness

to progress economically--can scarcely be exaggerated: pride, in their unaided victories over Europe's best, reinforced their traditional self-reliance; Pueyrredón was sent to Spain to inform the Spanish crown officially of the victory; Napoleon formally congratulated Charles IV on the achievements of his Buenos Aires subjects; the cities of Potosí and Oruro sent rich gifts of gold and silver to honor the capital; and the Río de la Plata accepted as truth (as the members of the London court martial--who had not been there--did not) the defense made by General Whitelocke that modern military history offered no precedent of civilian action equal to that of Buenos Aires where "every male inhabitant, whether slave or free, fought with a resolution and perseverance which could not have been expected even from the enthusiasm of religion and national prejudice, or the most inveterate and implacable hostility"; a sense of national identity developed, with its own symbols (like the blue and white cockades used by the elite creole patricios regiments which were later to be embodied in the national flag), and its own leaders, such as the hero of the hour, Santiago de Liniers, as well as creole military and political figures: Pueyrredón, Cornelio Saavedra, Belgrano; while the Spaniards split into two factions, those wanting independence (on terms favorable to Spaniards) and those prefering to remain loyal to the Spanish Crown, creoles in the Buenos Aires area became increasingly convinced that they could handle their own affairs better than the crown and tended to unite for independence, expressing their political differences in parties designed to offer different programs after independence--the May Revolution was less than four years in the future.

Economic effects, closely related to political ones, were momentous. British, through public proclamations, personal contacts, and the publication of La Estrella del Sur in Montevideo, in English and Spanish, convinced many Argentines that Spanish mercantilistic regulations placed unreasonable limitations on their growth and prosperity; and the forced sale, at cost or less, of British manufactured goods sent over following the news of Popham's successful opening of Buenos Aires to British trade strengthened this conviction as markets were flooded with more varied merchandise, of a better quality, and at cheaper prices than porteños had ever before been able to buy; finally, the fact that hundreds of Englishmen, of all classes, lived for months in daily contact with Argentine people, both in the port city and in the interior where many were interned may have contributed toward the easy relationship that soon developed between an independent Argentina and Great Britain, as they began to know each other and to exchange ideas, and the British went home to talk and write about their experiences in this new land of such rich potential. (See Martín de Alzaga; Sir Home Popham; John Whitelocke; Samuel Auchmuty; William Carr Beresford; Creoles; Santiago de Liniers; Juan Martín de Pueyrredón; La Estrella del Sur; etc.)

BRITISH PACKET AND ARGENTINE NEWS, THE. English periodical, published intermittently from 1826 to 1858 in Buenos Aires; devoted to giving full information about finance, commerce, immigrant arrivals, and official documents; political comment avoided; 1606 issues remain.

BRIZUELA, TOMAS (d. 1841). Caudillo of La Rioja during Rosas period. Born in La Rioja; in 1829 was serving as colonel of infantry in Quiroga's army; wounded and taken prisoner at battle of Tablada; took over La Rioja in 1831 as federalist, friendly with Rosas; after Quiroga's death (1835) Brizuela turned against Rosas; he joined with other governors in the Coalition of the North to fight against Rosas whom they considered to have betrayed the true federalist cause; they increasingly disliked and feared his foreign policy and were convinced that Rosas was no longer the guarantor of the economic development and political independence of the provinces; the Coalition of northern governors (under command of Lamadrid) and Lavalle's forces made common cause against Rosas following disaster at Quebracho Herrado; in an effort to rebuild their fighting strength, Lavalle led his forces into the llanos (plains) of La Rioja where he, with Brizuela and Peñaloza as his seconds in command, could keep the enemy occupied until Lamadrid was in a position to fight; in June 1841 the Rosas' forces closed the trap; Lavalle escaped safely but Brizuela refused to leave his province and was defeated and killed a few days later at Sañogasta.

BRONCA. Slang word for anger.

BROSSARD, ALFREDO DE. Secretary attached to French diplomatic mission sent to Buenos Aires in 1847 to clarify international matters with Rosas; returned to France after two months; published detailed study (in five books, Paris, 1850) about Argentine history and Rosas, giving a Frenchman's view of the latter (apparently influenced by unitarist ideas).

BROWN, GUILLERMO (William), Admiral (1777-1857). Naval hero of the Argentine war for independence and the early years of the republic. Irish-born Guillermo Brown was orphaned soon after reaching the United States; went to sea to make his fortune; devoted most of his career after 1814 to service and command of the Argentine naval forces. Highlights of his career: defeat of Spanish naval power at Montevideo (1814) forcing surrender to patriot forces under Alvear; commanded Argentine naval forces in war against Brazil (1825-1828); forced French to lift their blockade of Montevideo 1838-1840; served Confederación under Rosas. (See T. Caillet Bois, Historia naval argentina.)

BRUCE, JAMES (1892-). U.S. Ambassador to Argentina, 1947-1949. First of three business tycoons sent to Argentina as ambassadors in attempt to improve relations between the two

countries, tarnished during World War II and by publication of
the Blue Book; Bruce succeeded in winning Perón's confidence
and it was during his ambassadorship that Argentina came back
to active participation in inter-American system; hampered
greatly, however, by U.S. post-war preoccupation with Europe,
British success in establishing bilateral commercial agreements
with Argentina, and Argentina's own internal policies and
needs; published Those Perplexing Argentines (New York,
1953).

BRUCH, CARLOS (1869-1943).   Printer; entomologist.   Born in
Munich; educated in Nuremberg; came to Buenos Aires to install and operate printing press at Museo de La Plata; credited
with having introduced phototypography to Argentina; remained
at La Plata, closely associated with Francisco P. Romero; became distinguished national entomologist, setting up first collection of insects and butterflies in the museum; taught zoology
and entomology at the university at La Plata, along with the
use of photography in natural sciences; was last survivor of
original group of scientists responsible for development of the
Museo.

BRUIX BROTHERS.   Sons of French admiral; all Napoleonic veterans.
        Colonel Alejo Bruix; came to Buenos Aires in 1817; as-
signed to Army of the Andes in Chile; fought in San Martín's
regiment of Mounted Grenadiers at Cancha Rayada and following
major Chilean battles; accompanied liberating expedition to
Peru (1820); formed part of auxiliary force sent under Santa
Cruz to aid Bolívar in Ecuador; commanded remaining Argentine and Chilean Mounted Grenadiers at Junín; fought at Ayacucho and at surrender of Callao; died in Lima that same year
1826.
        Eustaquio Bruix, younger brother, also was assigned to
Mounted Grenadiers in Chile; killed in action, 1819, during
campaign commanded by Antonio González Balcarce in southern
Chile.

BUCARELI, FRANCISCO DE PAULA.   Governor of Buenos Aires,
1766-1770; lieutenant general of royal armies.
        Probably born in Sevilla, like his brother Antonio María
Bucareli who became viceroy of New Spain (Mexico); became
career military officer; imbued with new ideas circulating in
Spain (as well as rest of western Europe); as governor of Buenos Aires carried out royal orders to expel the Jesuits from
Buenos Aires, Córdoba, Santa Fe, the thirty-three Guaraní
missions, and from all other establishments within the area;
also dislodged the British from Port Egmont in the Falkland
Islands where they had established a small settlement in 1766;
(Spanish government later returned this to England to avoid
conflict); Bucareli asked to be relieved from his office before
the end of his term and returned to Spain where he died.

BUCICH ESCOBAR, ISMAEL (1888-1945). Journalist, historian, museum director; wrote largely about Buenos Aires life and history in latter nineteenth century.

BUEN AIRE, SANTA MARIA DEL. Virgin whose name was given to Buenos Aires by its founder, Pedro de Mendoza, in 1536. Cult of Santa María del Buen Aire as protector of men at sea apparently originated in Cogliari, Sardinia, and passed to Spain with conquest of island by Aragón. Especially strong in Sevilla at time of Mendoza's departure for New World.

BUENOS AIRES (City and Province). City of Buenos Aires. Located on southwest shore of Río de la Plata estuary (thirty miles wide there) in the Federal District, (approximately 75 square miles), surrounded on other three sides by suburbs extending into the pampas of Buenos Aires province; population of greater Buenos Aires in 1970 nearly 9 million, more than one-third of total Argentine population; national capital as well as hub of economic, cultural, and financial life of nation; transportation center for railroads, airlines, and all shipping--coastal, river, or trans-Atlantic.

Province of Buenos Aires. Area 118,800 sq. mi.; population a little less than 9 million; located in eastern Argentina, bounded by Entre Ríos, Santa Fe, and Córdoba provinces on the north, the Atlantic Ocean on the east, Río Negro province on the south, and Río Negro and Córdoba on the west; largely made up of pampas, traditionally used for grazing; capital city: La Plata.

Historical development. For three centuries the lines between city, province, and sometimes even the larger national area, are blurred in history; remote as they were, and unable for the most part to deal directly with Spain, those of the Río de la Plata area learned to look out for themselves, with municipal, provincial, or even volunteer unauthorized leaders accepting responsibility to solve problems dealing with public interest or community emergencies along with defense against Indian raiders and European attackers, as legitimate authority was not always at hand or effective; further confusion resulted from the casual relationships among the different administrative groups, particularly in the nineteenth century; for example, the cabildo (city council) of Buenos Aires initiated and took control of the revolutionary movement of May 1810 that resulted in national independence; the customhouse, belonging to Buenos Aires province, controlled all commerce at times; and the governor of Buenos Aires frequently (by agreement with other provinces) handled all foreign affairs.

A settlement was made at the port of Buenos Aires February 2, 1536, by Pedro de Mendoza, first adelantado of the Río de la Plata, and named in honor of the Virgin venerated by sailors, Santa María del Buen Aire; in 1541, after Mendoza had returned to Spain, the few remaining settlers were moved to Asunción where sedentary Guaraní Indians made survival possible; Juan de Garay, from Asunción, reestablished

the Buenos Aires settlement in 1580, with sixty vecinos (citizens), fifty of whom were American-born mestizos or creoles; formally organized the city, appointed cabildo members, allotted town lots and rural lands, and, in lieu of Indians for labor or in encomienda (hostile nomadic pampas Indians both unavailable and useless), distributed rights to the wild cattle and horses in the area; from this beginning, life in both town and country continued to be solidly formed by two factors:
1. the port--giving access to trade with outside world, and
2. the pampas, where a grazing industry--based first on wild horses and cattle, with mules added in the eighteenth century, and sheep in the nineteenth--provided food, clothing, transportation, housing, supplies, and a constant source of commercial wealth; although usually illegal, the trading of hides and fats (supplemented later by mysterious shipments of silver from Upper Peru) formed the basis of trade (permitted or contraband) with Portuguese from Brazil, as well as Europeans and (in eighteenth century) North American traders bringing in African slaves, European manufactures, and sugar, cotton, and tobacco from Brazil; royal authorities, both secular (Buenos Aires had its own governor after 1617, subject to Charcas audiencia in viceroyalty of Peru) and ecclesiastic, normally condoned the smuggling in interest of colony's welfare, if not actual survival, and generally took part in it; after meager markets of Argentina were satisfied, imported articles found their way to Chile and, along with hides, mules, and slaves, to the plantations and mines of the Perus; by eighteenth century, cattle had become semi-tamed on estancias, tended, slaughtered, or driven to market by gauchos; establishment in 1776 of viceroyalty of Río de la Plata, with Buenos Aires as capital, and opening of the port to trade, as well as the establishment (1794) of the consulado (commercial tribunal) increased the volume of trade; large numbers of Spaniards came to make their homes in Buenos Aires, as royal officials, military officers, and Spanish merchants, eager to profit by the new economic opportunities and hoping to establish a privileged position for themselves; the small Buenos Aires population of about 4000 in 1664, increased to 17,284 by 1744, and rose sharply to around 44,000 by 1788; creoles and Spaniards of Buenos Aires (both city and province) joined to fight off the British invasions of 1806-1807; then creole patriotic leadership in Buenos Aires gained control and led the entire nation to independence (declared July 9, 1816); and sought to set up the new government.

Meanwhile introduction of saladeros, meat-processing plants for drying salted beef, brought increased new wealth to both merchants and cattlemen at a time when serious differences in interests were developing between the porteños--who, accustomed from earliest times to large groups of foreign residents in town, found it easy now to draw closer to Europe in ideology and life styles, as well as in commerce; becoming "liberals" in their willingness to abandon creole traditional patterns and institutions ("barbaric") in favor of "civilized"

European ones--and the Buenos Aires provincials, like those
of the other provinces, who clung conservatively to the old
ways formed in their own land by their own people; with independence secured, this tension between provinces and Buenos
Aires overthrew the directorate government and resulted in
anarchy and civil wars during the early 1820s, with each
province practically autonomous, except for Buenos Aires
handling of international relations; the brief attempt at union
with the centralist constitution under presidents Bernardino
Rivadavia and Vicente López y Planes (1826-1828) ended in
civil wars that quieted only when the provinces decided to come
to agreement with the Buenos Aires estancieros and saladeros
who, under their leader Juan Manuel de Rosas, had gained
control of the Buenos Aires government and offered a loose
federal system under which Rosas remained nominally only
governor of Buenos Aires, with responsibility for national foreign affairs and defense; actually, through Rosas' use of armed
force, personal relationships with provincial caudillos, intrigue, and the economic power exerted by the port of Buenos
Aires over the national economy, he ruled the nation: the
economy, increasingly tied into the British market demands,
flourished but remained under control of pastoral interests;
sheep supplemented cattle on the pampas and refrigeration
made it possible to ship fresh chilled beef as well as dried.
      With fall of Rosas' government following Caseros (1852),
the traditional differences between Buenos Aires (especially the
city) and the interior provinces again surfaced but the situation was reversed; this time the provinces joined together in a
national confederation under a new constitution of their own
making (1853) and its own national capital at Paraná, while
Buenos Aires stayed out and formed its own government;
this unnatural situation, contrary to all previous Argentine historical development, was made all the more unrealistic by the
fact that leaders on both sides (Urquiza and Mitre, for example) knew that political union must come and that the national economy must be modernized, no longer dependent on pastoral interests; nevertheless, economic rivalries, personal ani-
mosities, and political differences brought opposing armies to
Cepeda (1859), after which Mitre and Urquiza agreed on union,
and then again (when this was rejected by Buenos Aires) to
Pavón (1860), a battle which ended in a draw but left Mitre in
command of the situation; two years later (1862), after appropriate political and constitutional steps had been taken,
Bartolomé Mitre became national president of the republic,
with the city of Buenos Aires as the provisional national capital (for five years), remaining at the same time the capital of
Buenos Aires Province.
      During presidencies of Mitre, Sarmiento, and Avellaneda
(1862-1880) Buenos Aires shared largely in the national progress; the city, as capital and port, played a key role in the
new prosperity, cultural development, and became a powerful
administrative center, with the growing bureaucracies of both
republic and province established there; in the province, estan-

cieros and farmers moved to occupy the new lands opened by
the "conquest of the desert," increased and improved their
herds of cattle and made sheep and wool important market
items; near close of Avellaneda's term, matter of federalization of the capital became critical as the national government
was forced to move to Belgrano on legal grounds that it had
overstayed its time in Buenos Aires; the situation demanded
immediate solution as both political and military violence
seemed imminent; on September 20, 1880, the city of Buenos
Aires, including Martín García Island, was formed into a
Federal District as the site of the permanent capital of the republic; and the province of Buenos Aires built a new, beautiful, and modern city, La Plata (q.v.), to serve as its capital; within a few years, La Plata had become not only the
seat of the provincial government but a cultured, cosmopolitan
city enjoying considerable varied economic activity but never
replacing Buenos Aires as the urban magnet of the nation;
Buenos Aires province has continued to play important, if no
longer the dominant, role in national political life--interesting
to note that both Juan Domingo Perón (president 1946-1955) and
his wife and political collaborator Eva Duarte Perón were born
and grew up in provincial Buenos Aires towns; economic prosperity has increased with the introduction of agriculture, new
improvements in the grazing industries; development of Bahía
Blanca as a major port with railroads transporting products to
the interland to it; and Scottish, Basque, and Irish sheepherders replacing the earlier gauchos and cattle on the coastal
pampas; industry increasingly important.
        Before World War I, the city of Buenos Aires rivaled
or surpassed in wealth, size, culture, and beauty the cities of
Paris and London on which it was modeled; but curiously
enough it had become a symbol as well as a vehicle for the
expression of the strongly nationalistic spirit of the republic
in the early and middle twentieth century; its population was
largely made up of people whose ancestors were neither Indian,
Spanish, mixed, or creoles, along with increasing numbers of
rural migrants from those traditional stocks; surpassed in size
in the western hemisphere in 1970 only by New York City,
Greater Buenos Aires shares with it the problems inherent in
the rapid growth of a modern, industrialized megalopolis:
those of providing adequate services and acceptable standards
of living for populations of unprecedented size and density.
        See James R. Scobie, Buenos Aires: Plaza to Suburb,
1870-1910 (New York: Oxford University Press, 1974).

BUFANO, ALFREDO R. (1895-1950). Prolific poet of Mendoza, po-
    ems widely published in newspapers, periodicals; style tradi-
    tional.

BULNES, EDUARDO PEREZ see PEREZ BULNES, EDUARDO

BULNES, JUAN PABLO (c. 1780-1850). Cordoban leader of revo-
    lutionary movement (1816), armed to depose the governor;

checked by division of Belgrano's army; decided to devote himself to education rather than politics; brother of Eduardo Pérez Bulnes.

BUNGE FAMILY.   Founded in Argentina by two German brothers, sons of a Lutheran pastor.

Carlos Augusto Bunge (1804-1849) came to Buenos Aires as a young man; married María Genara de la Peña; served as consul general for Prussia and later also represented the Low Countries; active in establishing the Congregación Evangelista Alemana in Buenos Aires; founded important banking house of Bunge Heretz and Co., 1830.

Carlos' younger brother, Hugo Enrique Augusto Bunge (1818-1891), joined him in Buenos Aires and moved into the banking business and consular positions that his brother had occupied; married Constancia Ramos Mejía y Basavilbaso and founded another distinguished porteño family; served as vice president of the German Red Cross in the war of 1870.

Continuing the family tradition were Carlos' sons: Emilio V. Bunge (1836-1909), lawyer, banker, and public official, centering his activities in the capital and Buenos Aires province; Octavio Bunge (1844-1910), also trained in law; devoted himself primarily to administration of justice in criminal and commercial law; became minister of the Supreme Court in 1894, served as its president for two years; and Rodolfo Bunge (1848-1927), served as officer in the national guard as well as in several elective positions, along with his major agropecuarian and commercial interests.

In the third generation, among the children of Octavio, intellectual and cultural interests predominated: Alejandro Ernesto Bunge (1880-1943), engineer and economist of international repute; professor in school of economic sciences, University of Buenos Aires; on law faculty, University of La Plata; author of several scholarly studies on economics; national director of statistics; and held other related national positions; made lecture tour of United States speaking on economic consequences of World War I; participated in international conferences; became known as moderate, but effective, advocate of Argentina's qualifications for exercising leadership, especially in Latin America.   Augusto Bunge (1877-1943), physician who became active socialist; exerted considerable influence, both as member of congress and as writer--for periodicals and in several published books--for social reform; interested in public health, workmen's compensation, improved educational facilities; welfare and social security, etc.   Carlos Octavio Bunge (1875-1918), intellectual, with degree in law from University of Buenos Aires; sent to Europe on national fellowship to study public education; his report, El espíritu de la educación, published in Buenos Aires (1901), appeared in revised edition entitled Educación, with prologue by Miguel Unamuno (Madrid, 1902); and the first edition of his Nuestra América, in which he attempted to describe and analyze the social, and political phenomena of Spanish America, came out in Barcelona, 1903,

with introduction by Rafael Altamira; having, with these two
books, established himself nationally and internationally as a
thoughtful, careful scholar and intellectual, and a writer with
both style and clarity, he devoted himself to his classes in the
science of education and introduction to law at the University
of Buenos Aires and elsewhere, and to further writing, including a critical biographical study of Sarmiento; although obviously interested in, and influenced by, the positivist ideas and biological theories of his contemporaries, his thinking was original and he converted to Catholicism shortly before his death.
Delfina Bunge de Gálvez (1881-1952) was a writer like her
brothers, Alejandro, Augusto, and Carlos (and also her sister
Josefina), but turned more to creative writing such as poetry,
newspaper inspirational articles, diaries, and travel descriptions; strongly religious (Catholic) like her novelist husband
Manuel Gálvez; prolific writer in both French and Spanish, left
large quantity of manuscript materials in addition to those published.

BURATOVICH, SANTIAGO (1846-1909).   Austrian military engineer
    with de Lesseps at Suez; moved to Buenos Aires, participated
    in the conquest and opening to settlement of the desert; strung
    first telegraphic wires across it; constructed forts; built rail-
    roads; installed trolley system in La Plata; later laid sub-
    marine cable from Buenos Aires to Montevideo.

BURCKHARDT, CARL (1868-1935).   Swiss geologist brought to the
    Museo de La Plata by Francisco P. Romero; along with his
    companion León Wehrli, he made several studies of the south-
    ern cordillera, the results then published by the Museum; he
    moved on to further geological work in Mexico where he died.

BURELA, ALEJANDRO, Lt. Col. (d. 1839) AND LUIS, Colonel
    (d. 1834).   Brothers born in Chicoana, Salta, who led their
    gaucho forces against the royalist invasions from Upper Peru
    from the early days until after victory had been won, 1825;
    closely associated with Martín Güemes' defense of the border,
    but also fought in other actions in the northwestern area.

BURGOS, JUAN MARTIN (1846-after 1893).   Porteño architect-engi-
    neer of many public works in Buenos Aires and other ports of
    republic; studied in Europe and United States; prepared plans
    for city of La Plata.

BURMEISTER, CARLOS GERMAN CONRADO (Karl Herman Konrad)
    (1807-1892).   Scientist; museum director.
        German scientist who devoted more than 30 years to
    study of Argentine paleontology and mineralogy.   After two
    preliminary research trips to South America, this distinguished
    professor and scientist at the University of Halle decided to
    move to the New World; applied for and received the position
    of Director of the Public Museum of Buenos Aires; from 1867
    until his death, he evidenced scientific knowledge of Argentine

paleontology, entomology, and ornithology through his prolific
scholarly writings and elaborate collections; founded the Sociedad Paleontológica; his studies fill three volumes of the Museum Annals; also wrote Atlas and Descripción físcia de la República Argentina.

BURTON, SIR RICHARD F. (1821-1890). British travel author of
Letters from the Battle-Fields of Paraguay (London, 1870),
based on trips to Argentina and Paraguay in 1868 and 1869
(while serving as British consul in Brazil); it contains much
descriptive material of the countries involved as well as reports of the war.

BUSANICHE, JULIO A. (1878-1942). Santa Fe intellectual, author,
and public official; published in 1923, Apuntes sobre la fundación y desarrollo de la ciudad de Santa Fe to commemorate
the 350th anniversary of the founding of Santa Fe.

BUSCHENTAL, JOSE DE (1802-1870). German-born banker and
naturalized Spanish citizen, he came to Argentina after fall of
Rosas; heavily subsidized Urquiza's Confederación government
and army; died in Paraná.

BUSCHIAZZO, JUAN A. (1846-1917). Italian-born architect, trained
in Buenos Aires, responsible for construction of many public
buildings in Buenos Aires; director of Public Works of the
Municipality (Buenos Aires) as well as important private structures.

BUSTILLO, ANTONIO (1732-1796). Spanish-born Jesuit who completed his studies in Córdoba; assigned at once to mission work
among the Mocobí Indians of Santa Fe, he assisted Father
Florián Paucke (q. v.) in the founding of a very promising mission at San Pedro in 1765, two years before they were both
expelled with other Jesuits; Bustillo spent his time in exile
writing about Argentina and his experiences there; died in
Faenza, Italy. (See Guillermo Furlong, Entre los Mocobíes de
Santa Fe.)

BUSTO, EUGENIO DEL (1800-1899). Born in Montevideo; moved to
Buenos Aires as a boy; captured by Indians on raid near Luján;
rescued years later (1825); spent next fifty years in military
service, important at first as guide and interpreter in fighting
along Indian frontiers; rose to rank of colonel before retiring.

BUSTOS, JUAN BAUTISTA (1779-1830). Career military officer;
governor of Córdoba.
Born in Punilla, Córdoba; entered military career; led
Córdoba auxiliaries to fight British at Buenos Aires; com-
manded arribeños in October 1806 against British; supported
May Revolution immediately and belonged to first Army of the
North; as colonel, took reinforcements from Buenos Aires to
Rondeau (1815) after defeat at Sipe Sipe; served under Belgrano

who sent him to put down Borges' uprising in Santiago del
Estero, 1816; then to occupy Córdoba, 1817, because of hostile developments in the Littoral provinces; defeated by Estanislao López and narrowly escaped disaster at Herradura
(1819); named chief of staff of Northern Army, revolted at
Arequito January 8, 1820; marched on to Córdoba where he became governor (1820-1828); hoped to make Córdoba a power
base from which to neutralize fighting and mediate differences
between Buenos Aires and the provinces; called for Constitutional Congress to meet in Córdoba to draw up constitution
satisfactory to both groups; unsuccessful in his plans he opposed the centralist constitution drawn up by Rivadavia's government, and came out fighting against what he believed to be
strategy forcing Córdoba and central provinces to accept it
along with Rivadavia's rule and ecclesiastical reforms; defeated and ousted as governor by former friend and colleague,
General Paz, at San Roque; fled to join Quiroga but suffered
new defeat at La Tablada 1829; left General Quiroga to march
to Santa Fe where he died September 18, 1830.

BUSTOS, MANUEL VICENTE (1805-1878). Political leader in native
province of La Rioja, holding many public offices, including
several terms as governor.

BUSTOS MORON, HORACIO (1885-1952). Founder of Argentine
Tennis Club; president for thirty years.

BUSTOS Y FERREIRA, ZENON, Monsignor fray (1850-1925). Cordoban Franciscan church administrator (Bishop of Córdoba) and
historian; left Colecciones de documentos históricos in archives
of Franciscan monastery where he had lived.

BYNON, SANTIAGO JORGE (James George) (1798-1883). British
naval officer who joined the South American fight for independence; fought under Lord Cochrane in the Pacific; later commanded the Argentine corvette Chacabuco in the war against
Brazil.

- C -

CAAGUAZU. Battle in which the invading rosista forces of the governor of Entre Ríos, General Pascual Echagüe, were decisively defeated by the brilliant strategy of the defending General
José María Paz and his Corrientes forces, November 28, 1841;
set free the province of Corrientes and opened way for General Paz as far as Entre Ríos.

CABALLEROS ORIENTALES (Cavaliers of the Eastern Province).
Secret society formed by Uruguayans determined to free their
country from Brazil; their commission signed two treaties of
offense and defense between the Cabildo of Montevideo and the
government of Santa Fe under Estanislao López in 1823;

played decisive role in winning Uruguayan independence.

CABAÑAS-BELGRANO ARMISTICE. Armistice signed between General Manuel Belgrano, following his defeat at Tacuarí, and the victorious Paraguayan general Manuel Cabañas, March 10, 1811, which paved the way for negotiations leading to Paraguayan independence (see Tacuarí).

CABECITAS NEGRAS. Derogatory term formerly applied by porteños to workers coming into Buenos Aires from the provinces; signified "hicks" as well as darker color; formed part of Perón's descamisado worker support.

CABELLO Y MESA, FRANCISCO ANTONIO (1764-c. 1814). Journalist, political activist, soldier.
    Born in Estremadura; educated as lawyer but entered military career; came to Peru in 1790; assigned to protect Indians along Jauja frontier, having attained rank of colonel; determined to bring ideas of Enlightenment to America, and, inspired by the Mexican El Diario Civil, he established in Lima in 1790 the first periodical to appear in South America, El Diario Curioso, Erudito, y Comercial, precursor of El Mercurio Peruano; also assisted in organizing the patriotic society Amantes del País.
    Moving to Buenos Aires, he started and became editor of the first periodical published there; with support of both the viceroy and consulado, the first issue of El Telégrafo Mercantil, Rural, Político e Histórico appeared April 1, 1801, under the sponsorship of La Sociedad Patriótica, Literaria, y Económica that he and Manuel Belgrano had cooperated in establishing; publication suspended, for financial reasons, with issue of October 15, 1802; because he accepted employment with Beresford's government and collaborated with British newspaper La Estrella del Sur during the British invasions, Cabello was sent as prisoner to Spain by the restored viceregal government; freed there, he participated in political activities of liberal party in Sevilla; shot by firing squad as result of bloody events accompanying the first restoration of Ferdinand VII to the Spanish Throne, 1814.

CABEZA DE TIGRE (Tiger's Head). Site, near Cruz Alta, of execution (August 25-26, 1810) of leaders of Cordoban conspiracy, including Santiago Liniers, by Juan José Castelli, acting under orders of patriot junta in Buenos Aires.

CABEZA DE VACA, ALVAR NUÑEZ (c. 1490-c. 1557). Second adelantado of Río de la Plata.
    Born in Andalusia of a noble family, Cabeza de Vaca joined Pánfilo Narváez' expedition to Florida in 1528; surviving shipwreck off the Texas coast, he and companions, including one black slave, spent the next nine years wandering through the lands of the Indians, with whom they became very friendly; arrived in Mexico City in 1536 where their report initiated the

search for the Seven Cities of Cíbola and resulted in Coronado's exploration of the southwestern part of the United States (1540-1542); meanwhile Cabeza de Vaca returned to Spain and received appointment as second adelantado of the Río de la Plata; arriving at Santa Catarina Island off the Brazilian coast, Cabeza de Vaca learned from Spaniards there that Buenos Aires had been abandoned and the colonists had moved to Asunción; decided to walk to Paraguay; with 220 men, only a few on horseback, he led the way for four months, discovering Iguazú Falls on the way, arriving in Asunción on March 11, 1542, to take possession of his government; a man of high principles, determined to rule justly, Cabeza de Vaca found himself in trouble almost at once, nothing in his previous experiences in Spain and North America had prepared him for the life-style worked out by Guaranís and Spaniards in Asunción for their mutual survival and comfort; his acts, designed to protect the Indians and to establish slightly different forms of authority, were considered dangerous and intolerable by residents there, or (as Cabeza de Vaca and his friends saw it) were opposed by his political enemies and those whose greedy profits were threatened; in any case, when the adelantado returned in 1544 from an important exploratory trip, attempting to open an overland route to Peru, he was met by a revolt of the citizens (including some royal officials) and imprisoned for ten months until a ship could be built to return him to Spain (1545); tried by the Council of the Indies he was exiled but later exonerated, called back, and granted a pension; still considered to be controversial, as well as extraordinary figure, Cabeza de Vaca's published commentaries form an excellent source for information about this early period; Argentines, as well as Paraguayans, point proudly to the 1544-45 revolt against him as the first demonstration in this area of the independent spirit of creoles against what was considered to be injustice, as well as of their determination to do things in their own way.

CABILDO.   Town council; basic unit of political, judicial, economic, social administration in Spanish American empire, governed as a collection of towns; church and Indians, as well as settlers, organized in this pattern.
      For two and a half centuries, from the founding of the first cabildo in the Plata area at Asunción by Domingo Martínez de Irala until independence had been won, the cabildos of the widely separated towns of the sparsely settled Argentine area constituted the traditional (sometimes the sole) source of authority and responsible action for their towns, as well as outlying areas--Cabildo of Buenos Aires, for example, exerted authority north almost to Santa Fe, across the pampas to Córdoba and south to the Indian frontier; in theory, royal authority was supreme, uniting all cabildos under its power, and governors and corregidores presided over cabildos in the towns in which they resided; but in practice, until the establishment of the viceroyalty in 1776, Argentina received relatively little

attention from the Crown and each more-or-less isolated cabildo had to fall back on its own resources to carry on the
functions of government.

From the very beginning, due to historical circumstances of settlement, members of the various Argentine cabildos were largely native-born, or already deeply rooted in
the life there; cabildos showed a strong sense of identification
with the land and the life style developed there by the Indians,
whose blood many cabildo members shared; fiercely independent in spirit and loyal to their own communities, they vigorously opposed threats from outsiders--whether Indians, British
or Portuguese, or even Spanish settlers, royal officials, or
the Church--into their land, their traditional prerogatives, or
their preferred way of life.

Each cabildo consisted of regidores, or councilors,
usually about six in number in Argentina, elected annually by
the cabildo, one or two alcaldes (magistrates) and various
other appointed officials to carry out necessary functions; cabildos supervised all political administration; exercised police
power; defended town and countryside; regulated food supplies,
weights and measures, market prices; distributed land and controlled land usage and transfer of property; levied municipal
taxes; proclaimed public holidays and planned public festivals;
were responsible for administration of justice, both criminal
and civil on first account; maintained jails, roads; inspected
hospitals, distributed welfare to poor and orphans; and generally listened to any complaints from the citizens, in addition
to representing the interests of the community to the royal
government; e. g. insistence for judicial independence from the
remote audiencia of Charcas brought the temporary establishment of audiencia at Buenos Aires 1661-1671; regulated both
rural and urban crafts and industries; even intervened in quar-
rels and lawsuits affecting community.

Cabildos faced changes in late eighteenth century with
establishment of viceregal capital at Buenos Aires (1776), introduction of intendancy system, opening of Buenos Aires to
trade; royal officials began to preside over most cabildos;
Spanish merchants became regidores; cabildos of the interior
like Salta, Tucumán, Córdoba lost importance while that of
Buenos Aires increased; centralization of power, with institutional changes and reforms under royal control, lessened local
creole power and responsibility, but, with the English invasions and the events leading up to the May Revolution and the
successful fight for independence, the cabildo of Buenos Aires
once more exerted leadership, attempting to take the place of
the viceroy for the whole viceroyalty, while other cabildos resumed traditional roles in the interests of their own communi-
ties--not always the same as those of Buenos Aires; because
of the problems involved in integrating the cabildos into the
modern governmental structures that he wanted to create, and
because their political activities interfered with national government, Rivadavia abolished the cabildo of Buenos Aires
(1821) and, as he had hoped, the other provincial governments

followed suit; abolition of this traditional core of local authority left an institutional vacuum that came to be filled by personal authority of caudillos or dictators.

CABILDO ABIERTO (Open Town Council). In times of grave emergency during colonial period, cabildo members would summon
the leaders of the community--ecclesiastic, civil, military,
professional, economic, and social--to meet in a cabildo abierto
to discuss and vote on action to be taken; not truly open, as
members came by invitation, it was representative and gave
experience in self-government; very important in late colonial
history was the cabildo abierto called in 1806 to consolidate
Liniers' reconquest of Buenos Aires from the British and that
of May 22, 1810 (often called the first Argentine congress)
that resulted in the establishment of the first patriot government, leading to full independence; in modern times, 1951, an
assembly of Perón supporters seeking to nominate Perón for
a second term in the presidency and his wife for vice president, claimed historical precedent by calling itself a cabildo
abierto in the revolutionary tradition of 1810.

CABOT, JUAN MANUEL (1794-1837). Military officer; commander
of northern wing of San Martín's army in crossing of the Andes.
   Born in Tucumán, educated in Buenos Aires, fought
against British invasions; joined patriot forces fighting for independence; commanding right column of the Army of the
Andes, he successfully occupied Coquimbo and Serena in northern Chile at same time that San Martín's main army was winning battle of Chacabuco to the south to secure Chilean independence; assigned to duty in Chile, Cabot remained there until his death.

CABOT, SEBASTIAN (c. 1476-1557). Explorer of Río de La Plata
rivers and area.
   Born in Venice; lived for long time in England; accompanied his father John Cabot on voyage that discovered coast
of North America; made other voyages in same direction; in
1518 accepted offer to become Pilot Major of Spain; Cabot prepared follow-up expedition in 1526 to that of García Jofré
Loaysa which had sailed through the Straits of Magellan the
previous year to the Moluccas; both Charles V and Sevillian
merchants were eager to strengthen Spain's hold on the Molucca
Islands and exploit their spice trade; leaving Spain with four
ships and 250 men, Cabot reached Brazilian coast where he
met survivors from Solís' expedition and heard increasing rumors of silver to be found in the interior of the continent (inspired by existence of Inca Empire in the Andes); finding himself short of supplies for planned transpacific voyage, and
seeking wealth for the king as well as royal favor for himself,
he marooned several rebellious Spanish officers along the Brazilian coast and entered the Río de la Plata for exploration in
April 1527; met with Indian hostility and hardships; vessel sent
up Uruguay river wrecked; many of crew killed, small fort on

Uruguayan coast built and abandoned; sailed up Paraná river, building first European base in Argentina at Sancti Spiritus where the Carcarañá flows into the Paraná (about thirty miles north of today's Rosario); remained there two years sending out exploring expeditions; Paraguay and Pilcomayo rivers discovered and explored; continued to receive new rumors of the silver, the first actual evidences of Inca Empire to reach Spain; Cabot found by Diego de García who was also sent out to support Spanish power in the Moluccas, but sidetracked; after some preliminary disagreements, both captains joined in exploration of area; Captain Francisco César sent out on final search for route to silver kingdom, returned empty-handed; Cabot and García returned to the coast, leaving their ruined fort (destroyed earlier by Indians) as landmark to future conquistadores who knew it as the Tower of Cabot; returning to Spain in 1530 to seek permission and support for a colonization of Argentina as a base from which to conduct a longer and more successful search for the fabulous empire to the west, Cabot ran into bad luck: the Crown had already given a grant to Francisco Pizarro and his partner Diego de Almagro to go to conquer the Inca empire by the Panama-Pacific route; and the dissident Spanish officials, left in Brazil, had returned to Spain to register complaints against him; exiled to northern Africa briefly, Cabot was called back to Spain in 1533 to resume his post as Pilot Major; preferring to return to England, he was back in the service of the English crown by 1549 and continued in it until his death, becoming especially interested in trade ventures in the Baltic.

Cabot's three years in the Río de La Plata area left their mark; the river acquired its present name from the hope of finding silver that had brought him there, and, in fact, the name Argentina is but another expression of that same hope; he had established the first Spanish base in Argentina; some of his men, apparently from the César expedition, had eventually made their way across the cordillera to Chile where they had met some of the Peruvian conquistadores in the first meeting of the two streams of Argentina colonization, and had returned to tell the tales resulting in the legend of the City of Caesars (q.v.) that inspired Argentine explorers for centuries to keep pushing back their frontiers.

CABRAL, JUAN BAUTISTA, Sergeant (d. 1813).   Heroic officer of San Martín's first Mounted Grenadier corps.

Born in Corrientes; sent to Buenos Aires with contingent of soldiers to support the revolution; made his mark in history by saving San Martín's life at the cost of his own; in the battle of San Lorenzo February 3, 1813, when San Martín's horse was shot from under him, Sergeant Cabral interposed his own body between the Spaniards and the fallen general until San Martín was rescued; by this act, Cabral has been credited with having also saved the liberty of half a continent (later led to independence by San Martín).

CABRERA, ALONSO.   Royal inspector who brought cedula from king
to Asunción, dated 1537, following Pedro de Mendoza's death
granting permission for citizens to elect their own governor in
absence of royal appointee; became practice in Asunción in
early years and was used several times in colonial period (by
Asunción as well as other Río de La Plata areas) to justify
actions of citizens (or comuneros) against royal governors
whom they considered to be acting against community interests.
  Cabrera accompanied Domingo Martínez de Irala to Buenos Aires in 1541, to complete the moving of these settlers to
Asunción; joined with other royal officials and citizens in im-
prisoning Governor Alvar Núñez Cabeza de Vaca and bringing
charges against him, 1544.

CABRERA, JERONIMO LUIS DE (1528-1574).   Soldier; conquistador
in Peru; founder of city of Córdoba.
  Born in Sevilla; came to America with his brother Pedro
de Cabrera y Figueroa in 1538; established himself in Cuzco
in 1549, with rank of camp-master; pacified areas of Ica,
Nazca, and established cities; appointed governor of Tucumán
(then all of northwest Argentina); reached his capital, Santiago
del Estero in 1572; made immediate plans to carry out project
of establishing city farther south to serve as base from which
to open Atlantic route to Spain for Tucumán as well as the
Perus; left Santiago in June with large group (approximately
100) of soldier-settlers, including members of his own family,
40 carretas of supplies, large herds of cattle and farm animals; moved southward to land of the Comechingones (already
explored the previous year by his captain Lorenzo Suárez de
Figueroa); passed peacefully through land containing more than
600 Indian towns; converted and baptized cacique in valley of
river known as Primero; established city of Córdoba de la
Nueva Andalucía on its banks, July 6, 1573, with cabildo and
all proper legal steps necessary to ensure its continued existence; then, with forty mounted attendants, pushed on to the
Paraná river where he built a fort, named San Luis de Córdoba
on heights overlooking old anchorage of Sebastian Cabot; met
with Juan Garay, coming south from Asunción to establish
Santa Fe; first clash of authority threatened over whether Santa
Fe should belong to jurisdiction of Governor of Tucumán or
that of Asunción; both leaders avoided trouble by deferring this
matter to royal authorities (decision made later favored Río de
La Plata authority); Cabrera returned to Córdoba to find that
he had been replaced as governor of Tucumán, by Gonzalo de
Abreu on grounds that he had disobeyed orders by using his
energies and resources to seek an outlet to the Atlantic (forbidden since the establishment of the convoy system through
Panama) instead of following his instructions to pacify the Indians of the Salta area, and occupying it to safeguard the commercial routes and royal highway from Peru to Santiago del
Estero; partly for these reasons, and partly for his own,
Abreu had Cabrera seized at once, taken to Santiago, and im-

mediately garroted; the city that he had founded, Córdoba, prospered and members of the Cabrera family continued through centuries to play important roles in it, as well as in the nation.

CABRERA, JERONIMO LUIS DE (grandson) (before 1595-after 1646). Governor of Río de La Plata, 1641-1646. Grandson of the founder of Córdoba (with the same name) and of Juan de Garay, who established Santa Fe; son-in-law of Hernandarias; wealthy, powerful hacendado; sent out expedition (1620-1621) from Tucumán in search of City of the Caesars, hoping also to establish settlements on the Strait of Magellan; expedition forced to return after reaching Río Negro; as governor of the Río de La Plata district, he strengthened the fort against increasingly numerous intrusions from Europeans, especially Dutch; carried expeditions against Charruas in modern Uruguay, and enforced the new royal policy against Portuguese residents; with Portugal independent and no longer under the Crown of Spain, and with the Portuguese-Dutch alliance of 1641 against Spain, the situation of Portuguese residents in Spanish territory was drastically changed, especially in Buenos Aires; Portuguese holding royal official positions were dismissed and they, as well as all other Portuguese residents, were forced to leave the country or to move inland at least 60 miles; affected were 375 Portuguese residents in a community that had only 1500 Spaniards and Spanish creoles.

CABRERA, JOSE ANTONIO (1768-1820). Lawyer and public figure in Córdoba; signer of Declaration of Independence.
        Born in Córdoba, descendant of founder of city; licentiate in law from University of San Carlos; supported the May Revolution; served as first alcalde of cabildo of Córdoba in 1811; represented Córdoba in attempts to reconcile Artigas' group with the Buenos Aires government; sent as delegate from Córdoba to Congress of Tucumán; signed the Declaration of Independence July 9, 1816; Cabrera's continued open loyalty to Artigas brought him into conflict with the other delegates; when Congress moved to Buenos Aires, he retired to private life in Córdoba.

CACERES, FELIPE DE (sixteenth century). One of first conquistadors; controversial royal official in Asunción.
        Born in Madrid; accompanied Pedro de Mendoza's expedition to Río de La Plata as royal official, 1535-1536; after returning to Spain made second trip to Argentina in Cabeza de Vaca's expedition as accountant; while Cabeza de Vaca went overland to Asunción, Cáceres commanded the ships that went up the Paraná and Paraguay to that settlement; for next three decades (1542-72) remained a powerful, tempestuous figure in local affairs of Asunción; joined, for personal reasons, with other royal officials and Asunción leaders in revolt against and imprisonment of the adelantado Cabeza de Vaca (1544-1545); quarreled with governor Domingo Martínez de Irala;

and, when left as governor (1569) in name of adelantado Juan
Ortiz de Zárate (who had returned to Spain), found himself opposed by strong Asunción group led by Bishop Pedro Fernández
de la Torre which eventually seized and imprisoned him (1572-
1573) and sent him back to Spain in chains, accompanied by the
bishop, his accuser; exonerated and freed by the Council of the
Indies, Cáceres remained in Spain where he apparently lived
several years longer.

CAFIERO, ANTONIO FRANCISCO (1923-   ).   Economist, cabinet
    minister; writer, graduate and later professor in Faculty of
    Economic Sciences, Buenos Aires; assistant minister of foreign
    commerce (1952-1954) and then minister of commerce (1954-
    1955) in cabinet of President Juan Domingo Perón; author of
    several works, including El drenaje de reservas de oro y
    dólares en la postguerra, El programa de lucha contra la in-
    flación en los Estados Unidos desde la finalización de la guerra,
    and Cinco años después...   (Buenos Aires, 1961).

CAGANCHA, BATTLE OF.   Uruguayan site of bloody battle in De-
    cember 1839 in which the Uruguayan forces led by Fructuoso
    Rivera, assisted by Argentine exiles, defeated Rosas' invading
    forces under Pascual Echagüe and forced them back to Entre
    Ríos.

CAGLIERO, JUAN (1838-1926).   Missionary, bishop, cardinal.
    Leader of first group of Salesian priests to Argentina (1875);
    finally departed from republic in 1904, having made major con-
    tributions to its religious life.
            Born in Italy; early became protégé of John Bosco (later
    Saint), joined latter's group that became the order of St. Fran-
    cis of Sales; established five Salesian houses in Argentina and
    Uruguay, 1875-1877; accompanied General Julio A. Roca on
    campaign resulting in Conquest of the Desert; became dedicated
    to task of converting and educating Patagonian Indians; appointed
    vicar apostolic of Patagonia and titular bishop of Magida in
    1883, he went to area as missionary in 1885, continuing work
    despite serious chest injury in Neuquén in 1887; by time of his
    departure from Argentina in 1904 he had established some 50
    churches, 164 missions, 140 convents for auxiliary Salesian
    Sisters, seminary in Viedma, agricultural colonies, a printing
    press, observatories and weather stations; and had, by personal
    negotiation, made possible Roca's resumption of diplomatic re-
    lations between Argentina and the Vatican (1903); returned to
    Italy and other assignments; made cardinal in 1915; died in
    Rome.

CAINGANG (or CAINGAG).   Small but very old group of Indians whom
    the Spaniards found living in the Argentine mesopotamia, espe-
    cially in Corrientes and Misiones; these had migrated south and
    west from the eastern highlands of Brazil; they were primitive
    in their hunting and gathering economy, with a special fondness
    for honey; their religion was largely animistic and the chief had

both spiritual and temporal authority; mate was used for magic
and for supernatural purposes; outnumbered by their more
civilized Guaraní neighbors, the Caingang (who belonged to the
Ge linguistic group instead) disappeared from the Argentine
scene about the middle of the sixteenth century although Caingang Indians in Brazil continued to maintain their identity (see
Indians).
　　　　See Julian H. Steward and Louis C. Faron, Native
Peoples of South America (New York, 1959).

CAJA NACIONAL DE AHORRO POSTAL (National Postal Savings
Bank).　Envisioned by Rivadavia and frequently urged by farsighted statesmen in the nineteenth century, the Postal Savings
finally came into being April 5, 1915, opening modestly with
government financing; by 1921 it had paid off its debt and had
begun the growth that was to make it one of the most solid
supports of the national economy; later laws have widened and
increased its operations.

CALCHAQUI, JUAN.　Famous Indian chief in valley of Calchaquí,
a wild, mountainous area in western Salta; when Juan Pérez
de Zorita arrived in Tucumán to establish Spanish towns, Juan
Calchaquí, already having become a Catholic, permitted and
even helped in the founding of Londres, Córdoba, Calchaquí,
and Cañete; hostilities between Spaniards and Indians were
minimized because of the mutual respect of the two leaders,
but the arrival of the new governor Gregorio Castañeda, with
his arrogant, brutal treatment of the Indians set off an Indian
conflagration, with Juan Calchaquí as its leader, during which
the towns were destroyed and Castañeda forced to leave;
later governors brought the Calchaquí under a measure of control; Juan remained the highly respected cacique of his people
until his death, apparently in 1612.

CALCHAQUI INDIANS see DIAGUITA

CALDEN (botanical name: Prosopis caldenia burkhart).　Very hard
many-trunked tree found in Chaco and La Pampa, especially;
related to mimosa and algarrobo; wood used for construction
of parquet, furniture, fuel, posts, etc.; its leguminous fruit
is edible.

CALDERON, HORACIO (1869-1950).　Lawyer and educator, public
official, hacendado, and entrepreneur.
　　　　Born in Buenos Aires and educated in law at the university there, Calderón spent much of his life as educator
and lawyer but was also active in public life and in various
economic enterprises; he participated in the revolt of 1890;
became deputy in Buenos Aires legislature in following years;
served as minister of agriculture, 1914-1916, in government
of President Victorino de la Plaza; as interventor in Tucumán, 1930-31; and was offered the appointment as minister
of justice by his old friend Arturo Rawson when latter became

president, briefly, after the GOU takeover in 1943; was conservative in politics; favored Allies in World War II; his business interests were reflected in his activities as hacendado and colonizer, his serving as legal counsel for several railroad companies (1898-1909), his active promotion of oil industry in Comodoro Rivadavia where he established the Compañía del Sol (Sun Company) for that purpose, along with his presidency of meat-packing plants and food distribution companies.

CALDERON DE LA BARCA, PEDRO (1794-1868). Military officer. Officer in General José Rondeau's Auxiliary army of Upper Perú; aide-de-camp of Governor Martín Rodríguez in 1821; served under Juan Lavalle; fled into exile in Montevideo in 1840; fought under generals Paz and Rivera but joined Urquiza at India Muerta (1845); after battle of Caseros, returned to Buenos Aires, retired from military service; became treasurer of Crédito Público Nacional (1852) and member of Buenos Aires legislature (1865).

CALDERON DE SANABRIA, MENCIA. Doña Mencia Calderón might be called the Spanish mother of Río de la Plata area, as it was her arrival in Asunción with Spanish wives for the conquistadors that began the establishment (with minor exceptions) of white--creole, not mestizo--families and the stabilization of familiar Spanish homelife.
      When her husband, Juan Sanabria, died before he could go to Río de la Plata to exercise his rights as adelantado (granted 1547), and his son Diego, who then received the grant, was unable to leave immediately, Doña Mencia, whose fortune was invested in the expedition, departed from Spain in 1550, in her son's name, with three ships under command of royal treasurer Juan Salazar y Espinosa and Hernando de Trejo, a small armed force, and approximately fifty Spanish girls, including her own daughters who hoped to find husbands in the new land; years later, groups of survivors straggled into Asunción by various routes to tell of hardships suffered: capture by pirates off Africa's coast, with release only after they had been robbed; storms at sea; illnesses and deaths, including that of one of Doña Mencia's daughters; ships scattered and lost along the Brazilian coast, survivors delayed there indefinitely by inability to get help to continue their journey; drowning of Diego Sanabria along Brazilian coast, in follow-up expedition; detention by Portuguese officials, etc.; Doña Mencia's group, led by Trejo, came overland from Santa Catarina and reached Asunción in 1556; later many members of her party went on to Santa Cruz de la Sierra, on western boundary of Paraguay, but most returned eventually to Río de la Plata area; in 1564 Doña Mencia wrote a brief account of her sufferings en route to Paraguay.
      Among the new families established, from whom future creole leaders came, were those of Doña Mencia's two daughters, who early married the commanding officers of the little fleet; Fernando de Trejo y Sanabria, later bishop of Tucumán

was son of María Sanabria and Hernando de Trejo; and Isabel, daughter of Isabel (also known as Mencia?) Sanabria and Juan Salazar y Espinosa became the wife (in Santa Cruz) of Juan de Garay who later founded Santa Fe (1573) and permanently reestablished Buenos Aires in 1580.

CALFUCURA, JUAN (d. 1873).   Powerful Araucanian cacique of the southern and western pampas.

Born in Llailma; belonged to Pehuenche group; his name is corruption of Indian callou (blue) and curá (rock); migrated from Chile to Argentina to establish the Piedra dynasty (piedra, Spanish for rock); governed an almost independent republic known as Confederation of Salinas Grandes near Epecuen, Neuquén; led, or was responsible for, nearly all raids or malones (q.v.) that troubled Buenos Aires province around middle of 19th century; in 1837 attacked Chilean Aucas and captured 100,000 head of cattle; attacked Rojas (1844) and Chivilcoy (1846); for a time Rosas bought peace by treaty and payment but in 1847 Calfucurá turned against him and attacked Bahía Blanca and other frontier towns; joined with Urquiza in fight against Rosas and became very close to former personally; during period of Buenos Aires' separation from other provinces, Calfucurá constantly kept province in a turmoil--worst attack was that on Azul, 1855--so that its forces had to be diverted against him; having defeated Mitre at Sierra Chica, he was himself defeated by generals Granada, Conesa, and Paunero in 1857 and again at Pigüe the following year; fought on side of Confederation in battle of Cepeda, 1859, and continued to raid Buenos Aires towns until defeated at battle of Pichi Carhüe March 8, 1872, with 200 Indians killed; this Indian terror of the pampas died the following year June 3, 1873, in his own toldo in Chilihué (near General Acha in La Pampa); at his peak he had commanded 3000 trained warriors and been chief of 20,000 Indians; at least eight of his sons had served as his officers; one of these, Manuel Namuncurá (q.v.), godson of Urquiza, became the new and last leader of these Indians.

CALIBAR.   Famous tracker and guide (rastreador) of the late eighteenth and early nineteenth century; his extraordinary gift and feats in following trails described by Domingo Faustino Sarmiento in Chapter II of his Facundo.

CALVO, CARLOS (1822-1906).   Jurist of international distinction; diplomat; prolific writer; author of Calvo Doctrine.

Born in Montevideo, educated in law in Buenos Aires; spent most of his life in diplomatic missions for Argentina to European governments; profound student of international law; enunciated (1868) what has become known as the Calvo Doctrine; that foreign investors had no recourse beyond the courts of the nation to which their capital had migrated--ruling out collection of debts by force; became a member of the Madrid Academy of History; among his prolific writings are: A complete compilation of treaties and other diplomatic agreements

of all the Latin American States, 11 volumes (Paris, 1862-
1869); Anales históricos de la revolución en la América Latina
(with accompanying documents) 5 v.; various theoretical works
on international law, and a legal, statistical study La instrucción en la República Argentina (1878).

CALVO, NICOLAS ANTONIO (1817-1893). Born in Buenos Aires;
   returned from consular appointment in France to take active
   role in political affairs in Buenos Aires province in 1850s;
   became leader of Federal Reform party (popularly called
   Chupandinos, (q. v.) that sponsored reunion of Buenos Aires
   with other provinces; edited La Reforma Pacífica 1856-1857
   to advocate this; unsuccessful in his attempts to win office, he
   spent several years in retirement and travel; returning in
   1880, served several terms in congress; in 1886 published a
   study of the constitutional decisions of the federal judges of
   the United States, with introduction comparing the constitution
   of the United States and that of the Argentine republic; while
   serving as Argentine representative in the Misiones boundary
   settlement with Brazil, Calvo died in Paris.

CAMAÑO Y BAZAN, JOAQUIN (1737-1820). Argentine Jesuit priest,
   geographer, historian, and linguist.
        Born in La Rioja; graduated in arts and theology from
   university of Córdoba; entered Society of Jesus in 1757; became proficient linguist in Latin and Greek, as well as such
   Indian languages as Quechua, Chiquita, and Guaraní; preferred
   mission work to further study and was working among the Chiquitos in the Chaco when the order for expulsion of the Jesuits
   came in 1767; Father Camaño found refuge, with many of his
   fellow Jesuits in Faenza, Italy; in exile, he studied Argentine
   history and geography and devoted himself to linguistic and
   cartographical works about his native land; only map remaining
   is that of the Gran Chaco, published by his fellow-Jesuit José
   Jolís (q.v.); this has been called the most scientific one remaining from the colonial period; unfortunately the comprehensive geographical and historical dictionary of the Indies
   (i. e., America) that he spent his last twenty years in writing
   has been lost; Father Camaño died in Valencia, Spain.

CAMBACERES, EUGENIO (1843-1888). Novelist and public figure.
   Born in Buenos Aires, served in both provincial and national
   legislatures, but too outspoken and too innovative in his thinking for successful public life; strongly supported separation of
   church and state; denounced fraud in elections of 1874; his
   writings, evoking and describing the harsh impact of Argentine
   environment on human life, as in the novels Sin rumbo (1885)
   and En la sangre (1887) were widely read despite harsh attacks by critics; today it is generally agreed that the modern
   novel of Argentina began with the writings of Cambaceres, one
   of the most important literary figures of the so-called naturalist school.

CAMINO REAL.   Royal highway extending from Lima, Peru to Bue-
nos Aires; entered modern Argentina at Jujuy from Potosí and
Charcas (Sucre, Bolivia), passed through Salta, Tucumán,
Santiago del Estero, Córdoba, to Buenos Aires; more a trail
than a real highway; apparently rarely called by that name in
Argentina.

CAMPANA, JOAQUIN (1783-1847).   Jurisconsult; public official.
Born in Uruguay; received doctorate at university at
Córdoba; as member of May 22, 1810, cabildo abierto voted
to oust viceroy; as supporter of Saavedra in patriot junta, Dr.
Campana became one of leaders in the "preventive" revolution
of April 5-6, 1811, which forced out the followers of Moreno,
leaving Saavedra in control; later returned to Uruguay where
he became a member of the first legislature there.

CAMPECHANO.   Argentinism used to describe a countryman without polish, i. e. , a "hick. "

CAMPESINO.   Rural worker; term has different connotation than
elsewhere in Latin America (see Campechano; Cabecitas negras;
Peón).

CAMPO, NICOLAS CRISTOBAL DEL (Marqués de Loreto)   See
LORETO, NICOLAS FRANCISCO CRISTOBAL DEL CAMPO,
Marqués de.

CAMPOMANES, PEDRO RODRIGUEZ, Conde de (1723-1802). Spanish statesman and political economist largely responsible,
through his teachings, writings, and position as minister of
Charles III, for liberalization of royal economic policies regarding the Río de la Plata area in the late eighteenth century.

CAMPORA, HECTOR JOSE (1909-   ).   President of Argentine Republic, May 25-July 13, 1973.
Born in Mercedes, province of Buenos Aires, of Geno-
ese Italian parents; graduated (1927) from Colegio Nacional
Florentino Ameghino, where he had been a leader in student
politics; received his dentist's degree in 1934 from the school
of Odontology, National University of Córdoba, where he had
continued and expanded his leadership in student political affairs; established dental practice in San Andrés de Giles (Buenos Aires) and in 1944 became municipal commissioner there;
supported Juan Domingo Perón loyally from this time until
latter's death thirty years later; his real function throughout
this period was to amalgamate the various political groups of
Peronists; elected to Chamber of Deputies from Buenos Aires
1946, served as its president 1948-1953; elected to Justicialist Superior Council in 1947; from 1946-1952 was comptroller
of Peronist party in Buenos Aires as well as party supervisor
for that province, Santa Fe, Córdoba, and Tucumán; in 1953
President Perón used him as special ambassador of missions

139 139   Cámpora

to Europe, U.S., Brazil, Peru, Venezuela, Colombia, Ecuador, Guatemala and Mexico; following the military overthrow of Perón's government in 1955, Cámpora, like many other Peronist officials, was imprisoned; escaped from Tierra del Fuego prison to Chile in 1957; returned to Argentina in 1960 to find Peronists excluded from participation in politics for another five years; in 1965 he again was elected to city council of San Andrés de Giles; during the next few years he played the leading role, as Perón's own representative; in the attempts of the national government to restore constitutional processes with Peronists participating; in elections of March 11, 1973, Cámpora was presidential candidate of Justicialist party and won the presidency with about 50% of the popular vote; inaugurated May 25, 1973, he continued to maintain close contact with Perón--viewed as a senior counsellor--and generally followed conciliatory program; used moderate Peronists in his cabinet, hoping to bind Peronists together and to bring them back into national acceptance; freed hundreds of political prisoners, resumed diplomatic relations with Castro's revolutionary Cuba, and made a two-year pact between labor unions and management to ensure industrial peace, revive the economy and to give labor a greater share in national income; on July 13, 1973, he and his vice-president resigned to open the way for Perón to return to presidency in elections held September 23, 1973.

CAMPOS, LUIS MARIA, General (1838-1907). Military officer, cabinet minister.
      Born in Buenos Aires, began military career 1859; fought in battles of Cepeda and Pavón under General Paunero; steady promotion followed as he fought in war against Paraguay, was wounded several times, fighting montoneros, sent against López Jordán in Entre Ríos in 1870, 1873; intervened for government against Tejedor in Buenos Aires, 1880; became general of division in 1882 and rose to lieutenant general before his retirement in 1900; special assignments and appointments; chief of staff, 1892 and then minister of war and navy under President Luis Sáenz Peña until 1896; same post under President Julio A. Roca in 1898; took part 1899-1900 in setting up Escuela Superior (War Academy) for training high command; was married to daughter of President Justo José Urquiza.

CAMPOS, MANUEL JORGE (1847-1908). General; military commander-in-chief of revolt of 1890.
      Born in Buenos Aires; began his military career in light artillery, 1864, and eventually attained rank of general of division; fought throughout the Paraguayan war, wounded at Curupaytí; sent to Mendoza to bring revolting caudillos under control; after the Paraguayan war, saw action against Ricardo López Jordán (q.v.), in Entre Ríos and the Taboadas in Santiago del Estero in extending the authority of the national government throughout the republic; accompanied Roca on his campaign to Río Negro; Campos' force was designated as escort

for the federal authorities in the federalization crisis of 1880; in early 1880s he was sent to establish frontier forts on southern Buenos Aires frontier; established his headquarters at Huitré-Huitré (today General Acha in La Pampa province); in 1890, as brigadier general, he became the military leader of the proposed revolt to overthrow President Juárez Celman; although news of the conspiracy leaked out and Campos was captured, he managed to gain his freedom quickly, and, apparently, to win supporters for ousting the president; Juárez Celman resigned and eventually Carlos Pellegrini came in as president; Campos had supported Mitre and this action, along with other events of the aborted revolt caused an alienation between him and civilian radical leaders of the revolution that caused political repercussions later; Campos was elected deputy to the national congress (1892), but preferred to accept the post of Chief of Police of the Federal Capital during the administration of Luis Sáenz Peña; in 1897 accepted seat in Buenos Aires Senate; promoted to rank of general of division in 1904; served as deputy in national congress from 1906 until his death.

CANCHA RAYADA. Chilean site of royalist rout of San Martín's army, March 19, 1818. Royalist reinforcements from Peru under General Mariano de Osorio entered Chile at Talcahuano in the south and moved north to Talca where they faced San Martín's patriot forces outnumbering them greatly; by daring night surprise attack under Colonel José Ordóñez, the royalists caught the patriots just in the process of shifting positions to prepare for attack and dispersed them; San Martín and O'Higgins (who was wounded in the arm) escaped, and Las Heras saved most of his division but nearly all the equipment and artillery of the army was lost; in spite of the panic ensuing in Santiago among both political and military leaders, San Martín inflicted a crushing defeat on the royalists seventeen days later at Maipú (q. v.), April 5; Chilean independence preserved and way left open for San Martín's continental plan of liberation.

CANDIOTI, FRANCISCO ANTONIO (1743-1815). Entrepreneur and public figure, late colonial and early independence period.
    Born in Santa Fe and educated in Franciscan school there; engaged in trade with Alto Perú, amassing fortune in mule trade (see Arrias); promoted agriculture; Santa Fe requested his appointment as lieutenant governor after May Revolution but Spaniard Manuel Ruiz named instead; collaborated with Belgrano's revolutionary expedition north in 1810, accompanying it to his estancia Arroyo Hondo in Entre Ríos where he furnished food provisions, wagons, and other necessary supplies; became partisan of Artigas and federal doctrine during period when General Eustáquio Díaz Vélez represented Buenos Aires' authority in Santa Fe; March 24, 1815, General Artigas-Colonel Mariano Vera, and Candioti moved into Santa Fe, forcing Díaz Vélez to leave; elected interim governor of Santa Fe

by cabildo April 2, 1815; died August 29, in office, two days
after arrival of General Viamonte's expedition, sent by Buenos
Aires directorate to take over; in addition to his activities in
promoting stockraising and agriculture, Candioti had attempted
to reduce Indian problem by establishing settlements as defensive barrier against invasions in northern part of city, while
at the same time sending missionaries to convert, pacify, and
civilize them.

CANDOMBE. African dance performed by blacks in Buenos Aires on
Sundays and special feast days until the close of the nineteenth
century, when blacks had practically disappeared as an ethnic
or cultural group; Juan Manuel de Rosas and his daughter,
Manuelita, frequently attended the candombes held in the barrio
of Mondongo, where the blacks received them with honor and
affection.

CANE, MIGUEL (father) (1812-1863). Writer and lawyer.
        Born on his father's estancia near San Pedro in Buenos
Aires province, Cané was educated in the capital; became part
of the Reading Room group of Marcos Sastre; anti-Rosas in his
feelings, went into exile in Montevideo in 1835, the day after
receiving his law degree; continued fight against Rosas in the
press and otherwise for a time, then settled down to a life of
writing and traveling; returned to live in Buenos Aires after
fall of Rosas; devoted himself to literary career, writing several romantic novels in addition to other works; among his
close friends were Juan María Gutiérrez, Félix Frías, Vicente
F. López, Luis L. Domínguez, Andrés Lamas and Juan Bautista Alberdi.

CANE, MIGUEL (son) (1851-1905). Public figure; diplomat; writer
and literary critic.
        Born in Montevideo while family was in exile; returned
to Buenos Aires at age two after fall of Rosas; attended Colegio Nacional, inspiration of his most famous book, Juvenilia
(an elegant but realistic reminiscence of school days); after
receiving law degree in 1872, entered the public life in which
he became not only the symbol but a leader in expressing
what the Generation of 1880, as well as the oligarchy, stood
for at their best as public official, literary critic, academi-
cian, writer and diplomat; his writings appeared in La Tribuna, edited by the Varelas for the autonomistas; El Nacional,
with Sarmiento and Vélez Sarsfield among the editors; and
later in La Prensa, La Nación and El País; Cané served in
congress as national deputy and senator; was appointed Postal
and Telegraph director, 1880; then went on series of diplomatic
assignments as minister to Colombia and Venezuela (1881),
Austria-Hungary (1883), Germany (1884), Spain (1886), and,
later, France (1901); meanwhile in 1892 he served as municipal intendant of Buenos Aires, and in cabinet positions as minister of foreign affairs, very briefly, in crisis of 1893, and
minister of the interior in government of Luis Sáenz Peña

(1892-95); in 1900 he became the first dean of the Buenos
Aires Faculty of Philosophy and Letters, in which capacity he
delivered two famous lectures "El espíritu universitario" and
"La enseñanza clásica"; as a member of the oligarchy (elite
government structure) whose spirit Cané defined as being "open
to the powerful, evolutionary forces of the century, with faith
in science and in human progress," he worked for the anticlerical Law of Civil Registration and Law of Publication in
1884; drew up the residence law designed against foreign labor
agitators, in oligarchy's interests of law and order, but regarded as a limitation on the freedom previously enjoyed by
foreigners in the republic; an admirer of English and French
literature, Cané's most important work of literary criticism is
considered to be his Henry IV, Spanish translation with critical notes of Shakespeare's play; in later years of his life, after
leaning strongly toward positivism, became a skeptical, nos-
talgic liberal who called for reemphasis of the humanities in
education, and sent leter to La Nación (1900) challenging
younger men to leadership in public life and letters; blamed
their apathy on the uninspired and dogmatic educational system
of which they were products, and hinted, that the prevailing
positivism implied the danger of cultural suffocating by brutal
opulence.
> See Ricardo Sáenz Hayes in Suggested Readings, Appen-
dix III.

CANELAS, MANUEL (1718-1773). Missionary; educator; writer.
> Born in Córdoba, Canelas entered Society of Jesus in
1730; after receiving his training, he was assigned to missionary work among the Mocobí Indians of Santa Fe province and
spent almost his entire career in this service; the expulsion
decree found him at the Colegio de Santa Fe and he was transported with his fellow Jesuits to Italy; he remained at Faenza
until his death six years later; during this period he wrote extensively about the character and customs of the Mocobís
among whom he had spent so many years; in 1921 the Jesuit
historian Father Guillermo Furlong found three of these manuscripts in a Barcelona library and made considerable use of
them in his own book entitled Entre los mocobíes de Santa Fe
(Buenos Aires, 1938).

CAÑETE. A garrison town named for viceroy of Peru, with 20-30
soldiers, established between 1558-1560 by Juan Pérez de Zorita to protect road north of Santiago del Estero toward other
Spanish settlements; Cañete was destroyed by Calchaquí Indians;
later, San Miguel de Tucumán was established on its site.

CANGAPOL, EL BRAVO. Indian leader. Since the early 1700s
Araucanian Indians had been pushing across the pampas, attacking cattle drives, and raising outlying towns in Buenos
Aires province; in 1740 famous cacique (Indian chief) Cangapol,
known as "El Bravo" (the fierce or magnificent) destroyed the
towns of Arrecife, Luján, Matanzas, and Magdalena; immedi-

ate ruthless Spanish retaliation persuaded Cangapol to sign, in 1741, the first treaty of peace between these Indians and the government; the boundary between the two peoples, which had previously been open, now established as the Río Salado.

CANNING, GEORGE (1770-1827). English statesman. Served as British secretary of foreign affairs twice: 1807-1809 and 1822-1827; then became prime minister; influenced Argentine historical development in early independence period by such actions as: firm opposition to efforts of Holy Alliance to aid Ferdinand VII regain his colonies; appointment of British consul to Buenos Aires in October 1823; de facto recognition of Argentine independence by treaty of friendship, navigation, and trade February 2, 1825, between British and Buenos Aires governments (largely due to Rivadavia's efforts and diplomacy), thus paving the way for British loans; intervened in settlement of Argentine-Brazilian war (1828), bringing peace and the independence of Uruguay.

CANTERAC, JOSE (1775-1835). Spanish military officer. Chief of staff of royalist army facing San Martín in Peru, 1820; forced back into sierra; defeated by Bolívar at Junín; commanded reserve at Ayacucho where he signed surrender; killed while trying to suppress mutiny in Madrid.

CANTILO, JOSE LUIS (1871-1944). Writer and political figure.
        Born in Buenos Aires, educated there and in Paris; centered his active political life around the Unión Cívica Radical party of which he was a founding member; elected as provincial deputy in 1896; involved in political disturbance of 1905; represented Federal District in national congress in 1912, 1916; founded daily newspaper La Época (1916) to defend his party; became controversial figure as interventor in Buenos Aires province--criticized as too political; from 1919 to 1928 served effectively as municipal intendant of Buenos Aires and was governor of Buenos Aires province 1922-1926; again intendant of Federal District until President Yrigoyen's government was ousted 1930; a decade later Cantilo returned to Congress, president of the Cámara (lower house); in 1943 led group of Argentine statesmen on visit to the United States.
        In addition to his political activities, Cantilo was deeply interested in historical subjects; elected member of the Academia Nacional de la Historia in 1910; his written works on these include Don Juan de Garay; Juan Gregorio de Las Heras; and the Quichuas.

CANTILO, JOSE MARIA (1816-1872). Pharmacist, writer, public figure.
        Born in Buenos Aires, became self-taught chemist and operated pharmacy until anti-Rosas activities forced him into exile; joined the Argentine Legion; opened new pharmacy in Montevideo, and became journalist; wrote in El Comercio del Plata (becoming editor after assassination of Florencio Varela)

and contributed to others; after fall of Rosas, returned to Buenos Aires; held various municipal and provincial appointments;
was member of Buenos Aires legislature and also of Buenos
Aires Convention, 1860; represented Buenos Aires in national
Congress, 1862-1866; elected again in 1872 shortly before his
death; served in various public health capacities, such as member of Sanitary commission in Paraguayan war, and of commission to fight yellow fever (1871); elected director of the
Crédito Público Nacional; continued to write; founder and editor
of El Correo del Domingo and La Verdad; left large number of
poems; translated and edited writings of North American scholars Joseph Story and George T. Curtis on U.S. constitution.

CANTILO, JOSE MARIA (1877-1953).   Statesman, diplomat, writer.
        After a long diplomatic career Cantilo became foreign
minister in President Ortiz' government during the critical
years from 1938 to 1940, when the problems growing out of
the Chaco War and the Spanish Civil War were suddenly overtaken and complicated by the outbreak of World War II; endeavored to steer a middle course for Argentina by cooperating with other American nations as much as possible without
sacrificing Argentina's traditional independence, while at the
same time bearing in mind the republic's close economic and
cultural ties with European nations; resulted in Cantilo being
equally vilified by those in United States who thought he was
being deliberately obstructive and by Argentine nationalists who
accused him of accepting U.S. domination.
        Born in Buenos Aires; law graduate from national uni-
versity at Buenos Aires with further studies in law in Paris;
began foreign service career as second secretary in Argentine
embassy in Rome; became first secretary of legation at Rio
de Janeiro 1908, then transferred back to Buenos Aires as
secretary of President Roque Saenz Peña; continued in assignments in ministries in Buenos Aires and a series of diplomatic
appointments in Latin America and Europe; served as ambassador to Italy 1933-1938; summoned home in 1938 to become
Foreign Minister in cabinet of President Roberto M. Ortiz;
unable to secure a postponement, on grounds of disturbed
world conditions, of the Seventh Inter-American Conference
scheduled to meet that year in Lima, Peru, Cantilo attended--
made one of the opening speeches, restated Argentina's traditional inter-American policy, supporting "continental solidarity, individual policy"--then departed, delegating his authority
to the other Argentine representatives; U.S. resented his absence but welcomed Argentina's signature of Declaration of
Lima reaffirming continental solidarity; largely at Cantilo's
suggestion, it was decided that a consultation of foreign ministers should be called in emergency as instrument to determine
measure necessary to resist a threat to hemispheric security;
Argentina (through Cantilo) joined U.S. and six other nations
in calling the first such consultative meeting in later 1939, at
Panama, following declaration of war against Germany by England and France in September; Cantilo's instructions to Argen-

tine delegation made this meeting a high point in inter-American World War II relations; in April 1940 Cantilo, in the tradition of Calvo and Drago, and in line with President Ortiz' policy, attempted to add a new dimension to international relations by substituting the more positive category of non-belligerency for that of neutrality, which created duties but gave no rights; Norman Armour (U.S. ambassador to Argentina) with whom Cantilo first discussed this (April 19, 1940) forwarded the proposal at once to the U.S. State Department; but Cantilo's repeated efforts during the next few months met with no success; when second meeting of foreign ministers met in Havana (1940) the matter was dropped, and Argentine delegation less cooperative; Cantilo already out of office due to President Ortiz' resignation because of bad health; Cantilo retired to private life and to his writing; had collaborated with Mercure de France and Revue de Paris, as well as several Buenos Aires periodicals; now edited Vuelta del Camino and Les Silences vivants (dealing with France's tragedy); emerged from retirement from public life to send U.S. embassy immediate assurance of his support following Japanese attack on Pearl Harbor; and again in support of U.S. Ambassador Braden, under attack from Perón.

    For detailed, scholarly study of Argentina's attempt to create non-belligerency policy, and Cantilo's role, see Joseph S. Tulchin, "The Argentine Proposal for Non-Belligerency, April 1940," Journal of Inter-American Studies and World Affairs XI (1969): 571-604.

CAÑUELAS, PACT OF. Agreement signed June 24, 1829 between General Juan G. Lavalle, provisional governor and captain-general of Buenos Aires, whose position had become untenable for various reasons (including his execution of Dorrego), and General Juan Manuel de Rosas, commanding general of the army that had recently defeated Lavalle at Puente de Márquez; in an effort to restore civil government and peace, the two generals agreed: 1) to end hostilities and re-establish normal relations between the city and province of Buenos Aires; 2) to proceed immediately with the elections of legislative representatives, who would select governor; 3) as soon as governor had been elected, both generals would turn over their forces to him; government was to reimburse Rosas' army for its expenses; every officer was confirmed in his rank and personal rights protected; and no person would be punished or persecuted for previous political opinions; eventually, after one false try and a new pact, these conditions were carried out a few months later but Lavalle's hopes of a permanent peace were scarcely fulfilled; by the end of 1829, Rosas was the new governor, beginning his long rule, and Lavalle was an exile, hated for his execution of the former governor, Dorrego.

CAPAYANES. This group of Huarpe Indians (q.v.) was living in San Juan and La Rioja at the time of the conquest; most of what is known about them comes from study of their artifacts

as they fought the first Spaniards so fiercely that those who
were not killed were scattered among the distant new settlements and the land left empty for the most part; it has been
discovered that they represented a well developed example of
the Andean (or Inca) civilization; their economy was based on
agriculture with irrigation and underground storage facilities;
llama wool made the beautifully woven and colored textiles
used for the Andean ponchos and shirts they wore; they were
advanced in ceramic work and design; also made round clay
ovens; the Capayanes were also familiar with copper, from
which they made personal ornaments.

CAPITAL, CAPITAL INVESTMENT   see   INVESTMENTS

CAPITAL (Question of)   see   FEDERALIZATION OF CITY OF
    BUENOS AIRES

CARAS Y CARETAS.   Popular illustrated literary review, 1898-
    1939; founded by José de Alvarez (who used pseudonym "Fray
    Mocho"), Eustaquio Pellecier, and the cartoon artist Manuel
    M. Mayol (or Mallol), its 2,139 issues brought its readers
    literary news and contributions as well as those representing
    the fine arts; among its contributors were numbered the most
    distinguished writers and poets of the international scene as
    well as of the Argentine republic.

CARBIA, ROMULO D. (1885-1944).   Historian and professor.
        Born in Buenos Aires; professor of history and director
    of library of arts and letters at University of Buenos Aires,
    also taught at the University of La Plata; among his many
    works are Historia eclesiástic del Río de la Plata (2 v., 1914-
    1915); Historia de la historiográfica Argentina (1925) and Nueva
    historia del descubrimiento de América (1936); his work on
    historiography initiated a new Argentine approach to critical
    use of original source materials.

CARBO, ALEJANDRO (1862-1930).   Educator and legislator.
        Born and educated in Paraná's Escuela Normal (Teach-
    ers College) where he also taught; served as director of Gus-
    tavo Ferrari institution 1889-1892; drafted programs and cur-
    riculums for girls' colegio in Patamá; as director general of
    schools and president of the Entre Ríos council of education,
    he expressed his pedagogical philosophy and ideas about meth-
    odology in his written reports; entering the political arena, he
    became one of the most prominent members of the National
    Autonomist party; elected in 1898, and for three successive
    terms, as representative to the national congress, over which
    he presided in 1906 and 1915; in 1916, his name, as vice
    presidential candidate, appeared on ticket of Democratic Pro-
    gressive Party, with that of Lisandro de la Torre as presi-
    dent; left politics after this; moved, for health reasons, to
    Córdoba (1920); directed programs of teachers college there
    (named for him after his death); held doctor's degree in sci-

ences of education, conferred on him "honoris causa" by University of La Plata with which he had been associated in later years.

CARCANO, MIGUEL ANGEL (1889-1978).   Lawyer, economist, and historian; public offical; diplomat.

Born in Buenos Aires and educated there; congressman from Córdoba 1929, 1931, 1934; member of Roca-Runciman commission that drew up Treaty of London (1933) regulating and encouraging trade between Argentina and Great Britain; member of restricted governing group 1936-1943; belonged to Círculo de Armas; succeeded Luis Duhau as minister of agriculture in President Agustín P. Justo's cabinet; and latter's favored candidate for the vice presidency; ambassador to Great Britain 1942-1946; notable among his writings were his Evolución histórica del régimen de la tierra pública 1810-1916 that won national first prize in letters (1917); books (1940s) about England during World War II; La fortaleza de Europa (1951); La presidencia de Carlos Pellegrini; política de orden, 1890-1892 (Buenos Aires, 1968); and La política internacional en la historia argentina, 2 volumes. Biblioteca Cultural Colección Argentina (Buenos Aires, 1972).

CARCANO, RAMON JOSE (1860-1946).   Jurisconsult, writer, estanciero, statesman.

Born and educated in Córdoba; doctorate in jurisprudence; taught at Colegio de Monserrat and university; served as secretary to governors Antonio del Viso and Miguel Juárez Celman; elected to national Congress, 1884; became Córdoba's minister of justice and public instruction (1886) and then director of post office and telegraph services; withdrew from political life 1890-1910; became congressman again in 1910, 1918; elected governor of Córdoba 1913 and again in 1925, showed himself especially interested in highways, public works, and practical schools; director of the Banco Hipotecario Nacional; president of Sociedad Rural; ambassador to Brazil, 1933; a prolific writer throughout his life; contributed frequently to La Nación, La Prensa, La Tribuna, El Diario, and to the review published by the faculty of agronomy and veterinary sciences that he served as dean, 1921-1924; his longer works deal with agropecuarian topics, the history of Argentine transportation and communication systems, current legal and social problems, historical topics--many of these dealing with nineteenth century events, such as his detailed scholarly study of the months following Caseros (fall of Rosas), the Paraguayan war, etc.; his Juan Facundo Quiroga won national first prize for literature, 1931; elected member of National Academy of History (1901), served twice as its president; affiliated with many other political and cultural groups; in later life wrote Mis primeros ochenta años supplemented after his death by Ramón J. Cárcano a través de diez escritores in which ten of Argentina's distinguished writers presented him as political figure and legislator, intellectual and statesman, writer, historian, estanciero, etc.

CARCARAÑA RIVER.   Known as the Tercero River, rises in sierras of Córdoba, becomes the Carcarañá as it passes through province of Santa Fe; empties into Paraná south of Lake Caronda; at this junction Sebastian Cabot established the fort of Sancti Spiritus in 1527, the first European colony in La Plata.

CARDENAS, BALTASAR (d. 1813).   Independence fighter.   Upper Peruvian leader of Bolivian Indian guerrilla fighters from Cochabamba and Chayanta; harassed royalists under Goyeneche; cooperated with Manuel Belgrano to make latter's invasion of Upper Peru easier (1812); promoted to colonel by Belgrano for his action at battle of Salta; continued cooperation with other patriot leaders, such as Arenales; undertook, under Belgrano's direction, to arouse Indians in royalist territory to revolt; killed at Ancacato September 27, 1813, in encounter with royalists while so engaged.

CARDIEL, JOSE (1704-1782).   Jesuit missionary, explorer, writer, cartographer.
          Born in La Guardia, Alava (Spain); entered Jesuit order 1720; assigned in 1729 to Guaraní missions where he served in many capacities for most of the rest of his career; accompanied Father José Quiroga along Patagonian coast to Straits of Magellan 1745; with Thomas Falkner, established Jesuit mission Pilar in southern Buenos Aires province near modern Mar del Plata, 1746; after further explorations returned to Paraguayan missions 1750; expelled with other Jesuits in 1767, he made his home in Italy (Bologna) until his death.   His writings include: Declaración de verdad, a defense of the Jesuit Guaraní missions, written while serving as chaplain of Guaraní auxiliaries accompanying General Pedro de Ceballos' army invading Rio Grande do Sul (1762), refuting vicious Portuguese accusations against the Jesuit missions made by Portuguese Gomes Freire (published in 1900); writings dealing with scientific observations and descriptions of his extensive explorations from northern Paraguay to southern Argentina; detailed, useful descriptions of life in the missions; and an impressive series of more than ten maps, including some of the best colonial cartography of Buenos Aires province.

CARHUE.   Fortified town in southern Buenos Aires province, established by Colonel Nicolás Levalle April 24, 1876 to serve as part of front line of defense in campaign against Patagonian Indians; site both before and after founding of several savage Indian attacks, including one led by Namuncurá; served briefly as field headquarters for both General Julio A. Roca and Minister of War Adolfo Alsina.

CARLES, MANUEL (1875-1946).   Teacher and political figure.
          Born in Rosario; received law degree from university

in Buenos Aires; taught in Colegio Nacional, Escuela Superior
de Guerra (War Academy), and in the faculty of Law and Social Sciences at the University of Buenos Aires; held various
political positions, including that of national congressman
(elected 1898); served as federal interventor in Salta and in
San Juan; chief interest was in Liga Patriótica Argentina
which he organized in 1919 to fight against workers' organizations and ideologies that he considered to be subversive (see
Liga Patriótica Argentina); continued active as director until
his death.

CARLOS I (of Spain)   see   CHARLES V OF HOLY ROMAN EMPIRE

CARLOS II (1661-1700).   King of Spain 1665-1700.   Last of Hapsburg line; his death without issue brought in the Bourbons and
set off war of Spanish succession; treaty of Utrecht (1713)
gave British right to import black slaves into Buenos Aires,
along with a few other Spanish American ports (see Asiento de
Negros).

CARLOS III (1716-1788).   King of Spain 1759-1788.   Bourbon mon-
arch during whose reign foreign threats against Spanish sovereignty over Río de la Plata area were effectively handled and
traditional political, economic, and social patterns and institutions of colonial period were tranformed into more liberal ones
of enlightened, prosperous viceroyalty that tied area more directly to Spain but also prepared it for independence.
Portuguese expansion from Brazil halted by Treaty of
San Ildefonso (1777) providing for appointment of joint Portu-
guese-Spanish scientific commission to draw boundary; most
of so-called Bourbon reforms, many of them already instituted
in Spain and in other Spanish American colonies, came to Argentina during this rule; several factors combined to focus
royal attention on Argentina, and especially on Buenos Aires;
the latter's proximity to Rio de Janeiro, new capital of Brazil;
the serious economic losses (increasingly in silver trade)
through contraband, and the rapid growth and obvious potential
of this neglected area, among them; legal changes followed in
rapid succession: 1767, expulsion of Jesuits, with their university and schools, estancias and plantations, missions, and
other religious establishments either placed under other clerical control or secularized, and their wealth turned into royal
treasury; creation of new viceroyalty (1776--made permanent
1777) of Río de la Plata, with capital at Buenos Aires, consisting of modern Bolivia, Paraguay, Argentina, and Uruguay;
intendancy system superimposed on old political framework
(1782); and in 1783 (1785 began operating) royal audiencia of
Buenos Aires was reestablished (first one brief--1661-1671);
Buenos Aires opened to trade, with Sevilla monopoly ended
1778; Buenos Aires permitted to trade with other Spanish ports
and with Spanish American colonies; customhouse established
in Buenos Aires 1779; and (after Carlos' death) consulado established in Buenos Aires 1794; liberal education encouraged;

Colegio de San Carlos established 1773 in Buenos Aires, along with Carolingian academies, medical tribunal, and other scientific and cultural institutions; Indian policy protected Indians but also expanded frontier line of settlements farther south; Spanish immigration encouraged along with agriculture; direct mail service with Spain and throughout viceroyalty established; disputes with Great Britain, 1766-1774, over Las Malvinas (Falkland Islands) ended in latter year with British abandoning islands, not to return for several decades.

CARLOS IV (1748-1819). King of Spain (1788-1808). Second son of Carlos III; born in Italy; came to throne on the eve of French Revolution in difficult international situation at time when royal authority was under attack everywhere; well-intentioned, but unable to cope effectively with either internal or external problems, abdicated in favor of son Ferdinand VII shortly before Napoleon entered Spain and placed his brother Joseph Bonaparte on throne; Carlos' ineffectual rule, ambivalent policies, and foreign alliances were refelcted in viceroyalty of Río de la Plata in several ways: British invasions (1806-1807) related to Carlos' French alliances; Buenos Aires defense against them revealed weakness of royal officials and gave local residents self-confidence and desire for independence; Spaniards who had moved to viceroyalty in large numbers as merchants, officials, residents, ecclesiastics, forced to make difficult decisions about new relationships with both Spain and creole leaders; during early days of patriot government, with a legitimate, constitutional, independent monarchy suggested by some leaders as desired form of government, Carlos IV, then living in Italy, was approached (1815) by Argentine Manuel Sarratea (unofficially, through Conde de Cabarrús) to aid in secretly taking the royal prince Francisco de Paul to Buenos Aires to be crowned as ruler there; having first accepted the project in principle, Carlos IV then withdrew when he failed to secure Ferdinand VII's approval; project doomed, in any case, as official Argentine envoys, Manuel Belgrano and Bernardino Rivadavia, opposed it completely; and Argentine people refused to accept monarchical government; Carlos IV died in Rome.

CARLOTA JOAQUINA DE BORBON Y PARMA (1775-1830). Proposed ruler of the Río de la Planta. As the eldest child of Charles IV and María Luisa de Parma, Carlota, who was ambitious, unpredictable, and passionate, came to play an important role in the early independence plans of the Argentine republic; married to João (later King João VI of Portugal), she had moved with the Portuguese court to Rio de Janeiro in January 1808; when word came of Napoleon's occupation of Spain, and the placing of his brother on the throne, Carlota asked Viceroy Liniers to recognize her as Regent of the Río de la Plata for the Spanish Crown offering to come to Buenos Aires at once with support of a British squadron; Liniers refused, but certain members of the independence group, led by Saturnino Rodríguez Peña (and including Manuel Belgrano later),

came to believe that independence could be most easily won
and order best maintained by the establishment of a constitutional monarchy under a legitimate Spanish ruler; Carlota favored the project but it was dropped because of lack of creole
interest and the vigorous protests of the English minister to
the court at Rio de Janeiro, Lord Strangford; later projects of
the same order resulted from vigorous and tortuous intrigues
among the various groups vying for power in the area but all
failed eventually because of British or Portuguese opposition,
or because Carlota insisted on her divine right to rule and
would not accept a constitutional offer, or did not like some
of the revolutionary ideas; ultimately failed because the creoles in Buenos Aires wanted to win their own independence and
rejected monarchy as form of government; in 1820, the Portuguese royal family, including Carlota Joaquina, returned to
Lisbon; by that time Ferdinand VII had been back on the throne
six years and the Río de la Plata had declared its complete
independence of Spain.

CARMEN DE PATAGONES. Town on north bank of Río Negro
    near mouth; connected with Nahuel Huapi by railroad; founded
    in June 1779 by Francisco de Viedma as fortified frontier set-
    tlement when residents of Mercedes (now Viedma) across the
    river were flooded out; during colonial and early national per-
    iod served as rendezvous for pirates and privateers of South
    Atlantic, used by Viceroy Santiago de Liniers for exile of
    leaders of Alzaga conspiracy, 1809; on eve of Brazilian war,
    town's defenses strengthened and placed under command of
    Juan Manuel de Rosas, in charge of southern Indian frontier;
    defeated Brazilian attack, 1827, with enemy loss of four ships
    and 600 men taken prisoner; stone watchtower that served to
    alert early residents of approaching visitors, either by land or
    by sea, has been made a national historical monument.

CARRASCO, PEDRO BUENAVENTURA (1780-1839). Army surgeon
    and public figure in Independence era.
        Born in Cochabamba valley, Bolivia; graduated in medi-
    cine in Lima; served as army surgeon for the Patricios
    (patriot regiments) fighting against the British invasions; took
    part in the independence revolts in Chuquisaca (1810) and
    Cochabamba; in 1812 was physician in Belgrano's army to Upper
    Peru; back in Buenos Aires he was elected to the Congress
    (1817); appointed by Pueyrredón to commission to handle diplo-
    matic relations with Brazil; named one of the fifteen members,
    and vice president, of the Academy of Medicine created by
    Rivadavia in 1822; died in Buenos Aires 1839.

CARRATALA, JOSE MANUEL DE (1781-1854). Spanish officer in the
    royal armies fighting independence forces.
        Born in Spain, educated in law at the university of Al-
    calá de Henares; joined with other Spaniards in the fight against
    Napoleon's invasion; organized resistance in his native city of
    Alicante; with rank of colonel accompanied General Pablo

Murillo to America; in 1817 he was fighting against Güemes'
border guerrilla forces in Salta and Jujuy; in latter city he
married the brilliant and well educated daughter of a prominent royalist family, Ana de Gorostiaga y Rioja Isasmendi, after a courtship of romantic interludes between fighting that has
become one of the literary legends of that area; served as
chief of staff to royalist general Canterac; became field marshal and governor of Potosí; took part in humiliating defeat of
royalists at Ayacucho and departed soon afterward for other
assignments in Spain; eventually rose to appointment as minister of war and also served as senator from Sevilla before his
death in Madrid, 1854.

CARRERA, JOSE MIGUEL (1785-1821).   Chilean president who became involved in Argentine internal politics.
    President of Chile (1814) driven out by royalist forces;
sought aid from Buenos Aires and then United States; returned
to Argentina in 1817 just as San Martín's Army of the Andes
was crossing the cordillera to liberate Chile; when Director
Pueyrredón refused to permit him to enter Chile or interfere
with this action, Carrera became real trouble-maker for Buenos Aires government, allying himself with various of its political and military opponents and leading marauding bands
across the north, when not engaged in military action; captured and shot near Mendoza; his two brothers, engaged in
similar activities, had already been executed--Juan José in
1817, Luis in 1818.

CARRERAS, FRANCISCO DE LAS (1809-1870).   Jurisconsult; chief
justice of Supreme Court.
    Born and educated in Buenos Aires; devoted himself to
law until after fall of Rosas; became minister of hacienda (finance) in government of Buenos Aires in 1850s; resigned to accept judicial appointment, continued to rise in the judicial hierarchy, preferring such appointments to political ones offered
him; became justice of Supreme Court and then, under Mitre's
united national government, became first acting chief justice
(Valentín Alsina given honorary title as president), and, in
1865, received full appointment as chief justice of the supreme
court.

CARRETA.   Large, heavy, two-wheeled wagon, drawn by oxen; carried most of the heavy freight throughout the country until
railroads were built in late nineteenth century; built of wood
(usually lapacho from Tucumán), with wooden or leather sides
and covered with a rounded leather or cloth top; often traveled
in trains of thirty or forty for protection, especially against
the Indians.

CARRIEGO, EVARISTO (1791-1836).   Military, political figure of
Entre Ríos.
    Born in Yapeyú, of Spanish parents; early joined forces
of caudillo Hereñú near Paraná; resisting Artigas, Carriego

was defeated and went to Buenos Aires, 1817; Pueyrredón made him sergeant-major in the militia; involved in civil wars in Entre Ríos on side of Hereñú, he rose to rank of lieutenant colonel (later colonel) and was elected delegate to the constitutional convention in Buenos Aires, where he was considered to be one of the abler men helping to write the unitarist Constitution of 1826; in 1835 became Echagüe's secretary, serving in his place as governor in latter's absence; in spite of Rosas' objections, Carriego remained in this position until his death in 1836.

CARRIL, BONIFACIO DEL (1911-).   Historian; editor; professor; political figure.

Born in Buenos Aires, educated in law, entered legal practice after his graduation but quickly became involved in cultural and public affairs; taught both law and history at the university and devoted much of his time to historical research, especially of the Argentine national period; in the early 1940s he became leader of the able young moderates in the Movimiento de la Renovación; when General Luis Perlinger became President Farrell's minister of the interior, Carril was brought in as undersecretary; supported Perlinger in his unsuccessful power struggle against Perón and left the cabinet in 1944 when Perlinger was forced out; he became protagonist of revolution of 1955 that ousted Perón as well as its historian in Crónica interna de la revolución libertadora (1959); also was named honorary judge of the Army of the Andes operating in Cuyo under Julio A. Lagos during the "liberating revolution"; later became general director of the Emecé publishing house and served (1962) as foreign minister.

Elected in 1960 to the national academy of history, Bonifacio del Carril already had an imposing list of historical writings including, in addition to the Crónica, La vida sanjuanina de Sarmiento (1938); Buenos Aires frente al país (1946); Los Mendoza (1954); Problemas de la revolución y la democracia (1956); El día siguiente de Caseros (1957); Bajo el imperio de la fuerza (1958); Estados Unidos y la Argentina (1959); in a later work ¿Qué nos pasa a los argentinos? (1963), he seeks answers to the contemporary (1960s) Argentine problems.

CARRIL, SALVADOR MARIA DEL (1798-1883).   Jurist and statesman; vice president of Confederation.

Born in San Juan; educated in civil and canon law at the university of San Carlos in Córdoba; student of Deán Funes, received his doctor's degree in 1816; spent the next few years in Buenos Aires as journalist and official in ministry of finance; returned to San Juan and became governor; during his time in office, took Rivadavia as his model and attempted to modernize San Juan; new public buildings were begun, bridges built, water supply improved, the city beautified; new towns were established; brought in a printing press; July 15, 1826, promulgated the provincial constitution Carta de Mayo; based

on liberal new British ideas, many of which were later incorporated into the constitutions of Rivadavia and that of 1853;
aroused clerical opposition of such force that Carril was temporarily forced out; shortly after resuming his post, he resigned to go to Buenos Aires; became minister of finance under Rivadavia; later, when Dorrego had been elected governor,
served as one of chief advisors of General Lavalle, who defeated and executed Dorrego; after Lavalle's own defeat and
departure into exile, Carril also left the country; became a
member of the Argentine Commission and aided Lavalle on his
return to fight Rosas in 1839; joined Urquiza early in his fight
against Rosas; after Caseros, Carril remained with the Confederation, was a delegate to the constituent congress and
signed the constitution; became vice president of the Confederation; used by President Urquiza to help in working out a reunion of Buenos Aires with the other provinces; after this, during Bartolomé Mitre's presidency del Carril was appointed to
the Supreme Court (1862), serving as its president from 1870
until his retirement from public life in 1877, four years before his death.

CARRIZO, NICOLAS (1521-c. 1582).   Conquistador of Tucumán; in-
    terim governor 1570-1571.
          Carrizo arrived in Tucumán in 1550 with Juan Núñez de
    Prado and spent the rest of his life serving the various gov-
    ernors in their task of conquest and establishing Spanish rule;
    unusually effective against the Indians, he paved the way for
    Pérez de Zorita to establish the town of Córdoba among the
    Diaguitas in 1559; when Governor Francisco Aguirre was ar-
    rested in 1570, he left Carrizo in charge as interim governor;
    in 1573 he was sent to La Plata to inform Viceroy Toledo that
    Governor Jerónimo Luis de Cabrera had succeeded in founding
    the city of Córdoba in the land of the Comechingones Indians;
    at the viceroy's request he awaited the arrival of the newly-
    appointed governor, Gonzalo de Abreu, and escorted him to
    Tucumán; Carrizo's death seems to have occurred around
    1582.

CARRIZO, NICOLAS (c. 1631-1700).   Creole missionary to the Indi-
    ans of Jujuy.
          Born in Esteco, he studied to become a missionary to
    the Indians; settled in Jujuy in 1660 and spent the rest of his
    life teaching, evangelizing, and ministering to the Indians of
    the northwest; remembered and honored for his sacrifices and
    the self-abnegation of his life, in contrast to the normal privi-
    leges of his class.

CARTAS QUILLOTANAS.   Name given to famous letters in polemic
    between D. F. Sarmiento and Juan Bautista Alberdi concerning
    policy of J. J. Urquiza following defeat of Rosas; Sarmiento
    collected his letters under title "Las Cien y Una" and Alberdi
    labelled his "Cartas Quillotanas" as they were written in the
    Chilean town of Quillota where Alberdi was then living in exile.

CASA DE CONTRATACION (House of Trade). Established in Sevilla, 1503; represented a kind of ministry of commerce for the Indies, with responsibility for all matters relating to navigation, commerce, and actual moving of people, ships and goods to the Spanish American colonies; important during the sixteenth and early seventeenth centuries; its functions were gradually assumed by the consulados and merchant monopoly; by time it was abolished in 1790 it had lost its significance; its role in Argentine history was relatively slight; except for its aid and direction in early explorations of Vespucius, Díaz de Solís, and Sebastian Cabot, all three of whom held office of major pilot in the Casa, and its assistance to Pedro de Mendoza, first adelantado, and other early settlement ventures coming from Spain, rather than other Spanish settlements in America, the Tucumán and Río de la Plata areas only felt the Casa's influence indirectly, through its control of galleons, and monopoly trade by way of Peru, to which the Río de la Plata merchants reacted with a highly developed contraband trade of their own; by the time Buenos Aires' consulado was established in 1794, the Casa de Contratación was no longer in existence.

CASA DE EJERCICIOS (literally, House of Exercises). Name commonly applied to a Retreat House where Ignatius Loyola's Jesuit method of spiritual exercises is performed; most famous in Argentina is that founded by Sor María Antonia Paz y Figueroa (also known as Sor Antulo) in 1794 on Salta and Independence streets in Buenos Aires; declared an historical monument in 1941. (Term sometimes also applied in Argentina to the correction home for women built alongside it originally by Sor Antulo.)

CASA DE MONEDA. The national bank, founded in 1826 but operating under serious difficulties, was converted by Juan Manuel Rosas, into the Casa de Moneda, in 1836, with limited banking functions; during the next ten years it was responsible for five successive issues of paper money, after the fall of Rosas' government, the Casa de Moneda became the provincial bank of Buenos Aires (1853); as such it stimulated and supported the industry and commerce of the province during the years of separation from the other provinces in Urquiza's confederation.

CASA ROSADA. Name applied to the executive mansion, located on the Plaza de Mayo in downtown Buenos Aires; name believed to have been bestowed by President Domingo Faustino Sarmiento, remembering the White House in Washington and applying to the Argentine equivalent the name taken from its own rosy-colored walls; construction started during Sarmiento's presidency and completed during that of Roca.

CASADO, CARLOS (1833-1893). Banker, merchant, wheatgrower.
          Born in Valencia, Spain; came to Rosario de Santa Fe in 1857 to engage in commerce; quickly extended his interests

to include railroads, shipping, banking, colonizing, and agriculture; formed great business empire along Paraná river; established agricultural colony at Candelaria; as it prospered, helped found Bank of Santa Fe, of which he became first president; succeeded in raising enough wheat to export it to Europe for which he was given a gold medal by the business community of Rosario, at request of President Avellaneda who considered this exportation of wheat a turning point in Argentina's economic life; Casado continued active in promotion of cereals for export; organized growers and built granaries, etc., served also in civic life--municipal councilman for Rosario (1864).

CASARES, CARLOS (1830-1883). Hacendado and public figure; alternated agricultural and stockraising activities with public service.

Born in Buenos Aires, son of Vicente Casares, first Spanish representative to Argentina after independence; educated in capital; entered public life after fall of Rosas; elected to Buenos Aires legislature in 1857 and several times later; active in party of Adolfo Alsina; his acceptance, as a moderate autonomist, of President Avellaneda's appointment as governor of Buenos Aires province marked important step forward in Avellaneda's policy of national conciliation; in 1879 he headed committee backing nomination of Julio A. Roca for the presidency; served in many other public, not necessarily political, capacities: one of founders of Club del Progreso, 1852, presided over Club de Cría (1868) and supported improved breeding of racehorses; also was active in administration of the Western Railroad (Ferrocarril del Oeste), president of the Sociedad Rural Argentina as well as president of the board of directors of the Banco de la Provincia.

CASEROS (sometimes known as Monte Caseros). Site, near Buenos Aires, of battle February 3, 1852, in which Justo José Urquiza, commanding an allied army of his own forces, anti-Rosas groups, Brazilians, Uruguayans, decisively defeated an army of equal size and strength led by Juan Manuel de Rosas, ending the latter's dictatorship; Rosas escaped and, after writing his formal resignation from office, took refuge on British ship that carried him into permanent exile.

CASTAÑEDA, FRANCISCO DE PAULA (1776-1832). Franciscan friar, educator, journalist, and public leader.

Born in Buenos Aires; educated and ordained in Córdoba; occupied chair of philosophy there; embraced May Revolution from the beginning; returned to Buenos Aires and became well known and highly regarded as public figure and educator; established school of design and drawing with support of cabildo and consulado; interested himself in all public education opposing some of the new secular ideas but enthusiastically accepting new methods such as Lancastrian teaching, etc.; considered himself in sympathy with those who would become unitarists but broke with Martín Rodríguez' government when Minister Bernardino Rivadavia began his reforms; Castañeda belonged to no party or group, but, with his pen as weapon, fought violently and passionately (sometimes even libelously) for what he believed to be the best interests of the nation; exiled from capital 1821-1823, returned in time to assume leadership of opposition of Rivadavia's ecclesiastical reforms of 1823; first to show power of press in arousing popular feeling; only the support of liberal churchmen enabled Rivadavia to get his measures accepted in Buenos Aires--but not in provinces; Castañeda escaped attempts to exile him again; made his way to Santa Fe where he continued his teaching and writing under the protection of Estanislao López and with salvaging of a printing press abandoned by José Miguel Carrera; died in Paraná, 1832; remains brought to Buenos Aires for burial following ceremonial funeral in which clergy, government, army and people vied in honoring him as great patriot.

CASTAÑEDA, GREGORIO DE (d. 1567).   Lieutenant governor of Tucumán (1561-1563).
Castañeda's first act was to seize his predecessor, governor Juan Pérez Zurita; immediately thereafter, he faced a great uprising of the Indians under Juan Calchaquí; unable to bring the Calchaquians under control, Castañeda abandoned the settlements of Londres, Nieva, and Cañete, delegated government authority to a Captain Peralta, and left for Chile; Castañeda died in a shipwreck on his way to Concepción.

CASTELLANOS, AARON (1800-1880).   Business entrepreneur; land promoter; colonizer.
Born in Salta, of old, aristocratic family; before reaching age of thirty, he had fought in Guemes' gaucho army, traded in the Peruvian mines of Cerro de Pasco, explored the Bermejo river, hoping to prove its navigability but ending up a prisoner of Francia in Paraguay instead; later, he took up ranching and farming in Buenos Aires province, establishing settlements for these purposes along the southern Indian border; sold out and went to France where he published a pamphlet (in French) describing Argentina and what it had to offer; designed to promote immigration, especially of farmers, it was one of the first of its kind, and widely disseminated throughout France, Switzerland, Belgium, and Holland; returned to Buenos Aires, but when he found the government of Valentín Alsina unsympathetic to his proposed project for colonization of European farmers, or for improving ports of Buenos Aires and Ensenada and building a railroad between them, moved to Santa Fe where his ideas for economic development found welcome and support; June 15, 1853 (a little over six weeks after the Constitution for the new nation had been signed there), Santa Fe signed a colonization contract, its first, with Aaron Castellanos to establish an agricultural colony, as part of its new drive toward stimulating the provincial economy in every way possible but with especial emphasis on agriculture;

Castellanos bound himself to bring over 1,000 families during the next ten years and Santa Fe agreed to give them land, farm animals and implements; contract confirmed by Urquiza for the Confederation; upon arrival in Europe on his recruiting mission, Castellanos found plenty of immigrants, all bound for the United States, but few available for the unknown Santa Fe; finally secured 200 families, about 1,000 persons in all, and embarked them from Dunkirk and Antwerp, with all their farm equipment and necessary supplies, at his own expense; after settling them at Esperanza (q. v.), in a farming area about twenty-five miles from Santa Fe, Castellanos turned to new projects; his bid to build the railroad between Rosario and Córdoba rejected by President Mitre in favor of that of William Wheelwright, Castellanos devoted himself to the improvement of the port of Rosario; served as member of first city council of Rosario; prototype of provincial entrepreneurs throughout the nation whose capitalistic enterprise and business initiative proved important factors in the rapid economic progress of the second half of the nineteenth century; in Santa Fe he had contributed to breaking the traditional hold of cattle interests, as well as the Buenos Aires monopoly of commerce, and had opened the way to the alluvial era (q. v.) that would so soon transform Argentine life and society.

CASTELLANOS, JOAQUIN (1861-1932).   Lawyer; political activist; writer.

Born in Salta, educated there and in Rosario; completed doctorate in law, Buenos Aires 1896; early became active in political affairs, receiving serious leg wound while fighting with Carlos Tejedor (1880) for Buenos Aires autonomist principles; as radical leader both fought and served to arouse public support for revolution of 1890; exiled, 1893, for following Leandro Alem; returned to be elected to Buenos Aires provincial legislature three times; became minister of government for Bernardo de Irigoyen in La Plata; opened law office in Buenos Aires 1903; represented Buenos Aires in Congress; taught at the university in Buenos Aires; as governor of Salta presided over centennial marking death of Martín Güemes; ousted for political reasons, moved to Paraná to organize the historical archives there; also taught at national Littoral university; elected to Argentine Academy of Letters.

His writings include such diverse works as La leyenda argentina, published when he was about seventeen, that made his name known; a large quantity of poetry of varying literary quality; writings about labor movements in the early twentieth century (sometimes under pseudonym "Darma"); and Güemes ante la historia.

CASTELLANOS, TELASCO (c. 1846-50-1897).   Catholic educator in Córdoba; militant leader against President Roca's secular reforms; public official.

Born in Atamisqui, Santiago del Estero; educated in Córdoba at Monserrat and received the licenciate of laws from

the Faculty of Law; served as Minister of Government in his
province (1879) then as national deputy from Córdoba (1880-
1882); taught philosophy of law in the university and was rector
of the Colegio Nacional de Córdoba (1884-1888); then became
rector of the university in 1891; there he made many reforms;
fought so vigorously against the secular laws introduced in the
1880s that President Roca is said to have counselled his minister Juárez Celman that further conflicts with Castellanos
must be avoided even at the cost, if necessary, of making "a
novena in your home and showing yourself to be more Catholic
than the Pope himself"; Castellanos died in Córdoba in 1897.

CASTELLI, JUAN JOSE (1764-1812).   "Paladín of the May Revolu-
    tion. "   Born in Buenos Aires; father a Ventian-born physician
    and apothecary; brilliant, destined for the church, attended San
    Carlos, then studied theology and philosophy at University of
    Córdoba; turned from ecclesiastical career to that of law; re-
    ceived doctor's degree in law from University of Charcas; re-
    turning to Buenos Aires, he established himself in his profes-
    sion; became preoccupied with economic problems and was,
    with Vieytes and Belgrano, one of first Argentines to promote
    industry, common education, agriculture and free trade; close-
    ly related to Belgrano by interests, family ties, more than
    once took his place in secretariat of the consulado; one of the
    first--along with Belgrano, Hipólito Vieytes and Rodríguez
    Peña brothers--to work for political change in the viceroyalty
    of La Plata; fought consistently to end peninsular political,
    economic, and even social discrimination against creoles; one
    of first to believe that independence was only answer; consid-
    ered British aid (but stood with other porteños against British
    invasions) and crowning of Carlota Joaquina in Río de la Plata
    among other possibilities; 1801 one of founders of Sociedad
    Patriótica, Literaria, y Económica; became collaborator in
    early periodicals to spread his progressive ideas; founding mem-
    ber of Real Sociedad Universal de la Argentina (early use of
    Argentina's name).
        Played leading role in action leading to May 1810 revo-
    lution--Castelli and Martín Rodríguez being appointed as com-
    mittee to persuade Viceroy Baltasar Hidalgo de Cisneros to
    call a cabildo abierto; finally succeeded; Castelli's brilliant
    refutation of royalist arguments credited with contributing to
    success of meeting.   Castelli's thesis: with royal power gone
    with flight of royal family from Spain, and Spanish representa-
    tive government no longer existing after dissolution of Central
    Junta, power legally reverted to the people and their local gov-
    ernments; regency illegitimate, hence Cisneros' position as
    viceroy no longer valid; only cabildo abierto (open town council
    including all municipal leaders) of Buenos Aires had right to
    set up government; Cisneros forced to resign.   Castelli became
    member of first patriot junta; firm, energetic, he believed in
    strong measures to crush all opposition; sent to Córdoba to
    execute Liniers and other leaders of conspiracy against the
    junta; continued on to Upper Peru (Bolivia) to join Antonio

González Balcarce's army as a war commissioner from junta and propagandist for the revolution; present at victory of Suipacha; continued to promote revolution, attracting considerable support from the Indians. Wanted to progress straight on through to Peru with cause but junta called him back to Buenos Aires; signed armistice at Desagüadero with royalist commander Goyeneche; royalists violated it, won battle of Huaqui and brought all Upper Peru back under royalist control; desperately ill with cancer of the tongue, which had to be removed, Castelli died October 12, 1812; poor, persecuted, and calumnated; came later to be greatly honored and his firmness missed; Argentine independence, to which he had devoted his life, declared in 1816.

CASTELLI, PEDRO (1796-1839). Leader, with Ambrosio Crámer and Manuel Pico, of revolt in southern Buenos Aires province against Rosas; attempt became hopeless when Lavalle's expedition, with which it was timed, invaded Entre Ríos instead of Buenos Aires, as planned; Castelli defeated and executed at battle of Chascomús November 7, 1839, by army led by Rosas' brother Prudencio Rosas.

CASTILLO, PEDRO DEL (b. about 1521). Conquistador and founder of Mendoza.
     Born in Villalba, Spain; served in Peru under Gonzalo Pizarro against viceroy Núñez de Vela; accompanied García Hurtado de Mendoza to Chile, participated in establishment of cities there, named as corregidor of Villarica; when decision was made to conquer Cuyo (q.v.), del Castillo was given command; accompanied by at least 50-60 Spaniards and 1500 Indian auxiliaries, del Castillo left Chile late in 1560, crossed the cordillera by Inca road to Cuyo; well received by Huarpe Indians, he formally established the town of Mendoza (named in honor of Hurtado de Mendoza) March 2, 1561, distributed lands to the citizens October 9, and after spending a year in the Cuyo area, returned to Chile.

CASTILLO, RAMON S. (1873-1944). President of Argentine Republic, 1941-1943; Catamarcan conservative political figure.
     Born in Catamarca, educated in law at Buenos Aires; advanced up the ladder of political posts, holding administrative and judicial appointments; 1930 national interventor in Tucumán; 1932 elected national senator from Catamarca; then in 1936 minister of justice and public instruction, followed shortly by ministry of interior; 1940 vice president on ticket with Dr. Roberto M. Ortiz; assumed interim presidency because of latter's illness; continued Argentina's neutrality in World War II; destroyed the Concordancia narrowing his own political support to such an extent that he was deposed by GOU (Grupo de Oficiales Unidos) on June 4, 1943; last president to represent the oligarchy.
     A prestigious attorney, he taught commercial law, in which he specialized, both in Buenos Aires and at the Univer-

sity of La Plata; received many honors, including honorary degrees from universities of Rio de Janeiro and Heidelberg; published (among other works) Tratado de derecho comercial.

CASTRO, FELIX. Financier. Important member of Buenos Aires financial community in early national period (1820s); served as a director of the Banco de Descuentos (Discount Bank) and became a member of the mining society formed in Buenos Aires to exploit the Famatina mines in La Rioja; was one of two agents (with John Parish Robertson) that conducted the successful negotiations for the first Baring Loan (see Baring Brothers) and signed the shares of stock; helped organize the new Banco Nacional in Buenos Aires.

CASTRO, MANUEL ANTONIO DE (1772-1832). Jurisconsult; writer; early codifier of Argentine law.
        Born in Salta; studied in Córdoba and in Chuquisaca where he was friend of Mariano Moreno; was serving as secretary to president of royal audiencia of Charcas there, Dr. Ramón García Pizarro, when patriot revolution of May 25, 1809, forced latter out; Castro moved to Buenos Aires, received permission to practice law there, but became suspect because of his close relationship with Viceroy Baltasar Hidalgo de Cisneros at time of May Revolution 1810; imprisoned in June, all his papers seized, he was exonerated on grounds that he had acted as official of old regime, never in opposition to new; in May 1813 he was appointed to Court of Appeals; edited (1816) El Observador Americano, devoted to political problems and social and juridical studies; became permanent director of Academy of Jurisprudence created in 1815; accompanied Deán Funes on mission to Córdoba and Tucumán, 1816; went on to peace-making interview with Güemes; named interim governor of Córdoba by Supreme Director Juan Martín de Pueyrredón in 1817, provided progressive administration, especially in field of education, before returning to Buenos Aires following the revolution of Arequito in 1820; became permanent president of tribunal of justice; edited La Gaceta de Buenos Aires; became active as elected member of Buenos Aires Constituent Congress (president of it 1824-1827); sent with Dr. Dalmacio Vélez Sarsfield on government mission to provinces of Cuyo 1827; returned to resume judicial duties as president of tribunal and director of Academy and to write; distinguished for his writings in law and jurisprudence, one of the first to attempt to codify Argentine national law, he is best known for his Prontuario de la práctica forense (summary of handbook of legal court proceedings, first published in 1834.)

CASTRO BARROS, PEDRO IGNACIO DE (1777-1849). Priest, educator, and public figure; signer of the Declaration of Independence.
        Born in La Rioja province; educated in Santiago del Estero and in Córdoba; received his doctorate in theology and was ordained in 1800; devoted his entire life to three professions,

those of the church, the school, and public service on both
provincial and national level.

Returned to La Rioja in 1804 and opened a preparatory
school there; after a year teaching philosophy at the University
of Córdoba, he was back in La Rioja on a church assignment
when the May Revolution broke out (1810); immediately declared himself in favor of the May Revolution; elected to represent La Rioja at the constituent Assembly of the Year XIII,
he distinguished himself in several debates and on the directing board of it; in 1815 he and Juan Ramón Balcarce were appointed to make a propagandizing tour for the revolution
throughout the interior provinces--traveled 1200 miles on
horseback to complete it; again represented La Rioja at the
Congress of Tucumán; signed Declaration of Independence (July
9, 1816) and continued to be active in the congress after it
moved to Buenos Aires; after helping to bring La Rioja through
the period of anarchy, he returned to the University of Córdoba, 1821-1828, serving as both professor of philosophy and
rector; brought in printing press to replace the one owned by
the Jesuits that had been carried away; opened Lancastrian
primary schools; established the periodical Observador Eclesiástico to fight against Rivadavia's church reforms; supported
General Paz and when latter was captured in 1831 was forced
into exile in Uruguay (1831-1841); spent remaining years in
Chile teaching philosophy and ecclesiastical history at the university of San Felipe.

CATAMARCA (Province and City). Location of province: Lies in
Andes, between latitudes 26° and 30° 4'S, and meridians 64°
54' and 69°6' W; bounded on the north by Salta, on the east
by Tucumán and Santiago del Estero, on the south by Córdoba
and La Rioja, and on the west by Chile. Area: 38,500 square
miles. Population (1970): 172,323; relatively few are foreign
born; Diaguita Indian background and blood evident. Density:
4.5 per square mile. Capital: Catamarca, located in eastern
valley. Population: 45,929.

Climate and terrain. Mountainous, with some pleasant
valleys running from north to south; little rainfall and southeast arid; with irrigation agriculture could be greatly increased; projects under way for this; climate varies from extremely cold in the high Andes to hot and dry in the valleys
in summer, and temperate on some of the plains in the foothills.

Remote, arid, and mountainous, Catamarca still has
one of the smallest populations (only La Rioja and some of
the Patagonian provinces have fewer inhabitants) but it has always had a strong sense of identity (even before it became a
separate province), an unexpectedly high cultural level, considerable prosperity at times, and has always endeavored to
make its own contribution to the national life in spite of its
name which denotes a people or town on the edge, i.e., a
border-state.

Historical development. Unlike many of the older Argentine provinces, Catamarca did not develop from a city center, in fact, it had been declared a province and attached to the kingdom (government) of Tucumán (1679) several years before the capital city was founded; many settlements had been made by conquistadores from Tucumán and Santiago del Estero including five named Londres (London); in 1559 Juan Pérez de Zurita (through his lieutenant Julio Sedeño) had founded the first of these in the valley of Quinmivil, naming it in honor of Mary Tudor, Queen of England and wife of Philip II; originally established as a frontier stronghold against the Indians, who proved too strong; town was abandoned, except as a legal entity; revived and relocated several times during the next 120 years, the fifth Londres finally took firm root in the valley of Catamarca to which it was moved, 1682-1684, by the governor of Tucumán Fernando de Mendoza y Mate de Luna, and rechristened San Fernando de Catamarca; its establishment there marked one of the few seventeenth century adjustments to the settlement pattern made in Argentina by the conquistadores in 1500s: in 1694 Bartolomé de Castro, the first lieutenant governor, arrived to lay out the streets, allot the land, dig the irrigation ditches, etc.; a church was begun; religious life established, and the city's name finally shortened to Catamarca.

For the next century and two decades, Catamarca lived a rather quiet and prosperous life on a simple scale; little actual money was in circulation, but there was plenty to eat and trade for needs; the population of the province reached approximately 30,000 by the end of the colonial period and consisted of some hidalgos (aristocrats) living off their encomiendas of Indians; a few farmers, mostly creole or Spanish; many peaceful Indians; a large number of mixed bloods: mestizos, mulattoes, zambos (Indian-black); a few Portuguese, and a few converted Jewish families; the economy was largely based on agriculture--cotton, ají (chili peppers), and corn, with some vineyards and cultivation of sugar; some mining--gold, silver, and copper; and a well-developed cottage textile industry; almost every home had a loom and spinning and carding equipment with which they made textiles (mostly cotton); both this prosperity and the presence of a large number of churchmen--Franciscans, Mercedarians, Jesuits, Dominicans, and other clerics assigned to the area or simply resident there--contributed to cultural interest in the remote province; schools were good and graduates from the colegio could go directly to the universities of Córdoba or Chuquisaca (now Sucre) without further preparation; an interesting note from the records of the rector of Monserrat in Córdoba reveals that one student from Catamarca was returning for his second year and had arranged for shipments of cotton and chilis to be sent to cover his expenses; education was available on a class basis; one story relates that a mulatto was whipped publicly because he had dared to learn to read and write; but Catamarca was not unique in this attitude at that time and the Franciscans, particularly, along with the other religious teachers, tried to work on every level; with the establishment of the viceroyalty

and the opening of the port of Buenos Aires to trade, Catamarca faced political and economic change: along with Tucumán and other areas, it came under the political administration of the governor intendant of Salta (1783) and by the early
1800s, it was evident that its textiles could not compete with
those with which Europe was flooding the market; Catamarca
knew hard times.

News of the British invasions brought 200 men from
Salta to help in the defense; the 1810 May Revolution was accepted as soon as the monthly mail brought the news; Catamarca was placed back in the province of Tucumán in 1814 by
Director Posadas; it supported the gaucho forces of Martín
Güemes, holding the northern frontier in the war of independence, and contributed men, money, and supplies to Belgrano's
army, San Martín's expedition and other national independence
needs; two delegates, ranking churchmen, represented Catamarca at the Congress of Tucumán and signed the Declaration
of Independence, July 9, 1816: the Salteño presbyter and educator Dr. Manuel Antonio Acevedo y Torino and the Tucumán
presbyter and public figure Dr. José Eusebio Colombres y
Thames; the province immediately ratified this declaration;
during the next few years, the northwestern provinces, including Catamarca, attempted, through their cabildos, to become
autonomous political entities in the face of breakdown of national government and anarchy; other forces attempted to create provincial alliances or unions; briefly Catamarca became
a part of the Tucumán republic, but when this was destroyed
Catamarca relapsed into anarchy from which it emerged to
elect Nicolás Avellaneda y Tula first governor of an autonomous
(within national framework) Catamarca, 1821 with a provincial constitution promulgated in 1823; despite decades of political unrest and civil wars, province retained its modern form;
during the Rosas period, Catamarca remained generally on
the federalist side, although there was a kaleidoscopic shifting
of governments under such leaders as Aráoz, Quiroga, Lamadrid, Heredia, caudillos, armies, both within the province and
without; in 1840, under leaders from Catamarca like Marco
Avellaneda (newly elected governor of Tucumán) and José
Cubas, the Coalition or league of the North was formed
against Rosas; with rebellion crushed by the latter, the leaders beheaded and their heads publicly displayed, Catamarca
was terrorized and returned to the Rosas regime; in 1845
Manuel Navarro y Sosa, who had been governor before, assumed the governorship again; a doctrinaire federalist and
deeply committed, in principle, to what Rosas was trying to
do, he nevertheless brought the province peace and the beginnings of modern progress; Navarro leaned heavily on churchmen as his advisors and officials; the Jesuits returned 1844 to
help in the restoration and development and when Rosas ordered them expelled again, Catamarca dissolved the order and
permitted the individuals to remain; Navarro refused Urquiza's
call to fight against Rosas and his already declining health was,
in fact, seriously affected by the latter's defeat at Caseros;

Catamarca accepted the new regime, however, and sent delegates to the constitutional convention at Santa Fe: Pedro Ferré, the Correntino general, and the churchman Zenteno from Catamarca; adopted the constitution in 1853; Octaviano Navarro, son of the former governor, became governor in 1856 and for three years moved Catamarca forward; immigration, especially of artisans, was encouraged; a printing press was finally brought over from Paris by the governor and a group of private citizens; a periodical El Ambato was published, along with other materials, but in 1862 the government took it over as the state press; another period of anarchy followed: (1862-1869) within seven years there were 23 governments, not counting invasions and the raid of Felipe Varela's montoneros, 8 revolutions (including one by the women who took over the government briefly), 5 interventions by the national government, 6 battles and 5 elections. The actions of Chacho (Angel Vicente Peñaloza) followed by the rebellion of the colorados in 1866-1867 when the nation was engaged in fighting Paraguay, complicated matters; finally, Catamarca was on its way again; in 1872 the telegraph service was established; (from 1874 to 1880, the Argentine Republic had a president--Nicolás Avellaneda--from Catamarca province); schools were established; towns were lighted and policed; a provincial bank was established; hospitals, a theater, and public buildings were erected; administration of José Dulce (1889-1891), founder of the provincial bank, included two very different events of interest both to Catamarca and the nation: the coronation of the traditional image of Nuestra Señora del Valle, the special patroness of Catamarca, whose cult had spread beyond the provincial boundaries; and on July 26, 1889, the arrival of the railroad to the capital city--a branch of the Argentino del Norte, government built, that united Córdoba with Tucumán, now had been extended to include Catamarca.

The tumultuous political life of Catamarca manifested itself occasionally in the twentieth century; marked by national interventions, like that of President Ortíz in 1940; Catamarca leaned toward the radicals and Yrigoyen and supported strongly the inauguration of the Perón regime in 1946; the province's economic problems remain basically the same as ever: mountainous terrain, remoteness from financial and political power centers, and, above all, lack of water where it is most needed for agricultural development; project for dams and extensive irrigation systems are underway to enable Catamarca to grow the grapes, olives, tobacco, nuts, citrus and other fruits, vegetables and, especially, the very fine long-staple cotton, for all of which its soil and climate are well suited; mining continues to be more promise than performance; for all of these reasons, Catamarca's population, although five to six times greater than at independence, is still sparse.

CATHOLIC ACTION (Acción Católica). Catholic organization, largely composed of laymen; became important following World War I; aims are spiritual for most part, as expressed in official

weekly journal El Criterio; tended toward fascist right;
clashed with Perón in 1950s, organizing open resistance following his attempts to reduce power of its members in government (see Asociación Católica Argentina).

CATHOLICISM   see   ROMAN CATHOLICISM; RELIGION

CATRIEL, CIPRIANO (d. 1874).   Patagonian Indian chief (cacique),
son of Cipriano the Elder; friend of government; lived in civilized pattern near Azul; had his own bank account, etc.; considering himself Argentine, as well as Indian, brought his
800 warriors to aid in the defeat of invading Chilean Indian
leader Calfucurá; honored by Sarmiento and given status and
uniform in army; joined General Rivas on Mitre's side in revolution in 1874; defeated at La Verde, Catriel, along with the
other leaders was captured; fell into the hands of the Indians
on the other side (including his brothers and other relatives);
considering him a traitor, they stabbed him to death at once;
his brother Juan José Catriel became chief and began preparations for the uprising of the Indians in Azul the following
year, which ended eventually in Roca's conquest of the desert
and final pacification of the Patagonian Indians.

CATTLE.   Livestock industry is oldest and historically most important in Argentina; cattle formed major portion of this for 350
years and still very important in Argentine life and economy;
its effects, deeply rooted and widespread, have been psychological, social and cultural, as well as often determinant in
political and economic affairs; curious as cattle raising industry was not indigenous, nor did it appreciably affect direction
taken by early settlement.
       Cattle introduced into area in 1550s: from Brazil by
Vicente de Goes in 1556, bringing one bull, seven cows to
Asunción; into Tucumán area from Coquimbo, Chile, 1557, by
orders of Hurtado de Mendoza; by settlers (conquistadores)
coming into Tucumán area from Charcas (now southern Bolivia),
and Peru; pampas provided extremely favorable breeding
ground and cattle multiplied so rapidly, doubling their numbers
every three years, that later settlement expeditions could bring
their own herds with them--Juan Garay brought 1000 cattle
from upriver occupied areas to refound Buenos Aires in 1580.
       Cattle industry in northwest tied to mines, textile indus-
tries, and agriculture; on pampas, everything centered around
it and "leather culture" developed; everywhere, whatever regional differences, beef was there for the taking and formed
basic ingredient of diet for everyone from nomadic Indians to
royal officials; secure from starvation, with their clothing and
shelter provided, and free to roam, Argentines developed independent, individualistic spirit; economically, every class
profited from cattle; plainsman had not only food, but trading
goods in the hides that he could exchange in town for other
necessities; shopkeepers benefited from this trade; gauchos
found their herding skills in demand by increasing number of

estancieros, who became wealthy on hides and tallow; these also provided urban port merchants with bulk of exports in both
legitimate and contraband trade; even royal treasury profited.
Economic changes toward close of eighteenth century had
political and social effects; enormous, increased foreign demand for hides directed royal attention to this area; formerly
sparsely settled lands, like Entre Ríos and Banda Oriental
(Uruguay) were now settled and royal authority strengthened
there; commercial competition grew up between Montevideo,
established in 1726, and Buenos Aires, as latter was opened
to trade; economic rivalry became political; in independence
period was a factor in separation of Banda Oriental from
United Provinces into independent Uruguay; foreign demands
for meat (still mostly beef in Argentina) resulted in establishing of saladeros, meat-packing plants for salting or otherwise
preserving meat for export primarily to Brazilian or Caribbean slaveowners and for use in increasingly large Spanish and
other European navies; gaucho class developed; with free meat
disappearing, nomadic horsemen attached themselves to estancieros in economic and personal relationship, marked by individual equality and personal loyalty that often became translated into military and political support; early independence
government supported and protected cattle industry on which
independence armies depended; during civil wars and Rosas'
period cattle interests ruled as saladero owners controlled
Buenos Aires government and economy; patterns of land tenure
and ownership developed according to these needs; displaced
gauchos made up fighting forces of caudillos; economy of Argentina was already tied to world market on basis of cattle
exports; spread of saladeros northward brought increasing
power to littoral provinces and determination to break Buenos
Aires economic stranglehold; fall of Rosas resulted (1852).
Important changes in cattle industry in last half of nineteenth century included: new processes, such as that of Liebig
for using meat juices, etc., made use of entire carcass, increasing value of trade; new industries--especially those of the
sheepraisers and the agricultural colonies--began to challenge
cattle supremacy; increased cattle rustling and trading activities of Araucanian Indians in Patagonia united cattle and sheepowners in determined effort to destroy Indian control of these
southern lands; conquest of the desert opened these to new settlers; search for solution to problem of providing palatable
meat for important markets in European industrialized nations,
especially Great Britain, found solutions in refrigerated ships
and new meatpacking plants with refrigerated processing (see
frigoríficos) and in shipment of live animals; new interest in
breeding; saladeros had opposed introduction of beef cattle with
more fat (preferred in European markets) as unsuitable for
salting; now such cattle began to be introduced; Sociedad Rural
Argentina (q.v.) formed in 1866 supported such efforts; and
shorthorns and Aberdeen Angus brought over in 1879 by Carlos
Guerrero began to appear; new interest in dairy cattle developed; railroads tied interior cattle lands to such ports as

Buenos Aires, Rosario, and Bahía Blanca; salted beef peaked
in 1880s, shipment of live cattle predominated in 1890s, but
after 1900, when England barred live Argentine cattle from its
ports because of hoof and mouth disease, the frigoríficos took
over; meanwhile government interest had manifested itself in
regulations, agencies, establishment of national veterinary
schools, usually attached to universities, laboratories for research, and other supportive institutions.

In twentieth century, agricultural products supplanted
those of livestock in first place as exports and sheep challenged leadership of cattle; desire for greater industrialization
and less economic dependence on foreign nations brought real
threat to cattle (and other livestock industries) in 1940s and
1950s when Juan Domingo Perón's government, for first time,
attempted to limit power of estancieros in favor of greater industrialization; experiment proved costly, for time being, at
least; since then, changes in world markets, the development
of plastics to replace use of leather and other factors compli-
cate role of cattle industry; cattle numbered nearly 50 million
head in 1971 and Argentines still have beef to eat and still enjoy it.

See Peter H. Smith, in Suggested Readings, Appendix
III; Emilio A. Coni, Historia de las vaquerías del Río de la
Plata (Madrid, 1930); 2nd ed. Buenos Aires, 1956); Horacio
C. E. Giberti, Historia económica de la ganadería argentina
(Buenos Aires, 1954; 2nd ed. 1961).

CAUDILLISMO. Term most frequently used by Argentine historians
to describe both the system and the epoch that marked the difficult transition from achievement of independence to establishment of constitutional national government, more or less from
the anarchy of 1819 to the inauguration of Bartolomé Mitre as
president of united republic in 1862.

It was a period characterized by preoccupation with internal affairs--the setting up of provincial governments, of interprovincial relationships, of sketching the guidelines for national organization--with little interest in foreign affairs, and
accompanied by determination of provinces to share in new economic opportunities; by personal assumption of power by caudillos (q.v.) in vacuum created by breakdown of traditional and
formal government; by savage civil and interprovincial wars,
alternating with the signing of pacts of peace and alliance; it
represents a constant struggle on part of provinces to resist
political hegemony of Buenos Aires, along with latter's orientation toward European political and social ideologies, life-
styles and institutions in contrast to the more creole, indigenous provincial preferences; also a resistance to Buenos Aires
domination over provincial economic life through its control of
customs and river navigation, favoring estancieros of Buenos
Aires area.

Evaluations of role and contributions of caudillismo to
national development vary greatly; negative aspects are described by contemporary writers such as Domingo F. Sarmiento,

who, in Civilization and Barbarism, deplores the barbarism,
ruthlessness, violence, etc., of such caudillos as Juan Facundo Quiroga in contrast to the more desirable civilization of
such European nations as England and France; and by José
Ingenieros who regards it as a period in which personal ambi-
tion for power found no restraints and was the dominating political factor. A more positive attitude is expressed by modern historians, who like Ricardo Levene and others, view this
as a continuation of the May Revolution, sweeping away the
last vestiges of the colonial hierarchy and as an indigenous
expression of Argentine federalism and democratic principles
that came to be reflected in the constitutional structure of the
republic.

More recently the terms caudillismo and caudillo have
acquired somewhat simpler and more varied connotations, being
used to refer to any personal powerful political leadership or
even to political control of patron-client nature. See Hugh M.
Hamill, Jr., Dictatorship in Spanish America (New York,
1965), especially Section III, for this.

CAUDILLO (from Latin caput, meaning head). Local or national
politico-military chief; leader of band, party, or group (often
in Argentina consisting of gauchos or other horsemen) over
which he exercises absolute personal power; common throughout Latin America, especially during the nineteenth century,
the caudillo in Argentina prevailed from the early independence period into the first decade of national reorganization
(1870s) and was usually a charismatic, heroic, personally ambitious leader whose success and power came primarily from
the fact that he represented and led the fight for the prime interests and principles of local groups (see Caudillismo for historical role and contributions of caudillos).

Among important Argentine caudillos of the nineteenth
century were: José Gervasio Artigas, generally considered the
first, from Banda Oriental (now Uruguay); Martín Güemes,
Salta; Estanislao López, Santa Fe; Francisco Ramírez, Entre
Ríos; in the anarchy of the 1820s the number increased rapid-
ly; Juan Bautista Bustos, Córdoba; Felipe Ibarra, Santiago del
Estero; Bernabé Aráoz, Tucumán; Juan Facundo Quiroga, La
Rioja; José and José Félix Aldao, Mendoza; and finally, after
national reorganization in the 1860s, El Chacho (Angel Vicente
Peñaloza, La Rioja and Tucumán; and the last great caudillo
Ricardo López Jordán in Entre Ríos in the 1870s (see individu-
al listings).

CAXIAS, LUIS ALVES DE LIMA E SILVA, Duke of (1803-1880).
Brazilian general and statesman; commanded Brazilian forces
in Paraguayan war under Argentine commander-in-chief General Bartolomé Mitre, who assigned his presidential duties to his
vice president Marcos Paz, 1865-early January 1817; with
Mitre called back to Buenos Aires, Caxias was in full command until Mitre's return for the last half of 1867; the death
of Paz January 2, 1868 brought Mitre back to the presidency,

resigning his command over the allied army; now that the war was no longer, as in 1865, being fought in Argentine territory and Brazil was bearing three-fourths of the war effort, the command logically belonged to a Brazilian; and Caxias became commander-in-chief until 1869; succeeded by Count d'Eu, the Brazilian emperor's son-in-law, who successfully brought war to conclusion in 1870 (see Paraguayan War).

CEBALLOS, PEDRO DE (1715-1778).   Habitually signed his name "Pedro de Ceballos o Cevallos."   First viceroy of Río de la Plata, 1776-1778; lieutenant general of royal army; royal official in Spain.

Born in Cádiz, entered military service in 1739; distinguished both by his courage and by his unusual military talents became lieutenant general in 1755; served as governor of Buenos Aires, 1757-1766; much of his time taken up with Indian frontier in the north and with fighting the Portuguese from Brazil; captured Colonia del Sacramento in 1762 and was driving into Rio Grande do Sul when peace treaty (1763) ended hostilities; returned to Spain where he was received with high honors, appointed a member of the supreme war council and made governor and captain general of Madrid; ten years later (1776) renewed Portuguese pressure on the Río de la Plata area brought Ceballos back to Buenos Aires, this time as viceroy; in order to give Ceballos all the military and civil power that he would need to put a definite end to this Portuguese intrusion into Spanish territory, he was made viceroy of a newly created viceroyalty of the Río de la Plata, including not only present Argentina, Paraguay, and Uruguay, but Bolivia (probably at Ceballos' suggestion, because of its close relationship to Brazil), with its capital at Buenos Aires; in November 1776 Ceballos sailed from Spain with an armada of 115 ships and an armed force of about 9500 men; coasting down Brazil he took Santa Catalina Island in February; then went down to Montevideo and recaptured Colonia, again in Portuguese hands; operations were well under way for the occupation of southern Brazil when news came again of a treaty signed--the Treaty of San Ildefonso, by which Portugal surrendered its rights to the Banda Oriental (today's Uruguay), while Spain gave up rights to Rio Grande do Sul and both agreed that a commission be appointed to define the boundary; Ceballos took up viceregal duties in Buenos Aires; recommended strongly to the crown that viceroyalty be made permanent, with Upper Peru included; on his own initiative, later confirmed by the crown, opened up trade among the various provinces and eased restrictions on other trade; freed mines of Upper Peru from Peruvian domination by insisting that silver and gold must be sent to Potosí for smelting, rather than Lima, and suggesting that mercury be imported from Spain directly to Buenos Aires for these mines, rather than from Huancavelica in Peru; fostered agriculture by promoting cultivation of flax and hemp that Spain needed and by regulations improving position of agricultural laborers; with his health failing, his military services no longer needed in the Río de la Plata, and the fleet lying idle, Ceballos begged to be relieved; Juan José de Vértiz y Salcedo was appointed to succeed him as viceroy and Ceballos returned to Spain in 1778, hoping to resume his former position in Madrid but death overtook him in Córdoba, December 26, 1778, and he was buried in the cathedral there.

CENTRAL ARGENTINE RAILROAD. First major railroad built in Argentina; its first link (now the Mitre) connected Rosario with Córdoba along traditional mule track in 1870; reached Tucumán (the Belgrano) in 1876 and Jujuy in 1900; planned by Confederation President Justo José Urquiza in the 1850s, under the direction of American William Wheelwright, builder of railroads in Peru and Chile, its original purpose was to tie northern interior provinces to Rosario, being developed as rival port to Buenos Aires while at the same time promoting westward expansion; reluctance on part of British capitalists delayed railroad building until Argentine nation was reunited and government in position to guarantee investment returns; in line with new government economic development policies, three mile strip of land on either side or railroad reserved for colonization; intensive colonizing efforts by British company, largely in Switzerland and Italy, brought farmers over to establish agricultural colony thirteen miles from Rosario; followed almost immediately by three others along Central's tracks; pushing north and northwest, railroad stimulated new sugar industry of Tucumán and opened area to agricultural and other new economic development, with much of its commerce funneled through Rosario; Central, with monopoly on northern regions, joined three other British railroads, Southern, Pacific, and Western, in early twentieth century to form the Big Four; decreased profits in early depression years brought inclusion of protocol in Roca-Runciman agreement (1933), designed to placate and reassure discontented British investors; Central, along with other railroads of Big Four, had become run-down when purchased by Perón's government for £120 million in 1948 (see Railroads).

CEPEDA. Glen, or arroyo, northwest of Buenos Aires in which two separate battles, each marking turning point in national history, were fought.
      1. On February 1, 1820, allied army of the riparian provinces under Francisco Ramírez defeated national forces under José Rondeau; battle brief but decisive, with important political consequences; it broke the last political bonds between the interior provinces and the directorate government of Buenos Aires; brought the downfall of that government; and, many Argentine historians believe, marked a victory for the democratic sentiments of the masses over the monarchical tendencies of the governing elite.
      2. On October 23, 1859, the Confederation forces, commanded by Justo José Urquiza, routed army of General Bartolomé Mitre, fighting for province of Buenos Aires, then autonomous outside national organization; Urquiza persuaded

Buenos Aires to accept Pact of San José de Flores, November 11, providing for incorporation of that province into nation, after congress had been called to amend constitution of Santa Fe in way suitable to everyone; Urquiza also demanded the resignation of Valentín Alsina, governor of Buenos Aires; unfortunately things did not move smoothly and another battle had to be fought at Pavón (1861) before union was achieved.

CEPEDA, ALONSO DE (1536-d. after 1586). Conquistador of Tucumán; interim governor 1584-1586.

Active in public life of province and its capital; Cepeda was one of those influential in the selection of the valley of Salta, rather than that of Calchaquí, also proposed, for the establishment of the town of Salta; his brief governorship took place in a period of peace and Cepeda's chief contribution, apart from administering the routine affairs and continuing to improve communications between Santiago del Estero and the newly established Buenos Aires on the Río de la Plata, was to draw up a memorial for the king, listing the services performed by the landholding citizens and encomenderos of Santiago del Estero.

CERVIÑO, PEDRO DE (1757-1816). Engineer, educator, writer, and public figure.

Born in Galicia, arrived in Río de la Plata as member of the Spanish-Portuguese boundary commission (1782); 1783 made scientific expedition to the Chaco; organized and commanded Galician regiment that fought against British invasions (1807); patriot member of cabildo abierto of May 22, 1810; became director of new nautical school and mathematics academy, 1812; two years later prepared topographical map (preserved in San Fernando Museum) of city of Buenos Aires; collaborated with editor Hipólito Vieytes in weekly newspaper Semanario de Agricultura; died in Buenos Aires, leaving numerous manuscripts dealing with his work and experiences, many of which were edited and published in 1911 by another Galician, Manuel Castro López.

CEVALLOS, PEDRO DE see CEBALLOS, PEDRO DE

CGT see CONFEDERACION GENERAL DEL TRABAJO

CHACABUCO, BATTLE OF (February 12, 1817). Chilean site (about sixty miles north of Santiago) where San Martín's Army of the Andes decisively defeated royalist troops in battle that had significant military and political results.

San Martín's main army came through various Andean passes from Mendoza to rendezvous near Chacabuco, the place at which he planned to join battle; uncertain of exact point at which to expect San Martín, Governor Francisco Marcó del Pont had deployed his Chilean forces all along the Andes; assigned Brigadier Rafael Maroto, commander of famed Talaveras, to hold Chacabuco area with about 2000 men; arrived there

February 10, establishing headquarters in hacienda; San Martín forces numbering around 4000 began arriving next day; battle opened early on morning of February 12, with royalists drawn up in favorable position on only level, clear ground available, to repel expected frontal attack; San Martín's battle plan called, instead, for simultaneous flank attacks by Bernardo O'Higgins coming from the pass to the left and Miguel E. Soler from the right, with himself in command and the center guarded; O'Higgins rushed into early attack when Soler seemed to be delayed overlong and the resulting furious fighting threatened success of plan; San Martín's personal intervention turned tide and Soler's forces arrived in time to join with those of O'Higgins in forcing Maroto's professionals in hand-to-hand fighting among the olive groves and vineyards in hopeless attempts to escape; patriot victory complete; royalists lost approximately 500 men killed, including many officers, with 600 taken prisoner; patriot losses few, totaling about 140 of whom only 12 were killed (most of these from battalion eight attacking with O'Higgins--many liberated black slaves "who had fought like lions and were ready to give their lives for their country"--and from the mounted grenadiers; Marcó del Pont attempted to flee the country but was captured and interned in San Luis with other prisoners; San Martín and O'Higgins victoriously entered Santiago a few days later.

Significance of Chacabuco noted both in South America and abroad: Chile regained the independence lost less than three years earlier at Rancagua; Mendoza, training ground of Army of Andes, was jubilant and Buenos Aires, according to Pueyrredón, "went crazy" when Manuel Escalada arrived with news February 26; fact that victory was due to careful planning and effective training of military units gave clear indication of new offensive under professional command in war for independence; opened way for rest of San Martín's continental plan of isolating royalist power in Peru for final defeat and provided a permanent base on Pacific for undertaking this; Pezuela in Peru recognized this change, as did the Earl of Fife in Scotland, who had known San Martín in peninsular wars; Spanish ambassador to Portuguese court in Rio de Janeiro also noted fact; while Henry Clay, in U.S. Congress, took news of Chacabuco as reason for insisting (unsuccessfully) on immediate recognition of Argentina; politically, victory saved the Buenos Aires revolution by relieving its fear of invasion; and strengthened Supreme Director Pueyrredón's government both in Argentine provinces and in its dealings with Portuguese in Montevideo.

See Leopoldo R. Ornstein in Suggested Readings, Appendix III.

CHACHO. Nickname by which famous caudillo of La Rioja, General Angel Vicente Peñaloza, was commonly known. (See listing for General Peñaloza.)

CHACO (Province). Apparently the name is derived from Quechua

word for Indian practice of closing in on vicuñas by circle of
hunters to capture them; word later applied to other hunts using similar technique.

Location: North central part of Argentina; separated by
Bermejo River from Formosa on the north; bounded on east
by nation of Paraguay and province of Corrientes across the
Paraguay and Paraná rivers; on the south by Santa Fe; and on
the west by Santiago del Estero and Salta. Population (1970):
566,613. Capital: Resistencia--population (1960): over 84,000.

Climate and geography. Hot, semiarid, subtropical
plains, alternately flooded or semidesert; scrubby forests in
comparison with Misiones' rainforests but rich in useful lumber; lands good, when watered, for cattle and varied crop agriculture.

Area first visited by Sebastian Cabot in 1528 (possibly
earlier by Portuguese explorer Alejo García); explored forty
years later by Captain Juan Gregorio Bazán coming from Talavera in Salta; also visited and explored by Asunción colonists;
attracted by Indian trails, early Spanish settlements, like Concepción del Bermejo, were established there; Indian attacks
increased in both numbers and ferocity as the agricultural Indians of the west, and the nomadic fruit-, nuts-, and honey-
collecting Indians of the east became transformed into horse-
borne raiding bands, numbering hundreds of well-armed Indians, similar to those of the Araucanians in the south; settlements abandoned and Chaco left to the Indians, except for punitive raids by governors of neighboring provinces; in late eighteenth century (1774) Governor Jerónimo Matorras signed peace
agreements with the Tobas and Mocovíes; and in 1780 Gabino
Arias went down the Bermejo to reach Corrientes, across the
Paraná, and attempted to establish reducciones in the area;
settlement remained sparse and unstable; small military company, fleeing from Lavalle's defeat at Famaillá traversed Chaco
to reach Corrientes in 1841.

It was not until after the middle of the nineteenth century that the government decided to settle the Chaco Indian
problem once and for all; Indian raids threatening the new agricultural colonies and sheep ranches in Santa Fe could not be
tolerated; and national demands for the quebracho resources
of Chaco mounted: for the rich tannin variety of the east,
needed by the growing leather industry, and for the iron-hard
woods of the western varieties of quebracho (widely used for
axles and wheels of carretas) to serve as fence posts, railroad
ties, telephone poles, and other uses in the treeless coastal
areas that were rapidly developing economically; following a
series of military expeditions, 1870-1883, Benjamín Victoria
imposed peace on the rebellious Indian chieftains at La Cangayé,
1884; Chaco territory was established administratively that
same year; first four agricultural colonies had already been
founded, 1875-1876; first newspaper, El Chaco, founded in 1881;
in 1870 Resistencia was established on site of old settlement
and in 1885 made the capital of the province; population grew
rapidly with agriculture and cattle as basic industries; a major

supplier of tobacco and cotton, Chaco also produces sugar cane, sunflower seeds, oats, and other cereals; industries based on provincial products have developed; shipping provided by river ports (such as Resistencia and the nearby Barranqueras on the Paraná), railroads and highways.

In 1915, Chaco territory was divided into eight departments and it became a full-fledged province in 1951, with its first constitutional governor Felipe Gallardo taking office on June 4, 1953; province named for President Perón but name changed back to traditional Chaco in 1955.

CHACO (Region). Includes provinces of Chaco, Formosa, Santiago del Estero, and parts of Salta and Santa Fe; lowland plains subject to high temperatures; rivers of region, among largest in nation, are of little economic value; chief products are quebracho, for lumber and tannin, and cotton; Japanese having success with introduction of tea and rice in the mid-twentieth century (see listings of individual provinces).

CHACRA (from Quechua word meaning corn-planting). Term originally applied to country estates dedicated to agriculture as distinct from estancias for stock raising; after the middle of the nineteenth century when large scale agriculture was practiced, usually in colonias, the term chacra came to be used to designate a small rural holding where agriculture predominated, usually with diversification of crops.

CHAPADMALAL (Araucanian name, meaning corral de barro--mud pit). Area in eastern Buenos Aires province, famous among paleontologists for richness of its fossil remains; study of these has greatly increased knowledge of Argentine natural history in the pampas; first described by Father José Cardiel in 1748 and made famous by studies of Florentino Ameghino in 1880s; has become fashionable beach resort.

CHAPULTEPEC CONFERENCE (February-March 1945). Mexican Foreign Office invited all American republics (except Argentina) to meet at Chapultepec (in Mexico City) February 1945 to discuss intensification of America's war efforts--World War II approaching end--and to prepare for postwar problems; among matters discussed was that of formulating united American policy toward Argentina, which had remained neutral; latter republic declared war against Germany and Japan, March 1945, was included in signing of Chapultepec agreement.

CHARCAS. Name taken from that of Indians in area--south central Bolivia--and applied to both colonial administrative area and to its capital city, also known as Chuquisaca (q.v.), La Plata, and Sucre.

Discovery of rich silver mines of this area, bringing threats from Spaniards in Río de la Plata area as well as from Portuguese in Brazil, caused establishment of audiencia of Charcas 1559, subject to viceroyalty of Lima; audiencia began to function two years later; all of modern Paraguay, Uruguay, and Argentina (just beginning to be settled), in addition to its own area and much of Chile, were attached to it; for over two hundred years all Argentine matters of political, military, judicial, or cultural concern came under its jurisdiction (except for the brief period following the establishment of the first audiencia of Buenos Aires in 1661); ecclesiastical authority followed same lines, all Argentine churches being under archbishop of Charcas; difficulties of communication made appeals costly and links of authority sometimes tenuous, but never broken or denied; commercial ties, however, easier to establish between Charcas and Buenos Aires than the legitimate ones between Charcas and Lima; resulting impossibility of controlling flow of Charcas silver to Buenos Aires contraband trade and difficulties of effective administration to remote but increasingly prosperous Argentine areas weighed heavily in royal decision to create viceroyalty of Río de la Plata, with capital at Buenos Aires, (1776) and to attach audiencia of Charcas to it, instead of Lima; with viceroy in Buenos Aires and establishment of Audiencia of Buenos Aires (1783) with jurisdiction over present Argentine territory, audiencia of Charcas lost much of its former significance, especially as Charcas had become (1783) one of the eight new intendancies in the viceroyalty, under strong intendant rule.

CHARLES V OF HOLY ROMAN EMPIRE (Carlos I of Spain) (1500-1558). Emperor, 1519-1556, and first Hapsburg King of Spain, 1516-1556.
        Born in Ghent, Flanders, grandson of Ferdinand and Isabel of Spain and of Emperor Maximilian I; was ruling Spain (as regent for his mother at first) during entire period of discovery, exploration, conquest, early settlement and establishment of royal government in Río de la Plata and northwestern portions of Argentina; his own international ties and responsibilities brought many non-Spaniards to this area, such as Magellan, Sebastian Cabot, Ulrich Schmidel, etc. ; failure to find mineral wealth and populous Indian societies in Argentine area caused emperor to place conquest and settlement in hands of adelantados; international wars, complicated by rise of Protestantism in northern Europe, laid bases for later foreign intrusions, especially English, French, and Dutch, into South Atlantic waters and contraband trade; worn out from his burdens of ruling, Charles began divesting himself of different realms of power, finally withdrawing to a convent after having abdicated the Spanish throne in 1556 to his son Philip (II), and retiring from imperial throne the same year.

CHARQUI (English "jerky", from Quechua word meaning thin and dry). Thin strips of meat prepared by exposing them methodically to sun and air to dry and preserve them; used in northwest and in north (in dry areas) from Indian times to the present (family recipes still available); when stewed with potatoes and beans or peanuts, and seasoned with pimentoes and spices,

known as charquicán; if meat is salted also, it is usually
called tasajo; with the increasing abundance of meat, especially beef, in the Spanish period, charqui came to be one of
first articles of export from Argentina for use in slave plantations in Caribbean and Brazil.

CHARRUAS. Nomadic Indians occupying area of modern Uruguay at
time of discovery and conquest; formidable fighters with boleadores, slings, and arrows; after arrival of Spaniards, Charruas
made effective use of horses and continued to raid Corrientes
and Entre Ríos until mid-nineteenth century (see Indians).

CHASCOMUS. City that grew up around blandengue frontier fort,
San Juan Bautista de Chascomús, against the Indians south of
Buenos Aires; moved to present location in 1781; became a
city in 1873; on November 7, 1839, site of battle of Chascomús, in which Prudencio Rosas, brother of the governor, with
an improvised army, delivered crushing defeat to the leaders--
Pedro Castelli, Ambrosio Crámer, and Manuel Rico--of rebellion against Rosas; left Rosas free to fight Lavalle's forces
in the littoral provinces which had counted on this diversion
in the south to give them an opportunity to get their campaign
underway.

CHAVES, NUFRIO DE (d. 1567); also known as Nuflo de. Conquistador; explorer and Indian fighter; founder of Santa Cruz de la
Sierra; first to bring sheep and goats to Río de la Plata region.
        Born in Trujillo, brother of Philip II's confessor, Di-
ego Chaves; accompanied Alvar Núñez Cabeza de Vaca to
Asunción, 1542; after having engaged in several missions for
the adelantado and accompanying him on his disastrous unsuccessful attempt to reach Peru, joined with other officials in
deposing Cabeza de Vaca and making Domingo Martínez de
Irala governor, 1544; closely associated with latter for next
dozen years; led explorations north into Mato Grosso, west
150 miles up Pilcomayo river to falls (1547); led party of four
(including Pedro de Oñate) on mission from Irala (who remained in camp near Chuquisaca) to Lima, 1548, successfully
establishing the long-desired contact between Asunción and the
viceregal capital; conferred with Pedro de la Gasca, then in
charge, delivering Irala's documents, messages, and requests
for such trade items as copper, oil, drugs, wine, flour and
others not available in Asunción; returned to Asunción, 1549,
bringing first sheep and goats to Asunción; also brought a
tailor named Alonso de Escobar; in 1545, late in 1549, and
again in 1556, Chaves was sent to Upper Paraná Valley to
pacify Tupi Indians raiding the Guaraní and Spanish lands and
making communication with Atlantic coast difficult; forced Tupi
to accept peace and opened route to São Vicente in Brazil along
which cattle, iron, textiles and other trade and travelers began
to come; also offered shorter, more direct communication
with Spain; following Irala's death in 1556, Chaves returned

to search in the west for Silver Mountain and easier route to
Peru; founded Santa Cruz de la Sierra February 26, 1561, on
what was then considered to be boundary between western and
eastern Spanish jurisdiction (today in Bolivia), to facilitate communications and perhaps, according to some stories, in the
hope of carving out a new jurisdiction for himself; distributed
Indians to Spanish encomenderos, among whom was Juan de
Garay, future refounder of Buenos Aires; in 1567 Chaves
started out on final exploratory venture, met death in Indian
ambush.

"CHE." Argentinism, used in place of "tú" (informal Spanish pro-
noun for "you"); cherished by Argentines as peculiarly their
own; believed to have been developed during colonial years of
relative isolation from Spain from formal expression for "you"
Vuestra Merced (Vd.) to Usted, then through gaucho use to urban street talk to "che"; attracted considerable attention in
1960s as nickname given Cuban revolutionary Ernesto (Che)
Guevara, denoting his Argentine birth.

CHE PATRON. Expression used by Northeastern workers to refer to
the landowner.

CHICLANA, FELICIANO ANTONIO (1761-1826).   Jurisconsult; independence leader.
        Born in Buenos Aires; educated in Santiago de Chile,
graduating in law from the university of San Felipe in 1783;
returned to Buenos Aires where he served as legal adviser to
the cabildo; during the British invasions he played active roles
both as legal counsel and as captain of the fifth company of the
patricios; became a member of the secret patriotic society that
met in the homes of Vieytes and Rodríguez Peña to plan revolution; played an active role in events leading up to and during
the May Revolution in 1810; belonged to the moderate group in
the cabildo abierto that favored letting the cabildo take over
power until government could be reorganized again under Spanish crown; commissioned as colonel and appointed judge advocate for the auxiliary army of the north by the patriot Junta,
he was diverted to Santiago del Estero as governor intendant
briefly, then went on to Salta in the same capacity; political
confusions there caused him to return to Buenos Aires; there,
after involving himself in the controversy between Moreno and
Saavedra, he became a member of the First Triumvirate,
along with Sarratea and Paso, following the dissolution of the
Junta, 1811; in July 1812 he was one of the judges for the trial
of the leaders of the Alzaga revolt; and in November he was
again serving as governor intendant of Salta, where he effectively aided Belgrano in the reorganization of his army; resigned in October 1813, to be succeeded by Fernández de la
Cruz; Chiclana returned to Buenos Aires but was sent back to
the auxiliary army by Director Gervasio Posadas to spend a
couple of years gathering supplies for the army; when that assignment ended, he joined those opposing Director Pueyrredón

in 1817 and was exiled to the United States; after a miserable
year in Baltimore, he returned to the Río de la Plata; following a delay of several months in Montevideo, he was given permission to reenter Argentina; in 1819 his rank of colonel was
restored and he was sent to negotiate a peace on the pampas
with the chieftains of the Ranquel Indians; he was successful
in this, his last mission for his country; in 1822 he retired
and died four years later; Chiclana is generally considered to
have made his greatest contribution in the early days of the
revolution that owed much of its success to his fiery, turbulent
spirit.

CHILAVERT, MARTINIANO (1804-1852). Military officer. Com-
    mander of Rosas' artillery at the battle of Caseros; born in
    Buenos Aires but brought up in Spain, he returned with his
    family in 1812 on the George Canning with San Martín, Carlos
    María Alvear and Zapiola; became mathematician and engineer,
    accompanied Alvear on campaigns; later fought with Lavalle,
    Pacheco, and Paz; served under Rosas 1847-52; Colonel Chila-
    vert's heroic and loyal action at Caseros postponed but could
    not prevent defeat; executed by Urquiza's orders immediately
    after the battle.

CHILE. Argentina's neighbor across the Andes to the west and to
    the south, on the Strait of Magellan; historical development of
    two nations has been closely bound up together from the begin-
    ning to modern times; Cuyo founded by men from Chile who
    used old Indian trails; various Andean passes used constantly
    throughout the colonial period; Uspallata Pass has linked Men-
    doza, Argentina and Santiago, Chile, closely together by mule
    path, fortified colonial road, railroad, modern highway, and
    airlines through more than four centuries; in 1776, Cuyo was
    detached from Chilean administration to become part of the new
    viceroyalty of the Río de la Plata; in October 1814 Chileans,
    led by two former presidents--José Luis Carrera and Bernardo
    O'Higgins--escaped to Mendoza, leaving Chile under royalist
    rule; less than three years later, the Army of the Andes re-
    turned to Chile to free it, with O'Higgins commanding a Chile-
    an division but with an Argentine general, José de San Martín,
    in command of an army supplied and equipped by the Argentine
    people and government; the liberating expedition under San Mar-
    tín, both military and naval, to Peru in 1820 was a joint Ar-
    gentine-Chilean operation; after South American independence
    had been won, Chile and Argentina combined forces to defeat
    Santa Cruz's Confederation of the Andes (which included both
    modern Peru and Bolivia); during the 19th century Araucanian
    Indians from Chile overran the Patagonian area and the south-
    ern pampas, settling them and creating serious problems for
    Argentine settlers and ranchers as well as new Indian problems
    from displaced pampas Indians; national expansion and develop-
    ment goals of both countries brought disputes over boundaries
    in the Andes and around the Strait of Magellan; after series of
    unsatisfactory preliminary agreements, Argentina and Chile

signed treaties settling the matter, largely through arbitration
of Edward VII of Great Britain, during second term of President Roca (1898-1904); in the south, Tierra del Fuego was divided between the two countries, Chile was given the banks of
the Strait of Magellan, with Argentine rights to navigation protected; along the boundary cresting the Andes the statue of the
Christ of the Andes was erected in 1904 with impressive ceremonies, with both nations participating, symbolizing their hope
that the peace established between them would be permanent.

CHILEAN MERIT ORDER. Established by Bernardo O'Higgins in
1817, following victory at Chacabuco to honor heroes of the
war for independece; first award bestowed on Supreme Director of the United Provinces, Juan Martín de Pueyrredón for
his effective collaboration in creating and supplying the Army
of the Andes that made this possible.

CHINO, CHINA. Derogatory term formerly used in Argentina by
upper classes to refer to uneducated, unskilled, often somewhat darker-skinned workers (see Cabecitas negras; Descamisados).

CHOELE-CHOEL. Island in Río Negro river traditionally used as
stronghold by Patagonian Indians when attacked by Argentine
forces; Rosas' defeat of them there in 1833 stabilized the
southern frontier for a time and brought him honors and a land
grant on the island from the grateful Buenos Aires legislature;
approximately half a century later the Conquest of the Desert
(q. v.) was completed when Argentine forces from Toay ended
the Indian control of the island forever, forcing all groups to
surrender or disperse permanently.

CHOLERA see EPIDEMICS OF DISEASE

CHORROARIN, LUIS JOSE (1757-1823). Priest, educator, legislator, patriot leader, and director of public library.
        Born in Buenos Aires, educated in scholastic tradition,
received doctorate in philosophy, and was ordained as priest;
named professor of philosophy at the Colegio de San Carlos
(q. v.); in 1873 and three years later became its rector; Chorroarín influenced both intellectual trends and the independence
movement by his lectures and his writings in such journals as
El Telégrafo; his lectures on logic in 1783 at the Colegio,
long believed lost, were rediscovered and published in 1911;
in these and his other lectures and writings, he declared that
while the authority of the church must be accepted in moral
matters, in the field of natural science that authority must
only be accepted when the holy fathers were themselves well-
versed in the scientific discipline involved.
        Breaking completely with his conservative background
and training, Chorroarín entered the revolutionary movement
and supported independence, exerting his influence especially
in the field of political organization; in the Cabildo Abierto

(May 1810), he presented a plan for the new patriot government, parts of which were accepted; as member of the Assembly of the Year XIII (q. v.) he collaborated with Pedro
Agrelo, Juan Hipólito Vieytes, and José Valentín Gómez in
drawing up a constitutional project for its consideration; later
as a Buenos Aires deputy to the national congress, he proposed adoption of the flag that became the national banner; one
of his most important contributions to Argentine life came in
his closing years when he became director of the public library, in which he had always been interested, and which now
made major progress under his administration; Chorroarín
died in Buenos Aires in 1823.

 See Manuel Juan Sanguinetti, Chorroarín, el prócer
olvidado (Buenos Aires, 1952).

CHRIST OF THE ANDES. Bronze statue of Christ holding cross
set high in Andes on boundary between Chile and Argentina;
celebrates peaceful settlement, through decision of arbitrator
King Edward VII of England, of the bitter, long-standing boundary dispute; dedicated March 13, 1904 (a jubilee year in Catholic world), with formal diplomatic and ecclesiastical ceremonies by both nations; statue created by distinguished Argentine sculptor Mateo Alonso from melted cannon; Chilean and
Argentine embracing figures at the base of the 25-foot monument emphasize the symbolic meaning.

CHRISTIAN DEMOCRATS see POLITICAL PARTIES

CHUBUT. Patagonian province lying between parallels 42° and
46°S, with Andes and Chilean boundary to the west and the
Atlantic Ocean on the east; bordered on north by province of
Río Negro and on south by that of Santa Cruz; became province
in 1950. Population (1970): ca. 190,000. Capital: Rawson;
population ca. 5000; located near mouth of Chubut River.
Other important cities: 1) Comodoro Rivadavia; pop. 36,000; oil
and natural gas center; located on bay of San Jorge.   2) Trelew; pop. 12,000; progressive commercial, cultural, transportation center on Chubut river.   3) Esquel; pop. 10,000; rapidly becoming one of most important cities in southern Andes.
4) Puerto Madryn, located on Golfo Nuevo, connected with
Trelew and other towns by railroads and roads, as well as
water transit.   Area: 86,700 square miles; Density: 2.2
people per square mile.
 Life of the province centers around the Chubut river
and its valley, including that of the Chico, its major tributary,
to the south; high winds sweep over its semiarid plains, brok-
en by deep canyons; climate cold, with snow replacing rain
but average temperature above freezing; Andes rise abruptly in
the west; population sparse; major industry is sheep raising
with millions of sheep grazing on the short grass of estancias
owned by absentee landlords and operated by professional managers of sheep stations from Scotland, New Zealand, or Aus-
tralia; Welsh farmers and cattle-raisers (near coast) give

cultural stamp to area; oil and natural gas industry at Comodoro Rivadavia under YPF (q. v.).

History. Although Magellan coasted Chubut in 1519, the remoteness, cold climate, and aridity of the area left it outside stream of Argentine historical development until Welsh interest in colonization in the 1850s; in 1852 Welsh captain Elsegood established a colony that failed; two years later Henry L. Jones (Enrique Libanus Jones, q. v.), long a pioneer in Patagonian colonization projects, secured Buenos Aires backing for a colony; entered Chubut river in January 1855, established settlement, but was forced to abandon it after a few months; a few years later, Welsh nationalists, inspired by the great Welsh leader Michael D. Jones, seeking a remote area where they could establish a colony in which their own language, customs, and religion could be preserved, approached the Argentine government for aid in the form of land, farm animals, grain, etc.; Dr. Guillermo Rawson, then Argentine minister of the interior, interested himself and the project got underway, with land granted in the coastal area of the Chubut valley as site of the colony; on July 28, 1865, the first contingent of colonists--153 Welsh men, women, and children led by Sir Love Jones, Parry Madryn, and Lewis Jones, in the Mimosa--landed on the shore of Golfo Nuevo, near present Puerto Madryn; while the men went overland to the Chubut Valley, seeking a proper site, the women and children continued by sea; on September 16, 1865, Julián Murga, military commandante of the area established the Welsh Chubut Colony on the river about three miles from its mouth (later renamed Rawson to honor memory of its benefactor); colony suffered great hardships; few knew how to farm or even to survive in alien land; in spite of aid and food supplies from Argentine government and passing British ships, colony would probably have had to be abandoned if Indians, friendly from the first, had not come to its aid, trading furs, meat, etc. , in return for Welsh flour and iron work, and teaching Welsh to manage horses, to use the boleadores and lasso, and to hunt wild animals, like the guanaco; when Welsh also learned to use river waters for irrigation farming, the colony at last began to grow; after the Conquest of the Desert (q. v.)--in which the Welsh refused to fight against the Indians--had eliminated the Indian menace in Patagonia, the Argentine government extended its authority throughout the area; creating new territories, including Chubut, in 1884, opening schools, and sending governors to administer and develop the new lands; Chubut's first governor (1885) was Lt. Col. Luis Jorge Fontana, both able and interested, with a doctorate in natural sciences, in his new assignment; simultaneously the spiritual conquest of the desert was begun by missionaries sent out by the archbishop of Buenos Aires, while the Salesian fathers were also active in missionary work among the Indians, as well as in laying the foundations of education; in 1886, the company of Luis Jones started work on a railroad to Bahía Blanca and Trelew (Welsh for Lewis' city, in honor of Luis Jones) was founded a few miles up the river; it served as capital until 1900, when Rawson was made formal capital; other settlements--Diez y Seis de Octubre (named for the date of the promulgation of the law creating the territories), Colonia Sarmiento, Puerto Madryn, Comodoro Rivadavia (1901), Esquel in the Andes (1906)--were established, along with government infrastructure; land distributed in several ways: to individual farmers; to cattle raisers; to groups; even to Indian caciques; and then, as sheep raising became the most profitable form of economic exploitation (to satisfy the British wool demands), land came into the hands of a few estancieros with immense holdings; towns increased rapidly in population but rural areas remained the domain of sheep, with the few men needed to tend them--mostly Scottish and Welsh; the Sociedad Rural engaged itself in upgrading the stock, as well as improving the industry in other ways, although severe and prolonged droughts were still a problem for sheep wool shipped north to Buenos Aires in coastal steamers; Chubut continues to grow as young men (always more males than females in population count until midtwentieth century) came to this new frontier to make their fortunes; banking houses, foreign consulates, international businesses, etc., sent their representatives; the discovery of oil in Comodoro Rivadavia in 1907 added a new dimension to the economy, converting the town into an El Dorado or boom town overnight and giving great impetus to the development of the southern part of the province; gas pipeline built by Perón extends 1000 miles from Comodoro Rivadavia to Buenos Aires; educational facilities have been fostered, although still less advanced than in some of the older provinces; imprint of Welsh culture and religion still remains clear, although many descendants of Welsh colonists have married Spanish-speaking Argentines and Italians and Argentine Catholicism has taken firm root; the first newspaper of the province, La Estrella del Sur, appeared in 1892 but had brief life; others have followed, the Chubut of Comodoro Rivadavia being one of the most important.

CHUCHO. Indigenous name for malaria (see Epidemics of Disease).

CHUPANDINOS (from chupar, to suck or smack lips). Nickname applied to political groups in Buenos Aires led by Hilario Lagos and Nicolás Calvo in 1850s, referring to its practice of holding political meetings at barbecues (asados), particularly in the south where it was popular; in the Buenos Aires elections of 1857, chupandinos stood for federal reform and conciliation with the Confederation (rest of Argentina); opposed (unsuccessfully) the election of Valentín Alsina as governor.

CHUQUISACA. Distant, erudite city in Upper Peru from which all royal and ecclesiastical power emanated for first two centuries of colonial rule of Argentina (see Charcas for administration); city (also known as Charcas, La Plata, and finally Sucre) founded on left bank of Cachimayo river by Pedro Aranzares,

Marqués de Campo Redondo, on November 30, 1538, acting under orders from Francisco Pizarro; Chuquisaca, Indian name for town, commonly used throughout colonial period, although La Plata was also applied to it because of early discoveries of silver there, and city sometimes called by name of audiencia of Charcas, established there in 1559; in 1839 the name was officially changed to Sucre in honor of Bolivia's liberator and first president.

Throughout colonial period, Chuquisaca was a relatively small but very wealthy, powerful, cultural center for all southern South America; in 1624 the University of San Francisco Javier was founded by the Jesuit Jaime Frías y Herrán on the base of the Colegio de San Juan Bautista, established two years earlier; primarily devoted to ecclesiastical studies under the Jesuits, it took a somewhat different turn after their expulsion in 1767; in 1776, the Colegio Real de San Carlos was established, related to university, and emphasis was placed on Indian and Spanish law; Chuquisaca became the gathering place of ambitious young law students from entire viceroyalty and attracted excellent teachers; its library was second only to that of Lima in South America, and promising students also had access to the rich library (exempt from Inquisition censorship) of Matías Terrazas, secretary of the archbishop, that included most of the writings of the European scientists and philosophers of the Enlightenment; many of precursors and participants of Buenos Aires May Revolution educated and trained in new political ideas and techniques there; among these: Mariano and Manuel Moreno, Juan José Castelli, Juan José Paso, Manuel Antonio Castro, Teodoro Sánchez de Bustamante, Agustín Gascón, Bernardo Monteagudo, José Valentín Gómez, Tomás M. de Anchorena, Mariano Boedo, José Darregueira, José Ignacio Gorriti; Pedro Miguel Aráoz, and Pedro José de Agrelo; revolution of Chuquisaca May 25, 1809, in which law students joined with audiencia judges and populace against president of audiencia and archbishop because latter seemed to favor regency of Carlota Joaquina (then in Brazil) until her brother Ferdinand VII could regain crown from French, was put down by royal force but had both immediate and later effects on Buenos Aires revolution; one of its leaders, Bernardo Monteagudo, escaped to play an important role in early patriot movements in Buenos Aires.

CHURCH   see   ROMAN CATHOLIC CHURCH

CHURCH-STATE RELATIONS.   The Argentine Republic is a Catholic nation, with the Roman Catholic Church supported by the government and both president and vice president required to be Catholics; on the other hand, freedom of worship has long been granted and practiced; except for brief intervals, the Catholic Church has had little or no participation in public education since the 1880s or, for that matter, in politics; and the government exercises legal control over civil marriage, vital statistics, cemeteries and tacit control over ecclesiastical patronage.

Throughout the colonial period the Argentine provinces, like all other Spanish colonies were governed by the Spanish crown with the patronato real (royal patronage) agreement with the Papacy giving it virtually complete control of appointment of church officials, collection of tithes, creation of dioceses or changes regarding them, and in fact practically all ecclesiastical matters except those of doctrine; for all practical purposes this royal patronage was replaced by national patronage in 1810 by the May Revolution; the constituent congress, or Assembly, of XIII, and directorate government's statute (1815) recognized the Argentine executives' right to that power as did Congress of Tucumán in its provisional regulation (1817), and Constitution of 1819; this view was not accepted in either Rome or Madrid; after independence the issue was already drawn between those who believed that the patronato real was inherited as a patronato nacional, by the newly independent states and those who insisted that it reverted from the Crown to the Pope; Argentine patriot governments repeatedly declared and acted on the first theory, 1810-1820; there was no Church-State issue involved in its independence movement; although a few bishops like Benito Lué y Riegas of Buenos Aires, Rodrigo A. de Orellana of Córdoba, and Nicolás Videla del Pino of Salta (qq. v.) refused to back the revolution, most of the clerics supported it, not only with their talents and energy, but with essential financial support; by 1819 new bishops were needed for all the dioceses; the constitution of 1819 provided for the president to fill such vacancies and for ecclesiastical representation in congress but its rejection and the following anarchy left the problem unsolved; for the next four decades, each of the provinces handled patronage according to its own preferences and new constitutions; in Buenos Aires province, where Bernardino Rivadavia had put through extensive ecclesiastical reforms in the 1820s and several legal conflicts between Church and State had arisen, the Church welcomed Rosas' protection although it finally learned that it had become his instrument and that he jealously guarded his own rights of patronage.

The 1853 constitution provided that the government should support the Church and that both president and vice president must be Roman Catholics; as first president of the Confederation governed under this Constitution, Urquiza entered into negotiations with the Papacy to reestablish religious relations but had no success; during this confederation period Bishop Mariano Medrano (q. v.) had died and the government of Buenos Aires (separated at that time from the other Argentine provinces in the confederation) had appointed auxiliary bishop Mariano Escalada Bustillos y Zevallos in his place; when Escalada attempted to impose his ecclesiastical authority over Corrientes, Entre Ríos, and Santa Fe (all part of the Confederation), Urquiza appealed to the Pope for the creation of a new littoral diocese, separate from that of Buenos Aires but the papacy remained adamant against making any changes as long as the Confederation remained firm in its insistence on

its constitutional rights to national patronage; Congress itself
created the new diocese; new hopes for regularizing Church-
State relations came with the reunion between the confederation and Buenos Aires; but, although the more liberal Confederation provinces attempted to modify their ideas to conform
with the more orthodox ones of Buenos Aires, stalemate again
resulted when neither Bishop Escalada nor the papal nuncio
would recognize Argentina's rights to patronage; one problem
of long standing, however, was solved: technically (as in the
colonial period) all Argentine dioceses still came under the
supervision and authority of the Archbishop of Charcas (Sucre,
Bolivia), but in 1865, with both Church and State support, Buenos Aires was elevated to a metropolitan see, with Mariano
Escalada its first archbishop.

      The next clash came thirty years later when the Church
attempted to deny the sacraments to Catholic parents who sent
their children to Protestant or public schools in which Catholic instruction was no longer permitted; this was serious in
that doctrine as well as patronage was involved; both sides refused to change their legal positions; passions became violent
and an apostolic delegate was expelled from Argentina; in
1892, with a more conciliatory secretary of state in the Vatican and an Argentine government willing to settle for less than
a concordat, a tacit acceptance developed of the practice whereby the national senate would submit three nominees ("la terna")
to the president who would then choose one to be sent to the
pope for his acceptance or rejection; acceptance was usual but
a crisis was threatened by papal rejection of a candidate for
archbishop in 1923; it was solved when both sides reaffirmed
their legal rights but President Alvear submitted a new candidate, who was accepted; during this period of relative peace
(that lasted until 1943 and was resumed in 1956), religion
ceased to be a political issue and diplomatic relations were
maintained with the Argentine accredited envoy to the Vatican
elevated to rank of ambassador in 1927; a subsecretary of
Worship in Ministry of Foreign Affairs and Cult handles ecclesiastical matters that relate to government; parochial
churches and church charitable institutions depend on fees and
contributions for their support but government makes an annual appropriation for expenses of the hierarchy, cathedral chapters, seminaries, and Indian missions; the Church is unre-
stricted in its acceptance of entailments and bequests and its
properties in real estate and other possessions are very valuable, only cathedrals having been nationalized; from 1888-1943
the church exercised no control over public education; in 1943,
President Pedro Pablo Ramírez reintroduced religious instruction into all federally supported public schools (repealed in late
1955); from 1943 to 1954 the Peronists sought effective alliance with the church and the latter gave its support to them,
largely because Perón seemed to give priority to traditional
Catholic values; the 1959 constitution did not change legal relationship between Church and State although it seems to favor
the Church more than Constitution of 1853; many Catholics,

both lay and clerical, were troubled by this close relationship
and relieved when Perón broke it in 1954 (see Roman Catholicism); after Perón's fall, the constitutional position of Argentine Church returned to the pre-1943 status occupying a somewhat middle ground between a full-fledged State Church and one
completely separated from the State.
    See John J. Kennedy, Catholicism, Nationalism, and
Democracy in Argentina (Notre Dame, Indiana, 1958); J. Lloyd
Mecham, Church and State in Latin America, rev. edition
(Chapel Hill, N.C., 1966).

CINTA PUNZO. Red ribbon or sash decreed by Juan Manuel de
    Rosas to be worn as sign of federalist loyalty.

CIRCULO MILITAR (Military Club). Social club in Buenos Aires to
    which most officers belonged; acquired increasing public sig-
    nificance as the military (q.v.) became active in national poli-
    tics.

CISNEROS, BALTASAR HIDALGO DE, Admiral (1755-1829). Last
    Spanish viceroy of Río de la Plata, 1809-1810.
        Born in Cartagena, father a naval officer, entered naval
    career in 1770; in battle of Trafalgar against British (1805) he
    was badly wounded and his ship destroyed; joined in Spanish
    resistance against Napoleonic invasion, May 1808; became pres-
    ident of junta and captain-general in Cartagena; received news
    there February 23, 1809, that he had been appointed viceroy of
    the Río de la Plata, to succeed Liniers who held an interim
    appointment and about whom the Central Junta had received
    complaints from the junta of Montevideo; long before he reached
    the viceroyalty, Cisneros had become aware, through contra-
    dictory evidence and instructions, that his task would be diffi-
    cult in a viceroyalty splitting all its seams and that he would
    have to use his own judgment for the most part; fearing that it
    would be dangerous to go to Buenos Aires directly, he went
    first to Montevideo, arriving at the end of June, 1809, and
    then, largely due to Liniers' actions, assumed his position in
    Buenos Aires early in August in a city that was quiet, but
    cold; keenly aware of the political, economic, and social rifts
    developing there and aware of the problems faced--the legiti-
    macy of his appointment challenged; his lack of military
    strength in comparison to the proud creole military groups that
    had recently defeated the British; his need for greater revenue
    opposed by Spanish merchants, and the increasing friction be-
    tween Spaniards and Creoles and between Montevideo and Bue-
    nos Aires (rivals for political and commercial supremacy)--he
    strove for a realistic, moderate path and proved himself to be
    an able administrator; he authorized the suppression of the
    patriotic revolt in La Paz (1809); granted amnesty to those who
    had been involved in the Buenos Aires rebellion of January 1;
    confirmed actions of Montevideo junta, but then dissolved it;
    established compulsory primary education; called special junta
    of residents to advise him on best policy with regard to legal-

izing trade with British and decided on a fairly liberal policy,
antagonizing the Spanish monopoly merchants and stretching his
own instructions, but winning support of Creoles and British,
as well as supplementing his revenues at a time when expenses,
especially for repairing damages during the invasions, were
very heavy; as dissident political activities became more overt
(from French party as well as creole independents), he established a court of political vigilance; in April 1810 word came
that Sevilla had fallen to the French and early in May this was
confirmed, as well as news of the establishment of the Regency
and Napoleon's complete control of the peninsula; Cisneros permitted this news to be made public, but made no confirmation;
when patriots demanded that cabildo abierto (open meeting of
City Council) be called to decide on action to be taken in this
crisis of political legitimacy, he called the famous cabildo
abierto of May 22, 1810; a compromise was reached May 24
for authority to be vested in a junta, composed of leaders of
various groups, with Cisneros as president; creole leaders,
with military force and public opinion to back them, refused
to accept Cisneros' appointment and on May 25, when the formal vote went against him, he resigned; the first patriotic
junta, with Cornelio Saavedra as president, was established.
　　　Cisneros retired to live quietly in the viceregal residence until changes in government in Spain should return him
to office; instead, the junta, alarmed by loyalist conspiracies
developing in the interior and learning that Cisneros' home
had become a center for such conspiracies, as well as rumored ones to make Montevideo the capital of a restored viceroyalty, sent Cisneros back to Spain; after holding various important naval positions there, he went home to Cartagena
where he remained as captain general until his death.

CITY OF THE CAESARS. Legend of the City of the Caesars pro-
vided for three hundred years both motive (greed combining
with humanitarian interests) and pretext for extension of
Spain's southern frontier through Patagonia to the Strait of
Magellan; its early promise of silver is tied in with the very
names of the republic and its great river system (República
Argentina and Río de la Plata). Name comes from Captain
Francisco César, leader of expedition sent out by Sebastian
Cabot from Sancti Spiritus to explore area to west where silver
had been rumored; no follow-up made after his return but it
came to be believed in America that his expedition had entered a rich, populous province, with gold, silver, many cattle, sheep from whose wool fine cloth was woven, and governed by a powerful lord; rumor strengthened through three
centuries by new "evidence" of city's existence offered by Indians; changed somewhat in later years as Caesar Indians were
said to be, in fact, impoverished white men held by hostile
Indians and needing rescue (doubtless based on stories of shipwrecked white sailors in the Strait of Magellan or Dutch or
English parties wintering near Port Julián) but these white
men quickly became metamorphosed into inhabitants of the

same great and wealthy mystical city firmly established in both
Chilean and Argentine folklore.

After central pampas had been explored and settled, by
Spaniards in the sixteenth century, interest in the Caesars
shifted southward, with major expeditions sent into eastern
Patagonia by Hernandarias (1604) from Buenos Aires and into
the western area, from Tucumán, by Gerónimo Luis de Cabrera (grandson of founder of Córdoba, of same name) (1620-
1621), with disappointing results; Argentine interest died down
temporarily, to be taken up by Jesuit missionaries in southern
Chile; Father Mascardi crossed the Andes and established a
mission on Lake Nahuel Huapi from which to continue the
search for the elusive City of the Caesars, carrying out extensive explorations of Patagonia before he was killed by hostile Indians in 1673; during eighteenth century, despite exhaustive
exploration of the area, Spanish Crown became interested for
first time as adventurers presented purported new evidence and
received permission to go in search of fabulous city; interest,
revived among Jesuit missionaries in southern Chile, was
taken over (after their expulsion in 1767) by Franciscans who
sent Fray Francisco Menéndez on at least eight expeditions,
the last four in the Nahuel Huapi area (1791-94) under orders
from the viceroy of Peru, without significant discoveries; the
matter was dropped.

Results of the legend: important in opening and settlement
of Córdoba and Cuyo area; led to colonial explorations of Patagonia that facilitated late eighteenth and nineteenth century settlement; played role in boundary disputes between Argentina and
Chile; toward end of nineteenth century, its history forms important commentary on the tempo and spirit of life along the colonial
frontier, as well as on human nature in general.

Legend survived into twentieth century; archeological
discovery of 1923 was interpreted to be the ruins of the City
of the Caesars. See Enrique de Gandía, La ciudad encantada
de los Césares (Buenos Aires, 1933); Robert H. Shields, "The
Enchanted City of the Caesars, El Dorado of Southern South
America," in Greater America (Berkeley, California, 1945).

CIUDADELA. Takes its name from armed camp established by San
Martín in 1814 to defend Tucumán; site of defeat November 4,
1831 of Lamadrid by Quiroga; resulted, along with capture of
General Paz about the same time at El Tío, in collapse of
unitarist resistance, for several years, to federalist control
under Rosas.

CIVIL WARS. Term usually refers to period of almost constant internal fighting 1820-1852, also known as age of caudillos;
sometimes applied to later fighting between Buenos Aires
province and Confederation at Cepeda and Pavón before final
reunion and national reorganization under President Bartolomé
Mitre in 1862; provinces were split within themselves and
fought against each other; provincial alliances and leagues
against Buenos Aires governments were formed; caudillos

fought their rivals.
Issues underlying apparent personal power struggles
were real--political, economic, and social; provincial federalists, representing a popular stream of Argentine democratic
ideals, supported a constitutional confederation of semiautono-
mous provinces, promotion and protection of provincial economies, and continuation of traditional creole way of life; unitarists insisted on strong, unified government, like those of Europe or U.S., centered around Buenos Aires; attempted to
"civilize" Argentina by imposing European patterns on culture
and society; and insisted on free trade policy which permitted
Buenos Aires to dominate economic life of entire nation to its
own profit; struggle complicated by personal and other elements as well as by fact that porteño federalists, including
Juan Manuel de Rosas who dominated nation during most of
this period, believed that Argentina was not yet ready for a
definitive constitution and preferred a pragmatic working arrangement for the time being.

COAL see MINES, MINING

COALICION DEL NORTE (Northern Coalition or League). League of
five northern provinces in important attempt to overthrow
Rosas; on April 7, 1840, Marco Avellaneda, newly elected governor of Tucumán, issued decree that, since the national government was a disgrace in its continued postponement of national constitutional organization, Juan Manuel Rosas was no
longer to be recognized as governor of Buenos Aires and the
authority granted him by the provinces to conduct foreign affairs withdrawn; about five months later, September 21, 1840,
a congress was held in Tucumán in which the provinces of
Salta, Catamarca, La Rioja, and Jujuy (all of which had taken
individual action against Rosas) joined with Tucumán to form a
league or coalition, under Avellaneda's leadership, to overthrow Rosas' government for political, as well as economic
reasons--strong resentment against Buenos Aires' continued
stranglehold on commerce and refusal to consider economic interests of interior provinces; coalition sent support to the unitarist general Juan Lavalle, then commanding an allied anti-
Rosas army in the littoral provinces; Lavalle's army was disastrously defeated at Quebracho Herrado in Córdoba, November
28, 1840, by General Manuel Oribe, commanding Rosas'
forces; after moving west in various unsuccessful attempts to
improve its position, Lavalle's army was destroyed at Famaillá, September 19, 1841, by Oribe who immediately executed
the captured leaders including José Cubas, former governor;
Avellaneda's severed head publicly displayed in Tucumán; coalition threat ended.

COCHRANE, LORD THOMAS ALEXANDER (1775-1860). Naval commander in war for independence.
Born in Scotland; entered British navy in 1793; had
brilliant career based on his courage, patriotism, and talents;

also served as member of Parliament; after becoming involved in a series of troubles (largely due to his own difficult personality), he accepted San Martín's invitation to come to Chile to serve as commander of the naval squadron being prepared to assist in the liberation of Peru; arrived in Valparaíso November 8, 1818; immediately named vice admiral; in 1819 he blockaded Peruvian ports and captured island of San Lorenzo in bay of Callao; returning to Valparaíso, he seized the Argentine ships of Hipólito Bouchard on his way home from a round-the-world trip (see Argentina, La), setting off a long and complicated lawsuit; when San Martín's expedition to liberate Peru sailed out of Valparaíso, August 20, 1820, Lord Cochrane was in command of the naval unit--eight fighting ships and sixteen transports; after making real and important contributions to the Spanish American cause of independence, Lord Cochrane quarrelled with San Martín--largely because the latter lacked funds to pay the crews--and, late in 1821, Lord Cochrane took some of the ships and returned to Chile, and thence to Europe; served briefly in Brazilian navy and elsewhere; then returned to Great Britain and reentered the navy; making admiral in 1854; had already, in 1831, inherited his father's title becoming 10th Earl of Dundonald.

CODOVILLA, VICTORIO (1894-   ).   Militant Communist leader in period between World Wars I and II.
    Born in Italy, naturalized Argentine citizen; one of founders and leaders of Argentina Communist party, orthodox Marxist organization both ideologically and politically linked with Moscow; author of numerous propaganda pamphlets and books.
    Codovilla's small but vigorous Communist party lost much of its effectiveness when Perón seized the leadership of the revolutionary movement in 1943.

COLEGIO DE LA UNION DEL SUR.   Short-lived secondary school, more modern than the Colegio de San Carlos that it replaced; founded in 1817 by Supreme Director Juan Martín de Pueyrredón, it opened the following year with Dr. Domingo Victoria Achega (q. v.) as first rector; French, English, and Italian were used, along with Spanish; its new orientation was typified by liberal teachings of its philosophy professor, Juan Crisóstomo Lafinur (q. v.); in 1823 Bernardino Rivadavia transformed this colegio into the Colegio de Ciencias Morales.

COLEGIO DE MONSERRAT.   Academy attached to the University of Córdoba that was one of the most important colonial educational centers; established in 1687 with funds and property left by Duarte de Quirós, Monserrat operated almost independently as scholarly center, although actually under royal patronage, as well as direction of Jesuit provincial; drew students from Chile and the Perus, as well as Río de la Plata.

COLEGIO DE SAN CARLOS (Buenos Aires).   Prestigious preparatory school during viceregal period; royal officials as well as creole residents deeply concerned by lack of educational facilities in Buenos Aires in middle of eighteenth century; situation worse after expulsion of Jesuits 1767; royal academy (colegio) of San Carlos established 1773 to fill need; by 1783 its students were able to enter University of Córdoba, like those of Monserrat, without further preparation; San Carlos the training ground for future leaders: Cornelio de Saavedra, Mariano and Manuel Moreno, Manuel Belgrano, Bernardino Rivadavia, Vicente López, and others; declined during early decades of nineteenth-century political activity and unrest; occupied by soldiers during British invasions; many of its younger students left school early to participate in national events.

COLEGIO DEL URUGUAY. This institution was founded in Concepción del Uruguay, Entre Ríos, on July 28, 1849, by Governor Justo J. de Urquiza as the capstone of the provincial system of education; it began to function in 1851, with Dr. Manuel María Erausquín as rector; in 1854, with the province of Entre Ríos federalized and Urquiza president of the new federal republic, the Colegio del Uruguay was placed under direction of French scholar, Alberto Larroque; during the next ten years-- known as its "golden age"--the colegio became a center for advanced studies, offering programs in literature, exact sciences, business, and law, and attracting students from all the provinces, as well as from Paraguay, Uruguay, and Chile (son of U.S. naval commander Thomas J. Page also attended); distinguished intellectuals--many of them French like Larroque and Alexis Peyret--as well as educational administrators like the English George Clark--made it into the most stimulating Argentine educational institution of its time; leaders of the next generation were educated there, including Julio A. Roca, Onésimo Leguizamón, Eduardo Wilde, Rodolfo Rivarola, Martín Ruiz Moreno, Honorio and Martiniano Leguizamón, and Victorino de la Plaza; the colegio declined after the national capital had been moved to Buenos Aires; with national support unavailable, it suffered serious financial problems, as well as a loss of prestige, as intellectual and educational emphasis centered on Buenos Aires; the low point came following the assassination in 1870 of Urquiza who had always supported it loyally; finally, however, it was converted into the Colegio Nacional Capitán General Justo José de Urquiza as part of the new national system; in 1942 the original building housing the Colegio was declared a national monument.

     See Beatriz Bosch, El Colegio del Uruguay, Sus orígenes. Su edad de oro (Buenos Aires, 1949).

COLEGIO MILITAR. Argentine equivalent of U.S. West Point; established 1869. Necessity of training military officers recognized by early patriot governments; preliminary temporary schools established in 1810, 1812; officers' training classes taught by San Martín at his headquarters in Buenos Aires, Tucumán, and at Mendoza in preparation of Army of Andes for fight for independence; Ignacio Alvarez Thomas opened military academy in Buenos Aires 1816-1820; others were attempted during the 1820s but efforts ceased during period of civil war; after fall of Rosas (1852), civil government determined to protect itself against future threats from caudillos and their gaucho forces; President Santiago Derqui was attempting to establish military academy in Confederation when his government fell and nation was reunited; President Bartolomé Mitre, himself a general, undertook to modernize and professionalize the army by sending young officers to French military school at Saint Cyr; unsuccessful in this he began plans (1865) for Argentine military school; disrupted by outbreak of war with Paraguay.

In 1869, President Domingo Faustino Sarmiento got congressional approval for similar project; under director Juan F. Czetz Colegio Militar opened in former home of Juan Manuel de Rosas in Palermo in July 1870; both admission and graduation governed by examinations under president's control; academy later moved to building in San Martín, 1892, and then to modern, fully equipped establishment at El Palomar, 1925; later administrations, especially that of José F. Uriburu (1930-1932) continued to support colegio as important part of greatly expanded training and educational program for officers of all branches of the armed services (see Juan F. Czetz; Military).

COLEGIO NACIONAL DE BUENOS AIRES. Important secondary school founded in 1863 as part of President Mitre's educational policy; its first director was Eusebio Agüero; it occupied the historic site of the first Jesuit headquarters (1622), then, in 1767, became the Colegio Máximo de San Ignacio, followed by the Colegio Convictorio y Universidad Máxima de San Carlos (1768), the Real Colegio de San Carlos (1783); in 1810 it served as barracks for the Patricios, in 1813 it was occupied by the colegio seminario and in 1817 this was followed by the Colegio de la Unión del Sur; it was used by the new University of Buenos Aires (1821) and by the College of Moral Sciences (1823); the Jesuits returned to it for a brief period in 1836.

COLOMBRES, BISHOP JOSE EUSEBIO (1778-1859). Ecclesiastic; signer of the declaration of independence; founder of modern sugar cane industry in Tucumán.

Born in Tucumán; received doctorate at Córdoba in 1803; ordained same year; assigned to parish duties in Catamarca; became enthusiastic supporter of May Revolution; elected to Congress of Tucumán; signed declaration of independence (July 9, 1816), resigned shortly after that to return to Catamarca; moved back to Tucumán where he played active role in political and economic life of province; reintroduced the cultivation of sugar cane, planting extensive fields and designing and building ox-driven sugar mills to process the cane; became victim of Quiroga's anger after Ciudadela (1831), his canefields burned, he, himself, imprisoned; later served as minister of government under governors Aráoz and Piedrabuena; strongly supported formation of Coalition of the North; defeat of unitarist forces sent him into exile in Bolivia until after the fall of Rosas; returned to hold ecclesiastical positions in Salta; died in Tucumán.

COLONIA DEL SACRAMENTO. Oldest city in Uruguay. Portuguese colony founded by Brazilians, 1680, on north bank of the Río de la Plata almost directly across from Buenos Aires, in what is today Uruguay; represented Portuguese (or Brazilian) thrust southward as well as their desire to participate in the active contraband trade in the estuary; Spain's answer to this intrusion into what it considered to be Spanish territory was threefold; establishment of Montevideo as a civil and military base (1726-1729) to the east of Colonia to pre-empt trade and hold land; military campaigns to capture Colonia (it changed hands several times in late 18th century); and the establishment of the viceroyalty of the Río de la Plata, with its capital at Buenos Aires and the latter's port opened to trade; treaty of San Ildefonso (1777) establishing boundary left Colonia in Spanish hands; it prospered during viceregal period; in Río de la Plata area first saladero (meat salting drying plant) established there; in wars of independence Artigas used it frequently in his attempts to separate the Littoral provinces from Buenos Aires political control; even after Uruguay had won its independence (1828) the civil wars of the Rosas period became entangled with those of rival Uruguayan leaders and Colonia was involved in Argentine affairs; finally, however, in the last half of the nineteenth century acquired its modern role of important, but secondary, Uruguayan port and city, proud of its unchallenged position as oldest town in Uruguay.

COLONIAL PERIOD (preferably known in Argentina as the Spanish Period--"Período Hispánico"). The three centuries (1516-1816) from discovery by Juan Díaz de Solís to the Declaration of Independence from Spain by the Congress of Tucumán, July 9, 1816, during which the area now included in the Argentine Republic was ruled by the crown of Spain, an integral part of the Spanish empire.

COLONIZATION. In the sense that this means planned, organized settlement with some government backing and control and usually, although not always, for government or national purposes, colonization may be said to have existed in the Plata before the arrival of the Spaniards with the planned settlements of the Northwest Indians within Inca empire; the sixteenth-century Spanish settlement, by conquistadores, as well as later creole ones, and the reducciones (Indian towns), especially the Jesuit Missions (q.v.); in the nineteenth century, colonization took on a special and greater significance as the republic's determination to populate the empty pampas and to develop its economy fully met with the desire of large numbers of people in oppressed nationalist, religious, or economic groups in other

countries, seeking greater opportunities elsewhere; capital
available from foreign as well as Argentine entrepreneurs to
supplement government aid in land and supplies; foreign capital could be borrowed quite readily from nations like England
and France, interested in seeing Argentina produce raw materials and food supplies for their own industrialized societies.

First Argentine statesman to promote colonization was
Bernardo Rivadavia, doing so as a member of the triumvirate
in 1812, as diplomat in Europe (1818), minister of Buenos
Aires provincial government, and president in the 1820s; Immigration Commission created in 1824 with Juan Pedro Aguirre
as president; interest in colonization among British commercial and financial houses rose to feverish pitch during this period (1820s) but, although Rivadavia's government attempted to
cooperate, the confusion of the political situation in Buenos
Aires and the province, the conflict of economic interests and
the sheer enormity of the problems involved in colonization for
which inexperience had few answers, resulted in failure, frustrations, misery on the part of the immigrant colonists and
disastrous financial losses; J. T. B. Beaumont, one frustrated
British would-be colonizing promoter, returned home to publish (London, 1827) a bitter attack against Argentina's government and colonizing possibilities; already the seasoned Anglo-
Argentine merchants, Wm. Parrish Robertson and G. P. Robertson had lost their fortune of 60,000 pounds in colonizing
ventures; creole attempts fared better in southern Buenos
Aires province; under Rosas' governments, colonization was
not pushed, partly because it ran counter to the economic interests of cattle and landed interests, but even more because
civil wars and unstable conditions within provinces made it impractical; Rosas early abolished Immigration Commission
(1830).

Great change came after departure of Rosas in 1852.
Anti-Rosas leaders, like Juan Bautista Alberdi, Domingo Faustino Sarmiento, and Florencio Varela so firmly believed that
lack of population caused most of the nation's problems that
constitution of 1853 included a clause making government responsible for bringing in new settlers (preferably European
farmers and artisans); in that same year Aaron Castellanos
established Esperanza with Swiss and French colonists in Santa
Fe, the first permanent colony; Urquiza lent his official support and gave some of his own best lands for colonization;
Corrientes contracted for a big French colonization but it fell
through; other provinces on their own or cooperating with the
federal government began offering incentives and advertising
throughout Europe; laws and government agencies were directed
toward fostering colonization; Nicolás Avellaneda wrote first important work on public land policy and, as minister in Alsina's
provincial Buenos Aires government, national minister in Sarmiento's, and during his own term as president (1874-1880),
worked to secure the land laws that would have important favorable effects on colonization and immigration; new government
immigration agencies set up to coordinate and support all such

activities. The flood began in 1870s and continued for half a century creating (along with immigration of individuals on their own) the so-called Alluvial Era (q. v.; see also Immigration) that changed the political life, economy, and society of Argentina; the Welsh nationalists moved into Chubut; Germans from Brazil settled Guadalupe, near Santa Fe; very successful vineyard, wine-producing colony established in Córdoba on former Jesuit properties; Russians and Germans established settlements in Entre Ríos, moving out to other colonies from General Alvear; Baron Hirsch and his Jewish Colonization Association established Jewish colonies in Santa Fe (Moisés Ville) and Entre Ríos; late in the nineteenth and early in the twentieth century important colonies were founded in Santiago del Estero by Near Eastern Syrians and Lebanese; by 1890 Buenos Aires province had 150 colonies, Entre Ríos 117, Córdoba 70, and Santa Fe (1900) had 400, not to mention smaller numbers elsewhere; toward the end of the nineteenth century the frontier areas began to fill: Misiones (created a territory in 1881) received large colonies of Poles, followed by Japaneses, Germans and Brazilians; northern Chaco has cotton planters, many of them from eastern Europe. (See Santillán II:342-365 for compilation of descriptive listings of these nineteenth and twentieth century agricultural colonies [Suggested Readings, App. III].)

With a national population of 23-1/2 million in 1970 and almost a century of successful agricultural exploitation, as well as a developing, diversified industry, Argentina in the mid-twentieth century has become more concerned with integrating its disparate elements into a people and a nation than attracting further colonization. (See listings for individual provinces, especially Misiones and Garuhapé for Japanese post-World War II colony in Misiones.)

COLORADO RIVER. Among several rivers and arroyos (streams running through valleys) of this name, the Colorado River in the south seems most important; formed by confluence of Río Grande and Río Barrancas, it marks part of the boundary between La Pampa and Mendoza and entire boundary between La Pampa and Río Negro provinces; crosses southern Buenos Aires province to flow into Atlantic in two parts, Colorado and Colorado Chico with delta between, at Bahía Anegada, south of Bahía Blanca; the Colorado frequently played role in Indian wars of nineteenth century.

COLORADOS   see   AZULES Y COLORADOS

COMAHUE. Northern region of Patagonia that offers rich opportunities for economic development; area extends from Buenos Aires province (Patagones) across Río Negro and Neuquén, including approximately 310,000 square kilometers (or nearly 116,000 square miles) traditionally used for sheep, the area, with its Limay, Neuquén, and Río Negro rivers, has potential for hydroelectric development similar to that of Tennessee Valley in the United States, along with mineral deposits of great value, including coal, iron (largest of country in the Sierra Grande), salt, kaolin, petroleum, and other minerals; the Chocón-Cerros Colorados enterprise was established in Neuquén to develop the power project.

COMECHINGONES INDIANS. Indians in hills of Córdoba, who already possessed a semi-agricultural economy and were easily absorbed as a labor force for raising sheep and mules, weaving woolen textiles, and cultivating crops (see Indians).

COMERCIO DEL PLATA. Anti-Rosas publication begun by Florencio Varela, owner and editor; first issue appeared October 1, 1845, in Montevideo printed personally by members of the editorial staff on their own press, dedicated to political opposition but also to the business of all the towns in the entire Río de la Plata estuary, along with all the countries trading with them; introduced new cultural features such as the Biblioteca del Comercio del Plata: literary and historical essays published on the last page, suitable for detaching and binding, beginning in the first issue with an English article by Washington Irving about Vasco Núñez de Balboa, discoverer of the Pacific Ocean; other cultural features included critical reviews and essays on the arts; almanacs, official documents, shipping news and notices, were also published; following Varela's tragic death, publication continued, with brief breaks and a move to Buenos Aires, until May 31, 1860, under successive editorships of Valentín Alsina, Miguel Cané and Nicolás Avellaneda (co-editors), and Juan María Gutiérrez.

COMISION ARGENTINA. Association formed by Argentine exiles in Montevideo, December 20, 1838, to unite and coordinate all forces against Rosas; leaders included Martín Rodríguez (president), Florencio Varela (secretary), Tomás de Iriarte, Félix de Olazábal, Valentín Alsina, Manuel Gallardo, Julián Segundo de Agüero, and Pedro José de Agrelo; joined with Fructuoso Rivera (who was seeking presidency of Uruguay) and diplomatic agents of France (then blockading port of Buenos Aires) to accomplish their various purposes by defeating their common enemy--Juan Manuel de Rosas; sought contacts and encouraged opposition throughout Argentina, in addition to giving support to Lavalle's army; Comisión Argentina played important role in final defeat of Rosas; its alliance with blockading powers, while professing sovereignty, still a subject of controversy among historians.

COMMERCE see CONTRABAND and TRADE

COMMUNISTS, COMMUNIST PARTY see POLITICAL PARTIES and VICTORIO CODOVILLA

COMODORO RIVADAVIA. Important petroleum and natural gas center in southeastern Chubut province; city, port, and capital of department in rapidly growing area of Patagonia.

Founded in 1900 or 1901 by Francisco Petrobelli as an
outlet for the produce of Colonia Sarmiento near Lake Colué
Huapi; attracted national attention in 1907 when a crew of well-
diggers struck oil instead of water; when the deposits proved
to be extensive, the government asserted its subsoil rights,
eventually established YPF (Yacimientos Petrolíferos Fiscales,
q. v.) to control and administer these first important Argentine
oil discoveries and placed the area under military government;
it was especially important during the 1940s as one of the nation's defense bases; after World War II, it developed rapidly
as a port and industrial center, based on its continuing large
petroleum and natural gas production; in 1949 a 1000-mile pipeline was completed from Comodoro Rivadavia to Buenos Aires
and in the 1950s this military area was joined with the national territory of Chubut to form the modern province of Chubut
(see Petroleum; Chubut).

COMPADRITO (derived from compadre, word denoting relationship
between father and godfather of child; also used colloquially to
refer to close friend or companion).
Compadrito refers quite specifically in Argentina to a
social type that emerged in the late nineteenth century from the
rapidly urbanizing, changing society in Buenos Aires; usually
a bully (and the word is still used to mean this), coming from
any of the various social classes, he combined the characteristics of a neighborhood dandy and sport; a gaucho's pride,
courage, gambling spirit, arrogant womanizing habits, and
readiness with knife or pistol to meet any challenge or enter
any adventure reappeared in city garb of tight black suit and
highly polished footwear; the compadrito flourished for a
couple of decades in suburbs of Buenos Aires and then disappeared into legend; has received literary and social recognition second only to that of gaucho.

COMUNEROS OF CORRIENTES. Twice in the eighteenth century
citizens of Corrientes took legal step of forming a commune
and, as comuneros, took over their own government in revolt
against government action considered to be unwarranted and
unjust; in March 1732, Governor Bruno Mauricio de Zavala ordered his lieutenant governor in Corrientes to recruit 200 men
to reinforce the Guaraní soldiers based in a position to threaten
the Asunción comuneros; refusing to fight the latter, the Correntinos revolted at Itatí and seized the lieutenant governor
Jerónimo Fernández; cabildo supported the comuneros, took
over the government and appointed a military commander of
their forces; in attempt to settle uprising peacefully, Governor
Zavala enlisted aid of Fray Juan de Arreguí, bishop of Buenos
Aires, to act for him; offering complete amnesty, bishop persuaded the comuneros to end their revolt in November only to
be visited with swift and harsh reprisals as soon as they had
surrendered and the bishop gone; leaders were sentenced to
years of hard labor in frontier posts and forts, under hardships never forgotten by Correntinos.

In 1764 Correntinos confronted powerful Governor Pedro
de Ceballos; already exhausted by military service against hostile Indians and on exploring and other military expeditions
that kept the men away from home and subjected to hardships,
they responded to Ceballos' demand for 200 men to accompany
a new expedition designed to open a road from Corrientes to
Tucumán; when this was diverted through hazardous difficult
terrain and Ceballos ordered that they place themselves at the
disposal of the Jesuits in support of his siege of Colonia (then
in Brazilian hands), the militiamen, who could not take any
more, simply deserted; cabildo had repeatedly complained formally to the government about the harsh and unjust treatment
from the lieutenant governor to which their men were being
subjected without redress, and now, when Ceballos demanded
an additional 200 men to replace the deserters, a cabildo
abierto (open town meeting) was called; it formally decided that
lieutenant governor should be suspended; notification was sent
to Ceballos of this action by the citizens of Corrientes; Ceballos did not even reply; later he ordered some citizens imprisoned and others executed and to impose his absolute authority appointed a partisan of the Jesuits, Manuel de Rivera and
Miranda, as lieutenant governor; on October 29, 1764, people
of Corrientes reacted violently against Ceballos; seized and
imprisoned the new lieutenant governor, put cabildo in charge
until a commune government could be established under José
González de Alderete (November 1764); this lasted until April
1766 when Irish-born Lieutenant Colonel Peter Murphy, sent
by Ceballos, appeared at Corrientes and demanded its surrender; 360 armed comuneros went out to meet him and peacefully laid down their arms; a long trial followed, presided over
by Juan Manuel de Labardén; thirteen Correntino leaders were
sentenced to death and more than fifty condemned to exile; arrival of Bucareli to take Ceballos' place as governor, resulted
in annulment of these sentences on grounds that evidence had
been falsified.
    These actions by comuneros of Corrientes point up very
clearly the irreconcilable differences between the creole comuneros defending what they believed to be their inherited rights,
by means that were sanctioned in law and custom, and Bourbon officials who viewed these same actions as rebellious
against authority that must be crushed ruthlessly lest they set
a precedent that would destroy authority, law, and order;
many Argentine historians also point to these comunero con-
frontations as clear evidence of revolutionary spirit of independence in the Plata area, even before creation of the viceroyalty.

CONADE (Consejo Nacional del Desarrollo). Established in 1966 by
    Onganía's government as national planning council for econom-
    ic development to supplement or balance Onganía's liberal pol-
    icy of private enterprise; both were designed to boost Argen-
    tina's still lagging economy; CONADE periodically publishes
    official five-year development plants of Argentine government.
    (See National Development Council.)

CONCEPCION DEL BERMEJO. Today an official historical site in
province of Chaco on south bank of Bermejo river approximately ninety miles from its emptying into the Paraguay, commemorating the founding of a city of this name there on April
14, 1585, by Alonso de Vera y Aragón with creoles, including
Hernandarias, from Asunción; played important role for nearly
half a century as meeting place of two currents of Spanish
settlement, from Northwest (Peruvian) and from Asunción; constantly raided by Indians, abandoned in 1633; became historical monument in 1943 after identification of correct site by
Ingeniero Nicolás Alurralde.
          A modern town in central part of province bears same
name.

CONCEPCION DEL URUGUAY. City and port of province of Entre
Ríos, on Uruguay River; approximately 200 miles north of
Buenos Aires; capital of department of same name; population
about 37,000 (1970).
          Established in 1783 by Tomás de Rocamora as part of
policy of Viceroy Juan José de Vértiz y Salcedo to civilize
and pacify nomadic Indians in empty lands by establishing
settlements, rather than by sending military expeditions; also
needed to handle increasing trade on Uruguay river; lay on
main route between Buenos Aires and Montevideo--overland
from capital to Santa Fe, across Paraná river and then across
province of Entre Ríos to Concepción del Uruguay, across the
Uruguay river to Banda Oriental and Montevideo--until about
1814 naval vessels brought much shorter, more direct, all-
water route across Río de la Plata estuary into common use;
served as capital of province 1813-1821, 1860-1883; elevated
to rank of city in 1826 at Urquiza's request; Colegio Nacional
there established by Urquiza.
          In the nineteenth century Concepción was stronghold of
federalism, with three leaders (all generals) having their base
there at one time or another: Francisco Ramírez, José Justo
Urquiza, and, finally Ricardo López Jordán; a plaque attached
to the monument in the center of Plaza General Francisco Ramírez sums up city's role as follows: "it was in this plaza
that on May 1, 1851 General Urquiza issued his pronunciami-
ento against the tyranny [of Rosas] that culminated in February
1852 with the victory at Caseros; here on November 21, 1852,
the people gathered to repel the invading army of General
Madariaga [sent from Buenos Aires to weaken Urquiza] and to
defend the meeting of the General Constituent Congress sanctioned by Argentine constitution of May 1, 1853, and promulgated by Urquiza in San José de Flores on May 25, 1853.
This constitution gives living expression (encarna) to the federal republican creed of General Ramírez."

CONCOLORCORVO (probably pseudonym for don Calixto Bustamante
Carlos Inca). Author of important late eighteenth century
travel work. Mystery shrouds identity of this author, as well
as circumstances under which it was published in Lima; still

controversial subject among literary and historical scholars, not likely to be settled as documentary evidence has not been found; from name taken, "Con color corvo" (translated "with the color of a raven") many have assumed the author to have been dark--a mestizo or cholo; others have suggested that both Concolorcorvo and Calixto Bustamante Carlos Inca are pseudonyms of the royal official Alonso Carrío de la Vandera, himself, whose identity and official mission have been documented; another theory suggests that although Alonso Carrío was the actual author, he used the name (and nickname) of a real person in Curzo whom he wished to flatter with a little publicity; no controversy, however, affects the contents of the six-volume work (of which the first volume deals entirely with Argentina); and its detailed observations are invaluable; its complete translated title is in itself a capsule description of the historical developments taking place in that area at that time: <u>Lazarillo (or Guide) of Blind Travellers from Buenos Aires to Lima with careful observations made along the itineraries with some useful information for new merchants trading in mules; and other stories taken from the journal of Don Alonso Carrío de la Vandera on the lengthy journey which he was commissioned to undertake by the court to organize the mail service, arranging for couriers and selecting sites for posthouses starting at Montevideo.</u> By don Calixto Bustamante Carlos Inca, alias Concolorcorvo, native of Cuzco, who accompanied the aforementioned commissioner on this journey and wrote his notes, with official permission, in Gijón, in the Rovada printing office; year of 1773 (see Arrias for description of new mule trade mentioned).

CONCORDANCIA. Loose alliance of established interests, conservatives and liberals, with a sprinkling of socialists that controlled political processes of Argentina between 1931 and 1943; tried to find central position attractive to conservatives of all movements; elected Agustín P. Justo as president in 1931 and Roberto M. Ortiz in 1937.

CONFEDERACION ARGENTINA. Name applied to nation under Rosas, actually a working arrangement among the various more or less autonomous provinces (in practice Rosas made his power felt); name officially chosen by provinces under the constitution of 1853 and Urquiza's presidency; when reunion was effected with Buenos Aires province through constitutional revisions of 1860 and Mitre's election as president in 1862, name of the nation became La República Argentina.

CONFEDERACION GENERAL DEL TRABAJO (CGT). First labor unions formed in Argentina in late nineteenth century (1891; CGT organized in 1930 as first national trade or industrial union; by mid-twentieth century it included approximately 135 widely assorted unions, with a total membership of at least 2-1/2 millions; feelings mixed among CGT leaders in early 1940s about supporting Juan Domingo Perón in his attempt to

build new political power base with labor as one of major supports; some leaders feared loss of labor's freedom of action
but most eventually came to welcome new political and economic opportunities offered; throughout Perón's presidency (1946-
1955) powerfully backed his policies and actions; after fall of
Perón's government, CGT weakened by government interventions and internal dissensions; reorganized in 1963--with Peronist, moderate, and Communist factions--but with Peronists
in control by 1964; pushed hard for legislation to aid workers,
such as price controls against spiraling inflation, fixed minimum wage levels, elimination of unemployment, and worker
participation in plant management; meanwhile CGT (as well as
individual member unions) had become national economic power
in own right; possessed of enormous wealth from membership
dues, investments, etc., it engaged in big business enterprises
with large capital resources available for use in banking, hospital, hotel and other holiday service, and consumer goods of
all kinds; constituted important factor in continuing inflation; after collapse of its strike operations in 1967, CGT split between
those wanting course of greater moderation and those determined on more violent action; return of Perón to the presidency
in late 1973 failed to improve role of CGT.

CONGRESS OF TUCUMAN (more properly called the Constituent Congress of Tucumán) 1816-1820. Declared the independence of
Argentina; supported Supreme Director in governing nation during four years of grave threat from royalist reconquest and internal anarchy; and wrote first formal national constitution
(1819); nevertheless its true importance has been subject of
controversy among Argentine historians on grounds of its representation and its achievements.
    Called by Director Álvarez Thomas to meet in Tucumán
to avoid fear of Buenos Aires domination, first session was
held March 24, 1816; eventually, all provinces of modern Argentina were represented, except for those of Corrientes,
Entre Ríos, and Santa Fe; Córdoba hesitated but finally sent
delegates; also represented were four provinces of modern
Bolivia (still part of the United Provinces); most of the thirty-
odd members were university educated lawyers or ecclesiastics; Congress faced grave situations, both externally and internally: Spaniards dominated Alto Perú and Chile; army of
the North in anarchy; Artigas (of Uruguay) dominated one-fourth
of nation (riparian and adjoining provinces); army of observation against them, itself in revolt led by Díaz Vélez; Spain was
organizing new expeditions to reconquer its American colonies,
backed by a Europe favoring dynastic legitimacy and opposed to
republican and revolutionary movements; even Great Britain,
bound by ties to Spain, could offer little help; with courage,
frankness and goodwill, and a sense of national vision, Congress of Tucumán debated and then enacted those measures
needed: a new supreme director, Juan Martín de Pueyrredón,
hero of the British invasions, was appointed to take up his duties in Buenos Aires immediately; a formal declaration of in-

dependence was finally made on July 9, 1816 (see Declaration of Independence); congress then settled down to its normal legislative and constitutional functions; because of increased royalist pressure along nearby Salta-Jujuy frontier, congress moved to Buenos Aires holding its last session in Tucumán January 17, 1817, and its first in Buenos Aires three months later April 19; after considering various forms of government, approved December 3, 1817, provisional regulations with which to govern until constitution could be written; in February 1818 made emblem of sun official part of national blue and white flag; held special session May 17, 1819, to honor San Martín publicly for victory at Maipú, final defeat of Spanish forces in Chile; proclaimed first constitution for republic May 25, 1819; accepted Pueyrredón's resignation as supreme director June 9, and appointed José Rondeau to succeed him; violent protests from riparian provinces (never represented in congress) led to battle of Cepeda, February 1, 1820, in which the allied forces under Francisco Ramírez defeated the national army commanded by Rondeau; Congress dissolved shortly thereafter--February 11; Argentina given over to anarchy and civil wars.

Modern Argentine historians tend to evaluate the Congress of Tucumán more highly than some of their earlier colleagues who considered the members to be mediocre because few of them played leading national roles during the following turbulent decades and because the congress never passed any major laws, and its centralist, aristocratic constitution of 1819 served as pretext, if not actually cause, of civil wars that followed; nevertheless, these men combined sound intellectual gifts with political wisdom and represented their provinces so well that Joaquín V. González has called it "the most national, most Argentine, and most representative Congress" that the nation has ever had; insofar as essential patriot legislation was concerned much of this had already been passed by earlier revolutionary governments, especially the Assembly of the year XIII, and this congress passed only such laws as were necessary and practicable in the given situation; unique contribution of the Congress of Tucumán lies in fact that it did save the revolution and had the glory of completing independence; in 1941-1943 the one-storied, patioed colonial house in which this historic congress held its first sessions and declared Argentine independence was restored by the national government.

See Leoncio Gianello, Historia del Congreso de Tucumán (Academia Nacional de Historia, Buenos Aires, 1966).

CONI, EMILIO ANGEL (1886-1943). Agronomist and economist, writer.

After graduating in 1905 as engineer in agronomy at the university of La Plata, became active as university professor, research scientist, and writer on subjects related to agropecuarian interests; specialist on rural administration and farm accounting; taught first at La Plata, then at Buenos Aires; because of his knowledge and contributions in these fields, he received many national and international appointments as adminis-

trator or consultant; served on permanent economic committee
of League of Nations, director of Banco Hipotecario Nacional
(national mortgage bank); elected to National Academy of History, 1927; among his best known historical works are La independencia económica argentina ante la historia (1918); La
verdad sobre la enfiteusis de Rivadavia (1927); Historia de las
vaquerías del Río de La Plata; and El estado contra la nación;
died in 1943, victim of a criminal assault.

"CONINTES PLAN." March 1960 elections were occasion for President Frondizi's announcing of this plan, which established
heavy penalties against internal subversion resulting from intensive terrorist activities that preceded the elections (see
Arturo Frondizi).

CONQUEST OF THE DESERT. Term commonly applied to the final
campaigns (1875-1879) ending Indian menace in Patagonia.
From the time of Mitre's presidency (1860s), popular pressure
mounted steadily, demanding that Patagonia be made secure
from Indian raids on towns, estancias, and cattle herds, and
safe for occupation by farmers and livestock raisers; problem
worsened during past century due to replacement of small
nomadic bands of primitive pampas Indians by larger groups of
Araucanians, more civilized--with well-organized economy
based on horses and the cattle which they captured and sold in
Chile, fiercely hostile, well-armed, and skilled in cavalry
warfare--even the gauchos little match for them; as the desired European immigration finally began and Indian raids intensified, all-out efforts were made by Adolfo Alsina, minister
of war in Avellaneda's government, and by General Julio A.
Roca to end the problem; Indian leader Manuel Namuncurú,
learning of plans, struck hard to ward this off, leading warriors of confederation of tribes, armed with rifles and revolv-
ers, in massive invasion during summer of 1875-76; defeated,
with serious losses, in five battles, withdrew behind line fixed
by Alsina; after Alsina's death, Roca continued operations according to his own plans, which called for massive strikes
against the Indians that would destroy their strength; by 1878
Indians had taken so much punishment that only about 2000
warriors remained; against these, Roca, in July 1878 sent
slashing raid of 6000 well-armed cavalrymen deep into the
semi-arid plains, killing more than 1250 Indians, capturing
more than 3000, including four chiefs, and accepting the surrender of 3300 others; Indian power broken forever; second
campaign, accompanied by photographers and news reporters,
searched the area in every direction, April-June 1879, and declared operation complete; only Namuncurú escaped--to Neu-
quén--where he surrendered himself in 1883; line of Río Negro
secured, and remaining Indians in south so scattered that they
would present little or no menace to settlement and exploitation
of "desert"--a misnomer for the semi-arid plains of Río Negro, Chubut, and Santa Cruz where farming was good in some
of the river valleys and grazing superb for sheep.

With these campaigns, Julio A. Roca not only became a military hero but also inherited Alsina's popular and political following that led to his election to the presidency, 1880, and again in 1888.

CONQUISTADORS. Name applied to first Spaniards who came to America to conquer an empire for their king, converts to their Roman Catholic Church (hence merit for themselves in hereafter), and fame and fortune for themselves; first, and most accurately, used to refer to conquerors of great Indian civilizations and kingdoms of Mexico and the Andean areas; in Argentina, only those Spaniards who came through the Perus to settle in northwestern Argentina in last half of sixteenth century, as well as some of those coming into Cuyo from Chile, belonged to this category; term has also been applied, however, to Spaniards who came into the Río de la Plata area before 1580, under the first four adelantados (see Ricardo de Lafuente Machain in Suggested Readings, Appendix III).

Attempting to use institutional patterns already set up in older colonies for establishing Spanish rule in new areas, including founding of cities, distribution of Indians in encomienda, land grants, and provisions for exploitation of natural resources, preferably mineral, these conquistadors quickly found themselves in totally new situation, remote from government rule, lacking aid from Indians, in area where few of their skills from Spain could be applied (except in pastoral pursuits), and where lack of minerals tempted settlers to try their luck elsewhere; the problem swiftly became that of survival both personally and as a society; most failed to solve it and died in misery; those few who found inner spiritual resources and physical stamina to create successful new life style in this alien land by making it their own in a true conquest, bred a race entirely different from their ancestors or their Spanish American neighbors (see Creoles); these first Spanish Argentines, many of them nobly born, also established the bloodlines for a united Argentine people; modern genealogies (see Lafuente Machaín) of prominent colonial families point out clearly the extent of intermarriage, beginning with the first three generations, between the families of such conquistadors as Jerónimo Luis de Cabrera (founder of Córdoba), Juan de Garay (Santa Fe and Buenos Aires), Diego de Villaroel (San Miguel de Tucumán), and Juan Ramírez de Velasco (La Rioja); at the same time integrated blood of diverse Indian groups from Salta to Buenos Aires into same society.

CONSERVATIVES, CONSERVATIVE PARTY see POLITICAL PARTIES

CONSORCIOS REGIONALES DE EXPERIMENTACION AGRICOLA (Regional Consortiums of Agricultural Experimentation). Grew up in 1960 through private initiative taken by educated leaders in field; formed groups of farmers and ranchers for practical action by employing agronomists and veterinary scientists to aid them in solution of specific problems and to furnish guidance in technical farm management.

CONSTITUENT CONGRESS OF SANTA FE, 1853   see   CONSTITUTION of 1853

CONSTITUTION. Argentine constitutional development into a nation was a painful process that took several decades; two factors remained constant: 1) the Argentine continuing demand for legal institutional national organization, growing out of its Spanish heritage of respect for law and tradition of civil government; and 2) the popular insistence that this constitution must be based on, and continually modified to satisfy current, as well as traditional, political, social and economic realities of the Argentine nation; difficulty of reconciling differences of various provinces and arriving at consensus of national direction kept nation in turmoil and without constitution 1810-1861.

On February 1811, the Great Junta (i. e. , original patriot junta of Buenos Aires expanded to include provincial delegates) approved a regulation or decree to serve as the legal basis of government; largely drawn up by Deán Gregorio Funes, it extended the May Revolution to all the provinces by providing for establishment of provincial juntas under that of Buenos Aires; Funes (from Córdoba) and other such provincial leaders as Juan Ignacio Gorriti (Jujuy) imposed the federalist stamp of the interior on this first attempt at national legal organization and postponed the calling of a national constituent congress; nine and a half months later, November 22, 1811, the new Triumvirate government replaced this decree with a brief statute of seven articles, issued in the name of Ferdinand VII, and abolished the provisional juntas; serious efforts to draw up a constitution had to wait until after the declaration of independence in 1816; meanwhile, however, much of the groundwork was laid by the legislative assemblies of 1812 and 1813 in destroying the colonial framework and establishing new legal institutional organization (see especially Assembly of the Year XIII).

CONSTITUTION OF 1819. After taking care of its immediate priorities, the appointment of Juan Martín de Pueyrredón as Supreme Director and the declaration of independence (both in 1816), the Congress of Tucumán addressed itself seriously to the form of government to be established; after prolonged debate, during which the congress moved to Buenos Aires, a committee was appointed on August 11, 1817, to draw up and present a projected constitution; members included José Mariano Serrano, Diego Estanislao Zavaleta; Teodoro Sánchez de Bustamante, Juan José Paso, and Antonio Sáenz; after making a careful study of previous Argentine legislation, and of such foreign constitutions as that of the U.S., France (especially its constitution of 1791), and the liberal Spanish constitution of 1812, the committee presented a constitutional draft in 1819; although it was generally believed that most of the members of Congress leaned toward a monarchical form of government, the constitution presented did not mention monarchy (q. v.) but would have served for either a republican or monarchical form of government; it called for a strong executive, or Supreme Director (elected by both houses of congress) with his own council of state; the legislature consisted of a lower house of provincial representatives and a senate composed of representatives chosen by the senate from nominations submitted by the provinces; important corporate bodies, such as the church, army, and universities were also to be represented; after some discussion, this constitution was approved by Congress and established as the governing law of the land May 25, 1819, meeting an enthusiastic reception from the people of Buenos Aires; in contrast, it was immediately rejected by the people of the provinces, who saw in its aristocratic bias, its strongly centralized power, and its concern with Buenos Aires' priorities, rather than those of all the provinces, a denial of all the democratic, federalist principles which they held dear; as a symbol of all the problems of the country that it had ignored, it served as the pretext, or spark, to tear the country apart in the anarchy of 1819-1820 (see Anarchy) and civil wars that followed.

CONSTITUTION OF 1826. In 1824, the local government of Buenos Aires requested each provincial government to express its views on what should be the bases for a new constitution and what form the new national government should take; 6 provinces--Entre Ríos, Santa Fe, Córdoba, Santiago del Estero, San Juan, and Mendoza--wanted a federation of autonomous provinces; four--Tucumán, Salta, Jujuy and La Rioja--preferred a unitarist pattern; Buenos Aires and Misiones abstained; the rest--Corrientes, Catamarca, San Luis, Montevideo, Tarija (now in Bolivia) expressed willingness to accept decision of a national constituent congress; provincial representatives (many of them veterans of previous congresses) began to gather in Buenos Aires in 1825; in addition to beginning work on a new constitution, this new congress also (probably illegally) began to function as a national legislative body; it created a national executive power of the United Provinces and immediately elected Bernardino Rivadavia as president; it also federalized the province of Buenos Aires; counting on the fact that most of the provinces had voted either for a unitarist constitution or to accept Congress' decision, Rivadavia pushed hard to get a unitarist constitution drawn up and accepted; this was violently opposed, not only by the interior and littoral federalist provinces, but also by the new federalists of Buenos Aires, for whom Manuel Moreno (q.v.) was a spokesman; they vigorously resented the federalization of Buenos Aires claiming Congress had acted illegally in taking over the provincial government; they also opposed sharing the wealth of their province and the port revenues to organize and maintain a national government; a majority of the delegates, however, accepted Rivadavia's arguments that this was the only way in which the

nation could be united, peace and order established, and the
planned national economic expansion and development could take
place; on December 24, 1826, the constitution (in many respects an updated version of the constitution of 1819) was
adopted by Congress by an overwhelming vote and confidently
sent to the provinces for ratification; with the single exception
of Montevideo, then engaged in the war against Brazil that resulted in its independence, every province rejected it; circumstances had changed; provincial federalism had gained strength
as Buenos Aires had shown its own determination to monopol-
ize, not only political power but especially economic resources;
the lines were drawn that were to keep the country without
complete political organization until 1861; during the intervening years, most of them under domination of Rosas and provincial caudillos, Rosas was adamant against any new attempt
at formal constitutional-making; over and over again he replied
to insistent provincial caudillos, who felt such a legal safeguard to be essential for provincial, as well as national, security, that the country was not ready yet for anything more
than the pragmatic, loose confederation under which they were
all operating (see Rosas); the individual provinces, for their
part, began a grassroots constitutional movement by debating
and then drawing up their own provincial constitutions.

CONSTITUTION OF 1853. The constitution of 1853, which is still
basically the one used, was the result of compromise to unite
the country then divided between the liberal porteño minority,
responsible for the constitutions of 1819 and 1826 (see above)
and the fundamentally more democratic federalist groups, of
which Juan Manuel de Rosas had been the most powerful representative.
     During Rosas' period of government and while provin-
cial federalists and others were writing provincial constitutions, young intellectuals (usually in exile) known as the Generation of 1837 (q. v.), had analyzed and attempted to interpret the Argentine problems; the views of these men were also
held by those who finally overthrew Rosas and determined to
obtain national unity; they were determined not to "depart
from practical grounds nor to lose themselves in abstractions"
(Esteban Echeverría in Dogma socialista, (qq. v.); in other
words, they wanted to find their historical roots, to sub-
merge themselves in Argentinism; many of them came to be
federalists and learned to know and respect the people and to
interpret their desires; this Generation of 1837, influenced by
French and German thought, believed that political solutions
must be tied in with the satisfying of social needs and solving
of economic problems; they had also learned that the Argentine solution was not to be found in the transplanting of laws
and institutions from other lands; this group, adopting the
name of Asociación de Mayo (q. v.), can be considered a precursor of the new social and political point of view, more
realistic and, as such, with greater possibilities of success;
with Juan Bautista Alberdi as their representative, especially

in political thought, they sought a combination of federalism
and unitarism to solve the problems; they also tried to counteract the colonial Spanish heritage by stressing the need for
Anglo-Saxon and French influences; many of the provincial
leaders, both federalist and liberal, had come during this same
period to share some of the ideas of the intellectuals in exile;
they had also become seasoned in Argentine politics, with its
underlying federalist and democratic trends; and the provinces
had matured politically and in their relationships with each other; many of the provincial caudillos supported Justo José Urquiza, who held the same ideas about constitutional needs, in
his effort to overthrow Rosas.

Urquiza's defeat of Rosas at Caseros February 3, 1852,
opened the door for a political program "based on the principles of order, fraternity, and a forgetting of the past, " in
Urquiza's words; most of the provincial governors signed the
Agreement of San Nicolás de Arroyos, April 6, 1852, by which
Urquiza was appointed Supreme Director and a constituent congress was called to meet in Santa Fe to determine the form
the new national organization should take; the agreement of San
Nicolás broke down with the formation of three groups: 1) the
Federal Urquiza group that favored national union; 2) the Alsinistas, followers of Valentín Alsina (q. v.), who insisted on an
independent Buenos Aires province; and 3) a middle group, led
by Bartolomé Mitre, that favored national organization, but only under the recognized leadership of Buenos Aires; although
the differences were not insurmountable, Buenos Aires broke
with the Confederation as a result of revolution of September
11, 1852, and drew up its own constitution (April 1854) to govern itself independently.

On schedule in November 1852, representatives from the
other provinces opened the Constituent Congress in Santa Fe
and immediately set to work to form the new constitution; with
Urquiza remaining aloof, the various member, including some
who had had experience in earlier constitutional debates, national or provincial, others who were young but enthusiastic,
and a solid core of mature intellectuals and seasoned political
figures such as José B. Gorostiaga, Juan María Gutiérrez,
Martín Zapata, Salustiano Zavalía, and Santiago Derqui; at hand
for their inspiration and guidance were copies of the U. S. constitution, as well as the Federalist papers written by James
Madison, John Jay, and Alexander Hamilton in its support; the
recently published book by Juan Bautista Alberdi, Bases y
puntos de partida para la organización política de la República
Argentina; as well as earlier constitutional deliberations and
constitutions, 1813-1826, and the Federal Pact of 1831; most of
the actual writing was done by José Benjamín Gorostiaga and
Juan María Gutiérrez; general discussion on the constitution
presented began on April 20 and on May 1 it was approved;
promulgated by Provisional Director Urquiza on May 25, it was
sworn into effect on Independence Day (July 9) for the entire
country.

This 1853 constitution provided for a federal republic,

more or less modeled on that of the United States, consisting
of executive, legislative, and judicial branches; executive powers were vested in a president, and a vice president; the legislative powers were vested in a bicameral Congress composed
of a Senate and Chamber of Deputies; a federal court system
headed by the Supreme Court made up the judicial branch; in
spirit this constitution attempted to reconcile both traditional
Argentine political currents; while strongly federalist in form,
it showed clear unitarist (or liberal) influences; the refusal of
Buenos Aires to participate had convinced most of the delegates
that a strong executive was necessary to hold the provinces together; therefore the president was given strong powers, including that of intervention (q. v.) in the provinces; powers were
divided between those granted to the federal government and
those remaining with the provinces; not only was the constitution intended to suit Argentine political traditions as well as
the social and economic realities of the current national scene
but its makers--strongly influenced by Alberdi and others of
the Generation of 1837--intended it to serve as stimulus and
guide for the nation's future progress; among its more important provisions were the reservation of civil, penal, and mining legislation to the national government; all residents were
made equal before the law and slavery (no longer used since
laws of 1813) was legally abolished; foreigners were given
equal rights with those of nationals; immigration was not to be
restricted as long as it was useful to the nation--in fact, it
was to be encouraged; free navigation of the rivers was declared; provincial constitutions had to receive congressional approval; Roman Catholic church recognized as official (or, more
specifically, promised government support) and both president
and vice president must be Catholic, but freedom of worship
was also established; presidential term to be six years, with
no immediate re-election; opponents of this constitution included
conservative Catholics who resented its liberalism and religious
freedom, a few provincial caudillos who preferred to retain
their local power, and Buenos Aires which remained outside the
Confederation; on March 5, 1854, Urquiza was inaugurated in
Paraná as the first president under the new constitution.
    Buenos Aires' refusal to rejoin the other provinces had
little to do with political differences but was based on economic motives--the Santa Fe Congress had wanted Buenos Aires as
the country's national capital and that city and province were
still unwilling to share their port revenues with the nation;
personal rivalry, growing out of the passions of the Rosas era,
between Urquiza and Mitre (qq. v.) and their supporters for
leadership of the new republic also played a part; increasing
tensions and misunderstandings brought civil war again, with
Urquiza's forces victorious at Cepeda, 1859; Buenos Aires
agreed to enter the Confederation if certain amendments were
made to the constitution; these included a provision that Buenos
Aires be temporarily the capital until a new one might be
chosen and that province was promised the port revenues for a
five-year period while the customs were being nationalized; on

October 21, 1860, the amended constitution was accepted but
new tensions became evident immediately; the credentials of
the Buenos Aires representatives to congress were rejected as
their number, determined by the provincial constitution, was
greater than that allowed by the national one, and revolutionary
movement in San Juan, costing the lives of José Antonio Virasoro and Governor Antonino Aberastain opened old wounds; Buenos Aires declared all agreements null and void and prepared
for war; Mitre's defeat of the confederation army at Pavón
September 1, 1861, brought the final union of all Argentine
provinces, with Mitre inaugurated as president of the republic
in 1862; national organization under the constitution was completed with federalization of Buenos Aires as capital in 1880
(see Federalization of City of Buenos Aires).
        See Leo Stanton Rowe, The Federal System of the Ar-
gentine Republic (Washington, D. C. 1921); Pavón y la crisis
de la Confederación, Equipos de Investigación Histórica (Buenos Aires, 1966); and Silvio Frondizi, Argentina la autodeterminación de su pueblo (Buenos Aires, 1973).

CONSTITUTION OF 1949.   "Constitución Justicialista." In 1948 Juan
    Domingo Perón's government felt it necessary to revise the
    constitution of 1853 in order to incorporate into it Argentina's
    new political and social realities and goals; a constituent con-
    vention, largely Peronist with a minority of Unión Cívica Radi-
    cal delegates, convened January 24, 1949 with Domingo A.
    Mercante as president; by March it had drawn up a constitu-
    tion that represented, according to its preamble, the "irrevoc-
    able decision to constitute a nation that was socially just, eco-
    nomically free, and politically sovereign"; this constitution
    went into force in March 1949; although it retained much of the
    form and wording of the constitution of 1853, it effectively
    strengthened the power of the federal government over the
    provinces, and over private enterprise and many phases of na-
    tional life; within the government (barely federal now, in name
    only) the executive branch--i.e., the president--became domi-
    nant over the legislative and judicial branches of government;
    among the changes were: the abolition of the electoral college,
    with president, vice president, and senators to be elected by
    direct popular vote; presidents now might succeed themselves;
    congressional terms of office were changed, that of senators
    increased in length, that of deputies decreased; Congress lost
    much of its autonomy and veto power over executive actions;
    the courts also were forced to surrender traditional powers,
    such as jurisdiction over controversies between provinces and
    national government, and judicial review of executive and leg-
    islative decisions; the president could appoint or remove
    judges by executive decree; increasing government control was
    extended over the national economy: it declared all minerals
    and almost all national sources of energy the property of the
    state, government ownership of all public services (somewhat
    vaguely); 1853 inviolability of private property was altered to
    read that private property has a social function and that it was

incumbent on the State to control distribution and utilization of
land; government intervention in economic affairs also authorized control of inter-provincial traffic and all foreign trade;
Perón's social program was written into the constitution with
new recognition of rights spelled out for workers, the family,
the aged, and the right of the public to culture and education;
a clause on education provided that all faculties of universities should establish compulsory courses for political formation (or indoctrination) of their individual students; the constitution retained old rights, duties, and freedoms of the individual; foreigners, however, were now required to have five
years of residence before applying for citizenship (reflecting
the fact that immigration was no longer regarded as the national priority that it had been a century earlier); the president
could establish a state of siege more readily, almost whenever
he felt that a disturbance or threat of public order required it.

    This new constitution, called by Robert J. Alexander
(in Perón Era, p. 83) a monument that Perón left to himself,
lasted only from 1949 until the fall of Perón in 1955; it was
cancelled by Pedro Aramburu by decree in May 1956 and the
1853 constitution reinstated; in July 1957 elections were held
for a constituent congress to draw up a new constitution; instead, it restored the old constitution of 1853, with a few
changes; it was generally hoped that its spirit of compromise
and conciliation could continue to be brought to bear as successfully on Argentine problems of the 1960s and 1970s as
those of a century earlier.

    For Argentine constitutional history, see Emilio Ravig-
nani, Historia constitucional de la República Argentina (3 v.
Buenos Aires 1926-1927); Ricardo Levene, Manual de historia
del derecho argentino (Buenos Aires, 1952; 2nd ed. 1957).

CONSULADO.   Commercial tribunal established by royal decree in
Buenos Aires, 1794.   Dating back to medieval Spain, consulado
was traditionally a kind of municipal merchants guild composed
of merchants engaged in commerce, particularly international
trade; interested in every phase of mercantile activity, its primary function was administration of justice according to maritime and merchant law; as royal authority united Spain and established its government over it, the officers of the consulado
came to be appointed by crown; in this form it was transferred to the American colonies, with its functions still primarily judicial, as in Mexico and Lima; in 1784 Charles III established a different kind of consulado in Sevilla, more in line
with new economic ideas and aims of his own government; ten
years later, when trade in Buenos Aires had become important
and the pressure of merchants there for a consulado too strong
to be ignored, royal government established (1794) this new
kind of consulado, modeled on that of Sevilla.

    Buenos Aires consulado had two functions: the tradi-
tional judicial one and that of serving as board to promote
economic development; in latter capacity it met twice a month
and was responsible for diversifying economy, increasing pro-

duction, encouraging settlement and exploitation of new lands,
establishing schools for technical and commercial education,
supervising public works and improvements, and, of course,
stimulating, regulating, and protecting commerce; officers consisted of a prior, two consuls, nine counsellors, a syndic, a
secretary (actually the executive director), an accountant, and
a treasurer, all originally appointed by the crown, but then
self-perpetuating, subject to royal approval; all merchants (except very small ones) were included in membership; although
no law provided against creoles, first prior was a peninsular
Spaniard and creole (native-born) merchants at first found it
difficult to hold their own against Spanish merchants (with close
ties to the merchant community in Spain) who had come over
in large numbers to new viceregal capital of Buenos Aires
that offered greater economic opportunities than could be found
in the older colonial establishments; first secretary, however,
was Manuel Belgrano (q.v.), born in Buenos Aires, educated
in Spain as an economist, and eager to put newest ideas into
practice for benefit of his native land; as secretary, he was
required to make annual report, including proposals for furthering economy; his reports, imaginatively conceived against Argentine realities constituted detailed blueprints for economic development of Argentina for rest of viceregal period, as well
as forming the basis for national development throughout the
nineteenth century; disillusioned, as were most creoles, by
firmness with which peninsular (Spanish) merchants protected
their own interests and those of the monopoly merchants in
Spain while ignoring, or considering secondary, interests of the
very area in which their own fortunes were being made, Belgrano continued to work toward his desired goals of promoting
agriculture, along with urban industries based on native products, free trade, including export of Río de la Plata products
to the best markets, and schools to train those engaged in
commerce, agriculture, and those needed in specialized industries, such as tanning chemists, etc., eventually, through creole pressure and as a result of royal law in the 1790s requiring that hacendados (landlords whose economic interests con-
flicted directly with those of monopoly merchants) be given
equal representation in the consulado, as well as the fact that
many Spanish merchants had become linked by family ties and
other interests to Buenos Aires, the consulado became liberalized to such an extent that it opted for free trade in 1798; as
commerce brought wealth and power to Buenos Aires, the city
acquired an almost autonomous life of its own, and the commercial leaders, i.e., officers of the consulado, came to be
considered community leaders and formed, with members of
cabildo, a ruling elite that supplied many of the fathers of the
new Argentine nation in 1810.

CONTRABAND (i.e., smuggling). Term comes from Spanish contra-
    bando, first used in sixteenth century to refer to illicit trade
    with Spanish-American colonies; trading in contraband goods
    constituted a major way of life in Buenos Aires and surrounding

area for most of colonial period; believed by most residents
there, and by many Argentine historians since, to have been
essential for survival.   Although Río de la Plata had been
viewed since discovery as natural gateway to interior of South
America--especially to wealthy Inca empire, since time of Sebastian Cabot who had been diverted upriver (1527-1530) by rumors of it--by time desired port on estuary was finally established with refounding of Buenos Aires in 1580, that door had
been firmly closed and locked by royal mercantilistic regulation of all trade; determined to safeguard Andean gold and
silver from increasingly numerous and more dangerous foreign
attempts to capture treasure vessels, and following current
European government practices of controlling commerce, Spain
in 1561 had formally established galleon system by which all
merchandise for South American colonies was handled by monopoly of Sevilla merchants in Spain, shipped annually under
galleon convoy to Portobelo in Panama, transported across isth-
mus for reshipment to Callao; from there overland transport
carried goods in limited quantities and selection, subject to
long delays--for sale at exorbitant prices at markets of Upper
Peru, Tucumán, and finally Buenos Aires; for first four decades Buenos Aires was granted intermittent trade concessions;
iron, sugar, manioc from Brazil were exchanged for hides,
skins, textiles of cotton and wool--along with some illegal sil-
ver--in the port or at markets in the interior to which they
were forwarded; in 1622, protests from Lima and Sevilla resulted in complete closing of port to trade (except for one
small ship a year) by the establishment of interior customs
barrier at Córdoba.
     Situation was unrealistic: porteños cut off from all
trade except from Peru and at same time left without access
to silver and gold with which to pay inflated prices of legal
goods; alternatives were inviting: neighboring Brazil, with
more than 120 sugar mills in operation and large black slave
population needing Argentine food, constantly pressed for trade,
offering sugar, slaves, European manufactures in return for
hides and dried beef; separation of Buenos Aires government
from Asunción, in 1617, made little difference in this trade;
in 1599 Dutch merchant ship discovered new route into estuary,
coasting along Argentine shore, instead of taking customary
route along Uruguayan coast; opened brisk trade with Argentine
merchants, accepting hides and tallow (available practically free
in abundant supply to latter) in payment for better and cheaper
European merchandise than could be obtained legally; other
European traders followed Dutch, eager to trade; colonists at
first divided between those loyal to crown and determined to
obey laws until they could be changed and those who felt that
survival was at stake and, since crown refused relief, Argentines had moral right to protect themselves; for most part, latter prevailed throughout seventeenth century, as evidenced by
moving of Córdoba customs farther north to Salta and Jujuy in
1676 (showing that Buenos Aires still dominated interior trade),
and by continued protests from Lima and Sevilla merchants;

Portuguese establishment of Colônia do Sacramento on the Uruguayan coast facilitated flow of slaves and merchandise across
the estuary; with the granting of the asiento (permission to
bring in certain number of slaves) to British in Treaty of Utrecht, 1713, latter's headquarters and base near El Retiro became distribution center for imported goods paid for in hides,
dried beef, and, increasingly in eighteenth century, with silver
smuggled from Bolivian mines; government and church officials
reflected division in popular attitude; throughout colonial period
there were no colonial officials, beginning with Governor Hernandarias, who valiantly attempted to stop illegal trading, but
there were others who decided that public interests (and sometimes their own private ones) demanded that contraband be allowed to continue; strategic coastal land grants went to merchants in the trade, other concessions were given, and restricting commercial laws were not enforced--latter impossible
anyway, considering geography of area, force of tradition, and
determined spirit of people; actually trade wide open with important political effects--one lieutenant governor of Buenos
Aires declared that contraband trade purchased every cabildo
office, and merchant class provided public leadership; disruption of galleon fleets by international wars of eighteenth century brought substitution of registered ships (1720s); new system very important for Buenos Aires as it broke Peruvian
monopoly, although not that of Sevilla, whose merchants used
these ships; increasing economic growth of area offered new
opportunities to contraband.
    Changes came in 1776 when government, alarmed by
size of silver flow from which no royal revenue was collected,
recognized realities and attached Upper Peru to new viceroyalty of Río de la Plata, with capital at Buenos Aires; first viceroy Pedro de Ceballos issued famous edict of free trade
(1776), permitting Buenos Aires to engage legally in trade;
followed by royal decree ending Sevilla monopoly (1778), and
opening of trade between Buenos Aires and other Spanish American and specified Spanish ports (1778), establishment of customhouse at Buenos Aires (1779) and consulado (1794); dramatic change in shipping: 1772-1776, five ships arrived in
port to trade (legally); twenty years later, 1792-1796, 395 arrived; some contraband continued, however, in protest of control exercised by resident Spanish merchants over both economic and political life (new phenomenon for Buenos Aires) in
port and interior cities; creoles demanded free trade, Spaniards monopoly or at least control; debate and power struggle
constant during last two decades of viceroyalty; by 1809, however, differences between creoles and Spaniards (many of them
now with creole families and interests of their own) were les-
sening; common interest in lucrative, burgeoning trade was
developing; last viceroy, Baltásar Hidalgo de Cisneros recognized this by calling an open meeting of prominent civic and
merchant leaders to advise him about granting additional trade
privileges to English merchants who had arrived in port; contraband gradually reduced to smuggling to avoid payment of

duties; brought under normal control by early patriot governments and reorganization of coastal patrol and customs services by Bernardino de Rivadavia in 1820s.

Contributions to historical development: contraband kept Buenos Aires alive and growing until legally permitted to fulfill natural function as port; unified area to become nation by economic ties reinforcing already existing family, cultural, and political bonds; established trade patterns and marketing demands that formed bases and directions for prosperous trade of nineteenth century; provided background for May Revolution and independence and determined economic life of new Argentine nation for more than half a century.

See Ricardo Levene, Investigaciones acerca de la historia económica del virreinato del Plata (2 vol., La Plata, 1927-1928; 2nd edition, 1952); Sergio Villalobos R., Comercio y contrabando en el Río de la Plata 1700-1811 (Buenos Aires, 1965).

CONTUCCI, FELIPE. Merchant and foreign agent. Italian merchant who come to Río de la Plata as a youth; owned trading vessels operating between Buenos Aires and Rio de Janeiro, as well as hacienda; became very active, 1808-1810, in cause of crowning Carlota Joaquina ruler of Río de la Plata (probably independent); generally considered a Portuguese agent, he established and maintained close relationships with the patriot independence group led by Rodríguez Peña as well as with viceroys Santiago de Liniers and Baltazar Hidalgo Cisneros; carried on correspondence with Venezuelan "precursor of independence" Francisco de Miranda; a master of intrigue, a man of rare talents and untiring energy, he failed in his project of placing Carlota Joaquina on an Argentine throne and also left no clear indication as to what his own final purposes or political convictions were.

CONVENTILLOS. Term applied to crowded downtown slums or lower class residential areas that grew up rapidly in 1880s in such cities as Buenos Aires and Rosario; buildings characterized by long corridors and honeycombed with tiny rooms-- hence the name.

COOKE, JUAN ISAAC (1895-1957). Jurist; cabinet member; diplomat. Born in Buenos Aires; graduated in law from university at La Plata; held several positions in provincial government; served as representative to national congress; taught constitutional and comparative law in faculty of law and social sciences, Buenos Aires; near close of World War II, President Juan D. Perón brought Cooke, a Radical, known to be pro-Allied in sympathies, into cabinet as minister of foreign relations and religion (1945-1946); joined President Perón in pre-Chapultepec talks with U.S. delegates, paving way for Argentina to resume its normal relationships in inter-American affairs; Cooke served as ambassador to Brazil 1947-1955; author of many legal studies.

COOPERATIVES. In late nineteenth century, European types of socioeconomic cooperatives--organizations of members banding themselves and their capital together for mutual and individual advantages not otherwise readily obtained--began to appear in Argentina; many of first actually founded by foreigners; came to be considered, especially in colonias, desirable alternative to government support and control; during first decades of twentieth century, cooperatives were formed to fill the needs of almost every phase of popular life, both urban and rural, from consumer purchasing to crop marketing to credit unions; multiplied so greatly in numbers, number of members, capital available, and scope of operations that federation, training in operation, and legal regulation and protection became necessary; in 1922, association of rural cooperatives (later known as Association of Argentine Cooperatives) formed in Rosario; in 1925, the faculty of economic sciences of Buenos Aires offered free courses about cooperatives and published many articles about them; in 1926, law regulating cooperatives was passed; at this time, there were 250 cooperatives (90 rural, 160 urban) with a total membership of about 90,000; by 1942, numbers had increased to 656 cooperative societies, covering interests of consumers, dairymen, agriculture (most numerous), credit, securities, and production of electric power; during administration of Juan Domingo Perón (1946-1955) president promoted growth of cooperatives, considered to be in best interests of workers and masses; wanted to cover entire nation's economy with cooperatives and hoped to stimulate production by replacing labor of wage earners by that of associated workmen; by 1960 societies numbered more than 3000, with more than 10% of the total national population in their membership; value of their financial operations made up nearly 15% of national total; agricultural production of all kinds by far most important cooperative sector; followed by that of dairy industry; especially useful--sometimes even essential--to success in development of agricultural colonies. (See Robert C. Eidt, in Suggested Readings, Appendix III for role of cooperatives in modern settlement of Misiones.)
        See Lázaro B. Grattaloa, Cooperativismo (Santa Fe, 1949); Adolfo Cavallone Brebbia, Cooperativismo (Buenos Aires, 1947); Juan L. Tenembaum, Agricultural Cooperatives in Argentina (Pan American Union, Washington, D.C., 1941).

COPELLO, SANTIAGO LUIS (1880-1967). Primate Cardinal Archbishop of Buenos Aires.
        Born in San Isidro, Buenos Aires province; studied at Gregorian seminary in Rome; doctorate in philosophy, 1899; ordained 1902, doctorate in theology, 1903; after holding other ecclesiastical positions in Buenos Aires became archbishop in 1929 and primate cardinal in 1935; became leader of so-called "right wing" of church that favored Juan D. Perón (1940s), prevailing over more liberal group led by Monsignor Miguel de Andrea.

COPPER see MINES, MINING

CORDOBA (City and Province). Location: Central province of Argentine Republic; bounded on north by Santiago del Estero and Catamarca; on east by Santa Fe; on south by Buenos Aires and La Pampa; and on west by San Luis, La Rioja, and Catamarca. Area: 65,200 square miles. Population of province (1970): 2,060,065. Capital: city of Córdoba--population (1960) 586,015. Density per square mile: 37.

Climate and geography. Climate pleasant and temperate; rainfall adequate; Córdoba lies at northwest corner of pampas, with its capital situated where plains meet foothills of Córdoba Sierras; mountains to west of city very popular for national tourist, vacation, and health resorts; pampas equally good for grazing or for agriculture; quarries of stone and marble important resources, valuable for construction and export; several mountain streams flow across province, Tercero and Saladillo uniting to form Carcarañú crossing Santa Fe into the Paraná; great depression fills northeastern area where several salt lakes are found, largest being Laguna Mar Chiquita.

Córdoba's historical development has always been governed by its location between the coastal and interior areas, its immediate and continued economic prosperity, and its strong and deep religious orientation; province developed around city.

Early in June 1573, the new governor of Tucumán, Jerónimo Luis de Cabrera (q.v.), set out from his capital, Santiago del Estero, with about 100 Spaniards, 40 carretas full of supplies, driving herds of cattle, as well as other farm animals, more than 240 miles south in search of good site for new town that would provide access to Spain for Peru as well as Tucumán by way of Atlantic; on July 6, 1573, he formally laid foundations of city that he named Córdoba de la Nueva Andalucía, on bank of Primero River; some Indian problems developed but Cabrera handled them well; explored eastward to the Paraná, met Garay coming from Asunción (see Juan de Garay for description of meeting), and was present at founding of Santa Fe; back in Córdoba he was replaced by new governor Abreu; largely due to their own efforts, settlers of Córdoba survived and area began to prosper; in 1584, the remote inland town had forty vecino-encomenderos with 6000 Indians, and more than twice that number available for good labor supply, easily trained for agriculture, stock-raising, or small industry such as weaving; in 1599 Jesuits officially established themselves there, primarily interested in work among the Indians, developing huge estancias, and in creating one of the finest centers of scholastic learning in colonial Spanish America-- University of Córdoba--in 1622, based on an earlier Jesuit academy established by Bishop Fernando de Trejo y Sanabria; in that same year the royal government established customhouse at Córdoba to serve as barrier to prevent trade from Buenos Aires (usually contraband) from reaching markets of interior provinces or Peru; by end of seventeenth century, Córdoba was wealthiest city in Tucumán government, due to its

superb location on all the commercial trading routes, its fertile lands as well as its remoteness from government pressures;
attracted settlers wanting peace and prosperity; for political
and religious matters, Cordobans looked to crown for guidance,
otherwise ran their own affairs; exported flour and mules; as
numbers of Indians decreased, blacks were brought in to take
their places (Córdoba, Buenos Aires, and Tucumán had largest
black population); Córdoba began to cobble its streets, build
government and ecclesiastical buildings, as well as some private residence, with stone; in 1761 printing press was imported for use at the university; publications, largely religious,
began to appear; after expulsion of Jesuits 1767, other orders--
Franciscans, Dominicans, Mercedarians--long established
there, took over many of their functions.

Creation of viceroyalty in 1776, followed by the opening
of Buenos Aires to more trade, caused some dislocation of
Córdoba's economy, to extent that it had been tied in with interior areas; but the establishment of intendancy of Córdoba in
1783 (splitting the Tucumán government in half) made Córdoba
a capital city for today's provinces of Córdoba, La Rioja, San
Juan, Mendoza, and San Luis; first governor-intendant, el
marqués Rafael de Sobremonte (1783-1797) improved the city,
built governor's mansion, laid out alameda (poplar-bordered
walk), constructed aqueduct to improve city's water supply,
strengthened Indian frontier, and organized and increased militia units; with population of 38,809 in 1785, Córdoba was not
only prosperous, but becoming most attractive (as well as certainly most cultured) city in what is now the Argentine Republic; Sobremonte had become viceroy at time of British invasions of Buenos Aires (1806-1807) and fled back to Córdoba to
organize defense (ineffectually as it turned out); last governor
intendant Juan Gutiérrez de la Concha (1807-1810) had commanded Cordobans at Buenos Aires defense, however; at news
of May Revolution (1810), Governor Gutiérrez immediately
called a meeting of his best qualified advisors May 29; all,
except Deán Gregorio Funes, agreed that authority of the Buenos Aires revolutionary junta should be disavowed, and that
militia should be placed on fighting basis; during next two
months the Cordobans sought to arouse the neighboring areas
to join them in remaining loyal to the crown (as Montevideo
had done) until situation was clarified; meanwhile Buenos Aires
junta prepared to export revolution throughout viceroyalty;
when its army, led by Ortiz de Ocampo approached Córdoba
early in August, the Cordobans, heavily outnumbered, withdrew; Ocampo occupied the city, sent searching parties after
the leaders, now in flight; following orders from the junta, he
executed all of them (including Santiago de Liniers, the hero
of the British invasions and former viceroy, Governor Gutiérrez de la Concha, V. Rodríguez, Alejo Allende, and J. Moreno) except the bishop Orellana; for most of next five years
governors of Córdoba were appointed by Buenos Aires, supported by those Cordobans who also wanted independence;
when Artigas strengthened his power in the Littoral, however,

and threatened Buenos Aires with war unless Cordobans could
be free to select their own government, Governor Ocampo
called a cabildo abierto April 19, 1815, and resigned; hailed
by Cordobans as a victory for provincial autonomy--more interested in breaking Buenos Aires control than in backing
Artigas; after five years of chaos in the province Córdoba
pulled itself together under General Juan Bautista Bustos and,
in early 1820s, entered into rivalry with Buenos Aires to be
organizer of nation that had fallen apart, with both executive
(directorate) and legislature (Congress) gone; differences between Córdoba and Buenos Aires both political and economic
in 1820s and 1830s: Buenos Aires under Rivadavia's influence
and later unitarists wanted strongly centralized constitutional
government with Buenos Aires the center; under Rosas, it
wanted a loose working arrangement among the provinces,
rather than a legal constitutional form; under both Buenos
Aires groups, economic interests of Buenos Aires merchants
and estancieros were primary; whereas Cordobans insisted on
national legal framework with constitution uniting semiautono-
mous provinces, protecting all provincial interests including
economic; Bustos had early congress set up but Buenos Aires
refused to cooperate on grounds that nation was not yet ready;
Bustos opposed Buenos Aires congress of 1824-1827 and the
1826 constitution was returned without even being considered;
after Rivadavia left and President Vicente López called new
congress, followed by Dorrego's election as governor of Buenos
Aires province, Dorrego and Bustos signed agreement to work
together but Dorrego's death and Lavalle's defeat of Bustos at
San Roque April 22, 1829, ended latter's long domination of
Córdoba; followed (1829-1831) by Cordoban General José María
Paz, hero of war of independence and of the war against Brazil, who had become a unitarist or centralist in his political
beliefs; briefly controlled all of interior, forming League of
the Interior (1830); Córdoba invaded by Quiroga and Estanislao
López; Paz out, and the federalist Reinafés (q. v.) came in to
rule Córdoba, backed by López but opposed by Quiroga; several years later, 1834, Quiroga, returning to Buenos Aires from
peace mission in Santiago del Estero was assassinated in Barranca Yaco, Córdoba; Rosas blamed the Reinafés, whose hatred
of Quiroga was no secret; removed governor and put in Manuel
López who coordinated his government with that of Rosas
(1836-1852); some disorder but Córdoba made considerable
progress under López rule; in 1839 Jesuits returned to Córdoba; in 1840 population of the province was given as 101,927,
with nearly 15,000 in capital city; the Coalition of the North
invited Córdoba to join in revolt against Rosas (1840) and Governor López's enemies, backed by Lamadrid's forces, took
over government briefly; after unitarist defeat at Quebracho
Herrado November 28, 1840, Manuel Oribe entered Córdoba
and replaced López in power; reprisals against unitarists so
excessive that López had to end them firmly; eleven years
later, the legislature rejected Urquiza's call to arms to overthrow Rosas, as treason, but after Rosas' fall at Caseros,

López attempted to cooperate with Urquiza but his long hold on Córdoba was over; for another decade and a half Córdoba continued to be torn with conflict, violence, and invasions from montoneras and neighboring caudillos interspersed with national interventions to maintain or restore order; finally in 1868, under provisional Governor Félix de la Peña, settled down to a century of growth, progress, and prosperity with return to its important role as educational and cultural center, and its traditional position as citadel of the Church.

University had already been nationalized in 1854, along with important Colegio de Monserrat; in 1869 President Sarmiento founded the national astronomy observatory there, bringing Dr. Benjamin A. Gould from the United States to direct it--opened October 24, 1871; Sarmiento also established faculty of physical and mathematical sciences at the university and sent Hermann Burmeister to Germany to recruit scientists; began classes May 1873 with seven scientists; Gould opened meteorological office attached to his observatory, but this quickly gained independent status (1885) and was moved to Buenos Aires in 1901, with other weather stations established throughout the republic; to stimulate economic growth, the first national exposition was held in Córdoba, with President Sarmiento to open it; result: thousands of visitors produced an industrial and social revolution; agricultural colonies were established and highways, railroads in the 1870s linked Córdoba to all major commercial centers; dams and water regulation provided; by 1889, 50,000 foreigners made their home in the province; before end of century, adult education classes and agricultural schools (1897) had been opened and agricultural courses were available elsewhere; cattle industry prospered, and Córdoba became major industrial center in twentieth century, as well as third largest city in the nation; religious conservatism and loyalty to Roman Catholic Church remained marked in Córdoba; showed itself in continued wealth of ecclesiastical establishments, in Córdoba clerical as well as popular opposition to secular laws of 1880s, and in its opposition against Perón's attacks on the church in the 1950s; juxtaposition of this rigid conservatism and clerical political attitude with radical ideas of large numbers of laborers of all kinds forming basis of Córdoba's prosperity have created political and social tensions in last few decades that have not only kept Córdoba in turmoil, toppling governments (Lonardi's Catholic-backed movement against Perón in 1955, for example), bringing national intervention often, but also may be early signs of a national revolutionary restructuring of institutions.

CORDOBAZO, EL (May 29, 1969). Term applied to action culminating violent Córdoba revolts of early 1969 that resulted in overthrow of government of Juan Carlos Onganía; on that day workers and students occupied center of city and committed acts of violent destruction; 14 persons killed.

CORN (Maize). Wherever it originated--in southern Mexico and

Central America, the Andean valleys of Ecuador, the Upper
Paraguay-Amazonas region or elsewhere--corn (maize) was
found in use among nearly all the Argentine Indians when the
Spaniards arrived; apparently they first utilized it as medicine,
later for food and beverages; by the 16th century, it was widely used as food--usually toasted--among the sedentary, semi-
civilized tribes of the Tucumán area and Santiago del Estero;
Indians of the Chaco ate corn roasted, boiled or otherwise
cooked, and valued it especially when made into the ritual
drink known as kawi; others made an alcoholic beverage of it
known as kiki by fermenting corn with araucaria fruit; the nomadic Querandí of the pampas added manioc and wild fruits to
this mixture for a drink; the Indians of Cuyo, like the Araucanians of Chile, used corn primarily as a cereal for nourish-
ment preparing it in many ways, using the whole grain, meal,
or flour; throughout the Spanish colonial period corn was used
in Argentina to supplement the meat diet; Tucumán also prospered through raising corn, along with cotton, rice, and wheat,
for export to the mines in Upper Peru (Bolivia).

Corn began to be grown commercially in Argentina in
the late 19th century, its cultivation spreading out from Rosario
into the pure-bred cattle land of Santa Fe, Córdoba, northwestern Buenos Aires, Entre Ríos, and Corrientes provinces that
provided sub-tropical humid climate, pampas soil, and easy
access to markets; flax was grown in same area, along with
some other cereals and cattle; by 1940 corn was rivaling wheat
as one of Argentina's chief exports and had made Argentina
chief Latin American corn exporter; varieties favored were
hard, small-kerneled ones, best for feed for poultry and farm
animals; by 1940 most corn was grown on large estates or
beef-cattle estancias by tenant farmers (many of Italian ancestry); constant efforts were made both privately and by government to improve the seed and cultivation, and to provide new
uses for the grain and other parts of the corn plants; in addition to corn flour and meal, Argentine factories and mills
produce: cornstarch; glucose; corn sugars; corn oil; alcohols
used in making liquors, medicines, paint solvents, vinegars
for local use or export to Great Britain for its distilleries;
the leaves, husks, cobs and stalks provide fibers and cellulose.

See Statistical Abstract of Latin America, published by
the Center for Latin American Studies, University of California,
Los Angeles.

CORREAS, EDMUNDO (1901-   ). Jurisconsult; professor; historian
of Cuyo.

Born in Mendoza; taught civics and Argentine literature
in the Colegio Nacional "Agustín Alvarez" in that city; served
as deputy in provincial legislature, 1935-1938, and as minister
of hacienda the following year; became rector of University of
Cuyo, 1939, 1943, where he was professor of constitutional
law; his historical writings on Mendoza and the Cuyo area include Historia de Mendoza; Sarmiento y sus amigos; Por la
cultura de Cuyo; he also wrote Biografía del doctor Manuel

Antonio Sáenz; Correas organized the first congress on the history of Cuyo and has lectured on Argentine subjects in various European and U.S. universities.

CORREGIDOR. Spanish royal official assigned to chief towns, entrusted with municipal administration and supervision of judicial affairs; in cities not capital of a district, or in areas of Indian towns, corregidor took the place of governor; area of responsibility called corregimiento; little real positive contribution to Río de la Plata colonial life; characterized by avarice, exploitation of inhabitants, and arbitrary action; their replacement, in 1782, by responsible, progressive intendants considered one of most important Bourbon political reforms in area.

CORREO DE COMERCIO. Weekly journal founded by Manuel Belgrano (q.v.) and used by him to foster the promotion of agriculture, industry, and education; each issue included usually one page devoted to port activities of Buenos Aires and Montevideo; lasted for 52 issues, March 1810 to April 1811; a facsimile edition of 412 pages, with introductory note by Ernesto J. Fitte, was published in Buenos Aires 1970, as part of the Biblioteca de la Academia Nacional de la Historia.

CORRIENTES (City and Province). Location: One of Argentine Mesopotamian provinces; separated from Paraguay on north by Paraná river; bounded on east by Misiones and Uruguay (across the Uruguay river); on south Mocoretá and Guayquiraró rivers separate it from Entre Ríos; Santa Fe lies across Paraná to west. Area: 34,500 square miles. Population of province (1970): 564,147. Density: 16 persons per square mile. Capital: city of Corrientes; population (1960): 97,507. Climate and geography. Hot and humid; subtropical weather and vegetation; rolling, grassy plains, crossed by rivers and interspersed with lakes, fine for stockraising and agriculture cover most of province, with heavy rainforests and swamps in northeast; forty to fifty inches annual rainfall; Paraná river navigable for ocean vessels as far as Corrientes, capital city and port; economy primarily stockraising and meat-processing but has important lumber-mills--exports quebracho and other hardwoods; agriculture produces large crops of cotton, tobacco, rice, yerba mate, and fruits for national market and for export.

Throughout its history Corrientes has had to fight for survival--not because of hunger, as its rich alluvial soils made that no problem--but against Indian attacks from Guaraní, Guaycurú, and Chaco Indians, so violent that the colony believed that only divine intervention--the miracle of the Cross, in the beginning and the continuing protection of the Virgin of Itatí--preserved them; survival of their own way of life against contrary pressures from Spanish and then Buenos Aires governments; and continued possession of their own lands against Jesuit missions, Brazilians, Paraguayans, who sought to take

possession of lands with boundaries still confused until late
nineteenth century; these struggles, lasting approximately four
centuries, along with economic richness of province have bred
a special blend of courage, pride, love of land (all of which
they held except Misiones, which became a national territory
in 1881), religious devotion, and spirit of independence that re-
acts immediately and violently against pressure.

Province grew up around capital, founded April 3,
1588, by fourth adelantado Juan Torres de Vera y Aragón,
with aid of his nephew Alonso Vera y Aragón ("El Tupí"),
Hernandarias, and other wealthy, experienced city-founders
from Asunción who brought their own resources of cattle,
horses to make new settlement self-supporting; violent attack
of 6,000 Indians against the 28 defenders of tiny fort seemed
certain to succeed when the Miraculous Cross (erected as sign
of possession) saved them; firebrands thrown to burn fort and
cross fell harmlessly at foot of wooden cross; instead, a light-
ning bolt struck already terrified Indians, killing some and
driving rest off (today a monument in the central plaza commemorates this; made a national historical monument February 2, 1942); having won this respite, town of San Juan de
Vera de las Siete Corrientes (name later simplified to Corrientes) was firmly established; throughout colonial period, province had to fight off Indians but increasing herds of wild cattle
brought in more settlers and colony remained stable as port
and center of area; by 1595 there were 152 landholders, with
number growing steadily; chapel of San Sebastián completed in
1593; Franciscans began to gather hostile Indians into missions in 1608-1609, with the great Jesuit missions farther up
the Paraná until mameluco slave-raids from Brazil forced
them south and west, some into Corrientes territory; in 1617,
when the Río de la Plata government was divided with governors at both Asunción and Buenos Aires, Corrientes was attached to Buenos Aires; by 1663 Corrientes (city and outlying
area under its authority) had more than 1000 settlers; eighteenth century characterized by change and turbulence; comunero revolts of both 1732 and 1764 developed out of intolerable
government pressures (due to problems in Paraguay and Uruguay) imposed on their own problems (see Comuneros of Corrientes); economy hurt by the shift of important river trade
from Paraná to Uruguay river, reflecting wealth and trade of
the Jesuit missions; in 1750 Corrientes had 300 landholding
citizens (vecinos), a curate and vicar, several resident clerics,
along with Franciscan, Dominican, and Mercedarian establishments and Jesuit Colegio; in 1782, Corrientes became part of
new Buenos Aires intendancy; scientist Félix de Azara made
two exploratory trips through Corrientes, leaving valuable new
geographic data in his diaries and maps; new towns and districts formed; some industry: Corrientes provided all tackle
and spars for viceroyalty and did considerable shipbuilding;
textiles also made for province and neighboring markets; at
time of British invasions (1806-1807), Corrientes responded to
Viceroy Sobremonte's appeal by sending one whole militia

regiment, well-supplied with extra mounts, to Montevideo;
while men from Corrientes who were residing in Buenos Aires
formed famous corps of Cazadores Correntinos under the command of Juan José Fernández Blanco.

Corrientes enthusiastically endorsed May Revolution
(1810) as soon as it learned of it; during next few decades,
its limits and its loyalties were sorely tested, defended, and
redefined: in 1814 provinces of Corrientes and Entre Ríos
(formerly combined and including Uruguay) were created;
Corrientes was delighted to have its own government in its own
capital city but resented loss of what it had formerly considered its territory (still included Misiones); province had difficulty deciding what its role should be in independent nation
and within next few years was at one time or another allied
with Buenos Aires in Federal Pact, or allied with Paraguay
for defense, especially commercially, against Buenos Aires
control of river commerce, or at war with Paraguay; influenced by Uruguay, both under Artigas and later, or invaded by
it or fighting it; considered formation of an intermediate nation with Entre Ríos to form solid buffer against Brazil; even
set up an independent nation briefly; actually always came back
to its goal of a united Argentina of fairly autonomous provinces under a constitution that guaranteed protection of Corrientes' commercial interests; meanwhile, in 1821, constitutional government was established in the province and under such
progressive governors as Juan José Fernández Blanco and
Pedro Ferré (q.v.), colonization, agriculture, and especially
education, were fostered; first newspaper in Corrientes La
Verdad sin Rodeos appeared 1828; in late 1830s, Governor
Génaro Berón de Astrada felt that time had come to force
Rosas out or to organize nation with constitution; allied himself with Rosas' enemies, foreign, exiled, and provincial--at
time of French blockade of Argentina but Rosas sent Echagüe
from Entre Ríos who defeated and killed Berón Astrada at
Pago Largo March 31, 1839; Pedro Ferré took up fight, particularly opposed to Rosas policy of free trade which benefited
only Buenos Aires; after defeats of generals Lavalle and Paz,
with whom Ferré had allied himself, Madariagas forced to go
into exile, while Corrientes saw some peace under Rosas-
controlled government, until Urquiza pronounced against Rosas
and Corrientes joined him; in 1852 a Corrientes revolution
placed Dr. Juan Pujol in as governor, 1852-1859; rapid progress was made; finances stabilized, public education advanced;
industry, especially lumber, improved; administration of justice reorganized and reformed, communications improved, first
postage stamp of nation created; museum founded under direction of elderly, distinguished Aimé Bonpland; new constitution
adopted but Pujol's rule was dictatorial and liberals came in
a few years later and revised consitution, 1864; in century
that followed Corrientes participated fully in economic, social,
and cultural development of the republic, in spite of frequent
political uprisings and federal interventions; new towns established; immigration and colonization fostered; steamship

service, with stops along the way, established between Rosario
and Corrientes; provincial bank established in 1880s but forced
into liquidation by banking crisis of 1890s; reestablished in 1912;
National University of the Littoral was founded with separate
faculties and schools in Santa Fe, Rosario, Paraná, and Corrientes, which appropriately had Faculty of Agronomy and Veterinary Sciences; classes began in 1922; marked important cultural advance; in 1900 the solemn crowning of the Virgin of
Itatí, patroness of Corrientes, took place and basilica (called
a "triumph of Argentine architecture on the frontier") was
later built as her sanctuary (see Itatí, Virgin of); political unrest continued to be a feature of Corrientes life in the 1960s
and early 1970s.

CORRO, MIGUEL CALIXTO DEL (1775-1851). Córdoba ecclesiastic
with doctorate in theology from University of San Carlos in
Córdoba; supported May Revolution 1810; elected as member of
the Congress of Tucumán, 1816, was prevented from signing
Declaration of Independence by his absence while serving as
peacemaker between Buenos Aires and Santa Fe; accepted other
political appointments but preferred to devote himself to teaching and religious responsibilities; book of his sermons published in Philadelphia, 1849.

CORSARIOS (privateers). Buenos Aires government made use of
these privately owned, privately manned ships to harass shipping of enemy, both in war of independence, especially under
patents and supervision of supreme director Juan Manuel
Pueyrredón, 1812-1821, and during war with Brazil, 1825-
1828; most of captains were North Americans, like David Curtis de Forest, or European; outstanding achievements by Hipólito Bouchard (q.v.) in his circumnavigation of the globe.
        See Teodoro Caillet-Bois and Lewis Winkler Bealer in
Suggested Readings, Appendix III.

COTTON. Known as oro chaqueño (Chaco gold) because of wealth
it has brought to Chaco region; cotton common to both old and
new world; indigenous in northwestern Argentina; when, around
1300, the Indian chief Tucma (from whom province of Tucumán takes its name--land of cotton according to another theory) asked the Inca Viracocha to incorporate his land into the
Inca empire, he sent robes of cotton, among other gifts;
throughout the colonial period the cultivation of cotton and production of cotton textiles remained important in this area; in
Jesuit missions area in northeastern Argentina, cotton was also important during seventeenth and eighteenth centuries; Jesuits discovered that a native tree cotton could be grown under
certain conditions to produce seven annual crops; more than
enough was raised for their needs and some export--it was in
fact, one of their major agricultural successes; during century
following expulsion of Jesuits, importation of cheap European
textiles, and emphasis on pastoral industries, especially the
turn to sheep, and preference for woolen fabrics, practically

eliminated cotton growing; in 1862, Thomas J. Hutchison arrived in Rosario as British consular representative and began to encourage new cotton plantings (needed for English textile factories); President Mitre took up cause, citing example of U.S. South, and his minister of interior, Guillermo Rawson, circularized all provincial governors urging high priority for introduction of cotton; few results, as Argentina was extending itself to utmost to develop pampas, including great agricultural revolution there; it was not until after two world wars and a depression between them, that attention was given to real development of marginal lands where cotton could grow; experiments with new seeds and scientific methods of cultivation demonstrated that cotton grows very well in the Chaco area and that Catamarca, with irrigation, can produce a high quality long staple variety; Misiones, on the other hand, has decided that other crops are more easily and profitably grown than cotton; by 1970 cotton, while not a major national crop, had become a notable new contribution to the national economy; production of cotton lint totaling 87,000 metric tons, cotton seed, 160,000 metric tons.

COUNCIL OF THE INDIES. Established by crown in 1524 to handle all matters relating to Indies (i.e., American colonies) following death of Bishop Fonseca who had handled these since Columbus' return from his first voyage in 1493; all political, military, and judicial matters of colonial Argentina came under its authority through audiencia of Charcas until 1783 when the second audiencia of Buenos Aires was established (first one 1661, very brief duration). Carlos III reduced Council's powers in 1770 and the Cortes of Cádiz abolished it, but Ferdinand VII reestablished it after his restoration in 1814; finally, with most of Spain's American empire gone, it was abolished in 1834.

CRAMER, AMBROSIO (1792-1839). Soldier and engineer.
        Born in Paris; veteran of Napoleon's army in Spain; after Waterloo came to Río de la Plata; assigned by Pueyrredón to Army of the Andes; fought at Chacabuco; returned to Buenos Aires and became aide-de-camp to Belgrano; later served with Governor Martín Rodríguez; became interested in surveying, defending, and developing Patagonian area; established himself at Chascomús, engaged in raising sheep; became one of three leaders in revolt against Rosas and was killed in battle against Rosas' forces led by latter's brother Prudencio, November 7, 1839 (see Chascomús).

CREOLE, CREOLE CULTURE (criollo, criollismo). Word derived from Latin creare, Spanish crear (to create); refers in Argentina to native-born person of European blood, although in early colonial period little distinction was made between white and (well-born) mestizos--both were creoles (in contrast to Indians).
        Creole culture was creation of these native sons; Span-

iards settling in Argentina in sixteenth and even early seventeenth century found themselves on far edge of western civilization; almost entirely on their own resources in alien land in which Spanish skills were of little use and Indians either hostile, not available, or of little help; survival, individually, or in isolated towns, became the simple goal; eventually on the new land and with importation of cattle, horses, sheep, and other farm animals that multiplied with almost unbelievable rapidity on it, the hardy survivors forged a new life style for themselves and their families--criollismo; royal and church authority and institutions accepted but, in this remote area, offered little threat to creole ways and were often themselves a part of it; by 1750s Argentines of all classes unified in spirit of pride in themselves, as individuals and as members of their own communities; love of their land and a close relationship with it; admiration for strength and even brute force, for their very existence had depended on it; a casual attitude toward bloodletting, common in town and in rural areas--every man his own meat butcher; and mystical faith in the God and saints to whose miraculous interventions so many early settlements attributed their survival; Argentines were comfortable in their way of life.

Establishment of viceroyalty in 1776 brought change; expulsion of Jesuits in 1767 had already separated many Creoles (who were members of the order) from their homes; new Spaniards in increasing numbers settled not only in Buenos Aires but in interior towns also, usually in dominant positions as royal or ecclesiastical officials, or as merchants with close ties to commercial monopoly of Sevilla; increased royal control over government and economy; introduction of new European ideas and institutions; creoles welcomed many of new political and economic ideas as leading to desired progress; shock came with realization, described vividly by Manuel Belgrano in his autobiography, that new goals for Argentina were to be determined, and advantages enjoyed, primarily by Spaniards; their feelings were further exacerbated by Spanish assumption of superiority over creoles in latter's own land; further disillusioned by viceregal inadequacy in face of British invasions, creoles welcomed Cornelio de Saavedra's remarks following victory over British: "I make bold to congratulate the Americans (creoles); to the proofs that they have already given of valor and loyalty, they have added this last--that by exalting the merit of those who were born in the Indies, they have given convincing evidence that their spirits are not kin to humiliation, that they are not inferior to the European Spaniards, and that they cede to no one in loyalty and valor"; creoles were determined to win independence, with their land, society, and government subject to their own control; provided political leadership for May Revolution and succeeding patriot governments and military command for armies of war for independence; anarchy and civil wars followed attempts of Rivadavia and others to centralize government and Europeanize Argentine life and society; most of leaders (in large part

caudillos) during period of civil war, especially federalists, including Juan Manuel de Rosas himself, were creole in spirit,
life style, and goals.
     Criollismo seemed to decline in closing decades of
nineteenth century, along with way of life of gauchos who came
to be its symbol and did, in fact, constitute one representation of it; gaucho literature began to appear (Fausto, 1866,
and Martín Fierro, 1872-1879) but public interest centered on
progress made in political, economic, and social development
fostered by government and private interests; foreign aid
sought in fields of finance, technology, education, and especially for promotion of agriculture; immigrants filled towns and
established new ones on pampas and Patagonian dry plains;
European and U.S. teachers, scientists, and artists directed
schools and institutes; intellectuals attracted to foreign ideologies such as positivism, social Darwinism, socialism, and
Marxism; nevertheless, in early twentieth century pendulum
swung back to strong revival of criollismo under new names
and taking new forms; gaucho writings and others of nativist,
traditional authors enjoyed new vogue; new writers vied in
studying and portraying Argentine life, customs, countryside,
traditions, folklore, and history in new literature; formed basis
for modern political and economic nationalism, as well as new
drive (often on part of second-generation Argentines) to discover national identity; term criollo usually applied now to customs, foods, fashions in clothing, etc., of traditional creoles
but spirit of criollismo--pride in being Argentine and stubborn
self-determinism--continues to be potent, if not dominant, factor in national life and international policy.

CROSSING OF THE ANDES   see   ANDES, CROSSING OF

CRUZ, FRANCISCO DE LA   see   FERNANDEZ CRUZ, FRANCISCO
   DE LA

CUBAS, JOSE (1798-1841). Catamarcan cattleman active in public
   life; served as governor on various occasions; backed Rosas at
   first; in 1839 became very active in anti-Rosas movement; one
   of leaders in formation of the Coalition or League of the North;
   suffered fate of other leaders by execution after its defeat.

CUENTOS DE FRAY MOCHO   see   ALVAREZ, JOSE SIXTO

CUITIÑO, CIRIACO (b. near close of 18th cent.--d. 1853). Mendoza-
   born police commissioner under Rosas; one of founders of Mazorca, the dreaded secret police society; after fall of Rosas'
   government, tried for political crimes related to his police activities and executed, along with Leandro Alén, in 1853.

CULLEN, DOMINGO (1791-1839). Political figure, Santa Fe governor and minister.
        Born in Canary Islands, of Irish father and Spanish
   mother, educated there and in Spain; moved to Montevideo,

1811, to become merchant; bought river boat, 1817, and traded
as far as Santa Fe where he formed friendship with Estanislao
López; returned to Montevideo, became active in politics;
joined Caballeros Orientales (organization opposed to Brazilian
domination); persuaded López to sign offensive-defensive alliance with cabildo of Montevideo to work for latter's emancipation from Brazil (March 4, 1823); Brazilian army force opponents into exile; Cullen, already in Santa Fe, remained there,
married a member of López's family, and established a cattle
spread; returned to politics as secretary for López in 1828;
became minister of government in 1833; was in Buenos Aires,
attempting to find peaceful solution to French blockade when
López died, June 15, 1838; Cullen had argued, for Santa Fe,
that blockade resulted from Rosas' application of Buenos Aires
provincial law and so provinces were not bound to support him;
Rosas denied this, invoking Article II of the Federal Pact;
López's death changed everything; although Cullen went back to
Santa Fe as governor, he faced opposition everywhere--from
personal enemies in Santa Fe to Rosas' followers outside; the
provinces, including Santa Fe, backed Rosas in his opposition
to the French and Cullen went into exile; the following year,
accused of conspiracy with the unitarists (Rosas' enemies) and
the French, Cullen sought asylum in Santiago del Estero but
was apprehended by Rosas' men and shot (June 21, 1839) on
Rosas' orders while being taken to Buenos Aires for trial.
(See José Luis Busaniche, Domingo Cullen.)

CUNEO, (ENRIQUE) DARDO (1914-   ). Writer and journalist; socialist.
        Born in Buenos Aires; became involved with labor and
socialist press at early age; formed part of editorial staff of
La Razón and La Vanguardia and contributed to various other
newspapers and periodicals in Argentina and abroad; served
(1958) as chief of press service for the presidency; also author
of longer, more formal works; as successor to enlightened,
liberal socialism of Juan B. Justo (q. v.), he wrote Juan B.
Justo (Buenos Aires, 1943), and the more complete Juan B.
Justo y las luchas sociales en la Argentina (Buenos Aires,
1956); other major works include El primer periodismo obrero
y socialista en la Argentina (1945); Sarmiento y Unamuno
(1948), for which he was honored by the Argentine Society of
Writers in 1949; Cuaderno de milicia (1952); El romanticismo
político (1955); Comportamiento y crisis de la clase empresaria
(1963); El desencuento argentino, 1930-1955 (1965).

CURUPAYTI (or Curupaity). Site of disastrous defeat (September 22,
1866) of General Mitre's allied forces in War of Triple Alliance; his casualties numbered over 4000 (said to be bloodiest
battle of the war), while the Paraguayans claimed only about
90; results of the battle: recriminations between Mitre and the
Brazilian naval commander for lack of coordination of actions
in battle; increased protests against government by Argentine
critics of the war; increased support of Paraguay by foreign

public opinion that now viewed Paraguay as heroic small victim of aggression from its colossus neighbors, Argentina and
Brazil; even Paraguay lost, as the overtures (the last one just
ten days before the battle) that its president Solano López,
had been making for a negotiated peace to the war no longer
had any hope of success; for the Allies, it had become a fight
to the finish (see Paraguayan War).

CUSTOMHOUSE. In an effort to curb Buenos Aires contraband trade
from entering the interior provinces, Chile, and Upper Peru,
customhouse was established at Córdoba 1622; Buenos Aires
goods had to pay 50% of regular duties before proceeding; customhouse moved northward to Salta and Jujuy 1676 for greater
efficiency, in tacit recognition of Buenos Aires continued control of interior trade: following royal decrees in 1778, ending
Sevilla monopoly and opening Buenos Aires to trade with other
Spanish and Spanish American cities, customhouse established
in Buenos Aires.

CUYO. Original name still in use, derived from the Araucanian
word meaning sandy land, it applies to Andean area comprised
of modern provinces of Mendoza, San Juan, and San Luis
(qq. v.); first visited by Francisco de Villagrá while returning
to Chile from a recruiting and provisioning trip to Peru (1550-
1551); following route east of the Andes, penetrated south as
far as site of Mendoza, taking possession of all the land in
the name of Valdivia, Spanish governor of Chile; returned to
Santiago crossing Andes by Indian trail leading through Uspallata Pass (over two miles high); a few years later Governor
García Hurtado de Mendoza sent men from Chile to occupy
Cuyo because of its fertile land and large number of peaceful,
farming Huarpe Indians; 1561 Mendoza established by Pedro de
Castillo; San Juan de la Frontera founded by Juan Jufré 1562;
and a few years later, 1594, San Luis de Loyola was added.
         For the next century and a half, these tiny towns (Men-
doza, for example, had only thirteen men to defend it) lived
on the frontier, developing a pattern of life of their own, cut
off from Chilean government and support for six months during
the winter; as large numbers of the Huarpe Indians were taken
to supplement labor force in Chile, and those that remained
stayed far away from whites, the populations remained largely
creole; in contrast to most of Argentina, Cuyo combined agriculture with the more common pastoral pursuits; economic and
social ties (especially through family migrations) began to link
the three economic centers of Tucumán, Buenos Aires, and
Cuyo together; Cuyo, on its own or jointly with Tucumán, sent
cattle to Chile and mules to Peru, receiving manufactured
goods in exchange; it needed Argentine markets for its dried
fruits and wines; and these were slowly established with the
other two centers, especially after trading among them was
legalized in 1690; by opening of the eighteenth century Cuyo
was part of the Buenos Aires-Tucumán system in every respect
but political; its inclusion in 1776 in the newly created vice-

royalty of Río de la Plata seemed logical and acceptable; fortunately its harness and dried fruits economy was less affected by competition from European imports than industries of other interior provinces; in 1777 Ceballos sent 523 Portuguese prisoners to Cuyo; most remained to become residents there; area was included in new intendancy of Córdoba del Tucumán, created 1783; after May Revolution, as patriot government attempted to reorganize country for independence, new provinces were created and Cuyo became a separate intendancy, including the provinces of Mendoza, San Luis, San Juan, responsible for protecting the border; raids from pampas Indians had been increasing since 1660 when Araucanians moving south and east had pushed them from their traditional campsites; in 1777, a punitive raid had been made against them and frontier forts of San Carlos and San Rafael held the line in the south; dangers of royalist invasions from Chile increased after reconquest of Chile in 1814; Cuyo, uneasy because of increasing pressures from Buenos Aires and fear of losing its local prerogatives to a strong Buenos Aires government was saved for the patriot cause by the appointment of José de San Martín as governor-intendant in 1814; for over three years, Cuyo was caught up in the fervor of cooperating with San Martín in the creation and provisioning of the Army of the Andes for the liberation of Chile and finally to complete the liberation of all southern South America; loyal to the patriot government, it became a political power base in itself; in the years following San Martín's departure, Cuyo (with a population in 1819 of 88,000, in comparison with 125,000 for Buenos Aires province) alternated, as did most of the other provinces of Argentina in the next few decades between progressive governors who attempted to modernize and improve the institutional life of their provinces, and to develop their economy, and caudillos who were apt to gain and keep power by force; Quiroga dominated in 1831 and the Aldaos had to be reckoned with until the 1840s; Cuyo had its share of violence and civil war; after fall of Rosas, as the nation approached union in 1861, all three Cuyo provinces had liberal governors; historical development from then on best viewed through individual provinces although, more often than not, these tend to act together politically and in many other ways; term Cuyo is still alive as denoting a cultural, economic, geographic unit--University of Cuyo, in Mendoza, for example.

See Kenneth D. Frederick, Water Management and Agricultural Development. A Cross Study of the Cuyo Region of Argentina (Johns Hopkins University Press, Baltimore and London, 1975).

CZETZ, JUAN F. (1822-1904). Military officer, cartographer, mathematician.

Hungarian-born military engineer, educated at Viener-Neustadt academy; after several years spent in traveling and living in England, France and Spain (where he married the daughter of General Prudencio Ortiz de Rozas) he moved to

Argentina in 1860; following year appointed to make survey for
Azul area; became chief of engineers in army; completed map
of Argentine boundaries with Paraguay and Brazil; made colonel by Mitre (1865); appointed by Sarmiento (1870), to organize and direct the newly-authorized Colegio Militar; remained
there until 1874; moved to Entre Ríos where he became head
of the provincial topographical department, performed services
for the colonies of Esperanza and San Jerónimo, and taught
mathematics at the normal school of Concepción del Uruguay.

- D -

DAIREAUX, EMILIO (1843-1916). Born in Rio de Janeiro; graduated in law in Paris; arrived in Buenos Aires in 1860s; fell
in love with the country and with Amalia Molina whom he married; established residence, purchased land around Caseros in
Buenos Aires province; validated his law credentials by attending University of Buenos Aires law school; practiced law and
devoted considerable time to writing about the rapidly changing
scene in Argentine during the last half of the nineteenth century; his great interest in the area combined with a gift of
vivid description to make his writings both useful and interesting to scholars studying this period; he also founded and edited
(1880-1883) L'Union française; later, Le Courier de la Plata;
died in Paris.
    Among his published works on Argentina are Buenos
Aires, La Pampa et Patagone (in French, 1883); La vida y
costumbres en el Plata, 2 v. (1886--French and Spanish); also
El abogado de sí mismo (1885).

DARIO, RUBEN (1867-1916). Nicaraguan poet; spent five years in
Buenos Aires (1893-1898); stimulated avant-garde reviews and
attracted such followers as Leopoldo Díaz, Enrique Larreta,
and Leopoldo Lugones to the new poetry that they called modernismo and to his insistence that new forms of literature and
cultural expression should be sought in Hispanic, Catholic tradition; became foreign correspondent for La Nación; this provided his living for rest of his life; celebrated Argentina's
centenary, 1910, in poetry.

DARREGUEIRA, JOSE (1777-1817). Judge; precursor of independence; signer of the Declaration of Independence.
    Born in Lima; brought up in Buenos Aires and received
early education there; graduated with doctorate in laws from
university at Chuquisaca; early allied himself with patriots in
Buenos Aires desiring independence; became one of judges when
the royal judges of the audiencia left; as delegate representing
Buenos Aires at the Congress of Tucumán, in 1816, he was
considered to be one of the most notable men there and signed
the Declaration of Independence; died the following year.

DARWIN, CHARLES ROBERT (1809-1882). English scientist, author

of Origin of the Species (1859). Darwin spent two years in
Río de la Plata and Argentine areas, 1832-1834, while accompanying Beagle expedition as natural scientist; this voyage,
which Darwin considered most important event in his life, determining his future career, was five-year (1831-1836) effort
to make accurate survey of southern coastlines of South America, determine geological relationships between offshore islands and mainland, and, continuing voyage around the world,
to take chronometric readings; at request of Captain Robert
Fitzroy for young gentleman with enough scientific background
to evaluate mineralogical possibilities of areas studied, Darwin
was attached to expedition; although his duties were primarily
geological, Darwin's own interests, which he was given ample
opportunities to pursue, embraced every form and manifestation of nature, including fossils, people, animals, plants,
weather, as well as geology; made contact with Argentine scientists, including Francisco Javier Muñiz (q.v.) whom he was
unable to meet but with whom he carried on correspondence
regarding Muñiz's studies concerning the vaca ñata (snub-
nosed--i.e., abnormal--cow); Argentine historians see relationship between this and Darwin's later ideas, especially those
expressed in his Variation of Animals and Plants Under Domes-
tication (1868).
    From time that Beagle anchored in Río de la Plata at
Montevideo in July 1832 until it entered Pacific two years
later, Darwin was engaged in exploring--at sea with Beagle or
on land on his own or accompanied by Argentine residents;
made several trips to Bahía Blanca, one by land, made possible by Juan Manuel Rosas who gave Darwin permission to use
horses and escorts posted along way, to his camp on Indian
frontier on Colorado river in southern Buenos Aires province,
where Darwin spent some time; visited Las Malvinas (Falkland
Islands), recently occupied by British; rode over pampas and
up along Paraná to investigate reports of fossilized bones at
Santa Fe; went up Uruguay river to see famous limekilns and
to explore Río Negro; studied entire Patagonian Atlantic coast
and went up Santa Cruz river to cordillera; spent considerable
time in Tierra del Fuego area--in straits at Cape Horn, cruising through Beagle channel--to which Captain Fitzroy returned
Jemmy Button (native purchased on earlier voyage for pearl
button) and several other Anglicized, Christian Indians to their
home territory, along with English missionary, emphasizing
British interest in and good will toward region through which
its ships passed frequently (hopes for settlement and successful missionary work dashed for time being, at least); Darwin's
comments in his Diary, Journal, Notebooks (various editions)
and private letters provide important source material for early
descriptions of Patagonian and other little-known areas and for
reactions and opinions of one educated (albeit provincial) young
Englishman to Argentine society of early 1830s, and especially
to political events of this critical period between Rosas' first
(1829-1832) and second (1835-1852) administrations in Buenos
Aires, and to leading participants in them.

235   Darwin

See Lady Nora Barlow (editor), Charles Darwin and the
Voyage of the Beagle, New York, 1946, for Darwin materials,
most of them previously unpublished, dealing with early, including Argentine, period of Beagle's voyage.

DAVILA, NICOLAS (1786-1876).   Officer of Army of the Andes;
    Governor and public leader in La Rioja.
        Born and died in Nonogasta, La Rioja; commandante of
    Famatina in 1816; ordered by San Martín to prepare two squad-
    rons from La Rioja to invade northern Chile in early 1817 in
    conjunction with crossing the cordillera by the Army of the
    Andes; captured Copiapó on schedule while San Martín fought
    battle of Chacabuco farther south; served as governor of La
    Rioja 1821-1823; became involved in civil wars and suffered
    persecutions from federalists; later (1854-1857) was minister
    in government of Francisco Solano Gómez; called by Joaquín
    Videla González (in Mis montañas) the strength ("nervio") of
    the La Rioja fight for freedom at the outbreak of the revolu-
    tion that led to independence.

"DAY OF THE THREE GOVERNORS."   June 20, 1820, "This was
    the famous day in the annals of anarchy of the year 1820,"
    said the historian Mitre, "which has become known as the 'day
    of the three governors' although no one of the three men was
    governor either in law or fact." (See Levene, History of Ar-
    gentina.)

DECKER, RODOLFO.   High-ranking official used by Juan D. Perón
    in 1945 and 1946 to head legal commission by means of which
    enemies of the government could be removed or silenced; co-
    chairman with J. A. Visca, their investigation of unfriendly
    newspapers resulted in suppression or oppression of many dur-
    ing the period from December 1945 to January 1950; in 1946
    he was appointed to carry on the political trials of the justices
    of the supreme court that resulted in the removal of all of
    them except Tomás D. Casares, appointed by President Far-
    rell and a supporter of Perón.

DECLARATION OF INDEPENDENCE.   Signed July 9, 1816, by 29
    delegates to the Congress meeting in Tucumán. When Con-
    gress of Tucumán held its first session March 24, 1816, the
    nation had been under self-rule for nearly six years, since
    May 25, 1810 Revolution (q.v.); patriot governments, set up
    in Buenos Aires during breakdown of royal government in
    Spain and Napoleonic invasion, had attempted with varying suc-
    cess to spread their revolution throughout the viceroyalty; a
    legal framework for independent government had been estab-
    lished but independence had not been declared and consequent-
    ly no constitution had been written; with Ferdinand VII back
    on Spanish throne, preparing expeditions to regain his Ameri-
    can empire, and the Army of the Andes poised in Mendoza to
    cross the cordillera against the royalist forces in Chile as
    the first step in San Martín's continental project to free the

people of Spanish South America, many leaders, including San
Martín himself and Manuel Belgrano, believed it essential that
such a declaration be made at once to clarify the situation and
lift the spirits of the people; overriding the objections of those
who felt it either unnecessary or too irrevocable a step to be
taken at this critical time (see Congress of Tucumán for background), the proponents of independence introduced the matter
before a crowded session on July 9, 1816, asking a standing
vote from delegates as to whether they wanted such a declaration prepared or not; received unanimous affirmative answer
amid applause from observers; Declaration drawn up at once,
brief and straightforward, declaring the United Provinces of
America (four provinces from Bolivia were also represented,
and several of the riparian Argentine provinces were not) to be
independent of Ferdinand VII and all future rulers of Spain, by
virtue of having reclaimed their right to rule themselves; it
was signed immediately afterward by Narciso de Laprida, delegate from San Juan, acting that day as president, and Mariano
Boedo, vice president.   Signatures of other delegates followed:
José Darregueira, Manuel Antonio Acevedo y Torino, Teodoro
Sánchez de Bustamante, Pedro Miguel Aráoz, Pedro León
Gallo, José S. F. Malabia; José Eusebio Colombres, José
Antonio Cabrera, José Mariano Serrano, Cayetano Rodríguez,
José Ignacio de Gorriti, Eduardo Pérez Bulnes, Esteban
Agustín Gascón, Pedro Ignacio de Rivera, Pedro Ignacio Cast-
ro Barros, José Ignacio Thames, Juan Agustín de la Maza,
Juan José Paso, Antonio Sáenz, Pedro Medrano, Pacheco de
Melo, Tomás Godoy Cruz, Pedro F. de Uriarte, Mariano
Sánchez de Loria, Jerónimo Salguero, Justo Santa María de
Oro, Tomás M. de Anchorena (see individual entries).
    On July 21, before the final oath-taking ceremony, Med-
rano proposed that to the section asserting independence of
Ferdinand VII, of his successors, and of the mother country
should be added a clause "and of any other foreign domination"
to discredit rumors that Congress was looking favorably toward establishing a Braganza prince or was involved in any way
in the threatened Portuguese invasion; Congress agreed to the
change.

DE FOREST, DAVID CURTIS (1774-1825).   Early Yankee trader in
    Río de la Plata.
        Born in Connecticut, U.S.A., early went to sea; one of
earliest North American merchants to establish firm roots in
Buenos Aires; after three trips to the Río de la Plata estuary
(1801-1805), he established first permanent U.S. business
house in Buenos Aires, 1806, and following year, wrote Secretary of State James Madison urging that a trustworthy U.S.
consul or commercial agent be sent to Buenos Aires, offering
on several occasions to accept such an appointment himself;
accumulated a fortune, partly from slave trade and privateering, acquiring a somewhat controversial reputation among other
American merchants; considered audacious, high-spirited, arrogant and/or dignified, affable, and gentlemanly; preparing to

retire in the United States in 1818, he accepted a commission from Supreme Director Juan Martín de Pueyrredón to act as Consul General for the newly independent Argentine nation in Washington; directed by Pueyrredón (February 24, 1818) to secure from President Monroe's government: recognition of Argentina's independence, appointment of a consul; curbing of activities of anti-Pueyrredón exiles in U.S.; additional privateering ships and an island base for them; and appointment of General William Winder of Baltimore as Argentine diputado (agent or representative) in Washington--Winder refused, after consulting with President Monroe, on grounds that he could be more useful as a private citizen; De Forest urged Pueyrredón's cause vigorously but had no success partly on personal grounds, but also largely because Secretary of State John Quincy Adams was giving top priority at this time to his negotiations for a boundary agreement with Spain and had no desire to antagonize the Spanish government until this was completed; relations between United States and Río de la Plata sank to a lower level for a time, but were placed on a firmer footing with the arrival of John M. Forbes (q.v.) in 1820; De Forest meanwhile retired to his home in New Haven, Connecticut (see Benjamin Keen in Suggested Readings, Appendix III).

DE LA PLAZA, VICTORINO   see   PLAZA, VICTORINO DE LA

DE LA TORRE, LISANDRO   see   TORRE, LISANDRO DE LA

DEL CARRIL, SALVADOR MARIA   see   CARRIL, SALVADOR MARIA DEL

DELFINA (d. 1839). Legendary Argentine Amazon. Beautiful, courageous woman who accompanied Francisco Ramírez (Entre Ríos caudillo) constantly and influenced him greatly; made colorful figure in favorite blue and red, booted riding costume, with ostrich plume in her chambergo (soft Argentine hat)--plume in official seal of Entre Ríos Republic a romantic gesture on part of Ramírez; nothing known of her past although rumor claimed her to be illegitimate daughter of Portuguese viceroy in Brazil; met Ramírez in 1818 or 1819; became his inseparable companion until July 10, 1821; fleeing from Santa Fe and Córdoba forces following his defeat at Fraile Muerto, Ramírez was overtaken in Río Seco and Delfina was momentarily captured by enemy soldier; returning to save her, Ramírez was killed; Delfina saved and escorted back to Entre Ríos by loyal followers of Ramírez; died in Concepción del Uruguay, 1839.

DELLEPIANE, LUIS J. (1865-1941). Career military officer; Minister of War (1928-1930); scientist and professor; called father of Argentine geodesy.
        Born in Buenos Aires; entered military college 1882; devoted himself to military studies and operations until his retirement as lieutenant general, 1925; accompanied military career with lifelong dedication to exact physical sciences, espe-

cially geodesy, science related to size and shape of earth;
graduated from university in Buenos Aires as civil engineer
1891; became director of military geographical institute; professor of topography in Escuela Superior de Guerra (war college for advanced officers); held various and continuing university teaching positions; elected member of national academy
of exact physical sciences 1915; sent as military attaché to
Berlin; returned with delicate new instruments for use in military geographical institutes; served as consultant on several
boundary commissions; published several scholarly monographs;
served as director of army engineers; held two appointments
as chief of police: 1909 interim appointment following death
of chief of police, and ten years later, as commander of all
civil and military forces in federal capital during violent
workers' outbreak in January 1919; served as minister of war
during Hipólito Yrigoyen's second presidency (1928-1930); resigned September 2, 1930, when Yrigoyen refused to permit
him to use stern measures against leaders of opposition conspiracy; Yrigoyen forced to turn government over to Uriburu
four days later; Dellepiane remained in retirement until his
death in Buenos Aires eleven years later.

DELTA OF THE PARANA RIVER. In Entre Ríos and Buenos Aires
provinces. Islands in river where Paraná joins the Río de la
Plata; economy based on softwood forests that support heavy
lumbering industry; poplars, eucalyptus, casuarinas supply the
sawmills and wood container factories of San Fernando and
Tigre, supporting thousands of families; tung oil plantations
have become important and various medicinal plants are cultivated successfully; beauty of area attracts heavy tourist trade
from Greater Buenos Aires.

DEL VALLE, ARISTOBULO see VALLE, ARISTOBULO DEL

DEMOCRACY. Defined politically as government by the people,
either directly or through chosen representatives, and socially
and economically as equality of opportunity and respect for the
individual within the community; democracy germinated in early
days of conquest and has been integral part of Argentine life
ever since; during struggle for survival of early colonial period, Argentines developed strong sense of individual independence; relative lack of Indian labor and abundance of horses and
cattle made for equality--no one very rich or very poor--in
isolated towns; constant revolts against unrealistic measures of
royal authorities or laws showed Plata insistence on self-determination in political and economic matters; liberal ideas of
Enlightenment, with emphasis on freedom and individual rights
widely accepted as basis for independence movement and establishment of new government; clash came when elite leaders
in Buenos Aires attempted to change established (i. e., criollo
and traditional) institutions for Western European ones, to
suggest monarchical form of government instead of expected
republic, and to increase Buenos Aires political and economic

hegemony over provinces; the period of anarchy, Rosas' dictatorship, and civil wars (1820-1862) today considered by many Argentine historians to be manifestation of violent and barbaric, but fundamental, democracy of masses; with establishment of national constitutional republic (1862), Argentina enjoyed several decades of economic and social progress under government dominated by old and increasingly wealthy elite that considered itself democratic in principle but found it difficult to accept new interpretations of democracy advanced by newly developing, highly literate, largely immigrant middle-class society; political participation widened, largely through efforts of Radicals, culminating with women getting vote in 1947; economic changes, especially rapid industrialization and depression of 1930s, prepared way for government sponsorship (especially under Perón) of greater economic and social democracy; following 1955 various authoritarian governments (backed by military) dispensed with or limited popular political participation but Argentina's traditional dedication to its own forms of democracy continues to manifest itself in demand for, and frequent restorations of, free and open elections.

DEMOCRATA PROGRESISTA, PARTIDO (Progressive Democratic Party).   Party formed in Santa Fe by Lisandro de la Torre of radical elements dissatisfied with Hipólito Yrigoyen's leadership of Radical party; de la Torre was the party's candidate for president in election of 1916; Yrigoyen won the largest number of popular votes but the new party played a decisive role in this first presidential election under the Roque Saenz Peña electoral law of 1912; when Yrigoyen failed to receive a majority vote in the electoral college, it was the Progressive Democrats who put him over, trusting his honesty and program more than those of the Conservatives; in the 1932 election the Progressive-Socialist slate of de la Torre and N. Repetto was defeated by that of Agustín P. Justo; in 1943, Socialists, Progressive Democrats, and Radicals joined to form the Democratic Union (see Unión Democrática).

DEMOCRATIC UNION see UNION DEMOCRATICA

DEMOGRAPHY.   Population (1970 Census): 23,364,431. Growth rate: approximately 2% a year. Density: about 20 per square mile. Literacy: 90%.
    Population almost entirely homogeneous racially--white, with majority of Spanish or Italian background; an estimated fewer than 100,000 Indians still conserve native culture and life style on remote frontiers; blacks and mulattoes have almost disappeared; Orientals--especially Japanese--increasing in number but still form very small segment of total population; concentration of population continues to flow toward Atlantic coast; 75% of people live in towns or cities with populations of 2000 or more; more than one-third of national population is found in Greater Buenos Aires area.
    History.   In sixteenth century population (Indian) of

Argentina estimated at about 300,000, many of these living in
Chaco, pampas, and Patagonia and not available as labor to
Spaniards following conquest; mestizos made up 80-90% of
founding citizens of Santa Fe and Buenos Aires; total population
in 1600 around 350,000; about the same in 1700, with apparent
dip in middle of century; Indians, even in missions, were declining in numbers due to wars, slave raids from Brazil, disease, etc.; new Spaniards, criollos, mestizos, blacks (brought
in from Brazil and Africa to provide necessary labor, especially in towns) and mulattoes increased; by 1750 population had
begun to grow, reaching approximately 500,000-600,000 by
1810, with 30% Indian, 10% black or mulatto and the rest white
or mestizo; Buenos Aires had population of 50,000 or about
10% of total.

First national census, taken in 1869, showed population
of a little more than 1,800,000 (a growth of 3 to 1 in six decades compared to U.S. growth of 7 to 1 in same period); Indians and mestizos made up 75%; whites 20% and blacks and
mulattoes had declined to 5%; Argentina still largely rural, with
urbanization given at 25%; during next five or six decades society was transformed showing rapid increase in total numbers,
largely due to influx of European immigration--census gives
populations of 2,600,000 in 1880, 3,955,000 in 1895, and
reaching 7,885,000 in 1914 (with 30% of these foreign born; almost complete disappearance of blacks and mulattoes, and rapid decline (due to miscegenation as well as occupation of Patagonia) of number of Indians; absorption of mestizos into white
race; concentration of people in coastal areas; Europeanization
of cities, where large numbers of immigrants made their new
homes; and migration from rural to urban areas--Buenos Aires
increased its growth rate from 28% to 46% while that of interior
declined from 40% to 19% (see Social Structure for discussion
of effects of this internal migration).

National population doubled between 1914 and 1947
(16,000,000) and has continued to grow although not as fast as
many Argentines would like--with current (1960s and early
1970s) growth rate of about 2% annually.

DEPRESSION (the great economic depression of the 1930s). The
world-wide economic crisis of 1929 that ushered in the depression of the 1930s caught Argentina in the early years of Hipólito Yrigoyen's second administration; his failure to attempt to
soften its impact frightened Argentines, who had taken continued economic progress for granted for over half a century
(with the exception of the 1890 crisis); and it was one factor
causing the overthrow of this government in 1930; generally
speaking, although Argentina's economy--based on exchange of
raw products for manufactures from Europe, for most part--
made it especially vulnerable to the changes brought by the depression, the latter was more responsible for accelerating
changes already underway than a prime cause of them; the
scare that Argentina had when World War I disturbed its trade,
was brief but the depression lasted long enough to make it clear

241   Depression

that change was necessary; trade of major nations dropped to
one-third of its 1929 levels within 5 years and both the value
and the volume of Argentine export trade declined; industrial
production of both Europe and U.S. fell by almost 50%; since
manufactured goods did not drop as much in price as agricultural and stock products Argentina suffered a double blow--
had to sell less at a lower price; for example in 1932 Argentina had to export 65% more agricultural products for the
same manufactured goods than 4 years earlier and pay more
for what it could get; economic nationalists who wanted economic independence, industrialists wanting to diversify the
economy, even landowners who hoped for a better return on
their money from industry than they were receiving from their
estancias, joined with consumers in trying to make Argentina
self-sufficient economically in as many ways as possible; most
agreed with other Western nations that the old laissez-faire
days (of so-called free trade) were over and that government
must play a stronger role in promotion and control of the national economy; even President Justo's government (1932-
1938), strongly backed by the oligarchy, increased this government control and did, in fact, see the economy begin to
improve rapidly.

    The economic situation strongly affected social and po-
litical development; mass unemployment throughout the rural
areas brought abundant labor into the cities to be used in industrialization; nationalism rose all over the world and Argentina was threatened with the loss of what was left of its traditional markets, as British nationalists (including investors who
had suffered heavy losses in Argentina) demanded that wool,
meat, hides, etc. be purchased from nations within the British Commonwealth; Argentina salvaged something with the
Roca-Runciman agreements but antagonized the United States
by so doing; industrialization brought new (renewed) demands
by factory workers, eventually to be matched by those of the
rural area; the middle classes were faced with insecurity,
even with loss of identity, crushed between the lower classes
and the oligarchy; inflation, devaluation of the peso, loss of
credit, decline of trade, all took their toll in the 1930s and
most of them remained problems for decades; economists,
statesmen, Argentine leaders still seek to understand why
their nation which for decades before the depression enjoyed
a higher gross national product and greater political stability
than most comparable nations has not been able to equal their
recovery since then; in this sense the depression marked a
break between the late nineteenth and early (pre-1929) twentieth century and the succeeding decades.

    See related entries such as Industrialization, Economic
History, Roca-Runciman Agreement, World Wars I and II; also the works of Henry S. Fern, Argentina (1969) and the Argentine Republic (1973); and Ysabel F. Rennie The Argentine
Republic (1945, 1975).

DERQUI, SANTIAGO (1810-1867). Lawyer; president of Argentine

Confederation (1860-61).

Born and educated in Córdoba; received doctorate in law, 1831; became professor of philosophy and vice rector of university; elected to provincial legislature; helped save General Paz from execution after capture at El Tío and became close associate of latter; as opponent to Rosas edited El Cordobés; forced into exile from Córdoba, first in Santa Fe, then in Uruguay; collaborated with Lavalle and other Rosas foes; sent by Rivera (1840) to negotiate with Pedro Ferré, governor of Corrientes, about fight opposing Rosas; joined Paz as secretary and, briefly, as his minister in Entre Ríos (1842); then alternated exile with return to fight, especially in Corrientes; after Caseros, elected by Córdoba as delegate to Urquiza's Santa Fe constituent congress (1853); elected vice president and then president of congress; one of signers of constitution; during Urquiza's term as president (1854-1860) served as minister of justice, religion, and public instruction, then as minister of interior; succeeded Urquiza as president in 1860; had participated actively in negotiations for reuniting province of Buenos Aires with Confederation; prospects seemed favorable but complications developed for a variety of causes: internal political problems faced by Derqui as well as by Bartolomé Mitre, who became governor of Buenos Aires at that time; personal friction arose between Derqui, who had his own ideas about government, and Urquiza, now governor of Entre Ríos but also commander-in-chief of the armed forces, who was determined that his work in forming the Confederation should not be lost; both opened personal negotiations with Mitre; Derqui's intervention in San Juan and consequent revolt there intensified bad feeling; on July 9, 1860, President Derqui, General Urquiza, and Governor Mitre met in Buenos Aires for a united celebration of Independence Day but the peace this symbolized deteriorated rapidly into open hostilities; on September 17, 1861, Mitre with army of 15,400 men, two-thirds infantry, faced Urquiza with 17,000, largely cavalry, at Pavón; Urquiza's cavalry routed Mitre's cavalry forces, but Mitre's center pushed through that of the Confederation; neither side had yet won, although much of the confederation's artillery had been captured, when Urquiza, who had no heart for the battle anyway, withdrew; Mitre, by default, continuing military action and show of force, negotiations with governors of Mesopotamian provinces, and political skill reunited the nation, becoming its first president in 1862; Derqui, totally without support after Pavón, resigned presidency in November 1861 and went into exile; returned to Corrientes where he died in 1867.

DESCAMISADOS (the shirtless ones). Name first applied in derision to the crowd of workers demonstrating on Perón's behalf (October 17, 1945) and demanding that he be brought back from detention on Martín García Island; following the success of this action both Juan and Eva Perón, their special leader and patroness, made political capital out of using the term affectionately to refer to the newly-organized group of formerly forgotten

workers now forming strong basis of Perón's power; in large
part made up of recent rural migrants to Buenos Aires and,
as such, outside the social and political framework, the descamisados also included other urban and rural workers of the
middle and lower classes who, whatever their economic status
had been (and for the most part, it was low), felt that the
Perón regime had for the first time brought them dignity and
participation in political life as well as a greater measure of
economic security.

DESERT.   Term commonly applied to Patagonian plains (see Conquest of the Desert).

DEVEREUX, JOHN.   Commercial agent.   U.S. merchant, requested
by President Madison to send report of his observations of political, economic situation in Buenos Aires on his trip there in
1816; exceeding his orders, Devereux took active role and
drew up contract for $2,000,000 U.S. loan, at 9%, to be paid
in full ten years after end of war with Spain; loan approved by
Congress of Tucumán and signed by Supreme Director Juan M.
Pueyrredón, who counted on this to finance San Martín's expedition to Peru; contract reached Washington after James
Monroe's inauguration; his acting secretary of state, Richard
Rush, disavowed Devereux's action and informed Pueyrredón
once again of U.S. neutrality policy making such support impossible.

D'HONTE SYSTEM (1963).   Law replacing Saenz Peña elector reform of 1912; combined previous electoral decrees of the
Guido government into a new system of proportional representation.

DIAGUITA.   Name generally applied to agricultural, town-dwelling
Indians living in northwestern Argentina at time of Spanish
conquest; several different groups included, all related to central Andean cultures and varying only slightly from each other
in language and customs; among most important of these were
the Diaguita themselves (in Catamarca and La Rioja), the Calchaquí (in Salta, Tubumán, and Catamarca), and the Pular in
northern Salta; together they occupied the triangle formed by
Córdoba, Mendoza, and Jujuy; although the Diaguita culture,
like its blood, has now become part of that of Argentina and
can no longer be clearly distinguished, Spanish chroniclers and
modern archeologists have contributed to a fairly clear picture
of it in sixteenth century.
        Living on semi-arid plateaus and in fertile mountain
valleys, Diaguita cultivated corn--which they ate either roasted
or ground--squashes, beans and peas, and the Andean cereal
quinoa; supplemented their diet with wild fruits, most important of which was that of the chañar tree (Gourliea decorticans--
similar to mimosa, with fruit tasting like jujube); terraced
their hillside farms and may have used primitive forms of irrigation; seem to have smoked tobacco in pipes; raised llamas,

and possibly vicuñas, for wool from which they made fine, many-colored textiles used in the ponchos and long tunics that they wore; partly to conserve limited water supply and partly for defense, Diaguita lived in densely populated towns with fortified center known as pucará, thatched houses and fort built of stone; Diaguita apparently engaged in frequent, fierce fighting, sometimes between autonomous towns, at other times with several towns united against common enemy; do not seem to have formed larger political organization; used bows and battle axes as weapons; armed forces sometimes included thousands of fighters (with women and children); Spaniards found conquest of these Indians difficult, costly, and lengthy; Diaguita and Calchaquí quickly learned to use horses and firearms against Spaniards and towns in the northwest were apt to be destroyed almost as soon as they had been founded; final occupation only became possible when Spaniards transported defeated Indians hundreds of miles away to mines in Upper Peru and to Buenos Aires in seventeenth century.

In spite of difficulty of conquest, this Tucumán area (as all northwest was known in sixteenth century) was most desirable part of Argentina for settlement because high level of Diaguita civilization made these Indians most valuable for use in encomiendas and in other labor; in addition to agricultural, military, and weaving skills, they worked metals, using copper and bronze for knives and tools, gold and silver for fashioning little bells; they were also famous for their pottery, especially that later known as Belén, made of reddish clay and decorated with geometric designs in black paint (see Indians).

See Smithsonian Institution's Handbook of South American Indians, edited by Julian H. Steward (6 volumes, Washington, D.C., 1946-1950); especially V. II on The Andean Civilizations.

DIAZ, CESAR (1812-1858).   Uruguayan general closely involved in Argentine affairs during Rosas and Confederation periods.

Born in Montevideo; attended military academy in Santiago, Chile, where his family was then living (1824); enlisted in Argentine army (1827); joined General Paz, and then went to interior to aid Lavalle (1829); after revolution of 1833, in which he supported Balcarce against Rosas who won, he returned to Uruguay; for most of the next twenty years he was part of the Uruguayan army and ready to fight Rosas whenever occasion offered; on December 4, 1851, he joined Urquiza's army at the head of the Uruguayan forces incorporated in it; leading these, as chief of the leftwing at Caseros against Rosas, he distinguished himself and was promoted to general; again in Uruguay, he served as minister of war and navy and then on the general staff; in 1856 he was a candidate for the Uruguayan presidency but not elected; two years later, while General Díaz was in Buenos Aires, the Uruguayan Colorado party offered him command of the armed forces, the president having been overthrown; invading Uruguay with at least the tacit approval of the Buenos Aires government, Díaz and his army were defeated by

the blancos and, in violation of the surrender agreement, Díaz
and 51 other leaders were executed; the fact that the blancos
had been aided by Urquiza's Confederation further embittered
relations between Buenos Aires and the providences of the Confederation.

DIAZ COLODRERO, AGUSTIN (1790-1829). Veteran of war for independence and civil wars.

   Born in Corrientes; joined militia accompanying Manuel
Belgrano to Paraguay (1810); fought in siege of Montevideo
(1814-1815); rejoined Belgrano in Army of the North (1816);
supported Bustos in revolt of Arequito (1820) but returned to
Corrientes soon afterward; joined General Paz and was placed
in charge of defense of Córdoba; died as result of wound received in one of Juan Facundo Quiroga's first attacks against
that city.

DIAZ COLODRERO, FELIPE (d. 1835). Priest. Born and died in
Corrientes. Educated in Córdoba; doctorate 1807 in University
of San Carlos; supported May Revolution enthusiastically, along
with most Corrientes ecclesiastics; devoted himself to church
ministry but accepted public responsibilities; brother of Pedro
Alcántara Díaz Colodrero (constituyente of 1853) who inherited
his library.

DIAZ COLODRERO, JUSTO. Conservative representative from
Corrientes; represented the anti-Peronists between 1946 and
1955.

DIAZ COLODRERO, PEDRO (1869-1942). Judge and political leader
of autonomista party in Corrientes province; after having held
several provincial positions, including those of president of supreme court, vice governor, and first magistrate, he was
elected to the national senate in 1941; died there very suddenly
of a heart attack suffered during a senate session.

DIAZ COLODRERO, PEDRO ALCANTARA (1787-1859). Jurisconsult;
public figure in Corrientes, 1820s-1830s; member of Santa Fe
Constituent Congress.

   Born in Corrientes; studied in Asunción (Paraguay);
made his home in San Roque where his family was engaged in
trade; became a judge and was then elected as deputy to provincial legislature; when Pedro Ferré (q. v.) was governor of
Corrientes he appointed Díaz Colodrero as his minister of finance and war; latter became involved in events and negotiations leading to the Federal Pact of 1831 (q.v.); in 1834 he
vigorously defended Corrientes' sovereignty over Misiones at
time of Paraguayan invasion there; as general minister of the
ill-fated governor Berón de Astrada (q.v.) he accompanied him
to battle and barely escaped with his life after the latter's disastrous defeat at Pago Largo; became rector and chancellor of
the university of San Juan Bautista established by Governor
Ferré in 1841; supported General Paz (q.v.) in Corrientes and

contributed to latter's victory at Caaguazú by his effective organization of Corrientes forces; served as judge advocate general in Paz's army; after Rosas' forces won the victory at
Arroyo Grande December 5-6, 1842 Díaz Colodrero fled to
Paraguay; returned soon afterward with the Madariagas (q.v.)
who regained control of the province; after the defeat of Rosas,
he became a prominent member of the Santa Fe constituent
congress that produced the Constitution of 1853; spent the last
few years of his life practicing law in Corrientes, serving as
State Attorney, and briefly in 1855, as interim governor of
the province.

DIAZ DE GUZMAN, RUY (d. 1629).   Military officer; first creole
historian of Río de la Plata.
        Born in or near Asunción around middle of sixteenth
century; parents were conquistador Captain Alonso Riquelme,
nephew of adelantado Alvar Núñez Cabeza de Vaca, and Ursula,
daughter of Domingo Martínez de Irala; after long, distinguished military career fighting Indians and assisting in establishment of towns (present with Hernando de Lerma at Salta's
founding, 1582) throughout the Río de la Plata, Tucumán, and
Paraguay areas, he returned to Asunción where he died while
serving as first alcalde.
        During his campaigning years, Díaz de Guzmán found
time to write a history of his native land, from discovery to
the founding of Santa Fe (1573), narrating events and conserv-
ing early legends, dated June 25, 1612, in La Plata, Charcas
(today Sucre, Bolivia), this work is known among Argentine
historians as "Argentina manuscrita" because several copies
existed; first printed in 1835; other editions followed, among
the best, that of Paul Groussac in 1914.
        Linked with Martín del Barco Centenera (q.v.) as one
of two first historians of Argentina, Díaz de Guzmán holds
distinction of having been first native-born historian and, according to Ricardo Rojas, the founder of Argentine historiography as there is an unbroken line from the Jesuits who used
his manuscript almost immediately to contemporary Argentine
writers in twentieth century.

DIAZ DE SOLIS, JUAN   see   SOLIS, JUAN DIAZ DE

DIAZ MELGAREJO, RUY, Captain (1519-1595).   Conquistador.
        Born in Sevilla of noble family; accompanied second adelan-
tado Alvar Núñez Cabeza de Vaca to Asunción 1540; was one
of few to back Cabeza de Vaca when Irala replaced him; spent
months in hiding, then continued to support Irala's enemies for
years; finally accepting established authority, became most important conquistador of Guayrá area (upper Paraná valley, east
of Asunción), fighting Indians and establishing Ciudad Real
(1556), Villa Rica del Espíritu Santo (1567) along with other
towns; few captains matched his tumultuous career for adventures and achievements; died in Santa Fe.   (See Lafuente Machain and Udaondo (colonial) in Suggested Readings, Appendix III.)

DIAZ VELEZ, EUSTOQUIO (or Eustaquio) (1790-1856). Military officer; hero of war for independence; one of earliest estancieros of Buenos Aires province.

Born in Buenos Aires; fought under Cornelio Saavedra against British invasions, 1806, 1807; took part in events of May Revolution and is said to have received first military commission given by junta; accompanied auxiliary army of Ortiz de Ocampo (1810) to bring Upper Peru into revolutionary movement under Buenos Aires government; after patriot victory at Suipacha, sent by Castelli to execute royalist leaders at Potosí; fought in battles of Huaqui, Tucumán, Salta, Vilcapugio, Ayohuma; in campaigns of the north (1810-1813); during next few years played dominant but changing and controversial role in province of Santa Fe which, determined to be autonomous, had come under influence of José Gervasio Artigas (from Uruguay) and was engaged in continuing, but intermittent, wars against Buenos Aires control; Díaz Vélez sent by latter government to become lieutenant governor of province (1814); in March 1815, Díaz Vélez was defeated and ousted by Eusebio Ereñú, Entre Ríos caudillo, who took possession of Santa Fe for Artigas' League of Free Peoples; Director Alvarez Thomas sent new "Army of Observation" back under General Juan José Viamonte, accompanied by Colonel Díaz Vélez to restore Buenos Aires power in Santa Fe and to block Artigas' advance; Viamonte took over Santa Fe in August 1815 with little opposition but was overthrown seven months later by revolt of Estanislao López, in one of latter's first public actions; after defeat of Viamonte, General Manuel Belgrano, who had arrived to take command of army of observation, sent Díaz Vélez to seek peaceful resolution of conflict; in surprising pact of Santo Tomé, signed April 9, 1816, by Díaz Vélez and caudillos acting for Santa Fe, it was agreed that fighting should stop, Díaz Vélez should replace Belgrano in command of army, and Buenos Aires forces should withdraw; like army revolt at Fontezuelas a year earlier, with which it is often compared, pact of Santo Tomé had immediate repercussions in Buenos Aires; Alvarez Thomas, unable to cope with multiple problems of directorate, forced to resign, replaced temporarily by General Antonio González Balcarce, and the pact made by Díaz Vélez accepted; curiously enough, in the confused situation that followed, Díaz Vélez, in apparent violation of the pact made a few weeks earlier, invaded Santa Fe again but his final defeat there paved way for Estanislao López to become caudillo of Santa Fe; after a brief term in 1820 as interim governor of Buenos Aires, following Juan Ramón Balcarce, Díaz Vélez left public life to devote himself for nearly two decades to creating some of largest estancias in Buenos Aires province, taking advantage whenever possible, of new land laws of emphyteusis, etc.; in 1839 he became involved in unsuccessful revolt in south against Rosas; imprisoned after fiasco of Chascomús, his property confiscated, Díaz Vélez was held incommunicado for several months until U.S. consul persuaded Rosas to permit him to go to Montevideo; returned to Buenos Aires after Rosas' departure (1852); died there in 1856.

DIAZ VELEZ, JOSE MIGUEL (d. 1833).   Patriot, public figure during independence period and 1820s.

Born in Tucumán in last quarter of eighteenth century;
studied at Colegio Real de San Carlos and later earned doctor's degree; when news of May Revolution reached Entre Ríos
he was serving as first Alcalde in Concepción del Uruguay and
was largely responsible for that cabildo becoming the first to
recognize the patriot junta in Buenos Aires; distinguished himself as early leader of revolutionary movement throughout
Entre Ríos; also served in that area as military commandant
1810-1814, appointed by Manuel Belgrano; was used by Buenos
Aires government on various missions; represented Tucumán
in the national congress briefly (1819) before it dissolved; supported Juan Lavalle and became his executive secretary in
charge of governmental affairs (1828) while Lavalle was engaged in military action against Dorrego and his supporters;
interceded unsuccessfully for Dorrego with Lavalle, urging exile rather than execution; served as Lavalle's minister of war
and navy (1829); following Lavalle's defeat, he retired to Paysandú where he died four years later.

DICKMANN, ADOLFO (1882-1938).   Socialist legislator.

Born in Finland (northwestern Russia); as a small child
accompanied his family to Jewish agricultural colony in Entre
Ríos; became naturalized citizen and joined Socialist party;
graduated in dentistry from medical school in Buenos Aires
and established practice in Morón, Buenos Aires province;
elected deputy to the provincial legislature, he gradually
abandoned professional practice to devote himself to public and
political life; served several terms in national congress (1920s
and 1930s), distinguishing himself by offering bills designed to
benefit both urban and rural workers; in later years entered
business world; wrote extensively on nationalism and socialism.

DICKMANN, EMILIO (1905-   ).   Engineer and professor.

Born in Buenos Aires; graduated as engineer from faculty of exact physical and natural sciences there; became member of that faculty and later taught legal engineering in faculty
physical sciences and mathematics at university of La Plata;
represented University of Buenos Aires at second world congress on energy (1930) and thereafter frequently served as
delegate to scientific meetings of this nature; contributed to
various scholarly and engineering journals, as well as to La
Nación and La Vanguardia; in 1938 he published La naciona-
lización de los ferrocarriles; active in public and political life,
Emilio Dickmann was leader of a small group of socialists who
early supported the Perón regime.

DICKMANN, ENRIQUE (1874-1955).   Militant socialist political leader and writer; physician.

Born in northern Russia near Riga; left home as young
teenager and eventually arrived in Argentina in 1890 as part of

group of colonists sent to Colonia Clara in Entre Ríos by the Jewish Colonization Association (q. v.); at age 20 he moved to Buenos Aires to advance his education; in 1904 graduated as physician from medical school there, having earned his own way by working on the colony's farm in the summers; by this time he had already become an Argentine citizen and was working closely with Juan B. Justo in the Socialist movement and party; combined his professional work with public and political activities, serving in Congress (seven terms between 1914 and 1943), as president of Biblioteca Juan B. Justo, and as a leader of Socialist Party, and with a prolific writing career, acting at various times as editor of the socialist journal La Vanguardia and publishing many books on socialist themes; a dynamic and controversial leader, he figured in the Socialist split (before 1928 elections) between personalistas (Yrigoyenistas) and anti-personalistas; in 1938, then deputy from the Federal Capital, he became alarmed at what he considered to be undue influence of propaganda from totalitarian European governments (especially Germany and Italy) and opposed this publicly; Dickmann was among the socialist leaders who tacitly acquiesced in the GOU (q. v.) takeover in 1943, feeling that any government might be preferable to a continuation of President Ramón S. Castillos's regime; in 1950s he was won over to Peronist regime.

One of his most important published works of historical interest is his Recuerdos de un militante socialista (Buenos Aires, 1949).

DICKMANN, MAX (1902-). Writer. Born in Buenos Aires; studied at Colegio Nacional Mariano Moreno; after a brief business career, he turned to writing, becoming a significant interpreter of the Argentine scene and spirit; founded Nosotros in 1926, a literary review for publishing Argentine and foreign writings; contributed to such journals as La Razón, Noticias Gráficas, La Vanguardia, and The Standard, as well as to some foreign journals; published his first book of stories, Europa, in 1930; his novel Madre América, an Argentine epic, won the municipal literary prize in 1935; in Los frutos amargos ("Bitter Fruits"), published in 1941, he explores what it means for both criollos and immigrants to be Argentine in a land that they love but which rewards their hard work with little more than monotony; in Esta generación perdida ("This Lost Generation") he depicts the spiritual crisis of Argentine writers seeking new values in post-World War II Argentina; later works include El dinero no cree en Dios ("Money does not believe in God") (1958) and Los Atrapados ("The Trapped Ones") (1962).

DIRECTORATE or DIRECTORY. Form of patriot government (1814-1820) (see Declaration of Independence) under which Argentina declared and won its independence; following Junta and Triumvirates, it was established by the Assembly of the Year XIII in order to place executive power in the hands of one man, to serve for two years, with a nine-man Council of State to advise

him and representative assemblies or congresses to be called
to perform legislative functions; actually no Supreme Director
served a two-year term; Gervasio Posadas, January 1814-
January 1815; Carlos María de Alvear, January-April, 1815;
José Rondeau appointed to succeed him but too preoccupied
with military duties for the time being so Ignacio Alvarez
Thomas was given interim appointment, serving from April
1815 to April 1816; Antonio González Balcarce took over director's duties briefly until Juan Martín de Pueyrredón, elected by the new Congress of Tucumán in May 1816 could arrive
in Buenos Aires to take over his duties; Pueyrredón successfully launched and supported San Martín's Army of the Andes
until Chilean independence had been rewon, thus securing Argentina's own (except for threatened northern border) and governed the nation firmly for three years; opposition and unsolved
internal problems brought his desire to be relieved from office; his third resignation finally accepted in June 1819; Rondeau reappointed and served until his defeat at Cepeda in February 1820 by the riparian forces under Francisco Ramírez;
cabildo of Buenos Aires took over power briefly; dissolved congress; anarchy resulted.

DISCOVERY   see   SOLIS, JUAN DIAZ DE

DI TELLA, GUIDO   see   TORCUATO DI TELLA

DI TELLA, TORCUATO (1892-1948).   Civil engineer; university professor; industrial magnate; estanciero; patron of arts and public figure.
        Born in town of Capracotta in mountains of Abruzzo,
Italy, May 15, 1892; moved with his family to Buenos Aires,
1905; continued secondary studies while holding part-time jobs
in stores, bank, brokerage firm, etc. in city; began his own
business career in 1910 in partnership to manufacture machine
for bakeries; company mushroomed into gigantic industrial
complex SIAM Di Tella Ltda. (q.v.); while giving SIAM full
direction throughout his life, Torcuato also managed to complete his education with engineering degree from Faculty of
Exact Physical and Natural Sciences, University of Buenos
Aires 1921; to play important public role both nationally and
internationally; positions held include: president of Board of
SIAM until his death; professor of economics and industrial organization of Faculty of Economic Science, University of Buenos Aires, 1944-1948; Argentine delegate to International Conference of Labor of Geneva and Chile, 1939; treasurer of
Board of Industrial Argentine Union (Unión Industrial--old and
well-established manufacturers association) and also secretary
of its Industrial Metallurgical section; president of institute
of Orientation of Argentine Social Museum; director of Popular
Argentine Bank; director of Commercial Argentine-Chilean Society; member of Committee of Help to Italy and Argentine Red
Cross; owner of estancia "Los Nogales" at Navarro near Buenos Aires, an important experimental dairy farm; combined

strong nationalist patriotism for Argentina (of which he became citizen in late 1930s and around which his business centered) and loyalty to his native Italy--returned to fight as Italian officer in World War I; contributed heavily to victims of Mussolini's dictatorship; worked steadily against Fascist propaganda in Argentina during World War II; traveled widely throughout Europe and Russia, the United States, and neighboring South American countries, always alert to contacts, new ideas, or innovations that might be useful to SIAM; always a patron of the arts, he had accumulated very fine art collection; among his published works were Two Themes of Work Legislation (1941) and The Post-War Problem (1943); contributed several articles to Revista de Economía Argentina.

　　Di Tella had married María Robiola in 1928; their elder son, Torcuato Salvador became sociologist at University of Buenos Aires, after study in Columbia University and in England; younger son Guido, with Ph.D. from Massachusetts Institute of Technology, returned to Buenos Aires to assume active role in SIAM, in managing the Navarro estancia, and in setting up Instituto Torcuato Di Tella (q.v.) as continuing memorial to his father's interest in learning and the arts.

　　See Thomas C. Cochran and Rubén E. Reina, Entrepreneurship in Argentine Culture: Torcuato Di Tella and SIAM (Philadelphia, 1962).

DI TELLA, TORCUATO SALVADOR see TORCUATO DI TELLA (his father)

DOBRIZHOFFER (sometimes spelled Dobritzhofer), MARTIN (1718-1791). Jesuit missionary in Chaco region; writer.

　　Born in Austria, began Jesuit training at University of Gratz (1745); received permission to move to America as missionary and to complete his studies at Córdoba; by 1750 was working with Chaco Mocoví Indians north of Santa Fe; after taking his priestly orders in Santa Fe, 1754, assigned for next eight years to missionary work in Paraguay; in 1762 founded one of last colonial Jesuit reducciones at site near west bank of Paraguay river between Pilcomayo and Bermejo rivers (not far from modern city Formosa) among the Abipón Indians; from mission, named Timbó, but also known as San Carlos and Rosario, Dobrizhoffer wrote long descriptive letters to his rector, Antonio Miranda, 1764-65 (published by Guillermo Furlong in number 35 of Boletín de Investigaciones Históricas); hard work, constant problems, attacks from neighboring Indians-- Father Dobrizhoffer organized successful Abipón defense of mission against attack by 600 Toba Indians, August 2, 1765, receiving several wounds himself--broke his health; had been transferred to Guaraní mission of San Joaquín when expulsion order came; departing from Montevideo with 150 colleagues, he reached Vienna in 1769; at suggestion of Queen María Theresa, spent five years (1777-1782) writing his three-volume history of Abipón Indians, published in 1784 (Vienna); English edition appeared in London, 1822 (New ed. Universidad Nacional...Argentina, 1970); died in Vienna (see Formosa; Jesuit Missions).

DODERO, ALBERTO A. (1887-1951).   Shipping Magnate.   Born in
Montevideo, became naturalized Argentine citizen; gained experience on his father's steamship line that represented Mun-
son line between Buenos Aires and New York; at end of World
War I acquired big river fleet of Nicolás Mihanovich line; incorporated it, retaining majority of stock; Dodero fleet dominated river shipping until nationalized by Perón; became interested also in aviation and took part in the C. A. U. S. A. that
linked Buenos Aires and Montevideo by air; his company became closely associated with Perón; died in Carrasco, Uruguay.

DOGMA SOCIALISTA (Socialist Dogma or Creed).   Statement of
principles and purposes drawn up in 1838 by Esteban Echeverría for Asociación de Mayo at its request; designed to serve
as intellectual and political platform for Generation of 1837
then becoming active in anti-Rosas activities, it has had more
lasting influence; growing out of romantic humanism and utopian socialism of 1830s, it expresses faith in cooperation as an
essential of Argentine democracy and progress; insists that
new society must conform to Argentine geographic, social, and
historical realities; first published in Montevideo in 1839; more
recent editions include those by Alberto Palcos, La Plata,
1940; and by Salvador M. Dana Montaño, Buenos Aires, 1948
(see Asociación de Mayo; (José) Esteban Echeverría; Generation of 1837).

DOMENECH, JOSE.   Secretary-General of Confederación General de
Trabajadores who opposed Perón's takeover of labor in 1943,
fearing that it would mean a loss of power and independence of
action for labor; the CGT had been torn internally since 1930
but in 1942 two major groups had emerged, one led by Domenech, largely based on the railroad unions, conservative and
socialist; the other under Francisco Pérez Leirós; Perón dissolved the latter as Communist but hoped to recruit Domenech
and his group; instead, when Perón intervened in his CGT,
Domenech resigned in protest and a new leader was appointed;
eventually the entire organized labor force came under Domingo
A. Mercante (q. v.).

DOMINICANS.   Members of religious order of friars established by
Domingo de Guzmán (St. Dominic) in early thirteenth century.
First Dominican friars entered Argentina from Peru in 1549
with expedition of Juan Núñez de Prado; leader seems to have
been Gaspar de Carvajal who had spent more than a dozen
years in Peru and had, as Gonzalo de Pizarro's chaplain, left
an original account of that conquistador's expedition to Land of
Cinnamon and exploration of Amazonian headwaters; Father
Carvajal returned to Peru four years after arrival, leaving
work of Dominicans among Diaguita Indians in Tucumán under
leadership of Alonso de Trueno; Dominicans established themselves with religious and teaching centers first in north and
west: Santiago del Estero and Mendoza (1563), San Juan (1590),

then moved toward Río de la Plata: Santa Fe (1604), Córdoba
(1604), Buenos Aires around 1609, and La Rioja (1623); in
eighteenth century, they moved into Corrientes; after Jesuit
expulsion in 1767, took over Jesuit house at Tucumán and their
estancia at Lules and undertook conversion of natives of Tierra
del Fuego (after 1768); throughout colonial period Dominicans
furnished large proportion of members of hierarchy in Argentina, many prelates also becoming important public figures;
in 1577 a Dominican, Father Francisco de Victoria, was bishop of Tucumán and brought in other orders, including the first
Jesuits, to help in work with Indians there; Dominicans
clashed with Jesuits in Córdoba after latter had established
university, with right to confer degrees; Dominicans claimed
same right for their school but audiencia finally decided that
Dominicans could not grant doctor's degrees; Church and monastery of Santo Domingo in Buenos Aires are important historically because the figure of Nuestra Señora de la Reconquista
y Defensa de Buenos Aires--special devotion of Santiago de
Liniers and Manuel Belgrano--is venerated there.

DON SEGUNDO SOMBRA see GAUCHO and RICARDO GÜIRALDES;
   also SOMBRA, SEGUNDO RAMIREZ

DORREGO, LUIS (1784-1852). Hacendado. Born in Buenos Aires,
   older brother of Manuel Dorrego; entered Colegio Real de San
   Carlos 1789, later earned degree in law from university in
   Santiago, Chile; returned to devote himself to his rural estates
   in Buenos Aires province; in 1815 joined Juan Manuel de Rosas
   and Juan N. Terrero in establishing "Las Higueritas," near
   Quilmes, the first saladero in Buenos Aires province; although
   he cared little for public life, in the 1820s he accepted the appointment as procurador síndico, and served in the legislature;
   when Rosas became governor as a strong Federalist, the former partners differed politically and Dorrego finally fled to
   Rio de Janeiro but returned to Buenos Aires before his death.

DORREGO, MANUEL (1787-1828). Federalist, democratic leader;
   governor of Buenos Aires province, 1828.
        Military and political figure from Buenos Aires; fought
   in wars of independence under Belgrano in Army of the North
   and later, with rank of colonel (1815), at Montevideo under Alvear; became leader of opposition to Pueyrredón's directorate
   government, fearing the latter's monarchical and centralist
   ideas; exiled by Pueyrredón in 1817 in interests of maintaining
   the peace and continuing support to San Martín's Army of the
   Andes; returning from the United States several years later,
   Dorrego joined Manuel Moreno in leading provincial efforts to
   prevent Rivadavia from federalizing the city of Buenos Aires
   (then both national and provincial capital); elected governor of
   Buenos Aires province, August 12, 1828, after fall of Rivadavia's centralized national government, Dorrego faced many
   problems, most critical being to find a way to end war with
   Brazil; peace agreement signed September 5, 1828, recognizing

Uruguayan independence, seemed unnecessarily close to surrender to the Argentine armies that had been almost consistently victorious on the battlefield; returning to Buenos Aires,
many units revolted and placed themselves under General Juan
Galo Lavalle (q. v.), independence hero, and prominent porteño;
as Lavalle moved on the capital, Governor Dorrego moved out
to join Juan Manuel Rosas and form an army with which to defeat Lavalle; latter entered Buenos Aires and was declared
governor; Dorrego, somewhat against Rosas' advice, met Lavalle in open battle at Navarro November 9, 1828, and was decisively defeated; captured in flight by one of his own officers,
Dorrego was sent to Lavalle's camp; after brief but heated
conferences with his advisors as to what should be done with
Dorrego, Lavalle accepted advice of unitarists who declared
that the federalist movement would end with Dorrego's death
and ordered Dorrego shot at once (December 13, 1828), declaring that history would be the judge of the correctness of
this decision; exactly one year after this execution, Dorrego's
remains were buried with impressive ceremonies and popular
demonstrations of appraisal in Buenos Aires, with the new governor Juan Manuel de Rosas presiding; Dorrego, as a man of
principle and humanitarian impulses, had become a beloved
martyr to the Federalist cause now led by Rosas; Lavalle went
into exile; many historians believe that Dorrego's death was a
tragedy for the new nation that needed his particular talents for
bringing the people together at a painful time.

DRAGHI LUCERO, JUAN (1897-). Historian, folklorist, writer,
professor; chief area of interest Cuyo.
        Born in Luján de Cuyo, Mendoza; early became inter-
ested in fostering bee culture in Mendoza; wrote about it in local periodicals, founded and directed school of scientific api-
culture in Mendoza; taught in Martín Zapata advanced school of
business (1915); turning his interest toward local history and
folklore, he served as secretary-general of first historical congress of Cuyo (1917); became secretary (and then director,
1941), of the Institute of Historical Research at University of
Cuyo; in 1945 he became professor of economic geography in
the Faculty of Economic Sciences, University of Cuyo; directed
the seminar of economic sciences for seven years; frequently
represented the University of Cuyo at conferences in Argentina
and traveled, studied, lectured, and did research in libraries
of Chile and the United States; a prolific writer, he published
works of poetry, drama, newspaper articles, edited academic
journals, etc., but his primary interest lay in history and folklore; among works in the latter fields are annotation of new
editions of Recuerdos históricos sobre la provincia de Cuyo
(1931); El Coronel Manuel José Olascoaga (1935); Cancionero
popular cuyano (1938), awarded a prize by the National Cultural
Commission; Cartas de Jesuitas mendocinos (1940) and other
writing about Jesuits in that area; introduction to new edition
of El eco de los Andes (1943); Integración de la ciudad de
Mendoza a través de su evolución histórica, 1561-1951 (1955).

DRAGO, LUIS MARIA (1859-1921). Jurist; writer; minister of foreign relations; author of Drago Doctrine.
  Born in Buenos Aires; grandson of Bartolomé Mitre;
worked on La Nación, becoming editor in 1881, one year before receiving his doctorate in Law; entered public life in province of Buenos Aires at once; elected to legislature in 1882,
then began two decades of service in the civil and criminal
courts of the province; became deeply interested in sociological and psychological factors and patterns of criminals; appointed foreign minister, 1902, in President Julio A. Roca's
cabinet, he showed unusual juridical abilities that gained for
him a place among world's leading jurists in his formulation of
what became known as Drago's doctrine--a statement of Argentina's position regarding foreign use of force to collect debts
(as in the British-German-Italian blockade of Venezuela)--and
in his conduct at the Second Hague Peace Conference, 1907;
accepted invitation of United States and Great Britain to become
member of the tribunal to arbitrate dispute over North Atlantic
fisheries, 1909; returned to Buenos Aires in 1912 to become
national congressman; invited to take part in Council of League
of Nations (1920) but ill health forced his refusal; received
many honors, including a conferred honorary LL.D. degree
from Columbia University in 1912 and award from Carnegie En-
dowment for International Peace, honoring him as "the highest
exponent of the intellectual culture of South America"; consistently working for a closer, mutually beneficial relationship between Argentina and the United States, he was leader of group
that sent President Woodrow Wilson a message of tribute and
sympathy upon U.S. declaration of war against Germany in
1917; his published works reflect his varied legal interests and
experiences.

DRAGO DOCTRINE. Statement from Argentine government of President Julio A. Roca to that of the United States (Theodore
Roosevelt, President) contained in note prepared by Foreign
Minister Luis M. Drago, December 29, 1902; in many respects
an expansion of earlier (1868) Calvo Doctrine, it was inspired
by the German-British blockade of Venezuela (joined later by
Italy) in attempt to force that Latin American nation to pay
debts owed to citizens of these countries; included the following: after statements repeating well-known facts that capitalists lending money to foreign nations must have assessed the
risks in advance, that a sovereign state is not unilaterally subject to executive and judicial procedure, that, although a nation
is bound to pay its debts, it cannot be forced to do so, declares that use of force in Venezuela threatens European imperialism and territorial occupation in that country, both contrary
to Monroe Doctrine; therefore Argentina would like to see the
United States or some other great nation publicly avow the
principle that public debt cannot occasion armed intervention or
even the actual occupation of American nations by a European
power; although John Hay, U.S. secretary of state, made only
a formal acknowledgment of receipt (and President Roosevelt

issued his own corollary to the Monroe Doctrine), this Argentine statement had been carefully worked out by the oligarchy and represented a change in Argentine policy, in some respects a rapprochement toward the United States in what was, in effect, an economic corollary to the Monroe Doctrine and a strengthening of it; hailed as such by newspapers and popular leaders throughout the United States and Argentina, the matter was dropped as the Venezuelan crisis was solved and neither government desired to push it further at the moment; United States endorsed it in principle at the Hague Conference in 1907 and without qualification in the 1936 Buenos Aires Declaration of Solidarity.

DUARTE, JUAN (d. 1953).   Brother of Eva Duarte de Perón; private secretary of President Juan Domingo Perón; suspected of having enriched himself illegally in government service; found dead, judged a suicide, April 1, 1953, at a time when he was being accused of involvement in serious meat scandal.

DUHAU, LUIS (1885-1963).   Wealthy and politically powerful estanciero of Buenos Aires province; minister of agriculture under President Justo; president of the Sociedad Rural.
            Born in Buenos Aires; graduated in engineering from university there; his training brought him appointment as delegate to irrigation congress held in Chicago, 1912; in 1922 became president of the commission in charge of water supply for Buenos Aires; his own extensive agropecuarian interests brought him a directorship in Banco de la Nación (1927) and the presidency of the Sociedad Rural Argentina (1928), with which he was always closely associated; during the late 1920s and early 1930s, a period of social and economic ferment in Argentina as well as elsewhere, Duhau seemed to represent conservative interests opposed to government regulation of meatpacking and agricultural production and distribution and to prefer to retain traditional economic ties, especially the close relationship with Great Britain; one statement attributed to him has been widely quoted as typical of his views and those of his class: "Hay que comprar a quien nos compra" (we must buy from those who buy from us); elected to the national congress in 1932, Duhau became minister of agriculture in President Agustín P. Justo's cabinet the following year; in this capacity he became responsible for defending the government's position against Lisandro de la Torre's accusations of government collusion with the refusal of the monopoly frigoríficos to submit their records to investigating senate committee, of which de la Torre was a member; in the violent protracted debate in the senate (1935), fighting broke out, one of de la Torre's supporters, Senator Enzo Bordabehere was killed, and Duhau was wounded in the hand; as the government forces were blamed for the outbreak, the entire cabinet, including Duhau, resigned so that a new cabinet could be organized; Duhau thenceforth devoted himself to his estancias in Buenos Aires province, specializing in the raising of shorthorn and Aberdeen Angus cattle

and to writing; he published Elevadores de granos (Grain Elevators); also Política económica internacional; Propósitos; Revaluación de la provincia de Buenos Aires.

DULCE, JOSE (1829-d. shortly after 1891). Governor of Catamarca province, 1888-1891.

Born in Catamarca; devoted his life to public service; his term as governor was progressive and marked the end of an epoch and beginning of a modern one; the Provincial Bank of Catamarca was established (1888) through his initiative; incentives were offered to stimulate agriculture, especially cultivation of cereals and grapes; civil marriage was established in 1889 and in that same year a branch of the Argentino del Norte railroad reached the capital city; on April 12, 1891, the coronation of the historic image of Nuestra Señora del Valle, patroness of the province, had national as well as provincial significance because of the widespread veneration in which she was held.

DURHAMS. Fine breed of shorthorn cattle imported from England; fast growers that fatten quickly; first Durham bull brought from England in 1848 by John Miller for another English estanciero named White; the half-criollo, half-Durham offspring of this bull Tarquin and the Argentine cows became known as tarquinos corrupted to talquinos and applied commonly later to all such cattle; for more than three decades Argentine cattlemen rejected the Durhams for commercial use as having hides too thin for leather and meat too fat for salting; with the introduction of refrigerated ships and the opening of the British market for meat, Durhams (along with other shorthorned breeds) came into great demand to improve the meat quality to suit British taste.

- E -

ECHAGÜE, PASCUAL (1797-1867). Military commander and public official; governor of Entre Ríos 1832-1841; Santa Fe, 1842-1852.

Born in Santa Fe; received a doctorate in theology at Córdoba; began his military-political career as secretary to Estanislao López, governor of Santa Fe, acting as lieutenant governor when López was on campaigns and representing him in treaty negotiations; joined Rosas and López in fight against unitarists led by Juan Lavalle, took part in latter's defeat at Puente de Márquez (1829); following year accompanied army of López to Córdoba to fight Paz who had just defeated Quiroga in battles of Oncativo and La Tablada; Echagüe distinguished himself by his chivalrous treatment of the captured, defeated Paz; 1832 sent as governor to Entre Ríos; gave province nine years of progressive administration; on Rosas' behalf, invaded Corrientes to put down allied revolt developing there and, at Pago Largo 1839, crushed it and executed the leaders, including the governor of Corrientes, Genaro Berón de Astrada (q. v.);

suffered disastrous defeat two years later (November 28, 1841) at Caaguazú from Paz, commanding the Corrientes and allied forces; returned to Santa Fe (leaving way open for his political rival Justo José Urquiza to become governor of Entre Ríos; joined Oribe's forces and became governor of Santa Fe; spent considerable effort in expeditions into the Chaco and pacification of the Indians there; fought on Rosas' side at the battle of Caseros (1852) but then left for a while to evade vengeance from the victors; in 1856, Urquiza brought him back into public service; Echagüe acted as minister of war in Urquiza's government; served as national interventor in Mendoza (1859); represented La Rioja at the constitutional convention of 1860; was interim minister of war and navy for Derqui; and offered his military services in the war against Paraguay, refused because of his age; died in Paraná.

ECHEVERRIA, (JOSE) ESTEBAN (1805-1851). Romantic poet; utopian socialist; intellectual leader of Argentine "Generation of 1837"; founder of Asociación de Mayo; center of opposition to Rosas.

Born in Buenos Aires province, son of Spanish Basque father and porteña mother; completed studies in Latin and philosophy at the university in Buenos Aires; then, after studying briefly in academy of Swiss artist Guth and working in business, went to Europe; spent four years (1825-1829) in Paris, studying and caught up in exciting intellectual and political ferment there--new romanticism in literature, especially poetry, liberal political ideas and events, secret societies formed to accomplish desired goals; uproar over Victor Hugo's latest play; Echeverría read works of Schiller, Goethe, Byron, Lamartine, and socialist ideology of St. Simon, who had just died at time of his arrival; imbibed nationalism of Mazzini's Young Europe and returned to Buenos Aires on fire with dreams of completing the May Revolution--bringing freedom, democracy, and happiness to his country through a government and institutions suited to its traditions and current realities and a spirit expressed through new literary forms.

Within a short time after his return to Argentina, Echeverría's poems--with the novelty of their romantic form and material drawn from Argentine customs and scene--made him famous; he found himself accepted as leader or master of new generation of intellectuals (see Generation of 1837) who were avidly reading about the cultures centered in the Paris from which he had just come; at first their interests were primarily literary and intellectual but soon, because of changing political situation under Rosas and Echeverría's own political ideals, group organized into Asociación de Mayo (q.v.), with formal political and social creed drawn up by Echeverría at its request (see Dogma socialista); when group, accused of conspiracy, came under persecution by Rosas, Echeverría fled in 1840 to Montevideo where he remained for the rest of his life; living in poverty and frequently ill, he continued to write; reorganized Asociación de Mayo, 1846; engaged in polemic with

Rosas' intellectual Pedro de Ángelis following new publication
of Dogma socialista; published in 1846, his manual of moral
instruction to be used in primary schools to teach principles
of May Revolution to Argentine children (Manual de enseñanza
moral para las escuelas primarias); died in Montevideo the
year before the overthrow of Rosas' government。
      Through his writings Echeverría made notable contribu-
tions to Argentine literature and to the development of a national spirit.   Considered the first romantic Argentine poet, he
introduced new form and substance into Argentine poetry with
such poems as Elvira: la novia de la Plata (Elvira: Argentine Bride), 1832; Los consuelos (Consolations), 1834; and
Rhymes or Rimas, including the famous La cautiva, poetic
story of a captive woman, published in 1837; although he first
came to attention with his poetry, some modern critics consider Echeverría's prose writing even more powerful, as demonstrated in his Dogma socialista, his philosophical and political
essays, and his hastily written and unfinished masterpiece
written in late 1830, first published in 1871, El matadero
(English translation by Angel Flores, The Slaughterhouse, New
Haven, Connecticut, (1942); in this draft of a novel, Echeverría
boldly portrays the Rosas regime in realistic terms of an Argentine slaughterhouse--El matadero still valuable for vividly
detailed description of customs and life styles of Rosas era;
Echeverría's complete works (Obras completas), edited by Juan
María Gutiérrez, published in 5 volumes, Buenos Aires, 1870-
1874; many later commentaries and later editions.
      Esteban Echevarría remains almost unrivaled as molder
of Argentine national spirit; every later generation has rediscovered him for itself and found in his writings inspirations
and reinforcement for its own Argentine idealism, nationalism,
and identity.
      See Alfredo L. Palacios, Esteban Echeverría, albacea
del pensamiento del Mayo (Buenos Aires, 1951).

ECO DE LOS ANDES, EL. Literary and political journal edited in
      Mendoza by Juan Gualberto Godoy; 71 issues appeared from
      September 23, 1824, to December 15, 1825; among its con-
      tributors were Francisco Borja Correa, Lisandro Calle, and
      José María Salinas; reprinted in 1943 with introduction by Juan
      Draghi Lucero.

ECONOMIC HISTORY. It is a paradox of Argentine economic history
      that although the name Argentina is derived from the Latin
      word for silver, and Río de la Plata means River of Silver in
      Spanish, and that early attempts to explore and settle the Ar-
      gentine republic grew out of belief that it provided greatest
      promise of easy access to silver mines of South America, in
      fact mining did not become important, and then was not based
      primarily on silver, until the twentieth century; a further dif-
      ficulty in establishing a prosperous stable economic basis grew
      out of fact that little or no labor supply existed; the Indian pat-
      terns of encomienda, mita, repartimiento, etc., used in other

areas of conquest, were possible only in the northwest sections
among the semi-civilized, sedentary Indians and even there only at cost of continued fighting; on the plains and in the coastal area, the Indians could not be caught and kept and had few
useful skills in any case; the colonial economy, then, had to
develop almost wholly from Argentine realities rather than
royal desires and needs, and differed from area to area; in
the northwest the economy was geared to subsistence and to
supplying the needs--in foods, textiles, and animals--of the
mines to the north, in modern Bolivia, and in servicing and
supplying the packtrains carrying the trade down the royal highway from Lima to Buenos Aires, stopping at intermediate
cities; Tucumán and Salta raised the oxen and built the carts
for freighting the goods across the pampas; labor was supplied
by gauchos with livestock, Indians for much of the rest, with
black slaves used extensively in sugar plantations and in the
towns; in the northeast Jesuit missions produced a surplus of
food supplies, especially yerba mate, shipped down-river in
exchange for needed goods; in the west Cuyo raised fruit for
exporting, in dried or preserved forms, to Chile and neighboring Argentine provinces; Buenos Aires and other coastal areas
desperately sought to become major port handling Spanish
trade with its southern American colonies but, after granting
a few concessions in the sixteenth century, royal government
closed Buenos Aires almost totally to legitimate trade, restricting all trade to the Lima route, in order to prevent flow
of silver and other trade from reaching foreigners; undaunted,
Buenos Aires developed flourishing contraband trade (q. v.) on
the pampas; wild cattle and horses provided food, mobility,
and leather for harness, clothing, shelter, and furniture, with
exportable hides that could be exchanged for other needed items;
the subtropical areas of the north as well as the cold, windswept plains of the far south had to wait nearly four centuries
before becoming integrated into the national economy.

Cattle formed the common basis of the area's economy
from the middle of the sixteenth century until forced to yield
priority to cereals toward the close of the nineteenth; together
livestock and grain continue to form important segment of national exports; very profitable, using little labor, all races
shared in finding their subsistence, providing labor, and dividing profits from this trade.

Many changes came in the eighteenth century: the Argentine population had begun to increase more rapidly and its
economy was prospering; Bourbon monarchs in Spain wanted to
increase revenues from the colonies while at same time developing resources of every area; increasing market demands for
hides and tallow brought pampas into greater economic significance; gauchos became important as necessary labor to handle
this lucrative industry; government controls were established to
regulate the trade by laws to prevent destruction of herds, illegal use or sale of hides by requiring branding, by outlawing
sale of unbranded hides, restricting mobility of gauchos by requiring them to show proof of employment, and by moving and

restraining Indians behind frontiers away from free access to
cattle; entrepreneurs in Santa Fe and neighboring areas had
begun massive mule drives (see Arrias) transporting thousands
of young animals across the Andes to be used in plantations
and mines of Peru; establishment of viceroyalty stimulated and
diversified the economy, opened new areas to settlement,
broke some old patterns and established new royal controls;
the establishment of viceregal capital at Buenos Aires, opening
of that port to trade with all Spanish possessions (along with
some concessions to foreign trade) and establishment of the
consulado there, made Buenos Aires very important economic
center but weakened traditional economic patterns of interior
areas; new Spanish monopoly merchants vied with creoles in
attempts to control and limit commerce for their own purposes,
while latter wanted free trade, with Argentine interests taking
priority; following the greater trade opportunities enjoyed during the British invasions, creole merchants like Francisco Escalada and such economists as Manuel Belgrano and Manuel
José de Lavardén expressed their desire for completely free
trade in consulado debates and in written form; these ideas
were summed up and forcefully advanced by Mariano Moreno
in Representación de los hacendados y labradores; economic
interests played important role in May Revolution and during
the early years of independence; with Spanish merchants becoming Argentines or being replaced by French and British
merchants, creoles had full control; meanwhile establishment
of saladeros--meatpacking plants for salting and drying meat
(charqui or jerky) to be sold, for most part, to tropical plantations in Brazil and the Caribbean to feed the slaves--had
boosted value of cattle; Bernardino Rivadavia, as minister in
various early patriot governments and then as president, made
strenuous efforts to improve and diversify the national economy;
believing two basic needs of Argentine economy to be manpower
and capital, he sought these abroad and integrated them into
his foreign policy as in his treaty of amity and commerce with
Great Britain in 1825; immigration and agriculture were encouraged, fine wool-bearing sheep were imported; and a capital loan was secured from Great Britain for construction of
public works; Rivadavia's plans failed, largely because they
were premature in their timing and geared to European ideas
and largely unsuited to Argentine realities of that time.
    During the Rosas period (1829-1852) a measure of pros-
perity returned to nearly all the provinces in spite of civil
wars and caudillo governments; many of the political leaders,
as well as ambitious businessmen were eager to take advantage of new opportunities and by the 1850s each province was
relatively economically independent (see listings of individual
provinces); development varied among the provinces; while interior provinces welcomed the freedom from Buenos Aires control and concentrated on renewing old trade ties with neighboring local provinces and with Chile, the coastal provinces devoted their energies to wresting a large portion of the hide,
jerky, and tallow trade from Buenos Aires monopoly; one

constant grievance, held especially by such provinces as Santa
Fe, Corrientes, and Entre Ríos was Buenos Aires' control of
all customs duties; Rosas' overthrow by Urquiza (both of them
cattlemen and entrepreneurs) paved the way for a healthy national economic development.

During the ten years of separation between Buenos Aires
and the Confederation (1852-1862), both governments pursued
similar economic policies, emphasizing attraction of agricultural colonists and the modernization of transportation and communications systems by use of the technologies already transforming Europe and the United States; united under President
Bartolomé Mitre, with the Buenos Aires customs nationalized,
the republic pushed forward rapidly; agricultural colonies began to flourish on the pampas; sugar plantations were reestablished in Tucumán and linked by railroads to coastal ports;
new ports--Rosario, Bahía Blanca, La Plata--were constructed
or improved; banking procedures were modernized; and both
immigrants and foreign capital began to enter the nation in
satisfying quantities; Indian lands in the Gran Chaco were
opened for subtropical crops and the Indians of the Patagonian
plains and Tierra del Fuego were forced to settle down and
take their places in the national economy as sheepherders,
farmers, or workers in towns, or face the alternatives of exile or death; wool and cereals began to compete with hides and
dried beef as leaders in exports; through efforts of individuals
and the Sociedad Rural the quality of Argentine beef had been
improved and made acceptable to European market after being
processed in new meatpacking plants and transported in refrigerated ships or shipped live to market; as a result of these
and other factors Argentina experienced, during fifty years preceding World War I, one of highest growth rates in the world
for such a prolonged period of time.

Although all Argentine governments had made it a policy
to exert every effort to create and protect foreign confidence
in Argentine financial responsibility, a crisis (known as the
Baring crisis, see Baring Brothers and Company) developed in
1890, bringing with it the downfall of the Juárez Celman government; major efforts by both governments and banking interests in England and Argentina managed to prevent further disaster and under new financing and a revised economic policy,
Argentina entered on a period of unparalleled national prosperity, still based on rural production of agriculture and livestock; the republic profited from World War I but in the 1920s
it began to question the desirability of having almost its entire
economy tied into a world market over which it had no control; rising spirit of nationalism resented foreign control over
public utilities and other vital parts of Argentine national life
and economy; industrialists, workers, economists, and political leaders pushed hard for a more diversified economy oriented toward the national as well as the world market; during
the depression years of the early 1930s, the threat of danger
materialized when Great Britain found it necessary to loosen
its more-than-century-old economic ties with Argentina to

strengthen its support of the various parts of its own empire; crisis was averted by the Roca-Runciman agreement in 1933 and Argentina was well on its way out of the depression in 1939 when World War II broke out in Europe.

Argentina's determination to remain neutral (until 1944) cut that republic off from sharing in the industrial and military development financed by United States for its Latin American allies; at the same time Argentina was almost totally cut off from its normal supply of European imports; the government of Juan Domingo Perón, elected in 1946, determined to use the accumulated funds, due to this imbalance of trade, to nationalize Argentina's economy and to make Argentina economically independent; the first plan called for the buying of the foreign-owned public utilities and railroads, nationalization of the Central Bank (largely controlled by representatives of foreign banks), the creation of a national market and an industry to satisfy it; the Instituto Argentino de Promoción del Intercambio (IAPI) was established to control all foreign trade; labor was given important role in political life and economic gains but was brought into a government-controlled union; despite violent protests from the agropecuarian interests that had been in control for so long and now became greatly reduced both in power and production, Perón's plans seemed to work for a few years, promising a more balanced national economy, but in 1949 troubles began; Perón altered his course but in spite of valiant attempts to bring agriculture and stockraising back into bull production and to attract foreign capital by offering various incentives, economic problems--dramatized by rapid rise in cost of living and wild inflation--continued to mount, contributing to the overthrow of his government in 1955; succeeding governments (1955-1976) have had recourse to various expedients, from austerity programs to those proposed by leading economists of the United States and England, but Argentina's continued growth of inflation baffled solution; on the other hand, inflation has become a universal problem of the modern industrialized nations.

In spite of its frustrations and restlessness, Argentina's Gross National Product (GNP) for 1970 was $25.4 billion, with a per capita income of $1,055, highest in Latin America; considerable progress has been made since World War II in development of natural gas and petroleum industries, mining, chemical and manufacturing industries, and in construction of hydroelectric installations to increase energy supply, in highway systems and nationally owned airlines and other transportation systems; private enterprise continues to dominate (1976) economy but the government owns or controls some industries in fields of natural resources, utilities, transportation, and communications; important trends show decline of importance of Western Europe and increasing significance of United States in Argentina's trade and foreign investment, along with emerging ties with the Eastern European nations and USSR.

See H. S. Ferns, The Argentine Republic (London and

Economic History 264

New York, 1973); Aldo Ferrer, tr. by Marjorie M. Urquidi, The Argentine Economy (University of California Press, Berkeley, 1967); Carlos F. Díaz Alejandro, Essays on the Economic History of the Argentine Republic (Yale University Press, New Haven and London, 1970); Statistical Abstract of Latin America, published annually by Center for Latin American Studies, University of California, Los Angeles; Publications by Inter-American Statistical Institute, Pan American Union, Washington, D.C.; U.N. Economic Commission for Latin America, El desarrollo económico de la Argentina (Mexico, 1959).

EDUCATION. Argentina's free national system of public education, from primary schools through university level, is one of finest in Latin America, with literacy (1970) at 90% and rising; largely an achievement of first three presidents of the Republic, Bartolomé Mitre, Domingo Faustino Sarmiento, and Nicolás Avellaneda, the roots of this system go back to the conquest in the sixteenth century and it has continued to grow and to be modified during the modern period.

According to recent studies, it appears that large numbers of the Argentine conquistadors were at least able to read and write and many of the leaders were well-educated; this interest in education was reflected in an early desire for schools in which to educate their children in the new land; members of religious orders reinforced this interest as they sought to educate Indians and new members for the ecclesiastical hierarchy; Hernandarias, as governor, probably established first schools in Río de la Plata area, with 150 students attending by 1609; Eduardo Madero has been called precursor of public education because of his proposed plan (1612) for public instruction and his efforts to collect the children scattered in the interior into schools where they could be taught; during next century and a half the religious orders, especially Franciscans and Dominicans, handled primary education, although municipal schools, varying greatly in quality, gradually became more common.

Accelerated support from both public officials and private leaders during viceregal and early independence years brought Buenos Aires public education system to a peak during Rivadavia years (1820s), with provinces attempting to create their own systems; civil wars brought decline of education to Buenos Aires (city and province); Rosas turned education back to Catholic Church, even brought back Jesuits in 1836 to improve quality of education, but expelled them in 1840 (after their apparent support of unitarist invasion led by Juan Lavalle and reduced budgets for schools; as Buenos Aires was losing its former distinction in field of education, the situation varied among the provinces and fluctuated within each, depending on the government in power; provincial histories show repeated examples of progressive governors building schools and otherwise promoting public schools, often using the British Lancastrian (q.v.) tutorial system for greater effectivness; Sarmiento's writings and those of other contemporary observers, however, bear vivid testimony to havoc wrought in public school systems by civil wars and caudillo governments; Entre Ríos was one province that continued to advance, surpassing Buenos Aires in the closing decade of Rosas' rule and establishing the famous Colegio de Concepción del Uruguay that was to supply many of the nation's educational leaders in the latter half of nineteenth century.

Argentina's modern educational system really began under Urquiza when the Confederation, despite its scanty revenues, established the first national educational system and began building and support of schools throughout the provinces; meanwhile, in autonomous Buenos Aires, Sarmiento was engaged in same process for that province; President Mitre (1862-1868) combined the two movements and established the national system firmly on the French system: seven years of primary school, five years secondary (colegio giving classical studies), with universities to offer professional or advanced work; French intellectuals and teachers resident in Buenos Aires and other national areas--often political exiles--provided excellent early leadership; President Sarmiento added some changes of his own; with his background as public school pupil and teacher, director of teachers college in Chile, observer of primary school systems in Europe and in the United States, he had selected as his model the public school system of Massachusetts under Horace Mann (with whom as well as with Mrs. Mann who translated his Facundo, Sarmiento had become acquainted), believing this the one best suited to educate Argentina for democracy and civilization; to produce more professional teachers, especially for primary schools, he established the distinguished Normal School at Paraná (Entre Ríos), with others following in selected areas soon afterward; these offered five years of teacher training to graduates of primary schools; believing that women teachers had strong civilizing influence, Sarmiento recruited many from the United States to aid in direction and teaching of normal and primary schools; both Argentine men and women were urged to enter teaching as career; Sarmiento also laid foundations for professional training in other fields: established national military academy (Colegio Militar), Naval Academy, Academy of Exact Sciences, School of Agronomy and Veterinary Sciences; also established first astronomical observatory (at Córdoba), first school for the deaf; began system of school inspection, broadened curriculums to include such practical subjects as physics and physical education, and encouraged opening of the evening schools that have become so important in modern Argentine cultural life; President Avellaneda, who had served as Sarmiento's minister of education, continued the work of his predecessor, expanding the system along the lines already laid down; by 1895 the literacy rate of 22% shown in 1869 census had increased to 46% and by 1914 to 65%, continuing to rise to its present high level above 90%; one serious problem was that posed by discrepancy between educational level in interior rural areas and those in towns, especially cities in coastal area, despite national laws making school attendance compulsory everywhere; by end of nineteenth century, however, both normal schools and colegios had been established throughout the provinces, along with special institutes offering vocational training in such practical subjects as agriculture, animal husbandry, and viticulture.

During the twentieth century development of educational system has been strongly influenced by such inter-related factors as: demands of increasing numbers of immigrants for better education for themselves and their children; surge (and reaction) of intellectual and popular interest in favor of more practical, positive studies such as the exact and social sciences and related technologies instead of traditional classical and humanistic studies; needs of an increasing population and changing economy; and by the changing role of Catholic Church in education. This latter has become a divisive issue during most of the last century; traditionally and constitutionally a Catholic nation, Argentina had naturally incorporated religious teaching into its national educational system, while broadening it by importations and innovations; in 1884, however, the Roca government, controlled by oligarchy that generally accepted secular ideas of contemporary European liberals, passed law forbidding religious instruction in schools during school hours and placing further limitations on it; despite vigorous protests that this violated Church-State agreements of 1853-1860, the law remained in force, with proliferation of public schools, until, under Perón's influence, it was declared unconstitutional and revoked in 1943; as president, Perón turned much of public education over to the Church and religious education was again included; this reversal of the practice of decades aroused criticism against Perón, eventually including even that of the Church when the president insisted that political, as well as religious, doctrines must be taught; in 1955, after Perón's ouster, public schools reverted to previous pattern and secular (and non-Catholic) feeling remained strong enough to protest vigorously against President Frondizi's gesture of goodwill toward the Church by offering to accredit Catholic educational institutions equally with national ones (see Universities for development of institutions of higher learning).

For research consult various publications of the Ministerio de Justicia e Instrucción Pública.

EJERCITO GRANDE (Grand Army). Urquiza's allied army that defeated Rosas at Caseros and overthrew his government; army consisted of about 30,000 men, of whom 24,000 were Argentine (largely from Entre Ríos and Corrientes), 4,000 Brazilian, and 2,000 Uruguayan; nearly all the division chiefs were federalists but some unitarists had also joined, such as artillery Lt. Col. Bartolomé Mitre and Domingo F. Sarmiento (qq. v.) who had an administrative post (see Caseros; Juan Manuel de Rosas; Justo José de Urquiza).

ELCANO, JUAN SEBASTIAN DE (1476-1526). Early explorer of Argentine coast. Spanish navigator who accompanied Magellan on his voyage to the Far East and accomplished the first cir-

cumnavigation of the globe by bringing Magellan's Victoria
back to Spain in 1522; accompanied by F. G. Jofré de Loaysa's
follow-up expedition to the Moluccas (1525) as Chief Pilot and
then briefly, after Loaysa's death in the Pacific, as commander of the expedition until his own death; on both expeditions Elcano sailed along Argentine Atlantic coast and during
the second one, because of bad weather in the Strait of Magellan, was first European to see certain new parts of that area:
January-May 1526.

ELECTORAL LAW OF 1912 see SAENZ PEÑA LAW

ELIO, FRANCISCO JAVIER DE (1767-1822). Governor of Montevi-
     deo 1808-1811. Career Spanish military officer whose action
as governor of Montevideo (and later as appointed, but un-
recognized, viceroy) threatened Buenos Aires hegemony following defeat of British invasions and posed serious problems for
early patriot governments.
     Arriving in Montevideo 1805 as military commander, he
aided Santiago de Liniers in defense of Río de la Plata against
British invasions (1806-1807) and was appointed governor by
Viceroy Liniers (1808); following Napoleonic invasion of Spain
and placing of Joseph Bonaparte on Spanish throne, Elío lost
confidence in Liniers, charged him with suspicious conduct but
refused to come to Buenos Aires to testify against him; allied
himself, instead, with those determined to overthrow Viceroy
Liniers' government, including the revolutionary junta in Montevideo (formed in 1808 and rejecting viceregal control from
Buenos Aires), and the Spaniards led by Martín Alzaga in Buenos Aires; involved were many issues, such as whether Spaniards or creoles were to dominate in new political situations,
Montevideo's jealousy of Buenos Aires' commercial control, increased since royal decision to establish only Río de la Plata
consulado in Buenos Aires (1794), and fact that burden of defending northeastern boundary of viceroyalty fell almost entirely on Banda Oriental (Uruguayan) forces; all these were complicated by personal considerations regarding Liniers and, after 1808, the fact that Viceroy Liniers was French-born and
might be suspected of favoring Joseph Bonaparte; even Liniers'
forthright declaration of loyalty to deposed Ferdinand VII
brought him into conflict with Elío who came to favor revolutionary junta government, under the Sevilla government, for
the entire viceroyalty; Alzaga revolt crushed in 1809; Elío
went back to Spain in April 1810 but returned early in 1811,
having been named viceroy of Río de la Plata by the regency
council to succeed Baltasar Hidalgo de Cisneros, ousted by
the May Revolution; when Buenos Aires junta refused to recognize him, Elío declared war, called in Portuguese aid from
Brazil, and blockaded port of Buenos Aires; with treasury already depleted, the junta imposed forced loans on resident
Spaniards, whom they blamed for this new threat to commerce,
and laid siege to Montevideo with patriot forces; armistice
signed brought withdrawal of Portuguese and end of hostilities;

by 1812 Elío was back in Spain involved in its civil wars until
his death ten years later by execution following court martial.

ELIZALDE, RUFINO DE (1822-1887).   Jurisconsult and statesman.
   Born in Buenos Aires; family of moderate means, father
sergeant-major in army; graduated from Law School at University of Buenos Aires, 1846, largely through his own efforts;
also studied drawing and opened own studio but was drawn into
public life; joined Urquiza in conspiracy to overthrow Rosas
and after 1852, following battle of Caseros, turned all his energies to government affairs; became closely associated with
Bartolomé Mitre, acting as finance minister in Mitre's cabinet
while governor of province of Buenos Aires; belonged to
Mitre's group desiring national federal union under leadership
of Buenos Aires; served in provincial convention of 1860
called to amend constitution to make this possible; during
Mitre's presidency, Elizalde was his foreign minister--often
called first foreign minister of Argentine republic, not only because of prior appointment but also as tribute to his abilities;
with firmness, energy, and considerable wisdom he set about
solving complicated problems left by the Rosas regime, as
well as those inherited from Confederation, and boundary disputes of even longer standing; through his treaties with Spain,
Chile, Bolivia, the formation of the Triple Alliance (Brazil,
Argentina, and Uruguay), as well as his firm insistence that
each American nation was individual and must govern itself in
its own best interests, rather than as a part of a hemispheric
political entity, Elizalde established an Argentine national foreign policy for the first time; hoped to succeed Mitre in presidency as candidate of Nationalists but lost out to Domingo
Faustino Sarmiento; practiced law; involved in several commissions for public works, and in building of Western Railroad;
contributed to Mitre's La Nación; became foreign minister
again in President Avellaneda's cabinet; then retired from public life; died in Buenos Aires.

ELMA   see   EMPRESA LINEAS MARITIMAS ARGENTINAS

EMIGRATION.   Emigration does not seem to have been a major factor in Argentine historical development although statistics are
   not clear; they tend to emphasize those foreign-born European
   or U.S. immigrants who returned to their former homes; little
   attention, until recently, has been paid to Argentine citizens
   who for personal, professional, or political reasons leave the
   country for periods of varying length or permanently; the record is further confused by inclusion of large numbers of European seasonal (see Golondrinas) and Latin American migrant
   workers who leave the country after season's work is over;
   most of the European colonists or immigrants who came to
   Argentina in the century following the 1870s (see Alluvial Era
   and Immigration) expected to return to their native homes after
   making their fortunes but fewer than half of them did; those
   who came to Argentina fleeing from insecurity at home tended

to remain in larger numbers than those primarily seeking economic opportunity; emigration increased sharply in times of political insecurity in Argentina or decrease of economic opportunities available; for example, large emigrations followed political revolt and economic crisis of 1890; outbreak of World War I caused 20,000-30,000 Italian reservists and others to return annually to serve their homeland in trouble; and emigration again increased after the military takeover of government in 1930, with Argentina already feeling the effects of the worldwide depression; since then, immigration has decreased, with a consequent lowering of emigration.

EMPHYTEUSIS (from Latin and Greek words meaning grant of long or permanent use of something immovable). Term applied by Bernardino Rivadavia to his agrarian reform bill for Buenos Aires province, 1822; later, in 1826, it was extended to the entire nation: the new nation had acquired from Spain vast tracts of public lands; Rivadavia sought to nationalize these and place land (except for that already in freehold) in a similar position as that of mineral resources in the colonial period: title remained with the crown but use was assigned to mine operators; as much of the land was pledged as security for foreign loans, and as government needed income from it, and wanted to stimulate the economy, it was proposed that long-term leases be made, with no restriction on size (except later in Santa Fe) with a rental to be determined by a land commission and reassessed every ten years; to encourage agriculture, the annual usage fee was to be twice as much for grazing use as for farming; in Buenos Aires province alone, 6-1/2 million acres granted 1824-1827; grants were usually made for 20 to 40 years and, as they were always negotiable, those held by farmers, cattlemen, immigrants, and other individuals began to be bought by speculators and combined into enormous holdings; Rosas, who disapproved in principle of this emphyteutic form of land tenure and was sympathetic to those estancieros desiring to own their own land, gradually phased the system out by changes in the law, 1833, 1838; lands could be sold; rents were raised while selling prices were lowered; and Rosas periodically called upon landholders to either buy or surrender their holdings; although emphyteusis was not legally abolished until 1857-1867, Rosas had virtually ended it by 1839; it had played a large role in the distribution of Argentina's basic resource--the land--but there is no real evidence that it promoted agriculture; this came later, for other reasons.

EMPRESA LINEAS MARITIMAS ARGENTINAS, LA (ELMA). Union in 1960 of two Argentine overseas state merchant fleets: the Flota Mercante del Estado (State Merchant Fleet) and the Flota Argentina de Navegación de Ultramar (see FANU) Argentina's overseas fleet); both companies had lost cargo and passenger business and were showing increasing deficits; by combining the two it was hoped that these deficits could be reduced and the line eventually be made profitable.

ENCOMIENDA (literally "that which has been entrusted"). Also
known as repartimiento in Río de la Plata. Spanish frontier
institution transferred to America to accomplish a double royal
purpose: to exploit human and natural resources of the New
World as fully as possible while at the same time protecting
the new subjects (Indians) in this world and the next (by converting them to Christianity); in theory and in law, an encomienda consisted of a group of Indians (from the same town or
otherwise related) entrusted to (or granted to) a conquistador;
this encomendero was responsible to protect, administer justice, and to give religious instruction to his Indians; in return,
he received a stipulated annual tribute from each adult male
Indian, payable in gold or silver; as times changed and as
places, needs, Indians, as well as colonists, varied, the encomienda took many forms, particularly in Argentina, where
it rarely (because of the lack of precious metals) conformed to
the original pattern; Domingo Martínez Irala is credited with
having granted the first Río de la Plata encomiendas in Asunción; he viewed it as a means of civilizing and converting the
Indians and preparing them for their place in a free society;
after a time the relationship between Indians and creoles in that
area was so close that encomiendas were neither necessary nor
desired; in Tucumán, on the other hand, Indian labor (largely
encomienda labor) provided the economic basis for the province;
in 1611, royal ordinances brought to La Plata attempted to eliminate the substitution of personal labor for tribute but, with
neither money nor metals readily available, both Indians and
encomenderos preferred the service alternative offered--30 days
labor instead of 5 pesos tribute; even in the pampas a few Indians were available but around Buenos Aires there were so
few that some city-founders were given hunting licenses for the
wild cattle in lieu of Indians; throughout the area encomienda
Indians steadily decreased in numbers through running away to
join wild tribes, disease, wars, forced labor in the weaving
and spinning workshops around Tucumán or the mines in the
high altitudes of Upper Peru to which they were sent.
        The table on page 271, based on census of 1673 taken
from Santillán III:161-2) reveals distribution, average size, and
relative number of encomiendas, etc.
        Attrition becomes more evident in comparison with
86,000 Indians distributed by Francisco de Aguirre in the Santiago del Estero area in the 1550s; even these were down to a
third of their 1673 number by the middle of the eighteenth century; encomiendas were ended by Charles III in the late 18th
century.

ENERGY RESOURCES AND FUELS. Throughout the colonial period,
wood (abundant everywhere except on the pampas), and charcoal made from it, supplied the necessary heat and light for
the sparse population of the scattered towns and rural areas,
with charcoal shipped downriver to supply Buenos Aires and
other pampas settlements; little change took place until the
last half of the nineteenth century when encouragement of

Town or Area	Encomiendas	Indians
Buenos Aires	26	354
Santa Fe	14	95
Corrientes	41	438
Córdoba	16	430
La Rioja	51	1390
San Juan de la Ribera	14	1117
San Salvador de Jujuy	9	1515
Esteco (former town in	9	10
Salta, abandoned after		
earthquake, 1692)		
Salta	20	1984
Santiago del Estero	34	3358
San Miguel de Tucumán	33	2303
Totals	267	12994

immigration increased the population of both rural and urban
areas, and the spread of network of railroads throughout the
republic, use of steamship on the rivers, and beginnings of industry brought new needs for more power and consequently
coal; although it was known that coal existed in Argentina, the
deposits were poor in quality and remote from areas where
they were needed; as a result, Argentina began the practice of
importing all its coal from Europe, most from Britain; World
War I disrupted this flow briefly and expensively but it was
quickly resumed; in the 1930s the world depression and Britain's responsibilities to its own Commonwealth members, that
were competing economically with Argentina, threatened to reduce the amount of coal available for Argentine trade at the
very time that increasing development of Argentine industry
and transport demanded more motive power; still, little effort
was made by either the government or private capital to provide it; World War II, cutting off coal supplies for a longer
period, encouraged the economic nationalists to push hard for
Argentine economic independence in energy sources; in 1943 the
Dirección Nacional de la Energía was created for the purpose
of intensifying search for new coal deposits, as well as other
sources of energy, and exploiting them.
    President Perón made the development of motive power
an important part of his economic program; he nationalized the
natural gas industry, promoted oil production (already under
government control), and established a huge electrical-power
plant in Buenos Aires; natural gas was piped into the cities,
with the pipeline from Comodoro Rivadavia to Buenos Aires being completed in 1949; later administrations continued the same
emphasis on search for new energy resources and power production; government agencies also turned to use of Argentina's
greatest power source, the water from its rivers; most of
these, in the Andes, upper Paraná and Uruguay rivers, and
in Patagonia had been considered too remote from coastal industry to be useful but they were now reconsidered; important

hydroelectric systems were established in the provinces of
Mendoza and Córdoba, at Salto Grande on the Uruguay (through
cooperation with republic of Uruguay) and a huge power complex at Chocón-Cerros Colorados, involving Río Negro and
Neuquén provinces; a 3 1/2 billion dollar dam is projected to
be completed by the mid-1980s by Argentina and Paraguay on
the upper Paraná river at Yacyretá-Apipé to provide additional
electric power; as a result, Argentina has multiplied its production of electric power, as well as other sources of energy;
since the 1940s, moreover, this has increasingly been distributed throughout the entire country instead of being available, for the most part, only in the coastal cities; the planned
(or at least government supported) creation of industrial centers in the provinces, especially those near available power resources, like Mendoza, Tucumán, Córdoba, and others, has
eliminated or greatly reduced the costs and problems of transporting that power (see Mines; Petroleum; and Yacimientos
Petrolíferos Fiscales (YPF).

ENGLISH INVASIONS see BRITISH INVASIONS

ENLIGHTENMENT, THE. The establishment (1776) of the viceroy-
     alty of the United Provinces of the Río de la Plata, with its
     capital at Buenos Aires, and the opening of that port soon af-
     terward to almost unlimited trade, brought with them the intel-
     lectual revolution known commonly as the Enlightenment; based
     largely on the writings of French philosophers and British and
     German political, social, and natural scientists, this called for
     new freedoms and reforms, through use of reason and scien-
     tific studies and methodology, in every phase of personal and
     social life; these ideas, not entirely new to Argentines, now
     flooded the area through books and other writings brought in,
     and through personal contacts with European and U.S. mer-
     chants, military and naval officers, scientists and naturalists,
     royal officials, travelers, and writers who came to Buenos
     Aires; increased prosperity enabled many young Argentines,
     like Manuel Belgrano and Manuel José Lavardén (qq.v.) to go
     to Spain and other European countries to complete their educa-
     tions, more often than not under professors espousing the new
     ideas.
          The church played an important role in the Enlighten-
     ment movement in Argentina; although in theory and to a cer-
     tain extent in practice it rejected and prevented diffusion of
     ideas considered harmful to church doctrine and authority, lead-
     ing members of the hierarchy and religious orders read widely
     and discussed vigorously all the new European ideas, often
     sharing their books and ideas with their more mature Argen-
     tine students; even the Jesuits, expelled in 1767, had played
     important role, controversial as it was; their supporters be-
     lieved that their long-established high standards of excellence
     in scholarship and emphasis on humanistic studies in their
     colegios and at university in Córdoba, had formed the intellec-
     tual basis for the Enlightenment; many royal officials, however,

felt that it was only with expulsion of Jesuits and the breaking
of their doctrinaire, scholastic hold on advanced studies that
the way was finally opened for new secular, rationalistic, scientific, and useful ideas; attempts to broaden curriculum of
university at Córdoba after Jesuit expulsion were made by such
intellectual leaders as the Franciscan José Elías de Carmen
and by Deán Gregorio Funes but the university of Chuquisaca
and the Franciscan monastery in Buenos Aires became much
more important as the new intellectual centers during this period.

Royal officials encouraged intellectual ferment and social and economic reform as long as Crown's interests and
authority were not threatened; Juan José de Vértiz y Salcedo
was especially influential, first as governor, then as second
viceroy (1778-1783); he established the royal Colegio de San
Carlos in Buenos Aires and projected a university there (not
opened until after independence); established a royal tribunal of
physicians (protomedicato) to supervise the practice of medicine as well as the education and accreditation of physicians;
viceroy found local talent available--such churchmen as Dr.
Juan Baltasar Maciel to serve as his advisor and Dr. Carlos
José Montero and Dr. Luis José Chorroarrín to add distinction
to the faculty of the Real Colegio de San Carlos--and among
the foreigners resident in Buenos Aires--for example, Irish Dr.
Michael O'Gorman (q.v.) to head the medical tribunal; Vértiz
also established a theater that enjoyed great popularity despite
some church opposition; among most famous dramas presented
was that about Siripo by Manuel José de Lavardén, a tragedy
based, as was so much of the new literature, on early Argentine history; the viceroy also brought the Jesuit printing press
from Córdoba to Buenos Aires and set it up in the Foundlings
Hospital, giving porteño authors their first opportunity to publish their works locally.

One of most important aspects of Enlightenment in Argentina was use of new ideas in practical areas such as expansion of educational opportunities through opening of more public schools and offering higher salaries and status to attract
better teachers; new kinds of educational institutions were created or projected, many of them by Manuel Belgrano, including his schools of navigation and design (short-lived for lack
of government support) and his proposals for schools of agriculture, commerce, and experimental chemistry (especially for
tanners), all refused by the government; learned academies on
Spanish and European pattern were organized--one of most
famous being the Carolingian academy associated with the university of Chuquisaca; composed of practicing lawyers this
academy offered advanced seminars in laws of the Indies, along
with other new courses that proved very attractive to ambitious
and patriotic young Argentine law students like Mariano Moreno; Río de la Plata also had its own patriotic and Literary
Society.

As reading public rapidly increased in size and interest, newspapers and journals appeared; the first issue of an

Argentine newspaper came out in April 1801, entitled El Telégrafo Mercantil, Rural, Económico e Historiógrafo, edited by
Francisco Cabello y Mesa; primarily designed for intellectuals, El Telégrafo included articles on science, literature, history and items of local or current interest; it was followed in
1802 by the more practical Semanario de Agricultura, Industria y Comercio, edited by (Juan) Hipólito Vieytes and Pedro
Antonio de Cerviño; it divided its attention between new ideas
and proposals for expanding Argentina's economic development
and news items of interest to public leaders and members of
the merchant community; ended publication at time of British
invasions but British publication of Estrella del Sur (Southern
Star), in both English and Spanish, increased Argentine exposure to ideas of greater political and economic freedom;
Manuel Belgrano and Vieytes had begun publication of Correo
de Comercio early in 1810 but were forced to suspend it when
both became involved with the May Revolution and new patriot
movement.

The first public library in Buenos Aires was created in
1810 by the patriot junta, largely as result of Mariano Moreno's influence; under the direction of Moreno's old professor,
Luis José Chorroarín, it exercised considerable influence on
cultural life; several extensive private libraries also contributed to intellectual ferment during this period; that of Father
Maciel was inventoried at more than 1000 volumes, including
many proscribed writings of French philosophers and others
that had come into his possession as head of Inquisition in
Buenos Aires; Bishop Manuel Azamor y Ramírez (who died in
1796) had a long shelf of such writings; both of these priests
were active in cultural life of community; much other evidence
may be found to prove wide circulation in Buenos Aires of
writings of European scholars: Rousseau's Social Contract was
published in 1810 with Spanish translation and introduction by
Mariano Moreno; similar works were read and discussed among
porteño leaders, along with such political documents as the
U.S. Declaration of Independence, Constitution, Washington's
Farewell Address and all the news about the French Revolution; Adam Smith's Wealth of Nations was being cited and discussed in Buenos Aires within twenty years after its publication in 1776; and ideas regarding free trade and diversified
economic development were not only freely discussed but powerfully supported in the consulado by creole merchants and
economists including Manuel Belgrano, Francisco Escalada and,
a little later, by Mariano Moreno.

To many Argentines of all classes, these new ideas of
freedom seemed to come as a natural extension of their own
historical development; political self-determination and self-
rule had been practiced as survival tactics from earliest settlement in such matters as selecting their own governor in
time of emergency or modifying laws unsuited to Argentine
realities; these had even been granted legal status under certain circumstances; the Crown's relaxation of trade regula-
tions--even the totally free trade (laissez faire) urged by creole

(and some Spanish) merchants and economists amounted to little more than legitimization and expansion of traditional trade patterns already established by contraband; and the new literature seemed best when based on Argentine tradition instead of the glorified classical or artificial native scene favored by European writers; the Enlightenment, therefore, helped to prepare both spiritual and legal background for Argentine independence movement.

ENSENADA. Port 25 miles south of Buenos Aires on estuary, with better harbor than Buenos Aires; in early nineteenth century proposed development to make it more effective rival to Montevideo failed; Ensenada remained neglected fortification attracting little attention from either residents or foes for several decades; in 1890s province of Buenos Aires built modern port (completed before that of Buenos Aires) as outlet for new provincial capital of La Plata; quickly attracted trade, but Buenos Aires supremacy remained unchallenged in long run.

ENTRADAS. Name applied to "entrances" or first penetrations into Argentine territory by parties of Spanish conquistadors from Chile or Bolivia in the sixteenth century (see Gran Entrada).

ENTRE RIOS (Province). As its name "Between Rivers" implies, Entre Ríos is entirely surrounded by rivers and it forms part of the so-called Argentine Mesopotamia; bounded on the south and east by the Paraná as it flows into the estuary of the Río de la Plata; on the east by the Uruguay that separates it from the republic of Uruguay; by the Mocoretá on northeast and Guayquiraró that form boundary between Entre Ríos and Corrientes; and by Paraná along entire western boundary.
    Area: 29,400 sq. mi.   Population (1970): 811,691; more than half of it urban.   Population density: 28 per sq. mi.   Capital: Paraná, Population (1960): 107,551; located across the river from city of Santa Fe.
    Other important cities are also riverports, connected by river transportation and often railroads and highways with towns across the Paraná river and to the interior behind them; such cities on the Paraná are La Paz (north of city of Paraná) and, continuing southward, Diamante, Hernandarias, and Ibicuy; going north on the Uruguay River are Gualeguaychú, Concepción del Uruguay, Colón, and Concordia; a highway bridge unites Entre Ríos to Brazil between Paso de los Libres and Uruguayana.
    Climate and Terrain. Softly rolling country with swampy, delta characteristics in south; climate mild and salubrious; rainfall not as abundant as in more tropical Corrientes and Misiones but adequate; rich, alluvial soil found almost everywhere.
    General comments. Stockraising and agriculture predominate, with Entre Ríos traditionally providing 25% of nation's cattle and horses and leading in production of linseed, along with high production of other cereals; although beef in-

dustry still very important, province's economy is becoming
increasingly diversified, with commercial raising of poultry in
southeast and sub-tropical citrus fruit, rice, and such other
crops as commercial fruits and peanuts; limestone deposits
extensively worked for cement.

History. At time of discovery, Entre Ríos was occupied by several different groups of nomadic, fierce Indians,
the Guaraní and Charrúa being the most formidable; settlement began late in the sixteenth century, coming then and
later from three directions: from Santa Fe across the Paraná
river; from the Jesuit missions to the north and east; and
from Buenos Aires in the south; Juan de Garay's grant included Entre Ríos and, after Santa Fe had been founded (1573) he
made some attempts at settlement in Entre Ríos, at Paso
Viejo, north of Hernandarias; followed during next few decades
by ambitious landholders from Santa Fe, some holding grants
from Garay, who carved out large estates for themselves
along the east bank of Paraná; oldest settlement in province La
Bajada (now Paraná) that grew up informally as settlers came
from Santa Fe; in 1607, Hernandarias crossed Entre Ríos in
campaign against Charrúas in the east; Jesuit activity in Entre
Ríos came in second half of seventeenth century with Jesuits
more interested in cattle wealth of area than in attempting to
establish missions; became owners of very wealthy cattle
ranches and haciendas, of which San Miguel was outstanding--
believed that this ranch responsible for continued veneration of
San Miguel Arcángel (archangel Michael) as patron saint of
Entre Ríos; in 1749 Governor José de Andonaegui of Buenos
Aires launched a two-prong expedition against the Charrúas of
Entre Ríos and Uruguay that almost annihilated them and eventually opened the land for settlement from Buenos Aires; Viceroy Juan José de Vértiz (1778-1783), deeply interested in promoting settlement of unoccupied areas and bringing them more
directly under government control, commissioned comandante
Tomás de Rocamora to report on possibilities of establishing
cities in area between Paraná and Uruguay rivers; Rocamora
used term "Entre Ríos" in his report; Vértiz adopted it; divided the area into two sections--west along Paraná, east
along Uruguay river toward which commerce was shifting--;
Rocamora sent to establish cities; first formal city-founding
in Entre Ríos took place in 1783 with San Antonio del Gualeguay Grande (had first cabildo in Entre Ríos), Concepción
del Uruguay (known for half a century as Arroyo de la China),
and San José de Gualeguaychú established in that year; served
as centers into which scattered settlers were brought by church
and government persuasion; other towns planned but project declined as Vértiz was succeeded by the marqués de Loreto,
Rocamora was transferred, and the powerful landlords along
the Paraná exerted pressure against the towns; economic progress, based primarily on cattle already in area, was rapid
and satisfactory; by end of eighteenth century and beginning of
nineteenth hides were shipped in large numbers; factories for
processing both meat and tallow also built; hardwood ñandubay

furnished posts and lumber; abundance of charcoal was produced for local and Buenos Aires markets; limestone of excellent quality was available there in large quantity.

For a combination of reasons, Entre Ríos immediately
espoused the cause of the Buenos Aires May Revolution and
cabildo of Concepción del Uruguay was first in the provinces
to adhere to it; Paraná river towns generously reinforced and
supplied Belgrano's expedition to spread the revolution to Paraguay in 1810; change came in 1811 when Buenos Aires triumvirate government signed armistice with Governor Francisco
Javier de Elío in Montevideo that seemed to sacrifice Entre
Ríos' political and geographical integrity to Buenos Aires' own
political needs; simultaneously Artigas brought his famous
"eastern exodus" across the Uruguay river into Entre Ríos at
Ayuí in protest; Entre Ríos became strongly federalist in political convictions ("anarchists" according to Buenos Aires government); its suspicions continued, even after Director Gervasio A. de Posadas made Entre Ríos a separate province in
1814; Director Juan Martín Pueyrredón encountered grave criticism from Buenos Aires and other provinces (1816-1819) because of his leniency in dealing with the upriver provinces--
hoping to win them back voluntarily or at least to prevent anarchy detrimental to San Martín's fight for independence; Entre
Ríos joined Santa Fe and Corrientes in refusing to send representatives to Congress of Tucumán, supporting that of Artigas
at Paysandú, instead; province continued to follow Artigas until its own Francisco Ramírez, military commander along the
Uruguay river, took over leadership of federalist cause; having
cleared his province of invaders, Ramírez joined forces with
Santa Fe caudillo Estanislao López and defeated Buenos Aires
forces led by Director José Rondeau at Cepeda, February 1,
1820; following the battle, the three provinces of Santa Fe,
Entre Ríos, and Buenos Aires signed the treaty of Pilar, which
has come to be recognized as the first interprovincial treaty in
succession of those that would lead to federal national reorganization in 1862; Artigas immediately attacked Entre Ríos because of this defection from his political leadership, i.e.,
Pilar agreement, but was defeated by Ramírez and fled for
safety into Paraguay where he remained, a virtual prisoner,
for the rest of his life.

Ramírez now became political as well as military leader of the Argentine Mesopotamia and united Entre Ríos, Corrientes, and Misiones into the autonomous República Entrerriana
into which he unsuccessfully tried to bring Paraguay; the purpose of this "republic" was to prepare the provinces politically,
economically, and in every other way to take their places in
an Argentine national federation when that could be formed; to
this end, the Entre Ríos caudillo promoted agriculture, stimulated more stockraising, and gave special attention to the establishment of public primary schools throughout the province;
Ramírez obtained the printing press (first one for Entre Ríos)
that Carrera had brought back from the United States and began printing textbooks as part of his program; unfortunately,

personal and political differences between Ramírez and the
Santa Fe López, complicated by civil wars raging in area,
ended in hostilities during which Ramírez was defeated and
killed; the República Entrerriana was dissolved due to pressure
from Santa Fe and Buenos Aires; Ricardo López Jordán, maternal half-brother of Ramírez, attempted to carry on government of Entre Ríos but was overthrown by conspiracy instigated
by Estanislao López, determined to establish a friendly government in this neighboring province to Santa Fe; after brief period of chaos, Lucio N. Mansilla (q. v.) became governor, followed in 1824 by León Sola (or Solas); during latter's administration Entre Ríos rejected the unitarist constitution adopted by
the national congress, but contributed support to the war
against Brazil; from the outbreak of this war until 1832, Entre
Ríos endured what is known in its provincial history as its own
"anarchy," as approximately 25 governors of various categories
came and went; Estanislao López finally brought order by placing Pascual Echagüe (q. v.) in as governor; Echagüe brought
Entre Ríos a measure of stability and kept it in Rosas' orbit;
new towns were founded and economy prospered; province, however, continued to attract armed forces opposing Rosas or otherwise engaged in civil wars of both Argentina and Uruguay; at
Caaguazú (November 28, 1841) Echagüe, leading Rosas' forces,
was decisively defeated by the Corrientes forces led by General
Paz; in the confused period that followed, however, Justo José
de Urquiza, leading estanciero of Entre Ríos and one of Rosas'
chief commanders, became the new governor of Entre Ríos.
    For next three decades Urquiza (q. v.) dominated life of
Entre Ríos; and because he came to view his province as the
key to satisfactory national political organization, Entre Ríos
did, in fact, play significant national role during this period;
Urquiza's first problem was to restore peace and order; in December 1842 he cleared the province of invaders by defeating
the combined Corrientes and allied forces commanded by Uruguayan Fructuoso Rivera; continued pursuit of latter into Uruguay where Rosas' forces were already besieging Montevideo
and inflicted decisive defeat on Rivera at India Muerta, March
27, 1845, leaving Oribe, Rosas' ally, in control of Uruguayan
government; Urquiza returned to Entre Ríos to find that Madariaga brothers had again aroused Corrientes against Rosas;
with a new alliance with Paraguay and Paraguayan auxiliaries,
and with the unitarist General José María Paz in command,
their forces were posed to invade Entre Ríos to secure aid
against Rosas; movement failed when Urquiza defeated and captured General Juan Madariaga; acting on his own initiative, Urquiza used the latter to bring his brother, Governor Joaquín
Madariaga, to sign the treaty of Alcaraz, by which both Paz was
exiled, peace established, Corrientes was reintegrated into
the Confederation and the Federal Pact of 1831 was reaffirmed;
a secret agreement was included allowing Corrientes to retain
its alliance with its neighbor Paraguay and freeing it from obli-
gation to fight former allies; Rosas reacted violently against
this treaty, partly because it violated the Federal Pact giving

the Buenos Aires government the sole right to conduct foreign
affairs and also because he resented Urquiza's increasing independence of action as shown by this treaty and by latter's offer to serve as mediator to end dissension between Uruguayan
political contenders, with whom Rosas was deeply already involved; Rosas therefore commanded Urquiza, who had for years
been serving as one of his chief military commanders, to
make a new treaty with Madariaga satisfactory to Rosas; when
this proved impossible, Urquiza invaded Corrientes and placed
a Corrientes friend of his, Benjamín Virasoro, in as governor,
november 1847; Governor Urquiza was now able to give internal provincial affairs, especially education, top priority; by
1848, building on bases already established, primary schools
were in operation in every rural district and those in towns
were being improved; free textbooks were printed in Concepción del Uruguay; grants and scholarships (favoring poor boys
and sons of veterans) were made available to bright students
wishing to undertake advanced and professional studies at Buenos Aires or Córdoba; a provincial board of public instruction
was established with Marcos Sastre as supervisor; secondary
schools were established in both Concepción del Uruguay and in
Paraná and Urquiza made some attempts, not always successful, to offer educational opportunities to girls also; in 1851 the
Colegio de Concepción del Uruguay (q. v.) was opened and became the first institution of its kind in Argentina to take full
advantage of the resident European intellectuals and to bring the
latest European ideas to Argentine students; together these educational reforms and innovations gave Entre Ríos the finest educational system in the nation in the 1850s and early 1860s.
      Under Urquiza, the press was also favored; in 1849 the
Federal Entrerriano, edited by Ruperto Pérez, was the only
journal published but it was quickly joined by others now, in
Concepción as well as in other cities; the economy also prospered; Urquiza, himself a successful and ambitious estanciero,
shipping merchant, and entrepreneur, was vitally interested in
developing the economy of his potentially wealthy province; he
created Estancias del Estado (State Ranches), with profits to be
used to provide loans, without interest, for industrial projects;
and for construction of public works; water supply was improved by building of dams and reservoirs; administrative and
financial changes provided better financial framework for colonization projects that were encouraged for agriculture; Governor
Urquiza gave full attention to further stimulation of profits and
production of estancias and saladeros that formed economic
foundation of province; the Anglo-French blockades of Buenos
Aires, 1838-1840, 1846-1848, had brought merchant ships up
both the Paraná and Uruguay rivers and Entre Ríos had enjoyed
taste of trade usually monopolized, to large extent, by Buenos
Aires; resentment when it was cut off by the lifting of the blockade formed important element, along with its traditional insistence on true federalism, in providing the essential provincial
backing needed by Urquiza when he decided, in 1851, to overthrow Rosas and unite the country under a new constitution.

Significantly, his proclamation was read in the main plaza of the provincial capital, Concepción del Uruguay, May 1, 1851, and stated that Entre Ríos was reassuming the powers formerly granted to Rosas and would conduct its own affairs until the provinces could form a union; within a few months Urquiza had put together a coalition of Rosas' Argentine enemies, ended the fighting in Uruguay, formed an alliance with Brazil and defeated Rosas at Caseros (or Monte Caseros) February 3, 1852; the constituent congress produced the constitution of 1853 (q. v.) that was accepted by all the provinces except Buenos Aires; Urquiza became the first president (1854-1860), with Paraná federalized as the provisional capital; during the following eight years--administrations of Urquiza and Santiago Derqui (qq. v.)--Entre Ríos experienced both gains and losses in its provincial life as result of this close involvement in national affairs; economically and socially, it was a period of progress but politically there were sacrifices and strains; in the face of Buenos Aires invasions attempting to prevent the formation of the confederation or to overthrow it, the entire province was federalized, to place its resources at the disposal of the republic; provincial government, under a new constitution, was reestablished in 1860, with Urquiza once more in the governor's seat and Concepción del Uruguay the provincial capital; Entre Ríos fought loyally for the confederation at Cepeda and Pavón but its strong spirit of provincial pride and freedom and its traditional resentment of Buenos Aires and fear of its control began to assert themselves after reunion of provinces into republic under President Bartolomé Mitre and transfer of national capital from Paraná back to Buenos Aires.

Urquiza's prestige and support remained strong enough to survive his withdrawal from battlefield at Pavón and his support of Domingo Faustino Sarmiento, rather than himself, as presidential candidate in 1868; by this time, however, young Ricardo López Jordán (q. v.) had become leader of powerful group of entrerrianos who opposed what they called the "sell-out to Buenos Aires" and labelled themselves the defenders of provincial sovereignty; in 1870 they took over the government by assassinating Urquiza and his two sons and electing López Jordán as governor; when President Sarmiento immediately sent a strong national force against these "rebels," as he considered them, almost the entire province backed López Jordán but he was defeated; for six years (1870-1876) Entre Ríos was torn apart at terrific cost by bloody civil war as the caudillo returned again and again to attempt to renew his control; meanwhile, however, nationalist feeling was growing stronger as the province prospered as part of the republic and by 1876 Entre Ríos had taken its place again in the Argentine Republic and was sharing in the national social, economic, and technological revolution underway.

During next half-century Entre Ríos saw increased establishment of agricultural colonies (begun by Urquiza), with new immigrants arriving to find homes and occupations in the

province; interior settlements were linked to riverports and to
Buenos Aires by network of railroads and (later) highways;
meanwhile, in educational field, the Normal School (q. v.) at
Paraná (q. v.) established by Sarmiento in 1871, offered significant leadership; first railroad was completed in Entre Ríos
in 1872 and its use of standard gauge became universal in
Mesopotamian provinces; in 1880s cereals spread into Entre
Ríos and Paraná, already a city of more than 10,000 in 1869,
replaced Concepción del Uruguay as capital of province in
1883; first British loan had already been placed in 1870s;
Bank of Entre Ríos opened in 1884; series of progressive governors in late nineteenth century encouraged economic growth;
first agricultural cooperative was established in 1900 and five
years later the province held its first agricultural exposition;
important Gualeguaychú frigorífico established in the 1920s and
in 1935 the province displayed its economic progress and initiative by holding an exposition of stockraising, agriculture,
and bellas artes for all the Argentine littoral provinces; government planned development of the Delta area and fostered
agricultural education and socio-economic reforms.

    Immigrant residents made up approximately 25% of its
population and tended to strengthen its democratic and liberal
political tendencies; following 1912, the Radical party had
strong support, frequently electing its candidates including its
first UCR governor, Miguel Laurencena, 1914; in 1933 the
stockraisers of Entre Ríos strongly protested the Roca-Runciman agreement (q. v.), with two brothers Julio and Rodolfo
Irazusto writing book entitled La Argentina y el imperialismo
británico; in 1943 the military government intervened in the
province to provide more favorable government and in 1946 the
province supported Juan Domingo Perón.

    See relevant entries, including those mentioned; also
historical writings of César Blas Pérez Colman on Entre Ríos
are useful; see also Leoncio Gianello, Historia de Entre Ríos
(Paraná, 1951).

EPIDEMICS OF DISEASE.   Full history of epidemics in Argentina
can hardly be written for lack of data; known, however, that
from time of conquest until twentieth century, recurring epidemics of various diseases have significantly affected Argentina's historical development; isolation of early settlements and
lack of large concentrations of sedentary, civilized Indian populations prevented epidemics from having the immediate, disastrous effects in early conquest period experienced in such
areas as Mexico and Peru.

    Most diseases responsible for epidemics were brought
into area from outside; malarial fevers, however, such as
chucho, were indigenous, with Incas better at treating them
than Europeans; malaria, in various forms, was widespread
across the north from Jujuy to Misiones during entire colonial
period; in sixteenth century, most diseases came from Europe;
Martín Barco Centenera, early chronicler, says that illness
suffered by Mendoza's men in Buenos Aires, along with hunger

and other miseries, was probably due to germs brought from plague (smallpox) raging in Spanish ports when they left; most Argentine epidemics of sixteenth century, due to smallpox or forms of typhoid and typhus (apparently endemic in Spanish fleets then), were equally destructive to all classes and ethnic groups; typhoid widespread in expedition of Ortiz de Zárate, 1573; fatal variety of smallpox swept Paraguay, 1589, with repeated attacks 1595-1499, killing almost all--creoles, mestizos, Indians--who caught it; similar epidemics attacked Tucumán, Córdoba, Santiago del Estero, as well as neighboring Bolivia and Chile in 1590.

Seventeenth century opened with colony's request to crown for permission to import more black slaves due to losses of native laborers from smallpox epidemics; in 1607-1608, novices in Jesuit Córdoba seminary stricken by typhus; followed by smallpox epidemic (1610) in Córdoba and entire area from Paraguay to Chile, apparently complicated by tabardillo (typhus), common in that area; originating in San Miguel de Tucumán, attacking Indians at San Ignacio, plague spread to Buenos Aires, claiming 700 victims in 20 days from its 1400 inhabitants; Buenos Aires suffered frequent epidemics from then on, as its importance as a port city increased: smallpox again, 1620-21; typhus twenty years later; troops from interior brought new smallpox to coast in 1660; etc.

In eighteenth century expansion into new territories brought killing epidemics to Indians in remote areas, and new diseases appeared; measles, smallpox, scarlatina swept through Jesuit Guaraní missions, 1738; Falkner found Patagonian Indians in 1742 decimated by recent smallpox epidemics; yellow fever came in from Brazil--often mentioned, but first authenticated death seems to have been in 1798; smallpox and African fevers brought in by slavers; bubonic plague (1720) and cholera began to be noted; in 1778, Viceroy Vértiz ordered Buenos Aires cleaned up from diseased, filthy port city it had become; established protomedicato (medical tribunal) for supervision of public health measures, training and certification of new physicians, etc.; placed distinguished resident Irish physician Dr. Miguel O'Gorman (q. v.) in charge; sanitation in city improved; new treatments for smallpox seemed to help in bad epidemics of 1790s; smallpox continued to be most deadly disease until introduction of Jenner's vaccination, sent over officially by royal government in 1805, but already known and in practice in Buenos Aires from Brazilian sources; cholera had spread from India to England and reached Buenos Aires by early 1800s; in 1818 there were several cases in Buenos Aires, including that of physician Dr. Ventura Salinas who, in 1833, published study of disease; in 1832, there was cholera in Corrientes, and thirty-four years later an epidemic spread from Rosario throughout the country; cholera epidemic in Buenos Aires in 1870 intensified by new infection brought in by Italian ship Barco in 1872; cholera epidemic in north and west believed to have followed railroad workers--1886-1887; in 1889 bubonic plague came downriver from Paraguay.

Yellow fever, usually brought in from Brazil, became
endemic in Buenos Aires in nineteenth century, with serious
epidemics in 1852 and 1859 and real panic in Buenos Aires in
1871 when, in four months, approximately 45,000 out of a population of 67,000 were stricken, with 13,640 of the victims dying, including the famous scientist and physician Francisco
Javier Muñiz (q.v.).
      Improvement of public health measures and medical dis-
coveries, diminished force and frequency of epidemics in
twentieth century. See Carlos Alvarado, Epidemias y estadística, Boletín del Departamento Nacional de Higiene (Buenos
Aires, 1937).

ERAUSQUIN, MANUEL MARIA (1804-?). Spanish priest and educa-
      tor who came to Argentina during the Rosas period; assigned
      to the parish of Gualeguaychú, Entre Ríos; became director of
      Urquiza's newly established Colegio de Estudios Preparatorios
      in Paraná and later was named director of the Colegio Nacion-
      al de Concepción del Uruguay; succeeded there by Alberto
      Larroque in 1854; attempted to introduce instrumental and vo-
      cal music into the new schools.

EREÑU, EUSEBIO   see   JOSE EUSEBIO HEREÑU

ESCALADA, ANTONIO JOSE DE (1753-1821). Merchant; public fig-
      ure and administrator in late viceregal period and early days
      of independence.
      Born in Buenos Aires of Spanish parents with both
      wealth and social prestige; devoted himself to commerce with
      his older brother Francisco; became one of best known citizens
      of Buenos Aires, holding office of regidor (councilman) in Bue-
      nos Aires cabildo, then becoming first alcalde, or mayor; also
      served in commercial tribunal, the consulado; in 1776 he mar-
      ried the niece of Juan José Vértiz y Salcedo and after her
      death in 1784 married Tomasa de la Quintana y Aoiz (1788);
      as chancellor of the royal audiencia Escalada was invited to the
      cabildo abierto of May 1810; showed himself to be one of most
      enthusiastic supporters of May Revolution; in fact his insistence
      on immediate declaration of independence and incorporation of
      provincial representatives into patriot junta government caused
      Cornelio Saavedra, head of government, to banish him for a
      time (in July 1810) to the frontier; back in Buenos Aires, Es-
      calada found his administrative talents in demand for organizing
      financial effort to secure necessary arms for Buenos Aires de-
      fense.
      Meanwhile new element had entered Argentine fight for
      freedom, with arrival of José de San Martín in March of 1812;
      long before this, Don Antonio's home near the cathedral had
      become favorite gathering place for all leaders in public and
      social life of community; San Martín was quickly introduced to
      Escalada and a strong friendship formed between these two
      supporters of independence--a friendship that was strengthened
      by the enlistment of Antonio's two sons, Manuel and Mariano,

in the new regiment of Mounted Grenadiers that San Martín was
recruiting and by the marriage of the Escalada daughter Remedios to the future liberator; by October of 1812, Escalada had
announced that his home would be center for receiving contributions necessary for formation of this new cavalry unit and
his wife, who has won lasting fame for her own patriotic efforts, as well as his sons and daughter, united their own
friends also in efforts to support this important new patriot
venture; after San Martín's war for independence had been
launched at San Lorenzo, and followed with assignments at
Tucumán and Mendoza, Escalada was next called into public
service (1815) as member and then president of junta of observation, in charge of trying to bring the river provinces into
cooperating with Buenos Aires' patriot government; he also
served on commission to protect freedom of the press; and as
member of first provincial junta of Buenos Aires ratified the
famous treaty of Pilar February 24, 1820, providing for peace
between Santa Fe and Buenos Aires for the time being; died in
Buenos Aires while serving as member of provincial legislature; buried in cathedral (see Francisco Antonio de Escalada
for evaluation of Escalada brothers by John Parish Robertson).

ESCALADA, FRANCISCO ANTONIO DE (1749-1835). Merchant; early
exponent of free trade; government official under viceroyalty
and patriot governments.

Born in Buenos Aires; parents Manuel de Escalada y
Bustillo de Zeballos and Luisa Sarría, both Spaniards; older
brother of Antonio José de Escalada; held various offices in
viceroyalty, including that of royal standard bearer, finding his
real niche as member of offices of the consulado (founded
1794); firmly upheld rights of criollo merchants against those
of Spanish representatives of Cádiz monopoly; when latter fought
to get new trade privileges among colonies revoked, Escalada
firmly challenged Spaniards to prefer instead "the interests of
the country which shelters them and which has perhaps produced their whole fortune," promising them a fierce, unending
fight from criollo merchants, if they did not; in a long mem-
orandum notable for its learning, logic, grace, and clarity,
Escalada expressed most of the economic doctrines of free
trade made famous years later by Mariano Moreno in his Representación de los hacendados; attended cabildo abierto of May
22-25 and became veritable champion (called "the paladín") of
May Revolution; while serving as first alcalde in 1815 of cabildo of Buenos Aires, he became briefly head of entire government, following revolt of Fontezuelas and overthrow of Alvear's
government, until new interim director Alvarez Thomas could
return to take over; again in September 1816, pending arrival
of new director, Pueyrredón, Escalada (along with Miguel de
Irigoyen) was in charge; it fell to him to read the formal declaration of independence--signed by members of Congress of
Tucumán July 8, 1816--to the people of Buenos Aires formally
assembled in Plaza de la Victoria, September 13, 1816; again
in cabildo of 1820, presided over junta of provincial repre-

sentatives; died in Buenos Aires in 1835.
John P. and William P. Robertson, in their Letters on
South America (3 v. London, 1843), praised the Escalada
brothers, Francisco and Antonio, very highly; saying that they
enjoyed the greatest respect among their fellow citizens because of their impeccable honor, integrity, personal talents,
and disinterested patriotism; and marvelled at the fact that they
were able to keep this respect through very difficult times, acquiring practically no enemies.

ESCALADA, MANUEL DE (1795-1871). Hero of war of independence
and colorful military officer and public figure thereafter.
Born in Buenos Aires; son of Antonio José de Escalada
and Tomasa de la Quintana y Aoiz; brother-in-law of General
José de San Martín; one of original officers of regiment of
Mounted Grenadiers; fought in its first engagement at San Lorenzo February 3, 1813; sent as captain to take part in siege of
Montevideo, 1813-1814; transferred to Army of North, he
fought in battles of Puesto del Marqués, Vuelta y Media, and,
following defeat of patriot forces at Sipe Sipe, 29 November
1815 covered rear of forces fleeing through ravine of Humahuaca to safety acting under orders of Colonel Juan Ramón Rojas; joined San Martín's Army of Andes in 1816 and took part
in its military actions from then until 1819; having become
colonel and commander of the regiment of Mounted Grenadiers,
Escalada requested retirement to return to Buenos Aires; had
meanwhile become national folk-hero as courier by speed with
which he had brought good news of victory of Chacabuco from
Chile to Buenos Aires--covering 90 leagues (about 270 miles)
over Andes to Mendoza in 48 hours, with another fourteen days
across pampas to Buenos Aires; and his exploit of riding 1000
miles in 12 days in 1818 to bring San Martín's report of victory of Maipú to government in Buenos Aires.
In 1825-26 Manuel de Escalada undertook delicate mission for Rivadavia in which is often called first intervention of
Argentine Republic in provincial affairs--that of preventing Ricardo López Jordán from taking over governorship of Entre
Ríos in conflict with José León Sala; Escalada fought in war
with Brazil; then joined Lavalle in fight against Governor Manuel Dorrego; is said to have been one of general's intransigent
unitarist advisors responsible for Lavalle's decision to execute
the captured governor, in spite of many appeals for clemency
received; served as minister of war for Lavalle, while governor, and again for interim government of General Juan José
Viamonte; retired into voluntary seclusion from public life
throughout entire period of Rosas' rule and was left undis-
turbed.
Following fall of Rosas' government in 1852, Manuel de
Escalada became minister of war under Buenos Aires provincial government of Vicente López--during which he organized
national guard--and minister of war and navy in that of Pastor
Obligado, until 1857; then took command of restless southern
frontier of province, forced Indian chief Cipriano Catriel (the

Elder) to sign treaty agreeing that raids would stop; for political reasons left Buenos Aires; became general under Urquiza; fought against Mitre at Cepeda October 23,1859; after resignation of Governor Valentín Alsina and signing of pact of November 11, 1859, looking to eventual union of Buenos Aires and confederation, General Escalada resigned from military service and withdrew from public life; became totally blind before his death in Buenos Aires in 1871.

ESCALADA, MARIANO DE (1796-1841).   Fighter in war of independence.

Born in Buenos Aires; brother of Manuel de Escalada and Remedios de Escalada de San Martín; became cadet in San Martín's regiment of Mounted Grenadiers and served as its standard bearer; took part in fighting at San Lorenzo, then was transferred to Army of North for several years, where he fought at Puesto del Marqués, Venta y Media, and Sipe Sipe; joined army of the Andes in Mendoza in 1816; accompanied it to Chile in its liberating campaign that included Chacabuco, defeat at Cancha Rayada, and following victory at Maipú; in 1819 requested retirement from military service because of poor health; returned to service in 1830, having spent some of intervening time in Misiones, engaged in cattle roundups, etc.; suspected by Rosas of being unitarist (although Mariano had been partisan of Dorrego and was married to sister of General Angelo Pacheco, rosista military commander), he was placed under house arrest in 1841, dying shortly afterward there.

ESCALADA BUSTILLOS Y ZEBALLOS, MARIANO JOSE DE (1799-1870).   First archbishop of Buenos Aires.

Born in Buenos Aires, educated at Academy of San Carlos, became priest 1822; rose in ecclesiastical hierarchy, becoming bishop of Aulón (in partibus) in 1835; entering political life as deputy in Buenos Aires provincial legislature (1836-1838), his opposition to Rosas brought him into trouble--confined within city limits for remainder of Rosas rule; after Caseros (1852), he was again elected to provincial legislature but refused to serve; in 1855 he became bishop of Buenos Aires and in 1866 was appointed first archbishop there; died in Rome in 1870 where he had gone to attend Vatican Ecumenical Council; following year his remains were returned to Buenos Aires for burial in the Iglesia Regina Martyrum (see Church-State Relations).

ESCALADA DE SAN MARTIN, REMEDIOS DE (1797-1823).   Wife of General José de San Martín; active supporter of independence movement in her own right.

Born in Buenos Aires, daughter of Antonio José de Escalada and Tomasa de la Quintana; brought up in home in which Buenos Aires society and patriots most often met, Remedios became involved in patriotic women's activities at very early age--joining with others in giving her jewels to buy arms for independence forces, pledging to buy equipment for indi-

vidual soldiers, etc.; after arrival of San Martín in Buenos
Aires in March 1812, Remedios' interests were even further
involved, with two of her brothers becoming Mounted Grenadiers and San Martín courting her; married to him November
12, 1812, Remedios remained with her family while San Martín fought battle of San Lorenzo and was assigned to command
of army of the north in Tucumán; after his appointment (1814)
as governor of Cuyo they established their home in Mendoza;
their daughter Mercedes Tomasa de San Martín was born
August 16, 1816; Remedios mobilized women of Mendoza to assist in preparation of Army of the Andes; they made uniforms,
sold personal jewels and belongings to buy military equipment,
and finally, at San Martín's request, just as the army was
preparing to start across the mountains, Remedios and several
of her young friends (most of them teenagers like her) created the famous Banner of the Andes from materials locally
available, formally blessed January 5, 1817, and proudly carried by army twelve days later as it started on its first step
toward liberating the southern part of the continent; her health
failing in 1819 as San Martín was ready to leave on Peruvian
expedition, Remedios returned to Buenos Aires to remain with
her family until war was over; died August 3, 1823, while San
Martín was on his way home from Peru; arriving in Buenos
Aires, he placed marker on her grave in new Recoleta cemetery with inscription "Here lies Remedios de Escalada, wife
and friend of General San Martín."

ESCALANTE, WENCESLAO (1852-1912).   Lawyer; educator and
    writer; cabinet minister; banker.
        Born in Santa Fe; educated in Rosario; graduated with
doctorate in law from University of Buenos Aires, 1873; from
then until retirement from public life held important academic
positions in addition to active political career; 1874-1881
taught philosophy at university; after law school created chair
of philosophy of law (1884) Escalante occupied this position for
twenty-three years, becoming one of first to teach this in Argentina; his Lecciones de filosofía de derecho, first published
in 1884, with revised editions in 1895 and 1901, became required text for Argentine lawyers for two and a half decades;
through this, his lectures and classes, and his continuing polemic with his positivist colleague Rodolfo Rivarola, Escalante
influenced more than a generation of law students with his
idealistic, moral, and ethical concepts, many of them derived
from his study of writings of German philosopher Karl C. F.
Krause (q. v.); Escalante also served as dean of law school
and vice rector of university.
        Meanwhile Escalante held such public positions as depu-
ty in congress (1886-1890); president of Banco Hipotecario
(1890-1893); four months as minister of interior (1893) in cabinet of President Luis Sáenz Peña; minister of finance (1897-
1898) during presidency of José Evaristo Uriburu--distinguished
himself by maintaining firm control during difficult period; director of Banco de la Nación Argentina (1899); minister of

agriculture (1901-1904) under President Julio A. Roca--organized teaching of agronomy and veterinary science at University of Buenos Aires; published works on education, philosophy of law, and biographical sketches Semblanzas de Guillermo Rawson, Domingo Faustino Sarmiento, y Juan Bautista Alberdi; Escalante also well-known as guitarist; died in Buenos Aires.

ESCUELA NAVAL (Naval School). Equivalent to U.S. Naval Academy at Annapolis, Maryland; founded in 1872 by President Domingo Faustino Sarmiento to improve professional training of Argentine naval officers; installed at first in steamship General Brown, with Major Clodomiro Urtubey as first director; after various mishaps and changes, Naval School established its headquarters on land, first in Buenos Aires but now in Puerto Belgrano, but continued emphasis on long training cruises to supplement its academic courses, largely emphasizing the sciences, especially in the early years.

ESCUELA SUPERIOR DE GUERRA. Advanced service school or national war college for higher officers; established in 1900 to raise professional standards of military training, provides a one-year course that officers must pass (since 1915) to gain rank of captain; courses taught by carefully selected superior officers.

ESNAOLA, JUAN PEDRO (1808-1878). Buenos Aires musician who studied abroad, then returned to his native city to become a leading musician of his period; said to have established first music conservatory in Buenos Aires; his arrangement of music for the national anthem has become accepted as the legitimate one.

ESPEJO, GERONIMO (1801-1889). Veteran of Army of the Andes; chronicler of events of San Martín's liberating campaigns in Chile and Peru.
 Born in Mendoza; joined Army of the Andes as cadet in engineering corps (1816); fought at Chacabuco; campaigned in southern Chile; took part in battles of Cancha Rayada and Maipú; embarked with liberation army to Peru; although still very young, he had won San Martín's confidence and was used on several special missions for him; accompanied Rudecindo Alvarado on the second campaign to the Peruvian intermediate ports and sierra; after San Martín's departure from Peru and Bolívar's assumption of command, Espejo returned to Buenos Aires; served as secretary for Martín Rodríguez and then accompanied General Carlos María de Alvear as aide in war against Brazil; fought at Ituzaingó; returned in division commanded by General José María Paz; became involved in the civil wars on unitarist side; served as chief of staff for Lavalle, fought at Puente de Márquez (1829), fought under Paz at battle of Oncativo; was chief of staff for Videla Castillo in Mendoza, fought at Rodeo de Chacón where Quiroga triumphed; was acting as minister of war for the League of the North when Paz was captured; re-

signed his post; shortly afterward, while serving as Lamadrid's chief of staff, he was caught in the defeat of the Ciudadela of Tucumán and fled to Bolivia where he was cordially received by President Andrés Santa Cruz (also a former officer in San Martín's army); after the overthrow of Rosas (1852), Espejo returned to Argentina, held several government posts under the Confederation and then under the national government in Buenos Aires; President Avellaneda promoted him to the rank of general in recognition of his services.

Espejo has been called the most notable chronicler of San Martín's liberating expedition and his writings have been extensively used by historians of the independence and early national period; he started publishing his memoirs in Revista de Buenos Aires and Revista de Paraná; continued with almost a flood of pamphlets, essays, and books covering various phases of military actions in which he had participated, and the leading figures involved; he also wrote an historical biography of Colonel Juan Pascual Pringles (1888).

ESPEJO, JOSE G. Labor leader. In 1939 he entered the syndicate of workers and employees in food industries; held various positions, including that of secretary of press and public relations; became protegé of Eva Perón in 1940s and in 1947 was appointed Perón's secretary-general of the Confederation of Labor (CGT); remained in this position, developing Labor's political and military power and potential until 1953; during this period he performed many services for the Perón government; was a member of the constitutional convention of 1949; served as chairman of board of editors for La Prensa after that newspaper was expropriated and turned over to the CGT for publication; official delegate to various conferences; member of national commission of culture, the Instituto Sanmartiniano, and national economic commission; removed from official responsibilities in 1953, as Perón sought to centralize power in his government.

ESPERANZA, LA. Agricultural colony (origin of city of same name) established in Santa Fe province, a few miles from the capital, on September 8, 1856, by Aarón Castellanos (q.v.) with approximately 1000 French and Swiss farmers whom he had brought over from Europe in 1854, in accordance with the contract signed with the Santa Fe government the previous year; after several years of severe hardship, colony finally began to prosper; as the first of these colonies from which so much was hoped, Esperanza has been called (by Godofredo Daireaux) "the cradle of national colonization and the grandmother of all Argentine colonies" (see Colonization).

ESTANCIA, ESTANCIEROS. A large Argentine landholding, either for ranching or agriculture, and its owners. In period of Argentine conquest, wealth consisted of encomiendas and hunting licenses for wild horses and cattle on pampas; only small plots of land were privately held; in seventeenth century, impover-

ished Spanish government was willing to sell, sometimes to
grant, large tracts of land that came into hands of creole sons
of conquistadors or merchants, desired for purposes of prestige as well as subsistence; some private individuals and church
groups (especially Jesuits and Franciscans) began to use these
lands for large-scale agriculture and raising of large herds of
half-tamed cattle and horses, with gauchos providing little labor needed; during viceroyalty, royal government concerned
about continuing decline in numbers of animals on pampas at
very time that demand for them was increasing due to growth
of population and lucrative trade in hides and tallow, sought to
improve the situation by giving estancieros greater privileges
and responsibilities with regard to animals; estancias became
processing centers for hides and tallow and estancieros began
to acquire wealth; introduction of saladeros (around 1810) making dried beef also important as export, increased wealth and
power of estancieros who rapidly brought most of wild herds
under control; in 1820s, while Argentina and Brazil were at
war, many merchants transferred their capital to investments
in estancias; during Rosas' period, 1829-1852, with an estanciero in power and the country wracked by civil wars, it was
the estancias that formed core of nation and made possible
later establishment of republic; estancia was primarily an economic and social institution--social because of the intricate relationships existing personally and socially between estanciero
and all the people on his land--practically all of same race--
as well as those tying estancieros into an elite group, through
their city residences in Buenos Aires, with common economic
and cultural interests, and usually family ties; during this same
period the estancia also became political institution; estancieros
eventually became the government itself, in guise of oligarchy
acting through constitutional forms; estancias largely responsible for high level reached (late 19th, early 20th centuries) in
economy--based on exchange of Argentine meat, wool cereals,
and other raw products for European manufactured goods and
luxuries--and in cultural development made possible by this
wealth and foreign economic ties: "as wealthy as an Argentine" (meaning estanciero) proverbial in Europe; estancias became elaborate country estates, centers of Argentine aristocratic society, as well as traditional commercial units of production for world market.

Power of estancieros was first seriously threatened in
political sphere, by Radicals (Unión Cívica Radical) with passing of electoral law of 1912 and election of Hipólito Yrigoyen to
presidency 1916; social and economic power greatly diminished
by Perón and his supporters, following first election of President Perón in 1946; estancias blamed for tying Argentine economy to world market over which nation had no control; for preventing or, at least retarding, normal industrialization, even
for national market, and other needed diversification of economy needed; for neglecting entirely too long the rights, needs,
and desires of all other social and economic groups and classes;
and for using whatever means necessary--including fraud and

corruption--to maintain themselves in power as the true leaders
of democratic Argentine republic, making a mockery of the
term; since late 1940s, however, nation has experienced great
difficulty in attaining high level of prosperity produced by estancia economy; causes not clear, but probably related to international economic problems as well as to national changes.

ESTECO, or TALAVERA DE ESTECO. Early town in eastern Salta
   that never really prospered, endured changes of location and
   of name, but continued to survive and be known as Esteco for
   more than 125 years; formally established in 1567 by Diego
   Pacheco, who named it Talavera, the new town was really
   based on a previous settlement named Esteco established there,
   without authorization, by Spanish soldiers who had mutinied
   while accompanying Francisco de Aguirre from Santiago del
   Estero to Charcas for trial; this town represented the Tucumán thrust toward the Chaco and, although badly located,
   ranked fifth in 1600 in terms of Spanish settlers, among the
   seven towns in the area now included in Argentina and Paraguay; in 1609 Governor Rivera moved the town to Madrid de
   las Juntas but the name Esteco persisted; the settlement still
   did not prosper; the climate was too hot and there were no Indians available for labor; when San Miguel de Tucumán replaced it on the route from Santiago del Estero to Charcas,
   Esteco was left almost isolated, with tropical forests encroaching on its outlying areas, with its population decreas-
   ing--by 1671 only about 20 very poor settlers remained, subject always to hostile Indian raids; these increased in violence
   in the 1680s in spite of the presidio and permanent garrison
   established there by Governor Mercado y Villacorta to hold the
   frontier against the Chaco Indians; while the fate of the settlement was still in doubt a terrific earthquake, September 13,
   1692, demolished the fort and the town had to be abandoned at
   last.

ESTRADA, JOSE MANUEL (1842-1894). Intellectual; professor,
   writer, orator. Militantly Catholic spokesman and fighter for
   democracy, freedom, and social justice.
      Born in Buenos Aires; attended San Carlos academy;
   early showed his intellectual brilliance and eloquence as orator; largely self-taught, without college degrees, was appointed
   teacher of political economics in the Colegio Nacional in 1865
   and professor of constitutional law in the law faculty of university in Buenos Aires (1876); considered first teacher of Argentine political science; founded the Asociación Católica, political group, to fight anticlericalism; dismissed in 1884 from university post because of his leadership of Catholic opposition
   to secularization policies of President Julio A. Roca and his
   minister Miguel Juárez Celman, Estrada publicly declared
   that "from the splinters of the professors' chairs destroyed by
   despotism, we will make rostrums from which to teach justice and preach liberty."
      "Freedom" (libertad) was central to his thinking; all

political science, he believed, was contained in idea of liberty;
to him freedom was basically Christian, enriched and invigor-
ated by religion, as the Church and religion were freed in a
Christian society; State omnipotence of any kind was essentially anti-Christian and he wanted religion to have its proper
role in all education; his ideas became widely known, through
his classes, public lectures, and writings.

At the age of 22, he challenged the ideas of the Chilean
intellectual Francisco Bilbao; founded and contributed to many
periodicals, such as Revista Argentina (1868-1872, 1880-1882)
and La Unión in which he and some of his friends defended
their political ideas and religious convictions against those of
Domingo Faustino Sarmiento and Eduardo Wilde (1882); his major scholarly works in fields of history and political science
include Lecciones sobre la historia de la República Argentina,
La política liberal bajo la tiranía de Rosas, Curso de derecho
constitucional, 3 v.; complete works (Obras completas de José
Manuel Estrada), 12 volumes, published in 1899, with introductory biography by J. M. Garro.

See Rodolfo Rivarola, El maestro José Manuel Estrada
(Coni, 1913); Salvador M. Dana Montaño, Las ideas políticas
de José Manuel Estrada (Santa Fe, 1944).

ESTRELLA DEL SUR (The Southern Star).   First periodical in
Montevideo; published weekly May 23 to July 4, 1807 in both
English and Spanish.

When General Samuel Auchmuty occupied Montevideo in
1807, he immediately set up the small printing press that he
had brought with him to print a newspaper in both English and
Spanish that would not only publish the news but could also be
used for propaganda purposes; The Southern Star constantly
stressed theme that Spanish commercial system kept Río de la
Plata unnecessarily impoverished; English edition directed by
M. Bradford, using pseudonym of "Veritas"; Auchmuty secured very able editors and writers for the Spanish edition:
principal writer was the highly respected intellectual Manuel
Aniceto Padilla; born in Cochabamba (Bolivia), he had lived in
Buenos Aires since 1802 as political representative of Francisco de Miranda (Venezuelan precursor of Spanish South American independence) and had also served as British agent before
the British invasions; another collaborator was Francisco Antonio Cabello y Mesa, founder and editor of Buenos Aires' first
newspaper El Telégrafo Mercantil; widely circulated throughout
the Río de la Plata area, The Southern Star posed a real
threat to the Buenos Aires government, but before effective
counter-measures could be adopted, the British withdrew, following Whitelocke's defeat.

ESTRELLA DEL SUR.   Name of first newspaper published (although
briefly) in Patagonian province of Chubut.

ETCHEPAREBORDA, ROBERTO (1923-   ).   Historian and public
figure.

Born in Milan, Italy; studied law and sciences in Buenos Aires; was president of law students' center 1952-53; became active in radical politics and in writing about radical leaders; he contributed to the editing and compilation of the works of Hipólito Yrigoyen (12 v. 1951-54) and annotated that of Leandro N. Alem (8 v. 1954-1955); he has written many books about Argentine history, one of them, Tres revoluciones, winning the National Prize in History; his most recent work on Yrigoyen appeared in 1972; throughout his career he has combined teaching and public service with his writing; he was director of the National Archives (1955-1964) and professor and rector of the Universidad Nacional del Sur (1967-1973); president of the municipal council of Buenos Aires (1958-1962); after that he served briefly as governor (interventor) of the province of Buenos Aires; appointed minister of foreign relations and then as ambassador to India (1962-1964); active in the Unión Cívica Radical, he later became the founder (1972) and president (1974) of the Partido Renovador Federal; in 1974 he became a Fellow at the Woodrow Wilson International Center for Scholars and in 1975 accepted appointment as J. R. Kenan, Jr. Visiting Professor in the history department, University of North Carolina, at Chapel Hill; member of the National Academy of History of Argentina; served as its secretary 1968-1970.

EVA PERON (City). Official name of La Plata, 1952-1955.

EVA PERON (Province). Name by which La Pampa Province (q. v.) was known 1952-1955.

EVA PERON FOUNDATION see MARIA EVA DUARTE DE PERON

EXCHANGE CONTROL COMMISSION. Established by law October 10, 1931, in attempt to give government strength and flexibility in dealing with economic problems of world-wide depression and Great Britain's action in going off gold standard, 1931; law provided that all foreign currency earned by sale of major Argentine exports, such as cereals, wool, meat, linseed oil, had to be delivered to commission (working through Argentine banks and Argentine branches or affiliates of foreign banks) in exchange for Argentine pesos at a slightly lower than current rate; failure to comply meant loss of loading certificates in Argentine ports; constituted, in effect, tax on exports; purpose: to provide Argentine government with foreign currency needed to service foreign bonds, etc.; and to maintain nation's international credit, government's first economic priority since 1857 when province of Buenos Aires had taken over payment of Baring loan of 1824; remainder of foreign currency to be auctioned off; commission used with restraint under conservative governments of Concordancia; more drastically by Perón; in 1930s probably aided industrialization by providing larger national market for goods manufactured in Argentina.

EXPORTS. For approximately two centuries Argentine economy was
based on production for export, with livestock and agriculture
providing 70-95% of its export earnings; principal exports include grain, meat, wool, hides, linseed oil, etc.; its major
trading partners have been Italy, Netherlands, Britain, U.S.,
Brazil, and West Germany, with other Latin American nations,
Soviet Russia, and Japan becoming increasingly important (see
Economic History; and Foreign Trade).

EZCURRA DE ROSAS, ENCARNACION (1795-1838). Wife and political associate of Governor Juan Manuel de Rosas.
      Born in Buenos Aires of Spanish father and French
mother; married Rosas 1813; bore three children, Juan Bautista and Manuelita (one child died in infancy) spent early years
of marriage on Rosas' estancias; after 1829 became active in
politics; during Rosas' campaigning in the south (early 1830s)
he wrote her constantly, along with other partisan friends,
about political plans and together, with Doña Encarnación rapidly assuming control, they prepared way for Rosas' return to
power 1835; Doña Encarnación organized propaganda activities;
widespread espionage systems--lower classes adored her and
brought all gossip to her home; was active in--and some believe most responsible for--organization of Sociedad Popular
Restauradora (known as Mazorca); aroused popular demonstrations for Rosas' return, etc.; after his resumption of power,
on basis of plebiscite giving him great authority, Doña Encarnación lived only three years; her funeral a public, religious
event of great importance dramatized by religious and political
ceremonial and by mourning of the Buenos Aires populace.

- F -

FABRICACIONES MILITARES see GENERAL DIRECTORATE OF
MILITARY MANUFACTURES

FACUNDO. Biography of Juan Facundo Quiroga, caudillo of La
Rioja, by Domingo Faustino Sarmiento; first published in Santiago, Chile, 1845, while Sarmiento was in exile from tyranny
of Rosas period; more than a biography, Sarmiento's classic
work is profound and colorful sociological and geographical
study of the land and historic roots that produced the gaucho
mentality that he considers largely responsible for the anarchy,
civil wars, and resulting tyranny; full title gives theme:
Facundo: o La civilización y la barbarie (translated into English by Mrs. Horace Mann with title: Life in the Argentine
Republic in the Days of the Tyrants; or Civilization and Barbarism; New York, 1868); as spokesman for one strong current
in Argentine culture, Sarmiento extols "civilization" of Western
Europe--with its centralization of government power and its
secular, educated, democratic orientation and cosmopolitan val-
ues--and deplores contrasting "barbarism" of indigenous Creole culture based on experience, intuitive and practical knowl-

edge, and including rural, emotional, and provincial overtones, along with strong loyalties to church, country, and authoritarian caudillos; he considers civil wars to be demonstration of clash between these two very different Argentine cultural currents and life styles; in developing his theme, Sarmiento has not only provided one of finest descriptions of Argentine customs, personalities, and events of Rosas' period but has also produced in Facundo one of nation's greatest romantic literary works, as well as one of earliest and best examples of Argentine gaucho literature (see Gaucho Literature; also Sarmiento).

See Suggested Readings, Appendix III for various Spanish and English editions of Facundo to 1970.

FAENZA. City in northern Italy where many of the Argentine Jesuits (both native and foreign-born) found refuge after their expulsion (1767) and spent their time studying and often writing valuable chronicles and descriptions of the Argentina that they had known, loved, and worked in.

FALCON, RAMON LORENZO (1855-1909). Career military officer; chief of police, Federal Capital 1906-1909; his assassination critical event in Argentine labor history.

Born in Buenos Aires; graduated from military academy in 1873 and named aide of President Sarmiento; served in various military capacities in events dealing with conquest of the desert, internal disorders, political uprisings; in 1906, with rank of colonel, became chief of police in Buenos Aires--Federal Capital; instituted many reforms, upgrading security operations; established training academy; raised morale by placing police in uniforms and giving them increased prestige; acted firmly against incidents growing out of labor unrest, often under immigrant labor leaders; on Sunday, November 14, 1909, returning with his secretary, Alberto Lartigau, from the funeral of Antonio Ballvé, director of the national penitentiary, Falcón's carriage was struck by bomb thrown by anarchist Simón Radowisky; both men died of wounds; tragic death of Falcón was mourned throughout nation and Congress passed law of social defense, giving president right to deport troublesome foreign agitators in the future.

FALKLAND ISLANDS (Las Malvinas). Group of islands in south Atlantic Ocean governed as British colony since 1833 but historically always claimed to be part of Argentina; British claims based largely on discovery and first occupation; Argentina disputes British discovery and claims to have inherited Spain's title to islands, with its sovereignty recognized internationally before first settlement was made.

Las Malvinas consist of two large islands: Soledad (East Falkland) separated from Malvina del Oeste (West Falkland) by San Carlos Channel, and about 200 tiny islets, with total area slightly more than 4600 square miles; they lie about 300 miles off the Patagonian coast and about 250 miles from entrance to Strait of Magellan; treeless, rocky areas, swept by strong west and southwest winds, the geography and climate resemble those of Patagonian provinces of Chubut and Santa Cruz, with which the islands have often been bound; moderate rainfall, temperature rarely over 70° F., and long winters produce grasses and vegetables like those in Chubut and Santa Cruz; islands given over almost entirely to British commercial sheep ranches with absentee landlords; scant population made up of about 2200 sheepmen and government employees; more than half of population lives in Stanley, British capital for islands and "Falkland dependencies" including British Antarctic claims; constitute financial asset with profits high and concentrated, expenses low, with value of exports annually averaging twice that of imports; hopes of finding mineral deposits or petroleum not yet fulfilled; labor shortage a problem as young men tend to leave.

History. British claim that Falklands were first sighted by English navigators: by John Davis in 1592 and by Richard Hawkins in 1594; Spanish and Argentine historians dispute these sightings and call attention to fact that unidentified--or identified by various names--islands in south Atlantic appear on many sixteenth-century Spanish maps, tending to prove that these may be islands casually mentioned by various early Spanish navigators from the time of Magellan on; first authenticated discovery made by Dutch merchant ship in January 1600; islands name Sebal or Sebaldinas in honor of ship's captain Sebal de Weert; French merchant ships from St. Malo also came by and left their name in the Spanish Malvinas; in 1690 English naval captain landed on islands and named them after Lord Falkland, treasurer of navy; first settlements on uninhabited islands came in latter half of eighteenth century, resulting from combination of factors: expanding whaling industries; new interest in natural sciences (British Admiral Anson projected scientific expedition to Falklands in 1749, but gave it up when Spain protested); international rivalries that made islands valuable as strategic base for naval stations, as well as for expansion into southern South America and Pacific coasts and islands. In 1764 the French, desiring a base for whale-fishing, established settlement at Port Louis in East Falkland, under Louis Antoine de Bougainville; in 1765 Commodore John Byron took formal possession of west island for England and founded Port Egmont; Spain's immediate protests at these violations of its sovereignty brought French cession of its claims to Spain and west island placed under Spanish governor subject to government of Buenos Aires; Governor Francisco de Paula Santander sent forces from Buenos Aires to expel British; negotiations between Spain and British allowed British garrison to return briefly in 1771 in face-saving move, with questions of sovereignty deferred; after 1774 Spanish garrison occupied Soledad (East Falkland) for remainder of viceregal period as part of Spain's policy to defend Patagonian coast and Strait of Magellan from foreign attack; also wanted to preserve fishing and whaling resources of island area for newly-chartered Spanish maritime company; in the 1820s, with independence won, Buenos

Aires government took over Malvinas as part of inheritance
from Spain; governor appointed in 1823 and grants made to individuals for settlement, land, cattle, and special fishing
rights; among those receiving such grants was Luis Vernet,
French-born, cosmopolitan adventurer; in 1828 he received new
extensive rights in Soledad and following year was appointed
military and political governor of Las Malvinas by Buenos
Aires governor Juan A. Lavalle; Vernet bluntly warned all
whaling and sealing captains that he would not tolerate illegal
fishing in Argentine waters (or infringements on his own monopoly); in August 1831 he seized three U.S. sealing vessels for
fishing in Argentine waters without a license, beginning controversy between Argentina and U.S. that lasted more than fifty
years; inflamed Argentine public opinion, inept, inexperienced
U.S. representation in Buenos Aires had aroused considerable
feeling in Buenos Aires against U.S. when U.S.S. Lexington
arrived in Buenos Aires, commanded by young, aggressive Silas Duncan; when Argentine government refused to yield to his
ultimatum, he raided the islands (December 1831-February
1832), looted them, scattered or removed most settlers, and
returned to Montevideo with his prisoners; U.S. public opinion
confused, but that of Argentina incensed at this flagrant violation of its sovereignty; diplomatic relations between U.S. and
Argentina broken; meanwhile, England, which had been considering for some time a new occupation of the Falklands now sent
an expedition to do so (late in 1832); Clio of the Royal Navy
arrived in the islands at same time that captain of Argentine
Sarandí was reestablishing Argentine authority at Puerto Luis;
British forced Sarandí to leave and Argentine garrison to surrender January 2, 1833, and took full possession of islands.
    Since then Argentina has consistently protested British
violation of its rights in Las Malvinas--even Rosas' tentative
suggestion that the Malvinas might be exchanged for cancella-
tion of the old Baring loan constituted statement of Argentine
ownership; England rejected Rosas' offer, as well as all Argentine claims; in following century, however, two nations became
bound together very closely by economic ties and other relationships; by mutual consent, Falkland controversy was not allowed
to spoil these; meanwhile British sheepfarmers moved in and
England thought briefly, toward close of century, of establishing naval base there but settled for coaling station instead; opening of Panama Canal 1914 decreased strategic and commercial value of islands to British empire although in 1914, Battle
of Falkland Islands, and in 1939 that of River Plata were won
by British naval squadrons based there; whaling declined; in
twentieth century international interest in Antarctica increased;
with Britain heavily involved; meanwhile Argentina and United
States resumed diplomatic relations in 1844, with Argentina re-
opening (1884) claims for indemnity for the Lexington raid; after
inter-American organization began to operate, Argentina used
almost every meeting to try to get hemispheric declaration recognizing Argentine sovereignty over Las Malvinas.
    By 1940s, it had become almost an obsession with all

Argentines to end this vestige of colonialism and in 1948 Perón government created the Antarctic and Malvinas Division under political subsecretary of Foreign Relations and Religion
(Culto) to have jurisdiction over Malvinas, Georgian Islands,
and other Argentine claims to Antarctica; later (1957) incorporated them into national territory along with Tierra del Fuego
and Argentine Antártida; in 1959 Argentina and eleven interested
nations signed treaty to suspend all territorial disputes and
claims in that area for thirty years; Falkland Islands Dependencies included but not Las Malvinas themselves; Argentine
government has continued--with universal Argentine support--
to press for repatriation of the Malvinas through action by
United Nations or Organization of American States; in 1966,
during presidency of Juan Carlos Onganía, 16 armed men and
one woman hijacked a plane, forced it to Falklands to proclaim
Argentine sovereignty there and to embroil Argentine government in trouble with Great Britain for nationalist reasons; effort failed but met with surprising approval by many responsible political leaders.

Argentina wants Malvinas because it firmly believes
that they have always been part of nation, but also as a base
for developing new fishing industries; possible exploration for
petroleum; for nationalist reasons; Great Britain would suffer
no great loss in giving islands up, nor would its inhabitants,
who have much in common with British sheepherders in neighboring Chubut province; its cession would help to dispel myth
of British imperialism in nationalistic Argentina; on the other
hand, Great Britain does not recognize Argentina's claims as
valid, does not welcome being pressured; and stands firmly on
principle of self-determination; in early 1970s Falkland Island-
ers showed no enthusiasm for becoming Argentine.

See Julius Goebel, The Struggle for the Falkland Islands
(Yale University Press, New Haven, Connecticut, 1927); Universidad de La Plata, Soberanía argentina en el archipiélago
de las Malvinas y en la Antártida (La Plata, 1951); and Harold
F. Peterson (Suggested Readings, Appendix III) for U.S. involvement in Falkland Islands controversy; and Cawkell et al.
for British account. (Suggested Readings, Appendix III.)

FALKNER, THOMAS (sometimes spelled Faulkner or Falconer)
(1702-1784). Jesuit missionary, physician, explorer, author
of first description of Patagonian interior.

Born in Manchester, England; educated in medicine under Richard Mead in London; apparently offered a grant by
Royal Society to study medicinal plants and waters in Río de
la Plata area, but took commission as physician and surgeon
with South Sea Company carrying African slaves to Buenos
Aires for sale under asiento; arrived in Buenos Aires in 1730;
gravely ill, he was nursed back to health by Jesuits; converted
to Catholicism and entered Jesuit order in 1732; studied in
Córdoba, ordained as priest in 1740; spent more than thirty
years ministering as spiritual counselor and physician to persons of all classes, including Patagonian nomadic Indians,
creole estancieros, merchants, Spanish royal officials, and

others; especially in demand among members of rapidly growing English colony in Córdoba.

   Assigned to open missions in Patagonia, he and Father
José Cardiel with aid of friendly caciques established the mission of Nuestra Señora del Pilar (1746) in southern Buenos
Aires province near present Mar del Plata, the first mission
in that area (later abandoned); Falkner spent most of next fifteen years traversing the Patagonian "Desert" from north to
south and east to west, making scientific observations and
notes while performing his religious responsibilities and functions; returned to Córdoba, 1761, where he was working when
expelled with other Jesuits (1767); by 1771 he was back in
England, warmly welcomed by English Jesuits and men of science eager to learn about Patagonia.

   In 1774 he published A Description of Patagonia and the
Adjoining Parts of South America in London (see Suggested
Readings, Appendix III) based on his own travels and studies
as well as countless interviews with Indians, captured Spaniards, and others encountered in that area; written not only to
provide scientific and geographic knowledge of an unknown land
but also to inform British readers of economic opportunities
there; Spanish version, with introduction and notes by Samuel
Lafone Quevedo, published in 1911 by University of La Plata.
See Guillermo Furlong's La personalidad y la obra de
Tomás Falkner, published by Instituto de Investigaciones Históricas (Buenos Aires, 1929).

FALU, EDUARDO YAMIL (1923-   ).   Folkloric guitarist and composer.   During the 1950s and 1960s there was a rebirth of Argentine interest in its own folklore; Falú became nationally
   and internationally known as one of the leading exponents and
   interpreters of folkloric music; his personal style of performance and his own compositions (more than sixty works for guitar and voice) brought him great popularity in his own country
   and then prestige in Europe and in the United States (1970) as
   a musician of great artistry and as an interpreter of the Argentine spirit through his chosen medium.

FAMA (Flota Aérea Mercante Argentina).   Air arm of Argentina's
   state merchant fleet (see Flota Mercante del Estado).
   Created in December 1945 to service Argentine international air traffic; began operations in 1946; inaugurated regular passenger service to Spain and Italy in 1947; to New York
   in 1950; became part of Aerolíneas Argentinas, the national
   airline.

FAMAILLA.   Site of final defeat in Tucumán (September 19, 1841)
   of remnants of Juan Lavalle's unitarist forces, supported by
   the Coalition of the North (q.v.), by Rosas' forces commanded
   by Manuel Oribe; Lavalle attempted to leave the country but
   was killed accidentally in Jujuy by federalist forces shortly afterwards; Coalition leaders, including Marco Avellaneda, were
   executed and opposition to Rosas in the northwest was ended
   for the time being.

FAMATINA. Extensive mining area in central western part of La
Rioja province. Exploited by both the Incas and the Spaniards
for copper, and smaller amounts of silver, the mines of Famatina have continued in operation, providing the industrializing
Argentina of the twentieth century with such minerals as iron,
manganese, wolframite, lead, uranium, and others, in addition
to copper; in various ways Famatina has affected Argentine
historical development; in the late sixteenth century the knowledge of these mines was one of the reasons for the Spanish
settlement of La Rioja; in the early national period (1820s)
Famatina figured importantly in both the provincial and national attempt to bring mines back into operation after the neglect
and damage due to the wars of independence; two rival companies were formed to work the mines: the River Plate Mining Company (q. v.) organized in London and authorized by
Buenos Aires government, and a company formed by a group
of Argentine politicians and land owners with a concession
from the provincial government of La Rioja; eventually this
was sold to the Famatina Mining company, organized by the
Robertson brothers with 250,000 pounds capital; for a time the
investors of this latter company seemed to dominate the financial life of Buenos Aires as they controlled the Banco de Descuentos (Discount Bank) and its successor the Banco Nacional;
both mining operations soon ended in failure because of unexpected difficulties; that of the Famatina Company was factor in
bankruptcy of the Robertsons (see Robertsons, J. P. and W.
P.); meanwhile a mint had been established in La Rioja by the
provincial legislature and in the 1840s it was issuing coins
from the mines stamped with "Cerro de General Rosas" as
Famatina was then known.

FANDANGO. Old folk dance (originally with singing), fiesta, and diversion that was immensely popular in colonial period, especially among lower classes; in 1748 Antonio de Ulloa described it as consisting primarily of heavy, disorderly drinking of wine and brandy followed by indecent and scandalous
dances; the church regularly opposed it as immoral and during
the years immediately preceding the establishment of the viceroyalty (1776) Governor Juan José de Vértiz and the reform
bishop Manuel Antonio de la Torre became involved in a serious dispute because of the governor's authorization of the
dance; eventually, the increasing violence of the fandangos resulted in so many injuries and deaths that Vértiz prohibited
them.
        Because of the nature of the dance, the word "fandango"
has also come to be applied to a situation or event characterized by wild confusion or disorder.

FANU (Flota Argentina de Navegación de Ultramar). Argentine overseas fleet created in 1949 after nationalization of Dodero shipping lines; established service to London and another that divided into two branches after reaching Europe, one to the north
and one to the Mediterranean; in 1960 FANU united with the

state merchant fleet (Flota Mercante del Estado) to form Empresas Líneas Martítimas Argentinas (ELMA).

FARRELL, EDELMIRO J., General (1887-   ).   President of Argentine Republic 1944-1946; career military officer.

Born in Avellaneda, province of Buenos Aires; graduated from military academy 1908; attended Superior War College 1918-1920; made distinguished service record, especially
in special forces assigned to Andean duty; awarded Cóndor de
Oro (Golden Condor) medal, in highest grade; had attained
rank of brigadier general by June 1943 when GOU revolt (q. v.)
overthrew government of President Ramón S. Castillo and established military dictatorship against background of World
War II; General Arturo Rawson, who left presidency almost
immediately, was followed by Gen. Pablo Ramírez; in this
government Farrell served as minister of war and also, after
November 1943, as vice president; internal tensions in military mounted between Perón and Perlinger groups until, in
February 1944, Ramírez was forced to resign in favor of Vice
President Farrell; became obvious that conservative leadership
of socially prominent, high-ranking officers in GOU had been
broken by younger men, known as "Colonels Clique" or "Young
Turks" led by Juan Domingo Perón.

As president, Farrell faced serious internal political,
social, economic problems of an industrializing, socially
changing nation, along with urgent need to improve Argentina's
international relationships; during two-year administration,
Farrell's government remained in control of situation, until
duly elected president could take over and Argentina's international situation had been normalized; early attempts to include
representatives of various military and political groups proved
unsuccessful; by July 1944 Perón, as minister of war, secretary of labor, and vice president, had become dominant figure
in government; in March 1945 President Farrell declared war
on Axis powers (relations had already been broken in January
1944 by Ramírez); U.S. had refused to recognize government,
accusing both Farrell and Perón of Nazi sympathies and acts--
U.S. disapproval seems to have strengthened Farrell in nationalistic Argentina; in April 1945 diplomatic relations were
resumed; meanwhile through negotiations and action taken at the
Chapultepec meeting of American foreign ministers (February-
March 1945, Mexico), Argentina had rejoined other hemispheric nations and was assured of seat in United Nations, then being organized; in July, at annual military banquet, President
Farrell announced that elections would be held before end of
year; a little later, free and open elections were held in February 1946, with Perón elected to his first term as president
and inaugurated in July; in 1947 General Farrell retired from
active military duty.

FASCISM.   Name given to totalitarian political system, with aspirations for world-wide domination, established in Italy by Benito
Mussolini in the early 1920s; by extension the term came to be

applied to any imperialistic dictatorship; in Argentina, anyone
espousing such a political system was known as a fascist, colloquially pronounced "fachista" (see Nazism and World War II).

FAULKNER, THOMAS see FALKNER, THOMAS

FAUSTO. Early gaucho poem that has become a classic. First
published in 1866 by Argentine poet Estanislao del Campo
(1834-1880) in pamphlet form, then included in author's
Poesías (1870); tells fanciful story of gaucho El Pollo (Chick)
who wandered into Teatro Colón in Buenos Aires and saw performance of the opera Faust by Gounod; tells story, believing
it to be true, to friend; unrealistic in plot, as critics claim
it to be, poem provides excellent vehicle for portraying Argentine natural scene, especially well-known description of sea at
sunrise; gaucho talk and comments authentic, revealing rural
life and spirit, as well as author's insights into human nature;
well-received at time of publication, when gaucho life style was
disappearing, Fausto held new significance for those intellectuals and writers of early twentieth century who were rebelling
against blind acceptance of European culture and searching for
native roots of their own; many editions of Fausto appeared;
translated into English by Walter Owen.

FEDERAL DISTRICT. Population (1970) about 3 million. Nationalized portion of city of Buenos Aires that serves as capital of
Argentine Republic (see Federalization of City of Buenos Aires).

FEDERAL INTERVENTION see INTERVENTION

FEDERAL PACT OF 1831. During latter half of 1830, representatives of riparian provinces (Buenos Aires, Entre Ríos, Santa
Fe, and Corrientes) met in conference at Santa Fe in attempt
to reconcile their political differences, to ally themselves
against common threat of League of Interior (eight provinces
under military command of General José María Paz), and to
provide basis for formal federal organization of government;
Federal Pact was result; signed January 4, 1831, by three
provinces, by Corrientes shortly afterward, and eventually by
all the provinces (after fall of League before end of year); it
has come to be regarded by many modern Argentine historians
as far more than treaty of alliance for defense and offense, but
rather as constitutional statement embodying fundamental national principles; replaced by constitution of 1853.
      Among its important clauses are those providing for:
alliance against common enemies; recognition of reciprocal independence, liberty, and rights of provinces; general declaration of rights for all inhabitants; incorporation of all provinces
as soon as they were in position to join; extradition of criminals between provinces; regulation of exports and imports; and,
most important of all (articles 15 and 16), a Representative
Commission (composed of governors or their delegates) to meet
regularly in Santa Fe (until national peace and order should

have been established) to handle all matters relating to foreign
affairs, to exercise control over military command in civil
wars, and to be responsible for calling national constitutional
congress at proper time to organize all Argentine political,
economic, and social life, and international relations on federalist basis; that time seemed to have come by close of 1831
with federalists in control of all provinces; Rosas, consolidat-
ing his power, considered the time premature; by various
means most of powers of representative commission, especially those regarding foreign affairs and economic matters, were
delegated to his government and a constitutional congress was
only called after Rosas left (1852).

FEDERALISM, FEDERALISTS. Doctrine and its adherents of political union of free states in loose national organization; in Argentine historiography most often used to refer to Rosas period, 1829-1852.
        Struggle between federalists and opposing unitarists
(centralists, unitarians) for control of national political organization tore Argentine violently apart during first half century
of independence--from May Revolution 1810 to inauguration of
Bartolomé Mitre as constitutional president of Argentine Republic (1862); differences were political, economic, and cultural; not clearcut along lines of geography, economic interests,
social background or status, or even ideology, but passions
ran high and differences were felt to be vital, regardless of
logic; generally speaking, unitarists desired a progressive,
modern, centralized government, with Buenos Aires as capital,
patterned somewhat along lines of such Western European nations as England and France, in republican, rather than monarchical (given up rather reluctantly by some early unitarist
leaders) form; constitution of 1826 represented their ideas and
goals, although many of the provinces had seemed ready to accept this constitution and had, in fact, helped to write it,
others--especially those in the littoral area--had long since become suspicious of Buenos Aires' willingness to sacrifice interests of provinces in favor of its own and now rejected the
constitution, as well as Rivadavia and his government; these
began fight to death for federal form of government; although
nation disintegrated into various kinds of autonomous groups,
anarchy, caudillismo, interprovincial alliances of short duration, federalists never gave up ultimate goal of a united nation,
including at least all of present Argentina, made up of semi-
autonomous provinces with rights clearly defined and protected;
differed strongly among themselves between those who demanded written constitution as best and, in fact, essential safeguard of this (like such provincial leaders as Pedro Ferré of
Corrientes and Juan Bautista Bustos of Córdoba) and those who
agreed with Juan Manuel de Rosas, actual ruler of Argentina
1829-1832, 1835-1852, although nominally only governor of
Buenos Aires province, that the nation was not yet ready for
formal institutionalization with a constitution and preferred a
de facto organization based on common interests to hold prov-

inces together until provincial ideals and institutions could be
more clearly formulated and prepared for national structuring;
economically, federalists, especially those in littoral provinces,
resented Buenos Aires control of rivers and rapidly increasing
lucrative international trade and demanded greater share in new
economic prosperity and more development of provincial resources; culturally, unitarists and federalists seemed to vie
with each other in establishing public education although some
federalist provincial governments (such as Entre Ríos) gave it
more support than did that of Rosas in Buenos Aires which had
excelled under unitarists; federalists rejected alien European
culture admired by unitarists, who, in turn viewed federalist
criollo culture as barbarism in comparison to contemporary
Western European civilization; federalists were also conservative with regard to Catholic Church and its role in their society, whereas unitarists were apt to view secularism as more
progressive and desirable; federalists believed that Argentina's
three centuries of experience counted more as guide to future
national development than did transplants of foreign ideas and
patterns and trusted more in their own historic institutions
than in those created by the logic of intellectuals; unitarists
countered this by accusing federalists of being opposed to all
forms of change and progress in Argentina; above all, federalists believed themselves to be guardians of traditional integrity
and entity of individual provinces which unitarists wanted to
destroy--in name of progress for everyone in nation was unitarist reply--and opposed government by elitest leaders and
groups in contrast to what they claimed to be traditional Argentine democracy; in the end, neither side prevailed completely
although many Argentine historians believe federalists to have
performed important contribution--although at great cost--to
saving of popular democracy and perpetuation of traditional elements in Argentine culture (see Unitarists; Criollismo; Juan
Manuel de Rosas; etc.) For economic aspects of federalism
see Miron Burgin in Suggested Readings, Appendix III.

FEDERALIZATION OF CITY OF BUENOS AIRES. The federalization
of the city of Buenos Aires in 1880 completed the organization-
al structure of the nation and secured its union; since then no
revolution has again threatened secession of disintegration--the
major problem of the first sixty years of independence; although Rivadavia urged in the 1820s that the city of Buenos
Aires be federalized, as part of his insistence on strong central authority, his proposal was so violently opposed by the
federalists of Buenos Aires province, led by Manuel Dorrego
and Manuel Moreno (who were considered by caudillos of other
provinces to be defending autonomous rights of all provinces)
that it fell through; during the Rosas period Buenos Aires continued to be the capital of the province of Buenos Aires and
served as the national capital only as the governor (Rosas) performed national functions delegated to him by other provincial
governors; for all practical purposes, however, it continued to
be the national capital; after the fall of Rosas, for the decade

(1852-1862) during which Buenos Aires province remained out
of the Argentine Confederation, there were two capitals: Buenos Aires, for the province, and Paraná for the Confederation;
with the approaching reunion of all the province, under adjustments made (1860) to the Constitution of 1853 adopted by Urquiza's confederation, the matter of the capital came up for
serious and heated discussion; there was no really satisfactory
alternative to Buenos Aires; federalization of the city of Buenos
Aires was again so violently opposed by the province, that considered the city to be uniquely its own capital, that the issue
was postponed, by compromise, in the interests of peace and
national progress; it was agreed that Buenos Aires should become national capital for a period of five years, after which
the capital question would be rediscussed; in 1880, during a
heated presidential campaign involving Carlos Tejedor, governor of Buenos Aires, and the administration's candidate Julio
A. Roca, civil war seemed imminent and Tejedor invoked the
law of the compromise and evicted the government of President
Avellaneda, which moved out to the suburb of Belgrano; determined to remove national government from pressure frequently
applied by government of powerful and wealthy province of Buenos Aires, on September 20, 1880, Congress federalized the
area included within the municipality of the City of Buenos
Aires into the Federal District, solely under the national government; the province of Buenos Aires, whose approval had
been gained, set about building itself a new capital that would
rival Buenos Aires in beauty, power, wealth, and culture (see
La Plata); with this action solving its last problem of national
organization, the Argentine Republic moved forward to surprising progress along political, economic, and cultural lines.

FERDINAND VII (1784-1833).   Last king of Spain to rule viceroyalty
of Río de la Plata.   Eldest son of Charles IV and María Luisa
of Parma; became king of Spain in March 1808 following father's
abdication; when Charles changed his mind and wanted to regain his throne, Napoleon came into the negotiations; invaded
Spain and placed his brother Joseph Bonaparte on throne; Spaniards revolted, called in Napoleon's enemies, and set up a
junta government; news of these events reached Río de la Plata
during July-August 1808; Viceroy Santiago de Liniers, despite
his French background, formally pledged allegiance to Ferdinand VII, then Napoleon's prisoner; nevertheless, for personal,
political, ideological, even economic reasons, this disruption
of royal rule opened rifts in viceroyalty and brought disputes
between Liniers and Elío (in Montevideo), Buenos Aires and
Montevideo, conservatives and liberals (as in Spain), Spaniards
and criollos; new viceroy Baltasar Hidalgo de Cisneros forced
to call cabildo abierto 22 May 1810 that resulted in May Revolution (q.v.); during next four years Argentina continued to
recognize sovereignty of exiled Ferdinand VII while actually
forming legal and institutional bases for autonomous government; return of Ferdinand VII to Spanish throne early in 1814
(with Napoleon's eventual defeat obvious), Ferdinand's rejection

of the Spanish liberal constitution of 1812, and his announced
intention to recover his American colonies by force, posed new
problems for Buenos Aires government; diplomatic negotiations
were begun along several lines; to seek British protection or
its influence with Spain's allies against forcible return of area
to Spanish colonial status; to establish separate Spanish kingdom in Río de la Plata viceroyalty under legitimate younger
Bourbon prince--project won some support from Charles IV
but after Napoleon's defeat at Waterloo (1815) and Ferdinand's
refusal even to discuss project, Charles withdrew; by 1816,
with army of the Andes ready to start its campaign to complete
war for independence, San Martín and others insisted that legal status of United Provinces must be clarified by formal declaration of independence to avoid appearance of rebellion
against king whom they still recognized as sovereign; July 9,
1816, Congress of Tucumán (with representatives from Argentine and Bolivian provinces) declared complete independence
from "Ferdinand VII, his legitimate successor and the mother
country"; expanded this a few days later to include "and of
every other foreign domination."

    While Ferdinand, with little more than moral support
from the Holy Alliance--due largely to British opposition to
forced retaking of colonies and to patriot victory of Chaca-
buco--prepared massive expedition at Cádiz to recover Río de
la Plata, Buenos Aires prepared to defend itself, continued
sending support to San Martín's expeditionary force for independence, and devoted itself to trying to establish a firm, liberal, centralized government; Spanish threat averted by revolt
of troops in Cádiz, led by Rafael de Riego; Ferdinand's government overthrown; king allowed to return to throne some
time later only after having agreed to accept liberal constitution of 1812; thereafter Spanish crown played little role in Argentine history--independence finally won at Ayacucho 1824;
Ferdinand VII died in 1833 and was succeeded by his daughter
Isabel II.

FERNANDEZ, MANUEL IGNACIO (d. 1790). Royal financial officer
who accompanied the expedition of Pedro de Ceballos to Buenos
Aires in 1777; later named intendant of army and hacienda
(treasury) in Buenos Aires; under viceroy Vértiz, Fernández
became general superintendent of the royal treasury and of war,
charged with responsibility for setting up procedures for handling all royal funds in the new viceroyalty in such a way as to
avoid abuses and prevent corruption; Fernández also proved to
be an able advisor to the viceroy and is credited with having
suggested many of the progressive measures that marked Vértiz administration, including the establishment of the first
printing press in Buenos Aires (see Foundlings Hospital and
Printing Presses); when his successor arrived in 1783, Fernández returned to Spain; he was highly honored by Carlos III
for his work in Argentina; died in Madrid.

FERNANDEZ, TEOFILO TOMAS (1858-1940). Veteran and historian

of the Conquest of the Desert.

Born in Buenos Aires; enlisted at age of 16 in the army; took part in Conquest of the Desert (q. v.) in 1879; retired from active duty with rank of colonel and devoted himself to study of his nation's history; was a founding member of the Center of Expeditionaries to the Desert; in 1910 he published La conquista del desierto in Rosario; died in Buenos Aires.

FERNANDEZ DE AGÜERO, JUAN MANUEL (1772-1840). Controversial priest and philosophy professor of early national period; strong supporter of Rivadavia's ideas and reforms.

Born in northern Spain, he was brought to Buenos Aires by his parents; studied at the Colegio de San Carlos and at Chilean University of San Felipe; was ordained as priest; he became very much interested in the new ideas of the Enlightenment, as opposed to the old scholasticism, and began teaching and writing about them; from 1822 to 1827, he occupied the chair of philosophy at the University of Buenos Aires; convinced that "it was necessary to create men who would be able to sustain the structure of the important reforms that Bernardino Rivadavia was planning and executing" rather than to react against them, he used his classroom for this purpose; although his thinking closely paralleled that of many patriot leaders at the time, his teachings brought shock waves to the conservative Catholics; the university rector attempted to suspend him for heretical teaching but was overruled by the government; following Rivadavia's departure, Father Fernández de Agüero retired (1827) to devote himself to his religious duties and to writing; at his death in Buenos Aires he left many unpublished writings; part of his Principios de ideología, elemental, abstractiva y oratoria appeared in 1824 and other works have since been published.

FERNANDEZ DE LA CRUZ, FRANCISCO (1781-1835). (Also called Francisco de la Cruz.) Officer in Wars for independence; cabinet minister; unitarist.

Born in Buenos Aires; studied at Colegio Real de San Carlos, then at nautical academy established by Pedro de Cerviño; fought against British invaders; supported May Revolution enthusiastically; remaining in the army, he took part in the siege of Montevideo 1812, served as interim governor intendant in Salta (1813); when San Martín's illness forced him to leave Tucumán, Col. Fernández de la Cruz was left in charge of Army of the North awaiting the arrival of Rondeau, the new commander; led patriot forces intervening at Puesto del Marqués (April 1815); wounded in arm at Sipe Sipe; in 1819 when Manuel Belgrano (the new commander in the north) became ill, Fernández de la Cruz took his place temporarily; on his way to Santa Fe to suppress the montoneras there, the revolt at Arequito (q. v.) put Bustos in command of most of his army; Fernández de la Cruz retired to Mendoza; suppressed revolt of Mendizábal in San Juan (q. v.); went to Buenos Aires to become minister of War and Navy in government of Martín Rodríguez, continuing to serve in cabinets of Las Heras and Rivadavia; organized war effort against Brazil (1827) and was promoted to brigadier general; became involved in events of 1828, supporting Juan Lavalle; after latter's defeat, General Fernández de la Cruz went into exile in Uruguay; returned eventually to Buenos Aires but took no further part in public life.

FERNANDEZ DE LA CRUZ, LUCIANO (1797-1842). Independence fighter; unitarist opponent of Rosas. Younger brother of General Francisco Fernández de la Cruz; captured by royalists in fighting in Upper Peru; sent to Peru to be imprisoned in casemates of Callao; freed by Las Heras in 1821, joined San Martín's liberating army; returned to Argentina in 1825 and joined the army, supporter of Juan Lavalle; in 1842 shot by order of Rosas as a "savage unitarist."

FERNANDEZ LONG, HILARIO (1925-). Engineer. Born in Bahía Blanca; graduated in engineering from Buenos Aires in 1943; taught there until 1951; returned to Bahía Blanca to teach in the University of the South; in 1957 returned to faculty of engineering in Buenos Aires; also taught in Catholic University Santa María de los Buenos Aires; has written extensively on his field and served as engineering consultant for many projects; in 1962 became dean of his faculty and vice rector of the university.

When President Onganía closed the University of Buenos Aires (1966) on grounds that student restlessness was Communist-inspired, Dr. Fernández Long, then Rector, spoke up boldly for the university and then resigned, followed by more than 1000 faculty members; as a result, the government turned to more thoughtful and conciliatory measures to accomplish the needed university reforms.

FERRE, PEDRO (1788-1867). Statesman and general. Born in Corrientes, educated as naval engineer; became first alcalde (mayor) of Corrientes in 1821; for next twenty years was key figure in Corrientes public life; served as governor 1824-27, 1830-33, and 1839-42; continued progressive work of previous governor Colonel Juan José Fernández Blanco; opened schools in every town and made education compulsory; introduced Lancastrian system of tutorial teaching; established school board; improved secondary education; opened courses in Latin and philosophy; planned new towns; regulated labor and promoted agriculture; largely solved the problem of Indian raids; made arrangements for compulsory smallpox vaccination (1827-28) avoiding an epidemic; during his second administration he fought off a Paraguayan invasion and annexed the eastern Misiones territory to the Argentine Republic; meanwhile he had been playing the role of an authentic federalist on the national level: loyal to both his province of Corrientes and to the nation, he consistently stood for a nation of self-governing provinces joined legally by and operating under a constitution; hailed the calling of the 1826 constitutional congress but then

pronounced against it because of its centralism; in 1830, when
Rosas feared isolation of Buenos Aires, Ferré signed uneasy
agreement with him although their political differences--Rosas'
preference for a working arrangement vs Ferré's insistence on
constitutional government--and their economic conflict between
Rosas' support of the free trade that the Buenos Aires merchants wanted for financial and international reasons and the
protection of provincial trade and industry that Ferré felt essential were clearly defined at this time; also, invited by Rosas, took part in the federal pact of the littoral provinces, January 4, 1831, establishing peace; elected governor again in
1839, Ferré decided that time had come to fight Rosas; joining
with Rosas' enemies and supporting the unitarist general Lavalle, he dramatically declared war on Rosas, January 1,
1840; less than two months later, with Lavalle defeated and on
his way to the western provinces, Ferré reorganized his almost helpless province, allied himself with the Uruguayan Rivera (opposing Rosas' backing of Oribe), and placed General
José María Paz in command of the allied army; Paz won magnificent victory over Pascual Echagüe (leading Rosas' forces)
at Caaguazú November 28, 1841; disagreements between Ferré
and Paz led to latter's departure to join Rivera's army, which
was then destroyed at Arroyo Grande; immediately Rosas' men
took control of Corrientes and all his opponents fled, declared
to be enemies; Ferré established himself at São Borja in Brazil and was planning to establish a new kind of city when he
learned that all his property had been confiscated; in 1848 he
returned to Corrientes and then went to Entre Ríos where he
took part in the founding of La Paz; after Urquiza's pronouncement against Rosas in 1851, Ferré joined his movement and
used his boat-building skills to prepare the river transports for
the cavalry forces, proud of his contribution to the overthrow
of the man whom he considered to be a tyrant; after Caseros,
represented Catamarca at the Constitutional convention in
Santa Fe, acting as a member of the committee to draw up the
constitution that would bind the provinces into a nation; signed
it in May 1853; in the following elections for president Ferré
received one of the few votes not cast for Urquiza; remained
in Santa Fe, now a full general in rank; engaged to direct the
building of boats needed; moved to Buenos Aires where he prepared a detailed map of a portion of the river there, just two
years before his death in that city; buried in La Recoleta
cemetery; widely eulogized as an "illustrious Argentine."

FERREIRA, J. ALFREDO (1863-1938).   Educator; writer; editor,
    regarded as one of important founders of modern Argentine
    public school system.
        Born in Corrientes province, at Rincón de Guayquiraró;
    graduated from Normal School at Paraná and later earned doc-
    torate in jurisprudence, largely through his own study; dedi-
    cated himself to creation of system of experimental, innovative
    public education that would free Argentine students from rigid
    limitations of classical education or that imported from foreign

nations, and would fit them to become citizens of a progressive, democratic republic; having studied Comte's positivism
under Pedro Scalabrini at the Normal School and familiar with
ideas of U.S. educators brought to Argentina by Sarmiento,
Ferreira took what he liked from both sources but insisted--as
had Echeverría and Sarmiento--that proper education of Argentine child and student must begin with Argentine realities and
be constantly oriented toward them.

As president of the superior education council and director general of schools in Corrientes (1893-1897), he determined to make his native province a model for other provinces
by establishing schools of this new type; he was assisted in
this by U.S. teachers Edith Howe and Cora Hill; later, his
Bases para un plan de educación primaria, designed for Corrientes, was used in other provinces; Ferreira also encouraged
practical education, including arts and crafts, and vocational
courses; strongly supported secular education and elimination
of religious teaching in public schools; with his former teacher
Pedro de Scalabrini, he further enriched life of Corrientes by
establishing the provincial museum there, as well as the Banco
de Corrientes--a private credit institution; moving to Buenos
Aires as deputy to congress from Corrientes (1901), Ferreira
became part of national scene; taught in various educational
institutions in capital and became vice president of national educational council in 1914; died in Buenos Aires.

Ferreira's influence on Argentine education was exerted
not only through his teaching, founding of schools, and other
contributions in pedagogical administrative posts, but also
through his writings; as editor of La Escuela Positiva, a journal devoted to educational and philosophical studies, he was
among the first to disseminate ideas of positivism throughout
the republic; later he founded El Positivismo to express his
ideas on role of positivism in Argentine political, economic,
and social life, as well as in education: among his books are
Creación del consejo nacional de enseñanza secundaria; La
separación de la iglesia católica y del estado; La escuela laica;
and Síntesis de la política positiva de Comte (see Positivism).
(See biography of Ferreira by his student Angel C. Bassi, J.
Alfredo Ferreira (Buenos Aires, 1943).

FERRER, ALDO (1927-   ).   Economist; professor; cabinet minister.
Born in Buenos Aires; received his doctorate in economic sciences, Buenos Aires 1949; served as economic counselor in Argentine embassy, London, 1956-1957; was minister
of economics for Buenos Aires province, 1958-1960; professor
of Argentine political economy in Faculty of Economic Sciences,
National University of La Plata, 1963-1966; member of the Inter-American Committee of the Alliance for Progress; executive secretary, Latin American Social Science Council; member
of national academy of economic sciences; was brought into
Roberto Levingston's cabinet as minister of Economics and
Labor in 1970; showed determination to reduce Argentine dependence on foreign capital and to promote Argentine industry;

presented a new development plan for 1971-1975; when Levingston's government was overthrown in March 1971 Ferrer was
maintained in his ministry by the Alejandro Lanusse administration.
      Among his published works are El estado y el desarr-
ollo económico (1954); La economía argentina (4th edition,
1963) was translated by Marjori M. Urquidi and published by
the University of California Press as The Argentine Economy
(Berkeley, 1967).

FERROCARRILES see RAILROADS

FIELDS, THOMAS (1549?-1625). Irish-born Jesuit assigned to early
      missions near Asunción; frustrated because of lack of support
      for work there from authorities in Lima, he wrote a letter to
      his superior recommending that the Jesuit work in the Río de
      la Plata-Paraná area be transferred from Peruvian jurisdic-
      tion to that of the Jesuits in Brazil; this letter (dated January
      27, 1601), was published in 1971 by Guillermo Fúrlong Cárd-
      iff, along with a biobibliographical study of Fields.

FIGUEROA ALCORTA, JOSE (1860-1931). President of Argentine
      Republic 1906-1910; jurisconsult.
      Born in Córdoba; educated at Monserrat and University
      of Córdoba, graduating with doctorate of laws 1882; began ca-
      reer as professor of international law and legal counsel for
      municipal government; quickly advanced in provincial political
      life, elected to legislature in 1885, 1887; serving as cabinet
      minister 1889-1892; sent as deputy to national congress 1892;
      governor of Córdoba, 1895-1898; national senator 1898; elected
      vice president on ticket with Manuel Quintana in 1904; seized
      in Córdoba sierras by radical revolutionaries in 1905; held as
      hostage and forced to attempt negotiations with president on
      their behalf; Quintana held firm, rescued Figueroa Alcorta,
      and revolt disintegrated shortly before death of president
      brought Figueroa to presidency March 12, 1906.
      Administration of Figueroa Alcorta characterized by
      political turbulence due to transition from half century of oli-
      garchical rule to new period of alternating popular and dicta-
      torial regimes; way cleared at last for real party government
      based on popular support but old leaders were gone--deaths of
      Bartolomé Mitre, Manuel Quintana, Carlos Pellegrini, and
      Bernardo Irigoyen in 1906, followed by that of Emilio Mitre,
      1909--and new leadership was uncertain, parties, confused;
      in this situation, Figueroa attempted to strengthen provincial
      political structures (six new provincial constitutions) and to
      gain provincial support for federal government; used presiden-
      tial political influence to secure succession of reformist Roque
      Saenz Peña to presidency; most dramatic, most popular act of
      president was dissolution January 25, 1908, of special con-
      gress called to approve appointments and appropriate funds for
      1908 budget; after two months of inactivity and obstructionism,
      congress was dismissed by Figueroa who thereafter governed

by decree; social unrest reflected renewed wave of immigration, accompanied by labor agitation; strikes and anarchical acts of terrorism culminated with bombing deaths of Chief of Police Ramón L. Falcón (q.v.) in November 1909; followed next year by law of social defense giving president right to deal directly with troublesome foreign labor leaders, deporting them if necessary; economy continued prosperous, based on traditional stockraising and agricultural export trade, accompanied with increasing industrial development; no startling international developments as president continued traditional foreign policy; Argentina broke off relations with Bolivia following violent Bolivian demonstrations against Figueroa Alcorta's arbitration decision of boundary dispute between Bolivia and Peru; negotiations with Uruguay concerning navigation rights in Río de la Plata system made progress; and Argentina and Brazil found themselves engaged in arms rivalry, during which relations between Argentina and United States became strained; Figueroa Alcorta had honor of presiding (1910) over Argentina's lavish centennial of May Revolution, with its accompanying special diplomatic missions and international conferences of scientists, intellectuals, and artists; after turning presidency over to Saenz Peña at end of term 1910, Figueroa went to Spain as ambassador (1912) and representative to centennial of junta of Cádiz; returned to private legal practice in Buenos Aires until his appointment to Supreme Court of Justice in 1915, position which he held for following sixteen years until his death in Buenos Aires 1931.

FIRST TRIUMVIRATE see TRIUMVIRATES, FIRST AND SECOND

FISCAL. Royal prosecutor; usually attached to audiencia.

FIVE-YEAR PLAN (Plan Quinquenal) 1947. Plan for economic and political reorganization and reform; developed by José Francisco Luis Figuerola y Tresols, Chief of Statistics in Department of Labor for use by President Perón during first administration; first five-year plan followed by second (see Juan Domingo Perón).

FLAG OF THE ARGENTINE REPUBLIC. The national flag, consisting of two horizontal stripes of celestial blue separated by one of white, with the golden emblem of the sun in the middle, took form in the early years of the fight for independence; when Belgrano found himself in need of a national banner in his expedition to Santa Fe and Rosario in early 1812, he devised one, using the heavenly blue and white of the Patricio's cockade; later used this same flag in expedition to northwest Argentina and Alto Perú; adopted by Congress in 1818 as official, with the addition of the golden sun (origin variously attributed to its relationship to celestial blue, ancient Spanish usage, or the sun of the Incas); executive decree of 1944 finally established exact shade of blue to be used and the symbolism of the sun as given above.

FLAX see LINSEED

FLORES, VENANCIO (1803-1868). Uruguayan general and political
    leader involved in Argentine affairs in 1850s and 1860s. After
    having been president of Uruguay, 1854-1855, Flores supported
    by the Colorados was overthrown by rival Blanco political
    party; fled across Uruguay river to Entre Ríos and then to
    Buenos Aires where he offered his formidable military serv-
    ices to the Buenos Aires government; fought at Cepeda and
    again at Pavón under Mitre; his defeat of General Cayetano
    Laprida at the Canada de Gómez November 22, 1861, de-
    stroyed military power of Confederation and left way open for
    reorganization of nation under Buenos Aires and Mitre's lead-
    ership; aid given Flores for his return to Uruguay in attempt
    to regain power brought President Mitre considerable opposi-
    tion from interior provinces who protested it was contrary to
    Argentina's declared neutrality; Flores got aid also from Bra-
    zil and became virtual dictator of Uruguay in 1865; Francisco
    Solano López, president of Paraguay, became alarmed and
    protested Argentine and Brazilian involvement in Uruguay; re-
    sult: Paraguayan war, or war of the Triple Alliance; Flores
    commanded the Uruguayan forces in allied army under Mitre;
    finally returning to Uruguay, he was assassinated by political
    enemies in 1868.

FLOTA MERCANTE DEL ESTADO (State Merchant Fleet). Estab-
    lished in 1941 in response to recommendation of Inter-Ameri-
    can Financial and Economic Advisory Committee that Ameri-
    can nations should expropriate any foreign vessels tied up in
    their ports by the war and use them during the current ship-
    ping crisis; Argentina immediately seized 16 Italian ships and,
    with this nucleus, gave high priority to the development of the
    merchant fleet; it proved to be one of the most successful
    features of Perón's first Five-Year Plan; in 1951, for the
    first time, more Argentine freight was shipped under Argen-
    tine flag than any foreign flag; the state fleet also competed
    for foreign freight with considerable success against the old,
    established lines; in 1960 it was reorganized and combined with
    other Argentine shipping into the Empresas Líneas Marítimas
    Argentinas (ELMA).

FONSECA Y CONTRERAS, MANUEL DE (d. 1612). General; public
    official; philanthropist. As the only son of conquistador Alon-
    so de Contreras, Manuel inherited a large fortune, including
    a huge encomienda, gained in the conquest; following his fath-
    er's death (1591), he married Leonor de Tejeda, daughter of
    his father's friend and companion in arms, Tristán de Tejeda
    (q. v.), who brought a wealthy dowry (1594); within a few years
    his health began to fail and Manuel de Fonseca y Contreras
    began to devote his attention and fortune to the endowment and
    establishment of the convent that his wife wanted to found in
    Córdoba; after his death in 1612, this was made possible by
    their joint efforts (see Leonor de Tejeda).

FONTANA, LUIS JORGE (1846-1920). Military officer; scientist,
early territorial administrator in Formosa; and first territorial governor of Chubut.

Born in Buenos Aires; entered military career in 1859
but after various assignments turned his attention to science;
studied natural sciences with Dr. Burmeister for several years
after 1865; following death of Urquiza in 1870, accompanied
national army against General Ricardo López Jordán in capacities of surgeon, secretary, and geologist; spent several years
on scientific missions in Río Negro area as naturalist for National Museum; taught physics and natural history in the university; sent to Chaco area claimed by both Paraguay and Argentina, in 1875, as secretary of Argentine government there,
acted also as interim governor and military commander; when
disputed area was awarded to Paraguay, Fontana selected site
for new capital, Formosa, and moved Argentine settlers and
officials there from old capital (Villa Occidental, now Villa
Hayes in Paraguay); acting under orders of governor of province Lucio V. Mansilla, formally established city of Formosa;
attempted to open road from Salta and Jujuy to coast through
Formosa; transferred in 1885 to become first governor of national territory of Chubut in Patagonia; continued scientific
studies and explorations; became concerned with boundary dispute with Chile; spent last twenty years of life in San Juan devoted to important scientific work; left fourteen major scholarly studies, in addition to minor writings; honored by Instituto
Geográfico Argentino with gold medal and citation as Bene-
mérito of Argentine geographers; promoted to rank of colonel
in 1917; died in San Juan (see Chubut; Formosa).

See Lorenzo Amaya, Fontana, el territoriano (Buenos
Aires, 1935).

FONTEZUELAS, REVOLT OF (April 3, 1815). Action taken by
commanding officers of Buenos Aires army, en route to Santa
Fe, with significant results.

His control of government threatened, Director Carlos
María de Alvear determined to regain badly needed support by
winning important military victory; José Gervasio Artigas had
proclaimed himself protector of riparian provinces against Buenos Aires control and was on his way to strengthen his position in Santa Fe; Alvear sent vanguard division under Colonel
Ignacio Alvarez Thomas to head Artigas off while director followed with main force to join battle later; instead, at Fontezuelas, in Buenos Aires province, about eighty miles from
Buenos Aires on the route along the Paraná to Santa Fe, Alvarez Thomas and his officers revolted, issuing manifesto that
civil war was over; this action won considerable support from
armies of Artigas, Rondeau in north, and San Martín in Mendoza; Alvear forced out at once, took passage in British naval
vessel for England; Rondeau called back to become Director,
with Alvarez Thomas acting until his arrival; historians note
that this revolt marked first time after May Revolution that
government had been interrupted in this way (but not the last);

and that it demonstrates at an early date that many porteño patriots shared provincial desire for federalism and felt need to reach agreement with caudillos to defend republican principles against grandiose plans of Alvear's Buenos Aires government; quite simply, it also showed impatience with civil wars when first priority should be fight for independence--not yet won.

FORA.   Federación Obrera Regional Argentina (Argentine Regional Labor Federation). Early anarchist trade union founded in 1901; remained only organized labor movement for several decades; disappeared in 1946 following development of CGT (Confederación General del Trabajo) as instrument of Perón's labor policy.

FORBES, JOHN M. (1771-1831).   U.S. commercial agent and diplomatic representative in Buenos Aires, 1820-1831.
      Born in St. Augustine, Florida, son of Anglican rector there; during the critical years in Buenos Aires from the anarchy of 1820 to Rosas' rule in 1831, Forbes, a former schoolmate of Secretary of State John Quincy Adams at Harvard, who had served as consul in northern Europe, was almost the sole U.S. official representative in Buenos Aires; sent as commercial agent in 1820, becoming secretary of the legation, and then, after Minister Rodney's death, chargé d'affaires, he placed his stamp on execution of policy, kept his government informed of critical events in Argentina, protected U.S. shipping and semen, brought Buenos Aires government the good news of U.S. recognition and of the Monroe doctrine's warning against intervention and colonization; became embittered by Argentina's increasingly close financial and commercial ties with Great Britain which he was powerless to prevent; died, having been in ill health for years, before he could return to the United States; respected in Argentina as well as by the government that he had served.
      John M. Forbes' notes and correspondence have been compiled and translated into Spanish by Felipe A. Espil: Once años en Buenos Aires, 1820-1831 (Buenos Aires, 1956).

FOREIGN AFFAIRS see FOREIGN POLICY AND FOREIGN AFFAIRS

FOREIGN INVESTMENT.   During most of the first century of Argentine national life foreign investment and capital, in form of private or public loans or specific investment in various business projects, was essential to Argentine economic development (see Economic History); railroad building was almost totally financed by European, largely British, capital; most of rest of credit went into loans to national, provincial, and municipal governments, and into land mortgage bonds; foreign private capital also invested heavily in banks, factories, tramways, gasworks, telegraph companies; disaster threatened when economic losses and bad management caused European investors to lose faith in Argentina in the 1880s, resulting in

the crisis of 1890; Argentine political and financial reforms
and Europe's need for Argentine meat and grain brought new
investment; although Argentine domestic capital became increasingly available, foreign investment rose from 31.8% of
the aggregate fixed capital in 1900 to a peak of 47.7% in 1913
and was still at 41.8% in 1920, two years after ending of
World War I; Great Britain, France, and Germany then had to
liquidate part of their foreign investments and United States
emerged as principal credit nation; during Perón's first term,
he brought all finances under government control and attempted
to buy out foreign interests; and, in spite of Perón's attempts
to invite it back, foreign investment had dwindled in 1955 to
only 5.1% of aggregate fixed capital; the decline was absolute
as well as relative as in the 1950s the inflow of long-term foreign capital into Argentina was only a fraction of what it had
been before 1930; the purpose for which it came also differed:
whereas before 1930 more than 20% had gone into public issues,
and 40% into social overhead, since 1950 foreign investment
has been concentrated almost entirely in those industries offering special advantages to foreign investors, such as automotive
and petroleum industries; after the Foreign Investment Act of
1959, there was a boom in in-flow of foreign capital and in the
1960s American investment increased sharply; 1970 American
direct investment estimated at $1,285 million, growing at rate
of 5% per annum; this amounted to 50% of foreign investment
in Argentina, with British holding 10% and French, Germans,
Dutch, and Italians holding most of the rest.

FOREIGN POLICY AND FOREIGN AFFAIRS. Following the initial
period of the wars for independence and the subsequent civil
wars, often complicated by political problems in neighboring
states--Brazil and former parts of the old viceroyalty: Bolivia,
Uruguay, and Paraguay--Argentina has attempted to follow a
consistent foreign policy based on its own economic needs and
cultural interests and to remain neutral (especially since the
Paraguayan War, 1865-1870) in other conflicts; its own fierce
sense of independence and local autonomy, manifested in its
early federalism and later nationalism, has been translated into a desire to permit other nations the same rights of self-determination according to their own interests; closely related to
this is the Drago Doctrine denying the right of foreign nations
to use force to collect debts or for redress of similar economic faults; much of Argentina's diplomacy in inter-American
meetings and during World War II was considered by Argentines
to be a continued application of this traditional policy (see Inter-
American Relations and World War II); on the other hand, Argentina would like to play a larger role in international affairs;
it joined Chile and Brazil in the ABC bloc; it briefly belonged
to the League of Nations; is a member of the Inter-American
Treaty Organization; the United Nations, the Latin American
Foreign Trade Associations, and has participated fully in these
and similar international relations; traditionally its closest ties
have been with Western European nations because of economic

and cultural ties, rather than its neighbors in the Western
Hemisphere with Brazil and the United States occupying special relationships; realities of changing world conditions as
well as economic, cultural, social, and political conditions in
Argentina have been reflected in Argentina's foreign policy
since World War II in its increasing attention to Eastern Europe, Japan, and Third World nations.
      See Argentina's Foreign Policy: 1930-1962, by Alberto
A. Conil Paz and Gustavo E. Ferrari, translated by John J.
Kennedy, Notre Dame, Indiana, 1966. Also see entries for
those countries with which Argentina has had closest relations,
such as Brazil, France, Germany, Great Britain, and the
United States.

FOREIGN TRADE.   (See Economic History for general role of for-
     eign trade; also Contraband for colonial foreign trade.)
          Traditionally Argentina's foreign trade, since independ-
     ence, has consisted of the exchange of Argentine rural produce
     from livestock and agriculture for manufactured articles or
     mineral and food products not readily available in Argentina;
     trade partners have been industrializing nations of Western
     Europe, United States, and Brazil; trade balance has usually
     been favorable, bringing prosperity to the nation and capital
     available for developing economy and for other national pur-
     poses; it is still true (in early 1970s) that livestock and agri-
     culture provide bulk of exports but changes in world market
     and in Argentina's own economic development, including many
     in rural industries, have greatly affected various aspects of
     foreign trade.
          During the period preceding 1930, Western Europe con-
     tinued to receive most exports and to provide most imports
     for Argentine market; beginning with hides, animal fats, etc.
     from the cattle industry, exports of latter industry progressed,
     during nineteenth century, through additions of salted, dried
     beef, and meat extracts, to include chilled and frozen beef,
     with some shipments of live cattle, to supply meat demands;
     sheep industry began to supply wool for export during 1830s,
     increasing its share in export trade to 50-60% in the 1880s;
     mutton and sheepskins also were exported; following political
     unification of the republic in 1862 and successful establishment
     of commercial agriculture by immigrant colonies, Argentine
     foreign trade increased rapidly during administrations of Sar-
     miento, Avellaneda, and their successors; by 1880s, cereals
     had begun to rival cattle products in export value; imports had
     changed somewhat in nature: textiles (cotton, wool, linen, and
     silk), manufactured goods, especially those of iron and steel,
     and fuels continued to furnish most of imports, but Argentina
     had begun to mill its own wheat flour and was well on its way
     toward providing its own sugar and wines; during the period
     preceding World War II, Argentine exports provided interna-
     tional market with 70% of its linseed, 60% of corn, 20% of
     wheat, 40% of its chilled and frozen beef, and 12% of wool.
          Since World War II, the Argentine republic has been

involved in a continuing industrializing revolution, aimed at
satisfying national market and producing national economic independence, with foreign trade more closely controlled by government and agropecuarian interests and exports suffering at
times because of diverted and diversified national economic interests; in 1970, exports were still dominated by grain, meat,
wool, hides, linseed oil, and other rural products, but imports reflected national economic change; machinery and equipment, iron and steel products, and chemicals, followed by traditional textiles and fuels, led import list: Western Europe
continued to account for much of Argentina's trade, but were
by no means as dominant as before; in 1970, U.S. received
8.7% of Argentina's exports and provided nearly 25% of its
imports, mostly machinery and electrical equipment; Argentine
export trade to its Latin American neighbors increased about
300% in the years from 1961 (organization of LAFTA) and
1968; and in 1969 exports to communist countries of Eastern
Europe were valued at $21,700,000 and imports from them at
$71,300,000; Argentina signed new trade agreement with Rus-
sia in 1971.

See H. S. Ferns, The Argentine Republic (New York,
1973); Aldo Ferrer, The Argentine Economy (Berkeley, Calif.,
1967); Carlos F. Díaz Alejandro, Essays on the Economic History of the Argentine Republic (New Haven and London 1970);
and Statistical Abstract of Latin America, published annually
by the University of California, Los Angeles.

FOREIGNERS, FOREIGN RESIDENTS. Foreigners came to the Río
de la Plata with the first Spaniards of the conquest, like the
German chronicler of early days in Asunción, Ulrich Schmidel
(q. v.) or to trade like Enrique (Hendrik) Ottsen (q. v.) at Buenos Aires in 1599, or as non-Spanish missionaries, like Martín Dobrizhoffer and Florián Paucke, but few established permanent residence there during the colonial period, except many
neighboring Portuguese Brazilians; with the establishment of
the viceroyalty and the opening of Buenos Aires to legal trade,
the numbers increased slightly; in 1810 foreigners accounted
for 10,000 in Buenos Aires' population of approximately
50,000; most of these were Portuguese, British, French, or
Italians and possessed wealth and influence far out of proportion to their numbers; following the May Revolution the patriot
governments encouraged foreigners to remain and to become
citizens; the treaty with Britain in 1825 guaranteed freedom of
worship and civil protection to British subjects resident in Argentina; this became the pattern for foreigners from other
countries and guarantees of this sort were specifically stated
in the 1853 constitution; during the first half century of independence foreigners came in larger numbers, most were single
young men, with some resources, who had come for adventure
and to make a fortune; many succeeded in the latter and returned to Europe; others decided to stay, sent for their wives
or sweethearts, or married Argentine girls, and established
Creole families; by 1850s, foreigners made up 45% of Buenos

Aires' population of 90,000 and 20% in the upriver towns along
the Uruguay and Paraná rivers; few occupied the rural areas,
except the sheepherders, or settled in the interior provinces;
traders and merchants, bankers, craftsmen, and shopkeepers
preferred the port cities; in the period following the fall of
Rosas' government both the Confederation and the province of
Buenos Aires sought eagerly to attract foreign immigrants for
agricultural purposes and for a skilled urban labor force; inducements were offered and the empty spaces in the republic
began to be filled (see Colonization; Immigration); the emphasis
on attracting immigrants continued until the depression period
of 1930s: earlier, however, labor violence instigated by foreign agitators had given the government authority to deal with
them in the Law of Residence and that of Social Defense
(qq. v.).

FOREIGNERS' RESIDENCE LAW   see   LAW OF RESIDENCE

FORJA.   Fuerza Orientadora Radical de la Joven Argentina (Radical
Orientation Force of Argentine Youth). Group formed during
mid-1930s of young political leaders and intellectuals, disturbed by fraudulent elections, vacuum of leadership, and desiring more democratic socialism; called by A. P. Whitaker
"small but vigorous dissident group ... which produced Argentina's first comprehensive program of popular nationalism";
numbered among its members were Luis Dellepiane, Gabriel
del Mazo, Arturo Jauretche, Homero Manzi, Arturo García
Mellid, and others; during 1930s FORJA led several abortive
revolutions; was apt to be anti-Yankee, neutralist, pro-Nazi,
anti-imperialistic in its nationalism; its political platform in
1930s foreshadowed that of Perón in the 1940s.

FORMOSA (Province and City).   North central Argentine province
(since 1955).   Location.   Lies between latitudes 22° and 27°S.,
longitudes 57°40' and 62°21'W.; rectangular area separated
from Paraguay on north by Pilcomayo river and on east by
Paraguay river; Bermejo and Teuco rivers form southern boundary with province of Chaco; and bounded on west by plateaus
of province of Salta.   Area: 27,800 square miles.   Population (1970): 234,075.   Density: 8.4 per square mile.   Capital:
Formosa; population (1960): 36,499.
        Geography and climate.   Heavily wooded areas or scrub-
forests alternate with grassy plains, often flooded during rainy
summers (December-April) by innumerable small Andean
streams tumbling or wandering across province to end in bogs
or lakes or to join Bermejo or Pilcomayo rivers on their way
through shallow, constantly changing channels to the Paraguay;
climate hot most of year, with tropical and subtropical temperatures and vegetation; heavy rainfall in east diminishes toward west; scrub forests provide both light and dark quebracho,
algarrobo, lapacho, along with medicinal trees and plants; chief
products: cotton, maize, peanuts, alfalfa, and tobacco.
        General comments.   Spanish determination following

discovery and conquest to link Río de la Plata settlements
(primarily Asunción) with Peru and settlements in Tucumán
area made Formosa, as apparently one of most direct routes
by land and river, center of explorations in sixteenth century;
unnavigability of Bermejo and Pilcomayo, except with small
rivercraft near junctions with Paraguay, combined with difficulties of terrain and fierce hostility of Indians to divert these
routes to north and south (especially after refounding of Buenos
Aires, 1580); Formosa left for about 250 years to Chaco Indians and their horses, and occasional scientific expeditions; in
late nineteenth century federal government became interested
in area for border defense and to promote national economy by
populating it and fostering economic development there; result:
rapidly growing province in 1970s; chief source of cotton for
Argentine market; experimenting with other subtropical agriculture; rapidly growing population is pioneer mixture of farmers
and other settlers from Argentina, Paraguay, various European
nations, Japan, and elsewhere, with descendants of original
Guaycuruans.

     History. Indians occupying Formosa at time of con-
quest belonged to two main groups of Chaco natives: Matacos,
or Mataguayans, in west; and Guaycuruan tribes--including Abipón, Toba, Mocoví, and related groups--in the east; they were
fierce, nomadic, practicing some agriculture and fishing; first
Spaniards to reach Formosa came with Sebastian Cabot and Diego García in 1528; in Spanish determination to reach silver of
Peru or to send it more readily to Spain via Atlantic, exploration for desired route followed in rapid succession: Juan de
Ayolas (from Buenos Aires, 1536); Domingo Martínez de Irala
(from Asunción, 1540, 1542); Nufrio de Chávez (1545-1546);
(1553-1557); Andrés Manso attempted it from Upper Peru and
almost reached Pilcomayo; in 1564-1565, various expeditions
were in Formosa, led by Felipe de Cáceres and Nufrio de
Chávez, by Governor Francisco Ortiz de Vergara and by Diego
de Pacheco, who left Santiago del Estero, crossed Formosa
from southwest to northeast to Asunción and returned by same
route; in 1580s Alsonso de Vera y Aragón left Asunción with
200 men on punitive expedition against Guaycuruans, who continued to make communication almost impossible between
Asunción and Tucumán; Concepción del Bermejo (q. v.) was established as a midpoint base; in 1590 missionary work was begun there by Alonzo Barzana and Pedro Añasco; the settlement
was destroyed by Indians in 1632; throughout the seventeenth
century, Formosa was abandoned except for occasional expeditions, like the official attempt under orders of Governor of
Paraguay to renew exploration of the Pilcomayo, 1682, as new
royal highways had been developed both in north and farther
south; missionary interests in eighteenth century brought Gabriel Patiño and Antonio Montijo from Bolivia in attempt to navigate down Pilcomayo (1721); reached marsh (estero) bearing
Patiño's name; another attempt made in 1751; finally, in 1763
first Jesuit mission (reducción) was established by Martín Dobrizhoffer (q. v.), among Abipón Indians, called Timbó, but also

known as Rosario, on site between present city of Formosa
and Puerto Bermejo in Chaco; progress made, but Jesuits expelled four years later; for more than a century the few expeditions into Formosa were apt to be either punitive expeditions against constant threat of horse-borne Indian raids
against neighboring Spanish settlements (Indians' favored
means of support) and scientific explorations; Spanish naturalist Félix Azara (q. v.) attempted to go up the Pilcomayo from
Asunción with small party and guide in river boat, 1785, but
abandoned effort after five days; area remained remote from
Argentine political, economic life for nearly another century;
Paraguayan war (1865-1870) brought renewed interest in entire
Chaco region, including Formosa; with constitutional national
organization finally established, the government was interested
in promoting economic development and immigration wherever
possible; public lands provided best national resource for ac-
complishing these purposes, especially in border areas occupied only by Indians; Formosa and Misiones held special significance as international areas also claimed by other countries (Paraguay and Brazil) with similar desires; by 1869 Argentina had officially claimed Chaco, including Formosa, and
three years later (1872) established province of Gran Chaco,
with capital at Villa Occidental (now Villa Hayes), across
Paraguay river from Asunción occupied by Argentine military
forces since end of war; Julio de Vedia, chief of occupation
force, became first governor; Paraguay protested and matter
submitted to Rutherford B. Hayes, president of the United
States; decision rendered November 2, 1878, favorable to
Paraguay, with Pilcomayo left as Argentina's northern boundary; Argentina accepted decision, turned disputed territory
over to Paraguay, and Governor Lucía V. Mansilla commissioned Lt. Col. Luis José Fontana to find best site on west
bank of Paraguay river, between Pilcomayo and Bermejo, for
new city to serve as capital and trade center; Fontana selected
high ground overlooking Paraguay river not far from old Jesuit
mission of Timbó, about 100 miles from Asunción and not
quite 200 from Corrientes; on April 8, 1879, with soldiers,
settlers, and government officials brought downriver from
Villa Occidental (see D. Abad de Santillán, III:728, for list
of original colonists), Fontana formally founded new capital,
retaining name Formosa (old variant for Spanish hermosa,
"beautiful") by which site had been known since Ayolas, upon
seeing it for first time in 1536, is said to have exclaimed:
"¡Qué vuelta hermosa!" (What a beautiful turn or bend);
country around capital good for raising beef cattle, subsistence
agriculture, and for growing cotton; by 1881 the city had 420
inhabitants; thirty years later, with population swollen temporarily because of workers on railroad to Jujuy, there were
2000; Fontana (q. v.) remained in command for five years and,
as a scientist as well as administrator and military commander, conducted and sent out several explorations; one of
most important sought fate of remnant of French scientific expedition led by Julio N. Crevaux, 1882, that had been attacked

by Indians, with many killed but others believed lost; in 1884
Formosa (using name of capital) became national territory, under its first governor Ignacio Fotheringham (1884-1891); (Fontana transferred to become first territorial governor of Chubut in Patagonia); provision already made in 1884 for military
occupation of Chaco territories, including Formosa, for protection of small interior settlements, and travel between Salta,
Tucumán, and Formosa from Indians or other attackers and
dangers; by 1914, Formosa's population had increased to
19,281 and the territory was divided into nine departments the
following year (1915); colonia San Francisco was established at
Laishi, about sixty miles from the capital for missionary work
among Indians and Europeans and Argentine settlers began to
establish colonias, along banks of Paraguay and Pilcomayo
rivers and in interior; in 1955, Formosa, along with other national territories became province; five years later population
reached 178,458; Formosa has continued to grow and prosper
as Argentina's most tropical frontier province.

FORT GUANACOS see GUANACOS, FORTIN

FOTHERINGHAM, IGNACIO (1842-1925).   Military leader and terri-
    torial administrator.
        Born in England, son of veteran of Waterloo; studied in
    England and Belgium; after two years in East India navy (1858-
    1860) he moved to Argentina; enlisted in army in war against
    Paraguay, beginning military career that lasted nearly forty
    years; saw action in Paraguay, accompanied General Paunero
    to Mendoza; after military action throughout the country was
    given border administrative posts; became governor of Chaco
    territory 1883; then of Formosa, 1884-1891; member of Su-
    perior War Junta 1895; war threatened along Andean border,
    sent him back to Mendoza as military commander of Cuyo,
    1897; placed in command of Fifth Military Region (including
    Cuyo); retired in 1905 after having been promoted to division
    general; died in Río IV, Córdoba.

FOUNDLINGS HOSPITAL (Casa de Niños Expósitos).   Home for
    abandoned infants and children established in Buenos Aires in
    August 1779 by Viceroy Juan José Vértiz, using a building
    that had formerly belonged to the Jesuits; the Jesuit printing
    press from Córdoba was installed there to provide necessary
    income for its support (see Printing Presses); later the in-
    comes from various rental properties and other funds were as-
    signed to the home but it regularly ran a deficit, usually made
    up by the war department; from 1779 to 1802, 2017 children
    were received and cared for; by royal decree, all those whose
    fathers were unknown were declared to be legitimate in birth
    for all civil purposes.

FRAILE MUERTO.   Site of two victories over invading armies by
    which Estanislao López maintained himself in power in Santa
    Fe and kept that province free from domination by the Buenos

Aires government; in 1818 he defeated Juan Bautista Bustos,
attacking from Córdoba with reinforcements from Belgrano's
army, thus immobilizing the government's forces; two years
later he again won a decisive victory over rivals by defeating
Francisco Ramírez, the Entre Ríos caudillo, and José Miguel
Carrera (former Chilean president, now involved in Argentine
civil wars and political affairs) at the same place.

FRANCE, AND FRENCH INFLUENCE. Unique relationships with
France have seriously influenced Argentine historical development since the beginning of the eighteenth century.
        When the Hapsburg line died out and a French Bourbon
prince was placed on the Spanish throne as Felipe V (1700-
1746), all the Spanish colonies, including the Río de la Plata,
felt the French influence in the centralization of political authority and use of intendancies and other political changes, in
the establishment of Carolingian academies, and implementa-
tions of economic, political, cultural ideas of the French philosophers and the Enlightenment; in the imperialistic wars of
the eighteenth and nineteenth centuries, largely between England
and France, the Family Compact between French and Spanish
Bourbon rulers kept Spain and its colonies involved; for Argentina this meant raising its boundary disputes with Brazil in the
Guaraní mission area and eastern bank of the Río de la Plata
(now Uruguay) to a new international level as the Portuguese
in Brazil were traditionally allied with England; the wars,
drawing of boundary (1777), establishment of viceroyalty with
capital at Buenos Aires, beginnings of Falkland Islands dispute;
British invasions of Río de la Plata (1806-1807), were all affected by this tie; on the other hand, when the French Bourbons
had been dethroned by the Revolution and Napoleon had gained
power, it was the French invasions of Spain to prevent England
from attacking France from that area, that brought alliance between Spanish patriot governments and England to defeat Napoleon and was reflected in Argentina by concessions that helped
to lay the foundations for future close relationship of new nation with Britain; French invasion of Spain and subsequent breakdown of Spanish government also provided spark that lit the
Spanish American independence movements, including the May
Revolution in Argentina.
        After the defeat of Napoleon, and restoration of Bourbon
monarchies in Spain and France, the latter tended to support
Spanish attempts to regain its colonies; after independence had
been clearly won, France continued to pressure Buenos Aires'
governments using pretexts that French subjects were mistreated, forced illegally into military service, etc.; French naval
vessels burned Argentine warships in Buenos Aires harbor during the revolution that brought Rosas into power and continued
to harass Buenos Aires and Rosas' government by giving military and financial aid to his enemies both at home and in Montevideo; this culminated in the French naval blockade of Buenos Aires and the rivers, 1838-1840, coordinated and allied
with Juan Lavalle's final unitarist attempt to overthrow Rosas;

the French withdrew after the Arana-Mackau treaty had been drawn up; French subjects were ultimately given the same privileges as those granted British residents in the treaty of 1825; for the next century France was second only to England in the financial, diplomatic support given Argentina; it sent the first refrigerated ship (Le Frigorifique) to Buenos Aires, beginning a revolution in the meat industry; it provided a minor portion of railroad financing and, later, a major portion of financing and skills for the western wine industry; much of the expense of developing Rosario as port was borne by French capital, as well as many other ventures.

France's most important contributions were cultural and intellectual; for a century and a half--from the late 18th century to the 1940s--Argentines looked to France, especially to Paris, for its ideologies, its literary patterns, its fashions and life styles; Paris was the Argentine cultural mecca and prominent and wealthy Argentines called it their second home; beginning with the ideas and institutions of the Enlightenment, the French influence continued with Esteban Echeverría's bringing of the Romantic movement from Paris to Buenos Aires and its subsequent influence through the members of the Asociación de Mayo and other Argentine unitarist exiles; it became dominant in the mid-nineteenth century as French intellectuals in political exile in Argentina were used in both the Confederation and Buenos Aires, and then by President Mitre to establish a modern system of secondary education throughout the republic; although this was somewhat modified later by Sarmiento's introduction of U.S. teachers and normal schools, the international prestige of Paris remained so high that Argentine intellectuals continued to make French their second language and to draw their inspiration from there, and wealthy members of the Argentine oligarchy spent much of their time and money there.

The economic depression of the 1930s and World War II changed this; the declining position of France economically and internationally, the rising preeminence, power and wealth of the United States, technological changes opening new opportunities, as well as competitions with its trade with France, coincided with rising Argentine nationalistic feeling to diminish the strength of this tie, as Argentina, with its heterogeneous population, moved to break its dependence on Western Europe and establish new international ties in accordance with its modern interests.

FRANCISCANS. Members of religious order founded by St. Francis of Assisi in early thirteenth century; Franciscan friars were first religious to come to Río de la Plata, as several accompanied Magellan on his voyage along coast in 1519-1520; other Franciscans came with nearly every expedition of discoverers and conquerors; first missionaries to Indians accompanied veedor Alonso de Cabrera to America but remained on Santa Catalina Island until arrival of Cabeza de Vaca whom they accompanied on overland journey to Asunción 1541; twenty-two more Franciscans, including Luis de Bolaños (q. v.) arrived with Ortiz de Zárate 1572; first missions in Paraguay and Río de la Plata were established by these Franciscans among Indians on Paraguay and upper Paraná rivers and maintained until eighteenth century; as missionaries, educators, students and scholars, prelates, founders of cities, artists and church builders, Franciscans have since been intimately linked to Argentine history; Martín Ignacio de Loyola, nephew of founder of Society of Jesus but himself a Franciscan, became bishop of Asunción; other Franciscans entered Tucumán from Peru, including Francisco Daroca who continued on to Asunción, joined Juan de Garay in founding of Santa Fe (1573) where he remained until his death in 1580; among other famous Franciscans in early period were San Francisco Solano (q.v.), famous missionary to Peru and Tucumán, Francisco de Zamora, and Juan de Rivadeneyra, present at Garay's refounding of Buenos Aires, 1580; Franciscan establishments served as centers of culture and benevolence throughout colonial period; after Jesuit expulsion (1767) Franciscans took over management of Monserrat academy and the university at Córdoba (until 1808); monastery at Buenos Aires had splendid library and was center of Enlightenment ideas and literature on eve of independence; many Franciscans aided cause of independence, including Father Cayetano José Rodríguez, active in May Revolution; Father Luis Beltrán, "Archimedes" (artillery engineer) of San Martín's Army of the Andes; others served in independence armies as chaplains or became members of national congresses.

See Fray Antonio de Santa Clara Córdoba, La orden franciscana en la República del Plata; Fray Pacífico Otero, Dos héroes de la conquista (about Luis Bolaños and San Francisco Solano), (Buenos Aires, 1905); also Diario y derrotero de sus viajes (1749-1753) by Fray Pedro José de Parras (Buenos Aires, 1943).

FRAY MOCHO, CUENTOS DE   see ALVAREZ, JOSE SIXTO

FREIRE, RAMON (1787-1851).   Guerrero of the war of independence.

Born in Santiago, Chile; was one of Chilean officers forced to flee across the Andes to Argentina, following the royalist reconquest of Chile at Rancagua; in 1815 accompanied Hipólito Bouchard (q.v.) on his Pacific venture; returned and joined Army of the Andes; sent by San Martín with small advance force to arouse southern Chile for independence, preparing the way for his approaching liberating campaign; rejoined main army after Chacabuco and took part in Las Heras' campaign to southern Chile and in the battles of Cancha Rayada and Maipú; with Chilean independence won, Freire became involved in political life there; succeeded O'Higgins as head of the government and occupied same position, briefly, on other occasions; spent most of years 1830-1842 in Peruvian exile for political reasons; returned to Chile and retired to private life; died in Santiago in 1851.

FRENCH, DOMINGO (1774-1825). Precursor, popular leader, and
demagogue of independence movement.

Born in Buenos Aires; post office employee until entering military service to fight British invasions, 1806-1807; one
of early proponents of complete independence; played dramatic
role in May Revolution by mobilizing and leading populace to
demand immediate action from Cabildo Abierto; displayed, with
Beruti, the blue and white colors of the patricios, later to be
used in national flag; became colonel in junta's revolutionary
army and carried out executions of the conspirators of Córdoba at Cabeza de Tigre; backed Mariano Moreno and his more
radical position; turbulent career; sent to Patagonia because of
political activities in revolution of April 5-6, 1811; restored to
command, engaged in successful siege of Montevideo, 1814;
led reinforcements to Rondeau's army of the North in 1815 and
assisted in reconciling differences between Rondeau and Martín
Güemes; back in Buenos Aires, 1817, exiled to United States
along with Manuel Moreno, Agrelo, etc. for opposing directorate; restored, 1819, by Pueyrredón to his rank and position in
the armed forces.

FRESCO, MANUEL. Railroad physician who served as governor of
Buenos Aires (1936-1940); powerful conservative leader in turbulent Argentine political life of late 1930s and early 1940s; a
strong nationalist, he represented and served as spokesman for
the extreme right wing of conservatives; he was determined to
maintain his group in power and to win popular support for
such leadership; ousted as governor and his province intervened by President Ortiz because of illegalities in elections of
1940; Fresco continued to be a political force, especially
through the pages of his Cabildo, a newspaper that sought to
attract wide readership through its publication of sporting and
racing news along with Fresco's political views.

FRIAS, ANTONIO (1745-1824). Argentine-born Jesuit, mathematician, astronomer (known as "el astrónomo santiagüeno"--the
astronomer from Santiago del Estero).

Frías entered the Jesuit order in 1764 and was still
pursuing his first course of study when he was expelled from
Argentina along with other Jesuits; went first to Spain, then
to Papal States where he completed his ecclesiastical studies
and was ordained; immediately began the study of mathematics
and astronomy to which he devoted the rest of his life; in collaboration with Fathers De Cesaris and Regia, he wrote the
monumental work that was published by the observatory of Milan and attracted interest in scientific reviews both in Europe
and in America; Father Gaspar Juárez (q.v.) wrote to friends
in Córdoba that Father Frías spent his entire time in such
studies so as to be of greater use to his native country when
he returned; contributed to astronomy journal Efemeridi Astro-
nomiche (Milan, 1775-1803); went to Spain in 1799, hoping to
go home but this was not permitted; returned to Italy after
having been captured by Anglo-Turks; when the Society of

Jesus was reestablished, Frías went to Rome and reentered the order (1814); died in Milan 1824, leaving many unpublished manuscripts, now apparently lost.

FRIAS, BERNARDO (1866-1930).   Historian from Salta.

Born in Salta and educated there at the Colegio Nacional; went to Buenos Aires where he received a doctorate in jurisprudence from the Faculty of Law and Social Sciences; returning to Salta, he immersed himself in historical research in the provincial archives and libraries, having two primary interests; the history of his native province and that of writing a comprehensive history of Argentina from a provincial, rather than the customary porteño (or Buenos Aires) point of view; supporting himself by teaching Argentine history in the Colegio and journalism, he published 3 volumes of his history of General Martín Güemes and the province of Salta (Salta and Buenos Aires, 1902-1911), along with other works on Salta and five volumes of Argentine traditions, published 1923-1930; left several works still in manuscript, including his Argentine history; new edition of Historia del General Martín de Güemes y de la provincia de Salta, o sea de la independencia argentina (4 v., Buenos Aires, 1971-1972).

After his retirement from teaching, Frías became minister of the Court of Justice; member of Junta de Historia; died in Salta.

FRIAS, EUSTOQUIO (1801-1891).   Military hero of independence war; career military officer; general.

Born in Salta; joined San Martín's army in 1816; fought in Chile, Peru, Ecuador; after taking part in campaign of Puertos Intermedios (intermediate ports, Peru), fought under Simón Bolívar at Junín (1824), distinguishing himself with group of guerrilla fighters; wounded at Ayacucho (1824); received gold medal from Bolívar; in 1826 returned to Argentina with mounted grenadier officers; fought in war against Brazil; joined unitarists against Rosas; captured, escaped from prison to Paraguay; joined Urquiza at Caseros against Rosas; in 1855 named second in command of northern border; engaged in war in Paraguay; became lieutenant general; attached to garrison at Federal Capital (Buenos Aires) until end of 1890; died following year.

FRIAS, FELIX (1816-1881).   Writer; intellectual; diplomat; militant Catholic lay leader.

Born in Buenos Aires; was preparing for a law career, in his family's tradition, when the accidental death of his father and Rosas' persecutions forced him to leave his studies and to go into exile in Uruguay; was one of founders of Asociación de Mayo, with Echeverría; while in exile in Uruguay he joined Juan Lavalle as private secretary and accompanied him across Argentina on his unsuccessful campaign of liberation (1839-1841); formed part of escort carrying Lavalle's remains to Bolivia for burial; went to Chile and then to Europe in 1848 where he interviewed General San Martín; returning to Argentina after the fall of Rosas, he edited the paper El Orden, devoted to discussions of the problems of Argentina; served also in the provincial legislature and later in the national senate (1863-1869); sent to Chile as Minister Plenipotentiary by President Sarmiento, he represented Argentina through the difficult period of the Paraguayan War, the War of the Pacific (opposed by Argentina) and the Andean boundary dispute between Chile and Argentina; highly praised in Argentina for his only partially successful efforts to solve the latter, he did make an important contribution to its eventual peaceful settlement by presenting a clear, carefully documented statement of the legal and historical basis of his nation's claims; returning to Argentina he refused Nicolás Avellaneda's offer (1874) to serve in his cabinet; also refused to accept election as vice governor of Buenos Aires province, believing that his influence could best be exercised through his oratory and writing; a prolific writer, he published essays, books, journal articles, etc., devoted primarily to two themes, politics and religion in Latin America and especially in Argentina; he was profoundly patriotic and, unlike many of his more secular, liberal friends, dogmatically Catholic in his public position; Frías was both predecessor and colleague of José Manuel Estrada in this field; joined latter in opposition to secular legislation of Roca period; his health failing, he went to Europe and died of a heart attack in Paris where he had gone for medical care.

Frías' works were published in Buenos Aires in 1884, consisting of four volumes, entitled Escritos and Discursos. His friend and militant Catholic colleague Pedro Goyena published Biografía de Félix Frías in Buenos Aires, 1889.

FRIGORIFICOS. Meatpacking plants using refrigeration; took name from first refrigerated ship in Argentine meat trade--Le Frigorifique (q.v.); successor to meat-salting factories (saladeros); as meat industry turned attention to new freezing processes in last two decades of nineteenth century, that of Carlos Tellier, used in Le Frigorifique, shipping meat at freezing point 32° F, chilled but not frozen, offered first promise but, after arrival of Paraguay (1877) with meat frozen and shipped at -22° F., latter process preferred because of long voyages and rudimentary technology; first frigorífico in Argentina built in 1882 at San Nicolás by Eugenio Terrasón (owner of Saladero San Luis); others followed rapidly financed primarily by Argentine and British capital; in 1884, 24 frozen beeves shipped to Europe, increasing to more than 113,000 quarters within five years; after 1900, frigoríficos handled most Argentine beef; by 1907 frozen beef constituted 51% of all meat exports; U.S. companies entered field; Swift in 1907, Armour, 1908; settlements grew up around frigoríficos, often taking their names, forming, in effect, new factory towns around ports serving as outlets for cattle areas.

See related entries on Cattle; Le Frigorífique; Refrigeration (detailed account of revolution that refrigeration brought to Argentine meat industry, with its economic and political effects); and Saladeros. Peter H. Smith (see Suggested Readings, Appendix III) has excellent material on frigoríficos.

FRIGORIFIQUE, LE. First refrigerated ship to carry meat to Argentina; revolutionized meat industry. Le Frigorifique left Rouen, France August 23, 1876, with six carcasses of beef, 12 mutton, 1 pork, and 50 fowl chilled to 32° F. according to method devised by Carlos Tellier, who accompanied voyage; French ship sailed on schedule, with full publicity; laid up in Lisbon 25 days for repairs to refrigerating equipment; arrived in Buenos Aires December 25; meat judged poor in quality but Tellier's method hailed enthusiastically; Le Frigorifique returned to France August 14, 1877, with cargo of Argentine meat furnished by members of Rural Society; this successful trial venture resulted from cooperative efforts of both governments, Buenos Aires province, and the Sociedad Rural Argentina.

FRONDIZI, ARTURO (1908-   ). President of Argentine Republic 1958-1962; lawyer and political leader.
        Born in Paso del los Libres, Corrientes; father Italian immigrant of 1890s; graduated as lawyer from University of Buenos Aires, 1930; had already become actively involved in Radical party (Unión Cívica Radical); 1936-1953 member of directing council and lecturer at Free University for Graduate Studies; during period 1946-1951 served as national deputy from Federal Capital; acquired great popular prestige; specialized in economic subjects; became known (after 1946) as one of most outspoken opponents of Perón's administration, although these differences were primarily about methods used, rather than economic and social goals; in 1951, Radical ticket with Ricardo Balbín up for president and Frondizi as vice president, won 2.3 million votes to Perón's 4.6 million; near close of Perón's administration, in 1955, Frondizi published Petróleo y política, strongly critical of Perón's calling in foreign oil companies; also broadcast speech criticizing Perón government but warning Conservatives that Radicals would never permit return to conservative rule of 1943; as national elections of 1958 approached, Radicals divided into two competing, conflicting groups: the more conservative traditional members followed Ricardo Balbín in Unión Cívica Radical del Pueblo; while leftist group--drawing support also from several provincial political leaders, university reformers, entrepreneurs, industrialists, and, briefly, some Peronists--took name of Unión Cívica Radical Intransigente and, under Frondizi, projected image of dynamic new political leadership with modernizing, industrializing goals; Frondizi and vice presidential candidate Alejandro Gómez won election, apparently with help of Peronists.
        Inaugurated as president May 1, 1958, Frondizi faced basic dilemma: although he wanted to govern as constitutional president, he could not forget that military forces (too divided among themselves to be predictable or easily won over) stood

ready to intervene; nevertheless he began work toward three
goals: to develop and stabilize Argentina's economy, dwindling since 1950; to effect conciliations of deep political, social,
and ideological hostilities to point that each group could at
least participate normally in political processes; and to restore international confidence in Argentina; optimistic, innovative, realistic, intelligent, experienced in politics, flexible and
willing to compromise, he worked for nearly four years toward these ends; hoped to bring republic forward without sacrificing gains made by earlier groups and governments; by end
of 1961 balance sheet stood as follows:

Internationally: confidence in Argentina had been restored, Frondizi had traveled extensively; visited U.S. in 1959
(first Argentine president to do so) and cooperated more closely with U.S. (although showing independence in matter of Cuba)
than any president since Sarmiento; Frondizi had taken lead in
organization of LAFTA (Latin American Free Trade Association, q.v.) and had urged greater coordination of various Latin
American national economic development plans and policies.

Economically: through contracts with foreign oil companies for exploration for new oil deposits and expansion of
processing capacity, Argentina had become self-sufficient in
oil; stabilization agreement signed with International Monetary
Fund 1958; through loans, largely also from IMF and other international sources, output of coal was increased to satisfy
one-fifth of Argentine needs; San Nicolás steel mill began production in 1960; energy crisis eased with power plants to service Buenos Aires, dams completed in Mendoza and Córdoba,
and plans drawn for use of falls on Uruguay and upper Paraná
rivers to provide power for needs of growing population and
expanding industrialization; austerity program imposed in 1959
to increase available national capital for new programs; wages
increased for labor to combat inflation.

Politically: democratic appearances maintained for
nearly four years; Peronists permitted to participate openly in
elections in early 1962; Frondizi's government had survived approximately 35 attempted coups against it; and urban terrorism,
largely politically inspired, had been somewhat abated by Conintes plan giving military courts right to exercise summary
justice in cases involving crimes against national security.

By March 1962, however, Frondizi's support did not
equal his opposition; his attempts to mobilize strong middle
class political leadership to balance old oligarchic ruling class
and new politicized masses failed--middle classes not ready
yet; his calculated risk in permitting Peronists to run their own
tickets in 1962 produced Peronist victories in several provinces, including control of Buenos Aires province, as well as
45 out of available 94 seats in Congress; nationalists were offended by his friendly attitude toward United States and foreign
capitalists; conservatives were appalled by Frondizi's public
reception of Cuban revolutionary leader Ernesto ("Che") Guevara, even though latter was Argentine-born, as well as by
Frondizi's continued friendly gestures toward Peronists; church

not appeased by Frondizi's offer of equal accreditation for ecclesiastical institutions of higher learning, while traditionalists
were offended by this departure from secular high status of
national universities; worst of all, economy still declining--
Frondizi accused of being too revolutionary and not revolutionary enough; finally, Frondizi's political wheeling-dealing had
lost him credibility and confidence in public opinion and support; when his last attempt to remain in office by intervening
the Peronist provinces failed and Frondizi still refused to resign, the military forces took action at end of March 1962,
overthrew his government, imprisoned Frondizi on Martín
García Island, annulled elections, and placed José María Guido,
president of senate, in presidency to preserve semblance of
civilian government; Frondizi was moved to more pleasant surroundings at Bariloche after few months and released by President Arturo Illia shortly after his own inauguration in July
1963; became active in the 1970s as leader of the Movimiento
de Integración y Desarrollo (MID).

FRONDIZI, RISIERI (1910-   ).   Philosopher; educator; writer.
        Born in Posadas, Misiones, brother of President Ar-
turo Frondizi; studied at Instituto Nacional del Profesorado
Secundario; received M. A. degree at University of Michigan
(1943) and Ph. D. at National University of Mexico (1950);
taught logic, history of philosophy, and esthetics at National
University of Tucumán, 1938-1946; organized the department of
philosophy and letters there, revised the curriculum, and introduced the doctorate in philosophy; during the late 1940s Professor Frondizi accepted appointments on the faculties of various U.S. universities, including the University of Pennsylvania,
Bryn Mawr, Yale, Columbia, and the University of Puerto
Rico; after his return to Argentina, he became rector of the
University of Buenos Aires 1957-1962; his scholarly writings
include a Spanish translation (1939) of A Treatise Concerning
the Principles of Human Knowledge by the eighteenth century
British philosopher George Berkeley, and in 1940 he completed
a Spanish translation of Alfred N. Whitehead's Nature and Life,
published six years earlier; throughout his career, in addition
to his major works, he has contributed to scholarly journals
of other Latin American universities, as well as those of Argentina; in the early 1970s he turned his attention to the mission of the university in a world of tensions.
        Among his writings that have gone into several editions
are 1) his study of values, translated into English as What Is
Value? :   An Introduction to Axiology (2nd ed. , La Salle, Illinois, 1971, and a new (fifth) Spanish edition published by the
Fondo de Cultura Económica, Mexico, 1972); and 2) his study
of personal identity Substancia y fundición en el problema del
yo, first published in Buenos Aires in 1952, translated into
English and published by Yale University as The Nature of the
Self (New Haven, 1953); new Spanish edition appeared in 1970,
entitled El yo como estructura dinámica.

FRONTIER, ARGENTINE.   Line or area separating lands used by
Spaniards and Creoles and those left to Indians; consisted
largely of semi-tropical lands of the north and northeast, as
well as the drier southern and western pampas, and Patagonia
and Magellan strait area; line had to be maintained by force
and Indian raids and punitive military campaigns were regular
features of Argentine colonial life; in 1751 the blandengues
(q.v.) were assigned to guard the Indian frontier; Viceroy
Melo de Portugal ordered Félix de Azara to make a study of
the various frontiers to see how Indian raids could be prevented; the early patriot governments were concerned with the
same problem; as lands became more valuable, pressure
against the Indians increased; Rosas in the 1830s stabilized the
pampas frontier farther south and west; it was not, however,
until the late 1870s that Roca's "conquest of the desert" (q.v.)
and similar campaigns in the Chaco region finally eliminated
the frontier, and brought all the land and Indians under the
civil government of the Argentine republic (see listings of various provinces, especially Buenos Aires, Chaco, Chubut, Formosa, La Pampa, Misiones, Santa Cruz, and the territory of
Tierra del Fuego).

FRUIT INDUSTRY.   During colonial period in Argentina Cuyo area
(including provinces of Mendoza, San Juan, and San Luis) engaged in extensive growing of fruits for shipping to Chilean or
Argentine markets after they had been dried or conserved;
Jesuit missions in subtropical northern areas also raised fruit,
especially citrus, on large scale; for the rest, most fruit was
provided by dooryard trees or small local orchards; commercial fruit growing developed in twentieth century to satisfy new
national and international demands; these resulted from many
factors, including, in Argentina, increasing size of population--
and different dietary habits of immigrant groups who helped to
swell the numbers, increasing urbanization, and development of
manufacturing and other industries taking rural laborers away
from farms; Argentines also (along with rest of Western people) were influenced by new health studies demonstrating value
of vitamins and other food supplements found in large measure
in various fruits; commercial fruit orchards and groves grew
up around Buenos Aires and other towns; colonias in Misiones
and other northern areas began to experiment with commercial
fruit growing; British railroad company financed irrigation system in Río Negro area in south, completed in 1920s; Mendoza
and other provinces added this traditional fruit industry to their
booming growing of grapes for wine; railroads and refrigerated
trucks on national highway systems brought fresh fruit to Buenos Aires, as well as all other markets; in 1936 government
interest and support was shown in establishment of institute of
fruit culture under auspices of Faculty of Agronomy and Animal Husbandry at the university of Buenos Aires with Isaac C.
Grünberg as first director; similar private institutions were
established for experimental and teaching purposes, such as
the school "Osvaldo Magnasco" near Dolores in province of Bue-

nos Aires.

Commercial fruit production reached more than a million metric tons annually by 1950s, with oranges leading, followed by table grapes, apples, peaches, and similar citrus and other fruits; production of citrus fruit alone given as 1,542,000 metric tons in 1971; approximately 90% of fruit was produced for domestic market; most of the rest exported to Brazil, United States, France, and Great Britain.

Argentina defines its six major zones of fruit-growing as follows: 1) Cuyo; Mendoza produces apples, pears, peaches, plums, olives, and some table grapes; San Juan leads nation in production of table grapes. 2) Southern region; Río Negro, Neuquén, and Chubut; Río Negro valley center of fruit production with Río Negro province providing around 70% of nation's pears and 50% of its apples, among other fruits. 3) Paraná Delta and surrounding area; warm waters of river coming down from tropics enable area to grow both subtropical and temperate fruits. 4) Atlantic region; coastal area of Buenos Aires province from estuary to around Mar del Plata; apples, pears, plums, peaches and fruits of this type are grown here. 5) Mesopotamia; largely citrus, with Misiones leading in national production of lemons, Corrientes in oranges and grapefruit, and Entre Ríos in tangerines. 6) Northern region; Tucumán, Salta, Jujuy; both subtropical and temperate fruits raised here, depending on altitude.

FUELS see ENERGY RESOURCES

FUERO. (A law, code of laws, jurisdiction; or exemption, privilege). As used in Spanish colonial Argentina, and in historical writings about it, the term is apt to refer either to the charter or constitution officially granted to a particular town or district specifying its legal rights and responsibilities, along with its special privileges--these charters were similar for all towns receiving them, but often contained special privileges jealously guarded by the citizens of the community--or to special rights or privileges given to a group or class.

FUERTE INDEPENDENCIA. Fort established on southern Indian frontier in 1823 by Martín Rodríguez; beginning of Tandil (see Tandil; Martín Rodríguez).

FUGL, JUAN (1811-1900). Danish entrepreneur and colonizer in Tandil area. Originally a schoolmaster, Fugl came to Buenos Aires from Denmark in 1843 seeking greater opportunities; after enduring many hardships in establishing himself as a dairyman on the outskirts of Buenos Aires, he learned that excellent land was available in eastern Buenos Aires province for agriculture and that so far no wheat farms had been established in the Tandil area; securing a government grant of land, he moved there, planted wheat, and rapidly became successful; established the first flour mill in that area and followed this by opening a bakery; having already become closely identified with the community life of Tandil (q. v.), he returned to Denmark in 1856 to bring back a group of Danish farmers to settle there; in 1871 he brought back a second contingent of Danish immigrants; Fugl remained in Tandil until 1875--active in constructing the church, establishing and encouraging the school there and remembered for his personal efforts in encouraging parents to educate their children--and then returned to his native country, a very wealthy man; died in Denmark, having left an indelible mark on one small area of Argentina.

FUNDAMENTAL LAW OF 1825 see CONSTITUTION

FUNES, GREGORIO, Deán (1749-1829). Churchman; statesman; historian.
    Born in Córdoba, from old, aristocratic families on both maternal and paternal sides; educated in Jesuit tradition at Montserrat and University of San Carlos, became active, liberal leader in education, ecclesiastical reform, patriot politics, and national organization, as well as influential writer.
    He became familiar with ideas of Enlightenment during four years (1775-1779) in Spain completing his education at University of Alcalá de Henares and other institutions; returned to Córdoba to become dean of cathedral and rector of university (1808); was involved in efforts to bring new ideas and programs to latter when May Revolution occurred; actively supported patriot cause, refusing to join Córdoba opposition; unsuccessfully urged clemency for Santiago de Liniers and other defeated conspiracy leaders; elected to represent Córdoba in Buenos Aires junta, Funes became militant leader and spokesman for deputies from interior provinces (1810); succeeded in getting latter integrated into junta, action that resulted in Mariano Moreno's resignation in protest and, later, the unsuccessful conservative revolution of April 5-6, 1811; active in junta affairs, Funes was responsible for first freedom of press law (1811); edited El argos de Buenos Aires; advised junta that royal rights over ecclesiastical appointments (in Patronato Real) devolved on junta after the revolution; in late 1816, following uprising of Artigas' supporters in Córdoba, Deán Funes took over government of province under Supreme Director Juan Martín de Pueyrredón; with other liberal churchmen, accepted Rivadavia's ecclesiastical reforms while strongly condemning excesses; elected to Las Heras' national congress in Buenos Aires in 1820s but no longer as active as in earlier period; strongly influential through his writings, both historical and those interpreting the contemporary scene and events; best known among his scholarly works is Ensayo de la historia civil del Paraguay, Buenos Aires y Tucumán (2 volumes, Buenos Aires, 1856).

FURLONG CARDIFF, GUILLERMO (1889-). Jesuit; historian.
    Born in Villa Constitución Santa Fe; received much of his higher education in the United States; became a Jesuit; taught English at Colegio del Salvador in Buenos Aires; became

a director of Academia de Letras del Plata and editor of its review Estudios.

Father Fúrlong Cárdiff became interested in the history of Argentina as made and written by his fellow Jesuits during the Spanish colonial period and has devoted several decades to research in the original documents remaining for this period; he has published, for the first time, or in new editions, the writings, maps, and other works of such missionaries as Thomas Falkner, Thomas Fields, Domingo Muriel, Bernardo Nusdorffer, Florián Paucke, José Sánchez Labrador (qq.v.), and others accompanying them with biographical data about the authors; widening his interests from the mission work, geographic explorations, and ethnological and linguistic studies of the various Argentine Indian groups with whom these missionaries had been involved, he published monographic studies of varying length on aspects and components of the Argentine colonial life and society as a whole, including such topics as music, libraries, architecture, mathematics, medicine and physicians, naturalists, the role of women (La cultura femenina), philosophy, and printing presses; various compilations and analyses of these individual studies were made and in 1969 he drew upon his researches of the past forty years to bring out his comprehensive Historia social y cultural del Río de la Plata: 1536-1810 in three large, illustrated volumes.

- G -

GACETA (also spelled GAZETA) de Buenos Aires, La (The Buenos Aires Gazette) 1810-1821. Newspaper established by the Junta shortly after the May Revolution (first issue June 7, 1810) to give the new patriot government an organ of publicity; originally under the influence and direction of Mariano Moreno, it was used to inform the public of government actions and of revolutionary activities elsewhere, as well as to educate the people into new democratic practices; after Moreno's resignation, the Gaceta was continued for a while by his followers; changing its name somewhat but always continuing as official organ of the successive governments, under distinguished editors--Deán Gregorio Funes, Pedro J. Agrelo, Vicente Pazos Silva and Bernardo Monteagudo (co-editors), Nicolás Herrera, Camilo Henríquez, Julián Alvarez, and Manuel Antonio Castro, until September 1821 when it was finally suppressed, apparently because the government felt that the Registro Oficial served the same purpose. The classic work on the Gaceta is that published by Antonio Zinny in 1975.

GACETA MERCANTIL, LA. Newspaper published continuously in Buenos Aires for 28 years; important source of information about Rosas period.

Publication was begun October 1, 1823, by printers Hallet and Company, with Esteban Hallet and Santiago Kiernan as editors; tabloid in size at first and devoted to commercial news and other matters of public information; after 1826 it was officially known as La Gaceta Mercantil, Diario Comercial, Político y Literario and the following year increased its size to large folio; in the Rosas period it supported his policies, was subsidized by him and tended to become largely political and literary; it published official documents, news items, especially political, from all the provinces and from Montevideo, announcements and literary contributions; among its editors were José Rivera Indarte, Manuel Irigoyen, Pedro de Angelis, Benjamín Gorostiaga, Bernardo de Irigoyen, and Avelina Sierra; its final issue appeared February 3, 1852 (date of defeat of Rosas at Caseros), but was not distributed.

A complete study of its 8472 issues was made by Antonio Zinny and published, after his death, in 3 volumes, 1912.

GAINZA, MARTIN DE (1814-1888).   Career military officer; cabinet minister; political leader.

Born in Buenos Aires; early became a soldier; joined his father (Mariano José de Gainza, 1789-1853, veteran of war of independence and unitarist) in army of Juan Lavalle (1840) and accompanied latter until final defeat of unitarist forces in northwest at Famaillá (q. v.); formed part of group returning through Chaco to fight against Rosas under leadership of General Paz in Corrientes, then as member of Argentine Legion in defense of Montevideo; went back to Corrientes but was forced into exile, in Paraguay; after the fall of Rosas, he returned to Buenos Aires and offered his military services to the province; took part in battle of Pavón and held various military appointments; in 1868 President Sarmiento named him minister of war and navy; he organized the Colegio Militar; directed campaigns (1870-1873) against López Jordán, rebellious caudillo in Entre Ríos; organized new naval academy created by Congress, and enlarged, modernized, and strengthened the navy; was replaced by Adolfo Alsina in 1874; retired in 1875 for political reasons; in 1878 called meeting to reconstruct the Autonomist Party; Partido Autonomista Nacional (PAN) formed; as minister of war for Buenos Aires Governor Carlos Tejedor (during crisis of 1880; see Federalization of City of Buenos Aires) he was deeply involved; demoted when Buenos Aires was federalized; brought back to active duty as division general in 1883, he died while serving as commander of 2nd division of 1st Army Corps; among several of Gainza's other achievements might be listed his winning of a medal for bravery in action against the French fleet in 1839, refused because it was offered by the dictator Rosas; his role in the founding of the Swiss colony at Baradero in 1856, and his services as legislator on both provincial and national level.

GAINZA PAZ, ALBERTO (1899-1977).   Newspaperman; lawyer; editor of La Prensa.

Born in Buenos Aires; studied there in Faculty of law and social sciences; although his career has been largely concerned with the editing of the daily newspaper La Prensa,

Gainza Paz has also been active in other newspaper and publishing concerns; served on committee governing pensions for newspapermen; was president of commission regulating distribution of newsprint; in 1951, La Prensa was expropriated by the Perón government, turned over to the Confederación General del Trabajo, and transformed into a trade union paper; Gainza Paz went into exile, spending considerable time in the United States where he was honored by newspapermen for his fight for the freedom of the press and by learned and academic groups; in 1950 he had received the prize of the Foundation of the Americas and was given honorary doctor degrees by several U.S. universities, including Northwestern and Columbia universities in 1951; after the overthrow of Perón's government in 1955, the provisional government of President Aramburu returned La Prensa and on February 3, 1956, it reappeared under Gainza Paz' direction and resumed its prestigious position in Argentine life under his continued leadership.

GALAN, FRANCISCO (d. after 1564). Conquistador; often confused with Francisco Ruiz Galán (q. v.).
    Born in Cádiz; accompanied Pedro de Mendoza's expedition to Río de la Plata 1536; took part in many of early activities of conquistadors; present at establishment of fort at site of Asunción 1537; also at Corpus Christi; accompanied Irala on search for Ayolas; back in Buenos Aires when settlers were moved to Asunción 1541; served as majordomo for second adelantado Alvar Núñez Cabeza de Vaca; remained in Asunción holding various responsible posts, not as high in political or social hierarchy as Francisco Ruiz Galán but also not as controversial. See Lafuente Machain in Suggested References, Appendix III.

GALLO, PEDRO LEON (1779-1852). Priest, active in independence movement; signer of Declaration of Independence.
    Born in Santiago del Estero; educated and ordained in Córdoba; supported May Revolution and represented his province in Congress of Tucumán; signed Declaration of Indpendence July 9, 1816; remained active in congress until it was dissolved in Buenos Aires, 1820; supported Juan Felipe Ibarra's government in Santiago del Estero as cabinet member and legislator; Ibarra's appointment of Father Gallo to head government of diocese of Santiago del Estero provoked conflict with Cabildo of Salta that had already appointed someone else; Father Gallo died in Tucumán in 1852 after a long illness.

GALLO, VICENTE CARMELO (1873-1942). Lawyer; university professor and administrator; political leader.
    Born in San Miguel de Tucumán; educated in law in Buenos Aires; his dissertation (1897), entitled Juicio político, won the faculty prize; taught in the university, serving as rector and dean 1934-1941; his teaching and writing on administrative law reflected the laissez-faire liberalism of the nine-

teenth century; becoming active in political life, he served as
Bernardo de Irigoyen's secretary (1898) while latter was governor of Buenos Aires; was elected to terms in congress as
deputy and as senator; resigned latter seat to become minister
of interior (1923-1925) for President Marcos T. Alvear but resigned for political reasons; Gallo became leader of the anti-
personalist group of the Unión Radical Cívica; was placed on
its national ticket in 1928 as vice president, with Leopoldo
Melo as presidential candidate; after defeat by Hipólito Yrigoyen, Gallo retired to private life and the practice of his profession, serving as lawyer for several large companies and financial groups; died in Buenos Aires.

GALVEZ, MANUEL (1882-1962). Writer; traditionalist, idealist of
early twentieth century, sought to call Argentina back to its
own Spanish, Catholic roots and values; believed these to be
still conserved in provinces in contrast to urban cosmopolitan-
ism of Buenos Aires with its active labor groups, floods of
immigrants, and liberal intellectuals.

Born in Paraná, educated at Santa Fe; graduated in law
in Buenos Airees; co-founder, with Ricardo Olivera, of literary journal Ideas; member of Argentine Academy of Letters;
in 1917 organized Cooperativa Editorial Buenos Aires; a prolific writer, his works widely translated into English, German,
French, and Portuguese; strongly influenced by Hispanidad
movement (literary revival with political overtones in Spain following latter's loss of empire 1898); El solar de la raza car-
ries this theme; his ideas of social justice (imposed by authority rather than revolution or clash of political parties or other
democratic action) appear best in his historical biographies of
Juan Manuel Rosas, Hipólito Yrigoyen (whom Gálvez admired
greatly and was himself inclined toward Hispanidad), and the
devout Catholic Ecuadorian reform president Gabriel García
Moreno; opposed university reforms; became more reactionary
as World War II approached, tending toward European fascist
ideals; Perón's justicialismo and peronismo, generally, may
reflect some of Gálvez's passion for Argentine and Catholic solution to modern social problems; his autobiography Entre la
novela y la historia. Recuerdos de la vida literaria was published in 1962.

GANDIA, ENRIQUE DE (1906-). One of Argentina's leading, most
prolific modern historians.

Born in Buenos Aires; he has devoted most of his career to historical research and writing, along with serving in
administrative and teaching positions in such Buenos Aires institutions as the superior school of Bellas Artes, the old municipal museum of colonial art and that of Cornelio Saavedra,
and the Universidad Libre de Olives; he has won many prizes
and been honored by many historical groups; was secretary of
commission for celebration of fourth centennial of founding of
Buenos Aires (1536-1936) for which his Historia de la conquista del Río de la Plata y del Paraguay, Los gobiernos del

Don Pedro de Mendoza, Alvar Núñez y Domingo de Irala,
1535-1556 (Buenos Aires, 1932) provided a comprehensive,
scholarly historical preview.

In addition to this history, Gandía's bibliography is extensive, consisting of monographic studies of varying length
based on both manuscript and printed sources, essays in scholarly journals dealing with the philosophy of history, the relationship between historical writing and political purposes, revisionism and other topics of interest to the historian's craft;
his early interest centered around colonial history, then moved
to the independence period and the national period; in recent
years (1960s-1970s) he has been especially interested in the
influence made by the ideas held by such men as Mariano Moreno, Juan Manuel de Rosas, Bartolomé Mitre, and Juan Bautista Alberdi; he served as codirector and contributor for the
Historia de la Nación published by the National Academy of
History.

A partial list of his other longer works includes:
Descubrimiento de América y crónica de la dominación española
(1939); Historia de la República Argentina en el siglo XIX
(1940); Historia de Cristóbal Colón (1942); Orígenes de la democracia en América (1943); Las verdaderas causas de la
renuncia de San Martín después de Guayaquil (1949); Orígenes
españoles de la independencia argentina and La revisión de la
historia argentina (1952); and Buenos Aires colonial (1957).

GARAY, JUAN DE (c. 1528-1583). Governor of Río de la Plata
1578-1583. Military officer, conquistador, explorer, founder
of Santa Fe and refounder of Buenos Aires.

Born in Spain, poor but related to wealthy, noble Ortiz
de Zárate family; accompanied uncle, licenciado Pedro de
Zárate to Peru in retinue of viceroy Blasco Núñez de Vela in
1544; went with Juan Núñez del Prado into northwestern Argentina 1549-1550, taking part in founding of city, which after several changes of locations, became Santiago del Estero, oldest
settlement in Argentina; joined kinsman Juan Ortiz de Zárate
in Charcas, engaging in pacifying the Indians there and assisting in establishing settlements; became encomendero and prominent citizen of Santa Cruz de la Sierra, on the boundary between settlements from Peru and those from Paraguay; married Isabel Becerra y Mendoza, granddaughter of Doña Mencía
Calderón de Sanabria (q. v.) and established family there;
moved to Asunción 1568 where he served as alguacil mayor
(chief constable or sheriff); delegated in 1573 to establish settlement on Río de la Plata estuary--considered essential by
both Paraguay and Tucumán for direct communication with
Spain; decided to establish Santa Fe first; while exploring sites
and making preparations, encountered Jerónimo Luis de Cabrera who had just established city of Córdoba in drive toward
Atlantic settlement; clash over jurisdiction threatened between
western and eastern streams of colonization but was avoided
by agreement between Garay and Cabrera to leave decision to
royal authorities; Santa Fe founded November 15, 1573, with

about 90 citizens, only nine of whom were Spanish born; shortly after this Garay met Ortiz de Zárate, returning from Spain
as adelantado, at Martín García Island; accompanied him back
to Asunción; Ortiz de Zárate, dying, made Garay guardian of
his only daughter, with instructions that, when she married,
her husband was to inherit adelantazgo; Garay went to Chuquisaca where he informed Juana de Zárate, then living with her
uncle, of her father's death and instructions in his will; saw
her married to Juan Torres de Vera y Aragón, oidor of audiencia of Charcas; latter immediately claimed his rights as
adelantado and appointed Garay governor and captain general of
the province; after Garay returned to Asunción, he immediately began plans to resettle Buenos Aires; delayed by campaign
to put down revolt of Guaraní under cacique Otera; finally arrived in 1580 in Buenos Aires, where city was first founded
by Pedro de Mendoza in 1536; expedition included 1000 horses,
500 cattle, 64 heads of families, 53 of them creole or mestizo, only nine of them Spanish, including three survivors of
Mendoza's original settlement who helped in selection of best
site; city formally established November 11, 1580; lands allotted later, with site for church selected; request sent to
Spain for priest; Garay forced to return to Santa Fe because
of revolt (apparently instigated by Gonzalo Abreu, governor of
Tucumán, determined to claim jurisdiction over it; order restored in Santa Fe, Garay returned to Buenos Aires; explored
overland as far south as modern Mar del Plata; distributed
600 Indians in encomienda at Buenos Aires on his way back to
capital, Asunción; after taking care of governmental affairs
there, was preparing expedition to City of Caesars (q.v.) from
Buenos Aires but was delayed by various events; surprised,
with small party on river, and killed by Querandí Indians; Garay had spent about forty years in America, the last five as
governor; regarded as one of most important founders of Argentina.

GARCIA, ALEIXO (died c. 1525). Historical or mythical Portuguese
adventurer whose exploits quickly passed into legends that significantly affected early patterns of exploration and settlement
in Río de la Plata area; surviving shipwreck off the coast of
Brazil while returning (1516) from Juan de Solís's voyage to
the Río de la Plata, García and several of his companions
reached Santa Catarina island; during the next few years he
learned Guaraní and became fascinated with the stories of the
White King (Inca emperor) who lived in fabulous wealth and
splendor far to the west; in 1524, he decided to go in search
of this king; most of his companions stayed behind but he gathered a force of several thousand Indians with whom he reached
the eastern edges of the Inca empire in Bolivia; had already
acquired considerable silver when the reigning Inca, Huayna
Capac, sent forces against him and García withdrew to Paraguay river for safety for himself and his loot; he sent message and some silver to his companions at Santa Catarina,
asking them to join him but they refused; meanwhile, García

and most of his companions were killed by the Indians and
their silver stolen; succeeding Spanish expeditions heard the
story, sometimes even claimed to have met his companions
and many were moved to change their course--like the seamen
who deserted from Loaysa's expedition to join in the search
for treasure, and such royal officials as Sebastian Cabot, Juan
de Ayolas, Domingo Martínez Irala, and Cabeza de Vaca whose
imaginations were fired by these stories, and actions taken,
both before and after Pizarro's discovery and conquest of
Peru.

Although the stories about García's exploits are so
hopelessly confused that some historians have doubted his very
existence, most believe that he did live and that he was, in
fact, the first European to cross the interior of central South
America; to form an alliance with Guaraní Indians; to see the
Iguazú Falls; to enter Paraguay and to cross the Chaco, as
well as the first to see any part of the Inca empire and one
of the first to die trying to reach its treasure.

GARCIA, DIEGO (1471-1535).   Early explorer of Río de la Plata;
participated in every Spanish expedition sent to that area 1512-
1535.

Born in Lisbon; experienced mariner and self-taught
navigator; sailed in service of Spanish crown; may have
reached Río de la Plata on early voyage in 1512; captained
caravel later in year in Juan Díaz de Solís's voyage of discovery; accompanied Magellan's expedition along Argentine coast,
returning to Spain in 1522 after circumnavigation of globe;
sought royal consent to continue exploration in Plata area;
may have sailed on brief voyage there early in 1525; set out
from Spain again in January 1526 in command of small exploratory expedition--some confusion as to whether purpose
was to explore the Plata or to serve as follow-up for Sebastian Cabot's expedition sent out a few months earlier to reinforce Loaysa's Spanish group in the Moluccas but turned to
Plata exploration instead; García entered Río de la Plata
1527, established first shipyard there near Colonia (Uruguay)
to assemble brigantine brought along for exploring in shallow
waters, then started up Paraná with sixty men; meeting Cabot's party, García persistently demanded that his authority be
acknowledged but eventually conflict was avoided; both captains
engaged in exploration of the Paraná and Paraguay rivers, and
eventually both groups returned to Spain, arriving in July
1530; when Pedro de Mendoza, as first adelantado of Río de
la Plata, was assembling his fleet to settle the area, García
was among the first to offer himself and his caravel Concepción; departed for last time from Spain August 26, 1535, became ill while in the Canary Islands, died at Gomera, left his
caravel and its command to his son-in-law Bartolomé Mendoza;
García's account of the 1526-1530 Plata expedition published
by Eduardo Madero in his Historia del puerto de Buenos
Aires (1892).

GARCIA, JUAN AGUSTIN (1862-1923).   University professor and
dean; sociologist; writer.

Born in Buenos Aires; received doctorate 1881 from
Law School in university there; professional life centered
around University of Buenos Aires as professor, Dean of
School of Philosophy and Letters, editor of university review
Anales de la Universidad de Buenos Aires; planned history of
university and published first volume, dedicated to Dr. Antonio Sáenz, first rector, in 1918; sought constantly, through
teaching and writing to create national sociology for Argentina,
growing out of its own historic roots of colonial period and
nourished by such traditional Argentine writers as Echeverría,
Alberdi, Mitre, López, and Gutiérrez, all but forgotten in
contemporary enthusiasm for positivism and other European
ideologies; García rejected materialism of positivism and
blamed ills of Argentine education and political life on acceptance of Spencer's ideas; insisted that nations creating new societies and economies, like Argentina from 1880 to 1914, and
caught up in the interests, challenges, and problems of current events to the neglect of history, actually had greater need
to study historical roots than did more tranquil societies; in
his Introducción al estudio de las ciencias sociales argentinas
published in 1889, he questioned validity of oligarchical rule
and emphasized that such upper-class rulers were responsible
to keep their own national goals and policies consistent with
those of the people; believed that this could only be done
through institutions of Argentine, not imported, origin; cau-
tioned also against making Argentina into national estancia or
attempting to limit intellectual freedom; searching for Argentine essence, he published in 1890 Ciudad indiana (literally Indian City--or City of the Indies--i.e., City of Spanish America), one of first scholarly attempts to study Argentine colonial society; distinguished four integrating characteristics: 1)
faith in future greatness of country; 2) criollo pride; 3) cult
of courage; 4) disregard for law; less important but pervasive
and significant were tendencies toward lack of persistence and
improvidence, due to situation in which land meant wealth and
individual effort nothing; because of these and other writings,
García was considered to have been one of most distinguished
of naturalist writers of Argentine "Generation of 1880."

GARCIA, MANUEL JOSE (1784-1848).   Jurisconsult; adminstrator;
diplomat; liaison and negotiator between early Argentine patriot governments and Portuguese court at Rio de Janeiro.

Born in Buenos Aires; studied at San Carlos Academy;
completed law course at Chuquisaca 1804; treasurer of Buenos
Aires cabildo 1812, along with holding other offices; 1814-1820
served as diplomatic agent for United Provinces to Portuguese
government at Rio de Janeiro; in somewhat mysterious "García
mission" in 1815, Carlos Alvear, then supreme director of
Buenos Aires government, directed García to open negotiations
with Lord Strangford, British representative in Rio de Janeiro,
for establishing British protectorate over Argentina, then fear-

ing new Spanish efforts to regain it; apparently Bernardino
Rivadavia, also in Rio de Janeiro, dissuaded García from delivering note; García named minister of finance in Martín
Rodríguez government, 1821 and minister of government under
Las Heras (1824); carried out financial reforms from which
Banco de Descuentos (Discount Bank) resulted; made first foreign loan for Argentina; signed treaty of friendship, commerce,
and navigation with Great Britain; aided Lavalleja's campaign
into Uruguay; sent by President Rivadavia on special mission
to Brazil; exceeded instructions by signing treaty of peace, so
unpopular in Argentina that Rivadavia was forced to resign
(1827); García returned to Buenos Aires and served Juan Manuel de Rosas and then Viamonte before retiring from public
life in early 1830s. See José María Rosa, La misión García
ante Lord Strangford (1951).

GARCIA, PEDRO ANDRES (1758-1833). Spanish military officer
who became active patriot in independence period and expert
in matters regarding Indian affairs on the pampas frontier.
          Born in province of Santander, Spain, García was at-
tracted to military career; accompanied expedition of Ceballos
to Río de la Plata; instead of returning to Spain after the
fighting against Portuguese was over, García again accompanied Ceballos to Buenos Aires where the latter assumed duties
as viceroy; continued in military service; took part in expedition of Juan de la Piedra (q. v.) to Patagonia (1778-1779);
served on various other royal missions; distinguished himself
in the defense of Buenos Aires against the second British invasion (1807); his actions in bringing his troops closer to the
city (following defeat of Liniers' forces at Miserere) lifted
spirits of porteños and contributed to success of efforts of
Martín de Alzaga (q. v.) to reorganize defense of the city; and
his stubborn fighting against Whitelock's forces when they arrived, July 5, brought him promotion to colonel and a grant
of land; thereafter, García, who had married Clara María
Ferreyra de Lima y Freyre de Landieu in 1783 and had already founded the family that would later contribute greatly to
Argentine political, military, and cultural life, identified himself with Creoles; joined Cornelio Saavedra in breaking up
movement against Liniers (October 17, 1808) and conspiracy
of Martín de Alzaga (1809); took active part in May Revolution
(q. v.) of 1810; later that year (October 21-December 22,
1810) Colonel García carried out government mission to the
Indian frontier in the South and made full report following his
return, recommending that line of defenses be moved farther
south (see La Pampa); imprisoned in Buenos Aires for nine
months following the mutiny of Fontezuelas (April 3, 1815);
restored to active duty, continued to urge government to stabilize frontier; November 15, 1821, after big Indian uprising,
he was asked to present plan to prevent future raids; March
1822-June 1823 conducted scientific commission to study terrain for best way to advance fortified frontier; recommended
shortest line possible would be best; wrote several studies

particularly about Indians and frontier; died in Buenos Aires.
His biography has been written by José Torre Revello,
Don Pedro Andrés García, coronel del ejército argentino
(1758-1833) and a brief biographical sketch included by Jacinto
R. Yaben in his Biografías argentinas y sudamericanas.

GARCIA DEL RIO, JUAN (1794-1856).   Patriot of Latin American
    independence movement; collaborator with San Martín in Peru.
        Born in Cartagena, Colombia; educated in Spain; while
    engaged in business in Cádiz during Napoleonic invasions
    heard of plans of José de San Martín and others for liberation
    of Spanish South America; in London on mission to secure rec-
    ognition of Colombian independence, had contacts with Argen-
    tines there on similar mission: Manuel de Sarratea, Manuel
    Belgrano, and Bernardino Rivadavia; accompanied José Antonio
    Alvarez de Condarco back to Chile in 1818; named secretary
    of foreign affairs in San Martín's expedition to Peru (1820);
    accompanied Tomás Guido to conferences of Miraflores and
    Punchauca, and became San Martín's minister of foreign af-
    fairs when he assumed duties of Protector of Peru; early in
    1822 sent to London with Dr. Diego Paroissien by San Martín
    to seek loan for Peru and to sound out feeling for recognition
    for an independent monarchy, if set up there; shocked to learn,
    while there, of San Martín's resignation and departure from
    Peru following July interview with Simón Bolívar in Guayaquil;
    published biography of San Martín in London 1823, using
    pseudonym of Ricardo Gual y Jaén; returned to native Carta-
    gena after several years in London; held diplomatic posts in
    governments of Colombia, Ecuador, Peru, and Bolivia; spent
    several years in Santiago, Chile, engaged in literary works;
    closely associated with Argentine exiles Juan María Gutiérrez
    and Domingo Faustino Sarmiento; moved to Mexico where he
    died.

GARDEL, CARLOS (1890-1935).   Composer and singer who popular-
    ized tango in 1920s.
        Born in Toulouse, France; arrived in Argentina with
    his family at age of three; began musical career very early;
    entered into partnership with José Razzano; acquired extraordi-
    nary popularity and fame with his interpretations of popular
    music, especially tangos, in Argentina, France and Spain, and
    the United States; appeared in several movies made in Paris
    and in Hollywood, California.

GARIBALDI, GIUSEPPE (1807-1882).   Italian patriot and revolution-
    ary leader; entered into Argentine history in the 1840s when,
    as commander of the Italian legion helping to defend Montevi-
    deo against Rosas' besieging forces, he fought alongside the
    Argentine legion, composed of the unitarist exiles, who consid-
    ered him to be also fighting their battle against Rosas' tyranny;
    the close friendship formed between the already famous Italian
    freedom fighter and the young Argentine artillery officer Bar-
    tolomé Mitre during the siege is said to have contributed to

the latter's political ideals and his development into the liberal national leader of the Argentine Republic.

GARRO, JUAN M. (1847-1927). Jurisconsult; journalist; cabinet minister; educator and historian.

Born in Renca, San Luis; graduated in law at Córdoba, 1872; remained there active in journalism, practicing law, teaching at the university, and entering politics; represented San Luis in the national congress for eight years; a militant Catholic and member of Estrada's Unión Católica he took an active part in the congressional debates regarding liberty of teaching in 1878; in 1892 he was proposed as vice president on the Unión Cívica Radical slate, with Bernardo de Irigoyen as presidential candidate; defended his Catholic position vigorously in his speeches and writings; among his historical works was the Bosquejo de la universidad de Córdoba with a documentary appendix (1882) and various monographs dealing with the same university's history; Garro served as minister of public instruction under President Roque Saenz Peña, 1912-1914; died in Buenos Aires.

GARUHAPE (or GARHUAPE) see JAPANESE

GAS see ENERGY RESOURCES; PETROLEUM

GASCON, ESTEBAN AGUSTIN (1764-1824). Jurisconsult; public official and financial administrator; signer of Declaration of Independence.

Born in Oruro, Bolivia; educated at academy of San Carlos in Buenos Aires; received doctor's degree in Laws from University of Charcas (Chuquisaca), 1791; returned to Oruro; practiced law and held various administrative posts, many dealing with finance; a leader in Chuquisaca revolt of 1809; supported Buenos Aires' May Revolution and, in 1813, became president of audiencia at Charcas; in that capacity, organized military aid for Manuel Belgrano in Upper Peru; fought at battle of Salta, in which his brother was killed; patriot defeats at Vilcapugio and Ayohuma in Upper Peru sent him to Buenos Aires where he immediately became active in public life; sent to Congress of Tucumán, he was one of those considered for post of Supreme Director; served on several commissions, signed the Declaration of Independence (July 9, 1816); when Congress moved to Buenos Aires, Gascón was used by Supreme Director Juan Manuel de Pueyrredón to organize finances of the new nation under the difficulties of fighting royalists in Upper Peru, collaborating in creation of San Martín's Army of the Andes, and contending against rise of provincial caudillos; established national financial depository (Caja Nacional de Fondos), predecessor of Banco Nacional; filled various other posts of public trust and responsibility in governments following that of Pueyrredón; was serving as judge in the tribunal of justice when he died in Buenos Aires, 1824.

GAUCHO. Argentine counterpart of cowboy in other American nations (also known as gaucho in neighboring Uruguay and as gaúcho in southern Brazil); name apparently comes from Indian word (huacho) meaning illegitimate, vagabond, or forsaken; applied in early colonial period to lonely nomads of pampas, needing only wild horses and cattle to support their simple, wild, free life; in intervening four centuries the gaucho has played varying roles in historical development of Argentina, becoming metamorphosed in the twentieth century into symbol of national identity just as gaucho himself disappeared from Argentine real life and scene.

During sixteenth century as part of struggle for survival in Argentina (see Conquest; Criollos) gaucho way of life developed outside normal Spanish pattern of town, church, government, farm and stock economy; individuals who, either by necessity or preference, exchanged amenities and securities of established society for free life on pampas, gradually formed viable alternative life style based almost entirely on wild horses and cattle found there; gaucho lived on horseback, using heavy leather saddle that formed pillow at night; armed with Indian boleadoras, leather lariat or lasso, and long lance with curved blade with which to hamstring cattle while riding and double-bladed dagger or knife with which to kill the animal, cut out desired meat, and remove hide to be sun-dried and used by gaucho, bartered in town for necessities or left for landowner; lived on diet of meat, with a little parched corn, and always yerba mate to drink; his roof was the sky or the thatch of the rude shelter that housed his family, visited occasionally; wore loose full pants, tucked into boots of colt-hide; breechcloth and poncho; loved to race his horses and to test himself in individual combat--and to gamble on both; engaged in rough sports, including team-games played on horseback (not too different from modern Argentine polo); joined in country dances at rural fiestas; always much given to poetry, especially to sentimental or melancholy ballads, usually accompanied by guitar; numbers increased during seventeenth and eighteenth centuries, with white, red, and black races--often in mixtures--represented, although Caucasian blood seemed predominant; frequent butchering and daily exposure to physical danger and personal injury brought indifference to bloodshed and acceptance of violence and brutality as normal, necessary, and even admirable if useful in securing desired aim; only hardy individuals would be apt to choose such a life and certainly only strong men could survive; gauchos developed powerful egos; gave their loyalty only, and then completely, to caudillo or leader who won their allegiance; under such captains, gauchos performed invaluable services in Indian wars, pushing frontiers back to expand area of settlement; joined other Argentine forces in defeating British invasions; fought valiantly in wars of independence; firmly held northern Argentine border (under Martín Güemes and other officers) against royalist forces until San Martín's armies and continental strategy could win independence; provided fighters for civil wars of

both independence and early national periods, usually following
leaders, such as Artigas, Estanislao López, Francisco Ramírez, Juan Facundo Quiroga, as well as Rosas and Urquiza,
who professed democratic and federalist principles; by eighteenth century Argentine economy depended on gaucho skills and
labor: to round up, kill, and skin wild cattle for flourishing
hide and tallow trade along coast; to handle stock on more conventional horse and cattle estancias of northwest; and to provide mule-drivers for profitable new industry in Santa Fe and
neighboring areas, raising mules for marketing in Peru and
Bolivia.

Economic changes in early national period brought disaster and eventual annihilation to the gaucho; introduction of
saladeros in early 1800s made meat valuable for export and
later developments used entire beef carcass; land came under
private ownership and free meat, mounts, and an occasional
hide were no longer available to gauchos riding by; as early
as Rosas period, gauchos who were not in armed forces, found
themselves once again fighting for survival, but this time
against the government, in armed bands of rural rustlers or
bandits or as individuals facing imprisonment for five years or
conscription into frontier military units unless they could prove
legitimate employment on estancias; eventually many young
men joined in rural move toward city to become military police or to join other security units; numbers dwindled with final crisis reached following Paraguayan war and conquest of
desert in 1870s when gauchos returned to find remaining pampas occupied by newcomers--vigorous, hard-working immigrant farmers or stock-raisers; gauchos forced to find employment or give up; only a few, like José Hernández, came to
their defense as Argentina was devoting all its efforts toward
creating the prosperous agropecuarian economy to which the
free gaucho way of life presented only a menace; by early
twentieth century gaucho had all but disappeared.

By this time reaction to changes had set in and gaucho
appeared in new guise, as traditional symbol of Argentine
people--an indigenous, authentic core of its national identity;
republic had been flooded with immigrants, largely from western Europe, bringing in new cultures, new economies, new
ideologies, and institutions; increasingly Argentines turned back
in search of their own historic roots; began to relate much of
it to gaucho life style which, in its relationship to the land,
its diet, sports, values, independent spirit of freedom, etc.,
seemed only an extreme form of their common criollo culture;
old gaucho classics were revived and read avidly and new poems, dramas, novels, centered around gaucho theme; many
Argentine intellectuals also found themselves rejecting European
positivism, secularism, and scientific ideas and values in fav-
or of traditional warmer, Spanish Catholicism, and humanism
to be found in deeper study of Argentina's own history; just as
criollos sought their identity in studies of gaucho culture, so
newcomers to the republic grasped eagerly at the gaucho as
a tangible symbol linking them to their new homeland; they all

read the same literature on every level; children of varied ethnic backgrounds played gaucho games together in Buenos Aires streets, and thronged the circus and folk-theaters to see gaucho Juan Moreira; by the time the gaucho had disappeared from the land, his essential spirit had been captured by Ricardo Güiraldes in novel Don Segundo Sombra and his way of life had been faithfully reproduced in gaucho idiom in novels of Benito Lynch (see Gaucho Literature).

See Madaline Nichols and Edward L. Tinker in Suggested Readings, Appendix III.

GAUCHO LITERATURE (including but not limited to specific literary genre known as gauchesca). On September 20, 1833, Charles Darwin wrote his sister Caroline: "I am become quite a gaucho, drink my mate and smoke my cigar and then lie down and sleep as comfortably with the heavens as a canopy as in a feather bed. It is a fine and healthy life; on horseback all day, eating nothing but meat, and sleeping in a bracing air; one awakes as fresh as a lark." In century that followed gauchos attracted attention of many different kinds of writers, with great gaucho classics bearing close relationship to historical development of that same period; two of most famous prose works by romantic writers drew on gaucho themes: El matadero, written by Esteban Echeverría in late 1830s as prose poem or probably draft of novel (first published in 1871), depicting Rosas' government as brutal tyranny in terms of operations in Argentine slaughterhouses; and Domingo Faustino Sarmiento's passionate Facundo, civilización y barbarie, based on life of gaucho caudillo Juan Facundo Quiroga, in which author made serious study of "barbaric" gaucho culture to learn how best to educate Argentina for civilized future; published in Santiago, Chile, 1845, during Sarmiento's exile there, Facundo has since become Argentine classic for its portrayal of Argentine life during Rosas era; in 1850s, with gauchos already losing ground fast, their own poems and writings about them began to be published; important among these was epic poem Santos Vega (1851), in which Hilario Ascasubi became one of first to express Argentine spirit as shown by gauchos and to describe them in detail; as pressure increased against gaucho, so did attention given them by writers; Estanislao del Campo published poem Fausto, a gaucho parody on Goethe's masterpiece (1866, 1870), and José Hernández distilled a lifelong admiration and defense of the gaucho into the two-part Martín Fierro, epic poem (1872-1879) that is still considered a great Argentine classic; on the popular level, prolific journalist Eduardo Gutiérrez serialized the adventures of gaucho Juan Moreira (1880) that had such appeal for the masses that Gutiérrez adapted it for dramatic presentation; appearing first in pantomine in circus, words were added, and play became so popular that this gaucho dramatic presentation has often been credited with having brought rebirth of Argentine theater, certainly of the folk theater; in early decades of twentieth century, sociologists, historians, and philosophers were studying the rapidly

changing nation to find its real unifying identity; historians
such as Ricardo Levene and Enrique de Gandía began to emphasize American elements (including gaucho) in Argentine culture
rather than European; both Argentine and foreign social scientists studied them; and distinguished men of letters, attracted to this powerful, durable theme, created an important body
of literature characterized as "gauchesca"; earlier Argentine
works, as well as important new Uruguayan gaucho studies
and literary works, were widely read; among the finest gauchesca works were two novels: Don Segundo Sombra, by Ricardo Güiraldes (1926) which presents the gaucho as a whole
man, rooted in Argentine scene and tradition, symbolic of
unique national character and identity; and El romance de un
gaucho (1930), by Benito Lynch; in this, as well as other novels, Lynch simply but effectively portrays gaucho culture as it
really was, using authentic idioms to do so; among Argentine
scholars who have made special studies of gaucho literature
are Martiniano Leguizamón, Ricardo Rojas, and Leopoldo
Lugones; it is impossible to gauge social and political effects
of this writing on later Argentine historical development but at
least one important political leader, President Juan Domingo
Perón, brought up in former gaucho country in Buenos Aires
province, has declared his fascination with gaucho literature,
which he read avidly, and seems in his later career to have
recognized nationalistic significance of gaucho spirit and human
values expressed there and to have attempted to translate these
into new terms in modern, industrializing society (see Gaucho;
also authors and literary works mentioned).

GELLY Y OBES, GENERAL JUAN ANDRES (1815-1904). Military
     officer and public figure.
          Born in Buenos Aires; took up military career in Monte-
     video where his family was in exile from Rosas; circum-
     stances dictated this choice but he remained in this profession,
     to become highly respected national military figure; command-
     ed Argentine Legion against Rosas, then went to Brazil, re-
     turning to Buenos Aires after Rosas' defeat at Caseros; be-
     came collaborator with Bartolomé Mitre; served as his minis-
     ter of war and navy in Buenos Aires provincial and later na-
     tional governments; showed his talent for organization as chief
     of general staff in war with Paraguay; became commander-in-
     chief of Sarmiento's forces against Entre Ríos caudillo Ricardo
     López Jordán; exercised various public responsibilities includ-
     ing that of president of council of war and navy at time of his
     death in Buenos Aires.

GENERAL CONFEDERATION OF LABOR see CONFEDERACION
     GENERAL DEL TRABAJO

GENERAL DIRECTORATE OF MILITARY FACTORIES (Fabricaciones
     Militares). Government agency formed during early 1940s to
     supervise supplying Argentina's new military needs during World
     War II; in 1943 President Castillo appointed military engineer

Manuel N. Savio (q. v.) as first head of it; under his leadership it pushed hard for the establishment of heavy industry in Argentina but costs were very high and available coal and iron still only found in short supply in the nation; in 1947 this was merged into the new Sociedad Mixta Siderurgia Argentina, created by Congress (see SOMISA).

"GENERATION. " Applying theories of Ortega y Gasset, Argentine writers have divided their history into 15-year intervals and have attempted to analyze the various factors unique to each period, as expressed by each "generation" of literary and historical writers (see Jaime Perriaux under Historiography); certain dividing points are more significant than others (see following entries for generations of 1837, 1880, and 1910).

GENERATION OF 1837 (sometimes called May Generation). Name applied to literary group of young Argentine writers in the 1830s, sometimes compared to New England transcendentalists of same period in their romantic idealism and interest in their own New World scene; Argentines, caught up in ferment and clash of European writings about romanticism and utilitarianism, which they read widely, often in French translation, and discussed vigorously, sought relationship of new ideas to their own troubled country, just emerging from civil wars and still without national organization; in 1837 group began to meet regularly under leadership of Esteban Echeverría who had just returned from five years in Paris in center of new literary and intellectual currents; turning from literature to politics, young Argentine writers determined to complete May Revolution by giving new philosophical and ideological guidance to political leaders then involved in shaping government and society; Generation of 1837 was radical in sense that it rejected both unitarists, as reformers without genuine social sense, and federalists, who talked of democracy but tended toward despotism; organized Asociación de Mayo (q. v.) with Echeverría's Dogma socialista (q. v.) as its creed; disappointed in failure to win Rosas' cooperation with their plans, several members of Generation of 1837 turned to anti-government action, unfortunately at time when all friends of France were under suspicion from Rosas, then desperately seeking support against French blockade of Río de la Plata; Rosas' immediate action against the "conspirators," sent all members into exile; fifteen years (1838-1852) spent away from Argentina--in Chile, Uruguay, Brazil, Europe and elsewhere; sometimes together, sometimes in individual travel--brought them individual maturity, both personally and intellectually; less optimism and consequently more willingness to explore both criollo past and old and newer European ideologies (such as positivism and role of science) more critically; but with strengthened convictions in need for determined search for institutions upon which to build a more progressive, better Argentine nation; many of them returned to Argentina (after Rosas' fall in 1852) to make their dreams approach reality in the constitutional reorganization of the nation (see Constitution), and its economic development, social and cultural progress of the last four decades of nineteenth century; public life of these leaders was accompanied and aided by their continuous flow of published works--poetry, philosophical essays, novels, scholarly studies in political and other social sciences (then new), memoirs, and all forms of journalism (see listings of following, usually included among others, as members of Generation of 1837, for individual achievements and contributions: Juan Bautista Alberdi; Miguel Cané; Esteban Echeverría, Juan María Gutiérrez; Vicente F. López; Bartolomé Mitre; Domingo Faustino Sarmiento; Carlos Tejedor).

See Félix Weinberg, El salón literario de 1837 (Buenos Aires, 1958).

GENERATION OF EIGHTY (1880). The brilliant group of intellectuals who began their careers around 1880 and quickly assumed a dominating role in the nation's educational, political, and economic life seemed to be the civilizing force for which Argentine intellectuals had dreamed and worked; representing a wide variety of interests and sympathies, members of this Generation of Eighty--including, among others, José Nicolás Matienzo, Juan Agustín García, Rodolfo Rivarola, Luis M. Drago, Norberto Piñero, Ernesto Quesada, José María Ramos Mejía, along with Carlos Octavio Bunge and José Ingenieros who came later but were influenced by it--drew most of their ideas from European positivism, supported the policies of the oligarchy, but also seemed destined to represent the new Argentine bourgeoisie; strongly influenced by ideas of Herbert Spencer, they considered themselves to be liberal, championing individualism and personal rights, especially freedom of speech and press and free enterprise, but believed that Argentine realities still required limited political democracy; hoped to turn Argentina from its traditional ways into a modern nation; prepared way for nationalism of twentieth century.

GENERATION OF 1910. The generation of writers that began to make its impact at the centennial of the May Revolution faced entirely different circumstances than its predecessors; Buenos Aires had become a cultural center, drawing intellectuals from all of Latin America as well as receiving new literary currents and ideologies from Europe; French cultural influence was at its peak; Ruben Darío had already introduced modernismo (symbolism), and poets, such as Leopoldo Lugones and others were using the new literary patterns; Marxism, socialism, anarchism called attention to needs for social justice and attracted intellectuals as well as activists; the flood of immigrants brought new European life styles as well as ideas at the same time that the writings of the Generation of 1898 in Spain--seeking its own national answers after loss of Cuba, Puerto Rico, and the Philippines following the Spanish-American war of 1898--called Argentine interest back to its neglected mother country and aroused feeling against "Yankee imperialism"; both old and new Argentines had a special need to learn

for themselves what Argentinism really meant; such men as
the literary critic and essayist Ricardo Rojas sought their
roots in Argentina's Indian and European heritage while others,
like novelist Manuel Gálvez emphasized Argentina's authoritarian traditions as expressed by the caudillos; many found their
own sources and styles; together, they began a real national
literature in contrast to earlier, isolated masterpieces, and
laid the foundations for the new Argentine nationalism.

GEORGE CANNING. Ship, named for British foreign secretary, that
arrived in Buenos Aires March 9, 1812 from London bringing
José de San Martín, Carlos María de Alvear, José Matías
Zapiola, Baron E. K. von Holmberg, and others who would
contribute new professional military leadership to the Argentine fight for independence and take their places in the political life of the new nation.

GERMANY, GERMANS. From the sixteenth to the opening of the
twentieth century, German relations were primarily economic,
expressed in trade and (later) colonization, or personal, as
shown by Germans who took part in the conquest (Schmidt), as
Jesuit missionaries (Dobrizhoffer and Paucke), or as educators,
scientists, intellectuals (Burmeister, Korn); by the late eighteenth century, German textiles were already in great demand
in the Río de la Plata area and rulers of the various German
states used every diplomatic means possible to keep this trade
open with Buenos Aires during the wars of independence despite Spain's opposition [see Karl Wilhelm Korner, La independencia de la América española y la diplomacia alemana
(Buenos Aires, 1968)]; during the Rosas period German trade
and investment increased although it never equaled that of the
British; after 1870, when both Argentina and Germany had become united into single nations, the relationship assumed new
aspects; large numbers of agricultural colonists came from
Germany; Argentina began to have grains to export, along with
meat, in exchange for German manufactures; Germany increased its investments in Argentina and established direct
shipping lines that competed effectively with older ones; in
1899, when Argentina was in the process of modernizing and
professionalizing its national army, it found most aid from
Germany; thereafter German military missions, advisors, and
weaponry predominated in the military (q.v.); and Argentine officers went to Germany for advanced training; during World
War I, President Yrigoyen, who wanted to reduce British economic power in Argentina, remained neutral and was meticulously correct in his treatment of Germans; in the period between the two world wars, Germany increased its trade with
Argentina and established an airline to Buenos Aires; in 1939
the Lufthansa became linked with the Argentine airline; many
nationalists who feared that English domination of Argentine
trade, investment, etc., might make the republic in fact an
economic, if not a political, dependancy of Great Britain, welcomed the return of German power and wealth under Hitler;

others admired his totalitarian government especially when this
information about it came from Franco's Spain with its echoes
of the Hispanidad movement; during World War II (q. v.) Argentina attempted to maintain its traditional policy of neutrality, in spite of the heavy propaganda disseminated from the
German embassy; trade was almost totally cut off as Allies won
control of the Atlantic; eventually, as the Axis (q. v.) faced defeat and Argentina wanted to be a participant in the new international organizations to be formed (United Nations and new
Inter-American Organization), Argentina declared war on the
Axis nations; it was also eager to seize the German assets and
patents in their country; following the war West Germany made
a strong recovery and was back in Argentine import trade by
1950; by 1952 it had passed Great Britain in this field and was
third to U.S. and Brazil; Perón seemed to be reviving the old
military affection for Germany and hoped to use it as a coun-
terpoise to the United States in his "Third Position"; Argentina continuing industrial development in 1960s and 1970s owes
much to its importation of German industrial machines.

GHIOLDI, AMERICO (1899-   ). Socialist leader and spokesman;
    writer and editor, educator, legislator.
        Born in Buenos Aires; graduated from normal school in
1920; wrote for educational journal La Obra and had become active in socialist movement in 1915; influenced in his thinking
by positivism of J. Alfredo Ferreira and Marxist socialism of
Juan B. Justo; became well known as orator on social and political matters; edited La Vanguardia intermittently after 1923,
also Acción Socialista; elected to chamber of deputies in 1931,
and again in 1936; engaged in vigorous debates, especially on
questions related to education and social matters; dramatically
led entire socialist delegation out of chamber in protest
against law giving British control of Buenos Aires transit system in 1935; criticized Perón violently in his journal and
joined other leftists in unsuccessful attempt to overthrow him
in 1951; exiled until 1955; returned to resume editorship of La
Vanguardia; joined faculty of philosophy and letters at university of Buenos Aires, and continued to write; among his many
writings, largely devoted to educational and politico-social subjects are two books about his socialist mentor and colleague,
Juan B. Justo; and Marxismo, socialismo, izquierdismo, y realidad argentina (Buenos Aires, 1950); and De la tiranía a la
democracia social (Buenos Aires, 1956).

GHIOLDI, RODOLFO (1897-1951). Militant Communist leader.
        Born in Buenos Aires; became one of most active lead-
ers of leftist political activities; wrote for leftist periodicals;
he was largely responsible for his party changing its name
from Partido Socialista Internacional to Partido Comunista
(1920); took part in most of the national and international communist congresses; was Communist candidate for national presidency several times; was killed by police in Entre Ríos during
violence of elections of 1951.

GINASTERA, ALBERTO E.   Music composer of international distinction.

Born in Buenos Aires; studied at national conservatory;
received grant from Guggenheim foundation; became internationally known as composer of many kinds of music for piano,
organ and orchestra, often using Argentine themes such as
Panambí (1937) Impresiones de la puna and Suite de danzas
criollas (1947); became director of conservatory of music and
scenic art of Buenos Aires province; clashed with the Onganía
government when his opera Bomarso, that had received public
honors in both Brazil and the United States, was banned in
Buenos Aires as immoral.

GNP (Gross National Product).   For 1970, Argentina's GNP was
$25.4 billion derived from trade and services (44%), industry
(35%), agriculture and livestock (16%), and mining, construction, and other activities (5%); major agropecuarian products
are meats, hides, wheat, corn, and fruit; annual GNP growth
rate 3.5%, 1960-1969.

Before 1929 Argentina's GNP's rate of growth was apparently well above the world average; from 1850 to 1928 it
was 4.5% to 5% annually; as late as 1950 it still exceeded the
average but by the 1950s it had become very uneven and was
lagging behind the world average; in the transformation of the
economy from its successful stock and agricultural basis to a
more diversified one including industrialization and an attempt
to become self-sufficient in minerals and energy, agropecuarian production declined badly before the new mining and industrial productions could get underway to take its place; progress
was being made, however, although not as fast as had been
expected; in 1970 Argentina's per capita GNP of $1,055 was
the highest in Latin America.

GODOY, JUAN JOSE (1728-1788).   Jesuit priest; precursor of Argentine independence.

Born in Mendoza, educated first by Jesuits there and
then in Chile, where he became a member of the order; returning to Mendoza he spent the years 1755-1767 as chaplain
of the Casa de Ejercicios (Jesuit religious retreat house) and
of the chapel of Nuestra Señora del Buen Aire; happening to
be at a neighboring hacienda when his fellow Jesuits were tak-
en into custody, he fled to Upper Peru disguised as a peasant
but was apprehended and sent on to Lima to be deported along
with the Jesuits there; after several years in Italy, supported
(as were the other four Mendozan Jesuits) by funds sent by his
brother, Father Ignacio Godoy; in 1781 Godoy went to London,
suffering an accident on shipboard that left him with an identi-
fiable face scar; in London he tried to interest the British
Government in his plans to win Spanish American independ-
ence--plans that are still vague, as are the rumors that he
had already been working for this in Italy; when Godoy disappeared from London in 1785, Spanish government alerted its
officials throughout the empire to look for him, especially in

newly-acquired British-American areas where priests were
needed and where he could organize liberating expeditions to
Spanish America; discovered in Charleston serving Irish Catholics there, he was persuaded to leave on grounds that he was
more greatly needed in Jamaica; instead, he was taken to Inquisition prison in Cartagena (Colombia) and then transferred
to prison in Cádiz where he died.

GODOY CRUZ, TOMAS (1791-1852).   Patriot, educator, signer of
Declaration of Independence, governor of Mendoza, agricultural pioneer.
          Born in Mendoza in prominent family, educated there
and at the University of San Felipe in Chile; returned to Mendoza in 1814; offered his support to Governor San Martín,
then beginning to prepare his Army of the Andes for liberation
campaign; turned over his own house to be used for powder
factory under Alvarez Condarco; member (1816-1819) of Congress of Tucumán; carried on famous correspondence with San
Martín about desirability of declaring independence, San Martín insisted that it was absolutely necessary to do so at once,
to clarify the anomalous situation in which the patriot government found itself--fighting against a Crown that it had never
disavowed--and said that all it took was courage; Godoy Cruz
expressed view that the formulation of a declaration of independence was not a simple matter, to which San Martín replied
that it was a thousand times simpler than other problems which
they had to solve; this view prevailing, declaration of independence was signed by Godoy Cruz and other members July 9,
1816; Godoy Cruz arranged following conference between San
Martín and Juan Martín de Pueyrredón in Córdoba, that resulted in their effective collaboration for liberation; as governor of Mendoza province, 1820-1822, during the years of law-
lessness and anarchy, he established order, defeated the invading forces of José Miguel Carrera and ordered the Chilean
leader executed; devoted himself to transforming Mendoza from
traditionally remote Spanish colony to active province in modern independent republic; created necessary institutions, dictated progressive laws, fostered education (tutorial system favored), encouraged the press, and established a theater; promoted agricultural industries along with others; turned governorship over to Pedro Molina amid provincial unrest; served
as deputy in Buenos Aires, 1825-1827; served again in Mendoza government but fled to Chile when threatened by Quiroga
and the Aldaos; while supporting himself there by teaching and
writing, his agricultural experiments induced General Aldao
(his long-time enemy) to invite Godoy Cruz to return to Mendoza for this work; died there of apoplexy while actively engaged in attempts to introduce the silk industry--by cultivation
of silkworms, mulberry trees for their food--and cochineal,
an insect-producing red dye (also used for black) and in experiments to acclimatize the tea plant.

GOES, VICENTE DE (16th century).   Conquistador reputed to have brought first cattle into Río de la Plata area. Son of a Portuguese nobleman with sugarmill at São Vicente, Brazil, Goes, who had heard of need for cattle at Asunción, departed overland from São Vicente (possibly with one or two of his brothers) in 1554 in expedition of Spanish royal official Juan de Salazar y Espinosa, driving one bull and seven cows; arrived safely in Asunción in October 1555 with the cattle, considered to be the founders of the cattle industry in Río de la Plata; apparently Goes remained as settler in Asunción as he signed legal papers there in 1580.

GOLD   see   MINES, MINING

GOLONDRINAS (Swallows).   Nickname applied to Spanish and Italian farm laborers, numbering 50,000 by 1890, who annually crossed the Atlantic to work the wheat and corn harvests of the pampas.

GOMEZ, INDALECIO (1850-1920).   Salteño lawyer, merchant, educator, diplomat, and statesman; played active public role in both provincial and national life.
Born in Molinos, Salta; educated in new secondary school in Salta and in the Colegio in neighboring Charcas (now Sucre, Bolivia); completed his law studies in Buenos Aires, then returned to his native city; taught civics, served as president of municipality, became member of provincial legislature; went into business with his brother Martín, organizing an important mule-shipping trade between Salta and Peru; lived in Lima for some time, married Peruvian girl Carmen Rosa de Tezano Pinto; during War of the Pacific he was acting as consul in Iquique; barely escaped death at hands of Chileans who accused him of being a Peruvian spy; returned to Lima where he formed close friendship with Roque Saenz Peña who had romantically gone to Peru to offer his services in the war; when the war ended he went back to Salta to enter politics there; not as successful as he had hoped, he accepted Carlos Pellegrini's invitation to come to Buenos Aires; became director of the Banco de la Nación; served two terms as Salta's deputy to congress; greatly influenced by Félix Frías and José Manuel Estrada--as well as being a strong Catholic traditionalist by nature and education--he joined them in fighting against Roca's secular legislation by means of Catholic Action (which published his book El episcopado y la paz in 1895); refused cabinets offers of ministry of education from both presidents Luis Sáenz Peña and José Figueroa Alcorta, but did become minister of interior under Roque Saenz Peña, with whom his name is linked in the electoral reform bill of 1912; meanwhile, Gómez had also been active in organizing and teaching in the Faculty of Philosophy and Letters; served five years as Argentine ambassador to Berlin and cultivated friendship with Kaiser Wilhelm II; maintained close ties with his home province; continued the anthropological and archeological research studies begun there by Juan Martín Leguizamón and made valuable

contributions to the ethnological museum founded in Buenos
Aires in 1904; served as member of commission to erect monument in honor of Martín Güemes; died in Buenos Aires; his
collected speeches and writings were published in 1953--Los
discursos de Indalecio Gómez.

GOMEZ, JOSE VALENTIN (1774-1833). Patriot churchman in early
national period; legislator, diplomat, educator.

Born in Buenos Aires, educated at San Carlos academy,
university of Córdoba, with advanced degrees in canon and civil law from university in Chuquisaca; while serving as curate
in Banda Oriental (modern Uruguay) accepted May Revolution
enthusiastically; joined patriot forces as chaplain; transferred
to cathedral in Buenos Aires in 1813, elected to national assembly of 1813; became well known as orator; member of committee to draw up constitutional project; advisor to Supreme
Director Posadas, meanwhile moving up ranks in church hierarchy; exiled briefly to Europe, 1815, by Director Álvarez
Thomas, returned to serve Pueyrredón's government as coun-
cilor of state; in 1818 sent on diplomatic missions to Brazil,
England, and France, replacing Rivadavia, to secure recognition of Argentine independence and to sound out European reaction to selection of Duke of Orleans as possible ruler of independent Argentine monarchy (see Monarchy); again sent to
Brazil, 1823, to discuss status of Banda Oriental then claimed
by new Brazilian empire; returned to Buenos Aires to support
Rivadavia's ecclesiastical reforms, while censuring his excesses; as one of porteño representatives at national constituent Congress of 1824 expressed his unitarist ideas and signed
constitution adopted; served two terms in legislature; succeeding Antonio Sáenz as rector of university at Buenos Aires, organized public and private primary school system, under direction of university, adopting Lancastrian tutorial system as
well as other progressive educational methods; also drew up
regulations governing newly created Sociedad de Beneficencia;
died in Buenos Aires.

GONGORA Y ELIZALDE, DIEGO (d. 1623). Spanish royal official
appointed 1617 as first governor of new province of Río de la
Plata, separated from Paraguay, with Buenos Aires as capital; arrived 1618 and remained until death 1623; concerned with
suppressing Indian revolt destroying settlements in Río Bermejo area; bringing contraband trade under royal control, and
establishing firm government over area accustomed to going
its own way; gave strong support to Jesuits turning Uruguay
over to their missionary efforts.

GONZALEZ, ELPIDIO (1875-1951). Statesman and militarist radical political leader; cabinet minister in both Yrigoyen administrations.

Born in Rosario; began his advanced studies in Córdoba
but they were cut short by revolution of 1890; he found in
Hipólito Yrigoyen a political leader whom he supported loyally

and ably for the rest of his life; participated actively in revolution of 1905 and was imprisoned; refused, in accordance
with Radical policy at the time, to accept political appointments offered; was elected national deputy from Córdoba in
1916 but was unable to accept because of illness; became
Yrigoyen's civilian minister of war; in 1919 he was appointed
chief of police in Federal District; in 1921 he was named
president of the Unión Cívica Radical and the following year
became their vice presidential candidate; he represented the
Yrigoyenist party as president of the Senate; during Yrigoyen's
second term (1928-30) he served as minister of the interior;
imprisoned for two years following the Uriburu revolt that
overthrew Yrigoyen's government; after Yrigoyen's death, Elpidio González played little role in politics except to join in
the party struggle in 1945; he lived quietly in poverty, refusing a government pension, supporting himself by a small business job; accepted violent changes of the period stoically;
when he died in Buenos Aires he was honored, especially for
the example of honesty in government that he had shown.

GONZALEZ, JOAQUIN VICTOR (1863-1923).   Intellectual and writer;
legislator and cabinet minister; university professor and rector.
        Unlike many of his contemporary intellectuals and
writers, Joaquín V. González was neither a porteño nor new
Argentine; rather he came from prominent provincial families
of long standing.
        Born in Chilecito, La Rioja; educated at Monserrat
Academy and University of Córdoba; interrupted his studies to
take up journalism, but completed his law degree in 1886;
elected immediately as deputy to national congress; from that
date until his death, González's career was bound up in his
law profession, activities as public official, dedication to writing, zeal as reformer (although he himself belonged to oligarchy and considered himself to be a conservative, he was
one of few to recognize that changed circumstances in Argentina must be met with new laws), and tasks as educator, especially as president of new and progressive university of La
Plata.
        During five years following his graduation, González
served as deputy to national congress, helped draw up new
constitution for La Rioja and was its governor 1889-1891;
married Amalia Luno Olmos 1889; established his place among
Argentine writers with publication of La tradición nacional
(1888); moved to Buenos Aires and opened law office 1891;
wrote for La Prensa (1891-1901); continued as deputy in congress; in 1893 published Mis montañas, considered by many
his greatest work; following year became one of first to teach
mining law in law school at university; at government's request, drew up mining reform laws, adopted in 1897; served
as member of national education council after 1896, continuing
traditions of Sarmiento and Avellaneda in that field; left congress in 1901 to become cabinet minister for presidents Roca

and Quintana; as minister of interior under Roca, largely responsible for unipersonal ballot law 1901; as minister of Justice and Public Instruction under Quintana supported and helped draft laws made necessary by increase of labor agitation and social unrest--the law of residence, giving government right, if necessary, to deport foreign labor agitators, and comprehensive labor law (1904) providing for major reforms in workers' situation; rejected as a whole by congress, the portions dealing with Sunday employment finally passed, 1905, to become first labor law in Argentina; González also successfully carried out negotiations with province of Buenos Aires to include University of La Plata in national system; resigned from cabinet at time of President Quintana's death, 1906.

Appointed president (rector) of University of La Plata in 1906, González began work with which his name is most often related--creation of a new kind of modern university in Argentina, based on latest concepts of university organization and curriculum programs in Europe and the United States, and dedicated to academic excellence, learning for its own sake, research, community service such as extension divisions, institutes, etc.; in this work, González formed close friendships with scholars abroad; important among these was Leo S. Rowe, professor of political science at University of Pennsylvania (later to become director of Pan American Union), who was at that time engaged in writing his classic study of the Argentine Constitution of 1853 (see L. S. Rowe in Suggested Readings, Appendix III) for which González wrote the introduction; retired from University of La Plata in 1918, leaving it already well known and highly respected both nationally and internationally, and having infused it with his own humanistic spirit; further enriched it with gift of his very extensive library.

During closing years of his life, González, whose strong nationalism and love of country had characterized his writings and actions, turned to wider view; became deeply interested in poetry and mystical writing of India and published Spanish translation of Rabindranath Tagore's One Hundred Poems of Kabir in Atenea as response to adulation following his retirement; became interested in world affairs--considered ABC agreement (1915) important innovation in Argentine foreign policy; strongly supported world peace and became admirer of President Woodrow Wilson and his peace efforts; became member of International Law Association, 1919; two years later, executive council of League of Nations proposed his name as member of court of international justice; 1922 named corresponding member of Royal Academy of History in Madrid; Dr. González died in Buenos Aires at age of sixty; a few years later, his remains were accompanied by large and distinguished official and academic entourage to his birthplace, Chilecito, La Rioja, for formal burial August 14, 1926.

Despite his busy career, González left a bibliography of more than 1000 items of his writings, including fifty books, in fields of law, pedagogy, history, and literature; University of La Plata completed publication of these in 25 volumes, 1937;

among the most important of these are Tradición nacional, 1888; Mis montañas, 1893; El juicio del siglo o cien años de historia, 1913; Patria y democracia, 1920, in which he declares that the congenital disease of Argentina is the hatred that vitiates its spirit and frustrates constructive reforms; and Estudios históricos.

See Pedro B. Franco, Ideario de Joaquín González (Buenos Aires, 1938), and Arturo Marasso, Joaquín V. González, el artista y el hombre (Buenos Aires, 1937).

GONZALEZ DE LA SANTA CRUZ, ROQUE (1576-1628). Early creole Jesuit missionary to the Indians, explorer, founder of missions, and martyr.

Born in Asunción of distinguished creole family, Father González early showed his preference for a life of religious devotion and service, educated toward that end, and ordained in 1598; offered various posts in the heriarchy, he joined the Jesuit order in 1609, instead; having spent much time as successful missionary among the Indians around Asunción, he was asked to take up the work of Father Lorenzana in bringing the Guaraní Indians into fixed mission towns (reducciones) in the area along the Paraná and Uruguay rivers; summoned to Buenos Aires for a conference with Governor Francisco de Céspedes who wanted to enlist his aid in extending Spanish authority over that area, he surprised everyone by making the trip from San Nicolás by the Uruguay river, opening it to navigation for the first time; returning he established several missions, including Yapeyú in 1626 (later to become the birthplace of the Liberator San Martín); his success aroused the hostility of the Indians who assassinated him at Caaró in 1628, along with two other martyrs, Alonso Rodríguez and Juan del Castillo; in 1928, honoring the third centenary of his martyrdom, he was beatified by the Church.

GORMAN, MIGUEL (or MIGUEL DE) see O'GORMAN, MIGUEL

GOROSTIAGA, JOSE BENJAMIN (1822-1891). Legislator, jurist, and statesman; one of writers of 1853 constitution.

Born in Santiago del Estero; received his doctorate from University of Córdoba 1846; entered public life as federalist; after fall of Juan Manuel Rosas (1852) became minister of finance in Vicente López y Planes' provisional government in Buenos Aires; formed part of advisory council established by Justo José Urquiza; elected to represent Santiago del Estero at national constituent congress of Santa Fe, 1853; formed part of commission to draw up draft of constitution and he and J. M. Gutiérrez given credit for actual writing of it; also, in 1853, assigned with Salvador María del Carril to conclude treaties with United States, England, and France providing for free navigation of Paraná and Uruguay rivers; became member of Confederation congress, then President Urquiza's minister of the interior; moved to Buenos Aires to open law office; served in both judicial and legislative capacities; in 1868-1870 acted as minister of finance in cabinet of President Domingo F. Sarmiento; was president of Supreme Court of Justice, 1877-1887; died four years later in Buenos Aires; had also been active in La Asociación Católica, founded by J. M. Estrada to combat anti-clericalism of 1880s.

GORRITI, JOSE FRANCISCO DE (1780-1830). Youngest of the three famous Gorriti independence leaders, commonly called "Pachi" or "Pachigorriti" and known historically as the "Guerrilla of Independence."

Born in Jujuy, brought up in Montevideo by paternal uncle; had personal and commercial contacts with José Gervasio de Artigas; fought in garrison there; assumed habit of Franciscan lay brother, in vow made following a narrow personal escape; back in Salta 1798, devoted himself to handling of family estates, his interests lying primarily in commerce and rural life; became totally gaucho in interests and life style; espoused May Revolution (1810) immediately; joined his brother José Ignacio in mobilizing intendancy of Salta (including Jujuy) in its support; in 1812 fought at Río de Piedras, second in command to Diego González Balcarce; from then until his death he and his gaucho cavalry were almost constantly fighting; in 1815 joined Army of North, his gauchos defending the Rosario de la Frontera line; March 14, 1817, dislodged royalists from Jujuy; continued to harass Canterac's invading royalist forces who came to greet him, still in Franciscan garb, on the battlefield, with the cry "Come on, little friar, we will make you general!" (¡Ven frailecito, te haremos general!); in 1820 forced General Canterac's army out of Salta; promoted to rank of colonel for this by Martín Güemes; fought closely with Güemes, and was with him in defense against new invasion of 1821 in which Güemes was killed; after escorting body of Güemes to funeral, Pachi placed himself under orders of Güemes' designate successor, Colonel Jorge Enrique Widt; armistice signed and independence won at Ayacucho, in Peru (1824), brought peace along border also; Pachi meanwhile involved in provincial politics and civil war; more federalist than his brothers in political convictions, he maintained contacts with provincial leaders such as Juan Bautista Bustos (Córdoba), Juan Felipe Ibarra (Santiago del Estero), and Estanislao López (Santa Fe), but did not enter into national political strife, out of respect for his brothers; in his province he took lead in overthrow of governor Juan Antonio Álvarez de Arenales, largely supported by forces from outside the province; 1827, but refused governorship; José Ignacio Gorriti was elected; Colonel Gorriti became commander of the frontier with rank of major general; died of pneumonia in Salta. Bartolomé Mitre, in praising his courage, characterized him as the "first lancer of the Salteño army, who neither gave nor asked quarter."

GORRITI, JOSE IGNACIO DE (1770-1835). Signer of the Declaration of Independence; statesman and administrator; political and military leader of Salta-Jujuy area during independence period.

Born in Jujuy; studied at Monserrat Academy in Córdoba; received doctorate at Chuquisaca in theology and jurisprudence; father's death made it necessary for him to devote his energies to family financial affairs; possessed fine library of philosophical, legal, and literary materials; interested in both provincial and viceregal public matters; in 1807, at his own expense armed and sent militia force to Buenos Aires to fight British.

Becoming known in 1810 at the Numen (inspiration and leader) of the Revolution in the North, he had already in 1808 and 1809 begun preparing the province for independence, while remaining on friendly terms with royal officials; accepting May Revolution of 1810, he immediately began mobilizing his area in its support; organized baqueanos (trail guides)--later incorporated into the army of the north; formed militia unit, placed under command of Martín Güemes; furnished supplies, money, horses, men to patriot military ventures in north; became officer in Güemes' force and accompanied latter back to Salta after disagreement with Castelli and Balcarce in Upper Peru; collaborated closely with Belgrano when latter became commander of the army of the north; with his gaucho cavalry covered Belgrano's withdrawal from Jujuy; fought in battles of Tucumán and Salta; when San Martín put Martín Güemes back in charge of defense of northern frontiers, José Ignacio became latter's political and military complement and associate until Güemes' death; from 1814 until 1825 (independence won) placed his prestige, personal energies and great fortune at the service of his country's fight for independence; represented Salta at Congress of Tucumán; signed Declaration of Independence, July 9, 1816; supported Belgrano's plan for monarchy under Inca; returned to Salta in 1817 and became acting governor 1819; turned authority over to cabildo late in 1820, raised new force with which to dislodge Olañeta's royalist forces from their sixth occupation of city of Jujuy; succeeded on April 27, 1821--known in history as "the Great Day of Jujuy" although Olañeta returned in new invasion that cost Güemes' life and resulted in harsh new occupation; José Ignacio Gorriti continued with Güemes' colleagues, carrying out his plans and policies; in 1821 a revolutionary movement overthrew governor José Antonio Fernández Cornejo and made Gorriti governor; latter restored order with firmness and turned government over at end of term (December 31, 1823) to Juan Antonio Alvarez Arenales; in 1827, revolution led by Pachi Gorriti and others who feared that Arenales was trying to succeed himself illegally, and resented the outside forces (some sent by Rivadavia) supporting him, forced Arenales out and José Ignacio was elected governor; two years later, succeeded by his older brother, Monsignor Juan Ignacio Gorriti; Gorriti lent full support to General Paz and anti-Rosas forces; their defeat at Ciudadela (fortress of Tucumán) combined with the actions of his political enemies forced Gorriti to flee into Bolivia for safety; 1832, all his property, as well as that of the rest of his family, confiscated by new government; embittered, he died in Sucre in 1835;

honored greatly by later historians for significant contributions
made to independence, especially in the north.

GORRITI, JUAN IGNACIO DE (1766-1842). Priest; independence
leader and legislator; governor of Salta 1829-1831; intellectual
and writer.
      Eldest of family; born at Los Horcones, family haci-
enda in Salta; studied at Monserrat Academy in Córdoba, then
went to Chuquisaca to receive his doctorate in theology, 1791;
ordained by Bishop Angel Mariano Troncoso; held ecclesiastical appointments for most of his life; widely known for eloquence in sermons and speeches; a liberal churchman, supported revolutionary cause before May Revolution, declaring that
Spanish royal power ended with French seizure of throne
(1808); shocked by harsh treatment given revolutionary leaders
in Upper Peru (Bolivia) in 1809, did not recognize Spanish
junta; urged independence with return to less centralized government, with provinces and cabildos recovering their traditional political rights, lost following creation of viceroyalty;
elected 1810 to provisional junta in Buenos Aires; played active role, always favoring democracy and justice.
      Strong critic of triumvirate government, returned to
Jujuy (1811); formed close relationship with Manuel Belgrano,
commander of Army of the North; as newly appointed vicar in
Jujuy, blessed Belgrano's blue and white flag May 25, 1812;
moved to Salta as canon of cathedral (1813); became member
of city's cabildo (1815); in same year joined Army of the North
and accompanied it as chaplain, 1815-1821; three years later
represented Salta in constituent congress (1824) in Buenos
Aires; in spite of his vigorous insistence that provinces should
be consulted on matters of national significance and his rather
negative feelings regarding Bernardino Rivadavia when he arrived in Buenos Aires, Dr. Gorriti came to support both Rivadavia's centralist constitution and him personally; voted for
war against Brazil; returned to Salta in 1827 following fall of
Rivadavia's government; became Jujuy's deputy to Salta legislature, over which he was elected president; appointed governor of diocese in same year (1828) and in 1829 Monsignor
Gorriti was elected governor of province of Salta to succeed
his brother, José Ignacio; joined with nine other governors
in signing anti-Rosas pact of League of Interior Provinces,
with General José María Paz placed in command of military
forces; defeats by Juan Facundo Quiroga's federalist forces
made life intolerable for Gorriti and he accompanied other
members of his family into exile in Bolivia; all Gorriti family
funds and property having been confiscated by political enemies (1832), he supported himself by teaching and church appointments, and devoted himself to his studies and to writing;
died in poverty, but widely respected, in Sucre 25 May 1842.
      Throughout his active career, Gorriti shaped public
opinion by his writings and his speeches, preparing the people
for independence and then orienting the new nation toward the
kinds of political organization and institutions to be chosen;

profoundly distressed by the anarchy and civil wars, he began
to probe even more deeply into the causes of these and his
Reflexiones sobre las causas de las convulsiones internas de
los estados americanos (Chuquisaca, 1834) links him to the
generation of Echeverría and Alberdi; most of his writings
were not published and many have been lost. See Miguel Angel Vergara, Papeles del Doctor Juan Ignacio de Gorriti.
Documentos para la historia argentina (Jujuy, 1936).

GORRITI, JUANA MANUELA (1816-1892). Writer and literary figure.
　　Born in family hacienda Los Horcones, Salta, six days
after her father had signed the Declaration of Independence;
parents Dr. José Ignacio de Gorriti and Feliciana de Zuviría
y Castellanos; educated by tutors and in convent school in
Salta; accompanied her family into exile in Bolivia in 1831; in
1833 married Manuel Isidoro Belzú, young military officer who
eventually became president of Bolivia and was killed by Melgarejo, his successor, 1866; long before this, Juana Manuela
had taken her two daughters and established her own home,
separated from Belzú; devoted herself to literary studies and
writing; moving to Lima, she opened a weekly literary salon
that became center of literary life as did her home in Buenos
Aires later; a prolific writer, her stories, historical sketches,
childhood memories, and novels appeared in literary journals
in Peru, other Latin American countries--including Argentina
after fall of Rosas--and in Paris and Madrid; her first novel,
La quena (from the Quechua word for an Indian reed flute) was
published in Lima, 1845.
　　Modern literary critics tend to attach more significance
to her amazing personality (called by one "the most unusual
(raro) temperament possessed by any woman ever born in Argentina") than to her literary contributions or talent; they find
her style less than elegant, her work disorganized, and even
sometimes crude, and prefer her historical sketches such as
the biography of Dionisio de Puch (Paris, 1869), those dealing
with her native Salta and childhood memories (especially La
peregrinación a la tierra natal (1889), because of their local
color but also their human interest as she reveals herself in
these personal memories; including Juana Manuela among romantic writers because of her imagination, critics also call
attention, however, to her unusual creative talent as revealed
in such works as Sueños y realidades edited by Vicente G.
Quesada (1865, later edition 1907); and Ricardo Rojas notes
that her novel El Pozo (Well) of Yocci may be considered a
precursor of the Argentine novel.

GORRITI FAMILY. Prominent, wealthy family of Jujuy and Salta;
three brothers, sons of Spaniard, Ignacio de Gorriti and María Feliciana de Cueto y Liendo, of Jujuy; made important con-
tributions--military, financial, administrative, political, and
ideological--to the defense and progress of their province and
to the nation during the war for independence; all three, as

well as most of the other members of the family became victims of the civil war of 1830 (see Juan Ignacio de Gorriti; José Ignacio de Gorriti; José Francisco de Gorriti).

GOU (Grupo de Oficiales Unidos--Group of United Officers). Secret society formed among officers of the army, March 1943; most had participated in the 1930 coup that placed Uriburu in charge of an elitist government, now wanted something better for their country; determined to strengthen military forces and power position, alarmed by the growing strength of neighboring Brazil under Vargas; they intended to assure that Argentine wealth should be used for Argentine purposes; and insisted that the military should be the arbiter in matters of public policy when civil authority failed; June 4, 1943, fearing the election of conservative estanciero Robustiano Patrón Costas, of Salta, as President, GOU junta took over the Argentine government, replacing President Ramón Castillo with General Arturo Rawson, and then, two days later, with General Pedro Ramírez as president of military dictatorship; policies of the government drew strongly on Roman Catholic support and placed religious teaching back in the schools; early in 1944 a "colonels clique," led by Juan Domingo Perón and desiring a much stronger social and economic revolution, gained control of the GOU and took over the government, with General Edelmiro Farrell as president, Perón as minister of war and vice president; GOU undoubtedly contained some Nazi sympathizers-- and was even rumored to be Nazi-inspired--but seems to have been primarily a manifestation of Argentina's neutrality and determined nationalism.

The initials GOU have been variously interpreted as representing Grupo de Oficiales Unidos; Grupo Obra de Unificación; Gobierno, Orden y Unión (or Unificación); Grupo Orgánico Unificado; Grupo Organizador Unificado, or others, but the official title seems to have been the first one indicated.

See Robert A. Potash in Suggested Readings, Appendix III; also study edited by Enrique Díaz Araujo, El G. O. U. en la revolución de 1943, (Universidad Nacional de Cuyo, Mendoza, 1970).

GOULD, BENJAMIN A. (1824-1896). Director of Astronomy Observatory in Córdoba.

Born in the United States, graduate of Harvard University, with doctorate in astronomy from University of Göttingen; spent fifteen years, 1852-1867, working with the U.S. Coast Survey; founded the Astronomical Journal and served as director of the Dudley Observatory; came to Argentina to direct the astronomy observatory that President Domingo Faustino Sarmiento founded in Córdoba in 1869; observatory opened October 24, 1871; later Gould created a meteorological office as an annex to the observatory; in 1885 it became separate and in 1901 was moved to Buenos Aires; meanwhile Gould had rendered important services in setting up weather stations in

other parts of Argentina; Gould's published studies of his astronomical observations in Argentina, especially his Urano-
metría argentina and his catalogs of southern stars were considered to be important contributions to the knowledge of the
heavens in the southern hemisphere.

GOVERNMENT. The territory now included in Argentine Republic
was under the crown of Spain from the Treaty of Tordesillas
(1494, between Spain and Portugal) until 1810; adelantados were
in charge of the conquest from the Atlantic and Spanish military commanders from Peru and Chile led the expeditions in
north and northwest; all were under the Viceroy of Peru; separate governors were appointed for Tucumán and the Río de
la Plata as civil government was established; and new governors and sub-governors were appointed as new areas were
settled, along with new audiencias; Cuyo, in Western Argentina, remained under Chile; all were subject to the royal audiencia at Charcas, remaining under the Viceroy of Peru until
1776; in that year the viceroyalty of the United Provinces of
the Río de la Plata was established with its capital at Buenos
Aires; it included modern Argentina, Uruguay, Paraguay, and
Bolivia; this was later divided into intendancies; following the
May Revolution in 1810, the patriot governments in Buenos
Aires attempted to hold the entire viceroyalty together in one
great independent nation but by 1829, Paraguay, Bolivia, and
Uruguay had broken away and set up their own governments.
        The first few decades of Argentine independence were
turbulent as federalists and unitarists, porteños and provincials from the interior sought unsuccessfully through constitutional conventions and on the battlefields to reconcile their differences and to bring the provinces together as one nation under organic law; eventually, with the election of Bartolomé
Mitre as president in 1862 under the revised constitution of
1853, the modern Argentine Republic was created.
        Still operating under the Constitution of 1853 (q. v.) the
republic has a three-branch--executive-legislative-judicial--
government similar to that in the United States; the 22 provinces have their own government, with the national executive
given authority to intervene under certain circumstances, and
providing government for the one remaining territory Tierra
del Fuego; local government has its own municipal government,
rights, and privileges.
        A new political element entered government in the twen-
tieth century; from 1930-1976 the military (q. v.) has intervened to overthrow the national government and establish a new
one more to its liking; for the most part these interventions
have come when the nation seemed imperiled by crises that the
existing governments seemed helpless to resolve and the new
governments established sought to obtain constitutional status
and govern constitutionally.

GOYENA, PEDRO (1843-1892). Militant Catholic lay leader; legislator; law professor; journalist and literary critic.

Born and educated in Buenos Aires, graduating in law
in 1869; in 1874 became professor of law in faculty of law and
social sciences; also entered politics, serving in Buenos Aires
legislature and national congress; became active, eloquent pro-
ponent (in congress and in public) of causes in which he believed
strongly, especially Catholic opposition to secular legislation
sponsored by liberals in 1880s; with José Manuel Estrada and
Achával Rodríguez founded La Unión, first paper to give regular organized logical expression to Catholic opposition to the
banning of religious teaching in public schools and institution
of civil marriages, publishing hundreds of articles in attempts
to bring popular pressure to bear on legislature; earlier, Goyena had engaged in journalistic controversy with Domingo
Faustino Sarmiento, Juan Carlos Gómez and others; he also,
in an entirely different field, became known as one of the cre-
ators of modern Argentine literary criticism, founding the Revista Argentina for essays of this kind (later compiled and published); Ricardo Rojas names him as one of those who contributed to the "civilizing" of Argentine prose following the
more florid style of the romantic writers exiled during the
Rosas regime; he died in his home in San José de Flores, Buenos Aires.

GOYENECHE, JOSE MANUEL DE (1775-1846). Military officer and
royal official.
        Sent by Sevilla junta (1808) as delegate to bring news of
Napoleonic invasion and Spanish uprising against it to viceroyal-
ists of Río de la Plata and Peru; remained in America six
years (1808-1814) during which, as commander of royalist armies for much of the time, he prevented Upper Peru from being integrated into Buenos Aires patriot government by either
popular revolution or military invasion from the junta.
        Born in Arequipa, Peru, his father a major in Spanish
army, José Manuel went to Spain in 1795 to begin his own military career; had risen to rank of brigadier when Junta of Sevilla sent him to two southern viceroyalties to win their loyalty
and strengthen their ties with Spanish government; during critical period of French attempted takeover he was received in
Montevideo and Buenos Aires with mixed feelings; although welcomed courteously by viceroy Santiago de Liniers, Goyeneche
ran into real trouble in Chuquisaca where Charcas audiencia refused to accept his credentials while its president and the archbishop did; difficulties grew out of political schism already in
existence along with widespread rumors that Goyeneche was involved in conspiracy to turn Upper Peru over to Brazil, largely
based on dispatches that he brought from João, prince regent
of Portugal (Portuguese court then in Rio de Janeiro), and
Carlota, offering to take the Upper Peruvian provinces under
their protectorate; moving on to Cuzco for a brief term as interim president of that audiencia, Goyeneche was sent back to
Bolivia to put down the revolutionary revolts of 1809; his firmness, amounting to harshness in punishing the leaders of the
famous La Paz revolution, by execution, imprisonment, or exile,

was largely responsible for bringing area back under royal control but when news of this reached Buenos Aires in March 1810, it served to crystallize creole determination to win independence from Spain; following May Revolution, as Buenos Aires junta prepared to send first army into Upper Peru, to incorporate that part of the viceroyalty into the new patriot government, Viceroy José Fernando de Abascal of Lima placed Goyeneche in charge of organizing and training army to defeat patriot force; General Antonio González Balcarce and Juan Castelli (representative of junta) won victory of Suipacha over royal troops November 27, 1810, and took over almost entire area for revolution; a few months later Goyeneche and Castelli signed a forty-day armistice, with battle lines drawn near boundary between two viceroyalties; violations claimed by both sides; and, in surprise attack near Huaqui, Goyeneche completely dispersed patriot army June 20, 1811; outbreak of revolts in Cochabamba delayed his invasion of northern Argentina until next year, when Goyeneche moved south to Potosí, sending advance force under Pío Tristán against Tucumán and northwest; General Manuel Belgrano, disregarding government orders to withdraw to Córdoba, repelled invasion by victories at Tucumán (September 24, 1812) and at Salta (February 17, 1813); Goyeneche withdrew farther north and submitted his resignation to viceroy Abascal; various reasons given by historians for this, including mounting difficulties, many due to his own repressive actions in quelling uprisings, but one story was that he had urged a cessation of hostilities after Salta, threatened to resign otherwise; viceroy refused and appointed Joaquín de Pezuela to succeed him; Goyeneche returned to Spain in 1814; immediately promoted to lieutenant general of royal armies and (1815) given grand cross of Order of Isabella the Catholic; died in Spain in 1846.

GRAHAM, MARY OLSTINE (1842-1910).   Educator; one of U.S. teachers brought to Argentina by Domingo F. Sarmiento.

Born in St. Louis, U.S.A.; came to Argentina about 1879 as part of Sarmiento's plan to introduce modern educational methods from United States, and to organize and direct Argentina's first normal schools (teacher training colleges); spent first few years learning language, and teaching at normal schools of Paraná, and at San Juan; moved in 1888 to become director of newly established school at La Plata; spent rest of her life there; organized complete elementary school, including one of first kindergartens in Argentina; in 1906 Mary O. Graham Center established and after her death her name was given to the school that she had created; emphasized learning by doing, rather than simply by rote.

See Juan Manuel Chavarría, La escuela normal y la cultura argentina (Buenos Aires, 1947).

GRAHAM, ROBERT BONTINE CUNNINGHAME (1852-1936).   Writer; adventurer; rancher.

Although born in London, Graham was Scotch in ances-

try, being descended on his father's side from Robert II; about
one-fourth his background, however, was Spanish and he always claimed that his basic approach to life was Spanish; his
idealism, passionate interest in humanity and in the rights of
an individual have caused him to be compared frequently to
Don Quixote; his adventures in the New World, from Texas to
Tierra del Fuego and those in Africa served as the background,
and often the main subject of his large number of writings.

Argentina was, in many respects, his first and last
love; having already acquired fluency in Spanish, an abiding interest and love for fine horses, and an education at Harrow
and in Brussels, Graham came to Argentina in 1870 to become
partner in a ranch; although this venture and others of the following eight years--failure to get concession desired for growing mate in Paraguay, another ranching venture near Bahía
Blanca, etc.--did not bring him the desired financial success
(although he was already wealthy in holdings in Scotland),
Graham acquired a love of the land, sharpened his observation
of all natural phenomena, became a gaucho among gauchos,
and gathered the material for many of his later works; following his father's death in 1883, Graham assumed the economic
and political responsibilities of the Scotch laird that he had become; the story is told of him during this period that he happened to recognize a horse pulling a tramcar in Glasgow as an
Argentine mustang bearing a brand with which he was familiar;
he immediately purchased the animal from the transit company
for £50, rode it to parliament as long as he attended it, then,
after twenty-five years of use, retired it to one of his country
estates; during World War I Graham went to Argentina to buy
horses for the British government, also to Colombia on government mission to buy cattle; in 1936 Graham returned to Buenos
Aires on a sentimental pilgrimage to the various areas in which
he had lived as a young man; died while there; his body was
taken to Scotland for burial.

Among his writings that deal most closely with Argentina are: The Conquest of the River Plate (London, 1924, reprinted 1968); A Vanished Arcadia (about the Jesuit missions
among the Guaraní Indians), (London, 1901); The Horses of the
Conquest (London, 1930, new edition, edited by Robert M. Den-
hardt, Norman, Oklahoma, 1949); Portrait of a Dictator (Francisco Solano López, the Paraguayan dictator at time of war
with Argentina), (London, 1933); and various short stories and
accounts, many of them included in Rodeo, edited by Graham's
very close friend and biographer, A. F. Tschiffely (q.v.).

See Tschiffely's Don Roberto (London, Toronto, 1937);
and Paul Bloomfield, The Essential Robert Bontine Cunninghame
Graham (London, 1952).

GRAINS.   After the political reorganization of the Argentine Republic in the 1860s, national leadership and resources were turned
to the development of a more diversified economy; the great
change came in the expansion of production of cereals; European immigrants with grain-growing skills, were brought over

to crop-farm, for the most part on Argentine-owned estancias
on the pampas; most of the grain was grown for export, moving from a negligible amount in 1870 to 50% of total export
values by 1900, with Western Europe its principal market; in
1932, with Argentina facing the serious world depression, the
Grain Commission was established by finance minister Federico
Pinedo in 1933 to regulate this trade; during the post World
War II period, grain-growing for export underwent many
changes along with other agricultural products (see Agriculture;
also individual grains such as corn, linseed, rice, and wheat).

GRAN ENTRADA, LA (1543-1546).   Name given to first Spanish
penetration from Peru into Tucumán to begin its conquest and
settlement.   In 1543 Vaca de Castro was attempting to restore
order in Peru following civil war there among the Spanish conquistadors;   in an effort to reward the soldiers as well as to
keep them busy he organized and subsidized several expeditions
to conquer new and presumably rich lands for Spain; Diego de
Rojas, a Spanish officer from Burgos, Spain, who had distinguished himself in the conquests of Nicaragua and Peru, was
placed in charge of an expedition to the southwest; well supplied and with at least 200 men, including officials and soldiers,
Rojas left Cuzco in May or June 1543, and led the "gran entrada" as it became known, across the Andes and south into the
subtropical lands of the Diaguita and Calchaquí Indians in northwestern Argentina; meeting constant Indian hostility, Rojas was
killed (1544) and Francisco de Mendoza took command; he
pushed eastward to the Carcarañá river, followed it to the
Paraná and reached the ruins of Cabot's fort at Sancti Spiritus;
the discovery of a letter, left buried there by Domingo Martínez de Irala for any Spaniards who came that way, with instructions on how to reach Asunción, caused considerable controversy among Mendoza's men; some wanted to go upriver to
the new Spanish town, others were determined to return to
Peru; the latter won.   Francisco de Mendoza was killed by disgruntled companions (1545) and eventually (1546) a remnant of
approximately 80 Spaniards reached Peru.
    The immediate accomplishments of the gran entrada
seemed negligible, but its long-range results justified its title:
although not actually the first Spanish expedition to enter northwestern Argentina--Almagro's men had passed through it a few
years earlier on their way to Chile--Rojas' expedition was the
first to open the way from Peru to the Río de la Plata; its information about lands, Indians, climate, natural resources,
etc. formed the bases for the success of later expeditions in
establishing Spanish settlements and government in Tucumán,
and one of its own survivors, Juan de Garay (q.v.) played an
important role a few decades later in the permanent settlement
of Santa Fe and Buenos Aires in the Río de la Plata area.

GRANADEROS A CABALLO.   Elite cavalry corps formed by San
Martín in 1812 under auspices of triumvirate government; Carlos
María de Alvear second in command.   Standards were high:

officers were selected from best families socially and for their
intelligence; both officers and men had to be tall, in good
physical condition, and excellent horsemen; San Martín used
this regiment as a training model and core of the Army of the
Andes; uniforms were simple, dark blue with red facings, a
red plume in helmet, and grenadier boots; weapons consisted
of curved saber, hunting rifle, and, on dress occasions, a
lance; name apparently chosen as reflection of San Martín's admiration for Spanish grenadiers; first battle resulted in victory
at San Lorenzo, a few miles north of Rosario, February 3,
1813, over Spanish forces that had gone upriver seeking supplies; during the next eleven years the Granaderos fought, in
areas now occupied by five republics, until the war for independence was finally won at Ayacucho December 9, 1824; disbanded shortly thereafter, seven of the original 125 that had
gone into the Army of the Andes in 1815, returned to Argentina under Colonel Félix Bogado; according to Bartolomé Mitre,
the Granaderos a Caballo had given the nation over 200 officers, including more than 16 generals.

In 1903 General Pablo Ricchieri reorganized the Granaderos a Caballo with similar uniforms and very high standards.

GRAPES see FRUIT INDUSTRY; VINEYARDS; WINE INDUSTRY

GREAT BRITAIN, BRITISH RELATIONS AND INFLUENCE. Throughout the nineteenth century Great Britain was the predominant
foreign power in Argentina's economic life and international
relations.

After its failure to take the Río de la Plata from Spain
in 1806-1807 (see British Invasions), Great Britain turned its
attention to securing economic privileges in that area; as an
ally of Spain during the Napoleonic wars it could not openly
sponsor the fight for independence but the presence of its diplomats in neighboring Brazil was a constant factor in Argentine
political life during the period preceding and following the May
revolution; and the British, for their own interests, gave Ferdinand VII little or no help in regaining his colonies.

In 1825, after independence had been won at Ayacucho,
the British signed a treaty with the Buenos Aires government
that established the legal basis for their relationship for the
next hundred years; primarily commercial and economic, it
paved the way for British investment (see Baring Brothers) in
the new nation and regulated their mutual trade; it also provided for the civil rights of British citizens in Argentina, ex-
empting them from military service and providing formally for
the freedom of worship that had been tacitly given them before
this time; other nations, such as France, later demanded similar treatment for their resident citizens; much of Argentina's
religious toleration (see Church-State Relations) may be attributed to this special British relationship, as well as to such
other factors as Argentine liberal ideas at the time, and its
need for immigrants later; during the following years British
investment capital flowed into Argentina for public works, mines

(see River Plate Co.), and especially for the stockraising industries; British shipping carried most of this trade; anarchy
and civil wars affected this commerce very little until Rosas'
campaign against Montevideo stopped the upriver traffic; Great
Britain (reluctantly joined by French) blockaded the estuary
1845-1848 to bring Rosas to terms but latter won out as British merchants forced their government to lift the blockade;
thereafter, the British government and Argentine economic, social, and political elite that formed the power structure known
as the oligarchy, worked closely together for decades for their
common interests; this tie was so carefully fostered that even
the continuing conflict over the ownership of the Falkland Islands (q.v.), held by the British but consistently claimed by
every Argentine government as part of its territory, offered no
threat.

The fact that "Britannia ruled the waves" and was determined to maintain a world at peace that would be good for
business, gave England's relationship to Argentina a special
meaning as Brazil, Argentina's most powerful neighbor, was also a protégé of Great Britain; British diplomacy on matters between them was always a factor, most notably in the establishment of Uruguayan independence in 1828; British merchants,
bankers, entrepreneurs, cattleraisers and sheepfarmers, young
adventurers and fortunehunters traveled throughout the country;
some took up residence permanently or for lengthy periods in
Buenos Aires and elsewhere; these made their impact on Argentine society and life-styles; although France continued to attract
the intellectuals and literary world, British governesses and
private academies were commonly a part of the life of younger
members of oligarchical families; it was through them (diaries
and memoirs published by British travelers) that the Western
World received much of its information and impressions of remote Argentina during the nineteenth century; British investment
capital in the latter half of the nineteenth century flowed into
railroad and other transportation systems, as well as into
sheepraising in Patagonia and grain cropfarming on the pampas.

Great Britain lost its preeminence in Argentina in the
1930s for reasons growing out of changes in Argentina, in the
British empire, and in the world situation; Argentine nationalists, especially those desiring economic independence, turned
the greatest part of their resentment against Great Britain,
simply and logically because it had predominated over the economy; creole nationalists were joined by the great numbers of
Argentines of immigrant stock, the majority of whom came from
nations with little or no affection for the British; furthermore,
they felt that Argentine economic development was stunted by
the limits of British interests; industry could not be developed,
even though almost all coal (for energy) was imported from England because that would compete with British industry; the weakness of Argentina's dependence on Britain for coal for all energy uses was demonstrated vividly in both world wars (q.v.)
when Germany effectively cut off shipping for considerable intervals; it also became clear that Argentine interests were not the

same as British interests; British discovered this to be true in
the depression of the 1930s when its dependencies demanded
that it buy wool, meat, grains, etc. from them, rather than
Argentina; the Roca-Runciman pact (q. v.) was an attempt on
part of British merchants and Argentine meat-grain interests
to preserve what they could of the old relationship.

After World War II this became impossible, if for no
other reason than that other nations, such as the United States
and West Germany were better able to supply the industrial
machinery, technological skills and advice, and capital needed
for the development of Argentine economic independence and
production for its national market that Perón's government
(1946-1955) and all subsequent ones have strongly supported.

On a reduced level, Argentine-British relations and
trade follow the outlines of the old pattern; one important result of this traditional relationship has been the continuing interest of British historians and social scientists in producing
excellent scholarly studies related to its historical development.

See Henry Stanley Ferns, Britain and Argentina in the
Nineteenth Century (Oxford University Press, Great Britain,
1960).

GREAT JUNTA, or JUNTA GRANDE see JUNTA

"GREAT WAR" (la Guerra Grande), sometimes called the "Great
Siege." Term applied to period of nine years, 1842-1851, during which the forces of Uruguay (largely Montevideo) struggled
to fight off those of Rosas from Argentina (see Montevideo).

GRELA, JOSE IGNACIO (1765-1834). Dominican friar who played active role in May Revolution and early days of independence.
Born in Buenos Aires; entered Dominican order 1784,
ordained 1792; supported the revolutionary movement whole-
heartedly and assisted Domingo French and Antonio Beruti in
organizing the popular demonstration that resulted in the deposing of Viceroy Cisneros May 25, 1810; his influence over the
Buenos Aires citizenry credited with having done much to maintain public order during this critical period; became a close
friend of José de San Martín; in 1815 was made provincial of
Dominican Order; served in legislature 1827-1828 and as director of public library 1829-1833.

GROSS NATIONAL PRODUCT see GNP

GROUSSAC, PAUL (1848-1929). Historian; director of national library; writer; literary critic.
Born in Toulouse, France; came to Buenos Aires in
1866; largely self-educated, devoted to French culture but became one of Argentina's foremost men of letters; accepted invitation from Nicolás Avellaneda, Sarmiento's minister of public instruction, to move to Tucumán, 1870; successively held
posts as teacher in academy, provincial director of instruction,
national inspector of education, journalist, director of normal

school; after visit to France in 1883, Groussac returned to
Buenos Aires and became director of national library, 1885;
devoted rest of his life to this post and to writing; his works
include fiction, literary criticism, historical studies and critical, sometimes iconoclastic, comments on Argentine historical
figures and events; often controversial, and evaluations of Argentine political leaders and intellectuals not always accepted,
his works are still widely read and quoted; even those most
critical had tonic effect on historiography in forcing historians
back to sources instead of accepting, uncritically, familiar
stories; included among his most scholarly works are his Ensayo histórico sobre el Tucumán, his very complete study of
the discovery and settlement of Río de la Plata, Mendoza y
Garay (Buenos Aires, 1916; 2 v. 1949-1950); the biography of
Santiago de Liniers; Estudios de historia argentina; los que
pasan (Buenos Aires, 1919); the published review of the library,
Los Anales de la Biblioteca (11 volumes) included many more
of his writings, especially historical essays; also edited Le
Courier Française, established in 1894.

GRUPO DE OFICIALES UNIDOS   see   GOU

GUAIRA (Guayrá in Spanish).   Region east of upper Paraná River,
    now part of southwestern Brazil; site of enormous Brazilian-
    Paraguayan hydroelectric power plant.
        After the base of the Spanish conquest in Río de la Plata
    had been moved north to Asunción, the Spaniards were eager to
    establish towns along a direct overland route through Guayrá
    to the Atlantic to avoid the long trip down the rivers; little
    progress made until early 17th century; in 1610 the Jesuits be-
    gan to gather the Indians of Guayrá into missions (see Jesuit
    Missions) and in 1617 the Asunción-Guayrá section was made
    into a separate political administration from that of Buenos
    Aires; Brazilian slavetraders, however, soon forced the Jesuits
    to move their Indians and missions south into what is now Ar-
    gentine territory and Guayrá was left to become part of Portu-
    guese Brazil; in the mid-1970s Brazil and Paraguay began con-
    struction at Itaipú (meaning "singing rock" in Guaraní) in the
    Guayrá area on the Paraná of the largest dam in the world to
    supply hydroelectric power to both countries; Argentina vigor-
    ously protested this project to various international bodies on
    the grounds that as a down-river nation on the Paraná river its
    rights were being violated, especially as it and Paraguay were
    building a smaller power plant down the river (see Energy Re-
    sources).

GUALEGUAY.   Name of town, river, and department in south cen-
    tral Entre Ríos province; town founded March 19, 1783, by
    Tomás de Rocamora, acting under orders from viceroy Vértiz;
    a curate or parish had already been established there; the
    name of the town is a vulgar corruption of guaribay or aguari-
    bay, the Guaraní name for the Schinus Molle (Brazilian pepper
    tree) found in the area (see listing on Entre Ríos).

GUALEGUAYCHU. Southernmost Entre Ríos port on Uruguay River;
    capital of largely urbanized department of same name; city
    dates from late eighteenth century, resulting from new royal
    interest in expansion into this area; in 1764-1765 a small set-
    tlement already existed on the site with a chapel attended by
    Uruguayan priests from San Domingo Soriano mission; in 1780
    a parish was established there and on October 18, 1783, Tomás
    de Rocamora, acting under orders from Viceroy Vértiz y Sal-
    cedo, formally established the city; the latter's location on the
    active river commerce and directly across the river from
    Fray Bentos (in modern Uruguay) involved the city in economic
    and political activities, provincial, national, and international,
    almost from its beginning (see Entre Ríos Province).

GUANACO (from Quechua huanacu). Animal belonging to wild vari-
    ety of camel tribe found in South America (lama guanicoe), re-
    lated to vicuña, and the alpaca and llama domesticated by the
    Indians before the arrival of Europeans; guanacos found in
    southern Andes, especially in Argentine Patagonia where their
    meat provided the nomadic Indians with food, and their skins
    were used for clothing, blankets, shelter, and thongs in their
    boleadoras; the guanaco stood about four feet high at the
    shoulder; covered with long, soft hair--reddish brown or fawn
    color on the saddle, white underneath; usually found in herds
    of from five to 30 animals; many place names indicate the im-
    portance of the guanaco in the Indian and early colonial periods;
    among these is the Guanacos River, a tributary of the Neu-
    quén.

GUANACOS, FORTIN (Fort Guanacos). Site of Indian massacre dur-
    ing conquest of desert. Fort established by Rufino Ortega near
    Río Trocomán in Neuquén national territory, December 1879,
    to facilitate advance of national forces; fort fought off several
    Indian attacks but on January 19, 1881, after having given ref-
    uge to seventeen muleteers carrying supplies to forward mili-
    tary detachments, the small garrison of a dozen cavalrymen,
    commanded by Lieutenant Alfredo Boerr, was attacked by over
    300 Indians, the fort captured, and all those in it killed; Indian
    casualties included 32 dead; in 1943 Fortín Guanacos was de-
    clared a national historic site.

GUARANI INDIANS. These were the only agricultural, semicivilized
    Indians whom the Spaniards found in eastern Argentina in the
    early sixteenth century; belonging to the extensive Brazilian
    Tupi-Guaraní linguistic group, they had wandered into Paraguay
    and the Paraná river area; some had spread into Bolivia; they
    lived in towns, in communal houses; using the slash and burn
    system, the men cleared fields in which the women then raised
    corn, sweet potatoes, squashes, and manioc; as rivermen,
    they were skilled fishermen and boatmen; the wild cotton of the
    area was woven into fabrics and their ceramic industry was
    well-developed; during the decades preceding the arrival of the
    Spaniards they had come into contact with Indians of the Inca

empire during raids through the Chaco to the eastern Andes;
although many of them remained there in Bolivia (becoming
Chiriguanos), most returned to their Paraná home, with news
of the "people of the metal" whom they had discovered; by the
time that Juan Díaz de Solís arrived and officially discovered
the Río de la Plata (1516) objects of metal were fairly plentiful among the Guaraní but it was becoming increasingly difficult to raid even the outlying areas of the Inca empire; they
therefore welcomed the arrival of Mendoza's expedition, looking to these Spaniards as possible allies in their raids to the
"Silver Sierra" as it came to be known; the Spaniards, for their
part, found the Guaraní indispensable as the only Indians in the
Río de la Plata area civilized enough to make the first permanent settlement possible--Asunción 1537; Guaraní warriors,
porters, and eventually Guaraní-Spanish mestizos accompanied
all Spanish leaders in explorations from Asunción and in final,
successful settlement of Santa Fe (1573) and Buenos Aires; unlike the conventional Spanish-Indian patterns established in Tucumán, including the use of the encomienda, a very different
life style emerged in the Río de la Plata; it would be unrealistic to say that the two races were equal in their relationships
as all authority rested in the Spanish crown and church, but
Guaraní and Spaniards lived together comfortably; both languages
were spoken (both even became official languages in Paraguay
centuries later); intermarriages, as well as miscegenation,
were common, with the children given the social and legal
status, as creole or mestizo, of their respective fathers; Spaniards accepted Guaraní diet and life style, based on the nature
of the land on which they were all living; Guaraní accepted the
teachings of the church; the Indians were expected to provide
all the labor but the encomienda system was not used very long;
there were, of course, instances of rebellions and examples of
unbearable exploitations; there were also many Guaraní who
lived outside this pattern; in the early seventeenth century
most of these were gathered into the Jesuit Missions (q. v.)
where their agricultural and other skills were upgraded by
European experts while they themselves were converted to
Christianity and acculturated into Spanish customs and institutions; the fact remains that the Guaraní who, on the one hand,
were more rapidly assimilated into the blood and pattern of
life of the Spaniards in the towns of the Río de la Plata area
and, on the other, were among those most completely dominated by the mission system, were the only large group of Argentine Indians to retain a sense of cultural identity, strengthened, as though by natural development, through the European
elements accepted (a situation rarely found among any other
American Indians throughout the hemisphere); they still live on
their ancestral lands with many elements of their ancestral life
style, and they still use their own language commonly; both in
Corrientes and Misiones it is gaining new currency from the
large number of Guaraní workers from Paraguay who daily or
seasonally cross the Paraná to work in the yerbales (groves or
orchards in which mate is grown), in other agricultural opera-

tions, or just to trade (see Indians).
See volume III of Handbook on South American Indians, entitled The Tropical Forest Tribes (Washington, D.C., 1948); and Elman R. Service and Helen Service's study of the acculturation of the Guaraní, entitled Tobati: Paraguayan Town (Chicago, 1954); although this deals primarily with Paraguay, much of it is relevant to northeastern Argentina; see also E. R. Service, Spanish-Guaraní Relations in Colonial Paraguay (Ann Arbor, Michigan 1954).

GUARANI WAR. Revolt of Guaraní mission Indians in the seven Jesuit missions (containing nearly 30,000 Indians) lying east of Uruguay river ceded by Spain to Portugal in treaty of 1750; remembering their traditional enemies, the bandeirante Brazilian slave traders, the Guaraní refused to live under Portuguese rule, claimed that the lands were theirs, refused to emigrate, and fought off Portuguese forces and the boundary commissioners; Governor José de Andonaegui of Buenos Aires, put down this revolt with aid of Portuguese forces (1755); Charles III annulled the treaty when he became king shortly thereafter, but royal officials continued to retain suspicion that Jesuits had been involved; some Guaraní already moved to other missions; missions never really recovered from this blow.

GUAYAQUIL, CONFERENCE OF see JOSE DE SAN MARTIN

GUAYCURUANS (Guaycurúes). These Indians made up one of the largest linguistic groups found in Argentina at the time of conquest and included the Abipón, Mocoví, Toba, Pilagá tribes, along with others, and the Mibaya and Payagua (river pirates) in Paraguay; although they were occupying the Chaco in the sixteenth century, the Guaycuruans had apparently moved north from Patagonia; fairly tall and vigorous, they made excellent fighters; before the arrival of the Spaniards they had lived by hunting and gathering what food they could find--with grasshoppers, peccaries (wild pigs), and honey favored items of diet; they had begun some agriculture, but were still nomadic for the most part; with the arrival of the Spanish horse, their entire life style changed; adopting the horse as an easier way to get around, the Guaycuruans (with exception of certain tribes) abandoned their primitive farms and based a new life and economy on raiding Spanish settlements and cattle herds, as well as other Indian settlements for provisions; they established their own herds and seized grasslands to support them; a military class system developed and everything in the tribal life was geared to the needs of this new, highly mobile fighting society; for over two centuries the Guaycuruans controlled the Chaco and terrorized its borders, forcing Spaniards to abandon or move several settlements; eventually the government brought them under control and the tribal units began to disappear as the individual Indians were assimilated into Argentine life, with only a few preserving the old Indian ways (see Indians; also individual listings of tribes mentioned).

GUAYRA see GUAIRA

GÜEMES, ADOLFO (1874-1947). Physician and political leader; philanthropist.

Born in Salta of patrician lineage; after graduating in medicine in Buenos Aires, 1898, Dr. Güemes went to Europe to spend several years studying in clinics in Paris, Vienna, Germany, and Russia; spent considerable time in Spain before returning to Buenos Aires in 1904 to establish his medical practice; became active in politics in 1920; joined the UCR, was elected governor of Salta in 1922 and gave his province progressive administration: imposed rigid code of political ethics, carried out public health program to stamp out malaria, supported railroad extension to Huayticina, and defended province's subsoil rights to petroleum; returned at end of term to Buenos Aires and resumed his medical practice there; appointed honorary professor by Medical Faculty; following the overthrow of Yrigoyen's radical government in 1930 by José Félix Uriburu, Güemes took an active part in reorganization of the Radical Party; signed Marcelo T. Alvear's Junta del City manifesto (q. v.) and was chosen as vice presidential candidate on ticket with Alvear as president (annulled as illegal as six years had not elapsed since Alvear's former presidency); took leading part in Radical uprising against President Agustín P. Justo and was imprisoned on Martín García island and in Tierra del Fuego; returning to political life in 1935, he published Tres discursos in which his strongly militant 'ideas were expressed, but, finding himself at odds with other Radicals, he withdrew to private life; died of heart attack in Buenos Aires.

During his life, Dr. Güemes was frequently called upon as consultant in the establishment of hospitals and other medical facilities; always interested in his own province of Salta, he had concentrated on beautifying its capital while governor and gave it his historic Chacra El Carmen de Güemes, hoping that a model school of agriculture would be established there; many of the fine old paintings of his home in Salta were also bequeathed to the Colonial Museum there.

GÜEMES, MARTIN (1785-1821). Governor of Salta; caudillo; military hero of independence era.

Born in Salta into wealthy, aristocratic family: father, Gabriel de Güemes Montero, Spanish royal treasurer of intendancy of Salta; mother, Magdalena de Goyechea y de la Corte, related to historic and currently powerful families of Salta and Jujuy, several of whom had subsidized the establishment of the royal treasury there in 1778; educated at home and in Franciscan schools, Martín Güemes entered military career at age of fourteen as cadet in Regiment of Buenos Aires, part of viceroy's permanent guard based in Salta; took his battalion to Buenos Aires to fight British invasions and distinguished himself as aide-de-camp to Santiago de Liniers in defeat of second British invasion, 1807; returned soon afterward to Salta because of his father's death; learning of May Revolution, he accepted it

enthusiastically and formed cavalry and observation units for
use of patriot Junta; carried out reconnaissance and espionage
missions in 1811; fought in Balcarce's army in Upper Peru;
assigned by Belgrano to duty in Buenos Aires where he took
part in siege of Montevideo, returned to Salta early in 1814
with reinforcements about same time that San Martín replaced
Belgrano in command of northern army; from then until his
death in 1821 was involved in defense of frontier and came to
be in command of it; accompanied General José Rondeau on
final and unsuccessful invasion of Upper Peru but returned to
Salta after victory over Pezuela's royalist forces at Puesto
del Marqués, April 1815, refusing, for personal and military
reasons, to accept Rondeau's command; in May Güemes was
elected governor of Salta by cabildo, an act that implied
Salta's independence and refusal to accept political control by
Buenos Aires junta; from then until his death, Güemes played
triple role as border captain, governor of province, national
officer and liaison between province and nation; as border captain he organized the gauchos and rural peasants into guerrilla
warfare that successfully rolled back at least seven royalist attempts at invasion of Salta, most of them commanded by Spanish officers who later became viceroys; in 1816, Pueyrredón's
first official concern, after having been appointed Supreme Director, was to go to Salta to solve the problem posed by quarrel between Rondeau and Güemes; Güemes placed in charge;
San Martín's continental strategy for winning independence for
southern Spanish America depended on his conviction that Güemes could immobilize royalist troops along northwestern Argentine border and to mount a counter-attack into Upper Peru when
San Martín's Peruvian campaign needed this; as governor, Güemes attempted to maintain order, to institute new taxes, especially for military reforms to modernize the force and adapt
it more effectively to its special functions, and to stabilize relationships between Spaniards and Creoles living in the area;
his own ability, along with his close ties with the families that
had dominated political and economic life of Salta for centuries, made him successful as long as he pursued goals also
desired by the establishment--i. e., strong defense against royalist invading forces and firmness toward Spanish sympathiz-
ers--but difficulties arose when he proposed new, democratic
land and tax reforms infringing on privileges of elite, and political opposition gained strength against him; meanwhile, Tucumán declared its independence and Güemes, attempting to bring
it back into the nation, found himself caught between this war
to the south and new royalist invasions from the north; killed
in one of latter, June 17, 1821.
        In modern period the traditional view of Güemes as
gaucho and guerrilla border captain and probably Argentina's
first caudillo has been broadened by both Argentine and U.S.
historians to recognize him also as one of the first regional
leaders and progressive governors, staunch in his loyalty to
the nation but determined that his province Salta should be permitted to play its own role in the new political economy.

See Roger M. Haigh in Suggested Readings, Appendix III, and Atilio Cornejo, Historia de Güemes (Academia Nacional de la Historia, Buenos Aires, 1946).

"GUERRA DE ZAPA, LA" see "ZAPA, LA GUERRA DE"

GUERRILLAS. Term usually applied to modern clandestine groups that represent different tendencies from extreme right to extreme left, from fanatical Catholicism to Communism; they are all violent, populist, idealistic, and opposed to economic oppression; one of the most important groups is the ERP (Ejército Revolucionario del Pueblo--Peoples' Revolutionary Army; also called montoneros); this was formed in 1969, claims to be Marxist-Leninist, and aims to trigger national revolution; its principal targets have been Argentine armed forces and foreign and local capitalists; among other groups are the FAL (Fuerzas Armadas de Liberación) and FAP (Fuerzas Armadas Peronistas); generally speaking, they have not aroused as much popular sympathy as they had hoped.

GUEVARA, ERNESTO ("CHE") (1928-1967). Argentine-born revolutionary; important leader of Cuban revolution that took over Cuba in 1959.
      Born in Rosario; graduated in medicine at Buenos Aires; became allergy specialist; attended medical conference in Mexico and remained there; joined Cuban Fidel Castro in latter's attempt to overthrow President Fulgencio Batista; spent two years with guerrillas in Sierra Maestra and became one of most prestigious leaders of Cuban revolutionary government established after flight of Batista (1959); as foreign minister he attended the inter-American meeting at Punta del Este (1961) for the organization of President Kennedy's proposed Alliance for Progress; declared publicly to the other Latin American nations that they owed this new U.S. interest and generosity to the Cuban revolution; met secretly with President Arturo Frondizi in attempt to persuade latter to support Cuban revolutionary government or, at least, not to oppose it; was given public reception by Frondizi because of his Argentine birth and background (see Frondizi for adverse Argentine public and military reaction to this); five years later Ché Guevara arrived in Bolivia with Cuban support to instigate and lead a similar Communistic revolutionary movement there; it was easily suppressed and Guevara was captured and executed.

GUIDO, JOSE MARIA (1910-1975). Provisional president of Argentine Republic, 1962-1963; lawyer.
      Born in Buenos Aires; moved to Viedma, capital of Río Negro province; practiced law and entered politics; became local leader of Radical Party; elected national senator from Río Negro in 1958; when Vice President Alejandro Gómez resigned in October of that year, Guido became pro tem president of the senate; still serving in that capacity in March 1962 when President Arturo Frondizi was ousted by the military,

Guido, as next in line of succession, was elevated to the presidency by the military in attempt to preserve continuity of civilian government and observance of constitutional forms; President Guido dissolved congress in November and ordered the reorganization of political parties; his administration was mainly characterized by open hostilities between rival political groups in the military; eventually General Juan Carlos Onganía gained control and established order; President Guido presided over general elections and, in July 1963, turned the presidency over to the duly elected Arturo U. Illia; in the early 1970s Guido was appointed by the Peronist government to a responsible position in a corporation developing southern Patagonia; after a brief period he resigned and died not long afterward.

GUIDO, TOMAS (1788-1866). Fighter for independence (general); government official; diplomat.

Born in Buenos Aires of Spanish parents; fought in Miñones regiment against British invasions (1806-1807); early joined patriot group desiring independence; went to London in 1811 as secretary of Mariano Moreno who died on the way; returning to Buenos Aires was appointed secretary of intendancy of Charcas (Bolivia); while in this area became acquainted with José de San Martín, then in Tucumán as commander of the Army of the North; began decade of cooperation with the Liberator by accompanying him to Córdoba in 1814; the following year, with San Martín now governor of Mendoza, Guido went to Buenos Aires to serve as liaison for San Martín with government in creation of Army of the Andes; after patriot victory at Chacabuco (February 12, 1817), rejoined San Martín in Santiago, Chile, becoming first aide-de-camp; while there, married Pilar Spano, daughter of defender of southern Chilean towns of Chillán and Talca; accompanied San Martín to Peru in 1820; remained there, collaborating with San Martín and then, after latter's departure, with Simón Bolívar until victorious completion of war of independence; became general and held several important military and civil positions, including cabinet appointments; awarded medal of Bolívar; returned to Buenos Aires in 1826; reentered government service; signed treaty of peace with Brazil, 1828.

Guido became active member of government of Juan Manuel de Rosas; served as minister (1829) and unsuccessfully urged Rosas not to resign in 1832; after Rosas' return to power, 1835, Guido was sent as ambassador to Brazil, 1840-1852; joined with Justo José Urquiza in attempt to unite Argentine under constitutional government; performed diplomatic mission to Paraguay; was vice president of Confederation Senate; wrote Memoria about the campaign of the Andes, published in Paraná, 1855; died in retirement in Buenos Aires, 1866.

See Felipe Barreda Laos, General Tomás Guido, vida, diplomacia, revelaciones, y confidencias (Buenos Aires, 1942).

GUIDO SPANO, CARLOS (1827-1918). Writer. Born in Buenos

Aires; son of Tomás Guido; held position in department of agriculture but devoted his efforts to writing; although deeply patriotic and tied in, by family and social relationships, to public affairs, his concern was to create literature for its own sake, not merely as a political tool; Ricardo Rojas has called him Argentina's first real literary artist; experimented with many forms and wrote on many topics, including historical; collaborated with Vicente G. Quesada's Revista del Paraná (1861); considered excellent dramatic and literary critic; in 1879 Ráfagas (Puffs), appeared containing two volumes of collected prose writings, and in 1911 Poesías completas was published.

GUILDS.   Organized craftsmen's guilds played little part in colonial Argentina and efforts to establish them in Buenos Aires during viceregal period met with limited success; in 1788 the silversmiths were organized, to regulate the proper training of those in this industry; forty-seven members were registered, 25 creoles, 15 Portuguese, and seven Spaniards; master shoemakers petitioned the government for permission to organize themselves into a similar guild to protect themselves and the public from the untrained workmen opening shops; this was opposed by those master shoemakers, such as foreigners and blacks who made up a considerable proportion of the total number but would have been excluded from management of the guild, and by Cornelio Saavedra, syndic of the cabildo, who wrote an opinion advising against formation of such a guild in the name of freedom of labor, saying that "the right to work is the most sacred and indestructible privilege known to humankind."

GÜIRALDES, JOSE LORENZO (1776-1861).   Priest; liberal intellectual and educator; patriot.
        Born in Mendoza and ordained as priest; Father Güiraldes became an enthusiastic supporter of San Martín's plans for winning the independence of Argentina and neighboring countries and had the honor of blessing the celebrated banner of the Andes in December 1816 shortly before San Martín started his army across the Andes to begin the campaign of liberation; with support of San Martín, governor-intendant of Mendoza, Güiraldes was able to open the Colegio de Santísima Trinidad November 17, 1817, for classes; he served as rector and professor of philosophy and the school was already accredited so that its graduates could be admitted into the universities of both Argentina and Chile; in 1822, Güiraldes welcomed another liberal exponent of popular education, Juan Crisóstomo Lafinur (q.v.), who succeeded him as rector of the colegio; his advanced ideas brought him into some troubles and he was exiled briefly but in 1826 he was elected member of the legislature; he also edited La Aurora Mendocina (Mendoza Dawn) and El Telégrafo; became one of most highly respected churchmen in central and western Argentina and was appointed canon in Córdoba; while serving there in 1855 he

was nominated for the bishopric of Cuyo; later moved to Chile where he died in 1861.

Güiraldes, Ricardo (1886-1927). Writer; author of Don Segundo Sombra, Argentine classic gaucho novel.

Born in Buenos Aires; grew up on family estancia in Buenos Aires province; studied architecture, social sciences in Buenos Aires but turned to writing as career; spent time in Paris, interested in modernism; became leader of Generation of 1922 "Florida Group" in Buenos Aires; after several earlier works in various forms dealing with creolism and Argentine life, published his famous Don Segundo Sombra (1926); a masterpiece of modern gaucho literature, giving authentic picture of modern gaucho and his rapidly disappearing way of life on pampas but serving almost as an Argentine Don Quixote in its presentation of Don Segundo "as a legendary symbol of a heroic type that was"--the ideal gaucho, lord of the pampas and of himself, the complete man, master of himself and of every situation, living gloriously and freely as lord of Argentine pampas.

GURRUCHAGA, FRANCISCO DE (1766-1846). Patriot financier, political leader; often called creator of Argentine navy.

Born in Salta, son of one of wealthiest merchants in the northwest area, young Francisco was sent to Spain, at age of eight, to be educated at the Colegio de Nobles in Madrid; later graduated in jurisprudence from university at Granada; when war broke out with England, he entered the Spanish navy, taking part in the battle of Trafalgar (October 21, 1805) on board ship commanded by Baltasar Hidalgo de Cisneros, later to become last viceroy in Buenos Aires; Gurruchaga also joined in the Spanish fight against Napoleon's invading forces, but he quickly decided to join his destiny with that of his native land and, in spite of French attempts to prevent his departure from Spain, escaped to accompany José de Moldes and Juan Martín de Pueyrredón back to Buenos Aires in 1809; returned to Salta where he and Moldes drew up Salta's statement of support of May Revolution (August 1810); from this time on Gurruchaga devoted all his fortune and his efforts to the revolution; on December 19, 1810 he took his place in Buenos Aires as Salta's delegate to the Provisional Junta of the Buenos Aires government; given responsibility to create an armed naval force, he had three ships ready for action by March 1811, and when these were lost after fighting valiantly at San Nicolás de los Arroyos, he immediately pledged to replace the little fleet at his own expense and did so in August of that year; during 1812-1813 he took part in Belgrano's campaigns in the north,

managing the financial affairs of the army; used up large part
of his own estate in the expenses incurred; supplied Martín
Güemes' gaucho army with clothing and other necessary items
from his own factories and warehouses; distributed 5000 pesos
of his own to victors at Tucumán on day following that critical
battle; he was elected to famous national constituent assembly
of 1813; five years later he was sent on secret mission to
Chile; during the civil wars following the winning of independence, Gurruchaga and Alejandro Heredia were charged with the
responsibility of making peace with the caudillo of the north,
Juan Facundo Quiroga, and they succeeded in drawing up an
agreement December 2, 1831; for thirty-three years (1813-
1846), Gurruchaga had held post in mail service in Salta; died
there in relative poverty, resulting partly from his own generosity, partly from changed circumstances, and considered by
Argentine historians as also a tribute to his honesty during
more than three decades in public office.

GUTIERREZ, CELEDONIO (1804-1880).   Fighter for independence;
    caudillo-Governor of Tucumán 1841-1853.

        Born in Tucumán; joined Army of North under Belgrano
in 1818; continued active in fighting along northwest frontier
until 1823 when he returned to Tucumán as commandante; with
independence won, he became embroiled in civil wars; joined
with Marco M. de Avellaneda (q. v.) in the Coalición del Norte
against Rosas, but went over to the other side; commanded
right-wing of General Oribe's forces in the defeat at Famaillá
of Lavalle's anti-Rosas' forces in 1841; Gutiérrez then became
governor of Tucumán; supported Rosas and suppressed the unitarists with speed and vigor, and began a dozen years of control of the province, being consistently reelected until after the
fall of Rosas; during this period Governor Gutiérrez attempted
to reform and reorganize administration of Tucumán; ordered
census of population taken in 1844, supplemented by one on agricultural production the following year; organized a police
force; provided for the administration of justice and that of finance; established public works program, with special emphasis on irrigation system; ordered first public clock to be
brought from England and placed on the town hall; and built a
pyramidal monument in honor of the winning of independence;
in 1852 he rejected Urquiza's call for governors to unite
against Rosas but, after Rosas had been defeated and exiled,
Gutiérrez took part in the meeting at San Nicolás and signed
the agreement (Acuerdo de San Nicolás) with Urquiza about future government; returning to Tucumán, Gutiérrez was ousted
from government, regained it briefly, then went into exile
(1853) in Bolivia; appointed a brigadier general by Urquiza he
returned to public life; attempted to regain power in Tucumán
several times but was forced out; finally retired to private
life; died in Alderetes, Tucumán.

GUTIERREZ, EDUARDO (1853-1890).   Novelist and journalist.
    Member of Gutiérrez journalistic family; served in army; be-

came preoccupied with plight of gaucho in 1870s and 1880s and other aspects of Argentine rural life; wrote prolifically about them for family papers La Nación Argentina and La Patria Argentina, as well as for other publications; made important contribution to Argentine cultural development through creation of semi-fictional gaucho figure based on career of historical Juan Moreira in his writings (see Juan Moreira); dramatized, first in pantomime, then with dialogue by the Podestá brothers, and presented in circuses and folk theaters, Juan Moreira popularized the gaucho as a national figure among the masses, at same time that Argentine historians and more literary authors than Gutiérrez were finding nation's identity in same traditional gaucho class.

GUTIERREZ, JOSE MARIA (1832-1903).   Editor, educator; cabinet
     minister.
          One of Buenos Aires "old patricians" who served in many official capacities in last half of the nineteenth century; began to write for public journals in 1852; held position as secretary of Buenos Aires provincial congress (1854-1857) and was a member of the constituent congress that drew up reforms in 1853 constitution making possible national union between the province and the confederation; took part in battles of Cepeda and Pavón as Mitre's secretary; in 1868 he founded and served as editor of daily newspaper La Nación Argentina to defend Mitre's policies; when this was replaced by La Nación he became its lifetime editor; served as legislator in national congress, minister of public instruction in cabinets of presidents Avellaneda and Pellegrini; in 1895 was appointed president of the national council of education; remained in this position until his death; Gutiérrez was distinguished for his interest in the development of fine arts in the community and was also himself a painter; a member of the French academy.

GUTIERREZ, JUAN MARIA (1809-1878).   Writer, poet, historian,
     intellectual of "Generation of 1837," one of authors of Consti-
     tution of 1853.
          Born in Buenos Aires; began writing at early age, but earned his way through university of Buenos Aires by working as surveyor in Topographical Department; studied mathematics and law, graduated in new university law program 1834; actively worked with group that started Literary Salon in Marcos Sastre's bookstore; then joined with Echeverría and others to create Association of May; worked from the beginning to overthrow dictatorship of Rosas; with them fled from Rosas' oppression to Montevideo; in 1843 traveled through Italy, France, Switzerland, and England; returning to South America, visited several countries, then took up residence in Valparaíso, Chile, where he spent his time in literary pursuits, teaching and serving as director of naval school; returning to Buenos Aires after Rosas' departure, Gutiérrez was one of porteños who strongly urged Buenos Aires to join other provinces in forming Argentine Confederation; when this failed, joined Alberdi

and other friends in backing Urquiza's efforts to form constitutional government, without Buenos Aires if necessary; elected
to Constituent Congress of Santa Fe as delegate from Santiago
del Estero, he played active role, particularly serving in the
writing (literary composition) of the constitution (usually
named, with José Benjamín Gorostiaga, as author of it); served
in Urquiza's cabinet as minister of Justice, Religion, and Education; then in 1861 was appointed rector of University of Buenos Aires by Bartolomé Mitre, a post for which he was emi-
nently suited by talents and experience; as part of President
Nicolás Avellaneda's conciliation policy following 1877 Gutiérrez was brought into the national cabinet again shortly before
his death.

Primarily famous as literary man, Juan María Gutiérrez also wrote historical and biographical works; exercised
great influence on Argentine culture; his historical works are
still frequently quoted; among the latter are Bosquejo biográfico del General San Martín; Noticias históricas sobre el orígen
y desarrollo de la enseñanza en Buenos Aires--a complete
treatise on that subject; Bibliografía sobre la imprenta de
Buenos Aires hasta 1810 and biographical studies of the poets
of the revolution; among his best known poems are A mi ban-
dera, A la juventud argentina, and the Canto de Mayo (for
which he won a literary award in Montevideo, May 25, 1841);
while still in exile in Chile, he published anthology of Spanish
American poetry (more voluminous than selective but very important as a first collection of American poetry) entitled
América poética (Valparaíso, 1846); and in 1870 published
Poesías, his own writings; among his novels one of best known
is El hombre hormiga; one of most prominent editors of his period; active especially on Revista de Buenos Aires (1863-1871)
and Revista del Río de la Plata (1871-1878); throughout his
writings the gaucho appears as favorite figure but gaucho language not used as in gauchesca literature.

GUTIERREZ DE LA CONCHA, JUAN (1760-1810).   Last governor intendant of Córdoba, 1807-1810.

Born in Spain, came to Río de la Plata as naval officer; led Cordobans and fought bravely against the British invasions; became intendant-governor of Córdoba in December
1807; upon receiving news of May Revolution, called meeting of
advisors, May 19, all of whom, except Deán Funes, favored
remaining loyal to Spain (as Montevideo was doing), and preparing the militia to fight, if necessary; meanwhile loyalists in
neighboring provinces were to be recruited; when the revolutionary army under command of Ortiz de Ocampo arrived in
August the leaders of what had come to be known as the Córdoba conspiracy were pursued by Balcarce, captured, and sum-
marily executed on orders of the governing Junta in Buenos
Aires; Gutiérrez de la Concha died, along with Santiago de Liniers, the royal assessor Dr. Victoriano Rodríguez, Colonel
Allende, Joaquín Moreno, only the bishop Orellana being spared;
the governor's family returned to Spain, and in 1864 his re-

mains, along with those of other royalists, were repatriated
to Spain with honors.

- H -

HACENDADO. Owner of an hacienda or large landed estate (see
    Estancia, Estancieros, terms more commonly used in Argen-
    tina, especially after independence).
        Among best known uses of term hacendado is in famous
    Representación de los hacendados y labradores, Mariano Mor-
    eno's fervent well-reasoned appeal for free trade and economic
    policy favoring Argentine interests, made during closing years
    of viceroyalty.

HAENKE, THADDEUS (1761-1817).   Bohemian naturalist and physi-
    cian.
        Born in Kreibitz, Bohemia, studied in Prague and Vien-
    na; appointed to accompany Alejandro Malaspina's scientific ex-
    pedition around the world; missed sailing in Spain; in later ves-
    sel, shipwrecked off coast, arrived in Buenos Aires where
    Viceroy Vértiz aided him to go overland to join his expedition
    in Santiago, Chile, 1790; during his crossing of the Argentine
    pampas and cordillera he collected approximately 1400 plants
    for study (many of them for first time); continued his botanical
    studies with the expedition; later settled in Cochabamba (Boliv-
    ia) where he served as physician and spent his time writing
    about his travels and scientific discoveries for sixteen years
    until his death there, 1817; some of his works published, others
    left unedited; in 1801 one of his articles appeared in the Telé-
    grafo Mercantil of Buenos Aires; and an article of his relating
    to curing of hides, sheepskins, etc. was published in volume
    XV of Revista de Buenos Aires (1868).

HAIGH, SAMUEL. British merchant and author of book of personal
    observations of leading personalities, events, and scenes of in-
    dependence era. At age of 22, Samuel Haigh arrived in Buenos
    Aires in mid-1817 as representative of British merchants eager
    to be among first to enjoy profits of new trade with Chile fol-
    lowing patriot victory at Chacabuco; went overland to Chile,
    sending his ship and cargo there by sea, where his vessel
    eventually became part of the Peruvian liberating expedition.
        During the next ten years, Haigh spent most of his time
    in residence in Argentina, Chile, and Peru, making three
    round trips from England for commercial purposes; during this
    time he met most of the patriot leaders--especially José de
    San Martín, whom he admired greatly, Bernardo O'Higgins,
    Bernardo Monteagudo and, later, Simón Bolívar--as well as
    many of his compatriots active in the independence movement,
    including physician James Paroissien, General William Miller,
    and others; escorted U.S. John B. Prevost to Chile when lat-
    ter had made himself unpopular in Buenos Aires; Haigh was
    eyewitness and minor participant in San Martín's victory at

Maipú; because of these unusual contacts and opportunities,
combined with Haigh's own personal interests and vivid descriptive ability, his writings constitute an important source for the
history of this period; first published in London in 1829 with
title Voyage to Peru, an expanded version came out in 1831
(London) as Sketches of Buenos Aires, Chile, and Peru; Argentine material has been translated into Spanish and appeared in
many forms, sometimes combined with writings of other English visitors at same time including those of Captain Basil
Hall.

HALL, SIR BASIL (1788-1844).   British naval officer who wrote
about his experiences in South America during war of independence.
        Born in Edinburgh, son of archeologist James Hall;
as young officer in British navy, served on missions to Far
East; came to South America in 1820; stationed along Pacific
coast during next two years; later left navy and continued travels, including those to North America in 1827-1828; died in
Portsmouth, England, after long illness.
        Sir Basil wrote extensively about areas visited; most
important work for Argentina is his Extracts from a Journal
Written on the Coasts of Chile, Peru and Mexico in the Years
1820-1821-1822 (2 volumes, London, 1824) that includes descriptive notes on San Martín and his liberating expedition to
Peru during those years; many Spanish editions have appeared,
including extracts of Hall's writings and combinations of his observations with those of other British writers such as Samuel
Haigh.

HALPERIN DONGHI, TULIO (1922-   ).   Historian.   Born in Buenos
Aires; graduated in faculties of law, philosophy and letters;
professor of history in universities of La Plata and Buenos
Aires; editor of new eight-volume history of Argentina; author
of several of the volumes; has written and lectured on modern
Argentine historiography; among his major historical works are:
Historia de la universidad de Buenos Aires (1962); Revolución
y guerra: formación de una elite dirigente en la Argentina
criolla (1972); The Aftermath of Revolution in Latin America,
translated by Josephine de Bunsen (New York, 1973); Politics,
Economics, and Society in the Revolutionary Period (Cambridge
University Press, New York, 1975).

HALSEY, THOMAS LLOYD (c. 1776-1855).   U.S. consul at Buenos
Aires, 1812-1818.   Providence (R.I.) merchant; moved to Buenos Aires as export-import merchant in early 1800s; appointed
U.S. consul in 1812; interested in improving economy of Argentina as well as furthering commercial ties between United
States and Río de la Plata; introduced first merino sheep into
Argentina (1813); worked for lower, reciprocal import duties;
assisted patriots in obtaining war materials; apparently on good
terms with Pueyrredón during first year of his directorate
(1816-1817); assisted Devereux in unauthorized plan to secure

U.S. loan for Pueyrredón's government; a controversial figure
because of his many diverse private business operations, as
well as public actions, Halsey found himself in early 1818 accused by Pueyrredón of being responsible for distribution in
Buenos Aires of inflammatory pamphlets and propaganda from
Baltimore, issued there by his exiled political enemies such
as Manuel Moreno, Vicente Pazos, and Pedro José Agrelo; also charged with meddling in the privateering system; and conspiring with José Gervasio Artigas in Uruguay against Buenos
Aires government; Pueyrredón demanded that U.S. recall Halsey but this was already underway due to rumors about him in
the United States; protesting his innocence Halsey retired from
public life; eventually, his financial claims against Argentina
were settled.

HEAD, SIR FRANCIS BOND (1793-1875).   Mining engineer; travel
writer.   English director of mining company (see Famatina);
traveled through Argentina and Chile, 1825-1826, making notes
on his observations; published them as Rough Notes Taken During Some Rapid Journeys Across the Pampas and Among the
Andes (London, 1826); descriptions detailed, objective, and
thoughtful; for example, his comparison of the laws and customs regulating the life and work of English miners in a competitive, industrializing economy, with those of a Spanish
South America emerging from a highly centralized, paternalistic rule indicates problems that nineteenth-century reformers
following European models would encounter.

HENRIQUEZ, CAMILO (1769-1825).   Chilean priest; propagandist for
independence in Chile and Buenos Aires.
          Born in Santiago, Chile; educated for the priesthood and
ordained in Lima; returned to Chile to become ardent supporter of independence from Spain, writing in La Aurora, Chile's
first journal; after the patriot defeat at Rancagua Father Henríquez came to Buenos Aires; spent eight years (1814-1822)
studying medicine and vigorously supporting independence of the
Río de la Plata provinces in his writings; served as editor of
the Gaceta de Buenos Aires (q.v.) in 1815; continued writing
after his return to Chile until his death in 1825.

HEREDIA, ALEJANDRO (1788-1838).   Governor of Tucumán; powerful leader in northern provinces in 1830s; commander of Argentine forces in war against Confederation of the Andes under
Andrés Santa Cruz.
          Born in San Miguel de Tucumán and educated at Co-
legio de Nuestra Señora de Loreto in Córdoba; joined patriot
army in the north after May Revolution; carried out diplomatic
mission to royalist general Goyeneche for Belgrano and was
sent by latter to give assistance to Santiago del Estero in 1817;
served as chief of staff for Martín Güemes; represented Tucumán at national constituent congress at Buenos Aires, 1824;
and Salta at congress of 1826; became governor of Tucumán,
his native province, in 1832; two years later, under provisional

government of Juan Vicente Maza in Buenos Aires, civil war
broke out between governors Heredia and Pablo de Latorre of
Salta; Maza (after consulting with Rosas) sent former caudillo
of La Rioja, Juan Facundo Quiroga, to mediate between them
but on the way latter learned that Latorre had been vanquished
by Heredia and had been assassinated (on his way back to Buenos Aires Quiroga himself was assassinated); Heredia now became central figure in north; imposed his brother Felipe as
governor of Salta; in 1837 Rosas, who was occupied with his
troubles with France (although somewhat doubtful of Heredia's
loyalty) placed him in command of Argentine forces against
Santa Cruz in Bolivia; Rosas not only feared development of
Bolivian-Peruvian confederated power to the north but also
wanted to crush anti-federalist conspiracies of Argentine exiles
in Bolivia against northern provinces; when hoped-for reinforcements from Rosas failed to arrive, Heredia undertook invasion
with his own forces but was defeated at Cuyambuyo June 24,
1838; soon afterward he was killed by army bandits while on
his way to Los Lules. See Newton, Jorge, Alejandro Heredia:
el protector del norte (Buenos Aires, 1972).

HEREDIA, FELIPE (1797-1852).   Independence war veteran; political
figure in northwest.
          Born in Tucumán, younger brother of Alejandro Heredia
(q. v.); in 1810 became cadet in one of companies raised in the
province for the Auxiliary Army of Upper Peru; for more than
ten years fought actively on the northwestern front against the
Spanish loyalists, gaining steady promotions; in January 1820
Lt. Col. Heredia led the escort that took General Belgrano to
Santiago del Estero, on his way, to die in Buenos Aires; Heredia returned to fight under Martín Güemes; took part in expedition that Governor Gorriti sent against Quiroga; in 1834, when
Pablo Latorre was assassinated in Jujuy, Governor Alejandro
Heredia of Tucumán sent his brother there to reestablish order;
named governor of Salta in 1836 and the following year appointed second in command and chief of staff of Rosas' army against
Santa Cruz in Bolivia; political turbulence surrounding his
brother's assassination forced Felipe Heredia to flee to Chile;
in 1839 he returned to accept Rosas' offer of a military command in province of Buenos Aires; died there a few months after
Rosas' defeat at Caseros.

HEREÑU (or EREÑU), JOSE EUSEBIO (born near close of eighteenth
century, died after 1831).   Fighter for independence and early
political and military leader in Entre Ríos province.
          Born in Entre Ríos; early joined group supporting Uru-
guayan leader José Gervasio Artigas as better for Entre Ríos
than increasingly centralist patriot government in Buenos Aires;
in 1814 Hereñú defeated army sent by Buenos Aires directorate
under Baron von Holmberg and thereafter was leading political
figure in province for several years; commanded vanguard of
Artigas' army invading Santa Fe in 1815 and kept Entre Ríos
loyal to Artigas' "league of free peoples" while Congress of

Tucumán was declaring independence of provinces from Spain; in 1817, however, rejected as new governor and jealous of Artigas' increasing preference for Francisco Ramírez, Hereñú allied himself with Director Juan Pueyrredón in unsuccessful attempt to bring Entre Ríos back into national allegiance; aided in placing Lucio N. Mansilla (candidate favored by Buenos Aires) in governor's seat, but was later exiled by him; thereafter Hereñú frequently fought in civil wars within the province, usually supporting Ricardo López Jordán (father) for the governorship; when latter went into exile in 1831, Hereñú seems to have disappeared from public life (see Entre Ríos).

HERMANDAD DE LA MESTA. Powerful Spanish organization or guild of sheepowners, with junta or council to safeguard their interests and represent them; never transferred to Río de la Plata but its establishment suggested seriously in 1790 by José Luis Cabral, the second alcalde of Buenos Aires, as a means of controlling the large number of vagrants--Spanish, creoles, mestizos, blacks, and Indians--roaming the rural areas of Buenos Aires province, with no way of earning a living but by stealing; viceroy backed it but proposal was rejected in favor of general reforms and greater pressure on the alcaldes de hermandad to do their job of maintaining order more effectively.

HERMANDAD DE LA SANTA CARIDAD (Brotherhood of Holy Charity). Founded early in 18th century in Buenos Aires to gather poor from the streets; became wealthy; included women's hospital, school for orphans, and other agencies; June 1, 1822 Governor Rodríguez issued decree signed by Rivadavia directing it to cease administering various properties and to place its philanthropic institutions under direct care of government; Sociedad de Beneficencia (q. v.) was formed to replace it.

HERNANDARIAS   see   ARIAS DE SAAVEDRA, HERNANDO

HERNANDEZ, JOSE (1834-1886).   Author of Martín Fierro; journalist and government official.
Born in Buenos Aires province; because of poor health, education limited; grew up in southern part of province on estancia of which his father was mayordomo; boy fascinated by life of gauchos; never forgot experiences with them; after brief military career, moved to Buenos Aires; became journalist on Nicolás Calvo's La Reforma Pacífica; favored political union of Buenos Aires with Confederation under Constitution of 1853; moved to Entre Ríos for political reasons 1858; held various government appointments and continued writing; in 1863 published Vida del Chacho (biography of "Chacho" or Angel Vicente Peñaloza, guerrilla leader in northwest), fought at Cepeda and Pavón; finally returned to Buenos Aires; established daily newspaper El Río de la Plata, dedicated to defense of gauchos then under severe attack by government; Hernández' violent criticisms of President Domingo F. Sarmiento resulted in end of

paper; his participation in Ricardo López Jordán's unsuccessful
revolt in Entre Ríos forced him into exile in Brazil; returned
to Buenos Aires to publish first part of gaucho epic poem Martín Fierro in 1872; sequel La vuelta de Martín Fierro came
out in 1879; also published new edition of Chacho, 1875; wrote
Instrucción del estanciero, 1884; served as deputy and senator
to provincial legislature; favored federalization of Buenos Aires
as national capital and took active part, with Dardo Rocha, in
establishing La Plata, new provincial capital (see Martín Fierro).

"HEROE DEL DESIERTO." Another title given Juan Manuel de Rosas
after his conquest of Indian country in southern Buenos Aires
province in early 1830s.

HERRERA, NICOLAS (1775-1833). Priest; writer, lawyer, early
supporter of independence in Río de la Plata area.
Born in Montevideo, Herrera studied at the university in
Chuquisaca and then completed his law studies in Spain; returned to Montevideo in 1801 but was sent back to Spain five
years later, to report the capture of Buenos Aires by the British and to represent Montevideo's interests; in 1808 he was
elected a deputy to the Cortes at Bayonne, called by Napoleon
for approval of Joseph Bonaparte as Spanish king; as soon as
he was back in the Río de la Plata area, Herrera dedicated
himself to the cause of independence; became one of early editors of the Gaceta of Buenos Aires; carried out delicate diplomatic mission to Paraguay (1813); became member of committee appointed by Assembly of 1813 to draw up project for a
constitution--Herrera's legal expertise considered to have been
significant in shaping of Argentina's laws at this time; became
minister of government under Posada's directorate, 1814; supporting Alvear in 1815, Herrera was in the midst of important
negotiations between the former and Artigas when Alvear was
ousted from the government; profoundly discouraged because the
early dream of the May Revolution had not yet come true,
Herrera became a leader of autonomous federalists in Montevideo, many of them supporters of Alvear and joined by José
Miguel Carrera (1818); their campaign of criticism against Director Pueyrredón caused him considerable embarrassment
and weakened his government; Herrera's later years were spent
at the Brazilian capital where he served as senator and on several diplomatic missions with great distinction before his death
in 1833.

HIDALGO. A member of the lower nobility; literally "the son of
someone" (hijo d'algo); many of conquistadors belonged to this
class, with others above and the majority below.
See Lafuente Machain in Suggested Readings, Appendix
III.

HIDALGO DE CISNEROS, BALTASAR see CISNEROS, BALTASAR
HIDALGO DE

HIDES AND SKINS. Hides and skins have played important role in
Argentine life from that of the guanaco used by the Indians to
the horses and cattle used by Spaniards at the time of conquest
and continue significant in the economy (see Cattle; Horses).
        During sixteenth and seventeenth centuries hides of cat-
tle and horses provided clothing, shelter, furniture, carts,
bridles, saddles, and other harness, lariats and thongs for
boleadoras and other purposes; all kinds of containers for
household and commercial use; and served as almost the only
item of barter for a countryman to sell or exchange in a store
for a knife or other needed article; they also formed basis for
beginnings of trade: hides transported from northwestern area
to mines of the Perus; and in Buenos Aires exchanged (often
in contraband) with Brazilians for sugar and slaves, with European traders for manufactured and other desired goods.
        During the eighteenth century political, economic, and
social changes in Argentina as well as in the world market for
hides significantly altered the commerce in hides, bringing,
in turn, revolutionary and long-range effects on Argentine life;
increased demands for hides became evident by 1750 as the
annual export from Buenos Aires rose from 75,000 (1700-1725)
to 150,000 in 1750; meanwhile, unnoticed, Araucanian Indians
had already begun to immigrate in large numbers into remote
pampas formerly sparsely populated by nomadic Indians, in order to take advantage of this increased trade, as well as to
use animals for other purposes (see Araucanians); increasing
value of hide trade (estimated at 8,000,000 pesos in 1794 by
landowners in their memorial presented to Minister Gardoqui
in attempt to exploit meat wasted in attempt to market hides)
had been important element in decision to create Viceroyalty
of United Provinces of Río de la Plata in 1776, with capital at
Buenos Aires and to open that port to trade; as government,
landowners, and foreign merchants began to explore greater
trade possibilities between Buenos Aires and the rest of the
world, the viceroys moved to handle the problem created by
the increased demand for hides--partly due to increasing populations and industrialization in Europe--causing the drastic depletion of wild herds on pampas--from an estimated forty-eight
million in 1748 in the Buenos Aires area to about six and a
half million in 1780; government control was established over
entire cattle industry: a branding system imposed; sale of unbranded hides and unauthorized sale of branded hides punish-
able by law; this incidentally brought about new socio-economic
groups--cattle-owners and raisers and cattle-herders and
workers, mostly gauchos; (blandengues assigned to southern
boundary to prevent Indian raids); during closing decades of
viceroyalty, its ports Buenos Aires and Montevideo were supplying much of the world market's demand for hides; saladeros
were beginning to be established to salt and dry the meat for
export; eventually these would become refrigerated packing
plants that would make meat more important than the hides but
for several decades hides continued to dominate the export
trade, with the saladeros handling them more efficiently in the

plants than skinning on the pampas had been; in 1837 hide exports made up two-thirds of Buenos Aires trade and in spite
of civil wars and foreign blockades hide exports trebled between that date and 1850; by this time sheepskins had been
added to those of cattle; in the agricultural and sheepraising
boom of the 1880s and 1890s, hides continued to increase in
volume and value, but dropped to third place in exports, providing only 16.9%, following wool (1st) and wheat (2nd); by that
time cattle-raisers who specialized in hides and salted beef
had already lost two battles: that against use of barbed wire
for fencing, hazardous to skins; and that against introduction
of expensive beef cattle for improving herds, but with little effect on hides; foreign experts had improved local leather industry, using Argentine skins and quebracho (in the tanning
process); in twentieth century this determined one direction
manufacturing would take with well-developed leather and shoe
industries among early factories to be established; during World
War I hides brought high prices and in succeeding decades continued to make approximately 8-9% of export trade; during
1951-1955 and again in 1962-1966 export value of hides declined, after having been 79 million dollars in 1961; since 1966
it has improved, reaching $69 millions in trade in 1970; 3.9%
of total trade.

HIGHWAYS.   Argentina's extensive highway system dates from the
early 1930s; projected by the Uriburu administration (1930-
1932), it was developed, as a government project, from 5,000
to 32,000 miles during the next decade, largely under Presi-
den Justo; it was designed to serve purposes of increasing demands for Argentine economic independence by competing with
foreign-owned railroads, trucking orchard and farm products
to local markets and busing passengers from city to city, fostering needs of new industry, promoting private and commercial tourism; also aided Argentina to recover more rapidly
from the world-wide economic depression; the program lan-
guished in the 1940s, somewhat over-built and handicapped by
unexpected shortages of gasoline, rubber for tires, and delays
in establishing automotive industries--largely due to World War
II; in the Perón period following the war, highway construction
was at first neglected in spite of the deterioration of the railways and their purchase by the government; during the latter
period of his administration, the importance of adequate investment in maintenance and expansion of the highway system
in this overall national economic development began to be recognized and in the 1960s Krieger Vasena (q.v.) finally placed
it in its proper role as part of the national passenger and cargo transport system, along with water and rail facilities.

"HIMNO NACIONAL."   The patriotic poem written by Vicente López
y Planes was declared by the Assembly of the Year XIII (q.v.)
to be the Argentine national hymn; Father Cayetano Rodríguez
had also written a patriotic hymn but withdrew it in deference
to López y Planes; the catalán composer Blas Parera wrote

the melody for it and it began to be sung at all public ceremonies; in 1860 J. P. Esnaola published a musical arrangement of Parera's composition that has become accepted as the
official one. According to tradition the national anthem was
first sung in the salón of María Sánchez de Thompson; an oil
painting by P. Soubercaseaux commemorates this scene.

HIRSCH, BARON MAURICE VON (1831-1896). Founder of Jewish
Colonization Association (q. v.). Born in Munich; died in Hun-
gary; district in province of Entre Ríos named for him.

HISPANIDAD. Literary and intellectual current that grew out of reaction of Spain's writers of "Generation of 1898" against national pessimism and self-doubt following Spain's loss of most
of its remaining empire in Spanish-American War; movement
emphasized Spanish and Catholic values, rejected secularism
and alien patterns of more powerful Western nations, and endeavored to tie all Spanish-speaking peoples together; many
Argentine intellectuals seeking national unity and identity for a
society inundated by non-Spanish immigrants, found in Hispanidad some elements of strength although few were drawn toward closer ties with Spain itself; Yrigoyen, as Radical leader
and as president, encouraged Catholicism and atmosphere favorable to ideas of Hispanidad; writers like Manuel Gálvez emphasized traditional Spanish and Catholic roots of Argentine
civilization; others found in it some basis for their fear and
dislike of United States; insofar as it became a part of Argentine nationalism it has also played a role in Peronism of middle and late 20th century.

HISTORICAL DICTIONARIES, ENCYCLOPEDIAS, AND REFERENCE
TOOLS. Argentina has produced several excellent reference
tools of this kind, most of them written by qualified professional historians; in addition to earlier ones, several have appeared during the mid-twentieth century; most important of
these seem to be Diccionario histórico argentino, edited by
Ricardo Piccirilli, Francisco L. Romay, and Leoncio Gianello
(6 v., Buenos Aires, 1953-1955); Diego Abad de Santillán, ed.,
Gran enciclopedia argentina (9 vols., Buenos Aires, 1956-
1963); and Enrique Udaondo, Diccionario biográfico argentino
(Buenos Aires, 1938); Diccionario biográfico colonial argentino
(Buenos Aires, 1945); and Grandes hombres de nuestra patria
(3 vols., Buenos Aires, 1968); a new project by Vicente O.
Cutolo, Nuevo diccionario biográfico argentino, 1750-1930,
with 8 volumes projected, began appearing in 1968-1969.
     For current bibliographical information, see Handbook
of Latin American Studies (University of Florida Press,
Gainesville) and a new bibliographical listing from Argentina;
in 1973 the Instituto Bibliográfico Antonio Zinny published vol.
I of Indice historiográfico argentino: 1970, an attempt to list
and annotate all historical items published in 1970; it is a
joint effort of Jorge C. Bohdziewicz (director), Guillermo Furlong, Abel R. Geoghegan, Vicente O. Cutolo, and Federico
M. Vogelius, who hope to continue it.

HISTORIOGRAPHY. From the time of the Conquest, Argentines have
always felt a sense of historical uniqueness and both native-
born and newcomers have been attracted to the study and writing of its history; consequently, its historiography has been
characterized by the great variety of interests among those who
wrote it; Renaissance writers accompanied early explorers and
wrote accounts, like Antonio Pigafetta with Magellan on the
first voyage along the coast and through the straits; business
agents and soldiers, like Ulrich Schmidel, sent back (1555)
valuable descriptive accounts; Martín Barco Centenera wrote
(1602) an early epic poem of the conquest; and Ruy Díaz de
Guzmán wrote the first historical chronicle of his native land
(1612), preserving in it the legends that had already taken root
following the conquest; in the seventeenth and eighteenth centuries the Jesuits kept meticulous records not only of their own
religious work but of the historical events taking place within
the entire area with which they were concerned; Jesuit missionaries were also famous explorers and wrote detailed descriptive accounts of the new lands into which they penetrated
and new Indian groups encountered; early in the eighteenth century Father Pedro Lozano devoted himself to research through
as many of the old accounts, Jesuit and government records,
etc., as possible and compiled them into the first comprehensive history of the area; the variety of these Jesuit writings,
the humanistic skills and interests displayed and the scientific
methodology and descriptive detail used--especially in the works
written by the Jesuits in exile, after 1767, provided much of
the basic material for both historians and social scientists of
the nineteenth and twentieth centuries; the establishment of the
viceroyalty (1776), with its capital in Buenos Aires, brought
royal scholars and scientists into the Río de la Plata and the
ideas of the Enlightenment became widespread.

  The patriot leaders of the independence movement were
well-read and keenly aware of the historical significance of
their political actions; out of this concern for the record came
Dean Gregorio Funes' two-volume civil history; in the decades
that followed much of the historical writing was done by men
who were also active political leaders; sometimes strongly personal, frequently controversial and polemic, their work also
maintained a high literary level and considerably high quality
of historical method as understood at that time; these writers,
many of them belonging to the Asociación de Mayo, prided
themselves on their familiarity with both the romantic writings
of the period in Europe and also with facts of Argentine history
and current Argentine realities; important historians of this
period include Bartolomé Mitre, considered to have been the
first modern Argentine historian, Vicente F. López, who valued style in writing and interpretation as much or more than
original research (according to Mitre, who insisted on research
in original materials), and Domingo F. Sarmiento, more passionate writer than professional historian; in the late nineteenth
century, especially after the organization of the Argentine Republic, there was renewed interest in the nation's history; Paul

Groussac, a Frenchman who had come to Argentina on a visit, remained to play an important role in its cultural life; as director of the National Library, he increased its holdings, studied its original materials, and began publication of the latter, reinforcing Mitre's call of historians back to the original sources, by making them more available.

Toward the close of the nineteenth century, several new influences appeared; the disappearance of the gaucho and other traditional elements of the criollo life style and the rise of a new cultural nationalism aroused in native-born Argentines a new interest in their past; at the same time the massive immigration movement had brought to Argentina thousands of new citizens eager to learn about the history of their adopted homeland; close economic ties with Great Britain were reflected in British historical writings about Argentina, supplementing the large, earlier body of travel writings; the National Academy of History became foremost organization of historians; provided guidance and encouragement and sponsored historical writing and the reproduction of source materials; Ernesto Quesada brought back the new German historical methodologies and the University of La Plata became a center for emphasizing them; from these, and other sources, Argentine historiography has matured in the mid-twentieth century; combining source and secondary, national and foreign scholarly materials with continued emphasis on literary style, it has broadened its scope beyond that of political history and important biography to include social materials and insights, the history of ideas and discussions of the philosophy of history, a cosmopolitan point of view in which Argentine historical phenomena are examined in comparison with similar movements and events elsewhere, and foreign scholarly writings about Argentina are consulted along with Argentine ones; the troubled Argentine political scene following the 1930s has had two main effects on the writing of history: in periods of threatened government takeover of the academic world, historians have emphasized research studies in earlier historical periods; whenever possible, however, historians have addressed themselves to a search for more satisfying historical answers to contemporary problems; the trend toward centering Argentine history around Buenos Aires has been reversed to a certain extent, with the universities in the provinces leading the movement to emphasize local history, with historical research centers modeled on those of the universities of Buenos Aires and La Plata.

Many Argentine historians have sought to distinguish patterns in the historical development of their nation; Sarmiento saw it in terms of decades--1810, revolution; 1820, dissolution of government, etc.; José Nicolás Matienzo considered three presidencies (18 years) a significant political unit for the period following 1862; R. Rivarola preferred to think in terms of thirty-year cycles--1792-1821, independence; 1821-1851, aspirations for a constitution, etc.; more interesting than precise, these offer clues to the thinking of historians in various periods; a modern work in similar spirit is that of Jaime

Perriaux, Las generaciones argentinas (Buenos Aires, 1970) in which the author attempts to describe the different Argentine contemporary scenes that molded each generation of historians; in recent years many historians have turned their attention to intepretation and philosophy of history, rather than attempting to discover patterns.

Two fields in which Argentine historiography has performed major services have been those of historical dictionaries (q.v.) and multi-volume comprehensive national histories; among the more important of the latter are Vicente F. López, Historia de la República Argentina (10 v., Buenos Aires, 1883-1893, later editions); Ricardo Levene, editor, Historia de la nación argentina (10 v., published by the Academia Nacional de la Historia, Buenos Aires, 1936-1942, with later editions and supplements); Vicente D. Sierra, editor, Historia de la Argentina, new multi-volumed history with volumes I-IX (through the Rosas period) published (1956-1972). The basic work on Argentine historiography is that by Rómulo D. Carbía, Historia crítica de la historiografía argentina, desde sus orígenes en el siglo XVI (La Plata, 1925; definitive edition Buenos Aires, 1940); see also Ricardo Caillet-Bois, "La historiografía" in Arrieta, Historia de la literatura argentina, VI, pp. 19-198; and Joseph R. Barager, "Historiography of the Río de la Plata Area," Hispanic American Historical Review, 39 (1959): 588-642.

See entries on historians mentioned and Suggested Readings, Appendix III; also, Pla, Alberto J., Ideología y método en la historiografía argentina (Buenos Aires, 1972).

HISTORY see HISTORICAL CHRONOLOGY, Appendix II; also specific historical topics

HOLMBERG, BARON EDWARD K. VON (1778-1853). Austrian military officer who accompanied San Martín and Alvear to Buenos Aires in 1812 to fight for Argentine independence and remained there for the rest of his life; became chief of staff in charge of artillery and engineers; served later in Uruguay and in war against Brazil; career thereafter varied, largely due to his involvement in Argentine politics, but throughout war of independence and period following, until his retirement in 1834, his engineering skills contributed to Argentine military and defense needs, especially in fields of artillery and fortifications; Baron von Holmberg died in Buenos Aires.

HOOF-AND-MOUTH DISEASE (Aftosa). The appearance of hoof-and-mouth disease in Buenos Aires herds of cattle in 1870 posed a threat to the cattle industry that was quickly recognized by the Sociedad Rural; its disappearance for the next three decades coincided with two new developments in shipping beef, freezing it and shipping live animals; the latter method met with greater success until a new outbreak in Buenos Aires of the disease, in epidemic proportions, in 1900 caused England to close all its ports to shipments of live Argentine animals; without this

competition, frigoríficos boomed and shipment of the animals
almost ceased; in 1927, when Argentine beef was trying to compete on the American market, the U.S. passed a sanitary regulation refusing it entrance because of possible hoof-and-mouth
infection; in 1959 a new sanitary order stopped the meat import again.

HORA DEL PUEBLO, LA (1971). Agreement signed between the
    UCRP and the Peronists to start political campaign against the
    military government.

HORNOS, General MANUEL (1807-1871). Lifetime fighter against
    whatever he believed to be tyranny.
        Born in Entre Ríos; almost completely illiterate, early
    became involved in military career; emigrated as a boy to
    Uruguay; returned years later with unitarist army of Juan La-
    valle; after latter's death in Jujuy Hornos returned home,
    crossing the Chaco with Indian aid; reached Corrientes in time
    to fight in defeat of Rosas' forces at Caá Guazú; also fought at
    Caseros, the battle that ended Rosas' dictatorship; despite his
    Entre Ríos birth, Manuel Hornos supported Buenos Aires
    against Urquiza (also of Entre Ríos), taking part in the revolt
    of September 11, 1852, following which Buenos Aires province
    reorganized an independent provincial government; in November
    1852 Hornos led one army of the two-pronged invasion of Entre
    Ríos mounted by Buenos Aires to decrease power of Urquiza
    and to prevent meeting of Santa Fe constitutional convention;
    Hornos landed at Gualeguaychú and was advancing on Concep-
    ción del Uruguay when word came of the breakdown of Juan
    Madariaga's companion invading force and Urquiza's strenuous
    military opposition, so he withdrew; two years later, Hornos
    commanded the Buenos Aires army that defeated and repelled
    the Confederation army sent against them by Urquiza; fought at
    Cepeda and at Pavón under Bartolomé Mitre; after his heroic
    action (that gained him rank of brigadier general) in Paraguay
    during war of the Triple Alliance (at second battle of Tuyutí
    November 3, 1867), Hornos returned to his native province to
    carry out his last commission--the national government's fight
    against the forces led by Ricardo López Jordán, rebelling
    against Buenos Aires control.

HORSES. The role of horses in the historical development of Argen-
    tina has been important; when Pedro de Mendoza went back to
    Spain (1537) and Buenos Aires was abandoned (1541), the re-
    maining five mares and seven horses of the seventy-two that he
    had brought with him were turned out on the pampa; within dec-
    ades these had multiplied into such large numbers of wild
    horses that some writers have hypothesized the undiscovered
    presence on the pampas of native horses; most historians ac-
    cept the fact that the pampas horses resulted from natural
    multiplication of those left by Mendoza and a few more brought
    in by Cabeza de Vaca (1541); Juan de Garay brought 1000
    horses with him to found Buenos Aires in 1580 and granted

licenses to its citizens to hunt the wild horses (all of whom belonged to the crown) for their own profit and use; Cabildo of Buenos Aires, 1589, refusing request of Spanish religious order to hunt wild horses, said that these were the rightful property of the sons of the conquistadors.

Effects of availability of large numbers of horses felt by Spaniards and creoles, mestizos, and Indians but in very different ways: wealthier creoles (and Spaniards) regarded them as wealth and transportation; to the mestizo or the white laborer, the horse offered escape from farm or town labor to the freedom of hunting on the pampa and living as he pleased, eventually to form the gaucho group whose mystique permeates all Argentine life and spirit; for the Indians, especially those of the Chaco and Patagonia, the horse brought a revolution in their social and political structures, their economy, their ways of fighting, and their style of living; now mobile, they abandoned small family or tribal units and roamed the pampas (as well as other areas) in large bands, usually numbering 100-500; but even as many as 1000; abandoning their primitive agriculture (in the Chaco area) they turned to hunting and lived off the meat of the wild cattle or other animals; in Patagonia, the horse provided all the necessities of life: food (meat and milk), housing, clothing, mobility and protection in fighting, and transportation of goods and property when necessary; Araucanians who took over the southern pampas and its horse civilization (abandoning former arts and skills) used horses also to round up cattle and drive the herds to market; as well as for extending their range of raiding operations.

To the gaucho, his horse was a loved companion, an inseparable part of himself and his life; innumerable stories of nineteenth century caudillos describe the strong attachment that such men as Chacho (General Angel Vicente Peñaloza), Quiroga, and Urquiza had for their horses and the care that they gave them; even Rosas, urban-born and bred, commanded the loyalty of his rural supporters largely because of his superb horsemanship; they tell the story that his last concern before boarding the British ship to take him into exile was that his horse be cared for properly; with the coming of agriculture, railroads, and industry to Argentina, the horse became more a symbol of Argentine life than a necessity; horse breeding for special purposes was introduced and improved; horse races and polo became national sporting interests, and the Jockey Club (which controlled the public races) symbolized the center of the social, economic, and political power structure until the middle of the twentieth century; horses numbered around 3,600,000 in 1971.

HOUSSAY, BERNARDO ALBERTO (1887-1971). Physiologist; educator; winner of Nobel Prize in physiology and medicine, 1947, the first South American scientist to be so honored.

Born in Buenos Aires, of an old Latin American French family; educated in the capital, graduating in pharmacy in 1904 and in medicine in 1910; certified as physician in 1911; from

1910 until 1919 served as professor of physiology in the faculty
of veterinary medicine at the university and also (1915-1919)
as laboratory chief of Bacteriological Institute of National Department of Hygiene; in 1919 he moved to the department of
medicine in the university and remained as professor there until he was removed in 1944 for political reasons--along with
many other faculty members, he had signed a political statement that won the disfavor of the current government; brought
back briefly in 1945, he was then asked (1946), again for political reasons, to retire; in 1955, after the fall of the Perón
government, he was fully restored to his academic position as
professor and director of the research institute.
        Throughout his life Dr. Houssay devoted himself to phys-
iological research, especially that related to diabetes, attracted by the recent discovery of the use of insulin in its
treatment; he established and directed an important research
center at the university of Buenos Aires that gained international recognition; during his exile from the university, he and
some of his ousted colleagues secured private funds with which
to continue their research in their new Institute of Biological
and Experimental Medicine, founded in 1944 with Houssay as
director; in 1947, his work involving the relationship between
the pituitary gland and the pancreas and the pituitary's role in
sugar metabolism (the "Houssay phenomenon") brought him the
1947 award of the Nobel Prize in physiology and medicine
(shared with the husband-wife team Carl F. and Gerti Cori,
biochemists, who had concurrently carried on similar research) and paved the way for further studies in diabetes; it
also made Houssay's research center very important, with as
many as 135 advanced scholars and research scientists working there at one time; Dr. Houssay remained active until illness overtook him in 1970 and retained his position as honorary president of Argentina's National Council for Scientific and
Technological Research, the principal scientific institution of
the republic, until his death in 1971; shortly before that, Dr.
Luis F. Leloir, one of his graduate students, a biochemist
continuing Dr. Houssay's line of research, had also won the
Nobel Prize in medicine (1970) for discovery of role of nucleotides in metabolism of hydrocarbons and in biosynthesis.
        Dr. Houssay probably received more honors from the
scientific world than any other Argentine to that date; and his
writings, especially his Fisiología humana (1945), have been
widely translated and published.

HOWARD, JENNIE E. (1844-1933). U.S. educator and writer in
        Argentina.
        Born in Boston, educated at one of first normal (teach-
er's training) schools established by Horace Mann, in Fram-
ingham, Massachusetts; showed outstanding teaching and administrative abilities in both elementary and high schools in
New England; selected by Clara Armstrong (q.v.) to become
member of group of American teachers going to Argentina in
1883 to organize and direct the new normal school being

established for girls during President Julio A. Roca's first administration; organized normal school for girls in Corrientes, then went (1886) as vice director to that of Córdoba; faced problems as people of Córdoba resented arrival of protestant teachers, especially at a time when government was pushing secularism in education; discouraged by such incidents as finding sign on school's entrance "This is the House of the Devil and the Gateway to Hell," she requested a transfer to San Nicolás in Buenos Aires province (1888); remained there as professor of mathematics and education until retirement in 1903, for reasons of health; died thirty years later in Buenos Aires.

Spent time writing poems and articles; one of latter appeared in La Nación in 1908 using Argentina to follow U.S. example of setting aside a memorial day for honoring all patriotic dead--both civil and military; such a day proclaimed that same year--October 31; in 1931 published book In Other Years and Distant Climes describing her own teaching experiences and those of her North American colleagues; translated into Spanish in 1951, Buenos Aires. See prologue to this book and La escuela normal y la cultura argentina by Juan M. Chavarría.

HUAQUI (or GUAQUI), BATTLE OF June 20, 1811. Bolivian site, between Lake Titicaca and Desaguadero river of first great defeat of armies sent to Upper Peru to incorporate that area of viceroyalty into Buenos Aires revolution; Auxiliary Army under General Antonio González Balcarce had totally defeated royalists at Suipacha and all four intendancies in Upper Peru had accepted the revolution but discipline in army broke down, volunteers could not be trained fast enough, situation became chaotic; Balcarce resigned; Castelli, revolutionary agent of junta, took over, moved north to boundary of viceroyalty of Peru and signed forty-day truce with General José Manuel de Goyeneche; both sides accused of violations; in surprise attack at Huaqui Goyeneche's well-trained, largely professional army of 7000 men totally dispersed the patriot forces, numbering around six thousand but with barely 2500 effectively trained men; cause of defeat attributed to lack of general's presence, separation of camps of two main divisions, but most of all to lack of discipline and training of army; Manuel Belgrano eventually sent to take over command, with Juan Martín Pueyrredón and others acting meanwhile; effects of Huaqui serious to revolution; all Upper Peru now in hands of Royalists to serve as base to invade northern Argentina; arrival of news of defeat in Buenos Aires brought fall of Cornelio Saavedra and his junta and formation of first triumvirate government; also responsible for lifting of first siege against Montevideo, leaving Banda Oriental also in royalist hands.

HUARPE. Indians occupying Cuyo region (provinces of Mendoza, San Juan, and San Luis) at time of Spanish conquest; peaceful, agricultural, at end of Inca road to the south (at Uspallata); the Huarpe showed Inca influence in their language, irrigation system, and polychrome decoration of their grey-black ceramics;

more peaceful than Diaguita Indians to north of them, the Huarpe disappeared rapidly after Spaniards arrived; many were given in encomienda to Spanish conquistadors across the Andes in Chile, to which Cuyo was attached at that time; disease took its toll, also; by middle of eighteenth century the Harpes, one of oldest cultures in Argentina, had disappeared.

HUDSON, WILLIAM HENRY (1841-1922).   British naturalist and writer.
    Born in Quilmes, near Buenos Aires; remained on pampas until 1874; went to England where he lived in considerable poverty, privacy, and frequent poor health until late success greeted his writings; considered himself to be field naturalist but his writings also showed sensitive understanding of human nature as well as keen observations of flora and fauna; wrote more than twenty books; several have become classics, such as Green Mansions (1904); A Hind in Richmond Park (1922); and A Purple Land (1885) for their literary quality; among his most important books about his native land, Argentina (still widely read), are Idle Days in Patagonia (1893); El Ombú (1902); Far Away and Long Ago (1918); and Birds of La Plata (1920); reminiscences, always written in English, these convey both scene and impact of the land with force and fidelity rarely equaled by other writers.

HUERGO, DELFIN B. (1824-1886).   Member of Santa Fe Constitutional Congress of 1853; government official and diplomat; legislator.
    Born in Salta; graduated in law, Buenos Aires, 1846; immediately joined opponents of Rosas; fled from Buenos Aires; became a member of liberation army of Urquiza and took part in battle of Caseros; as one of the younger, most enthusiastic members of the constitutional convention of Santa Fe, he signed the constitution that was adopted and held various appointments under the Confederation government; at the same time he vigorously supported peace and union with Buenos Aires and held appointments in the new united government formed; sent on diplomatic assignments to Germany (1859) and to Belgium; died in Buenos Aires.

HUERGO, EDUARDO.   Engineer; specialist in hydraulic engineering.
    Born in Buenos Aires; graduated from Faculty of exact, physical and natural sciences, 1896; worked on a branch railroad in Uruguay, then was sent to Bahía Blanca; after traveling through Europe and the United States, he returned to devote his skills (as inspector general) to the construction and use of the port of Rosario (1905-1906); in 1910-1911 he was back in Bahía Blanca directing the enlarging of its military port; during his presidency of the national engineering center, the first meeting of national engineers was held in Buenos Aires (1916); after having spent more than 20 years in practicing his profession, he turned his attention to teaching young engineers, first at the University of La Plata and then at the Faculty from which he

had graduated in Buenos Aires (1924); his work experience and personal interests had made him a specialist in hydraulic engineering, particularly with regard to maritime ports; in 1924 he led the Argentine delegation that attended the Pan American Scientific Congress in Lima; became vice rector of the university in 1926; died three years later.

HULLETT BROTHERS & COMPANY. London mercantile and banking firm with which Bernardino Rivadavia established close relations in early 1820s in his efforts to attract foreign capital for immigation and mining projects; active in floating stock for mining venture (see River Plate Mining Company).
    See H. S. Ferns, Britain and Argentina in the Nineteenth Century (Oxford Press, 1960).

HUMAHUACA. Name of largely rural department of province of Jujuy and of its small capital town (founded by Spaniards 1594) located nearly two miles high on Río Grande river (or stream) at northern end of narrow valley of same name; Humahuaca, or Omaguaca, Indians found there in sixteenth century belonged to sedentary, agricultural, semi-civilized but hard-fighting Diaguita or Calchaquí of northwestern Argentina; had been definitely affected by Inca empire but culture has disappeared so completely that it is not known whether they spoke Quechua or not; in 1908 Ethnological Museum of faculty of Philosophy and Letters of Buenos Aires began sending archeological expeditions to study sites and ruins remaining in spite of frequent earthquakes.
    Quebrada de Humahuaca extends from north to south in east-central Jujuy--a narrow valley or gap more than 100 miles long, varying in width from nearly 2 miles to less than 100 feet; the central one of three routes of access between Argentina and Bolivia, it was the one most commonly used by armies, especially in war of independence; guerrilla fighters under Comandante Arias honored by Buenos Aires government for daring exploit by which they captured entire garrison left at Humahuaca by royalist General José de la Serna on third invasion of Argentina.

HUMAITA or HUMAYTA. Fortified town on south bank of Paraguay river; following hard fighting here, March-July 1868, between allied Argentine-Brazilian-Uruguayan forces commanded by Duke of Caxias and the already weakened Paraguayan forces of President Francisco Solano López, the latter withdrew, leaving way open to Asunción and end of war of Triple Alliance.

HUTCHINSON, THOMAS J. (probably 1802-1883). Physician, diplomatic official, writer. British consul at Rosario, 1862-1871; father of Argentine cotton industry.
    Born in Ireland; graduated in medicine from University of Göttingen, Germany, 1833; gave medical care to victims of cholera epidemic in London; in 1854 undertook exploration of Niger and other African rivers using quinine to protect party

from malaria there; published description of trip after return
to England; came to Rosario 1862 as British consul for rapidly
growing new port; became deeply interested in plans for agricultural development, especially in that area, being promoted
by Bartolomé Mitre's government; decided to stimulate Argentine growth of cotton so badly needed by British textile factories at that time; explored valley of Salado river and neighboring regions of Santiago del Estero looking for suitable lands;
secured cooperation of government but success delayed; Hutchinson generally honored among Argentines as father of cotton
industry (see Cotton) gave generously of medical services in
Rosario, especially during cholera epidemic; also established
and maintained hospital; performed consular functions with
great personal interest, especially in meat shipments; left
Rosario in 1871; later served briefly in Callao, Peru as British consul before retiring; died in Bellinescar Lodge, 1883.

Hutchinson's writings, more valuable for their keen observations than literary quality, appeared in The Standard, The
Magazine of River Plate, and in La Capital de Rosario; published two important volumes based on his experiences, travels,
and observations while in Argentina: Buenos Aires and Argentine Gleanings with Extracts from a Diary of Salado Exploration in 1862 and 1863 (London, 1865--Spanish edition 1866, annotated by Luis V. Varela; new Spanish edition by J. Luis
Trenti Rocamora, biographer of Hutchinson, published in Buenos Aires, 1945); and The Paraná, with Incidents of Paraguayan War and South American Recollections from 1861-1868
(London, 1868).

HYDROELECTRIC POWER see ENERGY RESOURCES

- I -

IAPI see INSTITUTO ARGENTINO DE PROMOCION DEL INTER-
CAMBIO

IBARGUREN, CARLOS (1877-1956).   Jurisconsult; educator; historian; government official.

Born and educated in Buenos Aires, with doctorate in
law and social sciences; became professor, vice dean of Faculty of Law, University of Buenos Aires; minister of justice
and public instruction; president of University of Paris in Buenos Aires; proposed as vice presidential candidate by Democratic Progressive party in 1916; again in 1943; national interventor in Córdoba (1930-1931); supported President José Félix
Uriburu (1930-1932) in his insistence on use of constitutional
means for effecting reforms; served as legal advisor of major
financial institutions; active in cultural groups; member of National Academy of History; received many honors, including
membership in the French Legion of Honor; among his many
historical writings are his Juan Manuel de Rosas, su vida, su
tiempo, y su drama (Buenos Aires, 1930), depicting Rosas as

Argentine traditionalist and for which he received national literary award; San Martín intimo (1950); and his own autobiographical La historia que he vivido (Buenos Aires, 1955), impressions and observations on Argentine history 1880-1943.

IBARRA, JUAN FELIPE (1787-1851). Military leader; federalist caudillo of Santiago del Estero.

Born in Matará, Santiago del Estero; studied at Monserrat academy in Córdoba; entered military service 1811, forming part of expeditionary army into Upper Peru; later fought in battle of Tucumán; sent, as sergeant major, to hold northern frontier of Santiago del Estero for General Manuel Belgrano; returned from revolt of Arequito (in which he took part) to his native province; became its first governor later that year (1820) when Santiago del Estero declared itself independent of Tucumán; from then until his death more than three decades later, governed or controlled the province, except for brief intervals; defended himself and his government from internal attacks from political foes, and from attacks from neighboring provinces Tucumán, Catamarca, and Salta; maintained friendly relations with Juan Facundo Quiroga; latter persuaded him (1835) to sign treaty of peace and alliance (1835) with governors of Tucumán and Salta; five years later, always loyal supporter of Rosas, he fought against Coalition of the North; in 1848, overcome by illness, he appealed to Rosas for protection of his province; died three years later.

See Gabriel Antonio Puentes, Juan Felipe Ibarra (Instituto de Investigaciones Históricas, 1944) for Ibarra's career 1828-1832, and Jorge Newton, Juan Felipe Ibarra: el caudillo de la selva (Buenos Aires, 1973).

IGUAZU RIVER, FALLS, AND PORT. Iguazú river, approximately 30 miles long, flows west from southern Brazilian highland to join upper Paraná river; forms international boundary between Argentina (Misiones) and Brazil; spectacular waterfalls, about twelve miles from junction with Upper Paraná--drop of 200 feet, greater than that of Niagara; one of America's greatest undeveloped sources of hydroelectric power and increasingly attractive to both tourists and settlers interested in that remote, heavily wooded area; Puerto Iguazú near junction serves as outlet for sparsely settled northern Misiones area.

Iguazú falls probably discovered in 1524 by Eleixo García, Portuguese who had accompanied Juan Díaz de Solís, been shipwrecked at Santa Catarina island and had then struck west searching for the rich kingdom of which Indians had told him; Alvar Núñez Cabeza de Vaca, second adelantado of the Plata region had passed by falls on his journey from Brazilian coast to Asunción in 1542.

ILLIA, ARTURO UMBERTO (1900-   ). President of Argentine Republic 1963-1966; physician.

Born in Pergamino, Buenos Aires province; graduated in medicine from university at Buenos Aires; became active as

physician and political leader in small town in Córdoba; served
in provincial senate, 1936-1940, vice president of senate 1938-
1940; vice governor of province of Córdoba 1940-1943; became
Córdoba representative at national Congress, 1948-1952; undra-
matic but sound, long-time respected leader of more conservative branch of Radical Party; became its candidate for president in elections held by Guido government in July 1963;
planned as way of returning military government to traditional
democratic patterns, these elections--involving every elective
office in the nation--revealed unbelievable confusion and political ineptitude; as many as 39 separate political parties presented candidates and 21 of them won at least one election; Illia, candidate of the Unión Cívica Radical del Pueblo (People's
Radical Civic Union) received more votes for presidency than
any other candidate, but only about one-fourth of total popular
vote; with aid of minor parties, elected president by 51% of
electoral college votes; in spite of confusion, election well received; many believed that Illia's quiet political approach was
just what Argentina needed after hysteria and violence of previous decades; President Illia (who insisted on Italian pronuncia-
tion of his surname, i. e., accenting the first syllable rather
than the second) believed that the nation's problems called primarily for political solutions, with economic and social problems easy to solve once democratic processes were fully restored to control of national political life; underestimated continuing determination of both Peronists and the military to participate fully in government; in congressional elections of 1965,
and local ones of 1966, Peronists, permitted to vote, won victories that frightened large sectors of middle and upper class
Argentine society; meanwhile economic problems of inflation,
unemployment, etc. became worse; Illia cancelled (November
1963) petroleum contracts made by former president Frondizi
with foreign companies on grounds of unconstitutionality and
wanted to withdraw from International Monetary Fund commitments; whether because of his own failures in leadership or because the old Radical formulas and party procedures had lost
effectiveness in post-Perón era, feeling spread that Illia was a
do-nothing president; when triumvirate of military leaders of
three branches of service overthrew his government in late
June 1966, dissolved Congress, provincial legislatures, and political parties, calling on General Juan Carlos Onganía to take
over presidency, change was accepted by people with little protest; later historians tend to emphasize magnitude of problems,
which Illia saw clearly, rather than president's personal ineptitude.

IMMIGRATION. Argentina has ranked high among nations in the
world to receive immigration in modern period; from 1869
(first census) to 1970 its population increased from 1,800,000
to 23,400,000, most of it by immigration (in 1914, 30% were
foreign-born) and the ethnic content of its society was completely changed, along with its economy, but its cultural and
national identity has eventually been strengthened, largely along

Argentina's own traditional lines.

In the early national period, Bernardino Rivadavia, as minister for province of Buenos Aires, encouraged immigration to bring to the rural, cattle, and trading culture of Argentina, persons with new agricultural and urban skills to enrich Argentina's economic development as well as intellectuals, scientists, artists for its cultural development; an immigration bureau was established (1824) to promote this and several colonization projects were undertaken but they met with little success; Rosas abolished the immigration bureau in 1830 as useless and costly; turned the land over to grazing; during his rule there was no immigration policy; many foreigners came for their own personal, political, economic reasons, were welcomed, but received no special inducements; after the fall of Rosas' government (1852), the need for European immigrants to fill Argentina's empty lands and especially to stimulate agriculture was so great that Article 25 in the constitution of 1853 stated specifically: "The federal government shall promote European immigration and shall not restrict, limit, nor burden with any tax the entrance into Argentine territory of those foreigners who come to work the land, improve the industries, and teach the sciences and arts."

Meanwhile, in addition to this official interest, individuals in the Confederation, like Urquiza, Aaron Castellanos, were personally involved in bringing immigrants in; inducements and practical aids were offered to groups and individuals.

In Buenos Aires province, then (1850s) separated from the Confederation, the encouragement of immigration lagged, but only slightly; as the influx of Europeans began to pour into Buenos Aires (as well as into the Confederation towns and provinces) so many problems resulted that a group of private citizens (most of them estancieros) formed an Asociación Filantrópica de Inmigración (c. 1857) to see that newcomers were taken care of upon arrival, advised, and then directed to employment; the government found it necessary to appoint judges to handle some of their controversies (especially about debts incurred in transportation) and eventually to establish its own agency to take over the functions of the Philanthropic Association; after the provinces were reunited both Mitre and Sarmiento encouraged immigration; in 1868 a Central Commission of Immigration was created and in 1876 the Immigration Law was passed in an attempt to bring together, in one legal text, all previous laws regarding immigration and colonization and to establish a General Department of Immigration to set up and direct the necessary procedures; by 1880 the floodgates were open and Europeans came by the hundreds of thousands for the next four decades; from 1857 to 1941 more than 6-1/2 million came, although nearly half of them returned home eventually; some came on their own, some were brought by individual entrepreneurs or by organized groups; others came to projects sponsored by national or provincial governments; many went into commercial agriculture, others remained in cities; at first they were concentrated on the pampas and in coastal cities but eventually they spread throughout the provinces; as skilled artisans, farmers, miners, shopkeepers, industrial workers, teachers, and scientists, they made up a great middle class that eventually brought democratic political, economic, social reforms; by the opening of the twentieth century, some Argentines were alarmed by the foreign labor agitators and the laws of Residence and Social Defense were passed, but immigrants continued to be welcomed; personal and religious freedom and economic opportunity were the major incentives, with Argentina's Roman Catholicism and Mediterranean cultural background drawing many Italians and Spaniards (the predominating ethnic groups).

During the depression of the 1930s the flow of immigrants declined sharply and Argentina made citizenship slightly more difficult to receive; following World War II, however, a new wave of immigration has taken place; largely urban-oriented, with many from Eastern Europe and some from Asia; only the Japanese, East Europeans and Germans have sought out the agricultural frontiers in Chaco, Misiones, Río Negro. For details about specific aspects of this major movement, see related entries, such as Alluvial Era, Colonization, Emigration, Foreigners, Golondrinas, Jewish Colonization Association, Law of Residence, and various national groups, especially Italians and Japanese.)

Useful works dealing with immigration include those by Juan A. Alsina (early director of Argentine Immigration office), La inmigración europea en la República Argentina (1898) and La inmigración en el primer siglo de la independencia (1910); Mark Jefferson, Peopling the Argentine Pampas (New York, 1926; reprinted 1971); Carl C. Taylor, Rural Life in Argentina (Baton Rouge, University of Louisiana Press, 1948); Carl Solberg, Immigration and Nationalism: Argentina and Chile, 1890-1914 (Austin, University of Texas Press, 1970); Gastón Gori, Inmigración y colonización en la Argentina (1964); and José Panetierre, Inmigración en la Argentina (1970). See also Juan Schobinger, Inmigración y colonización suizas en la República Argentina en el siglo XIX (Buenos Aires, 1957).

IMPERIALISM. Many Argentine historians, and others, have frequently used the term "British imperialism" to refer to the close relationship existing between Great Britain (q. v.) and Argentina in the 19th century; the facts seem to indicate that, except for British unsuccessful use of force in blockading Buenos Aires during the Rosas period, these ties were based primarily on mutual economic interests; any political influence exercised by Great Britain-- and within the republic it was apparently slight--resulted from the desire of the Argentines to protect their lucrative trade; one exception must be made: the British insistence on taking possession of the Falkland Islands (q. v.) and refusal to recognize or negotiate Argentina's historical claims to those islands.

IMPORTS. Pattern of Argentine imports has changed greatly since depression of 1930s; before that time imports were divided

almost equally between capital equipment and consumer goods
but the proportion of consumer goods has steadily fallen as Argentine industry attempts to satisfy the national market, while
the proportion of machinery and equipment, iron and steel
products, and chemicals rose; some fuels are still imported,
also (see Energy Resources); Argentina's major trading partners have been Italy, Netherlands, Britain, U.S., Brazil and
West Germany, with other Latin American countries, Soviet
Russia, and Japan becoming increasingly important (see Economic History; Foreign Trade).

INCA EMPIRE. Although only the north and western parts of Argentina had come directly under Inca control, the existence of
this powerful, wealthy, civilized empire had very real effects
on the Spanish occupation of the nation and the original directions that it took; toward the end of the expansion of the Inca
realm, probably in the final decades of the fifteenth century,
the Incas spread their power east of the Andes, through western Bolivia, and into Argentina where the Diaguitas and others
of the Tucumán area were incorporated, either at their request
(according to one story) or, more likely, as an inevitable part
of the movement of extending the limits back across the Andes
to the central valley of Chile; as little silver or gold were
found in the Argentine provinces and the empire was already
over-extended, the rulers were not able to integrate these remote areas into their normal pattern completely; the royal Inca
highway was built, with its accompanying tambos or stations;
early Spanish chronicles and archeologists' discoveries prove
its existence and use from Jujuy to Mendoza, with some of the
most interesting Inca ruins in La Rioja; terraced and irrigated
agriculture became part of the pattern, as well as other features of Inca life; apparently native languages had not yet been
replaced by Quechua when the Spaniards arrived; during this
same period of Inca expansion southward, the Guaraní Indians
of the Paraná area had been raiding Indian tribes on the eastern fringes of the empire in Bolivia; for several decades these
raids continued, attracted by the silver, gold, and other
wealth found in this fabulous kingdom; it was from these Indians that Spaniards cruising along the Atlantic coast first heard
of the Silver Kingdom or Sierra in the west; following the reports made by Aleixo (or Alejo) García (q. v.), the first Spanish attempts to explore Argentina or to effect its occupation
came from Atlantic explorers, like Cabot and Diego García,
followed by Mendoza's captains Ayolas and Martínez de Irala,
and many others, all attempting to cut westward overland from
the Paraná-Paraguay rivers to the Inca wealth; the names of
both the Río de la Plata (River of Silver) and Argentina (from
the Latin word for silver) testify to the overwhelming importance attached to the eastern Argentine area as a base from
which to reach the coveted precious metals; meanwhile, on the
Pacific, slightly later on the timetable, Pizarro and Almagro
had entered the heart of the Inca empire and had captured its
capital at Cuzco and its emperor Atahualpa, had possessed

themselves of the Inca treasures and discovered new mines; as
the area filled up with landless and disgruntled Spanish conquistadors the latter were encouraged to find lands of their own
elsewhere; many of them, following Almagro's example took the
Inca road south into Tucumán and, among Indians somewhat
similar to those whom they had known in Peru, managed to establish permanent settlements in the old Tucumán region, using
the same institutions of church, city, and encomienda that had
worked in Peru; in fact, in some ways they continued practices
of the Incas themselves, as they forced the use of the Quechua
language on the Argentine Indians and even, in the seventeenth
century, adopted the Inca practice of transplanting rebellious
Indians to remote settlements; the Indians there provided excellent labor of the kind that the Spaniards had become accustomed to in Peru; while it may be argued that these patterns
were not due to the fairly recent Inca conquest of these lands
but dated back, rather, to common Andean civilizations that had
been shared from Colombia to Chile, the fact remains that
similarities and relationships and contact between Tucumán and
Peru made it possible for the first permanent settlement (Santiago del Estero) in what is now Argentina to be made there,
rather than on the eastern coast where the earlier attempts had
been made.
        The lasting power of the Inca name was demonstrated at
least twice during the colonial period: in the early seventeenth
century when Pedro Bohórquez (q. v.), posing as a legitimate
descendant of the royal Incas, roused the Calchaquian Indians
in two revolts that almost destroyed Spanish power in Tucumán,
and in the late eighteenth century when the rebellion of Tupac
Amaru II (q. v.) inflamed the entire Andean area.

INCAHUASI. Name of pre-conquest Indian town in northwestern Ar-
        gentina; famous for its gold mines worked by Atacama Indians
        in time of Incas; later the Jesuits exploited them and in the
        eighteenth century they came into the possession of the Isas-
        mendi family of Salta; mines fell into disuse after May Revolu-
        tion; reopened in 1936 by company with modern machinery; In-
        cahuasi ruins were declared a national monument in 1943.

INDEPENDENCE. On July 9, 1816, the Congress of Tucumán formal-
        ly declared the independence of the United Provinces from
        Spain and the anniversary of that date is annually celebrated as
        independence day in Argentina; most Argentines, however, con-
        sider their national independence to have begun more than six
        years earlier with the May Revolution when, on May 25, 1810,
        the cabildo abierto of Buenos Aires deposed the Spanish vice-
        roy and established a patriot government; it attempted to bring
        all the provinces of the former viceroyalty of the Provincias
        Unidas de la Plata under its authority but eventually Paraguay
        (1811), Bolivia (1825) and Uruguay (1828) became independent
        republics; in May 1822 the United States became the first non-
        Latin nation to recognize Argentine independence, with Great
        Britain following shortly afterward and signing an economic

treaty with the new nation; in 1858 Spain established diplomatic
relations with its former colony.

Much of the Argentine long war for independence (1810-
1824) was fought outside Argentine territory, except for the
vicious fighting in the northwestern area, and formed part of
the South American fight for independence from Spain, under
the command of an Argentine general, José de San Martín,
from 1813 to 1822; the classic Argentine historical account of
this continental struggle for emancipation from Spanish rule is
that by Bartolomé Mitre entitled Historia de San Martín y de
la emancipación sudamericana, supplemented by the same author's Historia de Belgrano for the early Argentine part of the
story (see José de San Martín; May Revolution; Declaration of
Independence; Manuel Belgrano; Juan Martín de Pueyrredón; and
related entries).

INDIA MUERTA.   Site in Uruguay of battle in which Rosas' forces,
commanded by General Justo J. Urquiza, defeated Uruguayan
General Fructuoso Rivera, March 27, 1845.

INDIANS.   At the time of Spanish arrival in Argentina, in the early
sixteenth century, the entire Indian population of the area now
included in the republic probably did not greatly exceed
300,000; these were divided among about twenty different
groups, ranging from the primitive fishermen, hunters, and
gatherers of the Tierra del Fuego area to the semi-civilized
agricultural communities on the southeastern fringes of the Inca
empire; although differing linguistically and in ethnic backgrounds, they were linked by the problems of living on the same
kind of land; they shared to a degree the same diet--at least
some corn and wild meat, and used many of the same weapons;
macanas, spears, sometimes bows and arrows, and, on the
pampas, boleadoras; in any given area the presence of Indians
and their cultural patterns determined the possibility of Spanish
settlement, with the hostility of the Charrúas diverting conquistadors to the south bank of the Río de la Plata and then 1000
miles up the Paraná-Paraguay to land occupied by semi-civilized agricultural Guaraní around Asunción; hostile Guaycuruans
kept the Spaniards from occupying the Chaco and establishing a
short route to link Argentine and Peruvian settlements; while
the civilized Andean Indians, although fierce fighters, provided
a skilled source of labor enabling settlements to be made in the
north and northwest; during the seventeenth century, both Indian
and Spanish population remained sparse, in widely separated,
sometimes isolated towns, but they survived and mixed their
blood and their life styles into what was to become the Argentine society; under the Spanish crown, church, and Spanish institutions for bringing the Indians into Spanish culture, and by
means of the encomienda (q.v.) and missions, largely Jesuit
but also operated by other orders (see Missions; Jesuit Missions), the Indians became converted, acculturated, and eventually bred into a mixed race; both Spaniards and Indians came
to use horses and cattle as the basis of their economy as well

as a new way of life; European agriculture supplemented that
of the Indians in the northwest to provide food, as well as
fibers for use in basically Indian textile industries in that area;
as Indians declined in numbers, blacks were imported from
Brazil and Africa to take their places in the fields, industries,
town labor, and transportation work.

During the eighteenth century the Indians along the frontiers became more active in raiding and destroying ranches
and settlements; forts were built along northern and southern
frontiers and a border guard, the blandengues (q. v.) created;
with the expulsion of the Jesuits in 1767, the formation of the
viceroyalty in 1776, and the stabilization of the boundary between Spanish and Purtuguese America along Argentina's northeast boundary, the Indians found their situation greatly changed;
royal authority was concentrated on keeping them under control
in order to develop and settle new lands, many of them formerly occupied by Indians; in the war of independence, as well
as in the civil wars that followed, Indians and mestizos frequently accompanied the forces, both as fighters and as laborers; during the first half of the nineteenth century, Indian action centered in the southern pampas and northern Patagonian
area; as these lands became valuable to raise cattle for the
new, thriving meat-packing plants, or saladeros, at the same
time that fierce and economically aggressive Araucanian Indians had taken them over from the earlier, more primitive
pampas Indians, bitter Indian wars were fought, first in the
Rosas period, and then, several decades later in the "Conquest
of the Desert" (q. v.), to bring the pampas and Patagonian
plains into use for agriculture, cattle and sheep raising.

During the same late nineteenth century decades the
Chaco Indians were finally brought under submission and the
land opened for settlement and development, largely by European colonists; much of the new agricultural wealth was based
on commercial production of Indian plants in their indigenous
habitats, such as corn and yerba mate both for national and
foreign markets, although European, Asiatic, and other imported agriculture played a very important role, also.

Today (1970s) officially there are no Indians recognized
in the national census--all are counted as Argentines; until recently it was customary to note that Indian blood was increasingly evident as one traveled into the interior from the coastal
cities--and certainly some Indian communities still exist along
the Paraguayan, Bolivian, and Chilean borders; the lines, however, are increasingly blurred as Indians migrate to the cities
and as the waves of foreign immigrants have changed the ethnic patterns throughout the nation; it still seems to be true
that, as migrant workers, service or factory workers in the
cities, or in farming, sheepherding, cattleraising, or used in
other labor, those Argentines closest to the Indian blood and
culture are apt to be at the lower end of the economic scale,
although this, too, is changing.

In addition to the contributions of their blood, plants,
labor, etc., the presence of Indians in Argentina has stimu-

lated national intellectual development and affected its cultural
history. During the colonial period, European scholars were
attracted to come as missionaries to the Indians; while teaching them the Catholic doctrine, they became interested in the
rich variations of linguistics and customs of the individual Indian tribes; as they established advanced schools for completing the education of their European novice missionaries, the
various orders (especially the Jesuits in Córdoba) were also
providing institutions in which native-born creoles could obtain
an education equal to that of any academy or university in
Spain; many of these same scholars explored new lands on their
missionary tours, like Falkner to the south, Sánchez Labrador
to the north, and others across the Chaco; their descriptions
of these missionary tours, with careful observations regarding
natural history phenomena as well as geographic and ethnic details, made it possible for later European and Argentine scholars to study the archeology and anthropology of the first Indians known to the Spaniards as well as their prehistoric predecessors in the land; writers of the late nineteenth and twentieth centuries have also become interested in the Indians as authentic Argentine figures, sometimes describing them in their
own habitat, as did Lucio V. Mansilla (q.v.), but more often
including them in gaucho literature (q.v.) or other works
about rural Argentine life (see entries on individual tribes).

  For more thorough detail, see writings of Salvadro Canals Frau, including Las civilizaciones prehispánicas de América (Buenos Aires, 1959, 2nd edition); Julian H. Steward, editor, Handbook of South American Indians (6 volumes, Smithsonian Institution, Washington, D.C.), especially volume I, Marginal Tribes (1946), for Indians of Patagonia, the pampas, the
Chaco, and most of Eastern Argentina; volume II, The Andean
Civilizations (1946), for Indians of the north and northwest, like
the Diaguitas and Calchaquians, Chaco-Santiagueño cultural
groups, and Comechingones, as well as the Araucanians in the
south and southwest; and volume III, The Tropical Forest
Tribes (1948), for Guaraní and Indians living in the Paraná
delta in the sixteenth century; a briefer work is Julian H. Steward and Louis C. Faron, Native Peoples of South America (New
York, 1959).

INDUSTRY, INDUSTRIALIZATION. Industry developed late in Argentina due to 1) lack of available fuel and easily worked mineral
  deposits; and 2) success of pastoral economy, augmented in
  nineteenth century by agriculture; industrial beginnings related
  to this economy, processing of food products, such as flour,
  sugar, yerba mate, for domestic market, meat packing for export, along with lumber mills; modern Argentine industrialization usually said to have begun in 1880s with establishment of
  first frigorífico for processing frozen meat (1882), organization
  of Unión Industrial Argentina (Argentine Manufacturers Association) in 1887 to promote and direct growth of industry, and, in
  same year, opening of Alpargatas (manufacture of cotton, rope-
  soled sandals), destined to become one of republic's largest

establishments in light industry; in succeeding decades industry has passed through many different periods, from government neglect in early period to heavy government support--and control--of first Perón period, leveling off in 1960s to become major competitive and supportive sector of balanced national free enterprise economy under government regulation and national planning.

Although constitution of 1853 had recognized need for industrialization and various public leaders had paid lip service to it, most people expected it to develop naturally along with progress of agropecuarian interests, as had happened in other nations; profits in traditional livestock and agricultural sectors continued so attractive until World War I, however, that traditional national and foreign capital continued to flow into them, confining industrial interests to new frigoríficos, etc.; industrialization was left to middle-class entrepreneurs, especially those of immigrant stock or foreign-born themselves (see Torcuato Di Tella), who seized on it as real opportunity for which they had come to America, and to representatives of European and U.S. companies; within less than twenty years (1895-1914) number of industrial establishments had grown from 22,205 to 48,779--of which only 24,203 were real factories, i.e., mills and meat packing plants; food processing still major industry but foundry products and iron manufactures were becoming notable.

World War I brought Argentina great prosperity but also frightening energy crisis, with coal cut off and no immediate substitute fuel; essential manufactured goods, as well as accustomed luxury imports almost stopped; import of machinery and needed parts cut off; immediately after war, government took lead in search for new fuels; petroleum discovered in northwest and in Comodoro Rivadavia; YPF (Yacimientos Petrolíferos Fiscales) national petroleum agency established 1922; search for new coal mines begun, along with plans for hydroelectric plants; industry burgeoned under desire for economic independence; world-wide economic depression following 1930 hurt Argentina somewhat less than more highly industrialized countries; tariffs imposed and after Exchange Control was established in 1931, imports were cut and industry encouraged to expand to satisfy national market; bigness became feature; foreign investment came in more rapidly and corporate ownership was introduced to make large enterprises possible; TAMET (Talleres Metalúrgicos San Martín, S.A.) first to offer public financing 1936; others followed; World War II brought new determination to become self-sufficient industrially; Argentina not only cut off again from import of European parts but found it difficult to secure machinery and parts from United States, which gave Argentina low priority in comparison with other Latin American countries such as Brazil and Mexico, due to Argentina's refusal to join other American countries against Axis until late in war; by this time Argentine industry strongly developed in food processing and meat packing; leather work of all kinds, including leadership in Latin America in shoe industry (established 1903 with U.S. machinery and advice); processing of vegetable oils; extraction of tannin from quebracho, for national use and export; clothing of all kinds for domestic market; chemical industries (supplemented with plastics after war); household appliances, electronic equipment, and farm machinery; foodstuffs, beverages, and tobacco, together, constituted largest industrial bloc, in number of employees and value of production, followed by textiles, machinery and vehicles, with metal manufacturing fourth; most industry concentrated along Plata river system in urban centers where both skilled and unskilled workers were apt to be found in mixed proletariat of porteños, immigrants or of immigrant stock, or migrants to city from the provinces; Argentine capital owned more than 60% of industrial manufacturing, with foreign capital more heavily represented in transportation and utilities; Union Industrial had continued to represent industry's interests before the government and public since its founding 1887 (following earlier Industrial Club 1875); skilled labor unions had existed since 1878 (see Labor).

President Juan Domingo Perón (1946-1955) determined to expand and strengthen industry under firm government control and direction; hoped to bring it into balance with agropecuarian interests for a healthier national economy and Argentine economic independence; at same time he planned to bring workers, industrial along with all others, into political action under his leadership; incentives and subsidies offered industry seemed to be reflected in increased progress for first few years but, after 1949, president was forced to reverse process, favoring other sectors over industry to get money needed for industrial expansion; after 1953 foreign capital invited back in as economy continued to deteriorate (see Foreign Investment); meanwhile problems with unions in Buenos Aires had brought about some decentralization of industrial complex; factories began to be built in provinces or near sources of raw materials; by mid-1950s both economy and society had been altered by industrialization: internal migration to coastal cities had accelerated and differences between latter and provincial interior were disappearing; new, more balanced social structure created as lines of communication and cooperation were opened among workers--skilled and unskilled, rural and urban, criollo and immigrant--and elite estancieros were forced to recognize power of new industrialists and difference of interests. (See works of Gino Germani in Suggested Readings, Appendix III.)

In 1960s labor continued to demand voice in industrial management; government continued search for new sources of energy--found coal in Santa Cruz and elsewhere; increased production of petroleum; developed hydroelectric plants; found better ways of exploiting lowgrade iron ores and other minerals; by late 1960s industry, no longer under protection, ready to compete on equal terms with most imported manufactures for national market; tariffs removed; loan credits extended to those industries with best records of production and for those projects offering most promise of production; in 1969 manufacturing contributed 35% of gross national product, compared to 15% for crop-farming and livestock combined, 43% in services, 5% for construction and 2% other. (See related entries; and works of George Wythe, T. C. Cochran, R. E. Reina, and Adolfo Dorfman in Suggested Readings, Appendix III.)

INFLATION. For several decades following World War II, economic inflation continued to be one of Argentina's most serious national problems (see Economic History; also entries on the presidents from 1945 to 1975).

INGENIEROS, JOSE (1877-1925). Psychiatrist; sociologist; writer and editor; professor.
    Born in Palermo, Italy; brought in infancy to Buenos Aires by parents; father, Salvador Ingenieros, was Marxist Socialist labor leader and journalist who took great interest in son's intellectual development; José was educated in Colegio Nacional, then entered both medical and legal faculties (1893) of University of Buenos Aires; became distracted by variety of political and literary activities; served in 1895 as secretary of Argentine Socialist Workers party founded that year by Dr. Juan B. Justo of medical faculty; drawn into orbit of young intellectuals around Nicaraguan poet Rubén Darío, living in Buenos Aires 1897-1899; with Darío's support, Ingenieros joined with Leopoldo Lugones and others in starting bi-weekly literary magazine, La montaña, devoted to revolutionary and socialist ideas; later, writers used El Mercurio; his medical studies were suffering, but under guidance of one of his professors, José María Ramos Mejía, director of clinic for nervous diseases, Ingenieros had his professional attention turned more firmly toward medicine, became associated in the clinic with Ramos Mejía; influenced through Ramos Mejía by "Generation of 1880," his intellectual interests turned away from Marxism and toward science and positivism; in 1899, under influence of second professor, Francisco de Veyga, who taught legal medicine, Ingenieros began to get firm sense of direction for studies and reading; became Veyga's editorial assistant on medical journal La Semana Médica; specialized in criminology; graduated in 1900 with degree in psychiatric medicine; immediately entered on double career combining professional interests as physician with those of scholarly editor and writer; from 1902 to 1913 edited review entitled Archivo de Criminología, Medicina Legal y Psiquiatría, bringing to Argentine attention writings of most distinguished scientists in those fields who wrote in Spanish; as criminologist, served as director of psychiatric observation for Buenos Aires police department 1904-1911; sent to Rome to attend international congress of psychology (1905), found his name already well known; in 1907 Ingenieros persuaded Joaquín V. González to establish first Argentine Institute of Criminology, as part of University of La Plata, and became its director; served as president of Argentine medical society (1909) and, with his former professor Francisco de

Veyga and Horacio Pinero, founded Psychology Society; disappointed in not receiving chair of legal medicine following Veyga's resignation, Ingenieros spent several years (1911-1914) traveling, studying, writing (Mediocre Man written during this period) in France, Switzerland, and Germany; returning to Buenos Aires he found a nation prosperous in World War I, optimistic about its national future, and a radical party (Unión Cívica Radical) that had pushed through electoral reform and would soon elect its first president; immediately after his return Ingenieros established the second scholarly review with which his name and influence are linked--Revista de Filosofía, which he edited and in which he wrote extensively from 1915 until his death in 1925; already acclaimed most widely read Argentine author, Ingenieros became, through Revista, acknowledged leader of positivism and scientific thought in Latin America; attempted to impress scientific principles and methods on all aspects of Argentine intellectual life; along with this he challenged the idealism of young Argentine and Latin American students to greater achievements for their nation and culture, to extent only rivaled by José Enrique Rodó of Uruguay, and Cuban José Martí; always revolutionary, Ingenieros became both leader and symbol of university reform in Argentine (1917-1918); continental nationalism became closely tied in with university reform and in the year of his death, 1925, Ingenieros, a convert to the movement, founded the Latin American Union.

By 1915 Ingenieros had already taken a strong stand regarding Argentine identity; unlike some of his contemporaries who were turning their attention to Argentine historical development in their search for this, Ingenieros turned to the new immigrants, integrating them into the historic process as those who would bring to fulfillment the dreams of Moreno, Rivadavia, and Sarmiento--Argentine true identity lay, he said, not in past with gaucho and criollo, but in future and was theirs to make; the new Argentine race, of which the founding fathers dreamed was now ready to take over--a white European race creating a new culture in a new land; moved greatly by Russian revolution of 1917, Ingenieros believed that all America should begin to prepare for the revolution that would eventually affect all nations; began his most important work to provide basis for Argentine acceptance and direction of such revolution; published first two volumes of his history of Argentine thought, La evolución de las ideas argentinas (2 v., Buenos Aires, 1918), and was at work on third when he died unexpectedly in Buenos Aires at age of 47.

An omnivorous reader and prolific writer, Ingenieros left a bibliography of several hundred items, including some 20 books, and more than 200 monographs on criminology, history, pyschology, psychopathology, ethics, as well as topics of current interest; his most widely read book was El hombre mediocre, first published in 1920; others of unusual note include Argentine Sociology; La simulación en la lucha por la vida; latest publication of his complete works, Obras Completas

(20 volumes, Buenos Aires, 1956).
See Sergio Bagú, Vida ejemplar de José Ingenieros (Buenos Aires, 1936); Hector P. Agostí, Ingenieros (Buenos Aires, 1950); Ricante Soler, El positivismo argentino (Panama, 1959).

INQUISITION, THE. The Tribunal del Santo Oficio, or Inquisition, was a Spanish institution transferred to its American colonies in the 1560s and 1570s; related to both Church and State, it was autonomous in fact and conducted its operations more or less in secret; its functions were to root out heresy and safeguard orthodoxy, serve as custodian or morals of the community, and incidentally to act as censor of all publications entering the colonies that would threaten the authority of either the church or the crown.

The Inquisition played a less prominent role in the Americas than it had in Spain and was even less important in the remote Plata area; a tribunal was established in Lima in 1570 and this supervised Inquisition activities in Argentina throughout the colonial period, with assistance of Inquisition official or commission located there; throughout the seventeenth century, there were frequent appeals to the crown, usually from church officials, with approval of royal officials, for the establishment of a tribunal at Buenos Aires, Tucumán, or Córdoba (frequently favored as most central site) to deal especially with the large number of Portuguese Jews (usually converts, but suspect) resident in or entering Buenos Aires and the increasing number of English and Dutch Protestant pirates (or contraband traders) in the area; the point was also made that it was unreasonable for an accused person to have to go 700 leagues (approximately 2200 miles) to Lima for trial by the tribunal; requests were denied as Inquisition was not self-sustaining and neither crown nor church would assume its support there; in eighteenth century Jesuits again urged establishment of a tribunal, due to almost total lack of enforcement of Inquisition activities--only one prisoner sent to Lima in 20 years and he escaped en route--and in the 1760s the archbishop called for a tribunal largely due to the increased influx and influence of Portuguese from Brazil, but these requests met same fate; as a result, as well as due to peculiar circumstances of Argentine life--including relatively small population of both civilized Indians and creole settlers and scattered nature of settlements--Inquisition operations consisted primarily of serving as watchguard over public morals and flagrant violations of private morals, and of rooting out religious aberrations and unorthodox fanatical leaders, of whom the most famous in Argentina was Angela Carranza of Córdoba.

Even in its role as official censor, the churchmen who served as officials of the Inquisition were more apt to be found among the intellectual leaders than the stiflers of creative thought (for example, see Juan Baltasar Maciel); during the closing decade of the viceroyalty, many of these, in fact, served as teachers of those who would lead the fight for independence.

See José Toribio Medina, El Tribunal del Santo Oficio de la inquisición en las provincias del Plata (Buenos Aires, 1945); also J. Torre Revello, El libro, la imprenta y el periodismo durante la dominación española (Buenos Aires, 1940).

INSTITUTO ARGENTINO DE PROMOCION DEL INTERCAMBIO (IAPI)--Argentine Institute for the Promotion of Trade. State marketing and purchasing agency established by President Juan Domingo Perón in May 1946 as core of program for controlling national economy and directing economic development; IAPI to buy all Argentine agricultural and pastoral products at fixed prices and to sell them on world markets; profits to be used by government for industrial development, purchase of foreign-owned railways and utilities, subsidies for shipping and national air line, building of hydroelectric plants, explorations for natural resources, such as coal and petroleum, etc.; during years 1946-1949, it seemed to function well with huge profits plowed back into new programs and projects and lid held on inflation; by 1949, however, with agricultural production in decline, involving less than 19 million hectares in comparison with an average of 21.5 million 1934-1944, with nation's population increasing, it became obvious that key sector of Argentina's economy was in trouble--agriculture and stock-raising; critics declared that initials IAPI actually stood for Institute for the Suppression of Agriculture; higher prices offered as incentive for greater production resulted in heavy financial losses absorbed by agency due to weakness of world market involving early 1950s and low prices received; IAPI continued to operate; in 1953, controlled 63% of exports, 20% of imports; served as buffer between national economy and disasters formerly experienced from such fluctuations in world market; criticism mounted, with IAPI blamed for all nation's economic woes and rapidly deteriorating national economy; certainly examples of inexperience, waste, graft and widespread corruption were to be found in its mammoth bureaucracy and some of its more unfortunate projects; shortly after Perón's ouster in 1955, IAPI was liquidated in hope that industry could secure needed foreign exchange that only increased production of agricultural exports could earn.

INSTITUTO NACIONAL SANMARTINIANO. Center devoted to the continued study and spreading of information about the liberator José de San Martín; instigated by José Pacífico Otero, one of San Martín's most important biographers, it was formally established in 1933 and in 1935 began publication of the review San Martín; in 1944 the institute was nationalized and placed under the ministry of war.

INSTITUTO TORCUATO DI TELLA. Non-profit research and cultural center established by family of industrialist Torcuato Di Tella on July 22, 1958, tenth anniversary of latter's death; reflecting the interests of the founder of S.I.A.M., its purpose was to sponsor innovation and creativity in the arts and in social science research; originally it consisted of three centers: Music; to finance new ventures in composition, etc.; Art--with Di Tella's own fine art collection deposited there as nucleus of Art gallery; and Economic Research Center (expanded to include all social sciences) to support research on problems in these fields; grants made to individual scholars to enable them to carry out their own research programs under most favorable circumstances; Instituto is financed and administered by family foundation but operates independently on all programs; Art and Music centers eventually turned over to Argentine government because of financial problems but research center continues active with grants and important scholarly publication program (see Torcuato Di Tella; S. I. A. M.).

INTENDANCIES (1782). One of most important Bourbon political reforms in the late eighteenth century was the creation of intendancies; these introduced the intendant, a new kind of official long used in France, who combined judicial, financial, and military (or police) powers with those administrative ones usually exercised by a governor; after the intendant system had proved its usefulness in Spain by adding mobility, greater centralization of power, along with quicker, more highly personalized governmental response than had been possible with the older bureaucratic methods, the Spanish government prepared to transfer it to colonial areas wherever it would be useful; Minister José de Gálvez drew up his plans with Mexico in mind but, with a few changes, they were first used in the new viceroyalty of Río de la Plata where the vast distances made tighter organization necessary and where a newer type of responsible official was needed to replace the corregidores, who all too often engaged in scandalous exploitations of the inhabitants in their region.
    Eight intendancies and four special governing districts divided the viceroyalty in 1782: the intendancies of Buenos Aires, Salta del Tucumán (including Tucumán, Santiago del Estero, Catamarca, and Jujuy), and Córdoba (including Córdoba, San Juan, San Luis, Mendoza, and La Rioja) in what is now Argentina; Paraguay and Cochabamba, La Paz, Charcas, Potosí, in Upper Peru (Bolivia); with subordinate military governments along the eastern boundary: Moxos, Chiquitos, Misiones, and Montevideo; intendants were expected to map each province as a basis for greater economic development, to introduce new agriculture and industries, to dispense a higher quality of justice, to be responsible for all financial matters, and generally to upgrade the colonial province in every sense and tie it in more directly with the royal government at Buenos Aires--i. e., with the viceroy who, after 1788 functioned as both viceroy and general intendant.
    It is difficult to evaluate the role and contributions made by the intendancy system in the Río de la Plata: for one thing, viceroyalty and intendancy system arrived so nearly at the same time that their individual effects cannot be distinguished; certainly the traditional powers and responsibilities of the cabildos

were decreased somewhat, as the intendant, or one of his delegated subordinates, presided over each cabildo, had to confirm
all elections, and maintained strict supervision over the collection and use of the propios and arbitrios (cabildo-levied
taxes for local use) as well as all municipal property; on the
other hand, the interests of the various regions received more
attention and often the administrative power of the cabildo was
extended farther than ever before; as a result, the area was
better organized, better governed, and, in many respects,
more prosperous than ever before, with the foundations laid
for the modern provinces, and the area generally growing up
to the point where national independence not only became desirable but possible.

INTER-AMERICAN AFFAIRS. Although the various American nations had been drawn close together (1776-1826) by the common
experience of winning independence from a European mother
country, these ties were loosened in the decades that followed;
Argentina, like most of the other Western Hemisphere nations,
was so engrossed in its own problems of economic development, national organization and identity that it had little interest in its neighbors; none of them, with the important exception of Brazil, offered lucrative trade opportunities equal to
those of Great Britain and other Western European nations and
the wars that took place in the early independence era largely
grew out of earlier colonial relationships or boundary disputes;
it paid little attention to various attempts at Pan American union, most of which were premature; Mitre refused to participate in the conference planned for Lima, 1864, because the
United States was not invited, the Argentine president insisting
that it also was an "American" nation; in the 1880s James G.
Blaine proposed the meeting of a Pan American congress that
finally got under way in Washington, D.C. 1889-1890; when a
customs union of the Americas was proposed, the Argentine
representative Roque Saenz Peña (later to be president of the
republic) vigorously opposed it, saying that Argentina could not
forget that in Europe were "Spain, our mother, Italy, our
friend, and France, our elder sister," not to mention Great
Britain, financier, best customer, and defender; the customs
union was dropped and Argentina remained a part of the informal group; at the third conference, in Rio de Janeiro, 1906,
the Argentine Drago Doctrine (q.v.) was unanimously adopted;
it was in Buenos Aires, in 1910, coincident with the Argentine
centennial celebration of independence that the fourth conference established the Pan American Union, to be located in
Washington, as a permanent clearing house of information regarding the Americas and to serve as the official agency of the
conferences; shortly after this, Argentina joined Brazil and
Chile in the independent ABC bloc (q.v.) to serve as a peacemaking agent in the Americas; during the 1920s and early
1930s Argentina's national mood of semi-isolationism, following disillusionments of World War I, was reflected in its inter-
American relations; changes came in the 1930s; the dynamic

foreign minister, Carlos Saavedra Lamas (q. v.) attempted to
wrest the Pan American leadership from the United States but
cooperated briefly with President Franklin D. Roosevelt's Good
Neighbor Policy, announced in 1933; a few years later, Argentina helped to bring the Chaco War to a peaceful end.
      As World War II (q. v.) approached, inter-American re-
lations entered a new phase; Argentina at first refused to join
the other American nations in common defense preparations and
later declarations of war against the Axis powers, insisting on
its traditional, popular policy of neutrality; finally in 1945, it
rejoined its American neighbors by a declaration of war and by
signing the Chapultepec agreement (q. v.); in 1948 it participated in the formation of the Organization of American States
(q. v.); in 1975 an Argentine, Alejandro Orfila (q. v.) became
Secretary General of the OAS.
      During the 1960s Argentina experienced a fresh aware-
ness of its identity and destiny as a <u>Latin</u> American nation and
took an active role in the organization and continued operations
of such regional groups as the Latin American Free Trade Association (q. v.). (In addition to entries cited, see United
States.)
      See Thomas F. McGann, <u>Argentina, the United States,</u>
<u>and the Inter-American System, 1880-1914</u> (Cambridge, Mass.,
1957); and general works on the Inter-American system by
Gordon Connell-Smith, Donald Dozer, and Ruth Karen.

INTERNATIONAL MONETARY FUND see INVESTMENTS

INTERNATIONAL RELATIONS see FOREIGN POLICY AND FOR-
      EIGN AFFAIRS

INTERVENTION. Right given by the Constitution of 1853 (q. v.) to
      the president of the republic to intervene, with force if neces-
      sary, to change the government or to restore order in any
      province in which internal conditions seem to threaten national
      security; it developed out of a determination on the part of the
      members of the constituent congress to prevent recurrence of
      the chaotic civil war period from which Argentina had just
      emerged; intervention has been used frequently from 1853 to
      the present and the supreme court has refused to accept ap-
      peals regarding it, on the grounds that intervention is consti-
      tutionally an executive power.

INTRANSIGENT RADICAL PARTY see UNION CIVICA RADICAL
      INTRANSIGENTE (UCRI)

INVERNADOR. Beef fattener in modern Argentine beef industry;
      buys calves at eight to 10 months, fattens them until they are
      ready for market, then sells them to the meat packing houses.

INVESTMENTS. (See Economic History; Foreign Investments for
      background.) By the late 1940s Argentina faced serious capi-
      tal deficiency for carrying out its plans for achieving the

economic independence desired; in 1949 Perón began attempts
to resolve direct conflict between economic necessity and political expediency and his successors have faced similar problems; Perón refused to deal with the International Monetary
Fund (IMF) as he regarded it as the "agency of the international capitalist conspiracy"; in the early 1950s he did succeed in
stabilizing the economy; he cut non-economic public investment
from 50.6% of the total in his first term to 27.4% and reduced
defense expenditures from 29.3% to 9.7%, diverting much of
this toward production of fuel, electrical energy, and telecom-
munications; during this same period overall capital formation
improved from 114 billion pesos in 1950 to 140 billion (at
1960 prices); in 1955 following the overthrow of Perón, the decision was made to join the International Monetary Fund and to
use its guidelines (Frondizi's stabilization agreement of 1958);
for political reasons, later administrations attempted to rely
more heavily on developing domestic investment capital or even
to attract funds from Soviet Union, to prevent monopoly by
Western Europe or U.S.; by the mid 1960s the capital investment pattern had changed significantly from that before World
War I; both national and foreign capital had increased but the
national was dominant; public investment capital had greatly increased in proportion to private; in 1973 a new investment law
was passed to regulate areas in which foreign investments
would be welcome and relationship between foreign and national
investments in the hope that this would prove economically beneficial and at least tolerable politically.

  See H. S. Ferns, The Argentine Republic, 1516-1971
(New York, 1973).

IRALA, DOMINGO MARTINEZ DE (c. 1509-1556). Conquistador;
  Governor of Paraguay 1539-1542; 1544-1556; explorer, colonizer, administrator; founder of permanent settlement in Río de
  la Plata area.

    Born in Vergara, Guipúzcoa (often called Captain Ver-
gara by his companions); father a royal notary of considerable
wealth; Irala sold his property to accompany Pedro de Mendoza's expedition to Argentina in 1535; participated in first
founding of Buenos Aires and other events in area; sent up the
Paraná, second in command to Juan de Ayolas, to find route
to Peru; continued up Paraguay river to natural port that they
called Candelaria or Puerto de Ayolas (about 125 miles north
of present Asunción); February 1537 Ayolas struck west across
Chaco leaving Irala in command of 33 men and the ships; appointed Ayolas' successor should latter fail to return; from this
time until his death Irala, with brief interludes, was leader of
Spaniards in Paraguay although not officially appointed royal
governor until 1544.

    After awaiting Ayolas for several months, Irala came
down the river to repair his ships and confer with Mendoza's envoys, Gonzalo de Mendoza (q.v.) and Juan de Salazar; (Ayolas returned during Irala's absence, set out again and was killed by
Indians); first clash of jurisdiction threatened when Francisco

Ruiz Galán, left in command of fort at Buenos Aires by Mendoza, disputed Irala's claim as successor to Ayolas; clash avoided and problem solved with arrival of Alonso de Cabrera, royal inspector, with royal decree (cédula), dated September 12, 1537, authorizing settlers to elect their own governor in view of Mendoza's death, without an appointed successor; on July 31, 1539, Irala became governor, supported by both Cabrera and Ruiz Galán, as well as the resident conquistadors; many Argentine as well as Paraguayan historians point to this as first instance of legal exercise of spirit of self-rule in area; meanwhile large settlement had developed at Asunción, bay on east side of Paraguay river, where Ayolas had anchored (1536), formed tenuous alliance with the local chief and secured food; the following year Mendoza and Salazar, on their way back to Buenos Aires, had built a stockade on the site and named it Nuestra Señora de la Asunción; Irala decided to make Asunción the center of Spanish settlement in this area; it was accessible from the Atlantic coast by water and eventually by overland route; located in midst of thousands of semi-civilized, sedentary, farming Guaraní Indians, whose way of life was satisfactory to the Spaniards and whose valor in fighting made them satisfactory allies; its rich land offered both pastoral and further agricultural opportunities; its location made it easy to defend from both Indians and foreigners and was much more favorable as a base from which to establish coveted communications and trade with Peru, with the hope of discovering new mines along the way; in 1541, after earlier unsuccessful attempts to persuade remaining settlers at Buenos Aires to come to Asunción, Irala and Cabrera went to Buenos Aires, destroyed all vestiges of settlement there and forcibly removed settlers to Asunción; on September 16, 1541 Asunción was formally established with a population of 600 Spaniards (including good number of other Europeans); royal officials appointed by Irala, apparently with the advice and approval of leading citizens--making this the establishment of the first cabildo in La Plata area; with base formally established, Irala began preparations for expedition to Peru; interrupted by arrival of second adelantado of Río de la Plata, Alvar Núñez de Cabeza de Vaca (q.v.); in March 1542 Irala welcomed Cabeza de Vaca, turned his authority over to him; spent the next few months exploring Paraguay river to Puerto de Reyes (Puerto de Irala) more than 300 miles north of Candelaria (penetrating deeply into what is now Mato Grosso, Brazil), then accompanied the adelantado on his ill-fated expedition in search of route to Peru; shortly after return to Asunción, royal officials, for various personal and political reasons, deposed and imprisoned Cabeza de Vaca (April 1544); asked Irala to resume governor's authority; conquistadors approving, Irala accepted and exercised this power for the rest of his life.

When he died in 1556, Irala left a well-established colony in Asunción of 1500 Spaniards and Europeans, along with their families, based on Guaraní life style but living under Spanish law, religion, and institutions; political institutions

included the cabildo (city council) and other traditional royal
offices; Irala himself finally received appointment as governor
in 1554; economic life had progressed from the exchange of
Irala's fishhooks for Guaraní food through more formal barter
economy to a normal monetary one; industries had been established; agriculture expanded, with some Spanish products added
to the indigenous ones; stockraising flourished, beginning with
the hogs and horses brought over by Mendoza, the goats and
sheep transported from Peru by Nufrio de Chaves on his return
from mission there in 1549, and the cattle driven overland from
the Brazilian coast in 1555 by Vicente de Goes; industry began
with shipyards built by Irala in early days of river exploration; textile industries established, with weaving largely done
by Indians; artisans, as needed, along with their necessary
tools and equipment, had been imported via Peru or the Atlantic coast; land had been distributed; and the religious and
cultural life of the colony was represented by two parish
churches, three convents, two schools, and, in 1556 by the arrival of Bishop Pedro Fernández de la Torre, marking the official establishment of the Church, and the beginning of building the cathedral; in fact, Irala is said to have been fatally
stricken while observing the cutting of timber for this; the
unique relationship established by Irala between Guaraní Indians and Europeans underlay much of this success; he led the
way in forming close family ties with the Indian leaders, with
several of their daughters bearing his children, who, legitimized by him, became leaders in making, as well as writing
(see Ruy Díaz de Guzmán), the later history of the Plata area;
close military and economic relationships, mutually satisfactory and productive, were also established; finally, reluctantly
(because of these traditionally close relationships) Irala yielded
to pressure from the settlers and established the encomienda,
distributing more than 20,000 Indians to approximately 320 encomenderos and promulgating the formal regulation governing
this institution in 1556; meanwhile peace and order had been
maintained--in spite of Indian revolts and wars on the frontier,
internal and external political rivalries and intrigues--by a
mixture of firmness, that made enemies, and a pragmatic,
humane approach that made him revered and loved, by all
classes, as the father of Paraguay.

Irala had also used Asunción as a base for exploration
and expansion of settlement; the coveted route to Peru had
been opened by going up the Paraguay river to Brazilian Mato
Grosso, thence across the northern Chaco through Bolivia to
Peru and Lima; alternate routes, such as Chaves' exploration
of the Pilcomayo had also been tried; the way east to the Brazilian settlement of São Vicente had been opened, the tribes
along the upper Paraná brought under control, the Portuguese
warned against slave raiding in this area, and Spanish towns
of Ontiveros (1554) and Ciudad Real (1556) established in Iguazú area to strengthen Spanish claim; his only real failure had
been in his inability to reestablish Buenos Aires, a continuing
purpose of Irala's despite his preoccupation with Peru; but

Asunción provided the base from which Juan de Garay accomplished this in 1580 and remained the seat of all royal government in that area until 1617.

See Ricardo de Lafuente Machain, El Gobernador Domingo Martínez Irala; Harris Gaylord Warren, Paraguay (Norman, Oklahoma, 1949), Chapter V.

IRIGOYEN, BERNARDO DE (1822-1906).   Lawyer, statesman, diplomat, estanciero.

For six decades, Don Bernardo, as he was popularly known in Buenos Aires, was respected as a public figure of stature, as well as one of the nation's ablest diplomats; his political orientation moved from federalist, in Rosas' time, to autonomist, to radical (UCR); served in lower house of Congress and in Senate; several times proposed as candidate for president or vice president of republic.

Born in Buenos Aires; graduated in law at university (1843); immediately called into government service by Rosas, to assist in settling strait boundary dispute with Chile; sent to Mendoza (1844-1850) where he established order and drew up an informal but comprehensive legislative plan for government providing for reforms and changes in policy, in justice, military organization, rural law, etc.; commissioned in Buenos Aires (1851) to collect documents justifying Argentine navigation rights and claims in Strait of Magellan; primarily involved in personal business for several years; not involved in Caseros; returned to serve as member of Buenos Aires convention 1860; refused, for personal reasons, nomination to Superior Tribunal of Justice but undertook other judicial assignments; served as legislator in Buenos Aires government (1870), as senator (1872); as chancellor in President Avellaneda's cabinet, promoted policy of conciliation and then as minister of foreign affairs signed boundary treaties, growing out of the Paraguayan war, with Paraguay and Brazil, and drew up basis of preliminary treaty on boundary dispute with Chile; held other cabinet posts under President Julio A. Roca, aiding president to reorganize nation after federalization of Buenos Aires as capital (1880) and serving four years as minister of foreign affairs; elected national senator 1884; active in Radical party (UCR); reorganized it after death of Leandro Alem; presidential candidate in 1880, 1896; from 1892 to 1902 served in La Plata as governor of Buenos Aires province; Irigoyen's influence strongly felt in the organization of the foreign office, in his support of oligarchical rule; on inter-American scene, his insistence that Argentina wanted peace at home and abroad, was not averse to joining an inter-American organization at proper time under proper circumstances, but opposed Blaine's early overtures toward Pan Americanism and refused earlier Colombian invitation to attend Pan American conference there; his early awareness of dangers posed to nation by foreign economic control due to investment foreshadowed later nationalism.

IRIGOYEN, HIPOLITO   see   YRIGOYEN, HIPOLITO

IRON   see   MINES, MINING

IRRIGATION. When the conquistadors first entered the Andean valleys of northwestern Argentina, especially in Mendoza and San
Juan, they found Indians (like Diaguita, Calchaquí, and Huarpe)
using irrigation in raising their corn, squash, beans, and potatoes; settling in these valleys the Spaniards introduced new
plants and improved irrigation techniques; more than 400 years
later, in the 1970s, the same process is continuing with introduction of new crops--alfalfa, fruit trees, etc.--and better
technology making possible expansion of new land to be exploited and intensive cultivation of the land already in use,
through control of the water supply; economy of interior area
somewhat neglected in 1860s-1880s as export agricultural
crops took over the pampas that had adequate rainfall; vineyards and fruit orchards largely found in western irrigated
areas; in the 1960s various irrigation projects were proposed
to stimulate the economy of the western provinces; most of the
limited funds were assigned to Córdoba; more recently the idea
of combining hydroelectric power plants with water for irrigation has brought new proposals, with La Rioja's potential considered most promising. (See Mendoza; San Juan; La Rioja;
also see Kenneth D. Frederick, Water Management and Agricultural Development. A Cross Study of the Cuyo Region of
Argentina (Baltimore and London, 1975).)

ISASMENDI, NICOLAS SEVERO (1753-1837). Governor-intendant of
Salta, 1809-1810.
        Born in Salta; studied at Monserrat in Córdoba, then re-
turned to Salta to devote himself to military career and the
management of his family's estate and encomienda; distinguished
himself in fighting against Indians of Atacama and in suppression of revolt of Tupac Amaru II; received military promotions
and political appointments; on trip to Spain in 1804 was captured by the British; returning to Salta, he was appointed governor of that intendancy by Viceroy Santiago de Liniers; Isasmendi's conduct at the time of receiving the news of the May
Revolution has aroused considerable historical controversy; he
called a cabildo meeting, informed them of it and seemed to
share in the general support of it; his loyalty was brought into
question, however, and the patriot junta sent Feliciano Chiclana
to replace him; after a brief stay in Buenos Aires where he
was suspected of being a royalist spy, he was permitted to retire to private life at his hacienda in the valley of Calchaquí
in Salta; died in 1837.
        His name is honored in Salta because of his military and
public career before the revolution and because of the extensive
program of public works for which he was responsible. Several historians, including Atilio Cornejo, Jacinto R. Yaben, and
Antonio Zinny have studied the career of Isasmendi.

ITAIPU   see   GUAIRA

ITALY, ITALIANS. Italy has always been an important trade partner of the Argentine Republic and Italian immigrants have made
up the largest single ethnic group in the nation. From 1857 to
1958 Italians constituted approximately 46% of the total immigration into Argentina, leading even the Spaniards who made up
33%; sharing a common Mediterranean cultural heritage, the
same Roman Catholicism, and speaking a closely related language, these newcomers found it easy to fit into Argentine life;
at the same time that they renewed and reinforced traditional
Argentine skills--fruit-growing, wine-making; irrigation, shipping, grain growing, shop-keeping, banking, they also brought
badly needed new industrial skills; throughout the republic Italians formed a large part of the growing urban and rural middle
class, serving as artisans, wheat and corn farmers on large
estates, rivermen, small vineyard and fruit orchard owners in
Mendoza and Río Negro, etc.; willing to begin humbly but working very hard to accumulate capital, land, and education, the
fathers and their sons made places for themselves; Italian
blood has given Argentina some of its greatest men in the past
century and a half, including the patriot general Manuel Belgrano in the independence period, intellectuals like José Ingenieros and Risieri Frondizi; several presidents, including Carlos Pellegrini, Juan Domingo Perón, Arturo Frondizi, and Arturo Illia; industrial giants and philanthropists like Torcuato
Di Tella, shipping magnates (Doderos), and generals of the
caliber of Pablo Ricchieri.
        Events and developments in Italy during World Wars I
and II period were reflected in Argentina; in World War I many
Italians returned to aid the mother country and in the period
between the two wars, many Argentines were attracted to the
new Fascist Italy under Mussolini; some saw in its totalitarian-
ism a kinship to Argentine caudillo rule and many felt that this
modern corporate form of government might offer new answers
to some of Argentina's political problems; a few accused President José Félix Uriburu (1930-1932) of attempting to create
such a government in Argentina; during World War II the large
number of Argentines, on every level, with close family ties
in Italy, was believed to have strengthened the traditional Argentine desire for neutrality in world wars instead of joining
the Allies against the Axis, including Italy; in the period following the war, Italian immigration was again renewed on an
intensified level.

ITATI. The name Itatí (meaning point of rocks) is applied to a modern department and its capital of province of Corrientes; historically interesting as one of the earliest settlements and site
of the origin of the cult of the Virgin of Itatí, patroness of the
province.
        Itatí, located on the Paraná just east of the entrance
of the Paraguay into it, was first visited by Sebastian Cabot in
1528 as he began exploration of the Upper Paraná River; it
was also known to Juan de Ayolas and other conquistadors;
when city of Corrientes was founded (1588), both settlers and

supplies for the new center came from Itatí; in 1615 the Franciscan missionary Luis Bolaños (q. v.) established a mission for Guaraní Indians there and built a church dedicated to Nuestra Señora de la Pura y Limpia Concepción de Itatí; according to legend, the image of the Virgin of Itatí had been mysteriously discovered lodged among the rocks of the river--perhaps lost or abandoned by residents of Concepción del Bermejo (q. v.) while fleeing from Indian attack--and her cult spread rapidly throughout Corrientes and neighboring areas, with the first pilgrimage taking place in 1618; during the seventeenth and early eighteenth centuries, both town and mission suffered severely from Indian attacks, particularly the devastating one of 1739; by mid-century, however, there were three hundred families living in Itatí with a prosperous economy based on the rich cattle lands surrounding it and its position as the point of entry for land travelers into Paraguay, offering supplies and ferrying services across the river; the mission was also apparently reestablished (1749), with its carpenters, weavers of cotton fabrics, farmers, mechanics, etc., and its special emphasis on music and dances.

The veneration of the Virgin of Itatí has continued into modern times, with her solemn coronation in 1900 and construction of magnificent basilica in her honor in Corrientes.

ITURBE, MARIANO (late 1700s-1852).   Military and political leader in Jujuy province.

Born in Jujuy; entered fight for independence in north in 1812 and remained in public service for rest of life; Governor Gorriti of Salta (of which Jujuy then formed a part) placed him in charge of defense of Jujuy (1821); Iturbe was one of those to sign Jujuy's declaration of independence from Salta, 1834; always a loyal supporter of Juan Manuel de Rosas; in 1837-1838 participated in war between Rosas' Argentine Confederation and the Confederation of the Andes led by Bolivian Andrés Santa Cruz; served as governor of province 1838-1840 but forced into exile when Jujuy joined northern provinces in revolt against Rosas; after Juan Lavalle's death in Jujuy in 1841, Iturbe returned to govern Jujuy for most of the following decade; as governor in 1842 supported Rosas rather than Urquiza and was executed by new governor after Rosas' defeat.

ITURRI, FRANCISCO JAVIER, S. J. (1738-1822).   Jesuit Argentine historian.

Born in Santa Fe, Iturri entered Jesuit order in 1753; deeply interested in the historical background of his native land, he divided his time between teaching assignments in Córdoba and Asunción (where the royal order for Jesuit expulsion in 1767 caught him) and scholarly research for the history that he was writing; he continued this work in exile in Italy and, with his close friend and fellow-exile Gaspar Juárez collaborating, completed what has been called the first civil history of Argentina, entitled Historia natural, eclesiástica y civil del virreinato de Buenos Aires; Deán Gregorio Funes, formerly

Iturri's student in Córdoba, paid tribute to the research and writing done by his former professor in this field in the prologue to his own historical essay on the same subject.

Iturri also showed his continuing interest in and loyalty by publishing in 1797 his Carta crítica sobre la "Historia de América" del Señor Juan Bautista Muñoz (reprinted in Buenos Aires, 1818), in which he criticized and pointed out the errors and distortions in the famous Spanish historian's work, due to bias or ignorance, so vigorously that publication of the later volumes of the history were delayed for a time; when Napoleon's forces occupied Rome in 1808, Father Iturri refused to swear allegiance to Joseph Bonaparte as king of Spain and suffered imprisonment; his closing years were spent in Spain and for some time the Santa Fe historian enjoyed a royal pension honoring his scholarly achievements; he died in Barcelona, shortly after having been threatened with new exile as the Spanish revolution outlawed the Society of Jesus in 1820.

ITUZAINGO, BATTLE OF (February 20, 1827).   Most important battle in war against Brazil.   Early in 1827 General Carlos María de Alvear moved his allied Argentine and Uruguayan army north from its encampment in Uruguay into Brazil, hoping that fighting would devastate Rio Grande do Sul rather than Argentine territory; for some time his "republican" army (as it was known to distinguish it from the imperial army of Brazil) advanced between two large Brazilian forces but battle was not joined until Alvear found his way blocked by difficulties in crossing Paso del Rosario (name by which Brazilians know this battle) and forced a confrontation with the army of Marquis of Barbacena (Feliberto Caldeira Brant Pontes); although Brazilian army was larger than allied army and both were well equipped, Alvear's forces had element of surprise and experience--Barbacena's men no match for veterans of wars of independence led by such generals as Miguel Estanislao Soler, Juan Lavalle, Lucio N. Mansilla, José María Paz, the Uruguayan Juan Antonio Lavalleja, and Colonel C. F. Brandsen (who was killed leading a charge in the battle); after considerable hard fighting, Barbacena withdrew from the field, leaving his materiel and armament behind; although Alvear made little or no attempt to pursue him, it was a complete victory for the republican forces; credit for this victory is variously assigned to Alvear's military skill, or to that of the individual Argentine commanders who took independent action in the somewhat chaotic situation that developed, or divided among them; fighting continued both on land and sea for a brief period until peace was made, largely through British mediation and unpopularity of war in Brazil.

IVANISSEVICH, LUDOVICO (1889-1957).   Engineer, university professor; writer.
        Born in Buenos Aires; studied at faculty of exact physical, and natural sciences; taught there 1914-46; planned and directed the construction of three dikes on the Tunuyán river

and other engineering works for the government of Mendoza
(1939); attended engineering congress in Chile as delegate of
the national sanitary works; wrote extensively in his field.

IVANISSEVICH, OSCAR (1895-   ).   Physician and surgeon; diplomat
and public figure.

Born in Buenos Aires; graduated from medical school
with honors, 1918; held various teaching and administrative
posts in his professional field; in 1945-1946 served as president of the Argentine Academy of Surgery; entered public life
in the 1940s, filling appointments as ambassador to the United
States (1946-1948), minister of education in President Perón's
cabinet (1949-1950) and serving on various special missions;
his honors include la Orden del Mérito, of Chile, and Gran
Cruz de la Orden del Sol, of Peru.

- J -

JACHAL.   Name of department and town in province of San Juan;
San José de Jáchal founded in early 1750s by Juan de Echegaray,
acting on orders from Domingo Ortiz de Rozas, captain-general
of Chile, to facilitate trade between Chile, Tucumán, and Río
de la Plata.

JACQUES, AMADEO (1813-1865).   French scholar who came to Río
de la Plata area in 1852 as political exile.   Although well educated in philosophy and sciences at French universities, and a
friend of Alexander von Humboldt, he was working in Tucumán
as a baker when someone discovered his background and made
him director of the San Miguel Academy there; in 1863, President Bartolomé Mitre, who was attempting to reorganize and
upgrade the secondary and university education offered in Buenos Aires, named Jacques director of the national academy in
Buenos Aires and professor of physics in the university; Amadeo Jacques, whose ideas of pedagogy were advanced, broadened scope of education to emphasize natural sciences as well
as humanities and arts, all designed to develop individual student's full intellectual potential and to make him effective citizen in the new era of Argentine development; his own philosophy and high idealism, as expressed in his teaching and writings, left important impact on Argentina's educational system
and on new generation of students in spite of the brevity of his
tenure; died in Buenos Aires in 1865.

See Juan Mantovani, Amadeo Jacques; escritos (Buenos
Aires, 1945).

JACQUES, FRANCISCA (1858-1948).   Educator; sometimes called the
dean of Argentina's education for women.

Born in Tucumán, daughter of French intellectual and
educator Amadeo Jacques; she dedicated her own life to teaching, much of it spent in Santiago del Estero where she received her first teaching position in the school founded by

Manuel Belgrano; when the normal school (teachers college)
was established there, she became member of the faculty
(1881), and then director; developed it into a model institution;
in 1899 she was appointed to the faculty of the normal school
in Buenos Aires, but returned to her old post in Santiago del
Estero after two years; retired in 1904 but continued her interest in education, especially in the bringing of French intellectual liberalism to Argentina, throughout the rest of her long
life.

JACQUES, NICOLAS   see   XAGUES, NICOLAS

JAPANESE. Since World War II Japan and Japanese have played increasingly important role in Argentine economy and society; in
January 1944 Argentina had broken off diplomatic relations with
Japan, to bring its policy in line with that of the other American republics and March 27, 1945, declared war against it;
in the post-war rehabilitation period the Perón government
signed an important new treaty with Japan (1952-53).
     In 1959 Japan began Garuhapé, a colonization project in
Misiones that both profited from the techniques learned in a
century of European colonization in Argentina, and also marked
a new beginning with modern social and economic innovations
and skills; Garuhapé was backed by the Japanese government
colonization agency, Kaigai Ijyu Jigyodan (KIJ), and thoroughly
planned before it was undertaken; a group of 100 Japanese families arrived in Misiones to establish an agricultural colony in
7500 acres that had been purchased from a private company;
KIJ had chosen Misiones because its remoteness and already
mixed ethnic pioneer settlements (including other Japanese residents) would reduce problems of cultural differences; site was
well located, bordering on upper Paraná river, about midway
between Posadas and Puerto Iguazú, and backed by Highway 12,
giving direct route to Buenos Aires; tract large enough to provide both subsistence and commercial agriculture; the Japanese
families, largely agricultural, had been carefully selected from
a wide range of Japanese regions, partly for their varied
skills and partly to make it easier for them, lacking close
community ties among themselves, to become integrated into
Argentine life; from the very beginning the newcomers attempted to dress, talk, eat, name their children, and otherwise act
like Argentines, in conscious abandonment of Japanese customs; they invited experienced pioneers of the region, especially those speaking Spanish, to join them and sent their children
to the public schools established there by the Argentine government.
     With yerba mate, Misiones' traditional export crop, in
a serious price decline, the Japanese turned to diversified
crops, experimenting with both Argentine and Japanese products;
they were quickly producing maize, manioc, and vegetables for
subsistence; and tung, tea, tobacco (with which they had great
success), rice, soy and mung beans, oranges and other fruits
for sale; they also used diversified labor, farming family style

in the rice paddies and vegetable gardens; imported migrant
Paraguayans from across the river to work the orchard and
tung crops with which they were more familiar, and used modern mechanized equipment whenever possible; they also turned
to lumbering and reforestation; a cooperative handled the financing of major construction and improvements and directed
labor and marketing operations; an experimental station was established for new developments in agriculture and stock raising;
the colony quickly began to ship fruit and vegetables to the
neighboring Paraná ports of Puerto Rico and Monte Carlo; by
1965, 300 tons of tobacco, 2000 of oranges, and increasing
cargoes of rice and mung beans were being sent annually to
Buenos Aires; by the 1970s Garuhapé was suffering growing
pains; it needed more land; its ambitious youngsters wanted
better schools to prepare them for the university, and problems of river contraband trade were arising.

Japanese are also to be found elsewhere in Argentina,
successfully raising tea and rice in the Chaco, and entering into the industrialization and trade worlds throughout the republic.

See Robert C. Eidt, Pioneer Settlement in Northeastern
Argentina (University of Wisconsin Press, Madison, 1971).

JAURETCHE, ARTURO M. (1901-   ).   Lawyer, militant radical political writer.

Born in Lincoln, province of Buenos Aires; took active
part in university reforms of 1918; in 1922 joined the Unión
Cívica Radical, supporting Yrigoyen's leadership; directed Radical reorganization in Federal Capital and Buenos Aires province during Uriburu's administration; took part in insurrection
of December 1933 against Justo led by Lt. Col. Roberto Bosch,
in Paso de los Libres; imprisoned for this, he produced a
book of gaucho verses entitled "El paso de los libres"; beginning to rebel against the Radical policy of abstention at the
polls, he joined with friends in organizing FORJA (q. v.); became active as writer and political speaker, attempting to reorient the Radical Party to its earlier ideals; when FORJA was
dissolved, he joined the forces backing Perón; in 1951 became
president of Bank of Buenos Aires province; among his major
writings are: El plan Prebisch, retorno al coloniaje (1956);
El medio pelo en la sociedad argentina (1966); and Los profetas
del odio (1967); and, in a lighter vein, Manual de zonceras argentinas (1968).

JESUIT MISSIONS. Term usually refers in Argentina to the thirty
Guaraní mission towns under Jesuit control (1610-1768) on the
banks of the Paraná and Uruguay rivers; ten other Jesuit missions included seven in Río de la Plata area and three in Tucumán.

Following the establishment of the first Guaraní mission
at San Ignacio Guazú in 1610 by Father Marcelo Lorenzana,
others followed in quick succession; when Brazilian slave
traders and gold hunters (bandeirantes) carried off 60,000

Indians and destroyed nine missions in the upper Paraná valley (Guayrá), the missions were moved south and west for safety; in 1644, royal permission was granted to arm the Indians and train them in military units; missions grew out of Jesuit zeal for spiritual conquest, creole desire for expansion of settlement (especially under such governors as Hernandarias who aided the Jesuits greatly), need for a bulwark against Portuguese expansion from Brazil, as well as against Indian raids from hostile, nomadic Guaraní Indians; proved to be an advanced experiment in religious communal living, as well as transculturation, resulting in over a century of unprecedented peace and prosperity for everyone involved, only to disappear completely within a few decades after the expulsion of the Jesuits.

Indians (around 100,000 of them), were gathered into 30 well-planned new towns, their lives, as well as their dwellings, centered around the church under royal government; mission area divided, 1617, into Guayrá, the northern part, subject to Asunción, and Río de la Plata, under Buenos Aires; each town organized as Spanish town, with Indian cabildo and municipal officers selected by mission dwellers; in fact, however, all control centered in two Jesuit priests, one in charge of religious life, one responsible for directing political and economic efforts, in a paternalistic society; Jesuits proved themselves to be excellent administrators; order maintained; schools taught most children to read and write; prepared them for various vocations as artisans, farmers, clerical help; artists--even printers as missions had printing press for their needs before Buenos Aires or Córdoba; yerba mate gathered and later cultivated; cotton plantations tended; subsistence farms and farm animals fed the community; all property (except personal effects) held in common; after needs of community families had been met, surplus sold for support of Jesuit order and for maintenance of missions; mission Indians frequently called on by royal officials to serve in exploring expeditions or for defense; effort made to bring Indians into Western civilization without destroying their own culture; Guaraní War (q. v.) when mission Indians refused to accept royal treaty transferring them to Portuguese rule, only serious outbreak; expulsion of Jesuits (about 78 of them) in 1768 by Governor Bucareli left missions without leadership and Spanish substitution of authority was poorly planned and ineffectual; within little more than a generation only ruins marked the site of the Jesuit empire-- with most of the Indians scattered, the cotton plantations gone and mate yerbales taken back by the wild woods, even the title to the land uncertain, being tossed around between Brazil, Argentina, and Paraguay until Argentina finally got it in 1860s after the war with Paraguay.

See Ludovico Antonio Muratori, A Relation of the Missions of Paraguay, an English translation of an earlier Italian work (London, 1759); and Robert B. C. Graham, A Vanished Arcadia (London, 1901).

JESUITS (Members of the Society of Jesus). The first members of Ignatius Loyola's Compañía de Jesús (founded in 1540) to enter Argentine territory came in the closing decades of the sixteenth century, as missionaries seeking spiritual conquest of the Indians simultaneously into the Tucumán area from Peru and to the Guaraní, in the Guayrá area, from Brazil; in 1607, the Jesuit province of Paraguay (including Argentina, Uruguay, Paraguay, and Rio Grande do Sul) was established, with the first provincial, Diego de Torres, in Asunción; by 1615, there were 122 persons (in 18 houses) attached to the group, with centers at Córdoba, Santiago del Estero, Tucumán, and Asunción, and shortly afterwards, at Buenos Aires and Mendoza; for the next century and a half, until their expulsion in 1767-68, Jesuits operated 40 Indian missions around which towns developed (see Jesuit Missions); controlled most of primary education in what is now Argentina, and all the secondary and university education--their University of Córdoba, founded in 1622, when the Jesuit Colegio Máximo received royal and pontifical charters to award accredited doctoral degrees in both secular and ecclesiastical studies, represented the flowering of Jesuit colonial culture in Spanish South America; they explored the land and opened it to settlement: Roque González de la Santa Cruz opened Uruguay river to navigation in the 1620s; Nicolás Mascardi explored Patagonia from ocean to ocean and may have penetrated south to the Strait of Magellan, 1660s and 1670s; Gabriel Patiño (with Lucas Rodríguez) charted the unknown Pilcomayo river area (1771), leaving diaries and maps for his successors; other Jesuits opened up central and southern Buenos Aires province, establishing Concepción near mouth of Salado river; Jesuits pioneered in Argentine agriculture, with sugar plantations in Tucumán, cotton plantations, as well as cultivated mate yerbales in Misiones, along with other agricultural production; their estancias, models of their kind, in Buenos Aires, Córdoba, Santa Fe, and Uruguay, increased pastoral welath; they pacified Indians and held northeast boundary against Portuguese expansion.

The royal command to expel Jesuits from all Spanish empire was carried out firmly in Argentina by Governor Francisco de Paula, leaving Guaraní missions until last; heavy mourning followed, especially for the large number of native-born Jesuits now forced to leave their homeland and families; total economic boycott closed Buenos Aires business down briefly, but no violence of consequence occurred as the 345 Jesuits finally departed; the thickly populated, prosperous mission towns soon emptied, with only ruins to be seen among the woods--as farmlands went untended and Indians wandered elsewhere; agricultural skills lost that had to be rediscovered decades later (sugar in Tucumán in early 19th century and cultivation of mate in Misiones area in early twentieth, for example); confiscated Jesuit property went into the royal treasury and helped finance many of the public works in the following years; many royal officials, members of the hierarchy, and merchants, who had feared their wealth, economic competition, and power,

welcomed the change as one opening up new opportunities; others found it a ground-clearing for the new ideas of the enlightenment to be transferred to the Río de la Plata area; exiled Jesuits devoted themselves to writing, many of them about their homeland, and at least one Argentine Jesuit, the Mendoza-born Juan José Godoy, died in a Spanish prison because of his attempts to foster Latin American independence; in two ways Jesuit expulsion is credited with having facilitated the May Revolution and following national independence: authority of Spanish Crown was weakened as Jesuits had been most powerful philosophical support of authoritarianism; and, as Vicente Fidel López mentions in his history of Argentina, if the Jesuits had not previously been expelled, they and their 10,000-15,000 armed mission soldiers would have constituted a formidable opponent to the independence movement; many of the Jesuits exiled from Argentina were distinguished by their writings about Argentina, both while in Argentina and in exile; these include Domingo Muriel, José Manuel Peramás, José Cardiel, Francisco Javier Iturri, Joaquín Camaño y Bazán, Pedro Juan Andreu, Gaspar Juárez, Alonso Frías, Antonio Bustillo, Florián Paucke, Manuel Canelas, and José Sánchez Labrador (qq. v.)
Following the restoration of the Jesuit Order by Pope Pius VII in 1814, Jesuits returned to Argentina briefly (1837-1841) under Rosas government; then came back to stay in 1852, with the strong support of Urquiza and his successor Derqui; opened houses in Córdoba (1852), Buenos Aires (1857), Santa Fe (1862), and Mendoza (1878); began to offer university courses in theological studies in their Colegio Máximo (Córdoba); the Colegio de Santa Fe, the oldest in the republic (founded in 1607 as a school) was returned to the original owners; additional houses have been added and Jesuit work, primarily religious and educational, continues to form part of the national life.
See Guillermo Furlong, Los Jesuitas: su origen, su espíritu, su obra (Buenos Aires, 1940); Magnus Mörner, The Political and Economic Activities of the Jesuits in the La Plata Region, translated into English by Albert Read (Stockholm, 1953); and The Expulsion of the Jesuits from Latin America (New York, 1965).

JEWETT, DAVID (1772-1842). U. S. naval commander who aided Buenos Aires government, 1815-1820, as privateer and as Argentine naval officer.
Born in New London, Connecticut, son of David H. Jewett, physician in American Revolutionary army; young David early acquired love of sea and was educated as navigator; fought for U. S. in undeclared naval war against France in 1790s; served as commander of U. S. Navy, April 1799-June 1801; entered service of the United Provinces de la Plata (Argentina) in 1815 as privateer, commanding armed brigantine of over 400 tons; took several Spanish vessels as prizes; in 1820 he was given command of Argentine naval vessel Heroína and in 1820 put into Soledad in the Falkland Islands; finding

British Captain Weddell there, Jewett formally raised the Argentine flag and took possession of the islands in the name of the independent Argentine government, calling upon the British captain to collaborate in the protection of the resources (whaling, fishing, etc.) of these Argentine islands, known as Las Islas Malvinas; this action firmly reinforced Argentina's claims to the islands as heir to Spanish territory that had been part of it in the colonial period (see Falkland Islands); returning to Buenos Aires, Jewett resigned his command, largely because of problems with Argentine officers and crews, and offered his services to the new empire of Brazil; became admiral of Brazilian navy and contributed greatly to the upbuilding of its strength and traditions; remained in this service for the rest of his life, spending much of his time in the United States obtaining and supervising construction of ships for Brazilian use.

JEWISH COLONIZATION ASSOCIATION. Philanthropic association established by Baron Hirsch in 1891 for resettlement and rehabilitation of persecuted European Jews in other lands, including Argentina.

Although enormously wealthy and living in great luxury, himself, Munich-born European capitalist and philanthropist Maurice von Hirsch continued his family's traditional interest in less fortunate fellow Jews; by the early 1880s he had become disillusioned about possibilities of any real success in Europe, especially in aiding the Jews of Czarist Russia; he therefore determined to change his tactics and established the Jewish Colonization Association in London, in 1891, for the purpose of colonizing Jews in parts of the world where they would not be persecuted and in which, through training in new occupations, they could create a whole new way of life that would promise usefulness, freedom, and human dignity; Argentina, eagerly welcoming farmers, was selected as a major location for colonization of Russian Jews who would become farmers; aware of the problems and failures of earlier colonizing ventures that had provided more promises and hope than careful planning and provisioning, the JCA emphasized the latter factors from the beginning; well-endowed with an initial capital of £2,000,000, it eventually became by 1899, following deaths of Baron Hirsch and his wife, one of the largest charity organizations in the world, with approximately £10,000,000 at its disposal.

In 1892 the Association set up its headquarters in Buenos Aires and began establishing the legal framework and realistic plans for the Argentine colonizing project; carefully avoiding the mistakes made by the earlier Jewish colonies, and, in fact, incorporating many of the remaining survivors of these into the new colonies, the Association established two colonies, Mauricio at Carlos Casares, Buenos Aires, and Moiseville in Santa Fe almost at once; these were followed by San Antonio in Entre Ríos and others in that area; in 1900 the Association was given status of a non-profit organization for charity and

colonization moved forward very rapidly; most of its earlier
settlers (before 1914) were Russian, followed a little later by
other eastern Europeans; by 1922 all of the colonies had been
established although a few hundred new families came later,
most of these from Nazi Germany; in 1940 the JCA became a
civil association; at that time there were 17 colonies--10 in
Entre Ríos, four in western Buenos Aires province and eastern La Pampa, two in Santa Fe, and one in Santiago del Estero, all based on an economy of agriculture and stock raising;
the colonists, with their families, totaled around 27,500 persons; more than 1,500,000 acres of land was held, most of it
in use, and most of it was now divided among several thousand small farmers.
     During its fifty years of experience the Jewish Coloni-
zation Association had become practically a laboratory in scientific rural colonization and had evolved a set of guidelines
for such operations and had come to provide services encom-
passing almost all the needs of the colonists--an exception
were the schools, operated, as were all public schools, by the
province in which the colony was located; homes were provided
and provisions and tools, to begin with; then the new colonists
had to be taught to farm as all were novices; eventually, by
the second and third generations these ranked among the best
farmers in the republic; successful tenant farmers were enabled to acquire their own farms; in 1900 La Agrícola Israelita
was established to become the forerunner of one of the most
important federated cooperative societies of the nation (see Cooperatives); each colony had its own cooperative, managed by
farmers, to provide agricultural and marketing services and to
serve in many ways as a center of community life; each colony
was also provided with a synagogue in which religious services
were held regularly and a community house; the Association also developed an Argentinization program to assist newcomers
in becoming adjusted to their new homeland and oriented toward Argentine culture; almost all of the Jewish colonists
quickly became Argentine citizens and the second and later generations were Argentine by birth.
     The annual reports published by the Association proved
very useful to others attempting colonization projects and to
later scholars studying this movement (see Colonization; Cooperatives; Jews).   More detailed studies may be found in Su
obra en la República Argentina, 1891-1941, published by the
Jewish Colonization Association (Buenos Aires, 1942); and Morton D. Winsburg, Colonia Baron Hirsch, A Jewish Agricultural
Colony in Argentina (Gainesville, Florida, 1964).

"JEWISH GAUCHOS." Term applied to small number of Jewish
     European colonists brought over to Esperanza (q. v.); unable to
     adapt to life in the colony they moved into the countryside of
     Santa Fe and adopted the life style of the gauchos.

JEWS.   Argentina has a large Jewish population in comparison with
     those of other Latin American nations; in the 1960s it totaled

around 450,000 Jews, with about 70,000 of these Sephardim
(largely urban) and the majority Ashkenazim--Russian or Polish by birth or ancestry.

There have always been Jews in Argentina since the
conquest, with Sephardic more important in the colonial period
and Ashkenazic more largely represented in the national period; all Jews were subject to legal limitations and came under
scrutiny by the Inquisition during the Spanish colonial period,
but religious freedom became more common in practice after
the May Revolution, and the Constitution of 1853 provided for
complete freedom of worship; this offered persecuted European
Jews a haven, with legal safeguards rather than limitations, in
a land that also promised economic and personal opportunity;
large numbers of them, mostly Ashkenazim, were accepted individually and in groups, and came to make their homes in Argentina during the following decades.

History. It is impossible to calculate the number of
Sephardic Jews (those from Spanish or Portuguese background
and ancestry, primarily) that entered Argentine territory during
the colonial era, either directly from Spain and Portugal or indirectly from Peru and Brazil; judging from Inquisition records
and repeated appeals for establishment of Inquisition tribunal
in Argentina to handle such cases more effectively (see Inquisition), the number must have been large and their presence significant in spite of the limitations imposed on them; during
most of the nineteenth century, Jews came individually and in
small groups but their number in 1889 was around 1000, almost all living in Buenos Aires or Santa Fe.

During the period 1891-1914 thousands of Ashkenazim--
Yiddish-speaking Jews from central and eastern Europe--came
to Argentina under the auspices of the Jewish Colonization Association (q.v.); non-colonist Jews also formed a significant
portion of the immigrant wave flooding the republic, and many
of these remained in Buenos Aires; organizations were formed
to take care of various needs, especially those for worship;
Aarón Castellanos (q.v.) had requested to build a synagogue for
Jews in Santa Fe province (1862) and in 1868, the Israelite Congregation of Argentine Republic was formed in Buenos Aires,
a temple built in 1875, and a very much larger one begun in
1897; meanwhile Rabbi Henry Joseph took over services after
1883; shortly afterward the congregation received legal right to
register births, marriages, and deaths; the establishment of the
Asociación Mutual Israelita Argentina (AMIA) in 1894 provided
Buenos Aires Jews with the kinds of services furnished rural
Jewish families by the JCA; by the mid-twentieth century the
AMIA had expanded its membership from the original 85 member families to 48,000 (1958) and was covering every phase of
Jewish life in Greater Buenos Aires, as well as many activities in the provinces; it had also become one of most important
and wealthiest mutual societies in Argentina; it maintained three
cemeteries, operated extensive welfare services, and had established an educational network extending from kindergarten
through secondary schools, with teachers from their own Normal

School to instruct all Jewish children, in both urban and rural
areas, in Hebrew religion, language, and culture; in 1940 the
AMIA opened a Hebrew seminary that was offering an accredited six-year course to around 700 students within twenty years
of its founding.

Jewish influence made itself felt in more scientific farming and the establishment of scientific institutes, the industrial,
financial, and professional worlds, and in literature and journalism; the first Yiddish newspaper appeared briefly in 1892,
followed by others; the Amanecer (meaning dawn or daybreak),
begun in 1957, claimed to be the first Jewish newspaper in
world published in Spanish, and was edited by Lázaro Schall-
man, who has written extensively about Jewish role and influence in Argentine colonization, history, and literature.

Anti-Semitism has from time to time become a factor
in Argentine life during the past century, despite laws and the
official position; special circumstances or times of stress,
growing out of internal affairs or reactions to foreign situations,
have resulted in anti-Jewish actions or movements; for example,
the opening of the Jewish Colonization Association headquarters
in Buenos Aires brought journalistic accusations in the 1890s
that the national culture would be submerged by the millions of
Jewish colonists to be brought to that still sparsely settled
country--but the public fears aroused by these stories soon sub-
sided as the JCA agricultural colonies got under way and, after initial period of hardship, began to make their various contributions to Argentine economy and society; the development of
several powerful grain, brewing, and textile industries under
Jewish control in Buenos Aires and other coastal cities nourished latent strains of anti-Semitism but did not lead to active
persecution; the situation worsened in the 1930s as changing
circumstances in Europe brought new immigrations of German
Jews fleeing Nazi persecution at the same time that Argentine
nationalism was reaching new peaks of resentment against what
was considered to be Western European economic and cultural
imperialism, and Nazi German and Fascist Italian achievements
were attracting attention and admiration in some sectors of Argentine society; as the American nations became actively involved in World War II, anti-democratic and anti-Semitic feelings were translated into overt acts by Nazi-type Argentine
rightist groups such as Tacuara (q.v.), sometimes with support
from the Catholic right.

Meanwhile Argentine Jews had been forming committees
to help the troubled European Jews; in 1933 these groups federated into the DAIA (Delegación de Asociaciones Israelitas
Argentinas); this eventually became coordinating agency for
nearly all Argentine groups formed to help persecuted Jews,
especially before and during World War II, to support Israel
afterwards, to maintain links with Jewish communities throughout the world, and to fight anti-Semitism through public information, education, political action, and legal process; generally speaking, the Argentine Jews are politically liberal; DAIA
cooperates with other organizations that seek to promote the

idea of human brotherhood, working with UNESCO and recognized by it, and aligning itself with other democratic Argentine groups with similar ideals and purposes.

See Boleslao Lewin, El judío en la época colonial (Buenos Aires, 1939); Pablo Schwartzman, Judíos en América (Buenos Aires, 1965).

JIJON, FRANCISCO BERNARDO. First graduate physician and surgeon to establish practice in Buenos Aires; after serving as physician in Potosí, he moved to Buenos Aires in 1607 or 1608, after having received permission to become a citizen there from the Buenos Aires cabildo; in 1608, he was formally given professional status (as a protomedicato de Madrid) by the cabildo and placed on a salary; before this time medicine in the Río de la Plata city had been in the hands of folk doctors, such as curanderos, and men with some training in medicine, such as barbers and those trained in bloodletting.

JOCKEY CLUB. Founded by Carlos Pellegrini and others in 1882 on the pattern of similar European clubs, based on decision reached by Pellegrini, Miguel Cané and one or two friends at dinner in Paris after a day at the Derby in Chantilly; controlled public horse racing in Buenos Aires and as it became more and more wealthy in early twentieth century, served not only as a center for private recreation of its members but became a treasure house of books and works of art; burned down and destroyed by Peronists in 1953 as symbol of social exclusivism and power of the oligarchy.

JOLIS, JOSE (1728-1790). Jesuit missionary, Chaco explorer, cartographer, philologist.

Born in Catalonia; while still a Jesuit novice, came to Río de la Plata in 1753 to work in missions; completed his studies in 1760 and dedicated his full time to missions in the Chaco until expelled with other Jesuits in 1767; he had made a good beginning by attracting large numbers of Indians into reducciones and had tirelessly explored the Gran Chaco during his ten years spent there; made his home in Italy after expulsion; planned four-volume natural history of Gran Chaco; published first volume in Faenza, Italy, in 1789, including important map of Chaco made by Father Joaquín Camaño y Bazán (q. v.); rest of Jolís' work never published but the incomplete work contained in volume I served, nevertheless, as important historical document in later years for establishing boundaries in the Gran Chaco and for studying the complicated social and cultural mix of the various Indian tribes in that area; Father Jolís died in Bologna, Italy.

JONES, ENRIQUE LIBANUS (Henry L. Jones). Explorer and early colonizer in Chubut.

Arrived in Buenos Aires in 1814; quickly identified himself with porteño life and society; married daughter of former first alcalde Martín de Alzaga (and, after her death, the daughter of Pío de Elía, prominent jurist and public figure); Jones, constantly preoccupied with colonization projects, explored coast between Colorado and Río Negro rivers; later (1820s) served as secretary for J. A. B. Beaumont (q. v.) who had come to Buenos Aires to further his plans for British colonization, but without result; Jones assisted in the establishment of the port and fort at Bahía Blanca (1828), conducting the sea support for the land expedition under Colonel Ramón Estomba; after Rosas' defeat at Caseros, Jones, now an Argentine citizen, renewed his colonization efforts; organization established, with Daniel Gowland as president; expedition sent out from Buenos Aires, August 4, 1854, with Jones in command of schooner Explorador with supplies for 50 persons on a voyage expected to last about 90 days; late in October, after difficult trip, Jones entered the Chubut River and at Potreros de las Lagunas established a base, setting up iron sheds and digging deep ditches for defense against the Indians; explored up the river for about 100 miles, as well as the peninsula de San José; situation became critical; in spite of aid sent by Gowland from Buenos Aires in January 1855, Jones decided to dismantle the settlement and leave, February 1855, the first attempts at settlement in Chubut (q. v.) frustrated.

JOVEN ARGENTINA (Argentine Youth) see ASOCIACION DE MAYO

JUANZARAS, VICENTE ANASTASIO (1745-1786).   Priest and educator.
        Born in Buenos Aires into family dating back to conquest; was committed to the priesthood and had advanced quite far with his studies to enter the Society of Jesus when the Jesuits were expelled (1767) from Argentina by royal order; continued his studies, graduating in theology at the University of Córdoba; taught theology (1775-1777) in school opened by viceroy Vértiz and in 1783 became, briefly, the first rector of the Real Colegio de San Carlos; died in Buenos Aires.

JUAREZ, GASPAR, S.J. (1731-1804).   Argentine Jesuit intellectual exiled for the last half of his life by the expulsion of Jesuits in 1767.
        Born in Santiago del Estero of prominent, wealthy family, Gaspar Juárez attended the Colegio de Monserrat in Córdoba; entered Jesuit order in 1748 there, continuing his studies in the university; served six years in the missions and then spent most of his time as professor of canon law in the university, widely known and esteemed in intellectual circles in both Córdoba and Santiago del Estero; seized and deported suddenly and secretly in the expulsion of 1767, Father Juárez was among those who remained in Italy; throughout the decades of his exile, his interests remained with his homeland and such friends as the Funes family in Córdoba (including Gregorio Funes who had been a student of his) and the revered Sor María Antonia de la Paz y Figueroa (Sor Antula) kept in touch with him, sending news and financial support; he wrote

constantly about his homeland; his writings include a biography of Sor María Antonia, and a briefer eulogy of the mother
of Deán Funes, Doña María Josefa Bustos de Lara; an account
of the expulsion from Argentina; wrote the natural history
part of La historia natural, civil y eclesiástica del Río de la
Plata, co-authored with santafecino historian Father Francisco
Javier Iturri (q. v.); spent twenty years on major work on law
but this manuscript has apparently been lost; in 1789, Juárez
was persuaded by some of his Italian friends to establish a
botanical garden of American plants in the heart of Rome;
known as the Orto Vaticano Indico; this attracted attention of
European botanists and natural scientists; it also served as
basis for scholarly botanical studies made by Father Juárez
and published by him and the Italian historian Felipe Gilli;
during the closing years of his life the Argentine Jesuit served
as director of the Roman curia in charge of beatification investigations; Juárez died in Rome.

JUAREZ CELMAN, MIGUEL (1844-1909).   President of Argentine
    Republic 1886-1890.
        Born and educated through doctorate in Córdoba; became
active in public life, taking lead in liberals' fight against
Catholics for secularization of education, etc.; after serving
as legal adviser, legislator, provincial minister and finally
governor, Juárez Celman moved to national scene; became
president 1886 as favored candidate of president Julio A. Roca
(his kinsman); as president, gave full support to immigration,
economic expansion and development under free enterprise and
private investment; also backed elaborate public works program, including port improvement, public schools, Teatro
Colón, government buildings, etc.; overexpansion, wild speculation, uncontrolled inflation, tripled public debt, irresponsible
emission of paper money, careless, even illegal banking practices combined with growing bureaucracy and widespread corruption on every government level to bring republic to almost
total loss of confidence in political processes, rapidly disappearing public credit, and imminent financial disaster; president attempted to get remedial financial measures through congress but was denied cooperation by his own supporters who
had profited most by system; early in 1890 angry investors and
others whose wages and savings had been eroded and, in some
cases wiped out, joined with Catholic activists and political reformers, especially leaders of new Unión Civica, demanding
greater democratic participation in political processes and return to political morality, in public demonstrations in Buenos
Aires and Rosario, especially; they culminated in three days
of fighting, known as the revolution of 1890; in attempt to restore order, Roca and other members of oligarchy insisted
that Juárez resign, in favor of more acceptable vice president
Carlos Pellegrini; August 6, Juárez Celman became first president in three decades not to finish his full term; retired to
private life.

445   Judicial System

JUDICIAL SYSTEM. According to the constitution of 1853, under
which the Argentine Republic still functions, with some modifi-
cations, the judicial system constitutes one of the three separate powers of the nation, along with the executive and legislative; its hierarchy of federal courts headed by a Supreme
Court functions very much like that in the United States; public respect for the role and authority of these courts, especially the Supreme Court, is great; military takeover governments
of the 1930s-1970s have been careful to secure its recognition
in order to govern constitutionally; Perón purged the federal
courts to make them more amenable to his policies but his
justicialist constitution of 1949 left the judicial system virtually unchanged (see Constitution).

JUFRE, JUAN (sometimes Jofré). (1516-1578). Conquistador of
Chile and Cuyo; discoverer of San Luis and founder of San
Juan de la Frontera, 1562, having been appointed lieutenant
governor of Cuyo by Governor Hurtado de Mendoza of Chile,
whose jurisdiction included Cuyo.
     See Alfredo Gargaro, Juan Jufré, fundador de Mendoza
(Córdoba 1937); César H. Guerrero, Juan Jufré y la conquista
de Cuyo (San Juan, 1960).

JUFRE Y MENESES, LUIS. Founder of San Luis. Born in Chile,
son of Juan Jufré, founder of San Juan; worked and fought
alongside his father; held various civil and military positions
in Chile, eventually becoming general; appointed lieutenant for
Cuyo by governor Martín García Oñez de Loaysa y Meneses
of Chile, Jufré y Meneses spent three years there, 1593-1596,
during which he moved the city of San Juan to a better location (1593) to avoid river floods; also, in 1594 established a
town in eastern Cuyo, formalized in 1596 with name of San
Luis de Loyola Nueva Medina de Río Seco de la Punta de los
Venados--or San Luis, capital of province of same name.

JUJEÑOS. Name by which inhabitants of province of Jujuy are
known.

JUJUY (Province and City). Andean province at northwestern tip of
Argentina; name of Indian origin--probably comes from Quechua word "xuxuyoc" used for special type of Inca official or
provincial governor whom Spaniards first encountered in this
area--hence referred to it as the valley of the "xuxuyoc" and
then shortened and modernized it to Jujuy. Location: Bounded
on north by Bolivia; on east and south by province of Salta; on
west by Chile and Bolivia. Area: 20,500 square miles.
Population (1970): 303,436, with a population density of 15
per square mile; most of population native-born; signs of Indian blood evident. Capital: San Salvador de Jujuy (old name
for city, reimposed since 1952--although Jujuy is often used
for convenience). Population of capital (1960 census):
44,188.
     Other towns of some importance include: La Quiaca,

on border with Bolivia; San Pedro, asphalt-petroleum center at
railroad junction in southeast; Rinconada, capital of department
of same name in northern mountains, Humahuaca and Tilcara
in valley of Humahuaca; and Ledesma in the west.

Geography and climate. Extremely mountainous terrain,
with semi-arid Puna of Atacama in west separated from eastern mountain ranges of Jujuy by deep, narrow valleys cut by
rivers, such as that of Humahuaca (q.v., for a description of
Indians in province), which served as historic ways of communication between Argentina and Bolivia, as well as Peru;
area subject to earthquakes; although Jujuy extends into tropics,
its climate is modified and for most part determined by its
high altitude: cold in mountains; hot but dry and healthful in
valleys.

Economy. Increasingly based on mining; Jujuy estimated to have 90% of mineral resources of nation; most important exploitation is that of iron of Zapla mines just outside
capital city; second comes tin, followed by lead and silver;
copper, gold (both placer and ore), lime, gypsum, kaolin,
salt, as well as asphalt and petroleum are also found in commercial quantities; in addition to mining, Jujuy has developed
extensive commercial agriculture, with sugar most important,
followed by cereals and tobacco, and some fruits and vegetables;
stock raising is also encouraged, especially that of sheep in the
high valleys; its increasing industrialization centers around
processing its own products.

Buenos Aires-La Paz railroad traverses province from
north to south and another line connects Perico with Salta; network of highways facilitates communication and transportation.

Historical Development. Although many explorers had
visited the area earlier, Spanish occupation of Jujuy began in
early 1590s under leadership of Francisco de Argañaraz y
Murguía, conquistador who had come to Tucumán with Governor
Ramírez de Velasco in 1586; after several plans for settlement had failed to materialize, Argañaraz got permission to go
to Jujuy as lieutenant governor to establish town needed at this
site to maintain open communication with Spanish towns in northwest Argentina and those in the Perus; settlement made (1593),
officials were appointed, land granted, and Indians given in
encomienda; Jujuy settlement very small and subjected to fierce,
coordinated attacks from neighboring Calchaquí and Omaguaca
Indians but citizens were alert, defended themselves, began to
raise cattle and grow sugar, rice, oranges, wheat, corn, tobacco, and cotton; Jesuit and Franciscan missionaries established themselves there; near close of seventeenth century--by
royal decrees in 1676 and 1696--the internal customhouse was
moved from Córdoba to Jujuy, making it the frontier of the
Río de la Plata area and, in effect, favoring economic integration of cities along route from Jujuy to Buenos Aires, uncon-
sciously establishing future limits for territory of national Argentine republic; during seventeenth and early eighteenth centuries, Jujuy remained a small but prosperous and cultural
community, its economy based on its location on the royal

highway, the fertility of its soil, and the sugar industry developed there by the Jesuits, working among the Indians; its population increased and diversified; from a total population of around 3000 (100 of whom were of pure Spanish blood) in 1628, San Salvador de Jujuy and its surroundings had come by 1779 to have a total population of about 13,500; most of these (11,200) were Indian or mestizo, about 620 were criollos of Spanish blood; while the rest were blacks, mulattoes, or zambos (mixture of black and Indian), 1150 of them free, the rest (about 350) slaves; cultural unity developed, centering around the Catholic Church; the historic cult of the Virgin of Rosario de Río Blanco y Paypayo--sometimes traced back to first Indians given in encomienda to family of Ortiz y Zárate--had become well established before 1698; recognized by Belgrano later in his honoring of this Virgin as Patroness of the armies of independence in the north; construction was undertaken 1761-1765 on the present cathedral to replace old church that had been destroyed by earthquakes; an intellectual core made up of descendants of conquistadors, new Spanish residents drawn to this attractive area, and members of Franciscan and Jesuit religious establishments there, along with their various fairly extensive libraries, conserved traditional cultures and provided a well-informed leadership for province.

Bourbon political and economic reforms in Argentina (1767-1810) brought traumatic changes to provincial life, and prepared jujeños for enthusiastic role in independence movement; expulsion of Jesuits (1767) was strongly resisted in Jujuy for reasons of religion, family ties, and economics--a century passed before sugar industry was restored; establishment of viceroyalty (1776), with its capital at Buenos Aires and subsequent opening of that port to trade effectively changed Jujuy from its position as front door to Argentina (at least legally) to that of back door or last stop on road as far as most commerce was concerned; cut off largely from European contacts (at very time that these were greatly changing coastal area) Jujuy became instead more strongly involved in Andean movements; in 1780 a violent revolt related to that of Tupac Amaru II in the north had to be suppressed by force; in 1783 the province became attached to new intendancy of Salta, losing its traditional ties with Tucumán; as population decreased and economy declined, the idea of independence--or at least autonomy--began to be expressed, with Canon Juan Ignacio de Gorriti as major spokesman; revolts in neighboring Bolivia (1809-1810) and arrival in Jujuy and propagandizing efforts of one of revolutionary leaders, Bernardo Monteagudo, strengthened their own sentiments; Jujuy cabildo, therefore, accepted Buenos Aires May Revolution and swore to support it (September, 1810); although still a part of Salta, area played its own active role in independence period, both in Buenos Aires patriot government through its cabildo representatives and in defense of the north; prominent among its leaders were the three Gorriti brothers (see Gorriti Family); represented by Canon Gorriti in the provisional Junta of 1810, the cabildo of Jujuy stood firmly in

favor of return to traditional government (before creation of
viceroyalty) giving more autonomy to cabildos and local governments; Canon Gorriti's brother José Ignacio de Gorriti played
active role at Congress of Tucumán, was one of signers of
declaration of independence; although Jujuy backed national centralist government at constituent congress of 1824 (as did Canon Gorriti, then representing Salta, who had changed his views
somewhat), Jujuy soon went back to earlier point of view about
local autonomy and declared its independence of Salta in 1834
(after Argentine independence had been won).

During war of independence, territory of Jujuy, as
northern bastion of Argentina proper, became a continued bat-
tleground; its total manpower--including some women and chil-
dren--was involved and its leading estancieros almost literally
beggared themselves to supply patriot armies on the way north
to fight royalists and in their retreats southward to regather
their forces following defeat; Gorritis were outstanding but also
typical of jujeño families who, on their own, or serving under
national armies or that of Martín Güemes held the northern
border for 11 years against royalists in Bolivia; city of Jujuy
occupied six times by royalists; in 1812, in which approaching
royalist forces brought about famous "jujeño exodus" of August
23, 1812, when General Belgrano, after having boldly forced
the citizens to make their choice between royalist and patriot
rule, led nearly all of them to Salta, to return and fight again;
and in 1814, 1817, 1818, 1829, 1831, each time patriots
forced royalists back into Upper Peru; finally, on what is known
as the "Great Day of Jujuy" ("El Día Grande de Jujuy"), April
27, 1831, Governor José Ignacio de Gorriti of Salta forced
complete surrender of last royalist forces, under Guillermo
Marchiegui.

During following decades, Jujuy continued to be battle-
ground for rival forces; Salta first opposed, then, after battle
of Castañares, accepted Jujuy's autonomy as separate province;
civil war continued between factions, usually representing themselves as federalists backing Rosas or as unitarists; Manual
Iturbe (q.v.) leader of those supporting Rosas, was governor
1838-1840 until revolt led by unitarists placed Jujuy in coalition of North in revolt against Rosas (1840); after defeat of
northern coalition and death of unitarist general Juan Lavalle,
killed in Jujuy by federalists while trying to flee the country,
Iturbe came back as leading political figure until after the fall
of Rosas; despite his federalist affiliations, Iturbe allowed unitarists to be represented in legislature and to carry out economic and social reforms similar to those made earlier in Buenos Aires by Rivadavia; in the 1820s educational beginnings
had been made with introduction of Lancastrian tutorial method
and establishment of primary schools and the short-lived Academia Jujeña; under Iturbe, largely as the result of the efforts
of Father Escolástica Zeygada y Gorriti, called one of the
most attractive and influential figures in history of Jujuy, more
schools were established, efforts were made (ultimately successful) to bring first printing press to province and to establish

journalism; a local Sociedad de Beneficencia (Benevolent Society) was established (1844); irrigation systems begun; an academy of Philosophy and Civil Law projected, and various other educational and social welfare institutions planned or gotten under way; in 1852, Iturbe placed his province behind Rosas and after latter's defeat at Caseros, Iturbe was overthrown and executed; with Roque Alvarado (q. v.) again in control, Jujuy accepted constitution of 1853 under Urquiza as president and joined its neighboring province in push for economic development.

Isolated as it was, Jujuy made fairly slow progress at first; sugar was reintroduced, along with other commercial agriculture and stockraising; the Ledesma sugar mill was established by the Ovejeros and English entrepreneurs opened a second, La Esperanza, at the end of the century; the big event for Jujuy was the arrival of the North Central railroad from Buenos Aires in 1900, its extension through Humahuaca to Bolivian border at La Quiaca in 1908 and its final link with La Paz in 1924, providing access to national and international markets for Jujuy's products; mining became increasingly important in twentieth century and province, especially during governorship of Benjamín Villafañe (1924-1926), made determined efforts to control exploitation of its own resources, especially petroleum; tourism became important enough by 1940s for Jujuy to establish an official tourist center as well as an Historical Museum, partly as attraction; in 1920s Jujuy had established Colegio Nacional, with special interests in local history and culture and in 1924 it had been host to first congress of national history; population statistics illustrate growth: 1895: total provincial population of 49,513; 1914: 77,511, more than 90% native-born; 1947: 166,700; 1970: 302,436--six times what it had been 75 years earlier.

In 1943 size of province was increased in the west by addition of department of Susques, formerly part of the Andes administrative unit. See historical writings by Miguel Angel Vergara about Jujuy.

JUNCAL, NAVAL BATTLE OF (February 8, 1827). With war declared between Brazil and Argentina, Brazil attempted to blockade Río de la Plata; in further attempt to prevent supplies from Entre Ríos from crossing Uruguay river to Alvear's camp in Durazno, Uruguay, Brazilian squadron went up estuary as far as island of Martín García; Admiral William Brown pursued them and, in battle of Juncal, not only completely defeated Brazilian squadron but was able to incorporate all its ships into his own fleet.

JUNTA. A Spanish or Spanish American governing committee, appointed for a special purpose or formed to take over government when normal political institutions have broken down; in Argentine history, most famous Junta was the first patriot junta formed after the May Revolution, May 25, 1810; after resignation of viceroy Baltasar Hidalgo de Cisneros, the Buenos Aires

cabildo abierto (open or enlarged town council) appointed a
junta to take over the government of the United Provinces of
the Río de la Plata in the name of Ferdinand VII; creoles predominated, with Cornelio Saavedra as president, Mariano Moreno and Juan J. Paso as secretaries, and Manuel Belgrano,
Juan J. Castelli, Domingo Matheu, Manuel Alberti, Miguel
Azcuénaga, and Juan Larrea as members; during its period of
rule, the Junta endeavored to unite all the provinces under its
authority and in the fight for patriot government; to reconcile
differences between Spaniards and creoles living in the Argentine area; to introduce, especially under Moreno's influence,
liberal reforms; and to prepare Argentina to fight any force
that opposed these objectives; gradually the Junta was enlarged
by representatives from the provinces (against Moreno's will)
to become known as the Great Junta; authority of Junta was extended throughout most of viceroyalty but rejected in Montevideo and Paraguay; Moreno resigned and sailed in diplomatic
mission to England in January 1811, leaving the more conservative Saavedra in power and in September following news of defeat at Huaqui, the Junta was replaced by the first triumvirate
(see May Revolution; also individuals named).

"JUNTA DEL CITY." Name popularly applied to group that met in
the City Hotel in downtown Buenos Aires in April 1931 with
Marcelo T. Alvear who had just returned to Buenos Aires to
resume leadership of Radicals; from the hotel Alvear issued a
manifesto demanding and providing for the reorganization of the
Radical Party and healing of differences between two main factions of Radicals; manifesto was signed by leaders of both anti-
personalistas and personalistas; Radicals won most of elections
of 1931 but they were annulled by action of Uriburu.

JUSTICIALISMO AND JUSTICIALISTA PARTY. Body of doctrine
with which Perón supported his proposed middle stance in both
internal and international affairs, called Third Position (q.v.)
and the political party formed to implement it (see Juan Domingo Perón; Peronism; Political Parties).

JUSTO, AGUSTIN PEDRO (1878-1943). President of Argentine Republic 1932-1938; career military officer; engineer.
        Born in Concepción del Uruguay, Entre Ríos, son of
former governor of Corrientes of same name; graduated from
military academy 1892; assigned to interior garrisons, but after 1897 almost entire career spent in Buenos Aires; graduated
as engineer 1904; taught mathematics and related subjects at
military academy; served as director of military academy (Colegio Militar), 1915-1922, resigning to become minister of war
in cabinet of President Marcelo T. de Alvear; made distinguished record, authorizing military construction including airplane plant at Córdoba, new barracks in Palermo, and new Colegio Militar at Palomar; modernized equipment and training
programs; temporarily served also as minister of public works
and of navy; as special ambassador headed Argentine mission

to Peru 1924 in celebration of Ayacucho centenary; after military overthrow of Yrigoyen's government, 1930, General Justo named commander-in-chief of army by President Uriburu; retired from active duty January 1932, shortly before being inaugurated as president; elected president through coalition of conservatives, largely anti-Personalist Radicals and Independent Socialists--political alliance known as Concordancia (q. v.) including representatives of all vested interests ruled Argentina 1931-1943; Justo pledged himself as president to restore constitutional government; raised state of siege, restored constitutional forms and prerogatives to federal, provincial, and academic institutions; directed immediate attention to most pressing problem: to restore Argentine economy to prosperity in midst of worldwide depression; traditional Argentine economy of more than century had found greatest success in producing raw products for European industrial nations in exchange for manufactures needed; increasingly Great Britain had assumed major share of this commerce as well as of foreign investment in Argentina--more than 2 billions dollars, including 70% of Argentine railroads; bases of Argentine economy faced traumatic shock in 1930s as Great Britain began turning to its own meat, wheat, and wool-producing dominions for relief in depression; Argentine mission headed by vice president Julio A. Roca (son of former president of same name) drew up Roca-Runciman pact (q. v.) in London preserving Argentine trade with Great Britain and giving latter preferred nation status for Argentine trade and almost monopoly on porteño transit system (1933, renewed 1936); with British help, but under Argentine government supervision Argentine central bank was established to handle national finance (1934); Justo's government reorganized and reformed internal tax structure eliminating interprovincial duties and establishing national economic system; also began construction of first nation-wide system and even further extending government economic control in contrast to former laissez faire principles--established federal boards for control of such commodities as meat, milk, cereals, and wine; by 1936 Argentina had regenerated its own economy and emerged from economic depression; internationally, moderate new departures were made under Nobel-prize winning Foreign Minister Carlos Saavedra Lamas (q. v.); in 1933 president visited Brazil at invitation of President Getulio Vargas; several agreements drawn up regarding cultural exchanges between two nations and anti-aggression pact made, with agreement not to recognize validity of title to any territory gained by force; at seventh Pan American Conference held in Montevideo that same year Saavedra Lamas and Cordell Hull (U.S. Secretary of State) persuaded other American nations to sign this non-aggression pact; Argentina resumed normal relations with League of Nations from which it had largely withdrawn (1921); hosted special Pan American conference in Buenos Aires (1936) attended by U.S. president Franklin Delano Roosevelt; in internal political affairs, Justo faced many problems: Radical revolt late in 1932 had to be suppressed; increasing authoritarian trend of formerly liberal oligarchical elite; death of old political leaders (Yrigoyen, Lisandro de la Torre, Manuel Rodríguez) and confusion among old parties and new political groups; committed to constitutional forms, Justo and his colleagues felt it incumbent on them to ensure election of "safe" candidates, using whatever means seemed necessary; Justo's critics violently objected to Roca-Runciman agreement as sellout to foreign power; to scandals charging corrupt business ties between foreign investors and Argentine government leaders--worst being deal involving British meat-packers and government officials--debate about this leading to fatal shooting in Congress; only less important was affair of French company constructing port of Rosario; they criticized almost total disregard of needs of rapidly increasing urban proletariat, rising power of middle classes, industrial sector, and labor movement; finally, fraud and corruption of electoral processes--election of 1937 bringing in Justo's candidates of Roberto M. Ortiz and Ramón S. Castillo, generally acknowledged to have been one of most fraudulent in Argentine history--made mockery of democratic processes; five years after completing term as president, Justo died in Buenos Aires, of cerebral hemorrhage, in 1943 just before the rising tide of discontent with government by the concordancia brought military intervention by the GOU (q. v.) and a new political era to Argentina.

JUSTO, JUAN BAUTISTA (1865-1928).   Physician, writer; congressman and senator; organizer of Argentine socialist movement.
      Already a distinguished physician, Juan B. Justo became important political figure in early decades of twentieth century; devoted himself to gaining for workers a fair share in prosperous economy, largely of their making, and to making "politics an intelligent and virtuous activity within reach of all men."
      Born in Buenos Aires; graduated from medical school at University of Buenos Aires with gold medal for thesis on aneurisms (1888); continued study in famous European clinics; returned to Buenos Aires to earn professional distinction for his services (especially in caring for wounded in revolution of 1890) and contributions to Argentine medicine, including introduction of new surgical techniques; while continuing his medical practice, he turned his attention to politics; formerly active in Radical Party, he now left it because he disliked directions it had assumed under new leadership of Hipólito Yrigoyen; became deeply concerned with plight of urban workers--both immigrant and native-born; related this to writings of Karl Marx, which he read in German, later translating first book of Das Kapital into Spanish (published in Madrid, 1898); determined to take action against injustices suffered, Justo joined with socialist leaders Alfredo L. Palacios, Nicolás Repetto and others to organize Argentine workers into what became known as Socialist Party (1895); although socialist in name, party came to be powerful force (especially in Buenos Aires) for progressive reform by democratic means, rather than revolution, largely through moderate, liberal influence of Justo who believed

strongly in action and called himself a Marxist, but tempered his thinking with Spencerian positivism, common sense, an understanding of Argentine traditions and current realities; Justo's ideas expressed in his Teoría y práctica de la historia, first published in 1909--later editions, including one in 1969; Justo established and became editor of Vanguardia (1894), scientific and socialist scholarly journal to serve cause of workers; also began workers' library and cultural society; visited United States to study its social problems and published his findings in En los Estados Unidos. Apuntes sociales en 1895 para un periódico obrero.

Returning to Buenos Aires, Justo's interests broadened to include all aspects of Argentine economic development; became economic nationalist, declaring that British capital had taken what British arms could not win in Argentina; promoted formation of cooperatives; founded cooperative El Hogar Obrero (Worker's Home), and served as its director in early years; in 1912, following electoral reform law, Justo was elected to Chamber of Deputies from Buenos Aires and after twelve years as deputy, elected senator; his personal and professional distinction, eloquence, and knowledge made him a leader throughout legislative career; Justo steadily supported cause of labor, no matter what it cost; always stood for honesty in government, fighting fraud and corruption constantly; died in 1928 at chacra in Pilar; eulogized by political leaders, intellectuals (including Alejandro Korn), and workers alike.

See biographical studies by his socialist colleagues Nicolás Repetto, Américo Ghioldi; also Dardo Cúneo, Juan B. Justo (Buenos Aires 1943), and Juan B. Justo y las luchas sociales en la Argentina (Buenos Aires, 1956); and Luis Pan, Justo y Marx. El socialismo en la Argentina.

- K -

KAPELUSZ, ADOLFO (d. 1957). Editor, publisher of textbooks and scholarly studies.

Born in Austria, arrived in Buenos Aires at age of eighteen; opened bookstore in 1905 and shortly afterward began the publication of textbooks, starting with those for elementary schools, then secondary; broadened his efforts to include scholarly studies, especially those in fields of education, psychology, history, and social sciences.

KAWI. Ritual drink used by Chaco Indians in preconquest era; made from Indian corn, it was served in a calabash by the Indian chief who passed it around to his warriors who were seated in a circle.

KIKI. Drink made by indigenous Indians of Argentina; consisted of corn fermented with the fruits or nuts of the araucaria tree.

KING, J. ANTHONY (1803-   ). U.S. adventurer who became colonel in Argentine armed forces and published book about his experiences.

Born in New York, King arrived in Buenos Aires seeking adventure in 1817; joined the Argentine army and eventually attained rank of colonel; personally witnessed many of the political and military events of the years from 1817 to 1841, the year in which he returned home; in 1846 he published, in London, an account of his observations and experiences, entitled Twenty-four Years in the Argentine Republic. Embracing the Author's Personal Adventures, with the Civil and Military History of the Country, and an Account of Its Political Condition before and during the Administration of Governor Rosas...; included among other items useful to historians studying this period are his comments on the defeat of Artigas, the actions and deaths of Francisco Ramírez and José Miguel Carrera, and descriptions of contemporary figures like Dorrego, Lavalle, Rosas, Quiroga, and Paz, as well as an account of the brief history of the Liga del Norte; translated into Spanish by Juan Heller it was published in Buenos Aires in 1921 by La Cultura Argentina.

KORN, ALEJANDRO (1860-1936). Psychiatrist; philosopher; great teacher. Argentine intellectual who, after successful psychiatric career of more than three decades, turned his full attention, in his mid-fifties, to study and teaching of philosophy, becoming leader in reaction against positivism and establishing new bases for study of Argentine philosophy.

Born in San Vicente, small town in pampas of Buenos Aires province, his father Adolfo Korn, former Prussian officer who ministered to area as country doctor, his mother Swiss-born; Alejandro graduated in medicine from University of Buenos Aires (1883), with thesis entitled "Locura y crimen" (Insanity and Crime); after several years as police physician, during which he founded medical society of La Plata and served as president (1888-1896), he became director of Buenos Aires provincial Hospital Melchor Romero for mental disorders; in his nearly twenty years there (1897-1916), he introduced many innovations, making it one of most modern institutions of its kind; taught various courses related to medicine and to philosophy in schools and universities in La Plata and Buenos Aires; became professor of history of philosophy in University of Buenos Aires (1906-1930).

After 1916, he devoted all his efforts to academic career and study of philosophy; in his maturity he found scientific positivism of his youth to be limited in scope and unable to supply satisfactory answers to questions such as those dealing with selection of moral, aesthetic, religious, and social values; believed that it must be supplemented by philosophy, and even this left metaphysics out; with his own thinking stimulated and reinforced by post-positivist European philosophy--especially Neo-Kantism--he began to emphasize the study of history of philosophy as necessary basis on which to build new philosophy centered around personality, liberty, and courage of individual;

this new approach, along with Korn's rare gift for human relations, attracted many serious students, among them such future leaders of Argentine philosophic thought as Francisco Romero, Aníbal Sánchez Reulet, and Eugenio Pucciarelli.

Although Korn's influence during his lifetime was largely exercised through personal contact, his writings (most of them published following his death) have become important in twentieth century development of Argentine culture and philosophy. Among those most often mentioned are: Incipit vita nova (his first philosophical work--New Life Begins, 1918); Las influencias filosóficas en la evolución nacional, written in 1919, published in Buenos Aires, 1936; La libertad creadora; Axiología (including his ideas on selection of values); Bergson en la filosofía contemporánea, and Apuntes filosóficos (published in 1935); all of his writings were published in Obras Completas, edited by Francisco Romero, La Plata, 1938; Buenos Aires, 1949.

See Francisco Romero, Angel Vasallo, Luis Aznar, Alejandro Korn, 1940; and Estudios sobre Alejandro Korn, Universidad de La Plata, La Plata, 1963.

KRAFT, WILHELM (Guillermo) (1839-1893).   Printer and editor; founder of important Kraft publishing house in Buenos Aires.

Born in Brunswick, Germany; determined to become fine printer and at less than twenty years of age went to Paris to learn lithography; moved to Buenos Aires in 1862 and two years later established a printing press in central Buenos Aires that proved immediately useful to the educational and cultural objectives of the newly reorganized Argentine Republic under President Mitre; since then it has continued to be closely linked with Argentine development in every field and has greatly improved the quality of the national graphic arts of the nation by constantly modernizing its equipment to include latest technological advances; its widely diversified publications include such items as scholarly bulletins, journals, and reviews; documentary series; historical monographs; literary works; the commercial guide Anuario Kraft (begun in 1885 as the Guía Kraft), and ¿Quién es Quién en la Argentina? (the Argentine Who's Who); through its prizes for best American and Argentine novels, its support of the Amigos del Libro, and its sponsorship of visiting scholars, the Kraft publishing house has further enriched the national cultural life; Wilhelm Kraft died in 1893 in Buenos Aires but his son, of the same name (1873-1936), continued the management of the family press.

KRAUSISM, the teachings of German philosopher Karl Christian Friedrich Krause (1781-1832).

An idealistic philosophy and metaphysical system of thought in which God is perceived as an essence, not a person, and Man and Universe form an organic whole; promises ideal society when man, through obedience to right or perfect law, as revealed by his conscience, perfects himself and continuing larger groups until man in his perfect society becomes one with God; French republicans, like Amadeo Jacques and

Alexis Peyret, brought Krausism to Argentina by the middle of
the nineteenth century; it dominated academic life for 20-30
years; especially influential in such schools as the Colegio de
Concepción del Uruguay, the Normal School in Paraná, where
Pedro Scalabrini taught philosophy, and in other similar institutions; later the scientific doctrines of positivism eclipsed the
more spiritual (or metaphysical) ideas in popular attention and
after 1880s Krausism, as such, was largely relegated to fields
of ethics and pedagogy; its influence in Argentina has rarely
been studied until recently but now it is being suggested that
Krausism, in a sense an extension or new form of the earlier
rationalism and romanticism of the Generation of 1837, should
be considered, along with positivism and traditional Catholic
thought, as one of important intellectual currents affecting social and political life in late nineteenth and early twentieth century Argentina; its emphasis on need and possibility of perfect-
ing society, even by violent means, if necessary, played some
role in the important changes that took place in that period;
Hipólito Yrigoyen, Radical leader and twice president of the republic, was most famous Argentine public figure strongly influenced by Krausism, which he discovered while teaching at
girls' normal school in Buenos Aires; among others influenced
by it were Wenceslao Escalante, Julián Barraquero, Carlos
Vergara, etc.; Argentine Krausism related to that of Spain but
was not drawn primarily from it; closely related to that of Uruguay.
    See Arturo Andrés Roig, Los krausistas argentinos
(Puebla, Mexico, 1969).

KRIEGER VASENA, ADALBERTO (1920-   ).   Economist and government official; minister of economy in President Onganía's cabinet.
    Born in Buenos Aires; received doctorate in economic
sciences, University of Buenos Aires, 1944; spent more than
twenty years in economic research, largely oriented toward the
republic's problems and needs, in various government positions
in which he dealt with the economy, and serving on various national and international commissions and seminars; in 1957 became a director of the Central Bank of the Argentine Republic;
in 1963 he became a member of the National Academy of Economic Sciences and began to use this as a platform from which
to publicize his views regarding the Argentine economy; in 1966,
when President Onganía was forced to reorganize his cabinet
because of economic crisis, Krieger Vasena was brought in as
minister of the economy; he immediately began to implement a
comprehensive, balanced economic policy based on the current
economic and financial realities, and rooted in his own somewhat conservative orientation toward a free enterprise system;
his program called for an immediate, massive devaluation of
the Argentine peso, with a heavy tax on major exports to prevent the creation of instant fortunes; along with this went the
organized development of the infra-structure of the economy,
largely financed by internal capital and including power plants,

steel foundries, road construction, and housing projects; by
1968, capital, much of it Argentine, had begun to flow into the
country and, in spite of labor's continued pressure for inflation and higher wages, the rate of increasing inflation declined
for a time; in 1968 Krieger Vasena became president of the International Monetary Fund (IMF). One of the best known of
his written works is Kennedy y la política de cooperación
económica, 1965.

KÜHN, FRANZ HERMANN (1876-?). German geographer who laid
foundations for modern geographical studies of Argentina.
     Born in Görlitz; began his advanced studies in Jena and
Halle and completed them in universities of Berlin and Paris;
after having taught in secondary schools of Berlin and Schön-
berg, he arrived in Argentina in 1909 to take charge of the
geography department of the Buenos Aires national institute for
training teachers for secondary schools; he remained in Argentina until 1927, traveling extensively throughout the republic;
his observations and conclusions appeared in numerous Argentine and European reviews; his major works on Argentine geography include Fundamentos de la fisiografía argentina (1922);
Manual de geografía cultural argentina (1933); and La nueva
Argentina, un análisis económico geográfico (1941); Kühn returned to Germany where he taught in the University of Kiel.

- L -

LA BAJADA. Old name for settlement on site of what is now Paraná, Capital of Entre Ríos.
     See Entre Ríos listing.

LA HORA DEL PUEBLO see HORA DEL PUEBLO, LA

LA NACION see NACION, LA

LA PAMPA (Province). Province occupies southwestern fringe of
pampas; great salt producer of nation.
     Location: Bounded by provinces of Mendoza, San Luis,
and Córdoba on the north; Buenos Aires province on the east;
separated from Río Negro to the south by Colorado river; and
bounded by Río Negro and Mendoza provinces on west. Area:
55,400 sq.mi. Population (1970): 172,029, still predominant-
ly rural. Density: 3.1 per square mile--only Patagonian
provinces of Chubut and Santa Cruz have lower population density.
     Capital and other cities. Santa Rosa de Toay, popula-
tion (1960 census) 25,273; Santa Rosa, largest, most important
city, followed by General Pico and General Acha, all three located on railroad lines in eastern part of province.
     Climate and terrain. Land for the most part consists
of softly rolling open plains; rainfall adequate for abundant
grazing for cattle and horses although both arid areas and

others with greater rainfall, as well as heavily wooded areas, are included; the Salinas Grandes, great salt beds, employing thousands of workers, are found in the west central part of the province; while the colder mountain slopes of the sierras, extending south from Córdoba, San Luis and Mendoza, provide grazing for millions of wool-producing sheep; climate usually moderate except for pamperos--fast-moving, windy, cold fronts, that strike from the south and west bringing violent temperature drops along with dust storms or chilly rains.

General comments. Many of its place names are Araucanian (see History below); La Pampa was organized as a territory with its present limits in 1884; in 1915, with approximately 100,000-110,000 inhabitants, it was divided into 22 departments; became a province in 1945; known as Eva Perón province, 1952-1955; its economy has been based primarily on cattle, horses, and wool-producing sheep; also provides most of salt used in Argentina; has important lumber industry; and has hopes of increasing mineral production and industrialization; cities of La Pampa linked by highways and railroads to port of Bahía Blanca, only half as far away as Buenos Aires.

History. This remote edge of the pampas, now the province La Pampa, has historically attracted exploration by both its mystery and its promise; in 1604-1605 Hernandarias (see Arias de Saavedra, Hernando) penetrated it seeking the fabled City of the Caesars (q. v.); later, missionaries explored it seeking new Indians to bring into missions but found the nomadic tribes unreceptive to their work; in the late 18th century, the Spanish government, eager both to keep foreign intruders (especially the English) out and to settle and exploit new lands, ordered the various viceroys to send expeditions to explore the area, bring the Indians under control, and open the lands to settlement; the greatly increased demand for salt also made the great saltbeds of western La Pampa very important; wagon-trains of hundreds of oxcarts periodically transported the salt from the Gran Salina (between Ríos Negro and Colorado in western La Pampa) through desert lands held by hostile nomadic Indians to Buenos Aires to supply the needs of the populace and army of the viceroyalty and of the meat trade; Viceroy Vértiz y Salcedo attempted to establish and maintain direct communications (1778-1783) with Salinas Grandes, and Pablo Zizur (q. v.) opened the road from Dolores to Carmen de Patagones in 1781; but two years later the viceroy abandoned the project as too costly; early patriot governments continued interest in this area; Mariano Moreno, secretary of the first junta, sent Pedro Andrés García (q. v.) on expedition (June 1810) to explore and report on the Indian frontier; García reported (November 1811) that settlements already extended far beyond the established Indian frontier and recommended that the latter be moved further south to protect them and to allow Cuyo and Córdoba to expand farther southward; Indian raids a few years later brought punitive expeditions and in 1822-23 García was sent down again with a scientific mission to study the terrain for most effective location of new fortified frontier;

in 1833 Rosas pushed the Indian frontier to the Colorado river and stabilized it there; for the next four decades Argentine government paid little attention to this area but important, almost unnoticed changes had taken place; Araucanian Indians had pushed east to take over the south and western pampas and had left their traditional farming habits to become herdsmen and traders of the wild horses and cattle found there (see Araucanians); by the 1870s wild herds had diminished to such an extent that Indians had taken to traveling great distances to raid estancias across the frontier for their animals; in the late 1870s a determined effort led by General Julio A. Roca, was made to end the Indian menace and open all the southern pampas and Patagonia to settlement and use (see Conquest of the Desert); with the final defeat of the Indians, more than a million acres of land became available; government was established, with La Pampa organized as a territory, with its present boundaries, on October 16, 1884; General Juan Ayala, of the Third Army Division, became its first governor; lands were distributed, often to veterans of the "Conquest of the Desert"; towns were established: General Acha in 1882, named for General Mariano Acha (q. v.), Toay, Victorica, all in the east; after preliminary attempts to establish the capital at one of the older settlements, it was finally permanently fixed at Santa Rosa; latter city was formally established in 1892 by Tomás Mason at a location near Toay (q. v.) but settlers had moved in several years earlier; the capital gradually became the active center of progress of the province that numbered about 26,000 inhabitants in 1895; a chapel had already been built in 1885 and a school established in 1893 under Enriqueta Schmidt; population more than quadrupled from around 26,000 in 1895 to between 100,000 and 110,000 in 1915 when the twenty-two departments were established; a flourishing economy developed, based first on livestock, with a crop farming, especially cereals, becoming important about 1920; related industries, such as leather tanning and dairy-farming were added to the already important salt production and the lumber milling that included the manufacture of furniture, parquet floors, etc., made from the abundant supply of wood from caldén (q. v.) and other trees; La Pampa produce is transported for the most part to Bahía Blanca for export abroad or to Buenos Aires for processing; education was promoted with the establishment of the Escuela Normal or teachers college (1909), Colegio de María Auxiliadora (1915) and Colegio Nacional (1917).

   In 1945 the territory became a province; in 1952 its name was changed from La Pampa to Eva Perón (q. v.) in honor of the memory of Evita's efforts, in the women's Peronist party, to have it constituted a province; that same year its constitution was drawn up and the first constitutional governor, Salvador Ananía, took over the government in 1953; two years later (1955) the province resumed its traditional name following the fall of Perón's government; by the 1960s, La Pampa was facing serious economic problems growing out of depletion of natural resources and reflected in a slight population loss in

contrast to its earlier rapid growth; its ecology had been disturbed by indiscriminate deforestation, exclusive monoculture,
superabundance of stock animals, and use of irrigating waters
that had robbed the soil of its essential minerals; the damage
was widespread: soil no longer consistently produced good
crops; alfalfa fields were disappearing; insect pests multiplied
and damaged or destroyed crops; grazing herds failed to get
enough calcium and produced poor meat or fell ill of decalcifi-
cation; weather changes became more abrupt and dust storms
were common; many springs and water holes dried up; programs of reforestation and recovery of the land were introduced and in 1964 the institute of economic and financial research, General Economic Confederation, drew up a plan for
industrialization of the province directed toward satisfying needs
of the national market and possibly some export; this included
a large meat-packing plant (frigorífico) for cattle, sheep, and
hogs; a dairy industry; expansion and modernization of traditional industries and establishing of new ones, such as shoe
factories, woolen mills, cereal processing plants; reactivation
of lumber mills; and the development of new mining and quarrying industries, in addition to those of salt, pegmatite and calcium.

See Enrique Stieben, La Pampa. Su historia, su geografía, su realidad y porvenir (Buenos Aires, 1946).

LA PLATA (known as Eva Perón, 1952-1955). Capital of Buenos
Aires province; located about thirty miles down the Río de la
Plata from Buenos Aires; population in 1970 over 400,000; important and beautiful administrative and port city; cosmopolitan
center of modern culture because of its academies, schools,
journals, university, and research institutions.

When the city of Buenos Aires was federalized in 1880,
a new provincial capital was needed; political leaders of Buenos
Aires province determined to create a new city that would rival
Buenos Aires for beauty, wealth, culture and power; under the
direction of Governor Dardo Rocha, the site overlooking the
port of Ensenada was selected, the name "La Plata" (probably
suggested by José Hernández, author of Martín Fierro) chosen,
plans drawn up, and the cornerstone laid and the city dedicated
in 1882; with settlers attracted by land and other incentives the
city grew at a miraculous pace; original (1882) population of
area, 7672, had increased to 27,643 by 1885, and to 90,000 by
1914; by 1884 the provincial government was established there
and municipal government was added in 1890; modern water and
sanitation systems installed; the port improved; the city beautified with parks, wide avenues, and the first public electric lighting system in Argentina (1888); in rapid succession cultural and
educational institutions took their places there: in 1884, the
cornerstone of the cathedral was laid and Dr. Francisco P.
Romero persuaded to establish and direct the Museo de La
Plata; followed by normal school, astronomy observatory, faculties of agricultural and veterinary sciences, a public library,
and, in 1905, the national University of La Plata, under Joaquín

V. González; increasing agropecuarian wealth of province, along with industrial development and port improvements, made this capital city an important financial center; while foreign workmen, business and banking representatives, scholars and artists, and consular and other representatives of foreign governments add to its cosmopolitan atmosphere.

LA PRENSA   see   PRENSA, LA

LA RIOJA (City and Province).   Andean province and capital with the same name; both taken from the Spanish birthplace of the city's founder, Juan Ramírez de Velasco.
          Location and Boundaries.   Province lies along the Argentine-Chilean border in the high Andes; bounded on the north by Catamarca, the east by Córdoba, and on the south by San Luis and southwest by San Juan province.   Area: 35,600 sq. mi.   Population (1970):   136,237, with density per square mile of 3.8 persons, lower than that of any of its neighbors.
          Cities.   Capital: La Rioja; population (1970): 35,431; located in central eastern area; hardly any other cities but a few population centers in the eastern area like Chilecito, Gobernador Gordillo, Patquia, Chepes, Cebollar and Chamical, most of them along railroad lines (see Communications below).
          Geography.   Mountainous, arid, for most part very high and sparsely populated; Andean cordillera and precordillera rise from high, semi-arid plains, known as llanos, some of them with altitudes of 4,000 meters (or nearly 2 1/2 miles); mountains rise as high as 5,565 meters (not quite 3 1/2 miles); in the southern part of this province the plains become almost a salt desert; valleys generally dry with rivers few and of little value; province possesses, however, greatest potential in nation for development by use of hydroelectric plants because of its almost inexhaustible subsoil water supply and the fertility of its soil when irrigated.
          Economy.   Agriculture possible only with irrigation; vineyards, established during 17th century, now constitute most important industry, with many wineries; second in importance to wines are olives, both cured and pressed into oil; with irrigation, agave (cactus varieties), cotton, dates, tobacco, and other crops could be produced; stock raising, especially cattle and horses, carried on in many areas; mining potential of La Rioja has always been believed to be great but successful exploitation of its mineral resources did not begin until fairly recent times; tourism is becoming more important in the province's economy.
          Communications.   Railroad from Serrezuela, Córdoba, has two lines going into La Rioja; the southern one passes through southeastern La Rioja by Chepes, and into San Juan province; the northern one goes, via Chamical, to Patquia, where it again divides into a short western branch to Chilecito, and a longer eastern one to the capital and then forks to Catamarca and Andalgalá (Catamarca).   Scarcity of rains and hardness of soil makes highways good for most parts of the prov-

ince; these are usually linked to the tourist hotels.

History. On May 20, 1591, Governor Juan Ramírez de Velasco founded the city of Todos los Santos de la Nueva Rioja in the land of the Diaguita Indians (q. v.), subject to the government of Tucumán, under the viceroy of Peru; after establishing the cabildo, distributing lands and Indians in encomienda, and checking the defenses of the new city, Governor Ramírez de Velasco turned it over, by prior arrangement, to the veteran Indian fighter and town founder Blas Ponce (q. v.); the new city began with 70 well-armed Spaniards, oxcarts, oxen, livestock, hundreds of war horses, and an abundance of supplies for defense and subsistence; in 1600, La Rioja ranked sixth among the seven largest cities in Tucumán and Río de la Plata, between Talavera de Esteco and Buenos Aires, numbering (1606) 62 vecinos, with about 6,000 peaceful Indians; several changes took place in the seventeenth century: repeated uprisings of the Calchaquí-Diaguita Indians (1638-1658) threatened to destroy all the Tucumán settlements (see Pedro Bohórquez); that danger overcome, the number of Indians available for labor declined very rapidly and riojanos found that survival depended on their working the irrigated farms alongside the Indians or on their own; in La Rioja, as in neighboring Catamarca, towns had no real role as there was little trade and a genuinely dominant rural class developed, unlike the situation elsewhere; early in the century La Rioja turned to the planting of vineyards and making of wines and brandies; during the eighteenth century, Indian population continued to decline and general population grew slowly; in 1783 La Rioja was attached to the new intendancy of Córdoba del Tucumán and the Marquis de Sobremonte (q. v.), designated as intendant; in 1785 he made a long report to Viceroy Loreto of the area under his jurisdiction; for La Rioja, he reported a total population of 9,887 of whom 2,287 were in the city, the rest scattered in areas of Arauco, Los Llanos, Guandacol and Famatina; about 1800 poorly trained, badly armed men available for military duty, only about eleven small tributary Indian villages left; the area produced corn, fruits, 1500 arrobas of wine and brandy, good cotton.

La Rioja supported the May Revolution and war of independence but soon came to feel that the interests of the Buenos Aires government differed greatly from those of the interior provinces and that the former was either uninterested in the welfare of the provinces or determined to dominate them; in the anarchy of 1820, La Rioja established itself as autonomous under Governor Diego Barrenechea, meaning that it was determined to set up its own government and laws but expected eventually to rejoin the national government when a truly federal government should be established; this process of withdrawing or revolting and then returning to cooperate lasted for several turbulent decades, even into modern times, with the federal government retaliating with interventions of the government or armed expeditions; for much of this time La Rioja was ruled by native-born (usually gaucho) caudillos, like Juan Facundo Quiroga, Tomás Brizuela, and Angel Vicente Peñaloza (El Chacho) (q. v.).

In the early 1820s the province hoped to bolster its declining economy by attracting European capital to exploit its mines at La Famatina and set up the legal and financial structure for it--Casa de Moneda, bank, chartered company--but this project failed (see Famatina; River Plate Mining Company); in 1826 La Rioja, led by Father Pedro Ignacio Castro Barros (q. v.) in a war against the enemies of the church and supported by the gauchos under Quiroga with banners "Religion or Death," opposed Rivadavia's ecclesiastical reforms; along with Córdoba, Santiago del Estero, and San Juan, La Rioja refused to recognize Rivadavia in 1827; in 1831, federalist Tomás Brizuela took over control of province; during the Rosas period, economic problems became so serious for La Rioja and its neighboring provinces that, in spite of agreement that Rosas should handle foreign affairs, they attempted individually to reestablish old commercial ties with Chile; disliking Rosas' foreign alliance and again resenting the preeminence of Buenos Aires in economic affairs, La Rioja refused to recognize Rosas' re-election in 1840 and became involved in uprising of the Coalition of the North against him; forced back into line by Rosas.

In 1854, after the fall of Rosas, the province accepted the constitution of 1853, and joined the confederation with Francisco Solano Gómez as first constitutional governor; La Rioja began slowly, but still turbulently, to move into the national stream; in 1858 the first printing press was brought into the province, under government sponsorship; La Patria, edited by Carmelo Valdés, was first periodical published; four years later, the print was melted down for bullets to fight off attack of montoneros; the national reorganization that united Buenos Aires to the other provinces under the presidency of Bartolomé Mitre (1862) brought the riojano gauchos out to fight to the death against what they considered to be a new form of Buenos Aires domination; eventually their leader (El Chacho) was killed and the movement suppressed; Sarmiento, from neighboring San Juan, was elected president (supported by La Rioja); in 1871 the Colegio Nacional was established, with 27 students, in the old Casa de Moneda building on site where later Colegio Nacional was built in 1906; most famous among its teachers was Joaquín V. González (q. v.) for whom the Colegio was named in 1926; finally, by mid-1880s La Rioja was linked to neighboring provinces by railroad; during the late decades of the 19th century and early 20th century, La Rioja still remained, however, out of the mainstream of national development; while other provinces were being inundated with immigrants, this province declined slightly in population as it ranked lowest in number and percentage of immigrants received and high in migration to Buenos Aires; with continued development of its wineries and cattle and horses, its increased agricultural and mining operations and its tourist industry, La Rioja by the early 1970s seemed to face a bright economic future; Argentina's twin objectives of industrialization and becoming self-sufficient in essential mineral products, especially important since World War II, make La Rioja's

mineral resources--copper, lead, wolfram, uranium, marble,
beryl, mica, etc.--vital to the national economy; modern technology seems to be bringing La Rioja's dream of exploiting its
special resources to reality at last.
       Its tradition of violence was, however, upheld by the
Tacuara terrorists (q.v.) who seized all public offices in the
capital in 1966, in an attempt to embarrass President Onganía;
the chief of police chased them out as delinquents and let them
escape into Chile.

LABOR. Spaniards faced unusual labor problems in the settlement
    of Argentine territory in the sixteenth century; except in a few
    western and northwestern areas they found almost no seden-
    tary, semi-civilized Indians with their own agricultural patterns
    and very few areas in which Spanish patterns and institutions
    could be effectively used; during the first two centuries much
    of their effort was spent in fashioning or adapting new tech-
    niques for survival; the life-style that emerged was based on
    cattle (q.v.); very little labor was required for this; agricul-
    ture existed primarily for subsistence of the small population
    and mining was almost non-existent; during the seventeenth and
    eighteenth centuries the Jesuit mission area in the northeast
    was an exception in that it maintained a labor-intensive econ-
    omy based on the use of the mission Indians; the rest of area
    had a subsistence economy, with some industry in the north-
    west and some agricultural exports to the mines in Bolivia; as
    the Indians in that area declined in numbers, black slaves
    were brought in (often smuggled) to take their place; as well as
    to serve as house servants and urban labor (see Blacks;
    Slavery); free labor was probably treated as well as its coun-
    terparts in Europe as it was always easy for any man of any
    color to escape to freedom on the pampas; during the closing
    decades of the eighteenth century, with the viceroyalty estab-
    lished, Buenos Aires opened to trade, fortunes easily made in
    the hide and tallow trade, and the population of Buenos Aires
    growing in size, sophistication, and wealth, new demands de-
    veloped for skilled and unskilled labor; guilds were established
    in Buenos Aires for silversmiths, shoemakers, hatmakers,
    etc., but problems developed: difficulties in getting enough
    supplies; controversies between criollos and Spaniards, white
    workers and those of other, or mixed races; and the fundamen-
    tal contradiction between new ideologies of individual freedom
    and the medieval labor guilds.
       With the independence came a thrust toward diversifying
    the economy and training free Argentines to take part in it;
    guilds lost prestige; slave trade was ended, slavery and forced
    labor abolished, and attempts to set up training programs for
    apprentices made; business houses and craftsmen were required
    to train a certain number of Argentine boys, instead of import-
    ing foreign skilled workmen; the programs had little success,
    partly because of resistance of foreigners who controlled the
    skilled labor; and partly because of controversy over the gov-
    ernment's role in regulating labor; in the early years of inde-

pendence the labor shortage became acute as thousands of men
and boys (especially blacks) were conscripted for the independence armies; after the 1820s the situation settled down for a
few decades, with gauchos (q. v.) handling the livestock industry, the basis of the economy; skilled craftsmen came from
Europe to open shops of all kinds, often training younger relatives in the trade; cities were not yet populous enough to demand labor in large quantities.

The encouragement of agriculture after the mid-century
brought hundreds of thousands of immigrant rural workers to
tend the grainfields, vineyards, orchards (qq. v.), etc.; fenced
estancias and fattening farms for beef replaced open grazing
fields and the gaucho labor disappeared before the end of the
nineteenth century, to be replaced by meat packing house employees, rural peons, tenant farmers, and the full parapher-
nalia of mechanical equipment and management organization;
some temporary migrant workers, like Italian golondrinas supplemented the regular labor force.

Most Argentine labor in the 1880s was foreign-born and
the first labor movements were inspired by foreign leaders
and ideologies; in the late 1880s members of a German club,
the Vorwärts, somewhat socialistic in principles, lent its club-
rooms to striking workers (not too many, but labor was hurt
by the financial crisis); organized mass meeting of over 3000
workers for celebration of May 1, 1890, designated as international labor day by Paris International in 1889; out of this
came the organization of the workers union and also the Socialist Party (q. v.; see also Juan B. Justo); the workers remained
largely international until after World War I; a recognition that
foreign leaders and agitators, some of them anarchists, had
been responsible for much of the labor unrest and violence resulting from hardships following financial crisis of 1890 resulted in first laws against foreigners, Law of Residence and Law
of Social Defense (qq. v.); there were a few gains, the labor
law of 1904, written by J. V. González was proposed and in
1905 a part of it, limiting work on Sunday, was passed largely
due to Socialist support; in 1907 a law regulating labor of wom-
en and children was passed; labor unrest began to mount, however, as the oligarchical governments refused to grant legislation protecting workers equal to that already accepted in most
Western countries; meanwhile the labor force had become
largely and self-consciously Argentine, by birth and citizenship
or as a result of new nationalist fervor; workers resented the
fact that neither they themselves nor their role as organized
labor was properly recognized in political, social, or economic
terms; after the electoral reform of 1912 had brought Hipólito
Yrigoyen into presidency with Radicals in power, labor hoped
for a change; Yrigoyen sent several proposals to Congress including projects for arbitration in labor disputes, minimum
wages, maximum working hours, and made some gains for labor, such as greater freedom of action for unions, beginning
of retirement funds, etc., but they were so far below expecta-
tions that, in the troubled inflationary years following World

War I, Argentine labor turned, for the first time, to use of
widespread strikes; these triggered the "Tragic Week" (q. v.)
in January 1919 that resulted in many unnecessary deaths
among both the workers and the police before it was violently
suppressed.

Tensions increased during the next twenty-five
years; in 1930 the Confederación General del Trabajo
(q. v.) was formed; rural workers, more poorly paid than
urban, poured into the coastal cities to live in abject poverty; world depression in the 1930s took its toll; Catholic
left wing attempted to help labor under Monseñor Miguel
de Andrea; finally, after the GOU (q. v.) takeover of the
government in 1943, President Ramírez determined to
crush the labor movement so that it could no longer constitute the foreign-led, socialist, communist threat that he
and his supporters believed it to be; unions and their
treasuries were taken over by the government and their
leaders sent to distant concentration camps; but the situation worsened, with multiple strikes breaking out and massive arrests ineffective; in October 1943, Juan Domingo
Perón (q. v.), one of the government leaders, suggested a
different labor approach; to win labor's political support
rather than its continued opposition; a department of labor
was created (later made into a ministry of labor) and Perón
was placed in charge of it; he won over most of the leaders of the CGT and, within two years, won more gains for
labor than it had received during the previous decades;
they also touched all kinds of labor, urban skilled and unskilled, rural workers (the most poorly paid of all) and
government workers, who were placed under protection of
civil service for the first time; labor responded by forming
one of Perón's most important political power bases; after
his election to the presidency in 1946, his wife Eva María
Duarte de Perón (q. v.) became responsible for matters relating to labor and welfare; for the first time laborers of
all kinds felt that they were a part of the Argentine nation
and recognized as such.

In the diversification of the economy since World
War II, emphasis has been placed on training Argentine
workers and business managers for the new demands of industry, power plants, mining, etc., to make the nation independent of foreign expertise as quickly as possible; foreigners coming in to work are apt to be at lower levels
such as migrant workers who cross the boundaries from
neighboring countries (legally and illegally) to work in new
agricultural developments for which they have special experience.

See Hobart A. Spalding, Jr., editor, Historia de la
clase trabajadora argentina, 1890-1912 (Buenos Aires,
1970); José Panettieri, Los trabajadores (Buenos Aires,
1967); Robert J. Alexander, Labor Relations in Argentina,
Brazil, and Chile (New York, 1962).

LAFINUR, JUAN CRISOSTOMO (1797-1824).   Journalist; philosophy
    professor; poet; patriot fighter.
        Born in La Carolina, San Luis; entered Colegio Mon-
serrat in Córdoba where he knew Juan Cruz Varela; graduated
as master of arts but his increasingly liberal and unorthodox
ideas cut short his academic career; fought for three years in
the Army of the North; acquired great admiration for both
Manuel Belgrano and José de San Martín; moving to Buenos
Aires in 1817, Lafinur entered enthusiastically into the new
artistic and intellectual circles there, writing for El Censor,
El Curioso, and El Americano; taught philosophy in the Colegio
del Sur, founded by the directorate; deeply influenced by such
writers as Condillac, Locke, Destutt de Tracy, and Newton,
he shocked the classroom by appearing in civilian garb
rather than the conventional gown and also, according to
Ricardo Levene, was the one who most clearly marked the
transition from scholasticism to the new era by seculariz-
ing the fundamentals of his philosophical teaching; opposition from the faculty and the Church caused him to leave
Buenos Aires for Mendoza where he joined with José Lorenzo Güiraldes and others interested in popular culture;
became active in various activities of Lancastrian society;
served as director of Colegio de la Santísima Trinidad
(1822); as editor of El verdadero amigo del país, expressed his own and his friend's advanced ideas and also published important documents from the liberating expedition to Peru; expelled, with Güiraldes, for their philosophic and economic ideas, Lafinur joined other Argentine exiles in Chile; died there from fall off horse; one
of his best known poems celebrated San Martín's victory
at Maipú.

LAFTA see LATIN AMERICAN FREE TRADE ASSOCIATION

LAGOS, HILARIO (1806-1860).   Federalist military commander for
    Rosas; after Caseros, led revolt of those in Buenos Aires who
    wanted to join Urquiza's confederation.
        Born in Buenos Aires, Hilario Lagos joined the Hussars
of that city in 1824 and spent almost all the rest of his life in
military career; during the 1830s he fought in the various campaigns against the Indians of southern Buenos Aires province;
in 1840 he was incorporated into Oribe's Rosas army to fight
against the unitarist invasions led by General Juan Lavalle; he
distinguished himself equally by his courage in battle and his
chivalry following the victories at Quebracho Herrado and
Famaillá; after returning to Buenos Aires, he was assigned,
with a division, to Urquiza's army in Entre Ríos; remained
there until latter pronounced against Rosas; unwilling to turn
against Rosas, Col. Lagos obtained a permit from Urquiza to
return safely to Buenos Aires; at Caseros he led a cavalry
division in Rosas' army; was one of last to flee from the battlefield; with Rosas gone, Lagos supported Urquiza and his

idea of a truly federal national organization of the provinces; called an "authentic federalist," Colonel Lagos was one of leaders of group called "chupandinos" (q. v.) consisting of Buenos Aires citizens who wanted to join its sister provinces in the confederation; in late 1852, when Buenos Aires province had refused to accept the agreement of San Nicolás and to cooperate in the constituent congress meeting in Santa Fe, a conflict broke out between the provincials of Buenos Aires and the porteños of the city; assuming the leadership of this movement, Lagos attempted to use this force to bring Buenos Aires into the confederation; by a coup d'état, he forced the resignation of Valentín Alsina as governor (for both political and personal reasons) and then presented the movement to Urquiza, inviting him to use these forces to bring Buenos Aires province into the confederation with the other thirteen provinces; Urquiza had hoped to use diplomacy and negotiation rather than force and was greatly embarrassed by this situation; the city of Buenos Aires was besieged, however, by Lagos for seven months; then the besieging forces melted away as the city, using its strongest defensive weapon--money--bought off Commodore John Halsted Coe, the American mercenary seaman who had commanded Urquiza's blockading naval forces in the Río de la Plata, and possibly some of the land besiegers; many of Lagos' soldiers had resented the federalization of Buenos Aires; the congress demanded that peace be negotiated and British and American diplomats offered their services in arranging this; some amnesty was given, but many of the most radical leaders were exiled; Colonel Lagos was exiled, stripped of his military rank, and deprived of his property; he went to Santa Fe; in 1857, the Buenos Aires government offered to restore his rank and all his military perquisites if he would aid in fighting the increasing Indian depredations in the south; he refused, preferring to share the fate of his fellow exiles; later he returned to his native city and died there in 1860.

LAISSEZ-FAIRE (from the French, meaning--very loosely--let them do as they please). Economic doctrine of 18th century advocating free trade, with the demands of the market place setting not only prices to be paid but ultimately also the wages paid for products sold; eagerly supported by Argentine leaders from creole patriots of the closing decade of the viceroyalty to the depression of the 1930s; Mariano Moreno upheld it in his Representación de los hacendados in 1809; Rivadavia attempted to create a new independent nation in the 1820s on a laissez-faire international economy; when Rosas briefly attempted in 1835 to establish tariffs to stimulate internal trade and domestic industry, his estanciero supporters forced him to abandon such efforts; he returned, instead, to free trade, establishing the firm foundations of a policy of exchanging Argentine raw products for European manufactured and mining ones that lasted for nearly a century; during this same period Argentina's trade partners had also moved more completely toward a laissez-faire economic policy; after the national reorganization in 1853-62, the government used subsidies and incentives to stimulate the economy and growth of population but this was not considered as any real modification of laissez-faire; after 1880s, authorities found themselves able to move even closer to absolutely free trade; in 1890, however, England was forced to move slightly away from it when the government stepped in to prevent the Baring crisis from becoming a national economic disaster; during the next few decades Argentina was undergoing so many social changes due to its massive immigration that economic and political pressures were developing; as these coincided with Argentina's "golden age" of incredible wealth and expansion, however, the economic policy remained unchanged; in the 1930s the depression brought an end to laissez-faire policy in both Europe and more slowly, to Argentina; President Perón, in his first address to the nation (1946) declared that his administration would make the state the primary agent for administering the nation's economy and economic policy; Perón did not find all the desired answers; nor have his successors, some of whom have tried to restore a measure of laissez-faire and others who have tried various measures of government control; nor, for that matter, have the governments of other capitalistic industrialist nations or those of Marxist nations; Argentina still seeks and is making its way toward an economic system that will allow the modern industrial nation to grow as effectively as it did under laissez-faire, at the same time creating a satisfactory life style for the great majority of its people.

LAMADRID (sometimes La Madrid), GENERAL GREGORIO ARAOZ DE (1795-1857).   Courageous and colorful military commander who played important role in war for independence and civil wars that followed.
        Born in Tucumán; joined provincial militia, commissioned as lieutenant in 1811; took part in most of fighting in north--in Battles of Vilcapugio, Ayohuma, Venta y Media, and Sipe Sipe, in which he saved wounded General Francisco Fernández de la Cruz (q. v.) from capture by the royalists; served as aide to San Martín in Tucumán; by 1818 he had become colonel; transferring from north to Buenos Aires, he fought in forces of directorate against those of mesopotamian caudillos Estanislao López, of Santa Fe, and Francisco de Ramírez, of Entre Ríos, in early 1820s; in 1825, Lamadrid was sent to northern provinces to recruit forces for the approaching war with Brazil; instead, as strong supporter of unitarist cause, he plunged into civil war in Tucumán, overthrowing Governor Javier López and generally arousing fear in northern provinces that Rivadavia (unitarist leader) intended to impose centralist power by force; Lamadrid continued his action in civil wars but was defeated and seriously wounded by Quiroga's forces at Tala, and fled into exile in Bolivia after next defeat at Rincón; returning to Buenos Aires in 1828, he joined unitarist forces of General Paz, fought at Tablada, San Roque, Oncativo, and, after General Paz was unexpectedly captured by royalists, Lamadrid, as his second in command, took over responsibility for

government of Córdoba and command of army; retiring to Tucumán, he was defeated at Ciudadela by Quiroga in 1831; Lamadrid went into exile in Bolivia again, remaining there for seven years; returning to Argentina, Lamadrid became one of leading generals under Rosas' federalist regime; sent back to his native Tucumán (early in 1840) to suppress rising revolt against Rosas, Lamadrid decided to join the opposition instead and was made commander-in-chief of forces of provinces that formed Coalición del Norte shortly after Lamadrid's defeat of Aldao at Pampa Redonda; in October, a revolt against government of Córdoba, as Lamadrid was approaching it, gave him command of that province's troops as well; joined Lavalle's forces to make united attempt to overthrow Rosas but latter, having made peace with France, was now able to send entire federalist army against Lamadrid and Lavalle; both armies, traveling together but under separate commands left Córdoba, retiring toward Tucumán where they hoped to gain reinforcements and supplies; on the way, Lavalle proposed daring stratagem that offered possibility of success: he would remain behind to keep federalists in province of La Rioja immobilized until Lamadrid could raise a new army in Tucumán; the desperate gamble failed and Lavalle was forced to flee to Tucumán in June 1841 and on to Jujuy where he was killed; Lamadrid opened campaign in San Juan, under his second-in-command General Mariano Acha but this failed (see Mariano Acha); Lamadrid, with most of the coalition forces, threaded his way between two federalist armies into Mendoza where the armies of Pacheco, Aldao, and Benavídez converged to defeat him September 24, 1841, at Rodeo del Medio; survivors, including Lamadrid, fled to Chile, where the Tucumán general received aid from Domingo Faustino Sarmiento, himself in exile from federalists; Lamadrid went on to Bolivia and then to Montevideo; joined forces against Rosas and distinguished himself as commander of right wing of Urquiza's army in defeating Rosas at battle of Caseros (1852).   General Gregorio Aráoz de Lamadrid died in Buenos Aires five years later.

LAMAS, ANDRES (1817-1891).   Journalist; historian; diplomat.

Born in Montevideo, Uruguay, while it was still considered politically a part of the Río de la Plata, Lamas' life and career reveal a dual loyalty, first in fulfilling important political and diplomatic responsibilities to his native country and then, when he felt that he was no longer so badly needed, retiring to devote himself, in Buenos Aires, to historical studies of the entire Río de la Plata area.

Lamas early associated himself with Argentine unitarist exiles in Montevideo whose political convictions he shared and with some of whom, including Bartolomé Mitre, D. F. Sarmiento, and J. M. Gutiérrez, he formed close lifetime friendships; he began his writing career as editor of El Sastre (1836) and contributed to similar journals; when all of these were suppressed by Manuel Oribe, he left Montevideo and joined Fructuoso Rivera's staff, returning victoriously with him in 1838; began

writing again, starting El Iniciador with Miguel Cané and contributing to such unitarist publications as El Nacional, El Comercio del Plata (edited by F. Varela) and J. Marmol's El
Conservador; meanwhile he had entered public life, heading
various ministries, including those of government, foreign relations, and Hacienda (treasury or finance); he consistently collaborated with Argentine unitarists against Rosas (who backed
Oribe's return) and enthusiastically supported Juan Lavalle's
campaign (1839) into Argentina; acted as chief political administrator in Montevideo during the "Great War" (q. v.) (1843-
1851) and siege by Rosas' forces; met with considerable success on diplomatic mission to Brazil seeking support against
Rosas' aggression; Lamas also found time for intellectual interests, establishing the historical and geographical institute of
Montevideo (1843) and beginning his own collection of manuscripts and documents for a comprehensive study of the history
and geography of the Río de la Plata.

After 1857 Lamas spent most of his time in Buenos
Aires, devoting himself to research and writing; one of his
greatest contributions to Argentine historiography was his publication, in Buenos Aires, 1873-1875, for the first time and
with a long introduction and notes, of the Historia de la conquista de la provincia del Paraguay, Río de la Plata y Tucumán
by the early eighteenth century historian, Pedro Lozano (q. v.);
among others of his works are a collection of previously unpublished documents, Buenos Aires, 1869; two books about the
discoverer of the Río de la Plata, Juan Díaz de Solís, 1871
and 1882; and an historical biography of the great unitarist
leader Bernardino Rivadavia, 1882; Lamas was engaged in a
study of the origins of the independence movement in America
when he died.

The Uruguayan historical and geographical institute began publication in Montevideo, 1922, of selections of Lamas'
writings and in 1944 the Argentine Academy of History published a bibliography of them, compiled by Guillermo Furlong.

LANCASTRIAN SYSTEM OF EDUCATION. System devised by English Quaker educator Joseph Lancaster and first used in his
school in Chelsea (London) in attempt to teach large numbers
of children more rapidly by having them help each other; system spread rapidly to the newly independent American nations,
eager to promote public instruction.

In Buenos Aires, the Lancastrian method was known and
discussed in 1816-17, but it really began to gain acceptance in
1818 with the arrival of Diego (James) Thompson, representative of the British Lancastrian Society as well as the Bible Society; in 1819, the cabildo authorized Thompson to establish a
model Lancastrian school and begin the training of teachers in
that method; by 1821 eight schools were operating in the Buenos Aires area, including one for girls, founded by José Ca-
talá and directed by an Englishwoman, Mrs. Hyne; a Lancastrian society was also founded, to keep the work going and to
promote related cultural activities; the Sociedad de Beneficencia

adopted the use of the Lancastrian method in their schools for
girls; when department of primary (or elementary) education
was established at University of Buenos Aires, the system of
"mutual teaching," or Lancastrian way, became compulsory;
the movement spread rapidly to the provinces (in fact, first
Argentine Lancastrian school had been established in Concepción del Uruguay (Entre Ríos) by Chilean Solano García); it
was introduced into Santa Fe under Pascual Echagüe; to Entre
Ríos, with a normal school to train teachers, at Paraná, 1822;
to Salta, under influence of Juan Antonio Alvarez de Arenales;
to Tucumán in time of Lamadrid; and to Mendoza (1822) where
it had one of its greatest successes under leadership of Dr.
Juan Crisóstomo Lafinur (q. v.).

In Buenos Aires, Rivadavia brought Spanish scholar
Pedro Baladia to coordinate schools but his methods were unpopular and he established his own private school, the Argentine Gymnasium; José Andrés García arrived in 1828, sent by
the London Lancastrian Society, and opened La Escuela Infantil en Buenos Aires (primary school); in that same year Pedro
de Angelis founded his Escuela Lancasteriana; in the early
years both government and the Catholic Church had encouraged
and supported the Lancastrian movement (in spite of Thompson's efforts in behalf of Protestants) because of their mutual
interest in education; but as Rivadavia's ecclesiastical reforms
began to attract opposition from the church and conservatives,
Lancastrian schools reflected the political losses of the liberals and declined in almost direct proportion to increase of
Catholic power; in Mendoza (see Sociedad de Lancaster) they
continued until 1883; although their impact was made throughout the nation in less than two decades, the widespread adoption of the Lancastrian system is still recognized as having
given the needed impetus to the new educational system.

LANDHOLDING, LAND SYSTEM.   Landholding in Argentina from the
conquest to World War II has been characterized by huge landed
estates, with the great landowners providing civic, political,
cultural, and economic leadership.

During Spanish period, all lands were considered to belong to crown by right of conquest; royal officials given authority to grant lands to the church (a very large landowner in colonial Argentina), to the towns--including rural lands extending
almost, if not entirely to those held by the neighboring towns--
and to individual conquistadors and settlers--each to receive
a townsite and a rural agricultural area, varying in size and
desirability according to his military rank or services performed; throughout the colonial period, the cabildo, or town
government, managed the lands reserved for common use (the
ejido) and continued to make grants from the public lands to
reward military or civic services; as land was the only available wealth, many landholders eagerly increased the size of
their estates by requesting additional grants, by eventually
claiming ownership of the lands on which their encomienda Indians lived (in the north where sedentary Indians had been

found) or where the cattle herds, to which they had been given
rights, grazed (as in Buenos Aires province), or by purchase;
many wealthy landowners took advantage of the legal provision
enabling them to convert their landholdings into a mayorazgo,
or entailed estate to be passed intact, indivisible and inalienable,
to one heir; large to begin with, these could always be increased
in size and established the pattern for great Argentin haciendas
and estancias; in a time and place where land was cheap, people
few, food free for the taking (beef from wild cattle), and
hacendados ready to take responsibility for defense and civil
and social needs, the system worked effectively.

Changes came with independence; in 1810, the patriot
government authorized the sale of public lands to supply needed
government funds; congress voted to give land grants to anyone
who would take and hold them along the Indian frontier or in
remote areas; in 1829 Viamonte increased this practice in
hopes of maintaining the southern Indian frontier in Buenos
Aires; after Rosas' successful pacification of that area, widespread use was made of such grants to reward the officers and
men who had fought with him, with Rosas himself receiving the
first and largest grant, the island of Choele Choel; meanwhile,
in the 1820s Bernardino Rivadavia had undertaken to reform the
land distribution policy completely; interested in establishing
agriculture and attracting farmers, as well as needing to use
the public lands as a financial resource, he revived the old
Roman lease system, known as emphyteusis (q.v.); ownership
of public land remained with government to be used as collat-
eral for loans, etc.; long term leases were given with rental
based on type of usage, agriculture being favored.

During the Rosas period the government of Buenos
Aires disposed of large amounts of public lands through the
grants to veterans, conversion of most land held in emphyteusis to land held by title, and by outright sales; proceeds of
latter divided between municipalities, provincial government,
and amortization of the public debt; two factors, in addition to
the government's need for money, favored this policy: the generally held belief that land was more productive in private ownership than under government control, and Rosas' use of land
as a powerful political weapon--giving grants to those whom he
wanted to favor and confiscating the lands of his opponents; on
a political basis, Rosas' estanciero supporters considered his
land policy completely successful: in a relatively brief period
of time he had fulfilled all the requirements of the federal economic program, by virtually eliminating emphyteusis, extending
southern frontier of province, and assuring an abundance of
grazing land at cheap prices; although Rosas was responsible
only for lands in province of Buenos Aires, policies similar to
his were followed in the other provinces, even though most of
these were not as completely given over to the hide, tallow,
and dried, salted beef trade as was Buenos Aires; so that
throughout the area great landed estates increased in number,
in size, and in the political power exercised by their owners.

After Rosas' departure, 1852, both Buenos Aires (au-

tonomous and separate 1852-1862) and the Confederation turned
their attention to land policies; in Buenos Aires some measures
were taken in revenge: confiscation of Rosas' lands and those
of his followers; invalidation of titles to land confiscated by
Rosas, etc., and return of lands confiscated in 1840 to original owners; a Topographical Department was created and ordered to survey all lands and to review all titles to lands
granted since 1821 as a basis for new policy; Urquiza, with
millions of acres of available land in the Confederation, offered a prize of 50 gold ounces for best study proposed for its
use; also commissioned Martin de Moussy (q.v.) to make geographical study in French to advertise Argentina's land opportunities to attract European farmers as immigrants; Description
geographique et statistique de la Confederation Argentine--3 v.
and atlas published in Paris, 1860-1864.

In the reorganized Argentine Republic a national land
policy took shape, culminating in the Land Law of 1876; public
land was to be granted for public purposes, such as colonization projects by individuals or companies, or for building railroads; only public lands in territories, opened up by "conquest
of the desert" in Patagonia, and military campaigns in the
Chaco, belonged to the federal government; these were disposed of in the 1880s by grants rewarding veterans, and land
auctions, of which the largest was that in which President
Juárez Celman opened offices in European capitals in 1889 to
sell 150,000,000 acres of land in Formosa, Chaco, and Patagonia in a vain attempt to prevent the financial crisis of 1890
that forced his government out of office; almost all of the public lands were sold in large tracts as this was financially more
feasible for the government and most of the grants given to
veterans were eventually bought out by large landowners better
able to develop them; even grants to colonizing entrepreneurs
often ended up as individual estates as colonists failed to appear; in fact, immigrations made little impact on the Argentine pattern of landholding by a few great estancieros; by the
1880s when farming immigrants began to come in large numbers, most good land was already privately held, largely by
Argentines, and most immigrants to rural areas came for economic betterment but did not count on owning their own land;
from the 1890s to the depression of the 1930s, Argentina
moved to an enviable position by extensive production of raw
products at low cost for the world market; mechanization, cooperatives, all modern techniques, and patterns were used on
estancias held by individual owners or by family companies;
in 1912 the electoral reform laws had broken the political power of the landholders, by introducing the secret ballot; in 1914,
however, 78.3% of all Argentine land was still held in farms
of 2500 acres or more; in the Radical governments that followed, some further land distribution was attempted, especially by Yrigoyen, but this largely concerned peripheral lands;
meanwhile land remained almost the only investment opportunity and it had risen so high in price that only the wealthy
could afford it; almost all classes agreed that Argentina needed

wider distribution of land ownership, especially of farm lands, for proper development of social and economic democracy but the old pattern was hard to break, especially as long as it continued to be so successful economically.

Perón attempted land reform but land was no longer profitable because of his economic measures; actually, his descamisados seemed satisfied by the improvement in their social, economic, and political position and there was no great demand for "agrarian reform" such as there was in Chile and in some other Latin American countries; meanwhile diversification of the economy was changing the pattern; the yerba mate industry in Misiones, the vineyards in Cuyo, the fruit orchards of Río Negro, for example, were more often worked by small farm owners than tenant farmers on large estancias; at the same time, industrialization, mixed companies (private-public) for mining and power projects offered new investment opportunities; the social status of the criollo landowner faded as other values became more important; in the mid-1970s, as Argentina's economic pattern has become more diversified and social democracy has made progress, the pattern of land ownership is becoming more like that of other Western industrialized nations.

See Miguel A. Cárcano, Evolución histórica del régimen de la tierra pública, 1810-1916 (Buenos Aires, 1925); and James R. Scobie, Revolution on the Pampas; A Social History of Argentine Wheat, 1860-1910 (Austin, Texas, 1964).

LANUSSE, ALEJANDRO AGUSTIN (1918-   ). Commander-in-chief of Argentine army; president of the Argentine Republic 1971-1973.

Born in Buenos Aires of French Basque parents, early entered military career and became interested in politics; imprisoned in south for four years (1951-1955) for his participation in the unsuccessful revolt against Perón in 1951; restored to rank in 1955, he served as major in command of the Granaderos a Caballo General San Martín (1955-57), special envoy to the Vatican (1956), colonel of cavalry and sub-director of Escuela Superior de Guerra (1957), and military attaché to Italy (1958); in 1962 he became a brigadier general; four years later he played active role in military coup removing President Arturo Illia from office (1966); appointed commander-in-chief of the army by President Onganía in 1968; during the next two years mounting terrorism and violence in Argentina--culminating in the kidnaping and murder of former President Pedro Aramburu--brought the overthrow of Onganía's government by a junta formed by the commanders-in-chief of the Army (Lanusse), Navy, and Air Force; the junta placed Roberto M. Levingston (q. v.) in as president but when he attempted to remove Lanusse as commander-in-chief of the army, he was himself ousted and Lanusse became president March 26, 1971.

Lanusse's accession to power was considered a victory for the traditionalist army group that wanted the army to return to a "moderator" role in politics rather than that of full authority; Lanusse also recognized the popular disenchantment with military rule and set himself to bringing political parties back into action to prepare for constitutional elections; these were held in March, 1973, with Héctor Cámpora (q. v.), the Peronist candidate, elected as the new president; Lanusse's term of office was marked by continued economic crisis, with inflation rampant, exports declining, the peso devalued, and even meat production in short supply; these problems were, for the most part, inherited from previous administrations and continued into the next ones.

After 1973, Lanusse retired and devoted himself to managing family properties.

LAPACHO. Common name for South American Bignoniácea; a tree with very dark leaves, lovely rosy or cream blossoms and very hard wood that grows in the subtropical forests of Misiones, Salta, Jujuy and Tucumán; indigenous, it was called by the Guaraní Tavib, which became Tajiba or Tajibo in the Jesuit lexicons; the word seems to mean sinewy tree, and many varieties of it are very hard; useful for furniture, carpentry, etc.; widely used in colonial period for building carretas; both bark and leaves contain tannin and have traditionally been used for medications, as well as in dyeing processes and for tanning leather; one variety, the lapacho negro is primarily used as ornamental plant, especially in Formosa and Resistencia; its lovely pink flowers appear before the leaves, unlike the other varieties; various varieties of the lapacho have been taken abroad and are now grown in subtropical areas like California and Florida, in the United States, where they are known as tabebuias, their Brazilian name.

LAPRIDA, FRANCISCO NARCISO DE (1786-1829). Signer of Declaration of Independence; governor of San Juan; member of constituent congress of 1825-1826.

Born in San Juan de la Frontera; both parents Spanish; educated at San Carlos, Buenos Aires, and at University of San Felipe in Santiago, Chile; returned to San Juan in 1811; served in various municipal and provincial positions (governor 1819-1820); became close friend of José de San Martín and contributed funds and efforts toward building army of the Andes; elected to represent his province at congress of Tucumán, was acting as president on July 9, 1816 when declaration of independence was signed; became active supporter of Bernardino Rivadavia's centralist constitution as member of constituent congress of 1825-1826; after Rivadavia's departure from government, Laprida returned to San Juan; fearing the caudillo Juan Facundo Quiroga, Laprida fled to Mendoza, joined defending force there against Quiroga; was surprised by Aldao near Pilar and killed while attempting to escape.

LARREA, JUAN (1782-1847). Spanish merchant; member of first patriot junta.

Born in Catalonia, Larrea came to Buenos Aires in the

early 1800s and established himself as a merchant; fought as
captain in battalion of Volunteers of Catalonia against the British invasions; became early leader for independence, belonging
at first to the so-called "republican party" dominated by Martín de Alzaga and other Spaniards of the area who controlled
the cabildo; some creoles, including Mariano Moreno and Julián de Leyva also belonged to this group that was largely responsible for ousting viceroy Sobremonte in 1807; Larrea was
active in the May Revolution and, by popular demand, became
a member of the first patriot junta; as a strong supporter of
Moreno (q. v.) and continued advocate of latter's ideas even after his departure, Larrea was a victim of the revolt of May
5-6, 1811, removed from office, his property confiscated, and
exiled to San Juan; with the establishment of the Second Triumvirate he returned to Buenos Aires; became one of the most
active members of the famous constitutional assembly of 1813
(see listing Assembly of Year XIII); when the first directorate
was created under Posadas, in 1814, Larrea became minister
of the treasury and was largely responsible for the creation of
the naval squadron that, under command of Admiral Guillermo
Brown, forced the royalists out of the Río de la Plata waters;
for political reasons he was again forced into poverty and exile in 1815; years later, he once more became a merchant in
Buenos Aires; was appointed Argentine consul general in
France; died in Buenos Aires 1847.

LARREA, RAMON (1789-1836).   Fighter in war for independence;
   one of first officers of San Martín's granaderos a caballo.
      Brother of Juan Larrea; born in Barcelona, Spain; came
to Buenos Aires at early age; fought against British; when San
Martín formed his regiment of granaderos a caballo in 1812,
Ramón Larrea was incorporated into it as an officer; after the
mutiny of Fontezuelas that deposed Alvear as director, Larrea,
as a supporter of the latter, was exiled; made his home in
Uruguay; married Manuela Sáenz Valiente there; back in Buenos
Aires in 1825 he was one of those who financed Lavalleja and
his famous band of thirty-three Uruguayan patriots on their
venture to expel Brazilians from their country; was restored to
his rank in the army by Alvear and later supported Lavalle but
was forced to emigrate again to Uruguay, suffering the loss of
most of his property; retired from public life; lived at his estancia in Paysandú where he died in 1836.

LARROQUE, ALBERTO (1819-1881).   French jurisconsult and educator; rector of Colegio del Uruguay, 1854-1864.
      Graduate in jurisprudence at University of Paris, Al-
berto Larroque came to Buenos Aires in 1841; a liberal politically, exponent of eclectic idealism, strongly influenced by
Krausism and other European intellectual currents of the time,
he quickly acquired prestige both professionally and among intellectuals; in 1854 he accepted Urquiza's invitation to become
rector of the Colegio del Uruguay (founded five years earlier
at Concepción del Uruguay, Entre Ríos); from 1854 to 1864, he

made it one of most outstanding educational institutions in the
confederation and placed his mark strongly on Argentine secondary education; influenced group of students who would be important leaders in future, including Julio Argentino Roca, Eduardo Wilde, Onésimo Leguizamón, and Victorino de la Plaza
(later president of republic, 1914-1916); in 1864 Larroque returned to Buenos Aires to resume his law practice; remained
deeply interested in Argentine political affairs (he had become
citizen under Rosas' government) but refused the various official positions offered him; in 1871 he took part in the founding
of the Centro Literario and also served on the commission to
fight the yellow fever epidemic in Buenos Aires and Corrientes;
in 1881 he agreed to serve on the National Council of Education, but died shortly afterward in Buenos Aires from a cerebral hemorrhage.

LA SERNA, JOSE DE (1770-1831). Spanish general in command of
royalist troops invading northwest Argentina just as San Martín
began his famous crossing of the Andes; last Spanish viceroy in
South America.
        Born in Jeréz de la Frontera, Spain; entered royal ar-
tillery corps in 1782; for next three decades fought in Spanish
armies against England and France, at siege of Ceuta in Africa, and against Napoleon's forces at Valencia and in second
siege of Zaragoza where he was taken prisoner (1809); making
his escape in 1812 he eventually returned to Spain; assigned to
duty in Peru, viceroy Pezuela placed him in command (1816)
of the royalist armies in Upper Peru (Bolivia) with orders to
take advantage of patriot confusion and weakness and invade Argentina at once; La Serna immediately opened action against
Jujuy and Salta, occupying Tarija, Jujuy, and Salta (1817); after finding himself practically besieged in the cities and unable
to advance further because of guerrilla resistance led by Martín Güemes, La Serna withdrew into Bolivia, remaining in field
headquarters at Tupiza for the next two years; depressed and
discouraged by his bad luck and loss of professional prestige,
he was considering resigning or requesting reassignment when
a combination of circumstances--loss of armed forces' confidence in Pezuela and political repercussions of Riego's liberal
revolt in Cádiz reflected in Peruvian royalist army (with La
Serna looked on as leader of liberals)--suddenly placed him in
political and military power as new viceroy of Peru and commander-in-chief of all royalist forces (1821); with San Martín
already entrenched in Peru and strong Peruvian independence
movement under way, La Serna invited San Martín to a series
of conferences at Punchauca, May-June 1821; both leaders explored possibilities for compromise--always based on Peruvian
independence--but no acceptable formula could be found; La
Serna withdrew his forces into the sierras and San Martín
eventually left Peru after his interview with Bolívar at Guayaquil in July 1822 in which he urged Venezuelan liberator to
bring his armies into Peru for a combined final, victorious
push against royalists; La Serna's defeat by these forces at

Junín and final defeat, his own capture, and surrender at Ayacucho December 9, 1824, effectively ended Spain's empire in
South America--by ironic coincidence La Serna had been made
Conde de los Andes (Count of the Andes) by royal government
on that same day; La Serna returned to Spain in 1825; retired
from public life; died in Cádiz in 1831.

LAS HERAS, JUAN (GUALBERTO) GREGORIO DE (1780-1866). Independence hero--called "right arm" of General San Martín;
governor of Buenos Aires province 1824-1826.
      Born in Buenos Aires of Spanish father, Argentine
mother; educated at Colegio de San Carlos; entered business
career that required him to travel extensively in interior provinces and to Chile and Peru; as officer of militia, fought in defense of Buenos Aires against British invasions of 1806, 1807;
in Córdoba at time of May Revolution, was appointed captain
of provincial militia there; then organized corps of Patricios
of which he became sergeant major; sent by Buenos Aires government in command of Argentine auxiliary forces, recruited
in Córdoba and Mendoza, to aid Chile maintain its independence in face of new royalist threats; fought under General Juan
Mackenna in several engagements but returned to Mendoza
when rift developed between José Miguel Carrera and Bernardo
O'Higgins; when Las Heras told the newly-arrived governor of
Mendoza, José de San Martín, that Chilean independence was
being destroyed by dissension among its own leaders, San Martín sent him back to aid Chileans; Las Heras arrived in time
to protect retreat from Rancagua to Mendoza (1814) where he
was placed in charge of 11th regiment, created by Buenos
Aires government to defend Mendoza's western frontier after
fall of Chile to royalists; his auxiliary force became corps of
Army of the Andes being organized by San Martín.
      When Army of Andes started across the cordillera in
late January 1817 to begin its continental fight for independence
from Spain, Las Heras commanded column of 800 men that
took direct route through Uspallata pass, convoying all the artillery and other equipment and supplies that could not accompany main body of army through Los Patos pass (to the north);
his force successfully fought engagements against royalist
groups posted in pass at Los Potrerillos, Guardia Vieja and
arrived on Chilean side to take possession of Santa Rosa on
February 8, according to schedule; fought in battle of Chacabuco (February 12, 1817) as part of General Miguel Estanislao Soler's division; after this victory, Las Heras was given
command of army to complete liberation of southern Chile; after victories at Curapaligüe and Gavilán, he occupied Concepción; then joined General Bernardo O'Higgins in unsuccessful
attempt to take fortified Talcahuano, now reinforced by new
royalist units from Peru; eventually O'Higgins withdrew forces
toward capital, Santiago, followed by royalists; at Cancha Rayada, where royalists routed patriot army by surprise attack,
Las Heras saved the day by preserving his entire force of
over 3000 men almost intact, thus making it possible for San

Martín to confront the royalists less than three weeks later at
Maipú; in this great patriot victory (April 5, 1818), Las Heras
commanded the right wing, confronting for the fourth time the
royalist general José Ordóñez who was taken prisoner; spent
next two years in collaborating with San Martín in preparation
of Liberating Army of Peru, with Las Heras as chief of general staff under San Martín; expedition to liberate Peru left
Valparaíso, Chile, August 20, 1820; on September 8, Las Heras had honor of leading first liberating forces onto Peruvian
soil to camp at Pisco near bay of Parracas; continued active
in liberation of Peru, becoming commander-in-chief of armed
forces when San Martín accepted political leadership as Supreme Protector of Peru; December 7, 1822 some months after San Martín's departure from Peru following his Guayaquil
interview with Simón Bolívar in July, Las Heras submitted his
own resignation from the army and returned to Buenos Aires;
on August 8, 1823, he was appointed minister plenipotentiary
by Governor Manuel Rodríguez of Buenos Aires to negotiate
with Spanish authorities in Upper Peru (Bolivia) but was prevented from carrying out this mission by Olañeta's revolt
against viceroy that confused situation there; on April 2, 1824,
Las Heras succeeded Rodríguez as governor of Buenos Aires
province, with responsibility for foreign affairs of all provinces, by agreement.

His two years as governor were marked by important
events in the national organization of Argentina as well as in
its international affairs; in many respects, his term represents
a continuation of reforms begun by minister Bernardino Rivadavia under Governor Rodríguez--in fact, Las Heras asked
Rivadavia to continue as his minister of government, but latter
refused as he had planned a trip to Europe--and a prelude or
preparation for Rivadavia's return as president in 1826; Las
Heras appointed Manuel José García as minister of government,
and General Francisco Fernández de la Cruz as minister of
war and navy; important events of his term included: placing
of Baring Brothers Loan July 7, 1824; calling of national constituent congress that held its first meeting December 16,
1824; ending of war of independence at Ayacucho December 9,
1824; given national executive power by congress January 23,
1825, he attempted to open negotiations with Bolívar for joint
action against Brazil if it should become necessary, but nothing resulted from this; signing of first treaty with Spain and
on February 2, 1825, Las Heras and his ministers signed
treaty of amity, commerce, and navigation with England; on
April 19, Uruguayan leader Juan Antonio Lavalleja attempted to
force issue of Argentine support of Uruguay by invading his
native province with 32 companions, known as the "Famous
Thirty-three"; in October, congress, after having provided for
defense of southern Indian frontier and port of Bahía Blanca under command of Juan Manuel Rosas, and having established an
army of observation under General Rodríguez, incorporated the
eastern province (Uruguay) into Argentina as it had requested;
Brazil immediately declared war in December; Las Heras

requested congress to provide for national organization in this
emergency and when law had been passed, resigned early in
1826, leaving way open for Rivadavia to assume presidency
February 6, 1826; as most experienced and distinguished general in the nation, many (probably including Las Heras himself) expected him to be given command of forces against Brazil, but Rivadavia passed him over--possibly for political reasons as many unitarists were suspicious of his federalist lean-
ings as shown in his willingness to allow Bolivia (formerly
part of Buenos Aires viceroyalty) to form independent nation
under Sucre, and by other actions--in favor of Carlos María
de Alvear, minister of war; Las Heras went to Chile where he
accepted a commission as general of division in Chilean army;
remained there, honored by both Chile and Peru, until his
death in 1866; his wife was a Chilean, Carmen Larraín; buried in Chile, his remains were repatriated in 1906, to lie
alongside those of José de San Martín in cathedral in Buenos
Aires.

LATIFUNDIO   see   ESTANCIA; LANDHOLDING

LATIN AMERICAN FREE TRADE ASSOCIATION (LAFTA). Argen-
     tina a charter member and President Arturo Frondizi one of
     major supporters of this regional organization drawn up in the
     treaty of Montevideo (1960) and ratified (1961) by Argentina,
     Brazil, Chile, Colombia, Ecuador, Mexico, Peru, and Uru-
     guay; later joined by Bolivia, Paraguay, and Venezuela; its
     purpose was to stimulate trade among themselves by lowering
     tariff barriers, integrating economic policies, and presenting
     a common front against European Common Market and Free
     Trade Associates; there were some suggestions that this eco-
     nomic association might also stimulate some closer political
     bonds.
          Progress toward economic integration proceeded so
     slowly that in 1969 LAFTA postponed the date for attainment
     of free trade among the members from 1973 to 1980; little
     evidence in early years of progress toward any political inte-
     gration.
          See Edward S. Milenky, The Politics of Regional
     Organization in Latin America: The Latin American Free
     Trade Association (New York, 1973); and Edward G. Cale,
     Latin American Free Trade Association: Progress, Prob-
     lems, Prospects (Washington, D.C., Office of External
     Research, U.S. Department of State, 1969); and Victor L.
     Urquidi, Free Trade and Economic Integration in Latin
     America (Berkeley, University of California Press,
     1962).

LAUTARO LODGE (Logia Lautaro), 1812-1820. Secret society
     founded by three Argentine-born Spanish officers--José de San
     Martín, Carlos María de Alvear, and José Matías Zapiola--
     who had returned to their native land to help fight for its in-

dependence; lodge named after heroic Araucanian Indian leader who had defended Chile against Spanish conquistadors in sixteenth century; modeled on Masonic lodges with which they had had contact in Europe and similar in purpose to the society for independence formed by Francisco de Miranda in London in 1797--although evidence indicates complete autonomy of Buenos Aires lodge, many historians still believe that relationships may have existed with one or both of the above; purpose of Lautaro Lodge was to provide core of ideological, political, military leadership to direct successful winning of independence and to guide political organization of new nation; only leaders of proved patriotism and liberal ideas were elected into the membership; after its first meeting October 8, 1812, Lautaro Lodge quickly assumed role of secret super-government, controlling all military and political appointments and policies; in 1814-1815, Alvear was able to use it to further his own political ambitions in the directorate but, after his defeat, the Lautaro Lodge again backed San Martín and his new continental strategy for independence; proved valuable support to Supreme Director Juan Manuel Pueyrredón 1816-1817 in latter's efforts to equip San Martín's Army of the Andes in the face of provincial revolts and other problems nearer Buenos Aires; Lautaro Lodge was dissolved in 1820; served as prototype of other secret military lodges formed in moments of emergency during nineteenth century, such as Belgrano's unsuccessful attempt to bring discipline back into the army with such a secret society in 1820--the unitarist lodge formed to bring Juan Lavalle to power that acted as decisive directing force bridging gap between Rivadavia's resignation and Lavalle's takeover (1827-28); and those of 1852--formed of 34 members in Buenos Aires to combat "Urquiza as same as Rosas" and the military lodge formed in 1890, that met in home of José Félix Uriburu, and was dissolved after it had prepared armed revolution that overthrew President Miguel Juárez Celman.

LAVALLE, JUAN GALO (1797-1841). General; military hero of war for independence and war with Brazil; anti-federalist revolutionary leader.

Born in Buenos Aires, belonging to aristocratic porteño family; became one of San Martín's early members of the Mounted Grenadiers; distinguished himself throughout the Chilean and Peruvian campaigns under San Martín; fought bravely under General Alvear in war against Brazil; unitarists looking for military leader to restore them to power after Rivadavia's fall and election of Manuel Dorrego as governor (1828) enlisted his support, as first porteño general returning home with his forces from Brazil; Lavalle, believing that he was leading a revolution to restore what independence had been fought for, and backed by an army that resented Dorrego's peace with Brazil as a betrayal of their victorious fighting, moved on Buenos Aires, then met Dorrego and Rosas at Navarro, November 9, 1828, routing their army totally; Rosas escaped, disguised, to join Estanislao López's forces in Santa Fe and return to fight

later; Dorrego, less fortunate, took refuge with a friendly
military unit, that turned him over to Lavalle; seeking advice
as to what to do with Dorrego, Lavalle meanwhile became provisional governor of Buenos Aires by a popular (controversial)
vote; accepted hard advice of some unitarists to effect that
Dorrego's death would end federalism and bring peace (although
many of his wiser advisors counseled that he be exiled, instead); Lavalle ordered Dorrego's execution, without trial; issued his famous statement that history must be the judge of
the wisdom of this decision (see Manuel Dorrego); conditions in
Buenos Aires deteriorated; federalists continued their opposition and unitarist support weakened as financial situation approached chaos; Lavalle tended to become dictatorial--lacked
both political talents and experience; arrival of General San
Martín in Buenos Aires roadstead (February 1829) after nearly
six years of self-imposed exile gave Lavalle hope; visited the
general and urged him to save his country once more by taking over the government; San Martín (also visited by federalist leaders--most of whom had, like Lavalle, served in his
Army of the Andes) saw the situation more clearly; declaring
that only a bloodbath could result from the present situation
before peace would be established and that he was not the man
to bare his sword against his own soldiers, he returned to
Europe; Lavalle had to fight against the united forces of Rosas
and López; hoped to join Paz and his Cordoban forces, but the
two generals could not work together; after his second in command, the Prussian Colonel Frederick Rauch, had been defeated and killed at Vizcacheras, Lavalle was decisively defeated
April 26, 1829, at Puente de Márquez, about twenty miles outside Buenos Aires; Lavalle realized his situation untenable and,
always a patriot as well as a porteño, he approached Rosas
(as a fellow porteño), instead of López, from Santa Fe, for an
agreement to work out a peaceful settlement; June 24, they
signed the pact of Cañuelas (q.v.) to restore peace and civil
government; elections held a month later (July 26) marked by
violence and fraud; Rosas threatened to renew fighting and
Lavalle, true to his pact, disavowed results; finally on August
24 Rosas and Lavalle signed new pact naming Juan José Viamonte provisional governor with extraordinary powers; both
Rosas and Lavalle withdrew from politics; Lavalle's situation
in Buenos Aires got worse rapidly; harassed by both sides,
and seeing the growing propaganda toward making Dorrego's
execution an act of high treason (so declared by all the provinces except Salta and Tucumán), Lavalle asked for his pass-
port and went into exile in Montevideo.

    Ten years later, he was urged to come out of exile to
save his country--this time from the dictator Rosas; unitarists
in Montevideo wanted him to lead their forces, in alliance with
the French, who were blockading the port of Buenos Aires,
and Fructuoso Rivera, the Uruguayan leader whose rival, Manuel Oribe, was supported by Rosas; Lavalle demurred, unwilling to join a foreign foe against his own nation, or to be
drawn again by unitarists into partisan politics; finally, con-

vinced that he was acting as a national liberator against a tyrant, he left Uruguay in August 1839 (at the head of a large
force) for what turned out to be more than two years of almost unrelieved disasters, ending in his own death; Rivera became president of Uruguay and could offer little aid while his
rival General Oribe became Rosas' able chief commander; the
Argentine Commission (anti-Rosas exiles) could not deliver the
aid promised; revolt in Buenos Aires province was crushed at
battle of Chascomús; with Berón Astrada's Corrientes revolt
destroyed by Echagüe and French aid decreasing, Lavalle's
situation became precarious; he moved to Entre Ríos from Martín García island and then to Corrientes but, after some victories, decided that he must get his army across the Paraná
river while French ships were still available (French talking
peace with Rosas); invaded Buenos Aires province but withdrew
to Santa Fe, rather than attack the capital at that time; on
October 20, 1840, the Arana-Mackau treaty was signed and
French withdrew; Rosas attempted to get Lavalle's acquiescence
to this and to agree to peace but he refused; Oribe sent with
10,000 men against Lavalle's depleted forces; at Quebracho
Herrado in Córdoba November 28, 1840, Oribe totally defeated
Lavalle; almost without moral and material support, Lavalle
made one last try: to move farther west--to join with the Coalition of the North and, by dividing his forces, to win a series
of small victories, to regroup and regain the initiative; instead,
his forces encountered a series of defeats; Lavalle himself was
defeated at Famaillá in Tucumán, September 19, 1841, by Oribe;
attempting to flee north to Bolivia with a few loyal companions,
Lavalle was killed (possibly by accident) in a private home in
Jujuy when a passing federalist group fired shots at it; when
his loyal followers learned of plans to desecrate the remains,
they secretly formed an honor guard to escort Lavalle's body
out of the country to Bolivia, where they deposited his remains in the cathedral of Potosí until they could be returned to
Buenos Aires in 1858 and buried in La Recoleta cemetery.

LAVALLEJA, JUAN ANTONIO (1784-1853). Uruguayan military officer and patriot leader; sought to use Argentine aid in his country's struggle for independence; became involved in Argentine
civil wars as general for Rosas.

Born in Minas, Maldonado (Uruguay); engaged in rural
activities on family ranch until entering military career in
1811; fought against Portuguese, being captured several times;
joined Artigas in his fight against Buenos Aires directorate
government; contributed to victory over latter at Guayabos January 10, 1818, but was later defeated and captured; in Portuguese takeover of Uruguay and its conversion into Cisplatine
province of the empire, Lavalleja was taken to Rio de Janeiro
as prisoner for three years; eventually freed, he made his way
to Buenos Aires where, early in 1825, while working as manager of saladero at Barracas, he learned of the victory of Ayacucho and determined to make another effort to liberate his
own country from Spanish power; Governor Las Heras seemed

reluctant to offer Argentine aid needed, so Lavalleja, in effort
to force issue, April 19, 1825, led band of Uruguayan patriots,
known as the "Famous Thirty-three" from their number,
across Paraná river into Uruguay where they quickly recruited
a force of several thousand to fight the Brazilians; in August
the province of Banda Oriental del Uruguay was organized,
with Lavalleja as governor, annexation to Brazil declared null
and void, and union with "other Argentine province" voted;
while Las Heras government hesitated, Lavalleja inflicted decisive defeat on Brazilians (who resented Emperor Pedro I's
venture into Uruguay anyway) at Sarandí, October 2; three
weeks later, October 24, 1825, the national constituent congress in Buenos Aires incorporated the new province into the
Argentine nation and recognized its delegates; in war with Brazil that followed, Lavalleja's Uruguayan cavalry made up vanguard of General Carlos María de Alvear's allied army and
contributed to victories won; appointment of Lavalleja as commander-in-chief of army to succeed Alvear caused division of
General Juan Lavalle to revolt, with lasting effects in civil
wars that followed; in negotiations following war with Brazil,
Great Britain (fearing Argentine control of estuary) intervened
in favor of Uruguayan complete independence--which had always
been Lavalleja's ultimate goal.

        Both Plata countries were torn by civil wars for next
two decades and rival factions in each sought aid from groups
in other country; Lavalleja, and later Oribe, were leaders of
Uruguayan Blancos, while the other great Uruguayan leader,
Fructuoso Rivera, led the Colorados; generally Rosas supported
the Blancos and used their exiled military officers, including
Lavalleja, in Argentina against his own unitarist enemies, Argentine exiles in Montevideo, on the other hand, supported Rivera and Colorados in return for aid against Rosas; Lavalleja
invaded Uruguay from Entre Ríos with Echagüe but was defeated at Cagancha December 19, 1839; later he took part in siege
of Montevideo 1843-1851; became member of triumvirate government of Uruguay in 1853 shortly before his death in Montevideo.

LAVARDEN, JUAN MANUEL DE (1727-1777).   Lawyer and public
    official.

        Born in La Plata, Charcas (today Sucre, Bolivia), of
French origin; graduated as doctor in theology and then as
lawyer at Chuquisaca; moved to Buenos Aires and in 1750 married María Josefa Aldao y Rendón; they became parents of
famous poet Manuel José de Lavardén, with whom later historians often confused the father because of similarity of names
and lack of records; Dr. Juan Manuel de Lavardén practiced
law throughout his life, but found time to serve as member of
Buenos Aires cabildo, military judge (auditor de guerra); consulted about law curriculum for new royal academy of San
Carlos to be established in Buenos Aires, he is remembered
for his emphasis on study of modern Spanish, rather than ancient Roman law; died in Buenos Aires.

LAVARDEN, MANUEL JOSE DE (1754-1809?). Poet, economist, estanciero.

Born in Buenos Aires, son of Juan Manuel de Lavardén; studied in Buenos Aires, Chuquisaca, and in Spain at Granada, Toledo, and Madrid; returned to Buenos Aires to take prominent role in intellectual, literary, and economic life during closing years of viceroyalty; regarded primarily as economist and poet, he joined Manuel Belgrano, Juan Hipólito Vieytes, and others in promoting economic progress of Río de la Plata area; as poet, attracted attention by his first poem Sátira, based on story about viceroy Marqués de Loreto; captured attention of entire porteño community by presentation of his drama Siripo, at theater Ranchería during carnival week 1789; said to have been Argentina's first drama, it takes its theme from legend, immortalized by Ruy Díaz de Guzmán, about tragic love of Siripo, Timbu chieftain, for Lucía Miranda, resulting in her death along with her conquistador husband, and Indian destruction of Cabot's Tower at Sancti Spiritu; presented in authentic costumes, the play apparently electrified the community with its reminder of traditional criollo and Indian culture and history and its expressed idea that both Indian and conquistador blood and culture had gone into making of Argentine history and culture and should be combined to make new race; Ricardo Rojas calls it first fruits although premature and bitter in taste, of Argentinism.

In 1792, after managing other estates in area, Lavardén received grant of estancia Sauce near Colonia del Sacramento (now in Uruguay) from viceroy Melo of Portugal; immediately began improvement of stockbreeding; brought over early merino sheep from Spain (1794) to increase production of wool in viceroyalty; established saladero, with contract to supply royal navy with dried beef; at beginning of nineteenth century he wrote memoir to government, urging development of port of Ensenada (downriver from Buenos Aires) as better port to compete with Montevideo; published his greatest poem, Oda al Paraná (Ode to Paraná River) in first issue of first periodical published in Buenos Aires, El Telégrafo Mercantil April 1, 1801; continued active in Buenos Aires public life and at estancia until 1808, then disappeared; believed to have died the following year; confusion of stories about his death has largely been replaced by legend that he was fatally gored on shipboard by bull that he was bringing back from Spain.

Whatever his role as progressive estanciero or as father of Argentine poetry and drama, or innovator of Argentina literature in his day, Lavardén, in his effective use of authentic Argentine material, is important as link between conquest and early historiography and romanticism of Echeverría's period and thence to its revival and transformation into twentieth century nationalism; Lavardén has been studied by Juan María Gutiérrez, the Uruguayan José Enrique Rodó, Ricardo Rojas, and by Mariano G. Bosch in his Manuel de Lavardén, poeta (Buenos Aires, 1944); through these and others much of confusion about his life--such as correct spelling of name, confu-

sion of his career with that of his father, loss of original Siripo manuscript, date, place, and circumstances of his death,
etc. -- has been clarified.

LAW. In general, Argentine law has a Roman basis; throughout
Spanish period the area was governed under the Laws of the
Indies, a combination of Roman, Spanish, and Indian laws that
Spain developed to meet the new situations in its American
colonies; compiled into one comprehensive code in 1680, these
laws were subjected within a few decades to numerous and important alterations by the Bourbon kings to suit the rapid economic development and scientific enlightenment of the eighteenth century; Charles III attempted to have a new codification
made but could not complete it; meanwhile, in Argentina by
the middle of the eighteenth century, the study of Spanish law
was being emphasized in contrast to the Roman and Canon
law previously taught in the universities; shortly after that Argentine youths who went to study in Chuquisaca, like Mariano
Moreno and other patriot leaders, were fully trained in laws of
the Indies and Spanish law, as well as classic laws; after independence, each succeeding congress in early days, and in later
constituent congresses, devoted itself to creating basic law for
the new Argentine nation (see Constitution).

See Ricardo Levene's writings on Argentina's legal history, especially massive compendium that he edited, Historia
del derecho argentino (11 v., Buenos Aires, 1945-58).

LAW OF RESIDENCE (1902). Congressional legislation giving the
executive power to act against certain classes of undesirable
foreigners. By the close of the nineteenth century, many Argentine leaders were seriously troubled by the changes being
brought to their country by the masses of foreign immigrants;
the increased activity of anarchists and labor leaders and some
initial anti-Semitic rumors regarding the plans of the Jewish
Colonization Association (q. v.), that later proved to be un-
founded, increased the tension; although there were all kinds of
demands for political reform, which the oligarchy was unwilling
to grant, the immediate danger came from violence in the
streets, led by labor agitators, most of them foreign; in this
emergency, President Roca revived a project that Miguel Cané
had presented to the Senate in 1899; using this as a basis, with
the cooperation of cabinet minister Joaquín V. González, a Ley
de Residencia (Law of Residence or Foreigners' Residence Law)
was drafted; passed by Congress in 1902, it authorized the executive to deport any foreigner guilty of criminal action or acts
against common law as well as those who threatened the national security or disturbed the public order; a state of siege was
imposed and Roca moved firmly to quell such disturbances and
to reestablish order; the law continued to be strictly enforced,
with numerous labor leaders imprisoned or deported; occasional abuses in its application gave it a bad reputation among immigrants (see Alluvial Era; Immigrants; Law of Social Defense).

LAW OF SOCIAL DEFENSE. Law passed in 1910, following the general strike of 1909 that included violence and the assassination that same year of the chief of police of Buenos Aires; strengthened the Law of Residence (q.v.), empowering government to deport undesirable immigrant leaders at once and take other measures necessary to preserve order.

LEAGUE OF NATIONS. As soon as the League of Nations was established following World War I, Yrigoyen had Argentina in its membership; terminated its active participation shortly afterward when the League refused to adopt certain principles that Argentina considered essential, including the admission of all states, even former belligerents against allies, and equality of treatment for all sovereign nations; in 1932, with the radicals no longer in power and the government attempting to strengthen its ties with Europe, Argentina again became active, with Carlos Saavedra Lamas (q.v.) playing a distinguished role and serving as president of the League of Nations assembly in 1936; Argentina felt very much at home in the League, not only because of its close relationships with various European countries, but also because it was able to play a desired international role without fearing U.S. domination as latter never became a member.

LEAGUE OF THE INTERIOR. On July 5, 1830, League of Interior was formed under leadership of Córdoban General José María Paz, unitarist determined to organize nation under constitution; signed August 31, by Córdoba, Mendoza, San Luis, San Juan, Salta, Tucumán, Santiago del Estero, Catamarca, and La Rioja, opposed by the Littoral League (coastal provinces), Estanislao López of Santa Fe, and Quiroga; Paz was accidentally surprised, thrown from his horse and taken prisoner; a federal government established in Córdoba ended the League of the Interior that had, in effect, represented the old Spanish colonial government of Tucumán against the coastal one of Buenos Aires.

LE BRETON, TOMAS ALBERTO (1868-1959)   Jurisconsult; statesman, diplomat.
          Born in Buenos Aires; graduated (1891) in law and social sciences there; his special interest was in copyrights and patent law; sent to Europe on confidential mission regarding boundaries with Brazil (1892); represented Argentina at international meeting on industrial patents in Berlin (1904) and artistic and literary copyrights in Stockholm (1908); served as national deputy representing the federal capital (1914-1920); as ambassador to the United States (1919-1922), he protested vigorously against the high U.S. protective tariffs of 1921 that would adversely affect 16% of Argentina's total exports; returning to Buenos Aires he was acting foreign minister briefly, then senator; President Alvear appointed him minister of agriculture; from 1922 to 1925 Le Breton vigorously protected interests of the estancieros; meat business faced crisis during

British and American "meat war" but Le Breton aided Alvear
in bringing Argentina successfully through it by moving toward
government regulation of entire meat industry and construction
of a government refrigeration plant (frigorífico) in Buenos
Aires; he also encouraged agriculture, emphasizing better seed
selection and new techniques to improve yield of cereals; increased acreage planted in cotton; organized railway tours for
agricultural propaganda purposes; and promoted improved methods for making cheese and butter in dairy industry; although
Le Breton was popular and trusted by the estancieros, Yrigoyen's radical followers hated him as a representative of traditional, conservative policies.

In 1936, Le Breton served on the commission to draw
up commercial agreement with Great Britain; became member
of permanent court of arbitration at the Hague (1938) and then
ambassador to Great Britain (1938-1941); he was a frequent
contributor to periodicals and also wrote Comercio de carnes
(1922) and Patentes y marcas, among others; died in Buenos
Aires.

LECOR, CARLOS FEDERICO, VIZCONDE DE LATURA (1764-1836).
Portuguese general; governor of Montevideo 1817-1825.
Born in Faro; took active part in fighting against Napoleon in the peninsular war; in 1815 he was sent to Rio de Janeiro with division of royal volunteer troops; assigned to carry
out Brazil's occupation of the Banda Oriental (Uruguay) to prevent disorders coming from Artigas' troops in that area; in
spite of Director Juan Martín Pueyrredón's protest against
this proposed invasion of territory claimed as part of the
United Provinces, Lecor occupied Montevideo in 1817 and remained there as its governor until 1825; meanwhile he had supported Brazil's declaration of independence (1822); died in Rio
de Janeiro (see Montevideo).

LEGENDS OF THE CONQUEST. Two, at least, of the legends that
grew up in the earliest days of Spanish settlement and are included in Ruy Díaz de Guzmán's La Argentina, have historical
value in showing what was already considered to be historical
truth by the first criollo generations and they give special insights and sidelights to the Río de la Plata area at the time
when first settlements were being attempted.

The first legend, that of Lucía Miranda, dates from
the expedition of Sebastian Cabot (1527); Lucía, the wife of one
of the accompanying conquistadors, attracted the attention of
Siripo, an Indian chief near the fort erected at Sancti Spiritus;
his determination to win her affections ended in tragedy, the
deaths of Lucía, her Spanish husband, and Siripo, and was
said to bear some responsibility for the Indians' attack on
Cabot's Tower; more than two and a half centuries later, the
legend was presented by the poet Manuel José de Lavardén
(q. v.) in Buenos Aires' first drama, Siripo, and served to revive the criollo memories of their beginnings.

The second legend comes from the early days (1536) of

the first founding of Buenos Aires, by Pedro de Mendoza; a
Spanish woman, known as "La Maldonado," found herself unable to bear the hardships of the new town's starvation period
and fled to the countryside, hoping to find a better life with
the Indians; taking refuge in a cave, she faced a native "lioness" (puma) in difficult birth pains; assisted the puma in the
successful delivery of two cubs; thereafter La Maldonado
stayed with the animals and was regularly fed, along with the
cubs, by the hunting lioness; sometime later, neighboring Indians discovered her and one of the chieftains took her back to
his camp as his wife; when the Spaniard soldiers found her in
this situation, they captured her, tried her, and then tied her
to a tree in the forest to be killed by the wild animals that
hunted in that area; three days later the Spaniards returned to
give her bones a Christian burial; to their surprise, they found
the woman still secured to the tree, but untouched; at her feet
lay a lioness and two cubs, acting as guard; freed, she is
said to have lived a long life in the community; her chronicler,
Ruy Díaz Guzmán, claimed to have known her.

LEGION CIVICA ARGENTINA (Argentine Civic Legion).   Paramili-
tary organization, strongly nationalist, formed in May 1931
with President Uriburu's support; designed to serve as an
armed forces reserve, the members received military training
under supervision of regular army officers and also enjoyed
many special privileges; Uriburu declared it to be an apolitical
group dedicated to the national defense and maintenance of order; he hoped its original membership of 10,000 would quickly
expand to 70,000-100,000; liberal critics and journalists proclaimed it to be a copy of European fascist organizations, especially when a youth movement was added to it and the Legión
became sharply critical of all political parties, Uriburu was
accused of attempting to use the Legión to replace Argentina's
constitutional government with a corporatist model; Alvear's
manifesto of the "Junta del City" (q.v.) was to a certain extent a leftist attempt to oppose this strong move to the right;
President Justo, who succeeded Uriburu, attempted to gain the
support of the Legión for his more moderate course but when
Juan Bautista Molina (q.v.) returned from Germany in 1936 he
reorganized it along the lines of the Nazi party.

LEGUIZAMON, DELFIN (1843-1917).   Governor, political and civil
leader in Salta.
        Born in Salta, son of Juan Galo Leguizamón; studied in
Buenos Aires; returned home at age of 18 to spend the rest of
his life as public figure in Salta; immediately elected to the
legislature; served in Tribunal of Commerce, president of legislature, minister of government, and several times as governor (interim, 1869; 1871-1874, 1893-1896); fought in the Salteño contingent in Paraguayan war and as colonel against the
invasion of Felipe Varela, 1867; in 1870, as representative to
the national congress, he was influential in securing improvements of navigation of the Bermejo river and the extension of

the railroad to Salta and Jujuy, from Tucumán via Córdoba; in 1886 was again a national deputy; his terms as governor were considered very progressive; carried out extensive public works programs, opened public libraries, and established an experimental farm; from 1897 to 1903 he represented Salta in the national senate; his services to his native community were so highly regarded that Udaondo declares that he has been ranked second only to Martín Güemes as Salta's most distinguished citizen; died in Salta.

LEGUIZAMON, HONORIO (1849-1921).   Educator, journalist, physician.

Born in Concordia, Entre Ríos; attended Colegio Nacional de Concepción del Uruguay, then went to Buenos Aires, graduating from medical school in 1874; while still a student, had cared for victims of yellow fever and cholera epidemics in Buenos Aires; also began journalistic career during this period; writing for La Prensa; joined the navy as physician, sent to Asunción; continued interest he had already shown in his thesis on yerba mate; left navy, settled down in Concepción del Uruguay where he taught physical and natural sciences in both the normal school for girls and the colegio (of which he was also rector); moved to Buenos Aires and became director of normal school there; retired from secondary teaching in 1893 because of his health; accepted various medical posts; in 1916 became professor of Argentine history in the faculty of economic sciences; one of founders of Instituto Geográfico Argentino.

LEGUIZAMON, JUAN GALO (end of 18th century-1853).   Merchant and military officer.

Born in Salta; studied Latin, grammar and poetry in Franciscan academy; supported May Revolution with enthusiasm; fought in independence war in the North, taking part in the Battle of Salta, campaigning with the Army of the North; distinguished himself at Humahuaca, follower of Güemes after this; in 1822 he was promoted to colonel by governor-general, Gorriti; meanwhile he had developed a very lucrative business in Salta; after independence was won, he became active in federalist groups, but devoted most of his time to his business house which had become the most important one in northern Argentina; after the defeat of Rosas at Caseros, Urquiza invited him to a conference at his Palacio San José in Entre Ríos and showed him great honor; returning to Salta, he died July 9, 1853, just as the national constitution (under which Urquiza became first president) was being sworn in.

LEGUIZAMON, JUAN MARTIN (1833-1881).   Writer, legislator, archeologist, businessman; civic leader in Salta.

Son of Juan Galo Leguizamón (q.v.); educated in Córdoba and in Buenos Aires where he studied under Alberto Larroque; returned to Salta to take over the family business; he spent most of the rest of his life there in active civic, cultural, and political roles, and devoting himself to scientific studies and writing; in 1853 he began to study the fossils of Salta and the Northwest; is usually considered to have been first to study Calchaquí archeology; began collection of fine private library that he eventually donated to the city as the nucleus of a public library; maintained scientific correspondence with Francisco Javier Muñiz (q.v.); meanwhile he served several terms in the provisional legislature; served twice as interim governor of Salta and held numerous ministries and other positions in provincial government; in 1867 he led armed forces against invader Felipe Varela (q.v.) from Catamarca.

In 1876 he completed L'Homme Blanc ("The White Man") a critique of Darwin's theory of evolution; sent manuscript to Paris where it won awards and brought him a corresponding membership in the Société d'Anthropologie; also sent exhibits to Paris from his archeological findings at Incahuasi, Salta; he was a founding member of the Argentine Scientific Society and published works in its Anales, including Descripción del campo de Pucará (Salta) and Cartas sobre antigüedades americanas; he created and was first president of Salta's council of education; fostered establishment of teachers' college; planned organization of Museo Histórico Regional; founded the local Sociedad de Beneficencia; in 1880 he was elected to the national senate; died in Buenos Aires.

LEGUIZAMON, MARTINIANO (father) (1814-1881).   Military officer.
Born in Santa Fe province; entered military service in 1830; fought in civil wars and against Indians until 1841 when he resigned from the army and moved to Entre Ríos; joined Urquiza in battle of Laguna Limpia, 1846; saved life of General Juan Madariaga (q.v.) when he was taken prisoner; fought with Urquiza against Oribe in Uruguay and Rosas at Caseros; joined Hilarión Lagos (q.v.) in his unsuccessful attempt to bring Buenos Aires into the Confederation; made his way, wounded, back to Entre Ríos; again supported Urquiza at Cepeda and Pavón; was given various military assignments in Entre Ríos; fought to suppress both of López Jordán's revolts; in 1880, as reward of 50 years military service was given rank of lieutenant colonel in the national army; founder of the Leguizamón family in Entre Ríos (see entries on his sons, Drs. Martiniano and Onésimo Leguizamón).

LEGUIZAMON, MARTINIANO (son) (1858-1935).   Writer and historian; lawyer.
Born in Rosario de Tala, Entre Ríos, son of Colonel Martiniano Leguizamón; studied at Colegio de Concepción del Uruguay; graduated in law in 1885; throughout his career was primarily interested in studying and writing about Argentine folklore and history; determined to separate fact from legend, as in traditional tale of Lucía Miranda (see Legends of Conquest) and in more recent historical lore, the vindication of Justo José Urquiza, under whom his father had served so long; before he left the Colegio, he had written a poem in honor of

Mariano Moreno and shortly after he arrived in Buenos Aires
(1880) he had begun journalistic work, writing for La Razón,
established by his brother Onésimo Leguizamón (q. v.); became
part of the intellectual and artistic life in the capital; in 1896
he published Recuerdos de la tierra, with introduction by J. V.
González, and ten years later a similar book on folkloric history appeared, entitled Alma nativa; in 1900 Montaraz, a historical sketch of the uprising of Entre Ríos against Artigas was
published.

Many of his greatest contributions lay in the field of
gaucho literature (q. v.); his gaucho comedy Calandria was a
sensation, marking a new departure for the Argentine theater;
he was among the first to recognize the significance of José
Fernández's Martín Fierro and to make scholarly studies of
gaucho language and idioms; his own writings were prolific and
his services in editing critical, annotated editions of other writings important; he has been called the patriarch of criollo literature and master of new generations of writers; among the
writers of gaucho and historical literature of the early twentieth century, few equaled his purity of literary style and meticulous scholarship.

LEGUIZAMON, ONESIMO (1837-1886).   Jurisconsult; statesman; pro-
    fessor; journalist.

    Born in Gualeguay, Entre Ríos, of parents closely re-
lated to Entre Ríos' caudillos Francisco Ramírez and Ricardo
López Jordán; studied at the Colegio Nacional del Uruguay; received one of two grants offered for study in Europe; returned
to Buenos Aires in 1860 and two years later received his doctor's degree in law from the University of Buenos Aires; was
given an interim cabinet appointment in Entre Ríos and then
elected to the provincial legislature (1864-1868); taught philosophy at the Colegio until 1870; disgusted by the assassination of
Urquiza, he moved back to Buenos Aires and became editor-in-
chief of La Prensa (1870-1873); meanwhile he taught international law at the University of Buenos Aires and served as national congressman from Entre Ríos; when Nicolás de Avellaneda became president (1874) he brought Leguizamón into his
cabinet as minister of justice, worship (culto), and public instruction; Leguizamón created normal schools (teachers colleges) for women; reformed the curricula of the national secondary schools (colegios); established a national commission for
the school system; regulated the functioning of the agricultural
schools, and made his detailed annual reports basic documents
in Argentine educational history; his efforts on behalf of the
Argentine public school system were so much talked about that
Sarmiento wrote him that he himself (always a sponsor of education) was beginning to be jealous; in 1877 Leguizamón resigned from his cabinet post and became a member of the Supreme Court (1877-1882); in 1882 he presided over the first
South American pedagogical congress, in Buenos Aires; during
one of his terms as congressman for Entre Ríos he became a
leading spokesman for Law 1420 providing free, compulsory,

and secular public instruction for Argentine children; in 1884
he was appointed federal interventor in Catamarca; he founded
and was still editing the newspaper La Razón at the time of his
death in Buenos Aires; Leguizamón was not only highly respected in Argentina but was also known abroad; had received
memberships in several international scientific societies in recognition of his intellectual achievements.

His writings--largely legal--include: Estudios sobre
Disraeli y Gladstone; Las leyes de la guerra internacional; La
cuestión de límites entre San Luis y Córdoba; and, with José
O. Machado, Instituto del código civil argentino.

LEIVA (or Leyva), JULIAN (1749-1818). Jurisconsult; public official; historical writer.

Born in Luján, son of one of founders of the Villa of
Luján; studied in Buenos Aires, then took his doctorate in law
at the University of San Felipe, Santiago de Chile, in 1783;
held legal post with audiencia of Charcas briefly, then returned
to Buenos Aires; involved the rest of his life with responsibilities with Audiencia and Cabildo in Buenos Aires, and as attorney for Luján; Leiva was also deeply interested in conserv-
ing and writing about early Argentine history, and collected one
of the richest libraries of his time for this purpose--including
the only manuscript copy found of Father Lozano's history and
a manuscript copy of La Argentina by Ruy Díaz de Guzmán,
which Leiva annotated; he placed his library at disposal of
Félix de Azara (q.v.) and worked closely with the latter on his
account of the conquest of the Río de la Plata and Paraguay;
his own historical writings commanded the respect of his con-
temporaries--Deán Funes asked him to criticize his historical
essay before publishing it and later Argentine historians cite
him as one of the first "modern" or "scientific" historians, in
contrast to earlier chroniclers; his very fine library was preserved for a time by his family and then given to the National
Archives.

Leiva faced a conflict of loyalties in the independence
movement; in 1808 he was one of the few creole (native) members of the Spanish republican group that dominated the Cabildo
of Buenos Aires and desired independence for Argentina, and
was a close friend of Mariano Moreno (q.v.); at the time of the
May Revolution he was serving as síndico procurador of the
cabildo and carried out faithfully his important responsibilities
for the calling of the cabildo abierto (open town meeting) and
its conduct; having been a royal official and said to have been
a close friend of viceroy Cisneros, however, he could not
bring himself to support wholly the revolution and ousting of
the viceroy; for the few remaining years of his life he lived for
the most part in retirement; in 1812 he was named president
of the tribunal of commerce; and other posts were offered him
but he refused them because of his poor health; died in San
Isidro, 1818.

LELOIR, Luis F. (1906-   ).   Biochemist; Nobel Prize winner in

medicine (1970).
    Born in Paris; naturalized Argentine citizen; graduated
from medical school in Buenos Aires in 1932 and spent next
ten years as research assistant to Dr. Bernardo A. Houssay
(q. v.); continued his research into the body's metabolic processes and became director of the research laboratories of Institute of Biochemical Research--Campomar Foundation; received considerable international recognition and in 1970 was
awarded the Nobel Prize in medicine for his discovery of role
of nucleotides in metabolism of hydrocarbons and in biosynthesis.

LENCINAS.   Family of colorful radical party leaders in Mendoza
    in early twentieth century; three of these are listed chronologi-
    cally below.
        Lencinas, José Néstor (1859-1920). Born in Mendoza;
    graduated in law from University of Córdoba; returned to Men-
    doza and became teacher of history in Colegio Nacional; be-
    came active in local politics as member of radical party; took
    over leadership of party around 1890 and began to offer effec-
    tive political competition to controlling liberals; led revolt of
    1905 against Mendoza government but radicals were forced out
    by national militia; in 1916 became national deputy and in 1917
    was made governor of Mendoza; ousted by federal intervention,
    he was immediately reelected; illness made his term brief and
    he had to face several strikes, along with other labor prob-
    lems following World War I; personal differences between the
    two radical leaders caused President Hipólito Yrigoyen to inter-
    vene in Mendoza's government; Lencinas was forced to resign
    (1920) and died the same year; Lencinas attracted passionate
    followers and equally powerful enemies; after his death his sons
    and followers made up the lencinista branch of the Unión Cívica
    Radical party.   See Dardo Olguín, Lencinas, el caudillo radi-
    cal.   Historia y mito (Mendoza, 1961).
        Lencinas, Carlos Washington (1889-1929).   Jurisconsult;
    political leader.   Born in Mendoza; graduated in law from Bue-
    nos Aires; under his father's (J. N. Lencinas') prestige and in-
    fluence, he became a popular radical leader in his own right
    with an especially large rural following; served as national
    deputy and twice was elected to the national senate; one of
    principal leaders of lencinista radicals; elected governor of
    Mendoza by direct popular vote in 1922; killed by political op-
    ponent in 1929; soon after his death friends and colleagues pub-
    lished a book based on important debate speeches that he had
    recently made in the Senate; it was entitled Lencinas e Yri-
    goyen.   Federalismo y unicato (1929).
        Lencinas, José Hipólito (1896-   ).   Lawyer, political
    leader, journalist.   Born in Mendoza; graduated from Buenos
    Aires law faculty (1919); held various government posts; served
    as national deputy 1922-1928; controversial political figure,
    centering his activities as director of the Unión Cívica Radi-
    cal lencinista in the Cuyo area; active in journalism both in
    Buenos Aires and in Mendoza; editor and publisher of La Pala-
    bra.

LERMA, HERNANDO DE (1550-1598).   Governor of Tucumán, 1580-
1584; founder of Salta.
    Born in Sevilla, licenciado Lerma was appointed gover-
nor of Tucumán in 1577 by Philip II; arrived in Santiago del
Estero (capital) to take up his duties in 1580; very quickly succeeded in making himself thoroughly disliked by arbitrary rule,
including abuses and outrages exceeding even those to which
the turbulent frontier province had become accustomed; one of
first acts was to seize and execute his predecessor Governor
Abreu--as the latter had done to Cabrera whom he had succeeded, and for the same reason: failure, because of Indian
hostilities, to carry out orders to establish towns in the valley
of the Calchaquí Indians to safeguard communications between
Santiago del Estero and Peru; Lerma also engaged in first
Church-State quarrel in Argentina when he challenged and succeeded in exiling dean Salcedo in dispute over right to confer
certain benefices; complaints from the people to the audiencia
brought arrest of Lerma (1584); while awaiting trial in Charcas
(seat of audiencia), he was taken back to Tucumán by the new
governor, Juan Ramírez de Velasco, tried there, convicted,
and would have been executed except that he appealed to the
Council of the Indies; back in Spain, he died in prison in Madrid (1598), still awaiting a decision on his case.
    Lerma's brief and unhappy administration had two con-
structive results: on April 16, 1582, he succeeded, where his
two predecessors had failed, in establishing a permanent settlement in the valley of the Calchaquí; he named the town Lerma
but in 1586 its name was changed to San Felipe de Salta; and
citizens of Tucumán had learned that, although under a centralized royal government they could not select their own rulers,
they did not have to remain under the authority of one whom
they found unsatisfactory.

LEVENE, RICARDO (1885-1959).   One of Argentina's most distinguished historians; professor of history for years in universities of La Plata and Buenos Aires.
    Born in Buenos Aires, educated in faculty of law and
social sciences there; for more than half a century thereafter
he put his mark on the study, teaching, and writing of the history of Argentina; throughout this period he taught in many
schools, including the Colegio Nacional Mariano Moreno, the
normal school Estanislao S. Zeballos, and the War Academy;
his academic career, however, centered around the University
of La Plata and in the faculty of law in that of Buenos Aires;
began his teaching career at La Plata in 1913; published his
Lecciones de historia argentina, a two-volume textbook that,
frequently revised in new editions, became widely used and
formed the basis for W. S. Robertson's one-volume translation,
A History of Argentina (Chapel Hill, N.C., 1937); in 1925,
largely as a result of Levene's initiative (and later named in
his honor), the Archivo Histórico de la Provincia de Buenos
Aires, was established at La Plata; Levene edited and contributed to the Historia de la Provincia de Buenos Aires y

formación de sus pueblos (2 v., 1940-1941); already he had
founded and edited the review Humanidades de La Plata (1920-
1923; 1926-1930); as dean of faculty of humanities, he established the humanities library and created chairs in Argentine
history and modern American history; and, as president of the
university, he added a faculty of medical sciences, the Argentine school of journalism; advanced the schools of astronomy
and of agronomy, and veterinary sciences.

Apart from those works growing out of his La Plata
work and relationships, Levene's early writings reflected his
interest in the independence period: Los orígenes de la democracia argentina (1911); the important Ensayo histórico
sobre la Revolución de Mayo y Mariano Moreno (2 v., 1920-
1921; 2nd edition 3 v., 1925, translated into French and Italian; 4th edition, 3 v., 1960); Investigaciones acerca de la historia económica del virreinato (2 v, 1927-1929; 2nd edition,
revised and expanded 1952); La anarquía de 1820 en Buenos
Aires desde el punto de vista institucional (1932; 2nd edition
revised and expanded 1954); Los primeros documentos de
nuestro federalismo político (1933); Las provincias del sud en
1811; consecuencias inmediatas de la Revolución de Mayo; and
La fundación de la universidad de Buenos Aires, su vida cultural en los comienzos y la publicación de los cursos de sus
profesores (1940); in the late 1930s, Levene's interest in comparing Argentine history with that of other American nations
had brought him attention from historians throughout the Western Hemisphere; in 1937 he was chairman of International Congress of History of the Americas that met in Buenos Aires;
became organizer and editor of the Historia de América project that produced about 14 monographs dealing with contemporary history of individual nations in an overall American setting (1940); during this same period he was hard at work directing the preparation of the monumental Historia de la nación Argentina published by the Academia Nacional de la Historia, 10 v. (Buenos Aires, 1936-1942; 2nd edition 1939-
1947; 3rd edition, 15 v. 1963).

In Buenos Aires Levene taught in the faculty of law
from which he had graduated; he became the leading historian
of Argentine law; founded the Instituto de Historia del Derecho
Argentino (that now bears his name) in the university there;
published his masterly Historia del derecho argentino (11 v.,
1945-1958); numerous shorter monographs or studies on legal
topics appeared, including La Academia de Jurisprudencia y
la vida de su fundador Manuel Antonio de Castro (1941); Introducción a la historia del derecho patrio (1942); Manual de
historia del derecho argentino (1952; 2nd edition 1957); and
Las indias no eran colonias (1952); other interesting works include Mitre y los estudios históricos en la Argentina (1944);
La realidad histórica y social vista por Juan Agustín García
(1945); El genio político de San Martín (1945); and El mundo
de las ideas y la revolución hispanoamericana de 1810 (Santiago de Chile, 1956).

Levene's honors include the Raza prize of the Academy

of History, Madrid; first prize in Argentine letters, 1920;
president of national academy of history and of the Historical
Archive of the Province of Buenos Aires; decorated by many
foreign governments, including those of Chile, Peru, Brazil,
and France; shortly after his death the Academia Nacional de
la Historia began publications of Levene's complete works, continuing in the 1970s; see biographical sketch of Levene by Ricardo Rodríguez Molas in first volume.

LEVILLIER, ROBERTO (1886-   ).   Historian; diplomat.
        Born in Buenos Aires; served in diplomatic posts in
Spain, Peru, Portugal, Poland and Czechoslovakia, and as ambassador to Mexico (1935-1937) and to Uruguay (1938-1941);
during this time he had become interested in historical research and published several books; after his retirement from
diplomatic service (1942) he devoted himself to historical writing; among his works are Nueva crónica de la conquista del
Tucumán (3 v. Buenos Aires, 1926, 1930, 1932); several other
works on Chile and Tucumán in the sixteenth century and colonial period; Biografía de los conquistadores de la Argentina
(Madrid, 1933); Don Francisco de Toledo, Supremo organizador
del Perú (3 v., Buenos Aires, 1935, 1939, 1942); in 1947,
1948, he published a two-volume defense of the naming of
Americas entitled América, la bien llamada and followed this
with publication of letters of Amerigo Vespucci; a later project
was that of preparing a series of more than 40 volumes of
16th-century historical documents relating to Argentina, Chile,
Peru, Bolivia, and Paraguay for the Argentine congressional
library.

LEVINGSTON, ROBERTO MARCELO (1920-   ).   Army intelligence
officer; president of Argentine Republic 1970-1971.
        Born in San Luis; entered Colegio Militar in 1938; after
a few years as cavalry officer he went into Army Intelligence
(1947) and most of subsequent assignments were in either military or civilian intelligence, assigned to Argentine State Intelligence Service 1956; while serving in Washington, D.C. (1970)
as Argentine military attaché to U.S. and representative on the
Inter-American Defense Council, Brigadier General Levingston
was selected by the military junta in Buenos Aires to succeed
ousted President Onganía; this choice seemed to have resulted,
at least partially, from the facts that he occupied a relatively
neutral position between the strongly nationalistic and liberal
factions of the divided military, had no personal following within it and had not previously been greatly involved politically;
taking office 18 June 1970 he immediately faced the aftermath
of the assassination of former president Aramburu, critical
economic problems such as rising living costs, financial losses,
especially in meatpacking industry, labor agitation, and pressure to carry out the junta's promises to restore constitutional
government; taking the initiative from the junta, he decided to
move toward economic solutions before political ones; appointed
economist Aldo Ferrer as his minister of economics and labor

and supported latter's program leading toward economic independence; his postponement of promised elections created popular unrest, widespread violence and protests increased and
when he attempted to remove Alejandro Lanusse (q. v.) as commander-in-chief of the army, the junta deposed him instead,
March 23, 1971, and Lanusse became president.

LEZICA, JUAN JOSE (1748-1811).   Merchant; chief alcalde of Buenos Aires at time of May Revolution.
     Born in Coripata, Yungas (Bolivia); educated in Buenos
Aires but left the classroom for the market place that interested him more; inherited the position of legal trustee of sanctuary at Luján; held various other public positions there and
in Buenos Aires while becoming one of most successful merchants in the viceroyalty; ironically, Lezica was serving as
chief alcalde of the Buenos Aires cabildo in May 1810 when the
breakdown of royal power in Spain took place; although he personally preferred recognition of the Cádiz junta, he responded
to the demand of the patriots and called a cabildo abierto and
also signed the official invitations to it and the communications
to the various towns of the United Provinces; Lezica attempted
to remain apart from the actions known as the May Revolution
that resulted in the establishment of the first patriot government, but his views were well known; he suffered property
losses and exile to Luján, where he died the following year.

LEZICA, TOMAS (1779-1830).   Merchant and financier.
     Born in Buenos Aires, son of Spanish merchant Juan
Antonio de Lezica y Osamiz, who became one of the first members of the consulado after it was established; in 1819, in
Spain, Tomás and another porteño, Andrés de Arguibel, apparently acting in communication with Director Pueyrredón,
used their influence to cause unrest among the Spanish liberal
officers of the fleet being assembled at Cádiz for the reconquest of the provinces of the Plata; Mitre, in his Historia de
Belgrano, gives them considerable credit for instigation of the
revolt that broke out in the fleet January 1, 1820, and prevented its sailing; he says that Argentina is greatly indebted to
them; Lezica made his way back to Buenos Aires where, as a
member of the financial power group, he supported Rivadavia's
reforms and progressive measures, and became one of the Argentine directors in the bank established by Rivadavia to
handle the nation's growing business and foreign trade; Lezica
died in Cádiz.

LEZICA VERA, SEBASTIAN (1791-1844).   Born in Buenos Aires,
son of Juan José de Lezica (q. v.); became a merchant; also
served as legislator in 1820 and several times later; commissioned to bring back from England the treaty of amity, commerce and navigation in 1825; that same year introduced first
colony of immigrants; took active part in business and financial
development; died in Valparaiso, Chile.

LIBERALS. Term usually applied to Argentine political leaders of
nineteenth century who favored adoption of European ideas, in-
situations and practices growing out of the eighteenth-century
enlightenment; Rivadavia and the unitarists, Mitre, Sarmiento,
were outstanding exponents; differing among themselves on such
political issues as the role of Buenos Aires (city and province)
in national life, they all stood for the freedoms that to Sarmiento (at least) constituted the desired "civilization" in contrast to criollo "barbarism"; their opponents considered this to
be a preference for secular European rather than traditional
Argentine Catholic values; during the 19th century the liberals
were responsible for giving Argentina freedom of worship,
freedom of expression, emphasis on popular, scientific education, secular control of public education, vital statistics, etc.,
and free trade and capitalistic economy; made Argentina a nation that ranked high in Latin America in desirability for immigrants, in growth of population and per capita gross national product, and in culture; provided constitution that has endured for over a century, political democracy, and political
stability for many decades; sponsored primarily by the aristocratic oligarchy, their leadership faltered before the twentieth
century development of Argentine nationalism, economic diversification, and demands for social and economic democracy.

LIBRARIES see BIBLIOTECAS

LIEBIG, JUSTUS VON, BARON (1803-1873). German chemist who
discovered process for making Argentine beef extract salable
to European market.
    Born in Darnstadt; determined to become chemist; at-
tended Bonn University, received Ph. D. at Erlangen; went to
Paris; through friendship with Alexander von Humboldt gained
access to best French laboratories; in 1838 turned to organic
chemistry and devoted rest of his life to it; returned to Gnies-
sen as professor of chemistry in university; remained there
for 18 years, 1852-70, developing one of finest chemistry laboratories in Europe, (university in Gneissen today--in Federal
Republic of Germany--bears his name); became interested in
food chemistry--baby foods a by-product of his research;
turned his attention to Argentine beef, still unacceptable to
European markets even though new foods, especially proteins,
were badly needed by increasing and industrializing populations;
in 1863 successfully devised technique for manufacturing palatable and nutritious beef extract by vacuum boiling juices, bones,
tissues and fats of beef; process well adapted for making use
of stringy Argentine meat; English company bought Liebig's
patent and began to process extract in both dry and liquid form
in Río de la Plata area, first at Fray Bentos in Uruguay, then
in Argentina; marketing met with widespread success throughout
Europe; beef production revolutionized in Argentina, especially
in Entre Ríos, with these increased demands and profitable use
of entire carcass; sale of beef extract continued for decades
after chilled and frozen processes became popular.

LIGA DEL NORTE (the Northern League)   see   COALICION DEL
NORTE

LIGA PATRIOTICA ARGENTINA (Argentine Patriotic League).
Founded in 1919 by Dr. Manuel Carlés (q.v.) to counteract
what he considered to be subversive activities; when labor
strikes of longshoremen (1916) and railroad workers (1917),
along with others culminated in 1919 in the announcement by the
Tenth Congress of Argentine regional workers of its sympathy
with Russia's Leninism and the terrifying events of the Tragic
Week (La Semana Trágica) January 7-13, Carlés organized
brigades of armed citizens to collaborate with the government
in establishing and maintaining order; the league was used both
in Buenos Aires and in the provinces, with Carlés as director
until his death.

LINIERS Y BREMOND, SANTIAGO DE (1753-1810).   Next to last viceroy of Río de la Plata, 1807-1809.
Born in France of noble blood, Liniers entered a naval
career at early age, spending three years as page to grand
master of Order of Malta where he received excellent training;
returned to France but decided 1774 to offer his services to
the Spanish crown; after sailing with O'Reilly's fleet to Africa,
he returned to Spain and entered the training school for marine
guards in Cádiz.
Accompanied Pedro de Cevallos to Río de la Plata in
expedition of 1776 but returned to Spain for years of naval action in the troubled period that followed; in 1788, he moved to
Río de la Plata as port captain responsible for guarding the estuary against enemy ships (usually British) and smugglers; his
first wife having died, he married the daughter of Martín de
Sarratea, prominent creole merchant and hacendado of the area;
from 1802 to 1804 served as political and military governor of
Misiones, but returned to Buenos Aires as chief of naval station there.
Two years later, when the viceroy Sobre Monte received
news of the approaching British invasion under Sir Home Popham and William Carr Beresford, he assigned Liniers to guard
the port of Ensenada to prevent British from landing there; instead British came in at Quilmes; on July 1, shortly after the
capitulation to the British, Liniers requested and received permission to visit Buenos Aires (as a foreigner he was not bound
by the terms of the agreement), hoping to gain an evaluation of
the British strength and the situation in Buenos Aires; as a devout Catholic he attended mass and, finding himself deeply
troubled by the changed atmosphere of the service (although
British had not curtailed Catholic worship), he is said to have
vowed to free the Virgin del Rosario from the captivity in which
she was being held; shortly afterwards he met Martín de Alzaga, powerful Spanish merchant and public figure, who convinced
him that all Buenos Aires was opposed to the British occupation, needing only a leader to rise up in revolt; Liniers agreed
to go to Montevideo to secure troops from Governor Ruiz Hui-

dobro to provide the professional skill and military equipment
needed, while the creole Juan Martín de Pueyrredón was arousing the peasants, and Alzaga mobilizing the porteños; on August 3, Liniers used his familiarity with the difficult waters and
winds of the estuary to slip his troops, supplied by the governor, across the river; one week later the combined forces
were in Buenos Aires and on August 12, forced Beresford to
surrender in the famous Reconquista; two days later, a cabildo
abierto was called to confirm the victory and to force the viceroy to confer all military power on Liniers; preparations began to meet the expected new British invasions and in early
February 1807, when it was learned that a new British force
had landed in Uruguay under Samuel Auchmuty, a cabildo abierto and a Junta de Guerra (War Council) called for emergency
action: viceroy Sobre Monte was deposed, civil powers vested
in the audiencia, and all military powers in Liniers; when
Whitelocke disembarked his forces at the port of Ensenada and
started up along the river to Buenos Aires, Liniers went out
to meet him in an ill-advised action that resulted in his defeat; he was able to regather his forces, while Alzaga organized the defense of Buenos Aires; and Whitelocke was forced
to surrender on July 6, after heavy fighting and losses; Liniers
was the hero of the hour, especially among the creoles who
considered him both their leader and the symbol of their victory.
          By early 1808, however, signs of trouble were evident;
Liniers was temperamentally better suited to emergency leadership than to sustained administrative work, and the viceroyalty was already rent with political, economic, and social differences; Napoleon's invasion of the Iberian peninsula (in late
1807) complicated the problem by bringing the Portuguese
court to Río de Janeiro, forcing the abdication of the Spanish
king, and making England an ally, no longer an enemy, of
Spain; in this confusion of intrigue with Carlota Joaquina (q.v.),
rivalry between Montevideo and Buenos Aires for political and
commercial primacy, conflict between free trade and monopoly
groups, and suspicion of Liniers' loyalty because of his French
birth, two major factions developed: Creole merchants and
estancieros who backed Liniers (confirmed as interim viceroy
in May 1808) and were, in some cases, willing to crown Carlota in an independent constitutional monarchy, wanted free
trade, and creole power; the Spanish party, led by Martín de
Alzaga, was determined to preserve privileged political, economic, and social position of Spaniards, probably in an independent republic, insisted on mercantilistic monopoly that favored them, and found their support in the cabildo, which demanded more power, and in Montevideo where Governor Elío
rejected Liniers' authority and denounced him to the Central
Junta in Spain; situation made worse by deteriorating personal
relationship between Liniers and Alzaga; Liniers publicly declared his loyalty to Ferdinand VII; steered a moderate course
in diplomacy with the Portuguese government and Carlota;
firmly refused to surrender viceregal powers to the cabildo,

and opened up the trade as much as possible; at the January 1,1809 meeting of the Buenos Aires cabildo, a cabildo abierto was called and Martín de Alzaga marshalled the Spanish militia groups and a public demonstration to force Liniers to resign; Liniers was willing but was persuaded by Cornelio Saavedra to put his resignation to the test; appearing before the crowd, accompanied by Saavedra and other creole officers, with their forces, in larger numbers than the Spanish units, also in the plaza, Liniers received an ovation; the leaders of the revolt were exiled; a few months later, he learned that the Central Junta in Spain had appointed Admiral Baltasar Hidalgo de Cisneros to succeed him as viceroy; on August 2, 1809, he turned over the government peacefully to Cisneros, having refused to permit creole leaders to use force to prevent it; probably greatly relieved, Liniers lived quietly until after the May Revolution of 1810 which he refused to support; having already been summoned back to Spain, he and the governor intendant of Córdoba Juan Gutiérrez de la Concha, Santiago Allende, and the bishop (see Rodrigo A. Orellana), determined to fight against the revolutionary forces and to remain loyal to Spain; the Buenos Aires government dispatched a liberating army against them with orders that the leaders be executed; having learned that the Cordoban conspiracy had links all over the interior provinces, and believing that the very existence of the revolution depended on the total suppression of this opposition, the junta stood firm on its decision in spite of widespread public protest; Liniers, whose followers had largely deserted him, attempted to flee to Peru but was pursued and captured by Colonel Antonio González Balcarce at Cabeza de Tigre and executed with the other leaders (excluding the bishop whose cloth saved him) on August 26, 1810, a martyr to the cause of the nation whose freedom he had assured a few years earlier; in 1862 his remains were taken to Spain and buried with honors (see British Invasions; William Carr Beresford).

   Paul Groussac's Santiago de Liniers, conde de Buenos Aires, published in Buenos Aires, 1907, is an old but detailed and scholarly study.

LINSEED (FLAXSEED). One of modern Argentina's most profitable export crops; most of flax raised in Argentina of oily variety, making nation (1920s-1940s) world's most important source of linseed oil, used primarily in paints, but also in varnishes, printing, and medically in topical ointments; grown in heart of cereal area, centering around Entre Ríos, where it forms major crop.
   Flax was apparently known in Argentina by end of sixteenth century, if not before conquest, with Andean Indians reported as spinning and weaving cloth from its fibers; its commercial cultivation in Argentina was urged (1778) by first viceroy Pedro Ceballos and by Manuel Belgrano (among others) in his Memoria of 1797: flax seeds were actually first introduced into Buenos Aires area in 1800 by Martín José de Altolaguirre, who cultivated them for both fiber and oily seeds; linseed

finally became important as commercial crop around 1880 after
railroads provided access to world markets; principal areas of
cultivation: provinces of Santa Fe, Buenos Aires, Entre Ríos,
Córdoba, with extensive sowing also in La Pampa, Corrientes,
and San Luis; as much as 90% of its production went to export
trade, with United States as principal customer, followed by
the Netherlands and Great Britain; peaked in production and
value between 1930 and 1945; governmental station established
in Pergamino to introduce new varieties and hybrids and to experiment with use of fibers in textile industry; early attempts
failed because of inexperience or inability to use fibers of oily
flaxseed; after 1938 new factories began using fibers for coarse
materials; Santiago del Estero and Tucumán seem to have had
most luck or best climatic and soil conditions in raising flax
for linen; demands for oil and coarse fabrics boomed during
World War II and immediately afterward, but small textile
factories were closed and linseed production dropped abruptly
to less than half of its former production by early 1950s;
causes not entirely clear, but doubtless include heavy U.S. import tax, increased wages of laborers and general decline of
agriculture during Perón period, along with changes in world
market; during 1960s and early 1970s linseed has been regaining much of its former importance in export trade.

See Raúl Ramella, El lino oleoginosas. Cultivo indus-
trialización y economía en la Argentina (Buenos Aires, 1944);
also Carlos Díaz Alejandro, in Suggested Readings, Appendix
III, for later material relating to its economic significance.

LITERARY SOCIETY OF BUENOS AIRES   see   SOCIEDAD LITE-
RARIA DE BUENOS AIRES

LITERATURE.   Relationship between Argentine creative literature
and historiography has been close, especially in the national
period, as many writers have selected historical themes for
their dramas, poems, novels, and essays, and historians have
been influenced by literary currents (especially French) such
as romanticism in the early nineteenth century (see Esteban
Echeverría) and modernism in the twentieth; works of literature have vividly depicted events and scenes of the historic
past and have also been deeply concerned with finding answers
for Argentina's various national problems; in this latter respect they have made positive contributions to the development
of nationalism and a sense of national identity; many writers,
throughout the national period, have also involved themselves
heavily in public life; Argentine literature, including that primarily historical in theme and interest, has often been international in appeal and widely translated.

Among historical works might be mentioned the first
Argentine drama Siripo, by Manuel José de Lavardén, three
novels of the Rosas' period: Echeverría's El matador, D. F.
Sarmiento's Facundo, and José Mármol's Amalia; in the late
nineteenth and early twentieth century the gaucho was featured
in many writings, including José Hernández's Martín Fierro

and Ricardo Güiraldes' Don Segundo Sombra; in the early twentieth century, many writers have sought Argentina's true identity in its past, some, like literary critic Ricardo Rojas, in
his Eurindia, looking into the European and Indian past; others,
like Manuel Gálvez, finding it in such historic manifestations
of authoritarianism as the Roman Catholic Church and caudillo
rule; modern Argentine authors, especially young and angry
ones, use literature as a medium through which to seek out
interpretations of their rapidly changing society and economy;
essayists have increasingly sought to discover Argentina's sense
of national purpose; in this spirit, Jorge L. Borges, one of
Argentina's leading literary figures, in 1970 edited a collection
of essays entitled, ¿Qué es la Argentina?
      See listings of names mentioned and of gaucho literature;
well-known surveys of Argentine literature are: Ricardo Rojas, Historia de la literatura argentina (4 v., Buenos Aires,
1917-1922; 4th edition, 9 v., 1957); Rafael A. Arrieta, ed.,
Historia de la literatura argentina (6 v., Buenos Aires, 1958-
1959); for briefer accounts in English, see Kessel Schwartz,
A New History of Spanish American Fiction (2 v., Coral Gables,
Florida, 1971-1972).

LITORAL (In English, littoral). From Latin word meaning coast or
      shore, i.e., land through which Paraná river and Río de la
      Plata flow in Argentina. In colonial period it was used to dis-
      tinguish Buenos Aires and its hinterland from the western
      mountainous areas; in modern times usually applies specifical-
      ly to provinces of Corrientes, Entre Ríos, and Santa Fe (qq.v.);
      Universidad Nacional del Litoral, for example, has faculties
      in cities of these provinces.

LIVESTOCK see CATTLE; HORSES; ARRIAS DE MULAS

LLAMA (lama guanicoe glama). The llama was the only domesti-
      cated beast of burden--almost the only domesticated animal of
      any kind--found in what is now Argentina by the first Spaniards;
      only in the northwestern part of the country, into which the
      Inca empire (q.v.) had been expanding were these used by the
      semi-civilized Indians in that area; as in Peru the llama fur-
      nished wool for an indigenous weaving industry, was a sure-
      footed burden-bearer, well adapted to carrying loads up to 100
      pounds on the mountain trails, and was a source of meat and
      leather.

LOAYSA, FRANCISCO GARCIA JOFRE DE (d. 1526). Commander
      of second Spanish expedition to sail the length of Argentina's
      Atlantic coast and through the straits (see Sebastián de El-
      cano).

LOGIA LAUTARO see LAUTARO LODGE

LONARDI, EDUARDO (1896-1956). President of Argentine Republic
      1955; career military officer--lieutenant general.

Born in Buenos Aires; educated at Colegio Militar and
Escuela Superior de Guerra; taught in both; artillery specialist
in anti-aircraft missiles; headed Argentine defense delegation
to Washington, D.C., commanded first army unit based in
Rosario; left military service in 1951 due to participation in
conspiracy against Perón, but continued to maintain close contacts with former military colleagues; in mid-1955, incensed
by increasing violence of Peronist government, especially
against Catholic Church (formerly supporter of Perón), Lonardi seized artillery base in Córdoba and assumed leadership
of new revolt against Perón; joined by civilian Catholic group
under Mario Amadeo and military and naval units under General Pedro Aramburu and Rear Admiral Isaac Rojas (who
feared Perón's move to make militia out of labor unions);
overthrew Perón September 19, 1955; Lonardi, to whose leadership and courage much of success of overthrow was attributed,
was sworn in at once in Córdoba, as provisional president,
with Rojas as vice president; five days later, on 24 September
Lonardi moved to Buenos Aires where he received a tumultuous popular welcome under flags of papacy and republic displayed side by side; Lonardi immediately announced policy of
conciliation--neither victors nor victims--but attempts to implement this brought immediate and continuing protests from
those who wanted sterner measures against the Peronists as
well as from those who wanted totalitarian (preferably church-
oriented) government; in November Lonardi was forced out of
office by fellow officers for his leniency; Aramburu became
president, with Rojas remaining as vice president; already ill,
General Lonardi died in Buenos Aires the following year, shortly after unsuccessful surgery in Washington.

During his eight weeks in office, President Lonardi
took remarkable steps toward trying to solve the complex of
problems that continued to trouble Argentina during several
later administrations: 1) Formulated policy of national conciliation revived three years later by Frondizi; 2) Moderated
harshness of military dictatorship by establishing civilian national consultative council--continued by Aramburu; 3) Began
economic reform by canceling Peron's Standard Oil contracts
and marketing agency IAPI; brought Raúl Prebisch, United Nations economist, into administration; latter had already filed
preliminary report on economic situation inherited from Perón
and was preparing plan for recovery--based on austerity, free
enterprise, encouragement of foreign investments; 4) Had dissolved congress and purged Peronists from Supreme Court and
embassies as well as from federal and provincial governments.

LONDRES (LONDON). Town founded (c. 1558) to control Diaguita
(or Calchaquí) Indians of Catamarca; first settlement made by
Julio Sedeño, acting under orders from Governor Juan Pérez
de Zorita of Tucumán; named in honor of marriage of Philip
II to Mary Tudor, Queen of England; surrounding area called
New England; first settlement, in valley of Quinmivil, about
180 miles from Santiago del Estero, destroyed by Indians and

name New England disappeared; town of Londres refounded and
moved several times, but always victim to Indian attacks;
finally, late in seventeenth century (c. 1683), San Fernando del
Valle de Catamarca (today known as Catamarca, capital of
province of that name) was successfully established.

LOPEZ, ESTANISLAO (1786-1838). Veteran of independence wars;
caudillo of Santa Fe province 1818-1838; federalist leader in
civil wars.
    Born in Santa Fe, educated in local schools; at age 15
was fighting Indians along northern border and learning montonera tactics useful later in confusing regular armies sent
against him; took part in reconquest of Buenos Aires from British (1806); as one of 100 Santa Fe blandengues (border fighters)
in Belgrano's command (1810), captured by royalists; imprisoned in Montevideo; escaped to engage in other patriot military
action; made first major appearance in history by leading his
men to revolt against Buenos Aires (1816), fought in campaign
forcing Buenos Aires' army of observation under General Juan
Justo Viamonte to surrender; although not in complete command,
and aided by Artigas, López became known as hero of campaign;
after victorious expedition against Indians in north, López returned to capital of Santa Fe to take over government and to
separate province from Buenos Aires control; until his death
twenty years later ruled Santa Fe by popular consent, elected
governor in 1819 and reelected regularly thereafter; allying himself first with Uruguayan leader José Gervasio Artigas and then
with caudillo Francisco Ramírez of Entre Ríos, raised great
new armies against Buenos Aires; posed such threat to directorate government that Pueyrredón ordered all forces back to
defend Buenos Aires, even San Martín's Army of the Andes
(San Martín refused to be diverted from war for independence
into civil wars); during temporary truce, Pueyrredón resigned
in 1819; López's rejection of elitest constitution of 1819 and his
suspicions (with some foundation) of monarchical tendencies of
Buenos Aires political leaders caused him to declare war
again; this time allied with federalist Francisco Ramírez, along
with Carlos María de Alvear (former director) and José Miguel
Carrera (former president of Chile) who had their own personal
fights against Buenos Aires government; on February 1, 1820,
at battle of Cepeda, López and Ramírez defeated forces of Buenos Aires, commanded by Rondeau, in what has become known
as victory for provincial federalism; brought end of directorate
government, inaugurating "Terrible Year Twenty" but peace was
briefly established between Santa Fe and Buenos Aires by
Treaty of Pilar February 23, and then more firmly secured by
Treaty of Benegas (q.v.) signed November 24, 1820; relations
remained close both personally and politically between Juan
Manuel de Rosas and Estanislao López from then on; in 1821
López refused to allow Ramírez (whom he had come to regard
as dangerous rival) permission to cross Santa Fe to fight Bustos in Córdoba; in fighting that resulted, Ramírez was killed by
a party of López's soldiers.

Rest of 1820s were fairly peaceful for López and Santa
Fe (see Santa Fe for provincial history) although caudillo
watched unitarist activities in Buenos Aires with constant suspicion; gave asylum to Fray Francisco de Paula Castañeda,
greatest opponent of Rivadavia's ecclesiastical reforms; honored by Santa Fe legislature (1822) with rank of brigadier general and award of diamond-studded gold medal; fought successful campaign against troublesome Ranqueles Indians; favored
granting Uruguay protectorate requested (1823) but did not insist; protected Rosas escaping from Juan Lavalle's defeat of
Manuel Dorrego's army at Navarro (November 1828); and
joined forces with Rosas to defeat Lavalle at Puente de Márquez
April 26, 1829; rift between López and Rosas narrowly avoided
by Rosas' determined efforts after latter had privately made
peace with Lavalle in Pact of Cañuelas--without López's knowledge or consent, which would probably not have been given due
to Lavalle's status as unitarist leader; in 1830 a new situation
prevailed, with Rosas, governor of Buenos Aires, and López,
of Santa Fe, leaders of riparian provinces against threat of
League of Interior (q. v.) under military leadership of unitarist
José María Paz; following months of conferences at Santa Fe,
four provinces signed Federal Pact January 4, 1831, of military alliance and provision for national federalist organization
(see Federal Pact of 1831); its clauses on representative commission with executive powers probably expresses core of Estanislao López's federalism; when Paz was captured a few
months later and his forces defeated in west by Quiroga, threat
of civil war disappeared for the moment and all provinces
came under federalist rule; strained personal relationships between Juan Facundo Quiroga and Estanislao López, two most
powerful provincial caudillos remaining, left way open for Juan
Manuel de Rosas, as governor of Buenos Aires to assume national leadership; López, prematurely aging and frequently ill,
cooperated with Rosas for most part; and in 1837 Rosas osten-
tatiously honored López in Buenos Aires, as citizen Beneméritus
in heroic grade and named him Illustrious Restorer (title also
held by Rosas) of the North; López died the following year at
critical moment in which Santa Fe, under Domingo Cullen
(q. v.) to whom López had delegated power, wanted to separate
itself from Buenos Aires because of French blockade against
Rosas; province shortly afterward came under control of Rosas.
See J. L. Busaniche, Estanislao López y el federalismo
del litoral (Buenos Aires, 1927).

LOPEZ, FRANCISCO SOLANO (1826-1870). President of Paraguay
1862-1870; both president and military commander of Paraguayan forces during Triple Alliance War.
Becoming president in 1862, following the death of his
father President Carlos Antonio López, Solano López determined to use Paraguay's well-equipped, professionally trained
army to help the nation break out of its relative isolation and
"make the voice of Paraguay heard" in southern South America; political and economic conditions in neighboring Argentina,

Brazil, and Uruguay convinced him that the time was ripe, if
Paraguay ever wanted to become a modern, prosperous nation;
when diplomacy seemed to break down, he invaded Corrientes
(early in 1865) on his way to Uruguay and precipitated the
Triple Alliance or Paraguayan War (q. v.) that resulted in his
own death and the devastation of his country; nevertheless,
however he may be regarded elsewhere, in Paraguay Francisco
Solano is regarded as a most important national hero and one
who uniquely embodied the Paraguayan spirit; one hundred
years after his death his nation is once again attempting to develop its own economy by international use of its natural resources (water power); this time force has been replaced by
use of international agencies and by reliance on diplomacy with
Argentina and Brazil.

See Charles J. Kolinsky, Independence or Death! The
Story of the Paraguayan War (Gainesville, Florida, 1965).

LOPEZ, VICENTE FIDEL (1815-1903). Historian; anti-Rosas member of "Generation of 1837"; public figure; cabinet minister.

Born in Buenos Aires, son of Vicente López y Planes;
educated in capital, receiving law degree in 1839; met with
other young intellectuals of "Generation of 1837" in Marcos
Sastre's literary salon; one of organizers of Asociación de
Mayo; exiled following 1840 because of opposition to Rosas; in
Chile (1840-1844) joined Sarmiento in founding lyceum and journal El Progreso; directed naval school at Valparaíso; continued
propaganda and efforts to arouse opposition against Rosas in
Rio de Janeiro (1844) and then joined exiles in Montevideo; returned to active political life in Buenos Aires in 1852, following Rosas' departure; became minister of public instruction;
joined his father and many other porteños in unsuccessful attempt to persuade Buenos Aires legislature to accept Acuerdo
(agreement) de San Nicolás and join other provinces under
leadership of Urquiza in forming national constitutional government; devoted next few years to writing, teaching, and scholarly research; in 1868 appointed rector of University of Buenos
Aires where he was professor of political economy; represented Buenos Aires in national congress, 1871-1880; was president of Bank of the Province, 1879-1883; joined with old
friends and former colleagues in group of political "notables"
including Mitre, Sarmiento, and Alberdi, among others, to settle problem of capital, resulting in federalization of Buenos
Aires 1880; was apparently present at meeting in 1889 in which
Unión Cívica was formed (later to become Radical Party), in
which his son Lucio V. López became active; brought (1890)
into coalition cabinet of President Carlos Pellegrini as minister
of finance; assisted president in critical task of drawing up and
getting congressional approval for new financial plan to pull
nation out of financial chaos that had played large role in overthrow of government of Miguel Juárez Celman; also created
Bank of the Nation and undertook tax reform; retired from
public life but continued writing until his death in Buenos
Aires, 1903.

Important among voluminous historical writings of Vicente Fidel López, still read and quoted by Argentine historians, are his editing of Acuerdos del cabildo de Buenos Aires
(6 volumes, Buenos Aires, 1886-1891); and his classic Historia de la República Argentina.   Su origen, su revolución, y
su desarrollo político hasta 1852 (10 volumes, Buenos Aires,
1883-1893; 5th edition, 8 volumes, 1957).

LOPEZ JORDAN, (JOSE) RICARDO (1793-1845 or 1846).   Fighter in
war for independence and in civil wars; father of caudillo Ricardo López Jordán; governor of Entre Ríos.
Born in Arroyo de la China (Concepción del Uruguay);
devoted himself to rural tasks on family estate; in 1810 joined
Rondeau's revolutionary force, along with his half-brother
Francisco Ramírez; in 1811 became officer in militia formed
in Concepción; two years later, he and 25 companions seized
two Spanish vessels that had come upriver and anchored at island nearby; after 1817 López Jordán belonged to group resisting Buenos Aires control of all provinces; in 1819, he was
left in charge of provincial government while Ramírez joined
Estanislao López (from Santa Fe) against Buenos Aires forces;
later, following Ramírez's death in 1821, López Jordán attempted to retain control of government, but López and Buenos
Aires authorities determined to establish friendly government
in Entre Ríos and overthrew him; during the next ten years,
López Jordán was alternately fighting in civil wars and organizing conspiracies against governments in power or serving,
himself, successfully, but briefly, as elected governor (as in
1825 and 1830); in 1831, with Pascual Echagüe firmly in office, López Jordán fled to Uruguay and remained there until
he returned in 1839 with Lavalle's invading army; captured in
the fighting that followed, he remained in prison in Buenos
Aires until finally released through efforts of his son who, as
a hero of the battle of Arroyo Grande, had come to Buenos
Aires in 1842 with its official report of the victory of Rosas'
forces; López Jordán died several years later in Uruguay.

LOPEZ JORDAN, GENERAL RICARDO (1822-1888).   Caudillo of
Entre Ríos.
Born in Entre Ríos, son of father of same name who
had been governor of province; joined provincial army 1841 to
begin long military career; rose rapidly through the ranks;
distinguished himself in fighting against Corrientes, and at
Caseros and Pavón, under Urquiza; became powerful political
leader in Entre Ríos; believing that province's best interests
were threatened by attempts of Urquiza and Mitre to unite Confederation and Buenos Aires province in national organization,
broke with Urquiza; in 1870 López Jordán led revolution to
seize Entre Ríos government, assassinated Urquiza and his
two sons, became governor in defiance of national government;
army sent by President D. F. Sarmiento defeated López Jordán
at Ñaembé January 26, 1871; latter escaped to Brazil but returned to invade Entre Ríos in 1873; again defeated, at Don

Gonzalo, in November 1876, he made final attempt to regain
power, but province no longer supported him; attempting to
return to exile by way of Corrientes, López Jordán was turned
in to federal authorities by someone that knew him; imprisoned
in Rosario, he escaped in disguise and made his way to Uruguay where he spent next decade as rancher; taking advantage
of new law of amnesty, he returned to Buenos Aires in 1888,
and was killed soon afterward by son of military officer Zen-
ón Casas whom López Jordán had ordered shot in 1873; Ricardo López Jordán often referred to as the last of the Argentine
caudillos (in the typical nineteenth century pattern) (see Entre
Ríos; Justo José de Urquiza).

LOPEZ Y PLANES, VICENTE (1784-1856).   Patriot and poet of in-
    dependence; president of Argentina, 1827-1828.
        Born in Buenos Aires; went into business after studying
    at Franciscan and San Carlos academies; one of first to enlist
    against British in 1806, became lieutenant in Patricio regi-
    ment; started poetic career with El triunfo argentino (Argen-
    tine victory over British) in 1808; following year abandoned
    business to enter University of Chuquisaca to study law; be-
    came active in independence movement from beginning; served
    as secretary of first liberating expedition to interior (1810);
    became one of secretaries of first triumvirate government;
    elected to national assembly in 1813, López y Planes became
    one of most prominent members and his verses, read to as-
    sembly May 11, 1813, were adopted as Argentine national
    hymn; also sang San Martín's praises after victory of Chaca-
    buco (1817); served as secretary for directorate governments
    of Balcarce and Pueyrredón (1816-1817); following downfall of
    centralist constitutional government under Bernardino Rivadavia
    in 1827, López y Planes became caretaker president until elec-
    tion of Manuel Dorrego as governor of Buenos Aires province
    in 1828; federalist national government established on de facto,
    not constitutional, basis by Juan Manuel Rosas in 1829 and
    continued, with brief break 1832-1835, until 1852; Vicente Ló-
    pez y Planes remained in Argentina during this period, filling
    various posts in justice department; immediately following
    Rosas' departure in February 1852, Dr. López y Planes once
    again was called on to take over interim government; this time
    as governor of Buenos Aires province (office held by Rosas,
    although through various agreements and means, he had acted
    for entire nation); serving in this capacity for several months,
    either through election by provincial legislature or by appoint-
    ment of Urquiza and returning after repeated resignations, Ló-
    pez y Planes supervised expropriation of Rosas' property and
    that of other proscribed rosista leaders; returned property that
    had been confiscated for political reasons; established freedom
    of press and that of Sociedad de Beneficencia, and generally
    attempted to restore society to normal and tranquil patterns;
    signed the Acuerdo (Agreement) de San Nicolás providing bas-
    is for constitutional national organization along federalist lines,
    urged Buenos Aires legislature to accept it and, when it re-

fused, finally resigned as governor in July 1852; died in Buenos Aires in 1856, with nation still divided between Confederation and Buenos Aires.

LORETO, NICOLAS FRANCISCO CRISTOBAL DEL CAMPO, Marqués de.   Third viceroy of the Río de la Plata, serving 1784-89.
        Born in Sevilla; a career military officer like other viceroys but, unlike most of them, had had no political experience in Spanish America before coming to Buenos Aires; proved to be honest, able administrator for the viceroyalty that was rapidly growing in importance; installed the Audiencia of Buenos Aires, August 8, 1785; was first to cope with the establishment of the intendancy system in Argentina (setting up eight intendancies) and working out the relationship between the head of this new system and the viceroy, with his traditional powers and prerogatives; fostered the economy on all levels, seeking to promote agriculture, while at the same time aiding the cattle industry; sought out new sources of good cheap salt to encourage the commercial salting of beef (introduced a decade earlier); improved port by building mole; fought contraband trade harshly in the interests of legitimate commerce; introduced new policy of peaceful coexistence and mutually profitable trade between Indians and other residents; turned his office over to Arredondo in December 1789 and returned to Spain.

LOS ANDES, TERRITORY OF.   Bleak, high, arid northwestern corner of Argentina, largely composed of the Puna of Atacama; governed as a national territory 1890-1943, then divided among neighboring Argentine provinces.
        Los Andes, populated by barely 1000 primitive Indians, remote from the capitals of Chile, Bolivia, and Argentina, was claimed by all three during most of the nineteenth century but little effort was made to push the issue; the sudden interest in the nitrates found in the Atacama areas of Chile and Bolivia sharply increased the apparent desirability of the Puna de Los Altos and Argentina began to insist on its ownership; its claim was largely based on the fact that Los Andes had been included in the intendancy of Salta de Tucumán and the latter's last governor, Nicolás Severo de Isasmendi y Echalar, had worked the mines of Los Andes; Argentina also claimed that its ownership had been recognized until the Bolivian occupation in 1826; Bolivia ceded its claims to Argentina early in 1889 and a few months later, with the arbitration aid of the U.S. Minister in Buenos Aires, William I. Buchanan, Argentina and Chile reached a boundary settlement, giving Los Andes to the former; immediately an Argentine Redemptorist missionary Luis Lorber entered the area and established (1889) the first school; the following year Congress provided for the government of Los Andes as a national territory, with its capital at San Antonio de los Cobres; during the next half century the area experienced some growth in population and economy; in 1943, with a population of barely 10,000 and an economy based almost entirely on sheep

and goats, the land of the territory was divided and attached
to the adjacent Argentine provinces, with Jujuy acquiring Susques, San Antonio de los Cobres and Socompa going to Salta,
and Antofagasta de la Sierra becoming part of Catamarca; region believed to be rich in archeological sites, especially of
Atacama tribes, and to have potential for economic development in mineral deposits, in the raising of fur-bearing animals,
especially chinchillas, as well as sheep and goats, and in encouraging a tourist industry.

LOZANO, PEDRO (1697-1752). Jesuit colonial historian.
        Born in Madrid into family with intellectual interests;
his brother in royal library; Pedro entered Jesuit order at age
fourteen and was soon sent to the Río de la Plata area; completed his studies in Córdoba and was ordained there; apparently spent several years in the 1720s working with the missions
in Santa Fe and beginning his writing career and travels and
research; in 1730, Father Lozano became official chronicler
for the Jesuits, continuing in this position until 1745; during
this period and until his death, he continued to make his home
in Córdoba, at the Colegio Máximo or the Santa Catalina hacienda, sometimes teaching philosophy and theology at the colegio and university but always writing; he was tireless in research and was known to have worked in the archives of Asunción, Santiago del Estero, Córdoba, Tucumán, and Salta, and
was the first to have plunged into this almost impenetrable
"Chaco wilderness" of documents, accumulated records, and
assorted manuscripts in an attempt to work them all into a
comprehensive, accurate historical narrative; it is little won-
der that his written style has been judged monotonous and
heavy but equally understandable that his writings form the basis of later Argentine historiography; his contribution was of
two kinds: the preservation of early historical data that might
otherwise have been lost; and his own interpretation of the materials; Father Lozano's scholarly skills and intellectual talents
were so highly regarded by his fellow-Jesuits that they entrusted him with the delicate and important task of preparing
the statement of the Jesuit claims to the mission territory surrendered by Spain to Portugal in the treaty of 1750; two years
later Pedro Lozano died in Humahuaca while on his way to La
Plata (modern Sucre).
        Among the many works of Lozano, some of the best
known are: the first geographical study of the Chaco, Descripción corográfica del Gran Chaco Gualamba (Córdoba, Spain,
1733); Historia de las revoluciones del Paraguay (Buenos
Aires, 1905); Historia de la Companía de Jesús en las provincias del Paraguay (including Argentina), volumes I and II, (Madrid, 1754-1755); the first part of the latter had been a civil
history of the area and this was first published, with introduction and notes, by Andrés Lamas, in Buenos Aires, 1873-75,
as Historia de la conquista de la provincia del Paraguay, Río
de la Plata y Tucumán--and has become one of the foundations
of Argentine national historiography.

LUCA Y PATRON, ESTEBAN (1786-1824).   Patriot and poet laureate
of independence movement.

Born in Buenos Aires; attended Colegio de San Carlos;
fought in Patricios against British invasions; in 1810 was appointed first director of national arms factory--scrounged area
for scrap iron from which to forge guns, handguns, sabers,
cannon, and horseshoes needed by revolutionary armies; became known as the civilian poet who most effectively memori-
alized the military events of the independence struggle; his
odes to the capture of Montevideo, San Martín's victories at
Chacabuco and Maipú brought him an official request from Rivadavia to write a poem in honor of San Martín's entry into
Lima (1821); Esteban Luca was an original member of the Buenos Aires literary society and contributed to such journals as
Argos, La Abeja Argentina; accompanied José Valentín Gómez
to Brazil as secretary; died in shipwreck on return voyage.

LUCERO, FRANKLIN (1897-).   Career military officer; became
Perón's top general and minister of War, 1949-1955.

Born in San Luis; educated at Colegio Militar and advanced military schools, including the War College; served in
various military posts until 1944; in that year, he became a
loyal supporter of Perón, convinced that the latter's dream for
Argentina was the same as his own, and was appointed chief
of the secretariat of the ministry of war; in 1947-1948 he
served as military attaché in embassy of United States; sent on
various foreign missions; became President Perón's top general and minister of war, 1949-1955; was given full responsibility for suppressing anti-Perón uprisings in 1955; put down the
June revolt with force; refused, as a military professional who
feared outbreak of civil war, to allow the arming of 6,000,000
members of the labor organization, CGT, as a citizen militia;
temporarily suppressed outbreak in early September 1955, but
its intensification finally forced downfall of Perón government;
in the court martial that followed, General Lucero was stripped
of his uniform and rank because of his collaboration with Perón.

LUCERO, JOSE CECILIO LUCIO (1791-1867).   Independence fighter
from 1815, when he became part of the Army of the Andes,
until 1824 following the battle of Ayacucho.

Born in San Luis; accompanied Army of the Andes to
Chile (1817) and then went with San Martín's liberating expedition to Peru in 1820; entered Lima with San Martín; fought in
campaign of the Puertos Intermedios and in battles of Junín
and Ayacucho; returning to Argentina he became (1826) an
aide-de-camp to Miguel Soler (q.v.); took part in the siege of
Montevideo; joined Lavalle in 1829 but was back in the northwest (1833) supporting Alejandro Heredia (q.v.) in his campaigns in Salta and Jujuy and against Santa Cruz in Bolivia,
1837-1838; thereafter he settled down to minor administrative
government posts in San Luis; in 1858 he was sent to the Confederation Congress at Paraná.

LUE Y RIEGA, BENITO (1753-1812).   Last of colonial bishops in
Buenos Aires.

Born in Asturias, Spain; became bishop of Buenos Aires
in 1802; considered to be hard and stern, he nevertheless attempted to improve his diocese by creating new parishes and
attempting to open a seminary; he also assumed his responsibilities as a public figure during this difficult period; in 1807
he lent financial aid to the hard-pressed government facing
British invasions; in 1809 he was appointed by the Spanish-
dominated cabildo to head the commission asking viceroy Liniers to resign (see Santiago de Liniers) as one of the most
prominent members of the cabildo abierto of May 22, 1810,
he opened the debate by defending Spanish authority vigorously
(see May Revolution); after the patriot junta had been appointed,
he made no further efforts to oppose the revolution but continued to be regarded by Buenos Aires government with suspicion; he was not permitted to leave the city on the grounds
that his presence there had a calming effect on the people;
actually it was feared that he might cause trouble elsewhere
if permitted to leave; restive under restraint, he died in 1812.

LUGONES, LEOPOLDO ARGÜELLO (1874-1938).   Writer; poet, biographer, novelist, essayist.

Born in province of Córdoba; attended Colegio Nacional
there, but was largely self-educated; primarily a poet but also
a prolific writer on widely varied subjects; his writings reflected his early anarchist and socialist thinking, as well as
his later (after 1918) conversion to a militant nationalism of
the right; his close friendship with Rubén Darío, with its styl-
istic effects on Argentine poetry; his ardent support of Allied
cause in World War I; and his love, knowledge, and understanding of the tradition, history, and psychology of his native
country; among works dealing with topics of latter type are
El payador; El imperio jesuítico; La guerra gaucha; the official biography of Domingo Faustino Sarmiento (written for the
centenary celebration, 1911); as well as El libro de los paisajes in which all the different birds of Argentina assemble to
sing its praises; later works include La patria fuerte y la
grande Argentina (1931); Política revolucionaria (1931); and
El estado equitativo (1932); considered to have been one of major builders of modern Argentine nationalism, Lugones died a
suicide, perhaps a victim to the troubled and confused era of
the 1930s in Argentina.

LUJAN.   Historical city and national religious shrine on pampa
about 40 miles west of Buenos Aires.

Modern department and its capital in province of Buenos
Aires; located on Luján river named in honor of Captain Pedro
Luján (q. v.) killed there in 1536 along with about 37 other
conquistadors in battle with Querandí Indians; settlement grew
up in this area, good for agriculture and stock raising, and
lying along commercial route from interior and north to Buenos Aires; bridge across river built in 1674 united town and

outlying rural areas; Luján acquired significance as religious shrine during seventeenth century as fame spread of miracles wrought by Virgin of Luján; legend relates that ox train en route from Córdoba to Buenos Aires in early 1600s was unable to continue journey after overnight stop in Luján until small terra cotta image of Virgin (in pyramidal shape similar to those used in Tucumán and Peru) was removed from carreta and installed in rustic shrine on site; as population grew and veneration of Our Lady of Luján became widespread, Luján became religious center, culminating (in modern period) in the building of a Gothic cathedral, with twenty-five chapels and spires rising nearly 350 feet, as her sanctuary.

During late eighteenth century construction of fine cabildo building and residence for viceroy emphasized Luján's growing political and historical significance. Viceregal treasury concealed there (1806) but captured by British and paraded in triumph in London; later, General William Carr Beresford and his officers were imprisoned there following Argentine reconquest of Buenos Aires; Luján cabildo first to accept May Revolution of Buenos Aires (1810); in succeeding years city served as center of various operations; General Miguel Estanislao Soler was declared governor of Buenos Aires province there (1820); Unitarist General Paz used it as headquarters for several years during Rosas period; Francisco Javier Muñiz conducted his scientific research in viceroy's home (1830-1845); Bartolomé Mitre imprisoned there following defeat of his attempt to overthrow election of 1874.

Luján declared to be national monument in 1942; its colonial official buildings house the historical museum of the province of Buenos Aires; created in 1917-1918, it has become one of the finest in the republic, largely as the result of the work done by Enrique Udaondo (q. v.).

LUJAN, PEDRO DE (d. June 15, 1536). Conquistador; as captain, accompanied his uncle, Pedro de Mendoza, first adelantado, to Río de la Plata 1535-1536; killed in battle of Corpus Christi against Querandí Indians; stream and settlement at place of his death perpetuate his name, somewhat unusual in conquistador practice.

LULES, LOS. Name applied to an area in northeastern colonial Tucumán centering more or less around the intersection of parallel 25°S and meridian 65°E, lying between Bermejo and Salado rivers; named for pre-conquest Indians there; Jesuit reductions were established in Los Lules in the early eighteenth century, along with a Jesuit estancia that cultivated sugar cane and made sugar (see Lule-Vilelas).

LULE-VILELAS. The Lules and Vilelas made up two small and separate (speaking different languages), but related groups of nomadic Indians in preconquest northeastern Tucumán; they were first seen by the Spaniards accompanying Diego de Almagro to Chile (1536) who named them "lules" because of their unusual

height and lankiness, reminding the Spaniards of ostriches;
they lived by hunting peccaries (wild pigs), gathering wild
fruits and honey, and digging roots; they used the bow and arrow, the macana (club), and poisoned dart; they made an alcoholic beverage from honey and the fruit of the algarrobo (q. v.);
these Indians were almost unique in having devised reservoirs
or cisterns for collecting and storing the precious rainfall in
their dry land; they vigorously attacked the early Spanish settlements in their area, but eventually withdrew to more remote
regions; when the Jesuits attempted to bring them into mission-
reductions in the early eighteenth century, many of them ran
away; by 1750, the Lule-Videlas, never numerous, had disappeared except for a few individuals left roaming in the Chaco.

LUNFARDO. The slang of the lower classes, the underworld, and
the streets of the city of Buenos Aires; born and developed
among the immigrants near the close of the nineteenth century;
today commonly used.

LUZURIAGA, TORIBIO DE (1782-1842).   Military and political leader
in war of independence, governor of Cuyo 1816-1820.
Born in Huaras, Peru; came to Buenos Aires in 1799
as page to viceroy Gabriel de Avilés y Fierro (marqués de
Avilés); joined volunteer regiment of Buenos Aires cavalry;
captured in viceregal forces while fighting British 1806; fought
in second defense of Buenos Aires 1807; as lieutenant colonel
in dragoons took active role supporting May Revolution 1810;
then spent several years with armies of the north fighting
against royalists from Upper Peru, with brief interval acting
for Buenos Aires government as governor of Corrientes to restore order there; named as secretary of war in 1815, he went
to Mendoza in 1816 to join San Martín (whom he had come to
know well in Tucumán) in Cuyo; joined army of the Andes, became intelligent, industrious collaborator with his former commander; placed in charge of government of Cuyo he remained
there for next four years in command of San Martín's home
base in Mendoza during critical years of liberation of Chile
across the Andes; as intendant governor of Cuyo, Luzuriaga became widely known as model for restoring order, fostering
economic progress, and generally bringing goals of revolution
to this interior province; his actions covered areas of administration of public funds, public school system, public health and
sanitation, police services, public works; at same time he continued vital support of San Martín's army; executed Luis and
Juan José Carrera (brothers of former Chilean president) in
April 1818, after their arrest for attempting to return illegally
to Chile and for disturbing order in Cuyo; in 1820 Luzuriaga
resigned as governor of Cuyo and accompanied San Martín's
liberating army to Peru as one of division commanders; after
performing various missions, both political and military for
San Martín in Peru, he returned to Buenos Aires on another
assignment in 1822; following San Martín's resignation from the
army and his departure from Argentina (1823), Luzuriaga found

himself without support from later Buenos Aires governments; retired to quiet rural life, wrote his memoirs which were approved by San Martín, then living in France; Luzuriaga died at his small country estate in Pergamino in relative poverty.

LYNCH, BENITO (1885-1951).   Novelist of Argentine rural life and gaucho culture.

Born in La Plata, son of one of founders of El Día; worked as journalist while engaged in early literary endeavors; published first novel Plata Dorada, 1909; continued writing, presenting life in Argentine countryside in tradition of R. B. C. Graham and W. H. Hudson; last and best known novel El romance de un gaucho (1930) reveals his empathy with those who lived on pampas and his understanding of psychology of gaucho and criollo; this novel considered to be most faithful representation of real gaucho life and culture (see Gaucho; Gaucho Literature).

See Nicolás Cocaro, Benito Lynch (Buenos Aires, 1953); Julio Gaillet-Bois, La novela rural de Benito Lynch (La Plata, 1960).

MACANA. Large wooden club used as hunting and fighting weapon by most Argentina Indians before and during the conquest; especially used by Indians of the northwest, Chaco, and northern and central pampas area (see Indians).

MACHISMO. Term commonly used throughout Latin America to denote possession, in a high degree, of such traditionally manly traits as courage, virility, unusual capacity to dominate one's self, others, and the situation involved, or the ability to accept the inevitable with stoicism; its roots lie in the Spanish heritage, but life in the sparsely settled, isolated colonial Argentina, especially on the pampas, soon revealed that only a man possessing such qualities could survive; Argentine machismo (not necessarily always called by that name) came to be accepted as a desirable, if not necessary, trait for Argentine men; by the end of the eighteenth century, this type was personified by the horseriding cattle worker--the gaucho; following the war of independence and in the civil wars that followed, all leaders who survived any length of time--from Artigas and Güemes to Rosas and Urquiza--came from this kind of background; the revival of the gaucho in folklore and literature (see Gaucho; Gaucho Literature) has continued this emphasis on machismo into modern times and it still plays a role in the selection of national or provincial political leaders although no longer the determining factor.

MACIEL, JUAN BALTASAR (1727-1788). Priest and church dignitary; educator; advisor of viceroys; intellectual of the Enlightenment; known as the maestro (schoolmaster) of Generation of May Revolution.
    Born in Santa Fe, educated at Córdoba and at San Felipe University in Santiago, Chile; returned to Buenos Aires where he discharged various ecclesiastical responsibilities; 1766, as vicar general and governor of diocese, following Bishop Manuel Antonio de la Torre, continued reform activities; member of commission of Holy Office of Inquisition; 1770-1787 supervised all education in diocese; served as advisor to viceroys; liberal in his own thinking and possessed of fine library (one of best in Buenos Aires) of more than 1000 volumes, including works of French philosophes and other writers of the Enlightenment period; advised Pedro de Ceballos that Jesuit main house in Buenos Aires and their wealth should be

519

used to establish colegio and university--beginning of San Carlos Academy (1772) of which Maciel became one of first faculty
members and the one who seemed to have greatest influence
upon such later patriot leaders as Cornelio Saavedra, Juan Hipólito Vieytes, Manuel Belgrano, Mariano Moreno, and Bernardino Rivadavia; collaborated closely also with Viceroy Juan
José Vértiz y Salcedo who named him first chancellor of education and for whom he drew up a memorial from the ecclesiastical cabildo setting forth his own ideas about liberal education; quarreled (1787) with next viceroy, marqués de Loreto;
died in exile in Montevideo (1788) shortly before royal answer
to his appeal arrived, exonerating him and restoring his positions and properties; left many manuscripts, among them a
gauchesca romance "Canta un guaso en estilo campestre los
triunfos del Excmo. Señor Pedro de Cevallos" (A gaucho sings
in country fashion of the triumphs of His Excellency Pedro de
Ceballos) that foreshadows later gaucho literature.

MACKAU, BARON ANGE R. A. DE   see   ARANA-MACKAU TREATY

MADARIAGA, JOAQUIN (1799-d. ca. 1847).   Governor of Corrientes;
    with his brother Juan, controlled Corrientes in mid-1840s and
    sought to take leadership against Rosas' kind of federalism.
        Born in Corrientes and educated there and in Buenos
    Aires; returning to his native province to devote himself to the
    business concerns of his rural estate, Madariaga found himself
    increasingly involved in politics; joined with his brother Juan
    in overthrow of government of Cabral and became governor of
    Corrientes in 1843; Madariaga, called by modern Argentine his-
    torians one of the "authentic" federalists--i.e., those insisting on
    autonomy of the provinces under constitutional national govern-
    ment, with a better and more equal economic policy for all prov-
    inces, began fight against Rosas by invading Entre Ríos, then un-
    der Justo José de Urquiza, one of Rosas' generals, as governor;
    while Urquiza was diverted into Uruguay by his campaign against
    Rivera, Madariaga formed an alliance with Paraguay and the
    brothers got ready to invade Entre Ríos; Urquiza's defeat and cap-
    ture of Juan Madariaga resulted eventually in the treaty of Álzaga,
    signed by Joaquín Madariaga and Urquiza, bringing Corrientes
    back into Confederation; Rosas had not been consulted and violent-
    ly rejected the treaty; ordered Urquiza to invade Corrientes; the
    latter delayed, in hopes that a new treaty could meet Rosas' ap-
    proval, but situation deteriorated; with peace apparently impos-
    sible at that time, Urquiza moved against his former ally and
    on November 27, 1847, defeated the Corrientes forces, placed
    Benjamín Virasoro in governor's seat; Madariaga fled to Bra-
    zil where he died shortly afterward; on May 6, 1927, his re-
    mains were repatriated and buried in the cathedral at Corri-
    entes, alongside those of Berón de Astrada.

MADARIAGA, JUAN (1807-1879).   Military figure; played active part
    in civil wars; political leader in Corrientes province and
    later in Buenos Aires.

Born and educated in Corrientes; became involved in civil wars at early age; joined unitarist Juan Lavalle in 1839; after latter's death, Madariaga returned to Corrientes where he enjoyed great prestige; commanded movement that overthrew Cabral's government and made his brother Joaquín Madariaga governor of Corrientes (1843); after freeing Corrientes of its enemies, he invaded Entre Ríos and fought a bloody but indecisive battle at Puntas del Palmar; when Urquiza returned from his campaign against Rivera in Uruguay and moved against the allied Corrientes forces, then under General Paz, Madariaga, in command of the latter's vanguard, was taken by surprise, defeated, and captured; during his stay as prisoner in Entre Ríos, Urquiza used him to establish peace with Governor Madariaga in Corrientes, leading to the signing of the controversial, but significant treaty of Alcaraz (see Alcaraz, Treaty of; Urquiza); Juan Madariaga returned to Corrientes; Rosas' rejection of the treaty and orders to Urquiza to invade Corrientes to bring it more closely under Buenos Aires control, brought new fighting with Urquiza victorious and the political power of the Madariagas destroyed in Corrientes; Juan fought, however, in the 1851 campaign of Urquiza's Great Army and against Rosas at Caseros; thereafter, he joined forces with Buenos Aires; participated in the revolution of September 11, 1852, in which Buenos Aires formally broke with Urquiza and the other provinces; commanded one of the Buenos Aires forces against Entre Ríos in November but was forced back by Urquiza; became member of legislature in Buenos Aires and later held other public positions; died suddenly in 1879 in town of San Justo while temporarily away from his home in Buenos Aires.

MADERO, EDUARDO (1823-1894).   Merchant and banker; creator of port of Buenos Aires.

Born in Buenos Aires; nephew of Florencio Varela, Argentine writer and foe of Rosas; Madero conducted business activities in Buenos Aires and Montevideo; served as representative in Buenos Aires municipal, provincial, and national governments and as president of the Bolsa de Comercio, Crédito Público, and Banco de la Provincia; served as government negotiator with Great Britain on financial matters; his name is linked with the development of the port of Buenos Aires to which he devoted himself for decades and which was named for him; in 1892 Madero published a documentary history of this port; he died in Genoa, Italy.

MADRID.   Strategic colonial city in northern Tucumán on road from Córdoba to La Plata (now Sucre, Bolivia); founded April 2, 1592, by Captain Jerónimo Rodríguez Macedo, by orders of Governor Juan Ramírez de Velasco; constantly raided by Lules Indians.

MAGELLAN, FERDINAND (c. 1480-1521).   Navigator; explorer of Patagonian coast; discoverer of westward route to the Far East through the Strait of Magellan.

Portuguese navigator; served in Portuguese East Indies; entered service of Charles I of Spain (soon to become Emperor Charles V); contracted with him to find the coveted westward route to the Orient; set out with five ships in 1519; entered Solís' Mar Dulce (Río de la Plata) in January 1520; named Montevideo and discovered Uruguay river; then continued coasting southward, wintering at San Julián where he suppressed a mutiny of his Spanish captains--first Spanish blood spilled on Argentine soil; on October 21, 1520, discovered strait that bears his name and today divides mainland Argentina from its only territory, Tierra del Fuego; passed through it and across the Pacific to the Philippine Islands where he was killed while participating in a native war; one of his ships, the <u>Victoria</u> commanded by Juan Sebastián de Elcano, after spending some time in the Moluccas, completed the first circumnavigation of the globe by returning to Spain in 1522 by the African route around the Cape of Good Hope.

Antonio Pigafetta, an Italian nobleman with Renaissance background and interests, accompanied Magellan's expedition as an observer and has left the best account of it that we have, including the first map and descriptions of the Patagonian coasts and of the natives (whom Magellan's men named Patagonians because of their big feet) and of the strait and lands through which it passed.

MAIPU, BATTLE OF (April 5, 1818). Critical battle that secured Chile's independence, relieved Argentina from threat of further royalist invasion, and opened way for campaign into Peru to complete San Martín's continental strategy for emancipating southern South America.

Following his defeat of patriot troops at Cancha Rayada March 19, 1818, General Mariano Osorio (q. v.) moved his royalist army of more than 5000 troops northward against Chilean capital, Santiago; San Martín, with army of same size, came down to meet him on plain of Maipú, just north of river of that name and about ten miles from outskirts of Santiago, effectively blocking Osorio's access to either Santiago or the port of Valparaíso; battle was joined April 5, 1818, with San Martín's forces opening attack; after six hours of very bloody fighting, San Martín's victory was complete, with practically all the royalist forces killed or captured; victory bought at cost of more than 1000 patriot casualties, including deaths of over half the blacks from Cuyo; credit given to San Martín's successful execution of brilliant battle plan, including use of oblique attack, that had wrested victory so soon after disastrous defeat at Cancha Rayada; (before battle, French general in Santiago had advised against battle, saying that even Napoleon could not have overcome military obstacles posed).

Although battle of Maipú forced viceroy of Peru to abandon further plans for reconquest of Chile and Argentina and to concentrate on strengthening defenses of Peru, two years passed before San Martín could undertake his expedition there, not only because of difficulties involved but also because

political leaders in Chile and Argentina--especially those in
Buenos Aires--felt it essential to turn to other, closer problems and developments now that Maipú had ostensibly removed
threats to independence.

MAIZE of INDIAN CORN   see   CORN

MALABIA, JOSE, S. F. (1787-1849).   Jurisconsult; signer of Declaration of Independence.
Bolivian, with doctorate in jurisprudence from Chuquisaca; elected to represent province of Chichas (then part of
United Provinces de la Plata, now in southwestern Bolivia) at
congress of Tucumán, with explicit instructions to favor establishment of constitutional monarchy after independence was declared; signed declaration of independence; went on to Buenos
Aires; served as member of legislature, secretary to governor
Juan Gregorio de Las Heras, and filled other government posts
before returning to Bolivia; eventually became minister of supreme court there.

MALARIA   see   EPIDEMICS OF DISEASE

MALDONADO, LA   see   LEGENDS OF THE CONQUEST

MALLEA, EDUARDO (1903-   ).   Novelist; intellectual.
Born in Bahía Blanca; educated in Buenos Aires; said to
have been first Argentine writer to master European techniques
of modern novel and to become author of first modern Argentine novel; belonged to generation that was deeply questioning
Argentine identity; becoming disillusioned with European forms
he sought a more natural and more genuinely Argentine cultural expression; his Historia de una pasión argentina (1935) combined his search for a personal identity as well as a national
one, contributing to an historical awareness although Mallea
himself remained more a literary figure than a political activist; considered by many to have been the foremost Argentine
novelist of his period, Mallea's works include Fiesta en novi-
embre (1938); La bahía del silencio (1940), which attracted
great popular attention; a pessimistic view of Argentina's cultural and spiritual decline, La vida blanca (written in 1942 but
published in 1960); a complete edition of his works (up to that
time), published in Buenos Aires in 1961, with prologue by
Mariano Picón Salas; a series of short stories in which Buenos
Aires is personified as the major character appeared in 1968;
and in 1969 Mallea brought out La penúltima puerta, dealing
with death; both in Argentina and abroad, the distinction of
Mallea's work has been recognized.
See John Polt, The Writings of Eduardo Mallea (Berkeley, California, 1959).

MALON.   Araucanian term that came to be commonly applied to the
violent Indian surprise attacks on towns and ranches that continued along the borders from the time of the conquest to the

late nineteenth century; the expression remained in the Argentine vocabulary to denote a "dirty trick" or sudden, unexpected
damage inflicted by one person against another.

MALVINAS, LAS   see   FALKLAND ISLANDS

MANSILLA, LUCIO NORBERTO (1792-1871).   Military hero of independence and of Anglo-French blockade; legislator; administrator.
        Born in Buenos Aires; fought against British invasions
1806-1807; entered military career as cadet in patricios (1810);
involved for next four years in fighting in Banda Oriental (modern Uruguay); wounded in chest (1813) while fighting Portuguese;
sent to Mendoza in 1815 to join forces of José de San Martín;
recruited and trained troops for Army of the Andes; second in
command of first vanguard division in crossing Andes and at
victory of Chacabuco; accompanied Juan Gregorio de Las Heras
as aide-de-camp on southern Chilean campaign; returned to
Mendoza at O'Higgins' request, then left Army of the Andes to
become part of government's force in Buenos Aires; once more
active in interior provinces as liaison between Pueyrredon's
government and upriver caudillos in attempt to reach understanding; joined Francisco Ramírez in final defeat of José Gervasio de Artigas ending his attempt to control interior; accompanied Ramírez on latter's final, disastrous campaign into
Santa Fe ending in caudillo's death; returned to Entre Ríos to
lead revolt against Ramírez's successor, demanding that new
government should be established by popular vote; elected governor, Mansilla gave Entre Ríos three years (1821-1824) of
progressive government, determined to make up for lost time;
established order throughout province; maintained peace with
neighboring provinces; promulgated provisional statute for government; forbade use of any but national flag; encouraged commerce (himself interested as saladero owner) by establishing
custom houses on Paraná and Uruguay rivers; organized or reformed institutions of justice, legislation, administration, even
of church; emphasized universal primary education based on
most modern methods; encouraged construction of schools,
public works, churches, and government buildings; refused second term as governor; accepted selection as delegate to national constituent congress called by Las Heras in 1824.
        Mansilla seems always to have been motivated by desire
for national organization; while governor of Entre Ríos declared publicly (and privately to Estanislao López, caudillo of
Santa Fe) that all progressive action in Entre Ríos was undertaken to form basis, needed in all provinces, for effecting national organization; supported and voted for Rivadavia's centralist constitution of 1826, saying that provinces lacked political
experience and (some of them) educated leadership; returned
to military service to distinguish himself in war against Brazil;
served as member of Buenos Aires legislature 1832-1844; as
Buenos Aires chief of police (1833-1835), placed security services of city on new, firm basis; made commander of reserve

army in late 1830s by Juan Manuel de Rosas (whose sister,
Agustina Ortiz de Rosas, he had married) at time of threatened
military action against Bolivian marshal Andrés Santa Cruz
and his Confederation of the Andes; sent by Rosas to General
Juan Lavalle, after latter's defeat at Quebracho Herrado, to
suggest armistice and to inform Lavalle of Mackau treaty
signed with his French allies; Lavalle rejected this; when British and French established blockade in 1845, Mansilla commanded by Rosas to prevent penetration of Paraná; chains
stretched across river, protected by mounted artillery at Vuelta
Obligado, eventually proved inadequate but Mansilla, severely
wounded in his chest again, became the hero of the day for his
attempt at defense; remained at home for next few years; in
1852, Rosas placed him in command of reserve force left in
Buenos Aires while he went to meet defeat by Justo José Urquiza at Caseros; following overthrow of Rosas' government,
Mansilla went to France where he was cordially received at
court of Napoleon III; returned to Buenos Aires in 1868 and
died in yellow fever epidemic of 1871.

MANSILLA, LUCIO VICTOR (1831-1913).   Military figure; cabinet
   minister; writer; member of intellectual "Generation of 1880."
      Born in Buenos Aires, son of Lucio Norberto Mansilla
and Agustina Ortiz de Rosas (sister of Juan Manuel de Rosas);
after being educated in Buenos Aires, became bored with work
in family saladero and, at 17, left for India; returned in 1851;
next year, following fall of Rosas' government, accompanied
family to France, where he continued his studies; returned to
Buenos Aires a few years later but found it difficult to overcome his kinship with former dictator; entered army and began
writing career; offered his services to Urquiza's Confederation
and became secretary to vice president, Salvador María del
Carril; formed close friendship with Dominguito, son of Domingo Faustino Sarmiento (whom he had earlier come to know);
continued writing and translating of French works; fought (1865-
1868) in Paraguayan war, being wounded in shoulder in battle
at Curupaytí in which he saw Dominguito killed; acted as
spokesman for group advocating candidacy of Sarmiento for
presidency and campaigned actively for him; sent as military
commander of southern frontier of Córdoba province; undertook,
with small party, to explore and study Indian country between
Cuarto and Quinto rivers; entered into friendly relations with
Indians; established Fort Sarmiento around which town of same
name grew up; as governor of Austral Chaco in 1878, founded
present city Switzerland in 1879, and then served in Congress
1882-1892; forced resignation of President Miguel Juárez Celman was rude blow to Mansilla's political hopes as he had supported Juárez; came back, however, as minister of war in
cabinet of José Evaristo Uriburu; sent to Europe in 1895 to
study military schools for ideas adaptable to Argentine academies; General Mansilla retired from army following year
(1896); represented Argentina at court of Kaiser Wilhelm in
Germany 1897; returned to Buenos Aires where he continued

his writing and was one of its best-known citizens; died in Buenos Aires in 1913.

Known as one of most characteristic voices of Generation of 1880, "a spiritual product of our time," one of Argentina's best story-tellers, his writings sometimes criticized but never boring, the Argentine writer most widely read in Paris, Mansilla's works have real significance for historians as well as for his contemporary readers; among best known are: De Adén a Suez (Paraná, 1855); Una excursión a los indios ranqueles, based on his Indian travels while commandant of Córdoba's frontier in 1869, first appeared in La Tribuna of Buenos Aires in 1870; many editions appeared later, one of first in Leipzig; translated into several languages; won award from International Geography Congress meeting in Paris; widely praised (as well as criticized for lack of depth by such contemporaries as Jorge Manuel Estrada); attracted public attention because of new interest in Indians, but even more because of Mansilla's gift for exciting writing and his careful descriptions of this almost unknown area and penetrating insights into society there; Retratos y recuerdos about the men of Paraná in 1852; and Mis memorias: Rosas. Ensayo histórico-psicológico, a thoughtful attempt to give objective portrait of uncle whom he knew well but whose memory was still widely hated in Argentina, appeared in Paris, 1898, with several later editions published elsewhere; finding himself deeply troubled about conditions in Argentina in early twentieth century and worried about the young people who seemed to be completely confused and contentious, Mansilla wrote En vísperas (Buenos Aires, 1910), expressing his ideas on the political and institutional life of his country about to celebrate centenary of independence; died in Buenos Aires, 1913.

See Enrique Popolizio, Vida de Lucio V. Mansilla (Buenos Aires, 1954).

MANUFACTURES see INDUSTRY

MAR DULCE, EL (Fresh Water Sea). Name given to the estuary now known as the Río de la Plata by its discoverer, Juan Díaz de Solís, when he entered it in February 1516.

"MARCH OF THE CONSTITUTION AND LIBERTY" (1945). Unprecedented combined effort of Perón's enemies from the far right and left that resulted in massive popular demonstration demanding restoration of constitutional government.

On July 7, 1945, President Farrell announced at annual dinner of Army, Navy, and Air Force officers that constitutional government would be restored by elections held before end of year; labor unions and other supporters of Perón immediately set up cry for "Perón for President"; August 6, the state of siege, existing since 1941, was lifted, taking advantage of this, Perón's opponents of the Radical, Conservative, Socialist, and Communist parties organized strikes, public meetings, and other demonstrations; then climaxed their efforts by uniting in an enormous march into Buenos Aires September 19, 1945; estimates of numbers involved vary from 70,000 to 800,000, but probably 250,000-400,000 people took part; they demanded an immediate end to military dictatorship and return to constitutional government, with the Supreme Court taking over until a new president could be elected; President Farrell replied by arresting the leaders and reimposing state of siege September 26; March remains proud memory of Argentine democratic action and served as dramatic prelude to violent events of October involving Perón's arrest and return and the restoration of constitutional government with his election in 1946.

MARCH PLEBISCITE (March 7, 1835). Following the assassination of Juan Facundo Quiroga in February 1835, the threat of anarchy and chaos became so real to the Buenos Aires legislature that it voted dictatorial powers to Governor Juan Manuel Rosas for five years; the plebiscite, called to confirm this action, resulted in 9,320 votes for it, eight against.

MARCO DEL PONT, FRANCISCO (1765-1821). President and military commander of captaincy-general of Chile at time that San Martín's army crossed the Andes into Chile.
        Born in Vigo, Spain, General Marcó del Pont had distinguished himself and been promoted to rank of general in Spanish military campaigns before being transferred to the New World; taken prisoner following the fall of Valencia (1809) he was tried by French military court and sentenced to death unless he swore loyalty to Napoleon; Marcó del Pont's refusal brought him respect from Joseph Bonaparte who commuted his sentence to life imprisonment; released in 1814 when the general peace was declared, Marcó del Pont was first named military and political governor of Plaza de Tortosa, then in September designated as captain-general of Chile and president of its royal audiencia; took up his duties there December 26, 1814, and ruled Chile for the Spanish crown until his defeat by San Martín at Chacabuco on February 12, 1817; taken to San Luis with other prisoners of war, he was later moved to the estate of Pedro Ignacio de Mujica, near Renca, where he died May 11, 1821 (see Chacabuco; José de San Martín).

MARMOL, JOSE (1817-1871). Romantic poet and novelist; journalist; one of most important anti-Rosas literary figures; public official and diplomat.
        Born in Buenos Aires; began his education there but his law studies were interrupted; after brief imprisonment by Rosas' forces, Mármol joined other exiles in Montevideo; spent his time writing, both for journals such as El Nacional, edited by Andrés Lamas, and El Comercio del Plata, under Florencio Varela, and, as a born poet, fighting Rosas with passionate, romantic verse of Spanish style; won poetry prize in 1841 and his poem "El Peregrino," 1847, is considered the great poem of the Rosas exiles; most of his poetry and even part of his novel Amalia first appeared in Montevideo.

Following the fall of Rosas, Mármol returned to Buenos
Aires, completing the first Argentine novel, Amalia (q. v.) contributing to various journals, etc.; he also became deeply involved with political affairs; after a diplomatic appointment to
Chile and Bolivia that he accepted from Urquiza fell through,
Mármol joined Mitre and the other porteño leaders who were
determined to keep Buenos Aires out of the confederation being formed by the other provinces under Urquiza; served in
Buenos Aires senate and on commission to revise 1853 constitution so that Buenos Aires could accept it and the republic
could be unified; was sent by President Mitre to Brazil on delicate diplomatic mission on eve of war with Paraguay; was Director of National Library until his death.

MARTIN DE MOUSSY, JEAN ANTOINE VICTOR see MOUSSY, V.
    MARTIN DE

MARTIN FIERRO.   Gaucho epic poem, written by José Hernández,
    in two parts 1872, 1879; often called most vigorous example of
    gaucho poetry; Martín Fierro personifies true Argentine gaucho
    who rises above every privation and injustice with physical and
    moral energy that inspire pride in all Argentines; poem writ-
    ten as appeal for aid of gauchos whose way of life was being
    destroyed and were themselves disappearing as a sector of Ar-
    gentine society; poem met with immediate success and was re-
    vived, two decades later, to receive even greater literary ac-
    claim and popularity as one of most important works of gaucho
    literature; has special value as historical study of gaucho life,
    customs, and psychology; so true to life that gauchos them-
    selves welcomed it into their own folk literature; English trans-
    lation made by Walter Owen, Oxford 1935; New York 1936 (see
    Gaucho; Gaucho Literature; José Hernández).

MARTIN GARCIA ISLAND.   Argentine island in the Río de la Plata
    that has played important role in the history of the area; dis-
    covered by Juan Díaz de Solís (1516) and named for the store-
    keeper of one of his ships, whom the Spaniards buried there;
    for the first four centuries following discovery, this small is-
    land, approximately 28 miles from the federal capital and less
    than 600 square miles in area, dominated all river traffic be-
    tween the interior up the Paraná and Uruguay rivers; all ships
    drawing more than six feet of water were forced to use either
    the eastern channel or the much more dangerous western chan-
    nel along the island, both of them within gunfire of artillery
    on the island; in 1765 the Spanish royal government, in control
    of both sides of the Río de la Plata, began to use the island
    as a detention center for prisoners; during the war for inde-
    pendence, however, and the various wars that followed--with
    Brazil, with the French, and civil wars--it was the strategic
    value of the island that mattered and its possession became a
    vital concern; Guillermo Brown captured it from the royalists
    (1814), Brazilians occupied it briefly in 1826, Rosas fortified
    it, Urquiza's Confederation and Buenos Aires province fought

over it and later Argentine presidents strengthened it and made
it a naval base; during the late nineteenth and early twentieth
centuries the island was a major bone of contention between
Brazil and Uruguay, on the one hand, desiring to internation-
alize the Río de la Plata and Argentina, on the other, claiming to be a national river; by the 1930s and 1940s, with the
western channel having been deepened and made the most important one and the navigation rights generally agreed upon,
Martín García island once again began to be used as a special
prison, usually for political prisoners, with Yrigoyen sent there
in 1930, Perón in 1945, and Frondizi in 1962.

See Teodoro Caillet-Bois, Historia naval argentina (Buenos Aires, 1944) for military and naval action involving island.

MARTÍNEZ, ENRIQUE (1789-1870). Patriot; hero of wars of independence; cabinet minister; member of Buenos Aires oligarchy.

Born in Montevideo; entered military career in 1801;
fought against British invasions 1806-1807; in 1810 was captain
of infantry regiment in Buenos Aires and part of the patriot
group that met at house of Rodríguez Peña; joined in patriot
activities that year along with José Darregueira, Manuel Belgrano, Tomás Guido, and others; campaigned against Montevideo (1814) and after its surrender joined the Army of the Andes in Mendoza (1815) as Lt. Colonel commanding 8th regiment
of line infantry; fought in all major engagements in liberation of
Chile: Potrerillos and Guardia Vieja (in Andes) Chacabuco,
Curapaligüe, Gavilán, siege and assault on Talcahuano, surprise
of Cancha Rayada, victory at Maipú; went to Peru in San
Martín's liberating army, fighting in assault on Callao, defense
of Lima, actions at Torata and Moquegua; by 1821 he was a
brigadier general, chief of staff and general-in-chief of the
Army of the Andes; later became field marshal; remained in
Peru after San Martín's departure, continued fight for independence under Bolívar, then returned to Argentina; on his way
home, in Chile, he was placed in command of the remnant
(76) of granaderos a caballo and led them back to Argentina.

In 1831 he accompanied General Juan Ramón González
Balcarce (q. v.) as chief of staff on campaign into Córdoba;
served as Balcarce's minister of war (1832-1833) when latter
became head of Buenos Aires government; the return of Governor Rosas after his victorious campaign against the Indians
in the south plunged Buenos Aires into political strife that became violent; in this struggle between Rosas' supporters and
his enemies, Martínez became the leader of those federalist
Buenos Aires landowners and others who opposed Rosas and he
persuaded Balcarce to give up his own preferred neutrality and
to oppose Rosas; eventually a break came--when Balcarce
threatened legal action for slander against a Rosas paper, Balcarce's government was ousted, with a new one under Viamonte
coming in to finish his term before Rosas' complete takeover
in 1835; Martínez fled to Montevideo where he remained until
1854; supported Fructuoso Rivera in his military campaigns
and also served as his cabinet minister; continued in responsible

military and government positions; after his return to Buenos
Aires, Governor Alsina appointed him military inspector general in 1857.

MARTINEZ, ENRIQUE (1888-1938). Vice president with Yrigoyen,
1928-1930; radical political leader; physician.
Born in Córdoba; graduated in medicine, Buenos Aires,
1910; became active politically in Unión Cívica Radical; elected
national deputy in 1918; won election for governor of Córdoba
in 1928 but gave it up to accept vice presidency with Hipólito
Yrigoyen, replacing Francisco Beiro who had died; when Yrigoyen, very ill, found himself unable to hold out further against
military revolt led by José Félix Uriburu, he formally delegated his power to Dr. Martínez September 5, 1930; immediately the latter imposed a state of siege to restore order but
it was useless; September 6 it was obvious that the Radical
government had no support and both Yrigoyen and Martínez resigned; latter retired to private life; was killed in an accident
while riding horseback.

MARTINEZ DE HOZ FAMILY. Family that played a leading role for
more than a century in the development of the agropecuarian
industries in Buenos Aires province that laid foundations for
Argentine lucrative trade throughout nineteenth and early twentieth centuries; founded by José Martínez de Hoz (d. 1819);
Spanish merchant, born in Madrid, who moved to Buenos Aires
late in the 18th century; became active in hide and tallow trade
and other rural pursuits; involved himself in public life, serving several terms as member of cabildo--first alcalde in 1797,
giving of his services and wealth to defense of Buenos Aires
against the British 1806-1807, and serving in the consulado; in
the cabildo abierto, May 1810, his Spanish loyalty caused him
to support the inclusion of viceroy Cisneros in the new junta
to be formed; a devout Catholic, he was a member of the
Third Order of St. Francis and active in the Hermandad de
Caridad (Charity Brotherhood).
A few of the later members of this family are: José
F. Martínez de Hoz (1823-1871), hacendado who devoted himself to improvement of stockbreeding; one of the most enthusiastic supporters of the founding of the Sociedad Rural Argentina (q.v.), he became its first president in 1866; forced to retire because of poor health in 1870; died in Córdoba.
Miguel Martínez de Hoz (1832-1868), military hero;
born in Buenos Aires; after attending primary school, devoted
himself to rural affairs in southern Buenos Aires province;
drawn into military action, fought at San Gregorio under Colonel Pedro Rosas y Belgrano; took part in defense of Buenos
Aires, 1852; in 1853 he went to Europe, returned to military
service in Buenos Aires the following year, in 1859 he was
serving as military commandant at Lobería when news of Urquiza's defeat of Mitre at Cepeda arrived; it touched off a revolt in which Martínez de Hoz, although seriously wounded in
an assassination attempt, distinguished himself in pursuit and

punishment of the rebels; as chief along the frontier, he engaged in many combats with the Indians; when war with Paraguay broke out, he presented himself as volunteer to General
Mitre (his friend); served on general staff, taking part in several engagements before he was assigned to the campaign in
Mendoza to suppress montoneros and caudillos Saá and Varela;
returned to Paraguayan war; taken by surprise at the Reducto
Corá (battle of Acayuazú) July 18, 1868, he was badly wounded,
but continued to fight off his opponents, until he dropped dead;
the story of Colonel Martínez de Hoz's dramatic and heroic
death was recorded by José I. Garmendía in a chapter of La
cartera de un soldado.

    Federico Lorenzo Martínez de Hoz (1865-1935), hacen-
dado and public figure; born in Buenos Aires, studied in Colegio Nacional; managed the family estates and added new ones;
pioneered in introduction of the modern cabañas (cattle-breed-
ing ranches) that made Argentine beef acceptable to foreign
markets; introduced extensive agriculture on his estancias and
interested himself in the economic situation of his tenant farmers; spent much of his time in Europe studying better methods
of cattlebreeding and improved living conditions of rural workers; exercised real leadership in these fields as president of the
Sociedad Rural Argentina; named a director of the Banco Hipotecario Nacional in 1930; active in conservative party and Liga
patriótica argentina; he was elected governor of Buenos Aires
province in 1931 but was ousted shortly thereafter for political
reasons.

    Miguel A. Martínez de Hoz (1867-1935), hacendado; edu-
cated in schools of France and England; returned to take charge
of famous family estancias--Chapadmalal, Las Tunas, Quequén,
Burzaco--most of them in southeastern Buenos Aires province
along the coast; these were devoted to extensive agriculture and
breeding of fine horses, cattle, and sheep.

    José Alfredo Martinez de Hoz (1895-   ), magnate in
meat business; born in Buenos Aires; educated in England at
Eton; was president of Sociedad Rural Argentina (1945-1950)
and of Argentine shorthorn cattle breeders.

MARTINEZ DE IRALA, DOMINGO   see   IRALA, DOMINGO MARTI-
    NEZ DE

MARTINEZ DE ROZAS CORREA, JUAN (1759-1813).   Early leader
    of independence movement involving both Argentines and Chile-
    ans; jurisconsult and royal official.
        Born in Mendoza; after attending local schools there, and
    Monserrat and the university in Córdoba, he went to Santiago de
    Chile to complete his doctorate in civil and canon laws at the
    University of San Felipe in 1786; taught philosophy, law, and
    experimental physics at the royal academy of San Carlos in
    Santiago; entered service of royal government, serving in both
    civil and military assignments, much of the time in the Con-
    cepción area, for over twenty-five years under succeeding vice-
    roys; Martínez de Rozas early began to think in terms of inde-

pendence for Spain's American colonies and gathered around
him a group of Argentine and Chilean patriots, working for a
new and better future for their native lands; he carried on correspondence with Manuel Belgrano and kept in touch with other
patriot leaders in Buenos Aires, especially after the May Revolution; when the Chilean revolution took place, he became a
member of the governing junta and eventually its provisional
president and leader of the more radical group; Ricardo Levene
considers him and Mariano Moreno the two great personalities
who gave the revolution (in Chile and in Argentina, respectively) a sense of direction and shaped its political character; and
Bartolomé Mitre credits his work with having helped to prepare
the way in Chile for the success of San Martín's continental
strategy for independence that began with his crossing of the
Andes a few years later; after the first couple of years of patriot government, Martínez de Rozas's bold actions and liberal
ideas had begun to be challenged by other patriot leaders, including those who resented his close ties to the O'Higgins family, and in 1812 he was exiled to Mendoza by the Carreras;
welcomed by his native city, he was immediately made president of its patriotic and literary society but illness, aggravated
by the mountain journey, prevented him from becoming active;
he died in 1813 and was buried in Mendoza; in 1892 his remains
were returned to Chile at the latter's request.

MARTINEZ ESTRADA, EZEQUIEL (1895-1964).   Poet and writer;
    one of ablest critics of twentieth-century Argentine society and
    culture.
          Born in Santa Fe; wrote for La Nación, La Razón, and
    contributed to such reviews as Nosotros, Plus Ultra among oth-
    ers; famous among his longer works is his Radiografía de la
    pampa, 2 volumes (Buenos Aires, 1933; many later editions);
    in this work, now considered a classic and increasingly re-
    spected because so many of its comments and observations have
    been borne out in succeeding decades, Martínez Estrada strips
    away the glittering, wealthy façade of Buenos Aires and other
    coastal areas and reveals the divisive forces at work through-
    out the changing society; he maintains that Argentina has no
    real culture of its own but simply reflects bits and pieces of
    European civilization; Alain Swietlick has translated Radiogra-
    fía into English with the title X-Ray of the Pampa (Austin,
    Texas, 1971); other essays with historical significance include
    Cabeza de Goliath: microscopía de Buenos Aires (Buenos
    Aires, 1940; 3rd edition 1957); Muerte y transfiguración de
    Martín Fierro (2 v., Mexico, D.F. 1948; 2nd edition 1960);
    ¿Qué es esto? Catalinaria (Buenos Aires, 1956); and Para una
    revisión de las letras argentinas: prolegómenos, compiled by
    Enrique Espinoza (Buenos Aires, 1967).

MARTINEZ PAZ, ENRIQUE (1882-1952).   Jurisconsult; university
    professor; writer.
          Studied and taught in Córdoba; represented liberal politi-
    cal thought and ethical concept of law; taught comparative civil

law, directed institute of American studies, and was dean of
law faculty; served as member and president of supreme tribunal of justice; president of academy of history in Córdoba
and of Instituto Deán Funes; traveled to United States and Europe to study institutions, historical and philosophical research,
especially in field of legal philosophy; is said to have introduced neo-Kantianism into Argentine studies of legal philosophy;
belonged to such learned societies as Argentine national academy of history, academy of political sciences in Philadelphia;
and institute of comparative law, Paris; honored by doctor's
degrees from San Marcos University, Lima, and University in
Rio de Janeiro, Brazil; published many works on law and history; among them is Dalmacio Vélez Sársfield y el Código Civil Argentino.

MARTINEZ PAZ, ENRIQUE (1908-   ).   Lawyer, professor, cabinet
     member.
          Born in Córdoba; received his doctorate in laws there,
     1933; taught in both the Colegio de Monserrat and University of
     Córdoba 1936-1946; became owner-editor of La Justicia; forced
     out of university for political reasons 1946-1955; returned af-
     ter Perón's government had been ousted; in 1966 became Min-
     ister of Interior, in charge of justice, education, police, and
     relations with provincial governments, in President Onganía's
     cabinet; resigned later in the year in a cabinet reorganization;
     wrote extensively on subjects dealing with history and law.

MARTINEZ ZUVIRIA, GUSTAVO (1883-1962).   Novelist, better known
     by pseudonym "Hugo Wast"; Catholic nationalist; public figure.
          Born in Córdoba; graduated from faculty of law and so-
     cial sciences at Santa Fe; taught for a time and served as na-
     tional deputy; served as president of National Commission of
     Culture and Director of the National Library; in 1941 he was
     national interventor in Catamarca; in 1943 he was drawn into
     politics further by the GOU (q.v.) and Peronists in their ef-
     forts to gain support from the Catholic nationalist right group;
     as minister of justice and public education in cabinet of Pres-
     ident Ramírez, he implemented the latter's policy of re-estab-
     lishing religious (Catholic) instruction in public schools; also
     clashed with students when he attempted to exert control over
     national universities, in effect nullifying the University Reform;
     in many ways, however, he helped to pave way for public ac-
     ceptance of Perón's national doctrine of justicialismo (q.v.),
     that sought to establish for Argentina a middle ground between
     collectivism and individualism.
          He was one of most popular Argentine novelists, a pro-
     lific and controversial writer of escape novels and adventure
     stories; many contained vitriolic attacks on democracy, com-
     munism, foreigners, and Jews; but they were well-written, de-
     scribing the sentimental, historical aspects of the nation; they
     brought him international fame, being translated into many lan-
     guages; among the best known of these are: La flor de durazno,
     (1911; marked beginning of his use of pseudonym Hugo Wast);

translated into English as Peach Blossom (New York, 1929);
Valle negro (1918), Black Valley (New York, 1928); Desierto de
piedra (1925), Stone Desert (New York, 1925; translated into
nine other languages); Los ojos vendados won literary prize of
1927; Lucía Miranda (1929), The Strength of Lovers (New
York, 1930); was a member of the Spanish Royal Academy.

MARXISM.   Karl Marx's ideology made its way to Argentina in the
latter part of the nineteenth century; working class Marxism
was sponsored by some early labor leaders; more important
was its appeal to the intellectuals led by Juan B. Justo (q. v.)
and his colleagues who founded the Argentine Socialist party
and newspaper, La Vanguardia; Justo translated much of Das
Kapital from German into Spanish; Marxist ideas, along with
those of positivism, interested Argentines looking for new realistic social political, philosophical alternatives to those of
Romanticism; the Communist Party was established on Marxist
principles by Victor Codovilla (q. v.); the Marxist stress on
importance of a working-class revolution to destroy or effect
radical change in existing institutions found little support in
Argentina where labor groups and the middle classes were more
divided internally than against each other (see Labor; Middle
Classes).
        See Luis Aguilar, ed., Marxism in Latin America (New
York, 1968); Silvio Frondizi, La realidad argentina, 2 v.,
(Buenos Aires 1955-56, and later editions); and Robert J. Alexander, Communism in Latin America (New Brunswick, 1957).

MASCARDI, NICOLAS (1625-1673).   Jesuit missionary, explorer,
linguist, and martyr.
        Born in Italy, entered Jesuit Order in 1638; came to
Chile in 1650 to become a missionary to the Indians as soon
as his studies were completed; learned Araucanian language
and was assigned to posts in southern Chile; while rector at
school there, became interested in plight of number of Indian
captives from eastern side of Andes, as well as in the story
told by one of the women captives who told him of the City of
the Caesars (q. v.) and promised to guide him to it; accompanying his charges to their home in Argentina (1670), he spent
the rest of his life exploring Patagonia from the mission base
that he established on north shore of Lake Nahuel Huapi, crossing it from the Pacific to the Atlantic and penetrating southward to the Strait of Magellan, never finding the elusive Caesars but making a name for himself as one of the greatest Patagonian explorers; killed by hostile Indians with their stone
boleadoras while on another missionary-exploring trip in 1673;
mission destroyed also; rebuilt a little later but only briefly
occupied.

MATACOS, MATAGUAYOS.   Short, primitive Indians found living in
western Chaco forests at time of conquest; had moved down
from north; hunters and gatherers as well as fishermen; knew
how to make dugout canoes from hollowed trunks of trees;

weaving of textiles was their most important industry; used bow
and arrow, macana, and spear; constructed houses of branches
set in ground and joined overhead in an arch; generally peaceful but joined other Indians in fighting Spaniards; Matacos did
not adopt the horse as did some of the other Chaco Indians;
many of them were gathered into missions--Centa, Nuestra
Señora de las Angustias, Orán, Saldúa, and Río Seco--during
Spanish period; the few remaining Matacos in modern times are
generally agricultural, often working in sugar cane fields, and
living with other workers; many have lived in the Protestant
(especially Anglican) religious colonies, like Algarrobal, Yuto,
San Patricio, and San Andrés.

MATE   see   YERBA MATE

MATERA, RAUL.   One of most respected Peronist leaders in 1960s.

MATHEU, DOMINGO (1765-1831).   Spanish merchant who became political and financial supporter of Argentine independence movement.
       Born near Barcelona, Spain; educated as a pilot; Matheu
   became associated with his brother Miguel who had obtained one
   of Cádiz monopolies for trade with colonies; after making several trips to Buenos Aires, Domingo Matheu located there in
   1793, establishing one of largest commercial houses in the city;
   in 1806-1807 he fought against British invasions as an officer in
   the Miñones corps; was strongly influential in Buenos Aires cabildo and became early supporter of independence; during May
   Revolution he was elected member of the patriot Junta in 1810
   and was acting as president of it the following year, during
   Saavedra's absence on army inspection tour, when the Junta was
   dissolved, September 23, 1811, and the first Triumvirate government was established to strengthen executive authority.
       During the early period of patriot government Matheu's
   financial support and commercial background proved invaluable;
   his financial generosity was largely responsible for the support
   of the early liberating expeditions sent to Bolivia, Paraguay,
   and Uruguay in attempt to bring all provinces into the movement;
   it was often his credit or his signature that kept the patriot governments from financial crisis, while his commercial contacts
   with the interior also proved valuable to the cause; following the
   dissolution of the Junta, Matheu became director of the gun factory and in 1813 he was also given responsibility for manufacturing military uniforms; retired to private life in 1817, he
   continued his interest and support of Argentine public affairs until his death in Buenos Aires in 1831.

MATIENZO, BENJAMIN (1891-1919).   Pioneer Argentine aviator.
       Born in San Miguel de Tucumán, son of distinguished
   Bolivian-born jurist of the same name; the young Benjamín entered a military career and, fired by the current enthusiasm for
   aviation, enrolled in the Escuela de Aviación Militar in El Palomar; in May 1919 the young lieutenant and two associates,

Pedro L. Zavani and Antonio Parodi, were in Mendoza, preparing to attempt the crossing of the cordillera of the Andes; on May 28, they took off but, finding the weather extremely unfavorable, Zavani and Parodi returned to Mendoza; Matienzo pushed on, determined to reach his destination; finally forced to land near Las Cuevas, he froze to death while attempting to walk to the town; his body was recovered months later; various monuments have been erected honoring his courage and heroic efforts.

MATIENZO, JOSE NICOLAS (1860-1936).   Jurist; historian; public official.

Born in San Miguel de Tucumán; after attending local schools, he continued his education in Buenos Aires, studying under José Manuel Estrada; received his law degree in 1882; Matienzo had already begun writing and publishing in a career that marked him as one of the most prominent members of the "Generation of Eighty" (q. v.); became a member of the Círculo Científico, formed in Buenos Aires in 1878; also a member of the Ateneo in 1892; from 1904 to 1927 he held various appointments in the Faculty of Philosophy and Letters in Buenos Aires; in 1906 he became dean of the faculty and began his important work of compiling and publishing the documents relating to the period of national political organization; this originated the history section that later became the Institute of Historical Research; his efforts also stimulated research in all archives, both personal and public, national and provincial, throughout the nation, thus making an important contribution to both the teaching and writing of national history.

Matienzo had meanwhile entered public service as legal adviser to ministry of public works in Buenos Aires (1885); member of commission to draw up laws regulating all railroads operating in Argentina (1889); civil judge in La Plata (1889-1890); he became involved in the revolutionary activities of 1890-1893, having been a supporter of President Miguel Juárez Cleman; strongly supported Argentine federalism in his writings and politics and opposed personalistas both in political life and in the interpretation of history; served as provincial senator in Buenos Aires; became president of the national Department of Labor (1907); strengthened its law and founded its publication, the Boletín; was attorney general of the nation, 1917-1922, and in 1923 became minister of interior in cabinet of President Marcelo T. Alvear; in 1932 Matienzo was elected national senator from his native province, Tucumán, and was serving in that capacity at the time of his death.

José Nicolás Matienzo left a long list of published legal and historical writings; Francisco Luis Menegazpi compiled a bibliography of them in Boletín del Instituto de Investigaciones Históricas de la Facultad de Filosofía y Letras, v. XXIV (1940); historians are particularly interested in his thoughtful interpretations of the political history of Argentina in the decades following national reorganization into the republic under Mitre (1862); troubled by the discrepancies between laws, especially reform laws, and political practices, he came to two conclusions that have been widely quoted: 1) that Argentine political history tended to fall into 18-year cycles--i.e., three presidential terms of similar leadership--during which a new political generation grew up and seized power to institute its own new ways; and 2) no reform laws could really change political life until a new social morality had been formed and this, he came to believe--close to Alberdi's position--could only come after Argentina was settled and educated; among his more important writings may be listed El gobierno representativo federal en la República Argentina (Buenos Aires, 1910; (expanded French edition, Paris, 1912); La política americana de Alberdi; cuestiones de derecho público argentino; responsabilidad judicial; and Proyecto de código penal, a plan for penal reform co-authored by Matienzo, Norberto Piñero, and Rodolfo Rivarola.

MATIENZO Y PERALTA, JUAN DE (d. 1580).   Oidor of Charcas; jurisconsult and legal writer.
        After having served for about seventeen years in the chancellery of Valladolid and having established his reputation as a writer on legal matters, Lic. Matienzo left Spain for South America; there he served as legal adviser to the viceroy of Peru and as oidor (judge) and much of the time as president of the audiencia of Charcas (to which the territory of modern Argentina was then attached); during this period (1561-1579), he pushed hard for a settlement and port on the Río de la Plata to avoid the dangerous voyage through the Strait of Magellan or the awkward transit across Panama that were the only acceptable routes from Spain to Peru; under his influence the audiencia sent strong recommendations for this to the crown, 1563, 1566, and 1567 and probably influenced the reestablishment of Buenos Aires in 1580 although it failed to become the major port of entry envisioned by Matienzo; he also aided Viceroy Francisco de Toledo in drawing up the legal ordinances and regulations to place the Spanish rule on a firm basis throughout the viceroyalty (then including all Spanish South America); these drafts, along with other papers, were included in the manuscript entitled "Gobierno del Perú," of which several copies remain; in 1910 the Faculty of Philosophy and Letters of the university in Buenos Aires used the one found in the British Museum to publish the first edition of this colonial legal work; Matienzo had brought most of his family to America and one of his daughters married Francisco de Aguirre, founder of Santiago del Estero; when the latter got in trouble with the Inquisition and was taken to Charcas for trial, Matienzo used his influence to see that the charges were dismissed and Aguirre restored to government favor; Juan de Matienzo is believed to have died around 1580.

MATORRAS, JERONIMO (1720-1775).   Governor of Tucumán, conqueror of Chaco.   Arriving in Buenos Aires about 1750 with a rich cargo of trading goods from Spain, Matorras quickly made a fortune and public place for himself; held various municipal and royal appointments and performed his public functions well; as alférez real (municipal standard-bearer with special honors and responsibilities in Buenos Aires), he organized and presided over the festivities marking the coronation of Carlos III; while back in Spain, around 1767, he succeeded in getting an appointment as governor of Tucumán, on condition that he would pacify and evangelize the Indians of the Chaco; on this same trip he was granted permission to bring his young cousin Gregoria Matorras (later to become the mother of the liberator José de San Martín) back to Buenos Aires with him; after various political difficulties, Governor Matorras in 1774 led an expedition of soldiers and missionaries nearly 700 miles east from Salta into the Chaco, defeated the Indians, gathered them into reducciones (missions), and finally made a peace agreement with Indian chief Paykin that brought a measure of security to the northeastern Indian frontier, especially to the province of Santa Fe; while organizing a new expedition for the Chaco, Matorras contracted a fever and died near the reducción of San Joaquín de Ortega (in Salta); meanwile he had commissioned artist Tomás Cabrera to paint the scene of the treaty-signing between himself and Paykin; this picture eventually was hung in the national historical museum and has been widely reproduced.

"MATORRAS, JOSE." Name used by José de San Martín, liberator, attempting to travel incognito on his return trip to the Río de la Plata, 1828-1829; Matorras was his mother's surname.

"MAY DOCTRINE." Statement of principles to which all Argentine governments have subscribed, at least nominally; it takes its name and its core substance from the official pronouncements of the first autonomous Argentine government, the Junta formed by the May Revolution in 1810; modified later, especially by the Assembly of 1813, it is essentially a national commitment to a free and open society; originally based on European ideas of the eighteenth century-Enlightenment and the ideology of the French Revolution, it won immediate acceptance in Buenos Aires but only gained favor throughout the provinces after it had been adapted to the realities of Argentine life and historical background.

MAY REVOLUTION, THE. Name given to series of events in Buenos Aires, culminating May 25, 1810, from which Argentines date their independence although it was not officially declared until July 9, 1816. Tensions had been rising in Buenos Aires ever since the British invasions of 1806-1807 during which the local residents and leaders (both Spanish and Creole) had had to defend their city with little or no help from the viceroy and royal government; the succession of political changes in Spain 1808-1810 had heightened these--the abdication of Charles IV and succession of Ferdinand VII, followed by Napoleon's capture of both monarchs and his occupation of Spain, placing his

brother Joseph on the Spanish throne; Buenos Aires accepted
the viceroy Cisneros sent over by the Spanish junta government
and he did his best to end the friction developing between creoles and Spaniards and to free trade from restrictions; news
arrived in May 1810, however, that Napoleon's troops had captured Sevilla, with the Junta dissolved; an attempt was being
made to establish a new one on an island near Cádiz but, for
all practical purposes, Spain was under French rule.

Revolutionary Argentine leaders had for several years
been discussing several alternatives to Spanish rule: they had
rejected both a British protectorate and the rule of the French
king Joseph Bonaparte; independence had been discussed, possibly as a monarchy under Ferdinand's sister Carlota Joaquina,
then in Brazil in exile with her husband King of Portugal; now,
with total breakdown of Spanish power, the time for action had
come as some formula must be established to legitimize government; the viceroy and other royal officials felt the disruption only temporary and wanted to carry on through regular
channels until Spanish monarchy was restored; creoles (and
some Spaniards), wanted more autonomy to set up a government consistent with what the viceroyalty wanted and needed,
rather than to satisfy desires of Spain, and many were eager
to pattern a revolutionary nation like that of the U.S. or
France, in its revolutionary days; legally, they insisted that
Argentina owed allegiance only to the Crown and when that was
gone, all power reverted to the people; the Cabildo of Buenos
Aires, the Patriotic Society and other groups insisted that Cisneros must call a cabildo abierto to decide what should be done;
reluctantly he yielded and called it for May 22.

Of the 450 invitations sent to prominent citizens, such
as military and naval officers, members of the Buenos Aires
cabildo and royal officials, including those of the audiencia and
consulado, leading clerics both of the hierarchy and of the religious orders, professional men (most of them lawyers), and
prominent merchants and landowners, 251 came to the meeting;
as soon as discussion was called for, Bishop Lué of Buenos
Aires rose and is reported to have declared that no problem
existed as Argentine remained under Spanish rule as long as
there was one Spaniard left there to rule it; Juan José Castelli
expressed the much more popular view that, in the absence of
Spanish authority, sovereignty resided in the people and their
representatives in the cabildo should be authorized to form a
new government on this basis; the royal fiscal Manuel Genaro
de Villota granted the legal validity of Castelli's argument but
insisted that the Buenos Aires cabildo had no authority to speak
for the entire viceroyalty; he suggested, therefore, that government go on as usual until national representation could be
achieved in a new congress; three major factions appeared:
1) those who wanted the viceroy to continue in power, with royal judges more closely associated with him; 2) those who
wanted the viceroy deposed and a new government formed either
by the cabildo or by the people; 3) a middle group that wanted
the cabildo to carry on provisionally; on May 24 a compromise

was close to acceptance--Viceroy Cisneros would head a new
junta composed of four members, including Saavedra, and Castelli; in the face of rising popular discontent, all resigned or
refused to serve; the following morning, the people of Buenos
Aires with armed units massed in the plaza in front of the cabildo building and two young men, Domingo French and Antonio
Beruti, brought a petition, signed by 476 prominent citizens,
to the meeting insisting that a junta must be appointed at once,
consisting of the nine men on the list presented; the cabildo
abierto took immediate action by deposing Viceroy Cisneros and
appointing a patriot junta, consisting of Cornelio Saavedra as
president, Mariano Moreno and Juan José Paso as secretaries,
and as members: Juan José Castelli, Manuel Belgrano, Miguel Azcuénaga, Manuel Alberti, Domingo Matheu, and Juan
Larrea, nearly all of them creoles.

For Argentines, the May Revolution has almost mystical
significance; not only was it the first step toward independence
from Spain--i.e., the end of the colonial era--but it also
clearly marked the beginning of a new era in which Argentines
could create their own kind of nation; although this May Revolution was the work of the enlightened minority of Buenos
Aires, it was quickly spread throughout the provinces, by force,
when necessary, but most of the provinces voted to support it
and sent representatives to join with the original members in
forming a national or "great junta"; it proved to be the only
Spanish American revolution growing out of the 1810 legal crisis of Spanish authority that was never suppressed, even temporarily, by the royalists; it also brought the breakup of the viceroyalty of the United Provinces, as Bolivia, Paraguay, and
Uruguay went their own ways.

See Rivardo Levene, Ensayo histórico sobre la Revolución de Mayo y Mariano Moreno (2 v., Buenos Aires 1920-
1921; 4th edition, 3 v., 1960).

MAYORAZGO see LANDHOLDING

MAZA, JUAN AGUSTIN DE LA (1784-1830). Lawyer; independence
leader in Mendoza; signer of declaration of independence.
Born in Mendoza; educated in law at University in Santiago, Chile; returned to Mendoza to enter public life; as member of cabildo was one of José de San Martín's most effective
collaborators in early (1815) organization of Army of the Andes;
represented Mendoza at Congress of Tucumán and signed declaration of independence July 9, 1816; in 1824 led popular junta
of mendocinos to overthrow Governor Pedro Molina whose administration had been unable to solve financial and other problems growing out of new situation; Maza popular hero and member of new triumvirate formed--but that lasted for only one
day; a strong federalist, Maza was member of Mendoza commission to bring request for federal government to national constituent congress; as member of federalist government of Governor Juan Corvalán, was forced to leave Mendoza (1830) when
Col. Videla Castillo, commanding advance force of General

José María Paz (unitarist) entered province; took refuge with rest of government party among Indians of Coleto's tribe, believed to be friendly; massacred in Chacay; Maza's remains buried in Mendoza year later; his wife was Lorenza Moyano.

MAZA, MANUEL VICENTE (1779-1839).   Jurisconsult; political figure; victim of assassination that inaugurated Rosas' reign of terror, 1839.
Born in Buenos Aires; educated at University in Santiago, Chile, as lawyer; as early enthusiast for independence, imprisoned by viceroy in Lima; following return to Buenos Aires remained in seclusion until 1815; emerged to preside over civil commission of justice; drew up regulation, bearing his name, for administration of justice; served as first alcalde in Buenos Aires cabildo (city council) 1816; during the next few years befriended young Juan Manuel de Rosas, beginning close personal and political relationship that ended finally in triple Maza tragedy; active in Buenos Aires politics in 1820s; temporarily exiled (1823) because of involvement in revolt against government of Martín Rodríguez; again exiled, to Bahía Blanca, as one of leaders in uprising against Juan Lavalle (1829); returned to take active role in Rosas' government; barely escaped with his life from Indian assassination on special mission for Rosas while accompanying latter to Córdoba against General José María Paz; as cabinet minister, protested British occupation of Las Malvinas (Falkland Islands); after Rosas' departure from government (1832) to carry out campaigns in the south, Maza served under his successor Juan Ramón Balcarce, took part in October (1833) revolution that brought latter's resignation, then was member of Juan José Viamonte's brief administration; when Rosas, and four other leading Buenos Aires political figures in turn refused to accept governorship because of chaotic and schismatic Buenos Aires political situation, legislature appointed Maza to serve as interim governor (October 1834-March 1835); no important innovations during his rule, although some interpreted his demotion of large numbers of high ranking military officers as perhaps unfriendly to Rosas; sent Juan Facundo Quiroga (most prestigious caudillo of north) on mission to end conflict between governors of Salta and Tucumán; Quiroga's assassination in Córdoba while returning from official mission brought Maza's immediate resignation; Rosas, offered almost complete power, overwhelmingly approved by plebiscite, now returned to governorship (1835-1852); Maza continued as president of house of representatives even though Rosas had exiled his son-in-law Valentín Alsina; also served as judge in trial convicting Reinafé brothers of Quiroga's murder; late in June 1839, Maza learned that his son, Colonel Ramón Maza, had been arrested and was suspected of conspiracy against Rosas; while seated at his desk, late at night, writing to ask his old friend Rosas to show clemency to his young son, Maza was murdered by assassins (believed to be from the Mazorca) who had entered his office, after having blocked off every entrance to the Legislature building in which it was

located; a few hours later Ramón Maza was shot in jail by
Rosas' orders; overwhelmed by double tragedy, Manuel Maza's
widow committed suicide by taking poison; Rosas' personal role
in Manuel V. Maza's death not clear, but Maza apparently had
no relationship with conspiracy; public shocked; assassination
set off wave of terrorism by Mazorca determined to stamp out
all conspiracy.

MAZA, RAMON (1810-1839).   Military officer, shot as leader of
conspiracy against Rosas.
        Born in Buenos Aires, son of Manuel Vicente Maza
(q. v.); entered army early; frequently engaged in military campaigns in south; accompanied Juan Manuel de Rosas in campaign
of desert, 1833; served in frontier garrisons, as well as in
capital; became involved, as leader, in conspiracy being organized by Asociación de Mayo against Rosas; betrayed by colleagues, popular Colonel Maza was arrested and shot in jail,
by orders from Rosas, June 27, 1839, few hours after his
father's assassination by Mazorca.

MAZIEL, JUAN BALTASAR   see   MACIEL, JUAN BALTASAR

MAZO, GABRIEL DEL (1898-   ).   Political activist in University
Reform; civil engineer; educator.
        Born in Buenos Aires; studied in faculty of exact, phys-
ical and natural sciences; became active in university reform
movement; was a founding member of Argentine university federation (FUA); served as its president 1919-1922; became head
of industrial and agricultural chemistry faculty at Littoral University, 1929-30; taught drafting and other subjects at university, La Plata; serving as its vice president, 1943-1945; earlier had become active in FORJA (q. v.); in 1958 he became Arturo Frondizi's minister of defense and later served as ambassador to Uruguay.
        His writings include La reforma universitaria, 3 v. ;
Significación argentina de Yrigoyen; and Historia y doctrina del
radicalismo.

MAZORCA.   Popular name for Sociedad Popular Restauradora (Popular, or People's Restoration Society), political organization
used by Rosas to maintain his government in power.   Established in 1833, during rule of Juan Ramón Balcarce by citizens
interested in returning Juan Manuel de Rosas to power; grew
out of irreconcilable differences between federalist groups but
came to be applied especially against "Unitarist savages" as
their political opponents were described; among early leaders
of Society in Buenos Aires were Colonel Pedro Burgos, first
president, Julián G. Salomón, vice president, whose brother
had been killed by unitarists, Doña Encarnación Ezcurra de
Rosas, guardian of her husband's interests during his absence
campaigning in the south, her parents, and other responsible
porteño citizens; general use of name "Mazorca" (ripe ear of
corn) explained in many ways, including suggestion that organi-

zation stood for indigenous, even earthy creole values and ways in sharp contrast to wordy foreign ideas and alien practices admired by unitarists; its enemies said that it means "más horcas" or more gallows.

One of first acts of violence occurred in 1834 as protest against return of former unitarist leader and president Bernardino Rivadavia to Buenos Aires; in 1835 Mazorca prepared way for Rosas' triumphant return to office and 25 young men in blue uniform harnessed themselves with scarlet cords to draw his carriage through the streets following inauguration; during Rosas' regime, Mazorca was responsible for creating public enthusiasm in his favor, organizing popular demonstrations of adulation; even inducing the Catholic Church to display portraits of Rosas on the altars as Argentina's sole unifying force; spies, hoodlums, and assassins made Mazorca synonymous for terrorism; following Maza conspiracy of 1839 Mazorca launched wave of violence against unitarists and other enemies of Rosas, precipitating flight of many intellectuals and other public figures; new wave of excesses--killings, beatings, kidnapings, torturing, and destruction of property, ordered or condoned by Rosas, made Mazorca both hated and feared; wave of assassinations in 1842 so scandalous that even Rosas protested; modern historians make no attempt to deny or to excuse these excesses, but some point out that political situation in Argentina following anarchy and threatened constantly with civil wars made Rosas believe them to be necessary; and that, barbarous as methods were, they had both roots and precedents in nation's recent political experiences, and were resorted to by all factions, in turn, becoming either executioners or victims as cirumstances permitted; after fall of Rosas, Mazorca abolished and leaders brought to trial, charged personally with crimes committed by Mazorca; documentation of trial preserved in Buenos Aires provincial archives; Manuel Troncoso, Silverio Badía, Fermín Suárez, Estanislao Porto, Manuel Leiva, Manuel Gervasio López, Leandro Alén, Ciriaco Cuitiño, Torcuato Canales, and Antonio Reyes convicted; several executed.

See Carlos F. García, El proceso de los mazorqueros de 1853 (Buenos Aires, 1938).

MBAYA.   Tribe of Indians living north of Asunción, Paraguay, belonging to the Guaycuruan linguistic group of the Argentine Chaco Indians; José Sánchez Labrador (q. v.) opened one of last Jesuit missions before expulsion among these people.

MBORBORE.   Battle in which Jesuit missions destroyed powerful bandeira (Portuguese slave-hunting expedition from Brazil) in 1640; put an end (for the time being) to such raids, assured safety of new missions west of the Uruguay, and demonstrated the military usefulness of arming the Indians.

MEAT-PACKING PLANTS   see   FRIGORIFICOS; REFRIGERATION; SALADEROS

MEDICINE. Medicine, both Spanish and Indian style, had its place
in Argentina from the beginning of the Conquest; a physician
named Hernando de Zamora accompanied Pedro de Mendoza's
expedition to the Río de la Plata (1535-1536); throughout the
rest of the century folk-doctors, Indian curanderos, barbers,
and farriers or horse doctors, had responsibility for medical
matters, with both European and Indian remedies used; by opening of seventeenth century, however, nearly every settlement
had at least one person that was recorded as "physician,"
such as Telles de Rojo in Córdoba and Manuel Alvarez in Buenos Aires; in 1607-1608 Francisco Bernardo Jijón (q.v.) was
given professional status as physician by Cabildo of Buenos
Aires and placed on salary; other physicians, such as Nicolás
Xaqués (q.v.), set up their practices in the rapidly-growing
port city; the religious orders, especially Franciscans and Jesuits, made important contributions in practice of medicine and
study and experimentation with various indigenous plants; Jesuit
Sigismundo Asperger (q.v.) was long remembered for his services during smallpox epidemics among Guaraní Indians during
early eighteenth century; and both he and Pedro Montenegro
(q.v.) left written descriptions of the Indian medicines that they
had used.

In 1779-1780 Viceroy Vértiz y Salcedo (q.v.) established
the Protomedicato (q.v.) under Dr. Miguel O'Gorman (q.v.);
from 1801 to 1808 it operated a medical school, with about 15
students in its opening class; from this time (1802) to about
1820 Dr. Cosme Argerich was the leading figure in medical
training, part of the time maintaining an institute of his own;
his students received a great deal of experience during British
invasions and war of independence; much of medical attention
was centered at this time on use of new smallpox vaccines and
treatment of victims of epidemics.

University of Buenos Aires opened in 1821 with department of medicine that quickly became a medical school; in 1822
Rivadavia established the Academy of Medicine (see Marcial I.
Quiroga, La Academia Nacional de Medicina de Buenos Aires
1822-1972, published by Academy in 1972 to celebrate its 150th
anniversary); during Rosas' period Argentine medical groups
were primarily concerned with developing national sources of
important vaccines and medicines; through British and U.S. contacts, use of chloroform and ether as anesthetics for surgery,
were introduced; throughout this century Argentine physicians
and surgeons received excellent training at home and many of
them supplemented this by further study abroad.

In twentieth century, Argentine medicine reached high
level with two Nobel prize winners in medical research, Bernardo Houssay, 1947, and Luis F. Leloir, 1970 (qq.v.; see also Epidemics of Disease; Smallpox; Vaccinations).

MEDRANO, MARIANO (1766-1851). Priest; controversial churchman
during early national period.
Born in Buenos Aires, brother of Pedro Medrano (q.v.),
member of Congress of Tucumán; graduated with doctorate of

theology and entered ecclesiastical career; held various posts in hierarchy of Buenos Aires and vigorously opposed Rivadavia's proposed reforms of the church; exiled in 1822 because of his insistence that Junta of representatives must support sacred, traditional rights of the church instead of reforms; after vicar apostolic Monsignor Juan Muzi had left Buenos Aires in 1825, he secretly appointed Medrano to take over in Buenos Aires; Medrano did not dare to exercise his full rights until after the fall of Rivadavia's government; in 1829 Viamonte became governor of Buenos Aires and Medrano was appointed Bishop of Aulón (see Aulón) with authority over Buenos Aires diocese; consecrated in Rio de Janeiro in 1830 he returned to take over his position in Buenos Aires, firmly swore to uphold the laws of the province; remained in this position under protection of Rosas until his death in 1851; his portrait was painted by Carlos E. Pellegrini.

MEDRANO, PEDRO (1769-1840). Lawyer, legislator, magistrate; signer of declaration of independence.
     Born in San Francisco de las Garzas, of porteño parents; educated at Monserrat academy in Córdoba and at university at Chuquisaca, receiving doctorate in laws; spent most of mature life in Buenos Aires practicing law and holding various official posts; member of cabildo abierto of May 22, 1810; supported May Revolution; delegate to congress of Tucumán, presiding over preliminary sessions in March 1816; offered amendment, adopted by congress, to Declaration of Independence clarifying nation's determination to be independent, not only from Spain, but from any other foreign power; signed Declaration of Independence July 9, 1816; remained in congress until its dissolution in 1819; elected to senate under new constitution but anarchy prevailed; served in provincial legislature five times during period 1821-1839; became judge in court of appeals, president of it in 1831; in addition to activities as legislator and magistrate, wrote considerable poetry, including Epopeya and La martiniana; died, greatly honored, in Buenos Aires in 1840.

MEJIA MIRAVAL, HERNAN (1531-c. 1592). Conquistador of Tucumán; probably first to introduce wheat and other Spanish agriculture there. Career of this active, prominent conquistador reflects the scope and turbulence of Tucumán's early decades; Mejía Miraval took part in the founding of the earliest settlements--Barco I, II, and III, as well as Cañete; accompanied Francisco de Aguirre at the establishment of the first permanent settlement in Argentina, Santiago del Estero (1553) and three years later introduced wheat, cotton seeds, and grapevines from Chile to strengthen the Indian agricultural base of that colony with Spanish plants; in 1565 he aided Diego de Villaroel in the permanent settlement of San Miguel de Tucumán and seven years later was with Jerónimo Luis Cabrera at the founding of Córdoba, of which he became first alcalde; meanwhile he was actively engaged, as leader or officer, in major conflicts with Indian tribes throughout the entire Tucumán area, suffering at least one very serious wound (1560); he also performed various military and administrative missions for several governors, including the escorting of rebellious conquistadors to Chile after political trouble; going in search of a rumored iron mine in the Chaco and coming back without iron but with a large company of captured Indians; saving San Miguel de Tucumán from annihilation by Indians (1579) by making forced marches from Santiago del Estero to the besieged area; for three decades Mejía Miraval seems to have avoided personal involvement in political violence but in 1580 his friendship with former governor Gonzalo de Abreu brought him into trouble with the new governor, Hernando de Lerma; he suffered exile and the confiscation of his property and that of his wife; spent the next six years in La Plata (now Sucre, Bolivia) and died some time later, probably around 1592 or 1593.

MELO, LEOPOLDO (1869-1951). Law professor; national political figure.

Born in Diamente, Entre Ríos; graduated from faculty of law and social sciences in Buenos Aires, taught there as professor of maritime and commercial law for more than thirty years; entered political life as national deputy from Entre Ríos (1914-1916) and then as senator (1917-1930); in 1923 served as special ambassador to Uruguay; anti-personalist party's candidate for national presidency in 1928, defeated by Hipólito Yrigoyen; held post (1932-1936) of minister of interior in cabinet of President Agustín P. Justo; won many honors in Argentina and abroad for his achievements and writings in field of international law; died at Pinamar, 1951.

MELO DE PORTUGAL Y VILLENA, PEDRO (c. 1734-1797). Fifth viceroy of Río de la Plata; career military officer and royal official. During his two-year rule, Melo was greatly interested in stabilizing the Indian frontiers and in exploring and settling the Patagonian coastal area; commissioned Félix de Azara to make report and proposal, based on careful investigation, for this project; Azara suggested that breaking up of large estates and forming settlements would be more effective than building more forts; Melo died before he could act on it; bread shortage, due to illegal export of wheat and flour, brought new legislation providing for storage of wheat and flour; viceregal residence improved and redecorated to serve as center of increasingly formal social and public events; ships from Manila and the Pacific now entering port; he supervised the strengthening of defenses in Montevideo against possible British attacks; he died at the age of 63.

MENDIZABAL, MARIANO (b. near close of 18th century-d. 1823). Independence fighter; leader of revolt in Army of the Andes, San Juan, 1820.

Born in Buenos Aires, son of silversmith Francisco Mariano Mendizábal and María Paula Basavilbaso; entered

military career at early age; fought hard against British invasions; at outbreak of May Revolution, he became a second lieutenant in the patriot forces; took part in many campaigns, finally (1816) becoming a captain in the Army of the Andes; in San
Juan married Juana de la Roza, sister of the patriot leader
and provincial governor Dr. Ignacio de la Roza; accompanied
Army of the Andes to Chile, taking part in battle of Chacabuco
and O'Higgins' campaign to liberate southern Chile; soon after
this, discharged for disciplinary reasons, he recrossed the
Andes to his home in San Juan; in January 1820 he became the
leader of the revolt known by his name (see Mendizábal, Revolt of) that overthrew his brother-in-law's government and
placed him briefly in military and political command of the
province, but was himself overthrown two months later; deported from the province under armed guard, he went first to La
Rioja, then Salta, Mendoza, and across the Andes to Chile
where O'Higgins sent him on to San Martín in Lima; after a
military trial, presided over by General William Miller, he
was judged guilty of treason and condemned to death; San Martín refused to pardon him in spite of the plea made by Dr. de
la Roza, his own close friend, and Mendizábal was publicly
executed as a traitor in the public square of Lima, January
30, 1822, the victim of his own passions as well as the travail
of the newly-born nation at that time.

MENDIZABAL, REVOLT OF (January 9, 1820). Military revolt that
temporarily imperiled San Martín's continental liberation plan.
In the difficult year of the Argentine anarchy, 1819, San Martín was torn between government orders that he return to Buenos Aires to place his army at its disposal to put down civil
wars or to continue preparations for carrying his fight for independence to Peru and victory; deciding on the latter, he recrossed the Andes to Chile with part of his forces, leaving
others in the Cuyo area for recruitment, reorganization, and
gathering of supplies and horses; the battalion of Cazadores
(hunters) was based in San Juan where it was reorganized for
the coming campaign; former Captain Mariano Mendizábal (q.v.)
was reincorporated in the Cazadores; toward the end of 1819
Mendizábal became the principal instigator of a revolt made up
of the soldiers who hated the harsh, uneven discipline of a new
commander, were uneasy about the disagreement between the
government and San Martín, resented the latter's departure to
Chile, and possibly hoped that a rebellion would enable them to
remain in Argentina; they were supported by federalists, personal and political enemies of the current government of San
Juan and opportunists with an eye on the public treasury; on
January 9, 1820, the army revolted under its sergeants, imprisoned its officers, moved into the city and took over the
government, placing Mendizábal in military and political control
of the province; Mitre has characterized this as originally a
spontaneous revolt, a federalist revolution of the kind found in
many of the provinces as a reaction against the centralism advocated in Buenos Aires; certainly the leaders had no program

and the provinces suffered from the unbridled excesses and
atrocities committed against both persons and properties by
the soldiers as the officers quarreled among themselves and
by the government itself; Mendizábal was forced out and eventually the other caudillos either joined the federalist forces
along the coast or formed marauding bands; San Juan regained
control of its own government and even declared independence;
San Martín sent a commissioner to attempt to salvage what he
could of the military units involved but had little success; although this uprising might be considered as one of many such
violent changes of provincial governments, the revolt led by
Mendizábal acquired a special significance in its threat to San
Martín's plans of liberation, because of its coincidence with
that of Arequito (q.v.) and to San Martín's return to Chile to
make his final preparations for the liberating expedition to
Peru, because units of San Martín's own army were involved,
and because of its unacceptable excesses even in a violent age.

MENDOCINOS. Natives of Mendoza province.

MENDOZA (Province and City)   Central Andean province and capital city with the same name; formerly part of the jurisdiction
of Cuyo, in colonial period; named in honor of Don García
Hurtado de Mendoza, governor of Chile responsible for its
founding; became separate province in 1820.
Location and boundaries.   Province lies in western Argentina along Chilean boundary, between 31° 57' and 37° 34' S.
latitude and 66° 30' and 70° 36' W. longitude; bounded on the
north by San Juan, east by San Luis, south by La Pampa and
Neuquén, and west by Andean cordillera. Area: 58,200 sq.
mi. Population (1970): 975,075. Density: 17 per sq. mi.
Capital: city of Mendoza, located at 785 meters (2574 feet)
above sea level; population 272,758, without counting surrounding settlements.
Geography.   Climate dry and temperate in summer,
cold in winter; arid landscape becomes luxuriantly green when
irrigated; since earliest times artificial irrigation has been
used in the region, facilitated by the fact that province is
crossed by five rivers: from mountains eastward flow the
Mendoza, Atuel, Tunuyán, Diamante, and the Colorado; the
Desaguadero flows from north to south forming boundary between Mendoza and San Luis; the eastern part of the province
is flat but the west rises toward some of the highest peaks in
the Andes: Aconcagua (23,215 ft.), Tupungato (22,440 ft.) and
the Juncal (19,215 ft.); the province lies in the earthquake
belt.
Communications.   Mendoza and Santiago, Chile, have
traditionally been linked through the Uspallata Pass--in modern
times by railroad, highway, air routes; the capital and other
cities, like Tunuyán, San Rafael, San Carlos are linked to
each other and the rest of the nation by rail and highway, as
well as direct air flights to Buenos Aires and other centers.
Economy.   Main industries include petroleum, wine, olive oil

and olives, hydrocarbon products, fruit production--especially
pears, apples, peaches, cherries and dried fruits; limestone
deposits are worked for cement, and Peugeot has a factory of
cars there. Political organization. Mendoza's executive is a
governor elected every four years, permitted to succeed himself once; its provincial legislature consists of House and Senate, with members elected at the same time as those for the
National Congress; provincial courts handle civil and criminal
cases and do not call for jury system; the province is divided
into 18 departments (including the capital), each with its own
local government.

History. (See also Cuyo, for colonial period). When the
Spaniards arrived in Mendoza they found the northern portion
occupied by the Huarpe Indians and the southern by the Puelches; the Huarpes clearly showed Inca influence in their irrigated agriculture, skills in ceramics, and other arts and
skills; on the site of the city of Mendoza stood an Inca fortification, known as the Pucará del Inga; another landmark was
found in the valley of Uspallata, today the property of the Army,
designating the southern end of the Inca road from Cuzco; region visited in 1551 by Francisco de Villagrá, from Chile; he
built a caserío (shelter) there but it burned; in 1560 the new
governor of Chile, García Hurtado de Mendoza, appointed Pedro
Ruíz del Castillo captain general of Cuyo (including modern
provinces of Mendoza, San Luis, and San Juan) with orders to
establish cities there; on March 2, 1561, Mendoza was founded
on the Huarpe site of Huantata; the following year it was transferred to its present location March 28, 1562, by Juan Jufré
who renamed it Resurrección; some Mendocino historians consider Jufré the true founder of their city, rather than Castillo
who had done little more than erect a fort; Mendoza became
the capital of a Chilean corregimiento, under the viceroy of
Peru.

During the 17th and 18th centuries Mendoza was definitely a frontier area; too small and remote to have royal officials,
it developed its own creole leadership in a few families that
provided food supply, defense against the Indians and continuity
of political and civil decisions and institutions even when royal
officials were briefly there; although thousands of Indians had
been given in encomienda, the Spanish encomenderos preferred
to live in Chile; the exorbitant tribute demanded of the Indians,
along with other unfair practices, caused them to decline rapidly in numbers, to such an extent that by 1613 the Cabildo was
requested the introduction of 1000 blacks to supply needed laborers; Indian raids against the city and outlying farms were a
common fact of life; in the late 1660s the city itself narrowly
escaped destruction from the raids of the Pehuenche Indians
led by Tanaqueupú; various irrigation projects were undertaken
by the local authorities, including the linking of the Tunuyán and
Desaguadero rivers in an attempt to make them navigable; the
building of reservoirs to store excess flood waters in the spring
and of a network of irrigation canals to make agriculture, especially growing of grapes, wheat, olives, corn and lentils, pos-

sible; in the Valley of Uco there were sheep, cattle, and horse
ranches; colonial Mendoza's main industry was production of
wine, with the manufacture of carretas (high-wheeled, mule-
drawn carts) for transport of goods between Mendoza and Buenos Aires second; with the opening of the port of Buenos Aires
to trade (1778), Mendoza wines and brandies could not effectively compete with European imports and lost their market;
education in the province was begun by the Dominicans (first
monastery in 1563), largely taken over by the Jesuits (1608-
1767), and then turned over to the Franciscans who maintained
the secondary school and opened the first school for girls in
1780; at the time that Mendoza was detached from Chile to become part of the Viceroyalty of the Río de la Plata (1776), the
province had a population of about 30,000 persons, including
Spaniards and creoles, Indians and mestizos and blacks (mostly
slaves).

　　With the outbreak of the May Revolution in 1810 Mendoza experienced a brief period of confusion; it had accepted
Spanish authority from remote Spain and then from the viceroy
but for the first few decades of independence, it was reluctant
to surrender its own local creole leadership for the domination
of Buenos Aires creoles; on June 23, 1810, however, its cabildo abierto gave its allegiance to the junta of Buenos Aires; the
latter appointed José Moldés (q.v.) as lieutenant governor but
both he and the following governor were resented as porteños
and followers of Mariano Moreno; in 1813 the province of Cuyo
(including Mendoza, San Juan and San Luis) was separated from
the intendancy of Córdoba and given its own first governor, Juan
Florencio Terrada (q.v.); in 1814 José de San Martín became
governor-intendant of Cuyo, with important results for himself,
the province, and the cause of South American independence;
San Martín reformed the customs and tax offices and improved
commerce and labor-management relations; his interest in the
province captured the loyalty of the people of Mendoza who became eager participants in his project of mounting the war for
liberation of Chile and Peru from Spain from this Andean base;
when power politics in Buenos Aires attempted to remove him
from the governorship, Mendoza supported the various movements against Director Alvear that brought the latter's downfall and kept San Martín in Mendoza; while governor of Mendoza
San Martín greatly influenced the declaration of independence by
the Congress of Tucumán as well as the selection of Juan Martín de Pueyrredón as Supreme Director of the United Provinces;
for San Martín personally, Mendoza provided the only home
that his family was to know; his daughter was born there and
he and his wife (see Escalada de San Martín, Remedios) enjoyed a happy rapport with the community; as the Army of the
Andes--in many respects created by the province--prepared to
start across the cordillera, a new governor, Toribio de Luzuriaga (q.v.) gave the province a constructive administration
(1816-1820), stressing education by increasing the number of
schools, including the founding of the Colegio de la Santísima
Trinidad (1817).

551   Mendoza

The anarchy and civil wars of the post-directorate period hit Mendoza very hard (1819-1831); in addition to the political confusions and conflicts between unitarists and federalists
shared by the other provinces, Mendoza's special closeness to
Chile throughout most of the colonial period and its unique relationship to San Martín's liberation expeditions brought acute
tensions at a time when Buenos Aires was attempting to establish political hegemony and to downgrade San Martín's efforts
to carry the fight for South American independence to a successful conclusion in Peru; military revolts, fratricidal civil war,
invasions by neighbor caudillos, _montoneras_, and forces of
Chilean leader José Miguel Carrera, alternating progressive
governors with military caudillos, renewed commercial ties with
Chile marked the period; some progress was made in 1820 when
Mendoza became a separate province and elected its first governor, Pedro de Campos; under Tomás Godoy Cruz (q.v.) the
first newspaper El Termómetro del Día was published; the Lancastrian educational system was introduced; agriculture, trade,
mining were fostered, and tax reform introduced; attempts were
even made to introduce the silk industry (see Godoy Cruz); the
Mendoza delegates to the Constitutional Congress, Tomás Godoy
Cruz, Juan Agustín Maza, and Juan Gualberto Godoy, voted
against the unitarist constitution adopted in 1826; government in-
terventors and unitarist forces attempted to impose their will
on Mendoza but succeeded only temporarily; Indians on the
frontier now took advantage of the turmoil and began heavy
raiding against the settlements and then became allies and mer-
cenaries in the forces of conflicting caudillos; finally, in 1831,
Mendoza became part of the Argentine Federation with Federalists remaining in power throughout most of the Rosas period;
Pedro Molina had a progressive government that created schools,
placed provincial finances on sound basis, signed commercial
agreements with Chile; maintained order by forcing unitarists
to flee in larger numbers into Chile; between 1840 and 1842,
General Lamadrid (then a unitarist) took over Mendoza and persecuted the federalists but in 1842, José Félix Aldao (see Aldaos), the frontier general, became governor and dominated the
area until his death in 1845; a strong but controversial figure,
hated by unitarist historians for his repressive measures and
unconventional life, General Aldao has nevertheless been characterized by Mendoza historian Edmundo Correas as the most
popular of the Mendoza 19th-century caudillos; under Pedro
Pascual Segura (1845-47) the provincial laws were codified; at
the time of the fall of Rosas, 1852, Mendoza was peaceful and
prosperous; continued under its own federalist governor and
signed the Acuerdo of San Nicolás.

A provincial constitution was drawn up and accepted and
Juan Cornelio Moyano (q.v.) served as first constitutional governor, 1856-1859; in the civil wars preceding the national reorganization under Mitre (1862), Mendoza supported the Paraná
government against that of Buenos Aires; even during Mitre's
presidency with the liberals in control (considered the same as
unitarists by Mendoza) a revolt in Mendoza, known as the rebel-

lion of the Colorados, a repercussion of the Chaco revolt in
the north, and largely due to resentment against the conscription of soldiers for the unpopular Paraguayan war, forced
Mitre to return to Argentina and to divert 3500 men to suppress
the revolt, at San Ignacio, March, 1867; meanwhile, in 1861,
the city of Mendoza had been almost totally destroyed by an
earthquake, followed by fire and other destruction, including
looting; at that time Mendoza was still a simple, colonial city
of 12,000 inhabitants living in one-story rural-type homes; in
1862 the rebuilding of Mendoza into a modern city began, centered around a plaza twenty blocks east of its earlier site;
Mendoza's economy was in a depressed state at the close of the
1860s but within the next three decades it had begun to develop
into the modern, cosmopolitan city that seems to be its destiny; in 1870 a teachers' college (normal school) was established, gas was installed for lighting purposes; first bank was
established in 1873; drinking water was piped in; watchmen
placed on security duty; a slaughterhouse was built and agricultural colonies attracted; in 1874 Mendoza again became involved
in national revolution as General J. M. Arredondo took over the
provincial government in the name of the Mitre revolutionaries
(nationalists) against the Alsinistas (Autonomists); Arredondo's
defeat by Colonel Julio A. Roca in battle of Santa Rosa December 7, 1874, ended the revolution as well as Mendoza's efforts
to overthrow national government.

During the 1880s the province was primarily engaged in
the problems of economic growth and social change; the railroad reached Mendoza in 1885 giving its wines access to the
coastal markets; large numbers of Italian vineyard farmers
moved into the area; importation of French vines, improved
technology, French capital to establish wineries made Mendoza
wines competitive in quality with imported ones and protective
tariffs made them competitive in price; a generous land policy
making small farms available to both European immigrants and
Chilean migrant workers, as well as progressive public services such as hospitals, schools, public health services (unable
to prevent cholera epidemics, however, apparently brought in
by railroads) etc., enabled Mendoza (along with Tucumán and
its sugar plantations) to share in the Buenos Aires-dominated
economy more effectively than other interior provinces; federal
intervention in provincial government continued frequently as
Mendoza never felt at ease with Buenos Aires liberals; 1890
revolution against the Unicato (q.v.) failed but the Radical Party
under the leadership of the colorful Lencinas (q.v.) began to
develop strong political competition with the liberals.

During the 20th century Mendoza has continued to know
frequent federal intervention in its provincial government but
its role in the national economy and cultural life have become
increasingly important; its diversified economy is seen as only
beginning to reach its potential as irrigation systems are expanded and improved; traditional crops, especially grapes and
fruits, have been supplemented by cereals and soybeans but
continue to dominate the provincial economy, with Mendoza

producing 97.7 of the wine consumed in the country and more than 50,000 hectares planted in apple, peach, pear, cherry, quince and plum trees; extensive petroleum deposits south of the city provide energy and a base for industry; the wine industry continues to be the most important but Mendoza seems on the verge of becoming one of the great industrial centers of the nation, with industrial plants not only in the city of Mendoza but scattered also throughout the province in its important agricultural centers such as Godoy Cruz, San Rafael, Rivadavia, Tunuyán, Lavalle, Malargüe, Santa Rosa, Maipú, and Luján; its mines, among the oldest in the country--copper, silver and lead, gold, iron, coal, some uranium with new minerals being discovered for exploitation--are expected to contribute to this industrial development; the establishment of the University of Cuyo in Mendoza in 1939 has made it once again a center of the cultural life of the Cuyo area, to which important national professional schools and private universities in the entire area contribute greatly; in 1910 the long dreamed-of trans-Andean railroad once more linked Mendoza with its earliest ties in Santiago, Chile, but succeeding decades have revealed that commercial ties with Chile had little to offer in comparison with those of the Argentine nation of which Mendoza has been an important, contributing part for the past two centuries (see Cuyo; Army of the Andes; José de San Martín; Vineyards; Wine Industry; Petroleum; Yacimientos Petrolíferos Fiscales).

See Agustín Alvarez, Breve historia de la provincia de Mendoza; Edmundo Correas, Historia de Mendoza; Damian Hudson, Recuerdos históricos sobre la provincia de Cuyo; Jorge M. Scalvini, Historia de Mendoza; and other writings on Mendoza and Cuyo area.

MENDOZA, FRANCISCO D.   see   GRAN ENTRADA

MENDOZA, GONZALO DE (d. 1558).   Conquistador: lieutenant governor of Río de la Plata 1556-1557.   One of ablest captains in Pedro de Mendoza's expedition; served in many responsible capacities in first twenty-two years of Río de la Plata settlement; said to have made one of most important single contributions to permanent settlement.

Born in Baeza, Spain, of noble family; forced to leave court for personal reasons; after arrival in Río de la Plata, commanded successful voyage to Brazil for needed supplies (1537); made many expeditions up the coast and upriver, exploring, seeking supplies; established fort at Asunción in 1537, on way downriver from search for Ayolas; later became leading citizen in Asunción, serving both Irala and then Cabeza de Vaca's government; joined other conquistadors and royal officials in replacing Cabeza de Vaca by Irala as governor; accompanied latter on exploratory expeditions in 1540s; served as lieutenant governor when Irala was away; elected governor at Irala's death 1556; died in Asunción following year; had married Irala's daughter and established important criollo family, includ-

ing Hernando Mendoza, one of refounders of Buenos Aires.
See Lafuente Machain and Udaondo (colonial) in Suggested Readings, Appendix III.

MENDOZA, PEDRO DE (1487-1537). First adelantado of Río de la Plata, 1536-1537; original founder of city of Buenos Aires.
Born in Guadix, Spain, of noble, wealthy family; little known about his early life, education, or career; rumored to have amassed fortune in sack of Rome but apparently never held military command; well-known figure in court of Charles V; when emperor determined to occupy lands explored by Sebastian Cabot and Diego García and to open land route through Río de la Plata region from Atlantic to Inca empire, then being conquered by Francisco Pizarro, Mendoza applied for and received the coveted contract for expedition; signed May 21, 1534, a few hours after that given Diego de Almagro for conquest of Chile, contract gave Mendoza title and privileges of adelantado, including appointment as governor and captain general, for life, over Río de la Plata region and extending across continent to include about 600 miles (200 leagues) along Pacific coast, beginning where Almagro's grant ended (geographically confused); he was to settle lands by establishing cities, especially along the Pacific coast after land route had been opened, and to convert the Indians to Christianity; promised a county or earldom (condado) and annual salary of 2000 ducats, with additional 2000, both to be paid out of profits of enterprise; project immediately attracted support and volunteers, among the first to apply being veteran Río de la Plata navigator Diego García, who captained his own caravel; departure delayed for over year due to Mendoza's illness, but sailed from Sanlúcar August 24, 1535 with 11 vessels, approximately 1200 men (numbers differ in various accounts) including about 100 Germans--Charles V had specified that foreigners be included; Diego Mendoza, brother of adelantado, sailed as admiral and chief posts were held by notables: Juan de Ayolas, Domingo Martínez de Irala, Juan de Salazar, Gonzalo de Mendoza, Francisco Ruíz Galán--destined to be numbered as conquistadors, or founding fathers, in early Plata history; also taken along were 100 horses, hogs, barnyard fowl, and tools, implements, supplies and equipment, to facilitate permanent settlement; fleet stopped at Canary and Cape Verde islands for supplies and reinforcements; reached Rio de Janeiro at end of November 1535; ill again, Mendoza turned responsibility over to Juan de Osorio, his second in command; charges brought to Mendoza against Osorio's actions resulted in the latter's immediate execution--an action generally considered hasty, illadvised, and illegal, with demoralizing effects on expedition; after two weeks in Rio de Janeiro ships continued on to Río de la Plata.
Early in 1536 Mendoza started upriver and on February 2, on south bank founded first settlement in Río de la Plata-- Puerto de Nuestra Señora Santa María del Buen Aire (Buenos Aires); built church, home for adelantado, and assorted mud

and thatched shelters (no wood or stone readily available) for
residents; Querandí Indians (about 2000 nearby) proved friendly for a while, exchanging fish and game for Spanish trading
goods, then disappeared; hungry Spaniards sent to find them
returned mistreated, and without food; with survival at stake,
Mendoza sent punitive expedition against Indians, led by Diego
Mendoza, consisting of 300 lancers and 20 cavalrymen; latter
met disastrous defeat from Indians June 15, 1536, on bank of
Luján river (named for Pedro Luján, one of Spaniards killed
there); horses bogged down in swampy area and crippled by
boleadoras; about thirty Spaniards killed, including Diego Mendoza; thereafter Spaniards defended themselves miserably in
Buenos Aires, living in fear of Indian attacks with flaming arrows and torches to destroy their shelters; waiting for reports
from Ayola's explorations seeking route to Peru, as well as
better site for settlement and food, and also waiting for food
supplies from Brazil; Mendoza, dying, turned command of
settlement over to Captain Francisco Ruíz Galán, until Ayolas
should return to reassume command, and departed for Spain;
died at sea June 23, 1537; left behind him those conquistadors
who would eventually carry out terms of contract: to explore
and settle country--from base at Asunción (Paraguay) for first
eighty years capital of Río de la Plata--and find desired routes
to connect Spain's Pacific and Atlantic colonies in South America; horses (72 of original 100 had survived voyage), left behind when remnant of Mendoza's Buenos Aires settlement moved
to Asunción (1541), multiplied rapidly on pampas to play significant role in criollo society and economy, as well as to
transform scattered nomadic Indians of pampas into well-organized, mounted bands of raiders who lived by raiding Spanish
settlements.

    Much has been written about Mondoza's expedition; brief
mention might include first account, by Ulrich Schmidel (or
Schmidt), one of Germans accompanying expedition, returned
some twenty years later to publish his memoirs in German,
1567; English translation by Hakluyt Society; early colonial historians such as Martín del Barco Centenera, Ruy Díaz de Guzman, and Pedro Lozano give accounts drawn from original
sources; R. B. C. Graham tells story in vivid English narrative form; Paul Groussac's Mendoza y Garay is scholarly study;
and Guillermo Furlong's article in Boletín de Academia Nacional
de la Historia, volume XLI, Buenos Aires, 1968, summarizes
recent research on original founding of Buenos Aires (see complete listings in Suggested Readings, Appendix III; see also entries on Buenos Aires (for discussion of name, etc.); Asunción;
and other related topics, especially those on Mendoza's officers
mentioned).

MENENDEZ, BENJAMIN, General. Active military figure in politi-
    cal affairs in 1940s and 1950s. By the late 1930s General
    Menéndez, a strong military nationalist, had become increas-
    ingly open in his admiration of Adolf Hitler; in 1941 he started
    one of the military movements (other led by Juan Bautista

Molina, q. v.) designed to keep Argentina neutral in World
War II and to counteract the influence of Justo's friends,
whom he believed to be tied to British imperialism; the discovery of the plot caused Menéndez, among others to be placed
on the inactive list for a time; in 1951 Menéndez, then in
command of cavalry school, joined Eduardo Lonardi in offering
military aid to the conspiracy brewing to overthrow Perón; the
plot failed and General Menéndez was court-martialed, convicted, and sentenced to prison for fifteen years, with less of
his rank and earned privileges; following the revolution of September 16, 1955, that ended Perón's presidency Menéndez was
freed and his rank and rights restored.

MERCADO Y PEÑALOZA, PEDRO DE. Governor of Tucumán,
1594-1600. Succeeded Francisco de Zárate as governor; his
term of office did not produce any significant new settlements
or achievements but it was remarkable for the firmness with
which he suppressed Indian uprisings--from the Calchaquians
in Salta and Tucumán and the Diaguitas in La Rioja--and used
the Jesuit missionary Gaspar de Monroy to pacify the Indians
of the valley of Humahuaca; he was able to pass on Spanish
authority to his successor, Francisco Martínez de Leiva, without serious problems.

MERCADO Y VILLACORTA, ALONSO DE (c. 1620-1681). Colonial
governor of Tucumán (1655-1660; 1665-1670) and pacifier of
northern Indian frontier; governor of Río de la Plata (1660-
1663) and president of first Buenos Aires audiencia.
Born in Spain; after having received some education in
Salamanca, he entered military service; had reached rank of
maestre de campo when he was appointed governor of Tucumán; his first administration there was highlighted by events
sparked by the Spanish impostor Pedro Bohórquez (q. v.); after
having accepted Bohórquez at his own value and given him authority over the Indians, Governor Mercado was ruthless in
suppressing the revolt instigated by Bohórquez; after having established peace, Mercado moved to Buenos Aires to take up his
new duties as governor there; he attempted to control contraband trade and to fortify Buenos Aires more effectively; the
governor strengthened Santa Fe against Indian raids and became
president of the new audiencia of Buenos Aires (see Audiencia);
accused of enriching himself at expense of the royal treasury
through corrupt relationships with foreign traders, Mercado
was removed from office but was soon exonerated and sent back
to Tucumán to serve a second term as governor; a second Calchaquí revolt, larger and even more dangerous than the first,
as it extended into western Chaco, and also led by Bohórquez,
was totally defeated in a nine-month campaign; this time Mercado executed Bohórquez, took thousands of Indians prisoner
and then relocated them--including men, women and children--
throughout Argentina as forced laborers in such places as Esteco, the vineyards and cotton fields of La Rioja and Catamarca, and on the fortifications in Córdoba and Buenos Aires;

forts and garrison were established along the Chaco Indian
frontier; by 1669 the Tucumán province was at peace; as a reward for his achievements, Mercardo became president of the
royal audiencia of Panama and was honored with title of Marqués de Villacorta; he died in Panama.

MERCANTE, DOMINGO A. (1898-   ).   Colonel of the army; Perón's
right-hand man from 1943 to 1951.
          Born in Buenos Aires; graduated from Colegio Militar
and had advanced studies at the Escuela Superior de Guerra;
specialist in artillery; Mercante was one of the colonels involved in the GOU revolt (q. v.) and one of Perón's chief associates from the beginning; became (1943) director general of
labor and social action; continued to hold other responsible positions with regard to labor and workmen's social benefits;
1940-52, served as governor of Buenos Aires province; meanwhile Mercante presided over constitutional reform convention
held in 1949 and guided the changes through it desired by President Perón; tensions between Perón and Mercante developed
and break was complete by 1951; Mercante had aspirations to
either vice presidency or presidency and Perón, who had come
to view him as a rival, had him expelled from the Peronist
party in 1951; aided Perón in revolt of 1955 that brought his
downfall and was tried in military court by the victors; retired from public life thereafter.

MERCEDARIANS.   Popular name for members of Order of Our Lady
of Mercy, from Spanish merced.   Founded in 1218 by San
Pedro Nolasco and others as a military order (Knights of St.
Eulalia) that took as its special mission the rescue of Chris-
tians held captive by Moors in Spain; it followed rule of St.
Augustine; later became a mendicant order, adopting new objectives as circumstances changed.
          Mercedarians were among first of the religious orders
to reach Argentine territory, coming with Diego de Almagro into northwestern Argentina (1535-1536), with veedor Cabrera to
Asunción in 1537; first monastery founded in Santiago del Estero, 1553; other centers were established throughout the area;
in these, primary and secondary schools were maintained;
from them missionaries went out to evangelize the Indians, often finding martyrdom; at first Mercedarian activities were directed from provincial of Cuzco, but by opening of seventeenth
century, Paraguay, Río de la Plata, and Tucumán came under
province of Santa Barbara del Tucumán (1594); after the expulsion of the Jesuits (1767), the Pope appointed Mercedarians to
take over many of their missions; during war of independence
Mercedarians were of great assistance to the patriots, continuing to be active in the republic; in 1957 the Mercedarian Convento, built in eighteenth century in Calle Reconquista, Buenos
Aires, that had served as base for Argentine troops defending
Buenos Aires against British and as a hospital in war with
Brazil (1827) and again in 1880, was declared a national monument.

See Bernardino Toledo, Estudios históricos, Provincia
Mercedaria de Santa Bárbara del Tucumán, 1594-1918.

MESOPOTAMIA, ARGENTINE. Name given by mid-nineteenth century French traveler, J. A. V. Martin de Moussy, to area between the Paraná and Uruguay rivers--comparing this to the
historical Mesopotamia watered by the Tigris and Euphrates
rivers (modern Iraq); the Argentine Mesopotamia, as it is commonly called, includes the provinces of Entre Ríos, Corrientes,
Misiones (qq. v.); rich farming and grazing country, subtropical to temperate climate; more than adequate rainfall; water
transportation accessible almost everywhere.

MESTIZO. Term used to designate a person of mixed Indian and
white parentage--usually, in Argentina, born of white father
and Indian mother, but not always; during the colonial period,
the mestizo paid tribute only if his father was Indian; during
most of the colonial period, the isolation of the Argentine settlements, the sparseness of population, and the fact that the
economy, lacking both rich mineral resources and commercial
agriculture was less dependent on forced labor supplies than
some other Spanish colonies combined, made for a closeness
between the two races as they worked together and gradually
fused; many descendants of oldest Argentine families proudly
claim both Indian and conquistador blood; the term "mestizo,"
however, came to be applied primarily to those persons caught
between the two cultures and integrated into neither, usually
those in lower economic and social strata in both towns and
rural areas (see Demography).

MIDDLE CLASSES. During the century between 1870 and 1970 Argentina's middle class grew from approximately 11% of the total
population to about 60%, with the nation on its way to becoming
a middleclass nation; originally largely Argentine creole, made
up of small farmers, urban shopkeepers, skilled artisans and
professional people, it suddenly became largely foreign, including merchants, professional people, bureaucrats, with the
new element of technologists and highly skilled workers and
specialists added during the industrialization thrust following
World War II; although most of the immigrants had been rural
in background, their desire to improve their own positions in
the society, economy, and political structure brought large
numbers to the cities where opportunities were greater; the
prosperity of the 1890-1914 period gave them economic resources with which to push their demands for greater and more
direct participation in the life of their new homeland; following
the reorganization and professionalization of the army (see Military) with promotion based on seniority and achievement, the
majority of the officers (such as Perón, etc.) came from the
middle class; the Unión Cívica Radical (q. v.) was formed to
represent the middle class political power; after the electoral
reform of 1912 the Radicals elected a middle-class president,
Hipólito Yrigoyen; during his administration the University

Reform (q.v.) brought democracy to the universities, where most of the students came from middle class families; in the 1930s the return of the oligarchy to power, the economic depression, and world-wide conditions culminating in outbreak of World War II sharpened the sense of insecurity felt by various groups making up the middle class.

The military takeover in 1943 followed Perón's two administrations brought many changes; at first his open championship of the descamisados ("shirtless"), or laborers on lowest level, frightened members of the middle class into fearing that their newly won status would be eroded between the oligarchy and lower classes; as time went on, they became more secure as much of their fear of the oligarchy disappeared when the latter lost power, prestige, and economic domination as a result of Perón's social reforms and attempts at economic nationalization and diversification; as the middle class continued to grow in size, wealth and power, many of its members became supporters of Perón or, after his departure in 1955, members of parties that favored continuing his policies without bringing Perón, himself, back; divisions among the various groups making up the middle class, along with ethnic ties linking them to the lower classes and, less often, to oligarchic families, have prevented serious clashes between classes; at the same time, nationalism has created a strong sense of pride in the fact that all are now Argentines; on the political level it is not yet clear what effect, if any, the middle class has made as its members are apt to be found scattered throughout the various modern political parties.

See John J. Johnson, Political Change in Latin America: the Emergence of the Middle Sectors (Stanford, California, 1958); Gino Germani, Política y sociedad en una época de transición; de la sociedad tradicional a la sociedad de masas (Buenos Aires, 1962; several editions); and Jean J. Kirkpatrick, Leader and Vanguard in Mass Society: a Study of Peronist Argentina (Cambridge, Mass., 1971).

MIERS, JOHN (1789-1879). English engineer, botanist, and entrepreneur; author of important descriptive book on Argentina. As friend of J. A. B. Beaumont (q.v.), Miers invested in copper mining industry of Chile, hoping to get in on ground floor in 1818; arrived in Buenos Aires in 1819 and went overland to Chile to inspect his holdings; mining venture failed and Miers returned to England; his detailed notes of his travels in pampas, Argentina, and events in Chile (including those involving San Martín and Lord Cochrane), published with title Travels in Chile and La Plata (2 v., London, 1826, with illustrations and maps) are highly valued among Argentine historians for their descriptions of the pampas and Mendoza in 1819.

See AMS edition of Miers' Travels (2 v., New York, 1970).

MILITARY, THE. The dominant political role of the military (used here to include all the national armed forces, but with army predominating, for the most part) in Argentina during the middle decades of the twentieth century is a new development in the nation's history which traditionally had seen the armed forces subjected to civil rule.

In the sixteenth century, as soon as a new era had been opened to settlement by the conquistadors, civil government under the Spanish crown was established; governors had small forces at their disposal but for the most part throughout the colonial period the citizens (vecinos) themselves, under the direction of the cabildos in each locality, were responsible for defense against Indians in the north and northwest, foreign pirates along the Atlantic coast, raids by Brazilian mamelucos into the northeast for mission Indians or new lands for Portugal, or the opening of new areas for settlements in Argentine territory; the only real "army" in the area was that formed by the Jesuits of their Guaraní mission Indians for defense against slave raiders from Brazil and occasionally used by royal officials in other emergencies; international warfare between Spain and European rivals in the eighteenth century brought larger royal armed forces to the Río de la Plata, the establishment of frontier garrisons against the Indians (see Blandengues), military units for exploring new lands for settlement, as well as more formal organization of the armed citizens' militia units; as late as the early 19th century, however, the Argentines had to use their traditional volunteer patterns of defense against the invasions of the British, 1806-1807.

The Argentine armed forces actually began with the May Revolution and the desire of the first Junta to spread the revolution to all the areas formerly included in the viceroyalty; various specific armies were created to carry out the government's policy as well as to fight for independence from Spain; with independence won, Rosas disbanded what was left of the national army (1829) and for more than two decades, Argentina was without formal national armed services as it was without constitutional national political organization; irregular armed forces, of varying sizes, usually held together by loyalty to caudillos who seemed to express their followers' own political or personal preferences, intervened constantly in internal political affairs of the various provinces as well as in civil wars between the provinces or against Rosas and Buenos Aires; after the defeat of Rosas (1852) and the establishment of the Argentine Confederation under the constitution of 1853, a national army was again created and a few years later under President Mitre, himself a general, the military was placed firmly under civil control and its professionalization and modernization undertaken; by 1880 a "new" national army had emerged: it had successfully defeated threats to the national government's authority from López Jordán in Entre Ríos and from military leaders in the northwest; advances in technology were represented by more modern weaponry, such as repeating Remington rifles, better artillery, some Gatling guns, and an expanding national telegraph system; its energies were primarily directed toward the final conquest and exploration of Patagonia and the

Chaco to facilitate their settlement and exploitation; provincial autonomy over its own armed forces and many of the "hold-over" officers from the old army had been eliminated by time or the casualties of the campaigns in the Paraguayan war, and the "conquest of the desert"; professional military schools had been established, the Colegio Miliar (military academy) in 1870; the Escuela Naval (naval academy) in 1872; and the general staff was reorganized in 1884.

Under President Roca and his Minister of War, Pablo Ricchieri (q.v.), the army was finally transformed into a centrally controlled, national institution, with compulsory military service, offering professional training and a successful, secure career to its officers and men; in 1899 the Germans responded to a request for professional assistance, and its military advisers remained important in Argentine military schools until the outbreak of World War II; their influence was especially strong in the Escuela Superior de Guerra (war academy for advanced military studies); during these decades (1890-1941) the army tradition was strongly professional, its goal being to serve the nation and its government rather than to control it; although there were many instances of revolts, both provincial and national, in which dissident military groups offered their aid to political leaders (especially involved with radicals as in 1890, 1905, etc.), the armed services generally regarded themselves, and were so regarded publicly, as an elite professional force to defend the republic and to assist the government in opening new areas for settlement; incidentally, the military also provided upward mobility, socially and economically, to many immigrants and poorer natives, served as a nationalizing and a cultural influence, and, especially after 1920, provided the best source from which directors for new national technological projects could be chosen (see Enrique Mosconi, first director of Y.P.F., and Manuel N. Savio, father of iron and steel industry).

This traditional civil control of the military had been re-emphasized by San Martín's dictum that a military leader should not intervene in political affairs, formalized by the constitution of 1853, and strengthened further by the professsionalization of the military, with its pride in both its unique function and its loyalty to the national government; the first real break came in 1930 when José Féliz Uriburu received support from enough of his fellow officers to oust President Hipólito Yrigoyen and become president himself, with approval from the supreme court (see Revolution of 1930); although personally inclined toward the political and social patterns being established by the new totalitarian governments in Europe, Uriburu insisted on holding constitutional elections in 1932, with the result that his own political and military rival Agustín P. Justo (q.v.) became president; throughout the latter's administration (1932-1938) increasing national and international tensions were kept under control and civil-military conspiracies were, for the most part, defused rather than violently suppressed (see Juan Bautista Molina; Benjamín Menéndez; Diego de Molinari); the military

continued to regard itself as an instrument and perhaps the
conscience of the Argentine government and continued, in spite
of Argentina's commitments to peace with its neighbors and
neutrality in international affairs, to command a unique place
in the pride and respect of the Argentine people; meanwhile,
officers shared the same pressures and changing interests as
the rest of the Argentines--the increasing popular demand for
social, political, and economic reforms; disillusionment with
corrupt practices and lack of leadership characterizing political parties and institutions; the strong nationalist movement and
tensions complicated by events of World War II (q.v.), between traditional economic and cultural ties to Great Britain
and France, on the one hand, and newer bonds with Italy and
Germany, on the other hand, growing out of recent immigration patterns, influence of German military missions, and personal admiration by some for new totalitarian governments;
sharp divisions along these lines within the military itself were
intensified by personal and professional rivalries.

On June 4, 1943, the military made its final and total
break with tradition when a group of young officers, organized
as Grupo de Oficiales Unidos or GOU (q.v.) took over complete control of the government to prevent the election of a
pro-British, pro-conservative government; for at least the next
three decades the military controlled the government to the extent that no national or provincial government regardless of the
manner in which it came to power--by military imposition or
election--could remain in office without support and consent of
the military; during this period constitutional and legal changes
advanced political, economic, and social democracy; foundations were laid for diversification of Argentina's economy, with
emphasis on industrialization, development and national control
of natural resources such as petroleum, coal, etc., building
of hydroelectric plants, etc.; in international affairs Argentina
sought a middle path between its former reluctance to join international groups and what it viewed as subservience to any of
the Great Powers; it belatedly joined Allies in World War II,
strengthened its position within inter-American organizations,
and took part in the organization of United Nations (See List of
Presidents, Appendix I and Historical Chronology, Appendix II).

In spite of these achievements, however, it became
more and more evident that the military had no greater success in solving current economic and political problems than
had its political predecessors; inflation soared and guerrilla
violence seemed uncontrollable; as it became increasingly clear
that in political affairs military leaders shared same problems
and difficulties in finding solutions as did their political counterparts, more and more officers joined the group that had always maintained that the military paid too high a price, in
terms of loss of its own professional attitudes and responsibilities, when it assumed political control; in this spirit of political withdrawal, reconciliation was effected with the Peronists and Héctor Cámpora was elected president in 1973; shortly
thereafter he resigned in Perón's favor and the latter was

elected president with his wife María Estela (known as Isabel)
as vice president; Perón's death in 1974 brought Isabel Perón
in as the first woman president of any American nation; despite Argentina's continuing serious problems with inflation and
guerrilla political (or semi-political violence, the military in
the mid-1970s was practicing restraint and attempting to use
its power traditionally for the support of the consitutional government, rather than in an attempt to take it over; on May
24, 1976, however, a peaceful coup, long delayed, overthrew
the government of President María Estela Perón.

See Robert A. Potash, Charles D. Corbett, and Marvin
Goldwert, in Suggested Readings, Appendix III.

MILLER, JOHN (1787-1843). Scottish cattleman who came to Buenos Aires shortly after May Revolution in 1810; married there
and by 1823 was well established as estanciero in Buenos
Aires province; made contribution to national economic history
in 1820 by introducing first shorthorn bull, Tarquino, to begin
improvement of cattlebreeding for beef in Argentina.

MILLER, WILLIAM (or GUILLERMO), General (1795-1861). British
veteran of Napoleonic Wars who aided San Martín and Bolívar
in emancipation of Spanish South America; author of memoirs
describing events of Argentine independence period.

Born in Kent, England; early entered military career;
fought under Duke of Wellington in peninsular wars (Spain)
against French; accompanied General Ross in campaign against
Washington, D.C. (1814) in War of 1812; shipwrecked on way
to New Orleans, he succeeded in returning to England in time
to fight against Napoleon at Waterloo; resigned from British
service (veteran officers in surplus supply) and arrived in Buenos Aires in 1817 to offer his services in the fight for independence; commissioned by Director Juan Martín de Pueyrredón
as captain of artillery in Army of the Andes, Miller immediately joined San Martín's forces in Chile; fought in various campaigns, both on land and sea; distinguished himself at victory
of Maipú; accompanied San Martín's expedition to Peru where
he played increasingly significant and active role; after the Liberator's departure from Peru in 1822, Miller fought with Peruvian patriot forces and then under Bolívar's command until
independence was finally won at Ayacucho (after which Miller
was made a grand marshal of Peru) and on to Chuquisaca
where he remained briefly as division general of Potosí.

In 1826 General Miller returned to England for family
reasons and in hopes of healing wounds incurred during South
American wars; during his stay there, his brother John Miller,
who had also traveled extensively in South America, began the
collection and editing of General Miller's voluminous notes and
memoirs; published in London in 1829 (2 v.), and immediately
translated into Spanish, the first volume constitutes a valuable
source of material for Argentine history of social and cultural
life, events, and public and military actions of the period between the British invasions and the end of the war for inde-

pendence (1806-1825).

Returning to Peru in 1831, Miller became involved in the civil wars and went into exile following the fall of Andrés Santa Cruz; he served for several years as British consul general on the Pacific coast; with his honors restored in Peru by Ramón Castilla, he went back to visit that country; died on board HMS Naiad in the bay of Callao, October 31, 1861.

MIN (Movimiento Integración y Desarrollo Nacional). Political party that appeared on the ballot in 1965 and won 6.2% of the national vote.

MINES, MINING, AND QUARRYING. From the time of its discovery Argentina has been believed to be rich in mineral resources; its important place names--"Argentina" and "Río de la Plata" (from Latin and Spanish words denoting silver) indicate this and the direction of its early lines of settlement and later explorations was largely determined by this hope; in fact, however, the serious search to find and exploit Argentina's mineral resources did not come until the twentieth century.

In the preconquest period Indians in the northwest had used copper and in the Andean areas, as well as in Misiones, Jesuits (and others) found enough minerals--iron, lead and copper to take care of their local needs; among the oldest mines in operation were those of Mendoza at Uspallata, from which lead and silver were mined and sent to Chile in the seventeenth century; scattered along the cordillera were also gold (see Incahuasi) and silver mines; although none of these were important in the area's economy, it is true that mines--from Bolivia--did control much of that economy; the Tucumán provinces supplied the miners in Bolivia with needed food, work animals, fabrics for clothing, carts, etc.; and the silver from the mines, transported along the camino real to Buenos Aires formed a major item in the colonial contraband trade and its loss to government was a determining factor in the decision to establish the viceroyalty of the United Provinces de la Plata, with capital at Buenos Aires, and to open that port to trade; during the viceregal period, revenue from the silver mines paid all government expenses.

Changes came with independence: mines were closed or neglected because of the fighting throughout the area, unsettled conditions, and lack of labor; Upper Peru broke away from the United Provinces to become independent Bolivia; in the early 1820s both the Buenos Aires government and those of provinces like La Rioja attempted to attract European capital (then readily available in a kind of mining boom stimulated partly by Jesuit writings about Argentina and especially by the needs of the industrial revolution); Rivadavia encouraged this and legislation was passed (1823) to provide the legal framework; a new problem developed as to whether the national or the provincial governments had rights to subsoil resources; in any case, civil turmoil, even wars, lack of transportation from mine to market, jurisdictional disputes, and unfamiliarity of British miners with

Argentine conditions, combined to make these ventures a fiasco (see Famatina; River Plate Mining Company); for several
decades thereafter the mineral most needed in Argentina was
salt for its meat-packing plants and adequate sources of this
had already been found in the salt flats of western Buenos
Aires province, in what is now La Pampa province, and in San
Luis; Argentina passed into a golden period of prosperity furnishing its cereals, meats and wool to Europe (especially Great
Britain) and importing its coal, iron, and all manufactured
goods.

A rude, but brief, awakening came in World War I
(1914-1918) when temporary disruptions of trade forced the nation to recognize its dependence on Europe; during the period
between World War I and World War II, economic nationalists
and enterprising industrialists determined to reduce that dependence, to diversify the Argentine economy by industrializing,
and thus also to break the power of the landowning oligarchy
over the political and cultural life of the nation; a determined
search for available mineral resources began; oil had already
been discovered at Comodoro Rivadavia and brought under government control (see Petroleum; Yacimientos Petrolíferos
Fiscales); extensive beds of coal (of varying quality) were known
to exist in the Río Turbio basin in the southern Andes of Santa
Cruz (discovered in 1887 by Agustín del Castillo); hardships
suffered during World War II (1939-1945), especially the lack
of coal (usually imported from Great Britain), increased the
Argentine desire to become independent in such energy sources;
Perón's interest in industrialization caused him (1943-1955) to
emphasize mining in every way and this emphasis has continued; mixed companies, i. e., financed by specified proportions
of private and government capital, were formed by General Directorate of Military Factories to explore for and exploit mineral deposits useful for military purposes; by 1950, such companies were engaging in every phase of mining and metallurgical industry; huge central smelting works were projected, like
the San Nicolás steel mill, financed with loans from Export-
Import bank 1955, opened in 1960; but there is also a tendency
to use smaller ones near the mining areas; unlike the agriculture and stock-raising industry that produced for export, the
mining industry was designed almost entirely for national
needs.

Argentina has become practically self-sufficient in petroleum production and is steadily approaching that goal with other
minerals; zinc and lead from Jujuy are most important for
heavy industry; copper comes from Mendoza; beryllium, an exception to the rule, is produced primarily for export; Argentina is an important producer of this mineral used in nuclear
physics, its supply coming largely from Córdoba, San Luis,
and Catamarca; manganese, for heavy industries and metallurgical factories, is mined in Córdoba, Mendoza, and Santiago del
Estero; uranium comes from Salta; tungsten, wolfram, tin,
gold, and silver are also produced; in addition to larger known
deposits of various minerals, small mines that can be used lo-

cally are also being developed and the government is attempting to make and maintain as accurate a survey as possible of mineral resources available throughout the nation; among the non-metallic minerals, salt is most important, but clays of all kinds, sulphur, borax, and construction materials--sand, granite, cement, calcium, and marbles are being quarried.

Argentina's mining engineers can be locally trained; as early as 1822 Carlos Ferrari, director of the Museum of Natural and Physical Sciences had begun mineral collections; in 1827 scientific studies in these fields were established at the university of Buenos Aires, attracting both European scientists and mining investors; in 1863 this became one of the Sciences in the Faculty of Exact Sciences and was emphasized by the rector, Juan María Gutiérrez; both in Catamarca and in San Juan schools were graduating mining engineers before 1900; modern geological and mineralogical studies came under the supervision of the Dirección de Minas and Geología, with centers at such national universities as Buenos Aires, La Plata, Córdoba, Rosario, Tucumán; much of Argentina's hope for future expansion of mining production is based on the new resources being discovered in Comahué (q.v.) in northern Patagonia.

MIR (Movimiento de Intransigencia Renovación). Successor to UCRI or Intransigent Radicals; one of major radical factions since 1945; represented at first national radical convention following Perón's fall (1955).

MIRANDA, FRANCISCO DE (1750-1816). Venezuelan precursor of Latin American independence who spent decade before 1810 attempting to get European support to free the Latin American colonies from Spain; his impact on Argentina consisted mainly in his role in the British invasions (q.v.) as Sir Home Popham (q.v.) had been impressed by Miranda's arguments in London to effect that Latin Americans would welcome an English takeover as a release from Spain and wrote enthusastically to Miranda from Buenos Aires shortly after his arrival there; and in the influence that Miranda had with young Argentines studying or traveling in Europe; several, like José Moldes (who seems to have had personal contact with Miranda) and others who did not, became early converts to idea of liberation and became members of secret organization in Madrid and Cádiz modeled on or similar to that of Miranda in London; these young leaders returned to Buenos Aires to join the patriot groups there and often to exercise considerable leadership.

MIRANDA, LUCIA see LEGENDS OF THE CONQUEST

MIRANDA, LUIS DE. Author of early chronicle of Río de la Plata. Spanish noble; officer in emperor Charles V's military campaigns in Italy; returned to Spain and became priest; accompanied Pedro de Mendoza's expedition to Río de la Plata, serving as priest in first settlement of Buenos Aires, then briefly in unfortunate settlement of Corpus Christi at mouth of Carcaraña before returning to Buenos Aires; moved to Asunción with other settlers in 1541 when Buenos Aires was abandoned; opposed Domingo Martínez de Irala and, continuing to minister in church in Asunción, became strong supporter and adviser of adelantado Cabeza de Vaca, upon his arrival a few years later; refused to join other royal officials in removal of Cabeza de Vaca from governorship and was temporarily imprisoned along with other friends of the governor; document in Archives of the Indies, sent to Spain in letter written by Miranda while imprisoned (1545) gives account of all Spanish settlements in Río de la Plata, from Cabot's expedition through that of Cabeza de Vaca, along with the poetic "romance" (tale) of the new land that the king had apparently requested him to write; may have been first verses written in that area (whatever their literary quality) and certainly one of earliest chronicles sent to Spain; combined by Enrique Peña into short work entitled El padre Luis de Miranda.

MIRANDA, MIGUEL (1891-1953).   Industrialist and financier; first chairman of President Perón's National Economic Council.
      Born in Buenos Aires, son of Spanish immigrants; largely self-educated, he began working at early age and had become picturesque, wealthy, powerful figure in national finance and industry by mid-1940s; first in President Farrell's administration, then as Perón's senior economic advisor; he dominated Argentine economic policy in the closing year of World War II and the following period; although his own success had come in the free trade (laissez-faire) economy, he strongly favored nationalization of transportation and public utilities; played important role in negotiations leading to government ownership of British railroads, other transportation systems, and public utilities in Argentina; convinced that living conditions of workers could best be improved by rapid industrialization, he moved in this direction, neglecting and sometimes even penalizing the agropecuarian industries on which Argentine's prosperous economy had been based; in 1946 he established Perón's Instituto Argentino de Promoción del Intercambio (IAPI) for handling all national foreign trade (q.v.); by 1948, Argentina had resorted to expanding the volume of paper money in circulation and inflation was becoming serious problem; it was obvious that Miranda's policies were in trouble, partly because of internal economic and political events and influences but also because of changing world situations; Miranda had believed that the European economies would fall apart soon after World War II and a new confrontation between U.S. and Russia would take place; instead, the U.S. Marshall Plan speeded European economic recovery, no new conflict took place, and Argentina's position in the world market abruptly changed, with the U.S. giving away what Argentina wanted to sell; Miranda resigned in 1949 and retired to private life; he continued to support Perón's economic policies, now more conventionally carried out in the first Five Year Plan; at his death, a few years later, he was given official honors.

MISCEGENATION   see   MESTIZO; DEMOGRAPHY

MISERERE.   Site of rout of Santiago de Liniers' forces July 2,
1807, by Whitelocke's British troops at beginning of second
British invasion of Buenos Aires.

MISIONES (Province since 1953).   Location.   Mesopotamian province
of Argentina, thrust northeast from Corrientes like a bent
thumb between Brazil on north, east, and south and Paraguay
on west; lying between latitudes 25°23' and 28°10' S and longitudes 58°39' and 56°4' W; takes its name from fact that 11 of
30 Jesuit Guaraní missions were in this central area between
Upper Paraná and Uruguay rivers.   Area: 29,821 square
miles; about the size of Haiti.   Population (1970):   443,020;
population density per square mile: 38.   Capital: Posadas
(q.v.).   Population (1970):   70,691.
        Geography and climate.   Bounded by rivers marking
Argentina's northeastern international boundary, Misiones pos-
sesses unique characteristics: rocky plateau in north, dropping
abruptly to river banks, extends through center of province to
plains in southwestern portion, forming watershed from which
many small tributaries flow into bordering Upper Paraná and
Uruguay rivers; waterfalls and cascades common; most famous,
those on Iguazú (q.v.), one of most spectacular sights in world;
climate hot and humid but relieved by cooler nights and occasional drops in temperature to freezing point, in southern portion; rainforest of north (La Selva) rich in hardwoods and other
exuberant subtropical vegetation; soil reddish lava like southern
Brazil coffee area; fairly fertile but easily eroded.
        Most important cities: Posadas, Candelaria, Apóstoles
(Jesuit mission in south now becoming important urban center),
Oberá, rapidly developing modern commercial center, and
Iguazú, port and outlet for north.
        Historical development.   Misiones area discovered and
claimed for Spain by Sebastian Cabot coming upriver from the
south in 1528, and again in 1542 by adelantado Alvar Núñez
Cabeza de Vaca entering from Brazil in the northeast; Spanish
government at Asunción kept Paraná-Paraguay river system
open for access to Atlantic; settlements made on upper rivers
in attempts to control Indians, but not in Misiones; finally, a
few years after Hernandarias' unsuccessful campaign against
Indians there in 1603, area turned over to Jesuits; in 1615
Itapuá mission was established at site of Posadas but moved
across river; 1619 Concepción mission founded near Uruguay
river, first permanent settlement in today's Misiones; by 1707,
30 Jesuit missions complete in area, 11 of them in Misiones
province, largely in southwestern part (see Jesuit Missions,
for period 1615-1767); after middle of eighteenth century Jesuit
missions declined due to border warfare between Portuguese
Brazil and Spanish Río de la Plata, loss of Jesuit influence at
Spanish court, and smallpox epidemic 1764-1765; Jesuits expelled
in 1767; limits of first Misiones province with capital at Candelaria by Governor Francisco de Paula Bucareli y Ursúa and

four lieutenant governors appointed, with commercial, religious, political matters all under Buenos Aires government; with creation of viceroyalty in 1776, and intendancies in 1782, Misiones became one of four frontier territories; in 1803 Santiago de Liniers became governor of the old Jesuit Missions jurisdiction, under Plan Avilés to establish royal authority more clearly; Guaraní Indians given freedom; a few years later 1809-1810 the area was placed under military governor, Tomás Rocamora, whose support of the May Revolution in Buenos Aires placed Misiones in precarious position, with its neighbors, Brazil, Paraguay, and Montevideo refusing to recognize it; in 1810 Belgrano, on Paraguayan mission, dictated a kind of constitutional document of 30 articles providing Misiones' first patriot government; during next twelve years Misiones almost completely at mercy of political currents and actions of its neighbors; Paraguay declared independence 1811 and claimed part of area; Artigas attracted support of rest of Misiones; 1814, Supreme Director Gervasio A. de Posadas annexed Misiones to newly-created province of Corrientes; 1815, it came under governorship of Andresito, son of Artigas; after defeat of Artigas by Francisco Ramírez and latter's establishment of republic of Entre Ríos 1822, Misiones became a part of it, with its own first governor, Félix de Aguirre, and with its boundaries recognized by quadrilateral treaty; delegates sent to constituent congress in Buenos Aires 1825; accepted centralist constitution; Misiones furnished 300 soldiers for war against Brazil.

For next half century while rest of nation tore itself apart in civil wars, in creating viable political institutions, and in opening new areas in pampas and Patagonia to agriculture and stockraising, Misiones, totally different topographically from rest of nation, lapsed into wilderness and solitude; raided by nomadic individuals or bands or crossed at will by military forces; sovereignty disputed at different times by Entre Ríos, Corrientes, Paraguay, and Brazil; its boundaries equally undefined; the Jesuit peak mission population of 150,000 in 1750 had dwindled to fewer than 2000 families, with little formal economy beyónd scattered yerba mate gathering; nevertheless rights and boundaries of Misiones as separate entity had never been denied even while it was part of Corrientes; government had frequently put itself on record promising to take action in behalf of Misiones when more pressing problems had been solved; in 1880s, following reorganization of nation, ending of Paraguayan war, that time had come.

After passing of National Law of colonization, 1876, federal government began to think of Misiones as possible site for such development; Corrientes tried to keep its control over area by establishing towns and making other gestures toward expansion; unable to divert federal government action, the province sold much of the land to 38 favored landowners and turned rest over to government when territory of Misiones was formed, 1881, with Corpus (renamed Ciudad de San Martín) as capital; three years later, Corrientes ceded Posadas to become the

new capital of the territory; and in 1895 the eastern boundary
with Brazil was settled by President Grover Cleveland as arbiter, with most of disputed area given to Brazil; decision finally accepted by all parties; federal government and private interests collaborated to encourage colonization and development
of area; colonias were established, usually with land grants or
sale at low prices, with cooperatives formed to aid in financial and marketing problems; settlers attracted first from Brazil and Paraguay, then in large numbers from Germany and
Central Europe, and eventually from almost everywhere; in
1903, in one series of colonias sixteen different nationalities
were represented; Argentines also quickly were attracted to pioneer in new lands and eventually outnumbered the foreign-
born, without destroying its international flavor; in 1915, territory was divided into departments; at close of World War I new
efforts were made to attract European immigrants through very
cheap land; in 1953 Misiones become a province, in recognition
of its stature and progress; first constitutional provincial governor was Claudio Arrechea; three years later, all federal
lands were placed under province's authority; following 1959
Japanese government strongly subsidized Japanese colonization
in Misiones (see Japanese); province turned efforts more and
more to expansion toward east along Uruguay river and in area
of Irigoyen plateau.

Economy on which this massive settlement movement was
based was primarily agricultural; some cattle, horse, sheep,
and hog raising but commercial agriculture most important; by
late 1960s, Misiones was furnishing Argentina with all its yerba
mate, producing 25° of its tobacco, 8° of its citrus fruit
(mostly oranges) much of its tung oil for paint (until 1950s U.S.
imported about 50° of its tung oil from Misiones); also profitable are tea, maize, manioc, sugar cane, rice, and more recently soybeans and essential oils; lumbering has always been
important because of the tropical hardwoods in the rain forest;
Misiones' hundreds of sawmills and number of plywood factories
supply more than half Argentina's demand for plywood; paper
factory established at Puerto Piray on Paraná; cedar, lapacho,
missionary pine, etc. used for lumber; reforestation represents
largest capital investment as industry aims to satisfy entire national market; mining has been disappointing as Jesuit reports
had encouraged early nineteenth century European investors to
believe that copper deposits, at least, would be valuable; some
copper found but not enough; tacurú, a lowgrade iron ore has
been found and a smelter built near Posadas to process it; and
there are small, but poor, coal deposits near Monte Carlo; one
entirely new industry--tourism--has become increasingly important, especially that to the Iguazú falls area, now rapidly being
developed.

Misiones in four and a half centuries has passed from
populous Guaraní indigenous society and economy through decades of fighting conquistadors, only to surrender rather peacefully to the spiritual, cultural authority and economic prosperity of the Jesuit father for a century and a half, undergone

decades of chaos, violence, and decline to emerge during the
past century as the newest, most international, perhaps most
vigorous and rapidly growing province in the Argentine Republic (see Jesuit Missions; Posadas; Iguazú; Japanese).
        See Robert C. Eidt in Suggested Readings, Appendix
III.

MISSIONS. The mission was one of the two most important Spanish
    institutions for converting the Indians to Christianity, civilizing
    (i.e., Europeanizing) them, and exploiting or using their labor
    and skills; the other was the encomienda (q.v.); both encomien-
    das and missions were introduced into the Río de la Plata and
    Tucumán area in the usual Spanish pattern but circumstances
    of the Argentine area and the diversified and sometimes unique
    characteristics of the Indians there forced changes; only the
    Indians in the north and northwest (Diaguitas, Calchaquians,
    Huarpes, etc.) were numerous and civilized enough to fit into
    satisfactory encomiendas; for a brief time the Guaraní also
    were granted in encomiendas in the early settlements of what
    is now Paraguay, but very soon this arrangement gave way to
    a unique life style in which the two races lived together in one
    society (see Guaraní); for the first few decades, following the
    conquest, however, encomenderos, friars, and secular priests
    were the agents attempting to bring the Indians into the Spanish
    faith and culture; and they met with varying success; the first
    missions in the Río de la Plata were founded in 1578 or 1579
    in what is now Paraguay by the Franciscans Alonso de Santa
    Cruz and Luis Bolanos (q.v.); the latter was responsible, as
    founder or cofounder, of a series of missions in Buenos Aires,
    Santa Fe, and Corrientes provinces; the Indians (Guaraní, for
    the most part) were gathered into towns or reductions and kept
    there while they were taught; because of their lack of support
    many of these missions disappeared, as did the early ones
    founded a little later in Tucumán by the Jesuit Alonso de Bar-
    zana; San Francisco Solano (q.v.) was also active in missions
    there; in the early seventeenth century the Jesuits began their
    famous series of missions in the Argentine mesopotamia and
    extending up the Paraná-Paraguay rivers (see Jesuit Missions);
    eventually Jesuits, as well as Franciscans moved into the Cha-
    co and other frontier areas and paved the way for the eventual
    assimilation of such Indians as the Guaycuruan tribes and oth-
    ers into the society and the pacification of the area; during the
    nineteenth century, especially after the campaigns in the south
    and final "conquest of the desert" (q.v.), the Salesians carried
    out similar tasks of converting and civilizing the conquered
    Araucanians, with missions that took on many aspects of the
    new agricultural colonies, as did those of the Catholic and Ang-
    lican churches established among the Chaco Indians in the twen-
    tieth century.

MITA. Derived from a Quechua word meaning "turn," mita was ap-
    plied to the special type of encomienda or repartimiento in
    which groups of Indians were forced to take turns in working

the mines; although there was relatively little mining during
the colonial period in the territory now included in Argentina,
important mitas were used in the mines of Potosí with which
northwestern Argentina had close political, economic, and social ties; the abuses of this system played a role in the Argentine fight for independence as manifested by the repercussions
of the Tupac Amaru revolt in Argentina and the thesis written
by Mariano Moreno (q.v.) on the personal service of the Indians in general.

MITRE, AMBROSIO (1774-1845).   Independence patriot; frontier military commander; government official; father of Bartolomé
Mitre.
        Born in Montevideo and educated there and in Buenos
Aires; joined militia and was sent to Mendoza; served as commandante on the Indian border along the Diamante River; in
1810 built crude fort at San Rafael; maintained order along the
Indian frontier by firmness and a gift for diplomacy; he supported the May Revolution and, after returning to Buenos
Aires, joined the Patriotic Society and (later) the Logia Lautaro; held various positions under the patriot governments; accountant for the weapons factory (1811); director of the public
theater (1813); commissary of war for the auxiliary army of
Peru (1819); commissary general of the artillery parque in
Buenos Aires (1820-1821); in 1822 Mitre accepted the position
of treasurer at the frontier post settlement of Carmen de Patagones, about twenty miles up the Río Negro river; his financial responsibilities caused him to exercise considerable influence in the little frontier settlement; he stabilized its financial
structure, aided in maintaining peaceful relations with the
neighboring Indians, encouraged the development of agriculture,
generally improved the cultural life of the community, emphasizing the need for education and the role played by reading for
self-education (meanwhile educating his own sons along same
principles); in 1827 Mitre was the central figure in the repulse
of the invading Brazilian squadron seeking to capture Carmen
de Patagones and became the chronicler of the event; some
time after this he decided to return to Montevideo; Uruguay had
become an independent nation and Mitre was appointed treasurer; except for a brief period of dismissal while Oribe was in
office, Mitre remained in this position until illness forced his
retirement; when Rosas' general, Pascual Echagüe, threatened
to invade Uruguay (1839), Ambrosio Mitre, who had always
considered himself a unitarist, gave half his meager property
toward the defense of Uruguay and enlisted his sons, with Bartolomé at 18 the eldest, in the army to fight against Rosas;
his letter to Bartolomé has become famous--saying that even
if he died in battle he would have fulfilled his mission in life,
as long as he was not shot in the back.
        See José Juan Biedma, Ambrosio Mitre (Buenos Aires,
1891).

MITRE, BARTOLOME (1821-1906).   President of the Argentine Re-

public, 1862-1868; statesman and diplomat; historian of independence movement; founder of newspaper La Nación; a dominant figure in Argentine public life from 1850s until his death
in 1906.
     Bartolomé Mitre was born in Buenos Aires of parents
Ambrosio Mitre (q.v.) and Josefa Martínez, both linked to old
families in Buenos Aires and Montevideo; he began his education in Carmen de Patagones, studying with his father who held
a post there; the boy quickly became an avid reader and, in
fact, thereafter practically educated himself through his reading, except for some instruction in English and French in Buenos Aires schools and in mathematics at the military academy
after the family returned to Montevideo; Mitre never forgot
one incident at Carmen de Patagones, as he personally witnessed
the Brazilian attempt to capture the small river settlement and
the courageous defense that defeated it; at the age of ten he
was sent to the estancia of Gervasio Rozas (brother of Juan
Manuel Rosas) to learn the ranching business; the boy was soon
returned to his father with the message that he could not be
used as he preferred reading to ranching; moving to Montevideo with his family, Mitre attended the military academy and
became an artillery officer in the militia of Fructuoso Rivera;
he first fought in the bloody battle of Cagancha (1839) against
the invading Rosas forces under Echagüe and barely escaped
with his life from the disastrous defeat at Arroyo Grande
(1842); from this time on he joined with Argentine anti-Rosas
exiles in a determined effort to remove Rosas from power--
the Mitre family had roots in Montevideo and had returned to
it voluntarily, not in enforced exile; the Uruguay years were
growing years for the young Bartolomé and contributed greatly
to his development as future Argentine military and political
national leader; he continued his military studies, published an
artillery manual, and engaged in the defense of Montevideo
against Rosas' siege, along with other members of the Argentine legion and foreign groups--Garibaldi of Italian legion became his close friend; Mitre began to write, belonged to the
Asociación de Mayo, admired Echeverría greatly, brought out
his own first volume of poems, and contributed frequently to
the various journals, especially El Iniciador, edited by Miguel
Cané and Andrés Lamas; joined the latter in his establishment
of the historical and geographical institute of Uruguay (1843)
and later founded a similar scientific center in Buenos Aires;
Mitre met, talked with, wrote with, and fought alongside many
of the older Argentine exiles who centered his scholarly interests on the independence period of Argentina (in which his
father and his godfather General José Rondeau had played parts)
as well as with the younger ones who were to be his colleagues
in the creation of the new, democratic, more strongly national
and prosperous Argentina of the future; during this time he also married (see Vedia de Mitre, Delfina M. L.) and began a
family; in 1846, following three years of siege by the Buenos
Aires government, Rivera became suspicious of the Argentines
living in Montevideo and forced them into exile elsewhere;

Mitre attempted to join his friend General Paz, then fighting
Rosas' forces under Oribe in Corrientes, but the complete rout
of Paz's forces turned him to Brazil, instead; after a brief
period there, he made his way to Bolivia, where he had
friends and where he had been offered a faculty appointment in
the military academy; spent some time in Bolivia as friend of
President Ballivián, active in writing and, when necessary,
fighting for democracy; eventually went to Peru, rather than
become embroiled in Bolivia's civil wars; unwelcome in Peru
because of his attacks on dictatorship, Mitre moved to Chile;
in 1851 news of Urquiza's manifesto against Rosas brought him
back to Uruguay and Entre Ríos to join in the final battle
against Rosas; Mitre's years of exile had matured his military
and writing skills and had given him a new perspective regarding Argentina's needs for the future and his own role with regard to these; democracy and national union had become more
important to him than unitarism versus federalism and he had
come to believe that Buenos Aires province must join with the
other provinces as only one part--an important one--of the new
national structure to be built.

Mitre quickly moved to a position of leadership in Buenos Aires in the 1850s; following the battle of Caseros, in
which he had commanded Urquiza's artillery division, he found
himself at odds with the general's plans for national reorganization; whether because he, along with many others, distrusted
Urquiza and believed that he would simply establish another
dictatorship like that of Rosas' or whether he feared too much
loss of political power to Buenos Aires in the federal plans
proposed by Urquiza, or for whatever reason, Mitre assumed
the lead in opposing Buenos Aires acceptance of the Acuerdo
de San Nicolás; he accepted military and ministerial appointments in the independent Buenos Aires government established
following the city's successful revolt alainst Urquiza September
11, 1852, in which Mitre, as commander of the national guard,
had played an important role; in December the provincial revolt led by Colonel Hilario Lagos broke out against the Alsina
government and, in the confused seven months siege of the city
that followed (see Hilario Lagos), Mitre repeatedly left his
desk, as minister of government and foreign affairs, to enter
into military action until he sustained a bad head injury that
required brain surgery and a prolonged period of recovery;
back in public life he served in the legislature and as inspec-
tor-general of arms; as minister of war in 1855 he carried out
an expedition against the Indians in the south and modernized
the armed forces of the province; in 1857 he published the first
edition of his Historia de Belgrano; meanwhile, feeling in Buenos Aires continued to be divided as to what its role should be
with regard to the thirteen other Argentine provinces, joined
in a constitutional confederation after 1853; a few porteños,
like Lagos, wanted to join the confederation; others, led by the
Alsinas, wanted Buenos Aires to become an independent American nation; Mitre became leader of moderate, middle group
that wanted to bind the fourteen provinces together under the

1853 constitution; the underlying suspicions and differences between the political leaders of Buenos Aires and those of the interior, complicated by personal hatreds, like that of the Alsinas for Urquiza, however, made reconciliation very difficult; for a few years emotions ruled, despite the efforts of moderate leaders on both sides, the obvious need that the provinces had for each other, and determined efforts of foreign diplomats to bring them together in the interests of trade; fighting between Buenos Aires and the Confederation had never completely stopped and at Cepeda, October 23, 1859, Mitre, as minister of war and navy and general-in-chief of the Buenos Aires armies, was totally defeated in a major battle by Urquiza and his forces; Mitre, who had favored negotiations rather than military action now became (1860) governor as well as commander; an agreement was made to join the province with the confederation on the basis of constitutional changes requested by the Buenos Aires constituent convention; Mitre was made a brigadier general in the confederation army; new problems led to a final battle at Pavón September 17, 1861, with Mitre and Buenos Aires the victors; the confederation government had fallen apart and the president Santiago Derqui had resigned and left; Mitre assumed the responsibility for forming the new nation; using diplomacy, patience, and fairness, he brought the provinces together at last and provided for presidential elections; Mitre, as unanimous choice, became first president of the Argentine Republic on October 12, 1862, with Marcos Paz of Tucumán as vice president.

As president, Mitre was able to attract the most talented men of the nation to his cabinet; in a spirit of compromise and conciliation he insisted on the law of compromise, making Buenos Aires the provisional national capital, and worked out national use of the waterways and ports; his attention was first directed toward establishing internal peace, with several provinces still in very unsettled conditions; determined to avoid personal government, he institutionalized political life as rapidly as possible; civil wars had delayed modernization and development of Argentina's economy and he turned his attention to building upon the foundations already established by both Buenos Aires and the confederation in the years since Caseros, by fostering immigration, agriculture, and trade, encouraging the building of railroads, establishing and subsidizing shipping lines; stabilizing the national financial base and generally creating a sense of confidence at home and abroad in the government and Argentina's future; national revenue doubled and population increased; at the same time Mitre vigorously encouraged the establishment of public schools, emphasizing secondary schools, and making use of foreign scholars and teachers already in the area, as well as attracting others from Europe; unfortunately, the president's attention was forcibly diverted from national to foreign affairs with the outbreak of the Paraguayan war in which he served as commander-in-chief of the allied Argentine-Uruguayan-Brazilian forces until the death of the vice president forced him to relinquish command to the Duke of Caxias (see

Paraguayan War); one of Mitre's most important contributions
came at the close of his term of office when he provided for
constitutional selection of his successor, Domingo F. Sarmiento.

Bartolomé Mitre never again became president but he
continued to be a powerful political leader, successful diplomat, deeply respected scholar, and profoundly revered public
figure for the rest of his life; in 1869 (first issue January 4,
1870) he founded the prestigious newspaper La Nación through
which he continued to express his views; as national senator
from Buenos Aires he engaged frequently in congressional debates, especially those dealing with matters of education, immigration, development of the Buenos Aires port, etc.; almost
lost his life in the yellow fever epidemic of 1871 due to his
visits to the hospitals and attempts to help in subduing it; sent
on diplomatic mission to Brazil to settle boundary and other
disputes growing out of the Paraguayan war, Mitre proved to
be a successful diplomat and was believed by the Argentine
people to have averted the outbreak of new hostilities between
the two nations (Mitre had always favored cooperation between
the two countries, rather than rivalry and tension); in 1874
Mitre ran for president again but was defeated by Nicolás Avellaneda; declaring that the election was fraudulent, Mitre resorted to force; government forces quickly defeated this movement and Mitre was imprisoned, spending most of the time in
the old cabildo building at Luján; at the court martial he was
censured, stripped of his ranks and honors, and condemned to
exile but Avellaneda immediately pardoned him and in 1883 he
was made lieutenant general; Mitre resumed his position as
public-spirited citizen, but devoted more and more of his attention to historical writing; caught up against his will in the political turmoil of 1880; in 1889 he was one of the founders of
the Unión Cívica and in 1890 he departed for Europe to avoid
becoming involved again in the political turmoil; refused to become a candidate for presidency in 1891, following the ousting
of Juárez Celman; again became national senator in 1894; his
last public position was that of president of the national senate;
his eightieth birthday was made a national holiday and he was
honored with great public ceremony as "the first citizen of the
republic"; Mitre died at his home in Buenos Aires January 18,
1906.

One of Bartolomé Mitre's greatest and most enduring
contributions was in the field of historiography; belonging to the
first post-independence generation, he bridged in his own lifetime and in his own actions the gap between the colonial viceroyalty and the modern republic needing to know its historic
roots; his love of reading, his skill in writing, his intuitive
sense of national needs, his lifetime bent toward seeking the
practical solutions, his self-taught sense of scholarly excellence, his long-practiced habits of hard work--all his abilities
--came to a focus in his historical writings and in his creation of an important school of historiography, one that demanded use of all available materials with especial emphasis to

original sources and conclusions drawn from those materials,
rather than for moral or national purposes; in these views he
clashed directly with his distinguished contemporary writers
and carried on long, public polemics with such men as Vicente
F. López and Dalmacio Vélez Sársfield about the purpose and
proper methodology of historiography; twentieth century historians are more apt to call him the founder of modern Argentine
historiography; during his lifetime Mitre had gathered an un-
surpassed collection of books and manuscripts to aid in his researches, especially those on Argentine history; after his death
this library was turned over to the nation; it remained housed
in Mitre's home on Calle San Martín--a famous colonial house
that the city of Buenos Aires had presented to him much earlier in appreciation of his work--and became the nucleus of the
Institución Mitre; it also houses the Academia Nacional de la
Historia; and ranks as one of the most important historical research centers in the nation.

The publication of Mitre's complete works was ordered
by law in 1936 and the first volume published in that year.
Among his most important historical writings are the classics
containing the story of Argentine (and Spanish South American)
wars for independence; Historia de Belgrano y de la independencia argentina (first edition 2 volumes, Buenos Aires 1859;
definitive fourth edition 3 v., 1887); and his Historia de San
Martín y de la emancipación sudamericana (3 v., Buenos
Aires, 1887-1890; many other editions, including an abridged
English translation by William Pilling, London, 1893).

See William H. Jeffrey, Mitre and Argentina (New York,
1952); Ricardo Levene, Las ideas históricas de Mitre (Buenos
Aires, 1948); and Enrique de Gandía, Mitre, hombre de estado (Buenos Aires, 1940).

MITRE, EMILIO, General (1824-1893).   Career military officer.
Born in Carmen de Patagones; brother of Bartolomé
Mitre; entered military career in Montevideo where family was
living in exile; first saw military action under Uruguayan general Fructuoso Rivera in battle of Arroyo Grande, 1839; won
promotion to sergeant major in defense of Montevideo during
siege; accompanied Uruguayan troops commanded by General
César Díaz in support of Urquiza against Rosas at Caseros;
fought in Buenos Aires forces at battles of Cepeda (1859) and
Pavón (1861); a general when war broke out with Paraguay,
Mitre commanded allied troops at Boquerón July 18, 1866;
fought at Curupayti, Humaitá, Angostura; replaced General
Gelly y Obés in command of Argentine army; commanded
troops sent by President Sarmiento against Ricardo López Jordán, caudillo in Entre Ríos (1871); elected deputy to national
congress in 1880; continued to hold high posts to military hierarchy; chief of staff in 1893; suppressed radical revolt of that
year; died in Buenos Aires in December of illness incurred
during that action.

MITRE, EMILIO (1853-1909).   Civil engineer; journalist; legislator and political leader.

Born in Buenos Aires; son of Bartolomé Mitre and Delfina de Vedia; educated in Buenos Aires; after graduating as civil engineer, became director of telegraph system of province of Buenos Aires; expanded its operations; went to Europe to broaden his own knowledge and to select foreign correspondents for La Nación, newspaper edited by his father; returned to Buenos Aires to divide his time between profession and family paper; took part (as captain in Buenos Aires forces in events of 1880 resulting in federalization of capital; member of board of directors of Western Railroad (later called Domingo Faustino Sarmiento); participated in revolutionary movements of 1890 and 1893; twice elected to provincial senate; in 1896 represented Buenos Aires province in national legislature and in 1906 represented Federal Capital there; largely responsible for legislation for construction of port of Buenos Aires and the channel (bearing his name) of the Paraná Delta; leader of Republican party in election of 1906; as editor of La Nación, from 1894 until his death in Buenos Aires May 25, 1909, he supported peaceful settlement of boundary disputes between Argentina and Chile; honored in death by military funeral (rank of brigadier general), naming of Buenos Aires street after him, erection of bronze statue (1931), etc.; his death marked virtual end of Republican party.

MOCOVI or MOCOBI.   Indian tribe found occupying the Chaco forest area between the Abipones on the southeast and the Lules to the northwest; all belonged to fierce Guaycuruan group (q. v.) linguistically and culturally; the Mocoví on their own, or allied with their neighbors, frequently attacked the Spanish settlements from Salta to Santiago del Estero and Córdoba; when Spaniards arrived, the Mocoví were hunters, gatherers, and fishermen, but they quickly adopted the horse and formed mounted bands of raiders over the entire Chaco as well as neighboring areas; in the middle of the eighteenth century the Mocoví numbered around 3000; those who remain today have become assimilated into the national economy and society as farmers, potters, and weavers.

See Lázaro Flury, Las tribus mocovíes del Chaco (Buenos Aires, 1945).

MOLDES, EUSTOQUIO (1783-1826).   Early independence leader in Salta.

Born in Salta; elder brother of José Moldes (q. v.); educated in Spain; returning to Salta on eve of May Revolution became strong supporter of liberating movement; as officer in Light Dragoons, joined Auxiliary Army; fought at Cotagaita, Suipacha, and Huaquí; gravely wounded in fighting at Tucumán, he was taken prisoner outside Jujuy; eventually released, he saw limited action under Arenales in Alto Perú and accompanied him in his campaign there in the closing years of the Bolivian fight for independence; returning to Salta, Moldes headed a revolutionary movement and was killed while resisting Arenales' forces sent to arrest him.

MOLDES, JOSE (1785-1824). Fiery salteño patriot who played important role in early years of independence movement, both in
Spain and in Argentina; strong exponent of localism.

Born in Salta; taken to Spain in 1803 to complete his
education; became cadet in bodyguard of king, an elite, privileged group; in Madrid became friends with Argentine patriots
Pueyrredón, the Gurruchagas, Zepeda, Lezica, Pinto, and Alvear; formed secret association in favor of Latin American independence; Moldes also in contact with and influenced by Francisco de Miranda (q. v.); in spite of French opposition (following Napoleonic invasion), succeeded in leaving Spain for Buenos
Aires, arriving there in January 1809; joined patriot group and
set himself the task of personally propagandizing the interior
in favor of independence; following the May Revolution he was
appointed to a series of responsible positions, both civil and
military: lieutenant governor of Mendoza, 1810; the following
year, he became intendant of Cochabamba and also performed
responsible military duties; joined Belgrano and distinguished
himself at battle of Tucumán; returning to Buenos Aires, he
was placed in command of city's police force and made responsible for defense of city, with rank of colonel; elected to
represent Jujuy and Salta at the general constituent assembly of
1813, then sent to aid in siege of Montevideo; the year 1814
seems to have marked the beginning of the decline of his relations with patriot leaders; apparently with the restoration of
Ferdinand VII to the throne, Moldes began to consider desirability of negotiations with the crown; his turbulent, individualistic spirit brought him into repeated conflict with authorities;
exiled to Patagonia in 1814 by Director Posadas; elected to
Congress of Tucumán by Salta and nominated by Córdoba for
Supreme Director, he broke his friendship with Pueyrredón
when latter was appointed instead; Moldes lost his civil rights
and was imprisoned through troubles with Godoy Cruz; he alienated his former commander, Belgrano, who banished him to
Chile where he was imprisoned by San Martín; in 1819 he escaped and returned to Buenos Aires where he charged the government with corruption and demanded justice; in 1826 he died
in Buenos Aires under somewhat mysterious circumstances.

Notwithstanding his excitable temperament, Moldes is
considered to have performed important personal and financial
services to the cause of liberty, especially during its earliest
years and has been called its alma or living soul.

MOLINA, JUAN BAUTISTA (1882-   ). Military officer; political activist in 1930s and early 1940s; strong nationalist.

Born in Salta, Molina was educated for his military career in the officer candidates school, school of ballistics, and
in the war academy (Escuela Superior de Guerra); also seems
to have served in the German army, 1911-1913; was a professor and company commander in the Colegio Militar (1915-1916);
held later appointments as commandante, professor, and chief
of battalion in the Ballistics School; became one of Uriburu's
key advisors in the planning of the coup of 1930 and his secre-

tary when Uriburu replaced Yrigoyen as president; strongly influenced Uriburu in such matters as the creation of the Legión
Cívica Argentina (q. v.), suggested, in fact by Molina, himself,
and Dr. Juan Carulla; although already tending more toward
the rightist and corporatist nationalists, Molina loyally supported and helped to implement Uriburu's decision to hold elections
(1932) to continue the constitutional political processes; he continued his military career during Justo's administration, serving as head of commission to purchase military equipment
abroad (1932) and as military attaché to Germany (1933); returned to Buenos Aires in December, 1933, greatly impressed
by the new German military techniques and eager to introduce
them into Argentina; became director of the school for noncom-
missioned officers and assumed active role as leader of ex-
tremist nationalists, especially those turning toward German
ties, rather than British; became leader of conspiracy designed
not only to oust President Justo but to create an Argentine
corporatist state under plan drawn up by Diego de Molinari
(q. v.); scheduled to take place July 9, 1936, the revolt was
aborted by Justo's discovery of its plans; Molina was transferred to the post of general director of engineers in the War
Ministry and other leading military conspirators were also
moved to innocuous positions; late in 1936 he was promoted to
brigadier general and in 1937 he was elected president of the
Círculo Militar; meanwhile his ultranationalistic and pro-German sympathies were intensified; he had reorganized the Legión
Cívica Argentina (q. v.) along lines of the Nazi party; later
sponsored another para-military organization, the Nationalist
Youth Alliance (Alianza de la Juventud Nacionalista) and served
as its president 1937-1943; in 1938 President Ortiz suspended
Molina from active duty because of political actions and in
1939 the latter retired from active duty rather than accept an
appointment to Bahía Blanca and increased his political activities; the national tensions arising from breakdown of political
parties and especially from the illness of President Ortiz and
the actions taken by acting president Castillo, added to the increasing probability of German victory in 1940 and early 1941,
convinced many ultra-nationalist, pro-German military officers
that the time was ripe to restructure Argentina completely
along more "modern," totalitarian lines; these officers lined
themselves up behind either Benjamín Menéndez (q. v.) or the
better-known conspirator Juan B. Molina; in many respects this
plot simply revived the plan of 1936 with Diego de Molinari
(q. v.) again the ideological master; Molina attracted promises
of support from many officers on active duty with forces and
the movement seemed to be reaching the take-off point in February 1941; instead, it disintegrated as various officers upon
whom Molina had counted (sometimes apparently mistakenly)
began to withdraw their support; this marked the end of Molina's political leadership as younger officers turned elsewhere;
Molina was involved for some time as a defendant in the federal civil courts as a result of the War Ministry's investigation
of the plot but apparently, for its own reasons, the government

was not interested in either punishment or publicity about the
conspiracy; Molina retired from the army in 1943 to private
life; by this time the entry of the United States and most of the
Latin American nations into the war on the Allied side had
made German sympathizers somewhat less open in their public
statements and positions.
    See Potash in Suggested Readings, Appendix III.

MOLINARI, DIEGO LUIS (1889-   ).   Historian; public figure; univer-
    sity professor.
        Born in Buenos Aires; educated at the university in fac-
    ulty of law and social sciences; became ardent supporter of
    Yrigoyen and entered public life at the same time that he was
    devoting himself to writing and historical research; served on
    diplomatic missions to Bolivia, Peru and Chile (1917), to Uru-
    guay (1919), and to Brazil (1922); as undersecretary of minis-
    try of foreign relations in 1920, he was concerned in the post-
    World War I years with the position taken by Yrigoyen's gov-
    ernment toward possible conflicts between League of Nations
    pronouncements and the traditional Monroe policy of the United
    States (which he viewed casually); in 1922 he undertook a dip-
    lomatic mission to Brazil and became president of the national
    labor department from 1924 to 1928 he served as a national
    congressman, and as senator 1928-1930 (again 1948-1950);
    meanwhile he had undertaken academic responsibilities--as pro-
    fessor of Argentine history in the faculty of philosophy and let-
    ters, 1933-1946, and economic history in the faculty of econ-
    omic sciences (1934-1946); in 1936 he drew up the political
    plan for the revolution led by Juan Bautista Molina (q.v.) that
    was supposed to begin on July 9; it called for a "national lib-
    eration" and restructuring of all government, most important
    economic enterprises, and professional and labor organizations
    into a new corporatist government, with strong nationalistic
    policies; when the revolution failed to take place because of
    prior discovery, Molinari kept his plan and published it in 1940
    in pamphlet form and then used it for the nationalist military
    revolution, planned for 1941 again led by Juan Bautista Molina,
    that also failed to take place; Molinari turned in 1942 to sup-
    port of Juan Perón, in weekly articles of Ahora; was closely
    linked with Perón's administration; carried out special mission
    to Mexico in 1946; visited several Latin American countries in
    1947 and led the Argentine challenge to the United States at the
    United Nations Conference on Trade and Employment held in
    Havana in 1947; the United States, along with other nations,
    strongly supported a draft for the forming of the International
    Trade Organization to ease flow of international trade; Molinari,
    as spokesman for Perón's bid for economic leadership, espe-
    cially in Latin America and among underdeveloped countries,
    countered by calling for a more flexible program and offered
    generous Argentine economic aid in its support; although his
    speeches failed to stop the organization of the International
    Trade Organization and Argentina refused to sign the Havana
    charter for it, Molinari had once again made Argentina's

nationalist position of independence against the United States
clear; in 1950 he visited Pakistan; in 1955, following the fall
of Perón's government, Molinari withdrew from public and
teaching responsibilities to private life.

In addition to numerous articles and monographs Molinari wrote several historical studies, including La "Representación de los hacendados" de Mariano Moreno (1914, 2nd edition 1939); La trata de negros (1914); El gobierno de los pueblos (1916); Un virrey (1923); La empresa colombina y el descubrimiento de América (1936); ¡Viva Ramírez! (1937--the
prizewinner in 1939 of the National Commission of Culture,
Littoral Region); La política lusitana en el Río de la Plata,
1877-1902 (1939); El nacimiento del Nuevo Mundo (1941).

MONARCHY. The idea of establishing an independent monarchy in
Argentina--or one to include the entire viceroyalty, or even
the viceroyalties of Río de la Plata and of Peru--was widely
discussed in patriot circles 1808-1820; its supporters, including Belgrano, Rivadavia, Pueyrredón, Valentín Gómez, San
Martín, and most of the members of the Lautaro Lodge, believed this form of government to be the one best adapted to
the life-style and historical practices of the people involved,
as well as the one most likely to attract international support,
first for the cause of independence and then for political recognition and economic aid in the development of the new nation;
during the period before 1814, the attraction of republicanism
was still strong, with the example of the United States (and,
to a lesser extent, Haiti) in their own hemisphere, with the
Spanish king forced into exile, and with the ideals of the
French Revolution still fresh in their memories; such creole
leaders and writers as Mariano and Manuel Moreno and Vicente Pazos Kanki never ceased to be ardent republicans; many
Spanish merchants in Buenos Aires, led by Martín de Alzaga,
also backed republican cause, as a way to break the tie with
Spain and establish an independent Argentina, unfettered by
Spanish regulations and different interests, to be ruled by the
Spaniards resident in Argentina, with creole leadership re-
duced to a minimum.

After restoration of Ferdinand VII to the throne in 1814
and the exiling of Napoleon the following year after his defeat
at Waterloo, Argentine thinking quickly began to reflect that of
Europe, with its return to the principle of legitimacy--i.e., the
insistence on placing the rightful kings on their own thrones;
with the United States still involved in settling its continent-
wide boundary with Spain to its south and west (resulting in
1819-1821 in Adams-Onís treaty), Europe offered Argentina's
only hope of support for independence, security, and stability;
in 1816 Belgrano, just returned from Europe, addressed the
congress of Tucumán and expressed the opinion that Argentina
could not expect any support from European nations unless it
also established a monarchical form of government; he remind-
ed the members that England, then the richest, most powerful,
and apparently most stable nation in the western world was

governed by a constitutional monarchy, to which he attributed
this success, as well as the freedom enjoyed by its citizens;
Belgrano wanted for Argentina a similar limited monarchy,
but with an American legitimate dynasty--the crowning of an
Inca prince as its ruler; such a move, he hoped, would unite
the Perus, Chile, and the United Provinces of the Plata in a
great Spanish-speaking nation in South America to balance the
size and power of neighboring Portuguese Brazil; French
writers and scholars of the eighteenth century had done much
to publicize and revive the ancient glory of the Incas so that
this would seem a "legitimate" move for Argentina, whose
northwestern portion had once belonged to the Inca empire.
  Other monarchical plans included the earlier (1808,
1814) attempts to crown Carlota Joaquina (q. v.) as regent or
as queen of an independent Argentina and Sarratea's project to
secure the Spanish crown prince, Francisco de Paula, as king;
the possibility of securing a French prince was discussed but
the French government felt that Argentina's choice, the Duke
of Orleans, was too liberal and Argentina rejected the suggested French candidate as too insignificant for its purposes; briefly the idea of finding an English prince was discussed; in 1819-
1820, it was seriously proposed that a Portuguese Braganza
prince (possibly with marriage to Inca princess) should become
the Argentine king, with hopes of reconciling traditional problems between Brazil and Argentina, but this was rejected by
Buenos Aires leaders as a kind of surrender to the Portuguese
who had occupied the Banda Oriental (today's Uruguay, but then
claimed as part of the old viceroyalty of Buenos Aires).
  Practically all of the members of the Congress of Tucumán (meeting in Buenos Aires from late 1816 to 1819), except
for Justo Santa María de Oro (q. v.) were willing to accept a
monarchical form of government as best for the nation although
federalists, especially those in the provinces outside of Buenos
Aires, opposed it; for various reasons each individual monarchical project failed and finally, with the dissolution of congress
in the period of anarchy of the "terrible year of 1820" the entire idea of establishing a monarchy was wiped out as unpopular, and not suited to Argentina's traditionally democratic spirit; natural as it had seemed to educated leaders of Argentina
at the time, oriented toward hierarchy in church and government and influenced by new European intellectual currents of
the period and, indeed, to many later historians who believe
that the establishment of such a government would have saved
Argentina several decades of bloody civil wars and repressions,
the idea of monarchy was never accepted by the people generally and many other historians regard this total defeat of the
monarchical principle as a victory won by the traditional Argentine forces for democracy that dated back to the days of the
conquest (see Conquistadors; Creoles; Democracy; Federalists).

MONROE DOCTRINE. In his message to Congress December 2,
  1823, President James Monroe stated the doctrine that bears
  his name and formed the basis of U.S. policy in the Western

Hemisphere: the American continents were henceforth not open
to colonization by any European power; the United States would
consider any attempt to extend European forms of government
to the Americas a threat to U.S. peace and safety; and U.S.
would not interfere with any existing colony but would view any
European intervention in any Latin American area in which
U.S. had recognized its independence, as an unfriendly act;
February 9, 1824, issue of the Gaceta Mercantil reported it in
Buenos Aires; published later in both El Avisador Mercantil and
El Argos, it received wide circulation; public officials, like
Rivadavia and Las Heras praised it, emphasizing its strong
statements against future European intervention and colonization;
the Argentine people, faced with instability of Rodríguez government in Buenos Aires, lack of national government and threat
posed by Quadruple Alliance in Europe received Monroe's message with enthusiasm; some doubted that it would have much
significance for Argentine because of its remoteness; in fact,
U.S. did not intervene when British occupied Falkland Islands
against Argentine protests; during most of the nineteenth century, with Argentina drawing closer to Europe in trade, economy, and culture, the Monroe Doctrine was only mentioned occasionally, as by Sarmiento while he was Argentine minister to
U.S. (1865-1867); Luis M. Drago considered his Drago Doctrine
(q.v.) an economic supplement to the Monroe Doctrine; by the
close of the 19th century many Argentinians felt that interpretation of the Monroe Doctrine changed from a defense statement
to a U.S. attempt to dominate the Western Hemisphere; the
diplomacy of the early (1933-1936) Franklin Roosevelt administration, designed to implement the Good Neighbor Policy and
provide for hemispheric defense in event of outbreak of war in
Europe, brought limited results, mainly the agreement among
the American nations to hold consultation about hemispheric defense if an American nation should be attacked by a non-Amer-
ican one, but this was hailed by many as the "Pan Americani-
zation" of the Monroe Doctrine (see United States; Inter-American Affairs).

MONSERRAT see COLEGIO DE MONSERRAT

MONTE CASEROS see CASEROS

MONTEAGUDO, BERNARDO (1785-1825). Revolutionary intellectual;
political leader, administrator, lawyer and judge; collaborator
with both San Martín and Bolívar in the wars of independence
in Spanish South America; a controversial figure, commanding
respect and admiration from many for his revolutionary ideas
and ideals, his eloquence in expressing them, and his administrative skills in putting them into practice; but arousing implacable hatred from others because of his doctrinaire rigidity and
ruthlessness, and the turbulence of his personal life.
        Born in Tucumán, Monteagudo was educated in law at
the universities of Córdoba and Chuquisaca; at the latter he became acquainted with many of the future leaders of Argentine

independence and revolution; he entered public life as a leader
of the Chuquisaca revolt, May 25, 1809; on his way back into
Argentina he aroused the patriot leaders of Jujuy and other
parts of the northwest (see Gorritis) against the Sevilla junta
in Spain; arrived in Buenos Aires in time to participate in the
May Revolution (1810); he accompanied the army to Upper Peru
as auditor de guerra (judge advocate) and became secretary to
Dr. Juan José Castelli (q. v.); following the defeat of the patriot
army at Huaqui (June 20, 1811), he returned to Buenos Aires
where he became the idol of the young porteño patriots through
his passionate revolutionary writings; as one of the editors of
the Gaceta de Buenos Aires, Monteagudo vigorously denounced
or supported various government actions according to his convictions and wielded considerable political power; in 1812, he
was a member of the commission that tried and punished the
leaders of the Alzaga conspiracy; in 1813 he became an active
member of the Assembly of 1813 (q. v.) that attempted to revo-
lutionize the institutional structure of the old viceroyalty; in
1815 he strongly supported Alvear as director but the fall of
the latter's government sent Monteagudo into exile in Europe
for two years.

Returning to Argentina in 1817, Monteagudo made his
way to Mendoza and Chile where San Martín at once made him
judge advocate of his army; for the rest of his life, he was
tied in with the wars of independence in Chile and Peru, except for a brief period in 1818, following the defeat at Cancha
Rayada, when he was back in Mendoza and played a principal
role in the trial and execution of the Carrera brothers, and
another period in 1819 when, living in San Luis, he had charge
of the trial of the royalist prisoners engaged in conspiracy
there; once more in Chile in 1820 he occupied his time in revolutionary writing until he accompanied San Martín's army,
again as judge advocate, to Peru (1820); there he became one
of San Martín's closest associates, especially in the task of
establishing the new revolutionary government, serving first as
minister of war and navy, then (January 1, 1822) becoming
minister of government and foreign relations; San Martín left
him in charge when he sailed to Guayaquil for his interview
with Bolívar, but the Peruvians ousted him July 25, largely for
personal reasons, and he went to Guayaquil; later (1824), Bolívar recognized Monteagudo's ability and knowledge of Peruvian
affairs and brought him back to Peru under his protection as
consultant; the following year he was assassinated in Lima.

Monteagudo's writings reveal him to have been both a
visionary revolutionary and a doctrinaire Jacobin; in the early
period following the May Revolution he belonged to the Moren-
ista group and later joined many of these in demanding reforms
and revolutionary changes apparently even at the cost of establishing a caudillo or dictator in power, if necessary; his ruthlessness and rigidity of principle were shown in his passionate
defense of Castelli's executions of Santiago de Liniers and other
leaders of Córdoba conspiracy (1811) and his own similar actions with regard to the Alzaga revolt leaders, and the Carrera

brothers; the breadth of his vision, on the other hand, is revealed by the fact that he, alone among the Argentine independence leaders, favored a federation of the new Spanish American nations and had assisted Bolívar in drawing up plans for
the Pan American congress, to be held later in Panama, before his death; many of Monteagudo's scattered writings have
been collected and published by Ricardo Rojas in Obras políticas de Bernardo Monteagudo (Buenos Aires, 1916); his biography has been written by Mariano de Vedia y Mitre, La vida de
Monteagudo (3 v., Buenos Aires, 1950); also by Eduardo M. S.
Danero Monteagudo (Buenos Aires, 1968).

MONTENEGRO, PEDRO (1663-1728).   Galician-born Jesuit physician
and missionary who came to Argentina in 1693; located in Córdoba and then moved to the Guaraní missions and across the
river to Colonia (Uruguay) after it had been captured by the
Spaniards from the Portuguese in Brazil; dedicated himself
throughout this period to the study of medicinal plants used by
the Indians; recorded his observations and conclusions in Materia médica (1710).

MONTERO, CARLOS JOSE (1743-d. after 1797).   Priest and educator; intellectual leader in Buenos Aires during early years of
the viceroyalty.
        Born in Buenos Aires and educated there and in Córdoba
where he received his doctorate in civil and canon law; ordained as priest in 1767; returned to Buenos Aires to devote
himself to his ecclesiastical duties and teaching; in 1773 he offered first course given in Buenos Aires in philosophy; because
of his prestige he was made chancellor of the royal studies at
the colegio de San Carlos; Dr. Montero represented a link between the scholasticism of the Spanish period and the more liberal education of the independence one, as he himself had studied under the Greek Jesuit Manuel Querini and was, in turn,
the teacher of Luis José Chorroarín and of Cornelio Saavedra
(qq. v.).

MONTEVIDEO.   Modern capital of independent republic of Uruguay;
for several decades at close of 18th and most of 19th centuries, Montevideo posed a rival threat to Buenos Aires' attempts
to dominate economic and political life of the Río de la Plata;
economic, personal, political, cultural relationships remained
very close, several times involving Buenos Aires government
in military action, even international wars.
        The bay on which the city of Montevideo is located was
first explored by Juan Díaz de Solís (1516) and later took its
name (and that of the city) from that given by Magellan (1520)
to a site several miles east along that coast; as Spanish settlement in the Río de la Plata began on the south bank of the estuary to avoid the hostility of the Charrúas, and moved up the
Paraná to Asunción among the more civilized Guaraní, the
Banda Oriental (eastern bank or shore of the Uruguay river as
Uruguay was then known) was left to the dwindling number of

Indians and increasing herds of wild cattle; its proximity to
southern Brazil, always seeking a base on the Río de la Plata
and its strategic importance for the defense of Buenos Aires
and the upriver settlements against foreign intruders, both
Brazilian and European, brought constant requests from Argentine governors for some kind of settlement or fortified outpost
to be established there; these went almost unheeded until imperialistic rivalries of 18th century finally caused Spain to
place a small garrison there and in 1726, in the face of real
threat from Portuguese Brazil and its settlement Colonia do
Sacramento westward on the river, Governor Bruno Mauricio
de Zabala established the city of Montevideo January 30, 1726,
giving it the traditional name of that site; the town grew slowly
but, as rivalry between Spain and Portugal increased, it was
given its own governor in 1750 and from 1763 (end of Seven
Years War in Europe reflected in increased Portuguese pressure against Río de la Plata) until Spain had lost the colony it
served as the base of Spanish military defense of that area;
the British invasions (q. v. , 1806-1807) demonstrated that control of Buenos Aires was difficult, if not impossible, without
first occupying Montevideo; it was from Governor Pascual Ruiz
Huidobro (q. v.) in Montevideo that Santiago Liniers secured
much of his army and equipment for the reconquest of Buenos
Aires; and the British took care to establish themselves first
in Montevideo as a base from which to undertake the second invasion of Buenos Aires in 1807.

Although this British conquest of Montevideo was surprisingly difficult, considering the small population and armed
force there, it became extremely important to the city, establishing in many ways the direction of its future development and
its unique characteristics; the city immediately began to prosper as the British opened the ports to trade and European and
North American ships filled the harbor to load their ships with
the plentiful hides and tallow; almost from its beginning the
city was cosmopolitan as the British (and other) traders came
to represent a large proportion of the inhabitants of this small
settlement that had not yet (in contrast to other Río de la Plata
and Argentine settlements) formed traditions and a life style of
its own but had been, from the beginning, a border outpost
against Portuguese-Brazilians and other Europeans; many British officers or merchants remained there or returned later to
become residents; the merchant class (both Uruguayan and foreign) acquired prestige and power; new ideas of political, economic, social and religious freedom became widespread through
personal contacts with the British, their publication of the
newspaper, the Estrella del Sur (q. v.), and their establishment
of Protestant churches and cemetery; by the time of the May
Revolution three years later in Buenos Aires, Montevideo felt
itself strong enough (and different enough) to refuse to accept
leadership from Buenos Aires; during the six years that Ferdinand VII was off the throne and Spain under Napoleonic domination (1808-1814), Montevideo became the center of Spanish
Royalist support; Buenos Aires, meanwhile, was thinking in

terms of a change--perhaps a British protectorate, perhaps an independent monarchy under Carlota Joaquina (q.v.), perhaps a semi-autonomous government under restored Spanish royal rule, or an independent American republic, like that set up in the United States; during 1808-1809: Governor Francisco Javier de Elío (q.v.) provided support or refuge to porteños opposing either viceroy Liniers (whom both he and the cabildo of Montevideo opposed) or the Buenos Aires cabildo's authority; this conflict between the two cities was an important part of reason for replacement of Liners by Cisneros as viceroy (1809); latter spent considerable time in Montevideo before going to Buenos Aires to assume his post; in May 1810 Governor Francisco Javier de Elío (q.v.) refused to accept the May Revolution (and its ousting of the viceroy); instead, in the breakdown of government in Spain (see May Revolution), he withdrew Montevideo from the viceroyalty and followed the example of European cities--and, in fact, of Buenos Aires, itself--by setting up a junta in Montevideo to act independently until normal Spanish government could be reestablished, and the port of Montevideo was closed to ships proceeding from Buenos Aires during 1810-1811; as governor, and then returning for most of 1811 as viceroy of the Río de la Plata, Elío successfully (sometimes with promise of Brazilian support) maintained Spanish authority in Montevideo both against patriot forces from Buenos Aires and against the Uruguayan revolutionaries, led by Artigas, and allied with the patriots in Buenos Aires; his successor Gaspar Vigodet (q.v.) continued the same policy until 1814.

For Buenos Aires it seemed essential in 1814 to bring Montevideo into the revolutionary movement; defeats of patriot forces in the northwest, the restoration of Ferdinand VII to the throne and his announced intention to bring the Spanish American colonies back under royal authority, the threat of a new Portuguese-Brazilian invasion into Uruguay, combined with the chaotic situation in Buenos Aires and the provinces, gave priority to the effort of bringing the stronghold (and first port of call for European vessels entering the Río de la Plata) of Montevideo under Buenos Aires control before the British should shift their support--or at least goodwill--to Spain; Director Gervasio Posadas exerted an all out effort under General Carlos Alvear and Admiral William Brown, who already held Montevideo under siege by sea, and forced Vigodet to surrender Montevideo June 23, 1814; although this gave Argentine patriot morale a great boost, with ballads sung and poems written to commemorate it, three years later Supreme Director Juan Martín de Pueyrredón (q.v.), totally engrossed in supporting San Martín's continental project for liberation and attempting to maintain authority and order in an Argentina torn by internal, provincial, and civil strife and unable to prevent guerrillas, often led by Artigas, from raiding southeastern Brazil (as well as Argentine riparian provinces), acquiesced in Montevideo's takeover by Portuguese-Brazilian General Carlos Federico Lecor in 1817; he hoped thus to prevent Ferdinand's forces from establishing a new Spanish base there, or its serving as a base from which

dissident provincial forces could threaten Buenos Aires; in
1821, after Artigas had withdrawn from the civil wars into
Paraguay, Montevideo and its hinterland--Uruguay--became the
Cisplatine province of Brazil.

For a few years Buenos Aires and the provinces were
also involved in their own anarchy and civil wars and Montevideo so concerned with its own changes--Artigas gone, Brazil
independent--that little or no overt action took place; Buenos
Aires was still determined, however, to wrest Montevideo from
Brazil and perhaps to bring it back under Buenos Aires domination; in April 1825 the famous 33, under the Uruguayan general, Juan Antonio Lavalleja, and supported by Buenos Aires
government, invaded Uruguay to join with other Uruguayan
leaders in freeing it from Brazil; as a result, Argentina found
itself involved in full-scale war with Brazil (1826-27) but after
peace was made, it was agreed (1828) that Uruguay should become independent, with Montevideo as its capital; British diplomacy has been given much credit for this, although Colom-
bians handled the negotiations; actually the fundamental differences between Uruguay and both its neighbors probably made
independence inevitable; during the Rosas period (1829-1852),
Montevideo presented a constant threat to the Buenos Aires
government; it served as a base from which both foreign and
Argentine enemies of Rosas could attack his capital; its estancieros and saladeros challenged Buenos Aires profits from
the new meat trade, as well as that in hides and tallow, and
provided a haven for unitarists, especially young intellectuals,
in exile from Rosas' rule; Rosas forcibly intervened frequently
in Uruguay's chaotic political life, backing Oribe and the Blancos against Rivera and his Colorado party; the nine-year siege,
known as the "Great War" (q. v.) attracted international attention, sympathy, and foreign volunteers to defend Montevideo,
popularly viewed as fighting the cause of freedom against that
of tyranny; this period also strengthened later ties between
Montevideo and Buenos Aires as many of the Argentine exiles
(later to become Argentine leaders--see especially Bartolomé
Mitre) married, established their families, reached intellectual maturity and acquired military, professional, and political
skills working and fighting alongside Montevideo colleagues;
ties already existing with these Montevideans who, like Andrés
Lamas (q. v.) had been born in days of the viceroyalty and continued to regard themselves as citizens (in spirit at least) of
the entire Río de la Plata instead of just Uruguay, were
strengthened, with rich cultural effects for both countries in
the future; it was Urquiza's ending of the siege of Montevideo
(1851) after his pronouncement against Rosas that ended the
Great War and marked the beginning of Rosas' fall (1852).

In the 1850s and early 1860s both Montevideo and Buenos Aires were preoccupied with their own national political
problems, but Montevideo's proximity to Brazil and their
unique relationship once more involved Argentina in an international war when, early in 1865 Paraguayan President Francisco Solano López, attempted to cross Argentina territory

without permission, to aid Uruguay against a threatened new
invasion from Brazil; Uruguay, Argentina, and Brazil joined
in Triple Alliance to defeat Paraguay in what has become commonly known as the Paraguayan war (q. v.).

By the end of this war the rivalry between Montevideo
and Buenos Aires to dominate the rich pampas was over; the
tragedies of the war, not to mention the long civil wars that
had preceded it, made everyone long for internal and international peace; more important, perhaps, was the fact that Montevideo, with its limited hinterland, could not hope to compete
with Buenos Aires, now the capital of a constitutionally united
republic and tied to all its provinces by railroads and modern
communications.

MONTONERA, LA. An irregular mountain cavalry unit usually led
by local caudillo; term most frequently used to refer to such
groups operating in the Andean provinces 1820-1870; these are
still controversial historically, being regarded by coastal Argentines as lawless, barbarous raiders, incapable of accepting
civilization; but considered by those of the interior to have
been consistent defenders of the interior's demand for local and
individual liberty against what they believed to be centralist attempts at control from Buenos Aires; the grievances and problems of the interior were real, but not all caused by government; the establishment of modern transportation and communication links between the western and the Atlantic port cities
brought the montoneras to an end with the defeat in 1869 of
Felipe Varela (q. v.) (see Montoneros).

MONTONEROS. Term originally applied to members of the Montonera (q. v.), marauding, political bands of the nineteenth century;
young Argentine leftists have chosen this name for their own
very numerous guerrilla bands, believing that only by violence
can the government be forced to make the changes that they
consider necessary; urban terrorists, they consider themselves
leftist Peronists; like their predecessors of the earlier period
the Montoneros of the 1970s aim their attacks against the national government in Buenos Aires which they accuse of favoring imperialism and a return to rule by oligarchy.

MORA, JOSE JOAQUIN DE (1783-1864). Spanish liberal; intellectual;
writer and educator.

Born in Cádiz; proscribed by Ferdinand as a liberal; in
London became closely associated with several Latin Americans,
including the Venezuelan Andrés Bello, and established a reputation for himself in South America through his writings published in London; under sponsorship of Bernardino Rivadavia,
he arrived in Buenos Aires in 1827 with Pedro de Angelis; devoted himself to writing and teaching and was said to have influenced young writers, such as Florencio Varela, by the purity
of his Spanish literary style; after Rivadavia's departure, Mora
went to Chile where he played an important role in that nation's
intellectual awakening and liberal movement; spent further time
in Peru and Bolivia before returning to Spain; died in Madrid.

MORAL, CYRIAC.   Pseudonym used by Jesuit historian Domingo
   Muriel (q. v.).

MOREIRA, JUAN (1819-1874).   Historic gaucho, one of last of disappearing breed, who has been romanticized in folklore and
   fiction; born of Galician Spanish father, brought up in Buenos
   Aires province by his Argentine mother, he early became
   gaucho; accounts of events of his life and his exploits (most
   of these outside the law) vary greatly; during his lifetime he
   aroused both panic and admiration by his utter lack of restraint,
   his fearlessness, and the boldness with which he acted; with a
   heavy price on his head, he succeeded in eluding Buenos Aires
   police for months until finally gunned down at Lobos on April
   30, 1874, at age of 55; a legend during his lifetime, Juan
   Moreira was popularized, shortly after his death, as romantic
   hero by Eduardo Gutiérrez (q.v.) in writings that mingled fiction and fact, but effectively caught and perpetuated the spirit
   of Juan Moreira as Argentines want to remember him.

MORENO, FRANCISCO P. (1852-1919).   Natural scientist and explorer of Patagonia, known as Perito Moreno.
          Moreno was born in Buenos Aires; his father had been
   exiled in Uruguay during the Rosas period and his mother was
   the daughter of a British officer who had been captured in the
   1807 invasion and had remained in Argentina; from his youth
   Francisco was fascinated with travel books; this interest was
   further kindled by his contacts with Germán Burmeister, director of the museum at Buenos Aires; before he was twenty,
   he had begun gathering the rocks, fossils, etc. that were to
   be the basis of his own great collection; in 1872 a friend sent
   him some important anthropological discoveries from the Río
   Negro valley in the south; from that time on he made repeated
   exploratory and scientific trips throughout Río Negro, Neuquén,
   Chubut, and Santa Cruz, opening up this unknown area not only
   to scientists but also bringing it, through his writings, for the
   first time to the full attention of the nation as a part of the
   republic that should be developed; as a result of his intimate
   knowledge of western Patagonia, he became the head of the Argentine commission to settle the boundary dispute with Chile;
   Moreno presented his very rich archeological and anthropological collection to the province of Buenos Aires; it became the
   basis for the museum of natural sciences of La Plata, with
   Moreno as its first director; remained there for many years;
   he also served as a national deputy in congress and as vice
   president of the national council of education; his name was
   linked with many educational innovations and reforms, as well
   as civic projects; Moreno died in 1919; twenty-five years later
   his remains were removed to the island Centinela in Lake Nahuel Huapi.

MORENO, MANUEL (1790-1857).   Patriot; journalist; legislator;
   diplomat.
          Born in Buenos Aires, younger brother of Mariano

Moreno; attended Colegio de San Carlos, became involved in defense of Buenos Aires against British and in the cause of independence; early in 1811 he accompanied his brother on latter's mission to England; buried his brother at sea and remained in London long enough to complete and publish Vida y memoria de Mariano Moreno (1812); returning to Buenos Aires, he became active in patriot group and was named secretary of the second triumvirate government (1813) and sent to Montevideo after its fall in 1814 to organize its new government; taking an active role as journalist, he and Pazos Kanki were the only ones to defend republicanism in the press during the discussions (1816) as to what form the patriot government should take, now that independence had been declared; Moreno collaborated with other radicals in La Crónica argentina in expressing violent criticism of Pueyrredón's directorate government; in 1817 Moreno was exiled along with his colleagues; going to the United States he spent the next few years attempting to propagandize Americans against Pueyrredón's government and in studying medicine in Baltimore (graduated as physician but never practiced); returning to Buenos Aires in 1821, he immediately became active in public life; serving as member of Buenos Aires legislature, 1821-1826, he was one of the few that defended federalism against the prevailing unitarist ideas of the time; as editor of La Abeja, published by the patriot literary society of which he was a member, he opposed Rivadavia's federalization of Buenos Aires and supported provincial autonomy; in 1822 he became director of the public library established by Mariano Moreno and was appointed as first chemistry professor at the university of Buenos Aires (1822-1828); was a member of the academy of medicine and contributor to its journal; in 1827 he filled the position of minister of government and foreign relations in Manuel Dorrego's government; sent as Argentina's minister to England in 1828, he remained there for about seven years, distinguishing himself in 1833 by issuing, in both English and Spanish, a clear, detailed defense of Argentina's legal claims to sovereignty over the Falkland Islands (q.v.) at the time of the British seizure of them; transferred to the United States, he was later reappointed to the post in London; in 1853 he returned to Buenos Aires and retired from public life; died there four years later.

Among his most important works were the biography of his brother, already mentioned, and Arengas en el foro y escritos del doctor Mariano Moreno (London, 1836).

MORENO, MARIANO (1778-1811). Jurisconsult; journalist and writer; statesman; his important role as organizer in government following the May Revolution has won him such titles as "the man of May" or the "soul of the revolution."

Born in Buenos Aires (date of birth somewhat controversial), his father Manuel Moreno, a Spanish official in the viceregal government, and his mother Ana María Valle, a Buenos Aires girl with an unusually good education, he himself received an excellent education, first in the King's school, then

at the Colegio de San Carlos where several of his professors
were impressed by his unusual intelligence and determined to
see that he was given every possible opportunity to use it; one
of them, Franciscan Father Cayetano Rodríguez, friend of
Mariano's father, opened the fine resources of his own monastery to the young student and, with others, prepared the way
for him to enter the Caroline Academy in the University of
Chuquisaca and to study under Canon Terrazas there; in Chuquisaca (today Sucre, Bolivia), Mariano was immersed in the
ideas of the Enlightenment and became imbued with a desire to
see Argentina progress along the lines indicated by Adam Smith
and Rousseau; graduated from the university with a disserta-
tion, reminiscent of the Tupac Amaru revolt a few years before, condemning Spanish legal practices of requiring personal
services from the Indians; Moreno returned to Buenos Aires
about 1805; quickly became involved in writing and public affairs; at first he was inclined to attach himself to the Spanish
liberal group, acting in legal capacity for the audiencia and
eventually aligning himself with the group led by Martín Alzaga;
in 1809, however, he was asked by viceroy Baltasar Hidalgo de
Cisneros to draw up a brief for the creole hacendados and
workers against the demands of the Spanish monopoly merchants
for restrictions on trade; his Representación de los hacendados
called unequivocally for the opening of Río de la Plata to free
trade for a period of two years; it was a clear statement of
what was to become Argentina's economic policy after independence and it brought Moreno the support of the creoles; with the
breakdown of government in Spain during Napoleon's invasion,
Moreno became active in the patriot group demanding that the
viceroy call a cabildo abierto (open town meeting) to deal with
the political crisis; as a member of the cabildo abierto, he
actively supported the deposing of the viceroy and establishment
of a junta chosen by the cabildo abierto, representing the people.
    In the new junta government that was formed following
the May Revolution, with Cornelio Saavedra as president, Moreno was appointed secretary, with executive responsibility for
political and military affairs; for the seven months during
which he held this position, he acted swiftly and firmly to carry
out his clear aims: to keep all the viceroyalty loyal to the
patriot government in Buenos Aires; to establish a healthy, free
economy, and to draw up a constitution that would legally establish institutions to preserve the personal, political, and economic freedoms of a new society; he thought of an autonomous
Argentina, either independent or under the legitimate Spanish
crown, but free of all the old restrictions and able to develop
in its own way; because he saw the revolutionary aims so
clearly and based them on the liberal ideas upon which both
Spanish and creole intellectuals had been educated, because he
had the strong support of most of the leading creoles, and because he himself worked indefatigably, he revolutionized the
nation; he founded and became editor of the Gaceta de Buenos
Aires, established a census bureau and a military school,

made plans for a national public library; reopened Maldonado, Ensenada, and Patagones, Río Negro, as ports and freed commerce and mining from old restrictions; equipped and sent out armies to various parts of the viceroyalty, especially Upper Peru, to fight the royalists; persuaded the Junta to let him deal firmly in suppressing the Córdoba conspiracy; won the respect of Lord Strangford, resulting in British goodwill toward the patriot government in Buenos Aires; carried on negotiations with the Vatican in attempt to define the matter of church patronage under the new situation; was largely responsible for the exiling of the viceroy and judges of the audiencia; in the Gaceta of November 6, he urged the Junta to adopt a constitution for the new nation that would insure institutions for the future; at the same time he insisted that a union or federation of all the Spanish provinces was impractical; by this time Moreno's influence had passed its peak; critics cited his harshness against opposition, his willingness to use intrigue to accomplish his purposes; many believed that Moreno and his progressive young creole supporters represented only the economic and political interests of the capital at the expense of the provinces; Saavedra and his group preferred a more moderate rate of change than the rapid revolutionary pace set by Moreno; such criticism spurred him to more radical measures: in December he decreed that only native born Argentines (creoles) could hold office, although Europeans were welcome as settlers, especially if they devoted themselves to agriculture; and, in an egalitarian move, that ceremonial honors formerly accorded the president of the junta must be abolished as the president no more deserved them than its other members; Saavedra was hurt and the break between the two patriot leaders became personal as well as political; when the provincial delegates, led by Deán Gregorio Funes, were incorporated into the governing junta by Saavedra (December 18, 1810) against Moreno's opposition--he feared that the more conservative Argentine provincials would dilute the revolutionary activities being carried out by the Buenos Aires patriots according to the most liberal European ideas of the period, he resigned from the junta; accepted a diplomatic mission to Río de Janeiro and London; departed early in 1811, with his brother Manuel and Tomás Guido as his secretaries; taken ill on the way to London, he was buried at sea; when the news of his death reached Buenos Aires, Corenlio Saavedra is reputed to have commented, "¡Era menester tanta agua para apagar tanto fuego!" ("How much water it took to put out that flame!").

Ricardo Levene has characterized the conflict between the Morenistas and Saavedristas as the first open clash between two Argentine historical forces: "turbulent democracy," that requires strong central government and "federal democracy."

Moreno's writings have been published by his brother, Manuel Moreno, Arengas y escritos (London, 1836); edited by Norberto Pinero, Escritos de Mariano Moreno (Buenos Aires, 1896); and by Ricardo Levene (1948); Manuel Moreno wrote the first biography of him, Vida y memorias de Mariano Moreno

(London, 1812); and Ricardo Levene has made a fundamental study entitled Ensayo histórico sobre la Revolución de Mayo y Mariano Moreno (2 v., Buenos Aires, 1949).

MORENO, RODOLFO (1879-1953). Jurisconsult; political leader and governor of Buenos Aires; diplomat.

Born in Buenos Aires; graduated in law there; practiced his profession and taught various aspects of law in the national universities of La Plata and Buenos Aires; was appointed, along with Eusebio Gómez, to codify penal law of Buenos Aires; edited seven volumes of Argentine penal law, writing one volume himself; Moreno became a public figure in Buenos Aires provincial politics, distinguished by his skillful speeches; held many positions, both elective and by appointment; after serving four terms as national deputy, appointments as provincial cabinet minister, etc., he was sent on diplomatic mission to Japan (1939-1941) leaving before the Pearl Harbor attack (December 7, 1941) to become governor of Buenos Aires (1941-1943); he attempted to reform the province's landholding laws by placing a large extra tax on estates of more than 10,000 hectares, hoping to break up the latifundia; at the same time he tried to increase the colonization budget to provide for new colonies on land that would become available; although these reforms had considerable support, they also offended many conservatives; for this reason, and because he was becoming a powerful contender against Castillo's choice of a successor to the presidency, the federal government intervened the province; he resigned and went into exile in Montevideo; continued his opposition to Ramírez and Farrell, after the military takeover in 1943; supported Allies in World War II openly; returned to Buenos Aires eventually and retired to private life.

MOSCA, ENRIQUE M. (1880-1950). Vice presidential candidate on ticket of Unión Democrática with José P. Tamborini for president, 1946.

Born in Santa Fe; graduated in law, 1906; became active politically as a Radical while still a student; held various provincial elected and appointed positions; in 1920 he served as interim governor of the province, then in 1924 became commissioner of Mendoza province; was serving as antipersonalist congressmen when Uriburi's revolt, 1930, took over the government; after brief imprisonment on Martín García island he returned to become active politically again; was proposed as vice president on radical ticket headed by Marcelo T. Alvear, 1937, but Ortiz won election; formed the Radical ticket, supported by Democratic Union, with José P. Tamborini in 1946; lost to Juan Domingo Perón; died in Buenos Aires.

MOSCONI, ENRIQUE C. A. (1877-1940). Military officer; first director of YPF.

Born in Buenos Aires of Italian father; educated at the Colegio Militar and with the faculty of exact, physical, and natural sciences; held administrative post in military arsenal

and served as director of army air service; in 1922 he was
appointed by President Alvear as first director of the new organization to control national oil production and reserves, the
Yacimientos Petrolíferos Fiscales (YPF); Mosconi remained in
this position until 1930, becoming a strong leader of those economic nationalists determined to keep Argentine resources under national control; also became known as leader of military
group favoring greater industrial development in republic; politically, he belonged to military group supporting Yrigoyen to
the very end of his unfortunate second administration; served
as president of the Círculo Militar in 1929; held rank of division general at time of his death; author of El petróleo argentino 1922-1930 y la ruptura de los trusts petrolíferos ingleses
y norteamericanos el 1° de agosto de 1929.
      See Raúl Larra's Mosconi, general del petróleo (Buenos
Aires, 1957).

MOTIN DE LAS TRENZAS (Pigtail Uprising) see REBELION DE
      LAS TRENZAS

MOUNTED GRENADIERS see GRANADEROS A CABALLO

MOUSSY, V. MARTIN DE (1810-1869). Name by which French
      physician and natural scientist Jean Antoine Victor Martin de
      Moussy was commonly known in Argentina; author of first im-
      portant physical geography of the nation, as well as other sci-
      entific studies.
            Born and educated as physician in France, Martín de
      Moussy combined his professional duties as military doctor with
      his own interests in scientific observations and studies; after
      having made a place for himself in France and neighboring
      countries, he came to South America, taking up residence in
      Montevideo in 1841, after a few months spent in Rio de Janeiro;
      he quickly identified himself with the community life of his new
      home; served as medical officer for the Uruguayan forces be-
      sieged by Rosas; stimulated the cultural life by supporting es-
      tablishment of astronomical and meteorological observatory and
      library emphasizing materials relating to natural history of
      area; perhaps most important for his future work, Moussy
      formed friendships with those who were to become the political
      leaders of both Uruguay and Argentina.
            Following the fall of Rosas in 1852, Moussy moved to
      Argentina and became very closely associated with Justo José
      de Urquiza and the Argentine Confederation of which latter was
      president; the French physician continued his scientific studies,
      largely with Urquiza's cooperation or under his order (although
      he seems also to have had some financial support from French
      government), exploring the Uruguay and Paraná rivers and
      neighboring provinces and taking copious notes for geographical
      and ethnological scientific studies; he urged the development of
      the confederation capital of Paraná into a commercial center by
      the cultivation of cotton in the adjoining areas; and, in many
      ways, strongly influenced the course of the newly developing

philosophical currents and educational movements.

Martín de Moussy's greatest contribution came as result of Urquiza's desire to have comprehensive and accurate
cartographical and geographical study made of the Argentine
provinces; Moussy appointed as director of commission; contract signed for four-year study, with bi-monthly scientific reports to be made; final report was published in Paris, 1860-
1864; under title Description géographique et statistique de la
Conféderation Argentine, with 3 volumes and an atlas; its importance lies not only in its unusually wide scope and scientific
approach (even though somewhat uneven), but also in the fact
that it was undertaken during the decade of Argentina's transition politically, socially, and economically from the Rosas'
period (or colonial and early national periods) into the modern
republic that it was to become; Martín de Moussy's descriptions and statistics have served later social scientists as at
least one, if not always the only, base of departure for modern social and geographical studies; his material on the agricultural development and rural life of the confederation in the
period 1855-59 are considered particularly valuable.

Before his final return to France Martín de Moussy had
performed other services for the republic; many other scientific studies were published, including his historical essay on
the decadence and ruin of the Jesuit missions in the Plata area;
he extended his explorations into Patagonia and the Andes area;
and served as director of Urquiza's board of public health and
hygiene for province of Entre Ríos in early 1860s; died near
Paris in 1869; his honors included his having been named as
Chevalier of Legion of Honor.

MOYANO FAMILY, MENDOZA. Family dating from conquest and
original settlement of Mendoza; among its members who have
figured significantly in the historical development of that area
and on the national scene are:

Moyano Cornejo, Pedro (1529- ?), conquistador and encomendero; came to Chile with Pedro de Valdivia; held various
military and civil positions of authority in Chile, such as factor of royal hacienda in La Serena (1558) alcalde ordinario
(1559); went to Cuyo with Pedro del Castillo's expedition of 100
cavalrymen to occupy lands of peaceful agricultural Huarpe Indians; took part in founding of Mendoza 1561, receiving townsite and farmland; served as regidor in cabildo, 1561, 1569;
in 1579 received royal land grant in valley of Uspallata and
encomienda of Indians in recognition of his services.

Moyano de Aguilar, Juan, 17th century city councilman,
chief justice, lieutenant corregidor; vigorous fighter against
Pehuelche and Araucanian Indians attacking Mendoza in attempts to free encomienda Indians under forced labor; distinguished himself in defense of Mendoza against insurrection led
by Tanaqueupú in 1658-1659.

Moyano, José Toribio (1732-1816), priest and educator;
born in Mendoza, educated in Córdoba and at University of
San Felipe in Santiago, Chile, where he received doctorate in

sacred theology; ordained as priest; returned to Mendoza; served as curate there from 1763 until his death; left money to establish a school of advanced studies in Mendoza; made possible the founding of Colegio de la Santísima Trinidad in Mendoza November 17, 1817, headed by José Lorenzo Güiraldes (q. v.).

Moyano, Juan Agustín (1787-1829), victim of anarchy and civil wars of the 1820s; served as judge in Villa Nueva de Barriales (1823); commander of local militia, he joined his forces with those of Colonel José Aldao in campaign to San Juan to oust Governor Salvador María del Carril (1825); then attempted to keep Mendoza out of the civil war; opposed and imprisoned the Aldao brothers in Barriales; led Mendoza movement supporting General Paz and was named commandant of Mendoza; in 1829 he led the unitarist movement that placed Juan Cornelio Moyano (q. v.) in office as governor for a brief period; Aldaos escaped from Barriales and after a victory over unitarist forces at El Pilar, gained control over Mendoza; the accidental death of Francisco Aldao (apparently caught in crossfire from his own troops) seems to have set off a bloodbath in Mendoza; Juan Agustín Moyano was especially hated by the Aldaos and when he fell into their hands (rumor at the time insisted that his close relative Juan Cornelio Moyano (q. v.) was involved in this), he was immediately tried and executed.

Moyano, Juan Cornelio (d. 1859), military leader; first constitutional governor of Mendoza; born in Mendoza; became governor of the province briefly in August 1829 after Juan Agustín Moyano (q. v.) had ousted Governor Juan Corvalán; General Alvarado elected governor but federalist victory at El Pilar put Corvalán back in office; at this time Juan Agustín Moyano, who had taken refuge with his kinsman, Juan Cornelio, was killed, probably in a trial and execution by the Aldaos, but suspicion has continued that Juan Cornelio was somehow involved; served as minister for Pedro Pascual Segura; got into trouble with Rosas, federalist governor of Buenos Aires, by executing, apparently without trial, a rebel official who was a close friend of Félix Aldao and one of Rosas' supporters; latter demanded that he be executed, but Moyano escaped to Chile; was granted permission to return in 1850; after Mendoza had signed the Acuerdo de San Nicolás and drawn up a provincial constitution, he was elected first constitutional governor of the province; his administration was not long, 1856-1859, but his policies were progressive; he began the distribution of land into fairly small holdings--a pattern still characteristic of the province; new taxes on land, water use (important) and mines established; rich mines were discovered at Payen; institutional life of the province was organized; freedom of the press emphasized and during this time Le Tupungato, the first French periodical of the interior, was published; completed interprovincial pacts with San Juan and San Luis; in 1858 he was promoted to general rank in the national army; political opposition from the legislature brought federal intervention (Mendoza's first under new constitution); Governor Moyano died as the interventor Pascual Echagüe was on his way to Mendoza.

Moyano, Francisco Borja (1801-1862), veteran of war
of independence; born in Mendoza; enlisted in Army of the Andes; fought at Chacabuco, Cancha Rayada, and Maipú; took
part in action at Bío Bío river, under General Antonio González Balcarce; accompanied San Martín's army to Peru; saw
action at Nazca, Mayoc, the capture of Jauja, and in Cerro de
Pasco; left Peru in October 1826 for political reasons; back in
Argentina, he joined in the fight against Brazil and then followed unitarist General Paz in battles of San Roque, La Tablada and Oncativo; after Quiroga's federalist victory at La Ciudadela, Moyano emigrated to Bolivia and did not return until
after the fall of Rosas' government; in 1856 he was given rank
of colonel of infantry in the national army; died in Salta.

Moyano, Carlos María (1854-1910), naval officer, explorer and cartographer of Patagonia; first governor of Santa
Cruz territory; born in Mendoza; remained there a short time
after the earthquake of 1861, then went to Buenos Aires to continue his education; joined the navy instead and served as midshipman on squadron sent up Uruguay River against López Jordán (1873-74); spent the next 10 years on assignments in the
south, exploring the coast, the rivers, lakes, mountains,
frozen plains of Patagonia; accompanied naturalist Francisco
P. Moreno on exploration up Santa Cruz river and into interior,
discovering Lake San Martín and the volcano Chalten; his maps,
charts, photographs, data of central and southern Patagonia
opened up this area for future developments; took part in final
pacification of Indian tribes; late in 1880 opened a route between Chubut and Santa Cruz; visited Welsh colony at Rawson,
helped it become more genuinely Argentine in feeling; when the
law creating national territories was passed in 1884, Moyano,
with rank of frigate captain, became first governor of Santa
Cruz territory, 1884-1885; his last exploration, a six-months
trip studying and mapping the pre-cordillera area from Chubut
almost to Buenos Aires was made at great physical cost; thereafter he served primarily as consultant or administrator on
naval staffs or boundary commissions where his expertise was
greatly valued; the nation granted him 10,000 hectares of land
in recognition of his services; among honors received was the
gold medal of the Institute Geográfico Argentino; many of his
writings appeared in the Annals of the Instituto; his photographs were used to illustrate the Second National Census
(1895); longer works include Patagonia austral, 1887; Viaje
de exploración a la Patagonia, 1931; his daughter María Cla-
risa Moyano has written his biography, Carlos Moyano, el explorador de la Patagonia (Buenos Aires, 1948).

Moyano, Francisco J. (1861-1929), political figure in
Mendoza; born in Mendoza two months after earthquake had destroyed his entire family except his mother; entered politics
early as a liberal; served as intendant of the city, then deputy
and senator in the provincial legislature; became governor of
Mendoza in 1895 under new provincial constitution of 1894; applied himself especially to problem of controlling the periodic

floods that were disastrous to the economy; created a superintendency of irrigation and, with help of national government, began construction of two dams; he also divided the province into three electoral districts; took a census that revealed a provincial population of 116,136 inhabitants; established a chemical office and laboratory to regulate quality of wines produced; began construction of Mendoza's city park, honoring General San Martín; reformed police and tax services.

Moyano, Juan Agustín (1891-1971), jurisconsult, university professor; born in Mendoza; studied in faculty of law and social sciences, Buenos Aires; minister of hacienda in Mendoza, 1923-1924; and of government, 1927-1928; devoted most of his life to teaching, usually history, in Colegio Nacional "Agustín Alvarez " Mendoza, 1922-1929; "Mariano Moreno," Buenos Aires, 1933-1937; advanced business school "Carlos Pellegrini," 1934- ; taught civil law in faculty of law and social sciences, University of Buenos Aires, 1937-1948, and served as librarian in same faculty; contributed to La Nación and Revista del Colegio de Abogados and was on editorial staff of the review Jurisprudencia Argentina.

Moyano, Federico J. (1897-), lawyer, specialist in commercial law, government official, educator, born in Mendoza; completed his studies in Faculty of Law and Social Sciences, Buenos Aires, 1918-1923; returned to Mendoza to become active in academic and public life; taught history and economic geography at Colegio Nacional "Agustín Alvarez," 1923-1939; became professor of economic history in school of economic sciences of faculty of sciences, Universidad Nacional de Cuyo, serving as director of the school and dean of the faculty, 1939-1941; general director of schools in the province 1940-1941, and minister of hacienda the following year; from 1943 to 1946 he was on board of directors of Yacimientos Petrolíferos Fiscales (YPF), serving as vice president; attorney for Banco de la Nación Argentina since 1923.

MOYANO LLERENA, CARLOS (1914-). Born in Córdoba; graduated in law in Buenos Aires; studied economics at Oxford University (England), 1937-1939; became professor of economics in Law Faculty, University of Buenos Aires; also taught in Argentine Catholic University, and other schools of advanced studies; discharged various public offices in his field; in 1953 became director of Banco Industrial and carried out extensive research projects dealing with regional economic problems; editor of the review Panorama de la Economía Argentina.

MULES, MULE TRADE, AND MULE TRAINS see ARRIAS DE MULAS

MUÑIZ, FRANCISCO JAVIER (1795-1871). Physician; military officer, public figure; paleontologist.

Born in San Isidro, Monte Grande, his entire life centered around his interest in military action, medicine, and natural science, pursued, for the most part in his own province

of Buenos Aires; in 1807 he fought the British, as a cadet, but
was quickly put out of action by a wound; while pursuing his
studies in Buenos Aires, became enthusiastic supporter of the
May Revolution and follower of Moreno; attended Colegio de
San Carlos, studying under José León Banegas, then began
medical studies at Cosme Argerich's institute, completing them
in the newly established medical faculty of the university in
1824; shortly afterward he began service as an army doctor in
Chascomús, with special duties related to the use of cowpox
serums for vaccination; while there he made some observations
of the cattle that later proved useful: his notes about the de-
generation and decrease in numbers of the vaca nata ("cow with
blunted or deformed nose") were later used by the naturalist
Charles Darwin (q. v.); and his discovery of "spontaneous
blisters" on the udders of many cows later brought him into
communication with the British Jenner society as his observations led him to somewhat different theories than those advanced by Dr. Jenner in his vaccination studies; his own experiments with vaccines made it possible for him, following
Rosas' prohibition of vaccine importation (c. 1838) for economic reasons, to develop a satisfactory Argentine one so that public health would not suffer.
        In 1828, after having served with distinction as chief
army surgeon in the war against Brazil, Muñiz accepted Dorrego's appointment as medical officer in Luján and two years
later Rosas added military duties to this assignment; the twenty
years spent in Luján were among the richest in Muñiz's life
as he found time to continue his researches into the paleontology, hygiene, and climatology of Buenos Aires province; it was
in the first of these that Dr. Muñiz won international recognition; acting as a link between Manuel de Torres (q. v.), who
had already discovered the richness of the Luján fossil deposits, and Burmeister and Ameghino (qq. v.), who were to study
them extensively later; his first enormous collection was
turned over to the Argentine government (1842) and given by
Rosas to Admiral Dupotel; these made their way to European
museums to be studied by paleontologists there; a later collection (1857) remained in Argentina and became part of its natural history collection.
        Moving to Buenos Aires in 1848, Dr. Muñiz became
professor in the university medical faculty (serving three times
as president) and began to take a more active role in public
life; served as judge in the medical tribunal (1849); attacked
Urquiza's manifesto against Rosas; after Caseros he was reincorporated into the army; in 1859 he was appointed chief surgeon of army of operations and was severely wounded and captured at battle of Cepeda; served as deputy and as senator in
Buenos Aires legislature at various times between 1853 and
1863; and as member of the congresses of 1853 and 1860 for
constitutional reform; in spite of his age and professional responsibilities, he immediately offered his services in the Paraguayan war and was at Paso de los Libres and the surrender
of Uruguayana; remained in Corrientes as head of hospital

services until 1868; the following year he retired completely
but in 1871, when Buenos Aires was devastated by a violent
yellow fever epidemic, he once more became involved as a
physician, contracted the disease and died.

Other contributions of Muñiz include the fact that his
interest in vaccines led him to become the first Argentine
physician to experiment with use of cowpox vaccinations for
skin diseases; as his special field in teaching included obstetrics, and health problems of women and children, he published
such works as a book on scarlet fever and the first Argentine
article (1864) on clinical obstetrics; he also published studies
on such diverse matters of local natural history as Voces usa-
das con generalidad en las repúblicas del Plata, la Argentina
y la Oriental del Uruguay; a scientific description of the
earthquake in the Argentina pampas, October 19, 1819; and the
best study that had been made up to that time on the ñandú--
rhea or pampas ostrich.

See Sarmiento, Domingo Faustino, Vida y escritos del
coronel don Francisco Javier Muñiz (Buenos Aires, 1885); and
Palcos, Alberto, Nuestra ciencia y Francisco Javier Muñiz, el
sabio--el héroe.

MURATURE, JOSE LUIS (1876-1929).   Jurisconsult and writer; foreign minister, 1914-1916.

Born and educated in Buenos Aires; graduated with doctorate in jurisprudence from university; turned to journalism
and teaching, becoming professor in the military college and
eventually editor of La Nación; in the growing social consciousness and social criticism of the early years of the twentieth
century, with such public and intellectual figures as Carlos
Pellegrini and Miguel Cané decrying the lack of moral leadership in public life on the part of young intellectuals, Murature
used the pages of La Nación to fling the challenge back to the
older generation, blaming them for the ills of the society that
the young folks had inherited; in 1914, President Victorino de
la Plaza asked him to become foreign minister and he served
in that capacity until 1916; he was active in the affairs of the
ABC powers (q. v.) and tried to get U.S. support for a unified
Pan American policy of neutrality during World War I but was
not successful; Murature did not otherwise support the inter-
American association very enthusiastically as he felt that the
previous meetings had not accomplished very much; this lack
of Argentine support was one of many reasons for the postponement of the Fifth conference, due to meet in Chile in 1914;
after 1916, Murature returned to journalism and other writing;
died in Hamburg, Germany, 1929; he was a member of the
Real Academia de Jurisprudencia of Madrid and the Academia
de Derecho y Ciencias Sociales of Buenos Aires.

MURIEL, DOMINGO (1719-1794).   Jesuit historian, educator, and
jurisconsult.

Born in León, Spain, Muriel entered Jesuit order at
age of fifteen; early showed unusual intellectual talents and was

assigned as teacher to colegios in Medina del Campo and Valladolid; he applied for missionary work in the Jesuit missionary
province of Paraguay and arrived in Buenos Aires in 1748;
while still there, he was placed in charge of newly arrived
Jesuit students and sent with them to Córdoba where he spent
the next few years teaching philosophy, moral theology, scholasticism in the university, as well as related subjects in the
colegio de Monserrat, of which he became rector in 1757;
later he became secretary for the province and was sent on an
inspection tour throughout all the Jesuit missions within its
jurisdiction; at the conclusion of this Muriel joined his superi-
or, the provincial, who had gone to the revolting Guaraní missions at request of Governor Cevallos; once more Muriel's request for missionary service was rejected on grounds that his
experience made him more useful as a teacher of novices in
Córdoba (1762); in 1764 he was sent to Spain as legal representative of the Jesuit province; the expulsion decree caught
him there and he eventually joined his fellow refugees from Argentina at Faenza in Italy and became their rector; Muriel remained there until his death, spending his time quietly at home
(especially after dissolution of the order in Italy) writing about
his work in Córdoba and scholarly legal studies related to the
patronato real and other aspects of Church-State relations; his
biography, written by one of his students, Father Francisco
Javier Miranda, was published by the University of Córdoba in
1916.
    Father Muriel made significant contributions to Argen-
tine history in two areas: his liberal and "American" (in contrast to Spanish) views, as expressed during his years of teaching, may have helped prepare (according to Ricardo Rojas) the
Argentine mind for independence; and his writings during his
retirement provide useful material for historians and other
serious scholars of the colonial period; his Fasti novi orbis et
ordinationum apostolicarium ad indias--written under pseudonym
Cyriac Moral and first published in Venice, 1776--contains the
edicts and decrees of the Spanish kings and of the popes concerning ecclesiastical administration of the Spanish colonies,
along with the author's comments, and is considered an excellent source of materials for both church and secular legislation
during the first two centuries following the discovery and the
conquest of the New World; his Historia Paraguensis, widely
used in manuscript, by his contemporaries, was largely an annotated and expanded translation of the work by Pierre François
Xavier de Charlevoix entitled Histoire du Paraguay (3 vols.,
Paris, 1756-1757).

MUSEO MITRE. Historical museum established by the Argentine
government as memorial to Bartolomé Mitre, following his
death in 1906, and using his own library and archives as basis
for an expanding collection; when the government expressed a
desire to buy Mitre's Buenos Aires home in Calle San Martín
to house the museum, the Mitre heirs presented it to the nation for that purpose; it opened June 3, 1907; through its use

by Argentine and foreign scholars, as well as its publication program, it has made an important contribution to the historiography of the republic; very important among its publications are: Archivo del General Mitre. Documentos y correspondencia (28 vols., Buenos Aires 1911-1914); Correspondencia literaria, histórica y política del General Mitre (2 vols., Buenos Aires, 1911); Sarmiento-Mitre correspondencia, 1846-1868, (Buenos Aires, 1911).

- N -

NACION, LA. One of the great conservative newspapers, founded by Bartolomé Mitre (q. v.) in 1870; in 1877 used telegraphic service for first time, and acquired its own linotypes in 1900; the first number in color appeared in 1902; today it has a circulation of almost 3 million and an international weekly edition (see Newspapers).

NACIONAL, EL. (1.) Buenos Aires newspaper, appeared between 1824 and 1826; published the discussions of the legislature, information about the historical background of the occupation of Uruguay (Banda Oriental), and news of the war with Brazil; its editors Valentín Alsina and Pedro F. de Cavia stated that El Nacional was published "to discuss primary political points, to promote the local and national rights, to sustain and advise the government, to move the spirit, and maintain the cause of civilization."

NACIONAL, EL. (2.) Anti-Rosas newspaper published in Montevideo between 1838 and 1846; editors were Andrés Lamas, Miguel Cané, Juan Bautista Alberdi, José Rivera Indarte; Domingo Faustino Sarmiento published "Facundo" in this newspaper as a serial story.

NACIONES. Early in the nineteenth century, following the May Revolution of 1810, blacks organized themselves into mutual aid societies, named after African places of origin; the Buenos Aires government, especially under the administration of Governor Martín Rodríguez, placed them under regulations, prepared by the police and approved by the governor; the greatest number of Naciones were in the Barrio Montserrat also known as Barrio Mondongo or Barrio del Tambor (Neighborhood of the Drum) as this was the favorite instrument of the blacks; the principal Naciones were: Cabunda (December 14, 1823), Banguela (December 6, 1829), Moros (December 14, 1823), Rubolo (December 6, 1829); Angola (March 20, 1825), Congo (March 20, 1827), Caricari (October 21, 1823). Others were Ombe, Mozambique, Mondongo, Alagumbani, Munanche, Los Bolos, etc.; the oldest was the Cabunda nation already formed in the 1700s, without regulation; the Naciones continued in existence until early 1900s when they began to disappear; during Rosas' rule, he and his daughter often attended the parties (candombes) given by the blacks who gave Rosas strong support; as in fact, they provided an important part of his very efficient net of spies; as late as 1903, the Court of Justice acknowledged the ownership of a house at Calle México 1271, by the survivors of the Banguela nation; the Naciones also had their own church which was still in existence in the late 1950s; it had been built by a free slave named Luciano Alsina; this church was used as a hospital during the cholera epidemics of 1868 and of yellow fever in 1871 (see Blacks; Slavery).

NADAL Y GUARDA (or GUARDIA), JAIME (1750-1846).   Merchant; public official; military officer.

Born in Catalonia; early entered into commerce; arrived in Argentina in 1777 and established his home and business in Salta; became officer in the foreign (non-Creole) militia there; took part in expedition commanded by Col. Francisco Gabinas Arias into the Chaco; ordered to open direct route through Chaco to Corrientes for transporting supplies; he did so, maintaining a diary account of the trail-breaking journey (c. 1780); this diary, along with other personal papers is deposited at the Historical Colonial Museum of Luján; expanded his business interests in Buenos Aires; commanded Catalán corps in fighting against second British invasion (1807); was serving in Buenos Aires in cabildo at time of May Revolution but refused to support it, remaining loyal to his native country; imprisoned briefly at Fort Ranchos (1811), he was released the following year and permitted to go to Salta; eventually he returned to Buenos Aires where he died at age of 96.

ÑAEMBE (JANUARY 26, 1871).   Ricardo López Jordán was defeated here in 1871 by the forces of the governor of Corrientes, and forced to go into exile for a time before his final defeat two years later (see Ricardo López Jordán).

NAHUEL HUAPI.   Lake in southern Argentine discovered in 1550s and explored in 1621; name, of Araucanian origin, means Tiger Island; became a National Park in 1922 (see Neuquén; National Parks).

NALE ROXLO, CONRADO (1898-   ).   Poet, newspaperman.   Best known for his poem El Grillo that won the poetry prize of Editorial Babel in 1923; also received the poetry prize of 1924 and his work Una viuda difcil won the municipal prize and the second national prize in 1943-44; the first national poetry prize was given to him in 1956 for Las puertas del Purgatorio; he wrote short novels, children's stories, and contributed to the newspaper El Mundo; Nalé Roxlo was the prototype for young intellectuals of the 1940s and early 1950s.

NAMUNCURA, CEFERINO (1886-1905).   Son of the Indian chief (Manuel Namuncurá) and grandson of Juan Calfucurá (q. v.).

Born in Chimpay (Neuquén); brought up by the priests of the Order of Don Bosco; studied with them and wanted to become

a priest but died in Rome before his ordination; he was buried
in the province of Buenos Aires; the lower rural classes re-
vere him as a saint and call him "the lily of the pampas"; a
movement has begun in the province of Buenos Aires to beati-
fy him.

NAMUNCURA, MANUEL. Last great leader of the Patagonian Araucanian Indians; defeated and his forces destroyed in the "conquest of the desert" (q. v.) by Julio A. Roca; surrendered in
1883; swore loyalty to Argentine Republic; given grant of land
and rank of colonel in the army.

ÑANDU. Argentine name for rhea or ostrich of the pampas.

NAON, ROMULO S. (1876-1941). Jurisconsult; political figure;
cabinet minister; ambassador to U.S. during World War I.
        Born in Buenos Aires; graduated in law from university
there, 1896, having studied under Aristóbulo del Valle; served
as secretary to Governor Bernardo Irigoyen (1902); elected national deputy, became minister of justice and public instruction in cabinet of President Figueroa Alcorta; founded first
rural normal schools in attempt to raise literacy in the countryside; emphasized training of all students for duties, obligations, and rights of citizenship in addition to academic and vocational studies; in 1910 began diplomatic career, carrying out
special missions in Chile and Uruguay, and attending Venezuela's centenary as Argentine minister of plenipotentiary; in that
same year he began eight years of diplomatic service in the
United States; worked to increase friendly relations and possibly an economic alliance between U.S. and Argentina, and
as an expert in international law, to strengthen Argentina's
role in international affairs; played a leading role in the negotiations whereby ABC powers (q. v.) assisted in bringing peaceful settlement between U.S. and Mexico (1914); with reciprocal upgrading of their legations he became first Argentine ambassador to the United States; formed strong liking for United
States and attempted, especially after U.S. was drawn into
World War I, April 1917, to secure Argentine collaboration in
some way, but this ran against Yrigoyen's policy of neutrality,
popular in Argentina; toward the end of the war, Naón became
alarmed about talk of new international organizations; although
at one time suspicious of Pan Americanism, he had come to
support it; feared that Wilson's talk of a League of Nations
threatened regionalism; also opposed a Latin American movement as a threat to Pan Americanism; resigned in 1918 and
returned to Buenos Aires; honored with doctor's degrees by
several U.S. universities, including Yale and Harvard; in late
1920s he successfully defended Standard Oil Company in a long
court fight against attacks from General Enrique Mosconi, Director General of Yacimientos Petrolíferos Fiscales (YPF);
named intendant (mayor) of Buenos Aires (1932) by President
Agustín Justo; taught constitutional law in university's law
faculty as well as in the Colegio Nacional.

Among his published works are: <u>Los ministros. Su
función y carácter constitucional</u> (1904); <u>Discursos</u> (1907-1910);
<u>Inviolabilidad de la propiedad mineral</u>; and <u>Nociones de derecho
comercial marítimo</u>.

NAPOLEON I (1769-1821).   Napoleon Bonaparte, Emperor of the
    Holy Roman Empire, 1804-1815. In his efforts to bring Europe
    under his French rule, Napoleon's wars with England and occu-
    pation of Portugal and Spain formed the background for Argen-
    tine independence movement, triggered its outbreak, and influ-
    enced direction of its national political and economic develop-
    ment.
        The Argentine impact of Napoleon's invasions of Portu-
    gal and Spain in 1807-1808 resulted largely from the difference
    in reactions of the two Iberian nations; the Portuguese court
    moved to Río de Janeiro, leaving its government intact and
    bringing with it ambassadors of all nations; for the first time
    Argentina had easy access to a high-ranking member of the
    ruling Bourbon family--Princess Carlota Joaquina (q.v.), sister
    of Ferdinand VII and wife of Joao VI, regent and then king of
    Portugal--and to foreign diplomats of ambassadorial rank; the
    Spanish royal government, on the other hand, went to pieces;
    Charles IV, who had abdicated to Ferdinand VII, changed his
    mind somewhat and Napoleon was asked to settle their differ-
    ences; he did so by holding both monarchs in custody and plac-
    ing his own brother Joseph on Spanish throne; the Spanish peo-
    ple revolted, established their own government for Spain and
    its empire, in the name of Ferdinand VII, and invited the Brit-
    ish forces into the peninsula to help defeat Napoleon; in the
    peninsular wars that followed, many Argentine military men
    who found themselves in Spain at that time, like José de San
    Martín and Carlos María de Alvear, received the excellent
    military training and experience in fighting against Napoleon's
    veterans, that later enabled them to become successful leaders
    of Argentina's fight for independence.
        When news of events of 1808 in Spain reached Buenos
    Aires it created turmoil and controversy among Spaniards and
    Creoles as to what course they should follow; public opinion
    was generally divided between those who wanted independence,
    with or without a monarch, and those who preferred to remain
    loyal to Ferdinand VII and to continue under existing Spanish
    rule until situation should be stabilized in Spain; no one wanted
    Joseph Bonaparte; the situation was aggravated by fact that
    Viceroy Santiago de Liniers (q.v.) was French-born and his re-
    ception of Napoleon's emissary, Marqués de Sassenay, aroused
    suspicions regarding his loyalty, not totally allayed by his for-
    mal recognition of Ferdinand VII on August 15, 1808; Governor
    Francisco Javier de Elío (q.v.) in Montevideo seceded that
    area from viceroyalty, setting up a separate junta there; and
    revolutions against Spanish rule occurred in 1809 in Chuquisaca
    and Potosí; in 1810 word that the last Spanish junta had fallen
    before the advance of Napoleon's forces brought the outbreak
    of the May Revolution (q.v.) in Buenos Aires and establishment

of first autonomous patriot government in name of Ferdinand
VII; Napoleon's final defeat in 1815, with Ferdinand VII back
in the throne, forced Argentina finally to face issue of submission to Spain again or independence; declared its independence
July 9, 1816, and prepared army, under José de San Martín,
to fight for it.
  During this Napoleonic period, ties between Britain and
Argentina were greatly strengthened, reflecting both the Spanish-English alliance against the French empire and the economic interests of the Río de la Plata area; British diplomacy,
largely directed from embassy at Rio de Janeiro, began to play
important role in political life of Buenos Aires area; its merchant ships called regularly at its port for the hides and tallow
--and increasing amounts of salted, dried beef--in exchange for
British manufactures; English colony in city grew in size as
seamen, resident agents, government officials, investors began
to appear, and often to remain, to handle these new interests
or improve their own opportunities; basis was laid, largely due
to mutual economic interests, but also because of personal and
political relationships formed, for close ties between the two
nations that continued and were strengthened during more than
the first century of Argentine national life.

NASERE.   Semispherical flute used by the Chaco Indians; contains
an air chamber with an upper and two side holes.

NASSERISTS.   Extreme leftist political group active during the 1960s;
named for Egyptian Nasser; supported authoritarian nationalism
based on military and workers.

NATIONAL ANTHEM   see   HIMNO NACIONAL

NATIONAL AUTONOMOUS PARTY   see   PARTIDO AUTONOMISTA
NACIONAL

NATIONAL BANK   see   BANKS, BANKING

NATIONAL CONVENTION OF SANTA FE.   In 1828-1829, a national
convention assembled in Santa Fe to select provisional executive and to draw up a republican, representative, and federal
constitution to replace Rivadavia's unitarist one that had been
rejected; representatives came from Entre Ríos, Banda Oriental, La Rioja, Santiago del Estero, Córdoba, and Santa Fe;
convention failed to achieve its main purposes; Córdoba withdrew, on grounds that all provinces were not represented but
probably because its governor Bustos was a contender for the
national power and wanted convention moved to Córdoba; convention accomplished the following: made peace with Brazil
following the war; recognized independence of Banda Oriental
(Uruguay) and removed its delegates from participation in congress; declared government of General Juan Lavalle in Buenos
Aires to be illegal and formed army under Estanislao López
that defeated Lavalle's forces at Puente de Márquez; convention
dissolved itself February 20, 1829.

NATIONAL DEMOCRATIC FEDERATION (1930). Coalition of political parties formed during Uriburu's period of government to defend democratic institutions.

NATIONAL DEMOCRATIC PARTY (Partido Demócrata Nacional-- PDN). Name of conservative party since 1930; led by oligarchy, this group had been in power for about a third of a century before being ousted by radicals 1916; returned to power 1932-1943; party accused by GOU leaders, who overthrew it, of responsibility for "fraudulent democracy" of Argentine political life; remained influential in some western provinces but its last two strongholds--Mendoza and Salta were defeated by Peronists in elections of 1973.

NATIONAL DEVELOPMENT COUNCIL. Its purpose is to determine policy and strategy directly related to national development, and to formulate national and regional long and medium range plans; it also directs short-term programs and issues the regulations by which the public sectors must abide; the Council is made up of government ministers and the 15 secretaries of state; its works is divided into eight development regions, staffed by eight regional bureaus (see CONADE).

NATIONAL FEDERATION OF PARTIES OF THE CENTER. Union of the Democratic party and other conservative elements, organized in 1958 for the election of that year; obtained only 77,796 votes.

NATIONAL GRAIN BOARD. Created by the government in the depression of 1930s to purchase grain for export at prices fixed by the government; replaced by IAPI in 1946 (see Instituto Argentino de Promoción del Intercambio).

NATIONAL PARKS. Argentina's national park system dates from 1903; it resulted from the initiative of its generous, farsighted natural scientist, Francisco P. Moreno (q. v.); having been given a very large grant of public land in appreciation for his services to the nation, he returned it to the national government, on condition that it be made into a permanent public park, with its vegetation and wild life preserved; this first park, Nahuel Huapi, in Neuquén and Río Negro provinces and including the lake, remains one of the largest ones; in 1928 a second park--Iguazú, in subtropical Misiones--was added; later, others were created; Perito Francisco P. Moreno, Los Glaciares, and Monumento Natural Bosques Petrificados, in Santa Cruz; Lanín, Reserva Nacional de los Copahues, and Laguna Blanca, in Neuquén; Los Alerces in Chubut; Finca del Rey in Salta, Río Pilcomayo, Formosa; and the Chaco; November 6, the date on which Moreno sent his letter ceding his lands to the government, has been designated National Park Day.

NATIONAL PUBLIC LIBRARY see BIBLIOTECA PUBLICA

NATIONALISM. This widespread twentieth-century political, economic, social, and cultural reaction against imperialism of preceding era, became very important in Argentina, which not only accepted its general tenets and forms, but added its own
Argentine elements.

Although it is frequently said that the term "nationalism" is more easily used than clearly defined, its emphasis on
self-determination in every phase of national life is readily accepted; this came naturally to Argentina, forced from its earliest days to create a new life style out of, but different from,
Indian and Spanish elements; its national characteristic of pride
grew largely from this experience, as did its determination to
use customs, values, and institutions growing from its own historic roots, rather than to accept European transplants; closely related to these feelings was a love of the land, inherited
from the Indians and especially strong throughout the northern
and western areas where first Spanish settlements were made
among large Indian populations; this commitment to independence and self-determination was a strong factor in the civil
wars that raged for decades following the winning of independence; in the twentieth century, it continued to manifest itself in
such traits (associated with nationalism) as xenophobia, abnor-
mal sensitiveness to foreign criticism or to suspected attempts
at foreign political domination, as in its opposition to U.S. in
inter-American affairs and rejection of foreign investment as
economic "exploitation."

By the 1890s, Argentina had emerged from its long
process of national reorganization and was politically united
and stabilized under the constitution of 1853 that had effected
a successful compromise between Argentine realities and desirable adaptations of foreign elements; railroads and river
steamers tied the provinces together and gave interior provinces
access to foreign markets and a share in the national economy;
the new great problems were social and cultural; close economic ties to western Europe had intensified cultural ties with those
nations at the same time that the gaucho and other traditional
Argentine figures were disappearing from the scene; while "old"
Argentines--creoles--were finding themselves cut off from their
own cultural and historic roots, the republic was being flooded
by hundreds of thousands of "new Argentines" (see Immigration), most of whom were not only eager to become truly Argentine in culture but also were determined to play as important a role in the social and political life of their adopted
country as they were already performing in the economic; in
late nineteenth century, such literary and historical writers as
José Hernández, Joaquín V. González, Juan Agustín García
were recreating Argentina's past for both groups and by the
time of the centennial celebration of independence in 1910,
many Argentine writers had begun eagerly to espouse the theme
of nationalism from both its native roots and new European intellectual currents; nationalism in Argentina fell into many,
varied forms of two major categories: 1. liberal such as
that of Ricardo Rojas who, while influenced by the writings of

Johann Gottfried von Herder, as had been the earlier Romanti-
cists (q.v.), emphasized the traditional Indian and colonial
roots of Argentina's past, especially in its interior provinces;
and 2. the more conservative, "integral" nationalism that
called for renewed dedication to traditional Spanish pattern of
loyalty to family, church, and fatherland; influenced by Spanish
Hispanidad movement (q.v.) and often by Fascist and Nazi ideologies that developed after World War I, integral nationalism
found such exponents as Manuel Gálvez and Leopoldo Lugones;
nationalism, in its different aspects, was taken up by public
leaders and in military circles; it was quickly spread throughout the country by newspapers, literary works, widespread public school system, and compulsory military service; it first
became important politically during Radical administration of
President Hipólito Yrigoyen (1916-1922); he showed its influence
externally in his insistence on Argentine independence of action
by its neutrality in World War I and his actions on behalf of
respect for sovereignty of all nations in early meetings of
League of Nations; within the republic, his nationalism manifested itself in broadening opportunities of middle and lower
classes to participate in national life; by 1930 liberal nationalism had become identified with the oligarchy--with its neglect of
the interests of the masses, as well as its close ties with
foreign trade and culture; at the same time, hatred of foreign
economic domination had become an increasingly important element in nationalism during depression of 1930s, accompanied
with a demand for economic diversification based on national
needs; integral nationalists, both military and civilian, demanding change, were largely responsible for the strongly populist
trend taken by GOU revolt in 1943 and Juan Domingo Perón's
later identification of nationalism with social justice, as well
as resistance to "capitalist imperialism"; policies of succeeding
governments have shown influence of populist nationalism in the
diversification of the economy, in the direction of making the
nation more nearly self-sufficient, in increased participation of
Argentina in international affairs on a wider geographic basis,
and the trend toward integration of all its citizens into an Argentine society (now largely middle-class) and culture; largely
remaining intact have been its traditional pride in itself and its
achievements, including new labor and social welfare legislation, and its continuing commitment, in spite of temporary inter-
ruptions, to constitutional government and its guaranteed personal and political freedoms.
        See Arthur P. Whitaker, Nationalism in Latin America;
Past and Present (Gainesville, Florida, 1962), and his later
writings on Argentina; for a Marxist view of nationalism in colonial and early national period, see Juan José Hernández Arr-
egui, Nacionalismo y liberación: metrópolis y colonias en la
era del imperialismo (Buenos Aires, 1969).

NATIONALIZATION OF TRANSPORTATION AND UTILITIES. Carried
out by President Perón in 1947; he purchased the foreign-owned
railroads, gasworks, and telephone companies; these expendi-

tures have weighed heavily on the budget of the country; Perón considered this move an "economic complement to San Martín's political liberation of Argentina"; the truth has often seemed otherwise as the country struggles to support the expenses of renovation, expansion, and modernization; by 1964 the deficit of the railroads reached 75 million pesos and they were carrying only a little more than half the freight load of 10 years earlier; it is said that it will take about 1.5 billion dollars to put the railroads back in service; steel, agricultural machines, and car plants are partly owned by the nation; the national airline Aerolíneas Argentinas, most of the river fleet, and part of the overseas transportation are also publicly owned; most of the country's means of production however are still in the hands of private firms.

NAUTICAL STUDIES, ACADEMY OF. Founded by Manuel Belgrano on October 3, 1799; its first director was Pedro Cerviño; the program included four years of study, three years of mathematics, and one year of navigation as such; the Spanish king ordered it closed in 1807; it reopened in 1810 as the Academy of Mathematics.

NAVARRO, BATTLE OF (December 9, 1828). Site of Lavalle's defeat of Manuel Dorrego; latter was taken prisoner and executed by Lavalle's orders on December 13, 1828 (see Manuel Dorrego; Juan Lavalle).

NAVARRO, MANUEL (1791-1852). Political leader in Catamarca. Born in Catamarca; became active in provincial politics; was elected interim governor of the province in 1834; this election was not recognized by the governor of Tucumán but the legislature appointed him governor for two years; the political life of the province was chaotic and Navarro was involved in several military problems; he was replaced in 1835; returned as governor in 1846, and remained in power until 1852; during this period maintained peace, promoted commercial and industrial activities; he ignored Rosas' orders to expel the Jesuits and permitted them to remain in the province; founded the first high school in the province, 1850; died March 5, 1852.

NAVARRO, OCTAVIANO (1820-1884). Military officer; government official.
    Born in Catamarca son of Manuel and Javiera Herrera, entered the army as career; elected first constitutional governor of Catamarca (1856-59); founded the Sociedad de Beneficencia, improved mining and public works; introduced the first printing press and published the first newspaper; he was appointed national interventor of Santiago del Estero by President Derqui; in 1866 helped to suppress the revolt of Felipe Varela; in 1868 was promoted to general; in 1869 served as general interventor of La Rioja; he was elected governor of the province in 1873 but for reasons of health he delegated his power in 1875; promoted to division general in 1882; in 1884 was elected senator

for the province of Catamarca but died before he could take his position.

NAVARRO MONZO, JULIO (1882-1943).   Writer and government official.

Born in Sevilla; after studying literature at University of Lisbon, came to Argentina as a young man; found ready acceptance in cultural circles and employment in the government served as private secretary to Dr. Indalecio Gómez in ministry of the interior (1910-1914); reporter for ministry of foreign relations (1914-1916); secretary to attorney general (1916-22); secretary of commission intervening in University of Córdoba (1918); was working as head of research division in ministry of foreign relations at time of his death; Navarro Monzó's interests were cultural and he devoted much of his time to writing; served as art critic for La Nación and on directorates of several cultural institutions; secretary of continental junta of Asociaciones Cristianas de Jóvenes (YWCA); his writings include Cataluña e las nacionalidades ibericas (1908); La Pampa y la Patagonia (1912); El renacimiento místico ante la tragedia europea (1916); La evolución religiosa en el mundo antiguo (1924), his most important work; La misión del arte en la cultura de América; and Los coloquios de Fu Lao Chang (1936).

NAVES AVISOS.   Fast, well-armed ships able to escape pirate pursuers, that acted as scouts for the fleets and galleons and were used to carry mail and sometimes merchandise; these ships served to advise the authorities of Portobelo and Veracruz about the arrival of the galleons; they were used during the 16th and 17th centuries; royal order of January 21, 1735, ordered naves avisos to leave six months ahead to advise departure schedule of the fleet.

NAVES DE PERMISO.   During colonial period the highly structured mercantilistic commercial system of Spain monopolized the commerce of its American colonies but some limited traffic with foreign countries was permitted; such foreign ships, allowed to enter the ports for business, were the naves de permiso; England obtained such a commercial permit in 1713 (Treaty of Utrecht); at the same time it received an Asiento de Negros—permission to bring in slaves; in 1790s, because of the pressure of European conflicts and the lack of ships, trade privileges were extended to neutral countries, and the naves de permiso disappeared.

NAVIOS DE REGISTRO.   King Philip V signed in 1720 the project for fleet and galleons for Peru (that served Argentina) and New Spain.   Included in the project we find the navíos de registro, so called because they had to be authorized by the Casa de Contratación de Sevilla; these ships could go to any port in America but they had to leave from and return to the port of Cádiz; the fall of Portobelo (1739) to the British practically ended the system of fleets and galleons and generalized the system of

of navíos de registro; authorities permitted the exportation of
hides in navíos de registro after 1766; this benefited Río de la
Plata area.

NAVY. At the time of the May Revolution in 1810, the royal naval
base at Montevideo made it essential for the patriot junta to
organize its own group of armed ships to defend the rivers
from Spanish attacks; the first "naval" unit consisted of the
brigantine 25 de Mayo, with 18 cannons, the sloop América,
with four, the schooner Invencible, with 12, plus six merchant
ships, with a crew of approximately 200, most of whom were
foreigners, under the command of Juan Bautista Azopardo; this
little fleet was destroyed in battle of San Nicolás March 2,
1811; for the next three years Spaniards remained in control of
the rivers; in 1814 Supreme Director Gervasio Posadas placed
Juan Larrea in charge of creating new naval unit to support Alvear's attempt to take Montevideo for patriots; Guillermo
Brown (q. v.) was given command of this navy and on June 23,
1815, the city and Spanish fleet fell to Buenos Aires patriot
forces; with the Spanish threat removed from the Río de la
Plata, interest in a national navy lagged until revived by the
war with Brazil (1826); Rivadavia established a Naval Academy,
created a Ministry of Navy in his cabinet, and sent a naval
commission to England to purchase ships; meanwhile Brown,
again in command, appealed for popular donations to buy ships
immediately (from appropriate ones in port) and bought four;
with the end of the war, the expansion of the navy was neglected for more pressing needs; during the Rosas period it was
used primarily to maintain Buenos Aires' control of the river
provinces and trade; most memorable event was Argentine defense of Vuelta de Obligado (q. v.); as the nation had no great
need for a navy, it was not until Sarmiento became president
that attention was given to it; he provided for a small river
fleet and founded the modern naval academy (see Escuela Naval), in 1872; by 1880 the nation began creation of a sea navy
to serve its needs along the Patagonian coast (then being occupied), to explore up its rivers, and to maintain Argentine rights
in the Strait of Magellan area, under dispute with Chile; naval
bases, like Puerto Belgrano were established, personnel were
trained in the Escuela Naval and Escuela Mecánica de la Armada (Naval Mechanics School), founded in 1897; in 1898 President Roca separated the navy from the ministry of war and
navy and appointed Commodore Martín Rivadavia, grandson of
first president of the republic, as minister of navy; although
problems with Chile were resolved by negotiations in Pactos
de Mayo (q. v.) in 1902, interest in the navy continued; submarines were added, as well as a greater variety of other vessels; in 1915 Argentina had the largest navy in South America;
following 1916, naval aviation units were included; Argentine
shipyards provided many naval vessels after 1936; traditionally,
naval officers came from liberal, upper-class families; traveled
more extensively than army officers and were closer to their
U.S. and British colleagues than were their counterparts in the

army, who tended to be more influenced by Germans and Italians.

Somewhat less political than the military, the navy, upon occasion, intervened; in revolt of 1890 it shelled government troops on behalf of insurgents; in 1943 the navy had acquiesced in the army takeover of Castillo's government; thereafter army and navy existed in a semi-harmonious relationship in which rivalry, cooperation, and opposition were revealed in national political life; in the 1950s the navy turned against Perón who had ordered retirement of a large portion of its officers, including thirty admirals and the minister of navy; became involved in the abortive June 16, 1955, movement to oust Perón, following which all active service admirals requested retirement; also took part in September revolt that successfully removed him from power; in the 1960s friendship between U.S. and Argentine navy was strengthened by loan of two submarines for training purposes; became stronghold of the Colorados and supported firm policies against the Peronists; after Onganía's defeat of the Colorados September 19, 1962, retired admirals Jorge Palma and Isaac Rojas (q.v.), along with several other senior naval officers made one last attempt to regain power April 6, 1963; after four days of fighting, the navy capitulated to the government's forces led by Onganía; ten days later the number of admirals was decreased from 26 to two and naval forces reduced by two-thirds; for the time being, the navy had lost its political power.

See Teodoro Caillet-Bois (Capitán de Fragata) Historia naval argentina (Buenos Aires, 1944); and Humberto F. Burzio, Armada nacional: reseña histórica de su origen y desarrollo orgánico (Buenos Aires, 1960).

NAZAR, BENITO (1801-1886). Military officer. Born in Buenos Aires, younger brother of Joaquín Nazar; began military career as cadet in artillery regiment at age of 11; studied at Academy of Mathematics and started up officer ranks; in 1825, as captain, he organized battery of artillery that he later commanded in war with Brazil; fought at Ituzaingó under Col. Iriarte; dismissed from army in 1835 by Rosas; placed under house arrest for remainder of Rosas' rule; in 1858 he was elected provincial deputy, Buenos Aires; served as minister of war and navy, 1859, in Buenos Aires cabinet; fought as chief of artillery at Cepeda and at Pavón; retired as division general shortly afterward; offered his services for war with Paraguay (1865) but met refusal because of his age.

NAZAR, JOAQUIN (1784-1820). Military man. Born in Buenos Aires and founder of the Nazar family of Mendoza that started a winery, at one time the best in the country; fought against the British in 1806; after the May Revolution, joined the Granaderos and served under San Martín; took part in the first siege of Montevideo and fought in Cerrito; in 1817, joined San Martín and fought with him in Chacabuco, Cancha Rayada, and Maipú; in 1818 became a lieutenant general in the army; in Mendoza married Juana Anzorena; in 1820 was killed during a convicts' rebellion while he was in the police station, offering his services against the riot.

NAZAR, LAUREANO (1816-1882). Political and military figure, Mendoza. Son of Joaquín Nazar; joined federalist forces in the province of Mendoza; became a lieutenant colonel in the provincial army; this rank was recognized by the national government in 1858; became governor of the province in 1861 but was forced by revolution to resign; Juan de Dios Videla replaced him; during Nazar's period of government the terrible earthquake of 1861 took place that practically destroyed the city; Nazar lost three sons in it; emigrated with family to Chile for a short time but returned to Mendoza, where he died.

NAZAR BLANCO, ROBERTO VALENTIN (1909-). Born in Mendoza; followed army career reaching highest possible rank of Army General Commander of Army IV Division (Mendoza, 1957); had earlier been Commandant of the second army in San Luis in 1956; member of the first expedition to the Aconcagua; active in revolution of September 1955 against Perón; federal interventor of Mendoza between September and November of 1955; retired from the army to his vineyards.
Wrote Guía para trabajos con tropas de montaña.

NAZARRE DE GANDIOLI, DIONISIA (1765-1860). Patrician dame of independence period.
Born in Buenos Aires; gave to the government all her jewelry and some money to organize the national army after the revolution of 1810; active in social welfare; the city of Buenos Aires has a street honoring her memory.

NAZISM. German political doctrine created by Adolf Hitler in 1930s; takes its name from political party National-Sozialist; similar to Fascism in its emphasis on militarism and authoritarianism, thought-control in political and intellectual life, but included new Germanic elements and racism; in Argentina, term "Nazis" was applied, often loosely, to those who emphasized any form of authoritarianism, Nazi or Fascist concepts of militarism, to ultra-nationalists and admirers of the revised Rosas' cult, as well as to those individuals and groups that genuinely followed the Nazi line, hoped for a Germanic domination of Europe, and engaged in anti-Semitic activities (as the Nazis did); in the passions aroused during World War II, most U.S. officials and many pro-Allies Argentines viewed government actions as pro-Axis rather than purely neutral, as claimed; in 1945, with war ended in Allied victory, suspicions of Nazi sympathies diminished and pro-Nazi rightist groups disappeared or were merged into new pro-Peronist groups.

NECOCHEA, MARIANO PASCUAL (1792-1849). Granadero a caballo under San Martín; director of mint, Lima.
Born in Buenos Aires of Spanish parents; in 1804 left

the country to study in Sevilla; returned and joined his father
in business; nothing is known about his activities during 1810
and 1811 but in 1812 appeared before General San Martín and
enlisted in the Granaderos a caballo as alférez (second lieutenant); fought for first time in San Lorenzo; later joined the army
of the north and, under Rondeau, fought against the Spaniards;
saved much of the patriot army after Sipe-Sipe; from there he
moved to Mendoza and rejoined San Martín; fought in Chacabuco, was sent to the southern part of Chile and involved in
the assault on Talcahuano; from there passed to Peru and participated in the Sierra campaign under Arenales, with rank of
general; Necochea remained in Peru and served under Bolívar
who appointed him in 1824 as governor of Lima; fought in battle of Junín where his bravery was noted; after this battle he
was promoted to general of division; but was wounded and
could not fight; after Ayacucho Bolívar appointed him director
of the mint in Lima; suspected of being involved in a conspiracy, he left Peru; upon his arrival in Buenos Aires he was
appointed by Rivadavia as head of the military reserves, he
requested to be sent to the Brazilian front but his request was
denied; in 1831 he returned to Peru taking advantage of an amnesty law; became director of the mint again; in 1834 the
Peruvian government awarded him the rank of Grand Marshal
again; political events forced him into temporary exile but
later returned to Peru where he occupied his old post; died in
Miraflores, Peru.

NEGRO BOZAL. Name given by the slave traders to a slave who
could not speak Spanish.

NEGROS see BLACKS; SLAVES; NACIONES

NELSON, ERNESTO (1873-1959). Lawyer; educator; writer.
        Born in Buenos Aires; studied at Columbia University,
New York; became professor in faculty of humanities and sciences of education, University of La Plata; served as inspector
general of secondary, normal, and special education; 1936-
1939 served in national ministry of justice and public instructions; retired in 1939 but continued to be active in cultural and
professional circles; represented Argentina at expositions in the
United States in 1904 (St. Louis) and 1915 (California); contributed to La Nación, El Mundo, and the review Nosotros;
two of his best known articles, written while he was a young
man, appeared in the Revista de Derecho, Historia y Letras:
"Posiciones respectivas de los Estados Unidos, y de Europa
en el comercio de la República Argentina" (Vol. 17, 1903) in
which he discusses rivalry, at that time, between Argentina
and U.S.A. for European food markets; and "Letter from E.
Nelson to Carlos O. Bunge" (issue of February 1904) that made
a penetrating early study of Argentine national characteristics
of that time, including individualism, excess of pride, melancholy, social unease, etc.

NELSSON, CHRISTIAN (1867-1947).   Danish geologist; agropecuarian specialist.

Born in Copenhagen, his mother a cousin of Queen Victoria of England; traveled and studied widely; turned his attentions to agropecuarian sciences; emigrated to Buenos Aires in 1895; moved to the Littoral and organized first milk cooperative in Santa Fe; made detailed study of economical possibilities of northern part of country; published La zona comercial del norte; moved later to Salta where he founded the History and Natural Science Museum; became its director and devoted himself to studying the Indian ruins of that area; maintained his contacts with foreign countries and scientists; died in Salta.

NEUMANN, JUAN BAUTISTA (1659-1703).   Jesuit missionary and printer.

Born in Vienna; entered Jesuit order in 1675 and was sent to the missions in Paraguay twenty years later; he founded the first printing press in Argentine territory, in what is now the province of Misiones; Mitre called this press an "original creation" as it was totally built from materials at hand in the remote mission by Indians under Father Neumann's instructions; later these same mission Indians operated the press (see Printing Presses); a street in Buenos Aires was later named in Neumann's honor; he died from illness and hardships encountered in attempt to open a road or trail between the Paraguayan missions and those in Chiquitos, in what is now Bolivia.

NEUQUEN (Province and City).   Organized as a province in 1955 with capital of same name, Neuquén lies against the cordillera, in Andean lake region; the name Neuquén is of Araucanian origin and means "torrential" or "turbulent," probably referring to the Neuquén river.   Boundaries: Mendoza, to the north and northeast; Río Negro, to the east and south; and the Andes to the west.   Area: 36,300 square miles.   Population (1970): 154,570; density of 4.3 inhabitants per square miles.

Capital and other cities.   Neuquén, capital of territory and province since 1904, located in extreme eastern part of province, joined by Southern railroad to Bahía Blanca (1899); other cities, Plaza Huincul, Chos Malal, San Martín de los Andes, Zapala.

Geography.   It is divided into two zones: the west, very mountainous, with fertile, colorful valley, and the east, flat mesa region, extremely arid; southern part of the province is covered with lakes that make the province one of the most prosperous tourist regions of the country; principal mountains are volcanoes; the climate is dry, cold, and healthy.

General comments.   Province is divided into sixteen political departments; throughout it flow such rivers as the Colorado that forms boundary with Mendoza, the Neuquén and Limay that flow together to form the Río Negro; the whole region is covered with coniferous trees, protected by government; the Lake Nahuel Huapi area as well as some others, constitute important part of national park system (see National Parks);

these, along with various thermal springs and other lake and
scenic areas, make tourism an important industry in Neuquén;
other important sources of income are: cattle and sheep raising; production of early fruit, such as apples and strawberries
(so abundant that they are fed to cattle); exploitation of oil and
natural gas, under national company, YPF (see Yacimientos
Petrolíferos Fiscales); gold, salt, solvay, and coal are also
found there; fishing is abundant.

History. The province was first explored from Chile;
Francisco de Villagra, who was looking for the Strait of Magellan, reached Huechu-Lauquen lake and the Limay river; between 1550 and 1552 Jerónimo de Alderete, one of Pedro de
Valdivia's men, visited the territory and described the lake for
the first time; this region of extraordinary beauty was later
traversed by explorers looking for the City of the Caesars
(q. v.); it is believed that the religious order of the Mercedar-
ios (Brothers of Mercy) had a mission on the shore of Lake
Nahuel Huapi, which is located on the boundary of this province
and Río Negro; in 1621 a Chilean military expedition was sent
to the region under the leadership of Diego Flores de León who
explored the beautiful lake of Nahuel Huapi; in 1645 Father Diego Rosales visited the region and collected data for his book
Historia general del reyno del Chile; various priests explored
the region and attempted to establish missions in several
places, but, until Father Felipe de la Laguna (Philip Vander
Meeren) came, these were unsuccessful; Father Vander Meeren
(q. v.) brought the first sheep to the region and the first apple
seeds; during the 1780s and 1790s several expeditions, generally of missionaries, explored Neuquén; Father Francisco Menéndez spent some time with the Pampa Indians in 1792 and described them as very friendly; the first expeditions from the
east came under the leadership of Pilot Basilio Villarino (q. v.)
who visited the Negro and the Limay in 1779 and 1783.

In 1856 a group of Germans settled in the area; during
the 1870s several army expeditions explored the region; in
1873 Francisco P. Moreno (q. v.) began his expeditions into
Patagonia; he visited not only Río Negro and Neuquén but also
the Nahuel Huapi, Viedma, Argentine and San Martín lakes;
the area, included in territory of Patagonia, was organized in
1862, and the Indian frontier established along the Negro and
the Neuquén rivers; in 1884 the national government established
Neuquén's boundaries and divided the new territory into five departments; the present capital was founded on September 12,
1904, by Carlos Bouquet; in 1909 the government reserved an
extension of 825,000 acres and created the national park of Nahuel Huapi which was inaugurated in 1922 (see National Parks);
in 1882 the national government appointed a survey commission
and in 1884 established the boundaries and divided the area into five departments; first governor, Manuel J Olascoaga (q. v.),
served from 1884-1890; at that time most of Neuquén was
sparsely occupied by Indians who had belonged to a paleolithic
culture until the invasion of the somewhat more civilized Araucanians in the late 18th and early 19th centuries; still largely

hunters, gatherers, and fishermen, they lived along the rivers and lakes or among the trees whose fruit they ate; early missionary efforts had left few lasting effects.

One of the most important pioneers in the settlement and development of the newly-opened territory was the Buenos Aires engineer Juan Alsina (1855-1927) who had been a member of the surveying commission; he returned to establish a cattle spread, La Porteña, near the cordillera; later set up a saladero in Codahué to make charqui (dried, salted beef) for export to Chile; after a brief absence, serving as cabinet minister in Buenos Aires provincial government, 1895-1898, he returned to Neuquén, constructed its first irrigation canal, using water from Lake Palau Mahuida; became governor of territory in 1902; retired to his estate at Las Lajas; introduced first Herefords into Neuquén, began working its mines, and built a sawmill, using water power, to convert pines and other trees into lumber.

Among the early settlements, Chos Malal, in the northwest, was the first and became the early capital; it received its name, meaning "yellow corral" because the location of its first fort, on top of a hill surrounded by yellow cliffs, resembled a ranch corral; although area around it is inhospitable, Neuquén's first school was built there in 1890s; other interesting towns include: San Martín de los Andes, an army town built in 1898; Zapala, an active industrial and commercial center; Plaza Huincul, center of active oil and natural gas exploitation; and the colorful village of Campana Mahuida where the wind blowing against the mountain sounds like bronze bells; the city of Neuquén, the present capital, was founded September 12, 1904, by Carlos Bouquet as the permanent capital; in 1909 the national government reserved a tract of 825,000 acres for the national park of Nahuel Huapi (see National Parks) that was opened in 1922.

Neuquén's population has doubled since 1940 in spite of the weather, the cold, and the wind that blows 360 days a year; several projects, including pipelines toward Buenos Aires, Bahía Blanca, and La Plata, are underway, as well as dams, irrigation canals, a petrochemical plant, and a Solvay Plant (for producing sodium bicarbonate); the railroad, in existence since 1899, that links the province with Bahía Blanca and Mendoza, needs to be extended to be efficient; as late as 1953 there have been discussions to extend the lines towards the east and towards Chile (Transandino del Sud).

The province's most important newspaper is Neuquenia; the University of Cuyo operates several schools, most of them mining schools, in the province.

NEW ARCADIA.   Name applied in 1806 to the region of the Río de la Plata by the British (see British Invasions).

NEWBERY, JORGE (1875-1914).   Pilot; pioneer of aviation killed in Mendoza while attempting to cross the Andes.
    Born in Buenos Aires; studied in the university and

graduated as engineer; early became interested in sports; was
Argentine fence champion (1901); became aviation enthusiast;
in 1907 flew in the balloon El Pampero with Aarón de Anchorena and crossed to Uruguay; founded the aviation Aero Club and
served as its president in 1908; in 1910 linked Buenos Aires
and Rio Grande do Sul (Brazil) by air; inaugurated the first
aviation school of the country (1912); in 1913 accompanied the
German pilot Enrique Lubbe on his flight between Buenos Aires
and Colonia, Uruguay (world record over water at the time);
that same year went back and forth between the two cities; the
government appointed him military pilot in 1913; later, in 1914,
went to Mendoza to study the possibilities of crossing the Andes,
but he died in an accident after his trial flight.

NEWSPAPERS. Argentine journalism began with the first issue of
the Telégrafo Mercantil, Rural, Político, Económico e Historiógrafo del Río de la Plata, April 1, 1801; it was followed the
next year by the Semanario de Agricultura (agricultural weekly);
in 1807 the first foreign language paper appeared, Estrella del
Sud, published by the British in Montevideo during their second
invasion of the Río de la Plata; with the founding of Belgrano's
Correo de Comercio and the Gaceta de Buenos Aires, official
organ of the first patriot junta, both in 1810, Argentine newspapers had begun to fulfill their continuing function of providing
news of current events at home and abroad, promoting study of
the country in attempt to bind it together, and spreading useful knowledge; two other characteristics were already evident:
each paper was founded for a special purpose, as well as that
of printing more general news, and non-Spanish journalism had
already appeared.
        By 1968 there were 200 significant dailies with a circu-
lation of more than 3 million, roughly one copy to every three
people over the age of 20; among these with largest circulation
we find: La Prensa, founded in 1869, (conservative newspaper); La Nación (independent and conservative), founded by
Bartolomé Mitre in 1870; Clarín (supported UCRI, especially
Frondizi); El Mundo (liberal-radical); La Crónica (Peronist);
Noticias Gráficas (Peronist); La Razón, afternoon paper that
claims to have the largest circulation in the Spanish-speaking
world, with more than 500,000 readers (independent).
        By 1900 each major immigrant group was publishing at
least one daily newspaper in Buenos Aires in its own language;
in 1968 the most important of these were: The Buenos Aires
Herald and the Argentinisches Tageblatt with a circulation of
20,000 each; L'Italia del Popolo is the oldest of the dailies published in a foreign language, founded in 1899.
        Although larger Buenos Aires newspapers have national
circulation, each province publishes its own; among the most
important of these are: El Litoral (Santa Fe); founded in 1918;
Entre Ríos founded in 1883 in the province of the same name;
El Diario (Entre Ríos, 1914); Los Andes (Mendoza) founded in
1922; El Zonda of San Juan; Los Principios of Córdoba, one of
the oldest of the interior newspapers founded in 1814; etc. (see
Press; and individual newspapers mentioned).

NEWTON, RICHARD BLACK (or BLAKE) (d. 1868). British rancher; arrived in Argentina while still very young; joined a British business company and later started work on a ranch; in 1834 purchased a ranch; in 1846 he introduced first wire fencing into the country; originally he used a very fine fencing around the living quarters of the estancia, to protect them from marauding animals--later in 1855, he brought coarser fencing with which he surrounded the entire estancia; he was also one of the founders of the Rural Society; died on his estancia.

NIETO, VICENTE (1769-1810). Royal officer and official; executed by patriots. Came to Río de la Plata in early 1800s on military assignment; won promotion for his fighting against British invasions; appointed military commander of Montevideo by Junta of Sevilla in 1809; then, with rank of division general, assigned to presidency of royal audiencia in Charcas (modern Sucre, Bolivia); repressed patriotic revolts in Chuquisaca and Cochabamba; is said to have conspired with other Spanish governors, like Gutiérrez de la Concha of Córdoba, to oust the patriot junta of Buenos Aires; defeated, instead, by the patriot army at Suipacha (q.v.), he was executed, along with other royalist leaders, by order of Juan José Castelli (q.v.), in accordance with his orders from the Junta.

NOBEL PRIZE WINNERS. By 1970 Argentina had had three Nobel Prize winners: Carlos Saavedra Lamas (1936), the peace prize; Bernardo A. Houssay (1947), the prize in medicine and physiology; and Luis F. Leloir (1970), the prize in medicine (see individual entries).

NONINTERVENTION, POLICY OF. This has been a tradition since the time of Rosas, who resisted foreign intervention into Argentine affairs; Yrigoyen, in early twentieth century, also resisted foreign economic penetration into Argentina; Argentinians are also strongly opposed to committing the country to involvement in foreign wars; thus during the first world war Yrigoyen's decision to remain neutral (see World War I) met with popular approval; during the second world war, Argentina again remained neutral for most of its duration; President Castillo's determined neutrality was interpreted by many pro-Allied Argentines and by United States as showing benevolence towards the Axis; the military, however, had a loud voice and many were pro-German; when the Japanese attack on Pearl Harbor took place, the president immediately declared a state of siege in the country to cripple popular opposition to his policies (see World War II); following the war Argentines reverted to their strong nonintervention sentiments, favoring noncommitment in the Cold War; this position reached its culmination with Perón's "Third Position" which he distinguished from neutralism; Perón claimed that "noncommitment permitted flexible participation in world affairs on terms compatible with Argentine national interests"; in its own way, Argentina believes that it has always been internationalist and isolationist at the same time.

NORDENSKIÖLD, ERLAND (1877-1932). Swedish scientist; pioneer in Argentine ethnography.

Born in Stockholm; arrived in the new world fir the first time in 1899, as a zoologist; his interest in anthropological studies of Argentine Indians was aroused on his trip of 1901 into the Chaco region in company with other scientists; directed several other expeditions there in 1904, 1908, and 1913; was considered a great friend and defender of the Indians; later became director of the Museum of Gothenburg, professor of ethnography in the University of Stockholm, where he received the degree of doctor honoris causa because of his research and studies about the Paraguayan and Argentinian Chaco; wrote several monographs and articles on the ethnography of South America; the best is a series called Comparative Ethnographical Studies.

NORMAL SCHOOL OF PARANA. Established in 1870 by Sarmiento to train the teachers needed to direct the desired mass education; based on Sarmiento's belief that order and progress could be firmly established on a base of individual will and that such responsibility must be brought about by an education along the lines of Comtean positivism and the ideas of British liberals; under the leadership of the Italian scientist-philosopher Pedro Scalabrini, and his best-known student, the Argentine J. Alfredo Ferreira, this school concentrated on developing teachers who thought for themselves, encouraged their students to do the same; they trained a new generation of Argentine teachers who based their teaching on observation of Argentine realities studied with the discipline of scientific method, rather than the rote of scholasticism; Paraná became a center from which positivism was spread but it was an Argentine selection of positivistic ideas, rejecting the Comtean religion, ideas about authority, and subjection of the individual to society as unsuitable for the nation (see Education; Positivism).

NORTHERN RAILROAD (Ferrocarril del Norte). Early railroad designed to serve suburbs and farms along the estuary; in 1860 it pushed out from Buenos Aires to a distance of 30 kilometers; built with Argentine money, it brought the outlying estancias within range of the market; land alongside this railroad multiplied in value, from about 600 pesos per cuadra (150 square yards) to approximately 35,000 pesos; this railroad was purchased by the Ferrocarril Central Argentino in 1890, for 6,585,000 pesos (see Railroads).

NOUGUES, MIGUEL M. (1844-1900). Jurisconsult; political figure.

Born in Tucumán, of French father and Argentine mother; studied in the University of Córdoba, where he received his doctorate in law; became active in political life in Córdoba; was member of the Constituent Convention of the province (1870) elected representative of Tucumán in 1873-1874; served as minister of government of Governor Tiburcio Padilla of Tucumán at the time of the inauguration of the railroad for

which he worked actively; became governor (1880-1882) of
Tucumán; emphasized public education and better water control;
elected national senator in 1883; during his term acted as provisional president of the senate; member of board of directors
of the Banco Hipotecario; died in Buenos Aires on April 19,
1900. Nougués married Dominga Saavedra, daughter of Cornelio Saavedra.

NOVION, ALBERTO (d. 1937). Writer, especially of dramatic comedies.
    Born in Montevideo (Uruguay); lived and studied in Bue-
nos Aires; his first play, Doña Rosario, opened in 1906; the
best known work is El vasco de Olavarría; other plays are:
La cantina, Bendita Seas, En un burro tres baturros, Los
provincianos, Misia Pancha, La brava, and others; all the
comedies depict popular characters and country life; they were
very popular during the 1940s and 1950s; Novión was active
member in the Sociedad Argentina de Autores (Argentores);
died in Buenos Aires on November 25, 1937.

NOVISIMA RECOPILACION. New legal codification compiled by order of Charles IV: included all royal decrees and orders for
the colonies issued after 1745; its 12 volumes were published
in 1805; it did not simplify the Spanish law as expected; several Argentine historians claimed that the Novísima Recopilación did not have legal force in Argentina because it did not
reach the Audiencia of Buenos Aires before 1810; others
claimed that it was applied (see Law).

NUEVA VISCAYA. Name given to Río de la Plata area by its third
adelantado, in honor of his birthplace; did not last (see Juan
Ortiz de Zárate).

NUFLO DE CHAVES see CHAVES, NUFRIO DE

NUNES, GUILLERMO J. (1857-1928). Naval officer and explorer;
public figure in Buenos Aires business world and society.
    Born in Buenos Aires; educated at naval academy; saw
action against Ricardo López Jordán in Entre Ríos, and in
revolution of 1874 and 1893; from 1891 to 1893 he withdrew
from active naval duty to serve as chief of police of province
of Buenos Aires; laid foundations for modern department, reorganized regulations, and introduced system of identification
based on French use of fingerprints, as demonstrated by Ber-
tillón; returned to active duty; commanded warships Belgrano,
Patagonia, and Almirante Brown; commanded various exploring expeditions along the Atlantic Coast to Antártica; given
Legion of Honor by French government for his services to
Juan B. E. A. Charcot's expeditions in the Antarctic and Order
of St. Olaf for his role as Argentine naval officer in aiding
Norwegian scientific expedition in southern waters; retired with
rank of captain; meanwhile he had established a large fishing
company that he managed until his death; served as one of first

625   Nunes

presidents of Marconi wireless company; directed installation
of Japanese gardens in Buenos Aires; was president of Argentine Yacht Club several times.

NUÑEZ, BERNABE F. (1839-1927). Military officer; government
   functionary.
      Born in Ensenada de Barragán, Buenos Aires; spent
most of his life in military service; took part in defense of
Buenos Aires under siege by Hilario Lagos (q.v.) and in battles of Cepeda (1859) and Pavón (1861); served on guard of
Customs House in 1877 and fought at Corrales and at Puente
Alsina (1880), under Colonel F. B. Bosch; operated government
hotel (reception center) for immigrants during Roca's administration; rendered services in national department of engineers
and in construction of sanitary works; died in Buenos Aires.

NUÑEZ, IGNACIO (1792-1846). Patriot; official; publicist.
      Born in Buenos Aires; studied there; at age of 14
joined Hussars regiment and fought in the Reconquista; his
military career was brief; by 1810 had joined the patriots; became a politician and a writer; was an official in general secretariat in the General Assembly of 1813, and assistant secretary of the Congress of Tucumán (1816); during Rivadavia's
government worked in the secretariats of government and foreign relations; in 1823, while secretary of the embassy in
London, signed the commercial treaty with Great Britain;
elected Buenos Aires representative in 1827; became editor of
El Argos de Buenos Aires, of El Centinela and of El Nacional;
after having retired to private life, was jailed by Rosas, 1837;
writings included Noticias históricas, políticas y estadísticas
de las provincias del Río de la Plata, con un apéndice sobre
la usurpación de Montevideo por los gobiernos portugués y
brasilero, published in London (1825); and other historical
works published posthumously by his son, with sponsorship of
Valentín Alsina; Núñez died in Buenos Aires.

NUÑEZ CABEZA DE VACA, ALVAR see CABEZA DE VACA,
   ALVAR NUÑEZ

NUÑEZ DEL PRADO, JUAN. Conquistador from Badajoz; founder of
   first Spanish towns in Tucumán (see Barco).

NUSDORFFER, BERNARDO (1686-1762). German Jesuit missionary
   and writer.
      Born in Bavaria, entered Jesuit order in 1704 and ar-
rived in Río de la Plata area in 1717; became Jesuit provincial in 1747; was serving as Superior of the Missions of the
Paraguay and Uruguay river areas when Spain and Portugal
signed the boundary treaty of 1750 providing that seven of the
Spanish Guaraní missions should be ceded to the Portuguese;
Father Nusdorffer was actively involved in this painful period
(see Guaraní War) and in attempting to make the transition as
painless as possible; he left a long account of the events; a

portion of this (Part IX) was published by Guillermo Fúrlong
Cárdiff in 1971, along with a well-documented biography of
Nusdorffer and a bibliography of his published and unpublished
writings; he died in 1762 in the Guaraní town of San Carlos.

- O -

OAS   see   ORGANIZATION OF AMERICAN STATES

OBARRIO, MANUEL DE (1777-1834).   Government official and merchant.
        Born in Madrid; arrived in Buenos Aires at early age
and worked in the royal treasury; during British invasion of
1806 he first made provision for safekeeping of books and funds
from his office, then fought against the British at Perdriel,
leading the forces whom he had helped Pueyrredón recruit; was
appointed one of three emissaries by Santiago de Liniers to
take letters to Spain following the Argentine reconquest of Buenos Aires; his ingenuity in evading the British made him the
only one to get through to Spain with the documents; returned
to Buenos Aires in 1807 with communications from Pueyrredón
for the cabildo of Buenos Aires and a new royal appointment;
in 1808 he married Josefa de Lezica, daughter of alcalde and
merchant Francisco de Lezica; vigorously supported Liniers
both in the January 1, 1809, revolution and in the May Revolution of 1810; forced to retire from public life because of his
continued loyalty to Spain, he went to Chile and then to Peru;
in Lima, viceroy Abascal appointed him treasurer of the national bank at Potosí; in 1819 he was placed in charge of customs at Lima and in 1820 awarded the royal American order
of Isabel la Católica (finally conferred in Río de Janeiro in
1821); by 1824, he was back in Buenos Aires engaged with his
father-in-law in trading with Europe and with the southern
Peruvian ports until his death ten years later; an oil portrait
of Obarrio, painted by the Peruvian Indian artist Julián Cayo,
was hung in the historical museum at Luján; and in 1916 his
great grandson, Manuel Augusto Lezica wrote his biography.

OBERA.   Guaraní Indian chief who revolted against the Spaniards
after Juan de Garay subjugated the Indians (1594); Oberá
claimed that he was the son of God and as such had been directed to redeem his people; the rebellion failed, Oberá was
killed, but the upheaval served to open the doors to new Indian
laws.

OBLIGADO, BATTLE OF VUELTA DE   see   VUELTA DE OBLI-
GADO

OBLIGADO, CARLOS (1889-1949).   Writer; philosopher.
        Born in Buenos Aires, son of the author of Santos
Vega; studied in Buenos Aires; in 1920 published his first volume of poems; in 1925 published his first anthology, translating

from the French romantics; taught literature in the University
of Buenos Aires until 1928 when he visited Europe; returned
to America in 1930 and became dean of the school of philosophy; in 1931 became member of the Academia Argentina de
Letras and of the Real Academia Española; translated for first
time all the works of Edgar Allan Poe; in the 1930s he published several anthological works, El poema del Castillo (his
best known book), Lírica de Shelby, Ausencia, etc.; in 1943
became president of the University of Buenos Aires and started
publication of a literary journal called Patria; received the order of Alfonso X, el Sabio, from the Spanish government; died
in Buenos Aires.

OBLIGADO, ERASMO (1842-1896).   Naval officer.   Born in the province of Buenos Aires; joined the army during the war with
Paraguay; at the end of the war fought against Ricardo López
Jordán; took part in the battle of Ñembé; was one of the insti-
gators of the Naval School founded by Domingo Faustino Sarmiento in 1872; spent some time abroad and then became head
of the squadron of Río Negro during the expedición al desierto
(see Conquest of the Desert) of General Roca; as captain of
the Río Negro, reached the river Limay and transported troops
to fight the Indians; returned to Buenos Aires, seriously ill,
and died on September 23, 1885.

OBLIGADO, MANUEL (1838-1896).   Military officer and public official.
       Born in Buenos Aires; joined the army during the revo-
lution of 1852; fought in Cepeda and Pavón; after his return to
Buenos Aires, worked in the ministry of war; fought during the
Paraguayan war and against the montoneros; in the 1860s he
suppressed the Cáceres uprising against the national government; fought against Ricardo López Jordán and by 1870 became
head of the frontier forces; helped in the establishment of colonies in Santa Fe and Córdoba; in the 1880s was transferred
to the Chaco where he became governor in 1885-87, after defeating the Indians; in 1886, was promoted to general and became under-secretary of the ministry of war and general inspector of cavalry; transferred to Santa Fe; died on May 26,
1896, in the house of the governor.

OBLIGADO, MANUEL ALEJANDRO (1767-1843).   Patriot; public figure.   First of the family to be born in the new world, son of
a Spanish merchant and hacendado, Antonio de Obligado, and a
creole mother; graduated in law at the University of Charcas;
became a regidor of the cabildo in 1809; embraced the patriot
cause and voted for the removal of the viceroy in the cabildo
abierto of May 22, 1810; became secretary of finance of Supreme Directors Alvarez Thomas and Pueyrredón and of Governor Balcarce; was member of convention that signed peace
between Buenos Aires and Santa Fe and Entre Ríos in 1827;
retired to private life because of political disagreements; died
in Buenos Aires.

OBLIGADO, PASTOR (1818-1870).   First constitutional governor of
state of Buenos Aires (1854); lawyer.
Born in Buenos Aires, son of Manuel Alejandro Obligado; graduated in law from University of Buenos Aires, 1845;
appointed judge for province of Buenos Aires the day after battle of Caseros; although formerly a Rosas supporter, he belonged to powerful Buenos Aires family and played important
political role during period of separation of Buenos Aires from
other provinces; elected governor of province in 1853 (provisionally, as he lacked a few days of being the specified age of
35); he proved to be intolerant toward his enemies and opponents but progressive in administration; founded numerous primary schools; appointed José Eusebio Agüero to head the Colegio Seminario that later became the Colegio Nacional; made
plans for several towns to be established on sites of small
forts; began construction of city water plants, and installed
first gas works; served on committee to form amendments to
national constitution of Santa Fe that would make national organization feasible; an intransigent separatist, he inclined toward views of the Alsinas rather than those of Mitre and his
colleagues; elected to provincial legislature in 1859; fought at
Cepeda and Pavón; became interim minister of war and navy;
served as national congressman in 1862-1870; died in Córdoba
while vacationing.

OBLIGADO, PASTOR SERVANDO (1841-1924).   Writer; poet; historian.   Son of the first constitutional governor of Buenos Aires;
born in Buenos Aires; studied in the university of Buenos
Aires, graduating as a lawyer in 1862; his interest centered
in the history of Buenos Aires and that of the north, especially Salta; traveled to Europe and the Orient in 1871-74; upon
his return he published Viaje al oriente; in 1876 he brought out
Una procesión de 1592; during his trip to the USA he pronounced his well-known speech Glory to the Two Americas and
wrote Los Estados Unidos tal cual son; after that he devoted
himself to his Tradiciones of which the first six volumes discussed Buenos Aires 1711-1861, the last volume was published
in 1888, other volumes of the Tradiciones were published in
1900 and 1903; became member of the Academia Nacional de
la Historia in 1910, became member of the real Academia de
Historia in Spain in 1916; past 70, he wrote the Biografía del
Gobernador de Buenos Aires don Pastor Obligado y Tejedor;
in 1921 he rewrote his previously published book Güemes en
Buenos Aires; died in Buenos Aires.

OBLIGADO, RAFAEL (1851-1920).   Early gaucho and nationalist
writer; member of "Generation of 1880."
Born in Buenos Aires, descended on mother's side,
from Spanish viceroy Antonio de Olaguer Feliú; studied in
Santa Fe and Buenos Aires, but abandoned university studies
at age of 20, for career in writing; an early nationalist, he
began writing his poem Santos Vega (1877-1885) about legendary gaucho of same name (see Santos Vega); although many

poems and other works had been written about the same character, some of them before his, Obligado's work, in literary Spanish, glorified the legend and is considered his greatest creative work; stimulated other gaucho literature (q. v.); was one of first anti-Yankee Argentine nationalists, publishing a bitter attack on United States in his Al mexicano Federico Gamboa (1892); among other literary works were El hogar paterno, El nido de Boyeros and La flor de Ceibo; in 1889 the Royal Academy of Madrid elected him a member; twenty years later he was granted an honorary degree by the school of philosophy in University of Buenos Aires and appointed professor of Argentine literature; retired for reasons of health, died in Mendoza.

OBRERO.   Blue collar worker.

O'BRIEN, JOHN TROMMOND (1786-1861).   Military officer; Irish
    hero of Argentine war for independence.
        Born in Dublin (Ireland); arrived in Buenos Aires in
1812; after brief attempt in business world, he joined the army;
fought in Montevideo (1813) and after capitulation of Montevideo,
returned to civil life; later he joined San Martín in Mendoza,
as officer in granaderos a caballo; while the army was being
trained to cross the Andes, O'Brien patrolled Portillo Pass;
became San Martín's aide and accompanied the general on his
campaigns in Chile and Peru; after battle of Maipú, he was
ordered to follow General Osorio, the Spanish commander and,
with 18 granaderos, he captured all the Spanish staff papers
and several prisoners; after battle of Callao (Peru) he was
sent to Buenos Aires with all the captured trophies of war;
later he went to Bolivia where he received a silver mine from
Bolívar for services given to the general in final fighting of
the wars of independence; went to Europe, hoping to bring immigrants back but returned to join Argentine army instead; in
1834 he retired; explored the Amazonas region and settled for
a while in Uruguay, where Rosas forces destroyed his ranch;
Rivera, at that time president of Uruguay, appointed him consul general to Great Britain and Ireland; while returning to
America for the last time he died in Lisbon (Portugal); in
1935 his remains were brought back to Argentina for burial as
an honored national hero.

OCAMPO, MANUEL (1810-1895).   Government official; public and
    political leader; banker.
        Born in Buenos Aires; quickly became active in government service and public life; in the course of his career he
held, or was candidate for, almost every kind of job or office
in the city or province--including those of treasurer, congressman, senator, and governor, as well as member of constituent convention (1860), city councilman, and national deputy--
and at age 75 was proposed as candidate for presidency of the
republic by a coalition of three parties; during Buenos Aires'
separation from the other provinces he was president of the
Bank of the Province several times.

OCAMPO, NICOLAS (1824-1889). Military leader. Born in Curuzú
Cuatiá, Corrientes; began army career with unitarist General
José María Paz, with whom he remained until 1844 when he
changed sides to join the federalists; later he accompanied General Urquiza in his campaign against Rosas; fought at Caseros;
joined militia of province of Buenos Aires and fought on the
side of the province in the revolution of September 11, 1852;
afterward he served on the frontier; fought in the Paraguayan
war as leader of the cavalry from the province of Corrientes;
fought against López Jordán and was again transferred to the
frontier; in command of the forces there, he defeated the famous cacique Calfucurá in 1872; two years later he supported
General Mitre in latter's revolt against 1874 election results;
taken prisoner, remained in Luján (Buenos Aires) until 1877
when he was reincorporated into the army; in 1880 he supported the province in the revolution preceding the federalization of
Buenos Aires, was removed from the army, and again taken
back in 1883; died in Azul (in province of Buenos Aires).

OCAMPO, VICTORIA (1891-   ). Contemporary writer and publisher.
Through her own early literary works and as editor of the review Sur and director of the press of the same name, both of
which she founded, Victoria Ocampo became very influential
among writers in Argentina and gained an international reputation; traveled extensively in Europe and the United States, becoming closely linked with literary and scholarly figures, as
well as cultural activities in these areas; served on intellectual
commissions of council of League of Nations; although not a
political activist, she organized the Unión Argentina de Mujeres
(Argentine Women's Union) and served as its president (1936-
1938); in 1953, in the series of arrests following the bombing
of a Peronist mass meeting she was arrested and spent three
weeks in jail--suspect as an anti-Peronist because she belonged
to the oligarchy and maintained close relationships with democratic writers in Western Europe and U.S.; later described her
experiences in Sur; the bibliography of her writings is extensive,
most of it devoted to purely literary themes; some of her later
works, dealing with Argentine personalities and scenes are:
the play Habla el algarroba (1960), Tagore en las barrancas de
San Isidro (1961), her extensive Testimonios, in several parts
and editions; and the lengthy dialogues published by her in Sur
with Jorge Luis Borges (1969) and Eduardo Mallea (1971).

OCANTOS, CARLOS MARIA (1860-1949). Novelist; belonged to real-
ist group.
    Born in Buenos Aires, studied in the university and
joined the foreign service; he became secretary of the consul
in Rio de Janeiro in 1884; in 1890 and 1895 was appointed
chargé d'affaires in Madrid and plenipotentiary minister of Nor-
way and Denmark; retired in 1918 and moved to Madrid where
he spent rest of his life; he became famous, however, as an
Argentine novelist; Rubén Darío said of him that he "wrote
Spanish novels that developed in the city of Buenos Aires";

his best known novels are: Promisión and The Danger (1911)
in which he discussed the assimilation of the immigrant into
the new environment and the resulting transformation of the
Spanish language; other novels, in the realistic style, include:
La cruz de la falta (1883), Entre dos luces and El candidato
(1900), Don Perfecto (1902), Marplatina, Flor de Lis, Fru
Jenny, La Princesa está alegre, El esclavo, Yo castigaré,
Carmucha, Memorias de un viejo verde, all after 1915.

OCLOYAS. Agricultural, Pacific Indian tribe; lived in region of
Humahuaca under leadership of cacique; little historical information is known, but excavations have shown that the Ocloyas
were familiar with metals and had an advanced neolithic culture; their best known industry was ceramics; they made tubu-
lar urns and decorated their houses with mosaics.

O'CONNOR, JUAN JOSE (1890-1942). Lawyer; judge; penologist.
Born in Entre Ríos of British father and creole mother;
studied in University of Buenos Aires, graduating as a lawyer
in 1915; served as civil judge in Salta from 1918 to 1922; appointed member of the superintendency of jails in 1925; became
director of penitentiary institutes in 1933; while in this position he rebuilt all the jails in the national territories (Chaco,
La Pampa, Santa Cruz, Formosa, Neuquén, Chubut and Río
Negro); in 1936 he founded the Revista Penal, official magazine of the Dirección General de Institutos Penales; appointed
criminal judge in Buenos Aires (1937); worked with young of-
fenders; published several articles and books on his specialty:
The Jails in National Territories, La carcel mínima, Censo
de las cárceles nacionales, Aperçu penitentiaire, and others.

OCTOBER 17. Considered a special day by Peronists, commemorating Juan Domingo Perón's triumphant return from Martín
García Island October 17, 1945, and his subsequent first election to the presidency.

"OCTOPUS, THE" (El pulpo). Nickname given to Buenos Aires by
the interior provinces.

OFICIOS VILES ("Degrading Occupations"). Term applied to manual labor and other pursuits considered inferior by the Spaniards; Spanish law said: "It is public and very well known
that they (the gentlemen) do not work as tailors, bakers, shoemakers, salesmen, merchants--thus leaving industry, commerce, blue collar work to Jews, blacks, foreigners, mulattoes, and mestizos."

OFRENDAS (offerings or gifts). Ceremonies carried on in the
northern part of the country on All Saints' Day (November 1)
also called "meal of the ghosts" or "ofrendas de las guaguas"
(offerings of the innocents); the offering, generally food, is
left during the night for the souls of the departed; on the following day the food is divided among the friends, part is eaten,

part is burnt, taken to the cemetery, or buried; the burial is carried on in the fogón (hearth) of the house or away in the working soil following the Indian custom of offering food to Pachamama, the goddess of the land; after the food is gone, the friends "send back the soul" by means of music and songs.

O'GORMAN, MIGUEL (or MICHAEL) (1749-1819).   Irish physician; became first royal physician of viceroyalty of Río de la Plata.
Born in Ireland; educated in medicine at Paris and Rheims, further accredited in Madrid; sent to England in early 1770s to study new methods being developed for treatment of smallpox; after several other public health assignments with military expeditions, Dr. O'Gorman accompanied Pedro de Ceballos to Río de la Plata (1777) as physician; appointed royal physician in charge of operations of medical tribunal (Protomedicato) established by Viceroy Vértiz (see Epidemics of Disease); Dr. O'Gorman introduced preliminary forms of vaccination and other treatments for smallpox and established isolation hospital at some distance from city; new measures enabled authorities to cope more successfully with smallpox epidemics in 1790s; after Jenner's vaccines had been brought to Buenos Aires in 1805, Dr. O'Gorman published explicit instructions for proper use of them in viceroyalty; cooperated with Cosme Argerich in establishing and teaching in first medical school and set up, with latter, first projects of preventive medicine; maintained his medical position until his retirement in 1816; took no part in political events following May Revolution but was one of first to offer his books and aid to Mariano Moreno for the public library project; died in Buenos Aires.
His niece and his nephew and their parents remained in Buenos Aires; the girl, Camila, who died in 1848, a romantic victim of the Mazorca, passed to the folklore of the country through the writings of Sarmiento; the nephew, Enrique, born in Buenos Aires, became chief of police in 1867 and remained in that post until 1874 when he resigned.

O'HIGGINS, BERNARDO (1778-1842).   Chilean patriot leader; collaborator with San Martín in liberation movement.
Born in Chile, son of an Irishman who was a royal Spanish official and later viceroy of Peru; as a young man, met Francisco Miranda (q.v.) in London, who imbued in him a desire to help South America gain its independence; late in 1814, O'Higgins, at that time leader of the Chilean army, was defeated by the Spaniards in the battle of Rancagua (October 1, 1814) and fled to Argentina; there, in the province of Mendoza, O'Higgins was selected by San Martín to command the Chilean division of the Army of the Andes; after the epic crossing of the mountains, San Martín and O'Higgins defeated the Spaniards in Chacabuco (February 12, 1817); three days later a cabildo abierto elected O'Higgins as Supreme Director of Chile; he declared the independence of Chile in 1818; remained in power for five years; during that time he supported San Martín's campaign to liberate Peru from the Spaniards; giving aid that

Argentina, involved in anarchy, was unable to supply; this included the creation of a modern navy under the leadership of
Lord Cochrane; while in power in Chile, O'Higgins angered
the conservatives and the Church with his reforms (abolition
of noble titles, freedom of religion, permission to bury non-
Catholics in cemeteries, etc.); these revolted against him in
1823, accusing him of becoming a tyrant; discouraged, he left
Chile and went to Peru; in the 1840s the Chilean Senate returned to O'Higgins all his titles and honors and requested his
return, but he was already too ill to travel; died in Peru; his
remains were transferred to Chile in 1869.

OIL   see   PETROLEUM; YACIMIENTOS PETROLIFEROS FISCALES

OLAGUER FELIU, ANTONIO DE (1740-1810).   Viceroy, Río de la
     Plata, 1797-1799; military commander.
          Born in Villafranca del Bierzo, León, Spain; after com-
     pleting his studies, entered military service; saw action in
     several international wars; sent to Buenos Aires as military
     technical specialist during governorship (1757-1766) of Pedro
     de Ceballos (q.v.); spent most of next four decades in that
     area, except for brief fighting assignments in the West Indies
     and elsewhere; took part in the capture of Santa Catarina is-
     land, off southern coast of Brazil, and siege of Colonia del
     Sacramento (1777); back in Buenos Aires, he was appointed
     military inspector (1783); in 1787 he married a creole girl,
     Ana de Azcuénaga Basavilbaso; two years later became gover-
     nor and military inspector of Montevideo; remained in vice-
     royalty on other military assignments; in 1796 he was named
     subinspector general of all troops in the viceroyalty of Río de
     la Plata; the following year he was appointed interim viceroy;
     confirmed, he held this position for nearly two years; his chief
     concerns were the threats of British and Portuguese forces
     against Buenos Aires and surrounding territory, and the desire
     to open Argentine trade further, by allowing neutral ships to
     carry import-export trade; replaced by the Marquis de Avilés
     as viceroy in March, 1799; returned to Spain and new military
     duties; served as commanding officer of province of Guipúzcua,
     inspector general of line infantry, secretary of state and of
     war; was promoted to lieutenant general and made a caballero
     of the Royal Order of Charles III; died in Madrid; his son re-
     turned to Buenos Aires and became the first director of the
     Serenos, the nightwatch security guards established in the city.

OLAÑETA, PEDRO ANTONIO (1789-1825).   Royalist general of Upper
     Peru; threat to northwestern Argentina during wars of inde-
     pendence.   Spanish merchant who settled in Salta and estab-
     lished extensive trade in the viceroyalty, primarily between
     Potosí and Buenos Aires; profoundly conservative and totally
     loyal to church and crown, he offered his services to the Span-
     ish army when patriot forces attempted to expand May Revolu-
     tion to the northwest and into Upper Peru (now Bolivia); his
     resources, unusual contacts, available manpower, knowledge of

the terrain, quick intelligence in learning military ways made
him valuable to Spanish army; became closely associated with
General Joaquín de la Pezuela (later viceroy of Peru); fought
against patriot forces at Salta, Tucumán, Vilcapugio, Ayohuma,
and Sipe Sipe; after 1816, with San Martín engaged in creating
Army of the Andes to carry out his continental strategy, the
fighting in the northwest border became a holding operation
rather than main theater of war; Olañeta invaded repeatedly,
occupying Jujuy in 1817 and establishing his headquarters there;
attempted to take Salta but was defeated by Martín Güemes; in
1821 he took Salta by surprise in action during which Güemes
was killed; by this time Olañeta was a general, in command
of royalist troops in Upper Peru; events following the revolt
of 1820 in Spain, had disturbed him greatly; La Serna, who
replaced Pezuela as viceroy and commander, and the new Spanish officers who came over supported the liberal constitution
of 1812 that Ferdinand VII had been forced to accept; for the
next five years, Olañeta found himself increasingly frustrated
as he continued to fight against the patriots but at the same
time developed suspicion and hatred against the new Spanish officers whom he felt to be disloyal to Ferdinand VII and the traditional role of the Spanish crown; his nephew Casimiro Olañeta attempted to win him over to the cause of Bolivian independence as a third alternative to Argentine patriot or liberal
Spanish rule; for a time Olañeta seemed interested--to the extent that Bolívar, now commanding the independence army,
considered him almost as another libèrator; Olañeta, however,
remained consistent in his loyalty to Ferdinand VII; early in
April, with Sucre in Bolivia to complete the conquest and hoping to gain Olañeta's support, the latter pronounced against
both Sucre and the royalists; deserted by most of his followers
he was met at Tumusla by forces led by Carlos Medinaceli, his
former second-in-command; in battle of April 1, 1825, he was
killed, the only casualty; ironically, two months later Ferdinand (unaware of his death) rewarded him with appointment as
viceroy of the Perus; and, equally ironically, most historians
believe that his actions in dividing the royalist forces at this
last critical moment may have contributed to Spain's final loss
of colonies in South America; unopposed by an Argentina preoccupied with internal problems and largely disposed, by this
time, to let individual portions of the viceroyalty work out their
own destinies, Bolivia won its independence shortly thereafter.

OLASCOAGA, MANUEL JOSE (1835-1911).   Military officer; first
     governor of Neuquén; writer.
          Born in the province of Mendoza; studied there and in
Buenos Aires, where he began his military career; when Urquiza pronounced against Rosas, Olascoaga returned to Mendoza
and joined the movement against the Rosas governor there;
while remaining in the army, he taught English in a secondary
school in Mendoza and was put in charge of a military newspaper La Constitución,   thus beginning his writing career; Olascoaga was transferred to Entre Ríos where he came in contact

with Urquiza and helped in the organization of the naval force
of the Confederación; in Rosario he founded El Comercio, a
political newspaper; he was back in Mendoza when the province
was destroyed by the earthquake of 1861; Olascoaga organized
the first aid services, helped with guard duty, restored the
mail service, and worked with the sanitary commission sent
out from the national government; moved to Córdoba and later
to Buenos Aires; fought with Urquiza in the battle of Pavón;
in charge of Indian frontiers, he presented the authorities with
a study for the defense of the frontier; sent to Chile in 1867 to
purchase war equipment he was forced by political changes in
Mendoza to remain there for some time; founded La Linterna
del Diablo, liberal newspaper; in 1869 joined Cornelio Saavedra
in his campaign against the Araucanians in southern Chile;
learned several Indian dialects that were useful to him later on;
returned to Argentina in 1873, was reincorporated in the army,
with general rank in 1877 and, as secretary of General Roca,
prepared plans for the Campaign to the Desert (Patagonia); in
1879 was appointed chief of the Military Topographical Office,
in 1880 published Estudio topográfico de la pampa y Río Negro;
for this work he received a gold medal from the government;
in 1883 he organized the Army Staff and became the first governor of Neuquén where he planned and founded Chos Malal,
the early capital of the territory; retired to province of Mendoza where he finished his study on the southern Andes, Los
Andes australes; died in that province in 1911.
          In addition to his topographical and journalistic works,
he also wrote fiction and poetry; some of his novels, interesting for the descriptions of the period, were: El brujo de la
Cordillera; El Club de las Damas; El gobierno de los locos;
Patria; Biografía de Bernardo de Irigoyen (biographical and
historical); El país del norte; etc.

OLAVARRIA, ANTONIO DE (1745-1813). Spanish officer; founder of
     Argentine family.
          Born in Vizcaya; entered military service; accompanied
Pedro de Ceballos to America on expeditionary force that captured Santa Catarina island (1777) and Colonia del Sacramento from the Portuguese; remained in the Río de la Plata
area; assigned to frontier service in province of Buenos Aires,
as officer in Blandengues; married Gertrudis Rodríguez Peña
and started large family; had risen to rank of lieutenant colonel
and was commander of border at Luján at time of first British
invasion; aided Pueyrredón in reconquest at Luján; he was ordered by Viceroy Liniers to escort Lord Beresford (then prisoner at Luján) to Catamarca; apparently he was tricked, instead, by his brother-in-law, Saturnino Rodríguez Peña, into
surrendering the captured British commander to him; this resulted in Beresford's escape to Montevideo and Olavarría's arrest and eventual imprisonment in Mendoza at time of second
British invasion; the first patriot junta following the May Revolution (1810) exonerated him, gave him rank of colonel in
patriot army; later he also received honorary citizenship; joined

Belgrano in expedition to Paraguay (1811) but had to leave because of illness; died in Buenos Aires after 47 years of military service; his sons José, Nicolás, and Rafael (qq. v.) followed their father in military careers.

OLAVARRIA, JOSE VALENTIN (1801-1845).   Hero of wars of independence.
        Born in Buenos Aires, son of Antonio; became a cadet
in the Blandengues at age of nine; joined Army of the Andes in
1815; fought in Chacabuco, Cancha Rayada and Maipú; returned
to the south of Chile and later fought in the Peruvian campaigns;
joined General Bolívar in continued fight for independence; after
the battle of Ayacucho requested retirement and returned home;
became part of Argentine forces during the war with Brazil and
joined Lavalle in 1828; after Lavalle's defeat, Olavarría emigrated to Montevideo; persecuted there by Oribe, he joined
Rivera's force against Rosas; died in Montevideo.

OLAVARRIA, NICOLAS DE (1797-1826).   Like his father and brothers, joined the army and fought for the independence of the
country; joined the Alto Perú campaign and fought in Huaqui,
Suipacha, Tucumán and Salta under the orders of Manuel Belgrano; taken prisoner after the battle of Ayohuma, it is believed he died in prison around 1825 or 1826.

OLAVARRIA, RAFAEL DE (1795-1827).   Like the rest of the family,
he joined the army as a cadet in his father's regiment; fought
in the campaign to Alto Peru from Cotagaita to Sipe Sipe; requested retirement from the army in 1818; returned to the army
as captain (1826) to fight in war with Brazil under command of
Juan Lavalle; died from illness during the campaign.

OLAZABAL FAMILY.   All five sons of Benito de Olazábal and of
Matilde Llorente followed military careers, fighting in the wars
for independence and in the civil wars that followed; the brothers were Benito, Félix, Gerónimo, Manuel, and Martín.
        Félix de Olazábal (1797-1841).   Born in Buenos Aires,
son of a military family; joined the army when he was only 16;
fought in the Alto Perú campaign; joined Army of the Andes in
1816 and was seriously wounded in the battle of Chacabuco; rejoined the army in 1818 and fought at Maipú; accompanied San
Martín to Peru; remained there as governor of Ica; in 1824 was
returned by Bolívar to Buenos Aires as leader of the remaining
members of the Army of the Andes; transferred to the observation army during the war with Brazil, General Dorrego appointed him military commander of the southern region; after
a short period under the orders of Lavalle, Olazábal joined the
federalist forces and fought against Paz; Rosas appointed him
colonel in the army and legislator, but he soon fell from favor
and had to emigrate to Montevideo where he died in extreme
poverty.
        Gerónimo de Olazábal (1801-1864).   Born in Buenos
Aires, like his brothers, joined the army as a young boy of

16; fought at Cepeda (1820) and in 1822 was appointed military commander of frontier forces against the Indians, under the leadership of General Balcarce; after being seriously wounded in the arm was discharged from the army; rejoined during the war with Brazil and made a career out of the army; became military attaché in Rio de Janeiro from 1842 until the fall of Rosas; offered his services to the Confederation, they were accepted in 1860; became a colonel in the army of the Republic died in Buenos Aires.

Manuel de Olazábal (1800-1872). Officer in Granaderos a Caballo; San Martín's aide. Born in Buenos Aires; joined Granaderos a Caballo in 1813; after taking part in siege of Montevideo under Alvear and fighting against montoneros, he rejoined San Martín in Mendoza in 1815; became chief of San Martín's personal escort; fought throughout the Chilean campaign, from Chacabuco to Bío Bío; returning to Argentina, he defeated José Miguel Carrera (q.v.) at Punta de Médanos (1821) following which the leader was executed; late in January 1823 having received word that his old commander José de San Martín was on his way back to Mendoza, Olazábal went up into the Andes to meet him at Cumbre in a deeply emotional scene later described in his memoirs; as military commander in Mendoza (1824), carried out expeditions against hostile Indians; captured while fighting against Brazil (1827) but soon released; supported Lavalle, 1828-1829; becoming a colonel following battle of Navarro; Rosas discharged him from national army (1835); Olazábal continued fighting with anti-Rosas, unitarist forces in Corrientes; in 1838 signed, in name of Governor Berón de Astrada, an agreement with Uruguayan leader Fructuoso Rivera; fought under latter at Pago Largo; continued to fight under Rivera while in Uruguay as political exile; returned to Argentina and was reincorporated into army of Buenos Aires province; later served as aid to presidents Urquiza and Derqui; his very important memoirs of the war of independence were published in Gualeguaychú in the 1860s; they were republished, along with some of his other writings, by the Instituto Nacional Sanmartiano in Buenos Aires in 1942, with prologue by Teodoro Caillet-Bois; Olazábal died in Buenos Aires.

OLIDEN, MANUEL LUIS DE (1783-1868). Patriot, public figure. Born in Buenos Aires; studied in the University of Charcas where he graduated as lawyer; joined in the militia in La Paz (in today's republic of Bolivia) and was active in the aborted revolution of 1809; after receiving the news of the Río de la Plata revolution of May 1810, he moved to Salta where he organized a militia that fought with Belgrano; became regidor of the cabildo of Buenos Aires in 1815, in charge of the police force; during the time he was in this position organized the finances, regulated use of firearms, forbade the useless killing of cattle, and attempted to apply sanitary laws to retail sales, etc.; later became minister of government in cabinet of Governor Sarratea (Province of Buenos Aires); retired

from public life in 1820 because of anarchy and moved to his
ranch in Chascomús (Province of Buenos Aires) where he died.

OLIGARCHY. Significant political label applied to the closely-knit
group of old, wealthy landowning families that dominated the
nation politically from the 1890s to the 1940s.

OLIVA, MOISES (1829-1889). Public figure; governor of Salta.
Born in Salta, from an old family; studied medicine in
the University of Buenos Aires; joined the army and fought in
campaigns against the Indians; in 1857, he published an essay
criticizing the mistreatment of the Indians and, as a result of
this, he resigned from the army and returned to Salta in 1858;
there he entered politics; was elected provincial legislator;
twice became governor of the province ad interim (1863-1864
and 1865); in 1879 was elected national congressman but remained in this position only a very short period because in
July of the same year he was elected governor of his province;
served in this capacity until his death.

OLIVERA, DOMINGO (1798-1866). Public figure; government official; progressive rancher and farmer.
Born in Ambato, Ecuador; educated in Quito and Lima;
moved with his family to Salta, in 1811; there young Domingo
and his father successfully exploited a gold mine; moved to
Buenos Aires in 1813; became clerk in office of chief of police;
attracted attention of Bernardino Rivadavia who used him in
many public and official capacities; Olivera was ordered by
Rivadavia to organize first school of agriculture and drew up
plans and governing rules for several public institutions established by him; after the latter's fall politically, Olivera turned
his attention to writing and to rural pursuits; contributed to
several papers and journals such as El Argos; El Mensajero
Argentino, El Censor, and others; his great love was the development of his diversified estancia; remained there during
Rosas period; established one of the first cabañas (breeding
farms) in Argentina; devoted himself to improving herd of his
merino sheep; devised a machine to separate wheat from the
chaff; was responsible for other progressive innovations; after
Rosas' departure in 1852, Olivera returned to public life; was
named justice of the peace in San José de Flores; served as
deputy and senator in Buenos Aires provincial government, as
well as member of government's advisory council; his last public act was to serve as member of National Convention of 1860
to reform the constitution; died at his ranch.

OLIVERA, EDUARDO (1827-1910). Estanciero and agriculture specialist.
Born in Buenos Aires; studied agriculture in Grignon,
France, and returned home to take care of his father's (see
Domingo Olivera) properties (1857); brought along Negrette
sheep to improve breed of his creole animals; opened several
agricultural banks to help farmers; attempted to install a

farming school and succeeded in establishing a model institution; Olivera revived Rivadavia's idea of a Rural Association and was one of founders of the Sociedad Rural in 1866 and an early president; appointed Director of Post Offices in 1874, he improved working conditions of the employees and installed iron mailboxes on the streets of Buenos Aires; President Luis Sáenz Peña appointed him federal interventor of the province of Buenos Aires in 1893; in 1910 he was elected dean of the first agronomical and veterinary school of the University of Buenos Aires; published Estudios y viajes agrícolas and Cartas de un estanciero while he lived in Europe.

OLMOS, EMILIO F. (1884-1932).   Politician; wealthy estanciero; governor of Córdoba.
          Born in Córdoba; graduated in engineering from University of Córdoba in 1912; joined the old Democratic party and became intendente municipal (similar to mayor) in 1925; as president of the party, was candidate for governor in 1928, elected in 1931, held the post until his death in 1932; Emilio Olmos represented the powerful politician of the provincial party that had almost complete power in the development of the party, nothing was approved without his knowledge and no candidate could run without his support.

OLMOS, RAMON I. DE (1861-1940).   Professional military officer; political figure in Córdoba.
          Born in Córdoba; became member of the cavalry; served on the frontier and in campaign to the desert in 1880, in command of two regiments; served on general staff of the army; became private secretary of President Figueroa Alcorta and Roque Saenz Peña; directed the office of military affairs; led national forces in La Rioja and Santiago del Estero; was elected provincial congressman for the province of Córdoba and senator in 1934; in 1938 became governor of the province of Córdoba; died in that province.

OLONGASTAS.   This long extinct group of Indians lived in the plains of La Rioja and Córdoba; very little is known about them; may have belonged to Huarpe group; they were hunters and gatherers, possibly planted some corn and squash; they ate ostrich (ñandú) eggs and cooked their food in ovens dug in the ground; it is believed that they used llama wool because loom weights have been found as well as stone containers with traces of vegetable dyes; they used bows and arrows and large stone balls; crude ceramics have been found; nothing is known of their housing and religious beliefs.

OLVIDO, LEY DEL (amnesty law).   Law issued on May 7, 1822, by minister Rivadavia permitting the return of those exiled for political reasons, enabling men like Juan Manuel Dorrego, Alvear, Sarratea, Pagola, etc. to return to Argentina.

OMAGUACAS (or HUMAHUACAS).   These Indians lived in the north-

western part of the country; were probably a separate ethnic
part of the Andean group; as such, they had the black-gray
ceramics, the burial in urns, and the Incaic type of ceramics;
they were short, long-faced, and practiced deformation of the
skull; cultivated the soil, using terraces and irrigation; em-
ployed shovel-like tools of stone or wood to plant potatoes,
squash, corn, and beans; supplemented their diet with meat
from guanacos, ostriches, and other animals; they also gathered carob fruit; they wore the Andean shirt, the blanket made
of wool, and used sandals (ojotas); houses were built of mud
brick and straw and were rectangular; ceramics were made in
several styles, the black-gray archaic and the black on red
background style in use at the time the Spaniards arrived;
Omaguacas were warlike, used sling shots, bow, arrow, and
boleadoras; they were strongly influenced by the Peruvian
groups; highest chief resided in Humahuaca with other caciques
subordinate to him; after the conquest, the Spaniards gave them
in encomienda to neighbors of Charcas and of Tucumán; the
oldest proof found is an encomienda granted to Juan de Villanueva in 1540; the Indians, however, opposed this institution
and were among the last tribes to submit to the Spaniards;
they twice destroyed cities founded in the valley of Jujuy--the
Ciudad de Nieva (1562) and San Francisco de Alava (1575)--
before the third city, San Salvador de Jujuy, was established
permanently.

OMBU (Phytolácca).   Argentine national plant.   Enormous tree-like
shrub that can grow to height of 42 feet, with massive truck (80%
water) attaining circumference of 100 feet and its shady spread
much more; it originated, according to Charles Berg, in Iberá
Lagoon of Corrientes and grows throughout northeastern, central
Argentina; it has a folkloric and literary tradition; it is used in popular medicine to cure rheumatism, drunkenness, and problems
related to love; its leaves were used to prepare soap during
colonial times; the Indian myth of its creation reads as follows:
Ombi, the wife of an Indian chief, took care of the corn plants
but under the hot sun, only the last plant, watered with her
tears, lived; God, feeling sorry for the woman who had no
more tears, transformed her into a tree to protect the corn
plants (on which the tribe subsisted) from the sun.
    Argentina has four different species of ombúes; three
are small but the last, the Dioica, is the large, more common
plant; there are several historical ombúes, including the Ombú
of Sobremonte, supposed to have been already full-grown when
viceroy Sobremonte founded the city of San Fernando, today a
suburb of Buenos Aires; the Ombú of Viceroy Vértiz, believed
to be five to six hundred years old; and the "Ombú of Hope"
under which San Martín and Pueyrredón are said to have discussed plans for achieving the independence of the country.
    See Arboles históricos de la República Argentina by
Enrique Udaondo.

ONA INDIANS.   One of the nomadic tribes that lived in Tierra del

Fuego; all but extinct now, considerable knowledge about them
is available through detailed studies made by Austrian anthro-
pologist, Father Martín Gusinde; members of the Chono group,
their lifestyle was primitive; hunters and gatherers, they used
the bow and arrow, stone and bone scrapers and knives; had
little housing except for shelters made from guanaco hides
draped on pole structures to protect them from extreme cold;
wore simple loin cloth, Andean blanket made from animal
hides, with hair side turned out, and moccasins; tall (averaging 1.74 meters in height), with wide, flat faces, with paint-
decorated bodies; social organization based on family as part
of patrilineal band; religion was monotheistic; buried their dead
on small mounds or hills; by the early eighteenth century Onas
had been affected by the presence of Spaniards in Argentina and
Chile; they adopted the horse; added the chiripá and horsehide
boots to their dress; also underwent social and cultural changes;
and made use of boleadoras; the Onas, along with other Chonos,
were subjugated by the Araucanians (q. v.) in the early nineteenth century; their numbers, never more than a few thousand,
began to decline; with the taking over of Tierra del Fuego by
white settlers and sheepherders in late nineteenth and early
twentieth century, the Onas practically disappeared, dying from
unaccustomed disease, in warfare, or becoming merged in other groups; the few remaining were placed on a reservation at
Lake Fagnano.

ONCATIVO, BATTLE OF (February 25, 1830).   Unitarist victory
     over federalist forces; led to signing of the Federal Pact (q. v.).
     After the defeat at Tablada, Juan Facundo Quiroga retired to
     the provinces of Cuyo and reorganized his troops; Facundo at-
     tempted to invade Córdoba but Juan María Paz attacked and de-
     feated him in the valley of Oncativo; José Félix Aldao, the
     caudillo of Cuyo fell prisoner to Paz, who treated him with all
     consideration.

ONELLI, CLEMENTE (1864-1924).   Scientist; cultural and public fig-
     ure.   Italian scientist from Rome; arrived in Buenos Aires in
     1884; appointed director of the zoo in 1904; promoted creation
     of trade schools for weavers and aviculturists; Onelli became
     secretary of the Patagonia explorer Francisco P. Moreno
     (q. v.); studied fossils of Patagonia and wrote essays about
     them; represented the Argentine government in Chile during the
     agreements negotiated about the Puna de Atacama (northwestern
     region of the country divided between Argentina and Chile by
     mutual agreement); Onelli wrote in newspapers and magazines
     and gave lectures to popularize his ideas; the variety of his in-
     terests is shown by the titles of his articles; these include:
     Alfombras y tapices y tejidos criollos (1916); Ensayo de hagio-
     grafía argentina (1916); Cartilla del criador de gallinas a
     campo (1917); Cartilla de la tejedora provinciana (1921); Ar-
     quitectura de la Antártica sumergida (1924); El cultivo del al-
     godón (1924) and others; died in Buenos Aires in 1924.

ONETTI, CARLOS MARIA (1894-1940).   Teacher; writer.
Born in Uruguay; studied in the University of Buenos
Aires and became a literature teacher; taught at the education
school of the university from 1927 until its disappearance in
1930; from then on he taught in the Escuela Normal Superior
of Paraná and in the Instituto Nacional del Profesorado Secundario; he was an active writer in education journals and gave
various lectures on literature and philosophy; some of his publications are: Novísimo diálogo de las sombras published in
1922 in Verbum; El barco de vela, poetry published in 1926;
wrote several essays which were not published like "Provinci-
anito con estrella federal"; "Cuatro clases con Sarmiento escritor"; "Tres Argentinos"; Onetti died in 1940.

ONGANIA, JUAN CARLOS (1914-).   Professional military officer;
president of Argentine Republic, 1966-1970.
Born in Marcos Paz in province of Buenos Aires, son
of agricultural worker who also operated a small store; studied
in parochial schools before entering Colegio Militar (military
academy); after graduation joined the cavalry and rose to brigadier general in 1959; he first attracted public attention in September 1962 when he led the Azules (moderate political faction
of military, preferring as little military intervention in politics
as possible) in their successful confrontation with Colorados
(authoritarian group, feeling military supervision over political
affairs necessary and desirable); appointed commander in chief
of the army by President Guido in 1962 he was dominant figure
in the administration; used his influence in early period to secure holding of constitutional elections and in attempts to unify
various factions in armed forces; resigned in September 1965;
in 1966 he supported a military movement to take over the Illia
government because of the increasing economic problems and
to prevent a Peronist victory in the elections that it was feared
would divide the military and bring new conflicts; in June became Argentina's 31st president in a bloodless coup d'état led
by the commanders of the army, navy, and air force; Onganía's
government recognized the Constitution of 1853 but subordinated
it to the new Statute of Argentine Revolution that gave president
virtually full federal and provincial powers; the eventual political goal of his military government was to restore electoral
system to Argentina; believed this must be preceded by thor-
ough-going three-stage revolution--economic development and financial stability, followed by social reform and integration, culminating in constitutional political processes; to bring this about,
he ruthlessly suppressed all opposition, dissolved congress and
provincial legislatures, removed governors and five supreme
court justices; confiscated property of political parties and
banned political demonstrations; and arrested Communist leaders;
in the beginning his support came largely from the military
(Azules), upper middle classes, and conservative Catholic
groups; most controversial early action was his heavy intervention into universities, on grounds that they contained Communists; many feared that this meant the permanent loss of hard-

won university reforms (q. v.) and freedoms; an exodus of professors, especially scientists, to U.S. and other countries resulted; his somewhat prudish attempts to regulate social morals brought approval from many Catholics but occasional excesses exposed the government to public ridicule; Onganía reshuffled his cabinet to obtain a balance between nationalists and moderates, attempted to win support from labor (with little success) and began the first stage of the revolution by appointing Adalberto Krieger Vasena (q. v.), an internationally known and respected economist, in charge of improving the national economy and financial structure; in spite of the fact that economic gains were made, oppositions continued and increased, from university students, labor, opposing military groups, and others; in May 1969, this violence peaked, much of it centered in Córdoba (see Cordobazo, El), and gave clear warning that national problems had no easy solution; in June 1970 a combination of factors caused the military to depose Onganía; largely on grounds that the kidnapping and killing of former president Pedro Aramburu by Peronist guerrillas, the slow pace of economic development and social reforms, and the continued violence throughout the country proved his government to be ineffectual; also there was some fear that Onganía wanted to replace Argentina's representative democratic government with a neo-corporativist system; also there continued to be resentment against his restrictions on political parties that had prevented their normal evolution; after his resignation, he retired from the army and became an estancia manager in Buenos Aires province.

ONGARO, RAIMUNDO (1939-   ). Leader of an extreme left-wing Peronist group; led several unions out of the Confederación del Trabajo (CGT) and formed an opposition labor union (1968); involved, with his followers, in the violent acts of 1969 against President Onganía, was arrested and imprisoned; freed by President Cámpora in 1973, joined a guerrilla leftist group fighting the government.

OPINION, LA. Political, commercial newspaper published in the province of Corrientes in 1857; came out three times a week, for 760 issues; was edited by Francisco Suárez and Pablo Coni; provides an interesting source for the study of the Confederation for three years; it also published the historical study of the Jesuit Missions written by Martín de Moussy (November 3, 1858) and botanical studies carried on by Bonpland; it was the only newspaper published in the province after El Comercio was closed by government order.

ORANGE TREE OF FRANCISCO SOLANO. Historical tree supposedly planted by the missionary priest in the province of Tucumán while he worked with the Indians of the region; the tree is about three hundred years old.

ORCADAS (South Orkney Islands). Archipelago in Antarctica, lying

to east and south of southern tip of continent, between 60° and
61°S. latitude and 44° and 45°W longitude; claimed by both
Argentina and Great Britain (see Antarctic Argentina); main islands are Coronación and Laurie; most of area desolate or
glacier-covered; used primarily for meteorological observations.

Discovered in 1821 by English expedition of Sir George
Powell; one group of islands still retains his name; two years
later, James Wedell visited and mapped them; after Dumond
D'Urville's visit to the Orcadas en 1838 they were forgotten
until a Norwegian captain Larsen stopped by; in 1903 a Scottish national expedition under William S. Bruce set up a
weather station, Osmond House, in Scotia Bay, off Laurie Island, while ships were iced in; later, in Buenos Aires, he
suggested that Argentina take over and continue this meteorological project; when Argentina agreed to do this, the British
government turned over its station to the Argentine Republic;
from that date (1904), Argentina has occupied and claimed the
Orcadas, maintaining an observation post there, issuing weather
reports and meteorological studies; sovereignty of the islands
remains in litigation between Argentina and England, although
Chile made claims to them, also; meanwhile Argentina enlarged the observatory in 1912, established radio station in
1926, and opened Patagones lighthouse and the airfield there in
1948.

ORDENANZAS DE CABILDO (city ordinances). Municipal ordinances
regulating the Cabildo; the first ordinances for the cabildo of
Buenos Aires were written by Alonzo de Solórzano y Velazco
in 1668; Charles III approved the ordinances written by Juan
Fernández Guillen and Juan de Reluz y Huerta written in 1695;
in 1812 the Regidor Antonio Alvarez de Jonte maintained that
the ordinances, in force since 1695, needed reform; the General Assembly of 1813 did not approve the changes, but Gervasio Antonio de Posadas, as supreme director, issued the new
ordinances for the Cabildo in 1814.

ORDENANZAS DE INDIOS (Laws About Indians). The systems of repartimiento and encomienda were applied in Argentina from the
time of Domingo Martínez de Irala; first ordinance issued on
May 14, 1556; the encomienda ordinance was changed in 1597
by Governor Juan Ramírez de Velazco; Hernandarias (q. v.) issued his famous ordinances in 1598 and 1603; the oidor Francisco de Alfaro issued the Ordenanzas de Alfaro, based on the
Peruvian ordinances, in 1612; these ordinances regulated the
government of the reducciones (q. v.), the relationship between
the pueblos (Indian towns) and the Spanish authorities, the work
to be done by the Indians, the way of life to be maintained in
the missions and reducciones and the form of justice to be
used with the natives; they were incorporated in the Ordinances
of October 10, 1618, issued by Philip III.

ORDER OF SAN MARTIN. Highest distinction bestowed by the Argentine Republic; established by law 13,202 of May 21, 1948; it is used to honor foreigners that have served the nation; order includes the following grades in descending order: 1) Collar; 2) Gran Cruz; 3) Gran Oficial; 4) Comendador; 5) Oficial; 6) Caballero; the president is the Gran Maestre and on the board with the minister of foreign relations, and the minister of war, navy and aeronautics; among the first foreigners to receive the order were General Dwight Eisenhower (1948) and President Miguel Alemán of Mexico (1950).

ORDER OF THE SUN (Orden del Sol).   Created by José de San Martín in Peru in 1821, to be bestowed on citizens and military men for distinguished services to the nation; the order had 28 articles, and three classes; founders, beneméritos and associates; among the founders (including many Argentines) were Bernardo O'Higgins, General Las Heras, General Arenales, Don Diego Paroissien, and Tomás Guido; the Marquis of Torre y Tagle, the Count of Valle Oselle and the Marquis of San Miguel were also founders of the order; the prerogatives of the order, as well as the pensions included with the honor, were inherited for two generations; Santa Rosa de Lima was the patron saint of the order; it was abolished in 1825; but reestablished, with changes, in 1921 to commemorate the one hundredth anniversary of the independence of Peru by President A. B. Leguía (see San Martín, José de).

ORDOÑEZ, JOSE (1789-1819).   Spanish royalist officer who fought against the patriots in Chile, led by San Martín and O'Higgins. Studied in Europe where he fought against Napoleon; fellow-officer with San Martín; sent to America in 1815 as intendant governor of Chile; while in Concepción he was defeated by José de San Martín's forces in Curapaligüe; after receiving reinforcements from Peru, he attacked again but was defeated by Las Heras in Cerro del Gavilán; retired to Talcahuano and although he failed to defend that port successfully was promoted to brigadier general of royalist armies, commanded attack of Cancha Rayada (q. v.) in which San Martín was defeated; Ordóñez himself was finally defeated by San Martín in battle of Maipú (q. v.); fell prisoner to the patriots and was sent as prisoner to San Luis; attempting to escape, with others, he was shot on February 8, 1819.

OREJANO.   Name given in Argentina to cattle without owner, which were marked by cutting the ear as a triangle; this was fashionable during the latter part of the 18th and early 19th century; Article 27 of the decree of August 24, 1852, says that the orejanos found on the property of a rancher belong to the rancher if the calf does not follow the mother cow (see Saladeros; Vaquerías).

ORELLANA, RODRIGO A. DE (1761-1821).   Bishop of Córdoba, involved in Liniers' conspiracy against May Revolution.
          Born and educated in Spain; before coming to America

taught in the University of Valladolid and acted as customs officer of the Cartuja; became bishop of Córdoba in 1809; that same year he was appointed dean of the University of San Carlos (later known as University of Córdoba); after the revolution of 1810 he collaborated with Santiago de Liniers and Gutiérrez de la Concha in the rebellion against the Junta of Buenos Aires; when the counterrevolution failed he was taken prisoner, but his life was spared because of his ecclesiastical character; he was sent to prison in Luján (province of Buenos Aires) and from there to the Convent of Pilar also in the province of Buenos Aires; in 1815 Orellana was sent to Spain where he became the Bishop of Avila; died in that city in 1821.

ORFILA, (WASHINGTON) ALEJANDRO (1925-   ). Foreign service officer; Secretary-General of Organization of American States, 1975-   .
      Born in Mendoza, son of prosperous wine-producing family; his first name (never used) of "Washington" reflects admiration of his father for George Washington; completed law studies at University of Buenos Aires; later studied political science at Stanford University (California) and foreign trade at Tulane (New Orleans, La.); entered Argentine foreign service in 1946; served in Moscow and Poland; became consul in San Francisco and New Orleans; moved to Washington where he held various posts in the Argentine embassy, including that of minister, and was director of information for OAS; in 1960-1962 he served as ambassador to Japan, spent the period from 1962 to 1973 in private business, mostly in U.S.; recalled to diplomatic service in 1973 by Perón's government; sent to Washington as ambassador; in May 1975 he was elected Secretary-General of OAS.

ORGANIC STATUTE OF POLITICAL PARTIES (1945). Decree signed by President Farrell calling for a committee to terminate political fraud within political parties; it provided for control of parties through electoral courts; all parties had to follow the directives of the statute; filing with the courts the program, platform, organization, and the officers of the party; a party could lose its permit if it failed to present a candidate in national elections or formed a coalition with other parties; "international affiliations" were also forbidden; it became law in 1945, but the opposition from the parties was so strong that the law was repealed by October of the same year.

ORGANIZATION OF AMERICAN STATES (OAS). Charter signed in 1948 in Bogotá was designed to place inter-American relations on firm treaty basis; Argentina did not ratify the treaty until April 1956; the country, at the time of the Bogotá meeting, was under the leadership of Perón who objected to the charter because he preferred bilateral agreements; he also opposed the establishment of a permanent military agency; in 1955 President Lonardi announced that Argentina would sign the treaty which provides a permanent framework within which political, economic and social questions are to be resolved; after the charter was signed Argentina joined the International Monetary Fund and cooperated with the USA armed forces; this relative friendliness of the late 1950s cooled again in the 1960s when, in Rio de Janeiro, Argentina, always a lukewarm member of the inter-American system, opposed the security structure on overseas threats; Article three of the agreement was proposed to read as follows: "An armed attack to any state shall be considered as an attack against all American states," but Argentina protested and an agreement was reached; as a result Article three says that if a country should be attacked from the inside the members are forced to assist the victim, but if the attack is made by a foreign country, the members should consult each other before taking action; also, as suggested by Argentina, Article 7 reads: "In event of conflict between member states the other members would try to solve it by peaceful means; for Argentina there is no greater evil than intervention; its policy is 'continental solidarity, but individual policy'; Argentines are inclined to view with suspicion any international organization, especially if the USA should appear to be stealing the limelight; in 1975 an Argentine, Alejandro Orfila, was elected secretary-general of the OAS (see Inter-American Affairs).

ORIA, SALVADOR (1883-1952).   Lawyer, journalist, writer, financier.
          Born in the province of Buenos Aires; studied in the university of Buenos Aires; began to write at an early age, in El Tiempo and El Diario; also published plays for the theater; taught finance at the University of Buenos Aires and was member of the board of the School of Economics; represented the province of Buenos Aires before the Supreme Court as judge for civil cases referring to the province; a founder of the Banco Hipotecario Nacional (National Mortgage Bank) and of the Banco Central in 1936; became president of the Bridges and Road Commission in 1938; Minister of Public Labor in 1940 for President Ramón Castillo; died in Buenos Aires; published: Legislación impositiva, Argentina; El problema actual de la moneda argentina; among his dramatic works are: Divina and La senda del mal.

ORIBE, FRANCISCO (1798-1866). Military officer. Born in Montevideo of Spanish parents; like his brothers Manual and Ignacio, he fought against the Spaniards during the revolutionary wars; transferred from the Húsares Orientales to Uruguayan army after this country declared independence; he was second in command when his brother (Manuel) became president and fought against Rivera under the orders of his other brother; after Rivera's triumph he emigrated to Argentina where he joined the forces fighting Rivera; after Urquiza defeated Rivera, Oribe returned to Uruguay.

ORIBE, IGNACIO (1795-1866). Military officer. Also born in Uru-

guay; supported Artigas, the caudillo, and opposed the forces
of the Supreme Director of Argentina; when Montevideo was
taken by the Portuguese, Ignacio moved to Buenos Aires where
he joined the army in Santa Fe; during the period of anarchy
(1820s) he returned to Uruguay, at the time part of the Brazilian empire; worked in agriculture until the Lavalleja forces
rebelled against the foreigners; after the battle of Sarandí he
joined the Alvear forces in war against Brazil; fell prisoner to
the Brazilians after the battle of Ituzaingó and was taken to
Rio de Janeiro where he remained until 1828; after obtaining
his liberty returned to Montevideo where he was appointed minister of war and navy during the government of Lavalleja; appointed General Chief of the army by his brother Manuel, the
president, to replace Rivera; emigrated to Buenos Aires in
1838 after the resignation of his brother; returned later to aid
in siege of Montevideo, but, after his brother capitulated to
Urquiza (1851) Ignacio retired from the army; lived at his
ranch until his death only five months after that of his brother,
Francisco.

ORIBE, MANUEL (1792-1857).   Uruguayan political and military
     leader, closely involved in Argentine internal politics, 1817-
     1851; second president of Uruguay.
          Born in Montevideo; early joined in patriot fight against
     royalists; fought at Cerrito (1812), a royalist defeat; joined
     José Gervasio Artigas, Uruguayan independence leaders, as
     gunner, and then supported Fructuoso Rivera; when Portuguese
     from Brazil took over Montevideo he went to Buenos Aires and
     joined government forces against rebelling provincial armies;
     fought at Cepeda (1820) under Balcarce; in 1825 became one of
     "Immortal 33" who accompanied Juan Antonio Lavalleja back to
     Uruguay to free their country from the Brazilians; in 1826 be-
     came part of Carlos María de Alvear's Argentine forces in war
     against Brazil and fought at Ituzaingó; when Uruguay became
     independent in 1828, Rivera became first president and appoint-
     ed Oribe as minister of war and navy; in 1835 was chosen sec-
     ond president, with Rivera remaining as commander of mili-
     tary; in a power struggle between them, precipitated by Oribe's
     attempt to remove Rivera from command, the latter won and
     resumed presidency (1839); Oribe fled to Buenos Aires where
     Rosas, antagonized by Rivera's welcome of unitarists and other
     Rosas opponents into Uruguay, recognized Oribe as constitu-
     tional president of that country and joined forces with him;
     Rivera declared war on Argentina.
          For more than a decade (1839-1851) the civil war of
     Uruguay and unitarist revolt against Rosas involved the Río de
     la Plata area in a prolonged struggle, with most of the fighting
     taking place on Argentine soil; Oribe fought in Santa Fe under
     Estanislao López, then was made chief commander of Rosas'
     armies; pursued unitarist forces of Juan Lavalle (q. v.) across
     northern Argentina, defeating them in Quebracho Herrado (Cór-
     doba) and finally at Famaillá (q. v.); returning eastward he
     crushed the anti-Rosas forces in Corrientes and Entre Ríos;

in latter province met his rival Rivera and thoroughly routed
him at battle of Arroyo Grande December 6, 1842; entered
Uruguay and began his siege of Montevideo from the landward
side while Rosas besieged it from the sea (see "Great War"),
eventually British and French attempted to help break the siege
(see Blockades) but the way was finally opened for Oribe, already in control of rest of Uruguay, to retake Montevideo in
1851; by then Urquiza had pronounced against Rosas and Oribe
(who had hoped to devote himself again to presidency of Uruguay) was forced instead to form government that joined Urquiza's (Entre Ríos forces) and Brazil in the effort that overthrew the Rosas government at Caseros (1852); Oribe went to
Barcelona, Spain, but returned a few years later; died in Montevideo.

ORKO-MAMAN. Quechua goddess of earthquakes and mountain mys-
teries; a blonde who combs her long hair seated on a rock
looking at herself in a calm lake; this Indian legend, popular
in Santiago del Estero, is part of today's folklore like Pachamama; Orko-Maman, of Indian origin, means "Mother of the
Hills."

ORO, FRANCISCO DOMINGO DE (1800-1879). Public figure. Born
in San Juan, studied in Buenos Aires at Colegio de San Carlos;
in 1820 attempted, unsuccessfully, to serve as intermediary
between San Martín and the rebellious forces of Mendizábal in
San Juan; returning, he was captured by another revolutionary
force and sent to prison in Jáchal (San Juan); while there was
sent to obtain aid against the Chilean caudillo José Miguel
Carrera who threatened to attack province of San Juan; Oro
forced Carrera to go back to Mendoza; after obtaining his freedom, moved to Entre Ríos where he served the governor General Lucio N. Mansilla; Bernardino Rivadavia sent him as secretary on Alvear-Díaz Vélez mission to obtain help from General Bolívar; after the failure of this mission he was sent to
Lima, Peru, as secretary of the Argentina legation; also appointed as representative to the first attempted Inter-American
congress in Panama; in 1826 he returned to Argentina and
joined San Juan forces to fight against Facundo Quiroga; later
moved to Buenos Aires; founded a newspaper El Porteño to attack Governor Dorrego's policies; accepted a post in the ministry of war and accompanied Juan Manuel de Rosas in his expedition to the south against the Indians; after his return he
visited Santa Fe and Corrientes and several other provinces;
for political reasons he moved to Chile in 1835; returned to
San Juan but was accused of treason and emigrated to Chile
again; there Oro published pamphlets against Rosas, one of
them, published in 1840, called El tirano de los pueblos argentinos; he returned to Buenos Aires after the battle of Caseros
and worked with Bartolomé Mitre and Domingo Faustino Sarmiento; died in the province of Buenos Aires.

ORO, JUSTO SANTA MARIA DE (1772-1836). Dominican priest who

played important public and religious role in independence and
early national periods; signer of Declaration of Independence;
first bishop of Cuyo.

Born in San Juan; taught at home, then sent to Santiago,
Chile, to be educated for Dominican Order; ordained there in
1794; won competitive chair of arts (including theology) at the
University of San Felipe, where he taught four years; having
become head of Dominican Order in Chile, he traveled to Spain
in 1809 to make arrangements for establishment of a more advanced seminary in Chile and reforms for the three Dominican
houses in Cuyo under his care; while in Spain, learned of the
May Revolution; returned to Chile to become supporter of Chilean independence movement under Bernardo O'Higgins, deported
to Mendoza, along with other O'Higgins supporters, by Carrera, Father Santa María de Oro was sought out by San Martín
desirous of accurate information about the current political situation in Chile; thereafter the two men became close friends
and collaborators; returning to San Juan, Dr. Santa María de
Oro aided in the organization of the Army of the Andes and
then was elected to represent his native province at the Congress of Tucumán, along with Francisco Narciso de Laprida;
during his year there, he put his mark on several political and
religious actions taken; commanding respect because of his
learning and administrative experience and abilities, and always
ready to speak eloquently in favor of his convictions as well as
to act on them, he became one of the most ardent supporters
of declaring independence; he offered the motion by which Saint
Rose of Lima was accepted by the Congress as patroness of
Spanish South America; and his greatest national contribution is
usually considered to be his adamant stand in the congress
against accepting any form of monarchy without first submitting
it to a vote of the people; his threat to resign if any other
course should be taken, as well as his arguments about traditional Argentine democracy may have been decisive; Joaquín V.
González, a later historian, declared that it was an irrefutable
historic truth to say that the republic owed its existence to Oro,
as otherwise monarchy would have been established in 1816;
after leaving the congress early in 1817, Oro returned to San
Juan, became involved in politics and went into exile in Chile
in 1818; served as provincial of Dominicans there for five
years; deported in 1825 to Juan Fernández Island, accused of
supporting his old friend O'Higgins against Freire government;
devoted rest of his life to religious responsibilities; became
first bishop of Cuyo, a diocese that he had been largely responsible in forming; devoted his energies to building cathedral in
San Juan, along with better educational institutions, including
one for women; buried in San Juan cathedral following his death
in 1836.

Domingo Faustino Sarmiento has paid moving tribute to
his fellow-citizen of San Juan in his Recuerdos de provincia.

ORO DE RODRIGUEZ, TRANSITO (1789-1856).   Teacher; librarian.
Sister of Justo Santa María de Oro, born in San Juan; founded,

with Domingo Faustino Sarmiento, the first high school of the
province of San Juan; inaugurated on July 9, 1839; acted as the
first dean of the school under the directorship of Sarmiento;
when Sarmiento emigrated to Chile, she remained as Interim
Director; died in the city of San Juan in 1859, after serving
the community not only as a teacher but also as organizer of
libraries.

ORTEGA, RUFINO (1847-1917).   Governor of the province of Mendoza; public figure; and member of the armed forces.

Born in Mendoza; started his military career in the
navy, in the ship Pampero; in 1865 fought in the Paraguayan
war and remained in the army as second lieutenant; was transferred to Cuyo, where he fought in the battle of San Ignacio;
in 1868 was transferred as captain to the service of the frontier; on the frontier of Mendoza he founded the General San
Martín fort from which he carried out several attacks against
the Indians; also took part in the Campaña al Desierto under
the orders of Julio A. Roca; in 1882 was second in command
of the army that went to Nahuel Huapi; became governor of
Mendoza, 1884; was elected national senator four years later;
before retiring from the army in 1912, Rufino Ortega was commander of several military regions; died in the city of Buenos
Aires while serving in the senate.

ORTIZ, FRANCISCO J. (1836-1932).   Lawyer; cabinet minister;
writer.

Born in Salta; studied law in the University of Córdoba
and graduated in 1857; returned to Salta in 1858 and entered
politics; wrote political essays in La Actualidad; in 1846 became general minister of cabinet of Governor Aguirre; in 1867,
when Felipe Varela attacked Salta, Ortiz was put in charge of
the defense of the city; as result of the siege, he wrote a
well-known poem, to which music was added, known as La
varelita; also wrote folklore classic La zamba de Vargas;
elected national senator by Salta in 1880; resigned in 1883 to
become minister of foreign relations and culture; bore some
responsibility for the expulsion of Papal Nuncio, Monsignor Luis
Mattera, from the country in the church-state school controversy; defended vigorously Argentine claims to the Malvinas Islands (Falkland Islands); after Miguel Juárez Celman was selected as candidate for president, Ortiz left for Europe; after
his return, he settled in Buenos Aires; in 1903 he wrote the
Rural Code for the province of Salta; became deeply interested
in project to build a railroad that would have joined the Salta
mountains through the Desert of Atacama with Chile, but
failed to obtain necessary cooperation from the government;
moved to Córdoba in 1913 and died in retirement at Villa Allende; before dying, he published Episodios del ataque a Salta
por las hordas de Felipe Varela el 10 de octubre de 1867, an
interesting short recollection of the attack; his remains were
taken to the Recoleta cemetery (Buenos Aires) in 1933 and a
street was named in his honor in 1934.

ORTIZ, JOSE SANTOS (1785-1835).   Political leader in San Luis in
    early years of independence.
        Born in province of San Luis; studied philosophy and
theology in the University of Córdoba; after returning home,
he was appointed captain of the militia; became president of
the cabildo when San Luis separated from Mendoza in 1820;
while attempting to organize the new province he was forced
to leave by the invasion of José Miguel Carrera in 1821; after
Carrera was defeated and killed in San Juan, Ortiz returned
to occupy the governorship again, and remained in power until
1829; while in power he signed several agreements with the
province of Mendoza, helped with the war in Brazil, and attempted to have a constitution adopted in 1826, but the legislature of the province refused to accept it; after his term ended,
Ortiz joined Facundo Quiroga, federalist caudillo of the north,
and fought in the battle of Oncativo against General Paz who
took him prisoner; regaining his freedom, he returned to Mendoza where he became minister of war for governors Lemos
and Nolasco Ortiz; in 1834 he went to Buenos Aires for vacation and agreed to accompany Quiroga on his mission of peace
to Santiago del Estero; on their way back he was murdered in
Barranca Yaco along with Facundo Quiroga.

ORTIZ, ROBERTO M. (1886-1942).   President of the Republic from
    1938 to 1942.
        Born in Buenos Aires; studied in the University of Bue-
nos Aires, medicine first, and law later, graduating as a lawyer in 1909; joined the Unión Cívica Radical and was elected
national representative in 1920; he was active in public economic and financial affairs, while winning distinction as corporation lawyer for foreign companies; in 1924 he was appointed director of the nation's internal tax offices and showed his
common sense and ability in administrative affairs; was appointed as minister of public works in 1925 by President Alvear; joined with latter in the Junta del City (q.v.) attempt to
reorganize the Radical Party (1931); in 1935 he was appointed
as minister of finance by President Justo; Ortiz resigned this
post in 1937 to become the Concordancia's candidate for president; like Justo, retiring president and leader of the Concordancia, he belonged to antipersonalist radical political faction;
after an election characterized by fraud and a probable secret
agreement between the radicals (who offered little opposition),
Ortiz became president in 1938; in spite of public disillusionment and political apathy at time of his election, as well as
the bad state of his health--he was a serious diabetic--Ortiz
was determined to restore honesty in government and constitutional elections by majority vote under Saenz Peña electoral
law; with firmness and considerable leadership, he imposed
this on the various provincial elections held in 1939 and 1940,
intervening when necessary, even in Catamarca (province of
his vice-president) and in Buenos Aires; progress toward this
goal was complicated by outbreak of World War II (q.v.) in
Europe and by his own worsening health; Germany invaded

Poland September 1, 1939, and three days later President Ortiz declared that Argentina would maintain its traditional policy of neutrality in this war; May 14, 1940, as Nazis invaded Western Europe, he repeated this declaration of neutrality but insisted that it did not mean either absolute indifference or lack of sensitivity toward the victims; Ortiz's sympathies were considered to be pro-allied and he modified slightly Argentina's somewhat anti-U.S. position in the Pan American meetings held in 1939 and 1940; his primary concern was to strengthen Argentina's own defenses as much as possible; took the initiative in establishing what would later become the General Directorate of Military Factories (q.v.); in July 1940 he was forced, because of blindness, to delegate his powers to vice-president Ramón Castillo; the following month the scandal about the sale of land for a military airport at El Palomar, adjacent to the Military Academy, in which many of the president's friends had illegally made enormous profits, reached its climax in congressional investigation; Ortiz offered his resignation but it was overwhelmingly rejected by Congress; in June 1942, with power having been delegated to Castillo much of the time, Ortiz resigned the presidency; died the following month; with Ramón Castillo's (q.v.) accession to the presidency, internal political policy became more conservative and authoritarian and the balance of power passed to uncompromising wealthy rightist group, preparing the way for the GOU military revolt of 1943.

ORTIZ DE OCAMPO, FRANCISCO ANTONIO (1771-1840). Military commander and public official during independence and early national period.

Born in La Rioja; fought for the first time during the Reconquista and defense of Buenos Aires against second British invasion (1807), as captain in the Cuerpo de Arribeños (Buenos Aires garrison); as a result of the invasions Ortiz de Ocampo left commerce and became member of the army; after the May Revolution of 1810 he was appointed commander-in-chief of the patriot forces being sent to Alto Perú (1810) "to carry the command of the people" to form new local juntas that recognized dependence on the Buenos Aires Junta; he was also expected to suppress any opposition to the idea of a national government; in Córdoba, Santiago de Liniers and the governor Gómez de la Concha, along with others, rebelled against the Junta of Buenos Aires; Ortiz de Ocampo took them prisoners, but when he hesitated in obeying the orders of the Junta to execute the leaders at once, he was replaced in command by Antonio González Balcarce; Ortiz de Ocampo remained for a short time as interim governor of Córdoba; transferred back to Buenos Aires he collaborated with José de San Martín in writing the army regulations; appointed president of Charcas, he remained in power until the defeats of Vilcapugio and Ayohuma lost Alto Perú for the patriots; in 1814, Supreme Director Posadas appointed him intendant governor of Córdoba; in 1815 he went to Mendoza to put himself under San Martín's orders; acted as governor of Mendoza when San Martín was ill; he left

the army in 1816 and became governor of La Rioja for a few
months; in 1819 he was again elected governor of La Rioja, remaining in power until removed by Facundo Quiroga; in 1826,
after trying unsuccessfully to obtain his past-due salaries, he
served under General Paz until he fell prisoner of Quiroga in
1831; he remained in La Rioja; died in the estancia of Angui-
non.

ORTIZ DE ROZAS, GERVASIO (1801-1855). Brother of Juan Manuel
Rosas and wealthy rancher; after acting as foreman for the
family's estancia that had been lost to Braulio Costa, Gervasio
purchased the ranch for the Rozas family again; his brother,
Juan Manuel, never trusted his political views and imprisoned
him in 1839; after escaping, he moved to Uruguay where he
remained until the 1850s when his brother called him back to
Buenos Aires; after the battle of Caseros, he was elected representative for the province of Buenos Aires, but died before
he had chance to serve.

ORTIZ DE ROZAS, JUAN (1868-1947).   Rancher and agronomist.
Born in Buenos Aires; member of the conservative
party; acted as undersecretary of the minister of agriculture;
president of the national commission of agriculture for ten
years, general director of agriculture, cattle and industry in
the province of Buenos Aires, minister of public works for the
province (1906); became representative in the national government in 1910 and senator in the twenties; while in Buenos Aires
was member of several Bank Boards of Directors (Banco de
la Provincia de Buenos Aires, Banco Español y del Río de la
Plata, and the Banco Hipotecario); founded several cattle establishments and received several prizes for his agricultural
studies and work; died in Buenos Aires.

ORTIZ DE ROZAS, JUAN MANUEL (1839-1913).   Public official.
Grandson of Juan Manuel de Rosas; born in Buenos Aires; accompanied his grandfather to Southampton when he was 12 and
remained with him until he was 19; at his return he worked
with British firms in the city of Buenos Aires; Urquiza gave
him a position in the Uruguayan legation; joined the army to
fight in the Paraguayan war; at his return, he moved to the
province of Buenos Aires and became quite wealthy; elected
several times as representative and once as senator for the
province of Buenos Aires; in 1880 was, under the presidency
of Sarmiento, General Director of Schools and founded 240
schools in the province of Buenos Aires; appointed minister of
finance and public works of the province of Buenos Aires in
1891; in 1893 and 1894 became president of the Provincial
Mortgage Bank; in 1910 was elected national senator and left
this post in 1913 to become governor of the province of Buenos Aires; died seven months later.

ORTIZ DE ROZAS, PRUDENCIO (1800-1857).   Military leader; estanciero.

Born in Buenos Aires; brother of Juan Manuel de Rosas; was early attracted to military career; in 1826 commanded garrison at fort at Barragán; fought against Lavalle in 1829; when Rosas became governor of Buenos Aires, he was appointed commandant at Chascomús; throughout the period of his brother's governorship he gave him political and military support, while continuing his own extensive, profitable ranching activities; owned an estancia near Azul and established fort there two years after town was founded; carried out punitive expeditions against Indians; successfully suppressed revolution of the south against Rosas at Chascomús (q. v.) in 1839; after fall of Rosas (1852), Prudencio Ortiz de Rozas went to Montevideo and then to Spain; immensely wealthy, he acquired a palace in Sevilla, where he died; in 1872 his remains were returned to Argentina to be buried in the family burial place in the Cementerio del Norte.

ORTIZ DE ZARATE, JUAN (d. 1576).   Third adelantado of Río de la Plata.
        Born in Vizcaya; in recognition of his services as conquistador in Peru, the viceroy there made him adelantado of the Río de la Plata area (1567), subject to royal approval; three years later in Spain, Ortiz de Zárate received the royal grant, good for two generations, making him responsible for settlement of at least 500 Spaniards, including artisans and farmers, and several thousand head of stock, while becoming the governor of the area, with unusual powers and land grants; after innumerable difficulties, many due to lack of funds, his expedition got under way in September, 1572; with hardships, leaking ships, bad weather, and desertions and deaths of many of those aboard, Zárate finally reached the American coast; on May 30, 1574, he established a short-lived colony on the Uruguayan coast, naming it San Salvador; formally renamed the whole area Nueva Vizcaya, in honor of his place of birth; finally reached Asunción, his capital, in 1575; died less than a year later, after having designated that his Adelantado title and rights should go to the future husband of his daughter Juana (q. v.).
        The story of Ortiz de Zárate's tragic voyage was told in the poem La Argentina by Martín del Barco Centenera (q. v.) who accompanied the expedition.

ORTIZ DE ZARATE, JUANA (1553-1584).   Tragic, legendary victim of Spanish conquest.   Daughter of conquistador Juan Ortiz de Zárate (q. v.) and Inca princess Leonor Yupanqui, she was brought up in Chuquisaca (modern Sucre), in traditions of both cultures; her father both legitimized her (1570) and protected her legal rights in his adelantado grant at his death by conferring them on the man whom she should marry; under guardianship and guidance of Juan de Garay, she married licenciado Juan de Torres de Vera y Aragón (see Torres de Vera y Aragón, Juan); her marriage, with the wealth and power conferred by her dowry, became immediate and long-enduring subject of social gossip and legal controversy, not ended by her death; her tragic, dramatic role in early Argentine history, kept alive in legend, has attracted attention from later historians; in Los adelantados del Río de la Plata, its authors, Pedro Acevedo, Tadeo and Ernesto J. Colombres, have published her biography.

ORTIZ DE ZARATE, PEDRO (1628-1683). Missionary; martyr.
Born in Jujuy; shortly after his wife died, at age 27, he began religious career; after studying at the Jesuit colegio and university in Córdoba, he was ordained as priest in Santiago del Estero by the bishop of Tucumán, Melchor de Maldonado y Saavedra; served for 24 years as curate in his native city; finally secured permission to enter the Chaco to establish two Jesuit missions; founded the first reducción, San Rafael, in 1683 with 400 families of Ojota and Taño Indians, and moved on to gather Tobas and Mocobíes into the second mission near the junction of the Jujuy and Tarija rivers; Indians killed him and his companions.
José Torre Revello made use of an extensive biography of him in Esteco y concepción del Bermejo (Buenos Aires, 1943).

ORTIZ DE ZARATE, RODRIGO (1554-1593). Conquistador. Born in Valladolid; came to Río de la Plata as alguacil mayor (head constable) in armada of Juan Ortiz de Zárate; filled this same post in Asunción, 1575, and two years later in Santa Fe; accompanied Juan de Garay on expedition north of Asunción; returned to Buenos Aires as captain and chief justice (elected by vecinos after Garay's death, 1583); was first to discover best route between Buenos Aires and Córdoba; in letter to king describing his services, mentioned that he had prepared defenses of Buenos Aires against possible English attack; shortly thereafter he went up the royal highway to Charcas and to Lima, where he died.

ORTIZ Y HERRERA, JOSE ANTONIO (1845-1911). Physician; public official; educator.
Born in San Juan; studied in Córdoba and the University of Buenos Aires; his studies were temporarily interrupted by the war against Paraguay, but after serving in the army, he completed his training; during the yellow fever epidemics of 1871 worked with the public commission to care for its victims; moved to Córdoba in the 1880s and was in charge of the Lazareto (charity hospital) during the cholera epidemics of 1884; while in Córdoba was elected provincial senator and served as vice-governor; elected governor in 1907; he was also dean of the school of medicine and president of the University of Córdoba; after retiring, he moved to Buenos Aires where he died.

OSORIO, MARIANO DE (1777-1819). Commander of royalist forces in Chile during parts of wars of independence; opposed San

Martín at Cancha Rayada and Maipú.

Born in Sevilla; became officer in Spanish army and fought in various campaigns, including those against French Napoleonic forces; in 1810 became director of Catalonian gun factory; in 1812 he took his place in the royal army in Lima; was transferred to Chile, and commanded the Spanish royalist forces at Rancagua (October 20, 1814); now a brigadier general, Osorio was given both political and military authority over reconquered Chile; his zeal against Chilean patriots brought so many complaints that he was replaced by General Francisco Marcó del Pont and returned to Peru; two years later, following the patriot reconquest of Chile at Chacabuco (February 12, 1817), General Osorio returned in command of the Spanish expedition to regain Chile; after defeating San Martín at Cancha Rayada (March 19, 1818) he suffered disastrous defeat at Maipú (April 5, 1818), but escaped and returned to Peru, although Viceroy Pezuela approved his military actions in Chile, public opinion went against him; leaving Peru for Panama, Osorio was forced, by pursuing Chilean privateer, to disembark along the coast where he contracted the tropical fever that caused his death upon his arrival in Havana (see Rancagua; Cancha Rayada; Maipú).

OSSORIO ARANA, ARTURO (1902-   ).   Military officer.   Born in Buenos Aires; graduated from Colegio Militar and became second lieutenant in artillery unit; later became artillery instructor in Colegio and took advanced studies at the Escuela Superior Técnica; continued these in Europe (1937-1940); in 1949 he was assigned to artillery school in Córdoba as director; two years later (December, 1951) he took part in unsuccessful attempt to overthrow Perón's government; in September, 1955 he accompanied General Eduardo Lonardi and other artillery officers in taking over the Artillery School in Córdoba as base of revolt against Perón; after military government under Lonardi replaced that of Perón, Ossorio Arana was used as interventor in Buenos Aires province and then, with rank brigadier general, in Lonardi's cabinet as minister of army; in 1957 assumed duties of commandant-general of army.

OTAMENDI, FERNANDO (1800-1866).   Rancher; important developer of southern part of Buenos Aires province.

Born in province of Buenos Aires; from youth was occupied with his rural interests; became very active in southern revolt against Rosas; fought at Chascomús (q.v.) and was taken prisoner by Prudencio Ortiz de Rozas; suffered persecution and torture from Mazorca (q.v.) and was called by Rosas a "salvaje unitario acérrimo" (an all-out, or very bitter, unitarist savage); obtaining his freedom, he went into exile in Uruguay; returned after Rosas had been driven from the country; was elected to provincial legislature in 1855 and to its senate in 1860 and 1866; he also served as justice of peace in his community, 1863-1866.

OTERO, JOSE PACIFICO (1871-1937). Historian. Franciscan priest
    born in Buenos Aires; entered convent in Córdoba, obtained
    his Ph.D. in philosophy and law; Father Otero first attracted
    attention through his sermons and his writing of Franciscan
    chronicles; his research for the latter took him to all the
    Franciscan convents, especially those of Mendoza, Salta, and
    Tucumán where the first Franciscans built convents and
    churches; in 1902 and 1903 he published the biography of Sor
    María Antonia de la Paz y Figueroa (q. v.) and Dos héroes de
    la conquista. La Orden Franciscana en el Tucumán y El
    Plata, about Fray Francisco Solano and Fray Luis de Bolaños
    (qq. v.); in 1907 he published El padre Castañeda. Su obra
    ante la posteridad y en la historia, publicizing the work of the
    pamphleteer of the May Revolution (see Francisco Castañeda);
    his last publication on Franciscan history, entitled La Orden
    Franciscana en el Uruguay, was published in 1908 and told the
    history of the Franciscan Order in Uruguay; after a trip to
    Europe he left the Franciscan order and a little later, in 1909,
    abandoned the priesthood; married in 1912 and left Argentina;
    in Europe he published La crisis de mi fe in which he ex-
    plained why he left the priesthood; worked as a lawyer and
    carried on extensive historical investigations; in 1932 he pub-
    lished in Buenos Aires the Historia del libertador José de San
    Martín, 4 volumes (8 vols., 1944-1945), a detailed and com-
    prehensive study for which he used much new, previously un-
    published material found in Europe; after his return to Argen-
    tina he became involved in founding the Instituto Sanmartiniano;
    divorced in 1935, he returned to the Franciscan Covent where
    he died two years later.

OTTAWA AGREEMENT (1932). Agreement signed in Ottawa, Can-
    ada, in 1932 between Britain and members of its Common-
    wealth, in effort to ease hardships of world-wide depression;
    it provided for an imperial preference system, with members
    of the Commonwealth assured a privileged share of British
    market for their food products in return for favored positions
    in Commonwealth markets for British manufactures; its effect
    on Argentine economy, based primarily, for decades, on free
    trade with Great Britain, was shattering; President Justo's
    government was forced to make immediate economic changes,
    of which the most important was the Roca-Runciman (q. v.)
    agreement (see Agustín P. Justo).

OTTSEN, HENDRICK (16th century). Dutch navigator who attempted
    to start trade with Buenos Aires in 1599; reached Buenos Ai-
    res in 1599 and attempted to negotiate trading rights from
    Governor Diego Rodríguez de Valdés but failed and was forced
    to return to Holland; it took him two hard years to reach his
    home country; there he published his diary under the name
    Corto y verídico relato de la desgraciada navegación de un
    buque de Amsterdam; in it he described the city of Buenos
    Aires and its customs as they were in 1599; the book pub-
    lished in 1603 (with facsimile Dutch edition in 1918), was

translated into Spanish and published in Buenos Aires in 1943 as Un buque holandés en América del Sud, 1598-1601.

OUTES, FELIX (1878-1939).   Pioneer of Argentine anthropological sciences.
Born and educated in Buenos Aires; Outes did his graduate work in Europe and the U.S.; published first monograph, about Querandíes, in 1897; his most important work was The Stone Age in Patagonia; contributed to the Bulletin of the Argentinian Geographic Institute, the Annals of the Argentinian Scientific Society, the Annals of the National Museum of Buenos Aires, Magazine of the Museum of La Plata; he also wrote in Revista Nacional and La Nación; founded first chair for Anthropology and Archeology in the University of Buenos Aires (1920) where he taught; later also taught and formed school of anthropology in University of La Plata; some of his other publications were: La viejas razas argentinas, 1910; Los aborígenes de la República Argentina, 1910; Las hachas, insignias patagónicas, 1916; and others; was a member in several national and international societies and took part in many national and international congresses; acted as secretary of the first Congreso Científico Latino Americano meeting in 1898 and again in 1901; in 1929 he prepared an economic map of the country for the School of Economics; in 1930 became director of the Museo Etnográfico of the University of Buenos Aires; in the same year he became honorary member of the Royal Anthropological Society of London and member of American Anthropological Society; he died in the city of Buenos Aires before he could assume the presidency of the university, to which he had been appointed, his last honor.

OYUELA, CALIXTO (1857-1935).   Writer and poet.
Born in Buenos Aires; he was basically a poet; won several prizes, the first in 1881 with his Canto al arte; in 1881 he published Estudio sobre la vida y escritos del poeta catalán Manuel de Cabanyes; in 1882 Eros, despedida de la infancia: Cuatro cantos, and a study on Andrés Bello; he founded the writers' journal Revista Científica y Literaria in which he published several critical works; as a member of the "Generation of 1880" (q.v.) he was a close friend and admirer of Rafael Obligado; before becoming a lawyer, a profession that he never practiced, he taught in high school and in the university where he taught Spanish literature; he visited the U.S.A. as Argentine secretary of the first Pan American Conference; at his return he published his most famous poem Canto al Niágara; his last publication came in 1910 with his Canto a la patria and Lecturas selectas; Oyuela continued writing but nothing further was published until after his death; became president of the Academia de Letras, founded in 1931; remained in that post until 1935; Oyuela is considered one of the best scholarly writers of early 20th century.

OYUELA, JOSE MARIA DE LA (1786-1849).   Military man.   Born

in Buenos Aires of Spanish parents; his father was regidor of
the Cabildo but was not invited to the open cabildo of May 22,
1810 (May Revolution); José María started his career during
British invasions and in 1807 was Liniers' aide-de-camp;
joined the patriot forces when the revolution broke out and
joined army of the north as an alférez (second lieutenant);
fought in Suipacha, Huaqui, and Cotagaita; in 1813 he was
transferred to company of Pardos y Morenos; captured by Spaniards in 1814; in 1816 he returned to the army of the north
where he served under Belgrano; in 1820 Oyuela moved to
Tucumán and served in the provincial militia while Aráoz was
governor of the province; in 1841 moved to San Juan with the
militia but when the government was taken by General Acha,
fought with federalists against the unitarists; in 1844 became
interim governor of San Juan, and in the same year, legislator for that province; and on the way to Buenos Aires was
robbed of all his possessions by an Indian malón (q.v.); remained in Buenos Aires until 1847 when, as a result of wounding the Portuguese chargé d'affaires in a duel, he was exiled
to Guardia de Lobos, where he died in 1849.

- P -

PACHAMAMA.   Mother goddess of the earth among Diaguita and Calchaquí Indians; invoked before planting, hunting, and in case of
sickness; name comes from pacha meaning "world," mama,
"the Mother"; the myth still exists in northwestern Argentina;
no longer of religious significance, but important in folklore,
as part of the land.   Today the word is used basically to refer to love of the land.

PACHECO, ANGEL (1793-1869).   Military commander, general.
          Born in Santiago de Chile; moved to Buenos Aires at
early age; became one of original officers in San Martín's
granaderos a caballo; fought at San Lorenzo and later, in
army of the Andes, at Chacabuco, Curapaligüe, Cancha Rayada,
Maipú, and Bío Bío; after his return to Buenos Aires he was
given command of a cavalry battalion in the war against Brazil;
took part, as a key officer, in Rosas' frontier war against the
Indians (1833); in 1834, after Rosas and several others had refused to accept the governorship of Buenos Aires province, it
was offered to him but he also refused it; accepted cabinet appointment as minister of war; later became legislator and arms
inspector; although a personal friend of Rosas, he refused to
become engaged further in politics; considered it his mission
to serve military purposes of whatever government was in power; fought against unitarists in Fraile Muerto, San Calá, and
Rodeo del Medio (q.v.); when Urquiza pronounced against Rosas
and organized an army to overthrow him, Rosas asked Pacheco
(after General Mansilla had refused) to take over command of
the government forces; after refusing at first he reluctantly accepted and moved to intercept Urquiza's forces as they crossed

the Paraná into Buenos Aires province; withdrew toward Caseros leaving delaying force behind; about that time a rumor
spread throughout the army and to Rosas that Pacheco planned
to defect to the enemy; Rosas immediately took over personal
command of the army; shortly before battle of Caseros Pacheco resigned, on grounds that Rosas' action proved lack of confidence in him; retired to his ranch at Talar; his biographer
Ernesto Quesada said of him that he was born a soldier and
died one; at his funeral Bartolomé Mitre, who had known him
well, delivered the eulogy.

PACHECO DE BORGES, JOSE FRANCISCO (1731-1809).   Priest;
historian.
        Born in Portugal; emigrated to Buenos Aires as a child;
entered the Franciscan order as a young adult and became
priest in 1756; in 1763 was sent to the Franciscan Convent in
Santiago del Estero where he remained until 1791; during that
period he wrote his Crónica del convento de San Francisco de
la ciudad de Santiago del Estero; in 1792 he was transferred
to the Convento of San Diego in Salta, there wrote a complete
description of the history of the first seven years of the city
founded by Hernando de Lerma; this history was published for
the first time in 1861 in the Revista del Paraná; in 1807 he
wrote and gathered documents about the first hundred years of
the province but could not finish due to his death; this Franciscan saved for posterity local documents and several of the
Actas of the province.

PACHECO DE MELO, JOSE ANDRES (1779-sometime after 1825).
Priest; member of Congress of Tucumán and signer of Declaration of Independence; government official and public figure.
        Born in Salta; schoolmate there of Martín Güemes, with
whom he maintained lifetime friendship; entered seminary of
Our Lady of Loreto in Córdoba; ordained as priest; was assigned as curate of town of Libi-Libi in province of Chichas
(now in southern Bolivia); became leader of independence movement there and organized resources of his province to support
revolutionary armies in Alto Perú; sent to Congress of Tucumán, he signed the declaration of independence and remained
active in it until it was dissolved (1819); was serving as its
president in April 1818 when the formal national celebration of
victory of Maipú took place; during the difficult years following
anarchy of 1819, his services were used as peacemaker in
Córdoba (1821) and San Juan (1825) and as cabinet minister in
Mendoza under governors Pedro Molina and José Albino Gutiérrez; retired from public life in 1825; died several years
later.

PACHECO Y MELO DE ANZOATEGUI, CELEDONIA DE (1789-1842).
Patriot in independence period.   Niece of the Spanish viceroy
Pedro Melo de Portugal, Marquis of Vilena, born in Salta,
and educated there; married in 1809 to José de Anzoátegui y
Alzaga, officer of the Cajas Reales of Salta and Tucumán;

when news of the revolution reached their province, she joined
the revolutionists, against the desires of her husband; offered
not only monetary help but her services also; the legend goes
that the gaucho Martín Guemes took refuge in her ranch many
times; died in the city of her birth.

PACIFIC RAILROAD (Ferrocarril del Pacífico).   Known today as the
San Martín railroad (see Railroads).

PACK, DIONISIO (DENIS) (1772-1823).   Irish officer who served in
British invading armies, 1806-1807.   Arrived in Buenos Aires
with the British invaders, in command of the Highlanders Regiment number 71; during the 1806 invasion was taken prisoner
with General Beresford (q. v.); escaped and returned to England; he took part in the second invasion (1807) and surrendered
in the church of Santo Domingo; after his return to Great
Britain, he fought in Spain against Napoleonic forces and was
in charge of a brigade in the battle of Waterloo; married
Beresford's daughter; died in London as major general.

PACKING HOUSES see REFRIGERATION

PACTO CUADRILATERO see QUADRILATERAL PACT

PACTO DE BENEGAS see BENEGAS, TREATY OF

PACTO DE 8 OCTUBRE 1851.   On May 31, 1851, Urquiza signed
an alliance between Entre Ríos (separated from the confederation since May of the same year), Brazil, and the government
of Montevideo to fight against General Oribe; Urquiza immediately invaded Uruguay; Oribe offered little resistance and capitulated on October 8; by the terms of the pact it was declared that there were neither vanquished nor victorious Uruguayans; as result of this campaign on November 21, 1851, a
new pact was signed between Brazil, Entre Ríos, Corrientes,
and Uruguay to end the domination of Juan Manuel de Rosas;
Urquiza received the military command of the forces; revisionist historians who consider Rosas a hero call this treaty
an act of treason against the country because it involved foreign forces in an internal Argentine struggle.

PACTO DE UNION Y ALIANZA (1830).   Agreement signed in Córdoba by the province of Salta to join the Liga del Interior, also called Liga Unitaria (see Unitarists).

PACTO DEL PILAR (February 23, 1820).   Agreement signed between governor Sarratea of Buenos Aires and Estanislao López
of Santa Fe, and Francisco Ramírez of Entre Ríos, in attempt
to end the war among those provinces and to work together
towards the formation of a national government and national
organization; the agreement established the way in which representatives should be called to the convention that would organize a federal regime, it established alliance against the

Portuguese in Brazil and Uruguay, free navigation of the
rivers, granted amnesty to political enemies, and declared
free trade between the provinces; the agreement was never
carried out because Artigas, powerful at that time, opposed
it, preventing its approval, and the war continued.

PACTO FEDERAL (November 20, 1852). Treaty signed among the
littoral provinces; it invited all the other provinces to participate in a Constitutional convention to be held in the province
of Santa Fe; this agreement served as the law of the nation
until the constitution of 1853 was sanctioned by the provinces.

PACTOS DE MAYO (May 28, 1902). Agreement signed with Chile
settling long-standing boundary problems, consisting of four
separate documents, it also provided for limitation of naval
armaments (canceled shortly afterward); the signers of the
agreement were José Antonio Terry, for Argentine Republic,
and the minister of foreign relations of Chile, José Vergara
Donoso; the British king was requested to name the technical
commission to draw the boundary between the two countries;
to commemorate the signing of the agreement the Christ of the
Andes was erected on the frontier between Chile and Argentina.

PADILLA, ERNESTO E. (1873-1951). Lawyer, writer, politician.
Born in Tucumán; graduated as a lawyer in the University of Buenos Aires with the highest honors; elected provincial legislator in 1900; elected national congressman (1902-
1906); his congressional speech opposing the proposed divorce
law has been published by the Catholic Church several times;
reelected congressman in 1911; became governor of his province in 1913; favored the founding of the University of Tucumán; returned to congress between 1918 and 1928; while in
congress tried to obtain funds to build a railroad to Chile; after the 1930 revolution, became minister of education and public instruction in President Uriburu's cabinet; resigned in 1931;
interested in folklore; wrote several monographs and books on
the subject like Cancionero popular I and II; La condición;
Huaytiquina; other books dealt with history and religion:
Apuntes sobre geografía histórica de Tucumán; San Francisco
Solano en la Argentina; La vida y obra pictórica de Ignacio
Bas y la iconografía Tucumana; died in Buenos Aires.

PADILLA, MANUEL (1856-1935). Physician and statesman.
Born in Jujuy; graduated from the University of Buenos
Aires in 1882; returned to Jujuy where he was elected provincial representative (1883); after three years of work and political activity (minister of government briefly in 1886), became
national congressman; in 1889 was for second time minister of
government in Jujuy; as such, he was part of the commission
that solved boundary problems with Salta; returned to the legislature in 1897 and 1906; elected national senator between
1911 and 1913; remained in Buenos Aires as director of the

national penitentiary until 1919; returned to Jujuy and became
governor in 1929; died in Buenos Aires.

PADILLA, MANUEL ANICETO (1765-d. after independence was won).
Early propagandist for independence.
    Born in Cochabamba (now in Bolivia); dedicated from
youth to spreading idea of independence from Spain; traveled
through Europe and America acquiring reputation as an intellectual because of his extensive knowledge of political science,
history, and literature and his familiarity with modern and
classical languages; became collaborator with Francisco de
Miranda, Venezuelan precursor of Spanish South American independence, whom he represented in Buenos Aires 1802-1806;
acted also as British agent before the invasions; joined independence group led by Juan José Castelli, including Saturnino
and Nicolás Rodríguez Peña, Manuel Belgrano, Juan Martín de
Pueyrredón, among others; Padilla and Saturnino Rodríguez
Peña held several conferences with British General Beresford
while latter was imprisoned in Luján, following the Argentine
reconquest of Buenos Aires; British fled to Montevideo; Padilla became one of the main writers of the Spanish edition of
Estrella del Sur (q.v.); after having spent some time in Rio
de Janeiro, he returned to Argentina after the war for independence and died there.

PADILLA, MANUEL ASCENCIO (1773-1816). Guerrilla fighter for
independence.
    Born in Bolivia; joined the revolutionary movement of
1810 and fought at Tucumán, Salta, Vilcapugio, and Ayohuma;
most active in guerrilla warfare; fell prisoner of the Spaniards
but escaped and established his headquarters in northwestern
Argentina to continue his attacks against the Spaniards; on September 16, 1816, was taken prisoner by General Aguilera who
shot and beheaded him.

PADILLA Y BARCENA, PABLO (1848-1921). Bishop; educator;
writer. Entered the Seminary of Loreto in Córdoba at age of
10 years; remained there until 1872, when he was ordained by
the Bishop of Córdoba; transferred to Salta as canon of the
Cathedral; also taught literature and theology; founded schools
for girls in Salta, Catamarca, Tucumán, and Santiago del Estero, orphanages in Salta and Jujuy; became bishop of the region in 1885; was founding editor of La Esperanza, religious
newspaper of Salta; transferred to Tucumán as bishop (1893);
founded there the newspaper Heraldo and a magazine called
Stella; established a seminary for priests in 1904; died in Jujuy
while starting another seminary.

PADRE FILBERTO (March 1827). The forces of the Provincias Unidas del Río de la Plata defeated the Brazilians at this place,
opening the Rio Grande do Sul region of Brazil to the Argentines in the war with Brazil.

PAGE, JOHN (d. 1890). River explorer. Son of T. J. Page (q.v.);
  born in the U.S.A.; accompanied his father during his explorations of the Paraná from 1857 to 1858; in 1861 joined the
  army as a lieutenant and dedicated his life to exploring the
  Pilcomayo, the Otoquis and the Salado; retired in 1885 but returned to navigate the Bermejo; visited London where he gave
  lectures about his explorations; in 1889 was in command of a
  military expedition to the Pilcomayo, where he died on February 8, 1890; reburied in Buenos Aires in 1896.

PAGE, THOMAS JEFFERSON (1808-1899). U.S. naval officer; explored upper tributaries of the Río de la Plata in 1850s.
          Born in Virginia; joined navy; sent to Argentina on com-
  bined scientific and official trip; arrived in Buenos Aires May
  15, 1853, on the Water Witch; with support of Urquiza, he explored the Río de la Plata, Paraná, Paraguay, and Bermejo;
  was exerting some influence on negotiations for treaty desired
  by U.S. for free trade and navigation of the rivers when President Carlos Antonio López of Paraguay became angered at actions of other Americans in area and closed all Paraguayan
  waters to U.S. ships; Lieutenant Page's action in sending the
  Water Witch (q.v.) up the Paraná from Corrientes precipitated the incident that curtailed his activities; returned to the
  United States; three years later he published, in New York,
  an account of his experiences in Argentina, 1853-1856, entitled La Plata, the Argentine Federation, and Paraguay; fought
  in U.S. Civil War, on side of Confederacy; returned to Argentina where Sarmiento appointed him naval inspector; later resigned and went to Europe; died in Rome.

PAGO. Term originally used to designate rural section with vague
  limits within a larger Spanish administrative district; it might
  or might not have settlers, and usually included water around
  or along which settlement would be possible; for example, the
  most important pagos of Buenos Aires province around the
  middle of the seventeenth century were: Arroyos, Arrecifes,
  Cañada de la Cruz, Luján, Las Conchas, Matanza, Magdalena
  and Monte Grande; in 1717 the cabildo of Buenos Aires appointed justices of peace for the rural pagos.
          Later on "pago" became synonym of "partido," the lo-
  cal geographical, political unit into which a province may be
  divided (similar to county in U.S.).

PAGO LARGO, BATTLE OF. Site in Corrientes of battle in which
  General Pascual Echagüe, governor of Entre Ríos and acting
  on behalf of Rosas, totally defeated the anti-Rosas forces of
  Berón de Astrada (q.v.) March 31, 1839; the latter was killed
  during the fighting and, with the execution of other leaders after the battle, the uprising was suppressed.

PALACIOS, ALFREDO LORENZO (c. 1879-1963). Socialist leader;
  intellectual; legislator; writer and educator.
          Born in Buenos Aires; graduated from law school there;

later became professor and dean; also professor in faculty of
economic sciences, in which he first held chair of labor legislation; served as professor and dean of faculty of juridical
and social sciences of University of La Plata and as president
of latter university until he resigned all his academic assignments as protest against Peronism (1944).

Palacios early involved himself in politics; became one
of founders of Socialist Party (q. v.); was elected to Buenos
Aires legislature in 1902 and two years later became the first
socialist deputy to the national congress, having been elected
from the Federal Capital; reelected at various times thereafter;
quickly earned recognition as pioneer in labor legislation, by
effecting passage of first laws benefitting workers (1905); these
regulated labor of women and children and forbade night and
Sunday labor; used his influence as dean of Buenos Aires Law
School to request Hipólito Yrigoyen (q. v.) to resign from the
presidency (September 5, 1930); elected senator (1935-1943);
consistently fought for social justice and against electoral
fraud and corruption in conservative government; wanted reform by legal, not revolutionary, means; in 1940 joined in
forming Acción Argentina (see Argentine Action); favored Allies during World War II; became active opponent against Perón in early years of latter's government and spent more than
ten years fighting him, although persecuted and in exile; in
1955 Lonardi's government designated him ambassador to Uruguay; in 1957 he served as member of congress called to reform constitution of 1853; although retired from active political
life he continued influential in the Socialist Party.

Alfredo Palacios was one of the great intellectuals of
his period; an early Marxist, he led those Argentine Marxists
who insisted on accepting only those Marxist principles that
could be usefully adapted to Argentine realities; his bibliography is extensive, dealing with his Marxist-Socialist ideas and
the concerns of his various careers as jurisconsult and law
professor, as legislator, and as political party leader; in 1954
he published La justicia social, summing up his fifty-year
struggle for social justice provided by law.

PALACIOS, PEDRO BONIFACIO (1854-1917). Argentine writer of
the generation of the 1880s who wrote under the pseudonym of
Almafuerte (q. v.).

PALERMO PARK. Former estate of Juan Manuel de Rosas in Buenos Aires; taken over by the government after Caseros, and
made into a great public park in the 1870s; today also a residential area; race tracks are located there and the annual
prestigious livestock shows of the Sociedad Rural Argentina
have traditionally been held there.

PALIN (or PILMA). Name given by the Araucanian Indians to the
ball used to play pali-kuden.

PALITO. Picaresque folk dance that originated in the pampas, a

mixture of Indian dance forms and Spanish music; in this popular dance, a man dances with two women partners; forbidden
in Buenos Aires in 1743 as immoral, it is still danced in social gatherings, along with the cueca, gato, and zamba.

PALLIERE, LEON (1823-1887).   Artist and author.
Born in Rio de Janeiro and educated in Europe, where
he lived most of his life; in 1856 he visited Buenos Aires and
remained ten years; taught art and in 1860, visited the Uruguay and Paraná rivers, making and leaving lithographs of that
region, showing how it looked during the mid-nineteenth century; gathered and reproduced his work in the Album Palliere,
Escenas americanas; in 1866 returned to France where he
died; among the paintings done in Argentina, the most important are: Porteña en el templo; La cuna; Riña de gallos (cock
fight), the best known: Un saladero; Un nido en la pampa;
La pisadora de Maíz; he also published his diary, Diario de
un viaje a América del Sud (1856-1866), translated into Spanish
in 1945.

PALOMAR DE CASEROS.   Historic house, built in 1799 by Bernardo
Casero, near site of battle of Caseros (q.v.) that ended dictatorship of Juan Manual Rosas and from which it got its
name; declared an historic monument in 1942.

PAMPA (or PAMPAS).   From Quechua Indian word for plains.
Grassy plains that form the geographical heartland of Argentina on the Atlantic side; in modern times also the economic
core of the republic.
Extending from the Atlantic to the pre-cordillera hills,
and from northern Patagonia to the heavily wooded subtropical
north, the pampas cover one-fifth of the Argentine area; they
include all or most of the provinces of Buenos Aires, southern
Santa Fe, southeastern Córdoba, and eastern La Pampa; treeless plains, covered originally with tall, heavily rooted grass,
the pampas have fertile soil, adequate rainfall except for the
dryer western portions; almost no rivers cross them, except
the Salado; when the Spaniards reached the pampas in early
sixteenth century, they found them devoid of the mineral wealth
for which they were looking and also lacking in civilized, sedentary Indians that would make satisfactory labor for colonies;
early attempts at settlement met with such hostility from the
Pampa and Querandí Indians (qq.v.) that the Spaniards abandoned these efforts for several decades; finally, from established towns at Asunción and in Córdoba-Tucumán area, new
towns began to be established, linking pampas and Buenos Aires with older settlements, and developing a life style and
economy based on the unexpected new wealth of herds of cattle
and horses that had grown from Spanish animals left on the
pampas; both Indians and creoles used them; throughout the
first two centuries of Spanish occupation, interior cities, like
Córdoba, dominated, with Buenos Aires a remote, small town,
and the pampas left to the wild horses and cattle, and occa-

sional solitary hunter; by 1750, pampas had entered the national economy and for next two centuries they dominated the national life as well as its economy; trade in hides and tallow was followed and supplemented by that of the salted, dried beef of the saladeros, and eventually, by the end of the nineteenth century, by refrigerated meat packing plants; mules and sheep were also raised; the Spanish and creole population increased and Indians were pushed off the pampas.

By the close of the nineteenth century, commercial agriculture, largely in hands of immigrants and aided by improved farming methods and equipment, was competing with livestock industry for pampas; railroads crossed them carrying produce to ports and grain elevators joined packing plants there; the frontier and gaucho disappeared as the pampas were transformed into the national economic core; in the middle of the 20th century this region contained three-fourths of the nation's cities with more than 100,000 inhabitants, 86% of the industrial plants, provided practically all the national exports, and had 60% of the railroads and 70% of the paved highways; its production included wheat, alfalfa, flax, corn, peanuts, cattle, horses, hogs, a dairy industry and even a small chicken industry; about two-thirds of the population live in the pampas, with five of the eight national universities located there; its economic dominance had become so great that James R. Scobie (Argentina, p. 29) says of it "the pampas today represent the nation. So much wealth and population has been drawn into the pampas, especially since 1900, that the other three regions of Argentina appear to serve only as frontiers."

In the period since 1950s Argentina's drive toward industrialization, its development of mineral resources (especially petroleum) and hydroelectric plants, and its attempt to locate industrial works in localities near production of raw products--all of these in an attempt to reorient production toward national, rather than export, markets--may be modifying the predominance of the role played by the pampas in the overall national economy.

See James R. Scobie, Revolution on the Pampas; a Social History of Argentine Wheat, 1860-1910 (Austin, Texas, 1964; Sp. trans., Buenos Aires, 1968).

PAMPA INDIANS. Name applied to primitive, nomadic Indians living in pampas at time of conquest and throughout 16th century; included the Taluhet, and Douihet Querandíes; lived in shelters made of hides or branches; were tall, painted their faces and bodies, and were clothed in garments made of hides; they used bows and arrows and boleadoras; made and used crude ceramics; religion was shamanistic; included belief in a father god named Soychu and in an evil spirit Gualichu; Spaniards first met these Pampa Indians when the Cabot expedition reached the Carcaraná in 1527; after the coming of the Spaniards, the Pampas adopted the horse and based much of their life-style on it; during the eighteenth century, they were overrun by Araucanians and became merged into them; all of them con-

tinued to be known as Pampas; these Indians were practically
extinguished by Julio A. Roca's campaign of 1879 (see Querandí Indians).

PAMPERO. Southwest wind, cold, dry, and violent, blows in November, December, February, and August; causes abrupt temperature drop as it sweeps across pampas.

"PAMPERO." A 1200 cubic meter balloon brought to Argentina by
Aarón Anchorena in 1907; after several successful flights, it
disappeared October 17, 1908 with its crew members, including Eduardo Newbery and Eduardo Romero.

PAMPIN, GREGORIO (1808-1886). Political leader in Corrientes.
Born in Corrientes; joined anti-Rosas forces formed in
Corrientes by Juan Lavalle and José María Paz; on at least
two occasions held governing posts, as member of provincial
governing triumvirate and as interim governor, in 1872 following defeat of Baibiene in Tabaco.

PAMPIN, JUAN VICENTE (1818-1876). Corrientes rancher and public figure.
Born in Corrientes; as result of his anti-Rosas activities, was forced to emigrate to Paraguay and then Brazil; returned after Rosas' defeat at Caseros to play active role in
provincial politics; always a liberal, he served as legislator,
cabinet minister and governor (1875-1876), and as bank director.

PAMPIN HOUSE. Colonial house built in 1838 in the city of Corrientes, used today as Historical Museum; its interior has preserved the primitive structure with the straw roof and wide
gables.

PAN see PARTIDO AUTONOMISTA NACIONAL

PANAGRA see PAN AMERICAN AIRWAYS

PAN AMERICAN AIRWAYS (after January 3, 1950, Pan American
World Airways). U.S. airline that first linked Buenos Aires
with the United States, establishing routes via both west and
east coasts; attempt made first to extend lines from Panama to
Peru and Chile; met opposition from both British interests and
W. R. Grace Company, a large U.S. trading company operating
a major shipping line on the Pacific; Pan Am (as the U.S. airline became commonly known), holding necessary U.S. airline
rights and W. R. Grace & Co., dominating banks and ware-
house facilities on Pacific coast of South America, combined
their interests in February 1929 to form the Pan American
Grace Airways (known as Panagra), with capital shared equally;
on March 2, 1929, Panagra received contracts to fly to Buenos
Aires and Montevideo from Cristóbal, Panama; started off with
flights down the west coast, then across the Andes, reaching

Buenos Aires in October 1929 with first airmail between U.S.
and Argentina; Panagra also operated flights between Buenos
Aires and Montevideo; in 1931, Pan American Airways linked
Buenos Aires directly with New York by a 6-day flight, having bought out the rights held by New York, Rio de Janeiro,
and Buenos Aires airline (NYRBA) along the Atlantic coast;
after the development of Argentine nationally subsidized aviation in the 1940s, both Panagra and Pan Am were prohibited
from carrying passengers and cargo within Argentina, but international flights continued.

PAN AMERICAN CONFERENCES, 1889-1948. Throughout the eight
Pan American conferences held by the inter-American States
from 1889 to the formal signing of the charter for the Organization of American States, as agreed upon in Bogotá, 1948,
Argentina asserted leadership in behalf of Latin American opposition to any policy or project that might lead to foreign intervention or loss of national sovereignty; the Argentine delegates boycotted the first sessions of the Washington Conference, 1889, until a regular delegate, rather than U.S. Secretary of State, James G. Blaine, had been elected as chairman;
they also refused to accept the customs union proposed by
Blaine; Drago (q.v.) evolved his doctrine at the Mexico conference in 1902, but it was not accepted until the third conference in 1906, held at Rio de Janeiro; fourth conference was
held in Buenos Aires in its centennial year of 1910; in 1923,
the long-delayed fifth conference was held in Santiago, Chile,
with no important actions taken and Argentina maintaining its
traditional independent policy; at the sixth conference, held in
Havana, 1928, U.S. recent intervention in Nicaragua came up
in discussion and Argentine delegates firmly restated their
non-intervention position; through this action and Argentine
policy expressed resentment of new U.S. tariff restrictions, a
break between U.S. and Argentina, with harmful effects on the
Pan American movement, seemed imminent, but conference
closed without overt action; at the seventh conference, in
Montevideo, 1933, Argentina's Carlos Saavedra Lamas joined
with U.S. Hull in obtaining approval for an agreement preventing intervention of one American state in political life of
another; and the republic signed the Declaration of Lima
(1938) reaffirming continental solidarity (see Inter-American
Affairs; Organization of American States).
          See Harold F. Peterson, Argentina and the United
States (New York, 1964).

PAN AMERICAN PEACE PACT. In 1915 President Woodrow Wilson
proposed that all American nations join in a Pan American
Peace Pact guaranteeing political independence and territorial
integrity of each state; Argentine ambassador Rómulo Naón
(q.v.) approved it enthusiastically and was supported in this
by his government; unfortunately, the project lagged, due partly to Chile's reluctance to sign it, because of the Tacna-Arica
dispute in which it was involved with Peru at the time; Brazil

was cool toward it; and U.S. became involved with border troubles with Mexico, and elections; with World War I over in 1918, Wilson turned his attentions to formation of the League of Nations, of which Latin American nations also would be members and the Pan American Peace Pact was dropped for the time being.

PAN AMERICAN UNION see INTER-AMERICAN AFFAIRS

PANDILLEROS (1.). Nickname given party that in mid-1850s favored Buenos Aires localism and separate government from that of confederation; opposed chupandinos (q.v.); pandilleros earned their name (meaning gangs or groups gathered for fun or mischief) from the youthful ebullience of many of its members and their habit of running noisy, lighted patrols through Buenos Aires streets in late night hour demonstrations; party considered itself to be the liberal party; leaders included B. Mitre, D. F. Sarmiento, José Mármol, etc.; elected Valentín Alsina governor of Buenos Aires province.

PANDILLEROS (2.). Young urban demonstrators and political activists of the 1900s; represented social unrest of the period; usually gathered in groups at corners of Buenos Aires streets to protest and criticize society's apathy to current problems, as well as their own.

PARADEROS. Semi-permanent campsites used by early nomadic Indians; provide archeologists and anthropologists with clues to lost indigenous cultures; apparently those along Paraná River served as refuge from river floods.

PARAGUARI (or PARAGUARY). Stream along which Belgrano's liberating force was defeated by Paraguayans January 19, 1811. Late in 1810 the Buenos Aires patriot junta dispatched a small liberating force under Manuel Belgrano (q.v.) to Paraguay to incorporate that part of the viceroyalty into the revolutionary movement; although Belgrano had had very little military experience it was generally believed that Paraguayans would enthusiastically revolt and support his small force in overthrowing the royalist government; in January 1811, having crossed the Paraná at Candelaria and penetrated to the Paraguarí, he was met instead by an army under intendant governor Bernardo Velazco; although heavily outnumbered, the Buenos Aires forces had a preliminary success but then were decisively defeated; Belgrano withdrew hastily to Tacuarí (q.v.) where the Paraguay venture ended.

PARAGUAY. Modern independent nation, about 1000 miles up Paraná-Paraguay rivers from Buenos Aires; its capital, Asunción, was first permanent settlement in Río de la Plata and seat of government for that area until 1617, when Buenos Aires was given its own governor; relationship remained close during colonial period, especially with Corrientes and Misiones;

following May Revolution, Paraguay firmly refused to accept
Buenos Aires authority, defeated the army under Belgrano sent
against it (1811-1812), and established its own independent government; boundary and river navigation disputes frequently
caused problems between Paraguay and Argentina, culminating
in costly, bloody Paraguayan War (1865-1870) between them;
a century later the nations were cooperating in hydroelectric
projects and Paraguayan laborers were contributing their skills
and energies to new farmers across the river in Argentine
Misiones (see Asunción; Paraguayan War).

      See H. G. Warren, _Paraguay_.

PARAGUAYAN WAR (War of the Triple Alliance), 1865-1870. This
    bloody war, involving Paraguay, Uruguay, Argentina, and Bra-
    zil, grew out of colonial and early national historical roots and
    rivalries and affected future development of all four nations.
        An unusual combination of events in the early 1860s
brought about this war that began with political civil war in
Uruguay, involved Brazil and Argentina in attempts to establish order, and quickly became transformed into a tripartite
agreement between these three countries to fight the president
of Paraguay until he was totally defeated; among the various
factors involved were: Argentina's new national reorganization
under President Mitre (1862), with national authority still pre-
cariously held and old provincial-porteño suspicions not yet al-
layed; simultaneous accession of new president in Paraguay,
Francisco Solano López (q. v.) who was ambitious to use his
nation's well-equipped, very large army to keep Paraguay independent and its territory undiminished; both Argentina and
Brazil claimed large portions of it and were believed ready to
fight for these lands; Brazil's increasing attempts at expansion
into the interior and along the Atlantic coast in areas claimed
by Argentina and Paraguay were strongly opposed by latter nations; Paraguay, in retaliation, had even interfered with Brazil's use of the Paraguay River, its only access to Mato
Grosso province, and Brazil could not tolerate this; the immediate problem was political unrest in Uruguay, with both
Brazil and Argentina interested because of their centuries' old
rivalry for settlement or domination in this area and because
opposing political parties in Uruguay had formed habit of calling in both of them for support against their own opponents; in
1863, Venancio Flores, the ousted former Uruguayan leader,
invaded Uruguay from Argentina, overthrew the existing government after bitter fighting, and became president; in this he
had at least the tacit support of Mitre who owed him political
debts; as Flores proved unable to maintain order in Uruguay
and much of Argentine public opinion opposed support of his
actions, Mitre adopted policy of neutrality and non-interference
in 1864; Brazil, however, declared that it would protect its
citizens living in Uruguay as well as its own borders constantly
being violated from South; when Uruguayan raids persisted into
Rio Grande do Sul, Brazil mobilized its forces along the border
and entered Uruguay; President López, seizing this opportunity

for Paraguay to strengthen its position against Brazil, and to
assert its rightful role in Río de la Plata affairs, denounced
this invasion, offered Uruguay its aid, declared war on Brazil
and invaded its territory in Mato Grosso and across the upper
Paraná; meanwhile Mitre's government and the new liberal government in Brazil had strengthened diplomatic relations between
the two countries and were working together to establish peace
in Uruguay under Flores' control; when Mitre refused to grant
López's request for permission to cross Misiones to go directly to Uruguay's assistance, López secretly declared war on
Argentina, occupied the city of Corrientes, and moved across
Argentina toward Uruguay; he assumed that he could count on
support from Urquiza, a close friend of his father, and other
Entre Ríos leaders, traditionally jealous of Buenos Aires' control; instead, Urquiza, and most of the others, strongly resented this Paraguayan infringement of Argentine sovereignty;
in May 1865, Argentina, Brazil, and Uruguay (under Flores)
signed a triple alliance agreement, pledging themselves to fight
Paraguay until Francisco Solano López had been totally defeated; Mitre was made military commander, all three nations
were to furnish troops, and the Brazilian naval squadrons were
given important role; although treaty provisions were secret,
it was generally believed, certainly by all Paraguayans, that the
Allies had bound themselves to destroy Paraguay's independence
as a nation and to divide up its territory.

The war lasted five years; during 1865-1866 a series of
hard-fought battles took place, with neither side really victori-
ous--Yatay, Uruguayana, Estero Bellaco, and Tuyutí (one of
bloodiest battles in South American history), Yataití-Cora,
Bouquerón or Sauce; in September 1866, López asked Mitre for
an interview to discuss peace negotiations; nothing came of
this, and shortly thereafter, the Paraguayans inflicted a crushing defeat on the Allies at Curupaytí; for the next two years
action was limited as Allies struggled with problems of transporting supplies, coordinating naval and military action, dealing (in Argentina's case) with internal disorders at home, and
recovering from the heavy losses already sustained; in early
1868 Mitre had to return to Buenos Aires to assume the presidency, due to the death of his vice-president Marcos Paz (q.v.);
with the Duke of Caxias in command, the Allies pushed through
Paraguayan fortifications at Humaitá and the last great battle
was fought at Lomas Valentinas, in which most of the remaining
Paraguayan army was destroyed; Allied forces moved up the
Paraguay River to occupy Asunción at the close of 1868; the
war dragged on, with Allies pursuing López and his loyal remnant of followers as they fled northward into the forest; war
ended March 1, 1870, when López was killed.

Treaty negotiations took several years; Argentina approved President Sarmiento's declaration that victory did not
give right to draw boundaries; eventually Argentina got Misiones
but lost, by decision (1876) of U.S. President Hayes who
served as arbiter, its claims in the Chaco; Brazil received
large grants of land from northern Paraguay; boundaries along

Paraná and Uruguay rivers were stabilized; Uruguay, responsible for triggering the war action, was least affected; Paraguay was prostrated: its population decreased by more than
half and only one out of ten persons left was an adult male;
agriculture neglected, cattle gone; most of leading families had
been destroyed by López in the last days; much of its territory lost to Argentina and Brazil; war had been unpopular in
Brazil and, even though Brazil gained territory and victory,
popular discontent with it was a factor in the fall of the imperial government two decades later; Argentina also had gained
territory but the war had been unpopular with the provinces,
which considered it Buenos Aires' war and with many groups
in Buenos Aires; national political reorganization had been
hampered; economic development had been delayed; flow of desired immigration decreased; cholera epidemics of that period
were believed to result from massive pollution of rivers by
hundreds of corpses--army casualties--floating downstream;
frontier defenses against Indians had broken down; positive results included the strengthening of national integrity and pride
by Mitre's refusal to accept López's insult of invasion; time
and heavy losses had removed large numbers of veteran military officers and soldiers, paving the way for organization of
a modern, professional army; perhaps most important result of
all was Argentina's consuming desire for peace, and its determination not to engage in future foreign wars.

See Pelham H. Box, The Origins of the Paraguayan
War (Urbana, Illinois, 1929, rep. 1967); Ramón J. Carcano,
Guerra del Paraguay (2 v., Buenos Aires, 1939-1941); José
M. Rosas, La guerra del Paraguay y las montoneras argentinas
(Buenos Aires, 1964); see also Charles J. Kolinsky, Independ-
ence or Death: the Story of the Paraguayan War (Gainesville,
Florida, 1965); and William H. Jeffrey, Mitre and Argentina
(New York, 1952).

PARANA, CITY OF. Capital of Entre Ríos province; river port on
east bank of Paraná; capital of Argentine Confederation, 1853-
1861.

In 1725 citizens of Santa Fe crossed the Paraná River
to establish the first permanent settlement (under Santa Fe control) in Entre Ríos; their purpose was twofold: to end the savage raids of the Charrúa Indians against Santa Fe by driving
them out of the area and to take advantage of the rich, unoccupied fertile alluvial lands; this settlement kept the name of
La Bajada, by which the area had long been known, as a travel stop on route to Corrientes and Asunción by travelers and
by earlier cattlemen who had used it; five years later the first
parish there was established and named Paraná for the river;
the settlement, having already moved to its present, more
healthy site, also adopted this name in 1732, and attempted to
get legal recognition as a city; finally, in 1813, this was accomplished and Paraná elected its own cabildo, with Andrés
Pazos as first alcalde; during the independence period Paraná
gave its support alternately to the Belgrano expedition repre-

senting the May Revolution of Buenos Aires and then (1814) to
the Uruguayan independence leader José Gervasio Artigas, and
finally to the Entre Ríos caudillo Francisco Ramírez and José
Miguel Carrera against the Buenos Aires government (1819);
in 1820 Paraná's first census showed a population of 4292; selected capital of Entre Ríos in 1822, the provincial government
was finally established there in 1826; after an initial period of
anarchy, Paraná came under federalist control of Pascual
Echagüe and, in spite of frequent involvement in civil wars of
littoral and interior provinces, began to show real progress by
the 1840's; after the fall of Rosas in 1852, Entre Ríos leader
Justo José Urquiza (q. v.) took over power; when Buenos Aires
refused to join other provinces in confederation, Urquiza established his government in Paraná; in 1854 it was declared
the national capital of the Argentine Confederation and two
years later Great Britain, France, and Brazil sent ministers
to Urquiza's government; during the next few years Paraná, a
rural town of about 7000-10,000, became the diplomatic and
political center of Argentine nation; the city was beautified and
modernized, with government buildings and a national museum
constructed; it served as base for important international diplomacy regarding navigation of the Paraná River (q. v.) and
for British efforts to reunite Buenos Aires with rest of nation;
newspaper publication, made possible by press brought by Carrera from the U.S., was begun in early 1840s with El Federal
Entrerriano and continued with the establishment of the official
paper El Nacional Argentino in 1853; others also were established, including the famous Revista del Paraná edited by Vicente Quesada (q. v.); with political stability assured by constitutional government, all-out efforts were made by President
Urquiza, the leaders of the various provinces, and by foreign
capitalists to develop Entre Ríos' rich economic resources,
with the capital as the business and political center of operations and chief port on Paraná River; in 1861, with the nation
reunited after the battle of Pavón, the capital was moved back
to Buenos Aires; Paraná lapsed into status of provincial town
until in 1883 it again became the political capital of Entre
Ríos and center of its burgeoning economic prosperity and new
cultural life (see Entre Ríos for economic development); education played important role in Paraná; in 1815 Artigas had
opened the first public school and by 1847 Urquiza had established an excellent secondary school; in 1870 President Sarmiento located the Escuela Normal (teachers' college) at Paraná
that was to be the prototype of other Argentine schools of education and became famous as the center from which new intellectual currents of positivism (q. v.) spread throughout the nation; nearly half a century later, following the University reforms of 1918-1919, one of the four parts of the new national
university of the Littoral was located in Paraná; by the middle
of the twentieth century, Paraná contained a population of over
100,000 and was continuing to grow rapidly as an agricultural
and livestock center, with most of its industries devoted to
processing products of the provinces--frigoríficos, flour mills,

fruit processing plants, dairy industries, etc.; tunnel connecting Entre Ríos and Santa Fe has given tremendous impulse to Paraná's commerce and industry (see Entre Ríos; Paraná River).

PARANA RIVER. Important river in Río de la Plata system; rises in mountains of Minas Gerais in Brazil; flows south and west to form international boundary between Brazil and Paraguay, and Argentine provinces of Misiones and Corrientes and Paraguay; after being joined by the Paraguay river, a few miles north of city of Corrientes, the Paraná flows directly south for several hundred miles to enter the Río de la Plata and then the Atlantic; its name means "like the sea" and was applied by the Indians to both Paraná and Río de la Plata; discovered by Díaz de Solís in 1516, it was apparently reached and explored a little by Portuguese soon afterward, but its real exploration began with the expedition of Sebastian Cabot (q. v.); at the confluence of the Paraná and Carcarañá Cabot founded the fort of Sancti Spiritus (q. v.); later joined with Diego García in further explorations; after the arrival of Pedro de Mendoza's expedition (1535-36), determined to establish settlements in the Río de la Plata area, the Paraná (with Paraguay) became the main route used between the Atlantic and early Spanish settlement at Asunción; other towns grew up along its banks, such as Santa Fe, Rosario (later), Corrientes, and Paraná, where its rich alluvial and delta lands brought economic prosperity to littoral provinces as they proved excellent for both stockraising and agriculture.

During the seventeenth and eighteenth centuries 13 of the 30 Jesuit missions (q. v.) were located along banks of upper Paraná but, after expulsion of Jesuits in 1767, the area largely was reclaimed by subtropical forests and the abandoned territory subjected to rival claims by Argentina, Brazil, and Paraguay; the Paraná was theater of naval action in war of independence, war with Brazil, and fortified at Vuelta de Obligado (q. v.) against Anglo-French blockading vessels; in the 1850s, as Paraguay emerged from isolation and the Argentine Confederation capital was established at Paraná, the matter of free navigation of the river, without control by Buenos Aires, became of prime importance not only to Paraguay and the confederation river ports but also to Brazil, which had to use this way to reach its own province of Mato Grosso, and to foreign nations, like Britain and France, eager to exploit new agricultural and commercial opportunities of the river provinces; treaties were drawn to establish principles of free navigation but somewhat imperfectly observed until after the Paraguayan War (q. v.); at the same time foreign capital became available to develop rival ports to Buenos Aires, such as Rosario and, later on the Upper Paraná, Posadas, Encarnación (linked to Paraguay by bridge); a fleet of river steamers carried the trade; in the late twentieth century attempts are being made to utilize the hydraulic resources of the Paraná (especially the Upper Paraná) for energy (see Energy Resources).

PARDO, PEDRO ANTONIO (1829-1889).   Physician; legislator; cabinet minister; diplomat.

Born in Salta; educated as physician and surgeon, he combined his professional career with public service in various ways; elected as congressman in 1856; he was coauthor of the citizen law project, 1857; directed medical relief in Mendoza following earthquake of 1861, and served as army surgeon during Paraguayan War; was appointed foreign minister in Avellaneda's cabinet; served as professor and dean (1884) of School of Medicine and as president of national health department; drafted national public health laws; occupied position of ambassador to Austrian empire and to Portugal, where he died.

PARDOS.   Name given to descendants of blacks and whites (mulattoes).

PARDOS Y MORENOS, BATALLON DE.   Infantry battalion of black and mulatto soldiers organized for defense of Buenos Aires during British invasions; retained afterward and given this name in 1810; fought heroically in the liberating expedition to Alto Perú and Paraguay; their bravery was commended by Belgrano after the battles of Tucumán and Salta; in 1826 the battalion consisted of six companies of 125 men each; the officers and sergeants used the famous Spanish alabardas (halberds) 6 1/2 feet long, the soldiers, muskets with bayonets.

PARERA, BLAS (1777-1820).   Musician; composer of music for national anthem.

Born in Barcelona, Spain; arrived in Buenos Aires in 1797; taught piano lessons; played organ in church; fought against British invasions, 1806-1807; in 1813 he was selected to compose the music for the words of the national anthem written by Vicente López y Planes; in July of that year he left for Rio de Janeiro to continue his studies under Marcos Antonio; returned to Spain in 1817 (see Himno Nacional).

PARERA, FAUSTINO MIGUEL (1857-1926).   Political and economic leader of Entre Ríos province.

Born in Entre Ríos; elected representative in 1894, served as provincial minister of government and their national representative; became governor in 1907 and promoted growth of agriculture; established several farmers banks and built roads linking rural farming areas with urban markets and centers of transportation; built schools and a theater, and presided over centennial ceremonies (of May Revolution 1810-1910).

PARI STREAM AND AREA.   Site in central Bolivia, near Santa Cruz, where Argentine guerrilla commander Ignacio Warnes (q. v.) was defeated by Spanish general Francisco Aguilera on September 14, 1816; Aguilera ordered that Warnes' head be cut off and publicly displayed, and shot more than 900 patriot prisoners, including men, women, and children.

Parish 678

PARISH, WOODBINE (1796-1882). First British diplomatic representative to United Provinces of Río de la Plata government.
Born in England, educated at Eton, closely tied to British foreign policy and Argentine commerce through his Parish and Robertson relatives, Parish was man selected to implement George Canning's foreign policy toward new and independent Argentine government; he arrived in Buenos Aires as consul-general in March 1824; remained there for nine years, from time of election of Las Heras as governor of Buenos Aires, through Rivadavia's election as first constitutional president, into the Rosas period; during this time he made two important contributions to Argentine history and historiography: aided by his family's close ties to Bernardino Rivadavia, he strongly urged British immediate recognition of independence and gave important assistance and direction to the close economic, as well as political and cultural ties established during this period between the two nations and lasting for over a century; in his diplomatic capacity, he was also largely responsible for the treaty provisions and practical applications regarding the rights and privileges of British Protestant residents and businessmen in Argentina, helping to create, or to strengthen, the pattern used effectively toward all foreigners by Argentine government throughout its national life; during his stay in Argentina, in addition to his official duties, Parish made careful studies of the natural science of the area, combined these with his observations of the political, economic, and social scene and published them in Buenos Aires and the Provinces of the Río de la Plata; Their Present State, Debt, and Trade (London, 1839; 2nd edition 1852; Spanish translations, Buenos Aires, 1854, 1958).
Parish, through his actions, interest, and ability to speak Spanish, had won both the respect and the affection of the Argentine people and, at his departure, he was made an honorary citizen of Buenos Aires.
See H. S. Ferns' comprehensive, scholarly Britain and Argentina in the Nineteenth Century (Oxford, 1960; Spanish translation, Buenos Aires, 1961).

PARISH ROBERTSON, JUAN AND GUILLERMO. Names by which the Robertson brothers have commonly been known in Argentina (see Robertson, John Parish; Robertson, William Parish).

PAROISSIEN, JAMES (or DIEGO) (1784-1827). British physician who played important role in Argentine independence movement.
Born at Harking (Essex), England of French Huguenot ancestry; received good general education with special training in medicine and surgery; some background in chemistry; sailed for Buenos Aires in December 1806, unaware that city had been recaptured from British; spent next eighteen months in Montevideo, apparently engaged in trade and aiding new British forces; in January 1808 went to Rio de Janeiro where he became involved in project of Saturnino Rodríguez Peña (whom he knew) to bring Carlota Joaquina to Buenos Aires; returning

to Río de la Plata area as courier for project, he was seized
and charged with high treason; imprisoned in Montevideo and
then in Buenos Aires for a total of 18 months, he finally secured Juan José Castelli for his defense and shortly after the
May Revolution was released by the Buenos Aires Junta; Paroissien accompanied Castelli in Balcarce's liberating expedition to Upper Peru and took part in his first battle at Huaqui
serving as aide to one of divisional commanders, in addition
to his duties as army surgeon and head of hospital services;
in Potosí he assisted Pueyrredón in evacuating the city and
transporting the wealth of the royal mint to patriots; as result
of Pueyrredón's commendation, Paroissien became the first
to be given naturalized citizenship by the patriot government
(confirmed by Assembly of 1813); remained with army in the
north until appointed director of the newly established gunpowder factory in Córdoba; during his three years there (1812-
1815) Paroissien began his collaboration with José de San Martín in latter's continental liberation plan, that was taking form
during San Martín's convalescence in Córdoba in 1814; the ex-
plosion of the gunpowder factory in April 1815 brought Paroissien back to Buenos Aires where he was appointed to the general staff and assigned in September 1816 to accompany battalion to Mendoza as chief surgeon to assume responsibility for
medical services of Army of the Andes; at the battle of Chacabuco Paroissien again combined military services with medical
ones, serving as aide-de-camp to General Miguel Estanislao
Soler; highly commended by San Martín for his performance;
became original member of Legion of Merit of Chile and was
appointed surgeon-general of army of Chile; came briefly into
personal conflict with former Napoleonic general Michel Brayer
who charged Paroissien with inefficiency and dishonesty, but
could offer no proof; Paroissien treated wounds of O'Higgins
after defeat at Cancha Rayada; Samuel Haigh has left vivid account of Paroissien's services at field hospital following patriot victory at Maipú; the surgeon's brief note sent to O'Higgins
gave the Chilean capital its first news of that great victory;
as result of his actions at Miapú, Paroissien was promoted to
colonel, awarded the Gold Medal of Maipú, and given an estate in Mendoza; as one of San Martín's principal aides, he
sailed with liberating expedition to Peru, August 1820.

During next five years, Paroissien's activities were almost entirely concerned with the Perus, first as very close
collaborator with San Martín in political and diplomatic affairs
and later as participant in mining ventures in Bolivia (formerly Upper Peru); on June 2, 1821, he accompanied San Martín to
meeting with new Peruvian viceroy General José de la Serna
at which the possibility of establishing an independent Peruvian
monarchy was mentioned; at close of 1821, Paroissien and
Juan García del Río sailed for Europe to seek recognition for
Peruvian independence and to conduct search for best-qualified
prince; at that time Paroissien had reached his peak: with
estates in both Mendoza and Peru given him by grateful governments, rank of brigadier general in Peruvian army, officer

of Chile's Legion of Merit, and founding member of San Martín's Peruvian Order of the Sun; by the time the envoys
reached London six months later (having had no success with
related missions in Chile and Buenos Aires) to establish what
was, in effect, the first Peruvian legation in England, San
Martín's interview with Bolívar had taken place in Guayaquil,
followed by the Argentine liberator's retirement from the independence movement; soon after receiving this news, the commissioners were informed by the new Peruvian government that
their mission had been disavowed; retiring to private life,
Paroissien became interested in the various British mining
ventures being planned for Bolivia; on April 27, 1825, he accepted a position with the Potosí, La Paz, and Peruvian Mining Association to take over direction of their mines in Potosí; after consultations with European mining experts, returned to South America, stayed briefly in Buenos Aires, then
went to assume his duties in newly liberated and economically
promising Bolivia; all his luck ran out: company had to be
liquidated; his American estates had been lost; his health
broken, a ruined man financially, Paroissien died at sea, on
voyage from Arica to Valparaíso, while attempting to return
home.
        See R. A. Humphreys, Liberation in South America,
1806-1827: The Career of James Paroissien (University of
London, 1952).

PARRAVICINI, FLORENCIO (1876-1941).   Actor; pilot and sports-
    man; public figure.
        Studied in Buenos Aires and Europe and represented
    Argentine theater well; belonged to Argentine association of
    actors, the Theater Guild, and was director of the Theater
    House; won national and international honors including Royal
    Order of Isabel la Católica in Spain, and doctor's degree in
    arts in France; he was also active in public life as president
    of the Aero Club and Honorary President of the Civil Aviation
    Center, member of the Red Cross, and member of board of
    aldermen for province of Buenos Aires.

PARTIDO (1.).   Political party (see Political Parties; also individ-
    ual entries).

PARTIDO (2.).   Term used in Buenos Aires province for political,
    territorial division usually known in other provinces as a de-
    partment; Buenos Aires has 113 partidos; these originated from
    the primitive division known as a pago (q. v.).

PARTIDO AUTONOMISTA NACIONAL (PAN--Nationalist Autonomous
    Party).   Political party, formed by union of Nationalists and
    Autonomists, in the 1870s, that controlled political life of Ar-
    gentine republic for nearly four decades of unprecedented
    growth and prosperity; after the election of Mitre as president
    in 1862, two parties had developed, the Autonomistas, led by
    Adolfo Alsina, and the Nacionalistas under Mitre and later,

Avellaneda; their major point of difference was whether or not Buenos Aires should be federalized as the permanent capital of the republic (see Federalization of City of Buenos Aires); Nacionalistas favored it, Autonomistas opposed it; in 1874 Alsina supported Avellaneda for presidency and the National Autonomous party was born; his death shortly after that and the federalization of Buenos Aires in 1880 completed the union of the two groups, called an "alliance of the elite"; although it originated as an attempt to unite rural leaders and voters, eventually the party became a political machine directed from the Executive Mansion; it tended to assure the privileges of the power-wielding aristocracy (of both Buenos Aires and the provinces) but was considered liberal, although not democratic; remained in control of government until 1916 (see Political Parties).

PARTIDO DEMOCRATA CRISTIANO (PDC).   First Catholic political party, founded in 1955 by Mario Amadeo; moderate center party, it favored a middle position on most economic issues, strong Congress based on proportional representation, and the right to private education; in the 1960s it moved to the left and split; this party had two major factions, a neo-liberal group centered in Buenos Aires formed by upper middle class men, anti-Peronist, and interested in the welfare of the middle class, and a younger group formed by young lower middle class, orthodox Maritainists, interested in the working class; this latter group counted with the Peronist vote; its leaders, like Horacio Sueldo and Raúl H. Matera, had been Peronists; in 1963 they elected their first congressman who vited with the Peronists in congress; the party did not develop as expected and disappeared by the 1970s.

PARTIDO DEMOCRATA NACIONAL (PDN)   see   NATIONAL DEMO-CRATIC PARTY

PARTIDO DEMOCRATA PROGRESISTA (PDP).   Name of party formed early in twentieth century as a union of the followers of Lisandro de la Torre and some small provincial parties; originally it represented the small farmers of the interior, but soon it appealed to the professionals and intellectuals of Santa Fe; it gained short new life in 1963 supporting the candidacy of Pedro E. Aramburu; it was a moderate, left of the center, slightly anticlerical party; by 1970 the party was virtually dead.

"PARTIDOS DE ENTRE RIOS."   Name applied by Tomás de Rocamora to four areas--Gualequay Grande, Arroyo de la China, Gualeguaychú, and Paraná--in what is now Entre Ríos province; in his letter of August 10, 1782, to viceroy Vértiz, recommending that these be combined under one command, Rocamora wrote that "with the partidos de Entre Ríos your Excellency would have the satisfaction of giving the King, without any expense, the best province of America"; shortly thereafter the province of Entre Ríos was created (see Tomás de Rocamora; Entre Ríos).

PASCO, CERRO DE. Site of Peruvian victory (December 6, 1820) of San Martín's troops, commanded by General Juan A. Alvarez de Arenales over royalist forces led by Brigadier General O'Reilly; patriot victory complete; O'Reilly captured, along with more than 300 prisoners, two cannon, muskets, all flags, and military equipment; victory celebrated in Buenos Aires with drama entitled "The Battle of Pasco" and San Martín's soldiers rewarded.

PASO, JUAN JOSE (1766-1833). Patriot, political leader; one of those most respnsible for revolutionary program and early patriot governments.

    Born in Buenos Aires where his father had a bakery; studied in University of Córdoba, graduating with doctorate in laws, 1779; appointed professor of philosophy at Colegio de San Carlos; in 1803 became fiscal agent of the Real Hacienda (royal treasury); in 1804 moved to San José de Flores as one of its first settlers; by 1806 had become active in the newly formed Independence group, including Juan José Castelli (leader), Saturnino and Nicolás Rodríguez Peña, Manuel Belgrano, Hipólito Vieytes, Juan Martín de Pueyrredón, and others; in cabildo abierto of May 1810, was strong spokesman for removal of viceroy Cisneros and establishment of patriot government; became one of two secretaries (Mariano Moreno, the other) in first patriot junta; in June 1810 was sent by government to Montevideo to win its support of May Revolution and Buenos Aires junta, but was unsuccessful; in new political divisions that were forming among patriots he supported Moreno against Cornelio Saavedra; served as member of first and second triumvirates; sent on secret, unsuccessful mission to Chile, 1814, and after his return was appointed judge advocate general of the army (1815); elected to the Congress of Tucumán where he became secretary and read the formal declaration of independence to the congress; later was one of those who signed it; like many of the others in the congress, he favored a limited monarchy as best form of government for the new nation; after congress moved to Buenos Aires, Paso assisted in writing the provisional by-laws for government; imprisoned briefly by Governor Manuel de Sarratea, his political enemy; reelected to congress in 1822 and 1824, he was influential in effecting legislation creating the first bank, organizing the army, and establishing the national printing office; served as president of the congress; after the constitution of 1826 was signed, Paso retired from politics; died in province of Buenos Aires in 1833.

PASO ALSINA. Ford across Colorado River used by Roca's forces (1879) in expedition into Patagonia; military leaders wanted to name it after their commander but Roca requested that it be called Paso Alsina in honor of Adolfo Alsina who, as minister of war a few years earlier, under President Avellaneda, had initiated this campaign to the desert; declared an historic site in 1943.

PASTOR, REYNALDO (1898-   ).   Political figure; writer.
Born in San Luis; quickly became involved in politics;
in his own province he served as deputy, jefe político, municipal intendant in Mercedes, president of council of education in San Luis (1934), minister of government (1935), and
governor (1942-1943); also represented San Luis in the national congress several terms and was minister of public education in Santa Fe; was active in conservative opposition to
Perón and, as result of his involvement in the unsuccessful
coup attempted in 1951, was imprisoned in Ushuaia with Lonardi, Menéndez, and other leaders; throughout his career he
contributed articles to such papers as La Nación and La
Prensa in Buenos Aires, La Capital of Rosario, and other publications in San Luis and Santa Fe; his longer written works
deal largely with politics, aspects of constitutional development
in San Luis or in the rest of the republic; freedom of the
press, rural codes, and Argentine democracy, and provincial
history, San Luis ante la historia.

PATAGONES.   Indians of Patagonia, found especially in Chubut
around Comodoro Rivadavia and in Santa Cruz; first seen by
Magellan's expedition, and given this name, according to Antonio Pigafetta who accompanied the expedition, because of
their very large feet and footprints (actually due to heavy hide
boots worn by them); the Patagones were characterized by large
size, a hunting and gathering economy, hide huts or shelters,
a polygamous society, and a religion that emphasized a god of
"Good" and one of "Evil."

PATAGONIA.   This land of windswept, cold plateaus, extending from
the Atlantic Ocean to the Andes, occupies one-fourth of Argentine territory; two theories are advanced about its name: 1)
most commonly accepted, that its name was applied by the Magellan expedition (see Patagones); 2) theory held by nativists
that name is of Indian origin, meaning wild coast; the region
extends approximately 1200 miles southward from the Colorado
River and includes provinces of Neuquén, Río Negro, Chubut,
and Santa Cruz, as well as the national territory of Tierra del
Fuego; the land slopes gradually from the eastern coast to high
plateaus and higher cordilleras; it is crossed by such rivers
as the Colorado, Negro, Chubut, Santa Cruz, and Gallegos;
most of it is arid except for a few inches of snowfall in June,
July, and August; in the western mountainous area adequate
rainfall sustains large forests; westerly winds blow most of the
time, often bearing dust clouds; the climate on the plains is
mild, especially along the coast, with the temperatures dropping below freezing only in the southern areas in winter months;
before the conquest this area was very sparsely inhabited by
primitive Indians, during colonial period other Indians, largely
Querandí, moved south from pampas; in late eighteenth and
early nineteenth centuries Araucanians immigrated into Patagonia from Chile and parts of western Argentina.
Although the Patagonian coast had been familiar to sev-

eral Spanish expeditions following that of Magellan, real exploration and attempts at settlement of the area first came
from Chile and Peru; Francisco de Villagra visited Neuquén
in 1553 and went up the Limay River; in the 1580s the famous
Pacific navigator Pedro Sarmiento de Gamboa was sent to the
Straits to explore that area and establish fortified settlements
to prevent England (then hostile to Spain) or other European
nations from gaining a foothold there and to prevent foreigners
from entering the Pacific, considered to be a "Spanish lake";
his efforts eventually failed; for most of the sixteenth and
seventeenth centuries Patagonia was left to the "giants" and
City of the Caesars (q. v.), believed to inhabit it and visited
rarely except by expeditions in search of the latter; one of the
first of these, led by Diego Flores de León, in 1621, explored
the Nahuel Huapi area; occasional missionaries, such as Nicolás Mascardi in the late 17th century and Thomas Falkner in
the 1740s entered, explored, and described the area; Patagonia
assumed new importance in the latter half of the eighteenth
century, with international European rivalries, imperial and
economic, being fought out all over the world, Brazilian expansion extending southward along the coast as well as inland,
and fishing and whaling becoming important in South Atlantic;
shortly after the creation of the viceroyalty of the province of
Río del Plata (1776), the government sent royal officials and
pilots down the coast to establish settlements, fortifications,
and to explore the interior for possibilities of economic exploitation; (see Francisco de Viedma; Basilio Villarino); Alejandro Malaspino made first map of Río Gallegos in 1789.

　　Throughout the first century of Argentine national life,
exploration and interest continued, especially as new economic
resources were revealed; in 1833 Rosas camped near the Colorado, found and claimed the salt beds needed for expansion
of saladero industry; as the Indian frontier was pushed farther
south and west, sheepherders moved in and Welsh settlements
were successfully established in Chubut, in the 1860s; most
other settlements had to wait until after Julio A. Roca's "Conquest of the Desert" (q. v.) and the establishment of government for territory of Patagonia in 1879 under Governor Alvaro
Barros; meanwhile the region had been explored by natural scientists, both from Argentina and foreign countries, including
British Charles Darwin (1830s), Captain Muster (U. S.), who
explored area from Limay River to Punta Arenas; in 1873 the
Argentine scientist Francisco P. Moreno (q. v.) began his
scholarly studies of the area; in the three decades following
1880, sheep raising was expanded throughout the region; as
boundary conflicts with Chile brought need for closer ties between interior and coast, in 1890s Southern railroad extended
its line from Bahía Blanca to Río Colorado and then to Neuquén; territory was divided into four new territories (provinces
after 1950s) of Neuquén, Río Negro, Chubut, and Santa Cruz
(qq. v.).

　　In modern Patagonia sheep raising is still a major industry but the discovery of important deposits of oil and natural

gas at Comodoro Rivadavia in 1907, followed by similar discoveries at Plaza Huincul, in Neuquén, and elsewhere have
stimulated search for other mineral deposits to satisfy national needs; coal has been found at Río Turbio, iron ore in Sierra Grande; varied mineral deposits at Comahué in northern
Patagonia give great promise; use is being made of the Andean rivers that cross the area to reach the Atlantic; irrigation
has made Río Negro and neighboring areas important fruit
producers; hydroelectric plants furnish new supply of energy;
and the magnificent scenery--water, heavy forests, and moun-
tains--are attracting increasing numbers of national and foreign tourists to this still wild, sparsely settled land.

    W. H. Hudson's description of this area is a classic:
Idle Days in Patagonia (London, 1893; many other English and
Spanish editions); see also his description of neighboring pampas, the autobiographical Far Away and Long Ago (New York
and London, 1918).

PATAY. Flour made from carob pods (algarroba tree); used by
    primitive Indians in northwestern Argentina to make bread un-
    til middle of nineteenth century; after that, only rarely seen.

PATO (Spanish word for "duck"). Gaucho game played on horse-
    back; first described in 1700s; two opposing teams would fight
    each other for possession of a large leather pouch with strong
    handles; the goal was to get hold of the duck (hence name of
    game) contained within the bag and the man holding it at the
    end of the game was the winner; the fighting was so rough and
    dangerous that Viceroy Sobremonte and, later, Rivadavia and
    Rosas forbade the playing of pato; it continued, however, as
    the occasion and high point of many rural social gatherings; in
    1909 it was recognized, given game grounds, and brought un-
    der government regulations.

PATRICIOS. Name given to young patriots and to the regiment that
    they organized in 1806 to fight against the British invasions,
    1806-1807; in military history this constitutes origin of Argen-
    tine infantry; but patricios also played important role in politi-
    cal directions taken in years immediately preceding and follow-
    ing May Revolution of 1810; under their commander Cornelio
    Saavedra they fought well against invading British; supported
    viceroy Santiago de Liniers against cabildo dominated by Mar-
    tín Alzaga (1809); the three original battalions were dissolved
    later that year by viceroy Baltasar Hidalgo de Cisneros and
    replaced by two new infantry battalions but the name persisted;
    and patricios helped with Argentina's first victory against roy-
    alists at Suipacha (q. v.); the Argentine national flag takes its
    colors from the blue and white plumes worn in the headgear
    of the patricios.

PATRIOTIC SOCIETY (Sociedad Patriótica). Organization of young
    patriot intellectuals in Buenos Aires, most of them followers
    of Mariano Moreno; formed in 1811, on pattern of French

revolutionary clubs; met in Café de Marcos and used device of
blue and white as its colors; viewed as a threat by the more
conservative group, the supporters of Saavedra (who apparently was not aware of the action planned) started a revolution
late at night April 5, 1811; supported by patricios and other
military units, they demanded that Nicolás Rodríguez, Hipólito
Vieytes, Miguel Azcuénaga, and Juan Larrea be dismissed
from governmental junta; also asked that various members of
the "Marco Club" be deported and Saavedra's power increased;
the success of this revolution temporarily halted the activities
of the Patriotic Society but it was revived early in 1812 by the
fiery leader Bernardo de Monteagudo (q. v.), then acting as
one of the editors of La Gaceta; its new president was Valentín Gómez (q. v.); it provided for two classes of members;
founders, with vote, and associate members, without vote; in
1812 the situation was complicated by the arrival of José de
San Martín, Carlos María de Alvear, and their companions
who formed the rival Lautaro Lodge (q. v.) as an elite group
to guide the direction of the political revolution and organization of the new government; although no longer editor of La
Gaceta, Monteagudo continued active in the Patriotic Society;
at the request of the second triumvirate government, the Patriotic Society, under Monteagudo's direction, presented a constitutional project for consideration by the Assembly of Year
XIII (q. v.); it consisted of 211 articles, declared independence
of the Provincias Unidas del Río del Plata, and suggested creation of association of Provinces of South America; nothing
came of this and after 1813 the Patriotic Society was over-
shadowed by, or absorbed into the Lautaro Lodge.

PATRIOTIC SOCIETY OF LIMA.   Created March 10, 1821) by San
Martín (q. v.) as a consultative government council, without legislative powers, for newly independent Peru; original 40 life
members selected by the government; vacancies filled later by
plurality of votes; its president served as a government minister; its action was only restricted by prohibition of attacks
against fundamental laws of the nation, and against honor of individuals; functioned until 1823 when San Martín left Peru.

PATRON COSTAS, ROBUSTIANO (1883-1953).   Powerful sugar industrialist of Salta; leader of conservative political power in the
interior.
          Born in Salta; graduated from school of law and social
sciences in Buenos Aires; returned to Salta where he founded
and managed the sugar refinery San Martín de Tabacal in Orán
(Salta) and plunged into politics; by 1916 he had held such provincial offices as treasurer, minister of government, governor
(1913-1916), and been elected to the first of several terms as
Salta's senator to the national congress; he was already exercising almost complete control over economic and political life
in Salta; now moved to national scene; president pro tempore
of the Senate, 1932 to 1944; he was responsible for Castillo's
candidacy as vice president with Robert M. Ortiz; in return,

after the death of Ortiz and Castillo's succession to the presidency, the latter made known his choice of Patrón Costas as
presidential candidate for the 1944 election; this met with immediate opposition by those who opposed Patrón Costas for
personal or political reasons, by the young military colonels
and by others determined to avoid another fraudulent administration; although the conservative machine (Concordancia)
backed Patrón Costas, opposition to his candidacy culminated
in the coup d'état of June 1943, overthrowing Castillo and
placing the GOU in control; remained as a senator; during
World War II had pro-Allied sympathies; after being defeated
by the Peronists he retired from politics and died in Salta
(see Ramón S. Castillo; Roberto M. Ortiz; GOU.

PAUCKE (or BAUCKE), FLORIAN (1719-c. 1780).   Jesuit mission-
     ary and writer.
          Born in Silesia; became a Jesuit in Bohemia in 1736;
     arrived in Buenos Aires in 1749 with Martín Dobrizhoffer
     (q. v.) and others; Paucke has left an excellent written descrip-
     tion of the city at that time; he was sent at once to complete
     his studies in Córdoba, then assigned to work among the Mo-
     cobí Indians of northern Santa Fe province and the Chaco; with
     the Indians at the mission of San Javier; the bands and orches-
     tras that he trained gave public performances in Buenos Aires
     and in Santa Fe; Father Paucke's skills as an artisan also en-
     abled him to establish industries of all sorts at the mission
     including a candle factory, carpenter shop, and smithy; he
     taught women to weave wool from the 1700 mission sheep into
     blankets to be exchanged in Asunción for yerba mate, sugar,
     and tobacco as well as for mission use; a smallpox epidemic
     in 1760 almost wiped out the mission but it survived; Paucke
     was attempting to establish mission of San Pedro, about forty
     miles west of his first mission, when he was expelled, along
     with the other Jesuits, in 1767.
          Back in Bohemia, at Neuhaus, Father Paucke wrote
     about his travels and experiences in Argentina, illustrating his
     story with over 100 colored sketches depicting the plants, ani-
     mals, and customs there; German editions of this work were
     brought out in 1829, 1870, 1908; Guillermo Furlong quoted
     from it extensively in his book Entre los Mocobíes de Santa Fe;
     and in 1942-1944, a complete Spanish translation, entitled
     Hacia allá y para acá: una estada entre los indios mocobíes,
     1749-1767, 4 v., was published in Buenos Aires; four letters,
     written by Father Paucke describing his labors among the Indi-
     ans of the reducción of San Fernando near Santa Fe, have been
     published by Guillermo Furlong Cardiff, Florián Paucke, S. J.
     y sus cartas al visitador Contucci: 1762-1764 (Buenos Aires,
     1972).

PAULA, FRANCISCO DE (1794-1865).   Spanish royal prince, son of
     Charles IV, who was considered by Belgrano, Rivadavia, and
     Sarratea in 1815 as possible king for an independent, limited
     monarchy consisting of the United Provinces; Sarratea approached

Charles IV, then living in Rome, for his approval and aid but
he refused as his other son Ferdinand VII had just been restored to the Spanish throne and he would take part in no action unfavorable to him and the crown; Sarratea was dissuaded
by the others from carrying out the project any further after
Charles' rejection; all returned to Buenos Aires convinced that
Ferdinand's determination to regain his American colonies
made fighting for independence inevitable (see Monarchy).

PAUNERO, WENCESLAO (1805-1871).   Military commander.
        Born in Colonia del Sacramento (Uruguay); studied brief-
ly at the Colegio de San Carlos in Buenos Aires, then went into commerce; in 1825 he was in Corrientes; finding war with
Brazil imminent, he offered his services and became part of
the Corrientes detachment, beginning a military career that
lasted more than forty years; fought at Ituzaingó and was taken
prisoner by Brazilians at Fraile Muerto (1827); in 1829 he rejoined unitarist General José María Paz (q. v.), under whom
he had fought in Brazil, and took part in the Córdoba campaign; fought in battle of San Roque and at La Tablada and Oncativo against federalist forces of Juan Facundo Quiroga; during following year he was assigned to fighting montoneros and
Indians under Lamadrid (q. v.); although he missed the battle of
Ciudadela (q. v.), he accompanied the remnants of Paz's army
into exile in Bolivia; spent several years there in business,
practicing journalism with Bartolomé Mitre, with whom he
formed close and lasting relationship; married sister of José
Ballivian (president of Bolivia); in Valparaíso, Chile, he
learned of Urquiza's pronouncement against Rosas and accompanied Mitre, Sarmiento, and others to join him; commanded
Uruguayan cavalry at Caseros; in formation of new government
after Rosas' fall, he supported that of Buenos Aires rather
than Urquiza's confederation; as officer in Buenos Aires (Argentine) army (1853), served at Azul on southern Indian boundary; held command assignments at San Nicolás de los Arroyos,
Bahía Blanca, and took part in expedition to Salinas Grandes
against Indians; in 1859 he served as Mitre's chief of general
staff; commanded center of line at Cepeda; after another assignment on southern frontier, he again commanded center of
Mitre's line of offense at Pavón; promoted to general following
this battle; spent most of next few years pacifying interior provinces, including quelling a liberal revolution in Córdoba and
campaigns against El Chacho (see Angel Vicente Peñaloza); in
the campaign of 1862 he came to believe that Peñaloza was the
best man to control the disorder in La Rioja area and made a
peace and loyalty agreement with him; when Peñaloza revolted
again the following year Paunero refused to negotiate, defeating
him completely; at outbreak of Paraguayan War (1865) he commanded the first army corps, recaptured Corrientes, almost
succeeded in cutting Francisco Solano López's forces off from
Paraguay and was, in fact, first Allied commander to penetrate
territory of that nation; after battle of Curupaytí, Paunero left
Paraguay to suppress the outbreak of violence in Cuyo, under

the Varelas and Juan Felipe de Saá, that posed challenge to
authority of Mitre's government; did not return to Paraguayan
action but went to Buenos Aires, for family reasons; became
minister of war in closing period of Mitre's term, was unsuccessful nationalist candidate for vice presidency in 1868;
concluded his lifetime of service to his country by serving as
Sarmiento's ambassador to Brazil; made important contributions to difficult peace negotiations following Paraguayan War
(q. v.) and strengthened Argentine-Brazilian relations in other
aspects such as exchange of postal services and the granting
of freedom to any Brazilian slave who entered Argentine territory; died in Rio de Janeiro.

PAVA.   Tea kettle used to boil water for serving mate; carried by
every gaucho on his saddle and found, in varying sizes, in
every creole home; the traditional kettle, originally made in
Barcelona and introduced by the Spaniards, was a rustic copper kettle with a narrow neck, two handles on the sides, and
a wide bottom; after 1810 enterprising British merchants introduced a new, highly polished model but this proved unacceptable to the Argentine market; British copies of the traditional
copper kettle quickly replaced them.

PAVON, BATTLE OF.   Decisive battle fought September 17, 1861,
on plains in Santa Fe province between national forces, mostly
cavalry, under Urquiza, and Buenos Aires strong infantry,
with weaker cavalry, under command of Mitre; Mitre's losses,
particularly among cavalry, were greater than Urquiza's, but
latter lost irreplaceable artillery and retired from the field;
friction between Derqui and Urquiza made this battle even more
important political than military victory for Mitre who soon
was able to effect national reorganization, through negotiation,
of Buenos Aires and Confederation governments.

PAYADOR.   Gaucho minstrel who wandered from place to place
playing his guitar and singing ballads; part of every fiesta;
his payada, or song, followed a formal pattern, with beginning
measures that had to be observed, and quatrains or ten-line
stanzas of verses that usually contained eight syllables, never
more; the payador sang of the life that he knew on the pampas,
of his dreams, his loves, and his fears, as well as of his
own epic achievements or those of other gaucho heroes; among
remembered payadores are Juan Gualberto Godoy, José Díaz
Trillería, Gabino Ezeizu, and José Betinotti; famous in Argentine literature are Santos Vega and Martín Fierro.

PAYAGÜE INDIANS.   Guaraní tribe that treacherously killed members of the Ayolas expedition sent up the Paraguay River in
1537 (see Juan de Ayolas; Guaraní Indians).

PAYRO, ROBERTO J. (1867-1928).   Writer; social critic.
Born in Buenos Aires; began his writing career as critic of El Interior of Córdoba, where he was teaching in high

school; disagreeing with the political orientations of the paper toward Juárez Celman, he moved back to Buenos Aires; became actively involved in the Revolution of 1890 (q.v.); eventually went to work for La Nación; in 1893 joined the Mitre group opposing the Unión Cívica during the political crisis of the 1890s; joined Socialist Party in 1896; in early 1900s went to Europe, remaining there throughout World War I; died in Buenos Aires.

His best known book is Las divertidas aventuras del nieto de Juan Moreira, a classic tongue-in-cheek sketch of a social and political climber; his first play Marco Severi was written as protest of Law of Residence (q.v.) that permitted expulsion of any foreigner considered undesirable; other writings include Los italianos en la Argentina; El falso Inca (novel); Cuentos de Pago Chico (short stories of criollo customs on the pampas and in frontier port town of Bahía Blanca), as well as several novels, plays, and diaries.

PAZ, BENJAMIN (1831-1902). Jurist; government official; dean of law school in Tucumán.

Born in Tucumán; graduated in law at University of Córdoba; returned to Tucumán to become legislator and judge; served as federal interventor in Jujuy (1881); following year became governor of Tucumán; was President Roca's minister of the interior; first dean of School of Law at national university of Tucumán; elected national senator in 1870s and again in 1886; resigned to become justice of the supreme court (1892); died in Buenos Aires.

PAZ, JOSE MARIA (1787-1857). Military general; leader of the Unitarists.

Born in Córdoba, where he started his law career, never completed as he joined army during the war of independence; fought in Tucumán, Vilcapugio, and Ayohuma under General Belgrano; in the battle of Venta y Media lost an arm and as a result he was known as el manco (one-handed or cripple) Paz; in January 1820, with Juan Bautista Bustos, Córdoba caudillo, revolted against the Buenos Aires government; later Bustos banished him to Santiago del Estero; in 1826, joined the army again to fight in the war against Brazil; was appointed army commander in 1827; by this time Paz had declared himself a unitarist and started his fight to have a multiprovincial power opposed to the Buenos Aires leadership; soon Buenos Aires, under the direction of Rosas, declared war against Paz; in 1829 latter reached Córdoba and defeated his old army general at San Roque; at the same time Facundo Quiroga marched against Paz but was defeated in La Tablada and Oncativo (June 23, 1829 and February 25, 1830); in this way Paz was able to transform Córdoba into the center Liga del Interior, league of nine provinces with a centralized form of government; in the meantime Estanislao López (q.v.) assumed the leadership of the federal forces and took Paz prisoner; Rosas ordered his execution but López refused to obey the order;

Paz escaped to Corrientes where he fought against Rosas, and defeated General Echagüe, Rosas partisan, in Caaguazú (November 28, 1841); in 1842 became governor of Entre Ríos, but soon disagreements with Ferré, the governor of Corrientes, and Rivera, from Uruguay, forced Paz to go to Montevideo; in 1844 the new governor of Corrientes, Joaquín Madariaga, invited him to return to lead the army against Rosas, and in 1845 signed a treaty with Corrientes and Paraguay to fight Rosas; he hoped to attack Entre Ríos but the triumph of Urquiza over Rivera at India Muerta changed his plans; Paz remained in Corrientes and attempted to face Urquiza but because of political complications he resigned and emigrated to Brazil; there, in poverty, he wrote his Memoirs; he remained in Rio de Janeiro until 1852 when the news of Urquiza's revolt reached him; immediately he returned to Argentina where he arrived at the time of the upheaval against Urquiza, following defeat of Rosas; Paz took part in the defense of the city of Buenos Aires; he was minister of war in Pastor Obligado's cabinet; in 1854, although in poor health, he was elected as legislator for the province and participated during the constitutional debates; Paz and Mitre opposed the signing of this provincial constitution; Paz died in Buenos Aires in 1854.

PAZ, MARCOS (1813-1868).   Lawyer and public official; vice president who assumed civic duties of President Mitre during latter's absence as military commander in Paraguayan War.

Born in Tucumán; studied in Buenos Aires, graduating in law, 1834; two years later, he was appointed secretary of governor of Tucumán, fought in battle of Caseros as aide of General Angel Pacheco; appointed representative to the constitutional convention in Santa Fe (1853) but resigned to become governor of Tucumán; occupied this post until 1860; his administration was one of order and progress; public buildings were constructed, public libraries opened, public welfare society was organized, and the first census taken; in 1861 Colonel Paz was called in by General Paunero (q.v.) to serve as temporary governor of Córdoba in unsettled conditions caused by split in liberals of that province; left this post in 1862, to return to Tucumán, as national commissioner, to make peace among the north-central provinces; he persuaded the governments of Tucumán, Catamarca, Santiago del Estero, and Salta to sign a peace agreement, March 3, 1862, that would have ended internal dissension and opposition to new national government in Buenos Aires, had it not been for new revolts led in the following two years, by Angel Vicente Peñaloza (q.v.); Paz had been elected national senator in 1861, and became national vice president in 1862; during the years from 1865 to 1868 (except for a brief period between February and July, 1867) Marcos Paz served as president pro tempore as Bartolomé Mitre delegated his executive authority to him while he commanded the Allied military forces of the Paraguayan War (q.v.); in this difficult period of national reorganization, Paz acted firmly and ably but was often frustrated by the popular desire to have the elected

president back in charge of government; offered his resignation
several times but continued to serve until his death, a victim
of the Buenos Aires cholera epidemic of 1868.

PAZ, MARCOS, hijo. (1843-1904).   Government official; chief of police, Buenos Aires.
   Born in Buenos Aires where he studied but failed to
complete his college career due to his father's death; served
as provincial congressman (1876) and as vice president of the
house; appointed by President Roca as undersecretary of the
ministry of justice, religion, and public instruction; became
chief of police of Buenos Aires in 1880 and in that position he
carried on his most effective work; improved the service, created a new school for officers, established patrols to walk the
streets, and created the system of regulations by which, with
only a few changes, the police still operate; during this time
the police department became a separate entity from that of
the army; Paz resigned from this post during the elections of
1885; later he was director of the port of Buenos Aires and
president of the Banco de la Nación; in 1891 he was elected
national congressman; both Tucumán and Santa Fe offered him
the post of governor but he declined; died in Santa Fe.

PAZOS, ANDRES (1765-1849).   Creole patriot.   Born in Buenos Aires
of Spanish parents; as a young man, moved to La Bajada of
Paraná where he was influential with the authorities in getting
that place declared a pueblo or village; in 1810 and 1811 helped
the army of the North under General Belgrano with funds and
as a commander of the Battalion of Pardos (q. v.); he received
recognition for the brave behavior of his soldiers in defense of
the Paraná River; Pazos also influenced the Assembly of 1813
in its granting of final separation of Paraná from Santa Fe;
was appointed Alcalde Ordinario of the new cabildo; he returned to Buenos Aires in 1813 and resumed management of
his private enterprises; died there.

PAZOS KANKY (or KANKI), VICENTE (1779-1853).   Name by which
Vicente Pazos Silva was best known.   Patriot newspaperman
and activist; priest.
   Born in Alto Perú (Bolivia) of Indian parents; studied in
seminary there; while serving as priest in La Paz, he met
Mariano Moreno (q. v.), and joined the patriot cause; moved to
Buenos Aires and succeeded Pedro José Agrelo as editor of
La Gaceta in November 1811; founded El Censor to defend liberal views; in 1815-1816, Pazos Kanki and Manuel Moreno
(q. v.) were the only ones to defend republicanism (vs. desire
for monarchy) in the press; exiled to Europe (1817) because of
his participation, along with M. Pagola, D. French, Agrelo,
F. Chiclana, Manuel Moreno, in the conspiracy against Supreme Director Juan Manuel de Pueyrredón; while in England,
he converted to Protestantism, leaving the Roman Catholic
Church; wrote America Argentina; returned to Argentina to become editor of Diario de Avisos; established a printing press;

published La crónica argentina; strongly opposed Belgrano's
idea of restoring Inca monarchy as government of independent
United Provinces; translated Gospel of Mark into Aymara language of Bolivian Indians; died in Buenos Aires.

PAZ Y FIGUEROA, MARIA ANTONIA DE LA (1730-1799); also known
as Sor Antula. Colonial religious figure, still venerated in
modern Argentina.

   Born in Santiago del Estero, in a prestigious family
descended from the founder of Córdoba, Jerónimo Luis de
Cabrera; decided at age of fifteen to join group of saintly wom-
en, called the beatas (the blessed ones) who performed Loyola's
Spiritual Exercises and devoted themselves to good works under
Jesuit supervision; when Jesuits were expelled in 1767, Sor
María Antonia dedicated herself to continuing use of the Spiritual Exercises in her country and to converting as many men
and women as possible to the same spiritual life; traveling as
a missionary thruugh the neighboring provinces she became
widely known and revered, gaining converts and effecting spiritual reform wherever she went; in September 1779 she approached Buenos Aires, barefoot, disheveled, bearing a heavy
wooden cross, arousing ridicule and even persecution from the
street urchins, from whose stone throwing she took refuge in
the old church of Nuestra Señora de la Piedad (Our Lady of
Piety) nearby; within the next twenty years she had won the respect, support, and veneration of the entire capital; she established the Casa de Ejercicios (Retreat House in which the Spiritual Exercises are performed), from which thousands joined in
her devotions, and a home where women in trouble could take
refuge and return to Christian life; everything supported by the
charity of the porteños; more than 100 years later, in 1905,
the archbishop of Argentina initiated action to have her beatified and canonized; action renewed in 1917.

   Sor María Antonia maintained extensive correspondence
with her Jesuit friends in exile; these letters, especially those
to Father Gaspar Juárez, also from Santiago del Estero, were
widely circulated in Europe.

PDN (PARTIDO DEMOCRATICO NACIONAL)   see   NATIONAL DEMO-
CRATIC PARTY

PEDERNERA, JUAN ESTEBAN (1796-1886).   One of San Martín's
granaderos a caballo; vice president of Argentine Confederation,
1860-1861.

   Born in San Luis; while studying in a Franciscan monastery in Mendoza, he learned that San Martín was organizing
an army to fight for independence; left the monastery and
joined it in 1815; fought at Chacabuco, Maipú, and in the campaign to Peru; although taken once to island of Chiloé as a
prisoner, he escaped and returned San Martín's liberating army
in Peru; in 1826 he returned to Buenos Aires in time to fight
in the war against Brazil; later joined unitarist general Paz
and fought at La Tablada; remained part of anti-Rosas forces;

spent some time in exile; after Caseros, returned to Buenos
Aires; became senator for San Luis; in 1856 he was appointed
commander of the frontier force of Córdoba and San Luis;
became governor of San Luis in 1859 and fought at Cepeda
(1860); elected vice president of the Argentine Confederation
with Derqui as president, and was president pro tempore during Derqui's absences; in 1882 he was made lieutenant general
of the armies of the republic; died in Buenos Aires.

PEDRAZA, MANUELA.   Heroine of British invasions.   Woman from
Tucumán who performed outstanding services among the wom-
en who fought alongside the men defending Buenos Aires from
the British (1806-1807); cited by Liniers for her valor; street
in north barrio of Buenos Aires named in her honor.

PEHUENCHES AND PUELCHES.   These two Indian groups that lived
in southern Mendoza and Neuquén formed part of the Huárpido
group; their economy was based on hunting--ñandúes, guanacos,
and, after Spaniards came, wild horses--and gathering wild
fruits, seeds, especially pine nuts from which they made
bread and an alcoholic beverage; they used skins for their
primitive shelters, clothing, and containers; in appearance they
were tall with long skulls (dolichocephalous), with darker skins
than other Indians; they used straw snowshoes, bows and arrows and boleadoras with two balls; later adopted the Araucanian spear; the men created featherwork of great beauty; also
produced simple ceramics; in the late eighteenth century Villarino found some of these Indians still living in the Río Negro
valley but they were rapidly being absorbed by the Araucanians
and their individual culture has been lost; during colonial period they had little contact with the Spaniards but were fiercely
warlike and occasionally sent violent raids (malones) against
Spanish towns; for example, they destroyed Chillán in southern
Chile in 1650 and La Arboleda, in Mendoza, in 1666.

PELLEGRINI, CARLOS (1846-1906).   President of Argentine Republic 1890-1892; Lawyer; part of "Generation of 1880."
        Born in Buenos Aires; known as "El Gringo" because of
his French-Italian father (see Carlos Pellegrini) and British
mother; early became involved in politics supporting Adolfo
Alsina's Autonomist Party; interrupted his law studies to fight
in Paraguayan War; ran unsuccessfully for congress, 1871,
1872; in 1873 became national congressman from Buenos Aires;
reelected for four more years; served as minister of government for province and in 1879 as minister of war and navy,
replacing Roca in Avellaneda's cabinet; occupied this sensitive
post during problem between national government and governor
of Buenos Aires over the federalization of that city (see Federalization of City of Buenos Aires); was responsible for selection and arrangements to move national capital temporarily to
suburb of Belgrano; in 1881 became senator, replacing Dardo
Rocha; in 1885, while he was in Europe on a financial mission, President Roca offered him ministry of war and navy;

in 1886 became vice president under Juárez Celman and when
latter resigned as result of revolution of 1890, Pellegrini succeeded to the presidency; faced national financial crisis boldly;
sent Victorino de la Plaza (q. v.) to London to confer with international bankers about refinancing Argentina's foreign debts;
created Caja de Conversión, placed currency on sound basis,
established Banco de la Nación Argentina to strengthen banking
system, and not only saved the nation from bankruptcy but began its period of greatest economic success; although his financial policy probably brought him greatest prestige and respect from Argentine public, he also made other contributions
such as the organization of the public health service, the creation of the Jockey Club, and his opposition to military intervention in politics; attacked corruption and called for social and
political reform but used traditional means to ensure election
of Luis Sáenz Peña to presidency to succeed him; it was said
of Pellegrini and Roca that they represented the "new oligarchy"
that combined the old estanciero power with that of new urban
leaders of foreign birth or ancestry; after his presidential
term was over, he was elected as senator for Buenos Aires;
refused PAN's nomination for presidency in 1898 and went to
Europe; returning, he founded El País, a morning newspaper
in which he began to express his new views about the urgent
need for social and political reform; extensive travel through
the United States in which he witnessed the election of Theodore Roosevelt as president in 1904 reinforced these convictions; Pellegrini published six letters about his U.S. experience in La Nación; along with his turn toward greater democracy he also broke away from his former European orientation
and urged closer relationships with the United States; his fight
against election fraud culminated in a dramatic scene in congress, when he grasped the hand of socialist Alfredo Palacios,
in his public acknowledgement of corruption practiced in oligarchical elections and the need for reform, and in his last public speech, in which he warned that "the floodgates must be
opened to the people"; died in 1906, along with Bartolomé
Mitre, Bernardo de Irigoyen, and President Quintana.
        See Agustín P. Rivero Astengo's biography published in
first 2 volumes of Carlos Pellegrini, Obras (5 v., Buenos Aires, 1941).

PELLEGRINI, CARLOS ENRIQUE (1800-1875). Engineer, artist.
        Born in Chamberry, France, and educated in Italy; while
working there in 1826 he met Juan Larrea who had been sent
by Bernardino Rivadavia to place a hydraulic engineer under
contract for Argentina; Pellegrini accepted; upon his arrival in
the Río de la Plata he found Buenos Aires besieged by Brazilian navy and remained in Montevideo; began painting; after
peace was established he moved to Buenos Aires; continued his
art work, producing water colors, lithographs, oils, and the
portraits for which he became best known; also known as an
early costumbrista, using gaucho theme; at the same time he
studied carefully the agricultural problems of Argentina, drew

up plans for railroads, ports, public works, the theater of
Buenos Aires (still standing), saladeros, and other engineering projects; became one of founding members of Instituto Histórico y Geográfico del Río de la Plata; died in Buenos Aires;
one son, Carlos Pellegrini (q. v.), became president of the Argentine republic and another, Ernesto, was a member of congress and a prominent lawyer.

PELLIZA DE SAGASTA, JOSEFINA (1848-1888). Writer. Born in
Entre Ríos; contributed to La Nación and other Argentine and
Uruguayan newspapers and periodicals; died in Buenos Aires;
among her best-known works are: Palmira; Margarita; El
héroe de Paysandú; La sirena de Ibercí; and La flor de la
laguna.

PELUCONA. Name of one-ounce gold coin used in eighteenth-century trade and other financial transactions between Río de la
Plata and Peru; usually stamped with sculptured head image of
one of Bourbon monarchs.

PEÑA, DAVID (1862-1930). Writer; lawyer; historian.
Born in Santa Fe; graduated in law at age of thirty;
held various public posts, including those of private secretary
to governor of Santa Fe, member of the province's constitutional convention, secretary of the May Revolution centennial
celebration, etc.; early entered field of journalism in Santa Fe;
founded the magazine Atlántida; became interested in history
and served as professor of history at university of Buenos Aires; considered one of first revisionist historians because of
his rehabilitation of Facundo Quiroga in his published study of
that caudillo; other historical studies include Marco M. Avellaneda sacrificado en Metán, and Dorrego; became interested in
writing drama; translated many of Shakespeare's plays into
Spanish; became a pioneer in the writing of historical dramas;
died in Buenos Aires.

PEÑA, JUAN BAUTISTA (1798-1869). Financier; government functionary; legislator.
Born in Buenos Aires; early engaged in business and
then rural pursuits; entered public life, holding such positions
as militia officer, justice of the peace, customs official (1822),
congressman (1830); caught up in the persecution of Rosas' enemies following the Maza conspiracy in 1839, Peña went into exile; returned in 1852, after Rosas' fall; having committed himself to Buenos Aires government, was appointed as chief of police of the province (1852); served as legislator and provincial
senator, various terms; minister of treasury under various governors; made available large sums of money to buy off Urquiza's
besieging naval force (1853); as delegated governor of Buenos
Aires province in 1854, proclaimed its constitution; following
national reorganization his prestige as financier and estanciero
(owned estancia in Balcarce, southern Buenos Aires) brought
him appointments as president of the bank and Casa de Moneda

(1863); refused Mitre's offer to serve as minister of treasury;
became president of Buenos Aires Municipal Commission;
died in Buenos Aires.

PEÑALOZA, ANGEL VICENTE (1798-1863). Known more commonly
by his nickname El Chacho (affectionate diminutive of mucha-
cho, "boy"). Caudillo of La Rioja.
        Born in La Rioja; fought with Facundo Quiroga (q. v.) in
the early days at El Tala, Rincón, Tablada, and Oncativo; returned to La Rioja and ousted the unitarist governor; in 1840
Peñaloza revolted against Rosas because he believed him to
have been responsible for the Barranca Yaco murder of Quiroga, for the poverty of the interior provinces, and the failure
to bring about national organization; continued to fight against
Rosas until 1845; spent much of his time attempting to change
or control political life in his own province as well as that of
neighboring provinces of San Juan, Tucumán, San Luis, and
Córdoba; offered his support to Urquiza in 1854; in 1861 he rebelled against the new national government of Buenos Aires,
reflecting and continuing the traditional, provincial federalist
fear and hatred of Buenos Aires; under his leadership the
whole area was in a turmoil that threatened the authority of the
new national government; army sent against him, with General
Wenceslao Paunero in charge; believing that El Chacho was only man able to control unrest in the area and that his loyalty
could be won, Paunero signed a peace treaty with him (1862);
later, El Chacho refused to grant certain government demands
and civil war broke out again in the provinces with El Chacho
carrying it to Córdoba, which he captured; Paunero again led
national forces, with aid from neighboring governors, against
him; on June 20, 1863, Peñaloza was defeated in Las Lomas
and at the bloody battle of Las Playas; a military dictatorship
was imposed on La Rioja; Chacho, who had escaped, attempted
to remove this military control; taken by surprise in the town
of Olta he was killed by Irrazábal November 12, 1863; this
blond, blue-eyed man was always a controversial figure; to
Sarmiento he represented the barbarism that had to be eradi-
cated before Argentina could become civilized; to President
Mitre and his officials he posed a threat to the new national
unity that could not be tolerated; but to the provinces of the interior he was a defender against the traditional danger of Buenos Aires control; and to the people who followed and loved
him he was an authentic gaucho caudillo, kind, illiterate but
courageous, and a master in guerrilla warfare, firm in his
loyalties--one of their own.

PENDLETON, JOHN S. (1802-1868). U.S. Chargé d'Affaires in Argentina at time of Rosas' overthrow. This perceptive Virgini-
an diplomat wrote to Secretary of State Daniel Webster, from
Buenos Aires in January 1852, to alert him that conditions
seemed about to change immediately in Argentina in a way that
might enable the U.S. to conclude the treaty of trade and
friendship that it had been trying to secure for the past thirty

years; the following month, after Rosas' defeat at Caseros,
Pendleton established cordial relations with Urquiza when he
entered Buenos Aires; became the only foreign diplomat to accompany him to the conference at San Nicolás and to receive
a copy of its proceedings; Webster sent U.S. minister to Brazil Robert C. Schenck to assist in drawing up the negotiations
(1853) and on April 9, 1855, the two treaties were proclaimed
providing for mutual freedom of commerce and most-favored-
nation principle applied to diplomatic and consular services,
as well as to commerce and navigation; soon afterwards he returned to the United States; retired to Virginia where he died
November 1868.

PENINSULARES. Term refers to Spaniards born in Spain as distinguished from Criollos, persons of Spanish or European
blood born in New World; political and economic differences
between these two groups were very important during early independence period.

PEON. Rural worker on an estancia; similar to campesino in other
parts of Latin America; traditionally, this term was applied to
a free worker, usually tending or herding cattle, who maintained a small garden near his living quarters; he was not
bound to the particular estancia where he worked; developed
close relationship with the land and animals; in modern times
the word has been used somewhat vaguely to refer to any agricultural or estancia worker who is paid daily wages.

PEPA LA FEDERALA. This historical figure of the Rosas period
has become the popular and literary prototype of the women
soldiers, common in the civil wars, who fought alongside their
men; Pepe la Federala was the widow of a sergeant-major,
who became an officer in her own right, commanding a company of mounted volunteers; her fighting career, of 35 years,
included her service with Pascual Echagüe (q.v.) fighting
against the unitarists in Entre Ríos, aiding the Rosas forces
to quell the rebellion in Chascomús (1839), and accompanying
forces of Manuel Oribe at Quebracho Herrado (q.v.) where she
was assigned to the field hospital; wounded many times; once
taken prisoner and sentenced to death, but escaped; in 1844
she submitted a petition to the government, describing her
services in detail, requesting her past due pay.

PERALTA RAMOS, PATRICIO (1814-1887). Wealthy rancher, founder
of Mar del Plata beach resort.
       Born in Buenos Aires; became owner of several es-
tancias in southern part of province; when his own fortunes
were seriously damaged by the overthrow of Rosas' government
(1852), he attempted to recoup his losses by new undertakings;
opened saladero and mill in Laguna de los Padres; in 1874 he
founded the city of Mar del Plata that became the tourist center of the south Atlantic coast; died in Buenos Aires.

PERAMAS, JOSE MANUEL (1732-1793).   Jesuit missionary, educator, and writer.

Born in Mataro, Spain; his father, in royal service, moved to Cartagena where José entered a Jesuit colegio at the age of 11 and in 1745 was accepted in Tarragona as a novice; in 1755 he arrived in the Río de la Plata area and went directly to Córdoba where he completed his ecclesiastical studies and made his final vows; was assigned the task of writing the annual Jesuit letters; he became known both in Córdoba and in Rome for his fine literary style and the detailed observations not only of Jesuit work in Argentina but of Argentine life and society of that period; served for a time in the Guaraní mission of San Ignacio but was called back to teach rhetoric and moral theology in Córdoba; expelled with his fellow Jesuits in 1767 he maintained a diary of the journey of the deportees from Córdoba to Faenza in Italy; Peramás spent the rest of his life there, engaged in religious and teaching assignments and in writing; various of his works about the Paraguayan missions and missionaries were published.

Guillermo Furlong included a brief biography of Peramás in his new edition (National University of Córdoba, 1937) of the Cinco oraciones laudatorias en honor del doctor D. Ignacio Duarte y Quirós (founder of Colegio Monserrat of Córdoba) a work now generally attributed to Peramás although earlier Bernabé Echenique had been named as author (see Printing Presses).

PERDRIEL.   Small farm about twelve miles from Buenos Aires where Pueyrredón's force of about 1000 peasants was routed by Lord Beresford's soldiers (see British Invasions).

PERDRIEL, GREGORIO IGNACIO (1785-1832).   Military man; chief of police; rancher.

Born in Córdoba; began his military career against the British invasions; later joined Belgrano's army; in 1815 personal and political differences between Supreme Director Carlos de Alvear and José de San Martín (qq. v.) brought latter's resignation and removal from military and political command of Cuyo; Colonel Perdriel was appointed to replace him; popular and official protest from Mendoza brought Perdriel's recall (before even reaching Cuyo) and San Martín remained in charge; Perdriel retired from army to devote himself to his cattle ranch at Cañada de la Cruz (Buenos Aires province); in 1827 became chief of police; regulated rural police, closed pulperías on holidays; died suddenly five years later amid unconfirmed rumors that he had been poisoned; a small town in Mendoza was named for him.

PEREZ, BENITO ESTANISLAO (1848-1916).   Public figure in Entre Ríos; legislator; cattle breeder; journalist.

Born in Entre Ríos; occupied such positions in the province as legislator, senator, president of the legislature, president of the senate, minister of finance; in 1900 elected as

national congressman; influential in improving the cattle breeds
in the area around Concepción del Uruguay, experimenting with
pure-bred cattle on his own estancias; also devoted much time
to journalism as editor of La Democracia, founder of La Razón (1895) and El Republicano; died in Entre Ríos.

PEREZ, GENARO (1839-1900). Painter. Many of his works are to
be found in the churches of Córdoba, including "The Mystery
of the Rosary" in the Jesuit church.

PEREZ, JOSE ROQUE (1815-1871). Lawyer; public figure.
Born in Córdoba; served as judge; professor of law at
university of Buenos Aires; wrote part of the national civil
code of laws; Argentine representative in Paraguay (1869);
president of Lawyers Association; died in yellow fever epidemic; his name given to rich agricultural district of province of
Buenos Aires.

PEREZ, SANTOS (d. 1837). Born in Córdoba; captain of military
party believed to have been responsible for assassination of
Juan Facundo Quiroga, acting under orders from the Reinafé
brothers; convicted in trial; executed in Plaza de Mayo December 24, 1837.

PEREZ BULNES, EDUARDO (1785-1851). Patriot; political leader;
signer of declaration of independence.
Born in Córdoba; educated at Colegio de Montserrat;
entered public life as officer of militia formed in Córdoba to
support May Revolution; served as regidor (1811) and as chief
of police; represented Córdoba at congress of Tucumán; played
active role in debates and as member of special committees;
signed Declaration of Independence; supported José Antonio Cab-
reta (q.v.) in his loyalty to Artigas; returned to private life
in Córdoba, refusing to accompany congress in its move to
Buenos Aires; years later (1824) represented Córdoba again at
the constituent congress and signed constitution of 1826; in civil wars that followed provincial rejection of this constitution,
he strongly supported General José M. Paz (q.v.); after latter
was overthrown as governor of Córdoba, Pérez Bulnes took no
further part in public life.

PEREZ COLMAN, CESAR BLAS (1874-1949). Lawyer; historian;
public figure.
Born in Entre Ríos, from a patrician family; studied in
the University of Santa Fe where he became a professor; became federal judge of Paraná and member of the Court of Appeals; elected to legislature of the province in 1901; retired and
wrote several history books; was elected member of the National Academy of History; some of his publications are: La ciudad de Paraná en el segundo centenario; Presidencia del General Urquiza; Historia de Entre Ríos (1520-1810), Época colonial (3 volumes); Los primeros 50 años de la vida nacional;
died in Córdoba in 1949 while on vacation.

PEREZ DE ZORITA (or ZURITA), JUAN (d. around 1595). Spanish conquistador; lieutenant governor of Tucumán 1557-1561.
    Born in Córdoba, Spain; sent from Chile to Santiago del Estero as lieutenant governor of Tucumán, in 1557, by Hurtado de Mendoza, with a small force of 60-70 men to strengthen and colonize the area; in 1558 he founded Londres (q. v.) among the Diaguitas of Catamarca; in 1559 on the ruins of Barco II in Salta, he established Córdoba de Calchaquí; and the following year he founded Cañete (q. v.) on site of former Barco I (where San Miguel del Tucumán was later established); by those strategically located settlements he hoped to hold the land for Spain and to strengthen communications between Tucumán and Peru, as well as with Chile; in 1561 governor Castañeda came from Chile to replace Pérez de Zorita; the latter refused to accept Chile's rule over Tucumán and was sent back to Chile as prisoner; shortly afterwards, his new towns were destroyed by Indians; he quickly got back into favor with Spanish authorities in Chile, and was used for important missions throughout Chile and Bolivia, but the well-known enmity between him and Francisco Aguirre kept him from further action in Tucumán (see Francisco Aguirre).

PEREZ VIRASORO, EVARISTO (1870-1950). Public figure. Born in Corrientes; became teacher, national representative (1910, 1918), minister of government for Governor Vidal, and national senator (1925); served as director of the savings and loans bank (1931), and governor of La Pampa (1934); was appointed federal interventor of San Juan (1941); director of the post office 1941-1948; died in Buenos Aires.

PERIBEBUY. Paraguayan fort taken by Argentines commanded by General Manuel Ocampo August 12, 1869; prisoners were divided among the Allies, flags given to Argentines.

PERICON. Folk dance that originated in the pampas, influenced by the Spanish quadrille; national dance.

"PERITO MORENO. " ("Honored specialist, or authority, Moreno"). Name and title by which scientist Francisco P. Moreno is commonly known in Argentina (see Moreno; National Parks).

PERLINGER, LUIS CESAR (1892-). Military commander; rival of J. D. Perón for political domination in GOU.
    Born in Trinidad, San Juan; studied at military academy and war college; had served as chief of general staff of 2nd army and commandant of 5th military region at time of GOU revolt in 1943; became minister of interior in President Farrell's cabinet; led opposition among GOU nationalist officers to prevent Perón's rise to political power as minister of war and then as vice president (1944); this Movimiento de Renovación (renewal or reform movement) failed; after having served as division general on new assignments, he retired from

active duty in 1948; received many honors, including those
from Chile, Spain, and Denmark.

PEROL.   Copper brazier for coal; used in better homes for heat
during nineteenth century.

PERON, JUAN DOMINGO (1895-1974).   President, 1946-1955; 1973-
1974.
          Born in Lobos, Buenos Aires province, his father a poor
farmer of Italian background and his mother Spanish creole,
Perón grew up in lower middle class social and financial insecurity, steeped in gaucho lore of freedom; entered the Colegio
Militar in 1911; deeply interested in Argentine and military his-
tory--submitted paper to Second International Congress of History
of America (Buenos Aires, 1937) on San Martín's crossing of the
Andes in 1817; entered public life in 1930, taking part in General
José E. Uriburu's takeover of Yrigoyen's government to establish
military dictatorship; spent 1939-1940 traveling in Europe, military attaché to Mussolini's Italy; returned by way of Spain, still
scarred from civil war.   Back in Argentina, became member
of military secret society GOU (Grupo de Oficiales Unidos)
and took part in its coup of June 4, 1943, overthrowing
government of Ramón S. Castillo and forestalling the probable succession to the presidency of conservative sugar plant-
er-estanciero Robustiano Patrón Costas of Salta; dissatisfied
with increasingly conservative orientation of the military government, Perón organized a colonels' military clique and exerted pressure placing General Edelmiro J. Farrell in the
presidency, February 24, 1944, with Perón in active role;
as Minister of War, he improved the army, as Secretary of
Labor, he protected workers and increased their wages; and
as vice president he attempted to mold public opinion in favor
of a new Argentina; ousted and sent to Martín García island
by his opponents, he was triumphantly brought back to Buenos
Aires a few days later (October 17, 1945) by the workers,
supported by the Campo de Mayo Army and some police
units.   Having created a strong political base from an alliance of his military following with that of the loyal workers,
Perón became candidate for the presidency in the approaching
elections; he was determined to find a new middle way for
Argentina, deeply rooted in its own historical past, avoiding
the extremes of fascism on the right (although his enemies
accused him of being fascist) and that of communism on the
left; to restore the constitution and to make it work; to incorporate all elements of society into participation in the public political and economic life, too long controlled by the landholding aristocracy; to make Argentina genuinely free from
foreign controls, both economic and international (i.e., resisted what he and many other Argentines believed to be U.S.
attempts at hegemony of Western Hemisphere); February 24,
1946, elected president in free election, largely by lower and
middle classes, but also supported by nationalists who resented what they considered to be U.S. attempts to influence

the election and those who hoped that Perón's political talents
could, in fact, bring greater social justice and national gran-
deur to Argentina, in a break from the past.

As president, Perón sought to centralize power in the
presidency and to establish control over every phase of public
life--military, political, judicial, labor, economic, moral,
and ideological--depending preferably on constitutional means
and popular support but using force, bribery and corruption,
and terrorism when these failed.   His administration falls into three periods:

1.   1946-1949--the high point of Perón's success; Argentina riding crest of post World War II prosperity; large
accumulation of capital on hand; nation proud to be under constitutional government again; Perón conciliatory and slow in
establishing controls; but quick to move toward his program:
established IAPI (Argentine Institute for the Promotion of
Trade) 1946; increased power, prestige, fringe benefits, and
gave higher wages to labor; social welfare benefits distributed
by Eva Perón; Five-Year Plan (500 pages) announced and im-
plementation of it begun--called especially for nationalization,
by purchase, of foreign-owned railways, river steamship
companies, and public utilities; acceleration and diversification of industrialization; and use of Argentine wealth, not only
for development of Argentina, but also to increase nation's
international power and prestige, claiming for Argentina a
"Third Position" of positive neutrality in Cold War developing
between Western powers and Russia.   Perón established his
power politically by organizing the Peronist Party (1949) and
by bringing Congress under his control; acting on his belief
that social justice was more important than the letter of the
law, he purged those judges who differed, and established
sympathetic courts; women received the right to vote in 1947,
and when the constitution was amended in 1949 to give the
president more power and to permit his reelection, women
were also given the right to hold office; political support
from church strengthened by law making religious instruction
in schools compulsory; after 1947 university rectors were appointed by president and all university fees were removed in
1949; size of the military expanded, as well as its budget;
salaries of officers raised and living conditions improved;
and a name, Justicialismo, (1949) given to the whole.

2.   1949-1952--decreasing rate of progress to point of
decline; Perón still popular with masses, but tensions increasing; economy, particularly in rural areas where the agropecuarian industries, that had supported Argentina for decades,
showed positive decline (in 1952 Argentina had to import
wheat), due partly to bad weather but attributed primarily to
government neglect and discrimination; labor strikes and an
abortive military uprising were easily put down but Perón
felt it necessary to place country under martial law (1951);
military pressure forced the withdrawal of Eva Perón's name
as vice-presidential candidate; nation decapitalized by high
prices paid for run-down foreign railways and utilities, by

Perón's extravagant government expenditures, and by flight of
estanciero capital; ideological controls were increased: press
censorship extended to powerful but critical La Prensa, expropriated and turned over to the CGT (General Confederation
of Labor), 1951; control over universities tightened and teaching of justicialismo required.

      3.   1952-1955--decline and fall of Perón and his re-
gime. Year 1952 was critical: re-election of Perón; death
of his wife and political colleague, Eva Perón; end of period
of strong expansion and generous use of government funds:
Perón's government apparently seemed strong enough and able
to find correctives: at end of year Second Five-Year Plan
was announced, enunciating principles for Argentina's future
economic growth as well as spelling out practical new measures designed to increase oil production and to restore confidence and prosperity to the agropecuarian industries; but fa-
tigue, both personal in Perón's case (accentuated by grief
over loss of his wife), and throughout the administration, became increasingly evident; financial scandals damaged government prestige; nationalists resented invitations to foreign
capital; labor contacts deteriorated with Eva gone; Perón's
political realism seemed to be replaced by irrationalism and
force; his acts alienated even further his long-standing enemies among the intellectuals (from communists to fascists)
and members of the oligarchic group; turned Church from
supporter to powerful foe by series of attacks--perhaps because Church approved formation of a Christian Democratic
party, perhaps in retaliation for Church's criticism of Perón's
insistence on teaching of justicialismo, perhaps even because
of the Church's stand regarding the popular demand for canonization of Evita; difficulties increased within the government,
growing out of the diverse interests of the groups within it,
as well as the problems involved in changing the old into
something new by constitutional, not revolutionary means;
powerful leadership, that Perón felt unable to provide at this
moment, was essential; his overthrow by the military came
September 19, 1955, and Perón went into exile leaving a nation that found it almost as difficult to live without him, as
with him.

      In 1972, upon invitation from the Argentine govern-
ment Perón returned to Buenos Aires in November for a
brief visit during which he refused to accept the nomination
for president by the Justicialist (formerly Peronist) party,
selecting Hector Cámpora in his stead, then returned to
Spain.

      Cámpora was elected president on April 15, 1973.
Péron returned to the country and after the resignation of
Cámpora in June 1973 became candidate for president.
Elected in September with 62% of the votes became president
for the third time in October 1973; his wife, María Estela
(Isabelita) Perón became the vice president of the nation;
died of a heart attack on July 1, 1974 (see GOU; Peronismo;
María Eva Duarte de Perón; María Estela Martínez de Perón;
Political Parties).

For early studies of Perón's first and second administrations see Robert J. Alexander, The Perón Era (New York,
1951, and London, 1952); George I. Blanksten, Perón's Argentina (Chicago, 1953); and Arthur P. Whitaker, Argentine
Upheaval: Perón's Fall and the New Regime (New York and
London, 1956); see also Alberto Ciria, Perón y el justicialismo (Mexico, D.F., and Buenos Aires, 1971).

PERON, MARIA ESTELA MARTINEZ DE (ISABELITA) (1931-   ).
President of the nation 1974-1976.

Born in La Rioja on February 4, 1931; youngest of six
children of a poor family; studied piano and dance and joined
a theater as a dancer; in 1956 she met Juan Domingo Perón
in Panamá; became his secretary and then married him in
exile in 1960; in 1964 as representative of her husband she
returned to Argentina and succeeded in destroying the movement directed by Augusto Vandor that wanted Peronism without Perón; in 1971 she attempted to reunite left and right
Peronists but failed; was elected vice president when Juan
Perón again became president in 1973; was made president
of Argentina on June 29, 1974, due to the serious illness of
her husband who died two days later.

Mrs. Perón became the first woman president in the
Western Hemisphere; her government was overthrown by the
military March 24, 1976, because of mounting economic problems and increasing guerrilla violence.

PERON, MARIA EVA DUARTE DE (EVITA) (1919-1952).   Wife and
political colleague of Juan Domingo Perón.

Born in humble circumstances in Los Toldos, Buenos
Aires, this beautiful, courageous, and determined woman rose
from an indifferent career as actress in Buenos Aires to become the symbol and agent of Perón's promised benefits to
the masses, or descamisados, with whom she readily related
and from whom she received loyalty and affection.

Devoted to Perón (whom she married in 1945 after his
return from Martín García island) and to his program, she
became responsible for uniting the labor groups into a powerful political force supporting Perón; accomplished this through
her charismatic personality, genuine flair for demagoguery,
and sheer hard work; during Perón's first term as president
(often referred to as a diarchy because of Eva's role) she
was in charge of all matters relating to labor; a new dimension was added when she became director of the María Eva
Duarte de Perón Foundation, ostensibly private, but drawing
from both private and public funds; spending several hours
daily at her office, she retained personal contact with the
workers, serving as ombudsman for their grievances; dispensed benefits of all kinds lavishly, but never as charity--
always dignified as earned benefits that Perón had secured
for them ("Eva dignifica" and "Perón cumple" slogans plas-
tered everywhere); kept political channels open between Perón
and labor and increased loyalty and support; but also

exacerbated the enmity of the oligarchy as her Foundation superseded the traditional Sociedad de Beneficencia (q. v.) through which the ladies of the oligarchy had dispensed charity since the 1820s.

Active leader in pushing for women's political rights, she was largely responsible for women getting the right to vote in 1947 and she herself took advantage of the constitutional change permitting women to hold office to become a candidate for vice president in 1952, but was forced to withdraw by military pressure and illness.

Died from cancer July 26, 1952, shortly after Perón's inauguration for second term; buried in Buenos Aires with great honors, amid mass hysteria; Eva Perón's body was secretly removed and sent to Italy after the revolution overthrowing Perón in 1955, and was returned to Perón in 1971; later placed in magnificent glass coffin in Buenos Aires.

It is generally believed that the decline in Perón's power during the second term was partially due to his wife's death: he missed her personally, especially her courageous spirit; without her sure touch he lost contact with masses when he needed them most and could give them less; and her death may have been an element triggering his final disastrous attack on the church, i. e., growing out of the refusal of the Church to take seriously popular demands for the canonization of Eva Perón.

PERONISM (Peronismo). Term applied to principles, policies, goals which Perón was believed to have represented; to his enemies and political opponents, this meant the introduction of abhorrent totalitarian ideas and methods, bringing economic chaos and social fragmentation to the country; to his supporters it stood for progress toward social, economic, political justice, and Argentine economic independence; Peronists were eager to continue the progress through political means but it was not until 1972, when they were joined by other Argentines, in the name of political harmony and justice, that they were permitted to form their own Justicialist party; their candidate, Héctor Cámpora, selected by Perón, won the election and was inaugurated May 25, 1973; presidents Juan Domingo and María Estela de Perón followed in 1974 and 1976.

PERONIST PARTY. Political party formed by Perón's followers in 1949; banned after 1955 revolution; attempted a comeback as Justicialist Party; formed again in 1970s under different name (see Political Parties; Peronism).

PERSONALISTS (Personalistas). Faction of Radical Party; followers and supporters of Hipólito Yrigoyen (q. v.); outlawed by José Félix Uriburu (q. v.).

PERTINE, BASILIO B. (1879-1963). Military career man.
Born in Buenos Aires; after completing his training in

the Colegio Militar, went to Germany for advanced military
studies; served as military attaché in Brazil (1909) and in
Germany (1910-1918); followed operations of World War I
from general headquarters of German army; returned to Argentina; after holding various military appointments, became
minister of war in President Agustín P. Justo's cabinet
(1935); considered to be sympathetic to the Radicals; president of Círculo Militar 1939-1944; after revolution of 1943
became municipal intendant of Buenos Aires; was leader of
governing board of Argentine Nationalism, a restricted group
formed by members of the Circle of Arms, very active in
politics until 1945; Pertiné was widely honored by foreign
governments as well as his own.

PETROLEUM.   Petroleum is the primary energy source in Argentina as it supplies nearly 75% of the nation's requirements
   (mid-1970s).   Production, refining, and marketing are controlled by Yacimientos Petrolíferos Fiscales (q.v.), the gov-
   ernment-owned oil companies; various contracts, however,
   have been granted to several private companies to supplement
   national needs and reduce imports, since the Frondizi government in the late 1950s.   These contracts were briefly canceled in 1963 during the short term presidency of Illia, but
   until the election of 1973 the political situation was still considered favorable to foreign investments; the oil industry is
   controlled by governmental decrees and YPF, which originally acted as an advisor, is now treated as any other company;
   the principal companies operating in Argentina are YPF,
   ESSO, Pan American, Cities Service, Shell, La Isaura, and
   Petroquímica.
       The major producing areas are Salta (Tartagal), Cuyo
   (Mendoza), Neuquén (Plaza Huincul), Gulf of San Jorge (Comodoro Rivadavia), Magellán (Río Gallegos) (see map, Appendix IV).
       All reserves are state-owned, and self-sufficiency has
   been the major goal of the late administration; YPF produces
   75% of the total, Cities Service 15%, Pan American 9% and
   all others 1%; petroleum consumption rose from 5 million
   barrels per year in 1925 to 50 million barrels per year in
   1962; it reached 200 million in 1970.   Self-sufficiency was
   attained by 1962, for a brief period, but imports were needed
   again to meet the evergrowing demand.
       Natural gas is being imported from Bolivia by pipe-
   line.   Some production is also sent from the south to Buenos
   Aires, but all discoveries have not been tapped yet; Argentina's refining capacity is well developed and adequate to
   meet demand, with 16 refineries operating in the country;
   locations: Luján de Cuyo (Mendoza), La Plata (Buenos Aires),
   and Salta; gasoline used to be marketed by YPF (60% of the
   total sales), Esso (15%), Shell (16%), Cities Service and a
   few small retailers (9%), but after President Juan Domingo
   Perón's death, in 1974, the Argentine government started to
   move toward complete control of all petroleum products

Petroleum   708

marketing operations; by 1973 the petroleum shortage affecting the rest of the world reached Argentina, and gasoline
shortage became critical; although the majority of automobiles
are small or economy size, the people-to-automobile ratio is
well ahead of those of the rest of South America.
        It is worthwhile noting the following: Buenos Aires,
Santa Fe, and Córdoba have 22% of the land area, 67% of the
population, 50% of the paved highway system, and 83% of the
automobiles; 50% of the population and 60% of the automobiles
are concentrated within 50 miles of the city.
        See Publications of Argentine Republic. Dirección
General de Yacimientos Petrolíferos Fiscales--Memoria--
1923, on; Arturo Frondizi, Petróleo y política (Buenos Aires,
1956); Marcos Kaplan, Petróleo, estado y empresas en Argentina (Caracas, 1972).

PEUSER, JACOBO (1843-1901).   Businessman; printer and publish-
    er.
        Born in Germany; immigrated to Argentina in 1860;
opened his first bookstore in 1868; began printing and publishing three years later with Trip to the Araucanian Country by
Estanislao Zeballos; today the family owns and operates one
of the largest bookstore and publishing companies of the country.

PEYRET, ALEJO (1826-1902).   Educator; administrator of agricul-
    tural colonies.
        Born in France; studied in Paris; was actively involved
in revolution of 1848 that deposed the king and proclaimed the
second republic; when this failed, he was forced, with other
republicans, to seek exile (1852); at his arrival in the Río de
la Plata, Urquiza immediately placed him as teacher in the
Colegio de Concepción del Uruguay; there, with Alberto Larroque (q. v.) he quickly became one of the intellectual masters
of what was to be the Generation of 1880 (q. v.); in 1857 Urquiza gave him management of the colony of San José; his
growing interest in the new agricultural colonies being established in Entre Ríos improved conditions in the colonies;
after several years he moved to Buenos Aires; taught French
at the university; in 1881 he was sent to Misiones to survey
possibilities of colonization; published Cartas sobre Misiones;
in the late 1880s he was placed in charge of all the colonies
and remained in that post for ten years; traveled extensively
through the interior visiting and reporting on all the colonies;
published Una visita a las colonias de la República Argentina
(1889); died in Entre Ríos.

PEZUELA, JOAQUIN DE LA (1761-1830).   Viceroy of Peru; mili-
    tary man.
        Born in Spain; entered military service; fought against
the French; sent to America as director of the royal artillery
of Viceroy Abascal in Peru; later was appointed to replace
General Goyeneche in army of Alto Perú; reorganized the

Spanish army after the patriots' triumph in Salta, and defeated General Belgrano in Vilcapugio and Ayohuma (1813);
entered the province of Salta and was attacked by the Güemes
forces and defeated in Puerto Márquez (1815); defeated the
patriot forces under General Rondeau in Sipe-Sipe (November
23, 1815); after this battle he was made Marquis de Viluma
and was promoted to rank of lieutenant general; was appointed
viceroy of Peru in 1815; as such, rejected San Martín's proposal to let the people of Peru decide their own destiny
(1818); deposed by the commanders and officers of the royalist army in 1821 and replaced by the energetic general, José
de la Serna; returned to Spain and in 1825 was appointed captain general of New Spain (Mexico); died in Madrid; his memoirs were published in 1947 in Sevilla as Memorias de gobierno.

PICAZZARRI, JUAN ANTONIO (d. 1843).   Pioneer musician. Born
in Buenos Aires; organized the first Argentine orchestra,
about 1811; played the national anthem in public for the first
time (1813); he is considered to have been the first to introduce Italian music into the country; in 1821 went to Europe,
and at his return opened the first academy of music (1822)
in his own home; taught there until his death.

PICCARDO, PEDRO (1870-1941).   Industrialist.   Born in Buenos
Aires; after studying at Colegio Nacional, went into business;
specialized in tobacco manufacturing; president of Piccardo y
Cía, Ltd. , that made the famous cigarettes "43" as well as
other brands; also had interests in glass factories, radio industries, as well as in insurance companies.

PICCIRILLI, RICARDO (1900-   ).   Historian.   Born in province of
Buenos Aires; held various appointments in normal and vocational schools and served as inspector of secondary education, 1945-1955; was active in several professional associations; in 1938 he acted as secretary of Second International
Congress of American History, held in Buenos Aires; his
two-volume Rivadavia y su tiempo, published in Buenos Aires,
1943, won second prize in 1940 and 1942 offered by Comisión
Nacional de Cultura; collaborated in writing of the Historia
de la nación argentina published by the Academia Nacional de
la Historia; among his other works are historical novels like
Jornada de Fuertes; essays, such as El caballo en la evolución sociológica argentina; other serious historical works are
Tacuaras que sangran; Rivadavia, precursor de los estudios
históricos en el país (1939); Rivadavia y la diplomacia.   Epi-
sodio de una tramitación monárquica frustrada (1945); Rivadavia y Canning (1946); Juan Thompson (1949); San Martín y
la política de los pueblos (1958); his major work, as general
editor of the Diccionario Histórico Argentino, 6 v. , published
in collaboration with Francisco L. Román and Leonicio Gianello (Buenos Aires, 1954-1955), has been invaluable to authors of this dictionary.

PICHI-CARHUE, ENCOUNTER OF (March 8, 1872). In this fight, the forces of Ignacio Rivas defeated about 3000 Indians under Juan Calfucurá; Indian casualties numbered over 200 dead; for the time being, Indians were pushed back in Buenos Aires province to a frontier beyond the settled districts of 9 de Julio and 25 de Mayo.

PICHINCHA, BATTLE OF (May 24, 1822). Battle on mountain overlooking Quito in which Bolivar's field commander, Antonio José Sucre, with the aid of 1000 men whom San Martín had sent from Peru to assist the common effort, defeated the Spanish forces, winning the independence of Ecuador and opening the way for collaboration between Bolívar and San Martín to complete the war for independence (see José de San Martín).

PICO, EDUARDO GUSTAVO (1838-1904). Military officer; governor of La Pampa in 1890s.
    Born in Buenos Aires, grandson and namesake of independence fighter; began his military career with battle of Cepeda (1859), fought at Pavón, in the Paraguayan War, against the Entre Ríos rebellion led by López Jordán (1870); took part in bloody campaigns against the Indians in the Southwest, accompanying Roca in 1876 to the desert and in 1879-1880 to Río Negro; served as governor of La Pampa three times, 1891-1899; town (General Pico) in northeastern part of the province named for him.

PICO, FRANCISCO (1803-1875). Lawyer; public figure.
    Born in Buenos Aires, son of Colonel Francisco Pico (1779-1819) who fought against British invasions and for independence; received degree in law in 1825 and entered government service; was in the ministry of government until federalists triumphed, following Lavalle's attempted takeover of government; moved to Montevideo; under Oribe, he and other opponents of Rosas (Rivadavia, Valentín Alsina, Juan Cruz Varela, etc.) were imprisoned on Isla de las Ratas and exiled to Brazil; after Oribe's overthrow (1838) he returned to Uruguay to join other Argentines in the Liberating Legion under Juan Lavalle; in 1844 became judge advocate of army in Uruguay; returned to Buenos Aires after Caseros; opposed Urquiza's desire to establish capital in Buenos Aires; attended congress of San Nicolás; defended the Acuerdo (q. v.); joined the Confederation group; appointed Confederation consul-general in Montevideo; 1858 appointed contador general de Confederation; President Derqui appointed him foreign minister (1860-1861); national senator in 1862; later, as Procurador General de la Nación, had four volumes of legal papers published by Ministry of Justice; collaborated with General Gerónimo Espejo in drawing up military code; died in Buenos Aires; father of engineer Octavio Pico (q. v.).

PICO, OCTAVIO (1836-1892). Engineer and cartographer.

Born in Montevideo of exiled parents; studied engineering there; after Caseros, returned to Buenos Aires; in 1870 was elected representative to Buenos Aires legislature; accompanied military expedition to Río Negro, 1878, as surveyor and cartographer; drew up topographical maps of area; made similar studies of Neuquén and Limay rivers in 1887; head of Argentine commission (1890) to negotiate with Chile over boundary problems; died while carrying out this mission.

PICO, OCTAVIO SERGIO (1867-1943).   Civil engineer, university professor.

Born in Buenos Aires; graduated as civil engineer from faculty of exact, physical, and natural sciences, 1892; taught in the central national academy and then in his own faculty; secured employment with government; in 1895 became undersecretary of justice and education, director of land and colonies (1898), adviser of Banco Nación; Uriburu brought him into his cabinet (1930) as minister of public works; in this capacity, he drew up plan for network of national highways and devised the gasoline tax to finance them; toward the end of Uriburu's administration, he served as minister of the interior and was responsible for the elections by which the Justo-Roca ticket was successful; President Justo appointed him president of National Council of Education; was founder and first president of Institución Mitre; served on many other boards of directors; died in Buenos Aires.

PIEDRA, JUAN DE LA (d. 1785).   Spanish official sent to explore and occupy Patagonian coast.   In the late 1770s Spain feared English expansion into South Atlantic waters and Patagonia as shown by its increased fishing and whaling industries there, its occupation of the Falkland Islands, and its threats to the unoccupied Argentine coast of Patagonia; Viceroy Vértiz y Salcedo was ordered to establish forts and settlements along the Atlantic coast; Juan de la Piedra arrived in Buenos Aires August 27, 1778, as commissary-general to establish forts as far as the Strait of Magellán; explored coast as far as Río Negro, then turned back; in 1784-1785 undertook to establish fortifications but was killed by Indians in a general massacre at Sierra de la Ventana; detailed account of explorations made by member of the party (see Basilio Villarino y Bermúdez).

PIFILKA.   Small vertical flute used by the Indians.

PIGAFETTA, ANTONIO (1481-1534).   Italian Renaissance scholar and traveler who accompanied Magellan's expedition on its voyage around the world 1519-1522, one of the eighteen survivors to return to Spain; his detailed report of the voyage, including the first map of South America and Argentina and first description of the Patagonian and Straits area, has been published in many editions and languages.

"PIGTAIL REVOLT"   see   REBELION DE LAS TRENZAS

PIGÜE.   Small town in southern Buenos Aires that gave its name
to defeat of Calfucurá's Indians May 15, 1858, by government
troops; temporarily stopped Indian raids (malones) in that
area.

PILAGAES.   These Chaco Indians still live in tribal fashion along
the right bank of the Pilcomayo river in central Formosa;
belong to Guaycurú linguistic group; originally hunters and
gatherers, especially of carob fruit; today they fish and raise
such agricultural crops as tobacco, squash, and corn; tend
their own livestock--donkeys, goats, and sheep--weave on a
vertical loom, and make simple ceramics; their early religion was primitive, with a belief in magic apparently showing
influence of Brazilian Indians (see Guaycurúans).

PILAR, TREATY OF (February 2, 1820).   Agreement signed between the Littoral Provinces (represented by Francisco Ramírez, Entre Ríos, and Estanislao López of Santa Fe) and
Buenos Aires Province led by its governor Manuel Sarratea,
in which they hoped to establish peace and a working arrangement by agreeing upon two principles: federalism, as the
provinces were declared to be autonomous; and nationalism,
with the provinces agreeing to send delegates to a national
congress to draw up a constitution for a federal form of
government; free navigation of Paraná and Uruguay rivers
guaranteed the signatories and a Paraná squadron turned over
to Ramírez.

PILCOMAYO RIVER.   River that originates in Potosí, Bolivia, at
2000 meters of altitude and flows tumultuously for 1000 kilometers to form delta at its entrance into the Paraguay river;
apparently takes its name from Quechua words meaning river
of the pilco (brightly colored Andean bird); became boundary
between Argentine Republic and Paraguay in 1878 as result of
arbitration decision made by U.S. President Rutherford B.
Hayes, following Paraguayan War (q. v.); its alluvial basin in
the Chaco region produces yerba mate, quebracho, tea, cotton, etc. ; in the 1950s an extensive project was drawn up,
apparently by engineer Juan Palacio, to create a new littoral
(coastal region) along the Pilcomayo by damming, dredging,
and rechanneling it to make it navigable; interior ports (like
that of Catoosa near Tulsa, Oklahoma, on the Arkansas
River), would provide direct access to overseas markets;
hydroelectric plants would furnish fuel and power for new industrial development and to take greater advantage of fertility
of soil by irrigation; eight provinces--Formosa, Chaco, Jujuy,
Salta, Tucumán, Santiago del Estero, Córdoba, and Santa Fe--
would profit directly; five others--Mendoza, San Juan, La
Rioja, San Luis, and Catamarca, indirectly; envisioned as an
Argentine project, Paraguay was also expected to benefit
from it and to be involved; in the mid-1970s this Pilcomayo

development remained in planning stages because of lack of funds.

PINAZO, MANUEL DE (d. 1792). Hacendado; civic leader in
Buenos Aires and Villa de Luján. Distinguished himself for
more than 40 years in defense of the frontier, and in establishing friendly relations with the nomadic Indians of northern
Patagonia; became a pioneer (1778) in working the great salt
beds (Gran Salina) in what is now central part of La Pampa
province and transporting the salt to supply the markets in
Buenos Aires and in the royal army camps; died in Buenos
Aires in 1792, the details of his long career almost forgotten
but his name remembered as one of those who prepared the
way for the eventual settlement and development of province
of La Pampa.

PINEDO, FEDERICO (1855-1928). Lawyer.
Born in Buenos Aires; consultant of the police (1880);
undersecretary of the ministry of interior (1882); secretary
of Pan American Congress (1889); minister of finance of the
province of Buenos Aires (1890); congressman (1902); minister
of education (1906); as congressman (1910) was influential in
creating the University of Littoral (q. v.).

PINEDO, FEDERICO (1907-   ).   Lawyer; statesman; historian.
Born in Buenos Aires of aristocratic family; graduated
in law; entered public life early; helped organize dissident socialists (1927) into Independent Socialist Party, tied in closely
with Conservatives and Antipersonalists; remained active for
the next fifteen years as government official or political leader behind the scenes as one of most highly respected and
brilliant representatives of moderate center; opposed Roca-
Runciman agreement in senate debate; as Justo's minister of
finance introduced a kind of New Deal economic program for
Argentina; joined Duhau in defending government's economic
relationships with Great Britain and role of meat monopoly
in violent congressional controversy led by Lisandro de la
Torre, whom he fought in a duel; again became minister of
finance in cabinet of acting president Castillo, 1940-1941; was
almost only leading Argentine statesman willing to support
U.S. and Allies in 1940-1941; resigned when he failed to secure congressional and moderate backing against Castillo's
increasing turn toward Axis and authoritarianism; retired to
private life; active as corporation lawyer, director on various
boards, and in writing; in 1946 he published his important,
4-volume political history En tiempos de la república; in
early 1960s he was called back into government service under
President Guido, but soon resigned in protest against military
influence and activities in government.

PIÑEIRO SORONDO, PATRICIO (d. 1935).   Pioneer of Río Negro;
founded village of Allen in 1910; owned one of the largest
sheep-apple farms of the region; acted as president of the

council house several times; died in Buenos Aires in 1935.

PIÑERO, NORBERTO (1858-1938). Jurisconsult; intellectual and writer of Generation of 1880; government official.

Born in province of Buenos Aires; received his doc-torate in jurisprudence from law school, University of Buenos Aires (1882); taught law for many years; collaborated with Rodolfo Rivarola and José N. Matienzo in drawing up reform of legal criminal code; served as interventor in San Luis (1896) and in same year went on special boundary mission to Chile; after spending some time studying in Europe returned to devote himself to establishment of the kind of technological education needed in Argentina to support industrial develop-ment; formed Sociedad de Educación Industrial and became dean of the new national industrial school founded; was brought into Figueroa Alcorta's first cabinet (1906) as minister of treasury; continued in this position under Roque Saenz Peña; in the 1910 centennial attended international congress of Americanists held in Buenos Aires; founded Colegio de Abo-gados (Lawyer's Academy) of Buenos Aires; served as presi-dent of Institución Mitre; wrote extensively, and was widely read, on Argentine past and role of new Argentina, as well as on legal matters.

PINO Y ROSAS, JOAQUIN DEL (1729-1804). Viceroy, 1801-1804; military engineer and cartographer who attained rank of mar-shal.

Born in Orán of distinguished family; entered military career, specializing in engineering and cartography; arrived in Río de la Plata, 1771, on assignment of that nature, in what is now Uruguay; five years later became governor of Montevideo; improved city and strengthened its fortifications, cooperating closely with Viceroy Vértiz (q. v.); also promoted establishment of towns in that sparsely settled province (then known as Banda Oriental); transferred to Bolivia, he served as captain-general of Charcas and president of La Plata (later Sucre) audiencia for nine years; and as president of audiencia of Chile, for two years; appointed viceroy of the Río de la Plata, he assumed that position in 1801 and served until his death in 1804; during this brief period his interests were primarily in developing the moral and material life of Buenos Aires, such as improvement of police services and construction of public works; during his administration the first periodicals--Telégrafo Mercantil and Semanario de Agri-cultura y Comercio--appeared, the schools of medicine and drawing were established and a French professorship estab-lished; was accused of improper dealings with Portuguese in Brazil but defended himself so well that he was exonerated; died in Buenos Aires; in 1783, having been widowed, he had married Rafaela Vera y Mujica, with whom he had 17 chil-dren, and who made an important historical impact of her own (q. v.).

PINTO, MANUEL G.   (1783-1853).   Military officer; political figure.
      Born in Buenos Aires; after studying at Colegio de
San Carlos, went to Spain to complete his studies; returned
in time to fight against second British invasion; voted in
cabildo abierto (May, 1810) for establishment of patriot junta;
joined auxiliary army under Balcarce that fought in Alto Perú
at battles of Cotagaita, Suipacha and Huaqui; returned to
Buenos Aires (1812) to become part of artillery regiment;
assigned to garrison in Montevideo; in January, 1815, he became colonel of artillery; during government of Martín Rodríguez, he served as president of the junta of representatives
of Buenos Aires (1821-1824); represented Misiones in the
constituent congress (1824-1827); after various military assignments, again became president of the legislature in 1833;
later served as vice president, in this capacity signed law
March 7, 1835 naming Rosas governor and captain general of the
province; retired to private life; after Caseros, again became
president of the provincial legislature; involved in power struggle against Urquiza; removed by latter; again served briefly as
interim governor following September 11 movement; General
Pinto remained active in Buenos Aires government until his
death June 25, 1853.

PINTOS, ANGEL (1856-1944).   Physician and public figure.
      Worked in province of Buenos Aires; served as mayor of city
   of Azul; created teachers' college; established courts of justice, built roads, installed running water, built hospitals, etc.;
   provincial senator (1918); national legislator (1924-1932).

PIRCAS.   Rock walls, from four to six feet high, built without
   mortar; used as boundaries between large properties; similar
   rock walls are used today to separate houses in the small
   villages, in regions where rocks and stones are abundant.

PISTARINI, JUAN (1882-1956).   Military engineer; strong supporter of Perón in first two administrations.
      Born in Victorica, La Pampa, of Italian parents;
   studied in Colegio Militar, Escuela Superior Técnica, escuela
   superior de guerra; completed his military training in Germany; in 1937 became general of division and eventually
   lieutenant general; accompanied Perón and Sosa to Italy as
   member of arms commission (1939-1940); served as director
   general of army engineers, national interventor in province
   of Buenos Aires; known to be pro-Nazi in World War II; in
   1943 became commandant general of internal forces and
   president of Círculo Militar; took part in GOU revolt of 1943
   and discharged duties of minister of agriculture and interim
   minister of navy, minister of public works, and minister of
   the interior, and vice president; known as one of Juan Domingo Perón's most faithful supporters; accompanied the
   president at his formal resignation from the presidency in
   1955; died shortly thereafter.

PISTARINI, PASCUAL ANGEL.   Commander-in-chief of the army
   under Illia; responsible for coup d'état that removed the
   president in 1966; one of the leaders of the Azules considered soft on the Peronists; forced the resignation of the
   minister of war and was accused of meeting with Peronists;
   this accusation started the coup intended to end all military
   takeovers, with Onganía installed as the new president.

"PLAN CONINTES" (1960) see CONINTES PLAN

PLAZA, VICTORINO DE LA (1840-1919).   President of Argentine
   Republic, 1913-1916; lawyer.
         Born in Salta, of poor parents; studied law in Buenos
   Aires; enlisted briefly in army to fight in Paraguayan War;
   bad health forced him to leave; in 1868 received his doctorate
   in laws; became secretary of Dalmacio Vélez Sársfield (q.v.);
   collaborated in writing civil code of laws; in 1876 Avellaneda
   appointed him minister of finance (hacienda); served as federal interventor in Corrientes (1878) and national congressman
   for Salta, 1880; drew up plan for Argentine monetary system;
   served during Roca's first administration as foreign minister
   (1882) and minister of finance (1883-1885); in 1890 went to
   London on official mission to discuss foreign debt problem
   with international bankers' committee headed by Lord Rothschild; served again as cabinet minister of foreign relations
   (1908); elected as vice president on National Union ticket
   headed by Roque Saenz Peña (1910); because of latter's illness, Victorino de la Plaza was frequently called upon to
   serve as interim president, 1913-1914, and then, at Saenz
   Peña's death, became president in his own right, 1914-1916;
   during this period the executive power was concerned chiefly
   with handling the possible political repercussions growing out
   of the electoral reform bill of 1912 (see Saenz Peña law) and
   the effects that the outbreak of World War I (q.v.) would
   have on Argentina; although he was primarily conservative in
   his convictions, President de la Plaza followed Saenz Peña's
   more liberal policies during interim presidency and throughout
   his administration carried out the law as written; the economic effects of World War I had not yet become fully evident
   during his term but he handled the situation effectively, just
   as he had the 1913 economic recession; the Caja Nacional de
   Ahorro Postal (Postal Savings Fund) was established; in 1915
   he published a book dealing with the unemployment situation
   in Argentina; in foreign affairs he followed traditional policy
   but broke some new ground; expressed formal disapproval of
   U.S. war against Mexico, 1913-1914; declared Argentina's
   neutrality in World War I; joined ABC bloc (q.v.), regarded
   by many as an emergence from recent Argentine isolation-
   ism; administered first election under new reform laws that
   brought Radical Party into power, 1916; retired from politics;
   died of pneumonia.

POBLADOR.   A kind of Argentine homesteader; name given to

person who is promised land as incentive for him to settle in
a given area and to develop that land; for example, when
Garay refounded Buenos Aires in 1580 and divided the surrounding land, he reserved 40 blocs (of 250) to be given to
pobladores; each was required to take possession of his land
and to begin cultivating it within three months or he would
forfeit it; pobladores were also given encomiendas of Indians
to help work the land; these prerogatives continued to the
eighteenth century; after independence had been won, pobladores were used to settle and hold the Indian frontier, with
additional prerogatives adding to landowning, like exemption
from military service.

POINSETT, JOEL ROBERTS (1779-1851).   President Madison's
appointment of South Carolinian J. P. Poinsett (1810) to go
to Buenos Aires, Chile, and Peru as commercial agent (acting as consul) marked two firsts in U.S. foreign policy: the
sending of a representative to a country whose independence
had not yet been recognized (and Argentina had not yet declared its independence) and Washington's first expression of
interest in the Latin American independence movement; presenting his credentials to the junta (February 13, 1811), Poinsett spent the next nine months representing U.S. interests in
the Río de la Plata area, and sending full reports to keep
President Madison informed; in November he decided to move
on to Santiago, Chile, leaving William G. Miller as U.S.
vice consul in Buenos Aires; after three years in Chile,
where he was closely related to the Carrera regime, Poinsett returned to the United States in 1815 to resume public
responsibilities, becoming the first minister to Mexico (1825-
1829) and serving as Van Buren's secretary of war.   Poin-
settias, which he introduced into the United States from tropical America, take their name from him.

POLITICAL PARTIES.   Argentine political parties appeared in the
first patriot government (1810) with the Morenistas, who supported the more radical European-oriented ideas of Mariano
Moreno and wanted government centered in Buenos Aires, vs.
the Saavedristas, the more traditional, conservative followers
of Cornelio Saavedra who favored greater provincial participation in government; after the declaration of independence in
1816, three major political groups were formed; the porteño
or Buenos Aires centralist republican group (led by Rivadavia),
the provincial group desiring a federalized government, and
the monarchical party that favored a constitutional monarchy
similar to that of Great Britain; the latter party disappeared
and from the 1820s to the 1850s Argentina lived (for most of
the time) without formal national government, bitterly divided
between Unitarists and Federalists; the Federalist governor
of Buenos Aires province, Juan Manuel de Rosas, was given
responsibility for handling foreign affairs in the name of all
of the provinces, and he also attempted to force the individual provinces to maintain friendly, federalist governments;

during the decade (1852-1862) between the defeat of Rosas
and the election of Bartolomé Mitre as constitutional president of the reorganized Argentine Republic, political parties
played active roles in the independent Buenos Aires province
and in the Confederation; most of the new political leaders
considered themselves liberals but fragmentation into individual parties, each believing itself to have a mission to
save the republic, developed very quickly; through responsible
leadership the two major groups, Autonomists and National
party combined to form the National Autonomous Party that
governed Argentina successfully for more than four decades,
1874-1916.

　　　During this period of political stability and economic
prosperity, important social changes--most of them related
to immigration--had brought demands for creation of new
parties to represent the needs and aspirations of the rapidly
growing middle classes, as well as of the rural and urban
laborers; the Radical party was formed in the 1880s (see
Unión Cívica Radical), the Progressive Democratic party of
Lisandro de la Torre, and the Socialist party, in 1890s and,
by 1920, the Communist party had been organized; following
the electoral reform bill of 1912, the Radical party came into
power, governing from 1916 to 1930; in the elections of 1932,
following José Félix Uriburu's military takeover in 1930, a
new group, largely conservative but with many old-time liberals, formed the Concordancia that remained in power until
1943, when the GOU took over.

　　　From 1943 until the mid-1970s, the history of Argentine political parties has been chaotic, and largely centered
around the issue of Peronism; for much of this time the
Peronist party, called Justicialist after 1955, was restrained
from participation in elections or given only restricted privileges; other leftist parties, including the Communist, suffered
the same limitations; the Argentine Communist party formed
by Victorio Codovilla (q.v.) had found its strength primarily
among foreign-born Argentines and declined in influence after
1943; when it became legal again in the 1960s (still under
leadership of Codovilla, by this time one of the oldest Communist leaders in the world), it generally sought to exert political influence through combinations with other leftist parties
(see Victorio Codovilla, Por la acción de las masas hacia la
conquista del poder, 1963); Communists became divided into
pro-Castro and pro-Russian groups; one new party, the
Christian Democratic party, gained national support during
this period; formed in July 1955 by a group of Catholics
under leadership of Mario Amadeo, the party sought to give
a Christian reform point of view; the church hierarchy immediately disavowed any connection with this new political organization and, after a brief initial period of influence, it
found itself caught up into the same pattern of fragmentation
and combination in which other Argentine political parties were
attempting to operate; for example, in 1965, 222 parties were
registered with the ministry of the interior but only the

Socialists, Christian Democrats, Conservatives, and two
chief Radical Parties (UCRI and UCRP) had national or mass
followings; in 1973, in a free election, the Justicialists, with
help of other Peronist and leftist groups, elected Héctor
Cámpora president and won control of the government again.
    For this confused later period see Jeane J. Kirkpat-
rick, Leader and Vanguard in Mass Society; A Study of
Peronist Argentina (The MIT Press, Cambridge, Mass. and
London, Eng., 1971); for ideology of modern Argentine Communist Party, see Alberto Kohen, Marxismo, estado y derecho (Buenos Aires, 1972); general reference: Robert J. Alexander, Latin American Political Parties (New York, 1973).

POLO. Ancient Persian stick-and-ball game played on horseback,
    introduced into Argentina in 1874 by the British, who brought
    it from India; became very popular in eastern horse-breeding
    area; first polo club founded in 1882; continues to be impor-
    tant Argentine sport.

PONCE, ANIBAL (1898-1938). Writer; psychologist.
        Born in Buenos Aires; studied medicine, specializing
    in psychology; studied under José Ingenieros and edited, with
    him, the Revista de Filosofía; from 1920 to 1930 was literary
    critic for Nosotros and El Hogar; one of founders, with Luis
    Reisig, A. Korn and others, of the Colegio Libre de Estudios
    Superiores; traveled extensively in Europe, including Russia
    (by invitation); taught psychology in national institute of
    secondary teachers; had gone to Mexico to teach in the na-
    tional preparatory school of University of Hidalgo when he
    was killed in an accident at Moreno; among his works of his-
    torical interest are: La vejez de Sarmiento (1927); Sarmiento,
    constructor de una nueva Argentina (1932); Educación y lucha
    de clases (1936).

PONCE, BLAS (1537-sometime after 1591). Conquistador in Tu-
    cumán; important leader in early days of La Rioja. Arrived
    in Tucumán in 1550's; became vecino of Santiago del Estero;
    involved for next forty years in pioneer activities of the area;
    took part in founding of Londres, Cañete, Córdoba (Calcha-
    quí), Talavera de Esteco (where he remained for three years,
    1567-1570), San Francisco de Alva in Jujuy, 1575 (destroyed
    the next year by the Indians); constantly fought the hostile
    Diaguita and Calchaquí Indians opposing Spanish settlements,
    and engaged in the political turmoil of the area, usually as
    a supporter of Francisco de Aguirre; entered into an agree-
    ment with Governor Juan Ramírez de Velazco that resulted
    in the founding of the city of Todos los Santos de la Nueva
    Rioja in 1591; Ponce received half of the neighboring valley
    and 600 Indians in encomienda, and was left in charge of the
    government and defense of the new city; biographical data
    about him is given in writings of Roberto Levillier.

PONCHO. Square piece of woolen cloth with slit for head; used by the peasants for protection against cold and rain.

PONSONBY, JOHN Viscount. British minister to Buenos Aires, sent to restore peace between Brazil and Argentina and to keep the Río de la Plata waters open to all navigation, is believed by Argentines to have been responsible for Rivadavia's government sending Manuel José García to Rio de Janeiro to begin his ill-fated negotiations regarding peace and the status of Uruguay (1827).

POPHAM, SIR HOME RIGGS (1762-1820). British naval officer (rear admiral) who captured Buenos Aires in 1806.
　　　　Born in Tetuan, Morocco, where his father was British consul; educated at Westminster School and Cambridge University; joined navy in 1778; on leave from admiralty (1787-1793), engaged in east China trade that ended in disaster with capture of his vessel and accusations of illegal trading operations (later proved false and damages awarded him); returned to navy and served in Flanders under Duke of York; in 1799 made Knight of Malta by Russian Czar for services in transporting Russian troops to Lowlands to fight against Napoleon; in 1800 was in African and Indian waters; served as aide-de-camp of British viceroy of India; three years later, back in England and serving as member of Parliament, he met Francisco de Miranda who converted him to cause of American independence; shortly after this, Popham became involved in the new outbreak of Napoleonic wars; after the battle of Trafalgar (1805) had destroyed the Spanish fleet, both Africa and America lay open to British; sent with expedition to south Africa, he saw surrender of Dutch Capetown, January 10, 1806; was informed there by American merchant captain that people of Montevideo and Buenos Aires would welcome British as liberators from Spanish rule; without any formal authorization from British government, but having been familiar with ideas held by many British officials, also probably influenced by Miranda, Popham decided to swing west across the South Atlantic to the Río de la Plata with an armed force under William Beresford to investigate and, if possible, to take advantage of the situation there; at the same time he would be able to secure the food supplies that his crew desperately needed before returning to England; captured Buenos Aires and began two years of British invasions (q.v.); leaving British force there, he returned to England to receive tumultuous popular welcome but was subjected to trial for having acted without orders; exonerated, he became rear admiral in 1814 and commander-in-chief of the Jamaica station; died in Cheltenham, Gloucester in 1820; author of signal code of British navy.

POPULAR UNION PARTY (1963). New name given to the Peronist party.

PORTEÑO. Term used to denote an Argentine resident of Buenos
    Aires (the "port"); traditionally there has been resentment be-
    tween porteños and provincianos (those living in provinces),
    growing out of early jealousy of Beunos Aires' political and
    economic supremacy, and cultural differences are expressed
    in such terms as "cabecitas negras" (q.v.) used by porteños
    for those from provincias denoting fact that in past many of
    the latter have been darker in skin than people of Buenos
    Aires with heavier infusions of European blood; the provinci-
    anos, for their part, often considered porteños more Euro-
    pean-oriented than truly Argentine; more recently, with all
    regions tied together by modern transportation and communi-
    cation and interior migration of population these differences
    are diminishing; even the local porteño slang is imitated or
    used throughout the nation.

PORTUGAL, PORTUGUESE. Spain and Portugal came into con-
    flict over respective claims in Western Hemisphere before
    Argentina had even been discovered; the line drawn by Treaty
    of Tordesillas (1494) gave Portugal its claim to eastern Bra-
    zil, with the rest of the Americas reserved for Spain; as no
    one knew, except theoretically, where the line lay, the whole
    interior of southern South America lay open to exploration,
    claim, use, and settlement by both nations, through Spain's
    Río de la Plata and Alto Perú colonies and Portugal's Brazil;
    Portuguese explorers may have discovered the Río de la
    Plata and Falkland Islands but made no claims; a Portuguese
    navigator, Ferdinand Magellan, was the first to sail and land
    along Argentina's Atlantic coastline and through the southern
    straits, but he was sailing under Spanish crown; Mendoza's
    expedition (1535-1536) was sent to occupy and make good
    Spain's claim to Río de la Plata; Cabeza de Vaca and other
    Spanish officials and conquistadors, before and after him,
    used route between Santa Catarina Island and Asunción, early
    capital of Spanish settlements, freely; both Spaniards and
    Portuguese attempted unsuccessfully to establish settlements
    in this area; the Jesuits, with their Guaraní reducciones, fi-
    nally did in early 1600s; meanwhile, during the period in
    which both Portugal and Spain were under same Spanish crown,
    Brazilians took advantage of this situation to push steadily
    westward into Upper Paraná valley and to trade, with some
    legality, with the refounded (1580) port of Buenos Aires; in
    1641 there were 108 Portuguese in Buenos Aires, most of
    them prominent and economically successful; constituted al-
    most 20% of the European population in the entire Río de la
    Plata area (370 Portuguese, 1500 Spaniards); during the early
    17th-century Portuguese encroachment had forced the Jesuits
    to move their missions downriver and in 1680, the Brazilians
    established their trading base and first permanent settlement
    at Colonia del Sacramento on north bank of Río de la Plata;
    during eighteenth century, new and closer ties between Portu-
    gal and Great Britain, both enemies of Spain most of the
    time, made Río de la Plata one of chief danger zones and

Portugal, Portuguese   722

forced Spanish crown to pay more attention to it; both nations
claimed southern Brazilian provinces of Santa Catarina and
Rio Grande do Sul, eastern Paraguay and Misiones, and Uruguay; all changed hands several times in 1700s; in 1777 treaty
of San Ildefonso gave what is now Uruguay to Spain and rest
to Brazil with a boundary commission appointed to survey
exact location of the line; although these problems were not
fully settled until after Paraguayan War (q.v.) nearly a century later, areas were very sparsely settled and there was
peace for a time; nineteenth century brought new situations;
Great Britain wanted better trade agreement from Portugal
and there is some evidence that Sir Home Popham's capture
of Buenos Aires in 1806 (see British Invasions) was partially
motivated by a desire to take over rich Portuguese slave
trade in Buenos Aires; Napoleon's invasion of Iberian peninsula put Spain, Portugal, and Great Britain all on the same
side and the signing of a much more favorable trade treaty
between England and Portuguese crown in Rio de Janeiro
(1810) put Britain in a position to exert much more influence
and pressure on Spanish America; for the most part, it used
this power to restrain Portuguese expansion into Río de la
Plata and to maintain a balance of power there favorable to
British commercial interests; outbreak of Argentine war for
independence and instability of Banda Oriental brought temporary Brazilian occupation of latter; the Brazilian empire,
after declaring its own independence (1822), continued same
policy; Portugal was one of first countries to recognize independence of United Provinces de la Plata, doing so in April
1821, about a year before U.S.; two wars involving Argentina and Brazil took place, War with Brazil in late 1820s and
Paraguayan War, 1865-1870 (in which the two countries were
allies, not foes); during the modern period Portuguese immigrants have continued to move to Argentina in search of
better economic opportunity.

POSADAS.   Capital of northeastern Argentine province of Misiones;
          population (1970): 70,691.
              Located in southwestern corner of province with port
on Paraná river; one of most rapidly growing cities in nation,
serving province not only as political capital but also as commercial outlet and supply center; connects entire province
with Buenos Aires and other cities by railroad (completed
1912); highways and trucking services (important since 1950s),
airlines; and river shipping companies; ferry service across
river to Encarnación, Paraguay; first settlement on site,
Jesuit mission Itapuá (1650s) but soon moved to Encarnación;
Posadas area neglected and unpopulated for nearly two centuries; by 1840s Paraguayan lumber and yerba mate traders
had established a semi-permanent camp there; informal settlement grew up around it known as Trincheras de San José,
from the nature of the camping quarters and shelters; Corrientes (of which this area still formed a part) formally established city, keeping name of camp, in 1870 as part of its

attempt to retain control of new expansion movement into
Misiones; name changed in 1879 to Posadas, in honor of
Gervasio Antonio de Posadas who, as Supreme Director of
government in Buenos Aires, had first made Corrientes (including Misiones) into separate province (1814); in 1884 Corrientes completed cession of Posadas to federal government,
to become capital of new Misiones territory (created three
years earlier); in 1893 federal government granted authority
for issuing of land titles in Posadas; for several decades
Posadas remained frontier city (population 4000 in 1884),
serving pioneering colonization centers and individual farmers
and other new settlers; today (1970s) a major interior city
rapidly becoming modernized; international in character reflecting recent historical development and ethnic complexity
of province; Paraguayans, Brazilians, Guaraní Indians, Englishmen, Japanese, Ukrainians, Germans, Swiss, and Argentines, mingle daily as farmers and business and professional
men (see Misiones for commercial interests).   See Robert C.
Eidt in Suggested Readings, Appendix III.

POSADAS, GERVASIO ANTONIO DE (1757-1833).   First Supreme
    Director (1814-1815).
        Born in Buenos Aires; studied in parish schools; be-
came lawyer; worked in law office of Manuel José Labardén;
during administration of viceroy, Marqués de Loreto, served
as secretary of government and war; in 1789 became notary
of the bishop; at time of British invasions he sent large donation to Santiago de Liniers to aid in equipping the army for
the Reconquest (q.v.); although invited, he was unable to attend the cabildo abierto that produced the May Revolution but
he supported the patriots; as a member of the Patriotic Society (q.v.) he was exiled to Mendoza (1811) for a time; returned to Buenos Aires to become the first supreme director
of the United Provinces (January 1814); resigned one year
later under pressure from Logia Lautaro (q.v.); during his
administration he had had to deal with royalist opponents,
sending army to Alto Perú, appointing San Martín (q.v.) as
governor of Mendoza, and attempting to end the siege of
Montevideo; authorized the naval expedition of Guillermo
Brown (q.v.) that ended Spanish domination of the Plata river
system; and accompanied his nephew Carlos María de Alvear
in the siege of Montevideo that ended with Montevideo's surrender; became involved in internal politics in 1815 and, as
a partisan of Alvear, was exiled to the province of Buenos
Aires; retired from public life; wrote his memoirs, published
in 1910 by the National Historical Museum, in which he gives
an excellent description of the events of year 1815.

POSADAS, GERVASIO ANTONIO DE (1809-1880).   General Director
    and reorganizer of National postal system.
        Born in Buenos Aires; grandson of Supreme Director
of same name; during second government of Rosas, joined
other Argentine exiles in Montevideo; became officer in

Argentine Legion defending Montevideo against siege by Oribe;
in 1853 formed part of Argentine diplomatic corps in Great
Britain; returned and was elected to Buenos Aires legislature; in 1858 he was appointed general administrator of the
postal system; retained in this position by presidents Mitre
and Sarmiento; after 1864, his title was changed to Director
General; he became largely responsible for organization of
the mail service in the newly united Argentine Republic; modified old systems, installed mail deposit boxes, improved the
services with courses of training for employees, drew up
formal regulations, organized the post office archive, etc.;
died in Buenos Aires.

POSITIVISM.   As expressed in the ideas of Auguste Comte and
Herbert Spencer, particularly, positivism had great appeal for
Argentine intellectuals of the post-Rosas period; its insistence
on the reconciliation of order and progress and its promise
that through the application of the scientific spirit and methodology to politics and social purposes a nation could revo-
lutionize itself into a Utopia seemed to offer intellectual independence and the first real philosophical base for national
life, replace the scholasticism of the colonial period; eagerly
accepted by Argentine intellectuals--but always critically and
selectively, with regard to what was believed to be the nation's needs; positivistic influences have varied greatly but,
in one way or another, have influenced almost every phase of
Argentina's historical development, from Alberdi's writing of
the constitution of 1853 to the peronismo movement of the
mid-twentieth century; such as: the establishment of the
Normal School at Paraná to make mass education possible;
the rapid economic growth and development of transportation
systems and beginnings of industry in the pre-World War I
period; the brilliant leadership of the Generation of Eighty
(1880); the program of university reforms and founding of new
and different universities in the early twentieth century; the
development of the social sciences, especially sociology, to
serve as useful tools for studies and analyses of the political
and social problems growing out of the immigrant inundation
of Argentina following 1880--also in response to positivist
aims; secularization of education and society (but little acceptance of Comte's Religion of Humanity); strengthening the
oligarchy's elitist political leadership and laissez-faire economic theories, but at the same time (through other exponents) laying the foundations for Argentine socialism, and
serving the drive of middle and lower classes to participate
more fully in the political life of their society; in the twentieth century, both Perón's revolutionary movement and Onganía's conservative government stressing civil order and
economic progress reflect positivistic influences.
        Positivism in Argentina had its critics: The Church
and devout Catholics feared increasing secularization; Argentine individualism always (except in the case of socialism)
rejected Comte's subjection of the individual to the authority

of society's needs; García and Alejandro Korn, among others, questioned the desirability of the strongly materialistic goals of positivism; and the historic breach was widened between those who felt that Argentina could only become civilized by making itself as much like European nations as possible (preferably the northern ones whose material progress and imperial success were assumed to have demonstrated their superiority) and those, like Ricardo Rojas, Alejandro Korn, and others, who insisted that Argentina could only become great by growing from its own historical roots in the land, religion, humanistically-oriented culture, etc. (see Normal School at Paraná; Generation of Eighty (1880); also individual entries on intellectuals of period covered).

See José Luis Romero, A History of Argentine Political Thought, tr. by Thomas F. McGann (Stanford, California, 1963); Ricuarte Soler, El positivismo argentino (Panama, 1959); and José Ingenieros, La evolución de las ideas argentinas (Buenos Aires, 1946).

POSSE, FILEMON (1831-1893).   Jurisconsult; public official; educator.

Born in Tucumán; educated in Córdoba at Colegio Nacional de Monserrat and the university, graduating with doctorate in law; from 1852 to 1855 practiced law in Buenos Aires, in law office of Marcelino Ugarte; moved to Santa Fe where he held several public offices; represented Tucumán at Confederation Congress in Paraná, 1856-1860; moved to Córdoba where he combined government service--minister of provincial government, provincial deputy (several times during his lifetime), minister of finance and fiscal of province-- with teaching of mathematics and physics at the university; in Tucumán, 1863-1865, he taught law and Argentine history while serving on Supreme Court; served as federal judge in Catamarca; returned to Córdoba, 1870, as municipal judge of small claims court; deputy of constituent congress; member of superior council of university, dean of latter's faculty of humanities, rector of Colegio Nacional (1876); in 1884 he was sent as Córdoba's representative to lower house of congress; demonstrated his liberal ideas by defending cause of civil marriage in historic debate; under President Juárez Celman, served as minister of justice, religion and public instruction until 1890; two years later he became president of criminal court of appeals in Buenos Aires; died in Buenos Aires; Dr. Posse's career was considered remarkable in the number of public projects that he initiated and carried to successful conclusion and in his continued, diversified efforts in behalf of public education on all levels, from kindergartens to most advanced graduate and professional schools in universities; also supported religious missionary schools among Indians.

POSSE, JOSE (1816-1906).   Businessman and journalist.

Born in Tucumán in 1840, while in Mendoza, took part in a political movement against Rosas; that same year,

as congressman of Tucumán, voted against the Rosas government; as a result of these activities he had to emigrate; in
Chile he became closely associated with Sarmiento; in 1844
he returned to Tucumán where he was justice of peace; in
1852 became minister of government of Celedonio Gutiérrez;
two years later became governor of the province; represented
Tucumán in the Paraná Congress (1856-1858) and was a member of the constitutional convention that reformed the constitution in 1860; director of the Colegio Nacional of Tucumán,
retired in 1882; he was editor of El Comercio, El Argentino,
and wrote in La Razón, El Imparcial, and El Liberal; during
much of his life he maintained a steady correspondence with
Sarmiento (1845-1888); this was published as Epistolario entre
Sarmiento y Posse, by the Museo Histórico Sarmiento; Posse
died in the province of Tucumán.

POTOSI. Wealthy colonial mining center in Bolivia, part of viceroyalty of Río de la Plata; the Ceca de Potosí (Casa de
Moneda or mint), established by Viceroy Francisco de Toledo,
around 1575, supplied the coinage for what is now Argentina
throughout the colonial period; also struck off first coins with
Argentine seal, 1813 and 1815; mines centering around Potosí
provided important market for livestock, agricultural products,
and small manufactures of colonial northwestern Argentina as
well as source of silver used in contraband trade; played important role in early years of war for independence, changing
hands several times, taken by patriots in 1810; one dramatic
incident was that following disaster of Huaqui (1811), when
Juan Martín de Pueyrredón (q.v.), president of Charcas audiencia, marched at once to Potosí, seized the wealth of the
mint and made hasty retreat with it to Jujuy before the
Spaniards could retake the city (1912).

POTRERO DEL CHACON (also known as Rodeo del Chacón). Site
of defeat of Mendoza unitarist forces on March 28, 1831, by
federalists led by Facundo Quiroga; after having defeated the
unitarist forces of Paz (led by Juan Pascual Pringles, q.v.)
in Córdoba at the battles of Río Cuarto (March 5, 1831) and
Río Quinto (March 17, 1831), Quiroga had moved westward
toward Cuyo, still under unitarist control; at Potrero del
Chacón he attacked and defeated Governor Videla Castillo's
unitarist forces, returning Cuyo provinces to federalist control and leaving General Paz isolated in Córdoba; following
this battle Facundo ordered all captured prisoners to be shot,
in revenge for recent unitarist murder of his friend and officer, Benito Villafañe.

PREBISCH, RAUL (1901-   ). Economist. Author of El pool de
los frigoríficos; necesidad de intervención del estado (1927);
member of Roca's commission signing the Roca-Runciman
Agreement (1933); head of Argentina's Central Bank; in exile
during Perón period, became chairman of the Economic commission for Latin America (ECLA), a United Nations body;

called in by President Eduardo Lonardi to serve as economic
adviser to the post-Perón government; presented report· analyzing difficult economic situation facing nation as result of
previous administration's policy and measures but offered a
plan for recovery and development, emphasizing austerity,
free enterprise, and attraction of foreign capital; political
considerations intervened to defeat much of this.

PREEMINENCIA. Name given to any one of several specific privileges granted during colonial times to government official or
group; for example, only a member of the cabildo could enter
its meeting place wearing a sword; not even a lieutenant governor could carry a walking cane when attending a cabildo
session, as that privilege was reserved for military men.

PRENSA, LA. Internationally known daily Beunos Aires newspaper;
founded October 18, 1869, by José Clemente Paz, during
presidency of Domingo Faustino Sarmiento; considered to be
one of ten best newspapers in the world; celebrated its centennial in 1969; has won several María Moors Cabot prizes
(see Newspapers; José Clemente Paz; Alberto Gainza Paz,
its long-time editor).

PRESIDENTIAL POWERS. The president is the supreme head of
the national government; his powers are defined by the constitution (q.v.) and are extensive; he can appoint or remove almost any member of the personnel of national administration
without senate approval; he can call special sessions of Congress; place nation under martial law, and issue decrees that
are enforceable as laws; the president himself must be a
native-born Argentine, at least thirty years old, and a com-
municant of the Roman Catholic Church.

PRESIDENTS. See Appendix I and entries on individual presidents.

PRESS, ROLE OF. Freedom of the press, based on a Supreme
Court decision of 1866 declaring federal laws of censorship
unconstitutional, was generally observed in Argentina until
1930; in 1932 that decision was reversed and press control
became part of Argentine life; during the earlier period press
played varying roles: acted as unifying force in development
of national identity, life style, and spirit; in early 1900s it
tended to strengthen an anti-Yankee spirit especially after
Theodore Roosevelt expressed his corollary to the Monroe
doctrine, arousing, in some parts of Argentina, a fear of
U.S. intervention; later it became a "Tower of Babel" (as
A. P. Whitaker expresses it) speaking with as many different
tongues as there were editors and financial backers; in 1930
President Uriburu curtailed freedom of the press; under President Justo, the Supreme Court decision (1932) placed press
under government control; in the 1940s, under presidents
Castillo and Farrell, repression of papers criticizing government action increased and during Perón's first administration

a systematic campaign against press freedom was carried on; in 1949, the ley desacato (law of disrespect) made it a penal offense "to offend the dignity of a public officer," further limiting the power of the press; although Juan D. Perón never officially destroyed the freedom of the press, he used various devices to punish offending newspapers, such as exercising control over their supplies, closing newsplants for violation of sanitary or building codes, etc.; at the same time he attempted to use the press for spreading his own propaganda; in 1950 many newspapers of the interior were closed because they failed to display conspicuously the official motto "The year of San Martín"; the most conspicuous act against press freedom was the closing of La Prensa (q.v.), the most highly respected Argentine newspaper, despite widespread international protests; during 1960s and 1970s, Argentine public, once one of the most widely read in the world, continued to have a controlled press; open attacks against the government were not tolerated; in late 1972 the government forbade use of foreign newsgathering services; and in March 1976, following fall of Madame Perón's government, all freedom of the press was cancelled for a few days.

PRINGLES, JUAN PASCUAL (1795-1831).   Officer in San Martín's Army of the Andes and in unitarist forces.
Born in San Luis; joined granaderos a caballo as lieutenant; fought with San Martín in Chile and Peru; taken prisoner at battle of Chancay; freed, he continued to fight for independence under Bolívar; received Order of the Sun for his bravery; returned to Argentina in 1826; joined unitarist forces of José María Paz, fighting against federalists in Córdoba; as Paz's second in command, was defeated by Juan Facundo Quiroga at Río Cuarto (March 5, 1831) and at Río Quinto (March 17, 1831), where he surrendered, but was killed shortly afterward; an historical biography of him was written by Gerónimo Espejo, 1888.

PRINTING PRESSES.   Jesuits brought printing presses to Argentina early in the eighteenth century; the first press known to have been used was not imported but built, around 1700, from materials at hand in Guaraní mission in what is now Misiones province; mission Indians under the direction of Juan Bautista Neumann (q.v.) built and operated it; several books dealing with Christian doctrine, Spanish-Guaraní language studies, and Guaraní translations of important Jesuit religious and devotional writings had been published by the 1720s, many of them including plates; remaining parts of this first press were eventually placed in the historical museum of Buenos Aires; the second Argentine press was also introduced by the Jesuits, imported in 1766, and set up in Córdoba for use in their important educational center; under the direction of Pablo Karer, its first book appeared in that same year, honoring the founder of the Monserrat Academy; in the expulsion of the Jesuits the following year, the press was left behind;

as the Franciscans, who took over the Jesuit establishments
in Córdoba had no immediate use for it, it remained in storage for a dozen years; officials in both Spain and Buenos
Aires were interested in its being used and in 1779 Viceroy
Vértiz had it brought to Buenos Aires; he installed it in the
recently established Casa de Niños Expósitos (home for foundlings) where it could supplement the income of this institution; José Silva y Aguilar was placed in charge, with the
boys from the home trained to serve as the first printers or
helpers; its first published work honored Viceroy Vértiz; for
years this press handled the printing needs of the Río de la
Plata area until it was replaced by the one that the British
left in Montevideo following their second invasion (1807); with
the coming of the revolution and independence, printing presses
proliferated in Buenos Aires and in the interior to serve the
demands of the new provincial and national governments,
newspapers and other periodicals, and increased publication
of literary, commercial, educational, news and current events
articles and books; Pueyrredón secured and sent San Martín a
press for use in the operations of the Army of the Andes;
Belgrano introduced the first press to Tucumán in the one he
brought for use of the auxiliary army in 1817; two years later,
José Miguel Carrera established the first newspaper in Santa
Fe, the Gaceta Federal, with a press that he had brought
back from the United States; abandoned by him shortly afterward because of political difficulties, the press was salvaged
in the 1820s by Father Francisco de Paula Castañeda (q.v.)
for use in his fiery political pamphlets against Rivadavia's
ecclesiastical reforms; by 1820 Mendoza already had three
presses in operation; that of Juan Escalante, the official provincial press, and the one operated by the Lancastrian society (see Lancastrian System of Education); as a result of
Bustos' efforts, Córdoba had its own press by 1823 and in
1824 the governor of Salta secured the old Niños Expósitos
press for his province and hired Hilario Ascasubi (q.v.),
just back from the United States, to put it into operation (in
1867 the type of this historic press was melted down to be
used as ammunition against the montonero Felipe Varela);
Governor Salvador María del Carril brought in San Juan's
first press in 1825 and in the following year La Rioja established its first one; Sarmiento brought a portable press to
Rosario in 1852, used in Urquiza's campaign against Rosas;
after the formation of the Confederation, both Catamarca and
Jujuy founded presses in 1856, the former an official press
obtained by popular subscription, the latter founded by Dr.
Macedonio Graz to print his newspaper; meanwhile in Buenos
Aires there were 26 presses by 1872 printing 94 newspapers
and periodicals; and the first strike of the printers' union
had already taken place, in 1868.

PROCTOR, ROBERT.   English traveler who arrived in Buenos
    Aires in 1823 and crossed Argentina, with his family and
    household, on his way to Chile and then to Peru; published

an account of the trip including much material about recent
events in independence war and descriptions about San Mar-
tín in Mendoza, etc.; this book was entitled Narrative of a
Journey across the Cordillera of the Andes and Residence in
Lima and other Parts of Peru in the Years 1823 and 1824
(London, 1825); translated into Spanish by Carlos A. Aldao
(Buenos Aires, 1920).

PROGRESSIVE DEMOCRATIC PARTY   see   DEMOCRATA PRO-
    GRESISTA, PARTIDO

PROPIOS.   Along with arbitrios (q.v.), propios served as only
    revenue resources possessed by towns and cities in colonial
    period; they varied in form, consisting of privilege or fee
    assigned by royal authorities for this purpose; among its
    many forms were: judicial fines; income from sale of cer-
    tain offices; rental from portion of common lands or use of
    repartimiento of Indians; in seventeenth century Buenos
    Aires' municipal income was practically reduced to licenses
    of a few liquor and tobacco retail stores; sometimes anchor-
    age fees or import duties on wine were included; total cabildo
    income in Buenos Aires rarely exceeded 400 pesos a year,
    although a propio, once granted, tended to become permanent;
    they were administered by the Depositario de Propios--with
    the establishment of the viceroyalty, Buenos Aires propios in-
    creased greatly; in 1783, with the establishment of intend-
    ancies, the propios were brought under the supervision of a
    General Auditing office in Buenos Aires (Junta Municipal de
    Propios).

PROTECTOR OF THE NATIVES.   Colonial government official re-
    sponsible for the defense and protection of the Indians; the
    first protector named in Río de la Plata was Don Pedro de
    Espinosa (1590).

PROTESTANTS, PROTESTANTISM   see   RELIGION

PROTOMEDICATO (Medical Examining Board).   Its establishment
    in 1779-1780 marked beginning of professionalizing of medi-
    cal practice in Argentina; before that time all doctors, sur-
    geons, and dentists came from Spain and were under super-
    vision of the protomedicato of Lima; the cabildos were re-
    sponsible for examining credentials and licensing procedures
    of those practicing in their areas after 1600; actually, how-
    ever, most of the sick were in the hands of medicine men,
    herbalists, and folk doctors; Argentine Indians knew some
    primitive medicine, such as use of native herbs to treat ill-
    nesses like malaria, dysentery, etc., and practiced use of
    fire and heat, hydrotherapy, cupping glasses, and scarifica-
    tion in other medical problems; after the conquest, Spaniards
    supplemented these with European drugs and new American
    ones, such as ipomea purga (jalap, a very strong purgative),
    quinine, cocaine, tobacco, sarsaparilla, etc. from other

Spanish colonies.

Apparently the first Spanish doctors were brought to Argentina in 1527, when medical men Pedro de Mesa, Fernando de Molina, and Hernando de Alcázar accompanied Sebastian Cabot's expedition; Córdoba had physician Telles de Rojo in 1598 and Buenos Aires cabildo records presence of Manuel Alvarez in 1605 with a salary of 400 pesos a year, and that of Flemish doctor Nicolás Xaques in 1619; Jesuit practical nurses, as well as more scholarly missionaries made careful studies and records of Indian medical lore; one of most important of these being Father Pedro Montenegro's Materia Médica; also important was Father Thomas Falkner's Description of Patagonia and of the Patagonians, that included descriptions of common illnesses, cures and treatments, with botanical and mineralogical data; first pharmacy in Buenos Aires was opened in 1680, bought by Dr. Angel Castelli in 1771; at latter date the city had eleven physicians and surgeons; when Pedro de Ceballos returned to Río de la Plata as first viceroy he brought with him a highly qualified Irish physician, Michael O'Gorman, who remained in Buenos Aires as first royal physician; was chosen by Viceroy Vértiz to head the new protomedicato established in Buenos Aires by royal authorization in 1779-1780; the other first members were Francisco Argerich, José Alberto Capdevila, Benito González Rivadavia, and Antonio Herrera, secretary; the protomedicato was responsible for all medical and public health concerns of the viceroyalty; these included provisions for medical training, examination of credentials, licensing procedures, maintaining high standards of medical ethics and practices, supervising public health measures, and attempting to prevent epidemics and treat their victims when they occurred; it also administered hospitals, homes for lepers, aged, mentally ill, and army medical facilities, and made regular physical checkups of black slaves imported for sale; also had supervision over sanitary conditions in slaughterhouses and other food establishments; in 1800 the first school of medicine was opened in the Río de la Plata area; under directorship of Cosme Argerich it offered a six-year course to produce qualified physicians; continued operating after May Revolution; in 1821, the University of Buenos Aires was created and, as it increased its medical training, the protomedicato disappeared (see Epidemics; specific diseases such as Smallpox and Cholera; also entries on individual physicians).

PROVINCES. Argentina has 22 provinces and 1 territory. See Buenos Aires, Catamarca, Chaco, Chubut, Córdoba, Corrientes, Entre Ríos, Formosa, Jujuy, La Pampa, La Rioja, Mendoza, Misiones, Neuquén, Río Negro, Salta, San Juan, San Luis, Santa Cruz, Santa Fe, Santiago del Estero, Tucumán, and territory, Tierra del Fuego; see also map, Appendix IV.

PROVINCIA ORIENTAL (modern Uruguay) see BANDA ORIENTAL;
MONTEVIDEO

PROVINCIAL POWERS (Autonomías Provinciales).   The role and
rights of provinces to self-government and to share in the direction of the central government; became matter of controversy immediately following the May Revolution; still unsettled.

PROVINCIANOS.   The people of the interior of the country; traditionally they have resented the capital of the country which
they say "stands on the coast looking to itself and toward
Europe keeping its back to the hinterland. "

PROVINCIAS UNIDAS DEL RIO DE LA PLATA.   First official
name applied to the former viceroyalty of the Río de la Plata
after the patriot revolution of May 25, 1810; the name was
used for first time on September 23, 1811; the name is still
legally applied to the geographical territory of the country.

PROVISIONAL STATUTE.   Designed to serve as legal basis for
government until a formal constitution could be written and
adopted (see entries below).

PROVISIONAL STATUTE OF 1811.   First attempt at writing national constitution; drawn up by Deán Gregorio Funes and
Juan Ignacio Gorriti for the provisional junta; proposed government with powers divided among executive, legislative,
and judicial branches; not accepted, as junta was replaced by
first triumvirate government.

PROVISIONAL STATUTE OF 1815.   After the overthrow of government of Carlos María de Alvear (q.v.) in 1815, following the
military revolt in Fontezuelas (q.v.), the cabildo of Buenos
Aires assumed authority, as the Assembly of 1813 had also
been dissolved; it created a "junta of observation" responsible to the people for governing and for calling a national
congress; this junta passed provisional statute, as basis for
government, that provided for appointment of a supreme director dependent absolutely on superior authority of junta;
this made clash of authority between them and the fact that
Rondeau, the director named, was still with army of the
north and interim director Alvarez Thomas had to be appointed, complicated national administration; provinces were
authorized to select their own governors and to continue ruling under their own institutions; it became obvious that a national congress should be called immediately, to meet in an
interior province rather than in Buenos Aires; this led to the
convoking of the Congress of Tucumán in 1816; meanwhile
the Uruguayan leader, José Gervasio Artigas, had already
called a national congress at Paysandú to which Entre Ríos,
Corrientes, Córdoba and Santa Fé sent delegates.

PROVISIONAL STATUTE OF 1817.   After its declaration of

independence July 9, 1816, Congress of Tucumán set itself
seriously to problem of deciding on proper form of government for new nation and creating national constitution; congress moved to Buenos Aires early in 1817 and, finding itself still unable to make final decision on national organization, on December 3, 1817, issued new provisional statute
that centralized executive and legislative powers in the Supreme director, insured independence of the judiciary, reduced power of provincial cabildos in national government but
provided that supreme director should be appointed by out-
going director from nominations made by the cabildos; Provisional Statute replaced by first national constitution, 1819.

PUBLIC LANDS   see   LANDHOLDING

PUCARA.   Indian fortification in northwestern Argentina used as
refuge in time of war; the interior resembled a labyrinth
with dwellings contained within the high walls on which guards
could be stationed; best known pucará is that of Jujuy discovered in 1908.

PUELCHE INDIANS   see   PEHUENCHES AND PUELCHES

PUENTE DE MARQUEZ, BATTLE OF.   Place, about twenty-five
miles from Buenos Aires, where Juan Lavalle's unitarist
army was defeated by federalist forces of Estanislao López
and Juan Manuel Rosas, April 26, 1829; pact of Cañuelas
(q.v.), providing for cessation of hostilities, followed shortly afterward; ironically enough, Rosas, with whom Lavalle
had made the pact, was defeated on almost the same site
February 3, 1852, in the battle of Caseros.

PUERTO BELGRANO (BELGRANO PORT).   Port authorized by
executive decree (1899) and created by the navy near Bahía
Blanca in Buenos Aires province; constructed by a British
firm, it contains five defensive batteries; since 1905 it has
been the main naval base of the country.

PUESTO DE MARQUES.   Site, on the property of Marquis of Yaví
in Salta, where strong Argentine patriot column, under
Colonel Fernando de la Cruz surprised and defeated Pezuela's
royalist troops stationed there, April 17, 1815; left way open
for Rondeau to advance into Bolivia.

PUEYRREDON, HONORIO (1876-1945).   Jurisconsult; university
professor; political leader; public diplomat.
        Born in San Pedro, Buenos Aires; graduated in law
in Buenos Aires in 1896 and taught in that faculty; became
active in politics of Unión Cívica Radical; appointed minister
of agriculture (1916) by President Yrigoyen, and as minister
of foreign relations (1917-1922); during this latter period he
led the Argentine delegation to the first meeting of League
of Nations in Geneva and served as vice president of its

first assembly (1920); in 1922 he was appointed ambassador
to the United States; also served as ambassador to Cuba;
president of Argentine delegation to Sixth Pan American conference, in Havana (1928); in 1930 he was elected governor
of province of Buenos Aires but elections were challenged
and finally annulled by President Uriburu; he continued active
in politics, considered to be best representative of Yrigoyenist tendencies; exiled because of these views; died in Buenos
Aires.

PUEYRREDON, JUAN MARTIN DE (1777-1850).   Patriot, precurs-
    or of the independence, supreme director.
            Born in Buenos Aires of French Basque father of
noble origin and Argentine mother of Irish ancestry; educated
in Paris; went into business; became a military man during
the British invasions; at first he acted as liaison between the
British and the cabildo, but soon realized that help for independence would not come from them and joined the patriot
defenders; together with his brothers he organized the regiment of Húsares in the outskirts of Buenos Aires; due to his
brave fight Pueyrredón was appointed lieutenant colonel of
the army by Santiago de Liniers and confirmed as such by
the king; selected as delegate of Buenos Aires to carry the
good news of the Reconquest (q.v.) to Spain and to request
help for the porteños; in Europe he witnessed the decadence
of the Spanish government and concluded that the best policy
for his country was absolute independence; convinced of the
failure of his mission he wrote to the cabildo in Buenos
Aires advising it not to recognize the viceroy (Cisneros) selected by the Spanish Junta; these letters were intercepted by
Martín de Alzaga who convinced the cabildo that Pueyrredón
was dangerous for the peninsulares; Elío, governor of Montevideo, was ordered to capture Pueyrredón; latter avoided capture and returned to Buenos Aires; joined his friends Belgrano,
Castelli, Vieytes, Berutti, and Rodríguez Peña in project of
appointing Carlota Joaquina (q.v.) as regent in Buenos Aires
during captivity of her brother Ferdinand VII of Spain; carried correspondence to this effect to Carlota Joaquina in Rio
de Janeiro but received little encouragement; returning to
Buenos Aires in 1810, he learned about the May Revolution
and immediately offered his services to the patriot junta that
appointed him as governor of Córdoba, which included at that
time not only the present city, but also the Cuyo region;
there he invited the criollos and the peninsulares to join
forces; in January 1811 he was transferred to the Audiencia
de Charcas (in today's Bolivia) as president and intendant;
while there he heard about the disaster of Huaqui; moved at
once to Potosí where he seized the mint and undertook a retreat to Jujuy and to Tucumán--a daring exploit that saved
silver for the patriotic cause; appointed commander-in-chief
of the army of the north, he reorganized the forces; relin-
quished his command later to Manuel Belgrano to assume new
position as member of the second triumvirate government;

this triumvirate fell in 1812 and Pueyrredón was taken prisoner to Matanzas and finally to San Luis; there in Cuyo, he
met governor San Martín in 1814; in 1815 he returned to
Buenos Aires; later in the year Pueyrredón was appointed to
represent the province of San Luis in the Congress of Tucumán; the Cuyo representation was Tomás Godoy Cruz, Justo
Santa María de Oro, Francisco Narciso de Laprida, and Juan
Agustín Maza; congress, influenced by San Martín and strong
support of Cuyo, Güemes, Buenos Aires and Alto Perú,
elected Pueyrredón as Supreme Director almost unanimously
(May 3, 1816), believing that, as hero of the Reconquest and
Potosí, he was best man to conciliate the differences and
secure independence; before returning to Buenos Aires to assume his new duties, Pueyrredón went to Salta to resolve
problems between Rondeau and Martín Güemes; he removed
Rondeau from the army of the north and named Belgrano in
his place, ending the provincial resistance; at a meeting in
Córdoba with San Martín (q. v.) he studied San Martín's
project to invade Chile and decided to give it top priority;
in the meantime the Congress of Tucumán declared independence.
        During his government (1816-1819) Pueyrredón exer-
cised tremendous influence on the nation; his determination
to support organization, equipment, and financing of San Martín's proposed liberating expedition to Chile and Peru (to
complete winning of Argentine independence) demanded political unity and financial sacrifice but Pueyrredón did not hesi-
tate to use both political and military power, when necessary,
to continue providing these; he governed during a very difficult period; Portuguese-Brazilian forces invaded the Banda
Oriental (Uruguay); Uruguayan leader José Gervasio Artigas
was attempting to divert loyalty of Argentine riparian provinces from Buenos Aires to himself; Pueyrredón also faced
serious political problems in the new nation involving personal rivalries and conflicts; civil wars were approaching between factions that eventually became centralists versus
federalists; as Supreme Director, Pueyrredón represented
central authority but he never identified with the porteños;
instead he attempted to reinforce national unity by using
moderation whenever possible; in spite of his good intentions
the problems against the directorate government flourished
everywhere; when he returned to Buenos Aires from Tucumán, he found Buenos Aires divided over the Portuguese invasion, and Córdoba and Santiago del Estero in rebellion; by
the end of 1816 he had recovered control throughout the
provinces except in the littoral, but signs of crisis existed
in the city of Buenos Aires, largely due to the increased
taxes to pay for San Martín's liberating expedition, the
forced loans made, and other economic and political problems; the number of dissidents and opponents to his government increased; a conspiracy was discovered in 1817 and its
leaders exiled; Carrera, the Chilean caudillo, appeared in
Buenos Aires, intending to proceed to Chile, but Pueyrredón,

fearing his interference with San Martín's operations, prevented him from going and gained the Chilean's enmity; Al-
vearistas (see Carlos María de Alvear) started a propaganda
war of libel against Pueyrredón; the Supreme Director attempted to suppress internal rebellions and made the mistake
of trying to defeat the Entre Ríos and Santa Fe caudillos
(Ramírez and E. López) thinking that the support of secondary
strongmen was going to be sufficient; in 1819 it was obvious
that the problem involved more than just a rebellious army;
on February 12, 1819, the forces of Estanislao López forced
the government forces to sign the San Lorenzo Armistice
which brought provisional and temporary peace.

Pueyrredón by this time had completed his term of
government; the constitution of 1819 had been signed, the
country was still independent, Chile was free and Santa Fe
was peaceful for the time being; wearied by continual opposition, suffering from poor health, Pueyrredón submitted his
resignation in April 1819; Congress refused to accept it but
finally yielded to his persistence June 9; while in power he
attempted to organize the public finances, founded the Caja
Nacional de Fondos, precursor of the first bank, the mint,
the customs regulations, several newspapers, reopened the
Colegio de San Carlos as the Academia de la Unión del Sur,
organized the army staff, military courts and refunded the
national debt; in 1820 he requested permission to leave the
country and went to Europe but returned after one year; attempted in 1829 to bring peace between Lavalle and Rosas,
but failed; thereafter he lived quietly on his country estate
in Olivos, Buenos Aires province, where he died and was
buried quietly as a private citizen.

General Bartolomé Mitre, president, historian, and
military man, said of him: "Because of his efforts the Argentine independence was guaranteed; the new nation acquired
respect abroad, the foundation of parliamentary government
was laid; the national armies were created, Chile was liberated by the crossing of the Andes ... and the laurels of
Chacabuco and Maipú were added to the Argentine emblem.... "

PUEYRREDON, MANUEL ALEJANDRO (1802-1865).   Hero of wars
of independence; political figure.

Born in Baradero, Buenos Aires, son of José Cipriano Pueyrredón and nephew of Juan Martín de Pueyrredón
(q.v.); moved with family to San Luis in 1812 and enlisted
in army as cadet the following year; after brief visit to Brazil to complete his education, returned to become officer in
granaderos a caballo (1819); fought against Araucanians and
royalists in southern Chile; remained there with Ramón
Freire instead of accompanying his regiment in San Martín's
liberating expedition to Peru; sustained many serious wounds,
once being left for dead on battlefield; in 1821 returned to
San Luis; became involved in the fighting against Francisco
Ramírez and José Miguel Carrera; reached Buenos Aires in
1822 and accompanied Martín Rodríguez in campaign against

Indians the following year; remained among forces along
southern Indian frontier until his old wounds forced him to
leave (1826); became actively involved in the political uprisings of 1833 that paved way for takeover of government by
Juan Manuel de Rosas and in 1839 fled to Banda Oriental with
Valentín Alsina and others; supported Juan Lavalle's unitarist
attempt to overthrow Rosas but differences arose between
them; hoped to encourage anti-Rosas revolt in south but found
it unfeasible; too ill to join Urquiza at Caseros, he returned
to Buenos Aires shortly afterward; out of sympathy with
Buenos Aires' separation from Confederation, he was exiled
by Pastor Obligado (q.v.) in 1853; five years later returned
to his estancia at San Nicolás; moved to Rosario and wrote
his memoirs, in which, in addition to his military and public
careers, he describes the years he spent as a young boy with
his uncle at the Aguada de Pueyrredón outside San Luis (a
national monument since 1941).
      See Memorias inéditas del coronel Manuel A. Pueyrre-
dón, edited by Alfredo G. Villegas (Buenos Aires, 1947).

PUEYRREDON, PRILIDIANO (1823-1870).   Painter; architect.
      Born in Buenos Aires; son of Juan Martín de Pueyrre-
dón; studied painting in Spain; graduated in engineering from
Polytechnical Institute of Paris; after returning to Argentina
became involved in restoration of historic construction such
as chapel of la Recoleta, the pyramid in Plaza de Mayo, and
the remodeling of the Casa de Gobierno; drew up plans for
the quinta de Olivos, the mansion built by Miguel de Azcuénaga and later given to the nation as a presidential residence;
became most distinguished for his paintings depicting the
people, scenes, and customs of the Argentina of his day;
helped to make the gaucho a familiar figure throughout the
nation; among his most famous paintings are: Blindman
(Cádiz, 1846), Portrait of Manuelita Rosas (Buenos Aires,
1851), Self-Portrait, The Siesta, Juan Bautista Peña, San
Isidoro, The Rodeo, Lavanderas del Bajo Belgrano (1865), Un
alto en el camino, Gauchos.

PUIGGARI, MIGUEL (1827-1889).   Chemist.   Born in Barcelona;
arrived in Buenos Aires in 1851; considered founder of
modern chemistry in Buenos Aires; taught in the University
of Buenos Aires; director of natural history of school of
physical sciences of the university, where he was dean (1865-
1868); published Inocuidad de los saladeros; died in Buenos
Aires.

PUJOL, JUAN GREGORIO (1817-1861).   Lawyer; political leader
in Corrientes.
      Born in Corrientes; graduated from University of Cór-
doba (1838); became professor of Latin and philosophy;
strongly opposed policies of Juan Manuel de Rosas; held various official positions in Corrientes; 1843 minister of war
and foreign relations for Madariaga; served as judge advocate

general in campaign in Entre Ríos; closely associated with
General José María Paz (q.v.); accompanied latter into exile
in Brazil in 1846; later Urquiza requested his aid against
Rosas and Pujol, joined by Governor Virasoro and the province of Corrientes, fought at Caseros; elected governor and
captain general of Corrientes; served 1852-1859 (see Corrientes); attempted to bring Corrientes into line with other
modern areas, drawing up its first constitution, founding
schools, libraries, colonies, museums, and building bridges,
roads, parks; founded towns, took first census, etc.; Dr.
Pujol was initiator of the meeting of governors with Urquiza
at San Nicolás de los Arroyos designed to bring about national union with Buenos Aires as capital; served as minister of
interior under President Santiago Derqui of confederation; in
1861 elected national senator from Santa Fe; died a few
months after his election (see Corrientes).

PULPERIA.   Name by which first commercial establishment in
new town was known; combined functions of country store
selling sugar, tobacco, liquors, a post office or message
center, saloon, social gathering place, etc.; origin of name
is variously given as coming from Spanish medieval fruit
stand (local fruit found market there); from the lean meat,
known as pulpa, often sold there; or from the Mexican pul-
quería where pulque was sold, as alcoholic beverages were
sold in the pulpería; for various reasons Spanish and early
Argentine national governments attempted to regulate the
sales, privileges, racial status of personnel of pulperías but
had little success; are rapidly being replaced, even in rural
areas, by more modern marketing centers.

PUMACAHUA, MATEO (1764-1815).   Indian chief that fought for
patriot cause from Cuzco, Peru, to northwestern Argentina.
Born in Cuzco; took part in Tupac Amaru revolt (q.v.)
in 1780; joined patriots in fight for independence; in 1814 became president of Cuzco; organized a revolutionary force that
defeated royalists at Picheuta, giving him possession of Are-
quipa (Peru), then was defeated by General Ramírez in Argentine territory, in Campos de Santa Rosa (Jujuy); he and his
twenty thousand Indians were captured and Pumacahua and
leaders executed March 17, 1815, ending the great rebellion
of Cuzco, the most impressive effort made by native Peruvians to win their own independence; Mitre and other Argentine
and Bolivian historians have devoted considerable attention to
Pumacahua's actions.

PUNA DE ATACAMA.   High, bleak desert plateau extending southward from Bolivian altiplano through western portions of
Andean provinces of Jujuy, Salta, and Catamarca; the puna
lies between the cordillera on the west and the lower Salto-
Jujeña sierras on the east; about 3500 meters above sea level,
it is crossed by higher mountains; its dry, salty soil supports little vegetation except occasional sparse growth of

thorny, drought-resistant shrubs; the only potable water
comes from occasional springs; the dryness, cold, altitude,
and lack of food and water have discouraged both animal and
human life; in preconquest period the Humahuaca Indians inhabited the northeastern portion of it; puna believed to have
rich mineral wealth.

PUNCHAUCA. Site of conferences in Peru (May-June, 1821) in
which San Martín (q.v.) attempted, without success, to persuade Viceroy La Serna to accept the independence of Peru
on the basis of establishing a liberal government there favorable to Spain--perhaps a monarchy with crown given to Spanish prince; La Serna's refusal led to resumption of hostilities
lasting more than three years before Ayacucho brought final
independence from Spain.

PUNTA ARENAS. Chile's southernmost city in which the Argentine-Chilean peace treaty was signed (1877) establishing the
boundaries between the two countries.

PUTAENDO. Valley on western slopes of Andes where Necochea
defeated and routed Spanish force under Miguel Atero February 7, 1817, and made possible patriot possession of San
Felipe de Aconcagua, according to San Martín's plan; one of
actions leading to victory at Chacabuco (q.v.).

- Q -

QUADRILATERAL TREATY (Tratado del Cuadrilátero), January 25,
1822. Another of the earlier pacts named in the preamble
of the national constitution; signed in Santa Fe by the representatives of Buenos Aires, Entre Ríos, Santa Fe, and Corrientes, it called for a Constitutional Congress to meet at
the first possible opportunity to organize a federal form of
government; the provinces involved declared themselves autonomous but members of one nation; important as a declaration of principles but did not immediately lead to national organization.

QUEBRACHO (the "axe breaker"). Scrub tree valued for hardness
of its wood and the tannin, used in the leather industry, that
can be distilled from its logs; one species, the colorado or
red quebracho (Schinopsis lorentzii) contains as much as 30%
tannin, but it is such a slow grower--said to take 100 years
to mature--that supplies are practically exhausted and reforestation plans impractical; the blanco or white variety
(Aspidosperma quebracho blanco) is more readily available,
but contains less tannin; this wood has in the past commonly
been used for telegraph poles, railroad ties, and fuel; it is
most commonly found in Formosa, Chaco, and to a lesser
degree, in neighboring provinces to the south; among the
earliest industries in the Chaco region were tannin extraction

plants; cotton was planted between the trees; in the late nineteenth and first part of twentieth century quebracho was so valuable that, in areas where it was found in abundance, most of the land was held either by big companies or in government reserves; its supply has diminished and substitutes and other products have been found so that quebracho no longer plays as important a role in the northern economy as it formerly did.

QUEBRACHO HERRADO. Battle fought at this place in Córdoba, November 28, 1840, successfully ended opposition to Rosas in the east and northeast for the time being; in 1839, in Paraná Rosas' Argentine enemies of the littoral provinces and in Uruguayan exile had joined with supporters of Fructuoso Rivera, Uruguayan leader against rival Oribe, and the French who had grievances against Rosas' government and had persuaded Juan Lavalle to take command of a liberating army against Rosas; the defeat of Lavalle's forces by Rosas' forces, led by Oribe, and their subsequent massacre, almost totally destroyed Lavalle's army; this defeat, followed almost immediately by news of the signing of the Arana-Mackau treaty (q.v.) with the French, and the later battle at Famaillá (q.v.) ended the joint action of the anti-Rosas rebellion; each group acted for itself thereafter, only General Paz was left to fight almost alone against Rosas (see Juan Lavalle; José María Paz; Manuel Oribe).

QUECHUA or QUICHUA (latter more commonly used in Argentina). Language used by Indians in Inca empire at time of conquest; its use extended across the Andes into Argentina as far as Tucumán.

QUENA. Indian flute of Quechua origin about 18 inches long, with five holes; apparently first made of bone, earthenware or metal (silver or gold), today it is made from cane; still used for folk music; various legends tell of its origin, all attributing it to loss of a loved one; in Jujuy the story goes that Maratec, son of an Indian chief, was so heartbroken when his sweetheart died that he used one of her shin bones to make a unique instrument, a quena, with which to express his grief; the Entre Ríos version says that when the Indian girl Picasú died, her lover Guazutí gathered her final cries in a tacuari cane, creating the first quena.

QUERANDI INDIANS. Group of Pampa Indians roaming the grassy plains that extended from northern Patagonia to the Río de la Plata in the sixteenth century; true nomads, they used primitive bow and arrow, sling, and later, boleadoras to hunt small pampas deer, guanaco and ñandús to supplement their roots and berries diet; also used fishmeal and made a flour of roasted locusts; were named Querandí (meaning eaters of grease) by their more civilized Guaraní neighbors because of their fondness for animal fats; little is known of their

language, only about a dozen words remaining; these were
the Indians that attacked and destroyed the first settlement
at Buenos Aires, made by Mendoza in 1536; they fought well
and many of them learned to use Spanish horses after the
conquest; remained wild, however, and conquistadors could
rarely use them for labor (see Pampa Indians).

QUESADA, ERNESTO (1858-1934).   Lawyer; historian; sociologist.
        Born in Buenos Aires, son of Vicente Quesada and of
Elvira Medina; studied in Corrientes, Buenos Aires, and
Germany; started writing while attending college; in 1881 published with his father the Nueva Revista de Buenos Aires;
taught sociology and law in the University of La Plata; in
1885 joined his father in the U.S.A., acting as his private
secretary; there he wrote Las islas malvinas; returned to
Argentina in 1888; taught in several universities (Buenos
Aires and La Plata) and in the Escuela Normal; widowed, he
married a German woman and spent much of his later life in
Europe; became member of faculty of University of Berlin;
died in Switzerland.
        Ernesto Quesada played important role in Argentine
historiography, having been one of the first to become familiar with the new German historical methodology; praised this
highly and used the new historical techniques in his revisionist
writings about Juan Manuel de Rosas, whom he had visited in
exile in 1873, and his rehabilitation of Angel Pacheco, his
wife's grandfather; in 1908-1909, at request of the faculty of
juridical and social sciences of the National University of La
Plata, he visited 22 German universities to study graduate
history programs; recommended that Argentina adopt the pattern of the institute of University of Leipzig, founded by Karl
Lamprecht; although his recommendation was not immediately
followed, it made considerable impact on young Argentine
historians.
        He wrote on history, law, sociology, literary criti-
cism, politics, criminology, and library science; published
Real Estate in Argentine Law; Los tiempos de Rosas; La
época de Rosas, su verídico carácter histórico (1898); La
enseñanza de historia en las universidades alemanas; La
sociedad romana en el primer siglo de nuestra era; Avellaneda irónico.

QUESADA, VICENTE (1830-1913).   Diplomat and scholar; juriscon-
        sult, librarian, and publicist.
        Born and educated in law in Buenos Aires; acted as
secretary of Vicente López y Planes, governor of Buenos
Aires in 1852 after fall of Rosas; the following year moved
to Salta and Tucumán where he began his historical researches;
then went to Corrientes; during years 1855 to 1857 he served
as adviser to Governor Juan Pujol, represented Corrientes in
the Confederation Congress, and published his first book, La
provincia de Corrientes; from March to May, 1860, he was
minister of interior for President Santiago Derqui; founded

La Revista del Paraná to encourage historical studies; in
1863, back in Buenos Aires, following national reorganization,
he began publication of La Revista de Buenos Aires; became
director of the public library of the capital, organizing its
collection of historical manuscripts; President Sarmiento sent
him to Europe to study library organization and to search
for documents that could be used in resolving Argentina's
delicate problems of boundary limits with Chile, Bolivia, and
Paraguay; published his official reports on his return: Las
bibliotecas europeas y algunas de América Latina and La
Patagonia y las tierras australes del continente americano;
was serving as national congressman (1878-1880) when the
federal government moved to Belgrano; when he refused to
leave Buenos Aires, he was expelled from the lower house
and retired from politics; wrote El virreinato del Río de la
Plata, 1776-1810 which supplemented his Patagonia report by
including critical historical data about the boundary; President Roca brought him back into public service as diplomat;
from 1883 to 1904, he lived in Rio de Janeiro, Washington,
D. C. , Mexico City, Rome, Paris, and Berlin, as well as
other European capitals; the six years (1885-1891) that he
spent as ambassador to the United States were notable in
several respects; he reopened the Falkland Islands (q. v.) controversy and requested, with no success, indemnities from
United States for part it had played in incident that caused
England to take them over; was appointed one of three Argentine representatives to first Pan American Conference
(1889-1890), along with Roque Saenz Peña and Manuel Quintana, but absented himself, apparently in effort to avoid com-
promising his usefulness as ambassador; served as minister
to Mexico in 1891 concurrently with his post in U. S. and
warned that nation against U. S. expansion; using the pseudonym Domingo de Pantoja, he published his bitterly critical
(for most part) impressions of the United States in Los Estados Unidos y la America del Sur: los yanquis pintados por
sí mismos (Buenos Aires, 1893).
        In addition to those works mentioned, Quesada left an
impressive bibliography; in 1881 he and his son Ernesto
(q. v.) had founded the Nueva Revista de Buenos Aires in
which he published Memorias de un viejo; in 1901 he began
publishing his diplomatic memoirs Recuerdos de mi vida dip-
lomática; among important historical works should be mentioned La sociedad hispano americana bajo la dominación española (1893); Los indios en las provincias del Río de la
Plata (1902), considered by many to have been his best work;
La vida intelectual en la América española durante los siglos
XVI, XVII, y XVIII (1910); Estudio sobre las leyes de indias;
Crónicas potosinas; Antecedentes históricos de Buenos Aires.

QUIJANO, HORTENSIO JUAN (1884-1952).   Lawyer; vice president
    of the Republic.
        Born in Corrientes; practiced law there; began his
political career as member of the Unión Cívica Radical;

defeated in his candidacy as vice governor of province; went
to the Chaco where he engaged in building a railroad along
the Río Bermejo that later became part of the national system; had been an ardent supporter of Yrigoyen; returned to
political life, after the 1930 revolution, as a collaborator
with Marcelo T. de Alvear; in 1943 he joined the Peronist
movement; served as President Farrell's minister of the interior in 1945; elected vice president on the Perón ticket in
both 1946 and 1952; died shortly after latter election.

QUILMES. Site, about 8 miles down the river from the center of
Buenos Aires, where British disembarked (June 25, 1806) with
about 1600 men to capture Buenos Aires in surprise attack
(see British Invasions); two naval battles in the war with
Brazil also took place here, one in July 1826, the second on
February 24, 1827; Brazilian navy withdrew after each encounter with Argentine ships.

QUINQUELA MARTIN, BENITO. Argentina's most famous modern
painter; specialized in watercolor scenes of port of Buenos
Aires; his works may be seen in the Metropolitan Art Museum in New York and in the Luxembourg in Paris.

QUINTANA, HILARION DE LA (1774-1843). Military officer; patriot leader and functionary.
        Born in the Banda Oriental; during the British invasions
represented Santiago de Liniers in the negotiations with General Beresford; in 1810 supported the revolution and joined the
army; took part in the campaign to the Banda Oriental (1811
and 1812); in 1814 was appointed commanding officer of Entre
Ríos forces; on August 3 of the same year was appointed
lieutenant governor of the new province created in 1814; joined
San Martín's army and fought in Chacabuco, Cancha Rayada,
and Maipú; in 1817 was briefly appointed delegate director of
Chile; when he became involved in the overthrow of the
Buenos Aires Directorate in 1819, was dismissed from the
army; the following year, however, the cabildo asked him to
take the military command of Buenos Aires; he did, for three
days, until calm was restored; emigrated to Montevideo and
returned to Buenos Aires during the governorship of Martín
Rodríguez; died in Buenos Aires.

QUINTANA, MANUEL (1834-1906). President of Argentine Republic, 1904-1906; jurisconsult; statesman.
        Born in Buenos Aires; grandson of independence vete-
ran Francisco Bruno de la Quintana; graduated in law; taught
in law school; served as dean of school of law, rector of
university; elected to several terms in chamber of deputies
and national senate; in 1888 acted as co-president with Roque
Saenz Peña of international South American law congress in
Montevideo; attended first Pan American conference in Washington (1889), exercised strong Argentine influence on matters
of form, procedure, and on arbitration plan for the Americas;

served briefly as minister of interior in cabinet of President
Luis Sáenz Peña; retired for a time but returned to restore
order in provinces of Tucumán, Santiago del Estero, and
Santa Fe; his firm action brought opposition from radicals
and others; retired to private life but was back in Congress
1900-1903; as the chosen candidate of the estancia oligarchy
and Roca government, Quintana was elected president of the
Argentine Republic in late 1904; almost immediately the political turmoil and social unrest broke out in revolt of 1905;
despite the fact that both Vice President Figueroa Alcorta
and Roca's son had been kidnapped and were being held as
hostages, Quintana was able to suppress the uprising and
restore order, temporarily at least; meanwhile his brief
presidency saw the beginning of an economic revival that
lasted until 1912, a doubling of immigration, improvement of
ports of Bahía Blanca and Quequén; the national university of
La Plata was established and the first labor law passed,
under Socialist leadership; opposition was mounting against
Quintana at the time of his death in March, 1906, and Vice
President José Figueroa Alcorta's (q.v.) succession to the
presidency.

QUINTEROS, LIDORO J.   (1847-1907).   Progressive political leader; business executive.
        Born in San Miguel de Tucumán; studied there; early
entered career of public service; elected to congress in 1874,
1878; became vice president of Chamber of Deputies (1881);
supported president's policy and federalization of Buenos
Aires as capital of the republic (see Federalization of City
of Buenos Aires); later became president of the Caja de Conversión (Conversion Fund), manager of the Northern Railroad, president of the Unión Azucarera (Sugar Board); also
held various offices in his province of Tucumán, including that
of governor; demonstrated administrative talents and progressive spirit throughout varied career; died in Buenos Aires.

Quirno Costa, Norberto (1844-1915).   Lawyer; vice president;
        liberal conservative statesman and diplomat.
        Born in Buenos Aires and educated as lawyer in uni-
versity there; became secretary of Argentine legation to Brazil in 1868 and undersecretary of ministry of foreign relations
in 1869; successfully carried out negotiations ending in signing of peace treaty with Paraguay; in 1871 was member of
commission for reformation of the Buenos Aires provincial
constitution; served as national congressman (1878); appointed
as foreign minister by President Juárez Celman, he played a
leading role in South American Congress of International Private Law that met in Montevideo in 1888; Quirno Costa addressed the assembly, more than once, stressing the need
for South American nations to strengthen their ties with
Europe by clearcut legal understandings and guidelines; ruled
out invitations to non-Latin American countries, such as the
United States; also served as minister of interior under

Juárez Celman; continued to serve under succeeding presidents: as minister to Chile, under Luis Sáenz Peña; minister of interior for José E. Uriburu; president of the convention to revise the constitution (1898), vice president during second administration of Julio A. Roca (1898-1904) and minister of interior in cabinet of Figueroa Alcorta; as a member of PAN (Partido Autonomista Nacional) he was a liberal conservative--belonged to the new oligarchy.

QUIRNO Y PIZARRO, NORBERTO (1837-1908). Rancher. Born in Buenos Aires; owned about 10 ranches in the province of Buenos Aires, Santa Fe, and Córdoba; brought Durham cattle from England; made his ranch La Estanzuela into a model; it won the national prize in the rural exposition of 1882; was one of the founders of the Sociedad Rural; while fighting in the battle of Pavón saved the life of Colonel Emilio Mitre; in 1880 was assistant of General Bartolomé Mitre; died in Buenos Aires.

QUIROGA, ADAN (1863-1904). Lawyer, writer, archeologist and folklorist.
        Born in San Juan but lived in Catamarca; graduated in law from university of Córdoba and founded La Propaganda with Joaquín V. González (q. v.); became member of Catamarca's supreme court (1890) and public prosecutor; in 1895 moved to Tucumán for political reasons; founded El Nacional and published several works; appointed judge; began his archeological studies in Tucumán with Antiguedades calchaquíes; returned to Catamarca where he divided his time between law, agriculture, and archeology; is best remembered for his poetry and archeological works; his verses appear especially in the collections Flores del aire (1893; 1913); his works in law and archeology include: Proyecto de código de policía y procedimientos judiciales (1892); Ley orgánica de los tribunales (1897); Defensas criminales y civiles; La cruz en América (1902); made important contribution through his preservation of folklore literature of the northwest, as in Folklore calchaquí (1897); El diablo en el norte, Tupay Miliko (1898); Huayrapuca o la madre del viento (1899).

QUIROGA, CAMILA (1896-1948). Actress who brought international recognition to Argentine theater.
        Born in Entre Ríos; began professional acting career under her maiden name Passera while still a teenager; attracted immediate attention; in 1912 she and her husband, Héctor Quiroga, formed their own company and toured the provinces; in 1914 was star actress in company of Pablo Podestá; performed in national theater; after 1917 she controlled her own company; became great favorite with Argentine theater and movie audiences, as well as with dramatists who preferred her for presenting their works; received enthusiastic welcome on her tours to various European and Latin American countries and in the United States (1927); her first

movie was "Mariano Moreno o la revolución de Mayo," with
Pablo Podestá; died in Córdoba.

QUIROGA, HORACIO (1879-1937). Short story writer.
     Born in
     Uruguay, Quiroga moved to Buenos Aires (1902) as a young
     man, following personal tragedy; became part of literary, in-
     tellectual circles there; formed close friendship with Leopoldo
     Lugones (q. v.); accompanied latter on trip through former
     Jesuit mission country; remained in Misiones, on a small
     cotton plantation near San Ignacio, for several years; had al-
     ready published poems Los arrecifes de coral (1901) and
     Cuento sin razón pero cansado; then turned almost completely
     to writing of short stories, of which he was a master; came
     to be known as the Edgar Allan Poe of the Río de la Plata;
     his tales of primitive nature, based on his stay and travels
     in jungles of Misiones and the Chaco, offered a vivid new
     panorama blended of reality and fantasy, to the nationalist
     literature; among his best known works are Cuentos de la
     selva; Cuentos de amor, de locura y de muerte; and Anaconda.

QUIROGA, JOSE (1707-1784). Jesuit missionary, explorer, mathe-
     matician, and cartographer.
          Born in province of Pontevedra, Spain; had already
     become advanced in scientific studies, through training in
     naval school and extensive travel and research while on voy-
     ages in Mediterranean Sea and Atlantic Ocean, when he de-
     cided to become member of Society of Jesus; encouraged by
     his Jesuit superior to continue his scientific and mathematical
     work, he was sent, in 1745, to Buenos Aires; assigned to
     accompany a fully-equipped scientific expedition to explore
     the Patagonian coast and interior with a view to establishing
     new missions there; for four months (December, 1745-April,
     1746) Quiroga and his companion scientist, José Cardiel (q. v.),
     as well as other Jesuits, all under Matías Strobel as super-
     ior, explored, studied, and carefully mapped the area; found
     so few Indians and such inadequate water supplies that they
     reported unfavorably about establishing new missions; Quiroga
     assigned to new duties; already, in 1745, while waiting to
     depart for Patagonia, he had drawn up plans for more accu-
     rate surveying of land held in Buenos Aires area, at request
     of cabildo; his guidelines became basis of law, 1746; after
     return from Patagonia, taught mathematics at University of
     Córdoba and, in 1749 completed his important Mapa de las
     misiones de la Compañía de Jesús en los Ríos Paraná y
     Uruguay, based on his own travels in the northeast mission
     area; map published in Rome four years later; following the
     treaty of 1750 between Spain and Portugal, Quiroga became
     involved in working out the boundary lines between Brazil
     and Argentina; left interesting account of commissioners' at-
     tempts to draw the line (1753); was living in Buenos Aires
     when Jesuits were expelled from Spanish colonies; went to
     Italy with other exiles; lived in Bologna with Argentine as-
     tronomer Ignacio Frías; devoted himself to cartographical

studies; his biography, written by Guillermo Furlong and entitled El padre José Quiroga, was published by the Instituto
de Investigaciones Históricas de la Facultad de Filosofía y
Letras.

QUIROGA, JUAN FACUNDO (1788-1835). Caudillo of the North;
denounced as barbarian by Sarmiento in his Civilization and
Barbarism: the Life of Juan Facundo Quiroga, and known as
Tiger of the Llanos (plains of La Rioja), Quiroga played
powerful role in the bloody wars and political life of Argentina 1818-1835.

    Born in La Rioja, too self-willed to accept the disci-
pline of the independence armies, he plunged dramatically into public life by prison episode in San Luis, 1818; Spanish
officers, captured by San Martín in Chile, sent there for detention, made break for freedom, liberating criminal prisoners, including Quiroga, to aid them; Quiroga, using either
a prison bar or a bayonet, turned instead on the prisoners,
killing several, and completely foiling the royalist plans; returning to La Rioja, a hero to his gaucho neighbors, he rose
rapidly to political power, meanwhile fighting in the various
wars of that area and period; fought against Rivadavia's centralist constitution but was defeated by Rivadavia's armies
under Lamadrid; by 1828, however, Quiroga controlled the
northern provinces from Catamarca to Mendoza; joined with
other caudillos in determination to establish federalism and,
especially after Dorrego's execution (December, 1828), to
destroy unitarist forces commanded by Lavalle, now governor
of Buenos Aires; Quiroga met defeat from unitarist general
Paz, at La Tablada June 23, 1829, and at Oncativo, February 25, 1830; temporarily prevented from returning, Quiroga
saw his chance to cut a way through to Cuyo in 1831 and
moved swiftly to Tucumán to meet the unitarist forces under
Lamadrid, in command since General Paz had been unexpectedly taken prisoner at Tío; battle at Ciudadela (famous fortress of Tucumán) November 4, 1831, resulted in a victory
for Quiroga and brought an end to the civil war as Rosas had
simultaneously overcome Lavalle in Buenos Aires.

    Moving to Buenos Aires Quiroga devoted the remainder
of his life to attempts (alone and with other federalists) to
secure the calling of a constituent congress to form the organic structure of a federal republic; Rosas opposed this vigorously, on grounds that such formal organization was premature and unwise until the provinces had created their individual political structures and healthy institutional life, citing
the example of the United States that would not admit a territory into full participation in national political life until it had
formed its own government; discussions interrupted in 1834
while Quiroga was sent on peacemaking mission in the hopes
that his power and prestige in the North would enable him to
prevent threatened civil war between the governors of Tucumán (Felipe Heredia) and Salta (Pablo Latorre); returning to
Buenos Aires after successful mission, he stubbornly ignored

warnings of conspiracy in Córdoba, was surprised and assassinated by force under Santos Pérez at Barranca Yaco, February 16, 1835; shocked public opinion divided blame between
Rosas, López, and the Reinafés, but José Vicente Reinafé,
governor of Córdoba, his brother, Santos Pérez, and others
were convicted of the conspiracy and executed (1836); death
of Quiroga left Rosas as only remaining power; realization
brought increasing uneasiness and fear to the people.

See Newton, Jorge, Juan Facundo Quiroga: aventura
y leyenda (Buenos Aires, 1973).

QUIROS, HERMINIO JUAN (1873-1931).   Lawyer, statesman.
Born in Entre Ríos; while still young, joined the Radical Party; at age of 19 acted as secretary of Dr. Leandro N.
Alem (q. v.); taught in the school of law (University of Buenos
Aires); served as national congressman for 3 periods, starting in 1920; during this time presented legislation for several
projects to improve his province; among these were the building of roads, improvement of railroads, colonization, public
school construction; tried to secure civil rights for women
but failed; in 1930 was elected governor of Entre Ríos; during his brief government, he stimulated agriculture, formed
cooperatives, recommended the reform of the provincial constitution, improved agricultural credit, created rural schools;
published several works, the most important being his college
text on administrative law; died in Paraná.

- R -

RADEMAKER, JOHN.   On May 26, 1812, this British army engineer, with rank of lieutenant colonel but acting with diplomatic credentials from Portuguese government in Rio de Janeiro, arranged a truce between the Portuguese government
and the first triumvirate patriot government in Buenos Aires;
this armistice, generally known as the Rademaker convention,
provided that both Portuguese and Buenos Aires forces should
withdraw to their own boundaries and that no further hostilities would be undertaken without three months' advance notice;
this represented a victory for British diplomacy, aimed at
maintaining a balance of power in the Río de la Plata, as the
Portuguese had been poised to send further aid to Governor
Elío in Montevideo and possibly to invade Buenos Aires; it
foreshadowed the eventual formation of an independent buffer
state (Uruguay) between Brazil and Argentina; convention significant in Argentine history as first international treaty with
foreign power signed by the Provincias Unidas del Río de la
Plata.

RADICALS, RADICAL PARTY   see   UNION CIVICA RADICAL
(UCR)

RAILROADS AND RAIL COMPANIES.   Although first Argentine

railroad was opened in 1857, in Buenos Aires province, and at the same time the Urquiza's (q. v.) government was negotiating with U. S. railroad engineers for railroad building in the provinces of the Confederation, real development of railroads had to wait until after national political reorganization had been completed.

During decades from 1862 to 1912, 20,400 miles of railroad were built, opening up the interior, linking interior to coastal cities, bringing demands (and opportunities) for thousands of new immigrants, making possible extension of livestock industry and development of new commercial agriculture, and successful marketing of products of both; strengthened unification of new republic and increased dominance and size of Buenos Aires and, to a lesser extent, those of other ports, such as Rosario, La Plata, and Bahía Blanca; greatly strengthened ties between Argentina and Great Britain; latter supplied engineers, rolling stock, all coal for fueling trains, and most of capital necessary; in many ways, the railroads did bring about the social and economic revolution that the Liberals had expected from them, but they also increased Argentine dependence on Great Britain, retarded economic diversification, and eventually created serious new national problems.

The first railroad built was the Ferrocarril Oeste (Western Railroad--today the Sarmiento); built by Buenos Aires entrepreneurs, with their own capital, to connect city with western suburb, it soon needed financial aid and was taken over by the government in 1863 and expanded; sold to British in 1890; running through densely populated area, it was very successful.

In 1862, Edward Lumb (British) received grant from government to build Ferrocarril del Sur (Southern Railroad-- today General Roca) to link city of Buenos Aires with southern part of province (Chascomús and, later, Bahía Blanca); in return Lumb was to receive free land, tax exemptions, guarantee that government would not interfere with rates, and a 40-year guaranteed profit of 7%; private capital failed and government forced to grant further support to complete it in 1867. That same year, President Mitre gave William Wheelwright (q. v.) concession for construction of Ferrocarril Central Argentino (Central Argentine Railroad--today the General Mitre) from Rosario to Córdoba; this railroad also received 40-year guarantee of profits, land to be used for colonization (q. v.); company agreed to transport mail and troops.

In 1870s, government began construction of Ferrocarril al Pacífico (Andean or Buenos Aires-Pacific Railroad-- today Ferrocarril General San Martín), dreaming of a trans-Andean railroad; (this railroad was sold to British company in 1909; it became international in 1910 when Chilean and Argentine workers completed more than 2-mile tunnel through the Andes).

By 1880s railroads stretched over 1,388 miles; the

pattern of financing, construction, and control had been established; resources of the state were used to encourage private companies (foreign) to build railroads; some government
ownership also existed; "golden years" of railroad building
included period from 1880s to 1916 when railroad fever was
rampant; as long as railroads traversed only the populated
pampas, costs and problems of construction were minimal
and profits from transportation on produce of area to market
were large; after 1890 railroads began to push into the more
difficult mountain area (as mentioned above in Andean Railroad), and government insisted that more remote areas also
be linked with coast, but not necessarily with Buenos Aires,
only, as had been the case until 1899; Central Norte (Northern Central--today Ferrocarril General Belgrano), was built
by the government; it ran into the northwest, from Santa Fe,
through Tucumán, reaching Jujuy by end of century; under
special contract the Southern (General Roca) Railroad extended its lines from Bahía Blanca to Neuquén in 1899; the
Central reached Bolivia in 1908; and in 1909 lines were extended into Patagonia; between 1907 and 1914, railroad mileage increased at average rate of 1100 miles per year, to a
total of 22,066 miles, with government support and encouragement of private companies (British); by this time practical
limit had been reached, however, and railroads began steady
decline, made worse in 1920s and 1930s by highway competition; the so-called Big Four--Great Southern (General Roca),
Central Argentine (General Mitre), Buenos Aires and Pacific
(old Andean, now General San Martín), and Western (Sarmiento) took over monopoly of railroad transportation with continued cooperation of laissez-faire governments.

   Meanwhile problems had developed forcing government
action and beginnings of regulation; difference in gauges used
by different lines made national service less satisfactory than
it should have been; by 1899 the imbalance that linked all
lines with Buenos Aires, and later with only other coastal
ports, was already evident; this made communication between
existing, or projected, interior industrial and agricultural
centers difficult; railroads practically destroyed markets of
interior and its weak or isolated industrial centers, although
it stimulated such provinces as Mendoza with its wine industry, and Tucumán, with its sugar; in early twentieth century,
service deteriorated further; companies (almost all British
by then) unhampered by competition or government control,
became lax in their practices and at same time demanded
higher rates; pampa producers, totally dependent on railroads
for marketing their products, put pressure on the government;
in 1891 Congress passed General Railway Regulation, giving
rate relief to large shippers but unfortunately no help to
smaller users; in 1907 the Mitre Law brought all railroads
under regulation; it asserted right of government to intervene
in rate fixing, abolished guaranteed profit on investment, and
established a tax on privately owned railroads; actually briefly stimulated some new private railroad building (British)

with continued government support; by this time, in spite of
oligarchic and government support and general national prosperity, Argentine public opinion, led by Nationalists, had begun to hate the railroads believing that they constituted a
foreign barrier to economic mobility and diversification and
strengthened oligarchy's control and its refusal to admit
middle and lower classes to political participation; economic
nationalists, especially, demanded that nation should recover
control of its own economy by ending British ownership.

President Yrigoyen planted seed of popular nationalism
and encouraged ousting of foreign control; in 1930s, President
Justo favored progressive purchase of the railroads (70%
British-owned at that time) that were suffering from neglect
and competition from new highway system with increasing
automotive traffic; but this policy was reversed by his successors or vetoed by their Congresses, even while popular
sentiment for it increased; finally, under Perón, steps were
taken to nationalize railroads.

In 1946, Perón's minister Miguel Miranda signed Mi-
randa-Cady agreement providing for takeover of railroads by
mixed British-Argentine company; pressures from U.S. forced
British to let agreement expire; instead, they sold their railroads to Argentine government for £150 million, May 1,
1948; it is generally agreed that this was a better deal for
British than Argentines as railroad tracks, rolling stock,
stations, equipment, etc., were in very poor condition and
use of blocked sterling pound at that time almost bankrupted
Argentine treasury; Wright (see citations below) says that
"the nationalization of the British-owned railways and other
foreign-owned utility companies contributed directly to the
economic crisis that has plagued Argentina since 1950."

Nevertheless, Perón's action was immensely popular;
railroads were reorganized in 1949; their workers form one
of most powerful unions in the nation; in 1960s Diesel engines
were introduced in Córdoba in hope of improving service;
railroads, however, in Argentina, as in most modern nations,
continue to suffer from air and automotive competition and
changed trade and travel patterns.

See Winthrop R. Wright, British-Owned Railways in
Argentina (Austin, Texas, 1974); Horacio Juan Cuccorese,
Historia de los ferrocarriles en la Argentina (Buenos Aires,
1969); Enrique Udaondo, Significado de la nomenclatura de
las estaciones ferroviarias de la República Argentina (Buenos
Aires, 1942).

RAMIREZ, FRANCISCO (1786-1821). Entre Ríos caudillo, entitled
El Supremo by his fellow entrerrianos who revered him as
their special leader and spokesman; early leader of provincial federalism against Buenos Aires unitarism and domination.

Born in Concepción del Uruguay (old name Arroyo de
la China) into prominent family; entered patriot movement in
1810 by acting as courier between Díaz Vélez and Rondeau;

in 1811 he joined Ricardo López Jordán (father) in supporting
Uruguayan leader J. J. Artigas in fighting against Spaniards
in Uruguay and on the rivers and then against the Portuguese
invasion from Brazil (1816); during next few years there was
an uneasy balance in the river provinces between Santa Fe,
led by Estanislao López, and Entre Ríos, under Ramírez,
both opposed to Buenos Aires domination; Supreme Director
Pueyrredón attempted a conciliatory policy, for the time being, to protect his first priority--that of supporting San Martín's continental project for winning independence from Spain;
in 1819 the situation changed dramatically when José Miguel
Carrera, former Chilean president, returned from U.S. exile
and was prevented by Pueyrredón from going to Chile, recently liberated by San Martín; Carrera joined forces with
Carlos María de Alvear (q.v.) who was eager to regain political power in Buenos Aires and they persuaded both López
and Ramírez to join them against the directorate government;
war broke out when López seized a government supply wagon
train passing through Santa Fe under protection of Marcos
Balcarce; Ramírez supported the Santa Fe caudillo, issuing
proclamation to effect that they were fighting to remove tyrants from government, reestablish popular liberty and equality of citizens--i.e., of provincials to porteños, and to remove Portuguese from the Banda Oriental; this "guerrilla"
warfare of riparian provinces against Buenos Aires posed
such a threat to Buenos Aires that San Martín was ordered
to bring his liberating army back to defend Buenos Aires but
refused; Ramírez and López commanded federalist army that
defeated Rondeau at Cepeda (February 1, 1820) and signed
treaty of Pilar shortly thereafter, marking triumph of provincial autonomy over Buenos Aires domination (see Entre
Ríos, for detailed sequence of events of 1819-1821 during
which Ramírez dominated Entre Rios as governor and military commander and exercised important influence on neighboring provinces).

　　　Rivalry between Ramírez and López for political leadership of the river provinces, along with their conflicting
purposes, eventually brought them to armed conflict; Ramírez
had never given up idea of ousting Portuguese Brazilians from
Banda Oriental and appealed to Buenos Aires for help; that
government was preoccupied with fighting Indians in southwestern part of province, aroused by Carrera, and could not
divert forces at once to Uruguay; peace had also been made
between Santa Fe and Buenos Aires (1820, Treaty of Benegas)
and plans were under way for a national congress to meet in
Córdoba; thus Bustos of Córdoba, López of Santa Fe, and
Martín Rodríguez of Buenos Aires opposed Ramírez and looked
on him as obstacle to national reorganization; Ramírez took
the offensive, crossed Paraná river to Santa Fe territory,
arranged with Carrera to take part in a pincers movement
against Córdoba to defeat their common foes; after some preliminary success, Ramírez and Carrera met crushing defeat;
they fled, separately, with a few followers, to recoup their

forces and renew the fight; in July 1821 Ramírez met his final defeat near Río Seco, where he had hoped to rejoin Carrera; escaped alive but, discovering that his constant companion, the famous Delfina (q.v.) had fallen into hands of an
enemy, returned to her rescue and was shot; his head was
severed and sent to Estanislao López who displayed it publicly in cabildo building; Ramírez's death brought an end to six
years of civil war and seemed to pave way for national unity;
actually the federalism for which he had fought remained a
vital force that played a role, decades later, in the constitution of 1853, national reorganization in 1861-1863, and federalization of Buenos Aires as capital in 1880.

　　　　See Aníbal S. Vásquez, Caudillos entrerrianos. Ramírez.

RAMIREZ, PEDRO PABLO (1884-1962).　General; president of Ar-
　　gentina, 1943-1944.
　　　　Born in La Paz, Entre Ríos, a meat packing center;
believed to have been descendant of Entre Ríos caudillo Francisco Ramírez; entered military career, studying at the military academy, ballistics school, and war college; by 1941 he
had become a division general, having had distinguished and
interesting military responsibilities and posts; in World War
I fought in German army and in 1930 served as military
attaché to Italy; became minister of war in 1942 and as a
member of the GOU (q.v.) took part in military overthrow of
government (1943); became president after Rawson's very
brief tenure; on January 26, 1944, he broke diplomatic relations with Germany and Japan (see World War II) and the following month turned the presidential power over to General
Edelmiro S. Farrell and retired to private life.

RAMIREZ DE VELASCO (or Velazco), JUAN (died c.1597).　Gov-
　　ernor of Tucumán, 1586-1693; governor of Río de la Plata,
　　1596-1597.
　　　　Born in Castilla, Spain, in province of La Rioja; belonged to old and distinguished family from which crown often
drew administrators (nephew and cousin of the Luis de Velas-
cos who served as viceroys in Mexico and Peru); served
about thirty years in military campaigns of Spain; appointed
by Philip II as governor of Tucumán, Ramírez de Velasco
assumed his duties there 1586 and during the next seven
years he devoted himself to completing the Spanish plan for
pacification of the Indians (Diaguitas and Calchaquís) and
establishing permanent towns; in 1591 he founded La Rioja,
which he considered to be a reconstruction of the older town
of Londres, established farther north in 1558 and destroyed
by Indians, and left Blas Ponce (q.v.) in authority there
when the formalities had been completed; in 1592 he founded
the Villa de Nueva Madrid; and Jujuy, in 1593, turning its
government over to Fernando de Zárate; his administration
marked the beginning of firm Spanish control in the Tucumán
area; he fostered the introduction of livestock, created

estancias, pacified the Indians, and encouraged the establishment of families; in 1594 he was named governor and captain-
general of Río de la Plata; unable to take up his duties there
at once, he delegated his authority to the Creole Hernandarias
(see listing Arias de Saavedra, Hernando); was governor and
captain-general of Río de la Plata (1596-1597); died in Santa
Fe about 1597.

RAMOS MEJIA FAMILY. One of traditional, powerful, wealthy
family of Buenos Aires province; founded by Gregorio Ramos
Mejía and Marina Cristina Ross y Pozo in late eighteenth
century, its members have continued for two centuries to
exercise leadership in economic, political, and intellectual
life of Argentine republic (see individual entries below).

RAMOS MEJIA, EZEQUIEL (1853-1935).   Statesman; financier.
        Born in Buenos Aires; early became involved in poli-
tics; elected to provincial legislature in 1880; toured Europe
with Paul Groussac, Roque Saenz Peña, and Carlos Pellegrini; in 1900 became congressman in national Chamber of
Deputies; appointed minister of agriculture by President Julio
A. Roca in 1901, but resigned after brief period because of
disagreement with president; in 1906 President Figueroa Alcorta appointed him minister of public works; remained in
this cabinet post until 1913, under President Saenz Peña; also during this period he vigorously supported the use of private, foreign capital for construction of such public utilities
as railroads, etc. ; later became president of the Mortgage
and Loan Bank; in 1933 served as ambassador to Italy; his
writings reflect his own interests and activities: Mensaje y
proyecto de ley sobre irrigación (1909); Organización bancaria
y soluciones financieras (1917); and his very important La
colonización oficial y la distribución de las tierras públicas
(1921).

RAMOS MEJIA, FRANCISCO (1847-1893).   Jurisconsult; sociologist;
historian.
        Born in Buenos Aires; graduated in law; served as
judge of criminal court in province and in the capital from
1877 to 1884; retired from the bench; became important member of group of lawyers introducing application of new theories
of positivism (q.v.) into Argentine criminal law; with Luis
María Drago and others founded Sociedad de Antropología
Jurídica in 1888; that same year read important paper to Society entitled "Principios fundamentales de la escuela positiva
de derecho penal" ("Basic Principles of the Positivist School
of Criminal Law"); became member of Unión Cívica and was
a popular leader in revolution of 1890; was serving as senator in Buenos Aires provincial legislature at time of his
death; made important contribution to Argentine historiography
in his Historia de la evolución argentina in which he claimed
that Argentina's devotion to federalism grew primarily out of
its Spanish heritage; first part, entitled El federalismo

argentino, published in 1887; the rest of it, with the full title given above appeared in 1921.

RAMOS MEJIA, FRANCISCO HERMOGENES (1773-1825).   Estanciero; sometimes called real founder of Ramos Mejía family's wealth.

Born in Buenos Aires province; older brother of Ildefonso Raimundo, son of Don Gregorio; lived more or less along the Indian frontier all his life; started economic career as manager of a general store (pulpería) but soon became involved in management of large landed cattle estates; living in an area where costly and savage Indian raids were a constant menace to successful ranch operations, he tried to turn the hatred and economic rivalry (Indians also cattlemen) of these neighboring Indians into friendship and cooperation; in doing this, he attempted to use religious teachings, claiming to find a common ground in a religion that mixed dogmatism, pantheism, and Christianity; this brought him into conflict with Catholic priests who resented his meddling in their work; government declared him a heretic, confiscated much of his property by force, and brought him to Buenos Aires where he was jailed for six days; returned soon thereafter to his estancias; died at one of them, Los Tapiales, in southern Buenos Aires province.

RAMOS MEJIA, GREGORIO (1725-1808).   Merchant; public official.

Born in Sevilla and educated in Spain; arrived in Buenos Aires about 1761; became member of Venerable Third Order of St. Francis in that year; immediately became active as merchant; following 1766 he also became deeply involved in political life of community; served as regidor or other cabildo member and officer for the next forty years; was interested in such municipal projects as the construction of recova (q.v.) building; firmly opposed (1798) free trade as dangerous to the colonies but was outvoted in cabildo; became influential member of Consulado established in 1794; retired to private life in 1805; died three years later in Buenos Aires; married María Cristina Ross y Pozo and founded the Ramos Mejía family (see Ildefonso Raimundo Ramos Mejía; Francisco Hermógenes Ramos Mejía).

RAMOS MEJIA, ILDEFONSO PRUDENCIO (1854-1924).   Mathematician.

Born in the province of Buenos Aires; received first mathematical degree granted by the university of Buenos Aires; taught at the university until his retirement in 1914; while teaching he served as adviser of the faculty, assistant rector of the Colegio Nacional of Buenos Aires and rector of the Institute of Free Teaching (1901-1921); in 1896 he was appointed general inspector of education (supervisor of national schools) with special responsibility for founding rural regional schools adapted to the demands of the specific region in which each was established.

RAMOS MEJIA, ILDEFONSO RAIMUNDO (1769-1854).   Patriot leader during early independence period.
        Born in Buenos Aires, son of Don Gregorio; began his
relatively brief political career in Buenos Aires as member
of the May Revolution cabildo abierto; continued to represent
interests of Buenos Aires province during independence wars
and early years of independence; proffered aid to Manuel Belgrano in closing months of his life, in Buenos Aires; became
a key figure that same year (1820) in the confused politics of
Buenos Aires; some historians believe that it was his resignation from the legislature that triggered the anarchy of that
year; the junta appointed him governor of the province and on
June 20 he was one of the three simultaneous (others, the
cabildo and General Miguel E. Soler) governors of Buenos
Aires; this resulted in a vicious power struggle with little
or no government (see Anarchy); a few months later, in
September 1824, representatives of important porteño families, led by Anchorena, called on Juan Manuel de Rosas,
then emerging as a political and military leader, to restore
order and government in the province by supporting one of
two candidates, Ramos Mejía or Martín Rodríguez; he chose
the latter; six years later, Ramos Mejía was a member of
the congress that adopted the constitution of 1826; died in
Buenos Aires.

RAMOS MEJIA, JOSE MARIA (1842-1914).   Physician; historian.
        Dr. Ramos Mejía's interests were divided between
those of his profession and those regarding the fairly recent
historical background of the Argentina in which he lived; as
a medical man he specialized in mental illness and treatment
of neuroses; served as president of the departments of public
hygiene and of public assistance; as president of national
council of education he attacked problem of current cultural
heterogeneity and supported more nationalistic education that
would incorporate immigrants into mainstream of Argentine
society; elected as national congressman in 1888 and again in
1890; although he advocated a more Argentine education in
the schools, he followed the somewhat more European style
of classic Argentine writers, like Echeverría, Alberdi, Vicente López, etc.; among his works medical and historic
themes alternate; some of these are: Rosas y su tiempo
(1907); Rosas y el Dr. Francia (1920); Las multitudes argentinas (1899); Las neuroses de los hombres célebres en la
historia argentina (1878); La locura en la historia (1898).
        See José Ingenieros, Personalidad intelectual del Dr.
José María Ramos Mejía.

RAMOS MEJIA, MATIAS (1810-1885).   Estanciero and military officer.
        Born on family estate, Los Tapiales in Buenos Aires
province; revolted against Rosas (1839) and was defeated;
went to Montevideo; joined Juan Lavalle's unitarist army and
fought at Quebracho Herrado, Sauce Grande, Famaillá, Don

Cristóbal, etc.; escorted Lavalle's body to Bolivia; after
Rosas' defeat at Caseros, he returned to his estancia; became colonel in the army and devoted much of rest of his
life until retirement to training military units to fight against
the Indians in the south; supported Buenos Aires government
in battles of Cepeda and Pavón, supplying mounts and food
supplies; a close personal friend of Bartolomé Mitre, he accompanied him in the 1874 revolution, sustaining an injury;
died at Los Tapiales.

RAMS Y RUBERT, ESTEBAN (1800-1867).   Spanish entrepreneur
and philanthropist.
        Born in Catalonia; came to Argentina for purpose of
making the Salado and Dulce rivers navigable; invested his
own funds; also, as director of railroad company, attempted
to increase track mileage; promoted education in Entre Ríos
and was one of founders of Spanish hospital in Buenos Aires;
died in cholera epidemic.

RANCAGUA, ACT OF.   Faced with the fact that anarchy in Buenos
Aires had destroyed San Martín's legitimacy of command as
well as continued government support for his projected liberating expedition to Peru, the officers in his army formally
drew up an agreement in Rancagua, April 2, 1819, authorizing him to continue with this expedition as planned; based
their action on old Spanish principle that ultimate sovereignty
resided in the people (see José de San Martín); Chile furnished much of the support for new expedition.

RANCAGUA, BATTLE OF.   Site, in town a few miles south of
Santiago, of defeat, October 2, 1814, of Chilean forces under
Bernardo O'Higgins, aided by Argentine Las Heras, by royalist forces commanded by General Manuel Osorio; O'Higgins
succeeded in escaping with his army across the Andes to
Mendoza; there they became part of San Martín's liberating
expedition that freed Chile from Spanish control in 1817-1818.

RANCHO.   Primitive rural house of adobe or straw and mud walls
covered by thatched roof supported by forked poles; building
materials vary according to those most common in the region; modern ranchos built of brick or adobe; face prevailing
winds or are sheltered against violent winds like pamperos
(q. v.); term "rancho" also used in slang, for crude straw
hats to distinguish them from more elegant Panama hats.

RANQUELES.   Araucanian Indians who established themselves in
territory between Quinto and Colorado rivers, from southern
San Luis and Córdoba to south of La Pampa province; raided
all attempts at settlement in that area until conquered in
latter half of nineteenth century; see listing of Lucio V.
Mansilla who was stationed on that frontier and wrote book
describing Ranqueles and popularizing usage of this name for
them.

RASTRA.   Gaucho belt ornament; usually made of gold or silver; consists of two or three chains suspended from the belt, each chain ending in gold or silver coins; considered a luxury article.

RASTREADOR.   Scout or tracker; most famous in Argentine history was Calíbar (q. v.), depicted by Domingo Faustino Sarmiento in Facundo.

RAUCH, FREDERICK (1790-1829).   Soldier; Indian fighter.   Prussian colonel who had fought with Napoleon; arrived in Buenos Aires in 1819; joined the army; fought in civil wars; in 1823 was sent against Indians of southern Buenos Aires; two years later penetrated area south of Tandil and took Indians there by surprise; incurred Rosas' jealousy because of his prestige; accused by former of being a unitarist; on March 28, 1829 he was in command of one of Juan Lavalle's divisions when he was attacked and defeated, with heavy losses, at Vizcacheras (Buenos Aires province); this left Lavalle open to attack and led to his defeat at Puente de Márquez less than a month later; Colonel Rauch was killed by Indians immediately after the battle at Vizcacheras.

RAVE, FRANCISCO (1837-1871).   German engineer and writer. Rave was working in Brazil when governor of Corrientes invited him to come to Argentina to make survey of yerba mate plantations; went on to Buenos Aires (1864) where he taught mathematics and physics; published geographical study of El territorio de Misiones; died during yellow fever epidemic of 1871.

RAVE OCANTES DE LAHITTE, MARIA (d. 1944).   Writer and civic leader.   A professional journalist, she contributed regularly to such publications as El Pueblo, La Nación, El Diario, El Tiempo; also wrote for La Revista de Derecho (Law Review); published historical novel Babylonia; served as president of Council of Women, worker in anti-alcoholic league and society of public welfare; organized the Third National Eucharistic Congress (1916), and performed other public and community services; died in Buenos Aires.

RAVIGNANI, EMILIO (1886-1954).   Historian; jurist; militant Radical political figure.
        Born in Buenos Aires; studied in faculty of law and social sciences and in that of philosophy and letters; meanwhile became active in Unión Cívica Radical; throughout his life he combined his professional life as a historian with that of a Radical political figure; his most important contribution as historian was made at the University of La Plata; this university had already been oriented toward historical studies by Joaquín V. González and Ernesto Quesada (qq. v.); Ravignani taught Argentine constitutional history in faculty of juridical and social sciences; sonstitutional history in faculty

juridical and social sciences; founded and became director
of its institute of historical research; edited the institute's
Boletín, one of Argentina's notable contributions to modern
historiography and methodology; continued his own writing
and research; during this period he had been active in public
life; served as undersecretary of finance for municipality of
Buenos Aires (1922-1927); as national congressman in lower
house (1936-1940, 1940-1943, 1946-1950); became involved in
founding and work of Acción Argentina (q.v.); twice served as
dean of faculty of philosophy and letters; during period 1944-
1954 spent considerable time at University of Montevideo, organizing its Institute of historical research.

His extensive bibliography includes: Nociones de
moral cívica y política (under pseudonym John S. War) (1908);
Una comprobación histórica, el comercio de ingleses y la
"Representación de Hacendados" de Moreno (1914); La socio-
logía, su importancia para los estudios históricos (1915); Historia del derecho argentino (1919); Cartografía histórica
americana; Un censo de la provincia de Buenos Aires en la
época de Rosas, año 1836 (1922); La constitución de 1819
(1926); Historia constitucional de la República Argentina (1926-
1930); El pacto de la Confederación Argentina (1938); El virreinato del Río de la Plata, su formacion histórica e institucional (1938); and his monumental 6 volume Asambleas constituyentes argentinas (1937-1940), that contains texts of constitutions, comments, etc.

RAWSON, AMAN (1794-1847). Physician. Born and educated in
his profession in the United States; arrived in Buenos Aires
in 1818 as a U.S. naval surgeon; was persuaded by his friend,
Dr. William Colisberry (who had been San Martín's physician
in Tucumán) to remain; established his practice in Cuyo area
and founded a family.

RAWSON, ARTURO (1885-1952). Leader of GOU military revolt,
1943; president pro tem of republic, 1943.
Born in Santiago del Estero; graduated from Colegio
Militar in 1907 and taught there; General Rawson was persuaded by military colleagues in GOU to lead the military
revolt ousting President Ramón S. Castillo, June 4, 1943;
served as president for about two days; during this period
differences among the various GOU officers, on matters of
internal policy as well as regarding Argentina's position
toward opposing sides in World War I, brought Rawson, who
favored improving relations with U.S. and Allies, to turn his
authority over to Pedro Pablo Ramírez, more representative
of militant nationalists, and inclined to be more sympathetic
to Axis powers although committed to policy of neutrality;
accepted post as Argentine ambassador to Brazil; reappeared
publicly in Buenos Aires in 1945 in the "march of the constitution and liberty" (q.v.); was brought before court martial
but exonerated; retired as division general; died in Buenos
Aires; author of Argentina y Bolivia en la epopeya de la
emancipación.

RAWSON, GUILLERMO (1821-1890). Physician. Born in San Juan
    where he worked in his profession until the 1850s; served as
    provincial legislator and was political opponent of Domingo F.
    Sarmiento; organized rebellion against Governor Benavídez
    (1853) that failed; represented San Juan in Paraná Congress;
    opposed Urquiza; after battle of Pavón he moved to Buenos
    Aires where he was elected in 1862 as national senator for
    San Juan; minister of the interior for President Mitre; while
    minister, Rawson established post offices, encouraged the
    building of railroad (signed contract with Wheelwright), and
    stimulated immigration, particularly the Welsh colonies in
    Chubut, whose capital bears his name; opposed federalization
    of Buenos Aires in 1880 and retired from politics; became
    university professor and taught first course in public hygiene
    at the University of Buenos Aires; died during a trip to
    Europe where he went for eye surgery.
          See Gregorio Aráoz Alfaro, Rawson ministro de Mitre
    (1938).

REAL PATRONATO see CHURCH-STATE RELATIONS

REBELION DE LAS TRENZAS (or "Pigtail Revolt"). Revolt of
    patricios, December 7, 1811, against government order to
    cut off their braids or pigtails as part of attempt to moder-
    nize and reform the military units; patricios refused to re-
    move what they considered to be the traditional symbol of
    their superiority over other units (see Patricios; British In-
    vasions); the rebellion was crushed by Manuel Belgrano, both
    the regiment and its leaders severely punished and the author-
    ity of the patriot government firmly established over the mili-
    tary.

REBELLION OF SPANIARDS IN SAN LUIS, 1819. During early
    nineteenth century, prisoners of war were frequently confined
    in city of San Luis on edge of the desert; San Martín had
    sent Spanish officers who had been captured in Chile (1817-
    1818) to San Luis; in 1819 these prisoners, unhappy because
    of changes made in their situation, or because they wanted
    to return to the war, organized an attempt to escape under
    Gregorio Carretero's leadership; the rebellion failed, large-
    ly because, as Sarmiento tells the story, Juan Facundo Qui-
    roga (q.v.), the future caudillo but then a common prisoner,
    led the other prisoners in a patriotic and violent fight to sub-
    due the Spaniards who had, in fact, freed them also; Spanish
    leaders were beheaded February 15, 1819.

REBELLIONS OF 1752. Uprisings in La Rioja and Catamarca in
    1752 in protest against arbitrary Spanish military conscrip-
    tion of peasants.

RECA DE ACOSTA, TELMA (1904-   ). Child psychiatrist. Born
    in Buenos Aires; studied there and in the United States, under
    a Rockefeller fellowship; director of children's psychology

center of University of Buenos Aires; has taught courses on
child behavior in several Argentine centers as well as
abroad; has published numerous articles in scientific journals; longer works include Delincuencia infantil (1932); De la
vida norteamericana (1932); Nuevos conceptos sobre etipato-
genia y terapia de la enuresis (1945); Psicoterapia en la infancia (1951).

RECOLETA, LA. Site of public cemetery established in Buenos
   Aires in 1822; property had originally belonged to adelantado
   Juan Ortiz de Zárate, but had changed hands several times
   until in 1717 it became property of Franciscans who built
   monastery of Recollect Franciscans and Church of Pilar there;
   when Bernardino Rivadavia was serving as minister of government and foreign relations for the province of Buenos Aires,
   he felt that it was essential for reasons of sanitation and
   public health to establish public cemeteries in cities and decided to use La Recoleta in Buenos Aires; Franciscans were
   moved, the land was consecrated for the purpose, and burials
   began in 1823, in the cemetery of the North, as it was briefly known before reverting to its old name; one of the best
   known burials during the first year was that of Doña Remedios Escalada, wife of the liberator José de San Martín; prominent public figures have been buried there; in 1881, it was
   modernized, declared non-sectarian, and placed under cus-
   todianship of municipal authorities; La Recoleta has become
   known as one of the most beautiful cemeteries in South America, visited by thousands of tourists every year.

RECONQUEST (La Reconquista). The recapture, August 7, 1806,
   of the city of Buenos Aires from the British through the
   mobilization of popular efforts under local leaders; the British, commanded by Lord William Carr Beresford, were
   forced to surrender themselves, their banners, and all their
   military equipment to the porteño forces led by Santiago de
   Liniers; this memorable event, in which the Argentine people
   still take great pride, proved also to be decisive in the direction taken by historical development in the independence
   period (see British Invasions; Santiago de Liniers; William
   Carr Beresford).

RECOPILACION DE LEYES DE LOS REYNOS DE LAS INDIAS.
   Collection of laws and regulations drawn up by Spanish royal
   government for the administration of the colonies in the
   Indies (Americas); designed to suit these new needs, differing often from those of Old Spain, this legal work has been
   called by Clarence H. Haring "one of the most notable documents of modern colonial legislation."
       Parts of it were published earlier, for example by
   Luis de Velasco, viceroy of New Spain in 1563; the complete
   collection (9 volumes) appeared in 1681, promulgated by
   Carlos II; the code is arranged according to topic: v. I:
   Church, ecclesiastical taxes, universities and learning;

v. II: Council of the Indies, audiencias, visitadores, and
other special royal officials; v. III: Viceroys, military matters, piracy, protocol and ceremony, and the mails; v. IV:
Discovery and settlement of new land, establishment of local
governments, sale and distribution of land, public works,
quicksilver and other mining operations; v. V: Governors,
corregidors, alcaldes and the jurisdiction of suits and judg-
ments, appeals, and the residencia (q. v.); v. VI: Indians--
their towns and reducciones, tributes, chiefs, encomiendas--
and postal service; v. VII: Miscellaneous, crimes and punishments, blacks and mulattoes; v. VIII and v. IX: Financial
matters such as auditing, royal treasury, and commerce;
during the Bourbon period (18th century) many changes were
made and a new compilation, or a part of it, was published
by Carlos IV in 1805, entitled Novísima Recopilación; despite all the good intentions of the Crown and legal expertise
that went into the making of these codes, the laws were frequently not enforced in what is now Argentina, especially
those relating to treatment of the Indians and those regarding
commerce, largely because they were unrealistic; Mariano
Moreno, on the eve of independence, called them a "monument of errors" serving only to demonstrate the need for a
new juridical regime.

RECOVA.   A public market, usually with several buildings connected by an arched, covered corridor or walkway, often front-
ing on main plaza; that of Buenos Aires had been in existence
on Jesuit property as early as 1757; one-third the rent was
collected as city tax; in 1803 Viceroy Del Pino ordered its
building constructed; Sobremonte paved and lighted its street
(1805); three decades later the Rosas government sold it to
the Anchorena family in satisfaction of a debt; after Rosas
was gone, the Buenos Aires government reclaimed the Recova as public property (1858) but the Supreme Court returned it to the Anchorenas; it was expropriated in 1884 and
demolished to make room for the new Avenida and Plaza de
Mayo.

REDHEAD, JOSEPH THOMAS (1767-1847).   Physician.   Born in
U. S. , educated in medicine there and in Europe; arrived in
Buenos Aires in 1803, commissioned by the British government to study natural science in South America; licensed by
protomedicato in 1803 to practice medicine; traveled extensively; studied vegetation of Jujuy and Salta; spent some time
in Rosario de Lerma studying typhus and malaria; in 1812
he moved to Tucumán where he acted as medical officer of
the army and personal physician to Belgrano; while in Tucumán he helped Belgrano translate George Washington's "Farewell Address" into Spanish; supported Rivadavia's ideas and
collected documents on Rivadavia and Belgrano; in provincial
revolution of 1819 he persuaded leaders Abraham González
and Bernabé Aráoz to refrain from putting Belgrano in prison
and permit him to go to Buenos Aires for medical attention

needed for his swollen legs; returned to Salta in 1820 as
physician of Martín Güemes; remained there until his death.

REDUCCION. Indian town founded by Spaniards for purpose of
civilizing and converting natives to Christianity; Indians were
concentrated in a town over which a corregidor ruled; no
Europeans, other than priests, were permitted to reside
there; it was believed that by forcing the Indians to adopt the
Spanish life style and to learn its skills and institutions, they
would become easier to govern and more ready to accept
Christianity; it was also believed that the reducción would
prove to be more humane than the encomienda (q. v.) system
(devised for the same purpose); in 1610 Governor Diego
María Negrón began this program in Río de la Plata with the
first reducción, San José along the Areco river; named Hernando Arias de Saavedra as protector of Indians; project
failed as Indians preferred their own ways and fled from the
town; eventually, missionaries, chiefly Jesuit and Franciscan,
were able to establish such reducciones under religious leadership; when successful, these religious reducciones (or missions as they became in fact and name) resulted from cooperative effort of government, military command in area, local
Indian chief or cacique, Spanish residents in neighboring
towns, and the Indian populace; varied in their origins; sometimes missionaries took initiative and persuaded Indians to
come into the new town; occasionally Indians requested such
a mission; government authorized land limits, political and
judicial authority, provided military security when desired;
eventually about 100 were established; with the increasing
secularism of the eighteenth century, and renewed pressure
of Creole townsmen against missions for land and labor, the
system of reducciones (except for those that were primarily
religious missions) was abandoned as unsuccessful (c. 1752)
and Indians allowed to disperse; the expulsion of the Jesuits
(1767) brought similar results eventually to the missions
(see Missions; Franciscans; Jesuit Missions).

REECE, WILLIAM ASHER (1883-1955). Electrical engineer. Born
in New Zealand; educated at Cornell University (USA); brought
to Argentina by General Electric Company of Buenos Aires
(1915-1930); spent later years in developing electrical companies and projects in such regions as Mendoza, Tucumán,
Patagonia, as well as the eastern provinces; his electrifica-
tion of the Tucumán sugar mills was considered his greatest
contribution; died in Buenos Aires.

REFRIGERATION. In the 1870s and 1880s the discovery of the use
of refrigeration in the processing and shipping of meat revolutionized Argentina's economy, life style, and society and
made serious impacts on its political development during the
next few decades.
        With the arrival of Le Frigorifique in 1876 carrying
chilled beef and the voyage of the Paraguay the following

year with frozen meat, such processing offered real possibility of sending Argentine meat to supply expanding markets of
European industrial nations; to make meat more palatable to
European taste, the estancieros of the Sociedad Rural began
to import bulls to breed for better beef; new controls were
exercised on both feeding and marketing; new grazing lands
had simultaneously been opened in the Conquest of the Patagonian Desert; and the rapid growth of railroad system provided transportation; although French had pioneered refrigeration of meat, British, with greater demand for meat and
more available fluid capital, quickly took over its control;
began shipping frozen meat regularly in 1880; the first meat
packing plant, or frigorífico (q. v.), The River Plate Fresh
Meat Company, for exporting lamb and mutton, was founded
by George Drabble in 1882; British capital also backed Las
Palmas in 1886 and others, controlling two-thirds of the refrigerated meat business by 1903; meanwhile Argentine investors had established the Sansinena Company (1884), the
Frigorífico La Blanca (1902) and, later, Frigorífico Argentino (1905); U. S. entered the competition in 1907 when Swift
bought the River Plate Cold Storage Company; Great Britain
countered this rivalry with anti-Yankee propaganda; World
War I caused some disruption of British trade with Argentina
and U. S. improved its position considerably; in 1920, however, chilled and frozen meat was still Argentina's leading
export, with 90% of it going to Great Britain; the prosperity,
largely brought by this new refrigerated meat industry, was
evident throughout the entire nation from the extremely wealthy, politically powerful estanciero aristocracy down through
the growing middle rural and urban classes, to skilled and
unskilled labor, as well as in the beautiful modernization of
Buenos Aires, and construction of transportation and technological improvements throughout the country.
　　Although the nation was enjoying economic prosperity
and political stability, and took pride in cultural flowering,
signs of internal conflict were already evident; many were
due to changes in Argentina's traditional livestock industry;
most of it was still conducted on the pampas but, even with
new lands open, free use of land was no longer available for
cattle; price of land increased; livestock industry had to compete with new commercial agriculture or farms for land; new
kinds of land and pasture, or special feed-crops, like alfalfa,
were essential for raising better beef cattle and sheep for
mutton; cattlmen divided into two groups: 1) breeders
(criadores), who produced calves, bred for best quality of
beef and cared for them until they were weaned at 8-10
months; these operations were concentrated in Corrientes,
Santa Fe, Córdoba, San Luis, and La Pampa where pasturage
was adequate; 2) fatteners (invernadores), who, by scientific
feeding, brought cattle up to weight and quality for sale at
two or three years; such ranches predominated in Buenos
Aires, southern Santa Fe, Entre Rios, and animals were
marketed directly from these ranches; labor changes involved

following: 1) disappearance of traditional gaucho cowboy who
had previously handled stock operations but were not suited
to the new demands; 2) development of several new kinds of
laborers, drawn from rural native Argentines as well as immigrants; varied in skills from the managers and technologists to the unskilled, known as peones in the country; frigoríficos also demanded more diversified range and larger
number of new laborers, from management and technicians
to unskilled, for processes of modern refrigerated meat
packing plants; provisions had to be made for importing experts or establishing schools to train various technologists;
the new, expensive shipping was almost completely in the
hands of the British and never quite adequate; a quota system
was devised by which frigoríficos fixed prices and controlled
market; criticism early arose that these were unfair and left
all Argentine stockmen at mercy of foreign monopoly; capital
for financing heavy costs of operations was largely furnished
by foreign investors; middle class ranchers, organized skilled
laborers, and Socialist leaders who demanded government
supervision and regulation for their protection were overruled by the cattle barons of the Sociedad Rural in the name
of the traditional laissez-faire (free trade) policy of Argentina; they also profited, with their English partners from the
system and firmly controlled government until World War I;
a few concessions were made: first national labor law passed
in early 1900s by Socialist pressure; electoral reform law
(1912) widened suffrage and opened way for election of two
Radical presidents; under Marcos T. Alvear in 1923, with
beef prices very low and a new president in the Sociedad
Rural, the government passed a law providing for a state
packing house and some government inspection for packing
house financial records; a meat war followed during which
British and American competition wiped out small companies
leaving foreign packing houses in more complete control than
ever; in 1927 discovery of hoof-and-mouth disease in some
Argentine cattle brought U.S. embargo against Argentine beef;
estancieros became more strongly pro-British than ever;
British strongly attempted to regain trade it had lost to U.S.
during World War I; Argentina sold its raw produce to Great
Britain but preferred to buy its manufactured and industrial
goods from the U.S. that bought less from it; in early 1930s
world-wide economic depression threatened Argentina with
complete disaster as Great Britain signed Ottawa Agreements
(q. v.) to transfer much of its buying from Argentina to its
own dominions; through the Roca-Runciman agreement (q. v.)
in 1933, Argentina recovered a substantial fixed portion of
this trade; nationalist public opinion resented the clear im-
plication of this pact that promised even more favorable treatment to British companies and investors; rumors ran wild
and the nationalist, anti-imperialist sentiment that had been
rising for decades and stimulated by labor leaders, historians, literary figures like Ricardo Rojas, and political leaders (usually Radicals), suddenly found expression in the

"Great Debate" in the Senate in June-July, 1935; it was set
off by a very critical report from the Senate committee in-
vestigating the packing house monopoly; Lisandro de la Torre
(q. v.), senior senator from Santa Fe, a Progressive Democrat, led the attack against the packers and the government's
corrupt alliance with them; considered himself to be championing rights of small and middle sized stockraisers against
monopoly; declared that the "most genuinely Argentine industry, the livestock industry, is largely in ruins because of
two factors: the extortion of a foreign monopoly, and the
complicity of a government which permits it to act"; accused
ministers Luis Duhau and Federico Pinedo (qq. v.) of profit-
ing from this relationship; latter defended both government
actions and their own; on July 23 violence erupted, resulting
in killing of Senator Enzo Bordabehere (q. v.) and wounding
of Duhau; this ended debate; President Justo reorganized his
cabinet and government created Compañía Argentina de Productores de Carnes (CAP-Argentine Company of Meat Producers), began auditing financial records, opened litigation
against Frigorífico Anglo (the great British company); for a
time peace reigned between packers and stockmen; meanwhile
breeders and fatteners combined to form the Confederation of
Rural Associations of provinces of Buenos Aires and La
Pampa (CARBAP) to break the power of the Rural Society
and to get favorable legislation passed; CARBAP remained
active, militant group until 1940s; new conflict broke out between fatteners and breeders as they fought to gain control
of CAP; latter won in 1941; packing house laborers also organized for power; became important in Confederación General del Trabajo (CGT formed in 1936) but did not gain real
power until 1940s; it was Cipriano Reyes (q. v.), leader of
the packing house workers, who gave Juan Domingo Perón
his first real labor support; after 1943 labor prospects improved as government began intervening in labor-management
problems; in 1945 compliance with minimum wage law was
enforced and a six-hour day established for frigoríficos; packing house workers joined with other labor groups in opposing
foreign control but favored continued emphasis on stockraising rather than the industrialization that others wanted; under
the Perón government, 1946-1955, labor's demands were
largely met at last but those who worked in ranching and
meat industry suffered as the government withdrew all support from it and subjected it to heavy regulation.
　　　The export of frozen and chilled beef continues in the
1970s to be important but the industry no longer dominates
the Argentine economy and life as it formerly did (see Beef;
Cattle).
　　　See Peter H. Smith, Politics and Beef in Argentina
(New York, 1969); James R. Scobie, Argentina, a City and
a Nation (New York, 1971); Ysabel F. Rennie, The Argentine
Republic (New York, 1945; reprinted, Westport, Conn. , 1975).

REGIDOR (ruler or governor). Member of cabildo (town council)

in Spanish period.   In theory the regidores were elected by
other council members once a year and took office subject to
royal approval; in practice the office was often inherited or
bought; the number of regidores varied according to the size
of the town, with 4-8 as an average; the Laws of the Indies
specified that a regidor must be a vecino (with a house and
family) and could never have been in debt to the Royal Treasury; they voted and carried out all the functions of municipal
government, except for administration of justice; this belonged to the alcaldes or magistrates (see Cabildo).

REGISTROS.   Registered ships allowed to sail individually with
special licenses (see Navíos de Registro).

REGLAMENTOS (regulations).   Governmental orders having force
of law, usually designed to handle specific problem or situation.   A few of these in Argentine history have acquired unusual significance; among these are: the Free Commerce
Regulation, signed by the king in 1778, opening 13 ports in
Spain and 24 in its American colonies to trade, with Buenos
Aires and Montevideo declared major ports; Regulation of the
First Junta, 1810, written by the cabildo to distinguish between functions of the cabildo and those of the junta; in a
sense it marks first attempt at making a constitution; Regulation of the Provincial Juntas, written by Deán Gregorio
Funes in 1811, provided for creation of provincial governments, with intendant governor and four elected members;
Organic Regulation (see Provisional Statute of 1811); Regulation for the schools of the country (1813) was brought about
by General Belgrano's donation of the 40,000 pesos, given
him by government following victories at Salta and Tucumán,
for the establishment of schools; drawn up in Jujuy, this
regulation provided rules for organizing and opening four
schools to be established in Tarija, Tucumán, Jujuy, and
Santiago del Estero; it also served as model for school organization in Córdoba (1813) and Buenos Aires (1816); Provisory Regulation of 1817 (see Provisional Statute of 1817).

REINAFE (or REYNAFE), LOS.   Four brothers who were in complete military and political control of Córdoba in 1835 and
implicated in death of Juan Facundo Quiroga (q. v.).   Family
name is believed to be Spanish version of Irish father's surname Queenfaith.
     In February 1835, Juan Facundo Quiroga was return-
ing to Buenos Aires through Córdoba, following successful
mission on Rosas' behalf in the northern provinces; at Barranca Yaco February 16, he was surprised and killed by
small armed party under Santos Pérez; the death of Quiroga
caused shock and suspicion throughout the northern and
western provinces where he had been caudillo and in Buenos
Aires where he was resident; accusations and rumors spread
blame from López to Rosas but finally centered on "los
Reinafé"; when Rosas' demands that they be brought to trial

brought no answer from the government of Córdoba, he placed the province under interdict, cutting off all its communications; Governor Reinafé was allowed to complete his term of office and, under a new governor, the brothers were brought to trial in Córdoba and judged innocent of Quiroga's death; Rosas immediately invoked the Federal Pact and ordered the brothers and their fellow conspirators brought to Buenos Aires for trial; after a lengthy judicial process, they were convicted of the assassination; on October 25, 1837 José Vicente and Guillermo Reinafé, along with Santos Pérez and about 10 others, were hanged in the Plaza Victoria; José Antonio had died in jail a few days before his scheduled execution.

The brothers, all born in Córdoba, are listed below in order of their birth:

José Vicente Reinafé (1782-1837). Caudillo and governor. Served as judge in court of appeals under Governor Juan Bautista Bustos; when General José María Paz took over as governor, José Vicente was imprisoned, but allowed to go free; in 1831 he was general commander of armed forces of Córdoba and in same year became governor of province; frequently, for military or health reasons, delegated these functions to his brother José Antonio; was serving as governor at time of Quiroga's death.

Francisco Isidoro Reinafé (1796-1840). Although primarily devoted to his own rural interests, he took part in political and military action of his period; for much of this time, he served under Estanislao López, caudillo of Santa Fe, in their mutual fight against unitarists and Buenos Aires; captured General Paz but refused to permit execution of his prisoner; was serving as commander of forces in Córdoba in 1835 and came under suspicion of conspiracy in death of Quiroga; escaped to Montevideo, the only one of his brothers not captured; spent next five years fighting Rosas; on March 26, 1840, following his defeat at Cayastá, he plunged to his death in Paraná river, apparently a suicide.

José Antonio Reinafé (1798-1837). Held administrative posts under Governor Bustos; after latter's fall, he moved to Santa Fe under protection of López; returned to Córdoba to cooperate closely with his brother José Vicente, then governor; led several expeditions against hostile Indians; implicated with his brothers in the Quiroga scandal, he succeeded in escaping through Bolivia to Chile but was captured at Antofagasta and sent to Buenos Aires for trial.

Guillermo Reinafé (1799-1837). Active in politics of Córdoba, took refuge in Santa Fe with López when Paz took over Córdoba; joined former in fight against Paz in 1831; in 1833 Quiroga invaded Córdoba in revolution to overthrow Guillermo's brother, the governor; following his victory at Río Cuarto Quiroga ordered that all prisoners, both military and civilian, be shot; Guillermo was known to have sworn undying vengeance against Quiroga for this; when Santos Pérez, an officer in his close confidence, killed Quiroga two

years later, it was generally believed that he had acted on
orders from Guillermo.

RELIGION. Religious development in Argentina may be divided into the following periods: 1) Indian religion; 2) Arrival and
diffusions of Spanish Catholicism; 3) Introduction of Judaism;
4) Union of Catholic Church and government to oppose non-
Catholic faiths; 5) Beginnings of "illegal" Protestantism;
6) Declaration of freedom of religion; 7) Development of real
religious freedom.
        Indians who inhabited Argentine territory before the
conquest were generally polytheistic; myths and beliefs varied
among tribes but many were related to material objects, with
gods for corn and algarrobo, for example, and such natural
phenomena as procreation, rain, the sun, wind, etc.; many
animals, such as pumas, jaguars, snakes, toads, and rheas,
were believed to possess supernatural powers; there was usually a god of war; a divine creator was recognized with
creation myths bearing similarities to the Christian story of
creation; there was some belief in immortality as southern
Indians, for example, visualized a paradise after death; Indians of the northwest were strongly influenced by sun worship of Incas; Argentine folklore reflects and has perpetuated
much of the ancient Indian religion.
        Christianity, in its Roman Catholic form and using the
ancient, strict mozárabe ritual, came to Argentina with the
conquest and dominated the life of the area from the sixteenth
to the early nineteenth century (see Roman Catholicism; Missions; also individual religious orders, as well as members
of those orders, for powerful, extensive role of church on
every phase of colonial life and development); the fact that
Argentina was so remote and one of last South American
areas to be occupied seemed to offer special opportunities to
Protestant adventurers and merchants from northern European
countries; Spain was determined for both religious and imperial reasons to keep these out and in Argentina the Inquisition
was established at Córdoba to discover and destroy all such
heresies; meanwhile many Jewish families had entered the
area, most of them as Christian converts, but all came under
the careful scrutiny of the Inquisition (see Jews; Inquisition);
by the close of the eighteenth century, the profits to be made
in the newly-opened trade with Protestant countries, along
with the liberal ideas of the Enlightenment, had relaxed the
persecution of heresy; freedom of religion was first established by British in their occupation of Buenos Aires in 1806;
after this time, foreigners who became residents of Argentina were rarely troubled by authorities in the discreet exercise of non-Catholic religious practices; British group included not only Anglicans, but also Presbyterians and followers of Robert Brown; this implied tolerance attracted Protestants of other sects; for the next few decades Argentine religious policy varied: in 1813 Assembly created a national
Catholic Church, independent from that of Rome, and abolished

Inquisition; provisory statute of 1817 recognized Catholicism
as state religion and made no provision for freedom of religion; constitution of 1819 did same; in 1823 San Juan province
established freedom of religion and two years later the British treaty of friendship, commerce, and navigation with Argentine government provided that British should be free to
exercise their own faith; other countries demanded and received same privileges for their nationals; the first Protestant church was established in 1825--an Anglican church with
John Armstrong as pastor; by that time religious toleration
was quite generally accepted; for example, in 1824 Bernardino
Rivadavia, in his capacity as minister of Martín Rodríguez's
government, had participated in Protestant burial ceremonies
for U.S. diplomat Caesar Rodney (q.v.) in Buenos Aires; as
the population grew during Rosas period, Protestants continued to arrive and were far outnumbered by new Catholics,
including many Irish (in 1840 Irish priests began to arrive to
minister to these; most famous was Patrick Dillon, who was
especially active in Patagonia); in 1853 the constitution recognized Roman Catholicism as the state religion but clearly established freedom of religion; this has remained the policy.
  This freedom of religion extends legally to all religious faiths, most of which are now represented in Argentina
with Protestant churches, Islamic mosques, Jewish syna-
gogues, Buddhist temples, etc.; most numerous are Protestant groups; these include, in order according to size: Anglican, Lutheran, Methodist, Presbyterian, and Baptist; Seventh
Day Adventists work in missions in the Chaco; a more recent
arrival is the Church of the Latter Day Saints (Mormon),
that has been successful in attracting a strong new group of
followers in western provinces; the Greek Orthodox and Russian Orthodox Christian churches are well represented in
Buenos Aires and in areas settled by Greek and Slavic colonists; other small Christian groups including Nestorians,
Egyptian Coptics, Jacobites, also worship publicly there (see
Church-State Relations).

REPARTIMIENTO. Assignment of Indians, in colonial period, for
labor considered to be of value to the community; in Argentina used primarily in the northwest among the semi-civilized
Indians, already familiar with similar labor patterns (the
mita, for example) in the Inca empire; in theory the Indians
were free men, subject to the crown and their labor was to
be paid with suitable wages; the Spaniards needed the help of
the Indians for cultivation of fields, labor in mines and similar work, but they began to put their own interests first and
often used the Indians so mercilessly that they were virtually
slaves; during the period in which Vértiz was viceroy the Indians of upper Peru (Bolivia) rebelled under the leadership
of Tupac Amarú (1780) against the Spaniards, with repercussions to Argentina; as a result the repartimientos were
abolished.
  Although legally the encomienda (q.v.) and repartimientos

were different, both were institutions designed to integrate the Indians into the Spanish communities in a useful way; in practice, as far as the Indians were concerned, both often resulted in forced labor.

REPETTO, NICOLAS (1871-1965).   Socialist leader; physician and surgeon.

Born in Buenos Aires; graduated in medicine; specialized in surgery; taught in university of Buenos Aires and represented Argentine surgeons at international congress at Budapest (1909); considered one of the founders of the Socialist Party; became its leader after death of Juan B. Justo (q.v.); elected congressman several times (1913-1943) representing the federal district; with Américo Ghioldi edited the Socialist paper La Vanguardia; nominated as vice president with Lisandro de la Torre heading the ticket (1932) supported by the Socialists and Progressive Democrats; suffered persecution and imprisonment during first Perón administration; a prolific writer, some of his works are Biografía de Juan B. Justo; Azúcar y carne; Los socialistas y el ejército; Mi paso por la medicina (1956); Mi paso por la política: de Uriburu a Perón (1958); Mi paso por la agricultura (1960).

REPETTO, ROBERTO (1881-1950).   Jurisconsult; president of supreme court.

Born and educated in Buenos Aires; in 1907 he was given post in ministry of justice and public education and following year named supply professor for civil law at the university in Buenos Aires; thereafter his career was on the bench: as magistrate of civil court in Buenos Aires (federal district), 1910-1916; member court of appeals for civil cases; minister of National Supreme Court (1923-1932); then, following death of José Figueroa Alcorta, president of the national supreme court; in that same year, he headed an international commission that solved current problems between U.S. and Belgium; was serving on Supreme Court in the years of the military takeovers of 1930 and 1943; belonged to Academy of Law and Social Sciences and was member of commission that projected reforms in code of civil law; retired for health reasons in 1946 (many thought his resignation was precipitated by fear of Perón's projected reprisals against court following latter's election); his resignation may have made Perón's suppression of supreme court opposition easier--but Repetto, in spite of his resignation, was charged along with his colleagues, with such violations of the constitution as the legitimization of the military governments that had come into power by force, 1930-1945; his defense of the proper role of the Supreme Court and of his own actions was masterly and widely quoted; died in 1950 in Buenos Aires where he was widely respected as the "arquetipo de juez" ("ideal or model judge").

"REPRESENTACION DE LOS HACENDADOS Y LABRADORES."
Document written by Mariano Moreno in 1809 in support of

creole ranchers' and farmers' demand for free trade against
opposition of Spanish monopoly merchants; represented new
liberal point of view of nineteenth century; this essay was
widely read and the influence of its doctrines was shown in
Viceroy Hidalgo de Cisneros' decision to permit British merchants in port in Buenos Aires to sell their ships' merchandise in spite of Spanish protests; this document was also
translated into Portuguese and English for wider distribution
(see Mariano Moreno; Hacendados).

REPUBLIC OF ENTRE RIOS (República Entrerriana) (1820-1821)
    see ENTRE RIOS

REPUBLIC OF TUCUMAN see TUCUMAN (province); TUCUMAN,
    REPUBLIC OF

REPUBLICA ARGENTINA. Official name of the nation; established
    by constitution of 1853.

REQUINOA. Site in southern Chile of defeat of superior royal
    force (100 men) under José Ordóñez by granaderos a caballo
    (60) of the Army of the Andes, commanded by Captain Miguel
    Caxaraville, March 30, 1818; encounter took place during
    Las Heras' southern campaign in attempt to stop the royalists
    from marching north to Santiago; although a victory for the
    patriots, it failed to stop the royalist movement that pro-
    duced the disaster of Cancha Rayada before San Martín's fi-
    nal victory at Maipú in May.

RESERO. Name given to worker who drives cattle (or horses) to
    new pastures on haciendas, meat packing plants or slaughter
    houses; in the northeastern area the term tropero (apparently
    an older term) is used instead; resero is derived from res
    (beast), term commonly used to denote one head of cattle;
    like the American cowboy, the resero led an extremely hard
    life but was a common and essential figure in traditional
    Argentine rural scene; has been idealized in such literature
    as Don Segundo Sombra (q.v.), Laucha, and Juan Nadie (John
    Nobody); a bronze statue by Emilio Sarniguet, commemorates
    the great historic contribution made by the resero in the
    slaughter house of Liniers (Buenos Aires province).

RESIDENCIA. Judicial process to which every royal official had
    to submit when he left a specific office; this Spanish institu-
    tion, transferred to its colonies in the New World, was de-
    signed to punish any crime of which official had been guilty
    or to redress any wrong committed against person or proper-
    ty; a special judge would secretly interrogate witnesses and
    hear all charges; latter had to be fully proved; outgoing offi-
    cial required to remain in area until residencia was com-
    pleted or leave a responsible agent and bond; in the eighteenth
    century the residencia, that had been generally applied to all
    royal officials in Argentina, began to be omitted for some

high officials; after the May Revolution, 1810, the patriot junta made special dispositions regarding this institution and the Congress of Tucumán kept it for governors and lieutenant governors.

RESTAURADOR DE LAS LEYES (Restorer of Laws). Title given by Buenos Aires legislature to Juan Manuel de Rosas (q. v.) early in 1830; at same time he was made brigadier-general; as governor of Buenos Aires and federal leader of the country, his power was virtually unlimited; this same title was used as the name of the official Rosas newspaper.

RETA, JOSE SALVADOR DE LA (1811-1897). Priest; public figure in Mendoza.
        Born in Mendoza of distinguished Mendoza family; appointed vicar of the province and then bishop of that diocese in 1882; involved himself actively in political life; served as member of provincial legislature several times, twice as president; died in Mendoza.

RETIRO. Northeastern portion of city of Buenos Aires; today a modern riverside suburb dominated by Plaza San Martín but traditionally a wild, somewhat swampy area set aside for special use; takes its name (place of retirement) from large house built there by governor in 1602; one hundred years later it became a slave market and was also used during the colonial period as a bull ring; Santiago de Liniers used this Plaza de Toros as one of his bases for reconquest of city from British (1806) and thereafter it was rechristened Field of Glory or Mars Field; a few years later, it was turned over to José de San Martín (whose statue stands there today) to become the military headquarters and training ground for his new granaderos a caballo, the nucleus of the Army of the Andes that liberated southern South America from Spain; today that area, surrounding the plaza named for the liberator, is still known by its original name, el Retiro.

REVOLT OF JUNE 7, 1956. Attempt at counter-coup by Peronists against military government of Pedro E. Aramburu; took city of Santa Rosa in La Pampa; martial law declared and revolt was suppressed at the cost of more than 48 lives, many of them civilian, and including execution of 28 leaders, following military trial; this revolt broke the long-standing pattern of bloodless coup d'états and was responsible for Aramburu's own assassination four years later in revenge.

REVOLUCION DE MAYO see MAY REVOLUTION

REVOLUCION LIBERTADORA (Liberating Revolution). Name by which its leaders designated the revolution of September 16, 1955, that overthrew government of Juan Domingo Perón.

REVOLUTION OF 1890. Civic-military revolt that led to resignation

of President Miguel Juárez Celman in July, August, 1890.
By 1890 Juárez Celman's government was in trouble politically, economically, and socially; formation of Unicato (q. v.)
had united estanciero oligarchy into one political group that
controlled government; protest developed from excluded and
dissenting groups, including elements of the old elite in
Buenos Aires, members of other political parties, urban
middle-class professionals and merchants, youth, and immigrants; in 1889 the young men had formed the Unión Cívica
de la Juventud under leadership of Aristóbulo del Valle and
Leandro N. Alem; with Bartolomé Mitre's support they transformed this into the Unión Cívica (q. v.) in April 1890; began
to plan revolution to force government to provide universal
suffrage, honesty in politics and government, and less federal interference in provincial and municipal affairs; economically Juárez Celman's government was leading the nation to
crisis; more than a decade of expanding trade and economic
development, financial boom, and enormous profits had encouraged speculation increasing the public debt irresponsibly
to handle great programs of public works, including bridges,
public buildings, dams, ports, parks, etc.; trade balance became more and more unfavorable, and inflation, welcomed
by estancieros and others in agriculture and stockraising,
placed intolerable financial burdens on the majority of people
who were not; increasing, often secret, emissions of paper
money made matters worse; for both political and economic
reasons, then, revolution was prepared; many churchmen also
favored a change, still furious about secular legislation of
1880s, and elements of the military, led by Manuel J. Campos and much of the navy also supported the revolution; national revolutionary junta was formed including Leandro N.
Alem, Aristóbulo del Valle, Mariano Demaría, Lucio V.
López, Juan José Romero, and Miguel Goyena; news of it
leaked out early but they began their fight July 26; for reasons not clear, revolutionaries permitted government to force
them on defensive at once; after two days fighting, with am-
munitions gone, they asked for an armistice; received it along
with promise of complete amnesty; revolution had failed but
Juárez Celman was forced to resign a few days later, August 6, to be replaced by his vice president, Carlos Pellegrini (q. v.).

REVOLUTION OF 1930. Term usually applied to overthrow of
Yrigoyen's second administration by military forces led by
General José Félix Uriburu and the establishment of a military dictatorship.
        The inertia and apparent inability of the elderly Radi-
cal President Yrigoyen to cope with Argentine social, political, and economic problems while confronting a world-wide
economic depression, made a change in government seem immediately necessary in 1930; for the first time, following
nearly seventy years of almost unbroken succession of constitutional presidencies, military officers talked of taking over

the government to effect the changes needed; divided among
themselves as to leadership and direction that the new movement should take, General Uriburu emerged as leader, with
support from both civil and military groups wanting strong,
authoritarian government; moving his forces into Buenos Aires,
without opposition and with the tacit, if not enthusiastic approval of the people, on September 6, 1930, he took over
the government, was made provisional president, and, after
having dissolved congress and established a state of siege,
attempted as a military dictator to create a political, social,
economic revolution somewhat similar to those underway in
Italy, Germany, and Spain at that time; this revolution did
not take place but the revolt of 1930 was in itself significant
as it marked the first time that the Argentine military made
itself completely responsible for national political affairs;
later military coups, beginning with that of 1943, were led
by young officers (including Perón) who looked to this action
of 1930 as a precedent but hoped to avoid its mistakes (see
Military; Hipólito Yrigoyen; José Félix Uriburu).

REVOLUTION OF THE SEVEN LEADERS (1580).   Early communal
    uprising in Santa Fe expressing criollos' determination to
    control their own local government.   When Juan de Garay
    left Santa Fe in 1580 to reestablish Buenos Aires, native-
    born Argentines determined to end Spanish domination of the
    cabildo; dissidents met in home of Lázaro de Venialvo, criol-
    lo alcalde of cabildo; appointed him military commander;
    joined by six other criollo leaders, including Cristóbal Aré-
    valo; Venialvo attacked and captured the Spanish officials, in-
    cluding lieutenant governor Simón Jacques, one of the al-
    caldes, and Francisco de Vera y Aragón, nephew of the
    adelantado Juan Torres de Vera y Aragón; Arévalo was
    elected governor but disputes about the division of power
    arose among the various leaders, weakening the popular gov-
    ernment to such an extent that the Spaniards regained con-
    trol and executed the leaders; Venialvo sometimes cited as
    precursor and martyr of Argentine independence.

REVOLUTIONS.   Term "revolución" usually denotes a movement
    with considerable popular support that attempts to take over
    government in order to make an important change in its na-
    ture, in contrast to more limited rebellions, uprisings, re-
    volts, or simple takeover of government by opposing group
    in a power struggle; Argentine legal scholars maintain that
    the people have a constitutional right to use any means neces-
    sary to effect such desired change, basing it on the principle
    that sovereignty resides in the people; this right to revolt to
    change government has been practised in Río de la Plata
    area for 400 years; among the more significant revolutions,
    in chronological order, are the following (see individual en-
    tries for those without annotation):

1580, Revolution of the Seven Leaders (Santa Fe).

March 1732 and October 29, 1764. Corrientes (see Comuneros of Corrientes).
January 1809. Buenos Aires (see Martín de Alzaga).
May 25, 1809. Chuquisaca.
July 16, 1809. La Paz (Bolivia). Patriot revolt suppressed.
May 25, 1810. Buenos Aires. May Revolution.
April 5-6, 1811. Buenos Aires. First revolution following
establishment of patriot government; conservative supporters of Cornelio Saavedra ousted Mariano Moreno
and his more liberal group.
1812. Spaniards, led by Martín de Alzaga, attempted unsuccessfully to take over government from criollos.
October 8, 1812. San Martín and Alvear, backed by their
regiments and other patriot leaders, presented people's
demand for overthrow of First Triumvirate; Second
Triumvirate formed (see Triumvirates).
April 15, 1815. Fontezuelas, Revolt of.
December 1, 1828. Juan Lavalle ousted Federalist governor
of Buenos Aires, Manuel Dorrego (see entries on both
men).
October 1833. Buenos Aires. Revolución de los Restauradores. Supporters of Juan Manuel de Rosas overthrew Governor Juan Ramón Balcarce and paved way
for Rosas' return as dictator in 1835.
February 3, 1852. End of Rosas' regime by defeat of his
army at Caseros by Justo José Urquiza's allied forces
(see Caseros; Rosas; Urquiza).
September 11, 1852. Uprising of Buenos Aires province
against Urquiza, resulting in separation of latter from
Confederation of other provinces for nearly ten years.
September 1874. Bartolomé Mitre's revolt against election
of Nicolás Avellaneda as president (see Mitre).
June 1880. Revolt in Buenos Aires (see Federalization of
City of Buenos Aires).
July 1890. Revolution of 1890.
February-July, 1893. New Radical attempt to win reform
and a share in political life; under Hipólito Yrigoyen's
leadership, Radicals took over government of La
Plata, capital of Buenos Aires province; other outbreaks deposed governors in Santa Fe and San Luis;
federal intervention recovered control of all three
provinces; revolution contributed to President Luis
Sáenz Peña's decision to resign in January 1895.
February 1905 Revolution. Unsuccessful Radical attempt
under Yrigoyen's leadership to arouse people against
oligarchic government; suppressed in Buenos Aires
and in Mendoza; in Córdoba Radicals seized and held
Vice President Figueroa Alcorta hostage but Quintana's government won; leaders sent to Ushuaia or exiled.
Revolution of 1930.
June 4, 1943 (see GOU--Grupo de Oficiales Unidos).
September 16, 1955. Revolución Libertadora (Liberating

Revolution) (see Juan Domingo Perón).

See Historical Chronology, Appendix II; also entry on
Military for instances of military takeover of government
during two following decades and for other revolts and rebellions.

REYES, ANTONINO (1813-1897).   Rosas' secretary and military
aide.   Accompanied Juan Manuel de Rosas on his expedition
into Indian country, 1833; served in militia; in 1836 became
secretary to Rosas and remained in this position until fall of
Rosas' government in 1852; after 1848 he was in charge of
secretariat established in Santos Lugares; accompanied Rosas
as aide on night before battle of Caseros; afterward moved to
Montevideo but returned to Buenos Aires during its seige by
Hilario Lagos (1853); captured, he was tried and condemned
to death, but escaped to Montevideo, where he remained until his death, although granted amnesty in 1855; published his
memoirs.

REYES, CIPRIANO.   Militant labor leader in 1940s.   Head of the
packing house workers; played important role in first winning
labor's support for Perón; organized, with Evita, Perón's
return from imprisonment at Martín García; after Perón's
election in 1946, Reyes began to turn against him as he realized that the independence of the labor party was being lost
to the government; he grew increasingly bitter against Perón
as he lost labor's support and found himself politically isolated; unable to defeat Perón, he attempted to rejoin him in
1948 but was accused of planning assassination attempts
against Evita and imprisoned until after Perón's downfall in
1955.
See Cipriano Reyes, Yo hice el 17 de octubre (Buenos
Aires, 1973).

REYES, MARCELINO (1845-1905).   Military man.   Fought in the
Paraguayan War; in 1868 went to La Rioja where he served
in such positions as chief of the city garrison, general accountant, congressman, minister of government, general inspector of the national guard, history teacher, adviser of a
loan bank, commander of the national guard; contributed to
several newspapers including La Situación, La Unión Nacional,
El Nacional, La Rioja, and El Autonomista; wrote historical
sketch of La Rioja from 1843-1867, published in Revista de
Derecho, Historia y Letras, Buenos Aires, June, 1902.

REYNA, PEDRO CELESTINO (1837-1908).   Born in Corrientes;
educated at Colegio de Concepción del Uruguay and in Buenos
Aires, graduating in law, 1865; became minister in Corrientes government and then member of Entre Ríos legislature;
after Urquiza's assassination, he moved to Uruguay (1870);
returned in 1875 and made his home in Rosario; served as
criminal judge, minister of government and finance (1878-

1880), and as national congressman from Santa Fe (1880-
1884); held other official and judicial positions, including
those of member of council of education and judge in Buenos
Aires where he died.

REYNAL O'CONNOR, EDMUND (1860-1908).   Physician.   Born in
Buenos Aires; studied medicine at University of Paris; while
intern in the hospital was secretary of the Argentine diplomatic corps; in 1885 was Argentine delegate to the Institute
Pasteur where his work was personally recognized by Dr.
Pasteur; while in Paris he invented a cannula (tube used in
surgery) that became widely used; in 1888 presented a paper
describing a new stethoscope and a speculum, both invented
by him; he returned to Argentina where he published several
medical books; left a dictionary of medicine unfinished at the
time of his death in an accident in Buenos Aires.

REYUNOS.   Name given to unbranded horses; during colonial times
these became property of the king; after the May Revolution
(1810) they were called "patriot" horses and belonged to the
new government.

RHEA   see   ÑANDU

RICCHIERI, PABLO (1859-1936).   Career military officer; considered to be organizer of modern Argentine Army.
          Born in province of Santa Fe, of Italian parents; at-
tended Colegio Militar on a scholarship; graduated in 1879,
commissioned as second lieutenant; sent to Europe to study
in Brussels; attached to Argentine embassy there; returned
to Argentina in 1886 and was assigned to general staff duty;
sent back to Europe in 1890 to purchase arms from Germany; upon his return he was appointed chief of staff; in
1898 became President Julio A. Roca's minister of war; was
given responsibility for creating a new national, professional,
modernized army (see Military); influenced the passing of law
known by his name (Ricchieri Law), the 1901 organic military statute (law no. 4301) making military service compulsory; purchased land at Campo de Mayo and Campo de los
Andes to serve as army headquarters of Buenos Aires and
Cuyo, respectively; divided nation into seven military regions;
reorganized the secretariat of war and reorganized the
granaderos a caballo (q.v.); in 1910 he became division general and retired in 1922 as lieutenant general; twelve years
later, in recognition of his distinguished military services,
President Justo named him general of the army; received
several foreign honors, including that of the Red Eagle in
Germany, merit medals from France and Chile, and was appointed a grand officer of the Crown in Belgium; died in
Buenos Aires; buried with full military honors.

RICCI, CLEMENTE (1873-1946).   Historian, journalist.   Born in
Italy; immigrated to Buenos Aires with his parents; wrote

for <u>La Nación</u>, <u>El Diario</u>; taught history in the University of
Buenos Aires; offered first course given there in history of
religions; created the Institute of Ancient and Medieval history in Buenos Aires; was a member of the Academia Argentina de Letras; published <u>The Historical Meaning of Christi-
anity</u>; <u>Origins of Christianity</u>; <u>Psychology of Jesus</u>; <u>Hellenic
Source of Christianity</u>; <u>Saint Francis and Communism in His-
tory</u>; <u>Descartes and Religion</u>.

RICE. Rice came to Argentina late despite its common use in
Spain; little, if any mention of it made in colonial period;
leaders of early 19th century, eager to develop Argentina's
economy in every possible way, began questioning desirability
of introducing it into northern Argentina's subtropical areas;
no real attempt made to grow it on a large scale until latter
half of nineteenth century when it became one of Tucumán's
chief products; found large domestic market partly due to
common use of rice and milk as dessert and increased numbers of new Spaniards and other rice-eating immigrants; in
1910 the Spanish author from Valencia, Vicente Blasco
Ibáñez (q.v.) attempted to raise rice commercially in Corrientes, using the Valencian rice and importing rice growing
farmers; although he had little immediate success, by the
1950s Corrientes and its neighboring provinces--Entre Ríos
and Santa Fe--with large flooded areas, had surpassed the
north-western provinces in production, with about 80% of the
rice planted in the nation; recent Japanese (q.v.) immigration and colonies since World War II, especially, have planted
extensive rice paddies in Misiones, using a longer grain
variety than the Valencian; results have been satisfactory,
with good production and excellent market reception.

RICO, MANUEL LEONCIO (1798-1841). Born in Buenos Aires;
lived on his ranch in Dolores in province of Buenos Aires;
fought in the campaign against Indians in the south, serving
as captain of militia; summoned to Buenos Aires by Rosas in
1837, he became infuriated at Rosas' delay in seeing him;
returned to Dolores and joined unitarists opposing Rosas; led
the uprising in Dolores against Rosas October 29, 1839; defeated by Prudencio Ortiz de Rozas at Chascomús; escaped
to Corrientes where he joined anti-Rosas army of Lavalle;
taken prisoner by the federalists, he was executed in Catamarca.

RIESTRA, NORBERTO DE LA (1820-1879). Lawyer; cabinet minister, diplomat. Persecuted by Rosas, fled to London, 1841;
returned to Río de la Plata in 1850; as a porteño he supported separation of Buenos Aires province from Confederation; served as provincial legislator, 1852-1855, then resigned to become Governor Pastor Obligado's minister of finance; continued in same capacity under Governor Valentín
Alsina; in the difficult period (1860) during which Urquiza,
Mitre, and President Derqui were trying to work out a

reunion between Buenos Aires and other provinces, Riestra accepted Derqui's appointment to serve as confederation's minister of finance but the tensions that were to produce Pavón (q.v.) soon brought his resignation; became senator of the national congress and in 1863 directed a mission to Paraguay; served as vice governor of Buenos Aires (1864), minister plenipotentiary to Great Britain (1865), director of savings and loan bank (1872); as part of his conciliation effort with the mitristas, President Nicolás Avellaneda appointed Riestra, friend of Bartolomé Mitre and old member of his nationalist party, as minister of finance in a time of financial crisis; Riestra served effectively.

RINCON DE VENCES, BATTLE OF. November 27, 1847. Site of critical battle between Justo José de Urquiza, commanding Rosas' forces, and Governor Joaquín Madariaga (q.v.) of Corrientes; Urquiza's total defeat of latter's anti-Rosas forces sent Madariaga into exile in Paraguay and marked the end of internal disturbance in the country for the remaining years of Rosas' rule; the federal government regards it as an historic site but the people of Corrientes still remember this battle between the federalists and the correntinos as a bloody nightmare because the winning troops looted, burned, and practically destroyed the town of General Paz after the victory.

RIO DE LA PLATA. River that flows past Buenos Aires (on its south bank) into the Atlantic Ocean (see maps, Appendix IV); name also applied to the system of rivers emptying into it, including Paraná, Paraguay, Uruguay, and their tributaries and, especially during the colonial period, to the entire area drained by this system.

Although it seems possible that Americus Vespucius was first to reach the Río de la Plata (in 1502), discovery is usually attributed to Juan Díaz de Solís who entered it in 1516 and named it Río de Santa María or Mar Dulce before his death from Indian attack along its north bank; twelve years later Sebastian Cabot (q.v.) called it Río de la Plata (River of Silver) and sailed up it hoping to find the legendary Mountain of Silver and White King rumored to be in interior (i.e., distorted rumors of the Andean Inca empire, not yet discovered by Spaniards); this name became official when used in Pedro de Mendoza's negotiations for grant with crown 1535-1536; the wide estuary (nearly 150 miles across at its mouth) became the Atlantic center of Spain's colonies in southern South America, with Buenos Aires as the hub; although the harbor at Buenos Aires was not very good, with its shallows, islands, multiple channels, and muddy shores, it became the main port, although greatly limited in its legitimate traffic by Spanish mercantilistic policies during seventeenth and most of eighteenth centuries (see Contraband; Trade); in the late nineteenth century the port was improved and in 1910 the new port (Puerto Nuevo) was opened; forming a great entrance to the southern continental hinterland, this river has played many different roles in Argentine history; throughout the colonial period Portuguese in Brazil and Spanish in Argentina rivaled each other for its political and economic control; this conflict finally ended with creation of separate republic of Uruguay in 1828 and eventual amicable agreement between latter and Argentina about navigation rights of the river (1909); the Spanish viceroyalty formed during the height of this rivalry (1776) was given name of the river (see Viceroyalty of the Río de la Plata); the French and British blockaded the river in the 1840s and 100 years later it was the scene of the pursuit of the Graf Spee in World War II.

The waters of the Río de la Plata have come, in the twentieth century, to be considered a very great source of hydroelectric power; improvements in the river system's flood control, irrigation uses, and navigation are greatly needed and possible only through international cooperation of Argentina, Brazil, Uruguay, and Paraguay; work has begun on these (see Energy Resources); the possibility of existence of underwater oil fields in the Río de la Plata has reopened disputes over river rights between Uruguay and Argentina, both claiming the new source of wealth and needed energy.

RIO DEFENSE TREATY (1947).   More formally known as Inter-American Treaty of Reciprocal Assistance.   Adopted at Rio de Janeiro September 2, 1947; U.S. and Latin American nations, including Argentina, pledged themselves to mutual assistance of any American nation that had become victim of armed aggression from any other nation; Argentina made valiant attempts to change form or limit this security system, but eventually signed it, in spite of Perón's preference for bilateral agreements, and finally ratified it.

See Harold F. Peterson, Argentina and the United States, 1810-1960 (New York, 1964).

RIO NEGRO (Province).   Largest and richest Patagonian province; takes its name from the Río Negro that crosses it from Andes to Atlantic; became province in 1959.   Boundaries: Bounded on north by province of La Pampa, on east by that of Buenos Aires and the Atlantic Ocean, on south by Chubut and on west by Neuquén and Chile.   Area: 78,400 square miles.   Population (1970):   266,622; density 3.4 persons per square mile.   Capital: Viedma; population c. 7,300 (1960); located on south bank of Río Negro about 25 miles from its mouth.

Geography.   Typically Patagonian with plateaus and pampas rising to Andes in west; crossed by navigable Río Negro; bounded on north by Colorado river separating it from La Pampa, and on west by Limay separating it from province of Neuquén; although climate is very dry, abundance of water in these river systems is available for irrigation and requires dams to control floods; in the south the lakes Nahuel Huapi,

Frías, Moreno, Gutiérrez, Mascardi, Martín, and others
form part of national park system (q.v.); pampas rise in
west to Andean cordillera; with highest peak in province being El Tronador, 3554 m. (11,660 ft.).

Economy. Río Negro is rich agricultural country,
with the economy largely supported by fruit growing: apples,
pears, peaches, grapes, and quinces; in recent years commercial growing of tomatoes for the national market has become important; industries related to processing of these,
such as jam, jelly, preserve factories, wineries, and industries for making glass and cardboard containers have grown
up in the area, particularly in the Upper Valley (Alto Valle)
where the water supply (from irrigation) is abundant and soil
and climate favor such crops; agriculture is supplemented by
livestock, largely sheep, and some mining in iron, gold,
magnetite (load-stone) gypsum, coal, salt, etc.; mining resources have only begun to be exploited but it is believed
that iron, especially, may be found in satisfactory quantity
and quality; in the beautiful southern lake area tourism is
very important, with skiing in the winter and water sports in
the summer; forests of the sierras provide lumber that is
processed in the various sawmills; hydroelectric plants on
rivers provide necessary energy; chemical plants, flour, sugar mills, and fish-processing factories add to industrial production.

History. Indians who inhabited area at time of Spanish conquest were Pehuelches or Patagones; first important
attempt to explore and settle area came in 1778 when Viceroy Vértiz sent expedition to the river to establish fort; (see
Río Negro River); Carmen de Patagones and Mercedes (later
renamed Viedma) were established as forts around which
settlements might grow; Francisco Viedma and Pilot Basilio
Villarino (qq.v.) continued exploration of the interior area
through which river flowed; Mercedes became a parish and
center of public life in that area; during the nineteenth century, various explorers and Indian fighters entered this area
and mapped it rather well; at same time, Araucanians moved
in from the west to occupy the land and to make it a base
from which outlying ranches could be raided; with Roca's Conquest of the Desert (q.v.), Río Negro was opened to settlement; from 1878 to 1884 it formed part of territory of Patagonia but was organized as Río Negro territory in 1884, with
Lorenzo Vintter as first governor and Viedma (as Mercedes
was renamed in 1878) as its capital; lands were distributed,
much of it to veterans of the Conquest of the Desert and to
agricultural colonies, and population in river valley began to
grow; a little later (1895-1903) el perito Francisco Moreno
(q.v.), the naturalist, made several trips to the Nahuel
Huapi lake region, studying it scientifically and publicizing
its beauty and resources.

Among interesting towns in Río Negro in addition to
Viedma, the capital, are: 1) General Roca, the largest city,
located east of Neuquén; lies near Río Negro, on highway and

railroad to Bahía Blanca; was established in 1879 as an army
frontier post; four years later it became first agricultural
colony in Río Negro, with arrival of about 700 Germans;
railroad came in 1889; flood of 1899 (that affected entire valley from General Roca to Viedma) destroyed the town and it
was rebuilt northwest of original site; 2) Choele Choel (q. v.)
was discovered by Villarino in 1782; became center of much
Indian fighting in Roca's campaigns; novelist Blasco Ibáñez
attempted to establish agricultural colony there in 1908 but
failed because of lack of irrigation; became a center for production of lavender; 3) Cinco Saltos (Five Falls) is in the
northwest on the Neuquén River; its location has made it a
fruit center, with hydroelectric power used for irrigation to
grow the fruit and to freeze it for marketing; 4) San Carlos
de Bariloche in the south, on Lake Nahuel Huapi is internationally known for its beauty and as a tourist center.

Early schools were established by Salesian priests in
the 1880s; today (1970s), Río Negro's schools form part of
the national system, with both public and private schools, national colegios in Viedma and other large towns, and normal
and vocational schools; the newspaper Río Negro was founded
in 1912. Since becoming a province in 1959, Río Negro has
grown rapidly in population and economic production.

RIO NEGRO (River). River, formed by confluence of Limay and
Neuquén rivers, which flows eastward across northern part of
province of same name, then at Choele-Choel, turns southeast into the Atlantic Ocean; Viedma, the provincial capital,
is located on its south bank near the mouth, Carmen de
Patagones on the north; known by many different names in the
past, the river has come to be known by the name given it
by Huiliche and Pehuenche Indians, Curú Leuvú, the Black
River, or Río Negro in Spanish; considered to mark the
northern boundary of Patagonia, it was first described fully
by Thomas Falkner in the account of his Patagonian explorations, published in London, 1774; a few years later, fearing
English attempts to occupy that area, the Spanish government
ordered Viceroy Vértiz to send expeditions down the Atlantic
coast to explore and fortify the area to hold it for Spain; expeditions commanded by Juan de la Piedra, with the Viedma
brothers (Francisco, Antonio, and Andrés) and pilot Basilio
Villarino reached its mouth but thought it impenetrable because of the sandbar there; Villarino proved river to be navigable and entered interior; after independence, succeeding
patriot governments and national governments attempted to
push the Indian frontier south of the Río Negro; finally accomplished by General Roca in his "Conquest of the Desert"
1877-1880.

In modern era, river has proved very useful for hydroelectric plants that provide energy and direct irrigation
waters throughout the entire upper valley; large tracts of
new land have been opened up for agriculture, especially
fruit growing (see Río Negro Province; entries on individuals

mentioned, and other related topics).

RIO PIEDRAS.   Small stream in Salta where encounter took place
between rearguard of Belgrano's troops withdrawing, by
government order, toward Córdoba after route at Huaqui
June 20, 1811, and vanguard of pursuing royalists; engagement relatively minor but fact that the patriots won had significant impact on morale of Belgrano's troops and influenced
his decision to renew the fight; victory at Tucumán resulted,
September 24, 1812.

RIVADAVIA, BERNARDINO (1780-1845).   Unitarist statesman who
attempted to develop and institutionalize new Argentine nation
along lines of early nineteenth century European liberal ideologies; first national president, 1826-1827.
        Born in Buenos Aires of Spanish parents; educated at
Real Colegio de San Carlos; married daughter of Viceroy
Joaquín del Pino; fought as officer in Galician corps against
British invasion; took part in May Revolution; during following period supported Mariano Moreno's liberal ideas against
the more conservative ones held by followers of Cornelio
Saavedra; following the revolution of April 5-6, 1811, in
which the latter took over the patriot government, Rivadavia
was sent on diplomatic mission to Europe, seeking aid for
Argentine independence; returned in time to become secretary of war with the First Triumvirate government (see Triumvirates); influential in passing a regulation that freed the
executive power of the triumvirate from the authority of the
Junta Conservadora in which provincial delegates were represented; in this he showed the commitment to centralized government and porteño (Buenos Aires) domination that were to
characterize his future policies and those of his Unitarist
policies and brought immediate opposition from federalists
and the provinces that resulted in civil wars; he also established the Museo de Historia Natural and a secondary school
for boys; firmly suppressed the patricios' revolt (see Rebelión de las Trenzas) and that of Martín Alzaga (q.v.); in
1814 he and Manuel Belgrano were sent to Europe by Supreme
Director Gervasio Posadas to seek aid for colonies' attempt
to establish independence from Spain, possibly through British
protection; they became involved in Manuel de Sarratea's unsuccessful project to establish independent monarchy of
United Provinces with Francisco de Paula (q.v.) on throne;
spent several years in London and traveling around Europe,
then rebuilding after Napoleon's defeat at Waterloo; returned
to Buenos Aires, convinced that Europe would not aid Spanish colonies against Ferdinand VII's determined efforts to
regain them; became dominant minister in Martín Rodríguez's
cabinet, 1821; determined to secure international recognition
of Argentina's independence, to place a nation, just emerged
from anarchy (1820) under a strongly centralized, constitutional government, and to institutionalize and develop its

political, economic, social, and cultural life according to
patterns and ideologies of contemporary Europe.

Within the next six years he accomplished the following: began with widespread amnesty law permitting Argentine political exiles to return; secured recognition of Argentine independence from several nations, including Portugal,
Brazil, the United States, and Great Britain and signed treaty
of amity, trade, and navigation with latter; abolished the
cabildo of Buenos Aires as a source of political disturbance
because of its recent involvements in national affairs; defined
limits of executive, judicial, legislative powers; called national constituent congress (1824) that elected him national
president (1826) and drew up Constitution of 1826 (q.v.); with
new Church-State relationship still uncertain, and Church discipline lax, he put through a series of ecclesiastic reforms
aimed at greater secularization, including abolition of special
legal rights (fueros), tithes and other special church taxes;
placed cemeteries under civil jurisdiction; created the Sociedad de Beneficencia (q.v.), on the model of the Junta de las
Damas de Madrid, and secularized the monastic orders; he
was aided by other Liberals like Manuel García, Cosme
Argerich, Manuel Moreno, and others, and supported financially by the Anchorenas, the Lezicas, the Sáenz Valientes,
McKinlays, and other wealthy, powerful Argentine and British
families; with British capital available, now that peace and
order had been established, he moved to strengthen Argentine
credit and to develop and diversify its economy; in 1822 declared State authority over personal property transactions and
public lands; established emphyteusis (q.v.) system of distribution and increased usage of land; created Banco Nacional,
arranged for loan from Baring Brothers; stimulated mining,
banking, agriculture, sheepraising, and trade; used loan
largely for public works program, especially in modernizing
Buenos Aires city; began construction of port at Ensenada;
meanwhile he had established the University of Buenos Aires
and stimulated teaching of new economic and philosophical
doctrines in Colegio de San Carlos; to speed up all these
processes of change, he attracted, often brought under contract, as many European experts as possible from technologists to professors; hoped to bring agricultural colonies to
occupy empty lands, and purchased ships for river trade;
during his years as president (1826-27) he was also fighting
a war with Brazil, brought on by rival claims in Uruguay;
although many veterans of war of independence were available to fight, the war was unpopular and Rivadavia sent
Manuel José García to arrange a peace; latter exceeded his
instructions and compromised Argentina's position, causing
Rivadavia, who immediately repudiated García's action,
great embarrassment; by this time Rivadavia had accumulated
too much opposition, even hatred; never very popular personally, he had alienated such leaders as José de San Martín and Juan Martín de Pueyrredón for personal reasons;
many Unitarists of the provinces resented his insistence on

Buenos Aires' domination and Federalists everywhere opposed
both this and the centralization of government in the Constitution of 1826 that was signed but never ratified; Catholics resented his Church policy; Tucumán, led by Facundo Quiroga,
had already reacted and, under motto of "Religion or Death,"
had defeated pro-Rivadavia forces in Catamarca, San Juan,
and Santiago del Estero; in 1827 Buenos Aires province was
infuriated by his federalization of the city of Buenos Aires,
resulting in the province's loss of capital and domination of
the national port; in July 1827 Rivadavia resigned as president, retired to his country estate and then, in 1829, vowing
permanent retirement from politics, went to Spain; attempted
to return in 1834 but was not permitted to disembark (ironically enough, his only defender at this time was Quiroga);
after brief stay in Montevideo and longer one in Rio de Janeiro, he went to Cádiz, Spain, where he lived modestly and
died in poverty; in 1857 his remains were returned to Buenos
Aires and buried, on September 4, in Recoleta Cemetery,
with great ceremony, under direction of Mitre, Sarmiento,
and Mármol; in 1932 his ashes were again moved into a
mausoleum built in his honor in the Plaza Once de Septiembre (later renamed Plaza Miserere) in Buenos Aires.

   Evaluation of Rivadavia's contribution to Argentine development remains as controversial among historians as
among his contemporaries; Unitarist and Liberal Argentines,
as well as many other Western scholars, hail him as a man
of vision, architect of the nation, and point to facts that
modern Argentine Republic has developed along lines that he
projected and that Buenos Aires has become both federalized
and dominant in all phases of national life; Federalists, nationalists, and others claim that much of Argentina's political agony of the nineteenth century should be attributed to
Rivadavia's insensitiveness to Argentine political and cultural
realities and his determination to destroy or distort its national identity to make it into a blueprint of European model
design and that, only decades later, when Argentina had created its own national political organization, and modern technology had tied the nation together and made possible the exploitation of its new land and mineral resources could Argentina comfortably adopt those foreign elements that it wanted
to use; in any event, he dreamed and worked to make his
country great and today is recognized and honored by his
compatriots.

   See Ricardo Piccirilli, Rivadavia y su tiempo (2 v.,
Buenos Aires, 1943); Nicanor Molinas, El precursor Rivadavia, su vida y su obra (Santa Fe, 1948).

RIVADAVIA, JOAQUIN (1811-1887). Military man. Born in
Buenos Aires, son of Bernardino Rivadavia; studied in Colegio
de San Carlos and later in Spain and France; returned to Río
de la Plata; joined Juan Lavalle's unitarist army in 1829 and
followed him until his death; formed part of the escort that
accompanied Lavalle's remains to Bolivia for burial; made

his way back to Montevideo by way of Mato Grosso, Brazil;
joined unitarist forces of General José María Paz; following
Rosas' defeat at Caseros he returned to Buenos Aires province; remained there until 1854 when he became embroiled in
uprising against Urquiza and was imprisoned; in 1865 he
joined army again to fight against Paraguay but illness forced
him to retire; died at his home in San José de Flores
(Buenos Aires).

RIVADAVIA, MARTIN (1852-1901).   Naval officer for whom city of
     Comodoro Rivadavia is named.
          Born in Buenos Aires, grandson of Bernardino Riva-
     davia, first Argentine president; entered military service as
     cadet in line artillery; as midshipman in navy fought in war
     with Paraguay; became involved in suppression of revolts
     along the Uruguay in 1870; after 1874 his entire time was
     spent in the navy, winning steady promotions; took part in
     Rosales' voyage to the South; in 1880, in command of caño-
     nera Constitución, charted the waters and buoy system of bay
     of San Blas; commanded the corvette La Argentina on its first
     training cruise; was sent to England to bring back the naval
     cruiser 9 de Julio; in 1893, he was largely responsible for
     preventing the navy from joining revolutionaries; reached
     rank of commodore in 1896; two years later he became min-
     ister of navy in Roca's cabinet; during his tenure of this post,
     service in the navy became included under the compulsory
     military service law; his name is perpetuated in the important
     southern petroleum city and port.

RIVAROLA, PANTALEON (1757-1821).   Priest; professor; poet-
     historian of criollo defense of Buenos Aires against British
     invasions.
          Born in Buenos Aires; studied humanities there; gradu-
     ated as doctor of laws in University of San Felipe, Santiago
     de Chile; ordained as priest in 1778; returned to Buenos
     Aires; became professor of philosophy in royal academy of
     San Carlos, 1779; in 1788 became chaplain of Third Battalion
     of Infantry; took part in military action against British in-
     vasions (1806-1807); wrote two extensive poems or rhymed
     chronologies about these, entitled Reconquista y defensa
     (events of 1806) and Gloriosa defensa (those of 1807); in addi-
     tion to the contribution made by the historical data contained
     in them, these poems have won for him the title of precurs-
     or of popular Argentine lyric poetry; written in a simple, al-
     most doggerel, style, these poems were designed to appeal
     to all classes, to be easily remembered, and easily sung in
     accustomed musical patterns; they won wide acceptance at
     the time; in 1808 he became royal assistant theologian to the
     viceroy; Dr. Rivarola attended Cabildo Abierto of May 1810
     and supported its action, insisting only that authority of
     Ferdinand VII be recognized; also supported patriot govern-
     ment's action in establishing a public library and freedom
     of the press; was appointed to commission in charge of

safeguarding this freedom of the press; died in Buenos Aires
and was buried in church of San Ignacio.

RIVAROLA, RODOLFO (1857-1942).   Jurist; university professor;
writer.
     Born in Rosario; attended Colegio de Concepción del
Uruguay; completed education in Buenos Aires, graduating in
jurisprudence in 1882; discharged judicial functions for next
ten years and then turned to teaching and writing; most of
his teaching took place in Buenos Aires as professor in faculty of philosophy and letters, from the time of its founding,
and professor of civil law in faculty of law; he also taught
juridical and social sciences in faculty of law at University
in La Plata, serving as dean of latter, 1905-1908; having
been trained as a positivist, but also having been exposed to
the more spiritual influence of José Manuel Estrada, Rivarola devoted the rest of his life--in his teaching and writing--
to attempting to bring his knowledge of law, and his intellectual training, to bear on the proper interpretation of Argentine historical development and the study of its social sciences; he also determined to evaluate the national political
system and policies on a scientific basis; making practical
applications, he brought news of daily happenings into his
classrooms for examination by himself and his students;
founded the Revista Argentina de Ciencias Políticas in 1910,
of which he was editor and important contributor, for this
purpose; he used its pages in an early issue to conduct one
of the first serious political polls in Argentina; convinced
that the government needed major reforms, he invited his
readers to send in their comments and recommendations as
to changes that should be made in the constitutional system,
form of government, electoral system, social organization,
economic system, relationship between Church and State, and
those growing out of a desire for a progressive nationalism
appropriate for the new ethnic compositions of Argentine
people; about 2,000 replies were received; after about four
and a half decades of such academic and public service, the
universities, cultural centers, and government authorities
united in honoring him publicly at a celebration in 1937 in
the Colón theater, as professor, penologist, sociologist,
philosopher, and interpreter of the national spirit and an active democrat.
     His bibliography is massive; only a few of his writings
can be mentioned; Fernando en el colegio (a kind of autobiography); Exposición y crítica del código penal de la República Argentina (3 v., Buenos Aires, 1890); Del régimen fede-
rativo al unitario (1908; defense of centralization of government again in Buenos Aires after 1880); Derecho penal argentino (Madrid, 1910); El maestro José Manuel Estrada (Buenos
Aires, 1914); "Mitre.   Una década de su vida política 1852-62,"
in Revista Argentina de Ciencias Políticas, Buenos Aires,
1921; his division of Argentine political history into 30-year
cycles (see Binayan, Ciclos en la historia argentina, B. A.

1933) is often cited: 1791-1821--independence; 1821-1851--
aspiration for a constitution; 1851-1880--consolidation of the
republic; 1880-1911--desire for representation and universal
suffrage.

RIVER PLATE MINING COMPANY. English mining company
    formed by Hullett Bros. & Company in London, December
    1824, to operate mines in Argentina, especially those of La
    Famatina (q.v.); encouraged by Bernardino Rivadavia's de-
    scription of mining resources and the speculating mood of
    the British public, convinced that new mineral wealth, equal
    to that of Bolivia, could be found in the Argentine Andes, the
    Hullett Bros. secured a charter from the Buenos Aires gov-
    ernment and sold stock on the London exchange for 1,000,000
    pounds; Sir Francis Bond Head (q.v.) became manager, Corn-
    ish miners and heavy equipment were transported to the La
    Rioja mining area (1825) but the venture failed in 1826;
    Buenos Aires and the company blamed Sir Francis but the
    latter, who had personally supervised operations both in
    Buenos Aires and at the mines declared that no such venture
    was economically feasible at that time; even if the rival
    claims to the mines could have been settled, political and so-
    cial turmoil of the area and heavy costs of transporting men
    and machinery to the remote mines ruled it out.
        See H. S. Ferns, Britain and Argentina in the Nine-
    teenth Century (Oxford Press, 1960).

RIVERA, FRUCTUOSO (1788-1854). Uruguayan caudillo deeply in-
    volved in Río de la Plata political and military affairs during
    independence and early national periods; opponent of Rosas.
        Born in Montevideo; joined Artigas in fighting for inde-
    pendence, 1811; took part in first and second sieges of Monte-
    video, 1811-1812; in 1816 became commander of Uruguayan
    forces fighting against Portuguese takeover from Brazil but
    in 1821 signed act incorporating Uruguay into Portuguese
    Brazil; served as military commander under latter for a
    time but became disillusioned and joined Juan Antonio Laval-
    leja and his famous Thirty-Three in fight to free Uruguay
    from Brazil; Buenos Aires congress gave him commission as
    general in Argentine forces in war with Brazil; in 1826
    moved to Buenos Aires but found that his federalist ideas
    clashed with political beliefs of the porteños; went to Santa
    Fe where he remained for several years under protection of
    Estanislao López; became governor of Misiones and estab-
    lished its boundary at the Cuareim river where it still re-
    mains; in 1830 Rivera was elected constitutional president of
    Uruguay; served his four-year term and turned government
    over to elected successor, Manuel Oribe; almost immediately
    military clashes developed from political differences between
    supporters of Oribe who came to be known as the Blancos
    and the Colorados, Rivera's men; from this time until his
    death, latter was constantly involved in this Uruguayan politi-
    cal strife; Argentina became affected as Rosas consistently

supported Oribe and fought against Rivera; Rivera, for his
part, joined with anyone who would aid him in opposing
Rosas, including Argentine unitarist exiles, provincial federalists of the interior, French forces blockading the Río de
la Plata; in 1839 Rivera again became president of Uruguay;
declared war against Rosas who supported Oribe as Uruguayan president and used latter to lead forces against his own
opponents in Argentina; Rivera signed agreement with Berón
de Astrada to join his Corrientes and other river province
forces against Rosas; in late 1830s and early 1840s fighting
took place both in Uruguay, where Oribe got possession of
most of outlying area and Great War (q. v.) began with Rosas'
siege, by land and sea, of Montevideo (1843), and in littoral
provinces where anti-Rosas forces, with Rivera and Paz,
vying for leadership, were opposed by Rosas' generals,
Urquiza and Echagüe; Rivera's defeat at India Muerta in
1845 forced him into exile in Brazil; returned briefly in
1846 but was forced back into exile; in 1853 he was named
as member of compromise triumvirate including Lavalleja and
Venancio Flores to form a new Uruguayan government; died
while returning to undertake this assignment (see entries on
individuals mentioned).

RIVERA, PEDRO IGNACIO DE (1753-1833).   Lawyer; patriot lead-
    er; signer of Declaration of Independence.
        Born in Bolivia; studied law at University of Chuqui-
saca; served as commander of militia and city attorney
(síndico) of cabildo in Mizque, his native town; took part in
revolt of 1809 against the Spaniards; in 1816 he represented
Mizque in Congress of Tucumán and served as its vice
president; urged greater support for patriots fighting against
royalists in Alto Perú; introduced law requiring compulsory
military conscription equal to 5% of population but could not
get it passed; remained in congress until its dissolution, participating actively in the debates leading to adoption of constitution of 1819; died in Buenos Aires.

RIVERA INDARTE, JOSE (1814-1845).   Writer and poet; opponent
    of Juan Manuel de Rosas.
        Born in Córdoba; studied in Buenos Aires; joined Ar-
gentine anti-Rosas exiles in Montevideo, 1832; founded El
Investigador and continued writing against Rosas; sent back to
Buenos Aires in 1834 by Manuel Oribe, he was imprisoned;
after his release, he traveled in Europe and the United
States; returned to Río de la Plata in 1839 and attacked
Rosas through his writings in El Nacional, Montevideo news-
paper; died on island of Santa Catarina off coast of Brazil.
        Rivera Indarte was considered by his contemporaries
one of ablest writers against Rosas and his best-known works
Tablas de sangre and Rosas y sus opositores, published in
Montevideo, 1843, obviously dealt with this theme; also wide-
ly known is his work entitled "Es acción santa matar a
Rosas"; Bartolomé Mitre published his other writings in

Buenos Aires in 1853, after Rosas' departure; Rivera Indarte
made another contribution to Argentine historical development;
it was his copy of The Federalist (collection of essays supporting adoption of constitution of United States by James
Madison, John Jay, and Alexander Hamilton) that had been
widely circulated and discussed among the men who were to
write the Argentine constitution of 1853.

RIVERO, FRANCISCO DE PAULA DEL (1770-1853). Spanish physician and surgeon; medical officer in patriot armies; accompanied Viceroy Baltasar Hidalgo de Cisneros to Buenos Aires
in 1809, having become latter's personal friend after saving
his life at battle of Trafalgar; became senior surgeon of
Residence Hospital in Buenos Aires; began, with Dr. Argerich, an immediate vaccination campaign against smallpox;
joined the patriots in 1810; served as army surgeon under
Sarratea and Rondeau during first siege of Montevideo; in
1814 became professor of surgery and joined Argerich and
Fabre in starting the Medical Institute; while continuing to
teach, he became president of the Academy of Medicine and
of the Medical Tribunal (Protomedicato); returned to military
duty during war against Brazil; retired to private life; died
in Buenos Aires.

ROADS see HIGHWAYS

ROBERTSON, JOHN PARISH (1792-1843).   Pioneer British trader
and financier (1809-1830); author of important books about
independence and early national periods.
        Born in Scotland; attempted to go to Río de la Plata
at age of fourteen but his voyage was diverted by news of the
British invasion going on there; reached Buenos Aires in
1809; established pioneer mercantile firm that eventually
operated throughout the country, buying produce and selling
manufactured goods, salt, mate, and tobacco, handling all
its own operations and finances; traveled to Paraguay (1811)
where he was well received and, with government help, succeeded in transporting a cargo of mate (1500 tercios) past
the Spanish river boats into Buenos Aires where he made a
small fortune by its sale; returning to Paraguay in February,
1813, he witnessed the victory at San Lorenzo, first American battle in which San Martín (whom Robertson had already
known in Buenos Aires) took part; John was joined by his
brother William Parish Robertson (q.v.) and they remained
in lucrative trade in Asunción until Francia forced them out
(1815); during next five years the Robertsons accumulated
another fortune, with aid of Irish gaucho Peter Campbell, in
the hide business, operating their own estancias in Corrientes;
in 1820 they crossed the Andes to make another fortune in
Chilean and Peruvian trade; back in Buenos Aires, with considerable capital to invest, the Robertsons cooperated with
Rivadavia in his desire to attract European capital (especially
British) and to diversify and develop Argentina's economy by

increasing mining operations and establishing agricultural
colonies; they advanced money to the government and aided
in securing the Baring Brothers loan; became stockholders in
both the Banco de Descuentos (Discount Bank) and in the
Banco Nacional; organized the Famatina Mining Company (see
Famatina) which turned out to be a fiasco; brought 220 Scotch
Presbyterian farmers and artisans over (1825) to establish an
agricultural colony at Monte Grande on 16,000 hectares of
land purchased near Buenos Aires; colony made excellent
progress during first three years but the anarchy and turbulence prevailing throughout the countryside in 1829 resulted
in violent raids against the colony by neighbors wanting the
land for cattle; this broke up the colony and dispersed its
members, again with heavy losses to their sponsors; shortly
afterward, the Robertsons had to declare bankruptcy, blaming
it on the disastrous mining and colonization ventures and the
Brazilian War; undoubtedly the deep and widely held resentment and violent competition of Creole entrepreneurs like
Rosas and provincial caudillos against such British commercial ventures especially in the interior also played an important role; in 1830 John Robertson returned to England; spent
a few years at Cambridge and then retired to the Isle of
Wight to work, with William, on their books on the Río de
la Plata and other portions of South America; for a combination of reasons, including the dramatic events of the period
of their stay, their own close relationship with the political,
military, and economic leaders of the period, and their gift
for gathering, analyzing, and describing their own adventures,
as well as public events, personalities, and Argentine customs and scenes, these works are invaluable primary sources
for the history of this period; they are contained in two major
works: Letters on Paraguay: Comprising an Account of Four
Years Residence in that Republic under the Government of
Dictator Francia (first 2 volumes appeared in 1823; translated into Spanish 1916); 3rd volume entitled Francia's Reign
of Terror, 1839; (translated into Spanish 1920); and Letters
on South America: Comprising Travels on the Banks of the
Paraná and Río de la Plata (3 v., London, 1843; Spanish
translation, Buenos Aires, 1952), covering their lives in
Corrientes and Buenos Aires, 1815-1820.

ROBERTSON, WILLIAM PARISH.   British trader, financier, and
author.   While living in Edinburgh received request from his
brother John to join him in his Río de la Plata trading ventures; did so in 1813 and collaborated with him from then on
(see John P. Robertson); when the Robertson bankruptcy took
place, he remained in Buenos Aires (having married there)
for about four years after John's return to England and then
joined him on the Isle of Wight, writing about their South
American experience.

ROCA, JOSE SEGUNDO (1800-1866).   Fighter for independence;
career military man.

Born in San Miguel de Tucumán (father Spanish);
served in Tucumán company of cazadores (hunters); fought under Belgrano in that area; in 1820 accompanied San Martín's
liberating army to Peru; fought in several engagements there;
formed part of San Martín's force sent to aid Sucre in Ecuador; his distinguished action at battle of Pichincha brought
him gold medals from Bolívar, cabildo of Quito, and government of Peru; promoted by San Martín to sergeant major;
fought under Santa Cruz and La Mar; took part in battle of
Junín, winning another gold medal; illness prevented his participation in final battle for independence at Ayacucho; returned to Argentina in 1826 in time to see service in war
against Brazil and then in Lavalle's forces; persecuted in
Buenos Aires for his unitarist sympathies he returned to
Tucumán; became involved in the civil wars of that area;
forced into exile after fighting against Quiroga; returned in
1837, became prisoner of Rosas for three years, 1839-1842;
was then allowed to return to Tucumán; after Caseros, in
1852, turned against Governor Celedonio Gutiérrez, Rosas'
man; became colonel in confederation army; at outbreak of
Paraguayan War Colonel Roca and his four sons, Julio A.
Roca (q. v.; later to become president), Rudecindo Roca
(q. v.), Celedonia Roca, and Marcos Roca (both casualties of
the war) joined in war effort; José Segundo Roca, division
commander, died unexpectedly in camp at Las Ensenaditas.

ROCA, JULIO ARGENTINO (1843-1914).   President, 1880-1886,
1898-1904; general in command of Conquest of Desert; statesman and dominant political leader at close of nineteenth century.

Born in Tucumán, son of José Segundo Roca; studied
at Colegio Nacional de Concepción del Uruguay; entered military career (1858) while continuing his studies; like many of
his fellow students joined Urquiza in battles of Cepeda (1859)
and Pavón (1861) that were followed by national reorganization; young Roca became secretary of his uncle Dr. Marcos
Paz, interventor in northern province; later became officer
in national infantry and fought against El Chacho's montoneras,
and in the Paraguayan War, distinguishing himself in attack
on Curupaytí; accompanied Paunero in campaign against guerrilla forces of Videla, Rodríguez, Sáa in Cuyo and the west;
won promotion to colonel by his courageous action against
López Jordán at Ñaembé (1871) and took part in second campaign against Entre Ríos caudillo; in 1872 was appointed military commander of Río Cuarto region and there married into
the Córdoba aristocracy; as commander of army of north he
forced Arredondo to surrender at Santa Rosa, ending revolution of 1874 and winning general rank for himself; fought always on side of national government; shortly after this, he
became commander general of the San Luis and Mendoza Indian frontiers; from this vantage point he turned his attention
to the plans for a final settlement of the Indian problem by
conquest of Patagonia and opening of all its lands to settlement;

supported by President Nicolás Avellaneda in whose cabinet
he served in 1877 as minister of war and navy, he crowned
his military career by the "Conquest of the Desert" (q.v.).
    In 1880, Julio A. Roca became president of Argentine
Republic at age of 37 and was elected again in 1898; for nearly twenty-five years he dominated political scene; a shrewd
politician, nicknamed El Zorro (The Fox), he used Partido
Autonomista Nacional to keep political power in the hands of
those favoring estanciero and foreign trade interests; the
nation prospered greatly during his administration; domestic
political tranquillity, the opening of immense tracts of new
Indian lands for settlement and exploitation and the establishment of a basis for ultimate peace with Chileans over boundary made rapid development possible; during his first term,
new expeditions were sent into Patagonia to complete the
conquest; mapping and scientific expeditions explored every
part of the republic, including the Antarctic; economic boom
of 1882-1889 began during his term and trade reached new
heights; railroad mileage more than doubled; population grew,
as nearly half a million immigrants entered Argentina to make
it their new home; public education was promoted and secularized (see Church-State Relations); a large public works
program improved ports, built river dams and public buildings, and beautified Buenos Aires; also created territory of
Misiones with its own government; turned presidency over to
Miguel Juárez Celman in 1886; spent some time traveling in
Europe; returned to serve as national senator for federal
capital; continued influential during succeeding administrations
following financial crisis of 1890 and development of Unión
Cívica Radical (q.v.) demanding political and social reforms;
elected again to presidency in 1898; during second term finally settled territorial disputes with Chile (see Pactos de Mayo);
continued modernization and professionalization of the army
(begun earlier) under minister of war, Pablo Ricchieri (q.v.);
increased size of navy and created separate ministry for it;
with his foreign minister, Luis Drago (q.v.), strengthened
Argentina's role in international affairs; improved national
credit position; faced increasing restlessness from labor,
students, immigrants, and other groups demanding more participation in government and economy as well as reform of
corrupt practices by which Roca's elite group maintained political domination; foreigners' residence law was passed (1903)
aimed at expulsion of undesirable aliens; Roca succeeded in
securing election of Manuel Quintana as his successor; retired
from politics but emerged to go to Brazil as ambassador in
1913.
    See José Arce, Roca, 1843-1914. Su vida--Su obra
(Buenos Aires, 1961); Courtney Letts de Espil, La segunda
presidencia Roca vista por los diplomáticos norteamericanos
(Buenos Aires, 1972).

ROCA, JULIO A., hijo (1873-1942). Lawyer; statesman, son of
President Roca.

Born in Córdoba; graduated as lawyer in 1895 from
the university of Buenos Aires; elected to the Chamber of
Deputies in 1904, 1908, and 1912; belonged to the conservative forces of the country and was member of the Democratic
party of Córdoba; Córdoba elected him as senator in 1916;
in 1922 was elected governor of Córdoba; in 1926 returned to
the House; resigned in 1928 to return to the practice of law;
in 1931 was elected as national vice president on the Justo-
Roca ticket; as vice president, was sent to London to sign a
commercial agreement, the result was the controversial Roca-
Runciman Agreement (q. v.); President Ortiz appointed him
ambassador to Brazil; in 1940 became minister of foreign relations and religion; resigned in 1941 and retired to private
life; died in Buenos Aires on October 8, 1942.

ROCA, RUDECINDO (1850-1903).   Professional military man; pub-
lic figure.
Born in San Miguel de Tucumán, son of independence
fighter Colonel José Segundo Roca, and brother of Julio A.
Roca; began his military career as cadet in artillery, 1864;
took part in Paraguayan War, fighting in battles of Estero
Bellaco, Tuyuty, Curupaytí, and Humaitá; in 1868 went to
Corrientes to suppress rebellion of General Cáceres; the
next two years were spent fighting, as aide to his brother
General Roca, against Indians on the southern frontier of
Buenos Aires province in "conquest of the desert"; served as
governor of Misiones territory, 1882-1890; was promoted to
brigadier general in 1886; named chief of national guard in
Buenos Aires, 1893; died in that city ten years later.

ROCA-RUNCIMAN AGREEMENT (May 1933).   Commercial pact between Great Britain and Argentine Republic.   As result of
world economic depression, England had been forced to
promise its distressed dominions a greater share in its market for meat, wool, and other products normally bought from
Argentina (see Ottawa Agreements); this loss of its major
trading partner threatened Argentina with economic disaster;
Vice President Julio A. Roca (hijo) was sent with commission
to negotiate with Walter Runciman, English minister of commerce; the pact drawn up in May 1933, known as the Roca-
Runciman Agreement, marked a serious departure from the
old laissez-faire system under which they had traditionally
operated (in theory, at least); Argentina was promised a
smaller, but substantial, share of British trade in return for
several concessions, including reductions on proposed Argentine tariffs on industrial items, continued free entry for
British fuel, adjustments in exchange control to advantage of
British investors, and commitment of 85% of its meat business to British frigoríficos; in Argentina only cattle barons
approved agreement; nationalists considered it a sellout; rising industrial group (both investors and workers) opposed it
strongly; its renewal three years later was even more controversial as Argentina had to pay the added price of forcing

private bus or jitney service in Buenos Aires out of business
to preserve the British transportation monopoly there; actually Roca-Runciman Agreement marked the beginning of the
end of the lucrative, preferential trade between England and
Argentina.

See Daniel Drosdoff, El gobierno de las vacas: 1933-
1956, Tratado Roca-Runciman (Buenos Aires, 1972).

ROCAMORA, TOMAS DE (1740-1819).   Founder of Entre Ríos;
patriot administrator.

Guatemalan-born Spanish officer, commissioned by
Viceroy Vértiz to draw up and then to carry out plan for
settlement of area between Paraná and Uruguay rivers and
to place it more directly under viceregal control; Rocamora
used term "Entre Ríos" (Between Rivers) in first report and
area became known by that name; three cities were established in rapid succession in 1783; Gualeguay, Concepción del
Uruguay, and San José de Gualeguaychú, each with cabildo;
others projected but with replacement of viceroy Vértiz by
the marqués de Loreto, interest in development of Entre Ríos
lapsed; Rocamora given other assignments; in 1810, as governor of Misiones, supported the May Revolution and independence; joined Manuel Belgrano on expedition to Paraguay; retired to Buenos Aires, where he died in 1819.

See César B. Pérez Colman, Entre Ríos, Historia, I;
María Cristina Demonte and Rosa Coralia Troncoso, Tomás
de Rocamora: pionero de la autonomía entrerriana (Santa Fe,
1972).

ROCHA, DARDO (1838-1921).   Founder of city of La Plata and of
university there; jurist; national public and political figure.

Born in Buenos Aires; interrupted his law studies
there in 1859 to take part in war between Confederation and
Buenos Aires province; received law degree (1863) after national unity was established; spent his life in public service;
held various administrative posts; was member, at various
times, of provincial legislature and national chamber of deputies and senate; his name is linked with such legislation as
that dealing with navigation of the Bermejo River, protection
of national industries, and first law regulating patents and
inventions; also served as justice of supreme court; fought in
Paraguayan War until severe wounds at Battle of Curupaytí
forced him to retire; became one of leaders of Partido Autonomista Nacional; after the revolution of 1880 that ended with
the Federalization of the City of Buenos Aires (q.v.), he became governor of Buenos Aires province (1881-1884) and
made some of his most important contributions; assigned responsibility for creating the new capital of the province, he
founded city of La Plata (q.v.); selected site and planned,
designed, and, by a furor of construction, dedicated this new
capital November 19, 1882, and moved provincial government
there; also ordered a census taken of the province; later established and became first rector of the University of La

Plata; hoped to succeed Roca as president of the republic in
1886 but Miguel Juárez Celman won; represented Argentina
on diplomatic assignments to Paraguay and Bolivia; died in
city of Buenos Aires.

ROCHA, JUAN JOSE ROMUALDO (1754-1821).   Public Notary;
first captain of Patricios.

Born in Buenos Aires; grandson of Victoriano Rocha,
one of founders of Villa de Luján; formed one of first companies of what became regiment of Patricios to fight against
British; remembered for his heroic defense action at the Real
Colegio de San Carlos, then converted into army barracks;
led his unit again in support of Liniers' government against
revolution of January 1, 1809; voted for removal of viceroy
in open cabildo meeting May Revolution, 1810; named secretary of public safety tribunal, 1811; exiled to Guardia de
Melincué in 1812, accused of participating in Alzaga revolt;
exonerated in 1813, he became a commandant of national
guard barracks; died in Buenos Aires.

RODEO DEL MEDIO, BATTLE OF.   Site, in Mendoza, of battle
in which federalist forces, under General Angel Pacheco,
aided by Aldao and Benavídez, defeated Lamadrid's anti-
Rosas forces September 24, 1841, and forced them to flee
to Chile.

RODNEY, CAESAR AUGUSTUS (1772-1824).   First U.S. minister
to Buenos Aires government, 1823-1824.

Born in Dover, Delaware; graduated in law; after
term in House of Representatives had been chosen in 1804 to
conduct impeachment trial of Judge Samuel Chase; served as
President Jefferson's attorney general, 1807-1811; selected in
1817 by President James Monroe as member of three-man
commission, along with John Graham and Theodorick Bland,
with Henry M. Brackenridge as secretary, to go to Argentine to determine whether that country merited U.S. recognition of its independence; commission arrived in Buenos Aires
in 1818 and returned to the United States about a year later
with varying reports; Rodney strongly favored granting recognition but other members presented less favorable reports;
no U.S. action taken until 1823 when U.S. recognized Buenos
Aires government, then acting for all the provinces in foreign
affairs, and appointed Rodney first U.S minister to that government; arriving in Buenos Aires in late November, 1823,
he was first diplomatic representative accredited to Argentina by non-South American country; had become ill on voyage to Río de la Plata and died there a few months later
(May 1824); buried in Buenos Aires with Bernardino Rivadavia giving the funeral oration; Argentine government placed
statue in his honor on his tomb in Anglican church.

See Henry M. Brackenridge's account of the Rodney-
Graham-Bland mission in Voyage to South America (several
editions).

RODRIGUEZ, CARLOS JUAN (1831-1892).   Lawyer; legislator and
   public figure in San Luis and on national scene.
       Born in San Luis; studied in Chile; returned to San
   Luis after Caseros and accompanied Governor Lucero to San
   Nicolás meeting (q. v.) as his secretary; held various provincial legislative and judicial appointments; served as deputy
   in legislature, general minister for governors Lucero, Pedernera, Maldonado, and Saá, and as judge of civil and supreme
   courts; acted as interim governor of provinces of Cuyo (1860)
   until end of confederation government; for political reasons
   went into exile in Chile for several years; returned to San
   Luis and public life in 1878; elected again to provincial lower
   house in 1879, he became its president the following year;
   again served on supreme court, as its president; in 1881 was
   elected national senator from San Luis but returned home two
   years later to become minister of finance, justice, and education in cabinet of Eriberto Mendoza; during this period he
   drafted education law and built many schools; reelected to national senate in 1887, he participated actively in the debate
   over civil marriage law; died in San Luis.

RODRIGUEZ, CAYETANO JOSE (1758-1823).   Franciscan friar; intellectual; patriot leader; author and signer of the Declaration of Independence.
       Born in San Pedro, Buenos Aires; entered Franciscan
   order at age of 16; ordained in Córdoba in 1778; taught philosophy and theology there; returned to Buenos Aires; continued his teaching in the Franciscan monastery; among his
   students was Mariano Moreno whom he influenced greatly and
   later supported politically; joined independence movement
   early and played important role in it; became first librarian
   of public library created by the patriot junta, serving at
   same time as provincial of his order; as member of the Assembly of XIII (1813) he was made responsible for the keeping and editing of its important proceedings (as Redactor de
   la Asamblea) until its dissolution in 1815; sent as delegate to
   the Congress of Tucumán, he was elected secretary and, in
   addition to recording its actions, wrote the Declaration of Independence; was one of its signers; he also wrote excellent
   poetry; his odes honoring Alvear, the crossing of the Andes,
   victory at Chacabuco were well known, as were his longer
   patriotic poems dedicated to Mariano Moreno and to José de
   San Martín and set to music; famous for his eloquence, he
   was selected to give the funeral eulogy of Manuel Belgrano;
   Fray Cayetano Rodríguez strongly defended the rights of the
   church against Rivadavia's secularism and proposed ecclesiastical reforms (early 1820s); debated these vigorously in the
   pages of El Oficial del Día, founded for that purpose, with
   the editors and writers of the Argos who spoke for the government; when the law passed in 1821 he retired from public
   life; devoted himself to religious duties until his death in the
   monastery in 1823.

RODRIGUEZ, GREGORIO F.   (1865-1922).   Lawyer; historical
    writer.
        Born in Buenos Aires province and graduated in law;
devoted his entire life to historical research, collection of
documents, and writing; among his works are: El general
Miguel Estanislao Soler--including previously unpublished
documents (Buenos Aires, 1909); La acción de O'Higgins en
Chacabuco (1912); Historia de Alvear, 2 v. (1913); La patria
vieja. Cuadros históricos (1916); and Contribución histórica y
documental, 3 v. (1921 and 1922), a collection of letters and
documents, including many related to diplomatic problems of
1811 and 1812 and one volume of Lavalle letters; his collection was purchased by the Jockey Club and destroyed in the
fire of 1953.

RODRIGUEZ, MANUEL FORTUNATO (1826-1892).   Governor of
    Catamarca; public leader.
        Born in Catamarca; rebelled against President Derqui
in 1861; filled various public offices; as congressman (1871),
governor (1879-1882); senator (1883-1892); appointed minister
of finance by Governor Terrari, but died before taking office;
his administration as governor was marked by settlement of
boundary dispute with Santiago del Estero, installation of running water in the city, promulgating of first law relating to
the press, and establishment of schools and hospitals.

RODRIGUEZ, MARTIN (1771-1845).   Military and public leader;
    governor of Buenos Aires, 1820-1824.
        Born in Buenos Aires; until 1806, devoted himself to
management of his rural estate; during the British invasions
joined the militia and was in charge of the famous Patricios
squadron that recaptured the convent of Santo Domingo from
the British July 5, 1807; joined the patriotic forces in their
fight against the Spaniards quite early; the first patriot junta
appointed him colonel and sent him to join the army of the
North; in 1811 he took part in the revolt of April 5 and 6 and
was imprisoned in San Juan; joined Belgrano's forces in 1812
and fought in the battle of Salta; three years later he commanded the vanguard of the army of the north; and in the
same year (1815) was elected president of Charcas; later returned to the army in time to share in defeat in Venta y
Media and Sipe-Sipe; transferred back to Buenos Aires, he
was placed in charge of the observation forces of Santa Fe
(1819); after Dorrego's defeat in 1820, Martín Rodríguez became governor of Buenos Aires; appointed capable ministers,
Bernardino Rivadavia and Manuel García, who began a large-
scale program of reforms; these included allotment of public
lands, development of agriculture, ranching and mining, ecclesiastical reforms involving both clergy and church organization, and military reforms; they also created the University of Buenos Aires, the Museum of Natural History, founded
the city of Tandil (province of Buenos Aires), established
forts, reorganized the police service, etc.; Rodríguez, who

owed his appointment as governor, at least partially, to support of Juan Manuel de Rosas, also signed the Benegas
Treaty with chieftain Estanislao López that established a truce
between Buenos Aires and the Mesopotamia provinces; in 1824
returned to military service; fought on the southern Buenos
Aires frontier against the Indians; between 1825 and 1827 he
was head of the Observation Army in Uruguay during war
against Brazil; in the 1840s Rodríguez turned against Rosas
and attempted to join José María Paz's forces but he was
already too old and sick; instead, he gave his fortune to the
Rosas opposition; died in exile in Montevideo (Uruguay); Rodríguez's Memoirs were published after his death in Montevideo (1849); a monument erected in his memory in 1910 stands
in the Recoleta cemetery of Buenos Aires (established during
his rule).

RODRIGUEZ, RICARDO (1877-1954).   Musician.   Born in Concordia, Entre Ríos; studied in Europe on government scholarship; became teacher and composer; among his best-known
compositions are Tu sais, Cinco miniaturas, Yu querí,
Atardecer en la tablada (for orchestra), Las mariposas, Gauchos, and Un vasco.

RODRIGUEZ PEÑA, NICOLAS (1775-1853).   Early independence
leader.   Born in Buenos Aires; educated at the Real Colegio
de San Carlos; briefly tried military service and later fought
against British invasions; became very prosperous merchant;
was one of organizers (1809-1810) of secret society working
for independence that met frequently in his home; as one of
wealthiest members of the group, his financial contributions
were important to final success of movement; supported May
Revolution and accompanied first patriot army carrying revolution to Upper Peru (Bolivia) in 1810 as secretary of Dr.
Juan José Castelli (q.v.); served briefly as governor of La
Paz; returned to Buenos Aires and replaced Mariano Moreno
in first patriot junta; exiled after the political events of
April 5-6, 1811; became part of First Triumvirate government (q.v.) in 1812; and was appointed president of council
of state by Assembly of 1813; was designated (1814) governor
of Banda Oriental (Uruguay) but exiled again, as supporter
of Alvear; he went to San Juan; there he aided San Martín in
organization and equipping of Army of the Andes; after Chilean independence had been won, he moved to Santiago where
he remained until his death; his remains were returned to
Buenos Aires in 1910, centennial year of the revolution that
he had helped to start and to which he had given his fortune.

RODRIGUEZ PEÑA, SATURNINO JOSE (1765-1819).   Jurisconsult;
early advocate of separation from Spain.
        Born in Buenos Aires, older brother of Nicolás Rodrí-
guez Peña (q.v.); studied in university at Córdoba, with José
Gaspar Francia, future dictator of Paraguay, as fellow student; also attended University of Chuquisaca (q.v.); served as

legal counsel of royal audiencia of Charcas; later became one
of first patriots to initiate idea of Argentine independence
from Spain; after reconquest of Buenos Aires from British
(1806) he entered into secret talks with British commander
Lord Beresford, imprisoned at Luján, about possibilities of
the Río de la Plata area becoming a British protectorate;
was joined in these efforts by other prominent Spanish and
criollo merchants and residents; Rodríguez Peña helped Beresford escape and accompanied him to Montevideo and then to
London; hoped to secure aid from Great Britain for Argentine
emancipation but failed; became involved in complicated, but
unsuccessful, plot to place Carlota Joaquina (q.v.) on throne
in Buenos Aires; returned to Buenos Aires briefly in 1815
but was exiled because of his support of Alvear faction; went
to London; returned to Rio de Janeiro; died in Buenos Aires
during visit to his family.

ROHDE, JORGE (1860-1903).   Military officer; cartographer.
          German-born officer who joined Argentine army in
1878; took part in expedition into Indian country and laid out
plan for town of Choele-Choel in 1880; the following year he
explored and mapped the area around Bariloche, Nahuel Huapi,
and Limay river, as well as that of the Río Negro; discovered
Bariloche Pass in the Andes; studied all strategic passes
along southern part of boundary between Argentina and Chile;
in 1885 prepared the New Map of the Gran Chaco; returning
to the south, he drew up descriptive maps of the new territories of La Pampa, Río Negro, and Neuquén; appointed as
member of commission that settled boundary problems with
Brazil (1886); after 1890 revolution became member of army
general staff and inspector of Patagonia; founded military
town San Martín de los Andes in Río Negro (1892); after serving, with rank of colonel, as military attaché in Washington
and London (1894-1895), he returned to Argentina; became director of the military academy of the capital's national guard
and published the Great Map of the Argentine Republic, drawn
up under his direction; died in Buenos Aires.

ROIG MATONS, FIDEL (1887-?).   Painter of historical scenes.
          Born in Gerona, Spain; studied art there and in Barce-
lona; moved to Argentina; made his home in Mendóza where
he taught art (1911-1931); dedicated himself to painting important scenes in the life of José de San Martín; received a
grant from national cultural commission 1941-1942 that
enabled him to spend most of his time in the cordillera,
painting the major passes through which the Army of the
Andes passed in early 1817 on its way to Chile to begin the
fight for continental liberation; in his drawings and portraits
of San Martín, the artist departs from the conventional Euro-
pean-style portraits and attempts to reveal the Liberator as
a powerful, heroic, and utterly Argentine leader; in 1952 the
government of Mendoza voted him a pension in appreciation
of his artistic contributions to its historical record.

ROJAS, DIEGO DE   see   GRAN ENTRADA

ROJAS, ISAAC F.   (1906-   ).   Naval officer; political leader in
         1950s and 1960s.
         Born in Buenos Aires; graduated from naval academy
in 1929; took advanced studies in artillery and international
law; became rear admiral in 1952; in 1955 he was director
of military naval school of Río Santiago; joined General Eduardo Lonardi in revolution to overthrow Juan Domingo Perón
in September 1955; attacked distillery of Mar del Plata and
his threat, as commander of the river and maritime naval
squadrons, to attack city of La Plata was considered turning
point in revolution; last Peronist forces surrendered on board
his flagship; on September 24, 1955, he became vice president of the republic in Lonardi's provisional government;
strongly anti-Peronist personally, he cooperated with Lonardi
in latter's attempt to establish conciliatory policy; in October
1955, he was made full admiral of the navy; became president of national committee of investigation into activities of
officials of Perón's administration; directed operations suppressing revolts in Buenos Aires, La Plata, and Santa Rosa
in La Pampa; in 1963 Admiral Rojas led a final attempt on
part of Colorados (see Azules and Colorados) to gain political
control but was defeated by General Juan Carlos Onganía;
during latter's presidency, Rojas continued to be spokesman
for those who opposed state planning and state enterprises.

ROJAS, RICARDO (1882-1957).   Writer; literary historian; roman-
         tic poet; nationalist.
         Born in Tucumán of very old Spanish-Argentine fami-
lies on both maternal and paternal sides; educated in Santiago
del Estero; moved to Buenos Aires to study law but in 1903
dedicated himself to literary life instead; in 1909 published
La restauración nacionalista urging Argentines to study their
past seriously and to teach it to all Argentine youth; the following year Blasón del Plata made a mystical appeal to nationalist pride; he followed these with Argentinidad depicting
democratic process involved in independence period, and
Eurindia that emphasized Argentine cultural debt to both Indian and European heritages; his greatest contribution was
probably his comprehensive La literatura argentina in 1917,
4 v. (Buenos Aires, 1917-1922; 4th ed., 9 vols., 1957); his
biography of José de San Martín, El santo de la espada, appeared in 1933 and was translated shortly afterward into English (see Rojas in Suggested Readings, Appendix III); he is
considered to have been father of literary school of nationalists;
a Liberal, he also criticized the "selfishness, arrogance and
the indolence, favored by the excessive national resources" of
the people, as well as general moral corruption and bribery
in government; died in Buenos Aires; in 1958 his widow Juli-
eta Quinteros donated his home in Buenos Aires (Calle Charcas 2837) to the government; it has been converted, with its
contents, into a museum and library.

For a listing of his works see Horacio Jorge Becco's
Bibliografía de Ricardo Rojas in Revista Iberoamericana, vol.
XXIII, núm. 46, Mexico, 1958.

ROJO, CAMILO (c. 1815-1886).   Rancher and political leader, San
    Juan province.
        Born in San Juan and educated in Chile at University
of Santiago; at his father's death, returned to manage his
rural estate in Pergamino; when this was confiscated for political reasons by Juan Manuel de Rosas in 1843, Rojo went
into exile until after battle of Caseros; in 1864 was elected
governor of his province; his progressive administration was
marked by establishment of several schools, a department of
education, the first public library in the region (named after
Benjamin Franklin and begun with four boxes of books sent
by Domingo F. Sarmiento from the United States), and compulsory education for ages 6-14; improved irrigation system;
had census made; resigned in 1867 to become national senator; after his retirement from public life he attempted to recover his lost property from the government but was unsuccessful; died in San Juan in extreme poverty.

ROJO, JOSE RUDECINDO (1780-1834).   Public figure and political
    leader, San Juan.
        Born in San Juan; studied in Buenos Aires at Colegio
de San Carlos; returned home; assisted lieutenant governor
José de la Roza (q. v.) in the organization of the Army of the
Andes; served as secretary of Governor Salvador María del
Carril; during that period the first provincial constitution was
signed, the judicial power was reorganized and supreme court
established; the position of minister of government was created and Rojo appointed; he promoted military and ecclesiastical reforms, established the first printing press, started the
first agricultural census, founded the Sociedad de Beneficencia
in the province, regulated craftsmen groups; when Rojo presented a project in the legislature known as the Carta de Mayo
declaring the rights of man, it was met by conservative opposition that resulted in ousting of del Carril and his minister
(July 1825); with aid from Governor Aldao of Mendoza they
defeated rebels in Las Leñas and returned to office; in September Rojo resigned to go to Buenos Aires as representative
to the constitutional congress; in 1830 he represented San
Juan in the meeting at which the League of the Interior was
organized by General Paz (see José María Paz); after federalists had destroyed the League, Rojo suffered persecution by
them; died in San Juan; had contributed to local newspapers,
1825-1830.

ROLDAN, BELISARIO (1873-1922).   Writer; orator; lawyer and
    public figure.
        Born and educated in Buenos Aires; graduated as law-
yer in 1895 but never practiced law; taught in colegio nacional in Buenos Aires; elected (1902) to national Chamber of

Deputies; served as minister of federal intervention of province of Tucumán (1905); carried out official missions in France and Spain; widely admired as an orator, he was invited to pronounce San Martín's eulogy when statue in his honor was dedicated in Boulogne Sur Mer (1910); distinguished as a writer and poet, he contributed to journals and periodicals, and published poems and dramatic works; was a member of Spanish Royal Academy; seriously ill, he committed suicide in Alta Gracia, Córdoba.

His speeches were published in three volumes after his death; other writings include poetry: La senda encantada, (1912); Letanías de la tarde (1919); and Bajo la toca de lino (1920); dramatic works such as El rosal de las ruinas, El puñal de los troveros, Los contagios, and others.

ROLON, CAMILA (1852-1913). Nun; social worker and benefactor.
Born in Buenos Aires; became well known for her untiring services during epidemics of cholera, 1867-1868 and yellow fever, 1871; entered Carmelite convent in 1876; later in town of Exaltación de la Cruz founded the Congregation (religious community) of the Poor Sisters of St. Joseph; established orphan asylums in Mercedes, Rojas, El Salto, and Muñiz (Buenos Aires); with funds donated by friends and relatives she expanded Congregation's activities to include serving in new hospitals and old people's nursing homes in many areas, including Mendoza, Río IV, and La Plata; died in Rome.

ROMAN CATHOLICISM; ROMAN CATHOLIC CHURCH. Argentina is a Catholic country; in the 1970s, after more than a century and a half of religious freedom, approximately 93% of its people continue to be Roman Catholic as they have been since the Spanish conquest.

Priests accompanied the conquistadores to the Río de la Plata and Tucumán areas; three primitive chapels were erected on the site of present Buenos Aires in 1536; and same pattern followed in other early settlements; almost immediately the hierarchical structure of the Roman Catholic Church was established to minister to the spiritual needs of its communicants, to supervise the moral life of the society, and to stimulate and direct the evangelization of the Indians to Christianity; the first diocese for the Río de la Plata was created in 1547 in Asunción, Paraguay; the first one in what is now Argentine territory was that of Tucumán in 1570; this included Tarija (now in Bolivia), Jujuy, Salta, Tucumán, Santiago del Estero (where the bishop resided as it was then capital of Tucumán province), Catamarca, La Rioja, and Córdoba; a Franciscan friar, Jerónimo Villacarrillo, was appointed to serve as its first bishop but died before he could assume his duties; the work of the church really got under way with the appointment of Dominican friar Francisco de Victoria (q.v.) in 1577 and his successors, including Bishop Fernando de Trejo y Sanabria, appointed in 1592; the diocese

of Buenos Aires was established in 1620; the Church's organization remained unchanged for the next two centuries, except for the transfer of the Bishop of Tucumán's residence
from Santiago del Estero to Córdoba in 1699; in 1806, the
Diocese of Salta was created.

Although the bishops and other members of the hierarchy were traditionally greatly interested in the conversion
of the Indians to Christianity, in fact this work was largely
carried out by the religious orders, first by Franciscans and
Dominicans, followed by Jesuits, Mercedarians, and others,
who arrived during the sixteenth century; throughout the colonial period, the Church was also responsible for the education, medical care, welfare assistance, and cultivation of
arts and skills (especially those needed in building their lovely churches) of the Argentine society; members of its orders
and hierarchy also wrote much of the scientific literature
and historiography, stimulated and enriched the economy of
the area (especially in mission areas), as well as played important roles as public leaders.

A new era began for the Church when Argentina won
its independence from Spain in early nineteenth century;
throughout the first century of independence problems of jurisdiction growing out of the old Spanish real patronato (Spanish crown's legal rights with regard to ecclesiastical appointments and finances), increasing secularism, Argentine establishment of religious freedom, etc., have periodically caused
disagreements that have been resolved more or less prag-
matically rather than by legal concordat; matters of dogma
have only rarely been part of the problem (see Church-State
Relations for this period).

Although legally the Roman Catholic Church has little
political power in Argentine Republic, it has great influence;
this became evident in the clash with Juan Domingo Perón in
1954-1955; in 1954 President Perón turned against the Church
that he had earlier favored so conspicuously; he accused it of
having "aristocratic and oligarchic" preferences and removed
the civil privileges that he himself had previously granted
(such as reinstatement of religious education in public
schools, 1943), imprisoned priests, suppressed Catholic newspapers, forbade religious processions, and even, at least,
tolerated (commonly believed to have instigated) public demonstrations that resulted in the burning of churches and other
violence against them; popular reaction to this attack on the
Roman Catholic Church was generally believed to have been
strongly influential in the success of the revolution that deposed him in September 1955; since then Christian (Catholic)
symbols have been widely used publicly and President Juan
Carlos Onganía and his followers adopted "Christus vincit"
(Christ conquers) as their slogan; Perón, however, had influenced the Church; in the mid-1970s its members are divided into three groups: 1) Conservatives who want to preserve tradition, stifle innovation, and refuse to adapt to new
situations; 2) Moderates who encourage some modernization;

and 3) Those who demand immediate, drastic social change
and are known as "the Third World priests" and considered
to be following Peronist policies; generally speaking, the Roman Catholic Church in Argentina still has little political
power; it also suffers from the universal Catholic problem of
lack of priests; there are only about 5000 Catholic clergymen
to serve almost 20 million people; these Catholic communicants are divided among 38 dioceses and 12 archdioceses;
Buenos Aires became the first archdiocese in 1865 under
Archbishop Mariano José de Escalada Bustillo y Zeballos; it
remains the primate, over those in Bahía Blanca, La Plata,
Santa Fe, Paraná, Salta, San Juan, Córdoba, Corrientes,
Mendoza, Rosario, and Tucumán; a papal nuncio, or special
emissary of the Pope, resides in Buenos Aires.

 The Roman Catholic Church has held two of its international Eucharistic Congresses in Buenos Aires, one in the
1930s, the other in 1944; both, involving the entire Argentine
nation, were considered successful (see Missions; Religion;
Catholic Action; also entries on individual religious orders
and priests).

 For further information see John J. Kennedy, Catholi-
cism, Nationalism and Democracy in Argentina (Notre Dame,
Indiana, 1958); Bruno Cayetano's multi-volume Historia de la
iglesia en la Argentina (Buenos Aires, 1966, 1971); J. C.
Zuretti, Historia eclesiástica argentina (Buenos Aires, 1945);
A. P. Whitaker, Argentina (New Jersey, 1964).

ROMANZO, ALBINO A. (1894-1947). Journalist. Born in Entre
 Ríos; founded Los Principios; editor of La Voz del Litoral;
 vice president of Circle of Newspapermen; contributed to La
 Crítica; wrote a book on yerba mate; founded Entre Ríos In-
 stitute of historical studies; died in Villa San José, Entre
 Ríos.

ROMAY, FRANCISCO (1853-1918). Educator. Born in Catamarca;
 graduated in 1874 from Escuela Normal de Paraná (recently
 established by Sarmiento); taught there; became director of
 schools in Entre Ríos; returned to Catamarca where he combined provincial public and legislative responsibilities with
 his teaching at the Colegio Nacional there; later served as
 vice director of normal school (teachers college) at Santiago
 del Estero, while teaching in the Colegio Nacional there and
 directing vocational school that he founded; moved to Buenos
 Aires and became vice president of the central teachers organization and inspector of the national schools in the province; died in La Plata; wrote text books especially in mathematics.

ROMERO, FRANCISCO (1891-1962). Philosopher; writer and teacher.
  Born in Sevilla, Spain; arrived in Buenos Aires at
 early age; although he has become widely known as one of
 Argentina's most distinguished intellectuals of the Positivist

Schooi, he first entered military career; graduated from Escuela Militar; resigned in 1931 as major in engineering
corps; had already begun teaching philosophy in universities
of Buenos Aires and La Plata; became titular professor in
Buenos Aires (1931) retaining this title until his death; continued to offer courses as guest professor at La Plata and
elsewhere throughout his career; a student and intellectual
follower of Alejandro Korn (q.v.) he himself came to have
large following of students, including Risieri Frondizi, Aníbal
Sánchez Reulet, Eugenio Pucciarelli, Juan Adolfo Vázquez,
and Norberto Rodríguez Bustamante; his ideas have inspired
many doctoral dissertations, both in his own country and
abroad; his own writings were extensive (see partial listing
below); founded and directed the Biblioteca Filosófica; served
as consulting foreign editor of Sur (journal of philosophy),
president of the Inter-American Philosophical Exchange, editor of journal Realidades; went into exile, 1946-1955, for political reasons; returned, after fall of Perón government, to
spend his remaining years teaching in various Argentine universities; died in Buenos Aires.

Among his published works are: Lógica, classic philosophy secondary text, co-author E. Pucciarelli, first published in Buenos Aires 1938 (latest edition, Buenos Aires,
1973); Alejandro Korn (with A. Vassallo and L. Aznar; 1940);
Sobre la historia de la filosofía (1943); Filosofía contemporánea (1944); Filosofía de la persona (1944); El hombre y la
cultura (1951); Teoría del hombre (1952; translated by Wm.
F. Cooper, with introduction by William J. Kilgore, Theory
of Man, Berkeley, California, 1964); Sobre la filosofía en
América (1953); and in 1959 ¿Qué es la filosofía?

See Hugo Rodríguez-Alcalá, Francisco Romero (New
York, 1954); Marjorie Silliman Harris, Francisco Romero on
Problems of Philosophy (New York, 1960); Solomon Lipp,
Three Argentine Thinkers (New York, 1969).

ROMERO, GREGORIO IGNACIO (1860-1915). Bishop; lawyer and
public figure, interested in labor legislation.

Born in Concordia, Entre Ríos; after death of his
parents was sent by his uncle to a Jesuit school; ordained as
priest in 1883; earned doctorate in both canon and civil law
at University of Córdoba; taught law at University of Santa
Fe; founded and edited newspaper El Lábaro (freely translated
as "Christian Banner"); as president of provincial council of
education, founded several schools while continuing his church
assignments; when diocese of Santa Fe was created in 1897
he became apostolic administrator of it, responsible for establishing its cathedral; the following year he was elected to
the lower house of the national congress; there he proposed a
law making Sunday a rest day for laborers; in 1899 was appointed titular bishop of Jasso; after his consecration in
Santa Fe, he returned to the Chamber of Deputies in rare
situation of bishop as elected member of Argentine congress;
when his second term was ended, in 1904, he and Federico

Grote suggested a detailed project of labor legislation to Congress, in the name of the Círculos Católicos de los Obreros (Catholic Circles of Workers--or labor groups) that paved way for passage of Joaquín V. González's labor code that followed; Bishop Romero died while serving as auxiliary bishop of archdiocese of Buenos Aires (1902-1915).

ROMERO, JOSE LUIS (1909-   ).   Historian; university professor and administrator.

Born in Buenos Aires; graduated from University of La Plata; began teaching career and writing of historical articles before receiving his doctor's degree in history in 1934; from 1942 to 1946 taught historiography in faculty of humanities at La Plata; an active Socialist, he lost his position for political reasons in 1946 and went into exile; taught philosophy of history in Montevideo, 1948-1955; returned to Buenos Aires in 1955; became interventor or rector of University of Buenos Aires when Perón's appointees had been dismissed; taught medieval history (to which he had turned during these troubled years) until becoming dean of school of Philosophy and Letters in 1962; he studied in Europe and in the United States (with Guggenheim grant) and served as visiting professor at University of San Marcos (Peru), Toulouse and Poitiers, Columbia University (New York City), as well as at universities of Chile, Puerto Rico, and Colombia; is a member of the Argentine group of International Academy of History of the Sciences; the Medieval Academy of America; and of Academy of Sciences of Buenos Aires; secretary of Argentine Society of Writers and founding-editor of review Imago Mundi, devoted to history of culture; his writings are concerned with attempts to analyze Argentine political expressions of economic and social forces--as well as to study formal political thought.

Romero's historical writings include, among others: Mitre, un historiador frente al destino nacional (1943); La historia y la vida (1945); Las ideas políticas en Argentina (Mexico, 1946; 3rd edition translated by Thomas F. McGann, A History of Argentine Political Thought (Stanford, California, 1963; 2nd edition 1968); Argentina: imágenes y perspectivas (1956); and El desarrollo de las ideas en la sociedad argentina del siglo XX (Mexico, D.F., 1965).

ROMERO, JUAN JOSE (1841-1906).   Statesman; governor of Buenos Aires; lawyer and financier.

Born in Buenos Aires; educated abroad, graduating from University of Paris and earning law degree in Rome; returned to Buenos Aires; events of early 1870s brought him into politics as enthusiastic supporter of Aristóbulo del Valle; involved in dispute over federalization of Buenos Aires; elected provincial senator in 1880; became interim governor the following year; appointed minister of finance in President Julio A. Roca's cabinet; took active part in revolution of 1890 overthrowing Juárez Celman; President Luis Sáenz Peña appointed him minister of finance to solve critical national

economic problems; Romero resisted uncontrolled inflation
and loose credit policies; insisted that Argentina must learn
to stand on its own feet financially; sent to London to reach
agreement with European creditors, he signed with Lord Rothschild (see Rothschild Committee) the agreement known as the
Arreglo Romero, July 7, 1893; regarded as a sound business
deal without political complications, its provisions included:
abandonment by bankers of their claims against Buenos Aires
Water Supply Drainage Company, thus easing the British
Baring Brothers who had underwritten the company; assumption of provincial debts by national Argentine government;
agreement by bankers to accept reduction in interest for five
years and to suspend amortization payments until 1901; ending
of system of guaranteed railway profits and railway claims to
be paid on basis of 50%; Romero operated on principle that
all debt payments should come from national resources rather than new loans; when Sáenz Peña resigned, Romero continued as minister of finance under his successor, José Evaristo Uriburu; later served two consecutive terms in national
congress; retired to private life; died in Buenos Aires.

ROMERO DE PINEDA, LUIS (c. 1635-1695).   Rancher and trader in
Santa Fe area; descendant of conquistadors; inherited land and
acquired more (including site of modern Rosario) through his
services to cabildos of river settlements; engaged in river
trade that took him frequently up and down the Paraná river
from Paraguay to Buenos Aires; concentrated on raising and
selling of mules; is believed to have been first permanent
resident on site of city of Rosario (q.v.).

RONDEAU, JOSE (1773-1844).   Military commander and political
leader during independence period.
        Born in Buenos Aires, father a French merchant;
moved with his family to Montevideo while very young; educated there; left his theological studies in second year to begin military career with Buenos Aires infantry regiment
(1793); fought against Indians and Portuguese Brazilians; took
part in defense of Montevideo against British invasion; captured by Whitelocke's forces, sent as prisoner to London;
regained his freedom and went to Spain; in La Coruña formed
the Buenos Aires battalion to fight against Napoleonic invasion; returned to Montevideo in August, 1810; joined patriots
of May Revolution immediately; commissioned lieutenant
colonel by patriot junta in Buenos Aires and placed in charge
of patriot forces in Banda Oriental (Uruguay); supported Artigas in first siege of Montevideo and fought in second siege;
his brilliant tactics at battle of El Cerrito against the royalists brought his appointment to command of Army of the
North to replace San Martín who had resigned because of illness (1814); served briefly as Supreme Director following
Alvear's removal (1815); returned to Upper Peru to win victory of Puesto del Marqués (q.v.) but to see his army almost
totally disintegrated by defeats of Venta y Media and Sipe

Sipe (qq. v.); turned command over to Belgrano August 7, 1816; returned to Buenos Aires; became interim Supreme Director during difficult period (June 9, 1819-February 11, 1820) following Pueyrredón's resignation; resigned after battle of Cepeda, determined not to become involved in civil wars that followed; returned to military duty in 1824 as brigadier general in command of forces fighting Indians on southern frontier; served as minister of war for Dorrego; later became provisional governor and military commander of new republic of Uruguay (December 1828-April 1830); performed other government functions but after the Uruguayans divided into two politically hostile groups (1836), withdrew from public life; before his death in Montevideo he gave his sword to his godson, artillery sergeant Bartolomé Mitre (q. v.) later to become a leading historian of events in which he had participated; buried in National Pantheon of Uruguay.

ROSA, JOSE MARIA (1846-1929).   Lawyer, financier.
        Born in San Fernando, Buenos Aires; graduated in law; accompanied General Paunero as secretary of legation to Rio de Janeiro (1869); returning to Buenos Aires, held several appointments as judge; retired from bench in 1881 to devote himself to private activities and teaching Roman law in the law school; served as administrator for Banco Nacional and as minister of finance in cabinets of presidents Roca and Roque Saenz Peña; served also as president of the Caja de Conversión; published a study on monetary reform in the Argentine Republic (1909); died in Buenos Aires.

ROSARIO.   City in Santa Fe province, second only to Buenos Aires in size and importance as trade center and port; located on Paraná River about 180-200 miles northwest of Buenos Aires, it is a river port, rail and highway hub, and important industrial center; although its history dates back to the late seventeenth century, its modern development largely began in 1850s.
        The first known resident on the site of Rosario is believed to have been Luis Romero de Pineda (q. v.) who established a home there in 1689 and gathered settlers and workers, most of them from Santa Fe that still suffered frequently from Indian raids; in 1725 Francisco Godoy used this site for an Indian defense post against the raiding Guaycurú tribe from the Chaco; in 1730 the Church established the curacy of los Arroyos there and in 1731 a church named Nuestra Señora del Rosario was erected and its first priest, Ambrosio Alzogaray, opened the parochial books; the settlement centered around this and began, slowly, to grow; apart from Indian attacks, Rosario enjoyed a smooth, peaceful life for next few decades; its economy was based mainly on sale of mules, but also on export of tobacco; the first school was founded in 1778 by order of Viceroy Vértiz; Pedro Tuella (q. v.) published first historical article about Rosario in Telégrafo Mercantil of Buenos Aires; by the May Revolution (1810) town's

population had reached 800; Rosario supported revolution enthusiastically, sending men, horses, and food supplies to support army of the North; when Belgrano arrived in the settlement to set up long-range guns along the river bank, he installed the Independence Battery on which he hoisted the Argentine flag for the first time, February 27, 1812; (in 1957
a massive monument to the Flag was dedicated in Rosario by
President Pedro Aramburu, commemorating this event); militia group defended Rosario and also fought at battle of San
Lorenzo (q.v.), February 3, 1813; during the period of civil
wars in which Santa Fe and other river provinces fought
against the government of Buenos Aires, Rosario's location
between capital city of Santa Fe and Buenos Aires subjected
it to many hardships; one of the worst was its total burning
by Juan Ramón Balcarce in 1819; this episode differed little
from the practice of military leaders on both sides in that
area and the armistice of Rosario was signed shortly afterward, but for some reason it served to fan and rekindle the
flames of littoral provinces' opposition to Buenos Aires for
several decades; meanwhile Rosario remained under power of
caudillo-governor of Santa Fe, Estanislao López (q.v.); on
December 2, 1823, it was constituted a villa, giving it the
right to its own municipal government; in Lavalle's attempt to
take over national government in 1829, Buenos Aires ships
on the river attacked and practically destroyed the city; from
then until the battle of Caseros in 1852 Rosario rebuilt but
grew very slowly; December 25, 1851, Rosario announced its
opposition to Rosas.

After Urquiza's overthrow of the Rosas government,
the provinces and their various cities acquired greater significance; on August 5, 1852, Rosario was advanced legally
to status of city; less than a year later, on July 9, 1853, the
constitution, drawn up in Santa Fe for the Argentine Confederation, was signed by Rosario; Rosario became the official
port of the Confederation as that of Buenos Aires was no
longer available to its provinces; Urquiza's government fostered its growth by encouraging ocean-going foreign vessels
to come to its very good natural harbor; the Banco de la
Confederación, Rosario's first bank, was established in
1854; that same year the first newspaper, La Confederación,
was published by Federico de la Barra; hostilities between
Buenos Aires and the Confederation involved Rosario; even
after Mitre's triumph at the battle of Pavón the people of
Rosario attempted to continue the fighting; in the 1860s, however, Rosario began to enjoy a new prosperity and this increased after Mitre inaugurated (1863) the construction of the
Central Railroad from Rosario to Córdoba, Rosario's first
rail link with interior; when the confederation and province of
Buenos Aires reunited to form the Argentine Republic, the
matter of the location of the permanent capital remained open
for future decision; in 1867 and again in 1876 Rosario was
seriously proposed as that capital, but both presidents, Mitre
and Sarmiento, vetoed it; Rosario continued to grow, becoming

chief port for new commercial agriculture being developed in
that area; its population of 23,000 in 1869 reached 40,000 in
1880s, and with arrival of large numbers of immigrants, multiplied to 220,000 by 1914; Rosario had long since become a
modern, industrialized, cosmopolitan city with the prosperity,
urban and economic problems, cultural and educational attractions and institutions, of such a city; more than half its residents were foreign-born; its natural harbor and port had been
improved in late 1870s by building of railroad sidings, chutes,
grain elevators, etc.; by 1890s Rosario handled 15% of export
trade, nearly 10% of import; development of new ports at Ensenada (La Plata), Buenos Aires, and Bahía Blanca began to
challenge Rosario's place; in early twentieth century, it reno-
vated its harbor facilities, with French capital; Rosario had
also become a force in national political life; it provided
center of Radical revolution under Leandro N. Alem (q.v.);
new revolutionary government was installed in Rosario but
movement failed to win rest of the country; Radical revolution again broke out in Rosario, along with other cities, in
1905 against Quintana's government, and there were later
similar actions and political conspiracies as growing middle
class tended to support Yrigoyen and Radicals; when National
University of the Littoral (q.v.) was founded in 1919, with
divisions in four major cities, Rosario received the faculty
(school) of economic sciences; by 1930 Rosario had become
not only the world's greatest grain port but a very prosperous, modern, cultural industrial center; in 1935 the port of
Rosario became the center of national political controversy;
according to the 40-year contract signed in 1902 as authorized by earlier law of congress, the French company Hersent
et Fils, Schneider et Cie. had the right to exploit the Port
of Rosario for 40 years after which all rights and installations should revert to national government without charge,
provided that the original loan had been amortized by that
time; this investment proved extremely profitable to the
French company and Argentine public, especially the nationalists, confidently anticipated the port's takeover by national
government in 1942, according to contract; in 1935, however,
the Justo government, for its own reasons and using techni-
calities in the contract, signed a new contract with the company, in spite of widespread protest and criticism, including
charge that new contract was illegal; in 1942 President
Ramón S. Castillo took over the port for the government.

By 1940s changes were clearly on the way; world economic depression, shift of British trade to members of its
own commonwealth, increased competition from other Argentine ports, diversification of economy following rise of Perón's
power, with dramatic change from government support of
agropecuarian industries to government regulation of these in
favor of support for diversified industrialization and national
self-sufficiency in mining, fuel resources, and manufacturing
industries, and World War II forcing of changes in trade patterns, brought immediate and continuing losses to Rosario; in

the 1970s Rosario, a city of approximately 900,000, continues to export grain, other agricultural products, and meat, and to support industrial plants processing these, as well as lumber.

See Agustín Fernández Díaz, Rosario desde lo más remoto de su historia (1941); Juan Alvarez, Historia de Rosario (1943).

ROSARIO, ARMISTICE OF (April 5, 1819). Preliminary agreement between Juan José Viamonte, commander of Pueyrredón's national forces and the leader of Santa Fe forces to end fighting; followed by more official San Lorenzo armistice (q.v.) a week later.

ROSAS, JUAN see ORTIZ DE ROZAS, JUAN

ROSAS, JUAN MANUEL DE (1793-1877). Military officer; caudillo; estanciero; controversial governor of Buenos Aires, 1829-1832, 1835-1852, who completely dominated all the provinces during that time and gave his name to that era of Argentine history of which he was both ruler and symbol.

Born in Buenos Aires March 30, 1793, of parents belonging to wealthy, powerful landowning families; grew up on family estancia near Salado; entered Francisco Javier Argerich's school in Buenos Aires at age of eight; interrupted his education to form company of boys to fight against British invasions (1806-1807); given choice afterward between returning to school or going to family ranch at Rincón de López (where his grandfather had been killed by Indians in 1783) he accepted latter, saying that he did not want anything out of life but to be an estanciero; remained there during eventful years following May Revolution; became manager of that estancia in 1811 and quickly proved himself to be adept at all the skills of the gaucho as well as those of management and marketing; in 1820 he married Encarnación de Ezcurra (q.v.); quarreled with his parents over a matter of honor related to his management of the family estate, changed and simplified his name from Juan Manuel José Domingo Ortiz de Rozas to that of Juan Manuel de Rosas, and began his successful career as an independent estanciero; joined with Juan Terrero to establish a saladero (meat salting plant), Las Higueritas, near Quilches; when the government closed it down; the partners purchased an estancia and began a new one; later founded Los Cerrillos on the Salado river near the Indian frontier; his first official action came (1818) with request of Supreme Director Pueyrredón that he assume responsibility for protecting southern frontier against Indian attacks; this he accomplished by treaties with the Indian leaders whom he knew well; the following year he sent the government a plan for the development, policing, and defense of the more remote pampas that foreshadowed the Conquest of the Desert sixty years later; joined Rodríguez's army in Buenos Aires to fight, with Manuel Dorrego, in campaign against José Miguel

Carrera, Carlos M. de Alvear, and Estanislao López in their
opposition to Buenos Aires government; in November 1820,
peace was established between Santa Fe and Buenos Aires,
largely through a gift of 25,000 cattle that Rosas promised to
deliver to Estanislao López, caudillo of Santa Fe; in 1821 he
resigned from army, with rank of colonel; returned to Los
Cerrillos and ranching; continued ready, with his armed peons
and gauchos, to hold frontier safe against Indians; installed
forts along new frontier line; made new agreements with the
Indians, but Rivadavia (then president) refused to accept
Rosas' terms; Indians renewed their attacks and Rosas, whose
ranch was on the frontier, became powerful opponent of Rivadavia; by this time he had become a Federalist, violently opposed to Unitarists led by Rivadavia; after Rivadavia's resignation (1827), Rosas became commander of the militia with
orders to make peace with Indians and establish settlement
in Bahía Blanca; succeeded in moving Indians farther south
and Bahía Blanca was founded; when Unitarist Lavalle ousted
Federalist Dorrego as governor of Buenos Aires, 1828, Rosas
led his own men against him; joined with Estanislao López of
Santa Fe to defeat Lavalle at Puente de Márques April 26,
1829, and in July Lavalle and Rosas signed truce; on December 8, 1829, Rosas became governor of Buenos Aires with
extraordinary powers; from then until February, 1852, except
for brief period 1832-1835, he dominated not only Buenos
Aires but also the provinces.

Rosas appointed able cabinet, including Tomás Guido,
minister of foreign relations, Manuel J. García, of treasury,
and Juan Ramón Balcarce, of War and Navy; one of his first
acts was to hold an elaborate public memorial service for
Dorrego, who had been executed by Lavalle a year earlier;
followed this with confiscation of property from those who
were proved to have taken part in the December 1, 1828,
revolution that overthrew Dorrego's government; used these
funds to compensate veterans of his "restoration" army and
rural farmers and peons who had suffered heavy losses in
the fighting; on January 4, 1831, a peace agreement was
signed restoring peace with the littoral provinces (see Federal Pact of 1831; also called Littoral Pact); when the commission, formed in accordance with this pact, began to plan
definitely for the national congress that it called for, Rosas,
who firmly believed that constitutional national reorganization
would be premature at this time, withdrew Buenos Aires'
support; on December 5, 1832, he was reelected as governor
but he refused, in spite of popular request to serve, as extraordinary powers were not granted him; Juan Ramón Balcarce succeeded to governorship of Buenos Aires but strong
rift developed between his supporters and those of Rosas;
ousted by latter by "revolution of restorers," Balcarce was
followed by Juan José Viamonte (1833-1934); meanwhile Rosas
had gone to south of province to lead expeditionary force into
heart of Indian territory southwest, west, and northwest of
occupied Buenos Aires; a three-year drought had been

disastrous to pasturage of livestock and new lands were essential; with about 2,000 men Rosas pushed the Indians ·far-
ther south, opening up new areas, destroying tribes of important caciques who had been raiding Buenos Aires settlements, killing or capturing several thousand Indians, rescu-
ing about 2,000 long-lost captives from them, and exploring
courses of the Neuquén, Limay, and Negro rivers to the foothills of the Andes; in the end, he made a peace with the Indians, promising necessary food in return for their withdrawal and other concessions, that lasted nearly 20 years; returning to Buenos Aires he was enthusiastically hailed as con-
quering hero; legislature conferred on him the title of Restorer of the Laws ("Restaurador de las leyes"), gave him
the island of Choele Choel (which he refused, accepting
430,000 acres of good grazing land nearer Buenos Aires instead); numerous other honors were bestowed on him; the
government was in shambles; Doña Encarnación and Rosas'
supporters had skillfully manipulated the political situation
against the governments in power during his absence; the secret police, Mazorca (q.v.) had already been created and,
by arousing popular support for Rosas and terrorizing his
opponents, had forced Viamonte out; Bernardino Rivadavia
had returned to the country, after exile of five years, but
was not permitted to remain; already the cinta or divisa punzó (vivid red ribbon or badge--color of uniforms worn by
Rosas' first military unit against the British and later by his
Indian fighters in the south) was beginning to be worn as emblem of Federalist loyalty (later it was required); Rosas'
greatest rival for power, Juan Facundo Quiroga, had been
killed in February 1835; on March 7, the interim governor,
Manuel Vicente Maza, resigned and Rosas agreed to become
governor providing that he be given virtually unlimited executive, legislative, and judicial powers and that a plebiscite approve his appointment; on April 13, 1835, he took office.
    For the first time since the May Revolution, Argen-
tine provinces were united under a central government (in
fact, if not in law) determined to enforce that authority by
whatever means necessary; Rosas immediately dismissed or
retired hundreds of government officials, employees and
army officers whose loyalty to him was not clear; throughout
his administration he crushed opposition--individual, group,
or institutional--ruthlessly and demanded constant demonstrations of loyalty; his purpose, he said, was to maintain peace
and order so that the nation could develop politically, socially, and especially economically. (See listings for events of
this period (1835-1852) included in Historical Chronology,
Appendix II).
    During this period the cattle industry dominated na-
tional life with its demands for more grazing lands, new
sources of salt for the saladeros (q.v.), and Buenos Aires'
increasing monopolization of lucrative trade of salted, dried
beef; in all of this Rosas, himself, was deeply involved as
estanciero, owner of slaughter-houses, saladeros, and salt

monopoly; even shipped his own beef to Brazil and Cuba, etc.;
any opposition or conspiracy against Rosas' government was
viewed as a threat to nation's welfare; Rosas' support came
from 1) the estancieros, especially in province of Buenos
Aires, who shared his interests; 2) the Roman Catholic
Church that he favored in many ways, in contrast to more
secular attitudes of some of his predecessors; and 3) the
poor people who adored him, from urban blacks to rural
gauchos and peons, and even to the Indians; opposition came
from 1) the Unitarists who hated Rosas for his brutal suppression of freedom, were not as deeply committed to cattle
economy as he was, and who believed that nation needed a
strongly centralized, constitutional government, drawn up
along lines of European liberalism and centered in Buenos
Aires from where these ideas and institutions could filter
down to, or be imposed on, the provinces; Rosas, for his
part, despised the Unitarists, blamed them for the civil
wars from which he had rescued the nation, and made "Death
to the Unitarist savage" a common motto; further, as a Federalist, he differed from them in political theory, believing
that national organization must develop from grassroots local
and provincial movements and that only after provinces were
individually ready and had reached agreements among themselves should a national constitutional convention be called;
2) intellectuals and literary writers who criticized him, his
policies and actions, and especially the Mazorca, in their
writings, speeches, and classroom lectures; an important
group was the Asociación de Mayo (q.v.) under leadership of
Esteban Echeverría; most of these went into exile, in Montevideo, Santiago de Chile, and Bolivia where they continued to
fight Rosas, often in novels that have endured, such as Sarmiento's Civilization and Barbarism, Echeverría's Slaughterhouse and Marmol's Amalia, perpetuating image of Rosas as
bloody assassin, tyrant and dictator; criticism of government
in the university brought severe regulation and education generally suffered neglect; 3) provincial caudillos who resisted
Rosas' authority and were immediately defeated and replaced;
4) other provincial caudillos, federalist like Rosas, who resented Buenos Aires' domination of the economy and lack of
interest in developing that of the provinces, and Rosas' refusal to call a constitutional convention; 5) Fructuoso Rivera's
colorados of Uruguay who resented Rosas' attempts to bring
Uruguay back under Argentine domination or sphere of influence; and 6) foreign powers, like England and France, determined to force their imperial control on Argentina to strength-
en their increasing economic domination; usually two or more
of these groups would unite against Rosas but all were defeated until 1852 (see Historical Chronology, Appendix II, for
various revolts, blockades, invasions, etc.).

    In 1851 Justo José Urquiza of Entre Ríos, long one of
Rosas' most important generals, announced his intention of
overthrowing the Rosas government; joined by Unitarists,
Rivera's forces, Brazil (with which Rosas had quarrelled over

Uruguay), and most of the provincial caudillos, Rosas' forces
were defeated at battle of Caseros (q.v.) February 3, 1852;
an era had come to an end, not entirely by force as Rosas'
support turned out to be surprisingly weak, but because it
had outlived whatever usefulness it may have had; within ten
years the nation was united under one president, Bartolomé
Mitre, and the federalist constitution of 1853, drawn up in
Santa Fe; Buenos Aires was forced to share its trade with
the new littoral ranching areas and diversification of economic
development throughout the provinces got under way (see Railroads; Agriculture; Refrigeration; Colonization; Immigration).
        Meanwhile Rosas and his family were taken to England
by British ship; made his home on a relatively small estate
in England at Swarkling near Southhampton where he lived for
nearly twenty-five years, largely on gifts from supporters in
Buenos Aires (even from Urquiza) as his enormous fortune
had been largely confiscated; died and was buried there.
        More than any other figure, Rosas dominates Argen-
tine historiography, which continues to be almost as controversial about his record as were the writings of his contemporaries; in the 1970s most historians tend to agree that his
cruelties were not unique in his period; that he did, in fact,
hold the provinces together until the Argentine Republic could
be formed and that his Federalist ideas are perpetuated in
the nation's constitution; that, in his firm stand against
French and British pressures, he upheld Argentina's sovereignty and dignity firmly (for this the Liberator, San Martín, left Rosas his sword); and that he improved tone of public administration and was personally honest; it has been said
of him that he "assumed power over an anarchy and left it a
nation"; also that he "consolidated what the revolution had
changed"; early histories of Argentina (following national organization) were largely written by those who had overthrown
and replaced Rosas; revisionism began with publication of
Adolfo Saldías' Historia de Rosas y su época, 5 vol., 1881-
1887 (later editions bear title Historia de la Confederación
Argentina); followed by Ernesto Quesada's important La época
de Rosas, first published in Buenos Aires in 1898; more recently there have appeared Clifton B. Kroeber's Rosas y la
revisión de la historia argentina (Buenos Aires, 1965); Emilio
Ravignani's Rosas, interpretación real y moderna (1970);
numerous essays by Enrique de Gandía; and extensive treatment in Vicente D. Sierra's multi-volume Historia de Argentina.

ROSAS, MARIANO.   Chief of Ranqueles Indians, part of Pehuenche
        group.   Captured as a boy, he had been brought up and
        trained as a peon on Juan Manuel de Rosas' estancial El Pino
        in the south; Rosas had served as his godfather when he was
        baptized and he had taken his name; became leader of the
        Ranqueles and dominated Mendoza, San Luis, and part of
        Córdoba; during Sarmiento's administration he signed a treaty
        of peace with Lucio V. Mansilla (q.v.) but later his Indians

fell victims to Roca's campaign to open the northern Patagonian area to settlement.

ROSAS, PRUDENCIO see ORTIZ DE ROZAS, PRUDENCIO

ROSAS DE TERRERO, MANUELA (1817-1898). Daughter of Juan Manuel de Rosas and Encarnación Ezcurra.
 Born in Buenos Aires; given good education, especially in music; popularly known as "Manuelita"; after her mother's death in 1838 she became official hostess for her father, governor of Buenos Aires and, in fact, dictator of all the provinces; talented, spirited, she made her own impact on Buenos Aires society and its many visitors; her father adored her and it was said that she often used her influence on him to soften verdicts and even to persuade him to change political decisions; accompanied Rosas into exile in England in 1852 after the defeat at Caseros; that same year she married Máximo Terrero; died in London.
 Several books have been written about her role in history, including Manuelita de Rosas y Ezcurra by E. F. Sánchez Zinny (Buenos Aires, 1941); Arte e historia by Antonio Dellepiane (1940); and Manuelita Rosas by Carlos Ibarguren.

ROSAS Y BELGRANO, PEDRO (1814-1863). Rancher; military officer.
 Born of white father and black mother in Azul (Buenos Aires); grew up on one of estancias of wealthy Ezcurra family; took part in military action in that area as federalist; acquired land of his own; during Rosas' rule, he served as head of the Azul frontier where he had many Indian friends; after battle of Caseros, he became colonel in command of the national guard; while engaged in defense of Buenos Aires (1853) against forces of Urquiza and Hilario Lagos, he was defeated at San Gregorio, captured, and sentenced to death; at request of diplomatic corps, he was imprisoned instead; his property was confiscated by the government.

ROSSELOT, NAPOLEON (1859-1919). Entrepreneur and public figure, San Juan.
 Born in San Juan of French father and Indian mother; rose from a cattle driver to Chile to financial, industrial leader; bought ranch in the Andes and engaged in his own cattle business; became banker; planted one of San Juan's first modern vineyards and established large winery producing fine wines; active in Radical Party; was campaigning for governor in 1919 when he died in Buenos Aires on vacation; buried in San Juan.

ROTHSCHILD COMMITTEE. International bankers committee, under chairmanship of Baron Nathan Rothschild, appointed to discuss Argentine economic problems with Victorino de la Plaza (q. v.), envoy of President Carlos Pellegrini; three solutions were proposed: the laissez-faire school called for

heavier taxation, a gold-based currency, and immediate payment of Argentine debts (unfeasible, if not impossible, at
that time); a second group offered a small loan to relieve immediate situation, cutting of volume of currency, bank reform,
and new taxes on land and imports; Lord Rothschild suggested
a new loan large enough to permit expansion of the Argentine
economy and to attract new capital; his plan was based on
sound analysis of the real situation in Argentina and recognized that Argentine economy needed a house cleaning to get
rid of corruption, loose credit practices, guaranteed profits
to railway companies, etc., but that the nation would have to
carry it out in its own way; the Rothschild decision was accepted and led to the Arreglo Romero (Romero arrangement
or agreement) signed July 3, 1893, with Argentine finance
minister Juan José Romero; this agreement was not popular
but it worked; seeming only to delay the day that Argentina
had to learn to stand on its own feet financially, it actually
provided the time needed to develop the financial resources
and structure to make this possible (see Juan José Romero
for further details of financial crisis with which this committee was involved).

ROWE, LEO STANTON (1871-1946). U.S. political scientist; Director General of Pan American Union.
        Born in Iowa; received law degree from University of
Pennsylvania (1895) and Ph.D. from German University of
Halle; taught political science at University of Pennsylvania
and international law at its Wharton School of Business; in
1917 resigned from teaching to accept government position;
served two and a half years as chief of Latin American section of Department of State; in 1920 succeeded John Barrett
as director-general of Pan American Union; meanwhile had
formed close ties with Joaquín V. González (q.v.) and with
University of La Plata that conferred doctor of laws degree
upon him; wrote The Federal System of the Argentine Republic (Washington, D.C., 1921), as well as briefer works about
Argentina.

ROYAL HIGHWAY see CAMINO REAL

ROZA, JOSE IGNACIO DE LA (1788-1835). Patriot leader in independence; lawyer.
        Born in San Juan; educated in Córdoba and Chile; ac-
tive in May Revolution; elected to Buenos Aires cabildo in
1812; formed close friendship with José de San Martín before
his own return to San Juan in 1814; served as governor,
1815-1820; during this period aided San Martín greatly in organization of Army of the Andes; founded a hospital and
schools for boys and for girls; promoted agriculture and mining; in 1820 was imprisoned and then exiled by revolt led by
Mariano Mendizábal (q.v.); joined San Martín in Chile and
Peru as judge advocate general of the army; died in Peru.

ROZAS, JUAN MANUEL DE   see   ORTIZ DE ROZAS, JUAN MAN-
UEL

ROZAS DE MANSILLA, AGUSTINA (1816-1898).   Sister of Juan
Manuel, married Lucio N. Mansilla; she was active during
the government of her brother and repudiated his violence;
her son Lucio V. , the writer, published in Paris (1898)
Homenaje a su memoria in her honor (see Lucio Norberto;
Lucio Víctor Mansilla).

ROZAS DE RIVERA, MERCEDES (1810-1870).   Sister of Juan
Manuel de Rosas.   Born in Buenos Aires; wrote a novel entitled María de Montiel (1816), under the pseudonym M. Sa-
sor, in which the novel's heroine is believed to be Mercedes
herself and the hero an officer who died in the battle of
Ayacucho; she died of a heart attack in Buenos Aires.

RUBOLO.   "Nation" of blacks formed December 1, 1826, in
Montserrat on Independence Street; a number of its members
withdrew almost at once and formed a second "nation" called
Ombé (see Naciones).

RUCA.   Araucanian simple shelter consisting of two parallel rows
of poles, those in front about 5 1/2 to 6 feet, those in back
somewhat shorter; hides or (later) sheets of heavy canvas
lashed to these poles formed the walls and roof.
        See Salvador Canals Frau, Las civilizaciones prehis-
tóricas de América.

RUCCI, JOSE (1940-1973).   Secretary-general of the CGT, 1970-
1973; a moderate, he believed in Peronism without Perón;
was killed by leftist Peronist group.

RUIZ DE MONTOYA, ANTONIO (1585-1652).   Jesuit missionary;
student of Guaraní linguistics.
        Born in Lima, son of wealthy Spanish military officer;
entered military service at early age but tired of it; in 1606
he was received into Jesuit order and devoted remainder of
his life to religious study and work, primarily as missionary
to the Guaraní Indians; in 1620 he made his final vows and
was placed in charge of the 23 missions on the Paraná, Uruguay, and Tapé rivers; wrote and published Conquista espiritual, describing the zoology and other features of this new
mission area; was one of the first to call attention to the
natural resource, yerba mate; also one of the first to prepare Guaraní linguistic studies, the Tesoro de la lengua
guaraní and, in 1640, a study of the art and vocabulary of
the language and a catechism that became commonly used;
more than 200 years later, historian Bartolomé Mitre said
of him that this almost forgotten man should be called the
"Bartolomé de las Casas of the Río de la Plata" and that his
linguistic studies of the Guaraní had immortalized him; Father
Ruiz de Montoya died in Lima and was buried near the high

altar of the Templo de los Desamparados; a biography of him
was written by Francisco Xarque (q. v.).

RUIZ GALAN, FRANCISCO (d. c. 1541). Born in Guadix, Spain;
hidalgo; accompanied lifelong friend Pedro de Mendoza to Río
de la Plata, as captain; when adelantado departed for Spain,
1537, he left Ruiz Galán as lieutenant governor of port of
Buenos Aires, subject to authority of absent lieutenant governor Ayolas; for next four years Ruiz Galán attempted to exert
authority as lieutenant governor of entire province, especially
after news of death of Ayolas; established his rule at upriver
forts and settlements of Corpus Christi and Buena Esperanza
but clashed with Martínez de Irala at Asunción; arrival of
royal inspector Alonso Cabrera and latter's recognition of
Irala as lieutenant governor in 1539, backed by the conquistadors there, ended Ruiz Galán's pretensions; he disappeared
from public scene; apparently died before February 1542 when
records show his heirs settling his estate; Ruiz Galán, in
Mendoza's name and in fulfillment of latter's contract with
emperor, had faithfully established churches in settlements,
using timbers from wrecked Santa Catalina for church in
Buenos Aires; and had worked diligently to secure adequate
supplies for his men from Brazil and the Indians; never became popular with conquistadors because of his harsh, unwarranted punishments of both Indians and Spaniards who incurred his wrath, and the general belief that his personal am-
bition led him to falsify official documents to his own advantage.
        See Lafuente Machain in Suggested Readings, Appendix
III.

RUIZ GUIÑAZU, ENRIQUE (1882-1967). Jurisconsult; university
professor; historian; diplomat and foreign minister (1941-
1943).
        Born in Buenos Aires and educated there, graduating
in the faculty of law and social sciences; served as professor
of finance and political economy in same faculty (1912-1930)
and of law in the faculty of juridical and social sciences at
La Plata (1924-30); meanwhile, was director of legal affairs
for the Banco Hipotecario Nacional and had begun publishing
scholarly legal and historical studies; from 1931 to 1941 he
handled Argentine diplomatic assignments in Europe, first in
Switzerland as special envoy and then as plenipotentiary minister (1931-1938), acting also as permanent delegate to the
Geneva Society of Nations; his next appointment was as ambassador to the Vatican, 1939-1941; from this, he was summoned back to Buenos Aires to become foreign minister in
the cabinet of Acting President Ramón S. Castillo; during the
next two years (1941-1943) Ruiz Guiñazú played a key Argentine role in the complicated international situation created by
World War II, especially after the United States had been
drawn into the war following the Japanese attack on Pearl
Harbor; Castillo was determined that Argentina should remain

neutral and his foreign minister adhered strictly to this poli-
cy, even though it brought him directly into conflict with the
United States at the conference of foreign ministers held in
Rio de Janeiro in 1942 (see World War II); after the fall of
Castillo's government by military takeover in 1943, Ruiz
Guiñazú returned to Europe as ambassador to Spain; during
his diplomatic career he had received honors from such
countries as Peru, Bolivia, Brazil and Spain.

Among his published historical works are La tradición
de América (1930); Lord Strangford y la Revolución de Mayo
(1937); Proas de España en el mar magallánico (1945); El
deán Diego Estanislao Zavaleta (1950); Mitre y el estado de
derecho (1957); El presidente Saavedra y el pueblo soberano
de 1810.

RUIZ HUIDOBRO, PASCUAL (d. 1813).   Spanish naval officer; governor of Montevideo (1803-1807); supporter of May Revolution
in Buenos Aires.

Born in Cádiz; entered naval career in 1769; eventually attained rank of lieutenant general; arrived in Río de la
Plata area in 1777 with expedition of Pedro de Ceballos;
named civil and military governor of Montevideo in 1803 and
remained in that post during British invasions (1806-1807);
supported Liniers in organizing his forces to reconquer
Buenos Aires from Lord Beresford in the first invasion; led
unsuccessful defense of Montevideo against British invasion in
1807, was captured and sent as prisoner to England; in 1808
he returned to Spain and was once again appointed governor
of Montevideo; refused this appointment and went, instead, to
Buenos Aires where he became inspector of the military forces
of the viceroyalty; as a member of the cabildo abierto of
May 1810, he was one of the Spaniards to support the cause
of the patriots; on his way to Chile he died in Mendoza, 1813,
and was buried there in the Cathedral; because of his contributions to the patriot cause, the government voted a pension
to his widow, María Josefa Morales de los Ríos.

RUIZ MORENO, ISIDORO (1876-1952).   Lawyer and law professor;
government official.

Born in Concepción del Uruguay; studied in universities of Buenos Aires and Córdoba; graduated in law and social
sciences; combined law career, usually teaching or acting as
legal counsel with government service, at first in Córdoba
and later (about 1909) in Buenos Aires; served as provincial
deputy, legal counsel for Banco Nación, minister of finance,
colonias, and public works, and professor of sociology in
faculty of law in Córdoba; went to Buenos Aires as national
deputy for Córdoba in 1908; in 1909 began teaching in law
faculty of University of La Plata; 1912-1935 taught international law at University of Buenos Aires with title of full professor after 1919; meanwhile (1912-1920) served as director general of national territories; served on university council, La
Plata, 1916; was ambassador and legal counsel for ministry

of foreign relations; wrote extensively on legal subjects; died
in Buenos Aires.
   His published works include: Finanzas públicas, gastos
públicos; Propaganda argentina en América (1912); El nuevo
derecho internacional público (1920); La teoría de la adminis-
tración nacional (1929); Lecciones de derecho internacional
público (1940); Manual de derecho internacional público (1943);
his papers and archives form important source for material
of his period.

RUIZ MORENO, MARTIN (1833-1919).   Political leader and historian.
   Born in Rosario, Santa Fe; became one of first to
graduate from the famous Colegio del Concepción del Uruguay;
graduated in law, taking his doctorate in Montevideo, 1861;
married niece of Urquiza and was closely linked to him politically; served as deputy in confederation congress; following battle of Caseros carried out confidential mission from
Urquiza to Mitre that laid basis for reconciliation; was member of first national congress; belonged to Adolfo Alsina's
Autonomist party; in 1864 presented project for repatriation
of remains of San Martín; opposed war with Paraguay; supported autonomy of Entre Ríos under López Jordán (q. v.);
became chief of police in Rosario and in 1866 defeated the
Indians threatening that city; moved to Entre Ríos for political reasons; served in its legislature until 1874, when he
was again elected to national congress; edited in Buenos Aires
the newspaper El Río de la Plata; returning to Entre Ríos
he held official positions in both Paraná and Concepción del
Uruguay; served as president of provincial constituent congress in 1909; devoted much of his later life to historical
research and writing, as well as legal subjects; his particular interest lay in the recent history of his own area, as
shown in such works as: his studies on life and works of
General Francisco Ramírez (1894); Cepeda y Pavón (1901);
La organización nacional (1906); La presidencia de Santiago
Derqui y la batalla de Pavón (1913); Contribución a la historia de Entre Ríos (1914), etc. ; died in Buenos Aires.

RUMBOLD, SIR HORACE.   British Ambassador to Argentina 1880-
   1881.   Six years after his return to England, published his
   observations in the Great Silver River.   Notes of a residence
   in Buenos Aires in 1880 and 1881, which has historic interest
   and serves to interpret an epoch.

RUZO, ALEJANDRO (1885-1939).   Jurisconsult.   Born in Catamarca; graduated in law, Buenos Aires, 1906; became secretary of Joaquín V. González, minister of interior; when national department of labor was created he was assigned to its
   legislative section; became president of this; taught finance
   in the law school, becoming full professor in 1924; lectured
   on labor law at the Sorbonne in Paris; received membership
   in French Legion of Honor; in 1925 became national senator

from Catamarca; removed by revolution of 1930; died in
Buenos Aires; published Origen de las asociaciones obreras
en la República Argentina; Legislación del trabajo; Curso de
finanzas y de legislación financiera argentina.

RUZO, EUSEBIO GREGORIO (1795-1828). Public figure; military
man.
     Born in Catamarca; educated in Córdoba; served as
governor of Catamarca 1822-1825; during his administration
the provincial constitution was signed; represented La Rioja
in national congress, 1826; reelected as governor of Catamarca in 1827 he resigned for health and political reasons;
died the following year.

- S -

SAA, JOSE FELIPE (1820-1880). San Luis caudillo during civil
wars; brother of caudillo Juan Saá.
     Born in San Luis, son of José Saá, of Galicia; joined
with his brother Juan Saá (q.v.) and other Unitarists in offering support to army of Lamadrid and Lavalle; after latter's
defeat at Famaillá, 1841, he joined his brothers in seeking
refuge with Ranqueles; emigrated to Chile; returned to Argentina after fall of Rosas; joined Confederation army and accompanied his brother Juan while latter was governor of San
Luis (1860-1861); fought in Pavón with Urquiza; again went to
Chile; returned to province and, in 1867, with Col. Juan de
Dios Videla, he organized revolution against President Mitre's
government; ousted Justo Daract as governor of San Luis replacing him with Videla; three days later Saá was defeated by
national forces; his brother Juan had just returned to the
province and renewed the fight; together they were defeated
at San Ignacio and emigrated to Chile; in 1877 José Felipe
returned to San Luis where he lived quietly until his death.

SAA, JUAN (1818-1884). One of pair of caudillo brothers in province of San Luis.
     Born in San Luis; joined Unitarist political party as
young man and fought under General Paz; after Unitarist
armies had been defeated at Quebracho Herrado November 28,
1840, and disbanded shortly thereafter, he fled with his
brothers to the Ranqueles Indians; united them under his
leadership and led them in savage raids against frontier settlements of San Luis and Córdoba for six years; later emigrated to Chile; returned to San Luis after fall of Rosas
(1852) and joined Confederation army; became governor of
San Luis in 1860; following the assassination of interim governor José Antonio Virasoro (q.v.) of San Juan, President
Derqui appointed Saá as interventor in that province, sending
two liberal negotiators, Colonels Paunero and Conesa to accompany him as sign of government's impartiality; Saá dismissed the latter, and joined battle with liberal forces,

defeating Aberastain in very bloody battle of Pocitos January
11, 1861; all prisoners were executed, including Aberastain;
execution of latter (for which Saá may or may not have been
directly responsible), a highly respected Liberal leader, was
unanimously condemned by Mitre, governor of Buenos Aires,
President Derqui of Confederation, and Urquiza; feeling ran
high throughout the provinces; while Derqui attempted to restructure situation in San Luis and Córdoba around Juan Saá,
Congress of province of Buenos Aires repudiated Pact of San
José de Flores; in Battle of Pavón that followed, September
17, 1861, Saá, as colonel, fought alongside Urquiza and,
after latter's defeat, went to Chile and then to Europe; returning in 1867, he took over leadership of the rebellion of
cordillera provinces against Mitre's government while latter
was commanding allied forces in Paraguayan War (q. v.);
forced to return to Argentina to restore order, Mitre's army,
under José Miguel Arredondo, defeated Saá in battle of San
Ignacio; he went back to Chile where he died many years
later.

SAAVEDRA, CORNELIO (1759-1829).   Hacendado and merchant;
    president of first patriot junta; commander of Patricios.
          Born in Potosí, son of prominent porteño father and
    mother from Potosí; family moved to Buenos Aires where
    boy attended Real Colegio de San Carlos, then entered busi-
    ness world; in 1801 he served as second alcalde of cabildo
    and in 1805 was appointed grain administrator; began his mili-
    tary career when British invaded Buenos Aires, 1806; organ-
    ized the Patricios (q. v.) and became their first commander;
    in January 1807 took them to Montevideo to help prevent
    British capture of that city but arrived too late; led them in
    fight against second British invasion, 1807, as well as in
    successful defense of Viceroy Santiago de Linier's govern-
    ment against revolution of January 1, 1809, led by Martín de
    Alzaga; was important leader in events that led to calling of
    cabildo abierto of May 22, 1810; his point of view, expressed
    both publicly and to the viceroy, was shared by the majority--
    that the viceregal authority should be dissolved as the time
    had come for Buenos Aires to assume responsibility for its
    own destiny and government; became president of First Junta
    (q. v.); rift developed between the younger, more radical fol-
    lowers of junta secretary Mariano Moreno, who wanted to
    create an immediate institutional revolution led and controlled
    by Buenos Aires, and those more conservative followers of
    Saavedra who preferred more gradual change, with powers
    shared by representatives of all the provinces; in revolution
    of April 5-6, 1811, the latter won; the Junta was already
    weakened, however, and the disastrous defeat of the patriot
    army at Huaqui (June 20, 1811) eventually ended it; on August
    26, 1811, Saavedra left Buenos Aires in personal attempt to
    reorganize the army of the North; eight days after his arriv-
    al in Salta he received word that political events in the capi-
    tal in September had resulted in his dismissal and a new

government; he was also ordered to turn over command of
the army to Juan Martín de Pueyrredón; for the next few
years Saavedra went through a series of vilification campaigns, charges and trials, and exile from the Morenistas
(see Triumvirates for government changes in period 1811-
1814); when Gervasio Posadas became Supreme Director
(1814) he attempted to force Saavedra to undergo traditional
residencia trial (Spanish judicial review of official at end of
term); Saavedra took refuge in Chile but San Martín, then
governor of Cuyo, permitted him to return to make his
home quietly in San Juan; in 1818 the national congress
cleared him of all charges and Supreme Director Pueyrredón
made him a brigadier general in the national army (retro-
active to January 14, 1811) and appointed him chief of staff;
undertook various military inspection tours and brought
Ranqueles Indians to peace terms; spent period of anarchy
(1820) in Montevideo but returned to Buenos Aires during
government of Martín Rodríguez; retired to private life; offered his services during war with Brazil--rejected because
of his advanced age; died in Buenos Aires; his memoirs were
published in 1910 and a statue erected in his honor in Buenos
Aires.

See Enrique Ruiz Guiñazú, El presidente Saavedra y
el pueblo soberano de 1810 (Buenos Aires, 1960); Guillermo
Furlong, S. J., Cornelio de Saavedra: el padre de la patria
(Buenos Aires, 1966).

SAAVEDRA, MARIANO (1810-1883). Hacendado; political and public leader during early years of national reorganization; governor of province of Buenos Aires.

Born in Buenos Aires while his father, Cornelio, was
president of patriot First Junta; after family's return from
exile, he grew up on its estancia in Zárate; joined enemies
of Rosas and, after two narrow escapes from assassination,
spent rest of Rosas period in exile in Montevideo; returned,
following Caseros, to become deeply involved in life of his
province; served terms in both houses of legislature and was
member of national congress; as governor of Buenos Aires
for two terms, he played constructive role in easing acceptance of Mitre's compromise formula by which Buenos Aires
served as temporary national capital at same time that it
remained provincial capital; during his administration he extended railroads to south, north, and west; regulated public
finances; founded several new settlements and established
many primary schools, as well as the department of exact
sciences in the university; drew up rural legal code; served
as director of major slaughterhouses in Buenos Aires and
was president of the Banco de la Provincia; a wealthy man,
he refused to accept compensation for public service and often contributed his own funds to public causes; during Paraguayan War Saavedra responded to government's request loan
of 500,000 from its citizens by placing 200,000 pesos at its
disposal; died in Buenos Aires where he was accorded respect

and honor usually only held by military heroes or national
political leaders.

SAAVEDRA LAMAS, CARLOS (1878-1959). Jurisconsult; statesman
and diplomat; Nobel Peace Prize laureate, 1936.
Born in Buenos Aires of aristocratic family; graduated
in law from university; married daughter of President Roque
Saenz Peña; devoted himself primarily to public service,
along with teaching and writing in legal field; taught in national universities of La Plata and Buenos Aires; as member
of Chamber of Deputies in 1912, he was largely responsible
for passage of protective tariff that saved national market for
Tucumán sugar industry; served as minister of justice and
public instruction in 1915; selected to preside over national
centennial of Declaration of Independence (1916) in Tucumán;
his great interest lay in foreign affairs; an ardent nationalist,
he sought to increase his country's prestige by strengthening
ties with Europe and by attempting to assume leadership in
Latin America; in 1928 he presided over the International
Labor Conference in Geneva; served as foreign minister for
President Agustín P. Justo from 1932 to 1938; during this
critical period Saavedra Lamas faced world depression, establishment of totalitarian powers in Europe, increasing interest of United States in hemispheric affairs, under F. D.
Roosevelt's Good Neighbor Policy, violent warfare between
neighboring Paraguay and Bolivia; he was determined that
Argentina should play an important role of its own in international affairs; opposed all U.S. intervention, preferred bilateral economic treaties, and hoped to work for international
peace through League of Nations rather than purely hemispheric agencies; U.S. Secretary of State Cordell Hull was
equally determined to push U.S. hemispheric policies, especially as U.S. did not belong to League of Nations; Saavedra Lamas pushed for an anti-war pact throughout Latin America and eventually got large number of signatures as well as
international recognition; through mutual collaboration between
Hull and Saavedra Lamas at Seventh Inter-American Conference, in Montevideo in 1933, much progress was made; by
1936, however, Saavedra Lamas had become disillusioned with
Pan American attempts to bring Chaco War to an end, Argentina had renewed its active membership in League of Nations
and Argentine foreign minister was serving as president of
the Assembly; through combination of efforts the Chaco War
was approaching peace settlement, and Nobel Peace Prize for
1936 was awarded to Saavedra Lamas in recognition of his
efforts in that direction; at the 1936 Inter-American Conference in Buenos Aires, Saavedra Lamas and Hull clashed;
former still held to faith in League of Nations; Roosevelt and
Hull wanted hemispheric solidarity in face of approaching
European War; former has been criticized for clinging too
long to traditional policies and hence delaying Argentina's
preparation for problems of World War II; when war broke
out, however, Saavedra Lamas criticized President Castillo's

pro-Axis neutrality; in the 1940s he went back to teaching, serving as rector of the University of Buenos Aires, 1941-1943, and professor of labor law, 1943-1946; supported U. S. ambassador Braden's stand against Perón; served as vice president and president of academy of law and social sciences, 1952-1954; was awarded many international honors such as Grand Cross of the Legion of Honor, Southern Cross (Brazil), Order of Merit of Chile, etc.; died in Buenos Aires province.

Among his many published works are Los asalariados en la República Argentina; Reformas orgánicas de la enseñanza pública; Los ferrocarriles ante la legislación positiva argentina; El carácter de los cursos intensivos; Las cajas de previsión social; Por la paz de las Américas; and El doctor Luis María Drago, su obra internacional.

SABATO, ERNESTO R. (1911-). Internationally recognized literary writer and intellectual.

Born in Rojas, Buenos Aires, son of immigrants; received his doctorate in physics at National University of La Plata where he later (1940-1945) taught mathematical physics after having done advanced work (1938-1939) in atomic radiations in Joliot-Curie laboratory in Paris and at Massachusetts Institute of Technology; as a student he had opposed corruption in government and its manipulation by party in power; had become a leader in Communist youth movement and attended International Communist Congress in Brussels; broke with party and returned to Argentina; continued interest in political affairs but turned from science to the humanities; when he lost his teaching position at La Plata in 1945, for political reasons, he began to devote himself almost exclusively to writing in many forms, from political and sociological essays for popular periodicals and newspapers, including La Nación, to philosophical treatises in scholarly journals, and to works of fiction; in 1955 he was removed as editor of Mundo Argentino because of his attacks on President Pedro Aramburu; in 1958 he was designated as envoy extraordinary and minister plenipotentiary; Sábato has visited and lectured in various U. S. universities and in Europe; received many international honors, including membership in the Club of Rome, Chevalier of Order of Arts, in France; won literature prize in Stuttgart in 1973 and Grand prize of Argentine Writers Society in 1974.

One of the earliest of Sábato's published works was an essay on cosmic radiation; two of his best known are his two novels, El túnel, 1948, and Sobre héroes y tumbas, 1961, considered among best Argentina has produced in twentieth century; in these he undertakes a search for Argentine identity and social morality through studies of various Argentine groups and customs; other works include Uno y el universo, 1946 (won municipal prize of Buenos Aires); Hombres y engranajes, 1951 (essays); El otro rostro del peronismo, 1961; El escritor y sus fantasmas and Absalón el exterminador, 1963; and Claves políticas, 1971.

SAENZ, ANTONIO (1780-1825).   Priest; lawyer and law professor;
    patriot leader and signer of Declaration of Independence;
    first rector of University of Buenos Aires.
        Born in Buenos Aires, son of wealthy Spanish mer-
    chant and public official; studied at Colegio de San Carlos,
    then took his doctorate in law at university in Chuquisaca,
    with Mariano Moreno, Teodoro Sánchez Bustamante and Mari-
    ano Boedo as fellow students; ordained as priest by arch-
    bishop in Chuquisaca; returned to Buenos Aires where he com-
    bined ecclesiastical duties with public responsibilities, serv-
    ing as lawyer for the poor in 1806, and attorney of cabildo
    in 1807; joined patriot cause in 1810 and voted in cabildo
    abierto of May 22 to remove Viceroy Cisneros; became a
    member of the Patriotic Society and Lautaro Lodge; was fre-
    quently called in to serve in government posts, as legislator;
    or for writing official statements and legal statutes; repre-
    sented Buenos Aires at Congress of Tucumán in 1816; exerted
    considerable influence in appointment of Pueyrredón as su-
    preme director; signed Declaration of Independence; in many
    respects his greatest contribution lay in field of education;
    strongly supported establishment of a public library and was
    one of first to contribute books toward it; during political
    anarchy of 1819-1820, he devoted himself to drawing up plans
    for organization and curriculum of University of Buenos Aires
    that Rivadavia wanted to establish and became its first rector
    when it opened August 12, 1821; taught courses in law there;
    as university was designed to be capstone of new educational
    system for educating Argentine youth for the new national
    independence, Dr. Sáenz interested himself in creation of
    primary schools, especially outside the city where they were
    lacking and in finding or writing adequate new text books; in
    1822 was one of founding members of literary society; died in
    Buenos Aires, and, as a special honor, was buried inside the
    church of San Ignacio where the university first held classes.
        His biography forms part of Monsignor Nicolás Faso-
    lino's history of the University of Buenos Aires (Buenos
    Aires, 1921).

SAENZ, MARIO (1879-1943).   Jurisconsult; legislator; professor.
        Born in Pergamino, Buenos Aires; took his doctorate
    in jurisprudence in law school there, 1906; served as private
    secretary to Norberto Piñero, minister of finance, and then
    as undersecretary in same ministry under Dr. Elodoro Lobos;
    became federal interventor in Jujuy; joined Unión Cívica Ra-
    dical and was elected to Chamber of Deputies (1936-1940),
    where he became chairman of Finance Committee; devoted
    much of his time to teaching in the law school, where he
    served as dean in 1921, and in school of economics; in 1925
    was vice president of the university; published several law and
    history books, including some textbooks; among his works are:
    Moreno y Rivadavia (1903); Curso de régimen agrario (1918);
    La filosofía del derecho en la enseñanza universitaria y en la
    vida; La vida y obra de Rivadavia; died in Río Hondo, Santi-
    ago del Estero.

SAENZ, MIGUEL ANTONIO (1782-1862).   Chief of police in early
national period; merchant.

Born in Buenos Aires; studied at Real Colegio de San
Carlos; began organization of police department in 1813, serving as chief of police of Intendencia de Policía until this was
closed in 1815 and replaced by sectional offices; served until
1821 as accountant in Buenos Aires government; returned to
police duty in 1826 when Rivadavia appointed him chief of
police again and then sent him to Montevideo to organize the
police force; returned to Buenos Aires, retired from police
department; became a commission broker from then on; died
in Buenos Aires.

SAENZ PEÑA, LUIS (1822-1907).   Lawyer; President of the Republic, 1892-1895.

Born in Buenos Aires; studied there, graduating in
law, 1845, with Bernardo de Irigoyen, Rufino Elizalde, Federico Pinedo, and Delfín Huergo; began his public life as
member of the Buenos Aires constitutional convention of 1860
where he supported Buenos Aires' incorporation into the Argentine Confederation; served as provincial senator (1870),
national congressman (1873) and was elected lieutenant governor of the province of Buenos Aires in 1874; served in
National Congress 1880-1882, then became member of Buenos
Aires Supreme Court, becoming its president almost at once;
served as president of Banco Provincial; in 1890, during
presidency of Carlos Pellegrini, he was named minister of
the National Supreme Court; as elections of 1892 approached,
there was feverish activity on part of Civic Union that hoped
to win presidency with Bartolomé Mitre and conservative
group that wanted to continue Pellegrini's policies; both
parties suffered divisions and a large new group of influential young Argentines (called Modernists because of their
desire for reform) broke away from the official Partido
Autonomista Nacional (PAN) and nominated their own candidate, Roque Saenz Peña; frightened at thought of change
latter's election might bring, Mitre, Roca, and Pellegrini
brought the more conservative groups together and proposed
a slate with 70-year-old Luis Sáenz Peña, young Roque's
father, for president and José Evaristo Uriburu as vice president; Roque withdrew his candidacy and his father became
president; he faced a nation in financial trouble--with the
crisis of 1890 not yet solved and nation still facing bankrupt-
cy--and political turmoil on every level from party to province to congress and cabinet; there were 23 cabinet crises
and several revolts by the Radical Civil Union group; in
spite of difficulties, progress was made in several areas;
ports of Buenos Aires and Rosario were improved, provision
made for permanent location of Colegio Militar and Escuela
Naval; navy increased in size; Buenos Aires was modernized,
a medical legal code passed, second national census projected and Dirección General de Estadística de la República
established; lack of personal political support became critical;

when he refused, as matter of principle, to follow advice of
Mitre and Roca, latter turned congress against him; his devout Catholicism had made him oppose some of Roca's secularization program and his long-expressed ideas about electoral reform (later carried out by his son, as president)
turned more conservative members of oligarchy against him;
as Radical opposition became more and more threatening he
decided to accept Pellegrini's suggestion and brought Aristóbulo del Valle (q. v.) into his government to reorganize the
cabinet in an attempt to create a reforming revolution from
the top; unfortunately, at this very time revolutions led by
Leandro N. Alem's Unión Cívica Radical followers, long
under way, broke out in provinces of San Luis, Santa Fe,
and Buenos Aires; Alem called on del Valle to join but latter
refused to fight against government of which he formed part,
but resigned along with rest of cabinet; revolution spread to
Corrientes and Tucumán, as well as other provinces; the
president placed entire nation under state of siege and by
end of the year, law and order had been restored and Radical leaders had largely gone into exile; pressures continued
on Sáenz Peña, now especially, from the leaders of the
acuerdo that had put him in office; it became increasingly
difficult for him to get cabinet ministers and, finally, when
congress insisted on passing a law of amnesty for leaders of
1893 revolt against his wishes, Luis Sáenz Peña resigned and
was succeeded as president in January, 1895, by his vice
president José Evaristo Uriburu; he retired to private life;
died in Buenos Aires.

SAENZ PEÑA, ROQUE (1851-1914).   Lawyer; statesman and diplomat; President of Argentine Republic, 1910-1913; one of leaders of intellectual Generation of 1880.
        Born in Buenos Aires, son of President Luis Sáenz
Peña; interrupted studies in law school to join national guard
in opposition to Mitre revolution in 1874; graduated in law,
1875, and entered political life as Autonomista; served briefly in lower house of Buenos Aires provincial legislature and
then resigned; when Pacific War broke out between Chile,
Bolivia, and Peru, he joined Peruvian army (apparently because of an unrequited romance) in 1879; wounded during defense of Arica, he was taken as prisoner but released shortly afterward; after a brief period as undersecretary to foreign
minister Bernardo Irigoyen, he toured Europe with his friends,
E. Ramos Mejía, Paul Groussac, and Carlos Pellegrini; returned to join in founding of Sud América, 1885, in which he
and Pellegrini, along with others of Generation of 1880 expressed their ideas about Americanism and Argentine inter-
nationalism, as well as their political opposition to Dardo
Rocha; began his diplomatic career (1884) by serving as Argentina's ambassador to Uruguay; one of Argentina's representatives at the Congress of international law in Montevideo,
1887, and at meeting of South American nations in 1888; in
1889-1890 he was spokesman for Argentine ideas at first

Pan American congress, Washington, D. C. ; his opposition to
U. S. efforts to establish a customs agreement within the
Americas, and to what Saenz Peña and many other Argentines regarded as a Yanqui attempt to dominate entire Western
hemisphere, found full expression in his speech of March 15,
1890, before the assembled delegates: rather than a policy of
"America for the Americans" as Latin Americans interpreted
U. S. policy, he demanded "Let America be for humanity!";
his words captured imagination of young idealists and political
leaders both in Europe and in Latin America and were widely
regarded as one of Argentina's most important foreign policy
statements; later, in 1910, on a trip to Rome, as newly
elected president, he was honored and given a gold medal
with these words inscribed upon it; in his own country, this
slogan was repeatedly used to express Argentina's determination not to accept U. S. provincial hemispheric policies but to
recognize instead Argentina's international obligations to both
Old and New Worlds; eventually, in 1913 shortly before Saenz
Peña s death, ex-U. S. President Theodore Roosevelt made
such an effective show of U. S. friendship in Buenos Aires
that La Prensa suggested that the two contradictory slogans
be combined into "the America of the Americans for themselves and for humanity"; meanwhile, for nearly a quarter of
a century Roque Saenz Peña's position affected inter-American
affairs and helped to develop Argentine sense of identity and
its foreign policy.

Returning to Buenos Aires from Washington, Saenz
Peña briefly served as foreign minister in 1890; in 1891 he
was selected by new group of "Modernists" as candidate for
president in the forthcoming elections; withdrew when his
father was nominated by a coalition group (see Luis Sáenz
Peña); after his father's election as president (1892) he moved
to Entre Ríos and retired to private life while his father remained in power; returned to political activity after 1895; in
1898 his strong attachment to Spain led him to denounce U. S.
actions in Spanish American War and to repeat his familiar
accusation of U. S. hypocrisy regarding the Monroe doctrine;
elected national congressman in 1906; served as president
of Argentine delegation to Second Hague Conference, 1907;
became ambassador to Spain in 1908; was elected president
of Argentine Republic in 1910; progress of many kinds was
made during his administration but his great contribution was
getting Congress to pass a satisfactory electoral law (see
Saenz Peña Law) in early 1912; in the elections of April of
that year, the Unión Cívica Radical returned to the polls
from its abstentions in protest and the law was given its
first trial, in provincial elections; the president was forced
by increasing illness to turn his authority over to vice president Victorino de la Plaza in October, 1913; died in Buenos
Aires in August of the following year.

See Felipe Barreda Laos, Roque Saenz Peña (Buenos
Aires, 1954).

SAENZ PEÑA LAW (1912). Group of election reform laws passed
in 1912 that became collectively known as Saenz Peña Law
because of the influential role played by President Roque
Saenz Peña in drawing them up and getting legislation passed
through Congress.
        For some time political leaders of various parties had
been seriously concerned about electoral reform; under the
oligarchy, elections had become fraudulent and corrupt, with
less than 10% of the qualified voters participating; Radicals
had abstained from voting as a protest and many others simply felt that elections were futile; in an attempt to make democracy genuinely effective, Roque Saenz Peña made the construction of major electoral reform the core of his entire political program as president; he and Indalecio Gómez (q. v.),
his minister of interior, wrote the laws that required new
and honest registration of voters--male citizens at age of 18
were required to register for military service with this listing also serving as voter registration; voting was made compulsory; secret ballots were to be used to prevent coercion
of voters such as that of workers by employers or tenants by
landlords; to ensure participation of minority groups in election, provision was included for an "incomplete ballot" with
a larger portion of posts going to majority party, a smaller
to minority, regardless of actual number of votes cast; this
was designed to encourage development of strong 2-party government as best safeguard for stable political development; it
failed to work out and was eventually replaced by a quota
system; in other respects, the Saenz Peña Law revolutionized
Argentine political processes; strictly enforced, at first, it
brought the voters to the polls in large numbers; the political power of the oligarchy was curbed and way was open to
middle and lower classes to participate in political processes;
Radicals won the next elections.

SALADEROS. Meat salting plants that for the first time made extensive commercial use of Argentine meat; dominated economic and political life of Argentina for more than half a
century following the May Revolution and independence movement.
        Argentines early used drying processes to make
charqui and tasajo (qq. v.) of some of the abundant beef available; as early as 1602 its exportation was authorized by
Philip III and in 1605 first shipload left Buenos Aires for
Cuba; pattern remained relatively unchanged, with most of
meat left unused, until some time after middle of eighteenth
century when a combination of factors brought the saladero
into Argentine life; the increasing demand for hides and tallow had resulted in slaughter of about 600,000 cattle annually; Argentine meat consumption used only one-fourth of
stripped carcasses; cattlemen were eager to find profitable
use for rest; at same time the development of larger European navies and more numerous tropical plantations in Brazil
and Caribbean areas created a need for preserved meat as

basic food for larger number of sailors and slaves; and the
Spanish Bourbon government was eagerly seeking new sources
of royal revenue that would also bring economic development
to its American colonies; in 1778 Minister José de Gálvez began urging the establishment of saladeros in Río de la Plata
area; he sent reports and experts to describe the process to
be used; salt could be imported from Spain while Argentine
sources were sought (and quickly found); as the operation required that meat be left in a salt brine, coopers were sent
from Spain to train creoles to make the barrels needed; first
saladero in Río de la Plata, actually a meat processing and
meat packing factory, was established near Colonia, Uruguay,
in 1784; in 1793 royal order provided for free exportation of
salted meat; first saladero in Argentina was established at
Quilmes in 1795; saladeros were established in all coastal
areas for salting beef, and in Santa Fe they were used for
fish; the business began to expand rapidly in Argentine independence period and estancieros gained considerable political
and economic power; most of them became federalists to preserve the important meat trade developed by saladeros as
monopoly for Buenos Aires province; provincial federalists
joined in their opposition to Rivadavia's unitarist government
and caused its fall; the Rosas era began, with Rosas the
leading exponent of saladero economy and a government directed towards interests of saladeros; system expanded until
fall of Rosas (1852) and continued dominant until replaced by
refrigeration processes in late nineteenth century; during
those decades the saladero had brought Argentina prosperity,
strengthened those groups that wanted easy access to world
markets, stimulated improvement of ports, roads from estancias to ports, acquisition of ships for trading, development of barrel industry, and exploitation of salt in Salinas
Grandes and elsewhere; it had also affected the pattern of
land tenure and delayed development of agriculture (see
Cattle; Charqui; Salinas Grandes; Refrigeration).

Suggested references: Alfredo J. Montoya, Historia
de los saladeros argentinos (1956); Peter H. Smith, Politics
and Beef in Argentina: Patterns of Conflict and Change (New
York, 1969); Miron Burgin, The Economic Aspects of Argentine Federalism, 1820-1852 (Cambridge, Massachusetts,
1946); H. J. Cuccorese, Historia económica argentina (Buenos
Aires, 1970); and James R. Scobie, Argentina, a City and a
Nation (New York, London, and Toronto, 1971).

SALADO RIVER (Río Salado). At least two rivers of historical interest in Argentina bear this name: one, in eastern Buenos
Aires province, flows into Samborombón Bay and formed
southern boundary between Argentine settlement and Indian
territory in late eighteenth and early nineteenth century.

Most important Salado river is that which rises in
Nevado de Acay in Salta and flows generally south and east
through provinces of Salta, Santiago del Estero, and Santa
Fe, entering the Paraná River near city of Santa Fe; its

unpredictable water flow has been a problem for Santiago del
Estero since its founding in sixteenth century as it needed
the water for irrigation, navigation, and even for hydroelectric power; it was not until the 1950s that these began to be
readily available.

River was first visited by Juan de Garay before his
founding of Santa Fe in 1573; during colonial period several
expeditions sought to navigate it; in the late eighteenth century the Italian doctor, Paolo Montegazza, called attention in
his Cartas médicas to its potential for giving new life to
province of Santiago del Estero (q. v.); on February 13, 1813,
Belgrano had his patriot Army of North swear allegiance to
the Argentine flag along its banks in Salta and the river in
that area is still known by name "Juramento" (the swearing);
in 1855 T. J. Page (q. v.) navigated 900 miles on the river in
a specially-built ship; but was forced to continue his trip
overland to Cueva del Lobo in Santiago del Estero; mapped
area traversed; in 1860s attempts were made to deepen channel or construct a navigable canal; Spanish engineer Esteban
Rams y Hubert (q. v.), made such a study and was enlisted
by Thomas J. Hutchinson (q. v.), British consul at Rosario,
for similar project in connection with his desire to promote
cotton industry in area; Hutchinson described his experiences
on the Salado in his various writings (see Santiago del Estero
for effects that these early failures to provide river navigation had on the economic development of the province).

SALALA, BATTLE OF (February 10, 1817). Site in northern
Chile of military victory by northern wing of Army of the
Andes over royalist forces; enabled patriots to occupy forti-
fied coastal town of Coquimbo, as planned, two days before
San Martín's victory over main Spanish force at Chacabuco
(see Juan Manuel Cabot, leader of San Martín's unit at Salala).

SALDIAS, ADOLFO (1850-1914). Historian; journalist; political
figure.
Born in Buenos Aires; studied under Amadeo Jacques;
graduated in law; attracted to politics, he became an Autonomista; elected to Buenos Aires legislature in 1877; became
involved in 1880 revolution and went to Europe; there he published Los minotauros in which he criticized revolution of
1880; returning to Argentina, he collaborated with Sarmiento
(who had admired his earlier Ensayos sobre la historia de la
constitución argentina) in La eneida en la República Argentina;
became interested in study of Juan Manuel de Rosas and
Rosas' family provided him with many documents for his research; published Historia de Rosas y su época (3 v. , Paris,
1881-1887); later editions of this masterpiece contain five
volumes and are entitled Historia de la Confederación Argentina; in 1888 edited Rosas' Las instrucciones para los estancieros: papeles de Rosas, 2 v. appeared in La Plata,
1904-1907; meanwhile he had been continuing a somewhat
turbulent political career; exiled again after his participation

in 1890 revolution, and later to Uruguay after criticism of
the government in newspaper El Argentino; became lieutenant
governor, 1890, and was elected to senate in 1894; in 1898
became public works minister for Bernardo de Irigoyen,
governor of Buenos Aires province; during this period he
wrote Cervantes y el Quijote, a work very well received by
critics; worked for constitutional reform in province of
Buenos Aires; in 1910 appointed federal interventor in La
Rioja; died in Bolivia while carrying out a diplomatic mission; other works by Saldías include Juicio político del Presidente Roca; La evolución republicana durante la revolución
argentina (1906); Estudio sobre Alberdi; Vida y escritos del
Padre Castañeda.

SALDIAS, JOSE ANTONIO (1891-1946). Writer; dramatist.
        Born in Buenos Aires; after studying in Colegio Na-
cional Norte, he entered Naval Academy; left it for career
in journalism and the theater; following 1939 he taught scenic
art and related studies in national conservatory of music; became director of national institute of theatrical studies and
of national theater museum; contributed to Crítica, La Razón,
La Ultima Hora, and La Nación; wrote about 60 works, including plays, novels, and short stories; included are Pecado
sin belleza; Un juramento de amor; La gringa Federika, Romance federal y provinciano, and El gaucho Robles; died in
Buenos Aires.

SALESIANS. Members of religious order La Pía Sociedad de San
Francisco de Sales founded in Italy in 1841 by Don Bosco for
purpose of educating and caring for young boys; made important contributions to education, especially in Patagonia, during century following 1875.
        The first Salesians, a group of 10 led by Father Juan
Cagliero, arrived in Argentina in 1875, followed by similar
groups almost immediately; the female auxiliary or coordinate group, Instituto de Hijas de María Auxiliadora began its
work among girls shortly afterwards; from the beginning,
Salesians turned their attention to the establishing of various
kinds of schools, with special attention to those needed by
Italian immigrants, whom they had come to serve; among the
early schools opened were the first vocational technical school
of Argentina, named Pío IX, in 1881 (still in existence), and
first agricultural school, 1894; meanwhile their attention was
turned to needs of Patagonia; Father Santiago Costamagna
accompanied Roca's expedition in 1879, beginning final conquest of the desert and, with all of Patagonia being opened
for settlement and Indians brought under government control,
the Salesians moved in to become preeminent in that area;
by 1894 they had reached Tierra del Fuego; missionaries provided schools, homes, and Christian religious teaching to Indians, as well as schools on all levels for white boys and
girls, many of them boarding schools to better serve the
families of the sparse, widely separated settlers; although

primary schooling and academic education were given full attention, the Salesians more and more began to place their emphasis on the new kinds of schools that Argentina needed, such as agricultural and teacher training schools, business colleges, etc.; several of these have become very influential in their various regions, like the vitivinicultural (wine growing and processing) school of Mendoza, the agricultural school of Pindapoy in Misiones and that of Viedma (Río Negro); much of this was due to initiative of Father José Vespignani (q. v.).

The Salesians also introduced the boys' organization Exploradores de Don Bosco, similar to that of Boy Scouts.

See Raúl A. Entraigas, Los salesianos en la Argentina (4 v., Buenos Aires, 1969-1972) for scholarly documentary study of early years, 1874-1885.

SALGUERO Y CABRERA, JERONIMO (1774-1847).   Government official; signer of Declaration of Independence.

Born in Córdoba, his mother a descendant of founder of that city; graduated from university there; supported May Revolution of 1810 and represented province of Córdoba at Congress of Tucumán where he signed the Declaration of Independence; most of his life was spent as government official in his native province until the political conflicts of the Rosas period forced him into exile; street in Buenos Aires named for him.

SALINAS GRANDES (great salt beds).   Name applied to various extensive salt deposits found from north to south along dry western and southwestern edge of pampas and elsewhere.

Historically, the name frequently denotes the Salinas Grandes nearest Buenos Aires, in southwestern pampas of that province and what is now La Pampa; during late viceroyalty and most of nineteenth century these were essential to the important meat industry (see Saladeros).

Although their existence was well known in earlier times, they first were exploited on large scale during period of viceroyalty (see La Pampa; Manuel de Pinazo; Pablo Zizur; and Pedro Andrés García); during middle decades of nineteenth century Araucanian Indians under Calfucurá (q. v.) established their rule there; after Conquest of the Desert by Roca (c. 1880), Salinas Grandes again became important source of salt for Buenos Aires; in modern times in industrial plant, la Compañía Introductora de Buenos Aires, S. A., has processed salt there for shipping throughout the country.

SALINEROS.   Name by which Indians living in area of the great salt lagoons (Salinas Grandes) in Córdoba were known in the sixteenth century; lived by hunting, food gathering, and a little planting of corn and squash; the tribal groups included Tobas, Quiningitas, Mogas, and Amanaes; several of these were conquered by Tristán de Tejeda in 1591.

SALTA (City).   Capital of province of Salta (q. v.).   For more
than two centuries (late sixteenth to early nineteenth) Salta
was commercial and cultural center of the northwest; its
wealth, prestige, and concentration of artists made it one of
the most beautiful cities in colonial Argentina; several of
these old buildings have been restored and named as national
monuments; pride in its historic past has led Salta to preserve this colonial type of architecture in new buildings; as
a result, Salta has unique attraction for tourists who come
also for other reasons.

City was founded in Valle de Salta, April 16, 1582,
by Hernando de Lerma (q. v.), governor of Tucumán; it was
named San Felipe de Lerma in honor of King Phillip II and
of the founder (name changed shortly afterward to San Felipe
de Salta); city was laid out, a church started, and corn and
wheat were planted; first flour mill was built in 1585; his
successor, Juan Ramírez de Velasco, ensured the town's
survival and promoted its growth; brought in new settlers;
established new towns, Jujuy to the north, and Madrid to the
south; cabildo building was begun in 1586 and finished in
1593; in 1676 the cabildo and jail were rebuilt as they appear
today; were declared national monuments in 1937; the Franciscans built the first church, started in 1582 and destroyed
by fire in 1680; in 1690 a new church was finished but the
present church was not begun until 1759; in 1586 a hospital
was begun by Governor Rivera; construction on the modern
cathedral began in 1858; in it is lodged the image of the
Cristo del Milagro (see Salta's Fidelity Pact with the Señor
del Milagro); other very old buildings still exist in the city.

The city of Salta came under the jurisdiction of governor of Tucumán; other cities grew around it, like Nuestra
Señora de Madrid de Estero (1609) and Nuestra Señora de
Guadalupe, founded to defend Salta from Indian attacks; the
city of Salta continued to grow in size, wealth, and in culture and the arts; its silversmiths and wood carvers became
well known; in the eighteenth century the city became the
capital of the Tucumán governors; among them was Gerónimo
de Matorras, cousin of José de San Martín's mother, and
pacifier of the Great Chaco; at that time the population of
the city had 4,020 inhabitants (see Salta Province, for historical role of city).

SALTA (Province).   Extreme northwestern province, with capital
of same name; dating from late sixteenth century, it has
conserved much of its colonial architecture and social structure but is again emerging, in 1970s, as powerful force in
national life; name is apparently of Indian origin, meaning
place of stones or place of rest.

Boundaries.   Lies between 22° and 26° 23' S. latitude
and 62° 21' and 66° 44' W. longitude; bounded on north by Bolivia and Jujuy; on east by Formosa and Chaco; on south by
Santiago del Estero, Tucumán, and Catamarca; and on west
by the Andes and Chilean boundary and Jujuy.   Area: 59,600

square miles. Population (1970): 509,803; population density is 8.5 persons per square mile. Cities: Salta, capital;
population 121,569 (1960); other cities are Metán, Embarcación,
Candelaria, Cafayate, Rosario de la Frontera, Rosario de
Lerma, Tartagal, and General Güemes.
          Geography and climate. There are two main geograph-
ic regions: a plain with marshes and forests; in the east
these share the Chaco characteristics; the other, in the west,
is mountainous, with lovely valleys like that of Lerma, in
which the capital city of Salta is located; the famous Puna of
Atacama, the dry, cold mesa or plateau where the Aymara
Indians live, begins in the northern part of Salta and extends
into Bolivia; most important river is the Salado (q.v.), known
as the Juramento in Salta, and the Bermejo (q.v.) flowing
through northeastern Salta on its course from Bolivia to the
Paraguay River; Salta's variations in climate--dry with mild
winters in the west, humid and subtropical in the east--make
it an ideal winter resort; agricultural development varies
with the climate.
          Economy. Tobacco and vineyards form important part
of agricultural development; latter produce a dry wine similar
to that from La Rioja, Spain; central valley produces sugar,
corn, rice, vegetables, cotton, citrus fruits, potatoes and
sweet potatoes; Salta has extensive forests, estimated at 10%
of all forests in Argentina; Western Salta has several mining
operations; gold in the Calchaquí valley, silver mixed with
copper pyrites in Cerro Bayo, salt in Salinas; petroleum and
natural gas have been found in several places; YPF engineers
believe that Salta has largest gas deposits in country and perhaps most extensive borate deposits in the western hemisphere;
small deposits of uranium and other minerals have been found;
Salta's industries process its own products: sugar-mills,
petroleum refineries, tobacco factories, wineries, and lime,
cement, and wood industries.
          History. First settlement in Salta was its capital city
of same name in 1582 and province grew up around it (see
Salta (City) for part of colonial history); as the city and
province developed in commerce, wealth, and prestige, it
constantly, during seventeenth century, also had to serve as
center of defense against attacks of Calchaquí Indians; by
1650 the city had 500 inhabitants, three conventos--Jesuit,
Mercedarian, and Franciscan--a cabildo, a public mill, and
a Jesuit secondary school; elementary education was in hands
of Franciscans; in 1692 earthquakes almost destroyed both
Salta and Jujuy; Indians from Chaco were causing trouble,
even invaded the city in 1736; after several expeditions they
were finally defeated in 1750s; expulsion of the Jesuits caused
new Indian uprisings; expedition into Gran Chaco in 1775 finally brought peace with Mocovíes.
          During eighteenth century Salta's growth in population
and its importance as a layover stop for trade and travelers
on the royal highway from Buenos Aires to Lima made it so
important that government took note; first it became the

capital for the governor of Tucumán (replacing Santiago del
Estero) and then, in 1785, it was made the capital of the
newly-created intendancy of Salta, including not only city of
Salta but also Jujuy, Tucumán, Santiago del Estero, Tarija,
Nueva Orán, and La Puna; first governor, Andrés de Mestre,
established a primitive postal service and built roads and
bridges to link the interior with the capital; Salta received its
first theater in 1789 and another secondary school was established in 1799; in 1806 Salta sent troops that fought effectively against British in Buenos Aires; several foreigners came
to live in Salta during early nineteenth century; Italians involved in agriculture; French, in commerce; British, like
José María Todd, pharmacist; and North Americans, like
Joseph Thomas Redhead, botanist and physicist; these gave
Salta aspect of cosmopolitan center.

Salta recognized authority of May Revolution and patriot junta, June 19, 1810, but differences arose at once between
local supporters of the patriots and those of the royalists;
Buenos Aires sent Feliciano Antonio Chiclana to take over as
governor but conflict continued; Belgrano's defeat of royalist
forces in battle of Salta (q.v.) February 20, 1813, finally
brought Salta firmly over to patriot side; province accepted
authority of General Assembly of 1813 and sent José Moldés
and Pedro Agrelo as its representatives; the following year
Director Posadas divided the intendancy into the separate
provinces of Salta and Tucumán; Salta included Jujuy, Orán,
Tarija, San Carlos, Valley of Calchaquí, Lerma, and Santa
María, and La Puna; first governor, Hilarión de la Quintana,
was disliked and soon removed; Martín Güemes became governor and combined his progressive civil administration with
heroic defense of Salta's borders against royalist invasion
(see Martín Güemes); defeated Spanish forces six times;
served as early exponent of Federalism and of new liberal
social ideas favoring the workers, especially the gaucho; sent
José Ignacio de Gorriti, Mariano Boedo, and José de Moldés
as Salta's representatives to Congress of Tucumán; Güemes
not only had to fight against the invading royalists and the
wealthy estancieros who protested his reform measures, but
also had problems with revolts in neighboring Catamarca and
with Bernabé Aráoz, governor of Tucumán, who wanted to
annex Salta; after Güemes' death in 1821, the Salteños continued fighting the royalists and won their peace with them a
few months later; Salta drew up its first constitution in
August 1821, and elected José Antonio Fernández Cornejo as
governor.

During the next dozen years Salta was torn by civil
conflict, largely between the former followers of Güemes who
were Federalists and those who supported the Rivadavia Unitarists in Buenos Aires; the Gorritis were active during this
period, with José Ignacio de Gorrita representing the Buenos
Aires group and his brother José Francisco de Gorriti (qq.v.)
on the Federalist side; in spite of political conflict, the province made progress internally, establishing new schools,

introducing compulsory smallpox vaccinations; under Juan Antonio Alvarez de Arenales (1823) the first printing press was
brought in and the Revista de Salta began publication under
direction of Hilario Ascasubi; census taken in 1825 showed
40,000 inhabitants; when Lavalle took over government in
Buenos Aires in 1828, Juan Ignacio Gorriti became governor
again of Salta (1829) and joined the League of the Interior;
opposed by the Federalists of Salta, the pro-Güemes gauchos,
and their ally, Governor Felipe Ibarra of Santiago del Estero,
who invaded the province, Gorriti fled to Bolivia; rivalries
between Pablo de la Torre and Alejandro Heredia (both having served as Salta governors) threatened such serious trouble
that former caudillo of La Rioja, Facundo Quiroga, was sent
from Buenos Aires to restore peace; succeeded in his mission but was murdered while returning; during the 1830s Salta
continued to suffer from conflict as it struggled toward progress; it lost territory (Valley of Balboa) to Catamarca and
Jujuy broke away to form separate provinces; rebelled
against Rosas in 1840 under Governor Solá; and in 1842
Lavalle and his Unitarist forces reached Salta; he was defeated by Manuel Oribe at Famaillá and the rebellion against
Rosas was crushed, with the leaders beheaded; in 1844 Manuel Antonio Saravia (q.v.), a patriarchal figure in Salta political life, became governor and progress began again; during
his administration Salta was struck by a series of earthquake
tremors that lasted fifteen days; during this terrible experience the people made a holy vow to commemorate annually
the divine intervention that saved them (see Salta's Fidelity
Pact with the Señor del Milagro); after defeat of Rosas in
1852, Tomás Arias became governor; he attended meeting at
San Nicolás; Salta sent representatives to the Santa Fe constituent congress and became part of the Argentine Confederation under Constitution of 1853; Salta still suffered from
strife between supporters of its liberal governors who attempted secularization programs and those Conservative
Catholics who opposed them, and attacks at the same time
from neighboring provinces led by La Rioja caudillo Angel
Vicente Peñaloza (El Chacho) and Felipe Varela from Catamarca; meanwhile national census of 1869 showed the province's population to be 88,933.

In the 1870s Salta finally gained peace and some progress; telegraph lines were installed in 1871-1873, hospitals
and public buildings were constructed; the first public library
was built in 1873; the first daily newspaper La Reforma, was
published in 1875; the first normal school was founded in
1880, the same year in which the telephone reached the city;
the provincial bank was founded in 1883; irrigation ditches
were dug to prevent floods; kerosene public lighting was installed in 1887; cholera broke out in 1887 and killed several
hundred people (one-third of the population), but as a result
the city built its first Health Center; the railroad reached
the capital on February 20, 1889; streets were paved in 1893,
and in 1896 the first electric lights were turned on in the

city; running water came to the capital in 1904 and was in
use throughout the whole province by 1920; the modern province of Salta is a winter resort because of its mild climate;
its cities are linked to the rest of the country by the General
Belgrano railroad that continues north to Jujuy and La Quiaca,
and east to the Paraná River system; airlines join it with the
populated eastern part of the country.

For decades modern Salta has maintained an almost
traditional society, relatively untouched by the radical changes
that have transformed the coastal area; recently, however, it
has given birth to the montoneros, originally an extreme leftist youth movement, that has become a powerful group dedicated to overthrow of the established government.

SALTA, BATTLE OF (February 20, 1813).   Important patriot victory over royalist forces invading northwestern Argentina from
Upper Peru; said to have been only instance of surrender of
complete royalist force, in pitched battle, to patriots during
Argentine war for independence.

Following Belgrano's defeat of royalists at battle of
Tucumán (September 24, 1812) latter retired and, under Spanish general Pío Tristán, entrenched themselves in Salta; Belgrano attacked him there and in a hard-fought battle so completely defeated the royalists that Tristán requested terms of
surrender; patriots took 3500 prisoners, 2 battle flags, 10
cannons, 2000 firearms, and 200 swords; Belgrano released
officers after pledge not to fight against patriots again; this
battle, along with the earlier one of Tucumán, under such
adverse circumstances, made Manuel Belgrano a national
hero and brought national honors to him and all his officers
and men; resulted in resignation of Goyeneche, royalist commander and cleared way for new patriot offensive into Bolivia,
and politically and militarily consolidated May Revolution in
northern Argentina.

SALTA'S FIDELITY PACT WITH THE SEÑOR DEL MILAGRO.
Declaration of faith carried in solemn procession by the authorities of Salta every September 15; custom began during
the earthquake of 1844; its accompanying festivities have
made Salta important modern tourist attraction.

SALVADORES, ANTONINO (1898-1953).   Historian; educator.
Born in Bahía Blanca; studied in La Plata, graduating
from faculty of humanities and sciences of education, 1920;
later received title of Doctor of History; was a founding member of Center for Historical Studies, National University of
La Plata, where he taught; was also active member of Sociedad de Historia Argentina de Buenos Aires, and of the Instituto Sanmartiniano; Professor Antonino was active in various
historical congresses, presenting monographs in several; contributed to Revista de Historia de América and was responsible for several chapters in Historia de la nación argentina,
published by Academia Nacional de Historia; also contributed

to Boletín del Instituto de Investigaciones Históricas of the
University of Buenos Aires and other scholarly journals; his
special field of research was the historical development of
public instruction in Argentina but he also wrote other historical studies, including Alberdi (1948); died in La Plata.

SAN ANDRES, SCHOOL OF. One of earliest private British
schools in Argentina; founded in 1840 under leadership of
John Rae and Miss Dick; at first a primary-secondary school
for girls, it later became coeducational; after other moves,
it was established in 1947 in larger, more modern quarters
on calle Nogoyá, Olivos, Buenos Aires.

SAN CARLOS (March 8, 1872). Another name used for battle in
which Ignacio Rivas inflicted final defeat on Indian cacique
Calfucurá; declared an historical site in 1943 (see Calfucurá;
Pichi-Carhué).
       See Manuel Prado, La guerra al Malón (Buenos Aires,
1960).

SAN CRISTOBAL DE BUENAVENTURA. Name of the first ship
that left Buenos Aires after Juan de Garay's refounding of
the city in 1580.

SAN FRANCISCO CHURCH IN SALTA. First church built in city
of Salta (1582). On the day after founding of city of Salta,
the Franciscan friar Bartolomé Cruz began construction of a
primitive mud and straw church on site designated for this
purpose; used until replaced in 1674; this second church structure was destroyed by fire (1757); present church was begun
in 1759 according to plans of Vicente Muñoz and dedicated for
use in 1796; throughout colonial period San Francisco church
and monastery served as center of Franciscan missionary
work among the Indians as well as providing religious ministry to creoles in area; declared historical monument in 1941.

SAN IGNACIO, BATTLE OF (April 1, 1867). Site, in province of
Mendoza, of battle in which vanguard of Paunero's national
army, commanded by José Miguel Arredondo, defeated rebellious forces led by Juan Saá and Juan de Dios Videla; this
ended the so-called "rebellion of the colorados" against President Mitre's government; to a certain extent this also marked
the end of internal political disputes prevalent there in 1860s
among former Unitarists in the Cuyo provinces with authority
of legal constitutional government of Mitre accepted.

SAN ILDEFONSO TREATY (1777). Agreement signed in Europe between Spain and Portugal to end hostilities in the Río de la
Plata region; this treaty preceded the Treaty of El Pardo
signed in March, 1778, that established the final boundaries
between Portugal and Spain in America.
       By the 1760s three European powers controlled the
Americas, while others like the French, the Dutch, and the

Russians possessed some land; the Spaniards and the Portuguese held power in South America, the British in North America; in the Plata region the Portuguese had established Colonia de Sacramento (q.v.) in modern Uruguay from which they attacked Martín García and Rio Grande do Sul (occupied by the Spaniards at that time); in 1776 Portugal attacked Rio Grande but was forced by foreign powers to suspend hostilities; Charles III, taking advantage of the British involvement in American Revolution and of the friendliness of the French, decided to determine control of Río de la Plata region once and for all; Spain's situation was also favored by the friction existing at that moment between Portugal and its ally Great Britain growing out of British minister's statement in Madrid that his government considered the situation in the Río de la Plata to be a simple boundary dispute; Charles then commissioned Pedro de Ceballos (q.v.) to take military action against the Portuguese in the Banda Oriental; Ceballos won a quick victory; the Portuguese left Colonia and Uruguay came under Spanish control, giving Spain domination of both banks of the river; Ceballos received news of the treaty before he could attack the Portuguese Brazilian colonies as planned; boundary commissions were appointed and the lines that they established between Brazil and the new Viceroyalty de la Plata (q.v.) were more or less accepted by the countries involved when they achieved national independence; they also formed basis upon which disputed boundaries were finally to be negotiated in the late nineteenth century.

A side effect of San Ildefonso Treaty was that it effectively ended, or at least postponed for several years, Charles III's early consideration of joining North American colonies in their fight against England to strengthen Spain's own cause against England's ally, Portugal.

SAN JOSE, PALACIO DE. Home of General Justo José de Urquiza in Entre Ríos on Uruguay River near Concepción del Uruguay; begun in 1848 and completed eight years later, it was the most sumptuous Argentine building of its time; history of province of Entre Ríos centered around it for many years; Urquiza signed his pronouncement against Rosas there on May 1, 1851, and was himself assassinated at San José April 11, 1870; it was declared a national monument in 1935 and became a property of the State in 1936.

SAN JOSE DE FLORES, PACT OF. Agreement signed between Argentine confederation and province of Buenos Aires on November 11, 1859, following defeat of latter at Cepeda, that provided for national reunion; Buenos Aires was to be incorporated into the confederation but was granted the privilege of studying the constitution and suggesting changes to be considered by a national constituent congress; this pact marked defeat of the Buenos Aires separatists like the Alsinas, Pastor Obligado, and Carlos Tejedor, but it took three more years of negotiations and fighting (see Battle of Pavón) before reunion was accomplished in election of Bartolomé Mitre as president of the Argentine Republic.

SAN JUAN (Province and City). San Juan Province is the most northern of the three western provinces forming the region of Cuyo; settled by Spaniards from Chile in middle of sixteenth century and governed from there until establishment of viceroyalty in 1776; described in writings of Domingo Faustino Sarmiento, its most famous native son.

Location and boundaries. Province lies between 28° 37' and 32° 20' S. latitude and between 66° 50' and 70° 35' W. longitude; bounded on north by La Rioja, on east by La Rioja and San Luis; on south by San Luis and Mendoza (the other two Cuyo provinces); separated from Chile on the west by the cordillera of the Andes. Area: 33,200 square miles. Population (1970): 384,284 with a density of 12 persons per mile. Capital: City of San Juan, estimated population (1970) 110,000; among other towns are Rawson, Rivadavia, Jáchal Caucete, Pocito Abardón, San Felipe, Pampa del Chañar, and Las Casuarinas, with urban and rural populations about equal.

Geography and climate. San Juan is mountainous in west where its ranges form part of the Andes on border with Chile; these mountains are rich in minerals and especially valuable for geological studies; fertile valleys, like those of Jáchal and Calingasta are in eastern part of mountains; farther east there are fertile plains in the north and desolate desert in the southeast; rivers are scarce but San Juan, Jáchal and Bermejo can be used for irrigation; thermal and medicinal springs, like those at Pismanta, Piedra Pintada, Zonda, Chaparro attract tourists; climate is very cold in winter and hot and dry in summer, with little rainfall; in the spring, the Zonda blows for days at a time, a hot, suffocating, dusty wind originating in valley of the same name.

Economy. From the time of the Indians San Juan's economy has depended on agriculture based on irrigation; in modern times growing of grapes both for table and for wine has taken up half the cultivated land; apples are grown in valley of Calingasta and elsewhere; other important crops are olives, for oil and table use, onions, and garlic; mining operations include exploitation of marble, magnesium, sulfur and sulfate, silver, quartz, malachite, and salt; some copper, iron, and gold ores are found there, as is petroleum.

History. In 1562 Juan Jufré y Montesa, sent by Governor Francisco de Villagra of Chile with small group of Spaniards, established a new city, north of Mendoza in valley of Catalve where Huarpe Indians lived; this city was named San Juan de la Frontera as it lay near the boundary of Tucumán and was formally dedicated June 13, 1562; later (1593) it was moved by Luis Jufré (son of Juan) south a few kilometers to avoid floods of the San Juan River; by the early seventeenth century San Juan was still small (24 vecinos) but was surviving and beginning to ship fruit and a little

wheat to neighboring areas; the Dominicans had already established their convento there, with a primary school almost
from the beginning; in 1732 they established a school for
training Dominican novices, in which Fray Justo de Santa
María de Oro (q. v.) began his religious training (see Cuyo
for general economic and social conditions during colonial
period); Jesuits arrived in 1655; planted vines, wheat, corn,
olive and fruit trees; produced alcohol; established a mill; at
beginning of eighteenth century, the Jesuits established a
center there with a church that eventually (nineteenth century)
became the cathedral of diocese of Cuyo; black slaves were
brought in to work the mines, replacing the Indians who had
disappeared or been sent to Chile; in 1776 city of San Juan
was almost destroyed by an earthquake and in that same year
it was separated from Chile and made part of the viceroyalty
of the Río de la Plata; some of the Portuguese that had surrendered in Santa Catarina were sent to San Juan where they
became active in agriculture and commerce; in 1784 San Juan
became part of Intendancy of Córdoba; prospered during closing years of viceroyalty; prisoners from British Invasions
were interned there, 1806-1807; many remained to become
citizens and establish families; when news of the May (1810)
Revolution reached San Juan, along with orders from Governor-Intendant against recognizing it, San Juan called a cabildo
abierto, read both communications, and then recognized the
Buenos Aires Junta July 28, 1810; in 1813 the triumvirate
created the intendancy of Cuyo, reuniting Mendoza, San Juan,
and San Luis; in 1814 José de San Martín became governor intendant, and the following year San Juan had a lieutenant governor who was a native of the province and a close friend of
San Martín's, José Ignacio de la Roza; during the next five
years, 1815-1820, San Juan cooperated fully in both civil and
military movements of independence; sent Narciso Laprida
and Justo José Santa María de Oro as representatives to Congress of Tucumán (1816); contributed more than 40,000 gold
pesos, 3333 mules, and large supplies of horses, food, and
clothing to San Martín's Army of the Andes; San Juan militiamen accompanied latter on crossing over the mountains to
Chile early in 1817 and returned with royalist prisoners from
battle of Chacabuco; at the same time Governor de la Roza's
government brought progress to the province; promoted agriculture, commerce, mining, and industry (wine, alcohol, and
mules); widened and paved streets in town; constructed roads
to the mines, irrigation ditches; established free education--
Escuela de la Patria; ordered compulsory vaccination against
smallpox; signed Agreement of Cuyo, 1819, with Mendoza and
San Luis for mutual defense against invasion; in January,
1820, Governor de la Roza was deposed by his brother-in-
law Mariano Mendizábal who was leading his regiment of
cazadores de los Andes in the famous revolt known by his
name (see Mendizábal, Revolt of); anarchy reigned in San
Juan for a few years; in 1820 the province declared its own
independence; in 1821 Chilean José Miguel Carrera invaded

847   San Juan

the province but was defeated by combined forces of Mendoza
and San Juan at Punta del Médano; in 1825, San Juan drew
up its Carta de Mayo, one of first provincial constitutions in
Argentina; written by Salvador del Carril, it has been called
a true "decalogue of liberalism"; Governor del Carril (1823-
1825) introduced first printing press into the city, published
first newspaper Defensor de la Carta de Mayo, founded the
welfare society, improved police department, ordered the
first agricultural census, and created the Justice department;
attempted to do for San Juan what Rivadavia was doing for
Buenos Aires but his revolutionary ideas brought about his
removal; in 1827 Federalists took over but anarchy continued
until 1836 when Nazario Benavídez assumed power; from 1836
to 1855 he governed province; schools were opened; newspaper El Zonda appeared; during this period Sarmiento and
Aberastain were young men; they joined in founding a cultural movement under the leadership of Manuel Quiroga Rosas,
a member of Asociación de Mayo.

In 1851 Benavídez declared the province an ally of
Rosas, but in 1852 gave his support to Urquiza; during late
1850s internal conflicts in San Juan became factor in delaying conciliation between Buenos Aires and the Confederation
as three governors in succession--Benavídez, Virasoro, and
Aberastain--met violent deaths as series of government interventions from Derqui's government were met with determined
opposition from people of San Juan, while Buenos Aires was
strongly critical of Confederation methods; Juan Saá, as interventor, defeated Antonino Aberastain's forces decisively
at La Rinconada January 1, 1861 but his subsequent execution of Antonino Aberastain, without trial, shocked the country; Domingo Faustino Sarmiento became governor of San
Juan in 1862; faced problems with El Chacho (Peñaloza) but
gave his home province excellent government; founded hospitals, schools, built roads, slaughterhouse, installed kerosene
illumination, and fostered establishment of agricultural colonies; resigned in 1864 to carry out diplomatic mission in
U.S.; Governor Camilo Rojo (q.v.) continued Sarmiento's
progressive policies; in the 1880s Governor Anacleto Gil
(1884) saw continued modernization of city and province; running water was installed, the telegraph and railroad came to
San Juan giving it access to coastal markets again; first
loan bank was established; in 1894 severe earthquake destroyed city of Albardón; political unrest, 1898-1903, brought
federal interventions but in early decades of twentieth century
the Cantoni brothers, Aldo and Federico maintained themselves in power for most of the time; antipersonalist radicals,
they opposed Yrigoyen's personal control and were popular
with people of San Juan; Federico granted voting rights to
women in 1923.

On January 15, 1944, San Juan was practically destroyed by the most severe earthquake in its history; it was
one of the nation's greatest catastrophes; tremors continued
for several months; victims buried in the ruins numbered

more than 10,000 and almost the entire city had to be rebuilt,
making it one of the most modern cities in Argentina, a few
historic buildings could be restored but, for the most part,
they had to be razed to the ground and new buildings constructed; San Juan's main products continue to be agricultural
(especially grapes and wines) and mineral (silver, petroleum,
copper); its people are mainly Spanish-mestizo with Italian and
German immigrants added; San Juan has distinction of contributing a large number of notable leaders in national political, literary, and scientific history, especially in period between May Revolution and national organization of all the
provinces; among these are: Antonino Aberastain, Salvador
María del Carril, José Ignacio de la Roza, Sarmiento, José
Alvarez, Saturnino Salas, Indalecio Cortínez, fray Justo Santa
María de Oro, Guillermo Cortinez, Guillermo Rawson, etc.

SAN LORENZO, ARMISTICE OF (April 12, 1819). In 1818 Supreme
Director Juan Martín de Pueyrredón sent government forces
under Juan Ramón Balcarce to suppress revolt of littoral
provinces; Balcarce faced guerrilla warfare in Santa Fe in
which Estanislao López's forces would fight and then withdraw, devastating the land through which they passed; after
varying initial successes and defeats, General Balcarce occupied Rosario but soon decided to withdraw and burned city
as he left; discouraged, he resigned, and Juan José Viamonte
was sent to replace him; meanwhile General Manuel Belgrano
was obeying government orders to bring most of his Army of
the North to aid in this pacification effort; sent reinforcements
ahead to join Viamonte; these troops were defeated at Barrancas March 10, 1819; without waiting for Belgrano and his main
army, Viamonte took initiative to seek armistice with Estanislao López, governor of Santa Fe; López, for his part,
wanted fighting to cease before further damage could be done
to his already suffering province; at the convent of San Carlos Borromeo (in San Lorenzo, north of Rosario), Viamonte
and representatives of López signed the provisional agreement known as Armistice of Rosario, April 5, 1819; this
agreement needed signature of Belgrano, as commanding general to become official; as latter had already become convinced that the littoral revolt was primarily a popular uprising of citizens determined not to have an unwanted government forced upon them rather than a military action, he was
also eager for peace; on April 12, 1819, the Armistice of
San Lorenzo was signed; replacing the preliminary one of
Rosario, by representatives of Belgrano and López; it provided that Buenos Aires national forces should leave Santa Fe
and Entre Ríos and that those of Santa Fe should also be
brought back more closely to their own territory; Pueyrredón accepted the armistice and peace was established; it
lasted only until new civil wars broke out the following
year.

SAN LORENZO, BATTLE OF (February 3, 1813). First battle

fought by San Martín's Mounted Grenadiers (Granaderos a
Caballo); resulted in patriot victory over royalists.

Royalist forces in Montevideo had been sending squadrons up the rivers to secure supplies and intimidate people
of those provinces; San Martín was commanded to protect the
west bank of Paraná River from such attacks; at battle of
San Lorenzo, north of Rosario, he took Spanish landing party,
under command of Juan Antonio Zabala, completely by surprise in battle at monastery of San Carlos there; Spanish
casualties and losses of equipment were heavy; even more
significant was the recognition by both Spanish authorities
and Argentine patriot leaders that the armed forces of Río de
la Plata had acquired a new kind of experienced, professional
military leadership; patriots also sustained losses, though
fewer than those of royalists; San Martín himself was
wounded and narrowly escaped death when his horse was shot
and fell, pinning him underneath; Argentine history proudly
recalls the names of Juan Bautista Cabral and Bautista Baigorria, who saved him.

By coincidence John Parish Robertson was traveling
in that area on a business trip to Asunción; he personally, at
San Martín's invitation, observed the battle and left a full
account of it in J. P. and W. P. Robertson, Letters on
Paraguay ... (London, 1839).

SAN LUIS (Province and City). Midwestern province, with capital
of the same name; most eastern of three provinces of Cuyo,
it marks the meeting place of the dry pampas and the first
pre-Andean hills and mountains; its historical development
has been slow because of its location, lacking the water abundant from snow-capped Andes that made Mendoza and San
Juan prosperous in colonial period and the rainfall that fed
the grassy pampas farther east.

Boundaries. Bounded on north by San Juan, La Rioja,
and Córdoba; on east by Córdoba and La Pampa; on south by
La Pampa; and on west by Mendoza. Communications. Highway from Buenos Aires to Mendoza crosses province, passing
through capital and other large towns; other highways link
San Luis with Córdoba and La Rioja; branches of General
Belgrano and General S. M. railroad also cross it; airline
communication with Buenos Aires. Area: 29,600 square
miles. Population: 183,460 (1970); Density 6.2 per square
miles; almost half the population is rural. Capital: San Luis;
Population (1960) 40,420; other urban centers include Justo
Daract, Santa Rosa, Bagual, Ramírez, and Villa Mercedes.

Geography and climate. Northern part of province
has low hills with green valleys watered by rivers and
streams; it has always been center of settlement and has become focus of tourist attraction; arid landscape in northeast
is a nitrous desert similar to that of Great Basin in U.S.,
with salt flats, scrub vegetation, and inadequate water to
support crops, stock, or human settlement on large scale;
central and southern portion is extension of dry pampas,

heavy winds cause serious soil erosion damage; San Luis has
few rivers--the Desaguadero forming its western boundary
with Mendoza, the Quinto flowing into Lake Amargo in Córdoba, and a few others; province has a few natural lakes, including Lake Bebedero, but new ones are being built in connection with hydroelectric projects; three main mountain valleys, running from north to south (largest and most fertile
the Concarán) from heartland of province.

Economy. Mining has been important industry since
pre-conquest period when Indians mined gold; during colonial
period mines continued to furnish quartz, onyx, marble,
beryl, lead, copper, salt, and in modern period tungsten,
uranium, vanadium, etc., have become important; livestock
was second in importance, with agriculture third; forests contain quebracho blanco, algarrobo, and caldén that are being
exploited; until modern times, San Luis has been a poor province in economic terms.

History. During pre-Conquest period, San Luis was
sparsely settled, with Diaguita Indians in the north and plains
Indians roaming the rest; first Spanish settlement was made
in 1594 near place known as Punta de los Venados, by Luis
de Jufré from Chile, acting on orders of Governor Martín de
Loyola; it was named San Luis de Loyola Nueva Medina de
Río Seco de la Punta de los Venados, honoring Jufré's name
saint, the governor of Chile, and the Spanish birthplace of
Jufré; latter returned to Chile because of outbreak of new
Araucanian Indian War and San Luis (as it quickly became
called) was abandoned; in 1596 it was rebuilt in present location; for many years the little settlement was at the mercy of
raiding Ranqueles and Pehuenches and even at that of neighboring Spanish Cuyo settlements; early in seventeenth century
San Luis protested to Chilean governor (under whom San Luis
was governed until 1776) that their few cattle were being
stolen by vaqueros of San Juan and Mendoza provinces; the
governor instructed Mendoza to give San Luis one-fifth of the
cattle from the annual roundup; in 1632 government help rebuilt the town but problems continued, especially from Indian
raids; a strong punitive expedition in 1711 quieted them for
a time but the following year town was burned and sacked; by
1750 situation was so serious that new forts were built along
Indian frontier.

In 1776 San Luis became part of the new viceroyalty
of the Río de la Plata and under Buenos Aires authority for
first time; change was reflected in greater royal interest in
defense and development of province; in 1782, San Luis and
other Cuyo provinces were placed under intendancy of Córdoba and in 1785 the Intendant Rafael Sobremonte (q.v.) visited San Luis and reported on its condition; he found it extremely poor, with about 7810 inhabitants in the city; the
cabildo operated without funds; there was no jail; the meager
economy of the area was based on weaving and work with
cattle and the mule trains; Sobremonte ordered roads constructed, mines opened, schools built (first one opened in

1793); meanwhile the first water-driven flour mill had been
constructed and fruit orchards and alfalfa had been introduced; province began to make impact on viceroyalty; joined
in defense of Buenos Aires against British invasions; on
June 13, 1810, its cabildo recognized the patriot junta of
Buenos Aires despite the opposition of its intendant-governor,
Juan Gutiérrez de la Concha (q.v.); was governed, 1812-1813,
by José Lucas Ortiz; its open areas had already come into
use for internment of military and political prisoners; in
1812 it received one of its most famous residents when Juan
Martín de Pueyrredón, member of first triumvirate, was
exiled there following movement of October 8, 1812; he acquired an estancia, built a stone house, planted fruit trees,
and had the famous "Ombúes de Pueyrredón" transplanted
there from his estate at San Isidro--still living and declared
an historic monument; in 1813 the intendancy of Cuyo was
created, with capital in Mendoza, and San Luis was once again
linked with its western neighbors in a single unit; when San
Martín was appointed intendant governor in 1814, he immediately appointed Vicente Dupuy lieutenant governor of San Luis;
during next six years Dupuy and province cooperated whole-
heartedly and effectively with San Martín's preparations for
continental liberation from Spain; established a military
camp--Campamento de las Chacras--where he trained thousands of recruits for Army of the Andes; established military hospital, arsenal, warehouses for military equipment,
etc.; in 1816, Pueyrredón, who represented San Luis at Congress of Tucumán, was elected supreme director, largely as
result of San Martín's influence; after San Martín opened his
liberation of Chile with victory at Chacabuco, he began sending royalist prisoners across the Andes to San Luis where
Dupuy cared for them; in 1819, he suppressed rebellion by
leaders of this group; meanwhile, Dupuy gave province good
administration and brought badly-needed water supply to the
capital; governor overthrown by popular revolt in 1820, reflecting the general political anarchy of 1819-1820 in Argentina; San Luis established itself as an autonomous province
March 1, 1820, under Governor José Santos Ortiz, who had
been president of the cabildo; in 1821 he was forced to fight
invasion by Chilean José Miguel Carrera (q.v.) and was defeated; Carrera occupied San Luis, using it as a base for
his campaign against western provinces and Córdoba; San
Luis regained its own government soon afterward under Leandro Ortiz; sent delegates to constituent congress of 1824,
with no commitment except to form of government that majority wanted; province became involved in civil wars between
federalists and unitarists; in 1830 Mendoza's Colonel Videla
Castillo, supporting Unitarist Juan José Paz, invaded San
Luis and appointed Juan Pringles (q.v.) governor; latter defeated by federalist forces of Facundo Quiroga (q.v.), caudillo of La Rioja, at Río Cuarto and Rodeo del Chacón,
March 19, 28, 1831; new unitarist governor of San Luis,
Luis Videla, captured and executed, and federalists took over,

issued provisional statute of 1832 and from then on, San Luis government was mere echo of that of Rosas in Buenos Aires; Pablo Lucero served as governor for many years, during period 1840-1854; began institutionalization of political life of province and signed the agreement of San Nicolás, although he had refused to fight against Rosas.

At close of Rosas' era, San Luis had made some progress; the state seal of the province was adopted in 1836; first printing press installed in 1848; by 1853 there were three elementary schools with a total of about 210 pupils, these taught reading, writing, arithmetic, and religion; a more advanced Latin School taught Latin, logic, and theology; the province's population of about 30,000 was largely rural, with only 5000 in the city; about 135 foreigners were included; in 1855 the first provincial constitution was adopted; Justo Daract, elected governor the following year, gave San Luis a progressive administration; established schools outside capital, first secondary school and welfare society; saw first news- paper published--La Actualidad, 1858; distributed public land and promoted irrigation; in 1860 Juan Saá (q. v.) became gov- ernor briefly; San Luis accepted national reorganization but had troubled existence for several decades as El Chacho in- vaded and civil war between political factions followed; cholera epidemic of 1868 took 182 lives; by 1873 one-tenth of its population was attending school; several newspapers had appeared; first railroad arrived in 1875 and the Banco Nación opened a branch there in 1877; in 1893 the Unión Cívica Radi- cal revolution broke out with San Luis joining other provinces in declaring Leandro N. Alem president, and was followed by a series of federal interventions, as was the Radical revolu- tion of 1904.

During twentieth century pattern of federal interven- tion continued but province has begun to prosper economically; mining remains important, with tungsten ranking high, along with wolfram, beryl, vanadium, and uranium that goes to na- tional commission of atomic energy in Córdoba; quartz, lime- stone, marble, and some lead, copper, and other minerals are exploited; system of dams throughout the province pro- vides adequate water supply; most important is La Florida, about 30 miles from San Luis that also provides energy for capital and Mercedes; other industries include flour milling, wine-making, tungsten processing, and a stock--cattle, sheep, and goats--industry; a lime and portland cement industry is found in sierra district and an important salt industry at Lake Bebedero, southwest of San Luis; a tourist industry has developed around San Luis.

SAN MARTIN, JOSE DE (1778-1850).   Argentina's national hero; liberator of Argentina, Chile, and Peru.

Born February 25, 1778, in former Jesuit mission Yapeyú (Corrientes) where his Spanish father, Lt. Juan de San Martín, was serving as governor of the mission town and territory; his mother was Spanish, Gregoria Matorras, who

had been brought to Argentina a few years earlier by her
relative, Jerónimo Matorras (q. v.); spent first five years
among the Indians of this community; as his father was transferred to new duty, moved briefly to Buenos Aires and then
(1783) to Spain with his family; attended the Seminary for
Nobles in Madrid for a few years; entered military career in
1789, as cadet in Murcia Infantry Regiment; engaged in first
combat 1791 at Orán in Africa; received commission as sub-
lieutenant in 1793; spent 22 years in Spanish military forces,
seeing service both on land and sea during Spain's international wars of the late eighteenth century and in the defense
of Spain during the Napoleonic invasion; during this time San
Martín rose to rank of lieutenant colonel in the cavalry and
had been given a medal for his courageous action at the battle
of Bailén; a combination of circumstances had turned his attention toward the fight for self-rule in Argentina; while
based in Cádiz, he had become acquainted with many of his
fellow countrymen, such patriots as Matías Zapiola, Carlos
María de Alvear, José Moldes, and Francisco de Gurruchaga,
and with their patriotic lodge in Cádiz; decided to return to
Argentina to help liberate his native country; in 1811 resigned
his commission and left Spain; travelled to England and sailed
in the George Canning (q. v.) for Argentina; arrived in Buenos
Aires March 9, 1812; presented himself to junta; was confirmed in his rank and given permission to form a new military unit; through his ties with the Alvears, and newly-made
friends in the merchant community led by the Escaladas, he
was able to recruit an elite corps of saberwielding cavalrymen, known as the Mounted Grenadiers (see Granaderos a
Caballo); their first engagement took place February 3, 1813,
at San Lorenzo (Santa Fe) and ended in a real victory against
the Spanish forces sent up the Paraná river for supplies.

Meanwhile San Martín had married María Remedios
Escalada, been promoted to full colonel, and had joined Alvear and others in forming the Lautaro Lodge to stimulate,
organize, and regulate the patriotic movement; in 1813, following Belgrano's defeat at Vilcapugio, San Martín was sent
to take over command of the Army of the North; he established a military training school at the citadel in Tucumán
and began military training of both men and officers on a
higher professional level than had previously been seen in
the Argentine area; during his months there he suffered acutely from the ulcers and other illnesses that periodically afflicted him and eventually (1814) went to the hills around
Córdoba for rest and convalescence; by this time San Martín
had made a critical military decision: already two attempts
had been made by the Buenos Aires patriot armies to carry
the revolution into Bolivia (and thence to Peru); both had
been defeated after initial victories--and a third under Rondeau in 1815 was to suffer the same fate; San Martín had
come to believe that final victory against Spain could never
be won by pushing up the old royal highway route to Peru;
the only hope of winning independence from Spain would come

by crossing the Andes to free Chile, then, using it as a base,
to create a navy to transport an Argentine-Chilean army to
Lima to destroy the heart of Spain's power there; the northwestern Argentine boundary could successfully be held by the
gaucho forces under Martín Güemes against royalist invasion.
In 1814 he secured the appointment of governor-intendant of Cuyo and there, in Mendoza, began his creation of
the Army of the Andes with which he proposed to carry out
his continental strategy; the Spanish reconquest of Chile
brought thousands of Chilean soldiers, under the two rival
presidents, José Miguel Carrera and Bernardo O'Higgins, into the Cuyo area; San Martín selected the latter to help in
the proposed new expedition and forced the rebellious Carrera
to leave the province--to go to Buenos Aires and then to
U.S.; in addition to his military activities, San Martín was
active politically in Mendoza and on the national scene; by
close of 1815 the cause of the patriots seemed lost throughout Latin America, with Ferdinand VII restored to the throne
and the royalists everywhere in control except in Argentina
and rest of Río de la Plata area; San Martín's plan gave almost only hope of final victory and he exerted his influence
strongly for a declaration of independence from the Congress
called to meet in Tucumán in 1816; met with Juan Martín de
Pueyrredón, the newly appointed Supreme Director, at Córdoba, in July 1816, and between them worked out plans for
implementing San Martín's strategy; Pueyrredón pledged complete support for the organization, equipping and supplying of
the army.
Early in 1817 the Army of the Andes started across
the Andes, the two main divisions going through passes of
Uspallata and Los Patos, with smaller forces going to the
north and south; at Chacabuco on February 12, 1817, San
Martín defeated the royalist forces, under Marcó del Pont,
so decisively that Chile's independence was assured; O'Higgins became supreme director of Chile and, while campaigns
in the south continued against royalist forces, San Martín returned briefly to Buenos Aires to make plans for the proposed Argentine-Chilean invasion of royalist Peru; delays followed: new royalist forces entered southern Chile at Talcahuano and, under command of Mariano de Osorio, started
northward to Santiago, the capital; routed San Martín's forces
at Cancha Rayada and Chilean independence was only saved
by San Martín's brilliant victory at Maipú, April 5, 1818;
although the Chilean and Argentine governments had acquired
ships for a naval force and Lord Thomas Cochrane, from
Scotland, to command it, internal political conflicts in Buenos
Aires and civil wars in the provinces had brought Pueyrredón's resignation and anarchy; not only was adequate Argentine support for the liberating expedition to Peru impossible
to secure at this time but the Buenos Aires government,
under Rondeau, ordered San Martín to place his army at its
disposal for the crushing of revolts, especially in the littoral
provinces, against the national government; San Martín refused

(as he had responded to a similar earlier request from Pueyrredón); this decision, often referred to in Argentine historiography as San Martín's controversial "disobedience," grew
out of the commander's conviction that his primary duty was
to win the nation's independence, as well as his unwillingness
to engage in civil war; moving quickly back to Chile, he prepared for the next step in his campaign, the liberation of
Peru from the Spaniards, with Chilean support.

On August 20, 1820, the liberating expedition embarked
from Valparaíso; on September 12, San Martín went ashore at
Pisco in southern Peru and began the organization of a combined Peruvian-Chilean-Argentine effort to complete the liberation of southern South America by driving the Spaniards out
of Peru, their final stronghold; by combined naval and military efforts, San Martín was able, early in July 1821, to enter Lima, and to declare its independence on July 28, having
forced the royalists to withdraw into the sierras, where they
could defend themselves more effectively and had ready access to food, recruits, and supplies; an independent Peruvian
government was established, for the time being; San Martín
became Protector of Peru with full civil and military authority; for the next year the military situation between patriots
and royalists remained relatively unchanged; in this stalemate,
conditions in Lima deteriorated; San Martín's earlier efforts
to reach a diplomatic solution at Punchauca with viceroy La
Serna had failed; patriot campaigns into the sierra and to the
intermediate ports in southern Peru had met with failure or
only limited success; Lord Cochrane had quarrelled with San
Martín and departed with his fleet; inaction bred conspiracies
and jealousies among San Martín's troops; for some time San
Martín had recognized that final victory for independence
could only come through a united effort in Peru between his
troops and those of Simón Bolívar in the north; he had been
in correspondence with Bolívar and had sent troops to aid the
latter in his liberation of Quito, Ecuador; it was not until
mid-1822, however, that Bolívar's campaign had reached the
point that a conference could be held and one was scheduled
for July 1822, at Guayaquil, seaport of Ecuador.

The famous Guayaquil conference that took place July
26-27, 1822, has been, especially in the past, the subject of
much controversy although its basic facts and results have
been clear; it began with an event considered by Bolívar to
have been a victory for him, but viewed by San Martín as
such a betrayal of trust as to place Bolívar's good faith in
question; one of the matters on the agenda for discussion had
been the future status of Guayaquil, whether it should belong
to Peru or to Gran Colombia (Bolívar's new confederation);
when San Martín was welcomed, upon his arrival in the port,
in Bolívar's name to Guayaquil, Colombia, before he had
even met Bolívar, he was shocked and considered returning
to Peru at once; instead, he continued on to the session; in
the private meetings between the two great liberators, it
quickly became obvious that their priorities were different:

San Martín (a professional soldier who believed that a military leader should play as small a role in political life as possible) had singlemindedly pursued the primary goal of winning the independence from Spain that would make it possible for each country to establish its own preferred form of government and had engaged in politics only when essential to this purpose; Bolívar, a political genius, was primarily interested in the establishment of democratic republics in the former Spanish colonies, and had engaged in military action-- bloody, prolonged, but eventually victorious--only as a means to that end; San Martín also discovered that if his purpose of uniting the two armies was ever to be achieved it would have to be under Bolívar's command, in spite of his own greater military experience; when Bolívar refused to accept such an arrangement with San Martín serving under him, San Martín immediately took the only course left to him to complete the winning of independence; he decided to withdraw completely, satisfied in his own mind that Bolívar and army would be called into Peru and that he would not give in until final victory had been won; San Martín has been greatly praised for this decision as a measure of his unselfish moral stature but it was also due to a realistic appraisal of the situation; if final victory could only be won by a union of the two liberating armies, it could probably only be done in this way; San Martín's forces were already in Peru and his personal departure would not affect their location; on the other hand, Bolívar's troops, strongly attached to him personally, would hardly have accepted willingly a mass transfer to another country and commander; in the end, both liberators achieved their purposes and formed a unique personal relationship, in spite of their very different personalities--as shown in their final toasts at the banquet: Bolívar: "To the two greatest men in South America: General San Martín and myself!" San Martín: "To the early end of the war; to the organization of the various republics of the continent, and to the health of the Liberator of Colombia!"--each recognized in the other the same dedication to independence and liberty and the unique roles that they had played in winning it.

San Martín returned to Lima, resigned his authority to the Peruvian Congress in September and left at once for Chile; remained there until January 1823; crossed Andes to his old home in Mendoza; he petitioned the government for permission to come to Buenos Aires but this was refused; Rivadavia, minister of government, had always been suspicious of San Martín and he insisted that the dangerous condition of the countryside (disorders, civil wars, etc.) made it perilous for San Martín to attempt the journey; feared the capture of San Martín by one of the guerrilla groups would have dangerous political consequences for the entire nation, already deeply troubled; San Martín bitterly resented being kept from his wife, who was dying in Buenos Aires, and felt that the danger of his being captured was merely a pretext; eventually he reached Buenos Aires December 20, 1823, following his wife's

death; left in February for Europe, taking his young daughter
Mercedes with him; established their residence in Belgium
where the retired general devoted himself to his daughter's
education and to receiving distinguished visitors.

In February 1829, San Martín returned to the Río de
la Plata; found Buenos Aires in aftermath of Lavalle's revolution and execution of Manuel Dorrego; refused to land; while
still aboard ship he was visited by such former Granaderos a
Caballo officers as Juan Lavalle, and Manuel Olazábal and by
Antonio Alvarez Condarco, among others; convinced that the
civil conflict in Argentina could only be resolved in a prolonged national blood bath, and equally sure that he could
never bring himself to lead such a fight involving his own
Army of the Andes veterans on both sides, San Martín returned to Europe, without setting foot on Argentine soil, although he spent a few months in Montevideo on the way back.

Eventually he made his home in Paris near Alejandro
Aguado, a former army friend in the Spanish war against
Napoleon, now a wealthy banker; San Martín's daughter, Mercedes, married Mariano Balcarce, the son of General Antonio
Balcarce, one of San Martín's closest friends in the fight for
independence; the young couple with their two daughters,
made their home with San Martín except for various diplomatic assignments given Balcarce by the Rosas government.

On August 17, 1850, at Boulogne-sur-Mer, where they
had gone for San Martín's failing health, San Martín died; in
his will he bequeathed his sword to Juan Manuel de Rosas,
then ruling Argentina; well aware of the unitarists' condemna-
tion of Rosas and of the violence of the period, San Martín
nevertheless felt that Rosas had put the seal on his own fight
for independence by forcing the British and French fleets
(1839-1840) to leave Argentina alone to determine its own
destiny; after Rosas' death, his family returned the sword to
the Argentine nation in 1897; it was received with great ceremony and placed in the Historical Museum; in 1880 San Martín's remains were transported to Buenos Aires and placed,
with solemn public ceremony, in a specially prepared crypt
in the cathedral.

Statues of San Martín are numerous throughout the
nations that he liberated as well as other nations wishing to
honor him; one of the most impressive, honoring both him
and his beloved Army of the Andes, is appropriately erected
in Mendoza (see entries on persons and events mentioned).

The bibliography of written works about San Martín,
on professional, literary, and popular levels is enormous,
even without the published documentary series and memoirs
of veterans of the war for independence; among the most important histories are the classic Historia de San Martín y de
la emancipación sudamericana by Bartolomé Mitre (3 v.,
Buenos Aires, 1887-1889; many later editions); translated into English, in somewhat abbreviated form, by William Pilling, London, 1893; reprint 1969; the later, even more fully
detailed and documented Historia del liberatador don José de

San Martín (4 v. , Buenos Aires, 1932; 8 v. 1944-1945) by
José Pacífico Otero; the somewhat romantic one-volume biography by Domingo Faustino Sarmiento; and the literary El
santo de la espada by Ricardo Rojas (Buenos Aires, 1933),
translated into English as San Martín, The Knight of the
Andes, by Hershel Brickell and Carlos Videla (New York,
1945); and a brief English biography by J. C. J. Metford,
San Martín, the Liberator (Oxford, 1950, reprint 1970).

SAN MARTIN DE BALCARCE, MERCEDES (1816-1875). Daughter
and only child of General José de San Martín and Remedios
de Escalada; born in Mendoza in August 1816, as her father
was training his Army of the Andes for its historic liberating
expedition that began by crossing the cordillera to Chile less
than six months later; mother and baby returned to home of
maternal grandparents in Buenos Aires; remained there following her mother's death (1823) until her father arrived in
1824 to take her to Europe where she was educated; in Paris,
in 1832, she married Mariano Balcarce, son of General Antonio González Balcarce; they had two daughters, María Mercedes and Josefa Dominga; although her husband served in
various Argentine diplomatic posts, they made their permanent home with San Martín in Paris and cared for him until
his death in 1850; the Liberator paid tribute to this devotion
in his will saying that, although he had dedicated many years
almost wholly to her education and rearing, "I must confess
that her honest behavior and constant love given me have
compensated richly all my efforts and made me very happy
in my old age"; Mercedes died in Paris.

SAN MIGUEL DE TUCUMAN see TUCUMAN, SAN MIGUEL DE

SAN NICOLAS, ACUERDO DE (Agreement of), May 31, 1852.
Fundamental organic precedent of the Constitution of 1853; reaffirmed principles of Federal Pact of 1831 (q.v.). Shortly
after defeat of Rosas at Caseros, Urquiza called a meeting at
Palermo to draw up plans for national political reorganization; the governors of Buenos Aires, Entre Ríos, Corrientes,
and Santa Fe, working with Urquiza, invited all provincial
governors to meet with them in San Nicolás de los Arroyos
for this purpose; by May 1852, eleven of them were there
(governors of Córdoba, Salta, and Jujuy missing, and Urquiza
acting for Catamarca); the old differences between Buenos
Aires and other provinces quickly reappeared but all agreed
on two major points: a general constituent congress should
be convoked in Santa Fe as soon as possible to draw up new
constitution that would clearly define roles of provinces and
Buenos Aires in representation and responsibility for financial
support as well as serving as legal basis of new government;
in interim, a provisional government was formed with Urquiza
given title of Provisional Director of the Argentine Confederation and important military powers as well as responsibility
for domestic and foreign affairs; the Acuerdo was signed

May 31, 1852; Urquiza called for the congress to meet in
Santa Fe and in 1853 it produced the constitution (see Constitution of 1853) establishing the Argentine Republic and used
from that date, with a few changes and lapses, until the
present (1970s); meanwhile the porteños had refused to accept
the agreement reached at San Nicolás; already suspicious of
Urquiza, they believed that it was unfair to Buenos Aires;
violent debates took place in the Buenos Aires legislature until Urquiza dissolved it and assumed power himself; hostilities followed, with result that Buenos Aires remained outside
the confederation formed by the other provinces until 1862
when Bartolomé Mitre was inaugurated as president of the
united nation.

Many historians, therefore, regard the San Nicolás
agreement as the starting point of the final national organization foreseen in 1810 May Revolution but delayed for more
than forty years of bloody internal strife and disagreement.

SAN NICOLAS, NAVAL COMBAT OF (March 2, 1811). Name given
to first battle fought by patriot naval forces; here, in the
Paraná river near town of San Nicolás, Argentine navy was
defeated and practically destroyed by Spanish naval squadron
(see Navy).

SAN NICOLAS DE LOS ARROYOS. City on Paraná River in northeastern Buenos Aires province, about 140 miles from federal
capital; population in 1960 approximately 50,000 and growing
rapidly.

First settlement made April 14, 1748, by Rafael Agui-
ar on lands belonging to his wife Juana Padilla de Ugarte;
town prospered and grew in size; served as concentration
point in 1806 for troops on their way from Córdoba and Paraguay to aid in defense of Buenos Aires, and as Belgrano's
base of departure to Paraguay, 1811; first naval combat of
Argentina took place in river adjacent to it (1811); was
granted title of city by national congress in 1819; although it
was involved historically in many events during war of independence and civil wars of early nineteenth century it acquired
a special significance as the "city of pacts" from the number
of agreements signed there; these included that of Benegas
(1820), and that of 1821 in which governors of Buenos Aires
and Santa Fe met to seek basis for peace in Entre Ríos, the
Pact of the Littoral provinces, 1831, and the most famous of
all, the Acuerdo de San Nicolás (qq.v.); during the nineteenth
century San Nicolás grew, counting 10,000 inhabitants in 1880;
served as outlet for new commercial agricultural development
in cereals and other products and attracted immigrants to its
city as well as its hinterland; in the twentieth century these
trends continued; during World War II 200-300 ships visited
its port primarily for corn but also to load linseed, wheat,
and other grains; by this time San Nicolás had already become the northern coastal center of Buenos Aires' industrialization; in 1955 this was recognized by beginning construction

of a great steel mill, financed partly by loan of $60,000,000
from Export-Import Bank; production began by 1960; at the
same time a powerhouse (superusina térmica) was built,
largest of its type in Argentina, that began supplying electric
power to Buenos Aires over high tension lines in late 1957.
        See José E. de la Torre, Historia de San Nicolás de
los Arroyos (Rosario, 1947).

SAN ROMAN, GUILLERMO (1842-1908).   Lawyer; political figure;
    governor of La Rioja.
        Born in La Rioja; graduated from University of Cór-
    doba; returned to native city and entered public life; became
    minister of government for Governor Julio Campos, National
    Congressman (1886-1890); was later elected national senator
    after serving again (1891) as minister in La Rioja govern-
    ment, became governor of province (1892-1895); moved to
    Rosario and held offices as provincial legislator and federal
    judge there; died in Córdoba.

SANAGASTA.   Name given to the geometrical decorative art used
    in pottery by the Diaguita Indians living in the northern and
    central western part of Argentina (see Diaguita).

SANAVIRONES.   Indians who lived in Santiago del Estero and in
    northeastern Córdoba, around Mar Chiquita.
        Following the establishment of Santiago del Estero in
    1550s (q.v.), the Sanavirones were given in encomienda to
    the Spaniards; twenty years later, many of them accompanied
    Jerónimo de Cabrera to assist in founding of Córdoba as In-
    dians of that area were uncivilized and too few in number to
    be useful; eventually were absorbed into creole life, disap-
    pearing as a separate ethnic group.
        Little is known about their language and culture; the
    word sacat, used for pueblo (people or town) has passed into
    Argentine use; differed in language and technology from neigh-
    boring Comechingones; may have had ties with other neigh-
    bors, Tonocotés; they seem to have practiced some agricul-
    ture and herded llamas (or guanacos); lived in large, com-
    munal dwellings; used bow and arrow and the macana club;
    apparently made pottery and seem to have made textiles;
    buried their dead in large urns.

SANCHEZ, FLORENCIO (1875-1910).   Dramatist; journalist.
        Born in Montevideo; began writing at early age; inte-
    rested in satire and social criticism; sometimes used pseudo-
    nyms, such as "Jack the Ripper," and later, Ovidio Paredes;
    moved to Buenos Aires in 1893; returned to Montevideo where
    he was active in International Center of Social Studies, an
    anarchist group; returned to Argentina in 1898 to write for
    Lisandro de la Torre's La República of Rosario; wrote for
    other newspapers and periodicals but his true vocation was
    the theater; bitterly attacked ethnic groups that resisted ac-
    cepting Argentine way of life; his most popular plays include

M'hijo el dotor, La gringa, Le gente pobre, Barranca abajo;
Gente honesta is a satire on life of middle class in Rosario; his
work greatly influenced development of theater in Argentina; died
in Milan, Italy, on his way to a tuberculosis clinic in Switzerland.
See Roberto Giusti, Florencio Sánchez: su vida y su
obra (Buenos Aires, 1920); Julio Imbert, Florencio Sánchez,
vida y creación (1954); and Luis Ordaz, Florencio Sánchez
(Buenos Aires, 1971).

SANCHEZ, MARIA (1786-1868).   Social and community leader in
Buenos Aires; affectionately known as Doña Mariquita.
Born in Buenos Aires, daughter of Spanish merchant
Cesáreo Sánchez de Velasco; reputed to be the wealthiest
heiress in the entire viceroyalty; married twice: to Martín
Jacobo Thompson (q.v.) in 1805 and, after his death in 1819,
to Juan Washington de Mendeville, French consul in Buenos
Aires; by 1810 her salon had become the popular gathering
place for the porteño political, social, cultural elite; according to tradition the national anthem was first sung there;
patriotic, musical, intelligent, interested in current events,
Mariquita came to have great influence and a kind of permanent club was formed in her home; in the 1820s Bernardino
Rivadavia was the dominating figure and formed the Sociedad
de Beneficencia there with her support; devoted much of her
life to community service, especially with hospitals for women
and children and the mentally ill and homes for the indigent and
foundlings; during Rosas' troubles with France (q.v.) María Sánchez de Mendeville went into exile in Montevideo, joining her unitarist son, Juan Thompson (q.v.); returned to Buenos Aires after
Caseros; in 1866-67 served again as president of the reorganized
Sociedad de Beneficencia; quarreled with Sarmiento for his failure
to promote education for girls and founded a school for them; her
portrait, painted by Rugendas, was hung in the National Museum;
her correspondence with leading writers of the period was published in 1952.

SANCHEZ, ZACARIAS (1852-1940).   Engineer; cartographer.
Born in Corrientes; studied at University of Buenos
Aires; returned to Corrientes and served in provincial legislature (1882); published first topographical map of Corrientes
in 1885; accompanied el perito Francisco P. Moreno, as map-
maker, during his Patagonian explorations; took Moreno's
place in boundary negotiations with Chile; also took part in
drawing of Argentine-Bolivian boundary; was appointed director
of international boundaries offices in 1906; in 1910 Sánchez
represented Argentina at Tenth International Congress of Geography in Rome and, in that centennial year, a map of Argentine Republic, prepared by Sánchez, was published; among
his other publications were: Geografía de Corrientes; a map
of railroads; La frontera argentino-boliviana and La frontera
argentino-brasileña; died in city of Corrientes.

SANCHEZ DE BUSTAMANTE, PLACIDO (1814-1886).   Government

official in Tucumán.

Born in San Miguel de Tucumán, son of independence leader Teodoro; studied at University of Sucre but was forced to leave because of ill health and the political conditions that caused his family to live in exile during Rosas' rule; returning to Tucumán, he became active in public life; serving as minister for several governors, senator to the Confederation congress at Paraná, Tucumán's representative at Constituent Congress to reform the constitution, 1860; elected president of Supreme Court in 1878 and governor of province in 1880; resigned from latter post because of disagreements with legislature; donated various important items from his father's library to the museum of La Plata; died in Jujuy.

SANCHEZ DE BUSTAMANTE, TEODORO (1778-1851).   Patriot leader; signer of Declaration of Independence.

Born in San Salvador Jujuy, a descendant of Francisco Argañaraz y Murguía, founder of that city; educated in Buenos Aires at Colegio de San Carlos and in Chuquisaca where he graduated in law; took part in revolution there, May 25, 1809, under Arenales; returning home, he was given legal posts in cabildo of Jujuy and then in Salta; in November 1810, Mariano Moreno, as secretary of first Junta, named him attorney for Audiencia of Buenos Aires; accompanied Belgrano in campaigns, was named secretary by San Martín (while in Tucumán), and served Rondeau as secretary on third expedition into Upper Peru (Bolivia) in 1815; from 1816 to 1820 represented Jujuy in Congress of Tucumán; signed Declaration of Independence (1816) and was serving as presiding officer of Congress in 1820 during events that dissolved it; joined Arenales in Salta as minister of government; in 1826 became lieutenant governor of Jujuy; political troubles with caudillo Juan Facundo Quiroga, who put a price on his head, forced him into exile in Bolivia where he spent the rest of his life; died in Santa Cruz while serving as rector of its Colegio Mayor; his remains were repatriated in 1916 and buried in Jujuy cathedral.

SANCHEZ DE BUSTAMANTE, TEOFILO (1868-1930).   Lawyer and political figure.

Born in San Salvador de Jujuy; studied in Buenos Aires, graduating from law school at university; returned to public life in his native province; was appointed president of the superior court; served as member of provincial legislature several times; distinguished by his interest in judicial reform; also served as lieutenant governor of province and cabinet minister; became national congressman (1902-1906, 1918-1924) and was national senator (1924-1930) at time of his death; took part in 1890 revolution, opposing the Unicato policies; joined Radical Party and when this split during government of Marcelo T. de Alvear, joined Antipersonalist group; died in Buenos Aires.

863   Sánchez de Loria

SANCHEZ DE LORIA, MARIANO (1774-1842).   Bolivian member of
Congress of Tucumán, representing Charcas, and signer of
Declaration of Independence.
Born in Chuquisaca, educated in law there; took part
in revolt of 1809; supported establishment of Inca monarchy
in independent United Provinces; returned to Bolivia; died in
La Paz after having retired to life of religious service.

SANCHEZ DE MENDEVILLE, MARIA   see   MARIA SANCHEZ

SANCHEZ DE THOMPSON, MARIA   see   MARIA SANCHEZ

SANCHEZ LABRADOR, JOSE (1717-1798).   Missionary; educator;
explorer.
Born in La Guardia, Spain, Sánchez Labrador entered
the Society of Jesus in 1731 and had begun his studies at the
colegio de Valladolid when he was sent to America; arrived
in Buenos Aires in 1734 and went at once to Córdoba to complete his studies; ordained in 1739; during the next 38 years,
he spent his time variously studying and teaching in the Jesuit
schools of Córdoba and Asunción; in missionary work among
the Mbayá Indians, attempting to learn their language (related
to Guaycurú) in order to teach and translate the catechism,
in establishing (with Father José Mantilla) the last new Jesuit
mission opened in the Río de la Plata area, Nuestra Señora
de Belén; and in exploring; during the final years before the
expulsion, his duties took him up the Paraguay River and in
1766, with five Indians, he struck out across the Gran Chaco
on an almost direct line to the northwest from Asunción to
Santa Cruz and discovered the route to Peru for which explorers had searched since the beginning of the conquest; the
new route shortened the distance by approximately 600 miles
from the circuitous one previously used; Sánchez Labrador
arrived back in Belén, his mission, early in August 1767;
delayed somewhat, he left the area in 1768 to join his fellow-
Jesuits in exile; during the remainder of his life, largely
spent in Ravenna, Italy, where he died in 1798, he devoted
himself to writing approximately twenty volumes about the
history, ethnology, and natural phenomena of the Río de la
Plata; his Paraguay católico was first published in Buenos
Aires, 1910, and Guillermo Furlong has edited some of his
studies and published them.

SANCHEZ REULET, ANIBAL (1910-   ).   Writer; university professor.
Born in Azul, Buenos Aires; studied in University of
Buenos Aires (faculty of humanities and educational sciences)
and at university in Madrid, 1934-1936; received Ph.D. at
National University of La Plata, 1939; moved to University
of Tucumán where he became professor of ethics and history of philosophy in faculty of philosophy and letters (1939-
1946) as well as dean (1945-1946); contributed articles to
Lorenzo Luzuriaga's liberal Revista de Pedagogía there;

lectured in other Argentine universities and contributed to
La Nación, Nosotros, Sur, etc.; came to U.S. as Guggenheim fellow in 1947 to study influence of philosophical ideas
on Spanish American development; taught at National University of Mexico, 1949; served as chief of Division of Philosophy, Letters, and Sciences, Pan American Union 1950-1958;
moved to University of California, Los Angeles, to teach
Spanish American literature and philosophy, 1958, served as
editor of Revista Interamericana de Bibliografía, 1952; and
member of advisory board of Handbook of Latin American
Studies; wrote Contemporary Latin American Philosophy,
1954; edited papers given at XIII International Congress of
Ibero-American Literature, held in Los Angeles, 1967, entitled Homenaje a Rubén Darío, 1867-1967, Los Angeles,
1970.

SANCTI SPIRITUS, FORT OF.   First Spanish fort and settlement
in Río de la Plata; established in June 1527 by Sebastian
Cabot.   On his voyage up the Paraná river Cabot (q.v.)
reached the mouth of the Carcarañá river late in May 1527;
anchored there for some time and, probably around June 9,
ordered fort built and small settlement established on left
bank of Carcarañá (Santa Fe province); gardens were planted
and good relations established with Indians; settlement at fort
lived fairly peaceful life for about two years while Cabot explored the rivers; during this time relations worsened between
Indians and Spaniards and situation was not helped by Cabot's
harsh reprisals against Indian offenses; in September 1529,
while Cabot was away, the Indians attacked the settlement,
destroyed it and most of the fort, and massacred all the
Spaniards except for a few who escaped in a brigantine to
Cabot's ship; Cabot returned to the site but decided not to
build a new fort or to attempt further settlement; returned to
Spain.

SANMARTINO, ERNESTO ENRIQUE (1902-   ).   Jurisconsult; Radical leader; writer.
        Born in Ramallo, Buenos Aires; graduated in law,
University of Buenos Aires; became journalist, editing El Diario of Paraná for six years and Nueva Palabra of the Federal Capital; in 1933 served as member of congress to reform
constitution of Entre Ríos; elected to national chamber of
deputies in 1936 and again in 1946; expelled two years later
for continued opposition to Farrell and Perón governments;
went into exile; returned after fall of Perón and in 1955
made notable radio address analyzing problems facing leaders of the liberating Revolution; warned of dangers from ex-
tremists of the right (whom he considered most dangerous)
and of the Peronist left; in 1958 he began publication of La
voz de Mayo, a journal devoted to political affairs, and was
again elected to congress; among his published writings are:
El infortunio argentino visto desde Europa; La verdad sobre
la situación argentina; Escuchemos ahora a las poetas;

Destierro (drama written while in Montevideo), and dramatic
poem San Pablo about life and work of St. Paul.

SANTA COLOMA, MANUEL DE (1826-1881). Sculptor. Born in
France where his father, Eugenio María de Santa Coloma
was serving as Argentine consul general, appointed by Rivadavia; devoted himself to sculpturing; first showed his work
in Paris, in 1863; won a prize for his Cavalier spagnol, a
bronze figure that remained in Europe; again in 1870 his
Poney de caza was awarded a prize; his best work was in
depicting animals and when French sculptor Albert Carrier
Belleuse was given contract to create the equestrian statue
of Manuel Belgrano for Palermo, Carrier selected Santa
Coloma to do the horse and the statue was unveiled by President Sarmiento September 24, 1873, with both sculptors being
honored; Santa Coloma died in Europe.

SANTA COLOMA, MARTIN ISIDRO DE (1800-c.1852). Officer in
Rosas's army. Born in Buenos Aires; began his military
career as second lieutenant in Blandengues regiment, 1824;
a few years later accepted honorable discharge to become
justice of peace at Los Corrales in Buenos Aires province;
returned to army in 1839, commissioned as colonel by Rosas;
was rumored to have been murderer of Manuel Vicente Maza,
president of Chamber of Deputies on June 22, 1839; remained
in Santos Lugares until 1840; then was sent to Santa Fe to
join pro-Rosas forces under Oribe against Rivera; in 1845 he
was seriously wounded when a division of Paz's troops, commanded by General Juan Pablo López, surprised and disastrously defeated his force; later he was placed in command
of defense of Paraná coast north of San Lorenzo; remained
in area of Santa Fe and Rosario during rest of Rosas' administration; fought for Rosas in battle of Caseros; died shortly
afterward; conflicting reports of his death include those saying that he died on that battlefield and the testimony of Domingo Faustino Sarmiento that Santa Coloma was executed
later by orders of Urquiza.

SANTA CRUZ (Province). Southernmost province, in Patagonia;
apparently gets its name from discovery (c. 1535) by Simón
de Alcazaba (Portuguese navigator, hired by Spain, to find
all water route to Peru) of a Spanish cross and note left
there by earlier Spanish expeditions (probably Loaysa's);
second largest province of nation, it is the lowest in population density; believed to be very rich in mineral potential;
became province in 1950s.
　　　　Location. Lies between Chubut on north and Territory of Tierra del Fuego in south, largely between latitudes
46° and 52° S.; bounded by Atlantic Ocean on east, and Andean boundary with Chile on west. Area: 94,100 square
miles. Population: 84,457; density: 0.9 per square mile;
most of the population lives in towns. Capital: Río Gallegos; Population in 1960: 14,439; located on right bank of

Río Gallegos; other population centers include Santa Cruz, San Julián, La Esperanza, and Los Manantiales.

Geography. Province consists of two very different regions: 1) the western or Andean, characterized by broken chain of mountains separated by large valleys, lakes, and transverse ranges; and 2) eastern plateau area that starts at the rough, irregular coastline and slopes westward in series of varied plateaus, steadily rising toward the west until it meets the Andean region; climate is cold and dry with little rainfall except in Andean area; violent winds blow constantly; vegetation is sparse; coastline has only a few natural harbors at the mouths of rivers that derive their water from melting ice of the Andes and flow across province; among the most important are Santa Cruz, that flows from Lago Argentino, Deseado, Chico and its tributary Shehuen, Coyle, and Gallegos; the largest lakes are the Buenos Aires, Belgrano, and Argentino.

Economy. Sheepraising continues to be major economic basis of Santa Cruz, although coal mining at Río Turbio, increasing petroleum production under government YPF (Yacimientos Petrolíferos Fiscales), and a little gold and copper mining also contribute; agriculture--potatoes, fruits and vegetables, wheat--has been attempted but without great success; sheep (numbering around 9 million in 1970) produce both wool and meat, processed in frigoríficos owned by government CAP (Compañía Argentina de Productores de Carne), Armour, or Swift in Río Gallegos, Santa Cruz (city), and other ports; much of transportation is handled by air as roads and railroads are few; paved highway finally linked province with rest of nation in 1951.

History. Ferdinand Magellan was first European to reach Santa Cruz, entering bay of San Julián March 31, 1520; after that time it appeared on most charts and was known to Spanish, as well as later foreign navigators as place to rest before entering the turbulent straits area or as a refuge from storms; frequently used by other Spanish expeditions on way to Philippines in early sixteenth century and by later maritime expeditions to Chile and Peru; Francis Drake stopped there in June 1578, on his circumnavigation of the world; with Spain's creation of restricted, armed convoy system of trade from Spain to America and limitation of trans-Pacific trade to Manila Galleons out of Acapulco, Mexico, Pacific was considered to be a private Spanish lake, with intruders sought and punished; straits traffic decreased greatly and Santa Cruz coast was only rarely visited until late eighteenth century; meanwhile Jesuit missionaries explored and wrote about interior of province; see listings of Matías Strobel, José Quiroga, José Cardiel and Thomas Falkner.

In 1778 Spain decided to explore, fortify, and settle the Santa Cruz coast and Las Malvinas (Falkland Islands) due to new British and French competition with Spanish whalers and sealfishers in South Atlantic, and their renewed interest in establishing settlements and extending their political

domination over this unoccupied tip of South America as a
base from which to strengthen their increasing trade with the
Orient as well as to trade with Spanish colonies; first expedition, under Antonio de Viedma, reached San Julián in March
1778; decided settlement could not be made there and moved
north to Puerto Deseado; spent bad winter there, with 30
colonists dying of scurvy; in 1781 colony was moved back to
San Julián and named Floridablanca, but lasted only three
years; during next few decades several attempts at settlement along the coast failed because of frigid weather and lack
of food; Puerto Deseado was resettled, briefly, in 1790 by
Real Compañía de Pesca Marítima as base for hunting seals
and whales; following May Revolution of 1810, development of
area stopped for a time; first new attention focused on area
at mouth of Santa Cruz river; in 1834 British natural scientist Charles Darwin (q. v.) accompanied Captain Robert Fitzroy in Beagle on voyage up that river to the Andes area; the
first Argentine settler in the province is believed to have been
Luis Piedrabuena on the island of Pavón, at mouth of Santa
Cruz River (1859), where he engaged in commerce and salvaging; two Anglican missionaries from Fort Stanley, in
Falklands, came in 1862 to a place in that area, later known
as Cañadón de los Misioneros, and remained there for a
year; a French colony established on same site eight years
later by Ernest Roquand also had to be abandoned because of
lack of food; in 1873 the Argentine government took possession of this port, erecting a casilla and leaving a force
there; after 3 months, supplies ran out and casilla was abandoned; almost immediately Chileans arrived to claim and occupy the site; naval forces of both nations were in those
waters but war was avoided by treaty of Pierro-Sarratea,
1877, that confirmed status quo, in effect accepting Argentine sovereignty over Atlantic coast, Chilean over Magellan
Strait area.

From this time on modern exploration, settlement,
and exploitation of Santa Cruz's natural resources began; El
Perito Francisco Moreno and Carlos Moyano (qq. v.) were already engaged in their extensive studies and travels of the
interior; sheep raising was introduced from Falkland Islands
(lying due east of southern part of Santa Cruz) in 1883 and
followed same pattern as in islands and other Patagonian
areas; breeding was improved by imported stock and British,
Australian, and Scotch sheep ranchers directed operations;
in 1884 the territory of Santa Cruz was created from southern
portion of Patagonian territory; Carlos Moyano was first governor and the settled area around present town of Santa Cruz
served as first capital; Río Gallegos, farther south, at mouth
of river of same name, was founded in 1897 by Governor
Ramón Lista and became capital in 1899; continued attempts
to establish Puerto Deseado, at mouth of Deseado River in
northern part of province met with failure due to inability to
secure food and fresh water supplies; finally these were
solved and both town and port were permanent by early 1920s;

in 1903 San Julián, with its relatively protected port, was
settled; by 1895 population of province totaled 1095; schools,
largely founded by Salesians (q. v.), numbered 26, with 340
pupils including some from other Patagonian territories; during the next few decades progress was rapid; in 1915 territory was divided into seven departments; in 1940s first high
school was opened and by 1947 the population had increased
to nearly 25,000; in 1950s a paved highway connected province with rest of the nation and the territory became a national province; the discovery of large coal deposits, of varying quality, at Río Turbio brought their exploitation by government company; in 1951 a railroad was opened between Río
Turbio and Río Gallegos.

Modern Santa Cruz is still largely underdeveloped but
its population increased to around 95,000 by 1970 and continues to grow; Río Gallegos continues to be its largest,
most modern city, and efforts are being made to exploit effectively its mineral and hydroelectric resources.

Many of the early explorers of the province published
useful descriptions of the land and its native people; the
first (not counting casual mention by sixteenth century coast
explorers like Pigafetta with Magellan) were those written
by the Jesuit expedition, edited by Lozano and published in
Madrid in 1747; Thomas Falkner's Description of Patagonia,
London, 1774, is useful study of interior; see also Charles
Darwin's Voyage of the Beagle, various editions; and account
written by first settler Luis Piedrabuena, Vida entre los
Patagones; Carlos Moyano's Carta general de la Patagonia
describes the geography of the province as he saw it in
1870s and 1880s, updated in 1894 by his Nuevos datos geo-
lógicos sobre la Patagonia austral; Carlos Ameghino, geo-
physicist, also wrote about his studies in southern Patagonia,
1887-1889.

SANTA CRUZ, ANDRES (1792-1865).   General in San Martín's
independence army; president of Bolivia.

Born in La Paz, Bolivia, son of Spanish colonial official and wealthy Indian woman; served at first in royalist
army after revolution began; captured by Martín Güemes at
Humahuaca and then exchanged; in 1820 he was again captured by patriots, led by Lavalle, in campaign of the sierra
in Peru; decided to join San Martín with his force; named
military commandant of Cajamarca; commanded division that
San Martín sent to aid Bolívar's forces in Ecuador; fought in
battle of Pichincha; later commanded second expedition to
Intermediate Ports and fought as grand marshal at both
Junín and Ayacucho; after independence was won, he served
as president of council of state in Peru and interim president during Bolívar's absence; replaced Sucre as president
of Bolivia (1828); organized administration, finances, educational system, and codified laws; attempted to reunite Bolivia
and Peru in Confederation of the Andes under his rule; both
Chile and Argentina protested; Rosas, occupied with French

blockade, put Alejandro Heredia in charge of Argentine effort but Santa Cruz easily took possession of port of Jujuy; defeat by Chilean forces at Yungay and internal political revolution ended Santa Cruz's rule in Bolivia and sent him to Europe where he remained until his death in Paris more than 25 years later.

SANTA CRUZ, ANDRES SIMON (1831-1911). Career military officer. Son of Bolivian president, left his country with his father in 1839; after attending polytechnical school he entered famous military academy of St. Cyr; fought in Crimean campaign in French army; requested discharge in 1856 to move to Argentina; Confederation government confirmed him in his military rank and President Urquiza (whose daughter he married) commissioned him to organize an artillery unit under his command; fought in battles of Cepeda and Pavón, and later fulfilled technical and administrative duties after having received honorable discharge; returned to military service in 1880 as director of the Colegio Militar for six years; collaborated in drawing up the Military Code; died in Entre Ríos.

SANTA ELENA. Name given by Juan Martín de Pueyrredón to the military prison camp called Las Bruscas located in the eastern part of Buenos Aires; no longer used after war with Brazil.

SANTA FE (Province and City). Littoral province extending along Paraná River north of Buenos Aires province; considered to be second most important province in the republic because of its large population and wealth.
    Location and boundaries. Lies between 28° and 34° 22'S. latitude and 50°54' and 62°52' W. longitude; bounded on north by province of Chaco, on east by Paraná River, on south by Buenos Aires, and on west by Santiago del Estero. Area: 51,300 square miles. Population: 2,135,583 (1970); density of 42 persons per square mile. Cities: Santa Fe, capital, with population of nearly a quarter of a million; most important city of province is Rosario (q.v.) (c.600,000 population), second ranking port of the nation; other cities include Esperanza, La Paz, Villa Federal, San Justo, Reconquista, San Cristóbal, and Casilda.
    Geography and climate. Several rivers cross the province, the Salado (q.v.) being most important; although not navigable, it is used to produce hydroelectric power; the San Javier, actually a branch of the Paraná, irrigates the fertile agricultural region north of the capital; amount of rainfall decreases from the northeast to the west; northern part of province has the algarrobo (carob) tree and quebracho; central area is flat, the heart of the dry forest area; in the south are the pampas where all cereals grow; subtropical foliage is found along the Paraná from north to south.
    Communications. Santa Fe is served by Mitre, Belgrano, and San Martín railroads and, additionally, the

Belgrano links it with La Quiaca in Jujuy and with Chile;
roads are extensive, most of them excellent, maintained by
local departments through which they pass; a modern tunnel
under the river now unites Santa Fe with province of Entre
Ríos.

Economy. Santa Fe was the first province to support
agricultural colonies; the first one was Esperanza (q. v.),
built in 1856; by 1860 there were five, by 1870, 36, and in
1895, 365; among most important products of Santa Fe are
cattle, dairy products--nearly 50% of butter and casein produced in republic, 48. 5% of the dulce de leche (caramelized
sweetened milk confection), 40. 5% of the cheese and 30% of
the canned milk processed in the country; most of this is produced by cooperatives (q. v.); cooperative movement has been
very important in Santa Fe, with more than 150 agricultural
cooperatives, 19 for cattle, and others; best known one is
San-Cor (group of cooperatives from Santa Fe and Córdoba)
that exports casein, dulce de leche, candies and powdered
milk; most important agricultural crops are wheat, corn,
flax, rye, oatmeal, and, recently, rice; other industries are
food canning, wood, cork, beer, textiles, paper, tobacco,
glass, ceramics, leather, and, of course, meat packing houses.

History. City of Santa Fe was founded by Juan de
Garay (q. v.) November 1, 1573; its jurisdiction included today's provinces of Santa Fe, Entre Ríos, and part of Buenos
Aires; while de Garay was absent on expedition to reestablish
city of Buenos Aires (1580), the Creole "revolution of the
seven leaders" (q. v.) broke out against the Spaniards but was
defeated; about 1650 the town of Santa Fe was moved to a
more favorable location, its present site, as the original one
had been too vulnerable to Indian attack, subject to water
erosion, and difficult for wagons traveling overland to reach;
in 1662 Santa Fe was declared a puerto preciso by the king,
requiring every boat navigating on the Paraná to stop at that
port; chief business of Santa Fe at this time was to serve as
distributing center for yerba mate from Paraguay to viceroyalty of Peru; Indian attacks continued to be serious problem although Santa Fe had series of good governors who coura-
geously fought off the repeated malones (unexpected, violent Indian attacks); in 1733, the city was almost deserted because
of these and a smallpox epidemic that killed both whites and
Indians; various attempts were made to establish Indian villages, like Concepción; in 1750, Governor Francisco Vera y
Mujica, descendant of earliest Santa Fe families, began campaign to end attacks of Charrúas, Guaraníes, and the Abipones
in Chaco; succeeded in making general peace agreement in
early 1770s; his successors, Melchor Echagüe y Andía and
Prudencio María de Gastañaduy, last two governors of colonial period, consolidated defense of the Indian frontier, improved the city of Santa Fe and governed it and other two
growing settlements of Rosario and Coronda efficiently; Santa
Fe became not only the administrative but also the trade center for the large territory it controlled; lost its rural aspect

as merchants and skilled artisans became residents; a thriving leather trade and industry developed as hides were converted into containers, roofing material, carts, hammocks,
furniture, and other manufactured trade items, and shipped
to market by the Paraná, as was the yerba mate; wheat was
planted and grew well but was only used locally, not as part
of trade.

News of May Revolution reached Santa Fe June 5,
1810, and the following month it recognized the Buenos Aires
patriot junta; when Belgrano's army reached Santa Fe in
October, on its way to Paraguay, the province provided
money, men, and food; among leaders of this patriot support
were Francisco Antonio Candioti, who offered his entire fortune, and Estanislao López, later to become caudillo of Santa
Fe and leader of its movement for autonomy; during next two
years province was scene of two important independence
events: on February 27, 1812, Belgrano unfurled Argentine
flag for first time and, at Convent of San Lorenzo, February
3, 1813, San Martín won his first military victory in his
fight for liberation from Spain; Santa Fe was strongly Federalist and determined to live under its own rule, rather than
that of Buenos Aires; in 1815 province joined forces with
Uruguayan leader Artigas and replaced the governor, appointed
by Buenos Aires, with their own Candioti; shortly after this,
Viamonte invaded Santa Fe with forces from Buenos Aires and
restored latter's authority; the following year Viamonte was
forced out by a popular revolution; situation rapidly grew
worse as Díaz Vélez, under orders of Belgrano and patriot
government in Buenos Aires, failed in peace efforts and then
captured city of Santa Fe August 4, 1816; Unitarists and
Federalists continued their conflicts; in 1818 a pro-Artigas
group began revolution; at this time anarchy was only avoided
by action of Estanislao López, who, as military commander
of province, seized the power; for the time being, hostilities
ceased as Balcarce, commander of Buenos Aires forces, was
forced to return to Buenos Aires (burning Rosario as he went)
and an armistice was signed by Viamonte and López at San
Lorenzo; in July, 1819 cabildo elected Estanislao López governor; he immediately gave Santa Fe its first constitution;
the twenty years (1818-1838) of López's domination of Santa
Fe were characterized by struggle against Buenos Aires government, complicated by rival ambitions of Francisco Ramírez, caudillo of Entre Ríos, to control the littoral provinces;
the rejection of the national constitution of 1819 at this time
increased tensions between the Federalists (called anarchists
by the porteños) and the Unitarists of Buenos Aires; Supreme
Director Rondeau attempted to concentrate a large force
against Santa Fe but was unable to do so as San Martín refused to divert his army from its purpose of national liberation to that of embroilment in civil wars; at the same time
revolts in the army--of the Cazadores de los Andes, led by
Mendizábal, and the Arequito group--left Rondeau dependent
solely on Buenos Aires' forces; Ramírez and López forgot

their differences long enough to join in defeat of Rondeau at
Cañada of Cepeda December 1, 1820; as a result, Rondeau's
government fell, Congress was dissolved and Buenos Aires
was plunged into its period of anarchy (q.v.); although a
temporary peace was established between Buenos Aires and
the littoral provinces by the Treaty of Pilar (q.v.), fighting
soon broke out again; López defeated Buenos Aires forces
under Miguel Soler in Cañada de la Cruz and those of Dorrego at bloody battle of Gamonal, followed by treaty of Benegas
(q.v.), November 24, 1820; this treaty brought new break between López and Ramírez; in fighting that followed latter was
killed (see Francisco Ramírez), leaving Estanislao López undisputed leader of littoral provinces for a time; on January
25, 1825, Quadrilateral Treaty (q.v.) was signed in Santa Fe
by Santa Fe, Entre Ríos, Buenos Aires, and Corrientes; this
recognized need for national union and promised to call a
national congress in Santa Fe to draw up such constitution;
congress failed in this mission but did give López power to
carry on diplomatic relations with foreign countries; also attempted to unite other provinces in military defense against
invading Unitarist forces of Juan Lavalle; latter invaded Rosario (1829) and was defeated at Puente de Márquez by López
and Juan Manuel de Rosas; in spite of Lavalle's defeat, Unitarists remained powerful in nine interior provinces and
formed Unitarist League under leadership of General José
María Paz; to counteract this, Federalist provinces signed
the Pacto Federal, January 4, 1831; López and others have
considered this to be the real beginning of eventual national
reorganization as its Article 15 called for provinces to organize country under federal system; peace and prosperity
prevailed in Santa Fe until death of López in 1838.

   Domingo Cullén (q.v.), who had served López as
minister, succeeded him as governor, but resigned to form
a coalition effort against Rosas that failed; Juan Pablo López
(brother of Estanislao) took over the government; destroyed
Unitarist forces commanded by Mariano Vera and attempted
to defend Santa Fe against new attacks by Lavalle; in 1840
latter captured city but did not remain in it; Juan López
formed alliance with Corrientes to fight against Rosas but
his poorly organized troops met defeats at Monte Flores,
Coronda, and Colastiné; López retired to Corrientes; Pascual
Echagüe (q.v.) ruled Santa Fe 1842-1852; Juan López attempted to return to power (1845) but was defeated at Mala-
brigo by Echagüe; in 1851 Santa Fe joined Urquiza against
Rosas, with Domingo Crespo replacing Echagüe as governor;
large numbers of Santafecinos fought in battle of Caseros, including Juan Pablo López who distinguished himself by his
bravery; a few months later the national constituent congress
met in Santa Fe and produced the famous 1853 Constitution
(q.v.) under which the republic is still governed; Buenos
Aires' temporary insistence on separation brought new fighting on Santa Fe soil in Cepeda and Pavón, before all the
provinces were united.

It was during the 1850s of the Confederation period
that the agricultural colonization program that was to transform Argentine national economic life began in Santa Fe with
founding of La Esperanza in 1854, followed by others (see
Colonization; Esperanza; Aarón de Castellanos); following the
reorganization Santa Fe set its political house in order with
a new provincial constitution and election of Patricio Cullén
as first constitutional governor; he was followed by very able
governor, Nicasio Oroño, who was, however, removed by
Catholic resentment against his institution of civil marriage;
by this time Santa Fe had begun to take on its modern aspect; public highway system was begun; Rosario was becoming important as a port and there was a strong movement in
1860s and 1870s to make it the national capital instead of
Buenos Aires (permanent selection of capital not made until
federalization of Buenos Aires in 1880); telegraph lines
reached Santa Fe in 1869, railroad extended to entire province by 1872, colonization continued expansion of commercial
agriculture; in 1883 Santa Fe's constitution was amended;
free, secular education was provided; in 1889 the University
of Santa Fe was established; this rapid growth and changing
pattern of life brought political repercussions; Santa Fe felt
the crisis of 1890 and was involved seriously in Radical revolution of 1893 (q.v.) that demonstrated the political unhappi-
ness of the growing middle class; federal intervention of
Santa Fe resulted; immigration continued and port of Santa
Fe was built in 1902 by its first Radical governor; Santa Fe
has continued to grow and prosper in the twentieth century;
commerce and industry have become increasingly important,
especially since the building of the tunnel under the river to
unite Santa Fe with Entre Ríos; this has made communication
with rest of Argentina easier.

Santa Fe has been called the granary of Argentina; its
major crop is wheat but corn, flax, rice, and other grains
are produced in quantity; the traditional cattle raising continues to be important, for dairy-farming as well as meat-
producing; industrialization is quite advanced; local products
are processed in dairy plants, meat packing houses, glass,
and beer factories; a tractor factory, half-owned by Italian
Fiat company, has also been established there, along with
other factories.

SANTA FE, CONVENTION OF (July 1828). National convention
    called originally by Vicente López y Planes who had succeeded
    Rivadavia briefly; provincial delegates met to draw up a fede-
    ralist constitution but conference was broken up because of
    rivalry for new presidency between Manuel Dorrego, new
    governor of Buenos Aires and Juan Bautista Bustos, governor
    of Córdoba; Bustos wanted conference moved to Córdoba to
    assure his own predominance but succeeded only in splitting
    the Congress and causing its failure.

SANTA FE CONSTITUTIONAL CONVENTION, 1852-1853. Convention, called by Urquiza, that drew up famous constitution of 1853, promulgated on May 25, of that year (see Constitution); Justo José de Urquiza was elected first president of new Argentine Confederation, with Buenos Aires remaining outside the union of the other provinces.

SANTA MARIA, CONSTANTE (1810-1893). Entrepreneur. Born in Gibraltar of Spanish parents; educated in London; accompanied his father to Argentina in 1831; quickly made a place for himself in porteño business and social world; among his friends were Juan Bautista Alberdi, Bartolomé Mitre, Quintana, Nicolás Avellaneda, Estrada and others; his home in Buenos Aires was a cultural meeting place of aristocracy; he and his father established the famous saladeros in Atalaya (Buenos Aires province) that operated under name of Llambí, Santa María y Cambaceres; supported building of Southern Railway and served on its first board of directors; returned to Europe as Argentine consul in Le Havre, Nice, and Pisa; died in latter city.

SANTA MARIA DE ORO, JUSTO see ORO, JUSTO SANTA MARIA DE

SANTA ROSA, BATTLE OF (October 12, 1870). Battle fought near arroyo of Santa Rosa in Entre Ríos in which national forces, commanded by General Ignacio Rivas, defeated the larger force of Ricardo López Jordán (q. v.), governor of Entre Ríos; latter was forced to retire from the battlefield and after defeat at Ñaembé (January 26, 1871), to flee into Brazil.

SANTA ROSA, BATTLE OF (October 2, 1874). Battle in Mendoza province that pacified entire country by ending Mitrista revolt following Avellaneda's election to the presidency, claiming that elections were fraudulent.
    Near village of Santa Rosa José Miguel Arredondo, leader of the revolutionary forces, twice clashed with government forces; in the first encounter the government leader, Colonel Amaro Catalán, was killed and his troops scattered; on December 7, the national troops returned to battle in the same place; led by General Julio A. Roca, they defeated their opponents and took General Arredondo prisoner; Roca himself was wounded; with the revolution over, the government granted amnesty to the rebels.

SANTAMARIANO(-A). Archeological adjective used to describe. special decorative art used by pre-Conquest Diaguita Indians; found in funeral urns of children; consists of stylized figures with symbolic significance, such as the rhea representing the wind, the serpent being the sun's rays, and the toad being water, with a human figure as suppliant.
    See El arte decorativa de los diaguitas by Serrano and Canals Frau, Prehistoria de América.

SANTIAGO, ACT OF (February 1953).   Bilateral economic agreement negotiated between President Juan D. Perón of Argentine Republic and President Carlos Ibáñez of Chile; provided
for elimination of custom duties and exchange differences.

SANTIAGO DE MOCOVI.   This Indian reducción, also called Cangayé, was located on the Río Bermejo and was founded in
1780; in 1943 it became a national historical site and has
been restored.

SANTIAGO DEL ESTERO (City and Province).   Interior northern
province centered around capital city of same name, oldest
permanent settlement (1551-1553) in what is now territory of
Argentine Republic; center of royal authority throughout most
of colonial period.
        Boundaries.   On the north, Salta and Chaco; on east
Chaco and Santa Fe; on south, Córdoba; and on west, Catamarca, Tucumán, and Salta.   Area of present province:
52,200 square miles.   Population: 495,419; density 9.5 persons per square mile.   Capital: Santiago del Estero; population approximately 100,000.
        Geography and economy.   Except for its mountainous
borders on west and south with Catamarca and Córdoba, the
province is a plain crossed from northwest to southeast by
the Dulce and Salado rivers; it was long hoped that the Salado River (q.v.) could be made navigable to provide province with outlet to Paraná and Atlantic but its seasonal flood-
ings and clogged channel made this unfeasible; attempts have
been made also to use waters of both rivers for irrigation;
large salt lakes are found in southwestern part of province;
the red and white quebracho forests of the Chaco extend into
the northwest portion of the province and have provided work
for poorly paid laborers who cut this wood and often made
charcoal from it for the Tucumán sugar mills; generally
speaking, the climate is that of a subtropical desert, hot
and dry, desperately needing water to stimulate agriculture;
cattle are found in small numbers, goats and mules in larger quantities.
        Communications.   Santiago del Estero linked with fed-
eral capital by highways, railroad, and airlines; the railroad
reached the capital city in 1884, finally linking it with the
coast and later with its neighbors; the General Güemes Highway links the capital city with San Miguel de Tucumán and
Santa Fe.
        History.   Following the conquest of Peru, Spanish con-
quistadores moved down old Inca highways into northwestern
Argentina by way of both Bolivia and Chile; groups from
these two areas contended for lands occupied by the Diaguita
and Calchaquí Indians who could be distributed in the familiar
encomienda (q.v.) pattern; Santiago del Estero became the
focus of these efforts and, after initial unsuccessful settlements (see Barco), the town was successfully established by
Francisco de Aguirre, 1553, near site of Barco III (1555) on

the Dulce River; approximately 12,000 Indians were distributed
among 48 encomenderos; the new town became the first center
of royal and ecclesiastical authority in Argentina; at first dependent on government of Chile, it was placed directly under
Viceroy of Peru in 1563 when the government of Tucumán
was created with Santiago del Estero as capital; in addition
to its administrative functions over what are now provinces
of Jujuy, Tucumán, Salta, Catamarca, and La Rioja, Santiago del Estero served as a base from which new explorations,
such as those seeking the City of the Caesars (q.v.), and new
settlements, like that at Córdoba, could be made; it was also
a trade center, designed to supply the mines of Bolivia with
food, mules, wagons, etc., and to link the interior with the
Río de la Plata estuary; in 1570 the diocese of Tucumán was
created with its seat at Santiago del Estero and in 1592
Father Fernando Trejo y Sanabria (q.v.) became bishop;
Franciscans, including San Francisco Solano, early established missionary work there; by early seventeenth century
Santiago del Estero had 400 vecinos, but was already surpassed by Córdoba, with 500; the small white minority ruled
a much larger number of Indians, mestizos, and black slaves,
all at mercy of hostile Indians on both sides of the narrow
trade corridor from Bolivia to Buenos Aires; by 1650 Córdoba had displaced Santiago del Estero as Argentina's major
urban center, largely because it was better located for agriculture; about the same time, town of Tucumán took over its
role of chief supplier for the mines as it was closer and
could more successfully produce the rice, mules, oxcarts,
cotton, etc., needed there; Santiago del Estero remained as
government center in a very slowly growing town with a considerable cotton and wool textile industry to support it.
        In 1783 the province became part of the intendancy of
Salta, along with latter province, Tucumán, Catamarca, and
Jujuy; its economy had already begun to suffer from economic
changes made following creation of the viceroyalty; Santia-
gueño woolen textiles could not compete in the lucrative coastal markets with those imported from England; not only was
the quality of the latter often preferred, but their prices
were cheaper due to the heavy transportation fees (100%)
from interior to Buenos Aires; in 1810 the town's population
numbered only 5,000; its cabildo, however, supported the
May Revolution, recognizing the patriot junta of Buenos Aires
June 29, 1810; shortly thereafter political conditions became
anarchic (1812-1822); in October 1814, the intendancy of Salta
was divided into two provinces: 1) Tucumán, consisting of
Santiago del Estero, Tucumán, and Catamarca; and 2) Salta,
with that province, Jujuy, and three Bolivian provinces of
Orán, Tarija, and Santa María; during the period from 1817
to 1820 many interior cabildos reclaimed political authority
for their individual provinces; attempt was made unsuccessfully in Santiago del Estero; in 1820 Tucumán intervened to restore order but the province finally seceded and came under
the control of the federalist caudillo Juan Felipe Ibarra (q.v.)

who governed it for most of the next three decades; joined
with other interior provinces, Córdoba, Santa Fe, La Rioja,
and Catamarca in opposing calling of new constituent congress in 1824, fearing that it would not recognize provincial
autonomy; sent representatives to the congress but refused to
accept Rivadavia, as president, or his centralized constitution; during Rosas' period Ibarra tried to persuade latter to
provide federalist constitution for the nation but latter refused, saying nation was not yet ready for formal organization; from 1835, when legislature was abolished, until 1851,
Ibarra ruled the poverty-stricken province; Santiago del Estero refused to support Urquiza's forces in the overthrow of
Rosas' government but on May 31, 1852, with Manuel Taboada
as governor, the province accepted treaty of San Nicolás; for
next thirty years Taboadas (q. v.) were in power most of the
time; in 1856 the first provincial constitution was written and
Juan Francisco Borges served as first constitutional governor.
        For next few decades federal intervention in provincial
politics was common, but in early twentieth century political
situation became more stable and more democratic; population
grew very slowly in spite of high birthrate as infant mortality
was abnormally high and few immigrants were attracted; economy developed very slowly because of lack of food and water;
railroad reached capital in 1884; first normal school, in
which Francisca Jacques (q. v.) and Juana Pérez served as
early directors, was established in 1881 (gradually expanded
to become Instituto Superior del Profesorado in 1953); and
Sarmiento public library was opened in 1893; by 1914 there
were only three towns besides the capital with a total urban
population of around 35,000; in the 1940s the province was
described as poverty stricken, with rural children hungry and
thirsty, and families living in mud huts; debt peonage was the
practice among quebracho workers in northwest, and the
people generally were at the mercy of the unpredictable climate that dried up their fishing streams and their crops and
reduced province's total livestock by one-third; since then,
there has been considerable progress; herds of livestock
have increased in size and great tracts of land near the capital have been brought into agricultural production by the
building of Los Quiroga Dam on the Dulce River (1950) with
its network of irrigation canals throughout the area; cotton
and alfalfa rank first in importance but fruits of all kinds,
including citrus, grapes, and olives are grown for the local
markets as well as vegetables; industry is being developed,
largely around raw products of area; among the most important towns outside the capital are Río Hondo, a winter resort
with thermal springs near mountain source of the Dulce River;
La Banda, just north of Santiago del Estero on the main highway, in which the national department of agriculture established an experimental station, largely devoted to cotton industry; and Loreto (San Martín), Frías, and Añatuya.
        Both city and province of Santiago del Estero are
still keenly aware of their historical role and seek to conserve

its memory in the archeological museum that contains a storehouse of relics from the pre-Columbian Indian cultures, in the popular and literary attention paid to rich folklore of province, and in restoring colonial buildings, especially religious ones, and declaring them to be historic monuments.

See Orestes di Lulio, Santiago del Estero, noble y leal ciudad, 1947, and El folklore de Santiago del Estero; also Actas capitulares de Santiago del Estero, Academia Nacional de la Historia, Buenos Aires, 1951, with introduction by Ricardo Levene.

SANTO TOME, ARMISTICE or PACT OF (April 9, 1816). Agreement signed by Eustaquio Días Vélez with Santa Fe rebels and supporters of Artigas; it provided for removal of Manuel Belgrano as commander-in-chief of the army of observation and his replacement by Díaz Vélez; Buenos Aires forces were to evacuate Santa Fe; Alvarez Thomas resigned as Supreme Director; Antonio González Balcarce became interim director; agreement was given to Artigas for ratification and Buenos Aires and Congress of Tucumán sent representatives to mediate but negotiations broke down and Santa Fe was again invaded in July 1816.

SANTOS LUGARES. Military barracks and prison during Rosas era. Site in San Martín partido of Buenos Aires where Franciscans established a mission and built a church in late eighteenth century; in 1806 English arrived there on way to confront Pueyrredón's forces at Perdriel; in 1840 Juan Manuel de Rosas established the general headquarters of his troops there near the church; barracks and prisons became notorious as rumors spread about brutal treatment and summary executions carried out there against suspected enemies of Rosas; after battle of Caseros, at request of people living in that vicinity, the government gave the settlement legal recognition as a village; renamed it San Martín (1856).

SANTOS VEGA. Legendary gaucho minstrel; invincible for years, eventually he was overcome by an unknown opponent (actually the Devil); became a favorite theme in Argentine literature with early short poem by Bartolomé Mitre (1838), epic poem in rural dialect by Hilario Ascasubi (1872), and shorter, brilliant poem by Rafael Obligado in literary Spanish (1877-1885); also theme of novel by Eduardo Gutiérrez and play by Juan C. Nosiglio, among others.

SANZ, FRANCISCO DE PAULA (d. 1810). Royal official; victim of May Revolution.

Born in Spain; came to Buenos Aires around 1780; was primarily charged with responsibility of establishing royal monopoly on tobacco there; served in several other capacities, including those of superintendent of war and navy and head of the Hermandad de la Caridad (Charity Brotherhood) (1784-1788); was transferred to Potosí, Bolivia; strongly

opposed the revolutionary movement of 1810 and when the
Buenos Aires auxiliary expedition reached Potosí, following
victory at Suipacha, Juan J. Castelli had him executed,
December 15, 1810, acting on orders from the patriot junta.

SARACHAGA, JUAN ANTONIO (1781-1840). Jurisconsult; able supporter of May Revolution and public figure during following
period; victim of Rosas' government.
     Born in Córdoba; in 1804 took his doctorate in both
civil and canon law at the University of San Carlos there;
enthusiastically supported May Revolution; served as secretary of governor of Salta and then of president of Charcas;
accompanied Juan Martín de Pueyrredón in latter's famous
retreat, following battle of Huaqui, back to Argentina with
funds from mint at Potosí; during next two years, served
patriot government as official in Córdoba, secretary of Chiclana, Junta's appointed governor of Salta (1811), secretary of
triumvirate government (1812); several times acted as rector
or vice rector of University of Córdoba; later supported
General José María Paz; became his foreign minister; reintroduced printing into Córdoba and founded various journals,
including the Unitarist El Montonero, in that province; became member of the society demanding freedom of the press;
also served on supreme court of Córdoba; selected by both
Córdoba and Salta as representative to national congress; contributed money, horses, and other gifts to cause of independence; performed important services in interpretation of civil
law during this early national period; had already retired
from all political activity in Buenos Aires when Rosas ordered him arrested as Unitarist; freed in 1833, he was later
arrested again, as political enemy, imprisoned, and executed
October 2, 1840.
     Although Sarachaga's role was largely supportive and
secondary, rather than as a leader, his contribution has been
recognized in writings of his contemporaries, such as Sarmiento and Paz, in his Memorias póstumas, and by such
later historians as Rivera Indarte, Bernardo Frías, and R.
Cárcano.

SARANDI, BATTLE OF (September 12, 1825). Defeat of Federico
Lecor's Brazilian force by Uruguayans led by Juan Antonio
Lavalleja; resulted in brief annexation of Uruguay to Argentina, with Lavalleja as governor (see "Treinta y Tres Orientales").

SARAVIA, JOSE DOMINGO (1782-1853). Patriot and military leader. Member of the distinguished Salta family; born and died
in Salta where he served the patriots' cause; news of the
May Revolution reached him in La Paz and he immediately
left to join Belgrano's army; Saravia commanded force that
took wounded from battle of Vilcapugio back to Jujuy; later,
under leadership of his father Pedro José, he took part in
the defense of Salta; in 1820 Martín Güemes promoted him

to sergeant major and sent him to Catamarca to buy horses
for the patriots; completed mission successfully, using his
personal funds for the purchase; served as member of the
legislature; emigrated to Bolivia when Facundo Quiroga took
over the government of Salta; returned to Salta and in 1853
he presided over the ceremony and festivities marking the
ratification of the new Argentine constitution; died a few days
later.

SARAVIA, JOSE VICENTE (1819-1883).   Lawyer and public figure.
        Born in Salta, son of José Domingo; graduated from
the law school of the University of Chuquisaca; his public
career began as a member of the provincial court (1845);
later, in 1854, he was elected criminal judge in Paraná;
Saravia represented Corrientes in the first congress of the
Confederation, of which he became vice president; as member of the supreme court he was visiting judge in Corrientes,
Entre Ríos, and Jujuy; in 1865 he was appointed district attorney and later national interventor of Jujuy; in 1876 was
elected provincial senator in Salta; died in the province of
Buenos Aires while visiting friends.

SARAVIA, MANUEL ANTONIO (1790-1879).   Patriot fighter for independence; governor of Salta.
        Born in Salta; left Salta in December 1810, with band
of 600 mounted men to offer their services to the patriot
junta in Buenos Aires; served first on Indian frontier in Santiago del Estero; was then assigned to Army of the North
under Belgrano; fought in battles of Tucumán, Salta, Vilcapugio, and Ayohuma; later, as sergeant major, served under
Martín Güemes; after war for independence had been won, he
continued military career, fighting against Santa Cruz of Bolivia in 1837-1838 and joining Ibarra against the Unitarist
forces in Salta and Tucumán; served as governor of his province between April and December 1842; during this period he
defeated a column of Lamadrid's forces led by Colonel Santos
whom he executed; in 1844 he again became governor and, in
spite of disturbances caused by Unitarist exiles in neighboring Bolivia, was able to make progress on construction of
public works in the capital, irrigation systems, roads, and
bridges; also introduced yerba mate plantations in district of
Orán; died at his estate in Payogasta (Salta) at age 89.

SARAVIA, PEDRO JOSE (1756-1832).   Military officer; hacendado;
patriot leader.
        Born in Salta; educated in Buenos Aires; in 1778 be-
came captain of dragoons in Salta; served as first alcalde of
the Salta cabildo in 1794; in 1803 he was appointed colonel
of volunteer militia regiment in Salta; his political, military,
and social prestige during closing years of the viceroyalty
brought him coveted appointment by Spanish crown as caballero of royal Order of Charles III; nevertheless, when May
Revolution took place in Buenos Aires (1810) he enthusiastically

supported it and became leader of patriot movement in Salta;
in August 1811, the Junta of Buenos Aires appointed him interim president of provincial Junta of Salta; later he aided
Belgrano in preparing for the defense of Salta against royalist invasion; reorganized his old militia regiment and fought
in the famous battle of Salta (q. v.), February 20, 1813, that
forced royalists to retreat to Bolivia; seven years later was
named civil and military prefect of Salta and furnished horses
from his own estancia, Castañares, for Governor Martín
Güemes' patriot gaucho force; in 1827 took José Ignacio Gorriti's place as governor very briefly; died in Salta.

SARMIENTO, DOMINGO FAUSTINO (1811-1888).   President of Argentine Republic, 1868-1874; literary writer; historian; statesman; diplomat; educator.
        Born in San Juan of relatively humble parents; studied
in native city and, with his uncle, Father José de Oro Albarracín, began his long career as an educator, teaching in
a mountain school in San Luis at same time that he was
studying; returning to San Juan, he obtained a government
position; joined Unitarists in fighting against Juan Facundo
Quiroga, 1828-1831; when latter won, Sarmiento fled into
exile in Chile where he was to spend much of his time during next two decades; taught school, learned English, and
worked for a time in mine at Copiapó; survived attack of typhoid fever; returned to San Juan in 1836, Quiroga having
been assassinated; entered into intellectual life of city, joined
literary society, and became acquainted with works of European Romantic writers that greatly influenced his own writing; in 1839 established a school for girls and published first
issue of controversial El Zonda (q. v.); on his way into exile
in Chile he inscribed his favorite motto on wall of hotel at
the resort of Zonda "On ne tue pas les idées" or "Ideas
cannot be destroyed"; from 1840 to 1852 he lived in Chile,
except for study trips to Europe, Africa, and America,
taken with aid of Manuel Montt, president of Chile; this was
one of his most active, creative periods; four of his most
famous works were written in Chile: the classic Facundo
(biography of Juan Facundo Quiroga--English title Civilization and Barbarism; see Facundo; also Sarmiento, in Suggested Readings, Appendix III); Recuerdos de provincia,
Argirópolis (q. v.), and Educación popular; wrote for various
newspapers, including El Mercurio, El Progreso, and La
Crónica, attracting wide attention from other Latin American
journalists; served as director of schools and was appointed
to reorganize the first teachers' training school in Chile;
Chilean government sent him to Europe and U. S. A. to study
school systems for this purpose; in Paris he was elected a
member of the French Royal Academy and, as his formal
paper for the academy, read a study of the famous and controversial (at that time, at least), interview between José de
San Martín and Simón Bolívar in Guayaquil, Ecuador, July
1822, based on interview with San Martín and with the

Argentine Liberator present at the Academy meeting; he later
wrote a biography of San Martín; in U.S.A. he met the educator Horace Mann and his wife (who translated his Facundo
into English) and brought back many of Mann's ideas for use
in Chile and later in Argentina.

Joined Urquiza and fought at battle of Caseros; differences between him and Urquiza forced him back into exile
in Chile; his Campaña en el ejército grande began his famous
polemic with Juan Bautista Alberdi (q.v.); Sarmiento's liberal
and democratic views and his commitment to importance of
education and immigration at this time show that U.S. influence had altered his earlier European orientation; in 1854 he
attempted to return to Argentina but was imprisoned in Mendoza, accused of conspiracy; released, he returned briefly to
Chile; both Tucumán, in the Argentine Confederation, and
province of Buenos Aires elected him to legislature but he
refused to serve; in May 1855, he returned to work for the
union of all the provinces; became editor of El Nacional;
spent some time that year in Paraná delta, introducing the
cultivation of wicker in that area; served briefly on governor's
advisory board and then was made director (1856-1862) of new
department of schools; also served as provincial senator, introducing legislation primarily concerned with agriculture and
education; was member of 1859 constituent convention; in
1860 became minister of government for Governor Bartolomé
Mitre; resigned because of problems between the confederation and Buenos Aires, including the death of his very close
friend Antonio Aberastain (q.v.), governor of San Juan; national reorganization under Mitre, following battle of Pavón
brought Sarmiento back into public life; as governor of San
Juan (1862) he improved education, mining industry, reformed
administration and judicial power; at same time widened popular suffrage and defeated montoneros of El Chacho (see
Angel Vicente Peñaloza); was appointed ambassador to U.S.,
Peru, and Chile; left for United States in 1864; traveled extensively there; in June, 1868, received an honorary doctor's
degree from University of Michigan; while in U.S. published
Life of Abraham Lincoln (1866) and magazine Ambas Américas, as a link between the two Americas; opposed Monroe
Doctrine, favoring international arbitration instead; was
elected president in 1868, while still away.

Was inaugurated as president in October 1868; continued to encourage immigration and to foster education;
founded military academy and naval school; established Normal School of Paraná (q.v.) to train secondary teachers; disturbed by census showing 71% of population illiterate, he
emphasized need for primary schools; number of children in
school increased from 30,000 to 120,000 during his six-year
term; brought U.S. teachers to train Argentine teachers;
founded school of science and mathematics under C. G. Burmeister at University of Córdoba; meanwhile he brought
Paraguayan War (q.v.) to an end; suppressed revolts of Ricardo López Jordán in Entre Ríos, 1870, 1872; intervened in

several provinces to maintain federal authority, with his own
province of San Juan causing him most trouble; was forced to
fight against revolt of Mitre after Avellaneda defeated him
for presidency in 1874; first national census was taken .in
1869; Central railroad extended to Córdoba; telegraph lines
were laid and roads, bridges, etc., were built; continued in
public life after his presidency, became senator from San
Juan in 1875; Congress gave him commission as general; became director general of schools of Buenos Aires province
and wrote daily for La Tribuna; served in Avellaneda's cabinet as minister of interior for a time; in 1881 became general superintendent of national education; returned to Chile on
visit; Argentine government authorized publication of his complete works, accomplished, under direction of his grandson
Belín Sarmiento, in 52 volumes; at age of 75, published Vida
de Dominguito, biography of his son who died in Paraguayan
War; died in Asunción, Paraguay, where he had gone in
search of a better climate for his various illnesses.
       One of the most famous and colorful leaders Argen-
tina has produced, Sarmiento is also somewhat controversial;
historians sometimes find his work more passionate than
scholarly; Argentine Nationalists have accused him of selling
out his country to foreigners, especially to the United States,
because of his proposal to import an American general to
end the Paraguayan War; or to the British to whom he
awarded generous construction grants for railroads, etc.,
thus making Argentina into a "British colony"; one such historian says of him 'El 'loco' Sarmiento es un espectáculo
permanente" (that crazy Sarmiento is a permanent sideshow);
his work as a romantic writer, however, has survived all
political differences; his Facundo, a masterpiece of romantic
writing as well as early gaucho literature, is still widely
read, as is Recuerdos de provincia about nineteenth century
San Juan; he made vigorous contributions to Argentine life
and development; above all else, in spite of his reiterated
devotion to urban (and often foreign) civilization, he himself
remained utterly Argentine.

SARMIENTO DE LENOIR, PROCESA (1818-1899). Painter. Born
    in San Juan; sister of Domingo Faustino; taught in several
    schools but is better known because of her paintings and
    portraits such as those of her brother, her daughters, Guil-
    lermo Rawson, and Monsignor W. Archával; other paintings
    include those of Saint Francis, Mary Magdalene, Our Lady of
    Perpetual Help, etc.

SAROBE, JOSE MARIA (1888-1946). Career military officer; his-
    torical writer.
         Born in La Plata (Buenos Aires); graduated from
    Colegio Militar in 1908; among his various assignments were
    those of military attaché at embassy in Rio de Janeiro, sec-
    retary of minister of war, secretary of commander-in-chief
    of army; military attaché in Japan; in the military events of

September 6, 1930 Sarobe was a leader of the group supporting Justo; later when Justo was elected president, Sarobe
held such positions as aide-de-camp to the president, chief
of staff of first division of army, commandant of fourth division, and commandant of first military region; represented
Argentine army at the Eighth Pan American Conference, Lima,
1938; received many honors and decorations; in the early
1940s, after outbreak of World War II in Europe, when military groups were forming for political action, Sarobe was
identified with those supporting liberal, professional military
tradition; attained rank of brigadier general and retired from
active service in 1943; died three years later.

Sarobe wrote several books of historical nature; his
Memorias sobre la revolución del 6 de septiembre de 1930
is considered to be the best chronology of the events (in
which he took part) that overthrew Yrigoyen and brought Uriburu into power; his study of the problems of Patagonia won
the General San Martín prize of the Círculo Militar in 1935;
he also wrote El general Urquiza y la campaña de Caseros
(1843-1852) and contributed to the Historia de la nación argentina edited by the Academia Nacional de la Historia.

SARRATEA, MANUEL DE (1774-1849). Political, military, and
diplomatic figure of independence and early national periods.

Born in Buenos Aires; educated in Europe; returned to
Buenos Aires to engage in early unsuccessful mission to Rio
de Janeiro in attempt to secure mutually advantageous agreement with Portuguese royal government and Buenos Aires
patriot junta; elected member of first triumvirate government
(1811) and then sent to command patriot troops in Banda
Oriental (Uruguay); in that same year (1811) negotiated armistice with Marquis de Casa Irujo of Brazil; confronted Artigas instead of conciliating him, as ordered, and clashed with
his own troops who overthrew him, largely because of his
lack of military experience, and replaced him with José
Rondeau whom he had appointed as commander of vanguard;
returned to Buenos Aires and was sent (1814) as diplomatic
representative to London and Madrid to seek British support
for establishment of constitutional monarchy under legitimate
prince (see Monarchy); mission failed largely because of
critical events during 1814-1815, including restoration of
Ferdinand VII to Spanish throne and defeat of Napoleon at
Waterloo; Sarratea returned to Buenos Aires and became minister of government and of foreign relations under Supreme Director Pueyrredón; resigned because of bad health; was accused of conspiracy in 1818 but quickly freed; on February 16,
1820, with anarchy and civil wars prevailing throughout the
provinces, Sarratea was elected governor of province of
Buenos Aires; a few days later, he signed treaty of Pilar
with Francisco Ramírez and Estanislao López to end civil
war in littoral area; as a result of the porteño dislike of
this agreement, he was overthrown by popular revolt; moved
to Entre Ríos where he made his home until Rivadavia

appointed him as minister to Great Britain in 1826; later
(1839) sent on special mission to Rio de Janeiro; went as
minister plenipotentiary to France in 1840; died there in
1849; his remains were brought back to Buenos Aires the
following year.

SASTRE, MARCOS (1808-1886). Educator; bookseller; writer.
        Born in Montevideo; moved to Concepción del Uruguay;
studied philosophy in University of Córdoba, 1826-1829; in
1833 opened bookstore in Buenos Aires that became a reading and literary center for young Argentine intellectuals, and
greatly influenced development of the romantic movement and
lives of those committed to it (see Esteban Echeverría; Generation of 1837; Asociación de Mayo) but had little impact on
his own career; after his shop was closed in 1837, he moved
to the river delta area where he wrote El tempe argentino,
considered by many to be his best work.
        Most of his life was devoted to education; he loved all
forms of teaching, from that of the children themselves, to
that of training their teachers in normal schools; created
schools; created better pedagogical methods and wrote better
textbooks; crusaded for more humane methods of teaching
children and opposed secularization of education; began his
career as director of the federal republican school (1844);
opened a primary school in San Fermando (1846) and in 1849
was in Santa Fe, teaching at Colegio de San Jerónimo and in
charge of that province's first public library, founded by Pascual Echagüe; also published textbook for reading and writing,
Anagnosia, adopted officially by Santa Fe, Entre Ríos, and
Buenos Aires; founded Santa Fe weekly, El Semanario; Urquiza brought him to Entre Ríos to edit El Federal Entrerriano and (1850) named him general inspector of schools of
Entre Ríos for which Sastre drew up general guidelines in
provisional regulation; returned to Buenos Aires following defeat of Rosas and became director of the public library and
then of the new Normal School, founded by Vicente Fidel
López; became involved in political conflicts between Urquiza
and Buenos Aires and was briefly imprisoned by latter, but
arrival of Sarmiento, in Buenos Aires, whose precursor in
education he is often considered to have been, brought him
into the mainstream of the new educational development,
first of Buenos Aires province, and then of the Argentine Republic; wrote textbooks on spelling, reading, instruction on
building of schools, etc.; unsuccessfully promoted creation of
agricultural school; again became director of normal school;
in 1880 he opened a new bookstore in Buenos Aires; served
several terms as member of national council of education,
position that he held at time of his death in Buenos Aires;
honored as one of Argentina's great educators.

SAUBIDET, FRANCISCO DE PAULA (1754-1829). Government official; first director of Buenos Aires provincial archives.
        Born in Sevilla, Spain; came to America in 1777 with

clerical position under Corregidor of Huaylas, Peru; hoped
to continue to Buenos Aires to become a merchant but was
persuaded by royal official Francisco de Paula Sanz to go into government administration; was appointed to go to Paraguay to stimulate growth and processing of tobacco there under royal monopoly of that industry; later became responsible
for collection of revenues from royal monopolies on both playing cards and tobacco in Buenos Aires; supported the May
Revolution and was given similar official responsibilities by
the patriots who valued his ability and experience; Assembly
of 1813 confirmed his citizenship in United Provinces of Río
de la Plata; when tobacco was placed on free trade list,
Saubidet was transferred to other duties; in 1821 he was appointed, with aid of Jerónimo Lasala and Mariano Yega, to
create and organize the archives of the province of Buenos
Aires; spent three years on this project until poor health
forced him to retire in 1824; died in Buenos Aires.

SAUCE DE LUNA, BATTLE OF (also known as battle of Cambay)
September 20, 1820.   Final battle in Entre Ríos in which
Francisco Ramírez defeated Uruguayan leader José Gervasio
Artigas and eliminated him from Argentine political life;
Artigas fled to Paraguay.

SAUCE GRANDE, BATTLE OF (July 16, 1840).   Site in Entre Ríos
where the Unitarist General Juan Lavalle was defeated by
Federalist Pascual Echagüe, effectively ending former's hope
of gaining control of the province of Entre Ríos as a base
for operations against Rosas; Lavalle was forced back across
Paraná River; Lavalle left some forces in Entre Ríos to
fight against Echagüe, but Governor Pedro Ferré of Corrientes considered Lavalle's movement treason since it left Corrientes open to Rosas' forces; this began the collapse of the
Unitarist coalition against Rosas.

SAVIO, MANUEL N.   (1892-1948).   Division general; military engineer; often called father of modern Argentine heavy industry.
        Born in Buenos Aires, son of Italian immigrant; chose
military career, entering Colegio Militar in 1809; attended
Escuela Superior de Guerra (advanced war college) and the
advanced technological school; supported Uriburu in revolution of 1930; became director of Escuela Superior Técnica,
making it a center for studying the technological problems
related to developing heavy industry and a promoter of economic nationalism; in 1941 Castillo appointed Savio as first
director of the newly created Directorate General of Military
Factories (q.v.), a mixed state and private company formed
to develop a national steel and iron industry, as well as
other war-related industries; Savio continued working for this
goal after World War II was over; the bill, finally passed by
Congress in 1947, providing for the creation of the Sociedad
Mixta Siderúrgica Argentina (SOMISA, q.v.) was given his

name because of his leadership in securing it; in addition to
his military and official contributions, Savio wrote several
books, including Movilización industrial (1933); Política argentina del acero and Política de la producción metalúrgica
argentina (1942); and Conceptos que fundamentaron el proyecto
de ley de fabricaciones militares (1944).

SCALABRINI, PEDRO (1848-1916).   Naturalist; educator; said to
have been first to introduce Positivism into Argentine intellectual life.
        Born in Italy; emigrated to Argentina for political rea-
sons in 1868; established close relationship with Sarmiento;
opened a private school, named Florencio Varela, in which
he applied one of his favorite pedagogical theories: the introduction of greater freedom and spontaneity into the classroom
through use of student self-discipline instead of authoritarian
rule; later moved to Paraná (1872) where he established another school and then became professor of philosophy in the
normal school established there by Sarmiento; introduced the
ideas of Auguste Comte--Positivism--and greatly influenced a
generation of Argentine leaders and trained the nation's best
teachers for the next few decades; his interest in archeology
and paleology brought increased interest into his classroom
lectures and was further reflected in the public museums of
natural history that he established in Paraná, Corrientes,
and Buenos Aires; moved to Corrientes where he founded and
became important writer for review La Escuela Positivista
that was used as guideline for development of educational system in Corrientes and also gave wide distribution to Positivist ideas; in 1899 became director of new Normal School of
Esquina (province of Corrientes); moved to Buenos Aires
where he continued his interests in science by promoting establishment of school museums, teaching science, and taking
part in scientific congresses held in Buenos Aires and Montevideo; founded and became president of National Teachers
Association; in addition to his many contributions and articles
in newspapers and reviews, he wrote longer works of which
one of the most important was Materialismo, darwinismo,
positivismo.

SCALABRINI ORTIZ, RAUL (1898-1959).   Nationalist intellectual
and writer.
        Born in Corrientes; studied at faculty of exact, physi-
cal and natural sciences in Buenos Aires, and at Sorbonne in
Paris; became a writer in both journalistic and literary
fields; edited La Nación (1926-1929), El Mundo, and Noticias
Gráficas; was founder and editor of the daily Reconquista;
his strong nationalist feelings manifested themselves in the
"muckraking" (Rennie), but detailed, studies of British control over Argentine economy, especially its railroads, that
brought him to public notice; these included Política británica
en el Río de la Plata (1936), Los ferrocarriles, factor principal de la independencia nacional (1937), and Historia de los

ferrocarriles argentinos (1940); in 1947 he was awarded prize by National Commission of Culture for his work Los ferrocarriles deben ser del pueblo argentino ("The Railroads Ought to Belong to Argentine people"); in 1940s he was among those intellectuals who opposed President Ortiz's attempts to establish a somewhat pro-Allied Argentine neutral position in early years of World War II; his literary works reveal a search for Argentine identity in the new society formed by recent influx of immigrants, especially in Buenos Aires; La manga (1923) is a collection of tales dealing with porteño scenes and types; most famous was his El hombre que está solo y espera (1931); the author himself describes this as "a psychological and esthetic guide to Buenos Aires"; in it he makes a brilliant analysis of porteño personality through depicting a man on street corner of Buenos Aires; in 1948 he published a book of poems Tierras sin nada, tierra de profetas.

SCHICKENDANTZ, FEDERICO (1837-1896). Chemist who contributed to economic and scientific development of Argentine Republic.
Born in Germany; studied in Heidelberg and Munich; continued scientific research at Oxford; came to Argentina, about 1861, under contract to work for mines in Catamarca owned by Samuel A. Lafone Quevedo; established himself there at Pilciao, 1862-1870, working to improve gold and copper mining operations; following this he studied alkaloids that might be extracted from trees in that area; in 1871 he moved to Tucumán as director of its agricultural school; also lectured in physics and chemistry; returned for a time to Catamarca where he directed the Colegio Nacional; in 1880s returned to Tucumán and made chemical discoveries that improved both the growing and processing of sugar cane and attracted attention of scientists elsewhere; he was placed in charge of chemical office of San Miguel de Tucumán; began publication of its Anales and worked with Miguel Lillo, later director of the chemical department; moved to Buenos Aires in 1892; taught in Colegio Nacional, then took charge of chemical section of the Museum of La Plata; left to become director of chemical office in Mendoza, where he died.

SCHMIDEL (or SCHMIDT), ULRICH (c. 1510-c. 1579). Early German chronicler of Río de la Plata conquest. Schmidel, a Bavarian soldier in employ of German banking house of Fuggers that helped finance expedition of Pedro de Mendoza, accompanied this expedition to the Río de la Plata; for his own reasons, or for his employers, he kept a detailed, descriptive diary or chronicle of events from 1534 to 1554; was present at first founding of Buenos Aires and then at that of Asunción; also describes political events of Cabeza de Vaca period in Asunción; returned home after 20 years, summoned back by his employers and carrying special communication from Domingo Martínez de Irala to Emperor Charles V; his mission accomplished, he went on to Antwerp, arriving there in January 1554.

The first German edition of his work was published in Frankfort-au-Main in 1567; an English translation was published by Hakluyt Society, The Conquest of the River Plate, 1535-1555, Vol. 81, Part I Voyage of Ulrich Schmidt to the River La Plata and Paraguay (London, 1891); a good Argentine edition is that translated by Samuel A. Lafone Quevedo and edited by Bartolomé Mitre, Viaje al Río de la Plata (Buenos Aires, 1903).

SCHULZ SELLACK, CHARLES (d. 1879). German physicist. Arrived from U.S.A. in 1871 to work in astronomy observatory in Córdoba; became a founding member of school of physical and mathematical sciences at University of Córdoba and of that city's academy of sciences; carried out important scientific research projects in Argentina during his brief stay; later published them in English and in German; also wrote description of The Factory of Meat Extract in Fray Bentos; left Argentina in 1874; died in Berlin.

SCHWARTZ, FELIPE (1850-1895). Industrialist. Born in Berlin; arrived in Argentina in 1854 with his parents; brought up on a ranch in Magdalena; his gift for mechanics and working with metal brought him employment as machinist on river boat to Santa Fe; made influential friends there who persuaded him to open blacksmith shop in Buenos Aires; this developed into the industrial ironworks known as Casa Amarilla; invented first iron safe, chain pump widely used in rural areas, and constructed first Argentine threshing machine; while supervising construction of tall building on Avenida de Mayo, he fell and was killed.

SCRIVENER, JUAN H. (1806-1884). Physician. Born in England; arrived in Buenos Aires in 1825 at invitation from his friend Dr. Diego Paroissien (q. v.); hoped to participate in Bolivian silver mining venture; when this failed, he remained in Argentina for several decades as physician in Salta and other cities; in 1857 served as secretary of British consul in Paraná; distinguished himself by unselfish services during cholera epidemics of 1866 and 1867; returned to England in 1871 and published his memoirs, describing Argentina in the middle decades of nineteenth century; translated into Spanish by Lola Tosi de Diéguez, published in Buenos Aires, 1937.

SECOND TRIUMVIRATE   see   TRIUMVIRATES, FIRST AND SECOND

SEIBO (or CEIBO).   Tree whose beautiful red blossom was declared the national flower of Argentina in 1942.   Belongs to Papilionaceae family of general order of Leguminosae plants (legume or bean); several varieties are found in Argentina, especially in the Paraná delta, pampas and northern areas; the trees are valued not only for their shade and beauty but for some usefulness; its wood becomes very hard when wet

and was used by Indians for boats and shields; medicines and
dyes have been extracted from its flowers; its seeds, bark,
and sap have also been used for medicines, balsams and healing salves; the blossoms vary in color, according to variety,
from brilliant scarlet to rosy pink.

SEMANARIO DE AGRICULTURA, INDUSTRIA Y COMERCIO. One
of first weekly newspapers published in Buenos Aires; founded
by Hipólito Vieytes September 1, 1802, it lasted until 1807
during British invasions; printed in the press of Niños Expósitos, the complete collection fills five volumes, numbering
218 issues; Manuel Belgrano and Pedro Cerviño were active
collaborators with Vieytes; this paper was devoted to economic
topics as indicated in its title.

SEPICH LANGE, JUAN RAMON (1906-   ).   Priest; philosopher;
writer.
       Born in Buenos Aires; studied in Buenos Aires, Rome
and Germany; taught philosophy and theology in the Seminary
and moved to the National University of Cuyo in 1943, where
he was dean of the school of philosophy and created the Institute of Philosophy; in 1944 taught in the University of Buenos
Aires and in La Plata; left Argentina during Juan Domingo
Perón's first period of government, and during his absence
was cultural attaché to the Argentine Legation of Switzerland,
1948-1949, and to the Embassy in the Vatican, 1950-1954; returned in 1955 to Mendoza to teach; in 1943 Dr. Sepich was
awarded second prize by the Comisión Nacional de Cultura for
his philosophical writings; his published works include La teología de la fe en la crítica cortesiana (1937); Lógica formal
(1944); Introducción a la filosofía (1942); La actitud del filóso-
fo (1952); La filosofía del ser y el tiempo de W. Heidegger
(1954) and others.

SERENOS. Nightwatchmen used in Argentine cities during middle
half of nineteenth century; name comes from their practice
of loudly announcing, throughout the night, the hour and
weather, for example "las doce han dado y sereno" or "twelve
o'clock and all is clear (and well)" or "lluvioso" on rainy
nights.
       During colonial period nightly security services in
towns were provided by citizens or soldiers directed by may-
or; in 1805 cabildo of Buenos Aires attempted to establish
regular night watchmen service but was unsuccessful; similar
attempt was made in 1815 and another in 1821 by police
deputy Joaquín de Achával but both failed; Governor Balcarce
reopened project in 1833 and the following year General Lucio
N. Mansilla, chief of police in Buenos Aires, established
first sereno corps; it consisted of 14 men who patrolled central 33 blocks of city, with salaries paid by city taxes; number soon increased and during governorship of Juan Manuel
de Rosas corps became so closely linked with his government
that it was disbanded after latter's fall; reorganized almost

immediately with serenos mounted for their nightly watch; in
Buenos Aires, as in other cities, their duties included handling of citizen emergencies, such as calling of doctor or
priest, relighting of flares and lights accidentally extinguished,
as well as maintenance of law and order; in early 1870s their
duties were assumed by the regular police forces; serenos
discontinued in Buenos Aires in 1872 but lasted until 1883 in
Rosario.

SERRANO, JOSE (1634-1713).   Jesuit missionary; author (or translator) of first book published in Argentina.
    Born in Andalusia, Spain; arrived in Río de la Plata
in 1658; spent next seven years in various religious posts
and in mastering Guaraní language; began missionary work
among Guaraní Indians in 1665; because the Jesuit missionaries were very eager to make the religious writings of
Spanish Jesuit Juan Eusebio Nieremberg available to the Indians, Father Serrano translated his De la diferencia entre lo
temporal y eternal and other works into Guaraní language; he
and Father Juan Bautista Neumann (q.v.) introduced printing
press into Misiones; published this first book in 1705; Father
Serrano performed other duties for the Jesuits, serving as
secretary general of Order in that area; rector of the colegio
in Buenos Aires (1696) and of that in Asunción later; he died
in Loreto, Guaraní mission town.
    Serrano's role in history of Argentine printing has
been studied by Jorge T. Medina in his Historia y bibliografía de la conquista en el Río de la Plata; a copy of the
book published in 1705 was included in collection made by
Pedro de Angelis, Rafael Trelles, and Enrique Peña and
copies of various pages of this appear in Francisco P. Moreno's Historia de la bibliografía de la imprenta en el Virreinato del Río de la Plata.

SERRANO, JOSE MARIANO (1788-1852).   Lawyer; signer of Declarations of Independence of both Argentina and Bolivia.
    Born in Chuquisaca; graduated from University there
(1811); joined independence movement in Tucumán (1812);
represented Chuquisaca in Assembly of 1813; two years later
he collaborated in drafting the provisional statute; represented Charcas at Congress of Tucumán where he was considered one of the most notable members; served as one of
secretaries; signed declaration of independence July 9, 1816;
when constitution of 1819 was signed, Serrano was vice president of Congress; resigned in November 1819, and was returning to Tucumán when he was captured by Francisco
Ramírez's forces; eventually freed; became adviser and secretary of governors Araoz and González; in 1825 he represented Chuquisaca in assembly of Alto Peru; became its president and wrote and signed the proclamation that gave Bolivia
its national independence August 6, 1825; when new Bolivian
courts were established Serrano became member and then
president of supreme court; served briefly as interim president

of Bolivia; exiled briefly for political reasons, Dr. Serrano
wrote the biography of General José Ignacio Gorriti, his
friend and fellow-congressman at Tucumán; also wrote poems
in honor of Andrés Santa Cruz; was serving as president of
supreme court when he died.

SEYMOUR, RICHARD ARTHUR.   Early British settler on Córdoba
Indian frontier; recorded his four years' (1865-1869) experience on the pampas area in the book Pioneering in the Pampas or The First Four Years of the Settler's Experience in
La Plata, published in 1869; describes his attempts to grow
sheep on his ranch; he also describes in detail the flora and
fauna of the region; cholera and continuing Indian attacks
(Ranqueles) forced him to leave the country; his book was
translated into Spanish by Justo P. Sáenz, Jr. and published
in 1947.

SHAYHUEQUE.   Chief of Christian Manzanero Indians of fruit growing area in Río Negro; joined with whites in fighting to defend
frontier from raiding Indians; the Manzaneros were semicivilized, working the soil and tending the apple trees; made a
drink called pulcú similar to hard apple cider.

SHEEP AND WOOL.   Although sheep were introduced into Argentina at the same time as cattle, they did not become important in the economy until the nineteenth century; for a few
decades at its close and at beginning of twentieth they were
dominant and have continued important.
        During 1550s various Spanish expeditions brought sheep
from Upper Peru through Chaco to Asunción; others brought
them into Tucumán from Peru and Chile; Indians in northwest
area had used wool of native animals of llama type and were
easily trained to care for sheep; wool was used in weaving
industries of that area; Garay took sheep from Asunción to
Buenos Aires in 1580 and some wool was exported from that
port to Spain in early 1600s but this was quickly forbidden as
Spain had its own superior and carefully protected wool industry; for two centuries the sheep industry centered in Andean area and Córdoba; lagged in the pampas as these had
neither proper grazing nor labor; there was no Argentine demand for the mutton; wool and sheep's tallow were used
locally, with the meat thrown away; in the 1800s British saw
in Argentina possibilities for commercial sheep raising (Popham spoke of wool and tallow as possible exports in 1806)
although wild criollo sheep produced wool too inferior for
market; sheep's tallow began to be exported; during Rivadavia's administration (1825) first 100 Merinos were imported
in attempt to improve breeding; cross between these and Argentine sheep still produced poor wool--too short, brittle,
fine; after commercial treaty of 1825 Irish, Scottish, English
sheepmen began to introduce better techniques and new breeds;
brought both skilled labor and capital; as a result, wool constituted 7% of total exports in 1830s; by 1880s this had risen

to 50-60%, with most of the sheep in Buenos Aires province
where they had pushed cattle farther south, and in Santa Fe
and Entre Ríos; with the Conquest of the Desert, all of Patagonia was open to sheep; Argentine sale of wool to U.S. had
increased greatly during U.S. Civil War but its end brought
lowered demand and high protective tariffs; fortunately British
demand for mutton increased and frigoríficos were better able
to handle these smaller carcasses than large beef ones at
first so estancieros turned to raising Lincoln sheep and other
good meat producers, along with those that furnished wool
for European carpet-makers; British capital imported sheep
for better breeding, built packing plants for shipping refrigerated mutton, and built railroads and established shipping
lines to bring Patagonian sheep to market; sheep industry
dominated economy until beginning of 1900s serving as transition from saladero to modern estancia economy; then a prolonged and serious depression in these wool markets combined
with disastrous floods in Buenos Aires that killed 14,000,000
sheep to break the sheepraisers' domination of the economy;
during World War I sheep were again very profitable but the
new pattern of agriculture, cattle, and sheep had developed
on the pampas; in 1970s sheep are raised for wool, meat,
fur (karakul), and milk (Romney Marsh and Lincoln); Argentina is world's fourth largest producer of wool (one-third of
this from Patagonia) and wool remains important Argentine
product; also produces mutton and tallow (see U.S. Relations
with Argentina for important role of wool).

SHIPYARDS (Astilleros). Shipyards scarcely existed in Argentina
until the nineteenth century and still do not provide boats
and ships adequate for the nation's naval and commercial
needs; during the colonial period boat and ship building was
largely confined to up-river areas, like Paraguay, Corrientes,
and Entre Ríos, which produced for the river traffic; individual carpenters or shipbuilders occasionally added to the
supply, and ships were commonly bought from traders who
had come into port; lack of lumber and naval stores in area
around Buenos Aires largely responsible; continued government sponsorship of shipyards since the early nineteenth
century at El Riachuelo and elsewhere produced cannonboats
used in the war against Brazil, steamboats for river trade,
and eventually ships of all kinds to handle a large portion of
national needs.

S.I.A.M. (Sociedad Industrial de Maquinarias Argentinas Di Tella,
Ltda.) Argentine industrial complex that manufactures and
distributes wide variety of industrial goods, including bakery
machinery and other heavy machinery, pumps, especially
gasoline pumps; electrical household appliances and electronic
equipment of all kinds; oil pipe and equipment for petroleum
firms; founded by Torcuato Di Tella (q.v.) in 1910, incorporated in 1928, remained under his personal control and
leadership until his death in 1948; by that time S.I.A.M. had

become one of foremost leaders in Argentina's new thrust toward industrialization and economic nationalism.

Company began as partnership between Di Tella and
Allegrucci brothers to manufacture new dough-kneading machine, perfected by Guido Allegrucci, to replace imported
machines not suited to Argentine flour; immediate success
with commercial bakeries in this venture brought expansion
into other fields; company took name of S. I. A. M. (initials of
department in which patent for kneader had been granted:
Sección Industrial Amasadoras Mecánicas; name S. I. A. M.
continued, with initials standing for different title after incorporation) with trademark showing Argentine gaucho strain-
ing to turn massive gear wheel; operations developed and
broadened through imaginative advertising, innovations, expansion, international licensing agreements with such firms
as British Motor Corporation, Kelvinator, Pomona Pump,
Wayne Pump; close relationship with YPF (Argentine national
petroleum company) brought S. I. A. M. into foundry operations
also; although Di Tella and many, if not most, of his managers and workers were European-born, company's production
and advertising programs were tied closely to Argentine interests and needs; spreading from original establishment in
Buenos Aires, new plants were opened in Rosario and La
Plata, as well as in other parts of republic; branches and
subsidiaries established in other Latin American countries,
with offices also in New York and London; Di Tella, whose
vast enterprise was run along lines combining patrón system
with most modern technological business and financial principles and procedures, opposed President Perón's policy of
government control of industry and labor; S. I. A. M. survived
during Perón period largely because of its ability to demonstrate that its own policies were already strongly nationalistic,
its capital and control Argentine, and its wages and benefits
to labor satisfactory.

After a lapse of about ten years following Torcuato Di
Tella's death in 1948, the younger son Guido returned from
study in the United States to take active part in managing
company; in 1958 the Di Tella Foundation was set up as a
form of non-profit trust to administer large part of capital;
members of Di Tella family included on boards of directors
to renew family ties with S. I. A. M. ; funds to establish Institute (see Instituto Torcuato Di Tella) for advancing learning,
research and the arts; S. I. A. M. became largely holding company for its various affiliates; in 1960s inflation, new competition, and world wide financial problems were reflected in
S. I. A. M. plans and operations.

See Thomas Childs Cochran and Rubén E. Reina,
Entrepreneurship in Argentine Culture.   Torcuato Di Tella
and S. I. A. M. (Philadelphia, University of Pennsylvania Press,
1962).

SICK, FEDERICO L. (1830s-1906). Physician, specialist in internal medicine.

Born and educated in Germany; came to Asunción under contract with President Francisco Solano López (1862); when Paraguayan War broke out he fled to Corrientes and then (1868) to Córdoba where he established his practice; became deeply interested in study of colitis, endemic in that area; blamed it on improper diet and treated it accordingly; also devised advanced treatments for respiratory diseases and inflammation; died in Córdoba following cholera epidemic.

SILPITOCLE. Famous leader of Calchaquí Indians in revolt against Spaniards in late sixteenth and early seventeenth centuries at time that San Francisco Solano came to region; war in area around La Rioja lasted about 30 years.

See Fernando Márquez Miranda, La antigua provincia de los diaguitas, v. 1, Academia Nacional de Historia; Pedro Lozano, Historia de la conquista del Paraguay, Río de la Plata y Tucumán.

SILVA DE GURRUCHAGA, MARTINA DE (1790-1873). Colonial dame of Salta.

Born in Salta of Spanish parents; married José Gurruchaga who was an ardent patriot like his brother Francisco; made many contributions toward Belgrano's victory over Pío Tristán's troops at Salta, February 20, 1813; she entertained Belgrano in her home before the battle; she led her friends in propagandizing the officers of royalist army in favor of patriot cause; embroidered the sun on the battle flag that she donated to patriot forces; on the morning of the battle, she appeared at head of guerrilla force that she had organized, armed, and equipped from her private funds for support of Belgrano's army; a week later, in return for her support, Belgrano gave her a beautiful tapada (cloak or large shawl) with inscription on its border "A la benemérita patriota capitana del ejército doña Martina de Gurruchaga," and along with it the commission for that military rank; at other times she made generous cash donations toward army expenses; died in Salta.

SILVER see MINES, MINING

SINSACATE. Colonial post house in province of Córdoba; an historic monument since 1941.

Posthouse 60 km. from Córdoba, was used in eighteenth century by travelers going by old road from Córdoba to Potosí; today road links Córdoba and Santiago del Estero; Sinsacate was built in 1709, probably by the Jesuits on estancia of Jesús María; consisted of chapel and several adjacent small buildings; parts of original chapel remain; rest restored by Mario J. Buschiazzo; both Manuel Belgrano and Juan Lavalle used Sinsacate in their travels in this area; most important historically was role it played in assassination of Juan Facundo Quiroga February 16, 1835, at Barranco Yaco, 9 km. away; it served as headquarters for those

involved in the murder and burial place for Quiroga and
those killed with him; in modern times the posthouse has become a museum displaying objects and antiquities relating to
the old post system as well as other relics of eighteenth and
nineteenth centuries.

SIPE SIPE, BATTLE OF (November 29, 1815). Site in central
    Bolivia, near Cochabamba, where royalist troops commanded
    by General Joaquín de Pezuela defeated patriot forces of José
    Rondeau (Spaniards called it battle of Viluma); considered the
    worst defeat suffered by Argentine patriot forces in war for
    independence; represented third, and last, time that patriot
    invading army into Bolivia was repelled; provinces of Upper
    Peru were lost to United Provinces; victory proved San Mar-
    tín's thesis that independence could not be won by fighting
    along the royal highway to Lima and opened way for his plan
    of crossing Andes and attacking Lima by expedition from
    Chilean port; proved to be important in developing Bolivia's
    desire for separation from Argentina in independence; royalist
    victor Pezuela became new viceroy of Peru; Spain hailed vic-
    tory as end of Spanish American War for independence in
    South America but less than eight months later Argentina de-
    clared its independence and in February 1817, the battle of
    Chacabuco, assuring Chile's independence, was won by San
    Martín's Army of the Andes.

SIVORI, EDUARDO (1847-1918).   "Painter of the pampa"; intro-
    duced etching to Argentina.
        Born in Buenos Aires; early entered business; on a
    trip to Italy in 1874 he became fascinated with the art that he
    saw there; returned to Argentina to dedicate himself to paint-
    ing; studied in the Academia de Bellas Artes; began winning
    prizes in European exhibits; a prolific painter, he had great
    popular appeal as his paintings of scenes from the pampa--
    the gauchos, the oxen and ox-carts, etc.--seemed to express
    to his countrymen the spirit as well as the reality of their
    land; his Tropas de carretas en la Pampa ("Wagon Train on
    the Pampa") is considered first etching made in Argentina;
    among his most famous paintings are Tormenta en la pampa;
    Puesto criollo, La pampa en Olavarría, and A la querencia;
    his influence in stimulating the arts in Buenos Aires is re-
    membered; one of the rooms of the Museo Municipal bears
    his name as does one of the prizes given to artists in annual
    art exposition; died in Buenos Aires.

SLAVERY AND SLAVE TRADE.   During colonial period Buenos
    Aires was important port for introduction of black slaves al-
    though for much of the time the trade was illegal; many of
    blacks (Indians used for labor but only black slavery was
    legal) were used for house servants in the Argentine towns
    or to perform other labor duties; they also replaced the dis-
    appearing Indians in the agricultural work and in caring for
    stock; many of them were sent across the Andes for sale or

to the mines and plantations of Upper and Lower Peru.

Slave trade in the Spanish American colonies was handled through licenses or asientos given to special merchants (usually Portuguese) by royal government; royal duties and bonuses provided source of revenue to crown; in the relatively free trading of the early days of Buenos Aires a royal cedula in 1595 authorized Pedro Gómez Reynel and Gonzalo Báez to bring in 600 black slaves annually for nine years and these Portuguese merchants took full advantage of their contract, with 5639 in five years; following this period, Buenos Aires was only rarely used as a legal port of entry to protect monopoly merchants in Lima; between 1606 and 1625, 8932 blacks were confiscated for having been brought in illegally; price of slaves at that time was between 60 and 70 gold pesos; during seventeenth century about 23,000 were brought into Buenos Aires, either legally or by contraband; in 1703 (with Bourbons on throne of both Spain and France) French received concessions (asientos) to bring in slaves in exchange for hides; between 1708 and 1712 approximately 3500 were imported by the French Company of Guinea; in 1713 treaty of Utrecht, England received similar asiento for thirty years; agents of its South Sea Company immediately appeared in Buenos Aires to set up proper facilities for operations, also using legal slave trade as an opening wedge to gain other trade; British developed active slave trade bringing in thousands of slaves, holding frequent public sales; shortly before the expiration of its contract, England was again at war with Spain; in 1750 the Spanish Crown bought out the South Sea Company's rights and attempted to return to its earlier special licensing policy; the result was chaotic and unproductive, and policy was gradually liberalized; in Buenos Aires slave trade continued on contraband basis; when Consulado (commercial tribunal) was established in Buenos Aires in 1784, one of its earliest concerns was control of the slave trade that formed important part of total commerce; in 1791 the new royal policy of free slave trade was extended to viceroyalty of Buenos Aires; movement to abolish slavery (and slave trade) began shortly after the May Revolution; first triumvirate forbade introduction of slaves (May 15, 1812) and announced emancipation of slaves; assembly of 1813 declared all children born in Argentina of slaves to be free, although they owed certain obligations to their master and he to them; any slave arriving in Argentina became a free man; blacks were given their freedom in return for fighting in Army of the Andes and large numbers were enlisted; none of these measures actually ended slavery or slave trade, however, and soon after he began his second administration in 1835 Rosas signed a treaty with England ending slave trade; many blacks, who adored Rosas, considered him to have been their emancipator; finally, the Constitution of 1853 legally abolished institution of slavery (see Blacks; Naciones; Social Structure).

Suggested reading: Diego Molinari, La trata de

negros: datos para su estudio en el Río de la Plata (Buenos Aires, 1916); Elena de Studer, La trata de negros en el Río de la Plata durante el siglo XVIII (Buenos Aires, 1958); Germán O. E. Tjarks, El consulado de Buenos Aires y sus provecciones en la historia del Río de la Plata (Buenos Aires, 1962).

SMALLPOX. Smallpox, brought to New World by Spaniards, broke out in Buenos Aires in 1588; it was followed by several epidemics, including a bad one in 1621; in 1701 several arriving slave ships were quarantined because of the disease but 400 lives were lost; Indians, possessing little or no immunity, feared smallpox so greatly that they often beheaded those ill with the disease to prevent its spread; in 1873 a smallpox epidemic swept through Indian tribes of Patagonia; in early nineteenth century government imported Jenner's vaccine from Europe and established vaccination program but even before that, other methods had been tried; experiments by Father Feliciano Pueyrredón and Dr. Francisco Javier Muñiz with Argentine cows afflicted with cowpox eventually produced an Argentine source of vaccine (see Epidemics of Disease; Francisco Javier Muñiz).

SOBREMONTE (or SOBRE MONTE), RAFAEL DE (1746-1827). Viceroy 1804-1807.
        Born in Sevilla; began his career in Spanish royal guards; served in Spanish colony of Puerto Rico; in Río de la Plata he became secretary of Viceroy Vértiz (1779) and successful governor of Córdoba (1797); succeeded Viceroy del Pino in 1804; began progressive regime; introduced vaccination for smallpox, improved production of mint in Potosí increasing royal remittances, badly needed in European wars in which Spain was engaged; promoted trade; concerned himself with navigation of Pilcomayo and Bermejo rivers and the gathering of Chaco Indians into settlements for greater control; in 1806 the diocese of Salta was created; in this same year the British attacked Buenos Aires; Sobremonte, with inadequate forces to defend city, withdrew to Córdoba, taking most of troops and royal treasury with him, to organize a counterattack; treasury was captured by British, Buenos Aires retaken by Argentine volunteer forces led by Santiago de Liniers; Sobremonte was deposed and kept under guard until 1809; returned to Spain, his career ruined; died in Sevilla (see British Invasions; Santiago de Liniers).

SOCIAL STRUCTURE. The complex and highly developed Argentine social structure has following characteristics: at least two-thirds of the people live in towns or cities; isolated rural populations play little part in national life; rate of social mobility is high; a large middle class, of European ancestry, exists; few real differences are to be found between middle and working classes but manual labor is still considered demeaning.

During colonial period Argentina had similar pattern
to that of other Spanish American colonies; conquistadors established their towns in midst of Indian communities that
could provide food and labor; society soon became divided into a hierarchy with Spaniards at the top and then came, in
descending order: creoles, born of European (usually Spanish)
parents in America, mestizos (Indian-white mixture), who became artisans and laborers in the towns, gauchos and herdsmen in the country; Indians followed, with Blacks at the bottom; royal census of 1760 showed the following groups in
Buenos Aires: Spanish, creoles, and mestizos, 26,000 Indians, 2000, and blacks and mulattoes, 9000; at the same time
in Misiones the report was that there were very few whites
and 80,000 Indians; at that time the average for the entire
Argentine area was 30% Indian, 10% black, and rest a mixture
of mestizos and creoles, with a few peninsular Spaniards.

At the time of independence geographic differences
were evident; the darker mestizos and Indians were largely
to be found in the hinterland, the blacks and mulattoes in the
cities; creoles and light mestizos predominated almost everywhere except beyond Indian boundaries; nineteenth century
brought changes that sharply affected the social structure;
for a combination of reasons whites increased greatly in
number and in proportional rating, and came to overwhelm
all other groups; Indian lands were conquered and placed
under government jurisdiction; Indians were exterminated in
wars, died from disease, or were, in large part, integrated
into Argentine life; mestizos were absorbed, blacks disappeared,
by absorption, death from disease (especially tuberculosis),
fighting in liberating armies, or by moving to plantation
areas and mines in Bolivia and Peru; at this same time the
flight from country to town became more important; total
population increased from about half a million in 1820 to 22
million 150 years later, in 1970; number of Indians and
blacks had decreased so greatly by the census, although some
Indian villages were still to be found along Paraguayan and
Bolivian boundaries; mestizos continue to be found in rural
areas of north and west but Argentina has been so whitened
by floods of European immigrants that race is no longer important; all are Argentines, from a melting pot of old creole,
mestizos, and new immigrant stock.

The rapidly growing population of Argentina has been
steadily shifting to coastal cities; in mid-1970s attempts are
being made to diversify the economy, with important commercial and industrial centers scattered throughout the country to aid not only the economy but a more healthy social
structure and distribution of population; contemporary divisions (mid-1970s) between middle class porteño and provinciano or between the factory worker of the city and the
laborer of the north or sheepherder of the south still tend
to divide and impoverish the nation (see Demography; Immigration; Creoles; Mestizos; Blacks; Indians).

SOCIALISM; SOCIALIST PARTY. Socialism came to Argentina in late nineteenth century both as an intellectual current from Europe and as an organized movement for social, economic, and political gains for lower and middle classes.

Immigrants coming from Europe, especially Spain and Italy, wanted to improve their economic positions as skilled urban laborers and turned to methods already in use in the home countries they had left such as strikes, unions, etc.; Argentine intellectuals, such as Juan B. Justo (q. v.), were equally eager to improve quality of life in Argentina and disillusioned with Unión Cívica Radical's proposed measures for establishing open, honest elections and for improving situation of immigrant laborers; in 1894 Justo and associates established La Vanguardia to express their socialist ideas; meanwhile socialist centers were being established in various barrios of Buenos Aires and the provinces; in 1896 representatives of these met at a Socialist Congress in Buenos Aires to form the Socialist Party to use political means to obtain its objectives and adopted La Vanguardia as its official organ; from the beginning the Socialist Party attempted to achieve its objectives through moderate, constitutional processes rather than by violence or revolutionary methods; its first political success came with election of Alfredo L. Palacios to Congress in 1904 from Buenos Aires; throughout its history it has been most effective in formulating and first publicizing many of the legislative reforms and programs that eventually were passed in Argentina; the party itself, however, never became a dominant political force as did many Socialist parties in Europe; instead it was constantly changing, splitting or reuniting for reasons of ideology, personal rivalries, differences of practices to be used, etc.; among its first competitors for labor votes were the anarchists whose violent ideas and actions terrified upper-class Argentines; later there were ideological splits between those who favored Russian Communism and those who did not, and those who supported an international labor movement and those who favored Argentine nationalism; the party lost much of its initiative in the late 1930s and 1940s when new ideas were badly needed but the new Socialist leadership had not yet emerged and the party offered only old answers to the new urgent questions; although Perón implemented many of the reforms desired by the Socialists, latter split in matter of supporting him; in late 1950s members of various Socialist groups (numbering in all about 500,000) constituted splinter parties that continued to be effective primarily in collaboration with other political groups seeking same objectives.

Among the many Argentine intellectuals and writers that were leaders in Socialist party or supported Socialism to some extent in their works were: Leopoldo Lugones, José Ingenieros, Enrique Dickmann, Nicolás Repetto, Angel M. Giménez, and Américo Ghioldi (qq. v.).

SOCIEDAD DE BENEFICENCIA (Society of Philanthropy). Founded

by minister Bernardino Rivadavia, in Manuel Rodríguez's
government, January 2, 1823, to bring the aristocratic women of porteño society into public social service and to provide a substitute for the Brotherhood of Holy Charity (Hermandad de la Santa Caridad) which had been forced to turn
its orphanages, hospitals, and other philanthropic institutions
over to the government, including its wealth, as part of Rivadavia's program for ecclesiastical reform; society became
active immediately and continued to maintain its social prestige as well as to control and dispense much of the charity
work and funds of Buenos Aires until the first Perón period.

SOCIEDAD DE LANCASTER (1822). Literary society in Mendoza,
closely related to Lancastrian system of education; composed
of local educators and intellectuals, it was organized to advance cultural achievements; published periodicals devoted to
politics, arts, and education; established several schools;
helped in founding of first library of province--that lasted only
a short time due to accusations that it was introducing foreign
revolutionary ideas to Mendoza; like other similar literary
societies it made an impact on the cultural development following the Revolution; many of its young members became
liberal political leaders, usually Unitarists (see Juan Crisóstomo Lafinur; System of Education).

SOCIEDAD LITERARIA DE BUENOS AIRES. Literary society
founded in Buenos Aires during governorship of Martín Rodríguez; an earlier society of this name, with such members as
San Martín, Monteagudo, Alvear, had been active politically
in the overthrow of the first triumvirate in 1812; the new
group, holding its first meeting January 1, 1822, in the
home of its leader and first president Julián Segundo de
Agüero (q. v.), dedicated itself more directly to cultural objectives; among its members were Esteban Luca y Patrón,
Vicente López y Planes, Antonio Sáenz, Manuel Moreno,
Cosme Argerich, Ignacio Núñez (qq. v.); among its major
projects were the publication of a monthly journal, La Abeja
Argentina (q. v.), that would accurately inform foreigners of
the Argentine situation and that would serve to formulate
public opinion in Buenos Aires and a weekly newspaper, El
Argos de Buenos Aires (q. v.); the society was also represented outside of Buenos Aires, as in Mendoza by Tomás Godoy Cruz and Remigio Castellano, in Salta by Joseph Redhead,
in Tucumán by José Molina, and in Chile by Camilo Henríquez; foreign members were welcomed and included Colonel
Duane, editor of the Philadelphia Dawn, and Joseph Laws
from Paris; Rivadavia, then most important government minister, lent his personal support to the group, as well as
some governmental financial aid; the society also made some
beginnings toward a national theater; the Sociedad Literaria
was dissolved in 1824, largely because its members had become too involved in public affairs to devote their time to it;
during its brief existence it made a real impact, never

completely forgotten, on the intellectual life of the new nation, on the relationship between scholars and political affairs; and it spread information about the country and stimulated literary currents.

SOCIEDAD RURAL ARGENTINA (Argentine Rural Society). Founded in 1866 by landowning elite to foster stockraising and agriculture. Although there had been earlier societies of this name, none lasted long enough to make an impact until that established in 1866 on bases laid during preceding years by Gervasio de Posadas, Sarmiento, and Eduardo Olivera; latter had drawn up organization plans and by-laws and these were accepted by the group of progressive estancieros led by José and Benjamín Martínez de Hoz, Francisco Madero, Jorge Temperley, Ricardo Newton (who had been first to use barbed wire fencing), Mariano Casares, and Luis Amadeo; José Martínez de Hoz became first president and the first issue of the Anales de la Sociedad Rural Argentina appeared in 1867, with Olivera as editor; its sole purpose was to promote anything that would improve the livestock industry and agriculture and to oppose anything that would harm it; it emphasized the raising of meat acceptable to the European--especially British--market; and promoted better breeding by importing pedigreed bulls and rams, introduction of more satisfactory feed, such as alfalfa, and control of stock by fencing; quickly accepted refrigeration for shipping; in 1875 the society held its first cattle show as an exhibit of what could be done; the following year this show was moved permanently to Palermo where the society maintained its headquarters in Rosas' old establishment; this annual livestock show became a national event and its eagerly sought prizes formed continuing incentives for upgrading quality of stock; although commercial agriculture was relatively new, the Rural Society was also deeply interested in promoting it; by the time of Julio A. Roca's election to the presidency in 1898, the nation was enjoying great prosperity for which the Rural Society was given much of the credit; the government's relationship with its members was very close; remained so until industrialization, developing in period of two World Wars, caused diversification of the economy and loss of prestige and political power to the Sociedad Rural Argentina.

SOICHU. Indigenous god of all good things of heaven and earth, in contrast to Gualicho, god of evil, responsible for sickness, plagues, infirmities of old age, death, and drought; pampas Indians venerated both as part of all life, apparently without special ceremonies or cults; a belief in them continues as part of the folklore and superstition; many people, especially in the interior, still wrap a red ribbon around a baby's arm to keep "gualicho" away.

SOLA, MANUEL (1798-1867). Merchant and soldier; twice governor of Salta.

Born in Salta; early entered business world; established textile factory (wool and silk) for which he brought
workers and machinery from the United States; joined gauchos
of Güemes in fighting against royalists; in 1826 organized expedition to explore Bermejo River; during war between Rosas
and Andrés Santa Cruz (q.v.) of Bolivia, Solá fought with
Argentine forces (1837); made peace with successor of Santa
Cruz, Velazco, on condition that Argentine territory be returned; elected governor of Salta, 1838; established schools
and defeated forces of Felipe Ibarra; joined with Avellaneda
in organizing Coalition of the North (1840) against Rosas and
demanding national political organization; defeated by Rosas'
forces led by Manuel Oribe, Solá fled to Bolivia where he
remained until after Rosas' fall; all his property was confiscated; returned to Salta in 1858 and served again as governor;
was member of Santa Fe congress, 1860, and voted for reuniting the provinces; died in Salta.

SOLANO, FRANCISCO (1549-1610).   Franciscan missionary to Indians in Peru and Argentina; canonized as saint by Roman
Catholic Church in 1726.
Born in Montilla, Spain; given good education; became
Franciscan friar in 1576; after having served in many religious capacities, he requested missionary duty among the Indians and, at age of 40, sailed to Peru; learning that the
most remote missionary work was in Tucumán (then including
all northwestern Argentina) he went there; became custodian
of all Franciscan houses in what are now modern Paraguay
and Argentina; for fourteen years he labored and traveled
throughout the area, establishing missions, learning Indian
languages so that he could communicate with the natives;
pacifying the rebellious Calchaquí Indians with music, diplomacy, and Christian love; his compassion and fondness for
music and poetry were noted by all; has been called the
"wonder-worker of the New World"; called back to Peru for
new responsibilities, he died in Lima (see Franciscans).
See José Pacífico Otero's Dos héroes (Solano and
Bolaños) de la conquista, La orden Franciscana en el Tucumán y el Río de la Plata (Buenos Aires, 1905).

SOLER, MIGUEL ESTANISLAO (1783-1849).   General of Army of
Andes; political figure in early national period.
Born in Buenos Aires; studied in Real Colegio de San
Carlos; became cadet in Regimiento Fijo at age of 12; his
bravery in action against British invasions brought him promotion to lieutenant and began his career in regular army;
supported patriot cause and in 1811 led regiment of Pardos
and Morenos against royalists in Entre Ríos and Banda Oriental; promoted to colonel following battle of Cerrito, May 12,
1813, and became governor of Eastern Province (Uruguay) in
1814; in 1816 he joined San Martín's Army of the Andes and
as brigadier general commanded main division, vanguard,
that crossed through pass of Los Patos; led right wing of

patriot army in victory at Chacabuco; was placed in command
of army of the Chilean capital in 1818; became actively involved in Buenos Aires politics and civil war 1819-1820; on
June 20, 1820, was one of three competing governors simultaneously elected by different groups in Buenos Aires; Soler
supported by cavalry and cabildo of Luján; his defeat by
Estanislao López and Carlos María de Alvear in Cañada de
la Cruz June 29, forced his resignation; in 1823 he went to
Montevideo on unsuccessful diplomatic mission to Brazilians
in power there; as major general, commanded third Argentine infantry division in war against Brazil; emigrated to
Montevideo during period of Rosas' rule; died in Buenos
Aires while on visit.

SOLIS, JUAN DIAZ DE (d. 1516). Traditionally considered the discoverer of the Río de la Plata, although earlier Portuguese
navigators had probably been in the area.
    Appointed Spain's Pilot Major in 1512 to succeed
Americus Vespucius, at the latter's death, Solís was commissioned in 1514 to explore the southern coast of South
America in the hope of finding a route to the Pacific (discovered the previous year in Panama by Balboa) and a possible route to the East Indies which the Portuguese had
reached by sailing around Africa; set out in October 1515
with three small ships provisioned for thirty months, carrying 60 men; coasted along Brazil and on January 20, 1516
(the height of summer) entered the estuary of the Río de la
Plata; named it El Mar Dulce (the Freshwater Sea) and
started up it; explored the bay of Montevideo and Martín
García Island which he named for one of his officers, taking
possession of all the land for Spain; invited ashore by apparently friendly Indians on the north coast (now Uruguay),
Solís and several of his companions landed, only to be immediately seized and killed in sight of their horrified companions still on board ship; with the loss of their commander,
the other members of the expedition returned to Spain in two
ships, the third having been wrecked.

SOMBRA, SEGUNDO RAMIREZ (1851-1936). Real-life, historic
gaucho whose life and stories formed basis of Ricardo Güiraldes' famous novel Don Segundo Sombra (1927).
    Born in Santa Fe, Segundo Sombra worked at several
ranches on the pampas, eventually taking up residence in San
Antonio de Areco, Buenos Aires; it was here, in the evenings,
that Güiraldes heard the gaucho tell the tales from which his
classic was born (see Ricardo Güiraldes).

SOMISA (Sociedad Mixta Siderúrgica Argentina). State organization
responsible for Argentine Airlines and iron and steel industries; organized in the late 1940s by Juan Domingo Perón as
part of his nationalization and industrial self-sufficiency plan;
its first important achievement was the national steel plant of
San Nicolás (that began operations in 1960), situated on the

bank of the Paraná river; after the 1955 revolution that removed Perón from power, SOMISA was placed under military
control until 1960s, when it became a "mixed" financial company, with the state the majority shareholder (in partnership
with Siemens Martín steel work); SOMISA has a deep-water
port at Ingeniero Zuitrago to unload raw ore and other materials; SOMISA uses both national and imported iron ore; high
costs and other problems of production at first prevented
SOMISA from reaching either its efficiency or production
goals; imports of semi-manufactured materials for the Argentine market continued necessary.

SOSA, DOMINGO (1788-1866). Military officer. Born a slave in
    Buenos Aires; joined the Batallón de Pardos y Morenos fol-
    lowing British Invasions; accompanied Belgrano on expedition
    to Paraguay; was with Rondeau at siege of Montevideo (1812)
    and decorated following battle of El Cerrito; in 1815 joined
    Army of the North, again under Rondeau; took part in defeat
    at Sipe Sipe, November 29, 1815; returned to Buenos Aires
    where he was placed in charge of training battalions of
    emancipated black slaves; remained in army, rising steadily
    in rank; suffered serious wounds at battle of Caseros; after
    recovering, he was given command of fourth battalion of in-
    fantry with which he supported Buenos Aires' revolt of Sep-
    tember 11, 1852; defended Buenos Aires during rebellion of
    Hilario Lagos; retired from army as colonel; later, when
    city of Buenos Aires was besieged by Urquiza, he was again
    among its defenders; served in provincial legislature and con-
    stituent congress; died in Buenos Aires.

SOSA MOLINA, JOSE HUMBERTO (1893-1960). Division general;
    member of GOU; close associate of Juan Domingo Perón and
    Edelmiro Farrell.
            Born in San José de Guaymallén, Mendoza; made the
    army his career; studied at Colegio Militar and Escuela Su-
    perior de Guerra; for more than two decades held teaching
    and command assignments in these and other special military
    schools; served as military attaché to Argentine embassy in
    Brazil, 1936-1938; accompanied Juan Domingo Perón and
    other officers on military mission to Italy in 1939; returned
    to command detachment of Cuyo montaña, 1940-1943; became
    active member of GOU (q. v.), belonging to group including
    Edelmiro Farrell and Juan Domingo Perón; after military
    takeover in 1943 he served as interventor in San Juan and
    in Entre Ríos; as commandant of Third Division of Infantry
    he kept his men confined to the barracks to prevent them
    from interfering with popular uprising against imprisonment
    of Perón, October 1945; became minister of war in Presi-
    dent Farrell's cabinet and continued in same capacity in that
    of Perón (1945-1949); remained strong supporter of Perón
    throughout his first two terms of office, usually holding high
    position in national defense; after fall of Perón, he was sub-
    jected to trial and suffered loss of military honors and

perquisites; died in Buenos Aires.

SOURIGUES, CARLOS TOMAS (1805-1870). Physician; engineer
and architect; educator.
Born in Bayonne, France; studied medicine in France
and Buenos Aires; arrived in latter city in 1835; taught
French, mathematics, and history at Colegio; his architectural skills brought him several appointments from Rosas;
served as architect of Buenos Aires, member of department
of architecture and of central commission of public roads; in
1845 moved to Gualeguay, Entre Ríos; worked there as teacher, physician, and engineer; directed a military school of
artillery and infantry; also taught surveying; served as surgeon in Urquiza's army at Cepeda and Pavón; laid out plans
for San José colonia (1857) and city of Colón (1861); after
1862 directed topographical department of Entre Ríos and
taught at Colegio de Concepción del Uruguay; after assassination of Urquiza, fought against Ricardo López Jordán; dying in defense of city of Concepción del Uruguay in 1870.

SOUTH ORKNEY ISLANDS see ORCADAS

SOUTHERN RAILROAD (Ferrocarril del Sur--today the General
Roca). Pushed south from Buenos Aires to Chascomús,
1865; continued south and west into pampas; by 1914 had
good network in southern pampas; became most profitable
line and made possible the development of this area with
rich resources; authorized originally by Buenos Aires provincial legislature and financed by British investors who were
guaranteed a 7% profit (see Railroads; also map, Appendix
IV).

SPAIN; SPANIARDS. For three hundred years after Juan Díaz de
Solís entered the Río de la Plata in 1516 the territory that
is modern Argentina was under Spanish sovereignty; the direction of settlements among the few Indians there, its political structure and the control of its economic life were all
determined by the ruler of Spain and his advisers; its church,
language, social institutions, and cultural heritage were
Spanish; during the long colonial period Spaniards in Argentina mixed their blood with the Indians; learned to survive in
a different land on a different diet--beef, corn, and mate--
and learned to defend themselves and to respect their own
new interests and priorities; their remoteness from Spain
forced them to find their own answers to problems not easily
understood in Spain; a basic creole independence and love of
land developed a new people; this was clearly revealed when
viceroyalty of Río de la Plata was established in 1776 with
Buenos Aires as capital; for the first time royal authorities
resided among the Argentines instead of hundreds of miles
away, the old patterns were more clearly stamped at the
same time that new ones were being created; royal control
was tightened but economy and culture were stimulated; large

numbers of new Spaniards came over as royal officials or to
make their fortune in trade; few clashes occurred between
peninsulares (as Spaniards were called) and creoles; many of
former, in fact, became permanent residents of the new
land; they fought together against British invasions and many
of the Spaniards supported the May Revolution, believing an
autonomous Argentina to be better for their own interests
than one under control of remote Spain; real clashes appeared, however, as to whether Spaniards or native-born
creoles were to control new independent government to be established (see Martín de Alzaga, Spanish leader of one revolt);
during the civil wars and Rosas period those Spaniards who
remained in Argentina usually became citizens of the new
country and, for a combination of reasons, easily became
part of the society.

During the last half of 19th century, Spanish influence
was renewed; in 1858 Spain restored diplomatic ties by recognizing Argentine independence; Spaniards formed a high percentage of the immigrants who came to Argentina to work in
the towns, agricultural colonies, stock ranches, vineyards,
etc.; intellectuals, writers, and artists renewed ties with the
mother country; the war between Spain and United States
(1898) revived old loyalties, all the more because many Argentines were resenting U.S. leadership of the Pan American
movement at that time; in the early twentieth century many
thoughtful leaders also saw in the revival of Spanish cultural
roots the greatest hope for bringing immigrants and creoles
to a common sense of national identity; others welcomed this
as part of a new nationalism seeking to free Argentina from
French and British economic and cultural domination; the
Spanish Civil War in the 1930s affected the republic in two
very different ways; many liberal republican Spaniards fled
to Argentina for refuge and contributed to its national cultural life; on the other hand, many devoutly Catholic, conservative Argentines saw in Francisco Franco the authoritarian caudillo leader that had played such an important part in
their historic heritage and some had faint hopes of emulat-
ing him in a troubled Argentina.

SPANO, CARLOS (1773-1814).   Spanish officer that joined patriot
cause.
Born in Málaga, Spain; began his military career
there, forming part of the Spanish garrison at Ceuta until
1791; after taking part in other actions in Spain, he arrived
in Chile, 1795, and served on the frontier; sympathizing
with the patriots, he became major of a battalion of grenadiers; was killed in royalist attack on Talca (1814) that he
was defending; one of his daughters married Argentine patriot
leader Tomás Guido (q.v.); from this marriage Carlos Guido
Spano (q.v.), the poet, was born.

SPORTS.   Argentines are devoted to sports, especially those involving teams; the most popular sport is soccer, with

basketball and boxing as close followers; polo, pato (q. v. , an
exciting combination of polo and basketball) and Rugby football are also popular; golf, yachting, etc. , have been adopted
by the upper class.

SQUIRRU, RAFAEL FERNANDO (1925-   ).   Jurisconsult; art
   critic; essayist.
          Born in Buenos Aires; studied law at university there;
   graduated from University of Edinburgh, 1948; served as director of cultural division of Pan American Union, Washington, D. C. ; since early 1950s he has written and lectured extensively on philosophy of the "New Man"; in 1957 founded
   'Ediciones del Hombre Nuevo" in which many of his poems
   and essays have appeared; has lectured in United States, England, and Scotland; in 1955 was appointed director of Museum
   of Modern Art of Buenos Aires.

STATUTE OF THE ARGENTINE REVOLUTION (Estatuto de la Revolución Argentina) 1966.   Charter for reorganization of Argentine government proclaimed by military junta that deposed
   Illia and installed Onganía as president; retained constitution
   of 1853 but subordinated it to new statute; stating that the
   government represented all the people, it abolished office of
   vice president, dissolved congress, provincial legislatures,
   and political parties to make way for new organization directly under president; enforced during Onganía's regime, it
   was revoked in 1970 when Levingston replaced Onganía as
   president.

STEAMBOATS.   Although an American, Thomas Llodi Halsey, received the first official concession to operate a steamboat on
   the river (in 1812), the first actual voyage was not made
   until 1825 when the Druid, backed by British capital, made
   its maiden voyage; aboard were forty passengers representing official and business interests of Buenos Aires; the brief
   trip to San Isidro, not an unqualified success, nevertheless
   marked the beginning of river commerce by steamboat.

STEVENSON, JOSEPH THOMAS (1865-1936).   Anglican clergyman
   and schoolmaster.
          Born in Capetown, South Africa; educated at Oxford
   University; ordained as minister 1888; sent to Buenos Aires
   in 1895 as chaplain of Anglican church in Quilmes; there he
   founded St. George's College, an English-type public school
   (1898) and became its headmaster; also established Santa
   Catalina school for girls and an elementary school for children; St. George's remains in use in modern times by
   Anglo-Argentine group and is considered one of best schools
   in the country; Stevenson died in Buenos Aires and was
   buried near his school.

STORNI, ALFONSINA (1892-1938).   Poet; teacher.
          Born in Switzerland; came to Argentina with her

parents; lived in Santa Fe; taught in Rosario; moved to
Buenos Aires in 1913 where she became part of literary
circle of capital; became associated with writers of Nosotros;
published her first writing in Caras y Caretas; continued
teaching in various institutions while writing; in 1916 attracted attention of critics with La inquietud del rosal; followed this with El dulce daño; Irremediablemente, 1919, and
Languidez, 1920; latter won second prize in national competition; one of her best works was Ocre, published in 1926; in
Versos a la tristeza de Buenos Aires, she depicts the sad-
ness of the great city's spirit; her last poem Voy a dormir
was written shortly before her death; original, tragic, somewhat uneven, her work was widely recognized throughout
Latin America.

STORNI, SEGUNDO R. (1876-1954). Naval officer; foreign min-
    ister in 1943 during World War II.
        Born in San Martín de Tucumán; educated in naval
academy and superior naval school; served as director of
naval academy (1922-1927); chief of secretariat of ministry
of navy, chief of general staff of fleet; director-general of
materiel; spent several years in Philadelphia supervising construction of battleship Rivadavia; represented Argentina at
several Pan American conferences and served also as technical adviser; reached rank of vice admiral in the navy and
retired from active duty in 1935; was nominated by Arturo
Rawson to be his minister of the interior and when latter
was succeeded within a few days by Ramírez, Admiral Storni
became minister of foreign relations and religion; during this
very difficult period in internal Argentine politics, as well
as in World War II events, U.S. Secretary of State Cordell
Hull demanded a clear statement from Argentina as to its
intentions regarding the Axis powers with which U.S. and
Allies were at war; Storni's reply attempted to state Argentina's position in terms of its traditional neutral policy and
to gain time, at least, for Ramírez's new administration to
formulate its policy; it satisfied no one and brought his resignation; he retired to private life; died in Buenos Aires;
Storni was author of several textbooks, technical works, and
studies dealing with Argentina's interests in the surrounding
seas.

STRAIN, ISAAC G. (1821-1856). U.S. traveler in Argentine, in
    1849; writer.
        Born in Roxbury, U.S.; corresponding member of
Academy of Natural Sciences, Philadelphia, and of Historic
and Geographic Institute of Brazil; he rode from Chile to
Brazil on horseback (1849) recording his observations and
experiences as he crossed from Pacific to Atlantic through
Mendoza, San Luis, and Santa Fe; in 1853 published these
in Sketches of a Journey in Chile and the Argentine Provinces in 1849; gives valuable data about life in Argentina in
closing years of Rosas era; Strain died in U.S.

STRAIT OF MAGELLAN (Estrecho de Magallanes).   Passage between Atlantic and Pacific oceans, at about 52° S. latitude;
separates southern Patagonia from island of Tierra del Fuego;
discovered by Ferdinand Magellan, Portuguese navigator sailing from Spain, October 21, 1520, and named for him; visited
again by Juan Sebastián Elcano (who had accompanied Magellan) as chief pilot of Francisco García Jofre de Loaysa's expedition to the Far East; by Simón de Alcazaba in 1535, and
by expeditions sent from Chile in 1557; in 1578 Francis Drake
startled Spanish South America by using the strait on first
English circumnavigation of the world; Pedro Sarmiento de
Gamboa was commissioned to fortify and occupy the area to
prevent further foreign intrusions into the Pacific where
Peruvian silver production was becoming vital to Spanish imperial needs; in 1584, a settlement named Nombre de Jesús
was established near Cabo de Vírgenes on north shore of Atlantic entrance to strait; a later settlement, farther west,
was made, near present site of Chilean Punta Arenas, and
named Del Rey Don Felipe, later known as Puerto del Ham-
bre (Hunger Port) and Puerto Magallanes; both colonies
failed from lack of food and attempt was abandoned; in 1615
W. C. von Schouten and Jacob Le Maire sailed farther south
and discovered the strait named for latter and Cape Horn
(1616); used by later Spanish expeditions but closed officially to
foreign expeditions for most of colonial period; after independence Chile and Argentina originally agreed to keep navigation open in the strait and leave actual settling of boundary
through this unoccupied area to later period; after decades of
discussion and near-conflicts, boundaries were established by
Pactos de Mayo (q. v.) in 1902.
        Early descriptions of the strait are given by Antonio
Pigafetta, who accompanied Magellan, and the scientist
Charles Darwin who studied on an expedition of the Beagle
in 1834 (see Tierra del Fuego, Territory of).

STROBEL, MATIAS (1696-1769).   German-born Jesuit missionary
and explorer.   Arrived in Buenos Aires in 1729; held various
posts in Guaraní missions and Jesuit colegios; in 1740 was
chosen to head mission among Pampa Indians, whose language he had learned; while there, selected to head Jesuits
accompanying José Quiroga and José Cardiel (qq. v.) on their
exploratory, mapping expedition along Patagonian coast,
1745-1746; returned to mission administration; died in Europe
two years after Jesuit expulsion from Argentina.

SUAREZ, JOSE LEON (1872-1929).   Jurisconsult; university professor; government official.
        Born in Buenos Aires, grandson of Uruguayan presi-
dent Joaquín Suárez; took his doctorate in law and social
sciences in Buenos Aires, 1897; held various posts as professor in Colegio Nacional, adjunct professor of international
law in faculty where he got degree; later became titular professor of diplomatic law, holding first chair in this subject

in Argentina and finally professor of international law in
faculty of economic sciences, which he had helped to establish and of which he was also dean (1921-1924); organized
sanitation and veterinary section of department of agriculture
(1898); served as second head of this department and director
general of national livestock industry until 1924; acted as private secretary of various ministers of public instruction; contributed frequently to newspapers and reviews; wrote several
works on juridical and historical themes; founded and edited
Revista de Derecho Internacional; twice served as editor of
Revista de Ciencias Económicas; and contributed to both; won
international recognition; was appointed by League of Nations
Council to serve on commission for progressive codification
of International law; taught in Guatemala; was awarded special
medal by Congress of Peru for his services to Peruvian justice; in 1925 Bolivia placed his portrait in the senate alongside those of Sucre and Morillo to show Bolivia's gratitude
for services to that country; public library in La Paz given
his name; served as president of Italian Union of La Plata;
was also decorated by Spain, Portugal, and Sweden.

Dr. Suárez's great interest, especially in the later
years of his life, was in the restoration of the traditional
cultural ties between Spain and Argentina as well as cultivating a closer relationship between Argentina and the other nations that shared its own heritage; because he believed this
heritage to be Iberian, rather than purely Spanish, he included both Brazil and Portugal in this special relationship;
he saw no conflict between this and the Pan American movement developing between U.S. and Latin American nations;
believed that latter reflected common interests of Western
hemisphere nations whereas former was a spiritual tie; Alfonso XIII of Spain, acting on recommendation of the Real
Academia de la Historia, awarded him the Grand Cross of
Isabel la Católica for his Carácter de la revolución, in which
he developed the thesis that the Spanish American Wars of
Independence constituted a liberal, civil revolution against
monarchical absolutism; in 1920, on the centennial of Riego's
liberal revolt in Cádiz, he wrote a long article in La Nación
expressing Argentina's gratitude to him; as advocate of Ibero-
Americanism, he lectured frequently, in hope not only of
strengthening national traditional roots but of using these to
integrate immigrants into Argentine society and culture; became honorary member of Spanish Republican Federation;
died in Buenos Aires.

Among his published works are: Bases y proyectos de
ley sobre policía sanitaria de los animales; Derecho público
eclesiástico; Apuntes de derecho internacional público; Diplomacia universitaria.

SUBLEVACION DE LAS TRENZAS (Pigtail uprising or mutiny)   see
   REBELION DE LAS TRENZAS

SUFFRAGE.   Universal male suffrage (for males over 18 years old) largely brought about by reforms of Roque Saenz Peña, 1911-1912; government of radical leader Hipólito Yrigoyen (1916) first to be chosen on this basis; in 1947 during first administration of Juan Domingo Perón, right to vote was extended to women; compulsory voting laws have been passed requiring all able adults to vote (see Saenz Peña Law).

SUGAR, SUGAR CANE. The wealthy sugar industry centered in Tucumán province and controlled by a few landholders and capitalists, with a virtual monopoly of the national market, is a modern development with historical roots.

Sugar came to Argentina in the middle of the sixteenth century: from Chile to Tucumán, probably brought by Francisco de Aguirre, 1553; from Brazil to northeast Argentina and Paraguay; Jesuits fostered its culture in their Paraná missions but were even more successful growing cane in the northwest, on the eastern Andean slopes; the sugar was processed in Tucumán; with expulsion of Jesuits (1767) the industry decayed for half a century until revived in Tucumán by Bishop José Eusebio Colombres (honored today as the father of the Argentine sugar industry); renewed the plantings and built new sugar mill, 1821, in Tucumán; others followed his example and by 1858 Tucumán had 13 sugar mills producing nearly 200,000 pounds of sugar annually; in 1858 General Justo José Urquiza and Baltasar Aguirre opened first modern sugar mill and within two decades 5,000 acres were in cane, 46 mills (most with metal grinders) operating; from 1876 to 1894 five railroads were completed, giving Tucumán sugar planters access to entire national market; by end of that time 135,000 acres had been planted; capital needs brought concentration of industry into hands of a very wealthy few, who also owned the major sugar processing plant at Rosario; a complicated protective tariff system secured the national market from foreign competition and ensured higher prices; sugar dominated the economy of Tucumán but the great wealth it brought did not filter down into all levels of society; the laborers, largely seasonal and migrant, in great numbers became poverty-stricken and Tucumán's economic suffering reflected itself in social unrest and political action.

Sugar cane cultivation was also renewed (in the 1870s) in the area of the former Jesuit missions in the northeast; Corrientes government offered attractive incentives to lure colonists to that area for that purpose but has had little success for a combination of reasons, including the Tucumán monopoly, the competition of Brazilian sugar nearby and the European colonists' unfamiliarity with subtropical agriculture.

SUIPACHA, BATTLE OF (November 7, 1810). First victory of patriot armed forces over Spanish royalists in Argentine War for independence. Auxiliary expeditionary force, commanded by Antonio González Balcarce, entered Alto Perú on its mission to win that area for the May Revolution; along the Suipacha river, Balcarce's forces joined battle with the royalists

under Generals Córdoba and Nieto; after half an hour of fighting, the patriots had won; the two generals, along with the
intendant Paulo Sanz, were captured and shot, in accordance
with orders from the governing junta in Buenos Aires; this
first triumph of patriot forces encouraged the spirits and
aroused enthusiasm of patriots throughout Alto Peru and Río
de la Plata and opened all of Alto Perú to the May Revolution; the patriot army became swollen with so many recruits
that adequate training was impossible and, within a few
months, the royalists had reorganized their own forces for a
crushing victory at Huaqui (q.v.).

SUPREMO ENTRERRIANO. Title given to Francisco Ramírez,
Federalist caudillo of Entre Ríos following his final defeat of
Artigas; used throughout duration of República de Entre Ríos,
consisting of Entre Ríos, Corrientes and Misiones (see Francisco Ramírez; Entre Ríos).

- T -

TABA. A game, somewhat similar to American practice of toss-
ing of coin for heads or tails, that is played with the ankle-
bone of a cow; this bone, called the taba and usually reinforced with metal to prevent it from breaking, is tossed into
the air by one of the players; if it falls with the curved part
(the suerte) uppermost, the thrower wins; the losing side is
called culo; this game was apparently brought to Argentina by
the Spanish conquistadors, and continues to be played in rural
areas.

TABARDILLO (Typhus) see EPIDEMICS OF DISEASE

TABER, SAMUEL WILLIAM (1780-1813). North American merchant who played active role in early Argentine independence
period. Member of distinguished New York family, Taber
arrived in Buenos Aires in 1810 while port was under royalist blockade; immediately offered his services free to junta
for construction of an underwater device to torpedo the Spanish ships; after investigation by Saavedra and Azcuénaga,
project was approved and was almost completed when blockade was lifted; Taber was then sent to Montevideo to study
situation there under Governor Elío; sent back several detailed reports (later very useful) about fortifications, etc.;
attempting to return to Buenos Aires, he was arrested and
imprisoned for four months; finally released as result of
bribery or efforts of U.S. consul (or both), Taber returned
to Buenos Aires to resume work on his submarine device
for possible use in Montevideo; became honorary (without
pay) captain of artillery in army of Banda Oriental; was
forced to abandon his explosive project as too complicated;
sent to Chile in 1812 as secret agent of Buenos Aires government; died shortly after his return of tuberculosis

contracted during his imprisonment; left his property to patriot government.

TABLADA, BATTLE OF (June 23, 1829). On this plain, north of Córdoba, the federalists led by Juan Facundo Quiroga and Juan Bautista Bustos were defeated by unitarist forces commanded by José María Paz; this hard-fought battle that began one day and continued on the next was witnessed and reported by visiting naturalist Théodore Lacaordaire (his account translated into Spanish and published by J. L. Busaniche); Quiroga rejected attempts of both Estanislao López of Santa Fe and Viamonte from the Buenos Aires government to persuade him to agree to peace terms; escaped, instead, to Cuyo; Paz entered Córdoba as result of this battle.

TABOADA, ANTONINO (1814-1883). Commander (General) of military forces that backed political power of Taboada family.
Born in Santiago del Estero; educated in primary schools in Buenos Aires; entered business there but unitarist sympathies forced him to emigrate to Montevideo in 1839; took part in Lavalle's unitarist campaign against Rosas in Entre Ríos and Córdoba; captured at battle of Quebracho Herrado; imprisoned at El Retiro, Buenos Aires; escaped in 1841 and returned to Montevideo; eight years later he went to Chile where he became closely associated with such exiled leaders as Mitre, Sarmiento, Paunero, and Gómez; returned to Santiago del Estero and led movement against caudillo Celedonio Gutiérrez, Rosas supporter who had retained governorship of Tucumán after Rosas' fall and had invaded Santiago del Estero in 1853; he was defeated by Taboada at Los Laureles; Taboada became military commander of the Chaco border area and successfully escorted U.S. scientific mission on exploration of Río Salado through this area to Santa Fe; decorated by Argentine government for this (1859); during the next few years he was offered political appointments within the province or on national level but either refused them or served very briefly, preferring to leave political leadership to his brothers, especially Manuel Taboada (q.v.), while he retained military command; during Mitre's presidency of the Argentine Republic, the Taboadas, liberals themselves, not only backed him politically but also supported him by restoring order in north and northwest, as in General Taboada's defeat of Felipe Varela and his montoneros at Pozo de Vargas; forced to emigrate to Tucumán in 1875 for this political reason, the general died there in poverty; department in his native province, General Taboada, is named for him.

TABOADA, ANTONIO MARIA (1787-1873). Political leader, public figure.
Born in Santiago del Estero, son of Spanish merchant; abandoned his studies to take care of the family's interests following his father's death; became active supporter of

revolution of 1810; in 1815 he became second alcalde of his
city's cabildo and was given command of a militia cavalry
battalion; continued in this until 1819; in the anarchy of 1820
he strongly favored Santiago del Estero's separatist movement
and was named first alcalde of the new cabildo formed;
served as member of the Constituent Congress in Buenos
Aires 1826-1827; after the death of his wife in 1840 he entered the priesthood; was elected national senator from Santiago del Estero in 1857; died in Rosario.

TABOADA, FELIPE (1821-1853). Painter. Born in Matará, Santiago del Estero, younger brother of Antonino and Manuel; in
spite of a general spastic condition that made it necessary
for him to steady his right hand with his left when he
painted, he became a well-known artist; his uncle, Juan
Felipe Ibarra, appointed him to decorate the church of La
Merced; his frescoes there and portraits of his brother Antonino, his uncle, and even a self-portrait may still be seen;
his most notable work, according to critics, was that of
Franciscan friar Cernadas; in spite of his physical problems
he joined other members of his family in fighting in the
civil wars; in 1853 he fought against the federalist forces of
Celedino Gutiérrez that had invaded Santiago del Estero; died
in political assassination in Cruz Grande November 17, 1853.

TABOADA, MANUEL (1817-1872). Liberal caudillo of Santiago del
Estero and national political figure, 1850s and 1860s.
        Born in Matara, Santiago del Estero; initiated his
public career in 1851 by leading movement that overthrew
government of Mauro Carranza; while latter fled to federalist
governor of Tucumán, General Celedonio Gutiérrez, for help,
Manuel Taboada placed Santiago del Estero behind Urquiza's
movement to overthrow Rosas; became governor and took
part in the Acuerdo de San Nicolás; during the 1850s and
1860s he was elected governor several times and during most
of rest of time, when he was not serving as governor, he was
active as political leader or government official while his
cousin Absalón Ibarra or brother Antonino was in charge of
government; in difficult transition period of 1859-1861, the
Taboadas, always friends of Bartolomé Mitre, came to sponsor latter's Unión Nacional proposal; Manuel defeated Governor Pedro Ramón Alcorta, already ousted by legislature,
when Derqui's confederation troops tried to replace Alcorta,
they were defeated; in 1861 the Taboadas took Santiago del
Estero out of the Confederation and joined Mitre; in the 1862
election latter was easily elected president of the new Argentine Republic; Manuel Taboada was proposed as vice president but lost to Marcos Paz; during 1860s he frequently
fought against invaders from neighboring provinces but most
of this military action devolved on his brother Antonino;
Manuel devoted himself to progressive reform and development of the province; spent considerable time on irrigation
canals that opened new lands to agriculture; reformed land

survey and taxation systems, reorganized administration and
financial structure of province; improved working conditions
for both private and public workers; built Indian forts in
desert area; both Antonino and Manuel were mentioned for
the national ticket in 1868 but Sarmiento was elected president; latter faced rebellion against national authority from
Ricardo López Jordán in Entre Ríos and feared similar action from Taboada in Santiago del Estero; in spite of latter's
affiliation with liberals, Sarmiento suspected him of perpetuating the barbaric caudillo system that he had hoped to out-
law from Argentina; acting with unexpected prudence, however, the president merely sent an official observer to Santiago del Estero; Governor Manuel Taboada viewed this as a
challenge to his authority; wrote Sarmiento a somewhat arrogant letter complaining of this action, and sent copies of this
letter to Urquiza and other leaders before original had
reached Sarmiento; the president answered with charges
against the Ibarra-Taboada tyranny, established for so long,
and wondered if Governor Taboada was trying to form his
province into a mini-Paraguay; both leaders, however, backed
off from confrontation; Manuel died in 1872; he had already
introduced a policy of moderation to the province and was
himself the last of the strongmen in political life of Santiago
del Estero.

     See Newton, Jorge. Manuel Taboada: Caudillo Uni-
tario (Buenos Aires, 1972).

TABOADA FAMILY OF SANTIAGO DEL ESTERO (including Juan
    Felipe Ibarra and Absalón Ibarra). Members of this family
    dominated political life of Santiago del Estero throughout most
    of nineteenth century; extended their power and influence
    throughout neighboring provinces and put their mark on na-
    tional political organization; Gaspar Taboada has edited and
    published the family archives in 5 volumes, entitled Recuer-
    dos históricos: los Taboada, in 1940s and 1950s (see entries
    on individual members of family and on Santiago del Estero).

TACUARA (lance). Name (of Guaraní origin), of an indigenous,
    flexible, very tough cane, similar to bamboo, from which
    deadly spears, or lances, surrounded with barbs and given
    very sharp points--called chuzas--were made in the 18th and
    early 19th centuries; these often formed chief weapons of
    armies of the caudillos and the militia; Bartolomé Mitre has
    described this method of combat and Argentines largely
    credit the chuzas for the defeat of the British invasions.

     See Mario López Osorno, Esgrima criolla (1942) and
Archivo del General Mitre (Buenos Aires, 1911-1913).

TACUARA (political group). Extreme rightist, nationalistic, anti-
    Semitic political action group, largely composed of young
    people, active in 1960s. Taking its name and symbolic em-
    blem from the lance used by Pampa Indians (see Tacuara
    lance), Tacuara was organized along lines similar to those

of earlier German-Nazi youth groups and had some of latter's
anti-Semitic views, but remained basically Argentine nationalist; used methods similar to those of Perón's street-fighters
(see Alianza Libertadora Nacionalista); the group received
little support from either the people or the government;
turned to dramatic action; in 1966 a group of sixteen men
and one woman hijacked a plane to take them to Las Malvinas
(Falkland Islands) where they landed and attempted to proclaim Argentine sovereignty in nationalist effort to provoke
quarrel between Argentina and Great Britain, as well as to
embarrass Onganía's government; police prevented this,
turned plotters over to Argentine authorities who took them
to Ushuaia; they were charged with theft of public property
(the hijacked plane) and jailed; the Tacuara (who used such
slogans as "For God, home, and country" and "Kill a Jew a
day" also tried to take over the government of La Rioja; succeeded in occupying the public offices of the city temporarily
but were driven out by the chief of police and then permitted
to go into exile in Chile.

TACUAREMBO, BATTLE OF (February 1820). Defeat of Artigas
and his forces by the Portuguese from Brazil, opening the
way for the latter to occupy the Banda Oriental (Uruguay).

TACUARI, BATTLE OF (March 9, 1811). Battle between Buenos
Aires liberating army commanded by Manuel Belgrano and
Paraguayan forces under Manuel Cabañas (also spelled Cava-
ñas) that paved way for Paraguay to become independent nation.
          After Belgrano's defeat at Paraguarí (q. v.), January
19, he moved south to the Tacuarí river near its entrance
into the Alto Paraná, on the traditional highway between
Candelaria and Asunción; he hoped to control the Paraná
river and to establish base from which new attacks on Span-
ish-held Paraguay might be made; his forces were divided
and completely outnumbered, however, by the Spanish-
Paraguayan forces that threatened him by land and from the
river; battle joined on several fronts on March 9; Belgrano
found himself in a desperate and indefensible position that
night, after fighting hard all day; refusing to surrender, he
requested negotiations for an armistice; Cabañas responded
and the two generals met; Belgrano explained that his primary purpose had been to bring the Paraguayans into the
patriot revolution, not to conquer them; Cabañas accepted
this and agreed to cessation of hostilities if Belgrano would
immediately withdraw his forces across the Paraná into
Argentine territory and promise to let Paraguay go its own
revolutionary way; Belgrano (and later the Buenos Aires government) accepted these terms, feeling that his mission had
been accomplished by negotiation and diplomacy where military action had failed.

TACURU. Low-grade iron ore found and processed near Posadas (province of Misiones).

TAFI.   Place name (from Aymara word for "place where the cold
wind blows") used in western Tucumán province for a department, the town that is its capital and that has been important for railroad shops, a river and its valley, and for an
archeological site that has acquired great interest for Argentine archeologists in the mid-twentieth century as the home
of an important prehistoric Indian culture that affected all
northwestern Argentine development before the Spanish conquest; since the early nineteenth century it has been known
that large monolithic stone pillars, often incised, were to be
found in Tafí del Valle, an unpopulated area about 6500 feet
above sea level; investigation more recently has revealed
something of the culture of these Indians, who apparently
reached northwestern Argentina before the fifth century A.D.
and seem to have belonged to the Tihuanaco pre-Incan civilization of the Central Andean area; they apparently practised
an advanced agriculture and must have had some social or
political organization in order to build andenes, terraces,
and other works for cultivating their crops; also made ceramics and had some metallurgical skills; they used llamas;
their buildings were well constructed of stone; apparently
they lived in rounded family homes in tribal groups, with
little evidence of real town living; Argentine archeologists
are seeking relationships between this early Indian culture
and later ones in Tucumán.

TAGLE, JUAN GREGORIO GARCIA DE (1772-1845).   Lawyer; public official; unsuccessful leader of conspiracies against Rivadavia's ecclesiastical reforms.
        Born in Buenos Aires, Dr. Gregorio Tagle (as he is
usually known in Argentine history) attended the Colegio de
San Carlos; graduated as lawyer in 1800; immediately entered
public life, serving as legal advisor or official to the royal
audiencia and then to early patriot governments; Juan Martín
de Pueyrredón appointed Tagle as secretary of state in his
directorate government (1817) and when Pueyrredón went into
exile, Tagle also left the country; returning in 1820, he led
two conspiracies opposing Rivadavia's church reforms; the
first, in late August 1822, was quickly crushed by Rivadavia
and Tagle was briefly imprisoned and then expelled from
Buenos Aires; in 1823, Dr. Gregorio Tagle became the leader of a much more important conspiracy combining both
church and lay Catholic movements against the reforms; on
March 19 armed demonstrators marched into the main plaza
of Buenos Aires, making dramatic appeals for popular support; demonstrators were immediately dispersed by government forces, most of leaders captured and executed or severely punished; Tagle escaped but Governor Manuel Rodríguez sent Manuel Dorrego (q.v.) in pursuit of him; captured,
Tagle expected death, but, in spite of Tagle's role in Pueyrredón's exile of Dorrego six years earlier, Dorrego now

assisted him to leave Argentina safely; in 1830 Tagle returned
to Buenos Aires and resumed his place in public life, serving
first as secretary and then as president of the court of appeals; became minister of government again in 1833 and in
same year was elected to provincial legislature; removed
from office in 1835 by Rosas, Dr. Tagle remained in Buenos
Aires until his death in 1845, suffering imprisonment again
in 1840.

TAJAMAR. Name applied to artificial water hole made for cattle
use where natural watering stations are not readily available;
apparently first used in 1764; by 1851, the government had
built 398 tajamares in Buenos Aires province.

TALAVERA DE ESTECO see ESTECO

TALITA (or TALITAS), COMBAT OF (December 8-9, 1873).
Arroyo in Paraná department, Entre Ríos, in which the vanguard of Ricardo López Jordán's Entre Ríos forces was defeated by those of the government, commanded by Col. Juan
de Ayala, with heavy losses of men and equipment; this defeat influenced strategy of López Jordán greatly, forcing him
to fight at Don Gonzalo, where he was defeated (see Ricardo
López Jordán).

TAMANDARE, BARON DE (Joaquim Marques Lisboa). Admiral of
Allied naval forces during first part of war with Paraguay.
When General (also Argentine president) Bartolomé Mitre became commander of the armed forces of the Triple Alliance
(see Paraguayan War), Brazil insisted that Baron de Tamandaré be made admiral of the almost autonomous Allied naval
force; Mitre and Tamandaré cooperated successfully in the
early military actions but differences of judgment regarding
strategy, along with military failures and defeats, brought an
end to the duality of command; the Brazilian admiral was relieved of his duty, Mitre was made commander of all allied
operations and the Duke of Caxias (q. v.) was placed in charge
of all Brazilian forces and made second in command to Mitre.

TAMANGO. Name given to the coarse heavy shoe made for soldiers of Army of the Andes for their crossing; apparently derived from the Portuguese word for wooden shoe, tamanco,
the term was early applied in Chile and Cuyo to the coarse
sheepskin wrappings with which the Indians protected their
feet on mountain trails; it came naturally to be applied to the
heavy-soled boots that San Martín ordered made in Mendoza
for his army and has continued to be used for similar military footwear; has come into common usage, through slang,
to denote any type of heavy shoe; somewhat like "clodhopper. "

TAMBO. Originally a Quechua name for the posthouses or stations providing supplies and shelter for the Inca messengers
and officials using the Inca royal highway; archeologists have

found remains of these in the north, especially in La Rioja; name was taken over by Spaniards for similar wayside inns of their own along the various oxcart routes linking the towns and trade areas together; during Rosas' time term also applied to colonies of blacks living in Buenos Aires; each tambo had its own king; regularly visited by Rosas and his wife or daughter; tambos supported Rosas loyally (see Naciones); in modern Argentina the name has come to be used to designate various aspects of dairy operations.

TAMBORINI, JOSE P. (1886-1955).   Porteño lawyer; Radical leader; public official.
           Born in Buenos Aires; early joined Unión Cívica Radical and was a youth leader in it while he was a student; presided over party's organization in the Federal Capital; served three terms in Chamber of Deputies and was minister of interior and of war in cabinet of President Marcelo T. de Alvear in 1920s; an Antipersonalist Radical, he signed the Junta del City (q. v.) through which the Radicals reorganized their party and won the election of 1931 (annulled by revolutionary government of Uriburu); because of his close ties with Alvear, he was confined in San Julián during Uriburu's administration; was elected Radical senator in 1940; nominated three times for presidency: in 1937 by Radicals; in 1946 by Unión Democrática, a coalition party of Radicals, Communists, Socialists, and Progressive Democrats; he received 44% of the popular vote but was defeated by Perón; nominated again in 1952 by Radicals, he lost to Perón; died in Buenos Aires three years later.

TAMET (Talleres Metalúrgicos de San Martín).   Major metalworking enterprise in Argentina; said to have been first manufacturing establishment to offer stock to public in 3,000,000 peso issue of debentures, 1937; issue heavily oversubscribed; TAMET constituted exception to general practice that most large Argentine foundries existed as subsidiaries of transport lines due to shortage of essential metals and fuel.

TANAQUEUPU see MENDOZA

TANDIL.   Commercial, industrial, and agricultural center in eastern Buenos Aires province, approximately 200 miles southwest of Buenos Aires and a few miles inland to the northwest of Mar del Plata; occupied by Indians, it was first described in 1746 by fathers José Cardiel and Thomas Falkner, who attempted to establish a mission there; later explored in 1770s and, in early independence period, plans were made to occupy area; in 1823, Martín Rodríguez established a town there around Fort Independence in effort to maintain a line against Indians; served rather to arouse them; by 1860s town really began to develop; a Danish colony was established by Juan Fugl, with school and church

facilities, in 1870, that has continued to make an impact on
the community; in 1883 the railroad reached Tandil and in
1895 it was given status of city; its economy is diversified,
with dairy industry, metalworks, cement factories, ranching,
agriculture, and tourism all contributing.

TANGO.   Modern Argentine dance that originated in the poorer
    suburbs or barrios of Buenos Aires toward the end of the
    nineteenth century and has acquired unique place in Argen-
    tine culture; often considered its national dance.
         As it has developed from its earliest crude and vio-
    lent forms to more aesthetic ones, the tango has created its
    own music, its own songs, and its own dance patterns; its
    origins have been subject of wide controversy, largely due to
    its humble first appearances, but most Argentine historians,
    musicians, and writers eventually came to defend the popular
    conviction that it is truly Argentine--created originally by
    lower-class creoles from elements of traditional Spanish
    dances, with some of the rhythms of African candombe
    added, and infused with the melancholy spirit of popular love
    songs of the pampas; its instruments are the traditional gui-
    tar, mandolin, Spanish lute (bandurria), harp, with others,
    such as accordion, added occasionally for special sound ef-
    fects.
         Although first tango is often said to have been "Dame
    la lata" (literally "Give me the can" but more colloquially
    "Please bother or pester me" meaning please pay me some
    attention), created in 1880 and immediately followed by many
    others, the tango was not accepted in respectable social
    circles in Buenos Aires until after it had enjoyed a great
    vogue in Paris following 1912; its popularity peaked in the
    1920s through the works and performances of composer and
    singer Carlos Gardel (q. v.); Argentines came to accept it as
    an expression of their unique national spirit; its unexpectedly
    quick acceptance and great success in other parts of the
    world, especially in urbanized areas of Japan and the United
    States, as well as France, indicate that it may rather be--
    as some Argentine psychologists and psychiatrists suggest--
    an Argentine expression of more universal human emotional
    moods and needs.

TARIJA.   Name of Bolivian city and department that lies along
    northern boundary of Argentine province of Salta, extending
    into the latter in the wedge bounded by Bermejo and Río
    Grande de Tarija rivers before they join; throughout the co-
    lonial period Tarija and Salta were closely related; having
    formed part of the intendancy of Salta, it remained a part of
    the province of Salta in 1814 when intendancy was divided;
    during the wars for independence in northern Argentina and
    Upper Peru (as Bolivia was then called), Tarija constantly
    changed hands between Argentine forces seeking to invade
    Upper Peru and royalist forces moving from there against
    Salta and Jujuy; after the final victory of Ayacucho in Peru

that sealed the liberation of Spanish South America from
Spain, some royalist forces still remained in Upper Peru and
in possession of Tarija; Sucre's capture of the latter brought
a delegation from Buenos Aires to Simón Bolívar, his superior, asking that Tarija be returned to the United Provinces;
Bolívar agreed, in spite of Sucre's protests, withdrew his
forces and on November 17, 1825, the cabildo of Tarija
turned province over to Argentine delegate; already Tarija
had sent representatives to the constituent congress in Buenos
Aires who were to help in framing the 1826 constitution (q. v.);
in the general breakdown of Argentine national organization
(1826-1827), Tarija turned again to Bolivia and was admitted
back into that nation in 1831.

TASAJO. Meat dried in strips and cured with salt for preservation and export; during early seventeenth century tasajo was
widely made throughout the provinces but it was costly in
comparison with charqui (q. v.) or jerked beef; latter more
commonly used until introduction of saladeros (q. v.) in late
eighteenth century; terms "charqui" and "tasajo" sometimes
used interchangeably.

TAXATION. During the four centuries of Argentine history since
the Spaniards entered the area in middle of sixteenth century,
the system of taxation has developed from the simple one
that they brought from Spain, suitable for an agrarian, early
modern European society and economy, to a sophisticated
program designed to support the heavy expenditures of an
urbanized, industrializing nation.
    The conquistadors brought with them the royal tax
system in which the almojarifazgo (q. v.; customs tax), alcabala (q. v.; tax on business transactions), sisa (tax on food),
were already established to supply royal revenues; local public services of defense, welfare, education, roads, etc.,
were provided, for most part, by efforts of citizens and
church; arbitrios and propios (qq. v.) were small local taxes
for cabildo expenses; the tithe, for support of the church,
was also collected by the royal government; new taxes included the tribute that every adult male Indian had to pay,
and others due to new circumstances such as the tax on
carretas (freight-wagons) to support the blandengues or frontier guard; sales at markets, such as La Recova, were
taxed; luxuries were taxed and royal monopolies such as
those on salt, playing cards, and tobacco added to royal
revenues.
    With the May Revolution, practically all government
revenue ceased; new tax systems had to be devised to pay not
only for government expenses but for the war for independence; while royal taxes, Indian tributes, the tithe, etc.,
were being specifically abolished legally by the patriot governments, new sources of revenue were being sought; experiments were made with taxes on bread sales, land taxes,
forced loans from Spaniards, especially, etc., but to a large

extent the early government had to depend principally on voluntary gifts and loans from patriots and larger customs income as trade increased.

Throughout nineteenth century customs duties continued to provide major source of national income; biggest problem was Buenos Aires' monopolizing of this for its own provincial purposes while other provinces suffered from lack of income; eventually, in national reorganization of 1862, port revenues were nationalized; meanwhile tariffs on interprovincial trade were legally abolished (constitution of 1853); taxation began to be used to serve national purposes as well as to provide revenue; for example, Urquiza attempted to divert trade to Rosario, instead of Buenos Aires, in this way; in early twentieth century, protective tariffs were introduced to promote such national agricultural industries as those of sugar, mate and wine.

In 1930s, because of increasing pressures of world depression, Argentine urbanization, and nationalist demands for economic independence, traditional revenues from foreign trade, even though increased, were no longer adequate to meet government expenses; new, direct taxes, such as income and inheritance taxes, were imposed; government welfare benefits were introduced and larger revenues were needed; taxes became a part of every individual's life; by 1970s taxes were also levied on profits and capital gains, real estate, public services (water, police, streets, irrigation, etc.); in early 1970s Argentina's tax revenue ranked very low (c. 6%) in proportion to Gross Domestic Product (GDP), as compared with other Latin American nations but it was running an increasing annual deficit of more than 20%.

TEHUELCHE.   Patagonian Indian tribe first described by Antonio Pigafetta, chronicler of Magellan's voyage; Tehuelche made up principal or best known group of Chonik or Patagones Indians; nomadic, relatively few in number, they roamed area from Strait of Magellan to Río Negro; Tehuelche were gatherers and hunters, using group hunting to round up and capture the guanacos and rheas; for weapons they had the bow and arrow, later acquired boleadoras and horses; tall people, averaging 6 feet for men, 5 feet and 5 inches for women; they lived in skin shelters, called toldos (q. v.) similar to those of the Pehuelches; used capes made of hides of guanaco for warmth and moccasins similar to the ones used by North American Indians were common; worked stone, bone, leather; no evidence of ceramics or weaving found; used only containers made of shells, armadillo carcasses, or leather; they were monogamous, lived in tribes of about 400 individuals; believed in one creator called Kooch Elel who created fire and revealed its secret to the Tehuelches; Kenos was the family god and there were also evil spirits; buried their dead on the top of hills and covered the bodies with stones; there are five known dialects; they used numerals up to 1000 but these

were of Quechua origin; Tehuelche culture and almost all
pure-blooded Tehuelche Indians had disappeared by end of
nineteenth century with Argentine occupation of southern
Patagonia.

TEISAIRE, ALBERTO, REAR ADMIRAL (1891-1970).   Naval officer; active Peronist political leader.
        Born in Mendoza; educated in Argentine naval academy
with advanced training in submarines and torpedoes in Argentina and in the United States; saw destroyer and submarine
duty with U.S. navy in World War I; continuing his naval career in various posts, of increasing importance, Teisaire became a rear admiral in 1944 and minister of interior in
President Farrell's cabinet; supported Perón strongly and
came to be considered most politically reliable Peronist; in
elections of 1946, as Perón was elected president, Teisaire
became senator from Buenos Aires, and, after eclipse of
power of Domingo Mercante, Perón's right arm; presided
over the constitutional convention of 1949; assisted in organization of the Peronist political party, of which he was for
years the acting president; in 1954 he became Perón's vice
president following the death of Hortensio Quijado; as director of the Peronists he suffered imprisonment and was subjected to trial; following the overthrow of Perón in September 1955; many felt that his statements at this time helped
to clarify public knowledge of the operations of the Peronist
party and of the deposed government.

TEJEDA, LEONOR DE (1574-c. 1640).   Founder and prioress of
first convent for nuns in Argentina; pioneer in education of
girls in Córdoba.
        Born in Tucumán, daughter of conquistador Tristán de
Tejeda, granddaughter of Hernando Mejía de Miraval (qq. v.);
was brought to new town of Córdoba, married in 1574 to
wealthy, distinguished Manuel de Fonseca y Contreras (q. v.);
both Leonor and her husband deeply interested in establishing
a convent of nuns in Córdoba; following General Fonseca's
return from official duty in Buenos Aires in 1598, already
ill with the infirmity that caused his death fourteen years
later, they began plans for the convent; Leonor had already
opened her home for the education of girls in Córdoba--
probably the first school for girls there--and her husband
now devoted himself to the building of a very large house that
might serve for the convent; after his death Leonor immediately enlisted the aid of Bishop Hernando de Trejo y Sanabria
who came to Córdoba and enthusiastically endorsed her project to establish (with her very great wealth) a convent for
nuns of the order of Santa Catalina de Siena in Córdoba;
despite the lack of precedents or even a copy of the rules
of this order, a conference of ecclesiastics was called and
guidelines improvised; on July 2, 1613, the Monasterio (convent) de Santa Catalina de Siena was opened with sixteen
nuns taking their vows, among them Leonor de Tejeda herself,

who became the first prioress; in 1625, this first convent in
Argentina received papal approval and a charter; between
1613 and her death, sometime after 1640, Mother Catalina de
Siena (as Leonor de Tejeda preferred to be known) divided
her time between this convent and that of Santa Teresa de
Jesús, founded by her brother Juan de Tejeda Miraval (q. v.)
in Córdoba in 1628.

See brief biography of Leonor de Tejeda in Juan Carlos Vera Vallejo, Breve historia del monasterio de Santa
Catalina en la ciudad de Córdoba.

TEJEDA, LUIS JOSE DE (1604-1680).   Writer, intellectual, soldier,
adventurer; first poet born in Argentine territory.

Born in Córdoba, grandson of one of city's founders,
Tristán de Tejeda; his early life reads like adventurous novel
of Don Juan type; attended university in Córdoba; had begun
military career by 1624; fought against Dutch pirate attacks
on Buenos Aires, Indian revolts in the Chaco, Tucumán, and
Córdoba; remained in Córdoba, active in public life as city's
attorney-general (1634), alcalde (1637), and public works official (1649) building dams on the river for flood control; in
1661, Tejeda's personal and public life changed completely;
following death of his wife and bloody campaign against Calchaquí Indians, he became involved in violent dispute over
militia with other authorities, who brought charges against him
in the royal audiencia; Tejeda's property was confiscated by
the government and only flight saved him from imprisonment;
in 1663, he took refuge in a monastery where he remained,
engaged in writing and religious works, until his death.

The poetry of Tejeda, influenced by the style of the
Spanish poet, Luis de Góngora y Argote, ranges from his
autobiographical El peregrino en Babilonia to his mystical
Soneto de Santa Rosa de Lima, considered the first Argentine poem to the American Virgin; others include Romances
al niño Jesús; El árbol de Judá; El fénix de amor; Sobre la
encarnación del verbo; and Soledades de María Santísima,
among others.   Tejeda's significance lies in the fact that,
while his poetry may not have equaled the best of that of
Spain's Gongorist period, during which he was writing, it
was a worthy example of it and almost the only one in the
semi-barbaric Argentina of that period, according to Ricardo
Rojas; preserved throughout the centuries, many of his poems
and prose writings were collected and published by the University of Córdoba in 1917, with title Coronas líricas.

TEJEDA, TRISTAN DE (d. 1617).   Conquistador; one of founders
of Córdoba; public official and commander of campaigns
against Indians throughout Argentine territory from Salta to
Buenos Aires.

Born in Old Castile in Spain; came to South America
and participated in expedition to Marañón river; accompanied
Jerónimo Luis de Cabrera (q. v.) from Peru to Tucumán; was
appointed councilman in first cabildo of newly-founded Córdoba

(1573); although Tejeda continued to serve later governors, in both military and civil capacities, fighting Indians, assisting in establishing of settlements in Salta, Tucumán, and Santa Fe, and accompanying Fernando de Zárate (q. v.) to Buenos Aires in 1593, he established his residence in Córdoba, took active part in its public affairs, and left a large family that made its own impact on that area (see Leonor de Tejeda; Juan de Tejeda Miraval; Luis de Tejeda).

See Roberto Levillier, Nueva crónica de la conquista de Tucumán; biografías de sus conquistadores (Buenos Aires, 1926; Madrid, 1937) and his other writings on early Tucumán and other Argentine areas.

TEJEDA MIRAVAL, JUAN DE (1575-1628).   Colonial merchant in Córdoba.

Born in Córdoba, son of conquistador Tristán de Tejeda and Leonor Mexía Miraval; acquired good education; devoted himself to military affairs and public office (held rare honor of being appointed lifetime member of cabildo); his marriage to María de Guzmán, only daughter of General Pablo de Guzmán, brought new wealth and distinction to the family; Tejeda engaged in such a lucrative commerce with Spain and Portugal, and with the principal cities of Peru, Chile, and Río de la Plata, that by 1612 his trading firm was reputed to be the wealthiest in the province; father of poet Luis José de Tejeda (q. v.).

TEJEDOR, CARLOS (1817-1903).   Jurisconsult and statesman; law professor and writer.

Born in Buenos Aires, graduated as doctor of jurisprudence in Buenos Aires Faculty of Law; early became involved in public affairs; throughout his life retained and acted upon liberal, porteño views held from time of Rivadavia to that of Mitre; became member of Asociación de Mayo (q. v.) but remained in Buenos Aires to fight Rosas while other members emigrated to Montevideo; became member of the Club de Cinco that organized the Maza conspiracy; when that failed (1839), he joined unitarist army of Juan Lavalle and eventually sought exile in Brazil and then in Chile, where he supported himself as lawyer and journalist and he and Domingo Faustino Sarmiento became close friends; after the battle of Caseros, Tejedor returned to Buenos Aires and immediately became active in politics and public life; was appointed editor of El Nacional and elected deputy to Buenos Aires legislature; following the Acuerdo de San Nicolás, Tejedor became strong supporter of group, led by Valentín Alsina, that refused to join the other provinces in their efforts to unite the nation constitutionally under Justo José Urquiza's leadership; and he and Dalmacio Vélez Sarsfield wrote the constitution whereby the province of Buenos Aires might govern itself as an independent state.

When Bartolomé Mitre became president of the United Argentine Republic, he charged Tejedor with the task of

codifying the penal code; in 1866-1869 he served as national
congressman and was reelected; became minister of foreign
relations under Sarmiento and taught courses in law at University of Buenos Aires; became director of national library
and in 1875 became Argentine diplomatic representative to
Brazil.

    Tejedor's election as governor of province of Buenos
Aires (served 1878-1880) and his subsequent backing by
Buenos Aires and Corrientes for national presidency in elections of 1880 precipitated what has come to be known as the
"Revolution" of 1880 and made necessary a final solution to
the problem of the location of the national capital; it resulted
in the federalization of the city of Buenos Aires and the establishing of the provincial capital at La Plata (see Federalization of City of Buenos Aires; La Plata); all the other provinces looked on Tejedor as a die-hard of the old porteño
school that demanded (according to federalist provincial opinion) protection of special porteño political privileges and economic profits from the port of Buenos Aires; although Tejedor, as governor of the province had taken the initiative in
1880 by mobilizing his forces and forcing the national government (on legal grounds, however) to move outside the city of
Buenos Aires, after fighting at Barracas, Puente Alsina,
and Corrales, with both sides wanting peace, he appointed
Mitre as his representative and as a gesture toward unity
as well as peace, resigned as governor of Buenos Aires and
withdrew his candidacy for election as president; retired to
private life, publishing in 1881 La defensa de Buenos Aires
(2d. ed. Buenos Aires, 1911) to explain facts of the 1880
uprising; in 1894 he was elected to represent the Federal
District in the national congress.

    Deeply respected both for his unusual talents and his
long career of devoted public service, Tejedor probably made
his major contributions to the Argentine republic in the field
of law--his teaching and writings, his codification of penal
law, and his contributions to the commercial and civil legal
codes--and in international relations as he dealt with the difficult legal boundary problems following the war with Paraguay.

TELEGRAFO MERCANTIL, RURAL, POLITICO, ECONOMICO E
    HISTORIOGRAFICO DEL RIO DE LA PLATA.   First news-
    paper in Buenos Aires.   Founded and edited by Francisco
    Antonio Cabello y Mesa (q.v.) sponsored by first Literary
    Society in Buenos Aires; the Telégrafo Mercantil aimed to
    provide detailed, accurate studies of the current situations
    and resources of the various provinces; published during ad-
    ministration of Viceroy Joaquín del Pino from April 1, 1801,
    to October 15, 1802; among its contributors were Gregorio
    Funes (under pseudonym of Patricio Salliano), Eugenio del
    Portillo (as Enio Tullio Grope), Manuel de Lavardén, José
    Joaquín de Araujo (under name Patricio de Buenos Aires),
    Tadeo Haenke the naturalist, Manuel Medrano, Domingo de

Azcuénaga, José Chorroarín, Juan José Castelli, Pedro Antonio Cerviño and others; a reprint of the issues appeared in
1914.

TEMPERLY, JORGE (or GEORGE) (1823-1900). English estanciero
and entrepreneur. Temperly arrived in Argentina at an early
age; settled on land in Lomas de Zamora, established town
there that still bears his name (in Buenos Aires province,
near the city) and began cattle ranch that became one of best
in the republic; strongly supported the building of railroads,
erecting a railroad station at his own expense when the Sud
(Railroad of the South) was projected; engaged in selective
cattle breeding to improve the quality of Argentine beef, making his ranch a model in this respect and other scientific innovations and introductions; Temperly was a director of the
provincial bank, an active member of the Rural Society; his
interest in civic affairs was displayed by his support of the
Teatro Colón, and his membership on public committees
formed to fight epidemics of yellow fever in the city of
Buenos Aires.

TEMPLE, EDMUND. Travel writer. British traveler that visited
Río de la Plata region in 1825; came as part of the expedition led by James Paroissien for the London mining company,
named La Potosí, La Paz, and Peruvian Mining Association,
to survey the area's mineral resources; in 1826 Temple
visited Córdoba, Salta, and Bolivia; after his return to England, he published Travels in Various Parts of Peru (London,
1830); those portions of greatest interest to Argentines were
translated into Spanish and published by the University of
Tucumán in 1920.

TEMPLO Y COLEGIO DE LA COMPAÑIA DE JESUS IN CORDOBA.
Jesuit church built in 1643 in Córdoba, center of Jesuit educational and scholarly work; built under direction of Felipe
Lemer, Belgian architect and painter; consecrated in 1671;
constructed in form of cross, with a center cupola and Roma-
nesque arches; its paintings are of rococo period; in 1941 it
was declared a national monument.

TERCIO DE YERBA. Weight measure used in trade of yerba
mate during colonial period; it takes its name from the
tercio or container made of uncured cowhide in which the
mate was packed and carried; in the north each tercio was
considered to be one-half the total load that a pack animal
could carry, i. e. , with one tercio hanging on each side;
these were commonly used for transporting the yerba mate
from Paraguay and Misiones to markets throughout viceroyalty of Peru (and later, that of Río de la Plata).

TERRADA, JUAN FLORENCIO (1782-1824). Independence fighter
and political figure.
        Born in Buenos Aires; took active part in fight against

British invasions and in May Revolution; belonged to early independence group led by Cornelio Saavedra; fought in siege
of Montevideo 1811; served as Director Pueyrredón's minister of war; first governor of the province of Cuyo after its
separation from Córdoba in 1813; retired to private life in
1817.

TERRERO, JOSE JOAQUIN (1741-1794).   Spanish physician who
        founded important Buenos Aires family.
        Born in Algeciras; came to Buenos Aires about 1770;
practiced medicine with great success; married socially
prominent and wealthy María Josefa Villarino, widow of Angel
Castelli (father of Juan José Castelli); their three sons, José
María, Joaquín Cayetano, and Juan Nepomuceno, and later
generations were prominent in political, economic, and ecclesiastical life of Argentina (see individual entries below);
Dr. Terrero died at posthouse of Bustos on his way to Mendoza.

TERRERO, JOSE MARIA (1787-1837).   Priest; teacher; public fig-
        ure.
        Born in Buenos Aires, son of Dr. José Joaquín Ter-
rero; studied at University in Córdoba; ordained in 1809;
named chaplain of cathedral by Bishop Lué; in 1816 received
doctor's degree in philosophy and theology from Córdoba;
named vice director of University of the South by Pueyrredón;
taught Latin in the Colegio de la Unión; held various posts in
the church; curate of La Concepción, 1822-1829; provisional
governor of the archbishopric in 1830 and then appointed
canon of the cathedral and eccesiastical attorney in 1831;
served several terms in Buenos Aires legislature in the
1830s and as director of public library during closing years
of his life; died in Buenos Aires.

TERRERO, JUAN NEPOMUCENO (1791-?).   Buenos Aires estanci-
        ero and political figure.
        Born in Buenos Aires, third son of Dr. José Joaquín
Terrero; with Luis Dorrego, formed partnership with Juan
Manuel de Rosas to establish first saladero in Buenos Aires
province, Las Higueritas, near Quilmes; account books of
this early packing house have been preserved, serving as important source for research into early operations of this important industry; Terrero increased his landholdings by acquiring vast tracts along Indian frontier; strong supporter of
Rosas against Unitarist policies of Rivadavia; in 1834, when
Rosas refused governorship of Buenos Aires, it was offered
to Tomás and Nicolás Anchorena who both refused it; Terrero, next to receive offer, also refused it.

TERRERO, JUAN NEPOMUCENO (1850-1921).   Priest; Bishop of
        La Plata.
        Born and educated in Buenos Aires; was about to em-
bark on political career when he suddenly entered the

priesthood; was ordained at Gregorian University in Rome
and completed his theological studies there in 1880; after
serving in various church positions, he was consecrated titular bishop of Delcos in 1898; appointed bishop of La Plata in
1900 where he remained until his death.

TERRERO, LUIS FEDERICO (1878-1962).   Engineer; hacendado.
Born in Buenos Aires; graduated (1902) from Faculty
of exact, physical, and natural sciences in Federal Capital;
in 1903 he was a part of boundary commission with Chile,
accompanying Generals Robertson and Thompson; thereafter
devoted himself to stockherding on family estancias in Los
Cerrillos and, later, on that named Reconquista, in General
Belgrano.

TERRITORIES.   Administrative units set up in 1884 by Law 1532
to govern remote, sparsely settled areas for purpose of developing them to point of becoming provinces; one prescribed
requirement was a population of 60,000; the governor and
two judges for each territory were appointed by the national
executive power but local officials were elected by popular
vote; originally there were ten territories: Misiones, Chaco,
Chubut, Formosa, Santa Cruz, Río Negro, Neuquén, La Pampa, Jujuy (or Los Andes, to distinguish it from province of
Jujuy) and Tierra del Fuego; in 1970 Tierra del Fuego remained the only territory; Los Andes had been divided up and
added to provinces of Catamarca, Salta, and Jujuy; the other
eight were provinces (see individual entries on provinces and
territories).

TERRITORY OF TIERRA DEL FUEGO, ANTARCTICA, AND SOUTH
ATLANTIC ISLANDS see TIERRA DEL FUEGO (Territory)

TERRY, JOSE ANTONIO (1846-1910).   Lawyer; financier; government minister and diplomat.
Born in Brazil of Argentine parents; graduated in law,
Buenos Aires, 1871; began public life as a journalist, writing for La Prensa, acting as one of editors of La Discusión
and then becoming responsible for political editorials in La
Nación; served as deputy and senator in Buenos Aires legislature and as congressman in national Chamber of Deputies;
held responsible positions in Banco Hipotecario (Mortgage
and Loan Bank), Caja de Conversión (conversion fund), member of commissions to supervise business corporations and
on that of railroads; served as minister of finance under
presidents Luis Sáenz Peña, Julio A. Roca, and Manuel
Quintana; also acted as interim foreign minister during Roca's
second term in absence of Roque Saenz Peña; designated by
Roca to prepare negotiations with Chile for settlement of
boundary and other problems; signed Pactos de Mayo (q.v.)
for Argentina May 28, 1902, in Santiago, Chile; began giving
courses on finance in law school 1898; his lectures were published under title Tratado de finanzas (1928); attended Third

Pan American Conference (Rio de Janeiro, 1906) and Fourth
(Buenos Aires, 1910) as Argentine delegate; was preparing to
go to Chile as minister plenipotentiary when he died in
Buenos Aires from a heart attack; had devoted much of his
time and interest to work with the deaf, organized institute
for them and published El sordomudo, su instrucción y educación.
     Most of his writings dealt with matters of finance:
La crisis; Cuestión monetaria; Exposición sobre el estado fi-
nanciero de la República Argentina (1893).

TERRY, JOSE ANTONIO (1878-1954).   Painter.   Born in Buenos
     Aires; studied there and abroad, in Chile, England, and in
     France; began by choosing European and religious subjects
     but eventually turned to painting scenes of primitive life in
     northwestern Argentina, working at his studio in Jujuy, and
     of Buenos Aires province; among his better known paintings
     of this type were Al bajar del cerro, La Emana Chepa con
     su cántaro; himself a deaf mute, he founded first elementary
     school in Buenos Aires for the deaf; died in Buenos Aires.

THAMES, JOSE IGNACIO (1762-1832).   Priest; patriot; signer of
     Declaration of Independence.
          Born in San Miguel de Tucumán; received his doctor's
     degree at University of San Carlos; became ordained as
     priest; after serving briefly in his native city, he became a
     canon of the cathedral of Salta (1813); represented Tucumán
     at congress there in 1816; was member of committee that
     drew up statute regulating government by supreme directors;
     signed Declaration of Independence; accompanied congress to
     Buenos Aires and remained active until 1818; resigned and
     returned to his clerical duties in Salta; returned to his home
     in Tucumán; was elected as provincial legislator in 1821;
     died in Tucumán; a street in Buenos Aires named in his
     honor.

THAYS, CARLOS (1849-1934).   Engineer; urban landscape archi-
     tect.
          Born in Paris; came to Argentina in 1891 under con-
     tract to design and construct the park in Córdoba that later
     became the Sarmiento Park; instead of returning to France,
     he accepted appointment as director of public parks, gardens,
     and promenades, in the federal capital, Buenos Aires; trans-
     formed its appearance, beginning with the Plaza de Mayo and
     beautifying or creating more than eighty parks and public
     walks; very important was his creation of the Botanical
     Garden in 1892, opened to the public in 1898; traveled ex-
     tensively throughout the interior, especially in Misiones, to
     gather specimens for growth and scientific study in the Bo-
     tanical Garden; in 1910 published El jardín botánico de
     Buenos Aires describing plants there at that time; planned
     other parks, including that of San Martín in Mendoza, in
     Argentina; died in Buenos Aires.

THIBON DE LIBIAN, VALENTIN (1889-1931). Painter. Born in
San Miguel de Tucumán; studied in Buenos Aires and in
Europe (Florence, Venice, Rome, and Paris); held private
shows in Buenos Aires between 1912 and 1924; won first
prize in the Venice exposition of 1923 with El violinista; his
favorite subjects were workers, dancers, or those taken
from the circus; his paintings have been compared with those
of H. P. G. Degas, an older French contemporary whom he
admired greatly; his style of painting varies, swinging between impressionism and romanticism, but always showing a
clear French influence until the last years of his life; among
his best known paintings are: Cabo Corrientes, La muerte
del clown, Jugando bambalinas en el café, Bebedor de ajenjo
(absinthe drinker), La fragua, Retrato de mi hermano; died
in Buenos Aires; an exposition was held in his memory in
1939.

"THIRD POSITION. " Name applied by President Juan Domingo
Perón to Argentina's foreign policy to be followed in Cold
War of post-World War II as well as to a middle position to
be taken with regard to Argentine domestic policy between
Communism and capitalistic free enterprise system; term
first used by Perón in Mendoza, April 1949, in an address
given before an international philosophy congress, dealing
with problem of collectivism versus individualism; justicialismo (q. v.) provided doctrine appropriate to this position; to
many Argentines, then and later, this meant a flexibility in
foreign affairs permitting Argentina to play a continuing role
in international affairs consistent with its own national interests without a forced commitment to either side; in many
respects, it was a continuation, or revised version, of Argentina's traditional policy of neutralism as practiced by
Yrigoyen in World War I and suggested by President Ortiz
in his "non-belligerence" policy at outbreak of World War II;
internally, it meant that Argentina intended to follow its own
pattern economically and socially; through justicialismo it
promised social justice at home and stood for justice internationally.
      Perón's argument in defense of his "Third Position"
was that underdeveloped countries had little real interest in
the Cold War between Russia and the United States because
neither pure Communism nor capitalism were adequate doctrines to solve their own social and economic problems; instead, they ought to look for some intermediate system combining good elements of both; he invited such international
leaders as Nehru of India and Pope Pius XII to join him in
forming a third power group on this basis in world affairs;
he also attempted to organize an Inter-American labor force
ATLAS (Agrupación de Trabajadores Latino-Americanos); his
efforts received initial support in Chile and Brazil but did
not acquire the immediate success that he had hoped for;
Perón's influence began to decline after this but the idea of
a "Third Position" continued to appeal to many Argentines

and other Latin Americans; meanwhile the Cold War began to thaw, changing the international situation; historically, the "Third Position" stands as a mid-twentieth century restatement of Argentina's determination to run its own affairs but at the same time to take its desired place in international community.

THOMPSON, DIEGO (JAMES) G. (1801-1864). English merchant and educator; appointed in 1818 as official representative of London Lancastrian Society to introduce the Lancastrian system of education into the Latin American countries engaged in winning their independence from Spain; arriving in Buenos Aires that same year, Thompson organized a society there to promote such schools; he was so successful that in 1821, with 16 Lancastrian schools already established in the area, the cabildo of Buenos Aires awarded him a letter of citizenship; Thompson (also representing Bible society) was equally interested in distributing Bibles and encouraging their use, taking advantage of the new religious toleration of this period; following his Argentine experience, Thompson spent seven years traveling in the other Latin American countries introducing and promoting the establishment of Lancastrian schools and societies (see Lancastrian System of Education).

THOMPSON, JUAN (1809-1873). Writer and journalist; lawyer; public figure.
    Born in Buenos Aires, son of Martín Thompson and María Sánchez; studied in Buenos Aires and Europe; graduated as lawyer in University in Buenos Aires; became member of the literary and intellectual group led by Esteban Echeverría; assisted in writing constitution of Asociación de Mayo, to which he belonged; kept a diary at that time that has been published; emigrated with his family to Montevideo in 1839; accompanied Lavalle in his campaign against Rosas the following year; later took refuge in Corrientes where he founded and edited El Sol de Mayo; returned to Montevideo and his law practice; in 1852 he was named Argentine consul in Madrid; returned to Buenos Aires in 1863; went back to Spain in 1870; died in Barcelona; a member of the famous Generation of 1837, Juan Thompson participated in intellectual life of every place in which he resided; he published several newspapers, in addition to one named above, such as El Grito Argentino, El Talismán, Muera Rosas, El Pueblo Libertador; continued his journalistic and literary writing in Europe.

THOMPSON, MARTIN JACOBO (1771-1819). Naval officer; patriot leader.
    Born in Buenos Aires, cadet at naval school in Spain, fought at Trafalgar; returning to Buenos Aires, he entered public life; fought vigorously against British invasions of Río de la Plata area in Montevideo, where he was wounded, in defense of Buenos Aires, as well as on the river where he

captured several enemy brigantines; Martín Thompson belonged to early patriot group including Rodríguez Peña, Castelli, and Cornelio de Saavedra; supported May Revolution as
member of the cabildo abierto (1810), and was appointed captain of the port of Buenos Aires by the first patriot junta,
with responsibility for protecting the city from river attack;
his home, presided over by his spirited and popular wife,
María Sánchez (q. v.) known in Buenos Aires society as
Mariquita, daughter of wealthy Spaniard Cesáreo Sánchez de
Velasco, became gathering place for patriotic leaders; it was
there that the Argentine national anthem was first sung and
popularized; in 1816 Colonel Thompson was sent by Director
Alvarez Thomas on diplomatic mission to the United States
to secure aid for the fight for emancipation from Spain and
recognition of Argentine independence; his mission met with
little success and Thompson was returning to Buenos Aires
in 1819 when he died on board ship.

TIERRA DEL FUEGO (Territory).   In 1957 changed to Territory of
Tierra del Fuego, Antarctica, and South Atlantic Islands.
Only national territory remaining in Argentine Republic in
1970s; consists of the Argentine one-third of the triangular
island of Tierra del Fuego, lying between Strait of Magellan
and Beagle Channel and includes the Malvinas Islands in
theory (actually still held by Great Britain; see Falkland Islands), and the Argentine Antarctica; takes its name from
that given to the island by Magellan's men in 1520 who saw
fires burning on its mountains; created a national territory
in 1943; later became a national park under the minister of
the navy.
     Boundaries. Chile on west and south; Strait on north
and Atlantic Ocean on east.   Area: Argentine portion of island 8070 square miles; including Tierra del Fuego, Antarctica and South Atlantic Islands, 490,000 square miles.   Population (1970): 15,698.   Capital: Ushuaia, located on Beagle
Channel on southern coast of Tierra del Fuego.
     Geography and climate of island. Consists of a
mountainous region with glaciers descending to the sea and
an eastern area with plateaus and valleys in which sheep are
raised; several small rivers, like the Fuego, Yrigoyen,
Grande, Chico, Varela, Oeste and others, flow across
the territory; very cold climate is tempered by the sea
and is very windy.
     Communications. Air transportation, especially ser-
vices of Aerolíneas Argentinas; private planes used, as well
as seagoing vessels.
     Economy. Largely based on sheepraising, with a
frigorífico at Río Grande since 1914; hardwood forests are
exploited by sawmills and factories that produce lumber and
plywood; there is very little agriculture; oil and natural gas
resources there are being developed and some gold has been
found on the island.
     History. In 1520 when Magellan's ships sailed through

Strait of Magellan (q. v.) the island of Tierra del Fuego was
inhabited by several very different, but all primitive groups
of Indians, including Ona, Yahgan, Alacaluf, and others; as
Ona were prominent, the island was known by the Indians as
Onisin, "land of the Onas"; remote Tierra del Fuego held
little interest for either Spain or its European rivals until
after the independence period; Anglican missionaries and
British merchants began to explore its possibilities as part
of Great Britain's general desire to establish a base in South
Atlantic and safeguard passage of its ships through strait;
from 1827 to 1830 British ships visited the area and Captain
Robert Fitzroy, of the Beagle, took four Yahgan Indians back
to London; he returned in 1833-1834 to bring the Indians, now
Christian, home along with Richard Mathews to establish a
mission; the mission attempt failed, but Charles Darwin,
scientist on the Beagle, left descriptive accounts of the area;
in 1850 the English Patagonian Missionary Association sent
Allan P. Gardiner and party to establish new Indian mission
there; all died of hunger; finally, in 1869 W. H. Stirling,
who knew some Yahgan, began an Anglican mission at Ushuaia
(Indian for tranquil bay) on bay of same name on Beagle Channel; joined in 1870 by Thomas Bridges, they developed the
mission into the first permanent settlement on the island;
Bridges made an intensive study of Yahgan and wrote a dictionary of Yahgan words; his own family was brought up
there and one of his sons, E. Lucas Bridges, later wrote a
classic study of the different Indian cultures found in Tierra
del Fuego at that time and the drastic changes that took place
in their lives during the following decades; missionaries
taught Indians Christian doctrine, reading, writing, manual
skills, and later, sheepherding and shearing.
          Meanwhile Argentine and Chilean interest in the area
was increasing, both officially and privately, by entrepreneurs and scientists; during first few decades of independence
both Chile and Argentina had paid little attention to their mutual boundaries along the Andes and in the south, as Patagonia was occupied only by Indians; in 1849 Chile established
Punta Arenas on the northern side of the strait and D. F.
Sarmiento, then in Chile, upheld its claim to both sides of
strait; in 1856 the two nations signed a treaty more or less
recognizing the status quo and Chile's sovereignty in the
strait but Argentina's rights to Atlantic coast; Chile denounced this treaty in 1865; in 1872 Argentina asserted its
claim to all of Patagonia south of Deseado river, and in following year an Argentine maritime subprefecture was established over Atlantic coastal area, under Augusto Lassere;
Chileans in Santa Cruz area were forced to leave, hostilities
almost broke out but peace was made December 6, 1877, by
treaty of Pierro-Sarratea, again observing the status quo, with
Chile in strait, Argentina on Atlantic; various scientific expeditions, some of them with joint Argentine-Italian cooperation,
had spent considerable time in Tierra del Fuego, exploring
island and studying its natural history; in 1881-1882 Luis

Piedrabuena was sent on official expedition to the island with Santiago Bove, head of scientific commission, naturalist Carlos Spegazzini and Captain Edelmiro Correa, who represented Argentine Geographic Institute; in 1883 Bove published his report Expedición austral argentina. Informes preliminares; the following year the territory of Tierra del Fuego was formally established with Captain Félix M. Paz as first governor and the Anglican mission, found flying a British flag, was asked to replace it with an Argentine one; in 1886 Ramón Lista and Salesian priest José Fagnano explored the area and Father Fagnano remained on the island to begin missionary work with the Indians while Lista went back to report; about this time Julio Popper, engineer, placer gold miner, explorer, and natural scientist, established himself in the area, with his own guard, postal service, and coinage system; sent reports of development potential to Argentine Geographic Institute, listing primarily sheepraising and gold mining as economic possibilities; in 1891 he published his observations, entitled Apuntes geográficos etnológicos, estadísticos e industriales sobre Tierra del Fuego; settlement was proceeding, largely centered around Ushuaia, with 300 in 1887, and Río Grande, a port on the north Atlantic coast, on northern bank at mouth of island's largest river, also named Río Grande; in 1890 Governor Paz was replaced by a naval physician and three years later Ushuaia legally became a town, and the official capital in 1904; (place where Argentine flag was first flown has been declared an historic site); meanwhile problem of Chilean-Argentine boundary in south had not been settled; in 1899, in bold attempt to allay Chile's fears that Argentina's increased naval power was designed for use in Pacific, along with other suspicions, President Julio A. Roca met with Chilean president, Federico Errázuriz Echaurren, in the Strait to reach an agreement; final decision was delayed, however, until the Pactos de Mayo, 1902, that confirmed Chile's right to both shores of the Strait but provided for free navigation of it, and to rest of archipelago at tip of continent, giving Argentina one-third of Tierra del Fuego, on Atlantic side.

During the twentieth century the territory has begun to contribute its share to national life; roads were opened in 1900 and schools and hospitals have been established; island continued to attract travelers, such as British traveler and writer Robert B. C. Graham and has, in modern times, developed into a summer (January-March) tourist attraction because of its spectacular scenery; among its most beautiful lakes is the Fagnano; before 1900 the public lands were opened for sale, in hope of attracting immigrants, but instead they have largely passed into hands of large landowners who have also secured timber and mineral rights; sheep ranchers dominate and Río Grande, founded by Salesians in 1887, has become important port for shipping wool and meat, with a frigorífico established in 1914; over a million sheep were grazing on the island by mid-century on the lands that

had been emptied of Indians; latter, who numbered about
10,000 in 1860, have practically disappeared through exter-
mination, in process of establishing sheep ranches, or in epidemics such as smallpox and measles, or by absorption into
the economy and society, many of them making excellent
sheepherders and shearers; as Indians have become less vis-
ible, interest in them has increased, with anthropologists
and archeologists finding Tierra del Fuego a rich site for research, especially in cultural anthropology; with the discovery
of petroleum, exploitation was turned over to government's
official YPF in the 1930s, but since then, other companies
have also been invited in; natural gas is also produced; hardwood forests supply sawmills and plywood is manufactured,
although forests are becoming somewhat depleted.
    Since 1900 government has been under minister of
navy; in 1946 the territory was declared a national park under
the navy; the penal colony long established near Ushuaia was
closed in 1950s; the increased strategic importance of Tierra
del Fuego with reference to Argentina's claims to Antarctica
and the Falkland Islands (qq. v.) caused the latter to be included, 1957, in the enlarged territory of Tierra del Fuego,
Antarctica, and South Atlantic Islands.
    See Antonio Pigafetta's account of Magellan's voyage
for first European impressions of Tierra del Fuego area
(many editions); for Indian cultures, see Julián Steward, ed. ,
Handbook of South American Indians, Volume I entitled Marginal Tribes, published by Smithsonian Institution, Washington,
D. C. , 1946; see also Darwin's Voyage of the Beagle and especially the classic Unto the Uttermost Parts of the Earth by
E. Lucas Bridges (London, 1948; New York, 1949); also, for
the earlier explorations, Samuel Eliot Morison, The European Discovery of America, Vol. II, The Southern Voyages
(New York, 1974).

"TIGER OF THE LLANOS" see JUAN FACUNDO QUIROGA

TIGER'S HEAD see CABEZA DE TIGRE

TIPOY.   Tunic without collar or sleeves made of white cotton;
    worn by the Chaco Indians; adopted also by Paraguayans of
    humble condition; used exclusively by women.

TIRABOSHI, ENRIQUE (1868-1948).   Swimmer.   Born in Italy;
    came to Buenos Aires shortly before outbreak of World War
    I and became citizen; attempted various distance swimming
    feats across the Río de la Plata; February 20, 1920, swam
    from Montevideo to within three miles of Buenos Aires,
    spending 24 hours 1 minute in the water, breaking the
    world's record; also swam from Colonia (Uruguay) to Buenos
    Aires and across La Mancha channel; after unsuccessful at-
    tempt to swim the British Channel in 1921, he broke the
    record in 1922 by crossing it in 16 hours and 23 minutes;
    returned to Argentina where he taught swimming; died in

Buenos Aires.

TIRO NACIONAL.   Military organization formed by porteños to re-
    sist the federalization of Buenos Aires in 1880; began street
    fighting under Carlos Tejedor against the government of
    Avellaneda; defeated by the national forces; as a result the
    congress nationalized the city of Buenos Aires as federal dis-
    trict (see Federalization of City of Buenos Aires; Carlos Te-
    jedor).

TOAY.   Name of town, capital of department of same name in
    northeastern portion of province of La Pampa, just outside
    the capital, Santa Rosa; site has long been known to the na-
    tives by this name, apparently referring to the fact that its
    fertile, wooded, well-watered valley area near a famous spring,
    was surrounded by sand dunes and semi-arid mountains; Toay
    apparently served as the base camp for the final expeditions
    and campaigns of the "Conquest of the Desert" (1875-1879);
    settlers early occupied the area and in 1881 it was linked to
    Bahía Blanca by a railroad and the town was formally estab-
    lished July 9, 1894 by Juan Brown on lands acquired from
    Benito Villanueva; Toay is linked with other cities in the
    province and to both Bahía Blanca and Buenos Aires by rail-
    road and highway (see La Pampa).

TOBACCO.   Tobacco was found growing in various areas of northern
    Argentina, especially the Chaco region, at the time of the
    Spanish conquest, and the Indians were accustomed to using it
    in various ways; by the 1970s it had finally become an impor-
    tant agricultural crop and had given rise to a large industry;
    during the colonial period tobacco was cultivated by the mis-
    sions and on small local farms for use by the neighboring
    community; throughout most of the colonial period, Argentine
    leaf tobacco could be freely traded, although the processed
    product came under royal control; in the late eighteenth cen-
    tury, especially after the royal monopoly had taken over all
    sales of tobacco in Peru and Chile (following 1752), tobacco
    became increasingly important in contraband trade between
    Argentina and those areas, and in 1779, an attempt was made
    to place Argentine tobacco also under the monopoly--never
    very successful but Argentina's production, especially after
    the decline of the Jesuit missions that had raised tobacco
    successfully for trade, was too small to warrant expensive
    enforcement measures; the importation of tobacco through
    Buenos Aires in the early decades of independence brought a
    further decline in its production in the interior provinces
    during the mid-nineteenth century.
        In the twentieth century, however, with increased na-
    tional interest in agriculture and the opening, or reopening,
    of the northern subtropical areas to settlement and economic
    development, tobacco began to play an important role in the
    national economy; a government agency was established to
    promote all phases of tobacco growing, processing, and

marketing; it has established experimental stations in most
of the tobacco growing provinces; the latter include most of
the Argentine area north of the 29th parallel, with Misiones,
Corrientes, and Chaco producing most of the Havana and
Bahía leaf tobacco, and the other more temperate provinces
growing the Virginia and Creole varieties; by 1960 Argentina
was about self-sufficient in tobacco; ten years later, in the
early 1970s, its annual production of 60,000-65,000 metric
tons of raw tobacco (about a third of it for export) placed it
third among Latin American countries, following Brazil and
Mexico; tobacco factories, both large and small, are concentrated in the Buenos Aires and littoral industrial areas
but others have been built in the tobacco-producing provinces
themselves.

TOBAS.   These Indians were among the Guaycuruans (q. v.) who
adopted the use of the horse and became fierce raiders of
Spanish ranches and settlements; by the seventeenth century
they had disappeared as a separate group and had become assimilated into other Indian or Spanish societies.

TOKI (or toqui).   Special ax used by chieftains of northwestern Argentine Indians and Araucanians as symbol of their authority;
Araucanians called it pillán-toki, or "magic ax" as it was
also believed to have supernatural powers; usually made of
metal, of a special form, tokis have been discovered in several places in Argentina, as well as in Pacific coast countries; similarity of its name with that used by Polynesians in
South Pacific for similar ax has led to increased interest in
possible early links between these areas.

TOLDO.   Primitive type of shelter among Patagonian Indians like
Tehuelche (q. v.), made of skins, originally guanaco, but
later horsehide and deerskin, sewn together with ñandú veins,
and supported by wooden poles; one side of the toldo was usually left open for smoke escape, light, and ventilation.   A
grouping of toldos was known as a tolderia.

TOMASO, ANTONIO DE (1889-1933).   Socialist leader.   Born in
Buenos Aires; graduated in law at University in 1914; elected
that same year as Socialist national congressman from Federal Capital; reelected for several terms; attended international Socialist congress in Geneva; published book about it after
his return; in 1930 led group that left Socialist Party to form
Independent Socialist Party; reelected by latter to Congress for
fifth term; Tomaso's party joined in revolutionary movement--
September 6, 1930--that brought Uriburu and military group
into power; defeated for seat in senate, he became minister
of Agriculture under President Agustín P. Justo (1932); began
program of reforms in rural agriculture and livestock industries but became ill and died in Buenos Aires; left his mark
on legislation relating to civil rights, penal and labor law.

TONAZZI, JUAN N. , GENERAL (1888-   ).   Career military officer; Minister of War, 1940-1942.

Born in Buenos Aires; educated at Colegio Militar and
Escuela Superior de Guerra; after various early military assignments, Tonazzi was assigned to the Colegio Militar as
commander of its battery (1918, 1920), professor of tactics
(1921), commander of the cadet corps (1922-1924); served as
military attaché to Italy (1925-1926) and as head of secretariat of Ministry of War (1927-1928); became close friend
and strong supporter of Agustín P. Justo and after Uriburu's
overthrow of the Yrigoyen government, was given assignment
to Uruguay as military attaché; during Justo's presidency he
served in various posts and became director of the Colegio
Militar (1936-1938); was commander of third division of the
army when he was appointed minister of war by Acting President Castillo; in this post he occupied key position (1940-
1942) during critical period following death of President Ortiz and entry of United States into World War II; Tonazzi represented strong Argentine neutral position along with Justo's
traditional oligarchical leaning toward the Allies; in 1942
President Castillo assigned him to the directorship of all military institutes and replaced him in the Cabinet with Pedro
Ramírez; in 1943 Tonazzi became commander of the Third
Army; the following year, Tonazzi was one of the sixteen
brigadier generals who signed a manifesto calling on the military government of President Farrell (March 1944) to hold
constitutional elections and to permit the army to remove itself from politics as soon as possible; retired in 1944.

TONELERO, PASS OF.   Easily fortified and defended site in
Buenos Aires province northwest of the city and near Ramal-
lo, along the Paraná river, from which government forces
have frequently attacked convoys attempting to ascend the
river or enemy forces descending by land or river to attack
Buenos Aires.

Among such incidents were the following: in 1841-
1842 General Urquiza made this his headquarters against the
Corrientes forces of generals Paz and Rivera revolting
against Rosas and moving toward Buenos Aires; on November
20, 1845, Argentine forces attacked an Anglo-French blockading squadron going up the river; a convoy of merchant ships
bound for Corrientes was prevented from taking on fresh supplies near Tonelero in November 1846 and finally reached its
destination after 112 days with a crew overrun with scurvy;
in mid-December 1851, a Brazilian squadron carrying the
first division of Brazilian troops and concealed exiled Argentine political leaders, including Bartolomé Mitre, Wenceslao
Paunero and D. F. Sarmiento, fought an hour's battle against
General Lucio Mansilla's artillery at Tonelero; losses were
light on both sides but Mansilla withdrew and thus missed the
main body of Urquiza's anti-Rosas forces approaching for the
battle that was joined at Monte Caseros a few weeks later,
February 3, 1852.

TONOCOTES. Sedentary Indians found living in area now occupied
by provinces of Santiago del Estero and part of Tucumán;
their language was adopted by Indians living in same area,
such as the Lules and some of the nomadic tribes; Tonocotés
were given in encomiendas during early Spanish conquest of
Argentina and eventually disappeared as a separate culture;
from the sixteenth through the eighteenth century, however,
they formed part of colonial life in interior Argentina, and
missionaries had studied them extensively; from their preserved works and studies made by modern anthropologists
and archeologists, much is known about these Indians.

Physically, Tonocotés were short, with wide, flat
faces, similar to Brasilid type; they were farmers, planting
corn, squash, and beans; supplemented their diet by hunting,
fishing, and gathering algarrobo fruit; they domesticated the
rhea and guanaco; their round or rectangular dwelling-huts,
with straw roofs, were built on artificial mounds and arranged in a village defended by a surrounding wall; the men
wore aprons of rhea feathers and women used garments made
of wool or vegetable fibers; the Tonocotés were effective
fighters and hunters, using a very large bow and large arrow, usually dipped in poison; also used the macana club;
they were skilled workers in ceramics, of which the best
found have been the funeral urns, decorated in red and black
on a white background; they believed in a Supreme Being,
Cacanchic, to whom they made offerings of alcoholic beverages and slain birds; there was also a special group of women dedicated to his service.

TORANZO DE ZAVALLA, BORJA. Wealthy patriot woman of San
Juan; honored for her contributions to patriot cause; in 1812,
gave liberally toward organization of patriot army; two years
later she became one of the first to liberate her slaves, providing for them financially as she did so; in 1835 she donated
land for the new municipal cemetery of San Juan.

TORCUATO DI TELLA, INSTITUTO see INSTITUTO TORCUATO
DI TELLA

TORRE, LISANDRO DE LA (1868-1939). Lawyer; leftist political
leader; successful estanciero; writer and journalist; fiery,
tragic public figure of the 1930s.

Born in Rosario, Santa Fe; educated in law in Buenos
Aires; de la Torre became involved in politics, as a young
idealist, and joined the Unión Cívica Radical; he worked with
Aristóbulo del Valle and supported Leandro Alem; took part
in and wrote detailed account of action in crisis of 1890 that
brought President Juárez Celman's resignation, was also involved in the radical revolution of 1893 in Santa Fe province;
became minister in Governor Candioti's administration there;
having had some journalistic experience in Buenos Aires, he
founded the political newspaper La República in Rosario in
1895, with Florencio Sánchez (later to become famous

dramatist) as editor; following deaths of Alem and del Valle,
Hipólito Yrigoyen took over leadership of the Radical Party;
refusing to accept this, de la Torre resigned immediately
and, after having fought a duel with Yrigoyen, retired to devote himself to his rural interests in Santa Fe; he spent
some time, 1900-1902, traveling in the United States to inspect scientific and technological advances being made there
in farming and ranching that might be useful to him in Santa
Fe; returning home, his success in these fields brought him
the presidency of the Rosario Rural Society in 1907.

Reentering politics, he was elected Congressman in
1912 and in 1914 he founded the Progressive Democratic
Party of which he remained leader; defeated by Yrigoyen for
presidency of the republic in 1915; again elected to Congress
in 1922; after the 1930 revolt led by José Félix Uriburu had
ousted Yrigoyen from his second term in office, Uriburu invited de la Torre to become minister in his cabinet but,
despite their close friendship, the latter refused; again in
1931 de la Torre was an unsuccessful candidate for the presidency, being defeated by Agustín P. Justo; elected to the
senate, he became powerful opposition leader against Justo's
government; he had always been a fighter for honesty in government and, as part of his basic commitment to democracy,
had always defended the political, economic, and social
rights of the average Argentine citizen against entrenched
privileges of the oligarchy; also part of his democratic beliefs was his conviction, reaffirmed by observations in the
United States, that municipal governments needed reform in
order to play their essential role in political defense of the
individual--a kind of extension of earlier provincial federalism; it was this strong sense of identity with the small rancher and farmer, combined with his own more extensive rural
experience, that brought him to the tragic climax of his career; after having vigorously, but unsuccessfully opposed the
Roca-Runciman agreement as a sellout of Argentine interests,
de la Torre in 1935 began a new, but related, attack on the
fraudulent practices of the meat-packing monopoly; as the
debate in the senate became heated, his Santa Fe colleague
Enso Bordabehere was assassinated in a scandal that rocked
the nation; Lisandro de la Torre resigned from the senate;
four years later, in protest against increasing corruption in
Argentine political and economic morality, and especially depressed because his own carefully cherished honesty in public
life was being questioned, he committed suicide in Buenos
Aires.   The speeches, political essays, and other writings
of Lisandro de la Torre were gathered together and published
in Obras completas (3 v., Buenos Aires, 1952).

See Raúl Larra, Lisandro de la Torre (BA, 1942);
Samuel Yasky, Lisandro de la Torre de cerca ... (BA, 1969).

TORRE REVELLO, JOSE (1893-1964).   Historian, professor, paint-
    er, engraver.
        Born in Buenos Aires; studied art in the Estímulo

association and in the National Academy of Bellas Artes;
commissioned in 1918, by the history department of the
Faculty of Philosophy and Letters, to go to Spain for research in its archives and libraries; took special courses in
the history of art at the university in Sevilla and attended
third congress of American geography and history, held in
that city in 1930; returning to Buenos Aires in 1935, Torre
Revello taught Argentine and American history at the Justo
José de Urquiza national academy and the history of art in
the Manuel Belgrano national school of plastic arts; directed
the historical research projects of the institute of research
in the Faculty of Philosophy and Letters in Buenos Aires and
also lectured there on American history; a member of various Argentine and international historical societies, Torre
Revello represented Argentina at international academic congresses on several occasions; he was also an engraver and
an artist of note, painting in both watercolors and oils.

Among his many publications, those of most interest
to historians include: El libro, la imprenta, y el periodismo
durante la dominación española (Buenos Aires, 1940, reprinted New York, 1973); the picturesque Crónicas del Buenos
Aires colonial (Buenos Aires, 1943); El marqués de Sobre
Monte, edition published by the Faculty of Philosophy and
Letters of the University of Buenos Aires (Buenos Aires,
1946); Colección de documentos relativos al libertador don
José de San Martín (Buenos Aires, 1954); and a book dealing
with secret Anglo-Spanish diplomacy about the Malvinas or
Falkland Islands entitled La promesa secreta y el convenio
anglo-español sobre las Malvinas, de 1771 (Buenos Aires,
1952).

TORRE TAGLE, MARQUES DE (1779-1825). Patriot leader in
Peru; important collaborator with San Martín in emancipation
war against Spain.

Born in Lima of aristocratic lineage; served as colonel in royal army in 1810, alcalde of city of Lima, 1813;
was appointed delegate to the Spanish Cortes of 1813; there
he vigorously defended the cause of American independence;
returning to Peru he became a brigadier general in Spanish
army (1820), in charge of inspecting the army in Peru; fulfilled his military function while still insisting that Spanish
America should some day be free; when José de San Martín
arrived in Peru with his liberating army in that same year,
Torre Tagle was serving as intendant-governor of Trujillo;
joined San Martín and led that intendancy in rebellion against
Spaniards; was a founding member of the Order of the Sun;
became president of Peru in 1823 but resigned because of the
Callao uprising in 1824; turned government over to Simón
Bolívar; the rest was tragedy: brought under suspicion, he
was forbidden to leave the country, accused of conspiring to
turn Southern Peru back to the royalists; he and his family
were imprisoned in Callao fortress; died there, ridden with
scurvy.

TORRES, MANUEL DE (1750-1819).   Priest; educator; pioneer in
Argentine paleontology.
Born in Luján, Manuel de Torres entered the Dominican order in 1765, was ordained as priest and from 1771 until his death made his home in the Dominican monastery in
Buenos Aires; rose in responsibility and rank to provincial
prior in 1795; always interested in teaching and learning, he
founded the Colegio de Santo Tomás de Aquino in Buenos
Aires (1797); ten years before that he was responsible for the
digging up, near his birthplace in Luján, of fossil remains of
a megathere (or megatherium), a very large, sloth-like, plant-
eating animal, now extinct, from the Pleistocene period; this
discovery aroused the interest of viceroy Marqués de Loreto
and, after having the bones carefully drawn for the record
in Buenos Aires, packed them in seven huge boxes and sent
them to Spain for study by the royal scientists; Manuel de
Torres thus began the continuing stream of Argentine (including F. J. Muñiz and F. Ameghino) and foreign scholars who
have carried out excavations to study the extraordinarily rich
fossil remains found in Buenos Aires province.

TORRES DE VERA Y ARAGON, JUAN.   Last adelantado of Río de
la Plata, 1578-1587.   While serving as aide of royal audiencia
of Charcas he inherited this title by marrying Juana, the
daughter of adelantado Juan Ortiz de Zárate and an Inca princess Leonor Yupanqui; because of various lawsuits as well
as Viceroy Toledo's annoyance with him for having married
the heiress to whom Toledo had hoped to marry one of his
own favorite courtiers, the adelantado was prevented for several years from going personally to his new domain to take
over; meanwhile he appointed Juan de Garay (q.v.) to go at
once to Asunción to rule in his name; during this period
Buenos Aires was formally reestablished; Indian wars were
fought, and new settlements were made, many of them in
today's Argentina; in late 1587 the adelantado finally reached
Asunción and April 5 of the following year he formally established the town of San Juan de Vera de las Siete Corrientes (today, Corrientes) on the east bank of the Paraná; shortly after this, he returned to Charcas and then to Spain; returning in 1591 to Chuquisaca, his home in Charcas, he discovered that he was no longer recognized as adelantado; actually his title had been acquired and held under unusual conditions and never confirmed either by the royal or the viceregal government; now the cabildo of Asunción had deposed
him under an action taken against him three years earlier
by the royal audiencia because of his flagrant use of his own
relatives in political positions in new cities founded, etc.;
left Río de la Plata area shortly thereafter, having appointed
his nephew Alonso de Vera as lieutenant governor (see Alonso
de Vera).

TOUNENS, AURELIO ANTONIO DE (1825-1878).   A "king" in Argentina and Chile.   Tounens was a late nineteenth-century

French adventurer who came to Chile in 1858 hoping to emu-
late there the conquests of Cortés and Pizarro more than
three centuries earlier; after two years of familiarizing himself with the Araucanian people, land, and customs, he won
the friendship of the Indian chief Quilapán in the province of
Valdivia and, with his help, as well as that of an old
prophecy that a white leader would liberate the Araucanians,
declared the independence of the kingdom of Araucania, with
himself as king; established a hereditary constitutional monarchy, widened the boundaries to include all of Patagonia,
drew up a constitution modeled on that of France, assuring
democratic guarantees and civil and political rights; a green,
blue, and white flag was designed, as well as a national
seal; King Aurelio Antonio I ruled for about a year with
Quilapán's support before the Chilean government of Manuel
Montt arrested him; French intercession, along with the general belief that he was insane, brought him deportation to
France.

 While in France Tounens published his memoirs (1863)
and aroused French interest in establishing a New France in
South America; apparently--or, it is believed that--the government of Napoleon III backed him as he reappeared on the
Patagonian coast in 1869, headed for Chile and the loyal
Quilapán; the Chilean government put a price on his head
and sent armed forces against him; Tounens fled and succeeded in reaching Buenos Aires, where the newspapers announced his arrival, and then went on to Montevideo and finally to France.

 A third attempt was organized, with new backing by a
London banker, but this was quietly suppressed by Chilean
diplomatic pressures on the French and British governments;
after the death of Tounens his cousin attempted to assume
the crown but the death of Quilapán (1875), the ruthless suppression of the Araucanians by Chilean forces as well as the
Argentine conquest of the desert made this a lost cause.

 France's real role in Tounens' ventures remains un-
clear; Chile preferred not to make an international incident
of it and Argentina was preoccupied during this period with
internal disputes and later with the war against Paraguay.

 See Armando Braun Menéndez, Pequeña historia pata-
gónica (Buenos Aires, 1936); Julio Marc, Un rey en la Argentina (Rosario, 1943).

TOURISM. Tourism, in the sense of individual or family travel
 has always existed in Argentina and in modern times it has
 come to be an important industry developing the economy of
 nearly every part of the republic in one way or another; Argentina's tourist attractions are widely diversified, with something of interest for almost everyone, and equally scattered
 geographically; beach resorts extend along the entire length
 of the nation's Atlantic coastline, and inland lake areas in
 Córdoba and the south offer alternative water sports and
 fishing; riverboats make excursions up the Paraná and

Uruguay rivers and to the delta islands; health resorts are
found throughout the country, especially in the sierras of
Córdoba and in higher, dry cordilleras; both national and international tourists are attracted to the magnificent scenery
at Iguazú Falls at border between Misiones and Brazil and to
the Andean southern lake country, especially to charming city
of San Carlos de Bariloche in Río Negro; historically, the
first collective tourist trade consisted of groups on pilgrimage to special religious shrines; such pilgrimages continue
but they have been joined by other, more secular, groups
going to sites of national historical interest or to places
holding annual fiestas or festivals with origins that derive
variously from religious feast, local historical events, harvest
festivals (such as the Wheat Festival of Córdoba, March 15-16
in Leones); the tourist trade is facilitated and encouraged by
splendid transportation systems, excellent accommodations,
resort facilities and sports, and the publicizing of interesting
events as in calendar of fiestas of interest to tourists.   (See
Abad de Santillán VIII:233 for calendario turístico.)
        In the decade 1962-1972, the number of foreign tour-
ists entering Argentina increased greatly, with more than
half a million entering annually and contributing almost $100
million U.S. to the national economy, approaching the estimated total expenditures of Argentine tourists abroad.

TRADE AND COMMERCE.   Shortly after the refounding of Buenos
        Aires in 1580 Hendrik Ottsen (q. v.) came from the Nether-
        lands to see about establishing trade with this new colony;
        although he was not successful he illustrates the recognition
        of Buenos Aires' natural advantages for trade; in the early
        years of the conquest, the Spanish government permitted some
        foreign trade--from Brazil and from Europe--but the mercan-
        tilistic policy of Spain, requiring it to control all trade, with
        special care given to that of gold and silver, caused the port
        in Buenos Aires to be legally closed for approximately 200
        years to foreign trade; contraband (q. v.) became a way of
        life in the Río de la Plata; nevertheless most trade from Ar-
        gentina was carried on the royal highway by oxcart across
        the pampas and Andean passes to the mines of Upper Peru
        (Bolivia) and to Lima where it was exchanged for goods
        brought from Europe by the monopoly merchants; cities along
        the highway, such as Córdoba, Tucumán, and Salta, profited
        greatly from this pattern, serving as stops, provision points,
        etc. for the wagon trains; this protective economic barrier
        also saved the coastal markets for the area's own agricul-
        tural products, milling, woolen, and cotton textiles, wood
        and leather crafts, sugar and salt refining, wines, olive oil,
        wagon-building; trade items varied, with black slaves, sugar,
        cotton, rice, spices, wax, brandy, and honey coming in from
        Brazil and manufactured items being exchanged for raw
        products; in the eighteenth century, the demand for hides
        and tallow (also soap made from animal fats) became so
        great that the government took steps to preserve the wild

herds; trade in blacks became increasingly brisk as Indian
labor disappeared; and the silver of Upper Peru was drained
off in increasingly large amounts in contraband trade; after
establishment of the viceroyalty, Buenos Aires trade was
made freer and the Consulado was established to control it;
new trade items appeared, such as the droves of mules that
annually moved from Santa Fe area to Peru.

     With independence, a policy of laissez-faire (q.v.) or
free trade was adopted; in their treaty of 1825 the British
got the right of trade for which they had invaded Buenos
Aires in 1806-1807 and, although other European nations later
made similar treaties, England dominated Argentine trade for
more than a century largely because it needed its hides and
tallow, jerked beef, and later, wool, cereals, and frozen
meats to support its industrial economy and could send in
return the coal, textiles, and manufactured goods that Argentina needed; trade was also carried on with the U.S. but protective tariffs and competition in meat and grain kept that
trade from rivaling Argentina's trade with Great Britain and
Europe; this trade brought a shift to the coast and real hardship to interior provinces unable to compete for coastal markets against cheaper, often better, European products, largely textiles, manufactures, wines, etc.

     This trade pattern of raw Argentine products--exchanged
for needed manufacturers and mineral products--brought so
much prosperity to Argentina that few--except economic na-
tionalists--wanted to change it; in the 1930s, however, the
increasing demand for Argentine industrialization and diversification of the economy coincided with the world economic depression that forced England to give trade priority to its dominions competing with Argentina for its markets; for a time
the Roca-Runciman agreement (q.v.) preserved part of the
British market for Argentina but in the 1940s World War II
disrupted flow of trade and Argentina was forced to intensify
its efforts to gain economic independence as well as to find
new trade partners; by the 1970s Japan, the LAFTA (Latin
American Free Trade Association), West Germany, and some
of the Communist countries were becoming more important;
main Argentine exports continue to be livestock products and
cereals making up about half the total; its main trade partners were the nations of the European Economic Community
(EEC), more than 60%, followed by U.S., West Germany,
and Great Britain; greatest change of all is the nation's shift
from all-important foreign trade to production for the internal market trade (see entries on various trade items and
important trading partners).

"TRAGIC WEEK," THE (La Semana Trágica). Second week in
     January, 1919. Name applied to week of violence, death,
     and destruction in Buenos Aires (and to a smaller extent, in
     Rosario) that culminated approximately two years of labor un-
     rest during first administration of Hipólito Yrigoyen; involved
     were the changing economic and social conditions and the

demands of industrial and other workers, increasingly led by
anarchist and (after 1917) Bolshevik revolutionary leaders,
for relief from the rapidly increasing cost of living and for
their legitimate share in the burgeoning Argentine economy.
    A series of more than eighty strikes had preceded
this; one of most important labor disputes had resulted from
attempts of workers in Armour and Swift meat-packing plants
to organize in FORA (q. v.); pressure from the establishment
(estancieros, Rural Society, and packing houses), supported
by British and U. S. diplomats, and accusations that foreign agitators were behind the workers caused Yrigoyen to intervene
with the navy to prevent the proposed workers' action.   The
specific outbreak of labor dissatisfaction that peaked in
January 1919 was sparked by a strike called by the metal-
workers in the Vasena mills; when this was met by police
action, FORA called a general strike and organized a mass
demonstration of 150,000 workers to assemble in the Congressional square; the president called out the armed forces
to disperse the crowd; violence resulted and for several days
central Buenos Aires was paralyzed, during which deaths, injuries, burnings and acts of violence and looting were common, before order could be restored; violence had also spread
to Rosario, by then Argentina's second city in size and commercial importance; a few labor reforms were made but un-
satisfied labor demands remained to play important role in
revolutionary movements of 1940s led by Juan Domingo Perón.

TREATY OF MAY 29, 1851.   Treaty of alliance signed in Montevideo under leadership of Justo José de Urquiza by which
Entre Ríos, Corrientes, Brazil, and Uruguay bound themselves to fight Rosas; led to downfall of Rosas' government
following battle of Caseros February 3, 1852.

TREATY OF MONTEVIDEO (1960).   Created LAFTA, the Latin
American Free Trade Association (q. v.), establishing basis
for an active trade between southern countries.

"TREINTA Y TRES ORIENTALES" (or the Famous 33).   An expedition of 33 Uruguayans, led by Juan Antonio Lavelleja (q. v.)
and supported by the Argentine government, that left Buenos
Aires April 11, 1825, to liberate the Banda Oriental (as
Uruguay was then called) from Brazilians who had occupied
it; on April 20, they crossed the Uruguay River and started
northward, their numbers increasing steadily with new volunteers; Uruguayan leader Fructuoso Rivera, who had been
serving under the Brazilians, joined the group with his cavalry division; defeated imperialist forces at Rincón de las Ga-
llinas, September 24, 1825; Lavalleja won victory at Sarandí,
October 12, 1825, and advanced toward Montevideo; established camp at Florida where congress met and annulled previous annexation to Brazil; Argentina then incorporated the
Banda Oriental into the Provincias Unidas del Río de la
Plata; this action by Argentine congress brought on war with
Brazilian empire that resulted in establishment of Uruguay

as an independent nation.

TREJO Y SANABRIA, FERNANDO DE (1554-1614). Franciscan
    priest; Bishop of Tucumán; creole colonial public figure.
        Probably born along Brazilian coast in San Francisco
    founded by his father Captain Hernando de Trejo in 1553; half-
    brother to Governor Hernandarias through his mother María
    de Sanabria, daughter of the adelantado and doña Mencía Cal-
    derón de Sanabria (q. v.); Fernando was sent to Lima to be
    educated (1568) and there entered Franciscan order; ordained
    as priest in 1576; in 1588 he became superior administrator
    of Franciscan province of Peru--first Creole to hold such a
    position; four years later, the king appointed him bishop of
    Tucumán and, after having been invested with this office in
    Quito, the new bishop took possession of his diocese, then
    seated in Santiago del Estero, in 1595; during the next near-
    ly twenty years, until his death in 1614, Bishop Trejo made
    a lasting name for himself in the sparsely settled and remote
    area, represented by Argentina at that time; his first con-
    cerns were for matters of the church; in 1599 he convoked
    the first general ecclesiastical assembly, calling for church
    and civil delegates from each town within his jurisdiction; at
    this synod and the two later ones held in 1606 and 1607, the
    ecclesiastical activities of Tucumán (as that whole area was
    known) were unified, reformed, and reorganized; Bishop Tre-
    jo was a staunch defender of the Indians, seeking to protect
    them from exploitation and from illegal use of their personal
    services; parish churches were established in the settlements
    and reducciones in rural areas to evangelize the Indians and
    tend to their spiritual needs; religious societies (cofradías)
    were formed for Indians, blacks, and mulattoes; the bishop
    promoted public instruction, is considered to have been
    founder of the university of Córdoba, through financial aid
    that he gave, and supported Leonor de Tejeda de Fonseca
    (q. v.) in her successful efforts to establish education for
    girls, including religious training for nuns, by founding of
    first convent, Santa Catalina de Siena, in Córdoba, in 1613.
        Bishop Trejo's concern for his community extended al-
    so to economic matters, as he was engaged in trade through
    Buenos Aires to exchange the products of Tucumán for those
    needed for survival by the struggling young settlements; he
    fought vigorously to keep Buenos Aires open for trade, but
    except for a brief victory--getting it reopened for a time in
    early seventeenth century--he could not change royal policy
    that required strict control of all trade, including use of
    Peru as only point of entry to Argentina.

TRELLES, MANUEL RICARDO (1821-1893). Research scholar;
    historian; archivist and writer.
        Born and educated in Buenos Aires; with his brother
    Rafael he contributed a work on American words to the Dic-
    cionario enciclopédico de la lengua española (1853); followed
    this with intensive research into and writing about Argentine

history; most of this was done while he held important public
positions; began his work in the Registry of Statistics for the
province, about 1857; during this time he discovered several
unedited documents about early Argentine trade; served as director of the National Archives, 1858-1875; edited and contributed to the Revista del Archivo General de Buenos Aires
(1869-1872), publishing also historical documents, including
viceregal memoirs; from 1879 to 1884 he was director of the
national library, personally financing part of costs of publishing its review; in the 1860s he began his important studies on
historical background of Argentina's boundary disputes with
Bolivia, Paraguay, and Chile; published many biographical
studies of varying length, including those about Fernández de
Agüero, Centenera, Francisco Trelles, Tomás Falkner, etc.;
he was one of first to react, on basis of factual historic
data, against the current anti-Spanish "Black Legend"; in
1888 was elected a member of the Academy of History in
Madrid, and in that same year founded Revista Patriótica del
Pasado Argentino; died in Buenos Aires.
    Among his most important published works are:
Apuntes para la historia del puerto de Buenos Aires; Indice
del archivo del gobierno de Buenos Aires, correspondiente a
1810; Cuestión de límites entre la República Argentina y el
gobierno de Chile; Cuestión de límites entre la República Argentina y el Paraguay; Cuestión de límites entre la Argentina
y Bolivia; Diego García primer descubridor del Río de la
Plata.
    See Rodolfo Trostiné, Manuel Ricardo Trelles, with
prologue by Guillermo Furlong (Buenos Aires, 1947).

TRIBUNA, LA.   Newspaper published in Buenos Aires from 1853
    to 1884.   La Tribuna was first published by Héctor F. and
    Mariano Varela, sons of Florencio Varela, printed at the
    government press and then on its own press, put together
    from the press units that had belonged to Urquiza; news, lit-
    erary essays, and articles of historical interest--often docu-
    mentary accounts--were emphasized in its pages; in 1872 an
    evening edition was started to compete with El Nacional; at
    the time its final issue appeared, June 30, 1884, Rodolfo
    Solveyra was its publisher and Mariano Varela editor-in-chief.

TRIPLE ALLIANCE, TREATY OF.   Treaty signed May 1, 1865, in
    Buenos Aires, by plenipotentiaries of Argentina, Brazil, and
    Uruguay; formed offensive alliance to make war against Para-
    guay; clearly stated that war was against the president, Gene-
    ral Francisco Solano López, and his government, not the
    people of Paraguay who were invited to join the allied forces;
    war to be waged until unconditional surrender of the Para-
    guayan leader, with no separate peace made; territorial in-
    tegrity of Paraguay guaranteed but disputed boundary settle-
    ments with Brazil and Argentina would be made after war;
    General Mitre to command allied land forces; Brazil to fur-
    nish naval support and command (see Paraguayan War).

TRIUMVIRATES, FIRST AND SECOND (1811-1814). Three-man
form of government in Buenos Aires that replaced patriot
junta and was succeeded by directorate.
    The First Triumvirate was created in September 1811;
it grew out of revolt of April 5-6, in which porteños and
more radical patriot group had been purged by Cornelio Saavedra's conservatives and provincial representatives of the
Great Junta; the Second Junta began with poor patriot support
and was further weakened in public confidence by the disastrous defeat of Army of North at Huaqui, June 20, 1811, and
by junta's attempt to contact Elio (newly appointed Spanish
viceroy in Montevideo) about course of action to be taken regarding Portuguese invasion of that area; many patriots of
Buenos Aires favored more revolutionary changes and resented domination by provincials, whom many considered
more backward than those who lived in the capital, cosmopolitan Buenos Aires; when Cornelio Saavedra, president of junta, left in August 1811 to supervise reorganization of the
patriot army, his opponents, largely led by Cabildo of Buenos
Aires, brought about creation of First Triumvirate as governing executive; its members were Feliciano Chiclana, Manuel
de Sarratea and Juan José Paso with José Julián Pérez, Bernardino Rivadavia (the guiding spirit of this group) and Vicente López as secretaries; the old Great Junta transformed
itself into a legislative body or junta of observation; it was
understood by latter that the triumvirate derived its authority
from the junta which in turn, retained a veto power over it;
the provincial statutes drawn up by Deán Gregorio Funes expressed this relationship but his statute was replaced by a
new one, drawn up by Rivadavia and put into effect November
7, 1811, made triumvirate sole authority until constituent
congress could be called to plan effective government for developing new nation; this action by triumvirate was largely
criticized as anti-liberal, undemocratic, and a manifestation
of absolutism and Buenos Aires' determination to control
provinces; with the junta dissolved as useless, its members
dispersed to their various provinces where they tended to
stimulate the rivalries and hostilities, already beginning to
form between the provinces and Buenos Aires, that were to
result in long period of civil wars.
    During year of First Triumvirate (September 1811-
early October 1812), some progress was made but government failed to win public confidence; internal disputes over
elections of members of triumvirates (renewed every six
months) and formation of factions, added to threat of invasion from Brazil and defeat again in Upper Peru frightened
people; when Belgrano disobeyed orders of government to
withdraw and won victory at Tucumán, triumvirate lost even
more prestige; arrival of San Martín, Alvear, Zapiola and
others from Europe in March 1812, brought new leadership
to patriot movement; on October 8, 1912, San Martín and
Alvear led their troops to the main plaza in a revolution c.-
rected by the Patriotic Society and Lautaro Lodge; they

demanded that a new government be formed for the purpose
of getting the revolution back on the track on which Mariano
Moreno had set it and that a new, representative constituent
assembly be called at once; this Second Triumvirate consisted
of Juan José Paso, Nicolás Rodríguez Peña, and Antonio Alvarez de Jonte; the situation, both in Argentina and Europe,
seemed propitious; with Napoleon in control of Europe, it
seemed unlikely that the Bourbons could regain the Spanish
throne and threatened autonomy gained by the Spanish American colonies; general military situation was good and made
even better by San Martín's victory at San Lorenzo February
3, 1813, and that of Belgrano over royalists in Salta February 20; a constituent assembly elected by popular vote was
convoked on January 1, 1813, and pushed through a splendid
body of liberal legislation although no constitution was drawn
up (see Assembly of the Year XIII); after a few months the
Second Triumvirate was in trouble; it had tried to do too
much too fast and as yet, no clear sense of direction had
developed; increasing opposition was met with suppression;
the military situation in Uruguay, with Artigas becoming a
powerful anti-Buenos Aires leader in Uruguay and littoral
provinces, and in Bolivia, with Belgrano's defeats at Vilcapugio and Ayohuma, became very bad; Ferdinand VII's return
to the throne brought clear threat of new Spanish invasion;
the patriots and provinces were divided among themselves; a
popular demand, encouraged by Carlos María de Alvear (q. v.)
who had gained control of the Lautaro Lodge, arose for a
unified, one-man executive to handle all these crises; in January 1814, the second triumvirate was replaced by a directorate form of government, with Gervasio de Posadas, Alvear's
uncle, as first director.

TSCHIFFELY, AIME FELIX (1896-1954). Swiss traveler, writer,
and educator. While living in London in his youth, Tschiffely became acquainted with Robert Bontine Cunninghame Graham (q. v.) and caught his infectious enthusiasm for the Argentine pampas; moved to Argentina, taught in a British
academy, and immersed himself in Argentine life and customs; conceiving the romantic idea of uniting Buenos Aires
with New York by horseback, he acquired two creole horses,
named them Mancha and Gato; on April 23, 1925, he departed
from the Rural Society's center in Buenos Aires, crossed the
pampas and then the Andes, and, taking his time, rode northward through the Pacific countries and on to New York, arriving there more than three years later, August 28, 1928,
with same two horses; after having covered approximately
10,000 miles; related his adventure in book called Southern
Cross to Pole Star (London, 1933, 1947; New York, with extended title, 1933); parts had already appeared in National
Geographic Magazine; he also wrote several other works
about countries through which he had passed, including
Coricancha about conquest of Peru (London, 1943).
    Tschiffely made another trip to Argentina, to see his

famous horses that had been returned there; on this visit he
explored Patagonia and Tierra del Fuego; in 1954 he died in
London but his remains were brought back to be buried in La
Recoleta cemetery in Buenos Aires, Argentina, the land that
he loved so much.

Among his writings of most interest to Argentine his-
tory may be included his fine biography of his friend, Don
Roberto, Being the Account of the Life and Works of R. B.
Cunninghame Graham, 1852-1936, published in both London
and Toronto in 1937, the year following Graham's death; The
Tale of Two Horses, with preface by R. B. Cunninghame
Graham (London and Toronto, 1934), Spanish translation by
Rafael Castellá Méndez entitled Mancha y Gato, los dos ca-
ballos criollos en su viaje por las tres Américas (Buenos
Aires, 1944); This Way Southward; a Journey through Pata-
gonia and Tierra del Fuego (New York, 1940; new edition
London, 1945), Spanish translations bore title Rumbo al
sur.

TUCUMAN. This name--derived from that of the Indian chief and
his town found there in 1545 by Diego de Rojas in his "Gran
Entrada"--may refer to any one of three political and geographic entities in history of northwestern Argentina: the
old colonial region and administrative unit of the Governa-
ción del Tucumán, the modern province by that name, or the
latter's capital, officially known as San Miguel de Tucumán;
the present province of Tucumán is only a small part of the
old colonial governing unit (see Tucumán, Gobernación del;
Tucumán, San Miguel de; and Tucumán Province).

TUCUMAN (Province). This present-day central Argentine province has retained the name of the larger Gobernación del
Tucumán (q. v.) of which it was a part; took modern form
as a province during period of directorate, 1814-1820.
Location. Lies between 26°6' and 28° S. latitude and
64°30' and 66°11' W. longitude; bounded by Salta in the
north, Santiago del Estero in the east, Santiago del Estero
and Catamarca in the south, and Catamarca in the west.
Area: 8700 square miles; smallest province in the republic.
Population (1970): 765,962, with a density of 88 persons per
square mile, highest in nation. Cities: San Miguel de Tucumán, capital (q. v.); other important towns are Tafí Viejo,
Lules, Montoneros, Famaillá, Concepción, Aguilares, Juan
Bautista Alberdi, Bellavista, Lamadrid, and La Cocha.
Climate and geography. Province consists of two regions: west is mountainous, including the Aconquija system
of two sierra ranges; the highest mountain, Nevado, rises
5000 meters high (16,404 ft.); the east is a well-irrigated
plain; the most important river is the Salí that, with its
tributaries--including the Tala, Chorromoro, Tapia, Lules,
Colorado, Valderramas, Seco, Medina, and Graneros--pro-
vides the waters that make possible Tucumán's rich agricultural economy; dams have been constructed to control the

water; important among them is that of El Brete on boundary
between Salta and Tucumán that furnishes irrigating waters
for both provinces; other dams are being built by federal
government to increase irrigation possibilities as well as to
supply hydroelectric energy.   The climate of Tucumán is hot
and humid with abundant rainfall, especially in the mountains;
it nourishes lush subtropical vegetation and heavy forests.

Economy.   Sugar cane industry predominates in Tucumán and produces 70% of the sugar used in the republic; citrus fruit, pears, and apples are also grown; cattle for local
use are raised.

History.   Tucumán was first visited (1535) by Diego de
Almagro, coming from Peru through Humahuaca on his way
to take over Chile; in 1543 Diego de Rojas made what was
known as La Gran Entrada (q. v.), the expedition that opened
up the territory, exploring it, meeting and fighting with the
Indians there; about 80 members of the expedition of 200 returned to report about the land and people; conquistadors
moved in quickly to take over the new land; the first two decades of Tucumán history were tumultuous, not only because
of Indian hostilities but also because of conflicting claims of
jurisdiction between Chile and Peru; attempts at settlement
were made briefly at Barco, Londres, Cañete (qq. v.), and
other sites, but the first permanent town was established, finally, at Santiago del Estero (1553) by Francisco de Aguirre;
Tucumán was assigned politically to Peru in 1563 and governed from Santiago del Estero under jurisdiction of audiencia
of Charcas; in 1565, San Miguel del Tucumán (q. v.) was
founded and the first bishop was appointed in 1570; although
life in Tucumán remained primitive and endangered throughout the sixteenth and seventeenth centuries, a foothold had
been made, and institutions and patterns for political, social,
economic development had been established; first Argentine
clash between royal and ecclesiastical authority took place in
Tucumán in sixteenth century (see Hernando de Lerma); Franciscans and Jesuits established missionary work among the
semi-civilized and fierce Indians throughout the area and
gradually Tucumán took shape; in 1600 there were seven
towns--Santiago del Estero, Madrid de las Juntas, Talavera
or Esteco, Jujuy, La Rioja, San Miguel de Tucumán, and
Córdoba--each with surrounding area; altogether they contained about 700 Spanish men, of whom about half had Indians assigned to them; total white population, with women and
children, about 2,000; these settlements, proudly called
"cities" and with all the infrastructure that this implied,
were actually poor collections of primitive dwellings, with
public buildings and churches little more pretentious, surrounded by cultivated lands and villages of Indians in encom-
ienda--the number of these, 24,000, a tribute to the achievement of the conquistadors of this area of hostile, warlike
tribes; although Indian wars continued throughout the colonial
period until the stabilization of the northern border in the

1770s, life in Tucumán took on a feudal and industrial aspect,
although cattle herding was always important; while their
creole masters stood ready to defend their lands and homes,
Indians raised corn and wheat, throughout the region, and
also cotton around San Miguel de Tucumán; they provided native natural dyes to be used for the cotton and woolen textile
industries and also the labor for other industries, both large
and small, of the northwest; hardwood forests provided abundant lumber for buildings, furniture, and especially for the
Tucumán carretas (large wagons or ox-carts) that carried
practically all the trade between cities in the colonial period;
cattle and mules were driven to Chile and Peru for sale
along with footgear, hosiery, bedcovers, candlewicks, hats,
etc., to be exchanged for imported, manufactured goods from
overseas for creole homes, clothes, arms, tools, and for
ornament; rapid decline in number of Indian laborers available in seventeenth century caused depression of economy
until blacks (q.v.) were imported to take their places; in the
eighteenth century, Tucumán's importance made it desirable
for the governors to establish themselves there instead of in
Santiago del Estero; at the time of the creation of the viceroyalty of the United Provinces of the Río de la Plata in
1776, Tucumán had a total population of about 20,000 with
Córdoba the largest and most important city and the intellectual center of all Argentina.

     With the coming of the viceroyalty, establishment of
its capital in Buenos Aires, and the subsequent opening of
that port to trade, a period of change began for Tucumán
during which its total life, politically, economically, and, to
a lesser extent, culturally, was reoriented from Bolivia and
Peru to Buenos Aires; in 1783, the old political unit of Tucumán was divided into the two intendancies of Salta del Tucumán and Córdoba del Tucumán, and governed by intendants in
these two cities, subject to viceroy; these intendancies were
subdivided into districts (usually a city and its rural territory), each governed by a subdelegado, or district governor;
from that time on, the term Tucumán frequently refers only
to the city of that name, governed as a district under Salta's
intendant and the nucleus of the modern province of Tucumán;
economically the establishment of the viceroyalty proved disastrous to Tucumán; its centuries-old position astride
the royal highway to the Perus, along which all legal trade
and official couriers had to pass from Argentina to Charcas
and Lima, lost its importance and its industries could not
compete against the cheaper, and often better, textiles and
other goods coming into the interior from abroad through
Buenos Aires; in spite of these problems, Tucumán (even before it became a separate province in 1814) played an important role in Argentine history during first two decades of
nineteenth century; in July, 1806, when it heard about the
British invasion of Buenos Aires, Tucumán organized a group
of volunteers to fight against the invaders (one of the groups
was led by Salvador Alberdi, the father of Juan Bautista);

Tucumán also received some of the captured British prisoners; and in 1807 it contributed about 10,000 gold pesos to defend Buenos Aires against the new British attack.

The news of the May Revolution reached Tucumán at the end of May and on June 11, 1810, Tucumán recognized the Buenos Aires junta government, as representative of Ferdinand VII, "beloved King and Lord"; in 1812 the First Triumvirate appointed Clemente Zavaleta lieutenant governor and at same time created the Court of Appeals; also, in that same year Manuel Belgrano won his decisive victory over the royalists at Tucumán, October 24, 1812 (see Tucumán, Battle of); Belgrano was offered appointment as captain-general of the city, but refused; the next governor was Antonio Luis Beruti who installed Tucumán's first public lighting system (by candles); the province sent Diego Zavaleta and Manuel Molina as its representatives to the general assembly of 1813; about this time José de San Martín (q.v.) arrived to replace Belgrano in command of Army of North that had suffered new defeats at Vilcapugio and Ayohuma, in Upper Peru; he established his famous military training school in the citadel of Tucumán; in 1814 the intendancy of Salta del Tucumán was divided into the separate provinces of Salta, Tucumán, Santiago del Estero, and Catamarca; Tucumán's first governor was Bernabé Aráoz; this separation led to new problems, many preferring the old, closer pattern, and others arguing, even fighting, about border communities such as Santa María, claimed by both Tucumán and Salta (today in Catamarca); Aráoz gave province a progressive administration, establishing schools, a market, public lighting and drinking water; during this period the Congress of Tucumán (q.v.), first important national congress to meet outside of Buenos Aires, opened its important sessions; Tucumán's own representatives included Pedro Miguel Aráoz, José Ignacio Thames, and José Serapión de Arteaga; on July 9, 1816, Congress declared Argentine independence (see Declaration of Independence; also Tucumán, San Miguel de, for more data about historic Casa de Independencia); national government appointed Feliciano de la Mota Botelho as governor and Belgrano installed him in power.

Mota Botelho's support of the centralist national constitution of 1819 set off a revolution that replaced him with Bernabé Aráoz as governor; so strong was the feeling of the local insurgents against Buenos Aires that their attempt to place General Manuel Belgrano, very ill at that time, in chains was prevented only by intervention of the general's personal physician, Dr. Joseph Redhead; Governor Aráoz took the lead in forming the Republic of Tucumán (q.v.), an expression of local federalist, autonomous spirit; Aráoz had hoped to include both Catamarca and Santiago del Estero in the Republic but latter refused; its governor, Ibarra, and Martín Güemes of Salta combined forces against Aráoz; latter was defeated, Catamarca withdrew from the republic and Aráoz resigned as governor (1821); during next few years

province was torn between those who, like Governor Javier
López, wanted to follow the revolutionary ideas of Rivadavia
in Buenos Aires--with sovereignty residing in the people, as
expressed in their representatives, any kind of government,
even centralist, could be accepted or rejected on its merits--
and others, like Aráoz, who favored as much liberty as possible and believed, on basis of Tucumán's long colonial experience, that this could best be achieved in a constitutional
federation established by democratic practices; the political
pattern was further disrupted by interference by leaders of
the neighboring provinces such as Quiroga from La Rioja,
Ibarra from Santiago del Estero; federalists gained power
and remained in until 1829; Javier López returned to office
that year and cooperated with José María Paz, joining his
league of the interior in 1831; the defeat of López and Lamadrid by Quiroga at La Ciudadela, November 4, 1831, marked
the end of unitarism in Tucumán; from 1832 to 1838, Alejandro Heredia (q. v.) governed; promoted irrigation, the sugar
industry, and maintained peace, except for his conflict with
Governor Pablo de la Torre of Salta; placed Tucumán in the
Liga del Litoral, aided Quiroga in his campaign to the desert;
reorganized municipal government, and presented a project
for a provincial constitution; after Quiroga established peace
between Heredia and de la Torre, the former was undisputed
caudillo of the north; resigned in 1837 but returned to lead
Argentine forces against Bolivian leader Andrés Santa Cruz;
Heredia was murdered November 12, 1838, on his way to his
estate; during next two years Tucumán swung toward hostility
against Rosas; in 1840 under leadership of its governor,
Marco Avellaneda, the Northern League (see Coalición del
Norte) was formed and declared war against him, joined Lavalle; following Unitarist defeats at Quebracho Herrado and
at Famaillá, Rosas' general Manuel Oribe occupied Tucumán
October 14, 1841; there he displayed the head of Marco M.
Avellaneda (q. v.) on a pike in the central plaza; Celedonio
Gutiérrez (q. v.) became governor and retained this position
until 1852; Tucumán was exhausted, tired of fighting, almost
without public spirit; Gutiérrez refused to join Urquiza against
Rosas but signed the Acuerdo de San Nicolás (q. v.) afterward;
ousted as governor, he made a brief comeback in 1853; then
left.

During the period 1853-1862, Tucumán experienced a
revival of its traditional public spirit and courage and entered
the new era with faith in its future; this was expressed in its
constitution of 1856 prepared under leadership of Salustiano
Zavalía; modern Tucumán began to take shape; streets were
paved in capital city in 1860s; first secondary school opened
in 1870; telegraph reached Tucumán in 1875, as well as kerosene lighting; in that same year the University of Tucumán
opened with a school of law and political science; in 1876
the railroad arrived, tying Tucumán with the coastal markets;
by 1886 running water was installed; banks, schools, social
welfare, and public health all advanced rapidly; the sugar

industry (see Sugar) became very important, breaking Brazil's
control of the eastern Argentine market; by 1910 sugar production had become the monopoly of the few families that
owned the 34 cane mills of Tucumán; this became a source
of political, economic, and social unrest; few European immigrants were attracted to the province--only 5% of the population in 1914; the seasonal aspects of sugar growing and the
need for transient or migrant workers made Tucumán a center of labor unrest, especially as little was done for the laborers; as the ownership was Argentine, the cry for relief
against "foreign exploitation" could not be raised; working
conditions differed little from those of slavery; Tucumán led
the nation in illiteracy, infant mortality, illegitimate births,
alcoholism, etc.; social legislation of the 1950s and changing
public attitudes have relieved this situation considerably;
other agricultural development, especially that of commercial
fruit raising has continued the traditional large estate pattern of land tenure; although small landholdings are still few
and small industries have little significance, Tucumán, in
1970s, has become one of the most modern and progressive
provinces in northern Argentina.

See historical writings of Manuel Lizondo Borda about
Tucumán from sixteenth through nineteenth centuries, 3 vol.,
Tucumán, 1949.

TUCUMAN (Republic, May 19, 1820-August 28, 1821). Political
entity formed in 1820 that was expected to include Tucumán,
Santiago del Estero, and Catamarca. Following the dissolution of the Buenos Aires national government in early 1820,
the provinces were free to make their own political arrangements; cabildo of Tucumán called for selection of three electors from that province to join with electors of Catamarca
and Santiago del Estero to write a constitution for proposed
new political entity; Santiago del Estero refused but Tucumán
and Catamarca produced a constitution, similar to the national one of 1819, for the new "Republic of Tucumán" with
Bernabé Aráoz as president; this was not designed to be an
independent nation but rather a self-governing province until
all the Argentine provinces could form a satisfactory national
federation; the use of the name "republic" was justified by
Tucumán on grounds of the formality and scope of the legal
organization; they considered it to be in fact, the first, if
not the only, province of the viceregal type; it had brought
two peoples, with separate cabildos and distinct areas, under
a single constitutional government; it therefore merited the
name "republic" to distinguish it from others formed by a
single group; it lasted until August 1821, when Aráoz was
removed as governor by Abraham González; Catamarca separated from Tucumán to form its own provincial government,
following example of Santiago del Estero; this left only the
modern province of Tucumán (q. v.), centered around San
Miguel de Tucumán.

TUCUMAN, BATTLE OF (September 24, 1812). Following the defeat of the patriot forces at Huaqui and the threatened Spanish invasion of the northwest, the Triumvirate government ordered General Manuel Belgrano to continue his withdrawal of the Army of the North back to Córdoba, fearing that otherwise his army would be lost; Belgrano disobeyed and determined, with the support of the northwestern provinces, to make another attempt to defeat the royalists and hold the northwest; at the battle of Tucumán, September 24, 1812, the patriots won a great victory over the royalist forces of General Pío Tristán; the results were significant for Argentina's future history: the northwest was successfully held for the time being and the threat of royalist conquest both postponed and reduced; politically, this victory gave the Buenos Aires government a breathing spell during which it could turn its attention to matters of reorganization and the creation of new autonomous institutions.

TUCUMAN, CONGRESS OF (1816-1819) see CONGRESS OF TU-CUMAN

TUCUMAN, GOBERNACION DEL. The establishment of the Gobernación del Tucumán and its attachment to the viceroyalty of Peru in 1563 represented an important, final step in bringing all lands and Indians formerly touched by Inca empire under Spanish royal rule; its jurisdiction included the present Argentine provinces of Jujuy, Salta, Catamarca, La Rioja, Tucumán, Santiago del Estero, and Córdoba, an area of 700,000 square kilometers, or approximately 271,000 square miles, and resulted from two Spanish colonizing streams from Peru and from Chile; this was the most heavily populated Indian area found in Argentina, incorporating the various groups of the semi-civilized Juries, Diaguitas, and Comechingones (qq.v.; see also various provinces for further information about specific tribes); this vast area was governed from the capital Santiago del Estero, under Audiencia of Charcas; by early 1600s approximately 700 Spaniards and 24,000 Indians in encomienda were under this jurisdiction; in eighteenth century, governors moved to city of San Miguel de Tucumán.

TUCUMAN, SAN MIGUEL DE (City). Capital of modern province of Tucumán; had population of approximately 287,000 in 1960s. Founded May 31, 1565, by Diego de Villaroel (q.v.) on site formerly occupied by Cañete in land known by Indians as Ibatin (or Ybatin), near the montaña; remained there for about 120 years; in 1607 the city numbered 300 Spaniards, many creoles, and 1100 Indians; by 1671 more than 2000 Indians were in encomiendas; San Miguel de Tucumán was moved eastward to its present location in 1685, by government orders because of constant Calchaquí Indian raids; in spite of vigorous protests from the settlers who disliked leaving their lands, Governor Miguel de Salas Valdés planted the symbolic tree of justice, brought from the old city, in the new site known as La Toma on September 27, 1685; in 1770 the town's population was given as more than 20,000, including creoles, mestizos, Indians, mulattoes and blacks (both free and slave); it came to be called simply Tucumán until it resumed its former name in 1952.

San Miguel de Tucumán contains many places of historic interest; one of most important is the Casa de Independencia, the residence belonging to Carmen Bazán de Zavalía, in which the Congress of Tucumán met from March 24, 1816 to January 17, 1817, and in which the Argentine Declaration of Independence was signed July 9, 1816; it is a typical colonial house located near the main plaza; in 1872 this house was purchased by Sarmiento's government and used as post office and telegraph center; later President Roca restored the congressional room but demolished rest of house; in 1940s house was restored to its historic form under direction of architect Mario J. Buschiazzo (see Congress of Tucumán; Declaration of Independence); another interesting building is that of the Church of La Merced that housed the historic image of La Virgen de la Merced that was commissioned a general by General Belgrano and declared to be protector of his army after the victory at Tucumán (see Tucumán, Battle of); this image was moved to Buenos Aires in 1912 to the temple of Nuestra Señora and the Tucumán church building was demolished in 1943 because of its poor condition; the oldest building in the city is often said to be the cathedral, established in 1685, but the present building dates from 1847-1856; in 1913 the governor of Tucumán declared the house in which Bishop Colombres had set up the first sugarmill to be an historic house (today a museum), thus saving from threatened destruction this precursor of Tucumán's modern sugar industry; one of the republic's most distinguished centers of botanical research, the Instituto Miguel Lillo, is located in San Miguel de Tucumán.

TUELLA, PEDRO (1738-1814). First historian, or chronicler, of Rosario; merchant and government official.

Born in Aragón, Spain; came to Río de la Plata about 1759; became an administrator and tax collector in tobacco industry in Rosario; wrote about history of Rosario in both poetry and prose; contributed article entitled "Relación histórica del pueblo y jurisdicción del Rosario de los arroyos en el gobierno de Santa Fe" (April 1802) to Telégrafo Mercantil (q. v.); other works published later; his royalist sympathies caused him problems with patriots of May Revolution but in March 1811, he contributed generously for construction of batteries to defend Rosario along river; died in Rosario.

TUPAC AMARU REVOLT (1780). Massive Indian revolt in Peruvian Andes that involved modern Argentine territory.

In 1780, José Gabriel Condorcanqui, of royal Inca ancestry, cacique of Tungasuca, near Lake Titicaca, became convinced that only force could bring relief to the Indians

from the economic repressions of the mita and the political
abuses of the corregidores; taking the name of the last Inca
emperor, Tupac Amaru I, who had been executed by Viceroy
Francisco de Toledo in 1579, he led the Indians in a great
uprising that spread throughout the cordillera area and posed
real threat to Spanish power throughout South America; viceroys of Lima and Buenos Aires (involved because Bolivia was
a very important part of the viceroyalty) immediately sent
forces; the rebellion was quelled from Cuzco and Tupac
Amaru II, members of his family, and other leaders, were
tortured and put to death; revolt continued alive in outlying
areas for another couple of years; forces sent from Buenos
Aires by viceroy Vértiz y Salcedo, under Colonel José Rese-
guin assisted in bringing peace to La Paz area against forces
led by Diego Tupac Amaru, brother of the leader; the legal
changes made to correct some of the abuses of the mita and
corregidor systems as well as the severe punishment meted
out to the Indians, in attempt to stamp out their culture and
prevent future uprisings, did not affect Argentina greatly, but
it is interesting to note that at the Congress of Tucumán, in
1816, one of the first forms of government proposed for the
newly independent nation was a revival of the Inca monarchy
in a more modern, constitutional form.

TURCOS.   Term applied indiscriminately to Near Eastern peoples
of Ottoman empire in late nineteenth century, whether they
were actually Turks or not; more than 100,000 of these immigrated to Argentina in period 1857-1941 and remained to
become residents.

TUYUTI.   Site in southern Paraguay where two military engagements were fought during War of Triple Alliance; the first,
a major battle, took place on May 24, 1866, when General
Bartolomé Mitre, commanding an allied force of about 30,000
men defeated 25,000 Paraguayan troops led by President Francisco Solano López after more than four hours of fighting;
losses were so heavy, especially on Paraguayan side, that
Tuyutí has been called bloodiest battle of South America; although Mitre was unable to take advantage of this victory immediately, it is generally conceded to have been the critical
battle leading to Paraguay's ultimate defeat.
On November 3, 1867, on same site, Paraguayan
troops attacked Brazilian forces and had gained advantage
over them when Argentine Colonel Manuel Hornos intervened
with his cavalry and forced the Paraguayans to withdraw.

TYPHUS   see   EPIDEMICS OF DISEASE

- U -

UDAONDO, ENRIQUE (1880-1962).   Historian.   Born in Buenos
Aires, studied in the British Academy and the Instituto

Sudamericano in Buenos Aires; director of the Museo Colonial e Histórico of Buenos Aires province (in Luján) from the time of its foundation in 1923; presided over exposition of historical religious art held in Buenos Aires at time of the thirty-second international Eucharistic Congress, 1934; member of the national academy of history; a prolific writer of historical works; believing firmly that Argentina needed to recapture a knowledge of its historical roots in order to understand its current self, Udaondo concentrated most of his attention on the colonial period.

Among his works are Los congresales de 1816. Apuntes biográficos (Buenos Aires, 1916), a study of the men making up the congress that declared Argentine independence; Arboles históricos; Actas del cabildo de Luján and Reseña histórica de la Villa de Luján; and his biographical dictionaries of historical figures: Diccionario biográfico nacional (1938); Diccionario biográfico colonial argentino (1945); and Grandes hombres de nuestra patria, prologue by Pedro Eugenio Aramburu (Buenos Aires, 1946).

UDAONDO, GUILLERMO (1859-1923).   Physician; governor of Buenos Aires province.

Born in Buenos Aires; graduated from medical school there in 1883; entered politics early; became member of Unión Cívica Radical and was one of the leaders of the revolution of 1890, as well as in that of 1893; was elected governor of Buenos Aires province, 1894; was candidate for election to Congress and to presidency; head of UCR following death of Mitre; taught in medical school and University of Buenos Aires, 1899-1904; died in an accident at home in Buenos Aires.

UDELPA (Unión del Pueblo Argentino).   Political party formed as personal vehicle for General Pedro Aramburu's bid to return to political power in 1963; drew about 7% of the total national vote; gave promise of becoming the party that could unite most Argentines under one leadership but assassination of Aramburu (1970) ended this.

UGARTE, MANUEL (1878-1951).   Writer and diplomat.

Born in Buenos Aires; joined Socialist Party and early became part of literary and journalistic circles; founded and edited the daily newspaper La Patria and the review Vida del Hoy; lived abroad a great deal, in Spain, France, and Chile; represented Argentine Republic as ambassador to Mexico (1946-1948), Nicaragua (1949), and Cuba (1950); strongly opposed foreign imperialism in Argentina; supported Pan Hispanism rather than Pan Americanism; his works include travel books, political writings, novels and short stories, and poems; among some of his best known non-fictional works are: Visiones de España (1904); Paisajes parisienses; El dolor de escribir; his political ideas are revealed in El porvenir de la América española; Mi campaña hispanoamericana;

El destino de un continente; La patria grande; one of his best
known works is La venganza del capataz, published in 1925;
among his last works were La dramática intimidad de una
generación and El naufragio de los argonautas (Madrid, 1951);
Ugarte died in Nice, France; remains brought to Buenos
Aires in 1954 for burial in La Recoleta.

UGARTE, MARCELINO (1822-1872).   Jurisconsult; public figure.
    Born in Buenos Aires; received doctorate in jurispru-
dence in Buenos Aires in 1852; exiled twice during Rosas
period; served as defense lawyer for Leandro Alen and Ciriaco Cuitiño, leaders of the hated Mazorca, on trial after
Rosas' defeat; again went into exile for political reasons; returning to Buenos Aires, he became professor of civil law in
the university (1857) and served on commission with Marcelo
Gamboa to draft proposed civil code; elected to Buenos Aires
legislature; served in the national congress during Mitre's administration and then succeeded Elizalde as foreign minister
in 1867; held judicial appointments in Buenos Aires; became
justice of National Supreme Court in 1870, position that he
held at time of his death.
    See Ricardo Zorraquín Becú, "Marcelino Ugarte" in
Revista de la Facultad Derecho y Ciencias Sociales, Buenos
Aires, January-April, 1952.

UGARTE, MARCELINO (1855-1929).   Statesman and legislator;
    governor of Buenos Aires province.
    Born in Buenos Aires, son of Marcelino Ugarte and
Adela Lavalle; grand-nephew of independence hero and Unitarist leader Juan Lavalle; studied in Buenos Aires; became
active in Conservative party politics; elected senator in
Buenos Aires legislature, 1888; served as national congressman, 1892-1902; played important role in financial life of
province by serving as president of the office to inspect and
guarantee national banks following crisis of 1890 and as
minister of finance for governor Bernardo de Irigoyen in
1898; served as governor of Buenos Aires 1902-1906; reformed educational and banking systems; during his administration, port of La Plata was nationalized and university
founded there; as governor of most important province, took
leading role in organizing Partidos Unidos that put Manuel
Quintana in as president, followed by Figueroa Alcorta; as
one of the last survivors of the conservative "Notables" who
had governed Buenos Aires and nation, he began to lose popular support in the new era following election law of 1912;
reelected governor in 1914, he was prevented by President
Yrigoyen's intervention of province from serving his term;
after an unsuccessful attempt to reunite the Conservatives,
he retired; died in Buenos Aires; in 1961 a statue was
erected in his honor in La Plata.
    See José Arce, Marcelino Ugarte. El hombre, el
político, el gobernante (1855-1929) (Buenos Aires, 1960).

UGARTECHE, JOSE FRANCISCO (1768-1834).   Jurisconsult; public
    official; early Federalist.
        Born in Villa Rica, Paraguay; studied in Buenos Aires
    at Real Colegio de San Carlos and then took his doctorate in
    law at university in Charcas (1791); returned to Buenos Aires;
    practiced law for many years and then became involved in
    public life; supported May Revolution in 1810; represented
    Chuquisaca in Assembly of 1812 (in which he was distinguished
    as one of its most brilliant members) and La Rioja in that of
    1813; became one of judges in military courts formed to in-
    vestigate causes of patriot defeats at Vilcapujio and Ayohuma
    (qq. v.); became governor adviser in 1818 and a member of
    commission to protect freedom of the press; in 1824, with
    Manuel Dorrego, published El Argentino, a newspaper in
    which he expressed his belief in federalism as best political
    form of government for Argentine provinces; as representa-
    tive of Santiago del Estero in Constituent Congress, 1826, he
    continued to support federalism; during early 1830s he held
    various judicial appointments, served as public prosecutor for
    Buenos Aires province, as member of lower house of its
    legislature, and as minister of foreign relations and finance
    for Governor Juan Ramón Balcarce; died in Buenos Aires;
    throughout his life he had maintained a personal and political
    correspondence with his boyhood friend, José Gaspar Rodrí-
    guez de Francia, counseling latter, after he became ruler of
    an independent Paraguay, to govern constitutionally.

UNICATO.   Name applied to the oligarchical government during the
    late nineteenth and early twentieth century; it referred to the
    one-party rule exercised by Partido Autonomista Nacional
    (q. v.) with power centralized in the executive branch of gov-
    ernment; Avellaneda had inaugurated this policy in the clos-
    ing years of his administration and Roca had continued it;
    under Juárez Celman the term began to be commonly used
    as he made it clear that there was only one power in govern-
    ment and as head of the party and that both were vested in
    the presidency; the term represented the unpopularity of the
    government and its loss of public confidence because of its
    reactionary politics and the corruption used to maintain its
    own group in power; this opposition was reflected by the for-
    mation of the Unión Cívica Radical; the Unicato was brought
    to an end by the Roque Saenz Peña electoral law of 1912.

UNION CIVICA RADICAL (Radical Party).   Party formed in 1880s,
    known as Unión Cívica, in protest against political control
    and corrupt practices of the oligarchy; the reformers, led
    by Leandro N. Alem (q. v.) and Aristóbulo del Valle de-
    manded "the guarantee of public liberties, honest suffrage,
    no government intervention in elections"; although their move-
    ment was primarily an urban, middle class one, it attracted
    a wide range of supporters dissatisfied with the government;
    they led the revolt of 1889-1890 that resulted in resignation
    of President Juárez Celman but little gain for the reformers;

at this point many of the leaders joined the Julio A. Roca group; the rest, the hardcore of the reform group, formed the Unión Cívica Radical in 1891; in 1892 it accepted the name by which it had already become popularly known: The Radical Party; in 1893 Radical revolts broke out in Buenos Aires and in Santa Fe province but failed; both Alem and Del Valle died in 1896; thereafter the party's leader was Hipólito Yrigoyen; he was determined to achieve the Radical objective of free, honest elections and felt that this could only be done by the secret ballot or by revolution; he adopted policy of in-transigency--total abstention of Radical Party from political action such as voting until free male suffrage with secret ballot had been granted; simultaneous revolts broke out in 1905 in Buenos Aires, Santa Fe, Córdoba, and Mendoza but failed; in 1912, the Roque Saenz Peña Electoral law (see Saenz Peña Law) was passed, giving Radicals what they had been working for; they went to the polls and elected Hipólito Yrigoyen president of the republic in 1916, along with several Radical members to Congress; during the next fourteen years, under Yrigoyen (twice president) and Marcelo Torcuato de Al-vear, Radicals controlled government; although their rule marked a real change, the Radicals seemed to have exhausted their political energy in having secured freer and more hon-est elections and had little to offer to the laborers and other groups demanding specific reforms to improve their situa-tions; it became evident that the nationalistic Radicals were more generally representative of the middle classes than of the masses and that they drew their strength from the criollo past rather than from the newer groups of immigrant stock; disappointed in Radicals, many of these groups later formed basis of Perón's rise to power; divisions within the party (Personalists-Yrigoyen, Anti-personalists-against Yrigoyen) further limited their power; the Radicals did, however, in-troduce stronger party organization and discipline, amounting almost to a political machine, into Argentine life and are given credit for creating atmosphere that produced the cele-brated University Reform (q. v.); in 1951 the Unión Cívica Radical presented a slate consisting of Ricardo Balbín for president, Arturo Frondizi for vice president but lost as Perón was reelected; after Perón left in 1955 the Radical party became active and in 1957 it split into two parties, the Unión Cívica Radical Intransigente (q. v.) led by Arturo Fron-dizi, candidate for president, who favored bringing Peronists back into political participation, and Unión Cívica Radical del Pueblo (q. v.) under Ricardo Balbín, who opposed this and hated Frondizi; although Frondizi was elected president, he was unable to complete his term; the Radicals continued to suffer in 1960s and 1970s from schisms and fragmentation that greatly reduced their political effectiveness, especially in view of revival of Peronist power (see Political Parties).

UNION CIVICA RADICAL DEL PUEBLO (UCRP--Popular, or
    People's, Radical Party).   Party formed by more moderate

sector of Unión Cívica Radical when latter divided in late
1950s; this split was partly personal involving power struggle
between Balbín and Frondizi, and partly sociological, between
old middle class that feared Peronist control (UCPR) and
Frondizi's group of new middle class and intellectuals favoring integration of Peronists into politics; in 1958 the Popular
Radicals supported Ricardo Balbín for president but his rival
Arturo Frondizi of UCRI won; UCRP claimed to be the nationalist group, opposing Frondizi's foreign policy; also maintained old UCR intransigency, opposing political alliances
(this attitude was later modified; in 1963 it was the only major party that refused to enter a coalition and its candidate,
Arturo Illia, won the presidency only with support of other
parties in the electoral college; see Arturo Illia for UCRP
policies as reflected in his administration); in the 1970s the
party was accused of offering only old men and old ideas to
a new Argentina.

UNION CIVICA RADICAL INTRANSIGENTE (UCRI). When Unión
Cívica Radical (q.v.) split in the late 1950s, the group led
by Arturo Frondizi took this name; it stood for the reintegration of Peronists into the political processes, sought support of labor, and promoted industrial development, with
foreign capital, if necessary; Frondizi became president in
1958 and attempted to carry out these policies; his forced
resignation in 1962 left the Intransigente Radicals demor-
alized; since then it has been important only in combination
with Peronists or other groups; many of its members became
involved in the Movimiento de Integración y Desarrollo Nacional, a political party that appeared on ballot in 1965.

UNION DEL SUR, COLEGIO DE (Academy of Union of the South).
On July 16, 1818, the Supreme Director Juan Martín de
Pueyrredón established this academy in Buenos Aires to
serve as a continuation, or replacement, of the royal Colegio
de San Carlos, now that Argentina was no longer under
Spanish Crown.

UNION DEMOCRATICA (Democratic Union). Coalition formed in
1945 to offer effective opposition to election of Juan Domingo
Perón as president; composed of radicals, socialists, communists, and progressive democrats, with conservatives cooperating but not formally joining, the group presented a
ticket with José P. Tamborini for president and Enrique
Mosca for vice president; divided by internal tensions and
with no positive program of reform, the Unión Democrática
slate was defeated by that of Perón-Quijano in February
1946.
     A similar Unión Democrática had been formed in 1943
but its effectiveness ended with the GOU overthrow of President Castillo's government.

UNION INDUSTRIAL ARGENTINA. Association of industrialists

organized to promote industry and its interests in Argentina.
Its origins go back to 1875 when a group of businessmen met
in Buenos Aires to discuss ways in which industry might be
promoted; they formed a society to accomplish this named the
Club Industrial Argentino; in 1877 they held first industrial
exposition in Argentina; three years later a group broke away
to form a separate Centro Industrial Argentino; both groups
continued same objectives and in 1887 they rejoined to form
the Unión Industrial Argentina; among its special interests
were customs legislation, the wine industry, wool and cotton
production; in the 1940s the smaller manufacturers separated
from the greater industrial magnates to form their own Confederación General Económica; neither included the workers;
because of its opposition to Perón, the Unión's activities
were suspended 1946-1955 but resumed after his departure
(see Industry).

UNION POPULAR.   Political party that came close to being official Perón party following 1955 overthrow of Perón government; either boycotted elections or was not permitted to participate until 1965 when it polled 30% of votes cast and the
largest portion of Peronist votes; supported primarily by
lower classes.

UNITARIOS, UNITARISTS (variously given in English, when Argentine form is not used, as Unitarists or Unitarians).
        Members of political group led by Bernardino Riva-
davia in 1820s; they advocated a strongly centralized government, given legal authority and institutionalized by a formal
constitution that would establish a government of the educated
elite, largely urban; Unitarists dreamed of converting the
newly independent Argentina into a progressive, liberal, free-
trading, free-thinking modern state according to the ideas of
the Enlightenment and examples of such European nations as
England and France; they expected to use European capital
as well as ideas to bring Argentina out of its Spanish colonial state as quickly as possible.
        Federalists, who opposed them, claimed that Unitarist
ideas were impracticable and constituted the substitution of
untried theory for practice developed out of experience; they
resented the abrupt abandoning of traditional Argentine institutions for new foreign ones; wanted a looser, federated
government in which provinces would maintain some local
autonomy over their individual problems; Federalists gathered
support from other opponents of Unitarists--those Catholics
who resented Rivadavia's reforms of the Church; provincials
who feared domination by Buenos Aires whose interests were
very different from theirs; rural people, from wealthy estancieros to their lowliest peons, who feared urban orientation of Unitarist leaders, and from poorer classes of towns-
people who felt that Unitarists ignored their interests; and,
finally, by many powerful leaders who disliked Rivadavia
personally.

The adoption of the Unitarist constitution of 1826, with Rivadavia, as president, marked the high point of Unitarist power; the following year Rivadavia's attempt to federalize Buenos Aires and use its customs revenue for the entire nation (that had no other source of income at that time) infuriated the powerful estancieros of Buenos Aires who intended to keep those revenues as monopoly of their own province; this, combined with Rivadavia's unpopular war with Brazil, forced the president's resignation; from 1827 until 1862, Argentina was without real national organization; for most of that time Juan Manuel de Rosas, Federalist, dominated; Unitarists went into exile and planned to return; did so twice, under Juan Lavalle (q.v.); meanwhile interior provinces, under their own caudillos, frequently went Unitarist, as under José María Paz (q.v.), desiring national reorganization, more liberal ("civilized") ideals, and a share in national trade; passions ran high as Dorrego's execution by Lavalle was followed by similar Federalist acts; one of Rosas' official slogans was "Death to the Unitarist savages" and the latter returned his hatred in kind; this had much to do with Buenos Aires' refusal to join other provinces under constitution of 1853, with Urquiza (a Federalist, formerly under Rosas) as president.

After the final reorganization of the republic under the federal constitution of 1853, with Bartolomé Mitre as president, in 1862, the name Unitarist was dropped; many old Unitarist ideals were eventually realized, as technology of communications and transportation drew interior provinces closer to coastal area and in 1880 Buenos Aires was federalized and secular education, marriage, and keeping of vital statistics brought under government, instead of church, control.

See Enrique M. Barba, Unitarismo, federalismo, rosismo (Buenos Aires, 1972).

UNITARISMO (Unitarism). Political theory of group in early Argentine national life that advocated a centralized, unitary system of government (see Unitarios).

UNITARIST LEAGUE OR LEAGUE OF THE INTERIOR see LEAGUE OF THE INTERIOR

UNITED PROVINCES OF LA PLATA. Name taken by the former viceroyalty of Río de la Plata after the revolution of 1810 (see Argentina).

UNITED STATES (relations with Argentina). From the days of discovery the areas now occupied by the United States and Argentina have been linked to some degree; in the early sixteenth century the name of Sebastian Cabot, who first explored Río de la Plata upriver area, was also associated with exploration along Atlantic coast of North America; for many reasons, including distance, lack of reason for contact, etc., there were few contacts between the small English

settlements and those of Argentina until the latter years of
the eighteenth century; by that time New England whalers,
merchant captains, and slave traders were in the South Atlantic seeking supplies for their crews and ships, hides for
their developing shoe industries, and animal fats (tallow) for
their candles; Montevideo and Buenos Aires were regular
ports of call; by 1810, Argentines were familiar--on every
level, as ships' officers and crews mingled with the towns-
people on their long layovers in port--with story and documents of American Revolution that produced independence
from England, and also drove American merchants to seek
new markets in Orient, Africa, and South America to replace those cut off as they lost their former favored position
in British empire; U.S. merchants, such as David Curtis De
Forest (q.v.), engaged in trade there; private individuals,
such as Belgrano's physician in Tucumán, Joseph Redhead
(q.v.), came to Buenos Aires on a visit and decided to remain there; during the period following the May Revolution,
Argentina's patriot governments sought and hoped to obtain
aid from the United States in fighting for its independence;
unfortunately the ending of the Napoleonic Wars in 1815 (U.S.
portion known as War of 1812) brought directly opposite effects to the U.S. and Argentina; while the former abruptly
turned its back on the Atlantic and Europe and devoted itself
for the next few decades to expanding its sovereignty over
territory as far as the Pacific, Argentina was forced to become more deeply involved with Europe as Ferdinand VII renewed his attempts to regain his American colonies; Argentina also desperately needed new trading agreements and its
best markets were in Europe; nevertheless, in spite of these
divergent, even conflicting, interests, both official and commercial contacts increased; from 1810 on, both sent numerous official expeditions to each other; in 1810 Joel Roberts
Poinsett was sent to Buenos Aires as agent for seamen and
commerce and to report on affairs; in early 1817 he was
followed by a U.S. fact-finding commission consisting of
Theodorick Bland, John Graham, and Caesar Rodney, that
spent about two months in Argentina before returning to report; their secretary Henry M. Brackenridge (q.v.) published
an account of their observations; in 1820 John M. Forbes was
sent as commercial agent to Buenos Aires; meanwhile Argentine patriot governments had sent their own representatives
to U.S., seeking recognition and aid; U.S. assistance, even
from volunteers, was forbidden due to neutrality laws still
in force, and because of the delicate negotiations underway
between U.S. and Spain that would result in Adams-Onis
treaty of 1819-1821, by which U.S. acquired Florida and established its southern boundary; U.S.'s recognition of Argentine independence was also delayed by conflicting reports
about stability of patriot Buenos Aires governments that
U.S. government received from Chilean exile, José Miguel
Carrera, and, later, Argentines exiled by Pueyrredón; U.S.
public opinion was divided but largely favored recognition,

with Henry Clay its champion in Congress; U.S. recognition
was formally accorded to Argentina in 1822 and in 1824
Caesar A. Rodney (q.v.) was received in Buenos Aires as
first U.S. minister to that government.

At about the same time, word of the promulgation of
the Monroe Doctrine (q.v.) reached Argentina; it was assumed
at that time that the doctrine applied to all the American nations but when Argentina appealed to U.S. with regard to
British settlement in the Falkland Islands (claimed by Argentina) in the early 1830s and again regarding the British-French
armed interventions in Río de la Plata area, 1838-1850, the
U.S. made no protest, apparently excluding Argentina; during
the first half century of Argentine independence, U.S. diplomacy in Buenos Aires was all too often handled by minor officials but, as a matter of fact, the dealings between the two
countries required little more; two disputes did arise: the
actions of U.S. naval commander Silas Duncan, in U.S.S.
Lexington at Falkland Islands (q.v.) in 1831-1832 and the dispute about free navigation of the Paraná-Paraguay rivers in
the incident of the Water Witch (q.v.) in 1854, involving both
Argentina and Paraguay; curiously enough, the latter aroused
more Argentine resentment at the time than the Falkland Islands episode.

Meanwhile, toward close of Rosas period, trade had
been increasing between the two countries; when Argentina
completed its national reorganization in 1853 it did so under
a federal constitution that bore many similarities to that of
the United States; and in that same year the first commercial
treaty between Argentina and U.S. was made; the U.S. Civil
War, 1861-1865, proved to be a windfall as a market for the
coarse Argentine wool that was beginning to seek new markets; unfortunately for Argentina the victory of the industrializing, tariff-committed North meant that its wool market
would be limited and less lucrative as U.S. used protective
tariff (1867) to develop its own sheep and wool industry;
tariffs began to be a real bone of contention and to this, in
the early twentieth century (1920s), was added the insult
(from Argentine point of view) of sanitary regulations forbidding entry of Argentine beef because of danger of introducing
hoof-and-mouth disease (q.v.); meanwhile, in 1890, James G.
Blaine had inaugurated his Pan American movement by which
he hoped to bind the nations of the Western hemisphere together in recognition and protection of their common interests
and hoped also to establish favorable trade agreements within
the area (see Inter-American Relations); Argentina refused to
accept U.S. leadership blindly; it countered that, while it
recognized American relationships, its own closest ties--his-
torically, culturally, economically--were with Spain, Italy,
France, and England; this point of view was strengthened by
the rise of nationalism shortly after this and a renewed interest in its Spanish roots (at time of Spanish American War,
especially); Argentine pride was also hurt by its feeling that
U.S. wanted to make foreign policy for all the other American

nations and paid too little respect to policy suggestions of
Argentina (such as Drago doctrine--later adopted) that wanted
to play its own role in international relations; its preference
for bilateral treaties, on basis of needs of individual nations,
its insistence on recognition of sovereignty of each nation,
seemed to be negated by U.S. demand for inter-American
group action; at the same time, especially in 1860s-1880s,
there had been many Argentines, like Sarmiento, who drew
democratic inspiration from the United States and looked to
it as a model from which much could be gained; a most conspicuous example of this was Sarmiento's importation of
American teachers to stimulate and organize the Argentine
public school program, and of scientists, such as Benjamin
A. Gould at the Astronomical observatory in Córdoba who contributed to Argentine cultural development; Generation of 1880,
however, rebelled and launched spirit and program of nationalism.

During the period between 1880 and World War I both
U.S. and Argentine were revolutionized socially, politically,
and economically by the floods of European immigrants that
came to both lands and by the transportation and communication technological advances that unified each nation; volume of
trade increased for each nation but their products tended to
be competitive, rather than mutually trade-producing; Argentina remained neutral during World War I but in the decades
and world-wide depression that followed, it became increasingly evident that Argentina was going to have to look to U.S.
for the capital funds and goods, and consumer manufacturers
that had previously come from Europe; in 1941, with U.S.
importing nearly all its linseed from Argentina in return for
fish, fresh fruit, automobile parts, lumber, radio receivers,
etc., a new treaty, removing obstacles to trade, was made;
at that time both nations were still maintaining neutrality in
World War II although U.S. was favoring the Allies; after the
attack on Pearl Harbor December 7, 1941, and the U.S.
declaration of war against the Axis, U.S. urged all Latin
American nations, at Rio de Janeiro Conference in 1942 to
break relations with Axis at once; Argentina refused to be
pressured, insisting on the right of each nation to follow
course best suited to its own sovereign interests (see World
War II); from then on, and especially after military takeover
in Argentina in 1943, relations between two nations worsened;
U.S. believed Argentina to be pro-Axis and totalitarian-
oriented, Argentina considered that it was following its own
traditional policy of neutrality; as Perón rose to power in
closing years of war, U.S. ambassador Spruille Braden almost openly challenged him for leadership of democratic Argentines and when Perón ran for president, U.S. issued a
"Blue Book on Argentina" accusing Argentine regime of Nazi-
Fascist orientation during war, that probably helped Perón
win.

Both governments attempted to improve relations and
a modus vivendi resulted; early Argentine attempts to

expropriate U.S. oil interests were eventually abandoned in
favor of government regulation of foreign business operations;
Argentina needed capital and U.S. has made heavy private investments and public loans to support its economic development program.

In January 1959, President Arturo Frondizi became
first Argentine president to visit United States (U.S. President Franklin D. Roosevelt had visited Buenos Aires in 1936);
on January 22, he addressed members of U.S. Congress,
stressing the similarities of the two countries in their political organization, dedication to individual freedom and democratic enterprise, their capacity to assimilate cultures from
other parts of the world and to defend national sovereignty;
he also praised U.S. for its early recognition of Argentine
independence and paid tribute to the stimulus that Sarmiento
had found in its system of public education; during this trip
he also sought investment funds and new bilateral agreements.

In 1970 no serious problems troubled relations between
Argentina and the U.S.; U.S. was receiving 8.7% of Argentina's total exports and providing 24.9% of its imports--most-
ly machinery and electrical equipment for its diversified industrialization program; three years later, these had decreased slightly, to 8% and 21.6% respectively; not only is
this balance of trade unfavorable to Argentina but another
drain to United States was causing concern; because of the increasing inflation and political uncertainties in Argentina,
there has been a growing emigration of young and ambitious
Argentine professionals and intellectuals to the United States
in search of greater opportunities; this represents an enrich-
ment for the United States but an impoverishment for Argentina.

See Harold F. Peterson, Argentina and the United
States, 1810-1960 (State University of New York, 1964); Arthur P. Whitaker, The United States and Argentina (Cambridge, Mass., 1954); and Thomas F. McGann, Argentina,
the United States, and the Inter-American System 1880-1914
(Cambridge, Mass., 1957). For recent Argentine interpretation, critical of U.S., see Miguel Angel Scenna, Como fueron
las relaciones argentino-norteamericanas (Buenos Aires,
1970).

UNIVERSITIES. The first university in what is today Argentina
developed in Córdoba early in the seventeenth century from a
Jesuit school; it remained the only university in the nation
but in the late eighteenth century after the Jesuits had been
expelled, it came under the control of the Franciscans and
stressed Thomistic teaching; students, eager for a more
modern education than it offered, traveled from Buenos Aires
or other provinces to the more liberal university in Chuquisaca (now Sucre, Bolivia) or to San Felipe in Santiago, Chile;
discussion of a university at Buenos Aires was common during viceregal period but actually it was not established until
after independence (1821); no others were founded until after

the national reorganization in 1860s; eventually a national system (nine universities in 1970s) developed, each created by
Congress and controlled by national government, with president having power to intervene (see Universities and Politics);
eventually in the late 1950s private universities were authorized and permitted to give accredited degrees; as in United
States and elsewhere, other kinds of universities were experimented with and other learned institutions permitted to offer
degrees.

The Argentine university consists of several different
faculties, usually separated physically as well as administratively from each other; administration (since the University
Reform, q. v.) is in hands of faculty, students, and alumni,
with government always able to intervene; during the half
century following the University Reform and later changes
making a university education more readily accessible to anyone desiring it--no tuition, class attendance voluntary, few
admission requirements--the student body has increased to
more than 12 times what it was; only a very small proportion of students complete the six years of study and take the
exams that will give them the professional degree for which
they have enrolled but Argentines are proud of the democracy
with which the opportunity to obtain these degrees have been
offered to its citizens. See individual national universities,
listed below in chronological order according to date of
founding.

Universidad de Córdoba: Founded in 1613 by Bishop
Fernando de Trejo y Sanabria who based it on the already
opened Jesuit Colegio Máximo and donated his fortune to create a theological university; classes opened in 1614, with
chairs in Latin, arts, and theology; degrees were granted
after 1622 but it was not accredited as a full university until
1664 after both church and royal government had approved it;
the university remained under Jesuit control, with all faculty
members Jesuit, and was essentially theological until the expulsion of the Jesuits in 1767; the Franciscans took over the
school, now under the patronato real, exercised by the viceroy, who appointed the rector; its teaching was largely scholasticism; a school of law was added in 1791 but many Argentines preferred to go to more liberal university of Chuquisaca; lay instructors began to be used along with clerics,
and civil, as well as canon, law was offered; largely through
the efforts of the Funes brothers, Ambrosio and Gregorio,
the university was reorganized, 1800-1808, into a major university with same rights and privileges of other such Spanish universities in Spain and America; in 1808 the Franciscans were removed from control and Dr. Gregorio Funes
named its rector; following May Revolution in 1810, it began
new orientation, emphasizing civil and public law; in 1854,
university was nationalized by President Justo José de Urquiza; school of theology disappeared in 1863.

It was in this oldest, most conservative university
that the famous University Reform (q. v.) originated in 1918;

in 1946 the university was intervened by Perón's government
and most of its faculty forced to resign; student protest
against political problems of the 1960s culminated at University of Córdoba in what is known as El Cordobazo (q. v.); the
university again experienced federal intervention, along with
other universities, in 1970s.

Universidad de Buenos Aires: On August 9-12, 1821,
the University of Buenos Aires was inaugurated by Bernardino
Rivadavia, minister in Governor Martín Rodríguez government; Dr. Antonio Sáenz, who had completed the general
plans, became first rector; this marked culmination of a project under way since the days of the viceroyalty, and eagerly
sponsored by patriot governments from time of Director Juan
Martín de Pueyrredón; it was organized into six departments
or schools; preparatory studies, exact sciences, medicine,
law, sacred sciences, and elementary education (Rivadavia
had hoped to place all education in the province under direction of the university); during the Rosas period, the university was closely supervised to keep it in line with government
policy and Catholic doctrine; in 1874 a new statute reorganized
the university integrating its various faculties more closely
under a general council and adding several new ones; when the
city of Buenos Aires became federalized in 1880, the university passed under control of national government in 1881; in
the 1970s the university had the following schools or faculties: Agronomy and Veterinary Sciences, Architecture, Economic Sciences, Physical and Exact Sciences, Law and Social
Sciences, Medicine, Philosophy and Letters, Sociology, Anthropology, and Dentistry; the University of Buenos Aires en-
joys a prestige and distinction not equalled by other universities; among its rectors have been many of the most distinguished intellectuals and professional men of the nation; its
students have become distinguished in the liberal professions
and able public leaders on political scene; the student body
is active politically, despite federal interventions and occasional loss of autonomy (see Universities and Politics). A
large oil painting depicting the day of the inauguration of the
university was executed by Antonio González Moreno, 1943-
1946, and placed in the Salón de Grados of the School of Law
and Social Sciences.

Universidad de Tucumán: This university, located in
San Miguel de Tucumán, dates back to 1875 but was formally
established in 1913 and opened in 1914; by provincial legislation a faculty of jurisprudence and political sciences was
established in 1875 but it disappeared as effect of national
law in 1881; in 1908 Juan B. Terán proposed a law creating
this university; it passed in 1912 and a council to form the
university was created; May 25, 1914, it opened, with Terán
as its first rector; it contains several faculties and serves
the northwest and central portions of the republic.

Universidad Nacional de La Plata: Shortly after the
founding of La Plata (q. v.) as the capital of Buenos Aires
province, provisions were made for the establishment of a

provincial university there; law proposed in 1889, the university opened in 1897 and soon offered courses leading to degrees in law, engineering, surveying, and pharmacy; in 1902-
1903, the province canceled its grant to the university and began to turn it and related facilities, such as the museum of
natural history, astronomical observatory, etc. over to the
national government to become part of the comprehensive
modern university projected by Joaquín V. González (q.v.);
the decree establishing this was dated January 24, 1906; Dr.
González became its first president and Dr. Agustín Alvarez
(q.v.), first vice president.

From its inception the University of La Plata differed
from other national universities; in contrast to the more traditional purposes of the others, dedicated primarily to the intellectual and ethical education of superior persons who were
to become leaders, this university attempted to follow new
educational trends in Europe and the United States and to include more emphasis on accumulation of knowledge (research)
in every field and to make that knowledge useful to the community; its various schools and related centers immediately
attracted large numbers of both Argentine and foreign students;
latter were especially drawn to faculties of agronomy, physical and mathematical sciences; by 1950s the new university
had nearly 22,000 students; by the 1970s this number had
doubled.

Universidad de Santa Fe: In 1889 Governor José de
Gálvez took initiative in establishing provincial university in
city of Santa Fe, closely related to the Colegio de la Inmaculada Concepción; it opened in 1890, offering only law; in 1911
the school of pharmacy was added; degrees of this university
were nationally recognized, with some reservations; in 1919,
with the creation of the Universidad Nacional del Litoral (q.v.),
the University of Santa Fe was nationalized.

Universidad del Litoral: Founded in 1919 during first
presidency of Hipólito Yrigoyen; this university operates
throughout the littoral provinces with major schools and related institutions in cities of Rosario, Paraná, Santa Fe, and,
formerly, Corrientes (before creation of University of Northeast).

Universidad Nacional de Cuyo: This university, centered in Mendoza, finally opened in 1939 after many years of
preparation and organization had been spent in bringing together the various cultural institutions of the old Cuyo provinces of Mendoza, San Juan, and San Luis to integrate them
into one national university; it has schools throughout the
provinces of the area; in Mendoza these include humanities,
philosophy, languages, medicine, history, engineering, architecture, art, agronomy; in San Luis education and sciences
are emphasized; in San Juan, schools of mining, engineering,
astronomy, and meteorology; school of atomic sciences in
Bariloche is also attached to it.

Universidad del Sur: Founded in 1946 in Bahía Blanca,
this university grew out of an earlier (1943) project of

University of La Plata to establish a technological institute there; as established in 1946, this new national university of the south included both technology and humanities.

Universidad del Nordeste: Established in 1956, this new national university is designed to serve the need for advanced education in provinces of Corrientes, Chaco, Formosa, and Misiones, with its center in city of Corrientes; its faculties are located in Corrientes, Resistencia (Chaco), Posadas (Misiones), and Formosa.

In the latter part of the 1950s a movement arose among conservative Catholics to reestablish Catholic universities in the traditional pattern, in spite of fact that earlier attempts in twentieth century had failed; congressional action now made this possible. The Universidad Católica de Buenos Aires was founded in 1958 and opened with faculties of philosophy, law and political sciences, and that of social and economic sciences. The Universidad Católica de Córdoba was inaugurated April 10, 1959, with Juan A. Camargo as its first rector, who expressed its philosophy in his inaugural address, "This is a Catholic university; that is to say, it accepts the responsibility to defend--and accepts it openly and specifically--a doctrine open to every person who is willing to accept it freely."

Universidad Obrera: Created in 1948 under sponsorship of National Commission of Apprenticeship and Professional Orientation, it was designed to give advanced technological training to provide employees for new national industrialization programs; in 1959 this was separated from the Commission, nationalized and created into an autonomous university known as the Universidad Tecnológica Nacional.

Universidad Popular de la Boca: Founded in 1917 by Tomás A. Le Bretón, it has trained many thousands in fields of diesel and steam engines, electronics, aviation, and other such new technical fields.

Universidades Populares: In 1948 these popular universities (or universities of the people, experimental in Argentina as in other Western nations) included about 60 cultural entities throughout the nation, many of them supported by leading Argentine political and intellectual figures; those of Buenos Aires and surrounding area were supervised by a Superior Directing Council; courses were offered freely but students contributed a minimum amount toward expenses; these popular universities provided advanced, specialized, courses, largely related to new technologies and economic changes in Argentina, not available in conventional schools or in all areas.

UNIVERSITIES AND POLITICS. Relationships between universities and government and between the university students and government remained close even after the University Reform (q.v.) that had made each university almost autonomous and placed most of its government in hands of faculty members and students; leaders of this 1918 reform movement had been largely nationalist, populist, anticlerical, antimilitary and leftist, rather than conservative; student generations succeeding to this heritage organized themselves into active political groups and entered the national political scene far more often than in the past; in 1930 they had a part in ousting Hipólito Yrigoyen from the presidency; during the next four decades, their increased numbers, close student organization within the individual faculties or schools, high degree of self-government, and increased interest in public affairs made them an important political factor; clashes between students and government were frequent and violent; professors, for their part, cherished their new role in determining university policy as well as their academic freedom and frequently opposed government policy; to all university opposition, the government used its traditional and legal weapon of intervention.

Most of the universities opposed the military takeover of 1943 and Ramírez's government, in 1943, attempted to overthrow the autonomy gained by the University Reforms but met with little success; Perón hoped to gain university support for his election as president but both professors and students viewed him as a right-wing dictator and opposed him violently; the result was the purge of most of the faculty members who were replaced by Peronists and the complete government takeover of university administration by University Law of 1948; new student outbreaks occurred in 1954; after Perón's departure in 1955, universities regained some, but not all, of their former status.

The period following this, especially that of the 1960s saw much political activity in universities but it tended to be expression of opposition to government policies, rather than a positive forward thrust; for example, students joined with many other groups in opposing President Arturo Frondizi's government's support for creation of private (such as Catholic) universities; by late 1960s it was obvious that universities needed both support and reform; overcrowded (by 1968 student body numbered 220,000), underequipped, and often incompetently taught by professors who were poorly paid, lacked full tenure, and often had been poorly trained; students were in constant rebellion against these conditions; in 1966 Onganía's rightist government, believing universities to be controlled by Communists, took immediate action; in accordance with decree of July 29 ordering reform of universities, police and troops closed the universities without notice; universities again lost their autonomy but a precarious order was established; the sudden flight of large numbers of professors to other American or European countries sobered the government and an uneasy truce was maintained with universities for nearly three years; the student unrest continued, however, and culminated three years later; students in Corrientes rioted in May 1969, when their food prices were increased; police killed a student during the resulting violence; student strikes followed; in Rosario another student (a 15-year-old) was killed during a demonstration; the CGT (national labor organization) at this time called a general labor strike throughout the country and joined forces with the students against the government; on May 5, 1969, Córdoba became the center of this opposition as students and laborers occupied the city and made it the victim of their pentup violence in what became known as El Cordobazo; with outbreaks threatened throughout the nation Onganía immediately declared a state of siege; he also turned to a more conciliatory policy toward universities but was himself replaced the following year; Onganía's university reform had been little more than an attempt to remove students from politics and to destroy the increasing radicalization of the students, and it had failed; universities regained their autonomy.

Since then, students have split into several leftist factions ranging from Communist to Peronist; a humanistic group that would restrict student political activity to the university level began to gain some influence among some groups of non-Communist students who had formerly been highly politicized; on the other hand, leftist groups, related to the guerrillas, were also growing more powerful among students; in 1973 President Juan Domingo Perón introduced new reforms, liberalizing attendance and exam requirements and giving students more control over faculty appointments and their own curriculums; later administrations have removed most of these changes.

UNIVERSITY REFORM (Reforma Universitaria). In Argentina this term, when used as a proper noun, refers specifically to the series of widesweeping reforms begun in University of Córdoba in 1918 that eventually affected university organization, teaching, and curriculums throughout Latin America.

In 1918 the universities represented an anachronism: all of them belonged to national government and reflected political interests as well as the elitist concepts of the oligarchy; times had changed and an expanded political suffrage had elected Hipólito Yrigoyen, a Radical, as president; there was widespread resentment within universities because faculty appointments seemed to be made for political reasons, rather than academic, and that these professors, often considered incompetent, could fail, or downgrade students on political, rather than scholarly grounds; a generally poor quality of education resulted; Yrigoyen's intervention of the University of Córdoba in March 1918, produced a student strike that set off the Reform; a University Congress was called, and as Santa Fe, Buenos Aires, La Plata, and eventually other universities, joined in, the Federación Universitaria Argentina (FUA) was formed (April 1918) to draw up guidelines and direct the fight to secure greater student and faculty participation in the governing of the University, to modernize and nationalize the curriculum; during the next decade many of these objectives were gained, with each university autonomous and governed by a council composed of members from faculty, student body, and alumni; class attendance was made more voluntary; the universities, for the first time, became available to middle class students, faculty members acquired appointment by public competition, and curriculums were modernized to suit Argentina's national needs; by 1930 Argentine universities were considered among the best in Latin America; in the troubled decades from the 1940s to 1970s, much of this autonomy was lost; the national government never gave up its right to intervene and intervention became common; some reforms, however, were added; Perón opened national universities to any student wishing to attend and abolished tuition fees; he also attempted to create full-time faculties, rather than those consisting of professional men who made their living off the campus and were recruited to give one or two special courses (see Universities; Universities and Politics).

UPPER PERU (modern Bolivia) see ALTO PERU

URBANIZATION. The city or town was the main agent or institution used by Spaniards in conquest and settlement of Argentina; Spaniards, coming across the Andes from the Perus or from Chile, or across the Atlantic from Spain usually carried official orders to establish permanent, legally organized towns in locations selected for their good soil, adequate water supply, number of available friendly Indians (for providing food and labor), and strategically placed for defense and for accessibility to older settlements as well as to new lands to be occupied; each town was laid out, lands apportioned for government and church, and provisions made for townsite and rural plot to be given each settler; by the close of the sixteenth century nearly all the present cities had been so established; fourteen of them, with the land over which each had jurisdiction, developed into modern provinces; the local city councils (cabildo) and the church provided leadership not only for the town but also for the surrounding area; in theory, these cities were governed by royal governors or lieutenant governors under the royal audiencias (q. v.) and ultimately, for most of the colonial period, under viceroy in Lima, but in practice they were so remote that only a few ever had royal officials in residence and the members of the cabildo were, in fact, city fathers responsible for the defense of the area (usually, but not always, from Indian raids), marketing conditions, labor supply, and other economic regulations, problems of law and order within the community, and care of sick, young, and old, as well as matters of public health; through the church, education was provided for the creole children and sometimes for others in town; missionaries evangelized the Indians and brought them into Spanish culture and often into creole society; the church also served as spiritual and moral guide and authority and provided, with its religious festivals, the great cultural, dramatic events of colonial community life.
        In eighteenth century, cities began to grow in size and

importance and by the close of the century, after viceroyalty
of Río de la Plata, Buenos Aires audiencia, and intendancies
had been established, Spanish royal officials were found in
most cities and newly arrived Spanish resident merchants took
their places in local cabildos; Buenos Aires, as viceregal
capital, began to be modernized and beautified into a city
worthy of its position and other cities undertook similar improvements; this movement continued slowly until the late nineteenth century, with cities, especially those along the Paraná
from Santa Fe to Buenos Aires, growing in size as early immigrants or people from interior, or foreign traders came in
as artisans, tradesmen, urban laborers, or as new merchants,
entrepreneurs, educators, scientists, etc.

The big change came in the period from 1880s to
World War I; the population of greater Buenos Aires quin-
tupled; the floods of immigrants, increasing commercial agriculture, new boom in meat business due to refrigeration,
revolutionized the coastal cities as new urban industries and
services brought demand for labor; Buenos Aires (the prototype and leader of coastal cities) was the goal of provincial
workers seeking greater economic opportunity; their darker
faces were reminders of the Indian and black labor used in
large numbers in the interior during colonial period; at the
same time new Europeans kept the city white in race but began to form a new social class in Argentina--the growing
mass of skilled workers and merchants who fell between the
upper class Argentines and lower class laborers and, in fact,
were to make up the great Argentine middle class; during the
three decades from 1880s to World War I, a massive public
works program in Buenos Aires made it the equal of a European capital, its port was improved; railroads connected
every part of the country to it or to the new cities of Rosario
and Bahía Blanca; cultural life bloomed; so did slums as the
cities found themselves unable to provide employment for all
the incoming laborers; their numbers were increased by migrant workers from Chile, Bolivia, Paraguay, and Brazil
who had come over to work in frontier areas and remained
in Argentina, eventually to be drawn by hope of better job in
coastal city; internal migration to Buenos Aires continued into 1940s and 1950s reaching nearly 200,000 annually following
World War II; the massive shift from interior to coastal
cities was accompanied by local migration from rural area
to town or city; in 1869 only 29% of population lived in towns
with more than 2000 inhabitants; by 1914 this had risen to
53% and in 1970 was estimated to be 75%; as in colonial period, these modern Argentine cities continued to be the vital
political, social, economic, and cultural cores of national
life; urban unrest, even with all its modern ideologies, demands, and practices of labor groups, had roots in comunero movements of colonial period and was effective in bringing change; it was largely responsible for the military takeovers of national government and the changes that characterized Perón's administration.

By the 1950s, the urbanization of the entire coastal
area had caused problems not only for those cities involved
but for the entire nation; since then Argentina has attempted
to decentralize its industry, establishing industrial centers
throughout the provinces; and new cities are developing, although still small, in the north and south, as centers from
which the national resources of the Chaco-Misiones subtropical area in the north and semi-arid Patagonian plateaus in
the south can be most successfully exploited; meanwhile coastal cities continue to attract money, people, business, and
power and to exercise great influence on life of republic.

The phenomenon of urbanization in Argentina is attracting considerable attention from historians and social scientists. See articles by Roberto Cortés Conde and Nancy López
de Nisvovich and by James R. Scobie in Urbanización y proceso social en América, edited by José de Matos Mar (Lima,
Peru, 1972) and Scobie's Argentina: a City and a Nation
(rev. ed., New York, 1971) and Buenos Aires: Plaza to
Suburb 1870-1910 (New York, 1974).

URIARTE, PEDRO FRANCISCO (1758-1839). Priest; legislator;
    signer of Declaration of Independence.
        Born in Santiago del Estero; early destined for the
    priesthood; completed his doctoral studies in canon law and
    was ordained; served as chaplain of the Casa de Ejercicios
    in Buenos Aires (1786); was also assigned as curate to Lo-
    reto; Dr. Uriarte concerned himself greatly with public edu-
    cation, establishing a school in Buenos Aires and another at
    Loreto; he was active in helping to get the Public Library
    started; he became an early supporter of the revolutionary
    cause; was one of the twelve provincial members to be taken
    into the junta in December 1810; he was selected to repre-
    sent his province at the congress of Tucumán and was one
    of the signers of the Declaration of Independence; repre-
    sented Santiago del Estero in the national congress of 1819;
    suffered imprisonment by Governor Manuel Sarratea, along
    with other members of congress; later was exiled briefly by
    Ibarra, caudillo of Santiago del Estero, for his political ac-
    tions; after being permitted to return, he devoted himself to
    his religious duties at Loreto; died there, in front of his
    chapel a few years later.

URIBURU, CASA DE LOS. Colonial house in Salta owned by the
    Uriburu family since 1773; José Evaristo Uriburu, son of the
    president of the same name, donated it to the government in
    1943 to be used as an historical monument.

URIBURU, DAMASO DE (1794-1857). Writer, political figure;
    entrepreneur.
        Born in Salta; studied at Monserrat in Córdoba, 1810-
    1811; returned to Salta to become active in journalism and in
    politics as his poor health ruled out military service; served
    as member of Salta cabildo; joined Facundo de Zuviría and

J. Marcos Zorrilla in establishing the Unitarist party in Salta; supported policies of Rivadavia nationally and Arenales locally; after Quiroga's triumph in the Northwest (1831), Uriburu emigrated to Bolivia in 1832.

Uriburu represents one of those Argentines of the northwest who matured while both Argentina and Bolivia were part of the same viceroyalty and relations with Chile were close; his career reflects this sense of unity even while the nations were drawing apart into separate national entities. He first went to Bolivia as representative of a mining group formed in Buenos Aires, backed by local and British capital, to exploit the Bolivian mines; this was an attempt (the first important one) to continue the traditional colonial economic ties between Argentina and Bolivia in their new independence; in spite of Dámaso de Uriburu's excellent relations with Bolivian presidents Sucre and Santa Cruz, as well as with the British General Miller, political and economic events of the 1820s and 1830s in both countries caused his efforts to fail; during the twenty years of his exile from Argentina, Uriburu maintained constant correspondence with intellectuals and literary figures of the three southern countries and performed government services for Bolivia and Chile, notably in his successful peace efforts of 1830s; at the same time he established a reputation as one of the finest journalists in Bolivia; returning to Argentina (1852) after Rosas' departure, Dámaso Uriburu represented his province as a senator to the Confederation Congress at Paraná; he died in 1857 in Bolivia where he had gone on business.

His most important historical writing, his Memorias, covering the years from 1808 to 1827 (the entire independence period), was published in 1936 by his nephew José Evaristo Uriburu.

URIBURU, EVARISTO DE (1796-1855). Veteran of wars of independence; three times governor of Salta.

Born in Salta; left his studies in letters and philosophy to fight for independence in Belgrano's army of the north, at Salta, Tucumán, Vilcapugio, and Ayohuma; later served under San Martín, recruiting in La Rioja, and fighting with the Army of the Andes in northern Chile and at Chacabuco; returned to Salta where he became very active politically, as well as in military life; promoted to colonel in 1825; became governor in 1831 but was forced into temporary exile in Bolivia, following Quiroga's victory in 1832; returning to Salta, he held public positions as judge, president of the legislature and of the convention that drew up the provincial constitution; created the tribunal of commerce and directed its action; became governor two more times, in 1837 and in 1842; in 1855 the Confederation commissioned him colonel in its infantry; Evaristo de Uriburu died in Buenos Aires, 1855.

URIBURU, FRANCISCO (1837-1906). Financier; public figure.

Born in Salta; more or less self-educated but well-read

and proficient in both English and French; he exercised considerable political power in province of Salta, serving as its
representative in the national congress and federal intervent-
or there; in April 1890 President Juárez Celman appointed
him minister of finance in a final desperate effort to find a
way out of the financial crisis in which the government and
nation was involved; Uriburu offered a program of stern reform and fiscal responsibility along with the purging of the
banks of corrupt bank officers and practices; when Juárez refused to implement this program and to request the necessary resignations, Uriburu immediately resigned (June of that
year) and shortly afterward Juárez himself was forced out of
office; in 1898 Uriburu became senator from Salta and was
still serving in that capacity at the time of his death.

URIBURU, JOSE DE (1766-1831).   Hacendado; educator; patriot;
first of that surname to come to Argentina.
        Born in Vizcaya, Spain; came to Argentina and settled
in Salta as royal customs official; quickly became involved in
life of community; acquired lands and went into agriculture
and cattle-raising; married Manuela Hoyos y Aguirre, descendant of Francisco Aguirre, founder and first governor of
Santiago del Estero; supported the May Revolution and was
declared a patriot in heroic and eminent degree by the junta
of 1810; when his activities took him to Catamarca, he established a school in Valle Viejo that had long been needed and
requested; José de Uriburu and his wife Manuela founded a
large family whose members would include two presidents,
José Evaristo and José Félix, as well as independence fighters, political leaders in Salta and the nation, financial experts, and scholars and writers (see entries on individual
Uriburus for some of these).

URIBURU, JOSE EVARISTO (1831-1914).   Lawyer and statesman;
president of Argentine Republic, 1895-1898.
        Born in Salta of old, aristocratic family; began his
studies in Chuquisaca, then moved to Buenos Aires and received his doctor's degree in law (1854); while still a student,
he worked in government positions in the Buenos Aires ministries of government and of war; after his return to Salta he
served, like his father before him, as member of a provincial constituent congress and was elected to the legislature;
in 1855 he founded the newspaper El Comercio and the following year he became secretary of the Argentine embassy in
Bolivia and remained there in various posts until 1860; returned to Salta where he became minister of the interior
(1861-1862) and then was elected as representative to the
first national congress after the provinces had been reunited;
reelected in 1864 he acted as president of the chamber in
1866; during Mitre's absence in Paraguay, acting president
Marcos Paz appointed him minister of justice, worship, and
public instruction in 1867 where he served briefly; in 1871
President Sarmiento appointed him treasurer of the nation; a

term of two years as federal judge in Salta (1872-74) was followed by a diplomatic mission to Bolivia and then by several
years in Peru; going there in December 1876 to represent
Argentina at an American congress of jurists; returned to
Buenos Aires in 1881 but was invited back the following year
to assist in solving diplomatic and legal problems growing out
of the War of the Pacific; with permission of the Argentine
government, Uriburu accepted the invitation from Bolivia and
Chile to serve as arbitrator on the mixed commission created
by their truce; fulfilled this mission with considerable success and returned to Argentina; in 1892, after a period of
complicated political maneuvering, the Civic Union and National parties, under leadership of Mitre and Roca, put together a ticket with Luis Sáenz Peña for president and Uriburu for vice president that won the national elections; three
years later Sáenz Peña resigned and on January 22, 1895,
José Evaristo Uriburu became president.

Uriburu's administration is usually included with those
that strengthened the central power of government; with a
measure of political calm prevailing, he was able to make
several important contributions: peace was made over the
boundary with Chile; the army and navy were reorganized in
the continued program of professionalization; military port of
Bahía Blanca was constructed; new naval units and land defense equipment were acquired; the Museo de Bellas Artes in
Buenos Aires was established, along with the industrial school,
the school of commerce, and the faculty of philosophy and
letters at the university; the study of natural resources along
the Patagonia coast and other marine studies were promoted;
the second national census was taken; and financial arrangements between the railroads and the government were adjusted
to the latter's advantage; in the elections of 1898 Roca came
in again for his second term; Uriburu continued in public life
--presiding over the senate; acting as president in 1903 when
both president and vice president were away; became candidate of the Republican party for the presidency in 1904 but
was defeated by Manuel Quintana; in 1910, when nearly eighty
years old, retired to private life and died in Buenos Aires
four years later.

URIBURU, JOSE FELIX, General (1868-1932).   Career military
    officer; president of Argentine Republic, 1930-1931.
        Born in Salta; early decided on military career; gradu-
ated from military academy; saw varied military actions; became involved in military revolt of 1890; served in province
of Formosa; acted as aide to his uncle José E. Uriburu (q.v.)
in 1893 and to president Luis Sáenz Peña; in 1905 supported
Quintana in suppression of radical revolt; became director of
Escuela Superior de Guerra (War College) in 1907 and then
was sent to Europe to observe military training programs and
equipment there; returning to Buenos Aires he attended the
scientific congresses of the centennial celebration and then
saw duty, as general staff officer, in frontier posts; in 1913

he returned to Europe as military attaché to Germany and
England; returning to Argentina Uriburu was elected a deputy
from his province to the national congress, 1914; in 1921 he
was made a general of division; the following year was appointed inspector general of the army by President Alvear;
was a member of the Consejo Supremo de Guerra (National
Security Council) from 1926 until he was retired from it by
Yrigoyen for having reached the official age of retirement.

On September 6, 1930 (see Revolution of 1930), Uriburu overthrew Yrigoyen's bankrupt and confused administration and established a military dictatorship; recognized by the
supreme court as president, Uriburu dissolved congress, declared a state of siege, intervened in provinces, and generally attempted to establish an elitist authoritarian government; although he publicly vowed to respect the constitution,
he personally felt that the nation needed a return to conservative government, perhaps similar to those that he had seen in
Europe (Nazi and Fascist) but essentially Argentine; he found
it impossible to gain political support for this; meanwhile his
imprisonment of political prisoners, his censoring of newspapers, his intervention in the universities, and his other
actions--often directed against the radicals--as well as his
prejudices against democratic practices, weakened his public
support; other critics feared that he was attempting to destroy
the constitution and electoral laws and force imported government patterns on the nation; both civil and military leaders,
ambitious for political power themselves, feared him and his
proposed plans; after permitting free elections in Buenos
Aires early in 1931 and then repudiating the results because
the radicals won, he was reluctant to allow national elections
but in November, these were held and Uriburu's military rival for political power, General Agustín P. Justo, was
elected to the presidency; Uriburu went abroad for reasons
of health; died in Paris, a few months later, following surgery (see Military; Agustín P. Justo; UCR).

URIBURU, JOSEFA ALVAREZ DE ARENALES DE (1807-1890).   A
    "Dame of the Argentine Revolution."
        Born in Salta, daughter of General Juan Antonio Alva-
rez and Serafina de Hoyos y Torres; although very young,
she supported the war for independence in any way possible
to her, including the donation of her jewels toward the purchase of military equipment for the Army of the Andes; this
brought her the award of a medal and a citation from San
Martín; both as the daughter of Arenales, a fighter and political leader in Salta, and as wife of independence fighter Evaristo de Uriburu, Josefa was constantly involved in public affairs as well as personal and family ones; one of her sons,
José Evaristo, became president of Argentina (shortly after
her death in 1890) and another, Napoleón, became a general
and conqueror and governor of the Chaco.

URIBURU, JUAN ANTONIO DE (1767- ?).   Merchant and hero of

first British invasion (1806) of Buenos Aires.

Born in Vizcaya, Spain; he came to Argentina about
1794 to help his brother José de Uriburu with his business in
Salta; in Buenos Aires at the time of the first British invasion (q. v.), he took part in the city's defense as a captain in
the Asturian battalion; his stubborn courage in attempting to
keep the British from crossing the Riachuelo, in spite of the
hopelessness of the defense and his own commander's orders
to fall back toward the city, won the respect of his British
opponent, who returned his sword to him after his capture
as prisoner; he was also offered parole but he refused to
give the necessary promise not to fight the British again; imprisoned in the fort at Buenos Aires, Uriburu became the
subject of a fervent appeal to Beresford, the British commander, from leading citizens and matrons of the city; again
he was offered his freedom but he refused to accept it unless
his comrades were also freed; moved by this chivalry (and
doubtless as part of his purpose to win the good will of the
porteños), Beresford freed them all and the story has become
a part of Argentine folk history; eventually Uriburu settled
permanently in San Juan.

URIBURU, NAPOLEON (1838-1895).   Career military officer; campaigned against Indians in Chaco and Patagonia.

Born in Salta; joined militia while still a boy; took
part in many local Indian campaigns, beginning his rise in
military rank that ultimately (1883) made him a brigadier
general; fought in Paraguayan War under General Paunero;
took part in such battles as Yatay, Uruguayana, Sauce, and
Curupaytí; in 1870 began his expedition into the Chaco, crossing it that year from Salta to Corrientes; 11 Indian caciques
submitted to him, with result that thousands of Indian laborers were sent as laborers to sugar mills of Salta and Jujuy;
in 1875 he became governor of the Chaco territory; further
pacified Indians of that area by defeating chieftains Noiroidike
and Silketroique; in 1879, as colonel, he commanded the 4th
division of General Julio A. Roca's expedition to the Patagonian desert; became president of the military court; his
active participation in the revolution of 1890 brought him
temporary demotion but from 1891 to 1894 he served as governor of Formosa territory in the Chaco; died in Buenos
Aires.

URQUIZA, CIPRIANO JOSE DE (1789-1844).   Hacendado and public
figure.

Born in Gualeguaychú, Entre Ríos, brother of Justo
José; educated in Entre Ríos and Buenos Aires; returned to
work on family ranch; joined militia and was commissioned
as alférez (subaltern or second lieutenant) by Viceroy Cisneros; joined patriot cause; became a federalist during period
of Francisco Ramírez (q. v.); edited first Entre Ríos newspaper, La Gaceta Federal; represented Entre Ríos in constituent congress of 1826; later fought against Unitarist forces

of Juan Lavalle; became general minister for his brother
when Justo José became governor of Entre Ríos; was assassinated in Nogoyá (Entre Ríos), in 1844 while acting as governor.

URQUIZA, JUSTO JOSE DE (1801-1870). President of Argentine
   Confederation, 1854-1860; governor of province of Entre Ríos;
   general, estanciero, and statesman.
          Born October 18, 1801, in Talar del Arroyo Largo
   (today, Urquiza), just north of Concepción del Uruguay; son
   of José Narciso de Urquiza y Alzaga, a Spanish-born estanciero and merchant, and a porteña mother María Cándida
   García y González; educated in Buenos Aires at academy of
   San Carlos during years 1816-1818 when independence was
   declared and the form and direction of the new nation were
   being decided; returned to Concepción to go into business and
   trade (especially that in hides); largely as result of family
   relations with Francisco Ramírez (q. v.) he became involved
   in turbulent political life of Entre Ríos; joined Concepción
   militia as officer; in 1823 joined the elder López Jordán
   (with whose family Urquiza's had close relationships) in conspiracy to overthrow Governor Lucio Mansilla; sent into
   exile; lived one year in Curuzú Cuatiá in Corrientes, engaged
   in business and forming friendships that would later be useful; he returned to Entre Ríos and was serving as head of
   provincial legislature when it rejected the national constitution of 1826; in 1832 he agreed with Estanislao López, governor of Santa Fe, to accept Pascual Echagüe as governor of
   Entre Ríos (q. v.) in order to end the anarchy there.
          In 1836, Urquiza accompanied Echagüe to Buenos Aires
   and met with Juan Manuel de Rosas who placed him in command of federalist division of observation on the Uruguayan
   border; for the next fifteen years, Urquiza, always a Federalist by conviction, served Rosas as military officer and political ally; aided in defense of Paysandú (1837); during next
   few years civil wars of Uruguay and of Argentine provinces
   of Entre Ríos and Corrientes were bloodily entangled; Rosas
   supported Manuel Oribe and his followers in Uruguay and his
   opponent Fructuoso Rivera was backed by Unitarists; Juan
   Lavalle, José María Paz, and Rivera commanded the Unitarists while Oribe commanded Rosas' federalist forces and
   Urquiza rose in importance as Federalist leader; in 1841
   Urquiza succeeded Echagüe as governor of Entre Ríos but
   was forced to delegate his power and move across the Paraná
   with his troops when eastern Entre Ríos was invaded and occupied by Unitarist forces from Uruguay; Paraná was taken
   by General José María Paz; finally, by 1845, peace had been
   made with Corrientes (that had aided the Unitarists briefly)
   and, after defeat at Arroyo Grande had forced Rivera back
   to Uruguay in 1843, Urquiza invaded that country and inflicted final defeat on him at India Muerta, March 27, 1845;
   returning to Entre Ríos he found that province threatened
   again by Corrientes forces led by the Unitarist Madariagas

(see Joaquín Madariaga; Juan Madariaga) and General Paz;
the defeat of these forces by Urquiza, followed by peace
agreement, marked beginning of differences between him and
Rosas (who resented Urquiza's independence of action in the
treaty of Alcaraz); Urquiza appointed a friend, Benjamín Virasoro, as governor of Corrientes; having been reelected governor of Entre Ríos in December 1845, he now (1847) became
dominant political leader of Argentine Mesopotamia.

The final break between Urquiza and Rosas began in
1851 with his manifesto on May 1, stating that Entre Ríos
was reassuming its sovereign rights and issuing a call for
national reorganization at last; he proposed that the last part
of the Federalist motto "Long live the Argentine Confederation! Death to the Unitarian savages!" be changed to "Death
to the enemies of national organization!" Only Corrientes
backed him at this time; on May 29, 1851, an alliance was
signed between Brazil, Entre Ríos, and government of Montevideo against Oribe (Rosas' ally); Rosas responded by declaring war against Brazil; after Oribe had been forced to come
to terms, Urquiza brought his army back to Entre Ríos; on
December 24, 1851, he crossed the Paraná with his Ejército
Grande Libertador and approached Buenos Aires; at the historic battle of Caseros (q.v.), February 3, 1852, Rosas was
forced to acknowledge defeat and to resign; Urquiza now dedicated himself to task of forming a national organization; on
May 31, 1852, the Acuerdo de San Nicolás (see San Nicolás,
Acuerdo de) was signed by most of the provincial governors
making Urquiza Provisional Director of the Argentine Confederation and calling for a General Constituent Congress to
meet in Santa Fe in August; in September Buenos Aires province withdrew from the Confederation, partly out of suspicion
on part of returned exiles that Urquiza might be another dictator like Rosas, partly because many porteños felt that national organization should be carried out under leadership of
Buenos Aires, and partly because of the long-standing desire
of Buenos Aires to keep the customs revenues of the port for
its own province; while open hostilities continued to break
out, the representatives of the other Argentine provinces met
in Congress at Santa Fe and drew up the federal Constitution
of 1853 (q.v.); it was accepted by most of the provinces and
in 1854 Urquiza began a six-year term as first constitutional
president of Argentine Republic, with its capital in Paraná,
Entre Ríos.

As president, he signed a treaty with Spain, 1858, by
which Spain recognized Argentine independence, and established diplomatic relations; encouraged immigration and the
establishment of agricultural colonies, one in Santa Fe (Esperanza) and one in San José, Entre Ríos; signed free navigation treaty with Brazil, recognized Paraguay's independence;
nationalized the University of Córdoba; through his efforts
public instruction, commerce, production, industry, sciences
and arts, transportation and communications received extraordinary stimulation and progress was made throughout the

provinces; the problem of bringing Buenos Aires into the
Confederation seemed to be approaching solution in 1859 although certain Buenos Aires leaders demanded that, as a
condition, Urquiza would have to resign; political events in
province of San Juan, resulting in murder of Governor Bena-
videz, reopened conflict; in the battle of Cepeda October 23,
1859, President Urquiza inflicted crushing defeat on Buenos
Aires troops commanded by General Bartolomé Mitre; on
November 11, 1859, the Pact of National Union was signed
at San José de Flores by which Buenos Aires was to be incorporated into the Confederation; in 1860 Urquiza turned
over the presidency to newly-elected Santiago Derqui and
again became governor of Entre Ríos (1860-1864); continued
earlier efforts to complete the reintegration of Buenos Aires
into the Confederation but new hostilities broke out; at Pavón,
September 17, 1861, Mitre, then governor of Buenos Aires,
defeated Urquiza (who was accused of retiring unnecessarily
from the battle), a peace was signed in which Urquiza agreed
to retire to Entre Ríos and remain apart from national politics; and the national organization, for which Urquiza had
worked so hard, was effected, with Bartolomé Mitre elected
as first president and Buenos Aires as capital.

War with Paraguay posed serious problems for Urquiza who had long maintained close business and personal
ties with its leaders; he tried to use his influence with Francisco Solano López to prevent outbreak of war but was unsuccessful; after Corrientes was attacked by López, he came
out against Paraguay and supported the Argentine cause, in
spite of the war's unpopularity in Entre Ríos; provincial Federalists in Entre Ríos, led by the younger Ricardo López
Jordán were rising again against Buenos Aires; Urquiza was
accused of selling out to the porteños; when López Jordán
(q. v.) was proposed as governor in 1868, Urquiza feared his
influence would be used against new national organization and
secured the governorship for himself; he also supported Domingo Faustino Sarmiento, from San Juan but closely associated with exiled Buenos Aires Unitarists, for president; in
February 1870, Sarmiento visited Urquiza at his governor's
palace; on April 11, 1870, the forces of López Jordán assassinated Urquiza in his home and killed his sons, Justo
and Waldino, in Concordia; López Jordán became governor of
Entre Ríos until ousted by national forces; Urquiza was buried
in parochial church of Concepción del Uruguay; this church
became a national monument; after his death the Colegio del
Uruguay (q. v.) was nationalized and converted into the Colegio
Nacional Capitán General Justo José de Urquiza; in 1942 the
original building became a national monument.

Justo José Urquiza has been one of most controversial figures in Argentine history; many contemporary and early
histories were still colored by passions of Rosas' period;
nevertheless, his contributions as successful leader of overthrow of Rosas and of national reorganization under federal
constitution have always been recognized; more recently his

clear vision of the cultural and economic needs, as well as
the political ones, of his country and his contributions in all
these areas have come to be known; modern historians of his
era tend to emphasize also his contributions to education,
freedom of the press, economic development--as a life-time
merchant, entrepreneur, and leading estanciero, Urquiza's
personal economic interests and those of his country played
important role, along with his federalist convictions, in his
insistence on both national organization and Buenos Aires' inclusion in it (see Entre Ríos, Urquiza's native province, with
which his career was so closely related and that formed
basis for his success in reuniting the nation).

     See writings of Beatriz Bosch on Urquiza and related
topics, especially her comprehensive, well-written, scholarly
Urquiza y su tiempo (Buenos Aires, 1971); Manuel E. Mac-
chi, Urquiza, el saladerista (Córdoba, 1971), invaluable study
of Urquiza as entrepreneur, landowner, and one of Argentina's most successful businessmen; Adolfo Saldías, ¿Cómo
surgió Urquiza? (Buenos Aires, 1973), taken from Saldías'
classic history of Argentine Confederation (5 v., Historia de
Rosas y su época, Paris, 1881-1887); and James R. Scobie,
La lucha por la consolidación, 1852-1862 (Buenos Aires,
1964); other studies include Juan A. González Calderón, El
General Urquiza y la organización nacional (Buenos Aires,
1940); Luis A. Calderón, Urquiza (Buenos Aires, 1949).

URQUIZA Y ALZAGA, JOSEF (1762-1829).   Estanciero; founder of
    Urquiza family estates in Entre Ríos.

     Born in Santander, Spain, he came to Buenos Aires at
the age of eleven to live with his uncle Mateo Ramón de
Alzaga y Sobrado, an alcalde and merchant in that city; during the next fifteen years he worked there, married a porteña, María Cándida García, and had his first three children;
in 1789 he became a pioneer rancher along the Uruguay river
in Entre Ríos establishing himself and his family at La Cen-
tella in Gualeguaychú, where his other children, including
Justo José (later to become first president of the Argentine
Confederation) were born; in 1794 he purchased royal land
near Concepción del Uruguay and began the ranch of San
José; in 1800 became an alcalde in cabildo of Concepción del
Uruguay; appointed by the viceroy as commander of the Entre
Ríos militia, he organized its forces to go to Montevideo to
fight the British (1807) but was unable to accompany them
there; signed the document by which the cabildo of Concep-
ción recognized the authority of the first patriot junta in
Buenos Aires; remained in Entre Ríos through the rule of
Francisco Ramírez (with whom Urquizas were related) but in
1822, when General Lucio Mansilla was appointed governor,
Urquiza returned to Buenos Aires where he died and was
buried in the Recoleta cemetery; thirty years later Justo
José brought his father's remains back to Entre Ríos and
placed them in the family crypt in the church of the Immacu-
late Conception in Concepción del Uruguay.

URUGUAY   see   BANDA ORIENTAL; MONTEVIDEO

URUGUAY, RIO. This river (its name meaning river of birds)
    forms the eastern boundary of Argentina, separating Entre
    Ríos and Corrientes from Uruguay and Brazil; about 612 km.
    in length, it rises in the Santa Catarina mountains of south-
    eastern Brazil and then flows westward and southwestward to
    empty in the Río de la Plata; it is not easily navigable be-
    tween Monte Caseros and Concordia but its falls could be
    used as source of hydroelectric power; the volume of water
    in the river varies greatly; it contains hundreds of small
    islands whose ownership was decided by treaty in 1961 be-
    tween Argentina and Brazil; between this river and the Pa-
    raná on the west lies the Argentine Mesopotamia; Argentine
    ports on the river include, from north to south, Paso de los
    Libres, Monte Caseros, Concordia, and Concepción del Uru-
    guay; during the earlier colonial period the Paraná and Para-
    guay carried most of the commerce from north to Buenos
    Aires but in eighteenth century, trade shifted to the Uruguay
    with the wealthy mission commerce coming down it to Buenos
    Aires; much of early Entre Ríos settlement and development
    came along this river and its two great leaders, Ramírez
    and Urquiza came from families with estates along it; since
    1853 the river has been declared free to all navigation; as
    part of the Pan American Highway a bridge, built by joint
    action of Argentina and Brazil, connects Paso de los Libres
    (Corrientes) and Uruguiana in Brazil.

URUGUAYAN PROBLEM (1864).   Considered immediate cause of
    Paraguayan War (q. v.).

USHUAIA. Southernmost city in Argentina; old penal colony, free
    port; became historical site in 1943 (see Tierra del Fuego).

USPALLATA, PASS OF. Natural pass across the Andes that pro-
    vided shortest, widest, most direct route from Mendoza,
    Argentina, to the Valley of Aconcagua in central Chile; used
    by San Martín for the movement of the vanguard of his Army
    of the Andes, commanded by Juan Gregorio Las Heras, on
    its first stage of the continental liberation project (see Andes,
    Crossing of the).

- V -

VACCINATION (for smallpox). Although vaccination was formally
    introduced into Río de la Plata by Charles IV in 1807, con-
    siderable use of it had been made before that time through
    work of Dr. Miguel O'Gorman and the Protomedicato (qq. v.);
    in 1805, a Portuguese slaver had arrived in Buenos Aires
    with two young blacks injected with fresh vaccines and "in
    excellent condition for the transmission of the desired pro-
    phylactic against smallpox"; a few days later Doctor García

Valdez and Silvio Gaffarot were able to show viceroy Sobremonte the first vaccines; Dr. Cosme Argerich and others offered their services and within a few weeks hundreds of children were inoculated, giving rise to the claim that Antonio
Machado Carvalho, owner of the slaves involved, deserved
credit as introducer of vaccination into Argentina; in 1810 the
patriot junta made vaccination compulsory but the regulation
was often ignored; meanwhile vaccine, imported from London,
became plentiful enough to be distributed into the interior;
San Martín personally paid the salaries of those sent to give
the vaccine in Mendoza; in 1821 Bernardino Rivadavia established official department of vaccination; during next few
years considerable progress was made toward eradication of
smallpox in Buenos Aires and the London Vaccination Institute elected both Rivadavia and Madera, administrator of
Buenos Aires vaccination program, as honorary members;
during Rosas' administration situation changed; imported
British vaccines were expensive and sometimes (during
British blockade, particularly) impossible to secure; through
work of Dr. Francisco Javier Muñiz (q.v.) Argentina developed its own source of vaccine; in 1880 the Vaccine Administration became part of the Public Assistance and Sanitary Administration under control of federal government; vaccination came to be required for every child reaching age
five (see Epidemics of Disease; Smallpox).

VALLE, ARISTOBULO DEL (1845-1896).   Lawyer; a major political leader of young leftists from 1870s through revolution of
1893; eloquent orator in Congress and in public; effective political writer; early nationalist and spokesman of growing
middle class.
        Born in Dolores, province of Buenos Aires; graduated
from law school, University of Buenos Aires, after having
interrupted his studies to fight in Paraguayan War; his thesis
was written on the subject of federal intervention in provincial territory, a problem that concerned him throughout his
career; early entered political life as follower of Adolfo Alsina; engaged in journalism with Sarmiento on El Nacional;
elected to legislature of province and to national congress;
served as minister of government in provincial administration of Barros and of Casares; elected to national senate in
1876 he became known as one of its most eloquent orators;
served as provisional president of the senate in 1880-1881,
in line to succeed to the presidency, if it should become va-
cant; made trip to Europe in 1885 and returned to take his
seat in senate; took active role in revolution of 1890 against
President Juárez Celman, resigning his seat in the senate
to do so; reelected the following year; helped form the Unión
Cívica Radical; agreed to form a cabinet for President Luis
Sáenz Peña to satisfy Radical demands; served briefly as
minister of interior, war and navy, and finance; taught constitutional law in faculty of law, Buenos Aires, and was engaged in writing a text for this subject at time of his death

in Buenos Aires.

VALLE, MARIA REMEDIOS (d. 1847). Black heroine of independence; called the "mother of her country" in Argentine folklore.
Born in Buenos Aires; she accompanied her husband
and two sons in the Auxiliary Army to fight the royalists in
the interior and northwestern provinces (1810); as a combat-
ant she fought in such engagements as Desaguadero, Tucumán, Salta, Vilcapugio, and Ayohuma; wounded six times,
captured and held as prisoner, she returned always to fight
in the patriot lines; her husband and sons were killed in battle; after independence had been won, an effort was begun
(1827) to recognize her services with the rank of captain and
an adequate pension but it dragged on for years and finally
passed too late to help her; she died in poverty.

VAN DER MEEREN, FELIPE (in Spanish, Felipe de la Laguna)
(1667-1707). Missionary and martyr. Young Belgian Jesuit
who arrived in Chile with group of missionaries near close
of 17th century shortly after the ill-fated mission at Nahuel
Huapi had been abandoned; having served as missionary for
some time in Chiloé, he eventually crossed the Andes and,
with Juan José Guillermo, reestablished Father Nicolás Mascardi's mission there in 1703; died four years later as result of poisoning by Indian cacique (see Neuquén).

VANDOR, AUGUSTO (d. 1969). Leader of metallurgical trade union
who acquired considerable power over other unions; represented neo-Peronism; favored conciliatory policies toward
government in 1960s; his assassination at his office in June,
1969, was one of most shocking acts during violence of labor
protest against Onganía's government.

VANGUARDIA, LA. Socialist newspaper founded in 1894 by Juan
B. Justo; has continued to serve as organ of the Socialist
Party.

VAQUERIAS. Organized roundups of wild cattle during colonial
period that formed the basis for the hide and tallow trade.
An expedition of hunters would secure permission from local
cabildo to round up the wild cattle, kill them, strip off the
hides and tallow and deliver them to the waiting ship captains at established prices; the gauchos, who shared in the
profits, would surround the wild herd, move in on it to hamstring the animals with a curved knife on the end of a lance
(known as the dejarretadero, or hamstringer), eighteen to
twenty men could handle 700-800 animals per hour; later they
would kill them and remove hides and tallow; during the
eighteenth century this trade peaked; then the herds began to
disappear so rapidly that in 1796 they were placed under
regulation by the viceregal government (see Hides and Skins;
Saladeros).

VARELA, FELIPE (1821-1870).   Andean caudillo from Catamarca;
led montoneras of 1860s.
        Born in Catamarca, Varela associated himself in the
early 1840s with the unitarists opposing Rosas; went with them
into Chile where he joined the Chilean army; after the fall of
Rosas in 1852, he returned to Argentina and joined the Confederation army; fought under Urquiza at Pavón; in 1862 he
joined El Chacho (General Angel Vicente Peñaloza, q.v.) in
his revolt against national authorities in Buenos Aires; as
El Chacho's protégé he was appointed chief of police in La
Rioja; invaded Catamarca in 1863, and fought in various battles such as Las Playas and Lomas Blancas; after the assassination of El Chacho, Varela took refuge in Entre Ríos,
serving again under Urquiza; then went back to Chile; Varela
had become a confirmed federalist and opponent of the Buenos
Aires government, then under President Bartolomé Mitre
and the revised constitution of 1853; as such he now became
the successor to El Chacho and leader of the revolt of the
Andean provinces against Mitre's government that they considered to be threatening their traditional, as well as their
new constitutional, provincial rights; from 1867 to 1869 Varela, assisted by such caudillos as the Saás of San Luis, Videla of Mendoza, and others, kept the northwest in turmoil;
his forces consisted of some Chileans and Argentine montoneros using violence freely to accomplish their goals; for a
time, 1867-1868, Varela was governor of Catamarca, and influential in power politics in the neighboring provinces, especially Salta and Jujuy; he and his montoneros have been
accused historically, especially by their enemies on the
coast, of committing all sorts of atrocities; to these accusations was added that of treason, as Varela increased his
military activities against the government during the Paraguayan War--which he and his followers opposed; Mitre was
forced to divert soldiers from Paraguay, even to return,
himself, to put down Varela's threat to national security and
authority; the latter's "lances and spears"--i.e., traditional
but antiquated weapons--proved no match for Mitre's more
modern military equipment and fire-power; the revolt was
defeated; Varela lost the battle of Salinas to Pedro Corvalán,
January 12, 1869, and, already ill, went back into Chilean
exile for the last time; died there in 1870.
        Felipe Varela has been called the last of the nine-
teenth century montoneros and his death marks the end of an
era--an era actually brought to a close by the introduction in
the 1870s of the railroads and telegraph lines linking the
west more closely to the coast and the increased use of
barbed wire fences and other innovations, all combining to
diminish economic and political differences between the interior and Buenos Aires; consequently modern Argentine historians tend to regard Varela as a political leader, the last
in the line of Artigas, Ramírez, Quiroga, Chacho Peñaloza,
all of whom resisted the political organization of the nation
from the federal capital at Buenos Aires (see Montoneros;

also entries on Andean provinces involved).
See Francisco Centeno, Las montoneras. Invasión a
Salta por el célebre montonero Felipe Varela (1921).

VARELA, FLORENCIO (1807-1848). Buenos Aires writer exiled
to Montevideo by Rosas; came to be unitarist spokesman most
greatly feared by Argentine dictator.
Born in Buenos Aires, brother of Juan Cruz Varela;
early attracted attention by the purity of his style in writing;
worked as newspaperman on several journals; received appointment in government of Rivadavia; graduated from Buenos
Aires law school in 1827; went into exile in Montevideo following overthrow of Rivadavia's government (1828); in Uruguay
Varela joined other Argentine unitarist intellectuals and writers in opposing Rosas by writing and by action; became influential member of the Comisión Argentina (q. v.); in the early
1840s he left Uruguay for two trips: in 1841-1842 he spent
several months in Rio de Janeiro for his health and in gathering documentation for a history of Argentina; he worked much
of the time there with Bernardino Rivadavia, who turned over
many valuable historical materials to him, some of which
were lost in shipwreck when Varela returned to Montevideo;
in 1843 he undertook for the Uruguayan government a diplomatic mission to England and France (where he also visited
San Martín); upon his return to Montevideo he began the
Comercio del Plata, first issue October 1, 1845, that rapidly became the newspaper most feared and hated by Rosas; on
March 20, 1848, Florencio Varela was stabbed to death in
the doorway of his home by Andrés Cabrera, believed to have
been acting for Manuel Oribe and Rosas.
See Leoncio Gianello, Florencio Varela (Buenos Aires,
1948).

VARELA, HECTOR FLORENCIO (1832-1891). Writer and journalist; traveler.
Born in Montevideo, eldest son of Florencio Varela;
unlike his brothers he did not return to his parents' homeland, Argentina, to make his life's career; instead he served
Uruguay in several official capacities, traveled widely
throughout South America and Europe, as private citizen, or
as diplomat, always interested in the political scene, always
writing vigorously about it and always fighting tyranny; his
chief contribution to Argentina was in the field of journalism
to which he brought new force and standards; cooperated with
his brother Mariano in the establishing of newspaper La
Tribuna in 1853; Héctor Varela died in Rio de Janeiro in
1891, a victim of yellow fever.

VARELA, JUAN CRUZ (1794-1839). One of first national poets;
journalist; prominent unitarist.
Born in Buenos Aires; sent to study at the Monserrat
academy in Córdoba, in the hope that he would become a
priest; he preferred to write; became one of the first poets

to celebrate in good literary style the achievements of the
revolution for independence; was elected a member of the
general congress in 1816; held a government post under Governor Rodríguez; wrote for several newspapers and edited El
Porteño, El Mensajero Argentino, El Tiempo, and El Pampero; supported Rivadavia's reforms in his articles; strongly
unitarist in his sympathies, he apparently backed Lavalle
against Dorrego and was among those who advised harsh
treatment of the latter in order to stamp out federalism;
instead, Rosas came into power, and Varela emigrated to
Uruguay; there he continued to write--newspaper articles,
poetic diatribes against Rosas, and two classic tragedies;
died in Montevideo after ten years in exile.

VARELA, LUIS V. (1845-1911).   Constitutional lawyer and his-
    torian.
        Born in Montevideo, younger son of Florencio Varela;
graduated in law from the university at Córdoba; held appointments in provincial courts of Buenos Aires as well as
federal courts; served as member and secretary for the reforming congress of the constitution of Buenos Aires; wrote
for his family's paper La Tribuna; also published several
volumes of constitutional history, as well as other historical
and legal works; died in Buenos Aires in 1911.

VARELA, MARIANO (1834-1902).   Jurisconsult; journalist; and
    public figure.
        Born in Montevideo, younger son of Florencio Varela;
graduated in law from the university at Córdoba; held appointments in provincial courts of Buenos Aires as well as
federal courts; served as member and secretary for the reforming congress of the constitution of Buenos Aires; wrote
for his family's paper La Tribuna; also published several
volumes of constitutional history, as well as other historical
and legal works; died in Buenos Aires in 1911.

VARELA, MARIANO (1834-1902).   Jurisconsult; journalist; and
    public figure.
        Born in Montevideo, son of Florencio Varela; came to
Argentina in 1852 to fight against Rosas at Caseros; became
active in public life of Buenos Aires province during its
separation from the other provinces; with his brothers he
founded La Tribuna in 1853, considered for thirty years to
be best newspaper in the country; acted as secretary in the
legislature and as minister of finance for Governor Alsina;
in the reunited republic he served as foreign minister for
President Sarmiento in the early period of the difficult negotiations following the Paraguayan war; later joined the
Unión Cívica Nacional and was elected senator in 1892; he
resigned this position in protest against a senate action regarding university degrees that he considered illegal and devoted himself to his legal practice; in 1901 President Roca
appointed him president of the court of appeals; Varela died

the following year in Buenos Aires.

VARELA, RUFINO (1815-1840). Journalist. Born in Buenos
Aires, brother of Florencio and Juan Cruz Varela; spent his
brief life writing and fighting against the federalism of Dorrego and Rosas; was killed while accompanying General Juan
Lavalle in his campaign into the Argentine interior.

VARELA, RUFINO (1838-1911). Journalist and government official.
Son of Florencio Varela, born in Montevideo; collaborated
with his brothers in editorship of La Tribuna; spent considerable time abroad in the 1870s; served as minister of finance for Buenos Aires province and then held same position
in cabinet of President Juárez Celman; later served in both
provincial and national legislative bodies and as administrator in the national tax division.

VARELA, RUFINO (1862-1939). Engineer; pioneer in Argentine
electronics.
         Born in Buenos Aires of Argentine father and Ameri-
can mother; began his career as apprentice in the workshops
of the Western Railroad; became assistant chief engineer for
the Southern Railroad as it was being extended to Bahía
Blanca; in 1888 he began operation of a small power plant to
supply electric power to about 100 neighbors; he provided
electric illumination of Calle Florida (heart of business district in Buenos Aires), was responsible for the power plant
that furnished electricity for the 1910 centennial celebration
of the May Revolution; went to Europe to study the telephone
system more thoroughly; returned to develop a microtelephone
that was adopted by the Ericsson factory; became manager of
the telephone company in 1930; promoted the various uses of
electricity throughout the republic; finally became vice president of the German Compañía Transatlántica of electric
power; died in Buenos Aires.

VARELA Y ULLOA, JOSE (1748-1794). Spanish ship captain whose
unusual knowledge of mathematics, astronomy, and geography
brought him a royal appointment as head of the first part of
the first division of the Spanish boundary commission appointed following the treaty of 1777 between Spain and Portugal; Captain Varela's special task was to determine the exact location of Montevideo and Buenos Aires in the surveying
of the boundary between Brazil and the Río de la Plata; during his various voyages to this area, he also drew up hydro-
graphical charts of the southern Brazilian coastal waters and
islands and the ports of the Río de la Plata; in 1794, in command of a Spanish naval squadron, he died in Havana, after
having transported a division of troops there.

VARGAS, PEDRO. One of San Martín's ablest spies in his preparation for crossing the Andes into Chile. A prosperous
farmer in Mendoza; Vargas gave up almost everything that

he had to aid in the fight for independence; posing as an out-
spokenly loyal Spaniard, he suffered many imprisonments in
Mendoza but established his credibility with the Spanish commander in Chile, Marcó del Pont, who was misled by his
letters purporting to reveal San Martín's plans for invasion;
when Vargas' wife threatened to divorce him for his Spanish
sympathies and actions, San Martín personally revealed the
closely guarded secret to her; almost no one else was aware
of Vargas' role and actual allegiance; in 1819, with Chile
freed, San Martín felt that his personal sacrifices were no
longer necessary and publicly vindicated him and made him a
lieutenant colonel in his army.

VASENA, ADALBERT KRIEGER   see   KRIEGER VASENA, ADAL-
BERT

VECINO, VECINOS.   Although in modern times the term "vecino"
means variously citizen, resident, or neighbor--as in the
Buen Vecino (Good Neighbor) policy--in the Argentine colonial
period it usually referred to a member of the ruling class of
a community in the Spanish legally stratified social pattern;
below the vecinos were domiciliados and the estantes; the
status was greatly desired, as only vecinos could vote or
hold office, expect to be invited to a cabildo abierto (open
town meeting), or--and this was very important economically
during seventeenth and eighteenth centuries--take part in the
vaquerías (q. v.); they were also responsible for the defense
of the community and expected to provide substitutes for this
service during any absence.
        See Ricardo Levene, Historia del derecho argentino
(volume I, Buenos Aires, 1945).

VEDIA, AGUSTIN DE (1843-1910).   Influential writer on public affairs.
        Born in Montevideo, he was brought to Buenos Aires
by his family; fought at Cepeda, he began his long journalistic
career with a literary review, El Iris, in 1859, then contributed to La Reforma Pacífica, founded by Nicolás Calvo on
the eve of Pavón; joined with Carlos Guido Spano in founding
La América February 1, 1866; this was closed a few months
later and its editors deported for having published and criticized harshly the secret treaty of the Triple Alliance; after
Sarmiento became president, Vedia and his associates resumed publication of La América; in the early 1870s he became actively involved in Uruguayan politics and for about a
dozen years shuttled back and forth between Argentina and
Uruguay, with a brief period of exile in Havana and the
United States; in 1885 he settled down in Buenos Aires and,
with his son Mariano de Vedia (q. v.), founded La Tribuna
Nacional (later known as Tribuna); in 1891 Vedia became an
editor of La Prensa; he also contributed to La Nación; died
in Buenos Aires.
        Vedia was not interested in holding public office or

responsibility but throughout his life he used his pen, in both
articles and more formal works, to educate the people about
public affairs and to attempt to shape public opinion politically. Among his longer works are: Historia financiera de
la República Argentina; La constitución argentina; Historia
del Banco Nacional; Martín García y la jurisdicción del Plata;
La neutralidad; La nación y las provincias; Soberanía y justicia.

VEDIA, MARIANO DE (1867-1941). Politician and journalist.
          Born in Buenos Aires; early entered newspaper work;
in 1884 he was working on La Nación and the following year
assisted his father Agustín Vedia in founding La Tribuna Nacional; served as private secretary to Bernardo de Irigoyen
during his period as minister of interior; after the fall of
Juárez Celman, he became secretary for General Julio A.
Roca, whose friend, adviser, and biographer he later became;
founded and became editor of El Nacional which became the
voice of the Partido Autonomista Nacional; served as national
congressman for several terms between 1896 and 1922, continuing his newspaper work in the meantime, especially with
El País and La Mañana; published several books, the best
known of which is his biographical study Roca, published in
Paris.

VEDIA, NICOLAS DE (1771-1852). Military hero of independence
     and early national period of Argentina; Uruguayan general.
          Born in Montevideo, then part of Río de la Plata
jurisdiction; early entered military career; captured during
the British invasions and sent to England; fought against Napoleon's troops in Spain; returned to Río de la Plata in time
to be member of Buenos Aires cabildo abierto of May 1810
that established first patriot junta and was among those who
voted to depose Viceroy Cisneros; Cornelio Saavedra, head
of new junta, appointed him his aide-de-camp; Vedia fought
in the war for independence, taking part in the first two
sieges of Montevideo against royalist control, fighting under
Belgrano and San Martín; in 1816 Director Pueyrredón sent
him to try to persuade General Lecor to withdraw his Portuguese-Brazilian troops from Uruguay but his mission was not
successful; in the anarchy of 1819 he supported Governor
Sarratea; in 1820 was minister of war; his later support of
Alvear brought him demotion in the army and he retired to
Montevideo to write his memoirs, but was called back into
active service; General Mansilla named him his minister in
1822; in 1828 he served under Dorrego; in 1834 Rosas placed
him on retirement and he returned to Montevideo where his
rank was restored and he resumed active duty, maintaining
close ties with other anti-Rosas persons; his daughter Delfina, married Bartolomé Mitre (future general and president
of Argentina); during the 1840s Vedia placed all his military
skill and experience at the disposal of those fighting Rosas;
directed building of fortifications to defend the besieged city

in 1843 (see Great War); the distinguished general later
served as president of the military court, head of the Council
of War and in 1852 was performing the duties of chief of
staff of Uruguayan forces; died that year in Montevideo.

VEDIA DE MITRE, DELVINA MARIA LUISA (1821-1882). Poet
and translator; wife of Bartolomé Mitre.

Born in Buenos Aires, daughter of General Nicolás de
Vedia and Manuela Josefa Pérez Castellano, said to have been
descended from Alfonso III of Portugal and the Inca Huayna
Capac; while living with her father in anti-Rosas exile in
Montevideo Delfina met and married Bartolomé Mitre who
was a captain of artillery there; in addition to her busy public life, as wife of prominent political and military figure
and her personal family concerns, she became a writer of
note; as translator she made several French and English
works available for the first time in Spanish, including a biography of George Washington and history of the United
States; among her poems were Los últimos momentos de mi
madre and Sobre las golondrinas; her personal diary includes
material about Mitre that is useful to historians; she died in
Buenos Aires.

VEDIA Y MITRE, MARIANO DE (1881-1958). Historian; writer
and professor.

Born in Buenos Aires where he studied law and social
sciences at the university; taught in national school of commerce (1905); served as supervisor of secondary schools
(1909-1911); and rector of the Colegio Bernardino Rivadavia
(1910-1916); held various advanced academic appointments,
including that of professor of history at the University of
Buenos Aires following 1908; represented his university at
many national and international academic congresses; Vedia
y Mitre held memberships in the Argentine academy of arts
and in the national academy of history; also received other
Argentine and foreign academic honors; he was active as writer or editor for many of the Buenos Aires periodicals, including his work as a contributor to La Nación.

Among his published works of greatest historical interest are: El Deán Funes en la historia argentina (1909;
also 1955); Derecho constitucional argentino (1921); La carta
de Mayo (1925); La revolución del 90 (1929); La vida de
Monteagudo (3 v. Buenos Aires, 1950); and Historia de la
unidad nacional (1953).

VEGA, AGUSTIN JUSTO DE LA (1805-1879). Lawyer and public
official.

Born in La Rioja of an old and prominent family;
graduated in law from university of Córdoba; with Salustiano
Zavalía appealed unsuccessfully to Governor Celedonia Gutiérrez (Tucumán) to spare Juan C. Alvarez, Mariano Villagrá, and Manuel Guerra from execution for supporting Urquiza against Rosas; served as governor of Tucumán, 1856-

57; during this period the provincial constitution was adopted, and an important program of public works, including cabildo building, public jail, hospital, the San Martín colegio, public irrigation canals, police headquarters, etc., was undertaken; earlier (1855) Vega had served as Urquiza's minister of finance and was national senator, 1858-1863; became a federal judge in Tucumán, 1863; died there sixteen years later.

VEGA, NICOLAS (1790-1879). Spanish officer who fought in Army of the Andes.
        Born in Granada, entered military career; fought against Napoleonic forces invading Spain; after restoration of Ferdinand VII found himself unpopular in Spain because of his liberal views; came to Buenos Aires and was sent to join San Martín's Army of the Andes; fought in battles of Cancha Rayada and Maipú and campaign of southern Chile; sent across to Andes to San Juan by San Martín to train recruits, Vega became involved and seriously wounded in the uprising led by Mendizábal, Corro, and Morillo (September 1820) and was unable to carry out further military assignments for a while; after several years of turbulent involvement in politics of San Juan, he went into exile, finally going into mining in Copiapó, Chile, where he was so successful that he was able to aid many anti-Rosas exiles; traveling in France, he received news of Caseros; immediately sent congratulations to Urquiza and returned to Argentina but did not reenter public life; died in Buenos Aires.

VEGA, URBANO DE LA. Military officer, closely associated with General Juan Bautista Molina (q.v.); Col. Vega was one of early leaders of GOU (q.v.) conspiracy that took over national government in 1943; engaged in later conspiracies that resulted in his being placed on inactive list with other militant nationalists; pardoned by President Ramón S. Castillo and given assignment in military intelligence.

VEGA BELGRANO, CARLOS (1858-1930). Journalist; public figure.
        Born in Buenos Aires, grandson of General Manuel Belgrano; studied at universities of Paris, Heidelberg, and Bonn; in 1875 founded El Plata Literario with Gregorio Uriarte; was attached to Argentine legation in Berlin, 1885, and served as consul general, 1886-1891; returned to Buenos Aires; founded and edited El Tiempo, 1893-1913; unsuccessful candidate several times for congressman; in 1907 he became librarian at the university in La Plata and served from 1907 to 1915 on the provincial council of education; wrote regularly for several periodicals; received many honors in educational and journalistic cricles; in 1890 he published two volumes, entitled Pensamientos, in Hamburg, that received favorable European comment.

VEGA DIAZ, DARDO DE LA (1895-1951). Historian of La Rioja; educator.

Born in La Rioja; after receiving his education and
having taught in the national academy in Chivilcoy (Buenos
Aires), he returned to his native province in 1923; spent the
rest of his life in educational work there, as teacher, dean,
and rector of the national academy in La Rioja, and writing
about the history of the province; founder and president of
the Junta de historia y letras of La Rioja; among his historical works are: Mitre y el Chacho (1939); Historia de La
Rioja in the Historia de la nación argentina (1942); Supersticiones riojanas (1945); Indianismos riojanos (1945) and many
others.

VELAZCO Y HUIDOBRO, BERNARDO DE (d. c. 1822).   Last Spanish governor of Paraguay.   Spanish military officer appointed
governor of the 30 mission towns in 1803; three years later
he was transferred to Asunción as intendant-governor; in 1807
he fought valiantly in defense of Buenos Aires against second
British invasion; when Asunción was asked to join the May
1810 Revolution the general assembly called by Velazco refused, and the governor immediately organized the army that
forced Belgrano's expedition, early in 1811, to return unsuccessfully to Buenos Aires; later that year Paraguay declared
its independence, deposed Velazco, established its own patriot government; after living for several years in retirement
and poverty, Velazco, along with many other resident Spaniards, was imprisoned by the dictator Francia; after about
eighteen months died in prison from hardships suffered there.

VELEZ SARSFIELD, DALMACIO (1800-1875).   Jurisconsult; statesman; author of Argentine civil code.
Born in Amboy, province of Córdoba; studied at Convento de San Francisco, Córdoba, and in Buenos Aires; represented province of San Luis at Unitarist Congress, 1824-
1827, and defended Rivadavia's policy of federalization of
Buenos Aires as capital; was already attracting attention because of his learning and talents; carried out mission to Cuyo
in behalf of new Unitarist constitution but the fall of Rivadavia's government in 1827 ended his public career for a
quarter of a century; remained in Argentina during most of
Rosas' period practicing, teaching, and writing about law; as
an authority in legal relationships between Church and State,
he was consulted by Rosas on several occasions in matters
dealing with the church; in 1835 became president of Academy
of Jurisprudence; in 1842 moved to Montevideo where he renewed his contacts with his friend from Córdoba, the Unitarist general José María Paz; met for the first time Domingo F. Sarmiento, on his way from Chile to Europe, with
whom he would later work; returned to Argentina to find his
properties occupied by strangers and almost destroyed but
they were returned to him by Rosas; after Caseros, Vélez
Sársfield joined with Bartolomé Mitre in opposing the Acuerdo de San Nicolás that agreed to calling of a congress to
provide constitution for national reorganization under Urquiza's

leadership; joined with Carlos Tejedor to draw up constitution for Buenos Aires province as a separate state; supported Buenos Aires government and in 1860 served on committee to frame amendments desired by Buenos Aires to Santa Fe constitution of 1853 before reunion could take place; became minister of finance in cabinet of Bartolomé Mitre (1862-1863); his commercial code, drawn up for Buenos Aires, was·nationalized in 1863; he was minister of interior in Sarmiento's cabinet (1868-1872); his great work was the drawing up of Argentina's Civil Code, begun in 1864 and completed in 1871; Congress adopted it without debate; Dr. Vélez Sársfield died in Buenos Aires.

See Joaquín V. González, Estudio biográfico-crítico de Vélez Sársfield, v. 22 in his Obras completas, and Abel Chaneton, Historia de Vélez Sársfield (2 v., Buenos Aires, 1937).

Vélez Sársfield's work Derecho público eclesiástico en relación al estado, written during Rosas period, was published in 1854 and a new edition appeared in 1919 under direction of Ricardo Rojas; among other writings was his Rectificaciones históricas: Belgrano y Güemes in which he defends contribution of interior provinces in fight against Spanish rule, and his translation of Virgil's Aeneid.

VENANCOURT, OFFENSIVE OF VISCOUNT OF.   French attack on Argentine vessels in Buenos Aires port May 21, 1829.   On April 1, 1829, Governor Juan Lavalle decreed that foreigners resident in Argentina should be subject to military service; British were exempted by treaty of 1825; the battalion Amigos del Orden was created, with French predominating; the French consul-general, M. Juan Washington de Mendeville protested; the Viscount Cornette de Venancourt, in command of a French squadron arrived in Buenos Aires to discuss with the French consul "the critical position of the French citizens"; together, they conferred with Minister José M. Díaz Vélez but were told that neither the naval commander nor consul general was authorized to deal with matters of diplomacy; also that the Argentine government was extending to the French residents the same protection and treatment that its own citizens received; Venancourt tried to persuade the French to refuse to serve in the militia, threatening them with loss of citizenship if they did but they ignored him; Venancourt departed for Montevideo to assemble larger naval force from French ships there and in Brazil; French protests and demands continued and Mendeville was asked to leave Buenos Aires; on night of May 21, 1829, French forces seized several Argentine ships and announced that they would hold them until the various French demands were met; one of Argentine ships was transporting about 200 prisoners captured at Vizcacheras; these were released; the negotiations that followed were long and complicated but ended amicably as France felt that Venancourt's action may have been hasty and based on inadequate

information and Rosas, about to begin his first period of rule,
having vanquished Lavalle, did not press charges; it was generally believed that Rosas had supplied the French ships with
large supplies of fresh meat and had turned their intervention
to his own advantage; Argentine ships were returned, along
with their crews and Venancourt departed.

VENCES, BATTLE OF   see   RINCON DE VENCES

VENDAJE. Commission of one real paid by bakers to the pulperías
for each peso's worth of bread sold by latter; after May Revolution, cabildo placed 50% tax on this, known as medio real
de vendaje, to increase municipal revenue; during next few
years price of bread rose rapidly, largely due to shortage
of flour and other causes, but public blamed high price on
tax and it was removed in 1821.

VENDIMIA. Annual festival in Mendoza that follows the gathering
of the grape harvest; as almost entire life of the area centers around grape and wine production, this is very important
national event with everyone in the community, from bodega
owner to grape-picker, taking part.

VENIALVO (spelled variously), LARAZO DE (d. 1580). Conquistador and martyr (see Revolution of the Seven Leaders).

VENTA Y MEDIA, BATTLE OF (October 21, 1815). Village in
Alto Perú (near Oruro, Bolivia) in which Spanish general
Joaquín de Pezuela defeated patriot forces commanded by
Martín Rodríguez; most of patriots were killed; it was in this
battle that José María Paz (q.v.) suffered loss of one arm.

VERA (Y ARAGON), ALONSO DE. Apparently there were several
conquistadors in the Río de la Plata area bearing this same
name, at least three of them related to the adelantado Juan
Torres de Vera y Aragón and named for their grandfather.
One was the son of the adelantado who has left various
records of his attempts to receive his full heritage. Another, Alonso de Vera, known as Cara del Perro (dog-face),
nephew of the adelantado, accompanied Juan de Garay to
Buenos Aires for its refounding in 1580; appointed lieutenant
governor of Asunción by his uncle at latter's departure, he
served until removed in 1592 by enforcement of audiencia's
rule that the adelantado could not use his relatives in such
positions without permission; during his administration, Alonso de Vera had founded the ill-fated town of Nuestra Señora
de la Concepción del Río de Bermejo, 1585, and had commissioned Ruy Díaz de Guzmán to occupy the area northeast
of Guairá (settlement of Santiago de Xérez founded finally in
1593 after Alonso de Vera was no longer governor). A
third Alonso de Vera, also a nephew of the adelantado, was
known as "El Tupí" to distinguish him from his cousin
conquistador in the same area at the same time; he prepared

the way for the foundation of the city of Corrientes and was
left there as lieutenant governor when his uncle returned to
Spain; he also took part in activities of the newly settled region.

VERA, FRANCISCO DE (1770-?).   Fighter for independence.
Born in Buenos Aires; became sergeant of infantry in
1782; was assigned to governor of Misiones in 1801; fought
against British invading in 1806-1807; in 1810 his political
activities with the patriots brought him into trouble with
Spanish authorities in Montevideo; sent to Cádiz in chains;
escaped to England and returned to Buenos Aires in 1812 on
the George Canning, with José de San Martín, Carlos M. de
Alvear, and others; took part in siege of Montevideo and
battle of Cerrito; appointed military commander of Patagonian
coast in 1814, with his base at Patagones; he quickly made
himself unpopular by his needless shooting of royalist commander Miguel Fernández del Olmo in 1815, his lack of command ability, and the ruthless way in which he sought to enrich himself as quickly as possible; complaints to the Buenos
Aires government brought his replacement and court martial;
Vera was released and returned to army; he was in trouble
again in 1820 when Dorrego imprisoned him as a friend of
Alvear; in 1822 Vera requested a discharge from the army
and disappeared from public scene.

VERA, JUAN CRUZ (1868-1950).   Lawyer and magistrate.
Born in La Rioja; took his degree, 1893, in School of
Law and Social Sciences, Buenos Aires; spent next three
years in Santiago del Estero as judge and legal attorney of
Bank of the Province; in 1896 he moved to Mendoza where
he lived for the rest of his life; served on court of appeals,
as member of city council, as district attorney, as
national senator from Mendoza, and as vice governor of the
province, 1935-1938; municipal intendant of city of Mendoza
(1939-1941); devoted much of his time to matters of industry
and of agriculture; taught poor children agricultural techniques
at his rural estate, Chacras de Coria, outside city of Mendoza; died in 1950.

VERA DEL PINO, RAFAELA (1753-1816).   Wife of Viceroy Joaquín del Pino, known affectionately, after his death, as the
Viceregal Dowager.
Born in Santa Fe, daughter of General Francisco Antonio de Vera y Mujica and Juana López Pintado; of royal
lineage through the Vera and Aragón families; as a lovely,
very wealthy, heiress she married Colonel Joaquín del Pino,
then military governor of Montevideo who, after serving in
royal assignments in Charcas and Chile, returned to Buenos
Aires in 1801 as viceroy; after her husband's death in 1804,
la Virreina Vieja, as she was generally called, remained in
Buenos Aires until her own death twelve years later.
In 1917 the historian Ramón J. Lassaga told her story
in a book entitled Una santafesina virreina del Río de la Plata.

VERA PEÑALOZA, ROSARIO (1873-1950). Woman educator and
writer, with two major interests: the training of teachers
for Argentina's new educational program and teaching Argentine children the story of their nation's winning of independence.

    Born in La Rioja of family linked to that province's
political and military history; taken as child to study in San
Juan; returned to La Rioja and studied in its normal school
under Mary Graham, one of U.S. teachers brought to Argentina by Sarmiento; completed her teacher's training at Normal
School in Paraná; took additional work in manual arts in
Córdoba and advanced courses in designs and crafts in Buenos
Aires; began her teaching career at Normal School of Paraná
in 1895; became vice-director of that of La Rioja and then,
in 1906, that of Córdoba, becoming director in 1910; in
Buenos Aires she was director of Escuela Normal de Pro-
fesoras (Normal School for Women Teachers) No. 1 Roque
Saenz Peña, 1912-1917, and director and founder of Escuela
Normal No. 9 Domingo F. Sarmiento; cooperated with Dr.
Carlos M. Biedma to establish the Argentine Model School;
her last educational work was the founding of the Museo Argentino para la Escuela Primaria in 1931 which she directed
until 1945; at the close of 1949 she installed her relief map
of South America in the Instituto Sanmartiniano de Buenos
Aires and conducted two or three tours there each week to
trace for school children the routes taken by the various liberating armies; died in La Rioja while on a visit there.

    Her writings were primarily on pedagogical subjects
but included some of "historical" interest, such as Lectura
del mapa en relieve de la República Argentina, Las seis ru-
tas del paso de los Andes, and La casa histórica de Tucumán.

VERA Y ARAGON, JUAN TORRES see TORRES DE VERA Y
ARAGON, JUAN

VERA Y MUJICA (or MUXICA) FAMILY. Prominent conquistador
and colonial family of Santa Fe that furnished military and
political leadership to that province and neighboring ones
throughout colonial period.

VERA Y PINTADO, BERNARDO DE (1780-1827). Lawyer; professor; patriot leader; poet.

    Born in Santa Fe where he received his early educa-
tion; accompanied his uncle, Marquis del Pino, to Chile in
1799 when latter became governor there; Vera y Pintado entered the royal university of San Felipe in Santiago and refused to accompany his uncle to Buenos Aires where he was
appointed its viceroy; in 1804 graduated in sacred theology,
canons, and law; appointed professor in university; influenced
by ideas of the French revolution he became one of first
precursors of Chilean revolution; jailed for conspiracy against
royal authorities in May 1810, he was quickly released in

response to overwhelming demand from the people, church authorities, and local Chilean officials; in 1811, the Buenos Aires patriot government appointed him as its representative to patriot government of Chile; when latter was defeated by royalists at Rancagua (1814), Vera y Pintado fled across the Andes to Mendoza; there he joined San Martín and became judge advocate general of the Army of the Andes; returned with it to Chile; wrote first Chilean national anthem, approved by the government in 1819; remained in Santiago, continuing to take part in public political life while devoting himself to writing until his death there; in earlier days he had edited the patriotic journal La Aurora and the Gaceta Ministerial (1812); in later years he devoted himself to writing poems, most of which were lost for lack of a printing press; a few, remembered orally or in manuscript remained extant long enough to be published.

VERGARA, CARLOS NORBERTO (1859-1929).   Educator; writer.
Born in Mendoza; educated at Escuela Normal de Paraná; immediately received position on faculty there; then became inspector of schools in Mendoza; founded educational review called El Instructor Popular; later, with Zubiaur and Sarsfield founded the La Educación en Paraná (1886) that influenced years of educational development; an innovator, Vergara experimented with popular libraries, free courses, individual programs and freedom of expression among students; ideologically, he was influenced greatly by the Positivist teachings at Paraná but later departed from the scientific bases of this teaching to include the more idealistic, spiritual ideas of Krausism (q. v.) becoming one of most important Argentine followers of this ideology or cult; died in Córdoba.

VERNENGO LIMA, HECTOR (1889-).   Naval officer; in politics.
Born in Goya, Corrientes; educated at Escuela Naval; taught English and artillery on training ship Presidente Sarmiento and held similar advanced naval appointments, as well as staff and command posts; in 1917-1918 operated in close contact with U.S. navy; became director of the Escuela Naval in 1939; on July 28, 1945, Vernengo Lima, as naval chief of staff, presented President Farrell with a formal document demanding immediate elections and the forbidding of any current government official to carry on political propaganda in his own favor or to use government facilities to promote his own candidacy; this obvious attempt, on part of navy, to force Perón's resignation failed for the time being; Vernengo also participated in the October uprising that forced Perón out of government temporarily.

VERNET, LEWIS or LUIS (1792-1871).   Merchant; cosmopolitan adventurer involved in Falkland Islands dispute between Argentina and U.S.   Of French origin, he had lived in Germany and U.S. before arriving in Buenos Aires in 1817; established business and then acquired land in Falkland Islands;

in 1824 he received rights of settlement, fishing, and hunting of cattle in return for a government debt owed him; by
1828 he had secured much of Soledad, or East Falkland, and
had established a colony; in 1829 Governor Lavalle appointed
him military and political governor of the islands; his attempts in 1831 to enforce his fishing monopoly brought trouble
between U.S. and Argentina over the Falklands (q.v.); Vernet and residents left islands, by force or voluntarily; back
in Argentina, Vernet was credited with discovering a special
preservative for the leather hides that were so much in demand; died in San Isidro, Buenos Aires.

VERTIZ Y SALCEDO, JUAN JOSE DE (1719-1799). Governor and
captain general of Río de la Plata 1770-1776; viceroy of La
Plata 1778-1783.
        Born in Mérida de Yucatán, Mexico, where his father
was royal governor; educated in Spain; early entered military
career; took part in various Spanish campaigns, including
those in Italy and Portugal, and had become a comendador
in Order of Calatrava before being sent to Río de la Plata;
served as interim governor in 1770, confirmed in 1771; during the next dozen years, with the exception of the brief
period during which the viceroyalty was established under
Pedro de Ceballos, Vértiz y Salcedo was in charge of government in Buenos Aires; during this period he revealed himself to be a better administrator than general; his efforts to
force the Portuguese out of Uruguay and back into Brazil
were unsuccessful and Ceballos, with his enormous army,
had to finish the job; but as Spanish civil ruler of Argentina
he was almost unequaled; his reforms and achievements, usually as result of royal policy, developed the whole area economically and culturally while expanding its defensible borders, beginning settlement of empty lands, increasing effectiveness of government, and generally improving quality of
life; during his administration, he completed arrangements
for the reestablishment of royal audiencia of Buenos Aires;
established intendancies throughout the viceroyalty; strengthened
the economy by the freeing of trade and regulation of labor
conditions; attempted to organize skilled artisans into guilds;
stimulated the traditionally important mining industry (in
Upper Peru, primarily); encouraged new meat-salting industry; attempted to foster development of agriculture, especially the commercial cultivation of indigo and flax for which
there was a growing, lucrative European market; he turned
his attention to the transformation of the city of Buenos Aires
into a proper viceregal capital; cleaned up the city, improved
its water supply, established street lighting, built alameda
(poplar-bordered promenade or walk) along the river, and
established bull-ring at El Retiro; took census of city and
province that revealed population of 37,679; made institutional provisions for vagrants, orphans, destitute or disorderly
women, beggars, etc.; revived the Hermandad de Caridad
(Brotherhood of Charity, precursor of later Sociedad de

Vértiz y Salcedo

Beneficencia); created Protomedicato to regulate practice of
medicine, make provisions for public health and for training
of physicians; his orderly disposition of wealth left by Jesuits (expelled in 1767) financed many of these efforts; Vértiz
y Salcedo was, in many ways, the first royal governor to
show interest in the cultural life of the community; he early
established the first theater in Buenos Aires, the Ranchería
(1771); opened the royal Colegio de San Carlos and had hoped
to establish a university (none in Buenos Aires until after independence); brought Jesuit printing press from Córdoba to
Buenos Aires and established it in the Casa de los Niños Expósitos, giving Buenos Aires its first press; in the establishment of all these new institutions, Vértiz y Salcedo sought
out qualified Creoles (perhaps because he, himself, was
American-born) to fill positions, along with newly-arrived
Spaniards.

His work extended throughout the viceroyalty; fortifications in Montevideo were strengthened; Indian· frontier in
Buenos Aires was pushed back and held by new fortified
settlements that later became towns such as Chascomús,
Monte, Rojas, Ranchos, Navarro; complying with royal orders that Patagonia should be explored and held against possible European intruders, the viceroy sent out several expeditions under Juan de la Piedra, Andrés and Francisco Viedma, and Basilio Villarino that explored the coast as far as
San Julián and the Río Negro and Río Colorado, and established such settlements as San José and Carmen de Patagones; in the north Jerónimo Matorras conducted expedition
into the Chaco, and navigation was opened on the Bermejo to
Salta; Vértiz y Salcedo assembled and equipped an army of
2000 men to aid in suppression of rebellion of Tupac Amaru
II in the high Andes of Peru and Bolivia (part of viceroyalty
of Río de la Plata); of far-reaching consequences to Argentina was his sending of Captain Tomás Rocamora (1783) into
almost unoccupied area between Paraná and Uruguay rivers
to begin settlements in what is now province of Entre Ríos;
established towns of Gualeguay, Gualeguaychú, and Concepción del Uruguay; in 1783 the viceroy requested transfer back
to Spain and his successor, Nicolás del Campo, Marquis of
Loreto, was appointed; exempted, because of his excellent
record, from the usual residencia, or judicial review, of
his administration, Vértiz y Salcedo turned his government
over to his successor in 1784 and returned to Spain, where
he died several years later.

See José Torre Revello's monograph, Juan José de
Vértiz y Salcedo, gobernador y virrey de Buenos Aires; and
his later comprehensive, La sociedad colonial: Buenos
Aires entre los siglos XVI y XIX (Buenos Aires, 1970).

VESPIGNANI, ERNESTO (1861-1925). Salesian priest and architect.

Born in Lugo, Italy and educated as architect in Academia Albertina de Turín; arriving in Buenos Aires early in

twentieth century, he established a center of architectural studies in the Salesian Colegio Pío IX that brought it wide distinction; also designed many churches and religious monuments not only in Argentina (including national sanctuary of Itatí, in Corrientes) but throughout South America; died in Buenos Aires.

VESPIGNANI, JOSE (1854-1932).   Priest; director of Salesian work in Argentina, 1902-1922.

Born in Lugo, Italy; in 1877 he arrived in Buenos Aires to become a part of the new Salesian missionary-educational work there; served in various capacities such as that of director of all Salesian operations in the nation and his leadership for the next twenty years is widely considered responsible for the remarkable growth and contributions made by the Salesians (q.v.); spent last ten years of his life in Turin, directing operations of Salesian industrial and agricultural schools throughout the world; died in Turin but his remains were brought back to Argentina in 1948 and buried in the crypt of María Auxiliadora in Buenos Aires.

VIAMONTE, JUAN JOSE (1774-1843).   Military and political leader in independence and early national periods; served briefly several times as governor of Buenos Aires.

Born in Buenos Aires; entered infantry regiment at age of 12; became artillery officer and fought in Banda Oriental against the Portuguese; as member of patricios and aide of Santiago Liniers, fought against invading British in 1806-1807; early joined the patriot movement led by Nicolás Rodríguez Peña, Manuel Belgrano, etc.; as sergeant major attended the cabildo abierto, May 1810, and voted for patriot cause; accompanied patriot army to Upper Peru and fought in battle of Suipacha and disaster of Huaqui (q.v.); as one of commanding officers in latter, he was subjected to military trial but exonerated; in 1813 Supreme Director Gervasio Posadas appointed him as governor intendant of Entre Ríos; protected forces of Dorrego retreating after defeat by Artigas; after fall of Carlos María de Alvear's government, Viamonte, by this time a general, was sent to Santa Fe by new director, Ignacio Alvarez Thomas, to establish order; occupied Santa Fe peacefully August 25, 1815; the following March the populace, led by Estanislao López, in his first important appearance in history, rose against him and forced him to surrender; in 1818, he was elected deputy to national congress but resigned to become general-in-chief of expeditionary army to Santa Fe in 1819, replacing Juan Ramón González Balcarce; following armistice of San Lorenzo (q.v.) he withdrew his forces to Buenos Aires province; returned to become president of the Congress in 1819; served as interim governor of Buenos Aires in 1821 for one month; after Lavalle's defeat and retirement from public life in 1829, Viamonte became governor of Buenos Aires for about three months; prepared way for Rosas' first administration; when

Rosas refused reelection in 1832, Balcarce was made governor; his short term was made difficult by the open conflict
between the doctrinaire federalists and those supporting
Rosas; after latter ousted Balcarce in the Revolution of the
Restorers, Viamonte again became governor; he quickly realized that the political conciliation he desired between the
two rival groups was impossible and concentrated instead on
matters of administration throughout this final governorship,
November 4, 1833-June 27, 1837; made good record for establishing bases for future progress in areas of ecclesiastical
patronage, public finance, regulation of civil employees' responsibilities, improvement of public works program, regulation of port traffic, creation of security programs in
Buenos Aires (see Serenos), and individual actions such as
those permitting religious marriages between non-Catholics
and establishing New Year's Day as a national holiday;
forced to resign by the Rosistas, Viamonte retired to private life and, soon after Rosas' return to power, emigrated
to Montevideo where he died; in 1881 his remains were brought
back to Buenos Aires to be buried in La Recoleta cemetery.
        Armando Alonso Piñeiro has published a biography of
this man who devoted a half century to public service; see
Historia del General Viamonte y su época, with prologue by
Carlos Sánchez Viamonte (Buenos Aires, 1960).

VICEROYALTY. The viceroyalty was the most important administrative, political unit of the Spanish colonial empire, with
the viceroy (literally vice-king) the apex of royal authority
in area involved; the first viceroyalty established in the
Americas was that of New Spain (Mexico) in 1535 that included all of Spanish North and Central America and Caribbean islands; the second was the Viceroyalty of Peru, established in 1542, with Vasco Núñez de Vela as first viceroy,
with its capital at Lima; this included all of South America;
for more than two centuries the area that is now Argentina
was governed as part of this viceroyalty; in the eighteenth
century the new Bourbon dynasty created two new viceroyalties on the southern continent, that of New Granada in the
north (including modern Colombia, Venezuela, Ecuador, and
Panama) and that of Río de la Plata (q.v.) in the south.

VICEROYALTY OF THE RIO DE LA PLATA (VIRREINATO DEL
RIO DE LA PLATA), 1776-1810.
        Created in 1776 by Charles III, this was last vice-
royalty established by Spain in America; it included present
republics of Argentina, Bolivia, Paraguay, Uruguay, and
part of Chile (Cuyo); in addition to the general desire of the
Spanish Bourbon kings to strengthen colonial administration
and defense and to increase royal revenues from the American colonies, there were special reasons that made it important to centralize power in Buenos Aires; among these
were: 1. unique defense problem in Río de la Plata; shifting balance of power in Europe had made France and England

strong contenders for supremacy as colonial powers; both
were interested in South Atlantic, especially Falkland Islands
and Strait of Magellan; Spain and France were joined by the
Family Compact, renewed in 1761 between two branches of
Bourbon family, but England's traditional ties with Portugal
combined with Brazilian expansion toward the Río de la Plata
to create a serious defense problem in the Buenos Aires and
northeastern Misiones area; 2. empire in South America was
too vast and complicated to be handled from one center; in
late eighteenth century, the Spanish lands east of the Andes
were too far advanced in size of population and development
of economy, with problems too complex, to wait for government aid and answers from Lima; 3. more royal initiative
and authority was needed to stimulate further development of
area, occupy new lands, as in Entre Ríos and Patagonia,
and increase production and royal revenues; 4. reality of situation forced refocusing of center of power; Buenos Aires
was natural trading center for this area and Spanish insistence on forcing trade through Lima, instead, had only resulted in growth of enormous contraband trade out of Buenos
Aires and resulting loss of royal revenue.

Establishment of viceroyalty, with capital at Buenos
Aires and Pedro de Ceballos (q. v.), then serving as captain-
general and president of royal audiencia there, as first viceroy, brought immediate changes to area; royal power was
strengthened and centralized in this new capital and by establishment of intendancies (q. v.) and military districts (on
frontiers) throughout the viceroyalty; during first twenty
years, trade increased, cities, especially Buenos Aires,
were beautified and improved; standards of living were
raised; hide and tallow trade promoted and regulated; medical tribunal was established (see Protomedicato); Patagonian
coast was explored, forts established; entire educational system, in confusion since expulsion of Jesuits, was reorganized;
the Royal Academy of San Carlos was established in Buenos
Aires; first printing press brought there; theater opened;
there were some losses, especially for the small industries
of the interior that could not compete with foreign imports,
and by end of viceregal period, in 1810, trade balance was
reversed as imports began to exceed exports; foreign trade
was liberalized and Buenos Aires became a cosmopolitan
center; Donald E. Worcester and Wendell G. Schaeffer sum
up this viceregal period (especially in its impact of earlier
years) as follows: ''Domestic and external trade increased
enormously, government revenues mounted, and social and
cultural life experienced a new birth. This was, in reality
the birth period of the Argentine nation. For the first time
the great region was brought together in a single political
entity with capable and aggressive political action.'' (The
Growth and Culture of Latin America, 2nd edition, New
York, Toronto, London, 1970, I: 354).

Viceregal government came to an end in Argentina in
May 1810, with the deposition of the last viceroy, Baltasar

Viceroyalty

Hidalgo de Cisneros (Buenos Aires did not accept authority
of later appointment of Elío in Montevideo); during the thirty-
four years of its duration, eleven viceroys had served, as
named below (see individual entries for events and contributions made during various administrations).   Dates are given
as of appointment, not the actual taking over of office.
    1776-1778   Pedro de Ceballos (or Cevallos).
    1778-1783   Juan José de Vértiz y Salcedo.
    1783-1789   Cristóbal del Campo, marqués de Loreto.
    1789-1794   Nicolás de Arredondo.
    1794-1797   Pedro Melo de Portugal y Villena.
    1797-1799   Antonio Olaguer Feliú (interim).
    1799-1801   Gabriel de Avilés y del Fierro.
    1801-1804   Joaquín del Pino.
    1804-1807   Rafael de Sobremonte.
    1807-1809   Santiago de Liniers.
    1809-1810   Baltasar Hidalgo de Cisneros.

VICTORIA, FRANCISCO DE (d. 1592).   Early bishop of Tucumán.
        Born in Portugal; arrived in Peru where he received
his education and became a Dominican friar; sent to Rome
by Dominicans in Peru as their legal representative; won
respect of church authorities there and was appointed bishop
of Tucumán (1577); took up his duties in Santiago del Estero
(seat of bishopric established in 1570) enthusiastically; visited
the scattered settlements and promoted expansion of missionary work among the Indians of the area; brought in first
Jesuits, from Peru, to join missionaries of other orders;
also bought ship and brought in missionaries from Brazil,
along with badly needed supplies for the Tucumán area;
because of this, he has been given credit for opening
Tucumán trade with Brazil; Bishop Victoria quickly became a
controversial figure, finding himself embroiled in tumultuous
politics of area in that period; in direct conflict with Governor Lerma, he was finally forced to leave; accusations of
greed and avarice were made against him and he made
counter-charges in what was Argentina's first Church-State
conflict; eventually both parties took their case to Spain
where Fray Victoria was exonerated; died in Madrid; his
memory remained honored in Tucumán's historiography for
the amount of work that he had been able to accomplish in
laying foundations for the orderly work of the church among
the settlers as well as evangelizing among the Indians.

VICTORIA, MAXIMIO SABA (1871-1938).   Educator; Positivist;
    writer.
        Born in Graneros, Tucumán; was educated there and
began teaching career in native town; received scholarship to
continue his studies at Escuela Normal de Paraná; studied
there under Pedro Scalabrini (q.v.) whose Positivist ideas
influenced Victoria throughout his life (see Positivism); was
appointed inspector of primary schools and then regent of

Normal School in Santiago del Estero; attempted to use new
Positivistic ideas of order and progress, based on laws of
science, not only in his teaching but in continuous journalistic writings that aimed to arouse a popular desire for cultural and civic progress; while in Santiago he learned to speak
Quechua in order to talk with the Indians in remote areas to
which he traveled on muleback trying to establish rural
schools; dismissed from his posts as result of his participation in 1893 revolution, he left Santiago and became director
of public school in Curuzú-Cuatiá, Corrientes; worked there
until 1897 when he became general inspector of primary
schools in Tucumán; his enthusiastic endeavors to educate
the public socially and politically as well as his students in
the classroom again cost him his position; taught briefly in
Esperanza (Santa Fe) and then, in 1899, returned to Santiago
del Estero as president of provincial general council of education; created schools and introduced educational reforms; a
change in government brought charges against him that put
him in jail; exonerated, he accepted an appointment from
national minister of public education to go to Catamarca to
serve as director of its Escuela normal regional; worked
with urban and rural schools there; from 1907 to 1923 he
was director of his own alma mater, the Escuela Normal de
Paraná; during this period he accepted temporary professional appointments in Buenos Aires and elsewhere; earnestly
tried to revive in the normal school the almost evangelical
spirit with which Scalabrini had inspired his students but
change had come and the school seemed to him to represent
only another bureaucratic category to the government and
public; left Paraná and organized the first professional
schools in Tucumán; also devoted considerable time to sugar
planting; moved to Buenos Aires where he died.

Among his published works are translations of Auguste Comte's works, such as Filosofía positiva; Discurso
sobre el espíritu positivo, etc.; among his original monographs are El socialismo y la libertad espiritual; Juventud;
El cooperativismo y la sociedad; Análisis positivo de la ple-
garia, dictated shortly before his death, after he had become
blind.

VICTORICA, BENJAMIN (1831-1913). Jurisconsult; general; frequent cabinet minister; writer.

Born in Buenos Aires, son of Bernardo Victorica who
had been Rosas' chief of police until they had disagreement
in 1845; Benjamín graduated from law school in Buenos Aires
and began his career, both political and military, in Buenos
Aires in 1849; served as secretary of Angel Pacheco; later
became closely associated with Urquiza and the new confederation; in 1854 worked with ministry of interior; from 1855 to
1860 he served Entre Ríos province as judge and as its representative in the national congress; in 1860 he was also
writing for Vicente G. Quesada's Revista del Paraná; served
as Urquiza's secretary; his combination of military, legal,

and administrative skills caused him to serve several presidents as minister of war and navy, in cabinets of Santiago Derqui, 1860, and later in those of Julio A. Roca, 1880-1884, and Luis Sáenz Peña, 1892-1893; meanwhile he was deeply involved in difficult process (1859-1861) of bringing Confederation and Buenos Aires into national union; was a member of national convention that studied constitutional reforms suggested by Buenos Aires in addition to performing in military service.

In 1861 Victorica returned to Entre Ríos; served as its president of supreme court, 1861-1869 and as national senator from Entre Ríos, 1869-1873; appointments followed making him member and vice president of National Council of Education, 1874, and attorney (fiscal) for court of appeals of Buenos Aires, 1875-1880; was also serving as legal counsel of supreme court and a member of the faculty of law; as minister in Roca's cabinet, he strongly defended Argentina's sovereign rights in the South Atlantic and Strait area; in 1884 led an expedition to the Chaco to subdue the Indians and to explore the Pilcomayo River; his account of this expedition was published in Buenos Aires in 1885; served as president of supreme court, 1887-1892; returned to political action in 1892-1893 as minister of war and navy for Luis Sáenz Peña; during next few years, continued to teach in law faculty of University of Buenos Aires, served as vice rector in the Free University; and retired as general in 1895; died in Buenos Aires.

VIDAL, JOSE RAMON (1821-1871).   Physician; public figure.
        Born in Corrientes; graduated in medicine in Buenos Aires; returned to Corrientes where he renewed the interest in politics he had shown as a youth; served in provincial legislature and as interim governor on various occasions; presided over convention that gave Corrientes its constitution; his greatest contribution was in his untiring selfless medical services during the cholera epidemic of 1868 and those of yellow fever 1870-1871; lost his life in the latter.

VIDAL, JUAN RAMON (1860-1940).   Lawyer; public figure; twice governor of Corrientes.
        Born in Corrientes and educated in Buenos Aires; became active in politics of Corrientes; at age of 24 served as minister of government in his native province; two years later he became governor; his administration (1886-1889) was noted for its founding of the Banco de la Provincia, promotion of education (including creation of superior council of education), and his public works program; in a second administration, 1909-1913, he continued his work in education, adding the industrial school of the province and a professional school for women; he also had a cadastral survey (public record of land ownership) of the province made; on the national scene, Vidal represented Corrientes in the Chamber of Deputies and twice in Senate; died in Corrientes.

VIDAL, PEDRO PABLO (1777-1848).   Ecclesiastic; supporter of
early patriot movement.
Born in Montevideo; studied at University of Córdoba;
received doctorate in theology; returned to Montevideo; Viceroy Joaquín del Pino appointed him to position in cathedral
there; Father Vidal early became attached to patriot movement; represented Jujuy in general constituent Assembly of
1813; carried out political mission in Montevideo with Saturnino Rodríguez Peña; was appointed to cathedral of Buenos
Aires; became supporter of Unitarists; cooperated actively
with the expedition of the Famous 33 (see Treinta y Tres);
served as legislator in Buenos Aires 1830-1834; suffered political exile from Buenos Aires three times, the last resulting from pressures of Mazorca during Rosas period; served
as secretary of Fructuoso Rivera; died in Montevideo during
its siege.

VIDELA, JORGE RAFAEL (1925-   ).   President of Argentine Republic, 1976-   ; career military officer.
Born in province of Buenos Aires; graduated from
Colegio Militar (1944) and took advanced work (1954) at Escuela Superior de Guerra; steadily moved up ladder of military rank and responsibility; became brigadier general and
director of the Colegio Militar in 1971; in 1973 he served as
chief of general staff; acquired increasing prominence during
presidencies of Juan Domingo Perón and María Estela Perón
(1973-1976), becoming commander-in-chief of the army in
1975; increasing internal problems of violence, inflation, and
charges of official corruption brought a military takeover of
President María Estela Perón's government in March 1976;
a junta was formed consisting of the heads of the army, navy,
and air force; a few hours later, however, General Videla
was inaugurated as president of the republic; his reputation
for honesty and integrity made him well received by public;
in his first address to the people he pledged to destroy the
Marxist-Leninist guerrillas terrorizing the country and to reduce inflation; both violence and inflation continued but economy approached stabilization and rate of inflation decreased.

VIDELA DEL PINO, NICOLAS (-1819).   First bishop of diocese
of Salta.
Born in Tucumán; became priest and served as dean
of cathedral of Córdoba and bishop of Paraguay before becoming first bishop of the new diocese of Salta; although a
creole, Bishop Videla del Pino remained strongly royalist
and opposed the May Revolution and establishment of the patriot junta; he continued in his post until 1812; the discovery
that he was in communication with the royalist military leader José M. Goyeneche brought his removal by Belgrano, who
then exiled him to Buenos Aires; Videla del Pino appealed
his case to both the Assembly of XIII and the Congress of
Tucumán but died in Buenos Aires in 1819 without recovering his position; his death marked the end of the line of legal

bishops (i. e. , those appointed under the <u>real</u> <u>patronato</u>) in Argentina.

VIDELA MOYANO, JUAN DE DIOS (1815-1880).   Military leader and public figure.
   Born in Mendoza; became part of Juan Lavalle's Liberating Legion that entered Argentina from Montevideo in Unitarist attempt to overthrow Rosas, 1839; after participating in most of the engagements that culminated in defeat of Lavalle's forces at Quebracho Herrado November 28, 1840, Videla went over to Federalists under Manuel Oribe; became colonel in Rosas' army; commanded cavalry division against Urquiza at Caseros; returned to Mendoza; elected governor in 1859 he refused to accept the position but continued very active in the political, military action of that province in the 1860s; following the earthquake that destroyed town of Mendoza March 20, 1861, the people were left at the mercy of unruly ruffians and looters; Colonel Videla, very popular and with undisputed authority, is given much credit for restoring order in the community, from which its main officials had fled or been victims, organizing the rescue squads, and punishing the pillagers; on December 16 of that year he forced Governor Laureano Nazar to resign and became governor for about 17 days; at opening of new year, Sarmiento appeared with forces from Buenos Aires to hold new election of governor loyal to new national government being established; in 1866 Colonel Videla led revolution against newly appointed Governor Melitón Arroyo in attempt to overthrow power of Mendoza oligarchy but also with popular support from those who opposed forced military service in the unpopular Paraguayan War and those who were disillusioned with failure of Buenos Aires government to improve Mendoza's situation; this revolt became part of the whole western uprising under military leadership of General Juan Saá (q. v.); after Videla's preliminary victories over Pablo Irrazábal at Fuente San Rafael and Julio Campos at Pocito, he shared in Juan Saá's defeat at San Ignacio, in which he had commanded the right division; fled with other defeated leaders to exile in Chile; later, he returned (1877) to care for his properties in Mendoza; died there.

VIEDMA, FRANCISCO DE (1737-1809).   Spanish naval officer; explorer of Río Negro and Patagonia; founder of early settlements there and first governor.
   Born in Jaén; became part of expedition sent by Viceroy Vértiz, under command of Juan de la Piedra, to establish forts and settlements along Patagonian Atlantic coast; Viedma was left in command of garrison at San José Bay in Chubut, January 1779; with pilot Basilio Villarino y Bermúdez (q. v.), made several exploratory trips in Río Negro area; built fort on right bank of river, April 1779, and named it Mercedes de Patagones; a second fort, Carmen de Patagones (q. v.), was constructed on the north bank where

higher ground protected it from the river's flooding; in 1784
he became the first to send the royal government a clear report on the strategic value of Río Negro as line of military
defense against Indians as well as the advantages that might
be gained for the viceroyalty by occupying these potentially
fertile lands; Viedma also established settlement at San
Julián; served as governor of Santa Cruz de la Sierra, 1785-
1809; manufactured gunpowder for use in defense of Buenos
Aires against British invasions 1806-1807 and was preparing
to send military force when invasion ended; died in Cochabamba; in 1878 the capital of modern Río Negro province,
the Mercedes settlement that he had founded, was renamed
in his honor, as well as a plaza and street in Carmen de
Patagones; Francisco de Viedma was an ancestor of the
Biedma family of Buenos Aires.

VIEYTES, JUAN HIPOLITO (1762-1815).   Journalist; economist;
early independence leader and official.
        Born in San Antonio de Areco, province of Buenos
Aires; studied philosophy and law at Colegio de San Carlos;
through his own reading, became an authority on agronomy
and political sciences; published the Semanario de Agricultura,
Industria, y Comercio (q. v.) September 1, 1802 to February
11, 1807; in this he constantly promoted agricultural development and free trade; its publication was stopped by the
British invasion of Montevideo; Vieytes fought against British
as captain of the militia but the spread of their free trade
ideas in the Río de la Plata reinforced those already expressed by Vieytes and Belgrano; about this time he established a soap factory in Buenos Aires, in partnership with
Nicolás Rodríguez Peña; also became very active in secret
patriotic society that often met in latter's home or at Vieytes' home or factory; with other members of this group, he
tried to enlist Carlota Joaquina (q. v.) in aid of Río de la
Plata autonomy; attended cabildo abierto of May 22, 1810,
and vigorously voted for removal of Viceroy Baltasar Hidalgo Cisneros; accompanied first patriot army, commanded by
Ortiz de Ocampo, sent to Upper Peru as judge advocate and
representative of the junta; when he attempted to persuade
the junta to countermand its orders to execute conspirators
in Córdoba, he was replaced by Juan José Castelli who ordered the executions at once; returned to Buenos Aires and
was appointed secretary of the First Junta to fill place formerly occupied by Mariano Moreno (q. v.); was removed by
the rebellion of April 5-6, 1811, and confined in Luján; when
First Triumvirate took over in September of that year, he
was permitted to return to Buenos Aires; served as one of
the commission of judges appointed to try Martín Alzaga
(q. v.) and other leaders of conspiracy in July, 1812; also
held appointment as member of court of appeals; with Juan
Larrea he wrote the Police Regulation and became chief of
police; represented Buenos Aires in general constituent Assembly of 1813, served as its secretary and on the committee

to present a "project for a constitution" to the assembly;
Vieytes was a victim of the political crisis that resulted in
overthrow of Alvear in 1815; along with Rodríguez Peña,
Monteagudo, Valentín Gómez and others who had supported
Alvear, he was condemned to exile; although Alvarez Thomas
suspended the sentence because of Vieytes' failing health, he
died in San Fernando a few months later.

VIGILANCIA, JUZGADO DE. Court of justice created by the last
viceroy, Baltasar Hidalgo de Cisneros, on November 25,
1809, to prosecute and detain anyone opposing Spanish rule,
or attempting, in any way, to destroy the public order; the
fiscal of the audiencia of Buenos Aires, Antonio de Caspe,
was appointed as judge but sentencing power remained with
the viceroy.

VIGILANTES. Name by which early policemen in Buenos Aires
were known; first appeared in police regulation of 1812, written by Juan Hipólito Vieytes and Juan José Larrea; in 1834
Lucio N. Mansilla created the vigilante corps as the first
police force assigned to patrol the city during the day (see
Serenos for night patrol duty).

VIGODET, GASPAR. Last representative of Spanish power in the
Río de la Plata area; named in 1809 by supreme junta in Sevilla to succeed Elío as governor of Montevideo; when Elío
returned to latter city in 1811 as viceroy of the united provinces of Río de la Plata, Vigodet remained to serve him in
political and military capacities; Elío departed after a few
months, leaving Vigodet in command again; he successfully
opposed attempts of the Buenos Aires government and of such
Uruguayan leaders as Artigas to incorporate Montevideo into
the revolutionary movement for more than two years but was
forced to surrender the city to the patriot forces commanded
by Carlos de Alvear on June 20, 1814 (see Francisco Javier
de Elío; Montevideo).

VILCAPUJIO (or VILCAPUGIO), BATTLE OF (October 1, 1813).
Defeat of Belgrano's second auxiliary army by royalists in
Upper Peru (Bolivia). After his victories in Tucumán and
Salta, Belgrano continued northward in a second attempt to
win war of independence for entire viceroyalty of Río de la
Plata by defeating royalists in control there; reached and occupied mining center of Potosí but was forced to fight large
royalist force under Joaquín Pezuela at Vilcapujio; for a
time the fortunes of this very bloody battle varied but
eventually Belgrano was forced to withdraw in defeat, his
forces dispersed and much of his military equipment captured; retired to Potosí to recoup his losses and reform his
army; met second defeat at Ayohuma (q. v.).

VILELAS see LULE-VILELAS

VILLAFAÑE, BENJAMIN (1819-1893). Writer belonging to generation of exiles from Rosas' rule; public figure; educator.

Born in Tucumán; as a young man (1839) while in San
Juan learned about the work of the Asociación de Mayo (q. v.);
returned to his home province to acquaint Marco Avellaneda
with its activities and to establish similar groups there and
in Salta (1840); took part in Lavalle's campaigns in the north,
writing many of its proclamations; was with Lamadrid when
latter was defeated by Rosas' forces and accompanied him
into exile in Chile but returned to rejoin Lavalle in the
north; after latter's death, he formed part of the escort accompanying Lavalle's body to Bolivia; remained there, along
with other exiles from Rosas, teaching, writing, and editing
various newspapers and journals; proved to be successful
businessman, making a fortune in Peruvian bark (cinchona--
source of quinine); returned to Argentina after Caseros and
reentered public life; while serving as senator from Jujuy to
the Confederation government in Paraná he edited El Nacional
Argentino in which he supported cause of union of provinces
against caudillo rule; he was deeply interested in possibilities
of navigating Bermejo river; in 1856 published in Salta the
book Orán y Bolivia a las márgenes del Bermejo; he was also said to have been involved in organizing a company for
shipping on Bermejo river in which he lost most of his fortune; became governor of Tucumán, 1861, and served as
provincial senator and rector of Colegio Nacional there; also
taught philosophy; returned to educational posts in Jujuy,
1880-1888, then retired; in his later years compiled his
Reminiscencias históricas, personal memoirs filled with
vivid accounts of his adventures with the montoneras and during exile; died in Jujuy.

VILLAFAÑE, BENJAMIN, hijo (1877-1952. Writer; legislator.

Born in Jujuy, son of writer of same name; educated
in law in Buenos Aires; returned to his own town; appointed
to the state court (1901); he also taught history and geography at the Colegio Nacional there; served as provincial deputy
several times, president of the provincial Council of Education (1916 and 1918); governor of Jujuy (1924-1927), director
of the Banco Hipotecario Nacional, and national senator from
Jujuy (1932-1941); he was an active fighter both in debate
and in writing for causes in which he believed; became quite
conservative, opposing Yrigoyen and his followers; led criticism against the "Palermo Scandal" regarding fraud in purchase of additional land for Colegio Militar; retired to private life in which he continued writing books that revealed
his deep affection for his native land and his concern for its
problems; he died in Buenos Aires.

His works include: Miseria de un país rico; Atraso
del interior; Yrigoyen el último dictador; Nuestros males y
sus causas; Pasado y presente; El petróleo y la constitución
nacional; Chusmocracia; Cosas de nuestra tierra; Motivos de
la selva y de la montaña (1952).

VILLAFAÑE, DIEGO LEON (1741-1830).   Priest; patriot.
Born in San Miguel de Tucumán; entered Jesuit order
1753; studied at University of Córdoba; exiled in 1767; continued his studies in Faenza (Italy) and lived in Rome 1785-
1798; although his nationalist position was well known he was
granted permission to return to Argentina (1799); lived in his
native city; when Spanish government attempted to reclaim
him as a Jesuit, the cabildo of Tucumán defended him successfully; he became an enthusiastic supporter of the fight
for independence, a close friend of Deán Funes and of Bishop
Molina; wrote ode honoring Manuel Belgrano following his
victory at Tucumán; died in San Miguel de Tucumán.

VILLANUEVA, BENITO (1854-1933).   Estanciero; financier; senator.
Born in Mendoza; educated in Colegio de la Inmaculada Concepción in Santa Fe and in school of law, Buenos
Aires; participated actively in Argentina's political, financial,
and banking life; operated large estancias in provinces of
Mendoza and Buenos Aires and derived much of his wealth
from breeding and raising Arabian horses imported from
England; entered public life, 1890, as member of national
chamber of Deputies from Mendoza; reelected in 1894; returned as deputy from Federal District in 1900; served as
president of chamber, 1901-1903; in 1904 he was elected to
the Senate by Federal District and remained there for many
years, being elected from Mendoza in 1913; served as its
president several times; his business interests included the
meat-packing plant La Blanca, several banks, and Central
Córdoba railroad; strongly promoted development of grape
and wine industries; member and twice president of Jockey
Club; also member of Círculo de Armas and Club del Progreso.

VILLANUEVA, GENOVEVA (1814-1890).   Heroine of Mendoza
Province.   Socially prominent, founder of the Sociedad de
Beneficencia (aristocratic social welfare group); her refusal
to wear Rosas' mandatory cinta punzó, the red ribbon of
Federalist loyalty, brought her, according to legend, time in
jail and the humiliation of being forced to ride astride a don-
key down main street of Mendoza.

VILLARINO Y BERMUDEZ, BASILIO (1741-1785).   Pilot in royal
Spanish navy; explorer of Patagonia.
Born in La Coruña; came to Río de la Plata in 1773
as assistant pilot in frigate Perpetua under command of Bustillos; in 1779 piloted first Spanish vessel up the Río Negro;
joined Francisco de Viedma (q.v.) at San José; their expedition departed from latter anchorage on February 13, 1779,
reached mouth of Río Negro nine days later and started up
the river on the 23rd; meeting Indians all along the way they
were finally forced on February 28 to return; Villarino remained in that area for several years, continuing explorations

on Río Negro, Limay, and other rivers in the territory, assisting in founding of Carmen de Patagones; left detailed diary
of his explorations; in January 1785, on new expedition exploring Sierra de la Ventana area, he was killed by Indians;
his contributions to the Río Negro area and to Argentina have
been recognized in many ways: his name has been given to
many places, including a fort in Río Negro, a point near San
Antonio port, a department in Buenos Aires, as well as a
plaza and street in Carmen de Patagones; in 1879 the first
Argentine naval vessel to cross the Atlantic, and transporting
José de San Martín's remains from France to their final
resting place in Buenos Aires, bore his name.

VILLAROEL, DIEGO DE (c. 1530-1580).   A conquistador of Tucumán; founder of San Miguel de Tucumán.
          Born in Villafranca, Spain; accompanied his uncle
Francisco Aguirre from Chile to Tucumán area in 1553;
served as regidor and alcalde in cabildo of Santiago del Estero, 1553-1554, then went to Spain to act as Aguirre's attorney; returning to Tucumán he found his uncle determined
to reestablish a town on site of former Cañete; after Diaguitas in that area had been pacified by captains Mejía and
Nicolás Carrizo, Villaroel was sent there with fifty Spaniards,
horses, cattle, arms, and provisions; on May 31, 1565, he
established San Miguel de Tucumán, laying out the town and
appointing the municipal officials, etc.; he may have remained there for a time but he died in Santiago del Estero
province at a place called Ybatín by the Indians.

VILLEGAS, ALEJO (1783-1857).   Jurisconsult.   Born in Córdoba;
received his doctor's degree in theology from university
there; later (1814) certified by cabildo to practice law; he
moved to Buenos Aires; became representative of Buenos
Aires to Congress; signed constitution of 1819; served as
secretary of general constituent congress, 1824; refused new
appointment as representative of Córdoba because of his Unitarist convictions that clashed with Federation of Córdoba; in
1828, after fall of Rivadavia's government, Villegas moved
to Montevideo; remained there, teaching civil and canon law
until after Caseros; became member of Supreme Court, and
was asked by Urquiza to serve on advisory board for civil
code that was being prepared at that time; died in Buenos
Aires.

VILLEGAS, CONRADO E. (1840-1884).   General; completed conquest of Patagonia.
          Born in Uruguay; joined Buenos Aires artillery regi-
ment in 1862; fought in Paraguayan War, campaigns against
Indians in southern Córdoba and rebellious caudillo López
Jordan in Entre Ríos; defeated Mitre's revolution in battle of
la Verde (1874); fought against Indians in Patagonia and
joined Roca in his campaign to Río Negro in 1879; founded
town first called Avellaneda, later Choele-Choel; led his

division in defeat of forces of Carlos Tejedor (q. v.) in struggle over federalization of city of Buenos Aires (1880); became
general; at end of that year commanded expedition sent back
to Patagonia in final campaign to assure pacification of the
Indians; became ill upon his return to Buenos Aires; went to
Europe for treatment; died in Paris; remains repatriated a
year later.

VILLOTA, MANUEL GENARO DE.   Jurisconsult.   Royal official in
closing years of viceroyalty; attorney for viceroy and audiencia 1799-1810; made courageous, shrewd, conciliatory (but
unsuccessful) appeal at the meeting of the cabildo abierto in
the May Revolution (q. v.) to continue viceregal government of
Cisneros until Ferdinand VII should be restored to the Spanish throne or at least until all the provinces of the viceroyalty could participate in decisions made; in June the patriot
junta decided to deport the members of the audiencia and Villota was sent to the Canary Islands.

VINARA.   Site in Santiago del Estero of signing of first treaty or
agreement on June 5, 1821, between that province and Tucumán; followed defeat of Juan Felipe Ibarra's forces by those
of Tucumán under Abraham González; at request of neighboring Córdoba, José Antonio Pacheco de Melo (q. v.) negotiated
this agreement.

VIÑEDO.   A vineyard farm.

VINEYARDS.   Whatever the evidence may be regarding existence
of indigenous grapevines in area now included in Argentina,
the record is clear that the nation's extensive vineyards developed from vines brought across the Andes from Chile
where they had been extensively grown since about 1551; Her-
nán Mejía Miraval brought the first ones to Santiago del Estero in 1557 and others were introduced shortly thereafter to
Mendoza (1561), San Juan (1562), and into La Rioja and Catamarca by the Jesuits; during this period the Spanish government was promoting the establishment of vineyards in new
settlements, considering their production of wine, vinegar,
verjuice (green fruit juice used in cooking at that time),
syrup, and raisins essential for their survival; vines were
also brought to Río de la Plata area from Brazil but they
flourished best in the west; in the irrigated deserts of Cuyo,
vineyards became the basis of a successful economy and the
center of community life and remained so from earliest settlement to modern times.
     In the nineteenth century European vines were im-
ported extensively to satisfy new market demands by supplementing or supplanting the creole stock; in Mendoza, for example, about 1885 Reinoud introduced the Malbeck, Cabernet,
Barbera Freisa, Grenache, Anamom, Mourdevre, and others
into what became the great Trapiche (see Tiburcio Benegas),
one of the most important of the vineyards of that area until

it was subdivided in the 1960s; in the twentieth century, the new emphasis on vitamins and nutritional values of fresh fruits, along with the development of new marketing procedures for handling them, made the commercial production of table grapes important, with extensive vineyards opened in other areas, especially Río Negro (see Fruit Industry, especially for table grapes; Wine Industry).

For historical development of vineyards, see Historia de la nación argentina, IV, La agricultura, ganadería e industrias hasta el virreinato (Buenos Aires, 1938); Carlos D. Storni, Descripción de viñedos que se cultivan en Argentina desde la época colonial (Córdoba, 1927); María Amelia Marrone, "El cultivo de la vid en Argentina," Revista Geográfica Americana XI: 64 (1939).

VIRASORO, BENJAMIN (1812-1897).   Estanciero, military and public leader; governor of province of Corrientes, 1847-1852.

Born in Corrientes; educated in Buenos Aires, then returned home to devote himself to stockraising; became military leader in Corrientes' opposition to Rosas and lost most of his properties when this failed; in 1839 joined Rivera and Unitarists and fought under Lavalle; later, fought with General Paz at Caaguazú; after battle of Arroyo Grande (1842) he emigrated to Paraguay and Brazil; became a supporter of Justo José Urquiza who appointed him governor of Corrientes after the Madariagas had been driven out (1847); cooperated, from beginning, with Urquiza's attempt to overthrow Rosas and served as Urquiza's chief of staff at Caseros; deposed as governor of Corrientes, he moved to Rosario; retired from the army but returned to support Urquiza at Cepeda and Pavón, and to mobilize troops from Corrientes and Entre Ríos for Paraguayan War; retired to private life in Buenos Aires where he died.

VIRASORO, JOSE ANTONIO (d. 1860).   Military officer during Rosas period; governor of San Juan province.

Born in Corrientes, son of Spanish pilot-cosmographer Juan Ascencio Virasoro and correntina Doña Mercedes Corrales; joined Unitarists under General Paz; fought at Caaguazú and elsewhere; later joined Federalist forces; fought under Urquiza from 1843 through his defeat of Rosas at Caseros in 1852, commanding Corrientes forces at this battle; in 1857 Urquiza appointed him a colonel in the army of the Confederation; as result of assassination of General Nazario Benavides in uprising in San Juan, Virasoro was sent as interventor and then designated as interim governor of that province in 1859; his unpopular appointment set off new revolution in San Juan, led by Antonio Aberastain; as this turmoil threatened the national unification agreed upon at San José de Flores (q.v.), Mitre, governor of Buenos Aires, President Derqui of the Confederation, and Urquiza met at San José to decide on policy; at very time that they were agreeing to invite Virasoro to consider resigning in interests of

national peace, Virasoro and several members of his family
were assassinated in his home, November 16, 1860; Aberastain took over but was replaced by Juan Saá and then executed; for national events growing out of Virasoro's assassination see Antonio Aberastain and Juan Saá.

VIZCACHERAS, COMBAT OF (March 28, 1829). At this site near
Salado River in Buenos Aires province, one of divisions of
Lavalle's army, led by Colonel Frederick Rauch encountered
montoneras led by Miranda, part of forces of Estanislao
López and Juan Manuel de Rosas; Lavalle's men were completely routed and Rauch and his companion, Colonel Nicolás
Medina, were later killed by Indians fighting with López; action at Vizcacheras made possible the defeat of Lavalle's Unitarist army by these Federalist forces a month later.

VIZCARDO, JUAN PABLO (1748-1798). Jesuit precursor of Spanish American independence.
        Born in Arequipa, Peru; had attained minor Jesuit
order when he was expelled with other Jesuits in 1767; after
a stay in Italy, he moved to London in 1782; devoted himself
to working for Spanish American independence apparently without contact with Francisco Miranda or Juan José Godoy, simi-
larly engaged; when French Revolution broke out, he moved
to France, hoping to find aid for his cause; wrote his famous
letter calling for independence there, in French, addressed
to Spanish Americans and signed "One of your fellow patriots";
not meeting with any success, he returned to London where
he died; his papers were willed to Rufus King, U.S. minister in London, who called them to Miranda's attention; Miranda published Spanish translation of Vizcardo's letter in
1801 (French version was printed earlier in Philadelphia,
1799); although this document was widely circulated by Miranda and others it seems to have made little impact on the
Río de la Plata patriots in early days of their independence
movement; in 1816, it formed part of the propaganda used
by those favoring a monarchy under an Inca prince.

VOTING LAWS see SUFFRAGE

VUELTA DE OBLIGADO. Site on Paraná river of defeat of Argentine land and river forces by British-French blockading
fleets, November 18-20, 1845; considered a glorious episode
in Argentine naval history because of heroism shown by the
defenders against insuperable odds.
        The Vuelta de Obligado, a deep, narrow turn in the
Paraná river north of San Pedro, had long been selected as
an ideal defense position against enemies seeking to reach
the upriver provinces; in 1811, following the Spanish defeat
of the patriot ships at San Nicolás, Hipólito Vieytes was
commanded to build defenses there; more than three decades
later, when British and French naval units determined to
open the river to Corrientes and Entre Ríos trade, Rosas

commanded General Lucio N. Mansilla to close the river at that point by stretching chains across it with artillery protection on shore; with fewer than 3000 men (soldiers, militiamen, farmers and other rural groups, and even including a considerable number of British residents) and no more than 21 cannons, Mansilla held off the largest fleet that had ever entered the river, armed with over 100 heavy guns; eventually the Allied forces broke through and captured the Argentine men and ships; Mansilla had been seriously wounded and other Argentine casualties were heavy; the allies found the victory to be an empty one as the estancias in the upriver provinces were too few to offer lucrative trade as yet; it also had little or no effect on the blockade that was lifted by arbitration shortly thereafter; Admiral Sir Charles Hotham, British commander, always regarded it as a symbol, if not an important cause, of the eventual treaty of free navigation of the rivers which he signed for England in 1853; Argentines remember it as an evidence of their determination to fight foreign domination; the Argentine ships, flags (very few captured), and prisoners were returned to the Rosas government.

- W -

WAIN (or WAINE), J.   U.S. sea-captain, master of the ship Elizabeth, who is said to have furnished Sir Home Popham with some of the information about the Río de la Plata that persuaded the latter to undertake the British invasion of 1806; Captain Wain had visited Montevideo and Buenos Aires several times and declared, in a secret communication, dated March 28, 1806, that the people of those cities were so eager for freedom to trade that they would welcome any foreign power that could liberate them from Spain and open their ports (see British Invasions; Sir Home Riggs Popham).

"WAR OF TRENCHES" see "ZAPA, LA GUERRA DE"

WAR OF TRIPLE ALLIANCE see PARAGUAYAN WAR

WAR WITH BRAZIL (1825-1828). War between the newly independent Buenos Aires government and Pedro I's empire of Brazil; grew out of colonial dispute as to whether the Banda Oriental (Uruguay) should belong to Portugal or Spain; specific cause: Lavalleja and Famous Thirty-Three attempted to make Uruguay (then the Cisplatine province of Brazil) a part of the United Provinces of the Río de la Plata; when latter accepted it, Brazil declared war. Fighting, on land and sea, continued for three years; most important battle Ituzaingó, Argentine victory at great cost; war unpopular with Argentines, Brazilians, Uruguayans, and foreigners; treaty (British influences strong) called for independent Uruguay as buffer state and cessation of hostilities; ended traditional, centuries-old boundary dispute between Argentina and Brazil.

WARNES, IGNACIO (c. 1771-1816).   Military hero of independence
   war.
        Born in Buenos Aires; joined Blandengues as cadet;
   fought against British invasions; joined patriot cause following May Revolution, 1810; accompanied Manuel Belgrano's expedition to Paraguay where he was captured and returned to
   Montevideo as prisoner; free again, he was commissioned
   lieutenant colonel and assigned to Army of the North commanded by Belgrano whom he served as secretary; took part
   in battles of Tucumán, Salta, Vilcapujio, and Ayohuma; Belgrano promoted him to rank of colonel and assigned him task
   of reorganizing forces in Santa Cruz de la Sierra (Bolivia) to
   renew fight against royalists and Spaniards; under command
   of General Arenales, he defeated royalists at battle of Florida and took possession of city of Santa Cruz; proved himself
   to be excellent organizer and trainer, forming effective military units from men of assorted races (freed the slaves to
   join the army), occupations, and weapons; with these new
   forces he was again able to hold the area for patriots until,
   in late 1816, another royalist force, commanded by creole
   colonel, Aguilera, attacked Warnes at the plain of Parí;
   trapped under his fallen horse, he was killed and his
   head severed from his body to be exhibited in plaza of Santa
   Cruz, where a monument was later erected in his memory.

WARNES, MARTIN JOSE (1775-1842).   Naval officer; fighter in
   war for independence.
        Born in Buenos Aires, brother of Ignacio; sent to
   Spain to study; as midshipman in royal navy, fought in battle
   of Trafalgar under command of Baltasar Hidalgo de Cisneros;
   returned to Argentina and became part of artillery regiment
   of San Martín's Army of the Andes, then fighting in Chile;
   fought at Cancha Rayada and Maipú; in 1818 he served in
   Chilean navy on the San Martín, under Blanco Encalada; rejoined land forces of San Martín and fought throughout war
   for independence in Peru; returned to Buenos Aires and
   joined Argentine navy in 1826; was commander of Sarandí,
   one of ships captured during war with Brazil; the resulting
   court martial absolved him of blame but he resigned, went
   back to Chile and joined its army; died there fighting the
   Indians.

WASHBURN, CHARLES A. (1822-1889).   U.S. diplomat, on special
   mission to Paraguay, 1861-1868.
        Born in Maine, a graduate of Bowdoin (1848), admit-
   ted to the bar in Wisconsin, Washburn moved to California
   in 1850 and became a newspaper editor; in 1861 President
   Lincoln sent him to Paraguay on a special diplomatic mission; he remained there until 1868, during the War of the
   Triple Alliance, always a controversial figure because of the
   mutual hatred between him and Francisco Solano López; after
   his return to the United States he published his observations
   in History of Paraguay (2 v., Boston, 1871); somewhat suspect

because of the author's bias against Solano López, the book
has considerable value for Argentine history because of its
detailed comments of the origins and events of the War of
the Triple Alliance, as well as the record of his dealings
with Bartolomé Mitre, then commander of the allied forces
besieging Paraguay, when the American wanted a pass to
proceed up the Paraguay river to Asunción as he was returning to his post from a leave of absence.

WAST, HUGO see MARTINEZ ZUVIRIA, GUSTAVO

WATER WITCH. American steamer used for commerce and exploring on the Paraná and Uruguay rivers in 1850s; played
important role in U.S. attempt to get treaties opening these
rivers, and others of the Río de la Plata system, to free
navigation and commerce; when Urquiza had to leave Buenos
Aires in 1853, he was given refuge on the Water Witch and
passage to his home in San José de Flores; when Paraguayan
President Carlos Antonio López closed all Paraguayan rivers
and Lt. T. J. Page (q.v.) sent the Water Witch to explore
the part of the Paraná that forms boundary between Corrientes
and Paraguay, it was fired on by the Paraguayan forces at
Itapirú and its pilot killed; this incident brought immediate
demands from U.S. for apologies and reparations and U.S.
naval units were sent to the Río de la Plata; through mediation by Urquiza with López, the U.S. and Paraguay settlement was finally signed in 1859.

WEDDELL (Island). An island in the Falkland group (Las Malvinas), named after the English seal fishing captain, James
Weddell, who discovered it in the 1820s; claimed by Argentina (see Falkland Islands).

WEDDELL, JAMES (1787-1834). Born in London; captain of early
seal fishing vessels in Antarctic (1819-1824); reached 74° 15'
S. latitude, a record unbroken for many years; wrote A Voyage Towards the South Pole (1825).

WEDDELL SEA. Large open bay, part of Antarctic Ocean, be-
tween Palmer Land and Coats Land; named in 1900 for James
Weddell who discovered it in 1823; forms part of Antarctic
Argentina (q.v.).

WELFARE. Problems relating to social security and welfare are
under Ministry of Labor and Social Security; government assumption of these programs has been for Argentina, as in
most newly industrialized, urbanized nations, a development
of the twentieth century (see Sociedad de Beneficencia, for
earlier history; Alfredo Lorenzo Palacios, for first such
legislation; Juan Domingo Perón and María Eva Duarte de
Perón (Evita), for important reforms of 1940s and 1950s).

WELSH. Important settlers and sheepherders in Chubut (q.v.) and other Patagonian provinces and in Falkland Islands.

WERNICKE, EDMUNDO (1867-1949).   Hacendado; writer.
Born in Swiss colony of Baradero; educated in Germany; returned to Argentina; became director of Unión Cívica
Nacional in Las Heras (Buenos Aires province); moved to San
Luis in 1902 and was active in agropecuarian interests there;
in 1908 founded the Sociedad Rural Río Quinto of Mercedes;
took part in convention called to reform San Luis' constitution and represented provinces at various geographic and historical meetings; moved to Buenos Aires in 1929 because of
financial reverses; became translator, contributed articles to
journals devoted to rural or historical interests; translated
Ulrich Schmidel's (q. v.) sixteenth century account of his voyage to the Río de la Plata and wrote Memorias de un portón
de estancia (Buenos Aires, 1918), a history of three generations of estancieros.

WERNICKE, JULIA (1860-1932).   Argentine painter who acquired
international recognition for her mastery of skills in oil
painting, water colors, and etching; received most of her
training in Germany; preferred to paint animals and birds;
many Argentines consider her "Los Toritos" (Little Bulls),
painted in Las Heras (Buenos Aires) in 1897, her best work.

WHEAT.   Although wheat was apparently successfully grown in the
late 1520s by Sebastian Cabot's men at Sancti Spiritus (q. v.)
it was not until three and a half centuries later that Argentina began to take advantage of its wonderful pampas soil
and climate to grow wheat commercially; by the 1580s some
of the Spanish settlements were growing wheat and milling
flour for bread but it was still being imported at the close
of the viceroyalty and during early national period; after the
fall of Rosas, 1852, agricultural colonies of European farmers began to grow wheat in Santa Fe and neighboring areas;
although their land had often been poorly chosen and they
suffered from Indian raids, locusts, droughts and floods, and
other hardships, enough wheat was produced by late 1870s,
during presidency of Avellaneda, to export some to Europe;
along with other cereals, wheat began to compete successfully against cattle for use of land in Santa Fe, Córdoba, Entre
Ríos, Buenos Aires, and later, La Pampa provinces; it
spread west as far as the rainfall would permit and the Argentine pampas became recognized as one of the finest wheat
growing areas of the world; railroads brought the wheat to
ports of Rosario, Buenos Aires, and Bahía Blanca for shipping abroad; during several periods before World War II, this
grain provided Argentina's largest export; nation became one
of world's major producers of wheat; by 1960s this had
changed, with wheat export decreasing from its high 1939
export of nearly 5 million tons to less than 2 million in
1949; its production and acreage also declined in 1950s and
1960s due to high cost of land, heavy competition for world

market, threats of discrimination from British and European
markets, government emphasis on diversification of the economy, and national emphasis on economic independence; the
national market for wheat had greatly increased due to the
predominance of wheat-eating immigrants; one of Argentina's
great industrial firms S. I. A. M. (q. v.) had its beginnings in
the invention of a doughkneading machine better adapted to
use of Argentine flour in making bread; bad wheat harvests
in the 1960s and early 1970s hurt Argentine economy but the
nation still ranks as one of world's great wheat producers
(see Agriculture; Agropecuarian Interests; Grains).

See James R. Scobie, Revolution on the Pampas. A
Social History of Argentine Wheat, 1860-1910 (Austin, Texas,
1964; Spanish translation, Buenos Aires, 1968).

WHEELWRIGHT, WILLIAM (1798-1873).   U. S. entrepreneur; early
railroad builder in Argentina.

Born in Newburyport, Massachusetts; studied at Andov-
er College; joined merchant marine; the ship of which he was
captain was wrecked along Quilmes coast, Buenos Aires, in
1823; although Rivadavia was minister of government at that
time and interested in improving ports and strengthening communications between interior and Buenos Aires, he did not
take advantage of Wheelwright's services; latter took passage
on ship sailing to Valparaíso; spent nearly two decades trading along west coast of South America, serving as U. S. consul in Guayaquil, Ecuador (1829), then returning to Chile to
undertake several projects; in 1840, with foreign capital, he
established steamship service between Valparaíso and Panama;
improved the ports, with waterworks in Valparaíso and Callao,
gas illumination in Copiapó; to provide easier way of getting
Atacama minerals (nitrates, phosphates, etc. , especially) to
port of Copiapó, he obtained concession from government and
built first railroad in Chile; secured services of American
engineers Allan and Alexander Campbell and opened railroad
for service in 1852; meanwhile Wheelwright had conceived
the dream for which he is best remembered in Argentina:
the construction of a railroad across the Andes and Argentine pampas to make Buenos Aires a direct outlet to foreign
markets for Chilean products; he arrived back in Argentina
during the period between overthrow of Rosas' government
(1852) and national reorganization in early 1860s; Urquiza,
president of Argentine confederation, asked Allan Campbell
to draw up plans and estimates for railroad from Santa Fe
to Córdoba and attempted to persuade Wheelwright and José
Buschental (q. v.) to build projected line; political instability
made it difficult to secure credit; in 1862, however, the new
congress authorized the building of this Santa Fe-Córdoba
railroad; President Mitre immediately gave contract (see
Railroads for concessions of contract, etc.) to Wheelwright
who had only copy of Campbell survey and was able to secure British capital; this Argentine Central Railroad as it
was called (today the General Mitre) was opened in 1870, the

first British-owned railway in Argentina; much of the land
for the right-of-way was directly purchased by Wheelwright;
other lands were made available for colonization projects to
provide produce for the railroad to carry; although his dream
of trans-Andean railroad did not come true until 1910 and
other projects for expanding railroad service to Tucumán and
thence to Bolivia were premature, he did construct a railroad linking Buenos Aires and port at Ensenada (opened 1872)
before illness forced him to leave the country; died in London in 1873; four years later, his very close friend, Juan
Bautista Alberdi, published a biography of him, The Life and
Industrial Labors of William Wheelwright in South America
(Boston, 1877).

WHITE, GUILLERMO (1844-1926).   Civil engineer; University professor; director of construction of much of Argentina's transportation system in late 1800s.
         Born in Dolores, Buenos Aires province; member of
first class (including 12) of engineers to be graduated in Argentina (1870); became member of the faculty of mathematics
when it was created in 1874 and retained this position
through various changes in university until 1905 when he resigned from the faculty due to pressure of other activities;
during most of the administrations of presidents Avellaneda
and Roca he was in charge of the national department of
civil engineers and, in that capacity, directed much of the
railroad and port construction throughout the country in
period 1876-1886; supervised the surveying of boundaries of
Buenos Aires, La Pampa, Córdoba, and San Luis; also constructed Casa de Moneda and was involved in Buenos Aires
transit system; in 1886 he was serving on board of directors
of the Southern Railroad and became its president; at same
time he held a similar responsibility on other railroads; was
largely responsible for government building port at Bahía
Blanca, constructed by him and later named for him; also
built other ports; was a founding member, in 1872 of the
Sociedad Científica Argentina and later (1877-1884) was its
president and editor of its Annals; served as president of
Engineers' National Association, member of Argentine Academy of Exact, Physical, and Natural Sciences, and of the
Civil Institute of London; his contributions in the technologi-
cal development of Argentina were publicly recognized by
President Julio A. Roca; Guillermo White died in Buenos
Aires.

WHITE, WILLIAM (GUILLERMO) P. (1770-1842).   Bostonian who
arrived in Buenos Aires in 1803 as supercargo on merchant
ship Príncipe; remained there, acquiring considerable wealth
as merchant trader; cooperated with British during invasions
and was tried by Spanish authorities afterward; supported
May Revolution; helped Posadas and Larrea finance, assemble, and equip first patriot naval squadron for use
against royalists in Montevideo, 1814; years later his

property was confiscated and he moved to Montevideo; eventually a settlement of his claims against Argentine government was made.

WHITELOCKE, LT. GEN. JOHN (1757-1833). Ill-fated British commander of second British invasion attempt on Buenos Aires (1807) that ended in disaster and complete British surrender (see British Invasions). At the court-martial that followed his humiliating return to London, General Whitelocke defended his course of action on humane and political grounds: he wanted to save the city from destruction so that normal life could be resumed at once and trade (on more favorable terms with England) established as soon as possible; he justified his defeat and surrender in a frustrated cry to the effect that his judges had never faced the ferocity of porteños defending Buenos Aires and consequently could not understand the situation.

WILDE, COL. DIEGO WELLESLEY (d. 1866). English-born military engineer who made his home in Argentina; father of Dr. Eduardo Wilde. Diego Wilde arrived in Buenos Aires with his father in the early days of independence; entered department of engineers in 1824 and followed military career thereafter; fought at Ituzaingó with Brandzen and was wounded; later joined armies of generals Paz and Lamadrid to fight against Rosas; went into Bolivian exile with his family following the battle of Ciudadela; engaged in mining until the fall of Rosas in 1852 made it possible for him to return to Buenos Aires; reentered military life, fighting the montoneras of El Chacho, studying prospects of colonization in the Chaco, and then becoming comandante of the Salta frontier until the outbreak of the Paraguayan War; he was promoted to colonel for his action in this but he also contracted a swamp disease from which he died in Buenos Aires, 1866.

WILDE, EDUARDO FAUSTINO (1844-1913). Physician; statesman; writer.
        Born in Tupiza, Bolivia, where his family was in exile from Rosas; son of Diego W. Wilde; attended the Colegio de Concepción del Uruguay, founded by Urquiza, where he met and formed friendships with Julio A Roca, Olegario Andrade, Victorino de la Plaza and others; this group later formed a special part of the intellectual and literary "Generation of Eighty"; it also became important part of the oligarchy that directed Argentina's political and cultural life until close of century; in 1864 he entered medical school in Buenos Aires but interrupted his studies to aid in the cholera epidemic of 1867-1868 and to serve as army surgeon in Paraguayan War; graduated in medicine in 1870; served as medical officer in the yellow fever epidemic in 1871 (1400 victims in Buenos Aires); filled various teaching positions in medical school during next few years, publishing two texts, Lecciones de higiene and Lecciones de medicina legal y

toxicología.

    Eduardo Wilde took his place in public life as a legis-
lator in Buenos Aires province, then as latter's deputy in national congress; an oligarchical liberal in politics he supported Avellaneda, Roca, and Juárez Celman; became minister of justice and education under President Roca in 1880s;
true to his frequently expressed belief that the best way to
improve the moral, intellectual, and material forces of a
nation was to strengthen its educational system, he reformed
its legal bases, increased number of primary schools, established the Colegio Nacional in La Plata and in other provinces that needed one, and restructured normal schools; he
vigorously supported lay education and civil marriage; continued his public service as minister of interior under President Juárez Celman; improved public health services and began construction of Madero port in Buenos Aires; after fall
of Juárez Celman's government in 1890 Dr. Wilde went
abroad and spent considerable time traveling through Europe;
published his impressions in Viajes y observaciones; became
president of national department of hygiene during Roca's
second administration; among other accomplishments, he organized a medical expedition under Dr. Carlos Malbrán to go
to Paraguay to help fight the bubonic plague in Asunción;
early in January 1900 he was appointed minister plenipotentiary to United States and the following year was sent to
Spain and then to Belgium; died while holding this latter appointment to Brussels.

    Throughout his lifetime Eduardo Wilde was a writer;
in addition to the works mentioned he contributed witty, sometimes sarcastic, articles to various journals; edited La República for four years; and wrote serious, as well as literary, longer works; among these were: Discurso sobre educación laica; Tiempo perdido; Prometeo y compañía (autobiographical); Aguas abajo, etc.; his works have been collected
and published.

    See Florencio Escardó, Ensayo sobre Eduardo Wilde
(Buenos Aires, 1943); Juan Antonio Solari, Eduardo Wilde y
el laicismo argentino (Buenos Aires, 1948).

WILLIAMS, ALBERTO (1863-1952). Musician; pianist; teacher;
    composer; orchestra director; called creator of Argentine
    musical independence.

    Born in Buenos Aires; studied there and then at con-
servatory in Paris under grant from Buenos Aires province;
returned to Buenos Aires (1889) to continue his musical career; almost at once began to write music interpreting the
Argentine scene such as En la sierra and Rancho abandonado
(1890); continued with many others in various musical forms,
including Aires de la pampa; these gave Williams the credit
for having for the first time freed national music from European models; meanwhile he had acquired national and international fame as a pianist, director, and composer in more
traditional musical patterns; in 1893 he had founded the

Buenos Aires conservatory of music; among the many honors
he received were gold medals from the Paris conservatory,
and in St. Louis (1904) and San Francisco (1915); he died in
Buenos Aires.

WINE INDUSTRY. The wine industry is one of the oldest in Argentina and remains concentrated in the irrigated western
provinces of Mendoza and San Juan where it first became important.

  Transplanted from Chile soon after the middle of the
sixteenth century (see Vineyards), the Cuyo wine industry
grew slowly at first but by the early seventeenth century was
not only supplying local needs, but also some of those of
Córdoba and Buenos Aires (where the western wines came to
be preferred to those locally made or brought down the river
from Asunción); wine was also a basic trade item between
Cuyo and the mining communities of what is now Bolivia; attempts of the Spanish government to tax the Argentine industry heavily, in response to pressure from the Cádiz wine
merchants whose Spanish wines sold for twice that of native
ones, were constantly protested by the Mendoza cabildo; finally the taxes were so commonly ignored as to be unen-
forceable; in 1768 wineries came under government supervision, with that of the Augustinians being the first to be inspected; with the creation of the viceroyalty and the opening
of Buenos Aires to more trade in the late 1700s, the wine
industry of the Andean area went into a decline; increasing
numbers of Spaniards and foreign merchants and other residents, especially in the coastal area, preferred their traditional European brands; Buenos Aires also found it more
profitable to take imported wines in exchange for its hides
and tallow; wine, as a trade item, suffered along with other
interior products from the newly opened rift and increasing
conflict between economic interests of the coast and the hinterland; independence from Spain and the consequent breakdown of the former centralized Spanish economic system further damaged Cuyo wine interests as they lost their former
markets to the northeast when Bolivia became independent;
for the first time in 250 years, the Andean wine producers
found themselves limited to a purely local market.

  During the last half of the nineteenth century this
trend was reversed; French and Italian vines were introduced; local infant wine industries, with legal protections,
were established in various provinces; immigrants with wine-
making skills arrived in increasing numbers throughout the
nation; once again the soil and climate of Mendoza and San
Juan and neighboring provinces proved most favorable for
the production of good wine grapes and, with the coming of
the railroads linking these areas with the coast in the 1880s,
Cuyo wines again sold in Buenos Aires 600 miles away;
meanwhile quality had improved to suit the new tastes; Tiburcio Benegas (q. v.) and Hilario Lasmastres were said to
have bottled the first fine wines; in the early 1900s the first

national school of enology was established for the study of
blending fine wines; most of the wine grapes are grown on
small privately owned viñedos (vineyard farms) or on large
estates worked by tenant farmers, with wine manufactured in
the bodega on the vineyard premises or in a larger factory;
most of the labor is of the family type and, although large
number of Italians are involved, a majority of the wineries
are still owned by Argentine capital in contrast to some other
industries; the vineyards, large and small, cluster around
small villages and form the core of the community life, as
well as of its economy, culminating in the vendimia (q. v.) at
harvest time; in 1953 government supervision was established
over the wineries, with its headquarters in Mendoza; among
the largest producers are Toso, Arizu, Bombal, Giol (owned
by the government), Escorihuela, Gargantini, Nazar Anchorena, and Bianchi; production more than satisfies the national market, with Argentines consuming 72 liters per capita
annually (or about 6 1/3 quarts a month) and in 1972 ranked
fifth in world production; Argentine wines are competitive on
the world market, both in price and in quality, and exports
are increasing, with the United States becoming a promising
customer.

     See especially Lucio Funes, Historia de la vitivinicul-
tura mendocina, II International Congress of American History, v. III (Buenos Aires, 1938).

WOMEN.   When Vice-President María Estela Martínez de Perón
(q. v.) succeeded her husband to the presidency, June 29,
1974, she became first woman to be president of an American nation.

     The fight for woman's suffrage in Argentina paralleled
historically that in United States but was delayed in being
legislated; it became part of Perón's program, sponsored by
his second wife, Evita Perón (q. v.), and the law of suffrage
giving all women the right to vote at age 18 was passed in
1947; in the political activities of Perón's first presidency,
women frequently appeared as Peronist candidates and a
special Woman's Peronist Party was formed.

     Women in Argentina had traditionally taken active part
in the pioneer experiences, defensive, civic, and philanthropic interests of their communities from the earliest days of
settlement; by heritage and historical experience, women
shared with the men and fostered in their children the strong
individualistic spirit that has characterized Argentines of all
generations; Spanish law and custom made a woman special
in her own right and place as she brought her own wealth
and strength of family relationships to her husband and children; women contributed personally to the winning of independence in many ways, including giving their jewels or their
own funds to buy arms, turning their homes into important
meeting places for patriot leaders or to be used as recruiting offices, making flags and uniforms for Army of the
Andes, and even, especially in the northwest, gathering and

leading armed forces against the royalists or accompanying
their husbands in the fighting; during nineteenth century, women were deeply interested in politics and public affairs, usually working with or for the men in their families, like
Doña Encarnación's efforts on behalf of her husband Juan Manuel Rosas (q. v.); in more modern period women have been especially active in arts and literature and large numbers of them
have become scholars and writers, lawyers, physicians, den-
tists, journalists, and other professionals. Many of these Argentine women's contributions have come down through folklore
and history as part of the national heritage (see Mencia Calderón de S. , Leonor de Tejeda, Maria A. de la Paz y Figueroa,
Martina de Silva de G. , María Sanchez, Francisca Jacques,
and Victoria Ocampo).

See "Women: the forgotten half of Argentine history"
by Nancy Caro Hollander, in Ann Pescatello, editor, Female
and Male in Latin America: Essays (Pittsburgh, Pa. , 1973).
See also Lily Sosa de Newton, Diccionario biográfico de mujeres argentinas (Buenos Aires, 1972).

WOOL see SHEEP

WORLD WAR I (1914-1918). In spite of Great Britain's primacy in
    its economy, Argentina declared its neutrality in World War
    I as part of a national commitment to peace and non-involve-
    ment in affairs of other nations--especially strong popular de-
    sire following Paraguayan War 1865-1870; approximately
    20,000-30,000 Europeans, many on reserve, returned annual-
    ly to fight for the mother country; the war made an immedi-
    ate impact on the Argentine economy and life style as war
    needs cut down drastically on the usual supply of manufac-
    tured goods imported; loss of customs revenue, one of the
    chief sources of national income, forced government to re-
    sort to floating short loans; almost total reliance on English
    coal, no longer available, for energy revealed Argentina's
    vulnerability, as did the lack of iron and steel industries,
    the neglected mining industries, etc. ; for a time England's
    place as prime supplier was taken by the United States; by
    the time Yrigoyen became president in 1916, the nation was
    enjoying great prosperity from the high prices commanded by
    its meats and hides; a thrust toward industrialization estab-
    lished many light industries, and the United States temporar-
    ily replaced Western Europe in supplying manufactured items;
    Yrigoyen firmly committed himself to continued neutrality in
    spite of considerable external and internal pressure; after
    the United States entered the war in April 1917 this policy
    caused U.S. -Argentine relations to deteriorate; for a time,
    diplomatic relations with Germany were also strained after
    the sinking of Argentine ships by German submarines (1917);
    when a German takeover of Uruguay by German settlers
    from southern Brazil was threatened in February 1918, Yri-
    goyen promised aid to Uruguay against such an invasion.
        Following the war, and largely as a result of high
    cost of living during the war, Yrigoyen faced serious labor

unrest; other events also indicated that the apparently successful Argentine agricultural economic pattern of the decades preceding the war had been definitely broken although briefly revived in the 1920s; World War I marks the beginning of clear
recognition that Argentina must create or develop enough industrial, energy, and mineral resources to supply its own
needs; Yrigoyen's neutrality policy, however, was considered
so successful economically even by his critics, that it served
as a precedent for Argentina's position in World War II.

WORLD WAR II (1939-1945). At the outbreak of World War II Argentina declared its neutrality and maintained this position
until the last year of the war; although public opinion was
widely divided both by economic sectors and social and ethnic groups, there were many exceptions within each category;
the oligarchy and the press generally favored the Allies because of their traditional, close, and profitable political and
economic ties with Great Britain and their admiration and affection for France, with Paris regarded for a century and a
half as Argentina's cultural Mecca; on the other hand, the
military, trained by Germans, admired the latters' professional skills, techniques, and attitudes and confidently expected
an Axis victory; Argentines of Italian blood (and they were
numerous on all levels) were divided between those who
hated everything that Mussolini stood for and those who regarded him as a glamorous caudillo whose counterpart they
would like to follow in Argentina; the Church, especially the
Spanish-born priests, tended to back such new totalitarian
governments as those of the Axis countries and that of Franco and to remember that he had been able to end the Spanish
Civil War only with help from the Axis powers; always anti-
communist, its influence became stronger against Allies after
Russia joined latter in 1941; nationalists of all political groups
tended to view Great Britain as Argentina's chief barrier to
economic independence--a view not changed by attitude of many
members of Buenos Aires British settlement who sometimes
tended to treat local Argentines as British colonials; in any
case, few feared the consequences of an Axis victory; some
wanted Great Britain humbled; and almost everyone felt that
the war was far away (in spite of the scuttling of the German
Graf Spee across Río de la Plata in Montevideo, December
17, 1939, following a naval encounter with the British naval
units in the South Atlantic); and almost everyone agreed that
neutrality was Argentina's traditional policy and had served
its interests well during World War I (q.v.); succeeding
presidents, from Ortiz to Ramírez, found more political support for continued neutrality than for any other policy.
      Argentina found itself more affected by the war than
it had anticipated and policy changes had to be made; after
the fall of Paris, President Ortiz (q.v.) began immediate efforts to strengthen Argentina's military defense; the quest
for additional arms continued with increasing pressure for
the next few years; the Allies could not furnish them, the

United States would not; and even Germany, approached somewhat secretly, was unable either to furnish or to transport
them; the Japanese attack on Pearl Harbor (December 7,
1941) brought expressions of sympathy and suggestions of aid
from President Castillo, but at the meeting of foreign ministers at the Inter-American defense conference in Rio de Janeiro (January 1942) Argentina's adamant opposition to U.S.
request that all member nations break off diplomatic relations with Axis powers forced the acceptance of a recommendation (rather than a decision to break relations) that each
member nation consider breaking off Axis relations in terms
of its own policy and interests; President Castillo seems to
have regarded this as a victory for each nation's freedom of
action as opposed to U.S. hegemony over all hemispheric
foreign policy; the United States, however, and many of Argentina's neighbors, including Brazil, apparently regarded it
as evidence of Argentine pro-Axis sympathy; within Argentina, various foreign groups--both Allied and Axis--continued
to operate freely as in a neutral country; tensions, already
high because of political problems, mounted as propaganda
from both sides spread among the people, shortages of manufactured goods became acute as national industry could not
satisfy markets formerly supplied by European imports no
longer available; Argentine meat sold for high prices but
money remained abroad as nothing could be bought and was
reflected in rapid inflation that hurt all wage earners--al-
ready dissatisfied with lack of labor reform; Argentine administrators became more and more concerned about national
defense, as German defeat became inevitable and Argentina
was left relatively defenseless with regard to such neighbors
as Brazil that had received great quantities of modern arms
from the United States; finally, January 26, 1944, Argentina
broke off relations with the Axis powers, partly because of
its increasing alienation from the American community but
specifically (although secretly) because embarrassing letters
being carried by an espionage agent from Argentine leaders
to German authorities had been captured by the British in
Trinidad and turned over to the United States, and partly because Argentine agents were known to have been active in
subversive movements in neighboring Latin American countries, especially Bolivia; in early 1945, as the American nations prepared for the end of the war and a new inter-American organization, Argentina was brought back into the group
by an arrangement whereby Argentina should declare war
against Germany and Japan and then be permitted to sign the
Chapultepec agreements; Argentina became the last Latin
American nation to declare war on the Axis powers, in
March 1945 (although several others had waited almost as
long), signed the agreement, and then also participated in the
organization meeting of United Nations at San Francisco a
few months later.
    World War II did not so much change Argentina's po-
litical, social, and economic development as accelerate

processes that had been under way for 100 years to integrate
its large immigration into an Argentine nation and society
and to change its agricultural, rural economy to an industrialized, urban one; the republic shared with the rest of the
world a new sense of social and political democracy and determination to implement it, and has been involved since then
in the economic woes of an industrial nation facing an over-
populated world of underdeveloped ones; internationally, World
War II forced Argentina to realize the difficulty, if not the
impossibility, of any one nation isolating itself and so it has
tended to play a larger role in foreign affairs.

WRIGHT, FRANCISCO AGUSTIN (1800-1849).   Journalist; political
    figure.
        Born in Buenos Aires; published small newspaper in
Ensenada where he had his ranch; as representative in the
provincial legislature, and an earlier supporter of Rosas, he
was one of few that opposed giving extraordinary powers to
Rosas; as result of this opposition, he was eventually forced
to emigrate to Montevideo; continued his journalistic work,
writing for Correo Político y Mercantil and then El Nacional
of Montevideo; took part in defending city against siege by
Oribe; in 1845 published Apuntes históricos de la defensa de
Montevideo; other works include a defense of immigration in Ensayo sobre la prosperidad de los extranjeros y de-
cadencia (1833), a biography of Tomás Espera (1835), and a
biography of Colonel C. F. Brandzen, included in collection
of historic documents, edited by Lamas in 1849; Francisco
Wright died in Montevideo.

WRIGHT, GUILLERMO CARLOS (1807-1868).   Naval officer.   Born
    in Philadelphia; began naval career in United States; arrived
    in Buenos Aires, 1825; joined forces of Admiral Guillermo
    Brown (q.v.); took part in war against Brazil; later favored
    Unitarists against Rosas and was demoted (1834); called back
    into service during Anglo-French blockade (1845); after Ca-
    seros, he took part in some of the fighting around Buenos
    Aires but devoted himself primarily to business and ranching.

                           - X -

XAQUES, NICOLAS.   Early physician in colonial Argentina.
        Born in Flanders, while that was still under Spanish
crown, Xaques came to Argentina probably early in the
seventeenth century; was said to have been the first physician in Salta; moved to Córdoba where he acquired considerable prestige in his medical practice; by 1619 he had become a vecino in Buenos Aires and had established his practice there.

XARQUE, FRANCISCO (1609-1691).   Jesuit missionary; writer.
        Born in Albarracín, Spain; came to Río de la Plata

as visitador of Jesuit missions in 1627; remained in the New World until middle of the century, serving as missionary to Guaraní and teacher; most of his time spent in Corrientes, Córdoba, and Santiago del Estero; he went to Potosí where he became rector and also held judicial appointment; returned to Spain on special mission for archbishop of Charcas; assigned to ecclesiastical duties in Albarracín; died there.

Father Xarque wrote at least two important accounts of the early Jesuit missions and missionaries in the South American area in which he had lived and worked; Insignes misioneros de la compañía de Jesús en la provincia del Paraguay (including Río de la Plata and Tucumán), published in Pamplona, Spain, in 1687, and a biography of one of his most distinguished co-workers there, Father Antonio Ruiz de Montoya (q. v.).

- Y -

YABEN, JACINTO R. (1887-).   Career naval officer and historian.

Born in Buenos Aires; educated in naval schools; reached rank of frigate captain before retiring in 1934; held various naval commands as well as teaching and administrative positions; was chief of personnel at Puerto Belgrano in 1934; after retiring from active duty he turned to writing; among his works were Biografías argentinas y sudamericanas (6 v. , 1938-1940); Los Balcarce, familia patricia (1942); Efemérides sanmartinianas (1944); and various monographs on naval matters for the Revista Militar, Boletín del Centro Naval, and other journals; in 1952 he was appointed president of the Instituto Nacional Sanmartiniano.

YACARE.   Name commonly applied to water reptile, smaller than the crocodile, found in the Paraná, Paraguay, and Uruguay rivers, as well as in Brazilian rivers; in length it varies from 6 to about 19 feet; its skin is frequently used in the making of purses, bags, footwear, etc.; in folklore medicine, and still quite commonly believed today, the fat of the yacaré is said to be useful in relieving muscular and rheumatic aches and pains; because of the early prevalence of the yacaré in the Argentine rivers, the name appears frequently as a place name, especially in the Mesopotamian provinces of Corrientes and Entre Ríos.

YACIMIENTOS PETROLIFEROS FISCALES (YPF--National Oil Fields).   Government agency established in 1922 to provide national control of development of recently discovered petroleum deposits; regulates all production, exploration, exploitation, including that of private companies to areas assigned, and processing; all petroleum reserves are property of the nation; five important producing regions are Comodoro Rivadavia, Neuquén, Mendoza, Salta, and Jujuy; YPF was logical

consequence of discovery of oil in Comodoro Rivadavis (q. v.)
December 14, 1907.

Signs of oil were discovered by accident in Comodoro
Rivadavia in 1903 while drilling for water; search continued
unsuccessfully, hampered by destruction of the tower by high
winds (90 to 100 miles); the foreman, J. Fuchs, forced the
workmen to rebuild the tower and to continue drilling until at
1780 feet they found, not water, but oil; the samples obtained from wells 1 and 2 were sent to the Dirección de
Minas (Bureau of Mines); since this oil came from public
land, the government automatically became owner of the
wells; President Figueroa Alcorta made at that time a declaration, that has continued to form the basis of Argentina's
national petrochemical and mining policy, to the effect that
ownership of subsoil resources was vested in the state, regardless of who owned the land above or who discovered the
oil, and that these must be used to benefit the people of the
entire country; within two years the government drilled seven
productive wells; the railroad arrived in Comodoro in 1909;
shortly after this President Saenz Peña refused an offer of
Rockefeller interests to help finance the oil wells; the first
official agency for the exploitation of petroleum was created
in 1910 and it was the Dirección General de la Explotación
del Petróleo de Comodoro Rivadavia; in 1913 the engineer
Luis A. Huergo sent to the minister of agriculture a study
on the problems caused in other countries by foreign investments; as a result, the minister canceled permits of exploration previously given to some private parties; by 1916 there
were 39 wells producing 137,500 cubic meters of oil annually; in 1922 attempts were made to establish refineries in
Comodoro Rivadavia and Buenos Aires; by that time there
were 128 producing wells.

The discovery of oil in Plaza Huincul, in Neuquén,
happened in a slightly different way; natural gas was found
in 1906 but the mining company exploring the region (an Argentine mining company called Picu Leifu) was not interested
in gas and the project was abandoned; the drilling of well
number one was carried out, 1916-1918; when oil was found
at 6900 feet, the government declared this region national
reserve zone.

On June 3, 1922, President Yrigoyen signed the decree creating Yacimientos Petrolíferos Fiscales; Enrique
Mosconi (q. v.) was appointed as first director; YPF introduced many modern social and labor policies and practices
earlier than other private and national institutions; these included medical services, extra salaries for maternity, pa-
ternity, and seniority, 13th month salary, dining rooms for
single employees, etc. ; in 1923 YPF signed a contract with
Bethlehem Steel Co. to produce gasoline and kerosene; by
1929 YPF controlled the internal market of fuels and established prices for gasoline and other products; at that time
the national tax on gasoline was 2 cents per gallon; in 1930,
80% of the employees were Argentine; meanwhile, the oil

industry was developing; in 1928 YPF started exploratory
work in Salta, in 1930, in Mendoza; and in 1930 natural gas
came into use for fuel; in 1932 liquified petroleum gas production was begun in Buenos Aires; the old rotary system of
drilling was largely replaced in 1935 by more efficient electrical logging; in 1937 gun perforation was used, in 1938
side-wall coring and in 1940 electric logging with automatic
recording; YPF continued to expand; it built tankers, and
produced gasoline, kerosene, and high octane aviation gasoline.

Decline came in 1940s due to the war; by the 1950s
YPF had about 600 wells in operation but was seriously in
debt and was still, after 30 years, unable to supply the national needs; in the early 1950s YPF had become flagrantly
corrupt and inefficient; in attempt to satisfy national oil
needs immediately, President Perón signed, in August 1953,
a contract with Standard Oil of California; this contract
marked the beginning of change; later, after the revolution
that had removed Perón, President Frondizi declared that
Argentina could not afford to continue paying 300 million dollars per year on petroleum imports and signed exploration
and production contracts with European and American companies; these companies operated only as agents of YPF, but
their contracts were criticized as a "betrayal" by the nationalists; President Frondizi's oil program, however, provided
quick results and Argentina became briefly self-sufficient
for the first time; when President Illia took power, pledged
to save "Argentine oil from the imperialists," he canceled
oil concessions paying United States $872,650,000 in compen-
sation; YPF's golden hour had passed and debt and inefficiency accumulated; later, under President Onganía (1966-
1967) a petroleum law opening investment opportunities to international capital was signed, YPF was reorganized so that
management would become professional instead of political,
and new exploration contracts to drill the continental platform were signed in the late 1960s.

In the 1970s YPF began to increase production, hoping to reach self-sufficiency by 1975; for this purpose, they
started the exploration of new possible fields in Salta, Jujuy,
Tucumán, southern Santa Cruz, Neuquén, and Río Negro,
as well as of the southern underwater basin; 60% of the nation's refineries are owned by YPF: La Plata, the most important, followed by Luján de Cuyo (Mendoza), South Dock
(Buenos Aires), San Lorenzo (Santa Fe), Campo Durán (Salta),
Plaza Huincul (Neuquén), and El Centauro (Tierra del Fuego);
in 1973 these processed more than 21 million cubic meters
of oil; the petroleum law of the Frondizi period will probably be abrogated; it provided for exploration, exploitation,
and transportation by the state and by private and/or mixed
enterprises; YPF will probably again exercise a monopoly
over all aspects of petroleum activities; private companies
will continue to operate but will be limited; in 1976 YPF
signed exploration contracts with Libya, Ecuador, and Bolivia;

these contracts will be paid with household products made in
Argentina and needed by the other countries (see Petroleum;
Fuel Resources).

YACYRETA-APIPE.   Project for joint Argentine-Paraguayan hydroelectric plant and system on Upper Paraná river.

YAGUARETE.   Guaraní name used for Argentine tiger; appears as
"yaguareté-abá" in missionary literature of Corrientes,
Misiones, and Paraguay; the yaguareté appeared in nineteenth-
century literature, as in Sarmiento's account of Facundo
Quiroga's attack by this animal and Darwin's earlier tale of
tragic episode of yaguareté walking into church in Santa Fe.

YAMANAS (also called YAGANES).   Canoe Indians that occupied
southern portion of Tierra del Fuego; said to have been there
by 2000-1500 B.C.; composed of several groups, each with
its own dialect of the related Yámana language; physically,
the Yámanas were small, dolichocephalous, with wide, flat
faces; their life was based on the sea with the entire family
engaging in collective fishing or seal hunting; boats or canoes
were made of bark sewn with vegetable fibers; they used a
harpoon with bone point; used leather or shell containers, no
ceramics, lived in primitive thatched or skin-covered shelters and used skins for clothing; believed in a father God and
both good and bad spirits; the Yámana culture is extinct but
a few descendants may be found working as peones in Beagle
Channel area.

YANACONAZGO.   Form of personal service required of certain Indians during colonial period.   Spanish conquistadors found
this system operating in Inca empire; yanacones apparently
were Indians who no longer belonged to any tribe or cacique
and were used as household servants or farm laborers, becoming the property of the master to whom they were assigned; in Argentina the system was criticized from the beginning because of the abuses involved; government regulations did little to improve the situation; Mariano Moreno attacked the institution in his "Disertación sobre el trabajo
personal de los indios"; in 1811 the Junta Grande abolished
it, publishing the decree in Spanish, Quechua, and Aymara
(languages of Indians in northwestern Argentina and Bolivia);
this decision was formally reinforced by the Assembly of
1813 that repeated it, adding a Guaraní version.

YANKELEVICH, JAIME (1894-1952).   Early Argentine entrepreneur
in radio-television broadcasting.
        Born in Sofía, Bulgaria, he moved to Argentina with
his parents in 1896; years later, he opened a small electrical business in Buenos Aires that led him to become one of
the leaders in this field; supplementing his knowledge and
training by trips to United States and Germany, he became
director (1924) of Radio Nacional (now Radio Belgrano) and

in 1951, one year before his death, had made that the first
TV station to operate in Argentina.

YAPEYU (from Guaraní word meaning "that which is ripe. ")
Jesuit mission town in Corrientes; birthplace of José de San
Martín; modern capital of department San Martín.
        Founded in 1626 by Roque González as reducción and
Jesuit mission town of Guaraní Indians; located near mouth
of Guaviravi river into Uruguay river; Yapeyú was administrative center for missions in that area and became very
prosperous, growing adequate food for its own sizeable population and shipping meat, hides, tallow, and yerba mate down
the river for sale; when lieutenant governor Juan de San Martín was assigned there a few years after the Jesuit expulsion,
it was still a thriving town, although Indians were beginning
to scatter and the economy showed neglect; José de San
Martín was born there in the governor's house (probably the
old colegio and headquarters of the Jesuits) in 1778 and remained there for a few years; in 1812, when San Martín was
organizing his granaderos a caballo, he recruited Indians
from Yapeyú to serve in it; the threat of Portuguese invasion from Brazil had been constant, especially throughout the
eighteenth century, and, during the wars with Artigas of
Uruguay, the Brazilians totally destroyed Yapeyú (1817) and
scattered its inhabitants; during the civil wars even the
name was forgotten but, with the death of San Martín in
1850 and attention called to Yapeyú as his birthplace, and
the ending of the Rosas' era at Caseros two years later, attempts were made to find and identify the actual birthplace
of the great liberator; eventually the ruins of the "casa natal
de San Martín" were found--or generally agreed upon--as
San Martín's birthplace and a protective covering placed
over them; in 1915 this became a national historic monument;
meanwhile Governor Juan Pujol of Corrientes had refounded
the town (1860), giving it the name of San Martín; Corrientes'
government attempted to grant some of the land to French
colonists but various land suits and conflicts developed between the newcomers and oldtimers living there, resolved finally by a new survey, 1884; eventually the town regained its
old name of Yapeyú and the department, of which it was the
capital, kept San Martín's name.

YATAITI-CORA, BATTLE OF. On July 11, 1866, the allied
forces of General Mitre defeated the Paraguayan army of
President Francisco Solano López at this place; López requested negotiations for peace but the allied governments
could not agree and this effort failed; meanwhile, Mitre was
not able to consolidate his gains after this victory as quickly
as desirable and the Paraguayans gained valuable time in
which to fortify at Curupaytí (q. v.) (see Paraguayan War).

YATES, WILLIAM. Irish adventurer who became involved in

Argentine civil wars, 1820-1821, as follower of José Miguel
Carrera (q.v.); took part in battles of Cepeda, Cañada de la
Cruz, San Nicolás, Pavón, and Gamonal; accompanied Carrera when he took refuge among Indians of Buenos Aires
province; continued fighting in Córdoba and Cuyo until Carrera was captured and executed in Mendoza; Yates was sent
as prisoner to Peru; pardoned there by San Martín, he went
to Brazil and joined army of Pedro I; published (1824) a detailed
account of his experiences with Carrera; of historical interest
as account of one of Argentina's most difficult periods.

YELLOW FEVER   see   EPIDEMICS OF DISEASE

YERBA MATE (sometimes known as Paraguayan tea).   Shrub or
    small tree, Ilex paraguariensis, related to common holly;
    native in small area of South America including Paraguay,
    northeastern Argentina, and southern Brazil; the tea made
    from its dried and roasted leaves was used by the Guaraní, who
    called it kaa-guazú (or "the splendid herb") and valued it pri-
    marily for its medicinal or magical qualities; it is considered
    be a diuretic, contains some caffeine and tannin, and prob-
    ably many vitamins; Spanish settlers in Argentina quickly
    adopted its use as a beverage; throughout the four centuries
    following the conquest it served as the universal Argentine
    beverage; gauchos popularized it, carrying their mate leaves,
    tied in bags to their saddles, along with primitive teakettles
    to heat the water to pour over the dry leaves; they sipped it
    through a straw or silver tube (bombilla) from a gourd
    (known as the mate) into which the leaves and boiling water
    had been poured; it seemed to provide the essential supple-
    ment to the meat diet of all Argentines and remains a sym-
    bol of Creole culture and life; yerba mate's economic im-
    portance was recognized in 1680 by a royal order imposing
    a duty of half a peso on every arroba (about 25 pounds) of
    Paraguayan yerba unloaded in Buenos Aires, usually in ex-
    change for hides; Jesuits brought yerba mate under cultiva-
    tion in Misiones and shipped it out regularly to supply Argen-
    tine demand, as one of their most important mission exports;
    when Jesuits were expelled, their yerbales, or yerba mate
    plantings, were neglected and eventually taken over by the
    forests; Argentina's increasing demand for yerba mate, as
    population grew, was satisfied by importing it from Para-
    guay, primarily, with some from Brazil, both countries hav-
    ing large supplies of it growing wild; in 1770s Viceroy Ce-
    ballos stipulated that mate must be served six times a day
    to soldiers and to workers; during nineteenth century gauchos
    and soldiers in civil wars relied on yerba mate and free
    meat for their diet; as gauchos were replaced on estancias
    by peon labor, the latter were assured their full supply of
    mate as part of their wages.
        During nineteenth century, it had come to be widely
    believed that yerba mate could not be cultivated, in spite of
    the Jesuit experience; attempts were made, however, along
    the Misiones side of the upper Paraná and in 1903 one proved

Yerba Mate   1046

to be successful; by 1930 its production (sold on domestic
market) was valued at 150 million pesos; 93% of Argentine
production came from Misiones, with Corrientes and part of
the Chaco providing the rest; when Argentines began to turn
to imported coffee and tea instead of the indigenous, Creole
mate, consumption declined as production increased; in the
late 1930s the government limited production in attempt to
maintain price levels; continued depression of prices made
profits marginal in this industry and during the next two or
three decades both its acreage and production declined; in
1971 an intensive publicity campaign was undertaken to increase consumption; in 1973 there were reported to be
35,000 hectares (over 86,000 acres) under cultivation with a
production of 128.6 thousand tons; the increasing use of mate
(or maté, as it is sometimes called in English) in the United
States, may offer a new market.

YERBALES (or YERBATALES). Term applied to commercial
    yerba mate groves; most commonly found in Misiones and
    Corrientes provinces.

YERUA, BATTLE OF (September 22, 1839). Site in Entre Ríos,
    just south of Concordia near west bank of Uruguay River,
    where Lavalle fought his first battle in his campaign against
    Rosas and won his first victory; the Unitarist forces of La-
    valle had been transported from Martín García Island by
    French ships to Entre Ríos; shortly after their arrival, La-
    valle's forces were attacked by a much larger army under
    Governor Pascual Echagüe, a general for Rosas; Lavalle's
    defeat of Echagüe was significant primarily because it opened
    the way for Lavalle to enter Corrientes to gain that prov-
    ince's support against Rosas (see Juan Lavalle).

YGOBONE, AQUILES D. (1901-). Lawyer; university professor;
    writer.
        Born in Santa Fe province and educated in law in
    Buenos Aires where he established his legal practice; taught
    in the faculty of economic sciences in Buenos Aires; he be-
    came especially interested in Argentine economic resources
    and policy; published over 300 articles and studies in various
    reviews and journals on historical and geographical themes;
    the predominant theme in his writings has been that of Pata-
    gonia, its historical background, its economic possibilities
    and development, and biographical studies of pioneers in
    opening up that area, with several works devoted to Francis-
    co P. Moreno (q.v.).

YOFRE, FELIPE (1848-1939). Lawyer and public official.
        Born in Córdoba and graduated from university there;
    served as national congressman from Córdoba, 1880-1884;
    took part in debates over federalization of city of Buenos
    Aires (q.v.) and was member of commission that planned
    creation of territory of Misiones; from 1886 to 1893 served

in court of appeals, Buenos Aires; became senator (1893-
1898); initiated laws creating department of mines and geology,
establishing Federal Courts of Appeal, and the National Lot-
tery; resigned to become minister of interior for President
Julio A. Roca; concerned himself with creating or reforming
legal bases of municipal organization, organization of national
territories, and the law of residence (q. v.) establishing some
government control over undesirable immigrants; established
first national Indian colony in the Chaco; also worked with
Roca as interim foreign minister during absence of Almancio
Alcorta due to problems related to boundary dispute with
Chile; proposed as candidate for presidency by groups within
Autonomist party in 1904; elected again to Senate in 1905; two
years later, he retired to private, professional life; died in
Buenos Aires.

YPF   see   YACIMIENTOS PETROLIFEROS FISCALES

YRIGOYEN, HIPOLITO (1852-1933).   Leader of Unión Cívica Radical (Radical movement); president of the Argentine Republic,
1916-1922; 1928-1930.   One of the most remarkable and original political leaders of Argentine history, he represented a
curious mix of democracy and personal authoritarianism (often
called a caudillo); Yrigoyen was a populist who made his political party organization into an effective means for gaining
desired political power.
      Born in Buenos Aires; he attended various schools
through the secondary level, then entered the school of law
but seems not to have graduated from it; always interested
in political life, Yrigoyen accepted minor clerical appointments in the government and then was made police commissioner (1872-1877) for one of the wards in Buenos Aires
through the influence of his uncle Leandro N. Alem (q. v.);
elected to Buenos Aires provincial legislature; following the
political turmoil of 1880 he spent several years in relative
political obscurity, teaching at the girls' normal school in
Buenos Aires where he apparently first became interested in
Krausism (q. v.), and engaging in the buying and fattening of
cattle for market on two small ranches from which he made
a good living; returning to politics in 1890, he served as
Alem's political lieutenant in the revolution of that year and
was appointed chief of police in Buenos Aires; by 1893 Yrigoyen was president of the Unión Cívica Radical organization,
or party, for Buenos Aires province and after the suicide of
his uncle Leandro N. Alem (1896), he became the undisputed leader of the party or, as he preferred to call it, the
Radical movement; in its struggle against the ruling oligarchy,
the UCR followed policy of abstention from participation in
either elections or government until its demands for wider
suffrage, free elections, and honesty in government were
met; Yrigoyen refused appointments from presidents Luis
Sáenz Peña and Carlos Pellegrini; after passage of the electoral reform law in 1912, the Radicals swung into political

action and elected Yrigoyen president in 1916.

His first administration (1916-1922) covered difficult period of World War I and its aftermath; he maintained Argentine neutrality but the nation suffered economic dislocations as its traditional European customers found themselves unable to provide transportation for trade items; when situation eased and demands for trade were increased, Yrigoyen, an early economic nationalist, attempted to make trade agreements that would benefit the Argentine farmers as well as the merchants; he also sent a representative to the League of Nations organization meeting but called him back when Argentine suggestions seemed to be ignored; internally, Yrigoyen's position was made difficult by fact that the congress and most of the provinces were still under conservative rule; he made full use of his constitutional powers of intervention, in twenty cases altogether, sometimes several times in the same province, if he considered its government to be illegitimate; his critics accused him of using this power for political purposes of strengthening the UCR; in 1919 social tensions snapped in a series of strikes that were suppressed ruthlessly by the government's use of armed forces (see "Tragic Week"); Yrigoyen aroused dissension in the armed forces by his apparent use of promotions to strengthen his party's political position; one important reform that took place during his first term was that in the universities; faculties (accused of oligarchical sympathies and support) were stripped of much of their power and university administration became much more democratic (see University Reform); in 1922 Yrigoyen turned the presidency over to Marcelo Torcuato de Alvear but remained politically powerful as head of the Radical Party; in 1928 the party split between the Personalistas, who wanted Yrigoyen for president again and the Anti-Personalistas (led by Alvear) who did not, but he was easily elected.

Yrigoyen's second administration (1928-1930) was brief and sterile, if not a fiasco; in the face of sharpening economic (world depression), social, and financial problems, and the increased political opposition of other parties, he offered little leadership and less action; blaming this on his advanced age and poor health, a revolt of military officers, led by Uriburu removed him from office September 6, 1930, with general public approval; imprisoned at Martín García island, Yrigoyen at first refused the pardon offered him but then returned to die in Buenos Aires in 1933; after his death his prestige among the people was largely restored.

In 1956, 12 volumes of his collected writings, Pueblo y gobierno, were published. See Félix Luna, Yrigoyen, el templario de la libertad (Buenos Aires, 1954); Manuel Gálvez, Vida de Hipólito Yrigoyen. El hombre del misterio (1939 and later editions); Luis V. Sommi, Hipólito Yrigoyen: su época y su vida (Buenos Aires, 1947); and Peter G. Snow, Argentine Radicalism: the History and Doctrine of the Radical Civic Union (Ames, Iowa, 1965).

- Z -

ZABALA, BRUNO MAURICIO DE (1682-1736). Governor and captain general of Río de la Plata; founder of Montevideo.
        Born in Durango, Vizcaya; entered army at age of
nineteen; after about sixteen years of fighting in Spain's international wars, during which he lost one arm and was made
a knight of the order of Calatrava, he was appointed governor
and captain general of the Río de la Plata; took office there
in 1717; Zabala faced two main problems: foreign intrusions
into the Spanish area and revolts of the comuneros in Paraguay; a French expedition that attempted to land a party near
Maldonado (in what is now Uruguay) was driven off; the chief
threat to Spanish power came from the Portuguese in Brazil,
who were then entrenched at Colonia do Sacramento (q. v.) also on the north bank of the Río de la Plata; fearing their
expansion eastward toward the Atlantic, he began fortifying
that area; his attention was then (1725) demanded by the
comunero revolt led by José Antequera in Paraguay; after
that had been pacified, Zabala returned to establish the town
of Montevideo formally on January 20, 1726, and spent most
of his time during the next few years in getting this new
settlement and port on a firm and prosperous basis; in
recognition of his work, he was promoted to the captaincy-
general of Chile (1734) but was forced to make another trip
up the river to put down a new outbreak of the comuneros
before leaving for his new assignment and died on the way
back to Buenos Aires; buried near Santa Fe, his remains
were removed (1737) to Buenos Aires and buried in the chapel
of the governors in the cathedral.

ZABALA, ROMULO (1884-1949). Historian; journalist.
        Born in Buenos Aires; served as Argentine consul in
Livorno (Leghorn), Italy in 1911, and in Newcastle, England
in 1914; his activities as historian and journalist then began;
in 1914 he was appointed assistant director of the Museo
Mitre; in 1917 he founded the Austral News Agency; was
manager of the newspaper Noticias Gráficas; served as secretary of editorial staff (dirección) of La Nación and head of
its archives; was active in several clubs and societies in
Buenos Aires; in 1923 he was elected a member of the Academia Nacional de la Historia; founded and became first editor of its Boletín; became director of municipal museum of
colonial art in 1937; organized several libraries; served on
national commission of museums and historic monuments;
became a corresponding member of the Real Academia de la
Historia in Madrid; Zabala died in Buenos Aires.
        Among his published works are: La enseñanza de la
historia en la escuela primaria; Historia de la ciudad de
Buenos Aires (2 volumes, in collaboration with Enrique Gandía); several other books dealing with early foundation of
Buenos Aires, and Numismática del virreinato del Río de la
Plata.

ZACCAGNINI, ANTONIO (1879-1932).   Socialist leader and writer.
Born in Italy; emigrated to Buenos Aires as a teenager; went to work as laborer; joined Socialist Party and became active in the labor union movement, founded and edited
small union paper El Progreso de la Boca; became manager
of La Vanguardia, largest Socialist newspaper; was elected to
national congressman from the Federal Capital in 1928; reelected in 1932, supported by independent Socialists; concerned himself in Congress primarily with legislation to improve situation of railroad and dock workers; also was responsible for creation of vacation camps for children and use
of mobile libraries; died in Buenos Aires.

ZAFRA (from Arabic word safar meaning time in which the crop
yellows or matures).   Name given to period of sugar cane
cutting, a time of great activity in the sugar region; since
1915 most of the old cane varieties have been replaced by a
Java variety that can tolerate more cold; still centered in its
original base at Tucumán, the important sugar industry has
spread to Salta, Jujuy, eastern part of Chaco, Formosa, and
northern area of Santa Fe, Misiones, and Corrientes; the
zafra takes place in May and migrant workers from Catamarca and Santiago del Estero and Indians from Bolivia and
Formosa provide most of the labor; the harvesting consists
of two parts, the cutting of the cane by machete, followed by
the stripping of the leaves and peeling of the stalk; the cane
is then carried to the sugar mills for processing; after the
strenuous work is over, a popular fiesta is held, with a Harvest Queen chosen to preside over it (see Sugar).

ZANNI, PEDRO (1891-1942).   Military aviator.   Born in Pehuajó,
Buenos Aires; graduated from military academy and then
from military school of aeronautics, 1913, with diploma #23;
taught in latter school; in 1914 flew from Buenos Aires to
Villa Mercedes (San Luis) covering a distance of 640 kilometers, setting a new record for South American flights;
made three attempts to fly across the Andes, succeeding in
1920; in 1924 undertook to fly around the world; he and his
mechanic Beltrame departed from Amsterdam in an airplane
named "City of Buenos Aires"; flew southeastward across
Europe and Asia for more than 10,000 miles but were forced
to abandon the flight at Karachi; served as air attaché in
France, Italy, Great Britain, Germany, and the United States;
died in an automobile accident near Buenos Aires.

"ZAPA, LA GUERRA DE. " Term applied by Mitre to the entire
complex of diversionary tactics used effectively by José de
San Martín (1815-1816) to deceive and confuse General Osorio,
commander of the royalist forces in Chile, so as to ensure
the success of his military expedition across the Andes early
in 1817; it takes its name from the sappers who were used
to dig military trenches or underground passages around the
fortifications of that period.

ZAPATA, JOSE VICENTE (1851-1897).   Lawyer; statesman.
Born in Mendoza and educated there and in Buenos
Aires; quickly entered public life; served as minister of government in Mendoza (1876) and president of the provincial supreme court (1877); elected to the national congress in 1878,
he played active role in the debate over the federalization of
the capital; became minister of government in 1881, resigning in 1883 to be national senator; in 1891 he became Pellegrini's minister of interior and made important contributions
through his efforts to reclaim lands that had been fraudulent-
ly sold and by proposing the creation of the Dirección General de Ferrocarriles; after having served as interventor in
Santa Fe province, he was asked by president Luis Sáenz
Peña to become minister of justice, worship, and public instruction; retired from public life because of illness; died in
Buenos Aires.

ZAPATA, MARTIN (1811-1861).   Jurisconsult; member of constituent congress, 1852.
Born in Mendoza; graduated in law from the university
of San Felipe, Santiago de Chile; as a Unitarist aided other
Unitarists in defense of Montevideo against Rosas' siege, then
spent rest of Rosas period in Chile; returning to Mendoza
after Caseros he was elected as one of the provincial delegates to the constituent congress of Santa Fe, 1852-1853;
took active part in debates resulting in the constitution;
helped form the first supreme court of the Confederation
(1854), and then served as senator from Mendoza (1856-1860);
died in Mendoza earthquake of 1861.

ZAPIOLA, JOSE MATIAS (1780-1874).   Independence hero; commander of Mounted Grenadiers during battle of Chacabuco.
Born in Buenos Aires, son of Manuel Joaquín de Zapiola, Spanish naval officer who accompanied expedition of
Pedro de Ceballos to Río de la Plata and of María Encarnación de Lezica y Alquiza; sent to Spain to be educated for
Spanish navy; graduated from Naval Academy in 1796; was
assigned to naval duty; sent to Buenos Aires in 1810, his
participation in the May Revolution caused him to be sent
back to Spain by royal authorities; there, in Cádiz he met
Carlos María de Alvear (q. v.) and José de San Martín (q. v.)
and joined with them in determining to return to Buenos
Aires to fight for independence; accompanied them to London,
then on the George Canning to Buenos Aires; upon their arrival, in March 1812, Zapiola immediately placed himself,
with them, at the command of the patriot junta; also joined
in establishing the Lautaro Lodge (q. v.); assisted San Martín in organization of the granaderos a caballo; served in
successful siege of Montevideo, 1814, under Alvear; rejoined
San Martín, then in Mendoza; became commander of the
Granaderos regiment in the Army of the Andes; fought at
Chacabuco, Cancha Rayada, and Maipú; captured city of
Chillán in southern Chile from royalists; in June, 1819, he

returned to Buenos Aires and the navy; commanded a river
squadron sent by Buenos Aires against upriver caudillos
(1821); in 1829 he withdrew from public life to devote himself to rural activities; remained in this situation until after
the fall of Rosas at Caseros, 1852; returned to active duty
as naval commander and to serve as minister of war and
navy in cabinet of Governor Valentín Alsina of Buenos Aires;
retired from navy; died in Buenos Aires.

    See Federico Zapiola, Zapiola, soldado de Chacabuco
y Maipo (Buenos Aires, 1956).

ZARATE, FERNANDO DE (d. 1595). Governor of Tucumán, Paraguay, and Río de la Plata (1593-1595); used resources of entire area to repel and fortify Buenos Aires against attacks
from corsairs (largely British); his health broke under the
heavy load and he died there after brief but successful administration; succeeded by Juan Ramírez de Velazco.

ZARATE, JUAN ORTIZ DE   see   ORTIZ DE ZARATE, JUAN

ZAVALETA, CLEMENTE (1760-1830). Political leader in Tucumán during early independence period.

    Born in Tucumán, brother of Deán Diego Estanislao
Zavaleta (q. v.); was serving as first alcalde of the cabildo
of Tucumán at time of May Revolution in 1810; because of
his position and his personal prestige, he was among those
that won Tucumán's support for the revolution; became director of gun-factory established in Tucumán by the First
Junta; from January to March, 1812, he served as lieutenant
governor of the province, then returned to service in the cabildo and legislature; he became provisional governor of
Tucumán, in 1822, replacing Bernabé Aráoz, but was replaced, himself, by General López that same year; retired
after having attempted for a dozen years to reconcile the
various groups during a very difficult period in Tucumán's
political history; Clemente Zavaleta died in Tucumán.

ZAVALETA, DIEGO ESTANISLAO (d. 1843). Priest and patriot
who played active ecclesiastical and political roles in early
decades of independent national period.

    Born in Tucumán; educated in Buenos Aires at Domin-
ican academy and at royal Colegio de San Carlos where he
later taught philosophy and theology; delivered sermon at inaugural session of patriot Junta May 30, 1810; his sermon
was printed in the Gaceta; in 1812 he was named chief canon
and shortly thereafter deán provisor and governor of ecclesiastical cabildo of Buenos Aires; Deán Zavaleta supported Bernardino Rivadavia's ecclesiastical reforms, while censuring
excesses, and carried out his refusal to acknowledge authority of the Apostolic Vicar, Monsignor Juan Muzi, sent to
Buenos Aires in 1823 to establish relations between the new
nation and the Vatican; in addition to ecclesiastical duties,
Zavaleta performed such public duties as serving in Congress,

1817 (served on committee that drew up Constitution of 1819) and in a mission undertaken for Rivadavia, persuading the citizens of Cuyo to cooperate in a general effort to restore peace within the individual provinces and to send delegates to a national congress to reunite all the provinces into one nation governed by a representative system; became a member of that congress when it met in 1825; served as member of Lavalle's state council (1829) and voted against granting extraordinary powers to Juan Manuel Rosas in 1835; Zavaleta died in Buenos Aires eight years later.

See Enrique Ruiz Guiñazú, El deán de Buenos Aires Diego Estanislao Zavaleta.

ZAVALIA, CLODOMIRO (1883-1959). Jurisconsult; university professor of law; writer.

Born in Tucumán; graduated in law and social sciences, Buenos Aires; became professor of federal and municipal law in same faculty and served as dean (1931-1936) as well as vice president of the university (1932-1934); also served as federal judge and as director of several commercial and business firms; wrote several works dealing with various aspects of Argentine law, including Historia de la corte suprema de justicia; Derecho federal (Federal Law); Derecho público provincial (2 v.); Jurisprudencia de la constitución nacional; and Defensa social de la nación; died in Buenos Aires.

ZAVALIA, SALUSTIANO (1810-1873). Jurisconsult; signer of 1853 constitution.

Born in Tucumán; graduated in civil law, Córdoba, 1829; became active in unitarist political life in his province (Tucumán); served as minister under Bernabé Piedrabuena, judge, deputy to legislature; joined anti-Rosas movement of 1841 but fled into exile after capture of its leader Marco Avellaneda; spent nine years practicing law in Lima; returned to Argentina after end of Rosas' government; became active member of constituent congress of Santa Fe and signed the constitution of 1853; also wrote the constitution of his province and served as its senator and provisional governor; died in 1873.

ZAVALIA, SALUSTIANO J. (1837-1914). Jurisconsult and justice of supreme court; journalist; cabinet minister.

Born in Tucumán; accompanied family into exile from Rosas; educated at Valparaíso, Chile, and then at university in Córdoba; began journalistic career by starting El Imparcial; later was editor briefly of La Nación Argentina; after holding various government positions, became a member of the national supreme court; later he was elected national senator and during administration of Juárez Celman served as minister of the interior and interventor in his native province; died in 1914.

ZEBALLOS, ESTANISLAO S. (1854-1923). Statesman; writer; lawyer; legislator; estanciero.

Born in Rosario; attended Colegio Nacional of Buenos Aires; early plunged into the life of public service and official positions to which he would devote all his energies, along with and closely related to his lifetime career as journalist; during his three terms as congressman, three appointments as foreign minister, and assignment as envoy to U.S., the unusual scope of his energies, interests, talents, and the force and volume of his writings on public affairs made a real impact on the nation's life, especially in its international aspects, for over four decades (from 1880 until his death).

In 1877, Zeballos refused to accept the conciliation plan made by the political leaders, including Mitre and Alsina, and although he attracted few supporters for this stand, he became a legislator in Buenos Aires' lower house in 1879; was elected to National Congress in 1880 by Federal District and again in 1884 by Santa Fe; and, much later, 1912-1916; during these twelve years in Chamber of Deputies he twice served as president; throughout his time as legislator he showed active interest in almost every kind of subject relating to national welfare and progress; among these were: reform of commercial and procedural codes, effective development of new national territories, all matters relating to the economy, such as agriculture, railroads, economic studies, monetary policy, the meat trade--he was himself an important estanciero and president of the Sociedad Rural, 1888-1894; also became involved in legislation related to sanitary regulations, the topographical mapping of province of La Rioja to show its potential geological and hydrographic resources; the Federal university of Rosario; development and regulation of wine industry; construction of highways; expansion of Argentine merchant fleet; and the law of civil marriage, which he favored.

Zeballos' most important contributions as a government official were probably in the field of international relations; resigning from congress to accept President Juárez Celman's appointment as foreign minister in 1889, he was first Argentine minister to be forced to create a national policy with regard to the new Pan American organization that the U.S. government was sponsoring; Zeballos' stand was firm: that Argentina would cooperate, within limits, as long as the sovereignty of Latin American nations was not violated by U.S. domination of the organization; refused to enter into any hemispheric economic agreement that would interfere with Argentina's close ties with Europe; Juárez Celman's government fell in 1890 and in October 1891, Zeballos became foreign minister in President Carlos Pellegrini's cabinet (1891-1892); in the difficult financial crisis facing the government, Zeballos supported Pellegrini's financial measures and, by his correspondence with Roque Saenz Peña and other prominent political figures, helped to create

confidence in new government's ability to improve its financial situation without foreign intervention; also gave instructions to Argentine delegates to second Pan American conference to be held in Mexico; from 1893 to 1896, Zeballos
served as minister to the U.S. government; continued fight
that his predecessors had carried on to get U.S. to modify
its tariff on wool imports that had hurt Argentina so greatly;
although he was not successful in this to any great extent,
trade between Argentina and the U.S. rose to new heights in
the mid-1890s; in Washington, Zeballos met defeat on matter
of Brazilian boundary; the boundary between Brazil and northeastern Argentina had never been clearly drawn; in 1889 both
nations agreed to abide by decision of president of U.S. as
arbiter; shortly after this, before decision was rendered,
the imperial government in Brazil was replaced by a republican one and Brazil's foreign minister and Zeballos made
an agreement by which the area in dispute was to be divided
between them; on February 10, 1894, Brazil and Argentina
presented their cases in Washington; in spite of Zeballos'
best efforts, President Grover Cleveland awarded entire disputed
area to Brazil; Argentine pride was hurt and Zeballos was
criticized in Buenos Aires but moderate papers, like La
Prensa and La Nación called the decision fair; in 1907 he
was appointed as one of the Argentine members of the Hague
Permanent Court of Arbitration; served again (1907-1908) as
foreign minister for President Figueroa Alcorta; in 1910 he
was a delegate to the Fourth Pan American conference held
in Buenos Aires on its centenary of May Revolution.

Thereafter, except for his last term in congress, Zeballos was no longer a public official; devoted himself to
teaching law at University of Buenos Aires (1912-1918) and
to his writing; his influence through his editorial work on La
Prensa and his own Revista de Derecho, Historia y Letras
continued to be great as he was generally regarded to be an
important authority on foreign affairs; in 1913 he criticized
President Woodrow Wilson's apparent intention to make U.S.
judge of constitutionality of political regimes in Latin America; in that same year, however, he presided over the ceremonies in Buenos Aires in which the University conferred an
honorary degree on Theodore Roosevelt who was visiting
there; praised former U.S. president for his corollary to the
Monroe Doctrine confining it primarily to Caribbean area,
calling this a recognition of fact that Argentina had attained
a level of civilization that made protection of Monroe Doctrine no longer necessary for it, but thanked U.S. for standing by in earlier days; in 1917 Zeballos firmly supported
Yrigoyen's policy of neutrality in World War I; following the
war there was a resurgence of Latin Americanism aroused
by U.S.'s new Pan American program, as expressed by
Charles Evans Hughes and Sumner Welles; in the closing
years of his life, 1921-1923, Zeballos again returned to
fight U.S. domination with his pen; he died in Liverpool; his
eulogy was pronounced a month later in Buenos Aires,

November 5, 1923, by Rodolfo Rivarola.

Zeballos was a writer all his life; contributed to various newspapers and reviews; his most important journalistic writing was done for El Nacional, which he founded, and La Prensa with which he was associated for many years; published several books of varied interest, such as Zálida (a novel), Viaje al país de los Araucanos (travel diary); El escudo y los colores nacionales (history), Misiones, Justicia internacional positiva (law), etc.; his Revista de Derecho, Historia y Letras (1898-1923) stands as a memorial to him; its 76 volumes (1898-1923), containing serious essays of scholarly or public interest written by Zeballos and his contemporaries constitutes a treasure trove for history, law, letters, and education; two large volumes of the Revista (1923) are devoted to the life and works of its founder and director.

For general background see Inter-American Relations; Pan American Conferences; United States (relations with Argentina).

ZEGADA Y GORRITI, ESCOLASTICO (1813-1871).   Priest; church and public leader in Jujuy province.

Born in Jujuy of a family largely devoted to sugar interests in the colonial period; his grandfather, Gregorio Zegada, had been a royalist governor of Jujuy and a colonel; his father Colonel Julián Gregorio Zegada, and the brothers of his mother, Ana María del Carmen Gorriti (see Juan, José, and Francisco Gorriti) were leaders in Jujuy for independence; the young Escolástico was educated in Jujuy and in Chuquisaca where he was ordained in 1836; returning home, he combined church responsibilities with his family's tradition of public service; served as curate; opened schools, including one for girls; aided in securing and paid for first printing press in Jujuy; was legislator, minister in provincial cabinet, federal judge, governor of province, and acting national senator (1862); gave Jujuy its first constitution; restored the monastery of San Francisco and became its first president; his Instrucciones cristianas were so widely used that several printings had to be made (see Jujuy).

ZELAYA, CORNELIO (1782-1855).   Veteran of war of independence; legislator.

Born in Buenos Aires; began his military career fighting under Juan Martín de Pueyrredón against British invasions, 1806-1807; after May Revolution of 1810, he joined Auxiliary Army, commanded by Ortiz de Ocampo, that was sent to Upper Peru; fought in battles of Cotagaita, Suipacha, Tucumán, and Salta; was wounded at Ayohuma; remained in Army of the North, fighting against montoneros in 1818-1819; did not participate in the Arequito revolt; left army of the North and entered service of Governor Bernabé Aráoz in Tucumán; in 1821 went to Mendoza at time of José Miguel Carrera's (q.v.) action there; after latter's defeat and death,

Zelaya returned to Buenos Aires; was appointed colonel in
the cavalry militia by Governor Martín Rodríguez; in 1826
he represented province of Buenos Aires at the Constituent
Congress and signed the Unitarist constitution; during rule of
Rosas whom he opposed, he absented himself from Buenos
Aires, living most of the time in Corrientes; after fall of
Rosas at Caseros, Zelaya returned to Buenos Aires; Urquiza
appointed him commandant of the Fortaleza; died in that post.

ZINNY, ANTONIO (1821-1890).   Educator; archivist; and historian.
        Born in Gibraltar; arrived in Buenos Aires at age of
twenty-one; became teacher, later sponsored by presidents
Mitre and Sarmiento; founded Colegio Argentino in Corrientes
and contributed to periodicals La Tribuna, El Nacional, and
La Nación Argentina; in 1864 he organized the archives of
foreign relations in Buenos Aires and in 1871, the municipal
archive; meanwhile he had begun his important work on the
history of Argentine journalism; in 1868 published his Efe-
meridografía argirometropolitana, listing alphabetically all
the periodicals that had appeared before 1851, with all available information about each; also published in Revista de
Buenos Aires, volumes X-XIII, with title "Bibliografía peri-
odística de Buenos Aires hasta la caída del gobierno de
Rosas"; Zinny made similar studies of the journalism of the
provinces, with special detailed histories of the Gaceta de
Buenos Aires, and the Gaceta Mercantil; in 1883 his history
of Uruguayan journalism (1757-1852) was published; other historical works include Historia de los gobernadores de las
Provincias Unidas del Río de la Plata, 1535-1879 (Buenos
Aires, 1879; reedited by José Ingenieros in 5 v., 1920); and
a richly documented Historia de las Provincias Unidas del
Río de la Plata hasta el fusilamiento de Dorrego (Buenos
Aires, 1887).

ZIZUR, PABLO (1743-1809).   Spanish pilot of royal armada; ex-
        plorer of Patagonia.
        Born in Pamplona, Spain, Zizur arrived in the Río de
la Plata area at an early age; took part in the expeditions to
survey the boundary between Portuguese Brazil and Spanish
South America; remained in Buenos Aires, married, and established his family there; sent to explore the Patagonian
coast to Cape Horn, he was shipwrecked in the icy waters;
he and a few companions built a boat that took them to Soledad (Falkland Islands) where he found means to return to
Buenos Aires; one leg was amputated due to frostbite in his
foot on that trip; in 1781 he went on successful mission to
establish communications between Buenos Aires and new
settlement at Río Negro, opened road from Carmen de Patagones to Dolores; and in 1786, acting under orders from the
viceroy and cabildo, made his way to Salinas Grandes (in
southwestern portion of province of La Pampa) and established a settlement there; his diary account of this trip was
published by Pedro de Angelis in his Colección de obras y

documentos relativos a la historia del Río de la Plata in
1836; Zizur became captain of the port of Buenos Aires in
1804, charted its waters and began the marking of its sand-
bars to make navigation easier; died in Buenos Aires.

ZONDA, EL. Periodical published briefly in mid-1839 in San Juan
     by literary society; almost exclusively written by Domingo
     Faustino Sarmiento, it was one of the causes of his political
     imprisonment and exile the following year.
          El Zonda takes its name from the harsh, hot, dry
     wind that frequently blows in valley of same name in San
     Juan.

ZORITA, JUAN PEREZ DE   see   PEREZ DE ZORITA, JUAN

ZORRILLA, BENJAMIN (c. 1840-1896). Jurisconsult; political
     leader.
          Born of Salteño family; graduated as doctor of juris-
     prudence from University of Buenos Aires; served twice as
     governor of Salta, 1869-1871, 1873-1874; founded its Normal
     school; was minister of interior for President Nicolás Avella-
     neda (1879) and provisional minister of foreign affairs (June-
     October, 1880); was elected president of the National Council
     of Education and vice president of first South American inter-
     national pedagogical congress, 1882; became minister of in-
     terior in cabinet of José Evaristo Uriburu but was forced to
     resign in 1896 because of bad health; died that same year in
     Buenos Aires.

ZUBERBÜHLER, CARLOS E. (1863-1916). Born in Buenos Aires;
     educated in Europe; entered business world; became active
     in public life; took part in early activities of the Radical
     Party; his learning in field of art brought him appointments
     as professor of art history at the Academia Nacional de
     Bellas Artes and at University of Buenos Aires; as director
     of the Museum of Fine Arts, he organized, classified, and
     catalogued all its works; at his retirement he gave to this
     institution his own very fine art collection; played active role
     in several societies formed to stimulate fine arts and to en-
     courage young artists; wrote La Unión Cívica del parque and
     Conmemoración del 10°aniversario de la revolución de 1890;
     also wrote several essays about the Casa de San Martín, the
     house in Yapeyú believed to have been birthplace of the
     Liberator José de San Martín.

ZUBIAUR, JOSE B. (1856-1921). Educator; writer.
          Born in Paraná; attended Colegio del Uruguay; studied
     law; devoted his life to teaching and promotion of education;
     held many positions such as those of rector of Colegio Na-
     cional del Uruguay, supervisor of secondary and teachers
     college education, adviser and member of National Council
     of Education, general director of 2 schools of Corrientes,
     etc.; in 1886 he joined with Carlos N. Vergara to found the

professional journal La Educación that greatly influenced development of Argentine educational system during its nearly
20 years of publication; he was one of first to introduce manual arts and technical training into public schools to balance
the traditional intellectual bias found there; Zubiaur's translations of works by American and European innovative educators, along with his own writings, often based on his observations of foreign educational systems, was given much
credit for establishment of the industrial, technical, agricultural schools in Argentina.

ZULOAGA, MANUEL ANTONIO (1797-1863).   Veteran of Army of
    the Andes; businessman.
        Born in Mendoza, belonging to an old family; son of
José Javier Zuloaga and María Godoy; joined the Army of the
Andes in 1816 and crossed the cordillera to Chile in Las
Heras' unit; fought at Chacabuco, Cancha Rayada, and Maipú;
was with the army in camp in San Juan, 1820, when the officers' uprising took place; Zuloaga went on to fight under San
Martín for liberation in Peru; took part in the attack on Callao in which he was promoted to sergeant major; requested
retirement after San Martín left Peru (1823); returned to
Mendoza in 1825; because of the many wounds he had received, he left military service and entered business; established a weaving factory in the convento of the Augustines, a
mill, and a free hospital in Mendoza; lost all his possessions
in earthquake of March 20, 1861; died in Mendoza two years
later as result of injuries received in the earthquake.

ZUVIRIA, FACUNDO (1793-1861).   Jurisconsult; president of Santa
    Fe constitutional convention, 1852.
        Born in Salta; graduated in canon and civil law in
Córdoba; became active in political organization of his native
province in 1820s; was first president of Salta provincial legislature; attempted to bring better schools and universal male
suffrage to Salta and to organize a provincial militia; as a
result of several attacks on him and the triumph of the
montoneras, he went into exile in Bolivia where he remained
throughout the Rosas period; lived in Sucre practicing law,
writing, and teaching; became general inspector of the universities there; returned to Salta after fall of Rosas and was
elected its representative to the Constitutional Congress of
Santa Fe; there he was chosen to be president; late in 1852,
after he had returned from an unsuccessful mission to Buenos
Aires, as member of Urquiza's mission to try to persuade
Buenos Aires to join the other provinces, Zuviría moved that
proceedings toward a constitution be postponed until Buenos
Aires could participate; this was voted down; became a member of the Supreme Court; in the new government, with Urquiza as president, Zuviría became foreign minister; later
he held other positions such as minister of justice and public
instruction in Salta, national senator from Corrientes, and
president of Supreme Court at Paraná (1860); published

several monographs: Discursos y escritos políticos; La
prensa periódica; La educación pública: Tiranía y demagogia;
and his most profound work El principio religioso (Paris,
1860) in which he reveals himself as a Catholic who believes
that religion must be a factor in national government; he died
in Paraná.

ZUVIRIA, GUSTAVO MARTINEZ see MARTINEZ ZUVIRIA, GUS-
    TAVO

LIST OF PRESIDENTS*

President	Administration	Vital Statistics	Native Province
Bernardo Rivadavia	1826-1827	1780-1845	Buenos Aires
Vicente López y Planes	July 1827-Aug. 1828	1785-1856	Buenos Aires
Juan Manuel de Rosas, Governor and Captain-General of the Province of Buenos Aires	1829-1833, 1835-1852	1793-1877	Buenos Aires
Justo José de Urquiza	1854-1860	1800-1870	Entre Ríos
Santiago Derqui	1860-1862	1846-1891	Córdoba
Bartolomé Mitre	1862-1868	1821-1906	Buenos Aires
Domingo Faustino Sarmiento	1868-1874	1811-1888	San Juan
Nicolás Avellaneda	1874-1880	1837-1885	Tucumán
Julio A. Roca (1st term)	1880-1886	1843-1914	Tucumán
Miguel Juárez Celman	1886-1890	1844-1909	Córdoba
Carlos Pellegrini	1890-1892	1846-1906	Buenos Aires
Luis Sáenz Peña	1892-1895	1822-1907	Buenos Aires
José Evaristo Uriburu	1895-1898	1831-1914	Salta
Julio A. Roca (2nd term)	1898-1904	1843-1914	Tucumán
Manuel Quintana	1904-1906	1835-1912	Buenos Aires
José Figueroa Alcorta	1906-1910	1860-1931	Córdoba
Roque Saenz Peña	1910-1913	1851-1914	Buenos Aires
Victorino de la Plaza	1913-1916	1840-1919	Salta
Hipólito Yrigoyen (1st term)	1916-1922	1852-1933	Buenos Aires
Marcelo Torcuato de Alvear	1922-1928	1868-1942	Buenos Aires
Hipólito Yrigoyen (2nd term)	1928-1930	1852-1933	Buenos Aires

*See Gustavo Gabriel Levene, Historia de los presidentes argentinos. 2 vols., Buenos Aires, 1973.

President	Administration	Vital Statistics	Native Province
José Félix Uriburu	1930-1932	1868-1932	Salta
Agustín P. Justo	1932-1938	1878-1943	Entre Ríos
Roberto M. Ortiz	1938-1942	1886-1942	Buenos Aires
Ramón S. Castillo	1942-1943	1873-1944	Catamarca
Arturo Rawson	June 4-6, 1943	1885-1952	Santiago del Estero
Pedro Pablo Ramírez	1943-1944	1884-1962	Entre Ríos
Edelmiro J. Farrell	1944-1946	1887-	Buenos Aires
Juan Domingo Perón (1st & 2nd terms)	1946-1955	1895-1974	Buenos Aires
Eduardo Lonardi	Sept. 20-Nov. 12, 1955	1896-1956	Córdoba
Pedro Eugenio Aramburu	1955-1958	1903-1970	Córdoba
Arturo Frondizi	1958-1962	1908-	Corrientes
José María Guido	1962-1963	1910-	Buenos Aires
Arturo U. Illia	1963-1966	1900-	Buenos Aires
Juan Carlos Onganía	1966-1970	1914-	Buenos Aires
Roberto Marcelo Levingston	1970-1971	1920-	San Luis
Alejandro Agustín Lanusse	1971-1973	1918-	Buenos Aires
Héctor Cámpora	May 25-July 13, 1973	1909-	Buenos Aires
Juan Domingo Perón (3rd term)	1973-1974	1895-1974	Buenos Aires
María Estela (Isabel) de Perón	1974-1976	1931-	La Rioja
Jorge Rafael Videla	1976-	1925-	Buenos Aires

Appendix II

HISTORICAL CHRONOLOGY

This chronology is designed to serve as a simple time
chart to be used as reference for listings in this dictionary. More
detailed historical chronologies may be found in Russell H. Fitzgibbon, comp. and ed. , Argentina: A Chronology and Fact Book,
1516-1973 (New York, 1974); and James R. Scobie, Argentina: A
City and a Nation (second edition, New York, 1971).

c. 1500s   Rumored Portuguese discoveries of Río de la Plata,
            including possible discovery by Amerigo Vespucci in
            1502.

1516   Traditional date of discovery. Juan de Solís entered
            Río de la Plata estuary and named it Mar Dulce;
            killed by Indians on Uruguayan coast.

1520   January-October. Magellan's expedition sailed and
            wintered along Argentine coast from Río de la Plata,
            discovering Uruguay River, to the strait that bears
            his name; first description of Patagonia and straits
            written by Antonio Pigafetta, accompanying expedition.

1527-29   June-end of 1529. Expedition of Sebastian Cabot ex-
            plored Paraná River; established first Spanish settle-
            ment, Fort Sancti Spiritus. Cabot joined there (1527)
            by expedition commanded by Diego García.

1531   Portuguese Martín de Sousa visited Río de la Plata
            and triggered Spanish decision to occupy the area.

1536   Expedition led by Pedro de Mendoza, first adelantado
            of Río de la Plata, officially founded city of Buenos
            Aires.

1537   Asunción settled by Spaniards.

1541   Buenos Aires abandoned; center of Spanish settlement
            and government established in Asunción; Irala major
            leader.

1542-44   New governor Alvar Núñez Cabeza de Vaca took over
            but was forced to return to Spain by Spanish settlers.

1543   La Gran Entrada--Rojas's first settlements in north-
            west Argentina.

1550   Juan Núñez del Prado founded first Argentine city near
            Tucumán but it was unsuccessful.

1550-70   Cattle and sheep introduced into Argentina from Brazil
            and Peru (grazing industry started).

1551-53   First permanent settlement of Argentina finally made;
            earlier settlement, Barco III (1551), by Juan Núñez
            del Prado moved (1553) to more favorable location
            and officially established as Santiago del Estero.

1558   Several cities founded in Province of Tucumán by
            Pérez de Zurita; destroyed by Indians.

1560   First Jesuits enter present Argentine territory.

1561   Spanish town of Mendoza is established by Pedro del
            Castillo; expedition came from Chile.

            Establishment of Sevilla monopoly of Spanish-Ameri-
            can trade, in effect closing Buenos Aires as a port,
            except under special circumstances, or limiting it
            strictly.

1562   Spanish town of San Juan established by Juan Jufré;
            expedition came from Chile.

1563   Royal Cédula established governorship of Tucumán,
            with its capital at Santiago del Estero, under authority
            of audiencia of Charcas; decision made to settle juris-
            dictional conflicts between Spanish settlers from Peru
            and Chile.

1565   Settlement of the town of Tucumán by Diego Villarroel
            sent by Governor Francisco de Aguirre.

1570   Bishopric of Tucumán established with seat at Santiago
            del Estero; later (1699) moved to Córdoba.

1573   City of Córdoba founded by Jerónimo Luis de Cabrera;
            Santa Fe established by Juan de Garay.

1578-79   First missions founded in Río de la Plata area by
            Franciscans.

1580   Second founding of city of Buenos Aires by Juan de
            Garay, restoring movement of colonization in Río de

la Plata to its original center.

Revolution of Seven Leaders in Santa Fe; often cited as first evidence of Argentine desire for self-government.

1582	Salta founded by Hernando de Lerma as place of communication and defense between Santiago del Estero and Peru.
1585	April 14. Founding of Concepción del Bermejo by Alonso de Vera y Aragón.
1588	Torres de Vera y Aragón founded San Juan de Vera de las Siete (Corrientes).
1590	Smallpox epidemic killed hundreds in Tucumán, Córdoba, and Santiago del Estero.
1591, '93	La Rioja and Jujuy founded by Governor Juan Ramírez de Velazco to strengthen defenses against Indians.
1594	San Luis founded by Luis de Jufré; moved two years later to present location.
1595	First permit (asiento) granted for importation of black slaves.
1600	Organization of vaquerías.
1605	First shipload of charqui (dried beef) left Buenos Aires for Cuba.
1613-14	Jesuit college at Córdoba established, later (1622) reorganized as the University of Córdoba.
1617	Buenos Aires became capital of the province of Río de la Plata, separated from Paraguay; first governor, Hernando Arias de Saavedra (Hernandarias).
1620	Creation of bishopric at Buenos Aires under archbishop of Charcas, with jurisdiction over part of Paraguayan territory also.
1622	Interior customhouse established at Córdoba to prevent entrance of imported products smuggled from Buenos Aires; moved to Salta (1651). University of Córdoba inaugurated.
1630-37	Calchaquí rebellion in Tucumán.
1650s-60s	Series of Indian revolts in Tucumán led by Spanish

adventurer Pedro Bohórquez posing as Inca prince.

1658   Second rebellion in Tucumán of Calchaquí Indians.

1661   Creation of a temporary audiencia at Buenos Aires; suppressed in 1671.

1666   End of Indian rebellions; Calchaquís removed from region.

1676   Customhouse moved from Córdoba to Salta and Jujuy in attempt to stop contraband trade from Buenos Aires entering interior markets.

1680   Colônia do Sacramento was established across the estuary from Buenos Aires to serve as a Portuguese base and port.

1683   Fernando de Mendoza Mate de Luna founded city of Catamarca.

1695   Academy of Monserrat in Córdoba came under sponshorship of the Jesuit Order; was first important secondary school in Argentina.

late 1600s   Bishop of Tucumán's residence moved from Santiago del Estero to Córdoba.

1713   First asiento for importing black slaves into Buenos Aires granted to Great Britain following war of the Spanish Succession.

1726   Montevideo established by Governor Bruno Mauricio de Zabala of Buenos Aires to serve as Spanish base in Uruguay against encroaching Portuguese Brazilians.

1730's   Revolt of the comuneros in Paraguay; first movement toward object of emancipation from Spain.

1732   March. Uprising of Corrientes comuneros against Governor Zabala's military conscription.

1750   Guaraní war; Indians rose against Spanish and Portuguese forces, refusing to accept transfer of certain Jesuit missions to Brazil.

1760s-74   Controversy between England and Spain over settlement in and sovereignty over Falkland Islands; England withdrew from islands, 1774, for several decades.

1761   Printing press imported by Jesuits for use in Córdoba.

1764   Revolt of comuneros of Corrientes against what they

considered to be unreasonable military demands of
Pedro de Ceballos (see 1732 for first such revolt).

1767   Royal expulsion of Jesuits from Argentina and confiscation of their property; most seriously affected were
Misiones and University of Córdoba.

1773   Royal academy of San Carlos (Colegio de San Carlos)
established in Buenos Aires.

1776   Establishment of Viceroyalty of the Río de la Plata
including modern nations of Bolivia, Paraguay, Uruguay, and Argentina, with Buenos Aires as capital
and Pedro de Ceballos as first viceroy.

1778   Buenos Aires opened to trade with various Spanish
and Spanish American ports; end of Sevilla merchants'
monopoly.

1779   Customhouse established at Buenos Aires.

1780-82   Revolt of Tupac Amaru II that inflamed entire Andean
area, involving Argentina, and threatened Spanish
power in South America.

1782-83   Division of viceroyalty into eight intendancies,
strengthening royal administration and collection of
revenues but at same time changing traditional political relationships; corregidores abolished.

1783   Buenos Aires became seat of new royal audiencia;
formally installed, 1785.

Founding of Concepción del Uruguay, Entre Ríos, by
Tomás Rocamora as part of Viceroy Vertiz' effort to
expand settlement.

1784   First saladero in Río de la Plata was established near
Colonia, Uruguay.

1785   Installation of an audiencia at Buenos Aires (decreed
in 1783).

1790   Serious smallpox epidemics.

1794   Consulado, or tribunal of merchants, established in
Buenos Aires.

1795   First saladero in Argentina was established at Quilmes;
saladeros were established later in all coastal areas
for salting beef and mutton (later); in Santa Fe they
were also used for fish; system expanded rapidly in
Argentine independence period to dominate economy

during first half of nineteenth century.

1795-97   Freedom of trade in Buenos Aires expanded to permit
            trade with Spain's allies (1795) and with neutral na-
            tions (1797).

1799   Schools of navigation and design were established by
            Manuel Belgrano.

1801   April 1-October 15, 1802.   First newspaper published
            in Buenos Aires: Telegrafo Mercantil, Rural, Politi-
            co, Economico e Historiografo del Río de la Plata.

1802-07   Publication of El Semanario de Agricultura.

1806   June 25.   Lord Carr Beresford's forces landed at
            Quilmes to begin first British invasion.

            August 12.   La "Reconquista," in which British were
            forced to surrender Buenos Aires to volunteer army
            led by Santiago de Liniers.

1807   February.   Second British invading force, led by
            General John Whitelocke, arrived in Montevideo in
            new attempt to gain possession of the Río de la Plata
            area.

            July 5-7.   General Whitehead forced to surrender to
            Santiago de Liniers in Buenos Aires, ending second
            British invasion.

1809   January.   Failure of conservative revolt led by Mar-
            tín de Alzaga to oust Santiago de Liniers as viceroy.

            Early revolutions in viceroyalty leading toward inde-
            pendence from Spain: May 25, Chuquisaca; July 16,
            La Paz (both in Alto Perú).

1810-11   Delegates from interior provinces joined patriot junta
            in Buenos Aires, creating the more widely based
            "Great Junta."

1810   May 22-25.   May Revolution; began with meeting of
            cabildo abierto May 22 and concluded with selection of
            a patriot junta to be governing body, after deposing
            viceroy, Baltasar Hidalgo de Cisneros; marked begin-
            ning of Argentine self-rule although actual independence
            from Spain was not declared until more than six years
            later; war of independence began at once as Buenos
            Aires attempted to bring entire viceroyalty under revo-
            lutionary government and was opposed by Spaniards
            and creole loyalists.

June 7.   First issue appeared of La Gaceta de Buenos Aires, official organ of the patriot junta, begun by Mariano Moreno.

August 25-26.   Execution at Cabeza de Tigre (Tiger's Head), near Cruz Alta, of leaders of Córdoban conspiracy, including Santiago de Liniers, by Juan José Castelli, acting under orders of patriot junta in Buenos Aires, against which they were revolting.

September 10-October 16.   Spanish forces of Montevideo imposed blockade of Buenos Aires as a result of May Revolution.

November 7.   Battle of Suipacha in Upper Peru--first victory of patriot forces over royalists in Argentine war for independence.

1811   January 19.   Belgrano's liberating force was defeated by Paraguayans along the Paraguarí.

March 2.   First defeat of the new Argentine navy at San Nicolás; Spaniards practically destroyed all the ships of the country.

March-September.   Blockade of Río de la Plata was renewed by Spanish forces at Montevideo, under new viceroy Elío, sent by government of Cádiz (allied with Great Britain).

March 9-10.   Battle of Tacuarí in which Buenos Aires' liberating army, commanded by Belgrano, was decisively defeated by Paraguayans under Manuel Cabañas; armistice was signed next day paving way for Paraguayan independence from both United Provinces of Río de la Plata and Spain.

April 5-6.   Revolt attempted by conservative Saavedra group to remove liberal group under Moreno.

June 20.   Battle of Huaqui (or Guaqui) in Bolivia; Goyeneche's royalist defeat of patriots commanded by General Antonio González Balcarce.

September.   First Triumvirate replaced patriot junta as governing body, with more conservative leadership.

December 7.   First Triumvirate established civil authority over military by crushing patricios' "Rebelión de las Trenzas."

1812   February 27.   Belgrano hoisted Argentine flag at Rosario for first time.

March 9. José de San Martín, Carlos María de Alvear and others arrived in Buenos Aires from Europe to give new leadership to independence movement.

July 1. Defeat of Martín de Alzaga's attempt to overthrow government of First Triumvirate and to replace creole leadership with that of resident Spaniards.

September 24. Manuel Belgrano's unexpected victory over royalists at Tucumán.

October 8. San Martín and Alvear, followed by their regiments, demanded, in name of the people, that triumvirs resign and a general congress be called; Second Triumvirate formed.

October 8. First meeting of Lautaro Lodge; formed for political and military purposes to aid in establishing independence.

1813   National anthem adopted.

Paraguay declared its independence under José Gaspar de Francia.

Assembly of the Year XIII; congress of provincial representatives in Buenos Aires undertook to provide legal and institutional basis for new revolutionary self-government whether or not independent completely from Spain.

February 3. Battle of San Lorenzo, first battle fought by San Martín's Mounted Grenadiers; resulted in victory over Spaniards under command of Juan Antonio Zabala.

February 20. Belgrano defeated royalists at Salta.

October 1. Vilcapujio--disastrous defeat of Belgrano's patriot forces by General Joaquín Pezuela; one of bloodiest battles in Argentine fight for independence.

November 14. Belgrano's defeat at Ayohuma in Alto Perú by General Joaquín de la Pezuela; resulted in Belgrano's replacement by José de San Martín and real fear that Alto Perú would be permanently held by royalists.

1814   San Martín took over command of Army of the North in Tucumán for a time; resigned because of poor health; became governor of Mendoza and began organization of Army of the Andes.

January. Gervasio Posadas became first Supreme Director in new directorate government that Assembly of 1813 had created to replace Second Triumvirate.

March. Naval encounter at Arroyo de la China between royalist river fleet and patriot squadron, under Tomás Notter; latter defeated.

October 2. Chilean patriots escaped from siege at Rancagua and crossed Andes to Mendoza; their leader, O'Higgins, joined San Martín in creating liberation army.

1815   Changes in Supreme Directors: Carlos de Alvear (January-April) and José Rondeau (April 1815-April 1816).

April 3. Revolt of Fontezuelas.

April 17. Puesto de Márquez; Argentine victory over royalists in Salta.

October 21. Battle of Venta y Media in which royalists under General Pezuela defeated patriot forces under General Rodríguez.

November 29. Battle of Sipe-Sipe in which Spanish army under leadership of General Pezuela defeated patriots under Rondeau; Upper Peru separated from the United Provinces of Río de la Plata as Spain regained its colonies north of province of Salta.

1816   March 24. Congress of Tucumán opened; shortly afterward Juan Martín de Pueyrredón selected as Supreme Director.

July 9. Formal declaration of independence by Congress of Tucumán.

September 14. Bloody patriot defeat at Parí creek in which Ignacio Warnes was killed.

1817-21   José Miguel Carrera, former president of Chile, joined with various opponents of Buenos Aires government (such as Ramírez and Alvear) to fight against it.

1817   January. Congress moved from Tucumán to Buenos Aires.

January 18. San Martín began invasion of royalist Chile, first step in his project of continental liberation from Spain.

February 7.   Necochea's defeat at Putaendo by
Spaniards led by Miguel Atero.

February 10.   Battle of Salala; Juan Manuel Cabot's
defeat of Spanish-Chilean garrison in Salala plains on
his way to occupy fort of Coquimbo.

February 12.   San Martín's decisive victory over
royalists at Chacabuco, assuring Chile's independence,
with O'Higgins as Supreme Director.

April 19.   First session of Congress after moving to
Buenos Aires from Tucumán.

1818   First battle at Fraile Muerto during civil wars; de-
feat of Juan Bautista Bustos by Estanislao López kept
Santa Fe province free from domination by Buenos
Aires.

Congress adopted the national flag of the Argentine
Republic devised by Belgrano in 1812.

March 19.   Royalist rout of San Martín's patriot army
at Cancha Rayada.

April 2.   San Martín's victory at Battle of Maipú that
ended Spanish threat to Chilean independence and
opened way for emancipation of Peru.

April 5.   Armistice of Rosario.

April 12.   Armistice of San Lorenzo.

1819   May 25.   Promulgation of first national constitution.

1820   "Terrible Year Twenty."   Later referred to as Argentina's year of national anarchy; followed by civil
wars and attempts of individual provinces to establish
autonomous governments either individually or in small
independent republics.

Estanislao López again won a decisive victory over
rivals by defeating Francisco Ramírez and José Miguel Carrera at Fraile Muerto.

January 8.   Revolt at Arequito of major portion of
Army of the North, that marked the beginning of the
end of the national government.

January 9.   Military revolt of Mendizábal that tempo-
raily imperiled San Martín's continental liberation plan.

February.   Battle of Tacuarembó, defeat of Artigas

and his forces by the Portuguese from Brazil, opening
way for the latter to occupy the Banda Oriental (Uruguay).

February 1.   Defeat of Rondeau's national forces at
Cepeda by allied army under Francisco Ramírez; followed by dissolution of Congress at Buenos Aires.

February 23.   Pacto del Pilar signed between Sarratea of Buenos Aires, Estanislao López of Santa Fe,
and Francisco Ramírez of Entre Ríos in attempt to
end the war among those provinces and to work together towards the formation of a national government
and national organization.

April 24.   Pact of Avalos formed alliance of Corrientes, Misiones, and Banda Oriental (Uruguay) to sustain
freedom and independence of Confederated Provinces
under leadership of Artigas.

June 20.   Known as the "Day of Three Governors" in
Buenos Aires.

August 20.   Departure of San Martín's expedition from
Valparaíso, Chile, to begin liberation of Peru from
Spain.

September 20.   Battle of Sauce de Luna (also known
as Battle of Cambray) in which Francisco Ramírez
defeated Artigas who fled to Paraguay.

December 6.   Battle of Pasco in Peru; early, important victory by San Martín's forces over royalists.

1821   Rivadavia abolished traditional cabildo of Buenos Aires.

Martín Rodríguez became governor of Buenos Aires
with Bernardino Rivadavia as minister; began period
of progress and development.

April 27.   Known as the "Great Day of Jujuy" when
Governor José Ignacio de Gorriti of Salta forced complete surrender of last royalist forces, under Guillermo Marchiegui.

May-June.   Conference in Peru at Punchauca in which
San Martín attempted, without success, to persuade
Viceroy La Serna to accept independence of Peru on
basis of establishing a liberal government there
favorable to Spain.

July 14.   Armistice signed by royalist commander
Olañeta and officials of Salta; resulted in royalist

evacuation of province, leaving it free for first time to establish constitutional government.

August 9-12.   University of Buenos Aires was inaugurated.

1822   United States recognized independence of Argentina, first non-Latin American nation to do so.

New land law passed for Buenos Aires province, embodying emphyteusis; extended to all provinces in 1826.

January 25.   Quadrilateral treaty (Pacto Cuadrilátero) signed in Santa Fe by the representatives of Buenos Aires, Entre Ríos, Santa Fe, and Corrientes.

May 7.   Ley del Olvido (amnesty law) issued by minister Rivadavia permitting the return of those exiled for political reasons enabling men like Juan Manuel Dorrego, Alvear, Sarratea, and Pagola, to return to Argentina.

May 24.   Battle of Pichincha (near Quito); victory of Bolívar's forces, led by Antonio José Sucre and reinforced with division sent by San Martín, over royalists; freed Ecuador.

July 26-27.   Conference at Guayaquil, Ecuador, between Liberators José de San Martín and Simón Bolívar.

1823   Alliance signed between Argentina and Colombia for friendship and mutual defense of their newly-won independence from Spain.

1824   December 9.   Battle of Ayacucho; final victory for independence of South America from Spain.

1825   One hundred Merinos imported to improve sheep breeding.

February.   Treaty of amity, navigation, and commerce made between Great Britain and Argentina recognizing, in effect, latter's independence.

April.   "Treinta y Tres Orientales" or the "Famous 33" crossed over to Uruguay to free it from Brazil.

September 12.   Battle of Sarandí: Brazilians ousted from Uruguay and latter integrated into Argentina.

December 10.   Outbreak of War with Brazil; Brazil imposed blockade on Argentine coasts and ports.

1826   Bernardino Rivadavia elected president.

              July.   Brazilian attack on Argentine ships at Quilmes.

              December 24.   New constitution, strongly centralist,
              promulgated.

1827   February 8.   Naval battle of Juncal in which Admiral
              William Brown not only completely defeated the Bra-
              zilian squadron but was able to incorporate all its
              ships into his own fleet.

              February 13.   Victory at Bacacay won by Juan Lavalle
              over Brazilians.

              February 20.   Major Argentine defeat of Brazilians at
              Ituzaingó.

              February 24.   Second Brazilian attack on Argentine
              vessels at Quilmes.

              July.   Rivadavia resigned as president largely due to
              provincial refusal to accept constitution.

              July-1828.   Vicente López y Planes serves as care-
              taker president until disintegration of national govern-
              ment and election of Manuel Dorrego as governor of
              Buenos Aires province, August 1828.

1828   Uruguay became an independent country, separated
              from Argentina, following war with Brazil.

              September 26.   Peace made with Brazil.

              December 1.   Juan Lavalle and other veterans of
              Brazilian War, opposing peace treaty with Brazil and
              loss of Uruguay, revolted against Buenos Aires govern-
              ment of Dorrego--in what is known as Decembrista
              Revolución or Revolution of December 1.

              December 9.   Lavalle's defeat of Manuel Dorrego at
              Navarro.

              December 13.   Execution of Dorrego by Lavalle.

1829   April 26.   Battle of Puente de Márquez, about twenty-
              five miles from Buenos Aires, where Juan Lavalle's
              unitarist army was defeated by federalist forces of
              Estanislao López and Juan Manuel Rosas.

              June 23.   Battle of La Tablada in which the unitarists
              under José M. Paz defeated the federalists under
              Facundo Quiroga for the first time; as a result of this

battle Paz entered the city of Córdoba and Quiroga escaped to Cuyo.

June 24.   Pact of Cañuelas signed between General Juan G. Lavalle and General Juan Manuel de Rosas in an effort to restore civil government and peace.

December 8.   Juan Manuel de Rosas became governor of Buenos Aires with extraordinary powers.

1830   February 25.   Battle of Oncativo in which the unitarists won a victory over federalist forces.

July-August.   League of the Interior formed by unitarist general José María Paz; represented unitarist desire for constitutional national organization and opposition of nine interior provinces to coastal domination.

1831   January 4.   Federal Pact, also called Pact of the Littoral, signed by Buenos Aires, Entre Ríos, Santa Fe and, later, Corrientes; provided limited basis for national unity and opposed League of the Interior.

March 28.   Defeat at Potrero de Chacón of unitarists of Córdoba, led by Juan Pascual Pringles, by Facundo Quiroga.

November 4.   Battle at La Ciudadela outside San Miguel de Tucumán in which Quiroga defeated López and Lamadrid; this marked the end of unitarism in Tucumán.

1832   December.   Rosas refused reelection as governor of Buenos Aires; succeeded as governor by Juan Ramón Balcarce.

1832-34   British scientific survey of Argentine coasts; Charles Darwin aboard.

1833   October.   Revolución de los Restauradores (Buenos Aires).   Supporters of Juan Manuel de Rosas overthrew Governor Juan Ramón Balcarce and paved way for Rosas' return as dictator in 1835.

1833-34   Indian frontier in southern Buenos Aires stabilized by Rosas.

1835   February 16.   Assassination of Juan Facundo Quiroga at Barranca Yaco.

March 7-April 13.   Rosas was again elected governor with "supreme and absolute powers" and confirmed by a plebiscite; inaugurated April 13.

1837-38   Rosas broke relations with and declared war on
            Bolivian-Peruvian confederation of Andrés Santa Cruz.

1838   March-October 1840. Due to disputes over govern-
            ment's treatment of French subjects resident in Ar-
            gentina, France blockaded Buenos Aires and offered
            aid to Rosas' opponents, without war being officially
            declared.

            December 31. Alliance signed between Province of
            Corrientes and Republic of Uruguay; treaty called for
            offensive and defensive alliance against Rosas and his
            government.

1839-42   Increased opposition to Rosas in Buenos Aires and
            provinces met with severe repression.

1839   March 31. Battle of Pago Largo, in Corrientes, in
            which General Pascual Echagüe totally defeated the
            anti-Rosas forces of Berón de Astrada, who was killed,
            and suppressed the uprising.

            September. Battle of Yeruá in which Lavalle defeated
            the governor of Entre Ríos, General Echagüe, parti-
            san of Rosas, shortly after entering Entre Ríos in his
            campaign against Rosas.

            November 7. Battle of Chascomús in which Prudencio
            Rozas defeated anti-Rosas forces led by Ambrosio
            Crámer.

            December. Bloody battle of Cagancha, Uruguay, in
            which the Uruguayan forces led by Fructuoso Rivera,
            assisted by Argentine exiles, defeated Rosas' invading
            forces under Pascual Echagüe and forced them back to
            Entre Ríos.

1840   July 16. Battle of Sauce Grande, in Entre Ríos, in
            which the unitarist General Juan Lavalle was defeated
            by federalist Pascual Echagüe, effectively ending for-
            mer's hope of gaining control of the province of Entre
            Ríos as base for operations against Rosas.

            September 21. Coalición del Norte formed in Tucu-
            mán to fight Rosas; included Salta, Catamarca, La
            Rioja, Jujuy, and Tucumán, under leadership of Marco
            Avellaneda.

            October 29. Treaty of Arana-Mackau ending the first
            French intervention was signed by Felipe Arana, for
            Rosas' government and Baron Mackau for France; rati-
            fied shortly afterward by both nations.

November 28.   General Oribe, Rosas partisan, defeated Lavalle at Quebracho Herrado, destroying Lavalle's army and leaving only General Paz to fight
against Rosas.

1841   August 16.   Victory won at Angaco by Mariano Acha
over José Félix Aldao in the civil wars of Cuyo.

September 19.   Final defeat at Famaillá, in Tucumán,
of remnants of Juan Lavalle's unitarist forces, supported by the Coalition of the North, by Rosas' forces
commanded by Manuel Oribe; Lavalle killed shortly
afterward in Jujuy.

September 24.   Battle of Rodeo del Medio, in Mendoza, in which federalist forces under General Angel
Pacheco, aided by Aldao and Benavídez, defeated Lamadrid's anti-Rosas forces and forced them to flee to
Chile.

November 28.   Battle of Caaguazú; General Paz defeated Echagüe, freeing Corrientes from fear of
Rosas' control.

1842-51   "Great War" between Rosas and Colorados led by
Fructuoso Rivera in Montevideo.

1842   December 5-6.   Alianza de Galarza, including Uruguay, Entre Ríos, and Santa Fe, opposed Rosas; its
military leader, Fructuoso Rivera, defeated at Arroyo
Grande by Rosas' forces led by Manuel Oribe and
Justo José de Urquiza.

1844   Englishman, Richard Newton, introduced barbed wire
fencing into Argentina, thus permitting the later development of wheat raising and breeding of better
beef cattle.

1845-48   Anglo-French blockade of Río de la Plata to protest
Rosas' intervention in Uruguay that was affecting their
trade as well as his treatment of their citizens resident in Argentina; blockade ineffectual against Rosas
but harmful to legitimate British and French trade in
that area.

1845   March 27.   Battle fought at India Muerta, Uruguay,
in which Rosas' forces, commanded by General Justo
J. Urquiza, defeated Uruguayan General Fructuoso
Rivera.

November 11.   Treaty of alliance between Corrientes
and Paraguay signed, in which Paraguay bound itself to furnish a well-equipped army to support

Corrientes in its fight against Rosas and Corrientes guaranteed recognition of Paraguay's independence and free navigation of the Paraná and Plata rivers; alliance soon fell victim to civil wars of rival provincial caudillos.

November 18-20. Defeat of Argentine land and river forces at Vuelta de Obligado by British-French blockading fleets.

1846   Treaties of Alcaraz between Urquiza and Joaquín Madariaga that attempted to establish peace between Corrientes and Rosas' Confederación.

1847   November 28. Battle between federalist forces under Juan José de Urquiza and Joaquín Madariaga of Corrientes at Rincón de Vences; the latter was defeated and emigrated to Paraguay. Urquiza's troops looted, burned, and practically destroyed the town of General Paz after the victory.

1849   July 28. Colegio de Concepción del Uruguay founded by Justo José de Urquiza.

1851   May 1. Urquiza stated Entre Ríos was assuming control of its own foreign affairs, no longer recognizing authority of Rosas.

May 29. Alliance formed between Entre Ríos, under Urquiza's leadership, Uruguay, and Brazil to confirm Uruguay's independence against Oribe and Rosas; widened in later treaty to include Corrientes and to emphasize freeing Argentina from Rosas.

1852   Intermittent civil war between Buenos Aires and the other provinces.

February 3. End of Rosas' regime by defeat of his army at Caseros by Justo José Urquiza's allied forces.

February 20. Urquiza's forces entered Buenos Aires and quieted the anarchy prevailing there.

May 31. Signing of Acuerdo de San Nicolás by Urquiza and most of provincial governors; reaffirmed Federal Pact of 1831 and provided for calling of a new constituent convention to draw up national constitution; rejected by Buenos Aires province.

September 11. Buenos Aires province rebelled against Urquiza's Confederation, resulting in separation of Buenos Aires from Confederation of other provinces for nearly ten years.

November 20.   Pacto Federal, treaty signed among the littoral provinces; it served as the law of the nation until the constitution of 1853 was sanctioned by the provinces.

November-May, 1853.   Constituent Congress met in Santa Fe; drew up constitution for Argentine Confederation, ratified May 1; declared fundamental law of land by Urquiza on May 25.

1852-59   Yellow fever epidemics.

1854   Buenos Aires adopted a separate constitution.

March 5.   Urquiza inaugurated in Paraná as first president under Constitution of 1853.

1856   Founding of agricultural colony La Esperanza, in Santa Fe; called grandmother of all Argentine colonies.

1857   First railroad (La Porteña) opened in Buenos Aires province.

1858   Spain established diplomatic relations with Argentina.

1859   October 23.   Porteño forces were defeated by Urquiza at Cepeda and Buenos Aires agreed to join Confederation.

November 11.   Pact of San José de Flores signed providing for the incorporation of the province of Buenos Aires into the Argentine Confederation.

1860   Mitre became governor of Buenos Aires province and Urquiza was succeeded in presidency of the confederation by Santiago Derqui.

1861   Bartolomé Mitre formed provisional government, moved capital provisionally to Buenos Aires.

March 20.   Destruction of city of Mendoza and surrounding area by earthquake.

September 17.   Battle of Pavón resulted from new differences between Confederation and Buenos Aires; Mitre emerged as victor and immediately began political organization of República Argentina under slightly amended constitution of 1853.

1862   October.   Mitre elected first president under new constitution; served until 1868.

1863   Rebellion of Angel Vicente Peñaloza (El Chacho) in La
              Rioja and neighboring provinces suppressed in inte-
              rests of national unity.

1864   Outbreak of Paraguayan War; brought on by Paraguayan
              attack on Corrientes; Triple Alliance formed by Argen-
              tina, Uruguay, and Brazil to defeat Francisco Solano
              López, president of Paraguay; Mitre in command of
              allied forces.

1865   Welsh begin settlement of Chubut.

              May 25.   Puente de la Batería, site of bitterest and
              most decisive fighting in the city of Corrientes during
              the Argentine recapture of the city from the Paraguay-
              ans who were holding it.

1866-67   Rebellion of los colorados in Mendoza and other cor-
              dillera provinces; led by Juan de Dios Videla, Juan
              and Felipe Saá, and Felipe Varela; suppressed by
              Mitre.

1866   May 24.   Battle of Tuyutí; critical battle leading to
              Paraguay's ultimate defeat in War of Triple Alliance.

              July 11.   Battle of Yataití-Corá in which the allied
              forces of General Mitre defeated the Paraguayan army
              of President Francisco Solano López.

              July 16-18.   Hard-fought, costly battle at Boquerón
              (formerly known as Potrero del Sauce) in Paraguayan
              War in which the allies emerged victorious; Solano
              López asked for talks about peace but negotiations
              broke down and war continued.

              September 22.   Disastrous defeat at Curupaytí of Gen-
              eral Mitre's allied forces in War of Triple Alliance
              against the Paraguayans.

1867   November 3.   Again at Tuyutí a battle was fought
              when Paraguayan troops attacked Brazilian forces and
              Argentine Colonel Manuel Hornos intervened with his
              cavalry and forced the Paraguayans to withdraw.

1868   Creation of Central Commission of Immigration.

              March-July.   Hard fighting at Humaitá (or Humaytá)
              between allied Argentine-Brazilian-Uruguayan forces
              and weakened Paraguayan forces; the latter withdrew,
              leaving way open to Asunción and end of war of Triple
              Alliance.

              October.   Domingo Faustino Sarmiento inaugurated as

president; served six years.

1869   First national census since May Revolution of 1810;
        showed total population of 1,737,000, with 28% living
        in Buenos Aires province.

        August 12.   Peribebuy Fort of Paraguayans taken by
        Argentines.

        October.   José Clemente Paz established La Prensa
        in Buenos Aires; it became one of world's great news-
        papers.

1870, '72   Rebellions of López Jordán in Entre Ríos put down.

1870   Completion of Rosario-Córdoba railroad.

        Escuela Normal established in Paraná by Sarmiento.

        Cholera epidemic in Buenos Aires and northwestern
        part of Argentina.

        January 4.   Newspaper La Nación founded by Bartolo-
        mé Mitre in Buenos Aires to express his views.

        April 11.   Assassination of Justo José Urquiza by
        forces of Ricardo López Jordán.

        July.   Colegio Militar opened in Palermo.

1871   Severe epidemic of yellow fever in Buenos Aires;
        more than 13,000 died within five months.

        January 26.   Ricardo López Jordán is defeated at
        Ñaembé by the forces of the governor of Corrientes,
        and forced to go into exile for a time.

        October 24.   National astronomical observatory opened
        in Córdoba, with Benjamin A. Gould as first director.

1872   March 8.   Battle of San Carlos (also known as Pichi-
        Carhué) in which the government forces under the
        leadership of Ignacio Rivas defeated the attacking In-
        dians led by Calfucurá, an Indian cacique of the south-
        western pampas.

1874   Nicolás Avellaneda elected as president; Bartolomé
        Mitre's revolt against election results ended in his
        defeat at Santa Rosa, October 2; entire country paci-
        fied.

1875   Salesians arrived in Argentina to begin active mission-
        ary work among Indians in Patagonia and to establish

schools offering vocational and technical training to both boys and girls in the various cities and rural areas.

1875-79   "Conquest of the Desert" by Julio A. Roca eliminated Indian menace in the south, opening Patagonia to settlement, agriculture, and stockraising.

1876   Immigration Law passed to bring together all previous similar legislation and to establish General Department of Immigration to set up and direct necessary procedures for future immigration.

            Le Frigorifique arrived in Buenos Aires with chilled beef.

1877   Argentine-Chilean peace treaty was signed at Punta Arenas establishing the boundaries of both countries.

            First voyage of Argentine ship Paraguay carrying frozen beef.

1878   City of Formosa founded by Lucio V. Mansilla.

            First cargo of wheat shipped from Rosario to Great Britain.

            November 2.   Pilcomayo River established as Argentina's northern boundary with Paraguay by decision of arbitrator, U.S. President Rutherford B. Hayes.

1880   City of Buenos Aires federalized as national capital after brief revolution by province against it; provision made for establishment of new capital (La Plata) of province; Julio A. Roca inaugurated as president.

1880-86   Administration of Julio Roca; consolidation of the oligarchy and of National Autonomist, or Conservative Party.

1881   January 19.   Destruction of Fort Guanacos in Neuquén and massacre of its force by Indians brings on final campaigns of Conquest of the Desert.

1882   Coastal city of La Plata was established on the pampa 50 miles southeast of Buenos Aires to serve as a new provincial capital.

1882-89   Beginning of economic boom, characterized by land speculation, railroad building, public works, agricultural development, and meat-packing.

1886-90   Administration of Miguel Juárez Celman; increasing

economic depression, huge public debt, and political
corruption brought public and congressional demand
for change.

1889-90   Argentina sent strong delegation to participate in first
Pan American conference held in Washington, D. C.

1890   April 13.   Organization of Unión Cívica de Juventud
under Leandro Alem.

May 1.   Laborers massed to celebrate international
labor day.

July-August.   Following unsuccessful civil-military
"Revolution of 1890" in July, Juárez Celman resigned
presidency on August 6 and was succeeded by his
vice president Carlos Pellegrini.

1890-92   Administration of Carlos Pellegrini during which Argentine credit and financial stability were strengthened.

1891   Jewish Colonization Association established by Baron
Hirsch to resettle persecuted European Jews; established many colonias in Argentina.

1891-92   Unión Cívica Radical organized in 1891; in 1892 began
using name Radical Party by which it was already
popularly known.

1892   October.   New conservative administration, headed by
President Luis Sáenz Peña, took office; general unrest
led to the president's resignation in midterm, in
1895.

1893   Radical revolts in La Plata, Santa Fe, and San Luis
in attempts to win reform and a share in political life;
suppressed by federal intervention.

1894-96   Socialists, led by Juan B. Justo, established their
newspaper La Vanguardia in 1894 and organized Socialist Party two years later.

1895-96   Administration of José E. Uriburu who, as vice president, succeeded to presidency when Luis Sáenz Peña
resigned.

1896   July 1.   Leandro Alem, leader of Radical Party, committed suicide; his nephew, Hipólito Yrigoyen took
over as leader.

1898-1904   Second administration of Julio A. Roca.

1899   Peso set at 0. 44 of gold peso, increasing financial stability.

1902   May 28.   Pactos de Mayo signed with Chile, settling long-standing boundary problems.

1903   Foreigners' Residence Law passed, aimed at deportation of undesirable aliens.

1904-06   Administration of Manuel Quintana who died in 1906.

1905   Partial labor law, written by J. V. González and supported by Socialists, passed, limiting work on Sunday.

            February.   Unsuccessful Radical attempt under Yrigoyen's leadership to arouse people against oligarchic government; suppressed in Buenos Aires and in Mendoza; in Córdoba Radicals seized and held Vice President Figueroa Alcorta hostage but Quintana's government won.

1906   University of La Plata founded.

1906-10   Administration of José Figueroa Alcorta who succeeded to presidency following death of Quintana.

1907   Labor law regulating work of women and children passed, largely due to influence of Socialist congressman Alfredo Palacios.

            Discovery of oil in Comodoro Rivadavia.

1910   Celebration of centennial of May Revolution that marked beginning of independence.

1910-12   Administration of Roque Saenz Peña who died in 1912.

1912   "Saenz Peña Law" passed, providing for secret and compulsory voting of adult males.

1914   August-1916.   Assumption of presidency by Vice President Victorino de la Plaza at death of Saenz Peña; faced at once with outbreak of World War I in Europe, de la Plaza announced policy of strict neutrality; national economic situation suffered further depression in early period of war.

1915   ABC treaty in which Argentina, Brazil, and Chile formed a permanent mediation commission to solve regional Latin American disputes.

1916-22   First administration of Hipólito Yrigoyen; continued policy of strict neutrality despite sinking of Argentine ships by German submarines; economy began to improve with meat shipments to Allies and local industry stimulated by reduction of imports of consumer goods.

1918	Movement for improvement of higher education began as famous University Reform in Córdoba and spread to Buenos Aires and La Plata; Universities of the Littoral and of Tucumán were founded; Argentine University Federation (Federación Universitaria Argentina--FUA) eventually formed to keep reform alive.
1919	First attempt to cross the Andes by airplane.
	Liga Patriotica Argentina formed by Manuel Carlés to combat workers' organizations and ideologies considered subversive.
	January 7-13. "La Semana Trágica" or Tragic Week of violence that resulted when government suppressed labor uprisings in Buenos Aires, and, to a lesser extent, in Rosario.
1919-21	Yrigoyen took Argentina into League of Nations but when the League declined to admit Austria and Germany Argentina withdrew.
1922	Creation of national oil agency (YPF).
1922-28	Administration of Márcelo T. de Alvear, Radical; post World War I era of prosperity with increased production and immigration.
1924	Split in Radical Party.
1928-30	Second administration of Hipólito Yrigoyen; breakdown in government and Yrigoyen's inability to cope with new problems growing out of personal opposition and world economic depression forced him to resign.
1930	Organization of first national trade union, the Confederación General Trabajo (CGT).
	September 6. Revolution of 1930; José F. Uriburu forced Yrigoyen out and established new government in first military takeover that served as precedent for many more in mid-twentieth century.
1930-32	Administration of José Félix Uriburu; nation under state of siege most of time, but national elections held in November, 1931.
1931	April. Manifesto issued by "Junta del City" as Alvear attempted to reorganize Radical Party.

October 10.   Exchange Commission established to aid government in dealing with problems resulting from worldwide depression.

1932	Radical Party revolt in Entre Ríos was suppressed.
1932-38	Administration of Agustín P. Justo.
1933	May. Roca-Runciman Pact signed with Great Britain, giving Argentina a continued share in British beef market in return for greater Argentine protection of British transportation investments.
1935	July 23. Heated debate in senate between Lisandro de la Torre and Luis Duhau over government corruption and meat monopoly practices resulted in death of one senator.
1936	Argentina played important international role with its foreign minister Carlos Saavedra Lamas presiding over League of Nations Assembly (in which Argentina had again become active in 1932); also over Inter-American Conference in Buenos Aires; Saavedra Lamas was also awarded 1936 Nobel Peace Prize for his contributions toward solving Chaco dispute.
1938-42	Administration of Roberto M. Ortiz; forced by illness to delegate powers frequently to Vice President Ramón S. Castillo, finally resigned from presidency June, 1942, shortly before his death.
1939	University of Cuyo was founded.
1939-45	Argentina attempted to maintain traditional policy of neutrality during World War II; refused to join U.S. and most of other American nations in declaring war against Axis powers until late in war.
1943	June 4. GOU Revolt; military government established with Arturo Rawson as president briefly (June 4-6).
	October. Department of Labor created at suggestion of Juan Domingo Perón who became its head.
	Latter part of year. Victoria Ocampo founded review Sur, a periodical designed to provide an open forum for world thought.
1943-44	Administration of Pedro Pablo Ramírez; accused by U.S. of being pro-Nazi, he maintained conservative authoritarian government internally and continued Argentina's policy of neutrality during World War II; broke relations, finally, with Axis in January 1944,

one month before being replaced as president by General Farrell.

1944-46   Administration of President Edelmiro J. Farrell; increased power gained by Juan Domingo Perón as head of labor department, Minister of War (May 1944), and Vice President (July 1944), in addition to other responsibilities.

1945   January. Earthquake destroyed city of San Juan.

March. Argentina declared war on Germany and Japan.

September 19. "March of the Constitution and Liberty," popular demonstration demanding return to constitutional government.

October. Perón forced to resign and placed under arrest on island of Martín García; mass rally of workers and supporters brought his return to Buenos Aires within a few days.

1946   Juan Domingo Perón elected president following restoration of constitutional processes; revolutionary social and economic changes made during first administration, 1946-1952; labor affairs and welfare delegated to his wife Evita Perón.

Argentina signed Act of Chapultepec; regained status in inter-American relationships and organizations.

Creation of IAPI to control trade.

1946-48   Nationalization of telephones, gasworks, railroads.

1947   First five-year plan announced.

Women given vote.

1949   March 16. New constitution approved; retained most of constitution of 1853 but contained much of Perón's justicialist philosophy and provided for immediate reelection of a president.

July 25. Formation of Peronist Party to serve as political vehicle for Perón.

July 26. Peronist Feminist Party, first women's political party; headed by Evita Perón.

1951   September. Military revolt, led by Manuel Menéndez, against Perón suppressed and "state of internal war" declared by government.

April. Government closed and expropriated newspaper La Prensa as climax to press-control measures;
turned it over to CGT.

1952-55   Second administration of Perón, following reelection;
death of Eva Perón from cancer.

1953   Jockey Club burned by Perón supporters; Perón sought
to improve oil production by negotiating with Standard
Oil of California.

February. Act of Santiago, treaty of cooperation and
trade, signed between Chile and Argentina; Paraguay
signed Act in August.

1954-55   Deterioration of economy, universities, independent
press, and political life combined with new opposition
from the Church to threaten Perón's position; violence
common; churches burned and pillaged.

1955   September 16-19. Military revolt, led by General
Eduardo Lonardi and known as Revolución Libertadora,
overthrew Perón's government, permitting him to go
into exile.

September 20-November 12. Lonardi headed provisional military government; constitution of 1853 reinstated.

November. Army coup ousted Lonardi and made
General Pedro E. Aramburu provisional president.

1955-58   Administration of General Pedro E. Aramburu; strong
effort made to eliminate Peronism from political
scene.

1956   June. Peronist revolt ruthlessly suppressed by President Aramburu; its leaders were executed.

1957   Creation of National Territory of Tierra del Fuego,
Antarctica, and South Atlantic Islands.

1958   May-1962. Administration of Arturo Frondizi; attempts to steer middle course toward economic, political, international progress interrupted by revolts
from both right and left.

1959   Frondizi visited U.S. , first Argentine president to do
so while in office.

June. Serious military coup, under leadership of
Peronists, suppressed.

December 1.   Thirty-year Antarctic Treaty signed in Washington, D. C. by Argentina and eleven other interested countries including U. S. , Chile, and Great Britain.

1960   Treaty of Montevideo created LAFTA, establishing basis for an active trade between southern countries.

June.   Military-civil revolt of Peronists in San Luis suppressed.

1961   LAFTA agreement ratified by Argentina.

1962   Self-sufficiency in petroleum attained for time being.

Peronists permitted to participate politically again, in 1962 elections.

March.   Military removed Frondizi as president, arrested him, and annulled elections.

September.   Internal conflict between Azules favoring nonpolitical professional military, under leadership of Onganía, and the Colorados who were helped by the navy: suppressed in April 1963 and September 1963.

1962-63   Administration of José M. Guido, former president of Senate, installed by military group that ousted Frondizi.

1963   December.   Threatened Air Force revolt averted.

1963-66   Administration of President Arturo Illia; economic problems continued and political unrest was aggravated by attempts of Peronists to return to politics.

1964   Peronist party (without Perón) organized by Augusto Vandor; acquired legal status and considerable popular support.

Perón attempt to return to Argentina (December) failed.

1965-66   Perón's wife, Isabelita, arrived in Buenos Aires to arouse popular sentiment for Perón's return.

1966   June 28.   Military coup, led by Pascual Pistarini, deposed Illia and took over all national and provincial government in attempt to give Argentina stronger direction toward economic development and to control increasing Peronist power in provinces; installed General Juan Carlos Onganía.

1966-70   Administration of Juan Carlos Onganía; strong govern-
           ment measures brought open rebellion from labor,
           universities, and church that resented its control.

1969-70   Labor strikes, violence, political unrest disrupted na-
           tional life.

1969   May 29-30.   Violence and deaths in Corrientes trig-
           gered general strikes and student protests in Córdoba
           ("El Cordobazo") and La Plata that cause more vio-
           lence when attacked by the militia.

           June.   Assassination of Vandor, moderate labor lead-
           er, at his labor headquarters.

           October.   Coup by army officers with Peronist sym-
           pathies; attempt to imitate Peruvian military takeover
           of 1968 was thwarted.

1970   Former president, Pedro Eugenio Aramburu, kid-
           napped and murdered by Peronist guerrillas in retalia-
           tion for execution of military leaders of revolt of
           1956.

           June.   Military removed Onganía from power; leaders
           appointed Roberto Levingston as president.

           June-March 1971.   Administration of President Ro-
           berto M. Levingston; marked by attempts to encourage
           production for national, rather than foreign, markets;
           continued strikes and public unrest; Levingston's at-
           tempt to exert his authority over military brought his
           downfall.

1971   March.   Levingston removed from power by military;
           Lanusse became president.

1971-73   Administration of Alejandro Lanusse; military attempt
           to return nation to normal constitutional political life,
           economic progress, and social order.

1972   November.   Perón returned to Argentina but recep-
           tion was not favorable and he left for Paraguay, Peru,
           and Europe in December.

1973   May 25-July 13.   Brief administration of Héctor Cám-
           pora, elected by Peronista Justicialista group; re-
           signed July 13.

           July 13-October 12.   Raúl Lastiri, former president
           of chamber of deputies, acting president.

           September 23.   Perón overwhelmingly reelected to

presidency with his wife Isabelita (María Estela Martínez de Perón), as vice president.

October 12-June 29, 1974.   Third presidential administration of Juan Domingo Perón; resigned because of illness.

1974   June 29-March 24, 1976.   Administration of Isabel (María Estela Martínez de) Perón, first woman president of Argentina (or of any American nation); her government overthrown by military after two years because of mounting economic problems and increasing guerrilla violence.

1976   General Jorge Rafael Videla became president of military government in Argentina following that of Isabel (María Estela Martínez de) Perón (March 24, 1976).

Appendix III

SUGGESTED READINGS

The following list is intended primarily to be a bibliographical checklist, rather than a detailed guide to further specific readings. The latter are to be found in individual listings, for the most part. See also Historical Dictionaries and Historiography.

Abad de Santillán, Diego, editor. Gran enciclopedia argentina, 9 vols. Buenos Aires, 1956-1963.
Academia Nacional de la Historia. Ricardo Levene, ed. Historia de la nación argentina. 10 vols. Buenos Aires, 1936-1942; second ed., 1939-1947; third ed., 15 vols., 1963.
Academia Nacional de la Historia. Historia argentina contemporánea. 7 vols. Buenos Aires, 1963-1967.
Albarracín, José M. Sarmiento. Buenos Aires, 1940.
Alemann, Roberto T. Curso de politica económica argentina. Buenos Aires, 1970.
Alexander, Robert J. An Introduction to Argentina. New York, 1969.
————. Communism in Latin America. New Brunswick, 1957.
————. Labor Relations in Argentina, Brazil, and Chile. New York, 1962.
————. Latin American Political Parties. New York, 1973.
————. The Perón Era. New York, 1951; London, 1952.
Almond, Gabriel A. and James S. Coleman, eds. The Politics of the Developing Areas. Princeton, N.J.: Princeton University Press, 1966.
Alvarez, Agustín. South America: Ensayo de psicología política. Buenos Aires, 1894. Various editions.
Alvarez, Juan. Estudios sobre las guerras civiles argentinas. Buenos Aires, 1914. Various editions.
Andrews, Joseph. Journey from Buenos Aires Through the Provinces of Córdoba, Tucumán, and Salta to Potosí. 2 vols. London, 1827; Spanish translation, Buenos Aires, 1920.
Angelis, Pedro de, comp. Colección de obras y documentos relativos a la historia antigua y moderna de las provincias del Río de la Plata. Reprinted with notes and prologue by Andrés M. Carretero, 8 vols. Buenos Aires, 1969-1972.
Anzoátegui, Víctor Tau. Formación del estado federal argentino, 1820-1852; la intervención del gobierno de Buenos Aires en los asuntos nacionales. Buenos Aires, 1965.

Arrieta, Rafael A. , ed. Historia de la literatura argentina. 6
   vols. Buenos Aires, 1958-1959.
Ayarragaray, Lucas. La anarquía argentina y el caudillismo.
   Buenos Aires, 1904. Various editions.
Azara, Felix de. Voyages dans l'Amerique meridionale depuis
   1781 jusqu'en 1801. 4 vols. and atlas. Paris, 1809; Span-
   ish translation, Buenos Aires, 1923.
Backhouse, Hugo. Among the Gauchos. London, 1950.
Bagú, Sergio. Evolución histórica de la estratificatión social en
   la Argentina. Caracas, 1969.
Bailey, Norman A. Latin America in World Politics. New York,
   1967.
Baily, Samuel L. Labor, Nationalism and Politics in Argentina.
   New Brunswick, 1967; Spanish translation, Buenos Aires,
   1971.
Barager, Joseph. "Historiography of the Río de la Plata Area,"
   Hispanic American Historical Review. November, 1959, pp.
   588-642.
Barager, Joseph R. , ed. Why Perón Came to Power: The Back-
   ground to Peronism in Argentina. New York, 1968.
Barco Centenera, Martín del. Argentina y conquista del Río de la
   Plata. Lisbon, 1602; fasc. ed. , 1912. Various editions.
Bealer, Lewis Winkler. Los corsarios de Buenos Aires. Buenos
   Aires, 1937.
Beals, Carleton. The Coming Struggle for Latin America. Lon-
   don, 1939.
Beaumont, J. A. B. Travels in Buenos Aires and the Adjacent
   Provinces of Río de la Plata. London, 1828; Spanish trans-
   lation, Buenos Aires, 1957.
Beltrán, Rafael. El papel político y social de las fuerzas armadas.
   Caracas, Venezuela, 1970.
Best, Félix. Historia de las guerras argentinas. 2 vols. Buenos
   Aires, 1960.
Biscay, Acarete du. An Account of Voyage up the River de la
   Plata, and Thence over Land to Peru. London, 1698. Vari-
   ous editions. Spanish translation, Buenos Aires, 1943.
Blanksten, George I. Perón's Argentina. Chicago, 1953.
Blasco Ibáñez, Vicente. Argentina y sus grandezas. Madrid,
   1910.
Borges, Jorge L. , ed. ¿Qué es la Argentina? Buenos Aires,
   1970.
_____ and Adolfo Bioy Casares. Poesía gauchesca. 2 vols.
   Mexico, D.F. , 1955. Includes works by Estanislao del
   Campo, Hilario Ascasubi, and José Hernández.
Bosch, Beatriz. Urquiza. Buenos Aires, 1967.
_____. Urquiza y su tiempo. Buenos Aires, 1971.
Box, Pelham H. The Origins of the Paraguayan War. Urbana,
   1929; reprint, 1967; Spanish translation, Buenos Aires, 1958.
Brackenridge, Henry M. Voyage to South America, Performed by
   Order of the American Government in the Years 1817 and
   1818. 2 vols. Baltimore, 1819; London, 1820; Spanish
   translation, Buenos Aires, 1927.

1095 Suggested Readings

Bradford, Sax. The Battle for Buenos Aires. New York, 1943.
Bridges, E. Lucas. Uttermost Part of the Earth. London, 1948;
New York, 1949.
Bruce, James. Those Perplexing Argentines. New York, London,
Toronto, 1953.
Bruno, Cayetano. Historia de la iglesia en la Argentina. 8 vols.
Buenos Aires, 1966-72.
Bryce, James B. South America: Observations and Impressions.
New York and London, 1912.
Bunge, Alejandro E. La economía argentina. 4 vols. Buenos
Aires, 1928-1930.
Bunge, Carlos O. Nuestra América: ensayo de psicología política.
Buenos Aires, 1903. Various editions.
Bunkley, Allison Williams. The Life of Sarmiento. Princeton,
N.J., 1952.
Burgin, Miron. The Economic Aspects of Argentine Federalism,
1820-1852. Cambridge, Mass., 1946.
Bustamante, Norberto Rodríguez. Los intelectuales y su sociedad.
Buenos Aires, 1967.
Cady, John F. Foreign Interventions in the Río de la Plata, 1838-
1850. Philadelphia and London, 1929.
Caillet-Bois, Teodoro. Historia naval argentina. Buenos Aires,
1944.
Canabrava, Alice P. O comercio portugues no Rio da Prata,
1580-1640. São Paulo, 1944.
Cantón, Darío. Elecciones y partidos políticos en la Argentina:
historia, interpretación y balance, 1910-1966. Buenos Aires,
1973.
_____. Military Interventions in Argentina 1900-1966. Buenos
Aires, 1967.
Carbia, Rómulo P. Historia crítica de la historiografía argentina: desde sus orígenes en el siglo XVI. Buenos Aires,
1939.
Cárcano, Miguel Angel. Evolución histórica del régimen de
la tierra pública. Buenos Aires, 1917; third edition,
1972.
_____. La política internacional en la historia argentina. 2
vols. Buenos Aires, 1972-1973.
Carlos, Calixto Bustamante (pseud., Concolocorvo). El lazarillo
de ciegos caminantes desde Buenos Aires hasta Lima. Gi-
jon, 1773; Buenos Aires, 1938.
Cawkell, M.B.R., D.H. Maling, and E.M. Cawkell. The
Falkland Islands. London: Macmillan and Co. Ltd.; New
York: St. Martin's Press, 1960.
Centenera, Martín del Barco. Argentina y conquista del Río de
la Plata. Lisbon, 1602; fasc. ed., 1912.
Chikhachev, Platon A. A Trip Across the Pampas of Buenos
Aires, 1836-1837. Translation by Jack Weiner. Lawrence,
Kansas, 1967.
Ciria, Alberto. Parties and Power in Modern Argentina (1930-
1946). Translated by Carlos A. Astiz with Mary F. McCar-
thy. Albany, N.Y., 1974.

_____. Perón y el justicialismo. Mexico, D. F. and Buenos
    Aires, 1971.
Cochran, Thomas C. and Ruben E. Reina. Entrepreneurship in
    Argentine Culture: Torcuato Di Tella and S. I. A. M. Phila-
    delphia, 1962.
Conil Paz, Alberto A. and Gustavo E. Ferrari. Argentina's
    Foreign Policy: 1930-1962. Translated by John J. Kennedy.
    Notre Dame, Indiana, 1966.
Connell-Smith, Gordon. The Inter-American System. London and
    New York, 1966.
Corbett, Charles D. The Latin American Military as a Socio-Po-
    litical Force: Case Studies of Argentina and Bolivia. Cen-
    ter for Advanced International Studies, University of Miami,
    Coral Gables, Florida, 1972.
Cortés Conde, Roberto and Ezequiel Gallo. La formación de la
    Argentina moderna. Buenos Aires, 1967.
Cuccorese, Horacio Juan. Historia de los ferrocarriles en la Ar-
    gentina. Buenos Aires, 1969.
_____, and José Pavettieri. Argentina. Manual de historia
    económica y social. Buenos Aires, 1971.
Cúneo, Dardo. Inmigración y nacionalidad. Buenos Aires, 1967.
    _____. El romanticismo político. Buenos Aires, 1955.
Cutolo, Vicente Osvaldo. Nuevo diccionario biográfico argentino
    (1750-1930). 4 vols. Buenos Aires: Editorial Elche, 1968.
Darwin, Charles. Journal of Researches into the Natural History
    and Geology of the Countries Visited during the Voyage of
    H. M. S. Beagle Round the World. 2 vols. New York, 1846.
    _____. The Voyage of the Beagle. London, 1839. Numerous
    editions.
Davis, Harold E. , Lamar C. Wilson, and others. Latin American
    Foreign Policies. An Analysis. Baltimore: Johns Hopkins
    University Press, 1975.
Davis, Thomas B. , Jr. Carlos de Alvear: Man of Revolution.
    Durham, N. C. , 1955; Spanish translation, Buenos Aires,
    1964.
DeFelippe, Bruno A. Geografía económica argentina. Buenos
    Aires, 1959.
Defense of Freedom. By the editors of La Prensa. New York,
    1952.
Denis, Pierre. The Argentine Republic: Its Development and
    Progress. Translated from French by Joseph McCabe.
    London and New York, 1922.
de Santillán, Diego Abad see Abad de Santillán, Diego
Deutsch, Karl W. and William J. Foltz, eds. Nation-Building.
    New York, 1963.
Díaz Alejandro, Carlos F. Essays on the Economic History of
    the Argentine Republic. New Haven, Conn. , 1970.
Díaz de Guzman, Ruy. La Argentina. Ed. by Enrique de Gandía.
    Buenos Aires, 1943.
Di Tella, Guido and Manuel Zymelman. Las etapas del desarrollo
    económico argentino. Buenos Aires, 1967.
Di Tella, Torcuato S. , Gino Germani, and others. Argentina,
    sociedad de masas. Buenos Aires, 1965.

Dozer, Donald M.   Are we good neighbors?   Three decades of Inter-American Relations, 1930-1960.   Gainesville, Fla., 1959.

Drosdoff, Daniel.   El gobierno de las vacas: 1933-1956, tratado Roca-Runciman.   Buenos Aires, 1972.

Eckstein, Harry.   Division and Cohesion in Democracy.   Princeton, N.J., 1966.

Eidt, Robert C.   Pioneer Settlement in Northeastern Argentina. Madison, Wisc., 1971.

Estrada, Juan C. Torchia.   La filosofía en la Argentina.   Washington, D.C., 1961.

Etchepareborda, Roberto.   Tres revoluciones: 1890, 1893, 1905. Buenos Aires, 1968.

Falcoff, Mark and Ronald H. Dolkart, eds.   Prologue to Perón-- Argentina in Depression and War, 1930-1943.   Berkeley, Calif., 1975.

Falkner, Thomas.   A Description of Patagonia, and the Adjoining Parts of South America.   London, 1774; Chicago, 1935; Spanish translations, Buenos Aires, 1911, 1957.

Ferns, Henry S.   Argentina.   New York, 1969.
_____.   The Argentine Republic 1516-1971.   (In series of national economic histories.)   New York, 1973.
_____.   Britain and Argentina in the Nineteenth Century.   London, 1960.

Ferrer, Aldo.   The Argentine Economy.   Translated by Marjory M. Urquidi.   Berkeley, Calif., 1967.

Feuerlein, Willy, and Elizabeth Hannan.   Dollars in Latin America: An Old Problem in a New Setting.   New York, 1940.

Fienup, Darrell F., Russell H. Brannon and Frank A. Fender. The Agricultural Development of Argentina: A Policy and Development Perspective.   New York, 1969.

Fillol, Tomas R.   Social Factors in Economic Development: The Argentine Case.   Cambridge, Mass., 1961.

Fitzgibbon, Russell H.   Argentina: A Chronology and Fact Book, 1516-1573.   Dobbs Ferry, N.Y., 1974.
_____.   A Directory of Latin American Political Parties. Tempe, Ariz., 1970.
_____.   A Panorama of Contemporary Politics.   New York, 1971.

Floria, Carlos Alberto and César A. García Belsunce.   Historia de los argentinos.   2 vols.   Buenos Aires, 1971.

Ford, Alec G.   The Gold Standard, 1880-1914; Britain and Argentina.   Oxford, 1962.

Fragueiro, Mariano.   Cuestiones argentinas y organización del crédito.   Buenos Aires, 1976.

Franco, Jean.   The Modern Culture of Latin America: Society and the Artist.   London and New York, 1967.

Frau, Salvador Canals.   Las poblaciones indígenas de Argentina: su origen, su pasado, su presente.   Buenos Aires, 1953.

Frederick, Kenneth D.   Water Management and Agricultural Development.   A Cross Study of the Cuyo Region of Argentina. Baltimore and London: Johns Hopkins University Press, 1975.

Frondizi, Silvio. Argentina: la autodeterminación de su pueblo.
    Buenos Aires, 1973.
_____. La realidad argentina. 2 vols. Buenos Aires, 1955-
    1956; second edition, 1957.
Fuchs, Jaime. Argentina: su desarrollo capitalista. Buenos
    Aires, 1965.
Funes, Gregorio. Ensayo de la historia civil de Buenos Aires,
    Tucumán y Paraguay. 3 vols. Buenos Aires, 1816-1817;
    third edition, 2 vols., 1910-1911.
Furlong Cardiff, Guillermo. Historia social y cultural del Río de
    la Plata, 1536-1810. 2 vols. Buenos Aires, 1969.
_____. Los Jesuitas y la cultura rioplatense. Montevideo,
    1933; Buenos Aires, 1946.
_____. Nacimiento y desarrollo de la filosofía en el Río de la
    Plata, 1536-1810. Buenos Aires, 1952.
Gallo, Ezequiel and Roberto Cortés Conde. Argentina: la repúb-
    lica conservadora. Buenos Aires, 1972.
Galmarini, Hugo Raúl. Negocios y política en la época de Riva-
    davia: Braulio Costa y la burguesía comercial porteña (1820-
    1830). Buenos Aires, 1974.
García, Juan A. La ciudad indiana: Buenos Aires desde 1600
    hasta mediados del siglo XVIII. Buenos Aires, 1900. Vari-
    ous editions.
Germani, Gino, ed. Britain and the Independence of Latin Ameri-
    ca: 1812-1830. 2 vols. Oxford, 1938.
_____. Estructura social de la Argentina. Buenos Aires, 1955.
_____. Política y sociedad en una época de transición de la so-
    ciedad tradicional a la sociedad de las masas. Buenos Aires,
    1962. Several editions.
Gianello, Leoncio. Historia de Entre Ríos. Paraná, 1951.
Giberti, Horacio C. E. El desarrollo agrario argentino. Buenos
    Aires: Eudeba, 1964.
Gil, Enrique. Pan Americanism and the International Policy of
    Argentina. New York, 1916.
Gillespie, Alexander. Gleanings and Remarks, Collected During
    Many Months of Residence at Buenos Aires and Within the
    Upper Country. Leeds, 1818; Spanish translation, Buenos
    Aires, 1921.
Goebel, J. The Struggle for the Falkland Islands. New Haven,
    1927.
Goldwert, Marvin. Democracy, Militarism, and Nationalism in
    Argentina, 1930-1966. Austin, Tex., and London, 1972.
González, Joaquín V. La tradición nacional. Buenos Aires, 1888.
    Various editions.
Graham, R. B. C. The Conquest of the River Plate. London and
    New York, 1924; reprint, Boston, 1973.
Greenup, Ruth and Leonard. Revolution Before Breakfast: Argen-
    tina, 1941-1946. Chapel Hill, N. C., 1947.
Groussac, Paul. Mendoza y Garay. Buenos Aires, 1916; 2 vols.,
    Academia Argentina de Letras, Buenos Aires, 1949-1950.
_____. Santiago de Liniers. Buenos Aires, 1907. Several
    editions.
Güiraldes, Ricardo. Don Segundo Sombra. Translated by Harriet

de Onis, with title Shadows in the Pampas. New York and London, 1935.

Gutiérrez, Juan M. Noticias históricas sobre el origen y desarrollo de la enseñanza superior en Buenos Aires. Buenos Aires, 1868; third edition, 1915.

Hadfield, William. Brazil, the River Plate, and the Falkland Islands. London, 1854; Spanish translation, Buenos Aires, 1943.

Haigh, Roger M. Martín Güemes: Tyrant or Tool. A Study of the Sources of Power of an Argentine Caudillo. Ft. Worth, Tex., 1968.

Halperin-Donghi, Tulio. The Aftermath of Revolution in Latin America. Translated by Josephine de Bunsen. New York, 1973.

_____. Historia de la Universidad de Buenos Aires. Buenos Aires, 1962.

_____. Politics, Economics and Society in Argentina in the Revolutionary Period. Cambridge Latin American Studies, 18. New York, 1975.

_____. Revolución y guerra--formación de una elite dirigente en la Argentina criolla. Buenos Aires, 1972.

Hanson, Simon G. Argentine Meat and the British Market: Chapters in the History of the Argentine Meat Industry. Stanford, Calif., and London, 1938.

Haring, Clarence H. Argentina and the United States. Boston, 1941.

Head, Francis B. Reports Relating to the Failure of the Río Plata Mining Association. London, 1827.

_____. Rough Notes Taken During Some Rapid Journeys Across the Pampas and Among the Andes. London, 1826; third edition, 1828; reprint, 1957.

Henríquez-Ureña, Pedro. A Concise History of Latin American Culture. Translated by G. Chase. New York, 1966.

_____. Literary Currents in Hispanic America. Cambridge, Mass., 1945.

Hernández, José. El gaucho Martín Fierro y la vuelta de Martín Fierro. Buenos Aires, 1872, 1879; critical editions, 1945, 1951, 1961; Madrid, 1971; English translation, New York, 1936, 1948, 1960, 1968.

Herron, Francis. Letters from the Argentine. New York, 1943.

Hodges, Donald C. Argentina, 1943-1976: The National Revolution and Resistance. Albuquerque, N.M., 1976.

Hudson, William Henry. Birds of La Plata. London, 1920.

_____. Far Away and Long Ago: A History of My Early Life. New York and London, 1918; Spanish trans., Buenos Aires, 1918.

_____. Idle Days in Patagonia. London, 1893; New York, 1917. Various editions.

_____. The Naturalist in La Plata. London, 1892.

Humphreys, R. A. Latin American History: A Guide to the Literature in English. London, 1958.

_____. Liberation in South America, 1806-1827. London, 1952.

Hutchinson, Thomas J. Buenos Aires and Argentine Gleanings, with Extracts from a Diary of Salado Exploration in 1862 and 1863. London, 1865; Spanish translation, Buenos Aires,

1945.
_____. The Paraná, with Incidents of the Paraguayan War, and South American Recollections from 1861 to 1868. London, 1868.

Ibarguren, Carlos. Juan Manuel de Rosas: su vida, su tiempo, su drama. Buenos Aires, 1930. Various editions.

Imaz, José Luis de. Los que mandan (Those Who Rule). Translated by Carlos A. Astiz with Mary F. McCarthy. Albany, N.Y., 1974.

Ingenieros, José. La evolución de las ideas argentinas. 2 vols. Buenos Aires, 1918-1920. Various editions.

Instituto Torcuato Di Tella. Relevamiento de la estructura regional de la economía argentina. 5 vols. Buenos Aires, 1965.

James, Preston E. Latin America. third edition, New York, 1959.

Jefferson, Mark. Peopling the Argentine Pampa. New York, 1926.

Jeffrey, William H. Mitre and Argentina. New York, 1952.

Johnson, Chalmers. Revolutionary Change. Boston, Mass., 1966.

Johnson, John J. The Military and Society in Latin America. Stanford, Calif., 1964.

_____. Political Change in Latin America: The Emergence of the Middle Sectors. Stanford, Calif., 1958.

Jones, Tom B. South America Rediscovered. Minneapolis, 1949.

José, James R. An Inter-American Peace Force Within the Framework of the Organization of the American States. Metuchen, N.J., 1970.

Joslin, David. A Century of Banking in Latin America: To Commemorate the Centenary in 1962 of the Bank of England and South America Limited. Oxford, 1963.

Karen, Ruth. Neighbors in a New World: The Organization of American States. Cleveland, Ohio, 1966.

Katz, Jorge M. Production Functions, Foreign Investment, and Growth: A Study Based on the Argentine Manufacturing Sector, 1946-1961. Amsterdam and London, 1969.

Keen, Benjamin. David Curtis DeForest and the Revolution of Buenos Aires. New Haven, Conn., 1947; reprint, 1970.

Kennedy, John J. Catholicism, Nationalism, and Democracy in Argentina. Notre Dame, Ind., 1958.

King, John A. Twenty-four Years in the Argentine Republic. New York, Philadelphia, and London, 1846; Spanish translation, Buenos Aires, 1921.

Kirkpatrick, F. A. A History of the Argentine Republic. Cambridge, 1931.

_____. Latin America and the War. Cambridge, Eng., 1918.

Kirkpatrick, Jeane J. Leader and Vanguard in Mass Society. A Study of Peronist Argentina. Cambridge, Mass., 1971.

Koebel, William H. Argentina, Past and Present. London, 1910; second edition, 1914.

Korn, Alejandro. Las influencias filosóficas en la evolución nacional. Buenos Aires, 1936.

Kroeber, Clifton. The Growth of the Shipping Industry in the Río de la Plata Region, 1794-1860. Madison, 1957; Spanish

translation, Buenos Aires, 1967.
───────. Rosas y la revisión de la historia argentina. Buenos
Aires, 1965.
Lafuente Machain, Ricardo de. Los conquistadors de la Plata.
second edition, Buenos Aires, 1943.
Lascano, Victor. Argentine Foreign Policy in Latin America.
Miami, 1940.
Latham, Wilfrid. The States of the River Plate: Their Industries
and Commerce. 1866.
Levene, Gustavo Gabriel. Historia de los presidentes argentinos.
2 vols. Buenos Aires, 1973.
───────. La Argentina se hizo así. Buenos Aires, 1960.
Levene, Ricardo, ed. Historia del derecho argentino. 11 vols.
Buenos Aires, 1945-1958. Stands as a masterpiece.
───────. A History of Argentina. Translated by William S.
Robertson. Chapel Hill, N.C., 1937; reprint, 1963.
───────. Investigaciones acerca de la historia económica del
virreinato del Plata. 2 vols. La Plata, 1927-1928; second
edition, 1952.
Levillier, Roberto, ed. Historia argentina. 5 vols. Buenos
Aires, 1969.
───────. Nueva crónica de la conquista del Tucumán. 3 vols.
Madrid, 1926-1928; Buenos Aires, 1927.
Lewald, H. Ernesto, compiler. Argentina: análisis y autoanalisis.
Buenos Aires, 1969.
Lieuwin, Edwin. Arms and Politics in Latin America. Revised
edition, New York, 1961.
Lipset, Seymour Martin. Political Man: The Social Bases of Pol-
itics. New York, 1960.
───────, and Aldo Solari, eds. Elites in Latin America. New
York, 1967.
López, Vicente F. Historia de la República Argentina. 10 vols.
Buenos Aires, 1883-1893; fifth edition, 8 vols., 1957.
Lozano, Pedro. Historia de la conquista del Paraguay, Río de la
Plata and Tucumán. 5 vols. Buenos Aires, 1873-1875.
Luparia, Carlos Horacio. El grito de la tierra; reforma agraria
y sindicalismo. Prologue by Juan Carlos Goyena. Buenos
Aires, 1973.
Lynch, John. The Spanish American Revolutions, 1808-1826.
New York, 1973.
───────. Spanish Colonial Administration, 1782-1810: The In-
tendant System in the Viceroyalty of the Río de la Plata.
Fair Lawn, N.J., and London, 1958; reprint, 1970; Spanish
translation, Buenos Aires, 1962.
MacCann, William. Two Thousand Miles' Ride Through the Ar-
gentine Provinces. 2 vols. London, 1853; Spanish transla-
tion, Buenos Aires, 1939; second edition, 1969.
MacDonald, Austin F. Government of the Argentine Republic.
New York, 1942.
───────. Latin American Politics. New York, 1951.
McGann, Thomas F. Argentina: The Divided Land. Princeton,
1966.
───────. Argentina, the United States and the Inter-American

System, 1880-1914.   Cambridge, Mass. , 1957.
Mackinnon, Lauchlan.   Steam Warfare in the Paraná.   2 vols.
    London, 1848; Spanish translation, Buenos Aires, 1957.
McLachlan, J. O.   Trade and Peace with Old Spain, 1667-1750.
    Cambridge, 1940.
Maeder, Ernesto J. A.   Evolución demográfica argentina de 1810
    a 1869.   Buenos Aires, 1969.
Mallon, Richard D. and Juan V. Sourrouille.   Economic Policy-
    making in a Conflict Society: The Argentine Case.   Cam-
    bridge, 1975.
Mansfield, Charles B.   Paraguay, Brazil and the Plate: Letters
    Written in 1852-1853.   Cambridge, Eng. , 1856.
Martínez, A. B. , and M. Lewandowski.   The Argentine in the
    Twentieth Century.   London, 1911.
Martínez Estrada, Ezequiel.   Para una revisión de las letras ar-
    gentinas: prolegómenos.   Compiled by Enrique Espinoza.
    Buenos Aires, 1967.
_____.   Radiografía de la pampa.   2 vols.   Buenos Aires, 1933.
    Several later editions.   English translation by Alain Swietlick,
    X-Ray of the Pampa.   Austin, Tex. , 1971.
Mayer, Jorge M.   Alberdi y su tiempo.   Buenos Aires, 1961.
Mecham, J. Lloyd.   Church and State in Latin America.   Chapel
    Hill, N. C. , 1934; revised edition, 1966.
_____.   The U.S. and Inter-American Security, 1889-1960.
    Austin, Tex. , 1961.
Metford, J. C. J.   San Martín, the Liberator.   Oxford, 1950;
    reprint, 1970.
Miers, John.   Travels in Chile and La Plata.   2 vols.   London,
    1826; AMS edition, 2 vols. , New York, 1970.
Miniati, Gino.   Argentina económica y financiera.   Buenos Aires,
    1966.
Mitre, Bartolomé.   Historia de Belgrano.   2 vols.   Buenos Aires,
    1859; definitive edition, 1887.   Several editions.
_____.   Historia de San Martín y de la emancipación sudameri-
    cana.   3 vols.   Buenos Aires 1887-1889.   Several editions.
    abridged translation by William Pilling.   London, 1893; re-
    print, 1969.
Molinari, Diego L.   La trata de Negros: datos para su estudio en
    el Río de la Plata.   Buenos Aires, 1916; second edition, 1944.
Moore, Barrington, Jr.   Social Origins of Dictatorship and De-
    mocracy.   Boston, Mass. , 1966.
Moreno, Francisco José.   Legitimacy and Stability in Latin Amer-
    ica.   New York, 1969.
Mörner, Magnus.   The Expulsion of the Jesuits from Latin Ameri-
    ca.   New York, 1965.
_____.   The Political and Economic Activities of the Jesuits in
    the La Plata Region, Hapsburg Era.   Translated by Albert
    Read.   Stockholm, 1953.
Morris, Arthur S.   The Regional Problem in Argentine Economic
    Development.   Great Britain, 1972.
Mulhall, Michael G.   The English in South America.   Buenos
    Aires, 1878.
_____.   Handbook of the River Plate.   Buenos Aires, 1869.

Nichols, Madaline. The Gaucho: Cattle Hunter, Cavalryman, and Ideal of Romance. Durham, N.C., 1942.
Noble, Roberto J. Argentina, a World Power. Translated by Marisa Martínez Corvalán. Buenos Aires, 1961.
North, Liisa. Civil-Military Relations in Argentina, Chile, and Peru. Berkeley, Calif., 1966.
Organski, A. F. K. The Stages of Political Development. New York, 1965.
Ornstein, Leopoldo R. La campaña de los Andes a la luz de las doctrinas de guerra modernas. Buenos Aires, 1929.
Ortega y Gasset, José. The Revolt of the Masses. New York, 1932.
Ortiz, Ricardo M. Historia económica de la Argentina. Buenos Aires, 1955.
Otero, José P. Historia del libertador don José de San Martín. 4 vols. Buenos Aires, 1932; 8 vols., 1944-1945.
Owen, Frank. Perón, His Rise and Fall. London, 1957.
Page, Thomas J. La Plata, the Argentine Confederation, and Paraguay. New York, 1859.
Paita, Jorge A., ed. Argentina, 1830-1960. Buenos Aires, 1961.
Palacio, Ernesto. Historia de la Argentina, 1515-1943. 2 vols. Buenos Aires, 1954.
Parish, Woodbine. Buenos Aires and the Provinces of the Río de la Plata. London, 1839; second edition, 1852; Spanish translation, Buenos Aires, 1854, 1958.
Parras, Pedro J. de. Diario y derrotero de sus viajes, 1749-1753. Buenos Aires, 1943.
Paso, Leonardo. Historia del origen de los partidos políticos en la Argentina, 1810-1918. Buenos Aires, 1972.
Pendle, George. Argentina. London, 1955; third edition, 1963.
Perón, Juan D. Peronist Doctrine. Buenos Aires, 1952.
Peters, Harold E. The Foreign Debt of the Argentine Republic. Baltimore, Md., 1934.
Peterson, Harold F. Argentina and the United States, 1810-1960. New York, 1964.
Phelps, Vernon Lovell. The International Economic Position of Argentina. Philadelphia, 1938.
Piccirilli, Ricardo. Rivadavia y su tiempo. 2 vols. Buenos Aires, 1943; second edition, 3 vols., 1960.
_____, Francisco L. Romay, and Leoncio Gianello, eds. Diccionario historico argentino. 6 vols. Buenos Aires, 1953-1955. 1955.
Potash, Robert A. The Army and Politics in Argentina, 1928-1945: Yrigoyen to Perón. Stanford, Calif., 1969.
Quesada, Ernesto. La época de Rosas. Buenos Aires, 1898. Various editions.
Quién es quién en la Argentina: biografías contemporáneas. Seventh edition. Buenos Aires, 1958-1959.
Rennie, Ysabel F. The Argentine Republic. New York, 1945; reprint, Westport, Conn., 1975.
Robertson, J. P. and William P. Letters on South America: Comprising Travels on the Banks of Paraná and Río de la Plata. 3 vols. London, 1843; Spanish translation, Buenos Aires, 1952.

Rocamora, José L.   La cultura en Buenos Aires hasta 1810.
Buenos Aires, 1948.
Rock, David, ed.   Argentina in the Twentieth Century.   Pittsburgh,
Pa. , 1975.
_____. Politics in Argentina.   The Rise and Fall of Radical-
ism.   Cambridge Latin American Studies, XIX.   New York,
1975.
Rojas, Ricardo.   Eurindia.   Buenos Aires, 1924.   Various edi-
tions.
_____. Historia de la literatura argentina.   4 vols.   Buenos
Aires, 1917-1922; fourth edition, 9 vols. , 1957.
_____. La literatura argentina: ensayo filosófico sobre la
evolución de la cultura en el Plata.   Buenos Aires, 1922.
_____. Las provincias.   Buenos Aires, 1927.   Various editions.
_____. El Santo de la Espada.   Buenos Aires, 1940.   Later
editions.   Translated into English by Herschel Brickell and
Carlos Videla with title San Martín, Knight of the Andes.
New York, 1945.
Romero, José L.   Argentina: imágenes y perspectivas.   Buenos
Aires, 1956.
_____. A History of Argentine Political Thought.   Translated
from third edition by Thomas F. McGann.   Stanford, Calif. ,
1963; second edition, 1968.
Rosenblat, Angel.   La población indígena y el mestizaje en Améri-
ca.   2 vols.   Buenos Aires, 1954.
Rowe, Leo S.   The Federal System of the Argentine Republic.
Washington, D. C. , 1921.
Royal Institute of International Affairs.   The Republics of South
America: A Political, Economic and Cultural Survey.   Lon-
don, 1937.
Ruiz, Jorge Comadrán.   Evolución demográfica argentina durante
el período hispano, 1535-1810.   Buenos Aires, 1969.
Rumbold, Sir Horace.   The Great Silver River: Notes of a Resi-
dence in Buenos Ayres in 1880 and 1881.   London, 1887.
Sáenz Hayes, Ricardo.   Miguel Cané y su tiempo (1851-1905).
Buenos Aires, 1955.
Salera, Virgil.   Exchange Control and the Argentine Market.   New
York, 1941.
Sánchez-Albórnoz, Nicolás.   The Population of Latin America.   Los
Angeles, 1974.   English edition by Sage, Los Angeles, Calif.
Saravia, José Manuel.   Argentina 1959, un estudio sociológico.
Buenos Aires, 1959.
Sargent, Charles S.   The Spatial Evolution of Greater Buenos
Aires, Argentina, 1870-1930.   Tempe, Ariz. , 1974.
Sarmiento, Domingo Faustino.   Facundo.   Santiago de Chile, 1845.
critical editions, Buenos Aires, 1938, 1941, 1955.   Trans-
lated into English by Mrs. Horace Mann, with title Life in
the Argentine Republic in the Days of the Tyrants; or Civili-
zation and Barbarism.   New York, 1868; Boston, 1960; New
York, 1961.
Scalvini, Jorge M.   Historia de Mendoza.   Mendoza, 1965.
Scheuss de Studer, Elena F.   La trata de negros en el Río de la
Plata durante el siglo XVIII.   Buenos Aires, 1958.

Schmidel, Ulrich. See especially Hakluyt Society. Vol. 81, Part I. The Conquest of the River Plate, 1535-1555. Voyage of Ulrich Schmidt to the Rivers La Plata and Paraguai. London, 1891. Many other editions.

Schmitt, Karl Michael and David Burks. Evolution or Chaos. New York, 1963.

Schwartz, Kessel. A New History of Spanish American Fiction. 2 vols. Coral Gables, Fla., 1971-1972.

Scobie, James R. Argentina. A City and a Nation. second edition, New York and London, 1971.

————. Buenos Aires: Plaza to Suburb, 1870-1910. New York, 1974.

————. Revolution on the Pampas: A Social History of Argentine Wheat, 1860-1910. Austin, Tex., 1964; Spanish translation, Buenos Aires, 1968.

Sierra, Vicente D. Historia de la Argentina. 7 vols. Buenos Aires, 1956-1965.

Silvert, Kalman H. The Conflict Society: Reaction and Revolution in Latin America. revised edition. New York, 1966.

————, ed. Expectant Peoples: Nationalism and Development. New York, 1967.

Smith, Peter H. Argentina and the Failure of Democracy, 1904-1955. Madison, Wisc., 1974.

————. Politics and Beef in Argentina: Patterns of Conflict and Change. New York, 1969; Spanish translation, Buenos Aires, 1969.

Snow, Peter G. Argentine Radicalism: The History and Doctrine of the Radical Civic Union. Iowa City, 1965.

————, ed. Government and Politics in Latin America: A Reader. New York, 1967.

Sola, Miguel. Compendio de historia de la cultura argentina. La Plata, 1959.

Solari, Manuel H. Historia de la cultura argentina. Buenos Aires, 1951; second edition, 1954.

Solberg, Carl. Immigration and Nationalism: Argentina and Chile. 1890-1914. Austin, Tex., 1970.

Spalding, Hobart A., Jr., ed. Historia de la clase trabajadora argentina, 1890-1912. Buenos Aires, 1970.

Steward, Julian H., ed. Handbook of South American Indians. Smithsonian Institution, Bureau of American Ethnology, Bulletin 143, 6 vols. Washington, D.C., 1946-1950. Especially volumes I, II, and III.

————, and Louis C. Faron. Native Peoples of South America. New York, Toronto, and London, 1959.

Street, John. Artigas and the Emancipation of Uruguay. Cambridge, Eng., 1959.

Szulc, Tad. Twilight of the Tyrants. New York, 1959.

Taylor, Carl C. Rural Life in Argentina. Baton Rouge, La., 1948.

Temperley, H. The Foreign Policy of Canning, 1822-1827. London, 1925.

Tinker, Edward Larocque. The Horsemen of the Americas and the Literature They Inspired. New York, 1953.

Torchia Estrada. Juan Carlos. La filosofía en la Argentina. Washington, D. C. , 1961.

Tornquist, Ernesto. The Economic Development of the Argentine Republic in the Last Fifty Years. Buenos Aires, 1919.

Tulchin, Joseph S. The Aftermath of War: World War I and U. S. Policy toward Latin America. New York, 1971.

Udaondo, Enrique. Diccionario biográfico argentino. Buenos Aires, 1938.

_____. Diccionario biográfico colonial argentino. Buenos Aires, 1945.

_____. Grandes hombres de nuestra patria. 3 vols. Buenos Aires, 1968.

United Nations' Economic Commission for Latin America (ECLA). El desarrollo económico de la Argentina. 3 vols. Mexico, D. F. , 1959.

_____. El desarrollo económico y la distribución del ingreso en la Argentina. New York, 1968; English edition, 1969.

Universidad Nacional de Cuyo. Wine and Wine Making. Argentine Republic. Instituto del Vino, Anales (several). 1949-1976.

University of California, Los Angeles (U. C. L. A.). Statistical Abstracts of Latin America. Los Angeles, Calif. , 1972.

Uriburu, José E. La republica argentina a traves de las obras de escritores ingleses. Buenos Aires, 1948.

Valaer, Peter John. Wines of the World. New York, 1950.

Vidal, Emeric E. Picturesque Illustrations of Buenos Aires and Montevideo. London, 1820.

Villalobos R. , Sergio. Comercio y contrabando en el Río de la Plata y Chile, 1700-1811. Buenos Aires, 1965.

Webster, C. K. Britain and the Independence of Latin America, 1812-1820. London, 1938.

Weil, Felix J. Argentine Riddle. New York, 1944.

Whitaker, Arthur P. Argentina. Englewood Cliffs, N. J. , 1964.

_____. Argentine Upheaval: Perón's Fall and the New Regime. New York and London, 1956.

_____. Nationalism in Latin America: Past and Present. Gainesville, Fla. , 1962.

_____. The United States and Argentina. Cambridge, Mass. , 1954.

_____. The United States and Independence of Latin America. Boston, 1941.

_____. The United States and the Southern Cone. Cambridge, Mass. , 1976.

White, John W. Argentina: The Life Story of a Nation. New York, 1942.

Wilgus, A. Curtis, ed. Argentina, Brazil, and Chile Since Independence. Washington, D. C. , 1935.

_____. The Historiography of Latin America: A Guide to Historical Writing, 1500-1800. Metuchen, N. J. , 1975.

_____. Latin America in the Nineteenth Century. Metuchen, N. J. , 1973.

Williams, Glyn. The Desert and the Dream: A Study of Welsh Colonization in Chubut, 1865-1915. Cardiff, Wales, 1975.

Williams, John H. Argentina International Trade Under Incon-

vertible Paper Money, 1880-1900. Cambridge, Mass. , 1920.
Williams Alzaga, Enrique. La pampa en la novela argentina. Bue-
nos Aires, 1955.
Willis, Bailey. A "Yanqui" in Patagonia. Stanford, Calif. , 1947.
Winsberg, Morton D. Colonia Baron Hirsch: A Jewish Agricul-
tural Colony in Argentina. Gainesville, Fla. , 1964.
Wright, Winthrop R. British-Owned Railways in Argentina. Their
Effect on the Growth of Economic Nationalism, 1854-1948.
Latin American Monographs, No. 34, University of Texas.
Austin, Tex. , 1974.
Wythe, George. Industry in Latin America. New York, 1945.
Yaben, Jacinto R. Biografías argentinas y sudamericanas. 6
vols. 1938-1940.
Zuloaga, María Angel. La victoria de las alas. Historia de la
aviación argentina. Buenos Aires, 1948.

APPENDIX IV

Maps

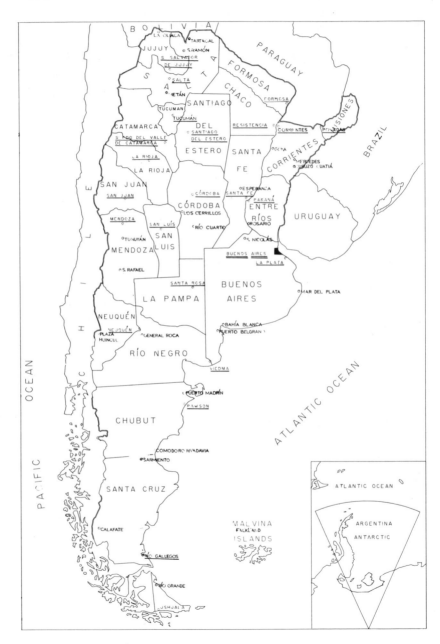

Political Divisions

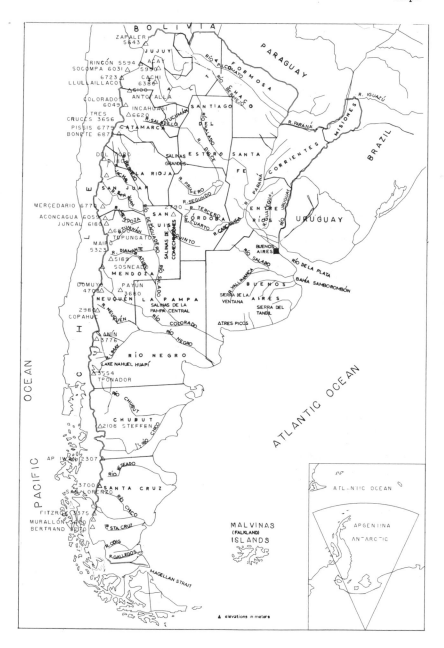

Physical Map (Rivers and Mountains)

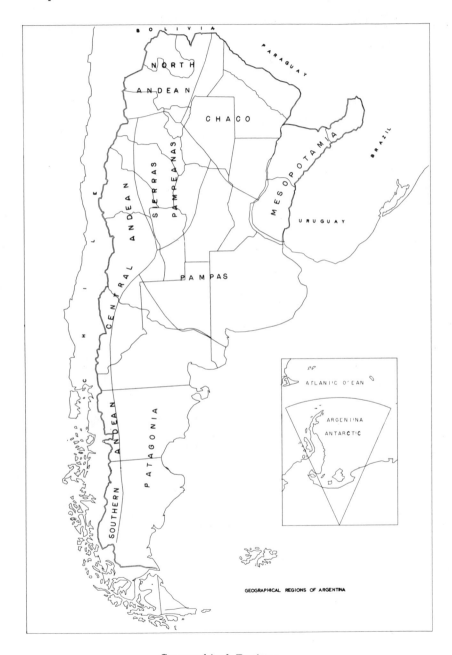

GEOGRAPHICAL REGIONS OF ARGENTINA

Geographical Regions

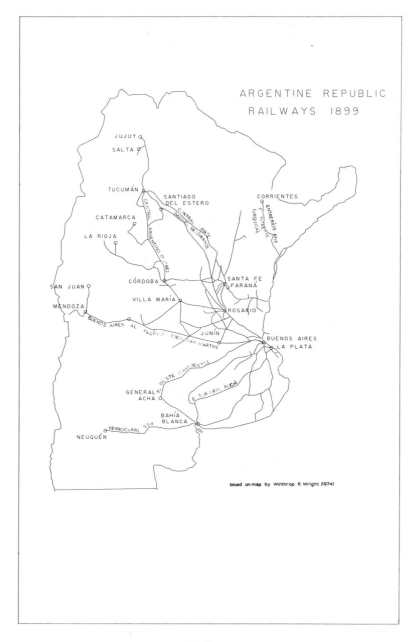

ARGENTINE REPUBLIC
RAILWAYS 1899

based on map by Winthrop R. Wright (1974)

Railways